An ABC of Indian Culture

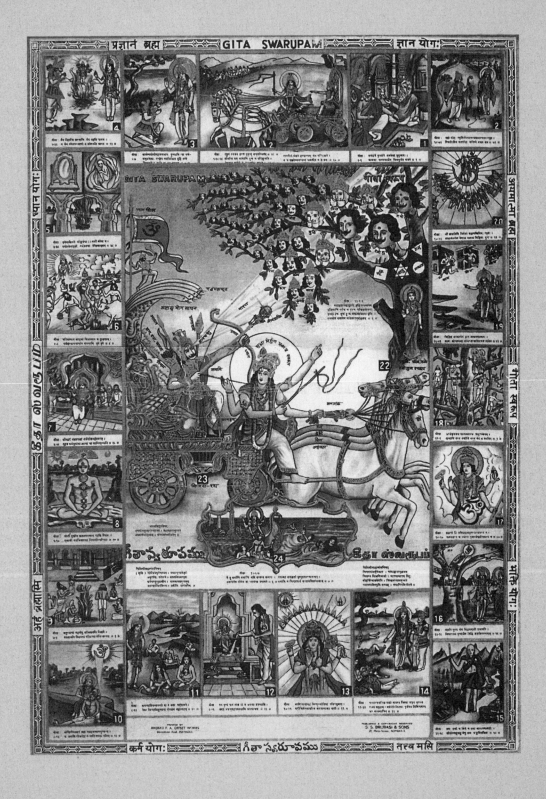

An ABC of Indian Culture

A Personal Padayatra of Half a Century into India

Peggy Holroyde

MapinLit

AN IMPRINT OF
MAPIN PUBLISHING

First published in India in 2007 by
MapinLit
An imprint of
Mapin Publishing Pvt. Ltd.

Simultaneously published in the
United States of America in 2007 by
Grantha Corporation
77 Daniele Drive, Hidden Meadows
Ocean Township, NJ 07712
E: mapinpub@aol.com

Distributed in North America by
Antique Collectors' Club
East Works, 116 Pleasant Street, Suite 18
Easthampton, MA 01027
T: 1 800 252 5231 ◆ F: 413 529 0862
E: info@antiquecc.com ◆ www.antiquecollectorsclub.com

Distributed in the United Kingdom, Europe and the Middle East by
Art Books International Ltd.
Unit 200 (a), The Blackfriars Foundry, 156 Blackfriars Road
London, SE1 8EN UK
T: 44 207 953 7271 ◆ F: 207 953 8547
E: sales@art-bks.com ◆ www.art-bks.com

Distributed in Southeast Asia by
Paragon Asia Co. Ltd.
687 Taksin Road, Bukkalo, Thonburi
Bangkok 10600 Thailand
T: 66 2877 7755 ◆ F: 2468 9636
E: rapeepan@paragonasia.com

Distributed in the rest of the world by
Mapin Publishing Pvt. Ltd.
10B Vidyanagar Society I
Usmanpura, Ahmedabad 380 014 INDIA
T: 91 79 2754 5390/2754 5391 ◆ F: 91 79 2754 5392
E: mapin@mapinpub.com ◆ www.mapinpub.com

ISBN: 978-81-88204-17-5 (Mapin)
ISBN: 978-1-890206-55-0 (Grantha)
LC: 2003100420

Designed by Amit Kharsani / Mapin Design Studio
Illustrations by Sanjeev Mishra
Editorial Consultant: Krishen Kak / Gayatri
Printed in India

Contents

Dedicated to my feisty mother known to the family as Granny E-B, who went without many personal comforts to give me a privileged education which enabled me to take full advantage of leaping beyond my own cultural grounding in those first steps onto Indian soil...

... and to gentle Scilla, patient ayah and 'other mother' of Michael, Caitilin and Christopher who also enabled me to leap many
Stepping Stones
along that Indian pathway beyond my own home

It is not some secret doctrine or esoteric knowledge that has kept India vital and going through these long ages, but a tender humanity, a varied and tolerant culture; and a deep understanding of life and its mysterious ways. Her abundant vitality flows out from age to age in her magnificent literature and art, though we have only a small part of this with us and much lies hidden still or has been destroyed by nature or man's vandalism.

The Trimurti, in the Elephanta caves, might well be the many-faced statues of India herself, powerful with compelling eyes, full of deep knowledge and understanding, looking down upon us. The Ajanta frescoes are full of a tenderness and love of beauty and life, and yet always with a suspicion of something deeper, something beyond.

Pandit Jawaharlal Nehru

From the first speech I ever heard Panditji give in the mid-1950s based on his 'search for India' while serving his longest term of imprisonment—his ninth of 1041 days—at the hands of the British in the prolonged Freedom struggle.

From this incarceration in the Ahmadnagar Fortress prison camp from August 9, 1942–March 28, 1945, came the writing of his famous book, **The Discovery of India**, a fortunate result of being able to mull over with his eminent co-prisoners their considered thoughts on India's long and sustained civilization. Wise and evergreen, the book on which his speech was based, is as relevant today as it was when Meridian Books published it in London in 1946.

FOREWORD

The first stepping stone

ABHAYAM, 'fearless in the sense of moral courage such as Gandhi and Socrates displayed'.

These are the words of an old Indian friend, Purushottam Mavalankar, the very first Indian whom my family came to know in London long back in 1949. As a student of Harold Laski at LSE he was addressing a large conference of Sixth Form students on World Citizenship and a mutual friend, David Ennals, later to enter Parliament as a Labour MP and complete his career in the House of Lords, had roped me in to be one of the group leaders. Our immediate postwar generation were full of high ideals and dedicated intentions to build a new world. Here was a young Indian speaking with articulate passion of his new freedom as an Independent India held its collective head high. He spoke with pride, doubly so as his father, G V Mavalankar was about to take on the responsibility of steering India's Westminster-style Parliament as Speaker of the first Lok Sabha or House of the People.

Purushottam suggested this word as symbolic of the task ahead of me when he considered my embryonic list of 'sign posts' I had finally assembled to help other travellers along the various routes into understanding India. Abhayam is a quality Gandhi demanded of all those, who in the civil disobedience campaigns underwent privations and imprisonment to release Indians from colonial rule.

A massive task to assemble one's own truth about India, each person's truth so different… And being a devotee of **GANESH,** with a home in Ahmedabad watched over by many gloriously carved or intriguingly minute images of this Lord of all Beginnings, Purushottam suggested Abhayam as taking appropriate pride of place as the very first word, the first indicator into India… removing obstacles for me in this pathway along the luxuriant but often devious and hidden byways of its terrain. And how many tripwires? …perhaps some triumphs!

This is after all a leisurely personal exploration through thickets and across hidden minefields where I am only too aware of the foolishness of rushing in where angels fear to tread. To have the temerity to try and encapsulate Indian culture, to compress what makes India sparkle and dilate as a dark pupil in the eye of the beholder with that distinctive sense of Indian-ness… what impertinence as a *firangi*–a foreigner! Not even Indians can compress India–this conglomerate of plural identities bulging like a globule of mercury–pushed on one part of the circumference of truth, it bulges immediately in another gigantic segment. Hundreds of books have been written by India's own great scholars, knowledgeable in Sanskrit, and profound in comprehending the symbols and myths that constantly transform into contemporary relevance, so resilient and constant is the continuum, the idea of Indian-ness, despite a lack of geopolitical unity many times during at least 5,000–possibly up to 10,000–years. However, the accumulation of that sense of being part of a mysterious 'way of life' is more readily understood if one uses the proper term for Indian–**BHARAT(A)** pronounced with emphasis on the first syllable, Bh*aa*rat.

'India' is a concept wished on a multitude of diverse peoples by non-Indians, the nation-state singularity having so possessed the European mind (but only since the 18th century) as the ideal, not recognising that India's pluralities have given its civilization such a resilient strength in the face of all the physical onslaughts it has endured from alien rule, that this seeming lack is in fact India's gain. For instance, under the overall direction of the Indira Gandhi National Centre for the Arts in New Delhi, a major groundbreaking project, running into volumes, is under way. An august array of India's scholars are compiling this multi-volumed series, the **Kalatattvakosa** (pronounced Kalaatattvakosha). Several volumes already in print since 1988, their vision is to explore 250 Sanskrit words as an essential core of the Indian view of life in a comprehensive series of articles (*kala* = the arts; *tattva* = fundamental core or quality inherent in something; *kosa* = lexicon or dictionary).

This is the erudite high ground. Its towering peaks dealing with diverse disciplines ranging from biology, medicine to mathematics and metaphysics stand guard at times over my own ground level of everyday life, **a compendium of over 310 words**, sayings, idiosyncrasies, startling events, even miracles… as overwhelming as **GANGA MA** in full flood—but that is India!

So Why Try? Why search out the middle ground between the straightforward guidebook language, the geographic and practical skeleton of a different country and an alien culture and the scholarly Himalayan tomes, peppered with diacritical marks and kangaroo-hopping between foot-notes and end-glossaries (enough to give you nausea on an Indian train!). Immediately one is in difficulties with pronunciation in even attempting such a **SADHANA**, a personally-imposed, almost devotional self-discipline (with its characteristic emphasis on the first syllable = saadhana, a stress which goes against the grain of most European speech). This is dealt with in a short note immediately after this on how to respond to the exactness of Sanskrit and its derivative languages which put considerable store on accuracy of sound.

That in itself is several stepping stones along the route, hence the system which worked itself out because of alphabetical orderings, of marking **STEPPING STONES** in the text in **BOLD CAPITALS** (and to note where fundamentally relevant, their inter-relatedness with other words further along the route, or, probably forgotten as the padayatra went over the next hill!)… and see in this regard **PRANA, SANSKRIT** and **VAC** (pr. vaach).

A Compendium Is Born. In searching out that middle ground I realised that India's greatest quality which the most unlikely people recall long after and which draws them back, is the magic humanity of Indians as well as the heritage embedded in the landscape. So often in guidebooks, almost of necessity, the psyche and the heart get left out; also the constancy of thought patterns, signals and symbolic shorthand transmitted by art forms, cultural impulses in the case of India transmitted through oral disciplines across at least 6,000 years of consistent development, are not highlighted. I always remember in my initial encounters an ebullient poet, Hirendranath Chattopadhya, larger-than-life at Delhi's gatherings. Pushing me into a corner at one of our first BBC receptions, this lively gentleman was not only telling me in his inimitable style that I must have been born in India in an earlier reincarnation, but with his charming poetic hyperbole imprinting on my mind this truism:

> India responds to those with heart. We can look you straight in the eye and 'know' if you are to be trusted with our truths that are not to be laughed at with the cool Western eye of total scientific rationality…. Or the superciliousness of some of your memsahibs!

And then he chuckled that infectious giggle I so recall as a mitigating factor to the rightful stiletto barb of truth!

And so an assembly not just of fundamental foundation stones in core concepts such as **DHARMA, KARMA, ARTHA, MAYA, MOKSHA**; matters to do with government; regional roundups of quite arbitrarily chosen areas of India which had special significance for my family; high philosophy and down to earth attitudes of minds, idioms and idiosyncratic behaviour such as the simple shaking of the head, the Indian wobble, began to take shape along with miracles that had come my way…. Not a Dictionary, nor a short, sharp Glossary but a very Indian narrative, quite uncontrollably so at times took me over—a headache for any editor!

By chance (or was it?) the fact is that during five decades or more in which this 'presence' swept into the fabric of my being a curious patterning implanted itself, hidden away at first with no conscious effort on my part. And yet what more unlikely for someone born Anglo-Saxon as far as I know to the core, in the heart of Leicestershire, with a staunch Christian mother who instilled strong Victorian verities into my upbringing along with a conventional Protestant schooling than to be so captured by an idea that insisted on becoming a reality? Gradually remarkable touches of serendipity, not all acceptable to my trained rational Western sense of reality, imposed a focus which took me unawares. There were sudden lurches onto crooked pathways which, part of the Indian paradox, were sequential logic now I look back bemused by the auspicious nature of the swastika emblem which had so disturbed me on coming across this symbol of India's logic so soon after my experiences of Nazi aggression.

The patterning now sends a frisson down the spine with its continuing influence as the last stepping stones were laid in this text, even to the almost meant-to-be learning curve with Mapin's editor guiding me over some very dangerous tripwires in harnessing such a volatile substance as India.

How Then Did All This Come About? Again an unexpected lurch… a chance request by a German business couple attending a residential orientation course at the Centre for International Briefing at Farnham Castle in Surrey where I had regularly lectured on the South Asia courses for 12 years on return from living in India. The patterning was beginning to intrude consciously by then. I found myself being invited back to Farnham Castle after an initial crucible of fire, yet another Sixth Form Conference. How to sum up India in six easy lessons? How I wished for an ABC then to pick up the out-of-the-way truths of India which are not part of general information, or too detailed for traditional guide books. But that could have involved 26 separate hours of talk through the alphabet to get to Z! However, **the idea was born in 1964**.

Not only groups of British business and governmental agency personnel and their spouses attended the week-long residential courses before appointments to India, Pakistan, Sri Lanka, later Bangladesh. There were a number of Dutch and German concerns, electronic ventures from Philips and Century Enka, pioneering factories in Maharashtra as the Indian transistor revolution began exploding. The continental members of the course appeared to be so well read (in English also) compared with their British counterparts and much more knowledgeable about Indian philosophy (was this an influence from Max Müller's era?). They certainly were keen to discuss ideas, an aspect British businesspeople seemed to shy away from. Talking about **DHARMA** and why Indian workers would want to open a factory by invoking the blessings of **Ganesh** or **Ganapati** were not exactly urgent topics for what Napoleon derisively called 'a nation of shopkeepers'! Tough questioning, however, even put the Indian speakers on their mettle. I went searching for the answers. Being a residential week-long course there was time to reflect and this process of challenge, a sharp learning curve, set into a pattern.

Reading the letters from course members 'out there' commenting on their initial reactions to the sub-continent and their assessments of our introductions, as well as the policy of the course planners in inviting returned personnel back for their own perspectives was salutary—but encouraging. That was a true **SADHANA**, tough, amusing, close to the bone! It was on one of those occasions before a civilizing dinner, mellowed by a strong gin and tonic in the resonating beamed Great Hall of the 11th century castle that these knowledgeable Germans suggested I try to pin India down in an A-Z in two hours flat!

Nothing venture… **Nothing do**… sprang to attention again deep within the depth of my mind. It had been a homily, slightly shifted in meaning, by the Protestant work ethic of my adventurous, slightly idiosyncratic mother. It was woven into my childhood upbringing… **ABHAYAM.** By the end of the week it was tried out… And **AHIMSA**… In the first instance I never got beyond **PALIMPSEST**, my favourite word in summing up India, a subject for a two-hour long dissertation on its own, learned from Pandit Nehru's famous book, **Discovery of India** written in and out of gaol incarcerations, enforced by my own Anglo-Saxon ancestors, or in third-class rail compartments travelling from one important Congress Party meeting to another while strengthening the struggle for freedom and independence. It was compulsory reading in New Delhi in 1954 soon after arrival in India.

1966–1973

At this particular period of my life, Britain was undergoing alarming challenges. Enoch Powell, MP for Wolverhampton, had delivered his 'rivers of blood' speech. Tempers were rising. Race riots exploded. Suddenly many professional people involved with a large increase in the UK of Asian immigration as well as Ugandan Asian refugees wanted background information. People realised despite all those centuries of imperial rule how very ignorant they were about Asian cultural backgrounds when dealing, for instance, educationally with Hindu, Sikh and Muslim children in increasing numbers in school—or medically with Asian patients, women for instance, who would not, could not, make eye contact with a doctor, whose children even had to be the interpreters for parents they should defer to.

1970s

That was when **EAST COMES WEST: A Background to some Asian Faiths**, written for the Community Relations Commission in London was published in 1973. Working closely with my Indian and Pakistani colleagues in Yorkshire at the time as editor of this project was yet another dimension in experiencing village India and people, most especially women unable to write in their own Urdu, Punjabi, Gujarati, the kind of Indians I had only infrequently met on their home soil, only fleetingly staying in villages in our many travels through the sub-continent.

Unknown cultural factors became everyday events not only for myself but intimately involving a very patient husband and children… especially when one of my Asian 'daughters', a Muslim, say, would run away with a Sikh boy—or vice-versa. As a result the Quaker Rowntree Trust requested a study in social change of 50 Asian families, Sikh, Hindu and Muslim. This was written for the Home Office, supervised by Leeds University where my husband then was pioneering educational television. I was plunged into yet another level of Indian society and social challenges.

1941

But There Have To Be Beginnings. The patterning had already begun 30 years earlier—unbeknown to me as a naïve English girl plunged unexpectedly into an American culture from the even flow of my school life until then. A shake-up of the system, as equally startling and unfamiliar then coming straight out of a very orthodox girls school at the age of 17, as India might be to a visitor nowadays. Our family were rejoining my British naval father in New York, sent earlier and urgently to help Britain re-arm. This was a result of Roosevelt's controversial Lend Lease policy to bolster Britain's severely depleted defences after the Fall of France. Pearl Harbor was only just three months away.

My formidable headmistress, Dame Emmeline Tanner, knew only of Radcliffe College and had negotiated my entry based on past exam results—and the fact that I had learned Latin! I knew none of this, being torn out of school before my final exams by the sudden war-time passage fixed by the Admiralty. Within weeks I was transferred from Brooklyn to Cambridge, Massachusetts. There I was to remain for four years until I gained my BA degree in English Literature and Fine Arts in 1945, all our professors and tutors being Harvard to a man because of wartime exigencies.

Serendipity, which has marked my life (my father would have put it down to my rare auspicious caul, a fine extra membrane which has to be peeled off the face of a new-born at birth and which is carried, dry as parchment, by superstitious sailors as an amulet against drowning) laid another personal stepping stone in 1942. I was brought face to face with H N Spalding, an English scholar deeply interested in Indian faiths, stranded at Harvard because of the war. He and his diminutive wife had befriended me and some of my Radcliffe friends when he discovered that Dr Annie Besant and Theosophy sourced in Adyar, a suburb of Madras (now Chennai) had become the unlikely cult figure of our student circle. It was only later that I learned of his eminence as the benefactor of the **Spalding Chair of Eastern Religions and Ethics** at Oxford University, Professor Sarvepalli Radhakrishnan its first incumbent in 1936.

Cocaine and marijuana, the Beatles and canny maharishis on the dollar trail were unknowns in those innocent student days at Radcliffe. Why Theosophy and Besant at this distance from the 1940s I am none too sure… certainly Aldous Huxley's concept of a 'perennial philosophy' was stirring as our questioning generation searched beyond the constricting views of orthodoxy–'ours is the ONE and ONLY truth' syndrome. Already known in the USA for her free-thinking radicalism, Besant had been praised by her close friend George Bernard Shaw as a fellow Fabian socialist and as a remarkable orator (there not being many women trained in the art). She inspired women to form their first trade unions, as well as advocating birth control long before its time. I knew none of this in the land of my birth! No wonder she upset the British establishment of the time and was somewhat of a heroine in my discovery of American attitudes.

In the USA I had anyway caught a whiff of a different perspective to the British Empire from my own conservative and patriotic 'service' upbringing, a stirring in the colonies for Independence. Annie Besant had fought vigorously for Home Rule, a courageous act for a woman born in London (mainly of Irish descent, however) 100 years ago. That led to her internment by the British in WWI and eventually her election as President of the Indian National Congress—which says something for India's natural bent towards a tolerant inclusiveness to strangers who show empathy, this also being well before the suffragette movement emerged in Britain.

H N as he came to be known to our Radcliffe group was himself deeply interested in Indian faiths, but disapproved of hybrid movements such as Theosophy and certainly of suspect figures like Madame Blavatsky 'who had gone all occult Indian'! Scholar that he was, he was concerned at our own gullibility. 'Go to the primary sources,' he gently prodded, chuckling in his spare frame. I clearly remember him exclaiming: 'Throw Annie Besant out of the window!' He thrust into my hands instead a translation of an Upanishadic text and then the **Bhagavad Gita** to follow. My mind was blown.

That text, those books have disappeared physically but like a tightly-bound ball of thread, the slow unwinding had begun, skeins wafting out into the intricate folded tissues of the brain, interlacing in lateral thinking across the synapses.

1942–1943

And then another skein rolled down into Boston Naval Harbor. I was an 18-year-old sophomore, my Englishness being prised open by American anti-imperial attitudes. **Gandhi**, suddenly came into my sights. I also foolishly thought I could help the war effort by providing hospitality at the British War Relief Club–an activity my Radcliffe friends were only too keen to share! There I met my future husband, a very dashing Englishman, every girl's dream, in naval uniform, his destroyer in for repairs from a collision in the Atlantic. There followed two and a half years wartime parting adding depth to such a brief haphazard meeting.

1945

My degree in hand as war was ending in Europe, the Admiralty suddenly found a passage for me to return to England. Within a month Derek and I were married as the atom bombs dropped, my husband on a shore course having survived being torpedoed in the Arctic Russian convoys… The war was over. A year later demobilization of service personnel presented a chance to renew disrupted education. Where to go for Derek, who was considering a degree in History at which he excelled, American History his concentration?

1946

At this point serendipity played its magic throw of the dice again, my elderly mentor surfaced unexpectedly after a year incommunicado due to erratic wartime communication. His six-month old letter re-directed by Radcliffe reached me miraculously. H N was back in Oxford… so it came about that another stepping stone was quietly put in place. On his advice, my young husband, released from the Admiralty Signals Division, found himself at Brasenose College in 1946–48, part of an extraordinary married generation of students, many with babies of the boom, a degree compressed into high-powered study of two years… impassioned ideals, a charged and changed world, pent-up yearnings to be rid of the old tired social divisions and narrow, inhibiting institutionalized religions.

And there, at All Souls College was Radhakrishnan (and Dr E Conze into the bargain, eminent Buddhist scholar and author of many books on Buddhism) occupying the Spalding Chair… inevitable therefore that I find myself literally sitting at the foot of this high-browed Tamil Brahmin, Upanishad-style… but on a 16th century sloping Tudor wooden floor, 'nothing venture' echoing its challenge once again. Surrounded as I was with graduate students (to a man) in Philosophy, with H N's amused encouragement I entered those hallowed corridors of All Souls (all **masculine** souls be it understood without question!) having cycled up from Folly Bridge with an 18-month-old son Michael strapped in his pillion basket, my babysitter husband dragooned next door in Brasenose College to hold the fort while I considered such subjects as Action and Contemplation, even writing a dissertation on the same between washing nappies and coping with a husband studying for exams. Action there was–but little to dilate on contemplation! And who then was to know that with his degree in hand in 1949 other stepping stones had been invisibly placed, moving ever onwards from my husband's first appointment as a current affairs producer in the Overseas Service of the BBC, to 1953–and promotion as BBC Representative to India and Pakistan, never envisaged in all those years of 'preparing the mind'…

Something I little understood then only to come into sharp focus 40 years later in Australia… a chance **ABC Science** broadcast, a discussion between Hubert Alyea, retired Professor of Chemistry at Princeton University, and the famous crystallographer Dorothy Hodgkin (awarded the Nobel Prize for protein research in 1964 and then President of the Pugwash Conference on nuclear matters). They were discussing the random nature of knowledge, of reaching the truth, sometimes erratically when Alyea, talking of Pasteur's own discoveries, let slip a phrase from the great man: **Chance favours only the prepared mind.** So chance it was, already the patterning prepared.

1953–1958

Our family lived in New Delhi, travelling widely all over the subcontinent, mostly by rail and car. That was India so soon after Independence, a golden era historically, incorruptible politicians, their personalities honed in integrity on the anvil of imprisonment by my people. I still remember with the utmost clarity after the 16-day sea journey from Southampton to Bombay by classic P & O liner (how civilized travel was then!) with Michael, then seven and Caitilin aged three, the crisp sheets of the khaki canvas bedrolls, a true Australian-style 'swag' but with the smell of starched pillow cases, boarding the immaculate coupé on the Frontier Mail of Bombay. Arriving in the evening at New Delhi railway station, India exploded in a cacophony around us. I had the strangest feeling however rippling through my being. I had 'come home'... and just before the beautiful festival of Diwali, November 1953.

1956

Our youngest son Christopher was born a Delhiwallah to return himself later aged 18 for a year's stint in voluntary service living very humbly, teaching at Mitraniketan in Kerala under his mentor and guide, Dr Visvanathan in a Gandhian-style education centre for poor rural and tribal students.

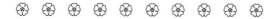

1992

An accumulation of this life-time pathway and so many recurring questions, my own as well as others, led me to wish I had been handed in compressed form a set of guidelines written along the lines suggested by that German couple, a format filling out the basic information of the regular guide books—but which was human as India so decisively is. A month after my husband died unexpectedly I decided with valour to defy discretion! **ABHAYAM**... a discipline for grieving.

The 55-year-old journey continues, the first stone laid by H N... or was it in my own karma as a diffident young student just 17, feeling very homesick all of a sudden, torn from all my friends at school in England, in a strange American culture, and on my own for the very first time, to sink or swim, parents way down in New York, and sipping coffee in that Brattle Street Café off Harvard Square with its red gingham cloths, impulsively to go up to this strange Englishman and his wife on overhearing their accents and, with fearlessness, abhayam, introduce myself as English also! A very un-English thing to do. To this day, I cogitate upon that hidden impulse which is all of a piece with this padayatra reaching the last stepping stone.

And so it has been a continuing journey, a resplendent lifetime enhanced and expanded by all of India's explosive joys, anguished yearnings, perturbing humanity, perplexing paradoxes! Thus warmed at the edges and in the heart by that quality of Indian friendship—loving care and overwhelming hospitality, naughty humour and unexpected miracles, I dare to commence with the first A.

Peggy Holroyde
Perth, 2007

ACKNOWLEDGEMENTS

Usually those who work at the tedious and often physically straining task of helping an author make a manuscript readable as well as coherent appear with appreciation rendered in the final paragraph of the acknowledgements.

I am, however, fully aware with a heavy conscience of how four women worked flat out to get a very lengthy and heavy manuscript in some order to be despatched in documentation boxes to India as their own family countdowns to Christmas 2000 ominously stood on the calendar for the following week. They deserve therefore to be showered with the first accolades of my gratitude—and wonderment that despite professional situations of their own in the day they ever completed this most demanding task.

First, **Joy McGilvray**. This book could never even have reached completion without her valiant and steadfast application in wading through a slough of pages originally handwritten, myself sometimes forgetful in the hurry to capture a sudden inspirational sentence, or oblique passing thought, to put Indian words familiar to me in readable caps for her to decipher. Initially Joy knew very little about Indian cultural attitudes, or even much of the geography or current politics. When I look at those original pages blobbed with whitener, sometimes a gap remaining blank as the mind raced ahead of replacing the right word needed, I marvel at Joy's capacity to read my thoughts as deletions and amendments snaked around the paper edge like haphazard Urdu graffiti rolling its calligraphy around Mughal palace walls in northern India! It has been a long partnership. Her loyalty and concern about the outcome of this manuscript deserves praise. She, indeed, carries 'good dharma.'

Pat Bosley of Curtin University in Perth came to the rescue several times at moments of real stress and urgency. I salute her too in difficult circumstances when the heat was on for a finished text as flu struck. That too calls for special recognition when India's way of life was still a mystery.

In the last months of coping with a blown-out book despite culling an abundance of pages in response to editorial suggestions which rightly called for literary circumspection (why is it that whatever is involved with India explodes in one's face from population to descriptive verbiage?), a partnership of two heroic battlers, **Lyn Smolarek** and **Samantha Warren** toiled well into summery nights to get the 800 pages slashed down into neat typing. Again Indian words were unfamiliar and unresponsive to culturally-dominated computerised western 'spell checks', something Asian IT processes need to address.

And now to India...

The very nature of the privileged position enjoyed by my husband, as Representative of the BBC allowed a ready access to so many Indians of all walks of life most especially the creative artists, writers, musicians, intellectual planners and concerned politicians and economists who thronged the capital in those heady days soon after Independence was gained.

So many who belonged to this vibrant culture of a golden era when those in government were not tarnished by self-serving hidden agendas and civil servants were blessed with great integrity, were very willing to drop by our house informally and sit on the lawn to cool off (this was before air-conditioning and when the desert-cooler and its fragrant smell of **khus khus** vetiver roots was not much help in the summer humidity).

As a result I owe debts of gratitude to countless Indians whose names frequent our guest books, who were mentors as well as friends, some who held high positions, others, though of more humble backgrounds, all extending helping hands, many giving me a gentle push into unknown territory.

Right from the very beginning, **the staff of All India Radio** who obviously shared a professional bonhomie with my husband, were generous enough to include me in as well. **K S Mullick**, then Station Director, often telephoned to put an important event in my awareness before it happened.

The late **Dr Narayana Menon** had already organised our initial introduction into 'classical Indian music—the Diwali concert at Rashtrapati Bhavan in the presence of President Rajendra Prasad on my fourth night in Delhi. The leap across the Great Divide which then still existed, a decade before Pandit Ravi Shankar, Ustads Alla Rakha and Ali Akbar Khan, initiated Europe into rethinking its own tight cultural musical boundaries happened that night. Shimmering sound exploded in my ear and I have to thank also AIR's chief recording engineer **Krishnamurthi** who encouraged my initial baptism of fiery enthusiasm with the secret discipline of allowing me to sit quietly cross-legged in the corner of the recording studio (surely impossible today!) after he had alerted me to the presence of renowned musicians in rehearsal, many of them never having themselves been to Delhi before, because of those subtle colonial constraints of the immediate decade before.

And here **T K Jayaram Iyer**, resident Carnatic violinist at AIR played a significant part, coming quietly to our house with **Ramnad Eswaran**, spending hours explaining complex musical systems; and even more so, **Pandit Ravi Shanker** who cared to write the preface to my book *Indian Music* in 1972.

To return to beginnings. Not only **Purushottam** (and **Purnima**) Mavalankar played their part (mentioned in the Foreword) to make us feel at home with a blessing from one of their many murtis of Ganesh but three lively Indian women, **Jamila Verghese**, **Suvira Kapur** and **Kanta (then Gupta) Reddy** and their respective husbands **George**, **Shiv** and **G K** watched over our extended education. **Jamila** and **Suvira** literally held my hand leading me through the crowded Talkatora Gardens Diwali Fair on my third night in India! They with Kanta and **Sanam Singh** who with her respected Army husband, the late **General Harbukhsh Singh**, had shared a shipboard journey back from India to the gloom of Tilbury docks as wet snow fell, all have contributed over 45 years of shared joys and sorrows, and the deadly bore of getting children to 'eat up' three times a day on board ship before adult meals are served and children banned from the dining room! Oh, joy!

I pay especial respect and affection to a score of elderly Indian men to whom it was only too easy to lose one's heart. Their charm, impish humour and depth of intellect are beyond compare. The seduction—fascinating conversations—of a depth and challenging complexity achieved nowhere else in my global sojourns that it can easily become an intoxication of the spirit!

Prof. George Verghese, retired Editor and member of the Centre for Policy Research normally a very private person, has given me such sound political advice over decades, shared vital insights, and allowed me to test out new ideas in periods of great volatility, such as the Emergency of the 70s when our youngest son, on a year's voluntary service in Kerala, aged 18, needed surrogate parents when riots broke out. Jamila became his Indian mother.

Shankar Pillai, cartoonist extraordinaire, sharpened my political senses along with his old mate, **M Chalapathi Rau** over many an idli and dosa in his home in Delhi; **Dr V Raghavan**, eminent scholar and then Sanskrit professor in Madras University had the grace to clarify my overloaded brain and allow me hours of his time in his own home while I plied him with questions and formative thoughts that had been stirred before I ever set foot in his country by another of his colleagues and contemporaries, **Professor Sarvepalli Radhakrishnan** (later President of India).

And for the joyous and enlivening discussions of Gandhi's role, Islam, basic education and its importance for all the neglected millions I remember the gentle duo, the late **Professor M Mujeeb** of **Jamia Milia** and the late **Dr Zakir Husain**, also eventually to become President of India, but both humble spirits who taught me loyalty to India's concept of the secular society.

And then of course there is always nonagenarian author, commentator, Sikh historian, **Khushwant Singh** who despite the flagrant image he deliberately creates about himself, has the innocence of a young boy and a heart of gold for some who have fallen on hard times. Despite all the ribaldry and riposte, I shall for ever retain especial affection—and not for anything a voyeuristic or cynical public might expect! Into my third weekend into Delhi life he took me off bird-watching with the gaunt white-haired American, Horace Alexander, another constructive Quaker like Agatha Harrison working behind the Indian scenes as their kind are wont to do. We drove way out to Miss Jackson's jhils (and which spinster English woman had she been?) near Meerut to discover Painted and Adjutant Storks. I still can see the scene of a delicate phantasmagoria—the early morning mist curling around these strange Jacobean birds, first obscuring, then half-revealing delicate pink and white ruffles against the verdant green of sugar cane and barley... and then into a predominantly Muslim village. He made me sit down on my first rickety charpoy to drink milky tea brought by a peasant farmer (probably straight from the cow as there was straw in the bottom of the glass!). And all the women gathered around—and stared—and then laughed. Kaval Singh had kindly asked her darzi to run up a traditional shalwar-kameez, the real baggy pant, waistline three feet wide pulled in on cotton tape. A very unfamiliar angrezan fit for ribald remarks! In those days the expression was still used—here was a white memsahib 'gone native'. I learned the first lesson in being the object under scrutiny, not the English ruler surveying the world with upper-crust hauteur. A lesson learned. Thank you Khushwant for the out-of-the-way places to which you have introduced me. And to the late **R L Agarwal** who taught me more than just Hindi at which I failed conspicuously because we always ended up in lively political or philosophic discussion instead. He saved me in many unusual bazaar (and bizarre) situations from being parted from my money by Kashmiri astrologers and sales merchant spinners of seductive words.

And on the subject of words and what they represent, I owe a particular debt to **Dr Kapila Vatsyayan** an old friend from those Delhi days of the 50s but a pioneering intellectual when India was having to rediscover itself in an all-India way, not often appreciated by younger Indians of today who inherit a totality of a nation in which Indians can in their millions join the tourist roundabout themselves. In the early 50s the south was virtually an unknown quantity and Kashmir a world unto itself.

Kapila Vatsyayan sharpened my mind to many of India's cultural paradoxes as well as introducing me in latter years to the immensity of the **Kalatattvakosa**—the lexicon of core-concepts words, an expansive project undertaken by leading Sanskrit scholars.

Indo-UK sources…

Again those who cleared the pathway with very different perspectives on the country they had left behind to settle as new citizens in Britain, many unable to write in their own languages, are legion. Often from poor rural backgrounds, they were very different sub-cultures held traditionally close to the heart. Here was an India I did not know from the inside, wholly different from urban Delhi. I thank those families and individuals who worked alongside many of us pioneering the organisation **Springboard** which was unique in Britain, functioning under the Yorkshire Council of Social Service, helping primarily not only Indian women (and their menfolk) but Pakistani and West Indians also to gain confidence and put their own viewpoints orally in public forums. I became intimately involved with 50 Asian families for a British Home Office study in social change.

Dr Cathie Ballard, **Dr Owen Cole** and **Professor Tom Nossiter** in Leeds, and **Professor Ursula King** of Bristol University were all in their own way pioneering in social involvement with Hindu and Sikh communities. They helped me immensely in late night talkfests which involved many young people as well especially **Vijay Malik, Asha Chand Glendenning, Surinder Manku, Manjit Bhogal Dhanjal** (their names then). **Apa Pant**, then High Commissioner for India gave our organisation great support and very generously organised my month-long tour around India in 1970 as guest of the Indian Council for Cultural Relations to collect artefacts for a major educational exhibition—East Comes West—another 'first' in Britain, jointly conceived by **John Thompson**, then Director of Bradford's famous 'industrial revolution' Art Gallery and Museum, Cartwright Hall, **Margot Tennyson** and Springboard.

There are two other South Indian families who stand out in those days, who enlightened me, provided sustenance of mind and body, straddling continents like myself. Both in England—and now retired from ambassadorships and to Mysore and Thiruvananthapuram respectively—**A Madhavan** and **his wife Girija**, and **Lakshmi** and **Shankar Menon**. I used to share lecturing sessions with 'Madhu' at Farnham Castle's Centre for International Briefing in Surrey. His wry humour and in-depth philosophic comments on his own people's foibles as well intricacies of language usage were staple diet when we met.

The USA…

and first **Phillips Talbot**, President of the **American Asia Society** in New York after his years in India, for much sharing of ideas and information supplied on major Indian cultural events and visiting artists. But it is to **Cathie Gamble Curran**, such an old friend from those earliest Delhi days and our mutual circle mentioned in the India section, that I owe a very real debt. She has over nearly 50 years shared the joy and the pain (and the laughter in retrospect) of many joint Indian experiences and most generously gifted to me beautifully produced Indian exhibition catalogues, books and vital articles not readily accessible in Australia... another perspective seen through the American prism.

Australia

Because of the nature of proximity to India since Perth, Western Australia has become my home for the last 30 years (subsequently becoming an Australian citizen) visits to the sub-continent have increased as well as awareness of developments, for better—and worse. Inevitably the numbers of people from Indian origins are large in WA. Now also new citizens of this spacious and generous country, they have given of their time, thoughts and constructive help as the specific idea of this book grew and people read sections of my manuscript. Another learning curve!

Sadiq Bux for background advice on Urdu spelling, Arabic calligraphy and the Islamic faith; **Maya Chatterjee** for reading part of the manuscript. As a good Bengali should be—expert in English grammar, often far more knowledgeable than native born English currently careless in school of past participles and possessive nouns ('its' a fatal stumbling block) and parsing (who knows about that today? my own grandchildren don't) her remarkable eagle eye for spelling mistakes put me on my mettle. Her husband **Professor Samir Chatterjee**, Shourik and Jishnu have cared for me since the death of my husband nearly a decade ago, allowing me to live in their home until I found my smaller villa—Chidambaram—a shrine of peace and contentment. Maya in true Bengali tradition brought me a camp bed, yoghurt, to sleep one night with Ganesh watching over me from a shelf and a blessing with tika mark on my forehead in a completely empty home. In so doing I imbibed Bengali family traditions and the rituals, intelligently maintained, of the great times of celebration. Here is India from the inside and an intimate awareness of the power of the Goddess—Devi, Durga, Kali, Shakti and the role She plays no matter how advanced intellectually, how modern, in the exterior appearance a family might be.

Lakshmi's tiny feet delineated in white rice paste on the Australian tiles and doorway at Puja time have rounded out those 50 years of 'being Indian', experiencing that joyous Diwali time on arrival in India, home for five years. I thank them profoundly.

In recent times **Shakuntalla Devagnanam** has provided wonderful hospitality and help in travel along with her daughter **Rekha** of Travel Emporium, in my many forays into India—most especially when all 10 of my family and an Australian friend Georgia Efford (on her own padayatra of healing hands, ayurvedic massage and herbal study) landed, exhausted for New Year's Eve in Keti down a difficult hill road in mist in the Nilgiris near Udhagamandalam. We had travelled 11 hours up from the coast, leaving Kochi in the early morning. And **James**, a truly Indian Jeeves, deserves thanks too at over 70 years scurrying around bringing me 'bed tea' (such a spoiling joy in India).

Jemma Dacre, **Maggie Baxter** and **Pam Gaunt** of Perth, all textile designers involved with the SRUJAN project in Bhuj (before the terrible earthquake) have enlarged my knowledge of Gujarat and the economic imperatives of craft in these distant places.

Michael Kile of Perth Mint vetted the sections on Buddhism as a practising Buddhist, and with searching conversation on a whole array of philosophic, political and economic themes gave me expert advice on gold. **Eric Moxham**, a cricketing aficionado, dealt likewise with the section devoted to the sport. **Anu Madan** deserves special mention. So many times I phoned, straight from the manuscript, for help with the Sanskrit words and the Devanagari script. No matter if she was preparing the family meal or otherwise occupied she patiently searched her Sanskrit dictionary and with gentle humour dealt with many other queries as well, as did **Naga Narayanan**, one-time lecturer in Economics, ever busy as brahmin priest-mentor for his community. Long philosophical discussions and the precious gift with which he surprised me once on return from Chennai—the Gayatri chant on cassette in a beautifully serene rendering—have given me much food for thought as have the truly learning-curve discussions into physics, infinity, zero, the genome project and other scientific matters—all clarified in language I could understand by my gifted neighbour, **Tim St Pierre**, professor at the University of Western Australia in this very subject, and **Wanita Chua-Anusorn**, Thai medical scientist.

In that regard his seniors, **Professor John de Laeter** of Curtin University and **Professor David Blair** of UWA, both physicists of standing, had also in earlier decades patiently heard me out on Hindu philosophical concepts of the cosmos and provided insights into the changing horizons of astrophysics.

The Indian High Commissioners in Canberra, **G Parthasarathy** and his textile designer wife, **Shanti**, as well as **Mr Ravindranathan** and **Devi** overwhelmed me with home hospitality, books, conversations providing in-depth assessments of their homeland politically and economically.

Jeya Ponnuthurai, Australian-Tamil born in Malaysia and musician has been a great travelling companion to the Tiruvaiyarur Tyagaraja annual gathering or aradhana near Thanjavur, a commemorative festival in January 2000 but she has also been a longtime friend, extolling Tamil culture and Carnatic music much neglected by many tourists who concentrate their visits in northern India only. As a State librarian at Perth's Alexander Library, she has been of great help in searching the internet and discovering much information wholly unknown to many people as it emerges from Indian input of NRIs around the world. As a sister Virgo she has been meticulous in checking most of the book references.

As a result of her persistence, my miniature Ganesh, a gift from a wayside stall some 30 years earlier from a Sanskrit scholar, standing in the east gopuram of Chidambaram was offered up by a dikshitar priest to the famous murti of Shiva Nataraj in that very same temple shrine where Shankaracharya, Tyagaraja and a legion of Tamil saints, women as well as men, have also presented themselves, some over a thousand years ago at Thillai. That is history sparking with auspicious electrical impulses across aeons of time!

Professor Surendra Rao, visiting Fellow at Curtin University in the late 90s and his wife **Geetha Rao** then Manager of the Air India office in Western Australia, have been very helpful 'sounding boards' as I began to immerse myself in the manuscript as also Keralites, mathematician **Dr K Vijayan** of the University of Western Australia and his wife **Sita**.

Two people who have links with Pakistan, **Sarlu Sujan**, lecturer in psychology in Perth universities, helped in translating idiomatic Hindi and Fillum songs (with good laughs in so doing) but she also has given me a rare view as an Indian of Indian-Pakistani relationships, some of her Hindu relatives still residents of Sindh province from where the late Pakistani PM Bhutto hailed. **Proffesor Samina Yasmin** is Australian of Pakistani heritage, lecturing in politics at UWA and occasional broadcaster as well. I am mindful that Samina made phone calls to a Karachi Persian/Urdu scholar on my behalf to check on the translations of Empress Nur Jehan's epitaph as well as that melancholy verse composed by the last Mughal Emperor for his own grave.

And lastly to both **Joyce Westrip** and **Louise Howden Smith**, my Australian friend, respected arts exponent, who as a Sydney-sider has reached out to Asia. Cultures with great sensitivity, shared the enrichment, the tribulations and triumphs of our pioneer Indian Ocean Festivals 20 years ahead of their time. She completed my pathway by tracking down an old colleague of my husband's, **Professor Roderick Mac Farquhar** now of Harvard University and China expert. It was he who first hoisted me over the stile into Farnham Castle Centre and many lifelong Indian connections. Joyce Born in South India, now an Australian author of books on India, expert in Indian cuisine presentations, and Charles her husband, just for their love of India... and their fabled gift of sharing it, their home, their hospitality with just about everybody who cares for India, and visits Perth.

And to the editor for Mapin of this particular manuscript, **Dr Krishen Kak**—it is exhilarating to encounter an Indian mind that challenges with very real subtlety. To see the red-noted 'Sure?' succinctly resting in the margin halted my loquacious flow every so often and sent me scurrying back to source material. That was a gentle nudge that caused me to exclaim out loud, a wide smile of admiration wreathing my face because 90% of the time he was right, saving me from stumbling over many a tripwire. A remarkable internal conversation built up in the ether between India and Australia and I feel nothing but a sense of privilege that he reined me in from my own enthusiasms and excesses as well as alerting me to new trends so immediately germane to the reconstruction, still a matter of controversy, in early Indian historical beginnings.

Despite my responding to the initial culling of the text according to his suggestions the editor has had the unenviable task of applying the red slash marks even further. I must have surely tested his patience, but then at times the totality of India does also to most people who really care about this overflowing land which not only suffers an explosion of population but a surfeit of expression. I remember only too well the words of Khushwant Singh on first meeting me. With a mischievous glint in his eye he chided me for loving all 360 million Indians (in 1953). "The trouble with India is too many **words**, not enough **work**. The greatest single heavy industry in this country is talking!"

A NOTE TO THE READER

Almost within moments of taking the very first step along the boulder-strewn pathway there is the dilemma of appropriate behaviour towards another civilization, and its own daily cultural expression. In the burgeoning life of India from the tropical south to the world's highest peaks where most, in the pristine white snows of this 'Abode of the Gods', have fortunately remained free of humanity's footprints, the eye of Divinity is ever watchful.

Those of us if only nominal Christians, agnostics, a few atheists who come out of the Western world now heavily overlaid by secular scepticism have, nevertheless, developed within Christian-Hebraic-Islamic roots deep within a 2,000-year civilization. These Semitic religions think in terms of a masculine Creator external to individual humans and whatever is believed as soul or spirit. In Christianity especially the Trinity is acknowledged as Father, Son and Holy Ghost. Consequently throughout scripture the words used for Deity are Lord, Father, He with a capital H. Transfer one's self into the Indian framework. There is also a male Trinity—the Trimurti examined in the graphic section, **PANTHEON**. Brahma, Vishnu, Shiva. These are the deities of what anthropologists refer to as the Great Tradition in contrast to the village level of the Little Tradition.

They are paramount, above all the other gods and goddesses who have 'come down to earth;' and been elaborated upon in hundreds of parables to make the abstract, almost incomprehensible cosmic concepts more understandable to ordinary humanity struggling to comprehend. But unlike Christendom and its human female presence of the intercessor, the Virgin Mary, the Hindu recognises the biological truth of universal creation—nature = **PRAKRITI**, itself of feminine gender. There is a She!—in our terms for want of a better word but a feminine principle to a Hindu believer. Therefore male deities are complemented by equally or more powerful female entities to combine the ultimate abstract truth of creation into the androgynous Whole, depicted in Indian imagery as half male, half female... but ultimately without and transcending gender, that Impersonal Absolute = **IT**.

I was very moved wandering the distant tracks of the Tamilnadu outback on my last journey finalising this padayatra, literally so this time, paying homage to an 18th century charismatic musician-saint-composer (see **TYAGARAJA**). Impoverished women bent down in the filmy morning mist rising from the surrounding sugarcane crops to weave auspicious *kolams* (designs) of coloured rice-paste before the lintel to their simple wattle and redbrick thatched homes—a daily act of dedication for blessing from some power beyond their reach—at the doorstep... abstract symbols of the divine presence.

So Indians address these multiple forms which are only the human mind's way of acknowledging complementariness with appropriate honorifics: Iswara or Isvara also sometimes spelled in compound nouns as Mahesvara—the Great Lord Shiva.

Whereas in south India, certainly in the Tamil-speaking lands, the genderless Sri of this manifestation of the one is addressed as Thiru, Thevam or Peruman (Vishnu's name in Tamil can be Perumal—the big entity). Male deities are also addressed as **BHAGAVAN** (or **BHAGWAN**), Hari (especially for **VISHNU**) the remover of humanity's 'cloud of unknowing' or **NARAYANA**, imbued with the amniotic fluid, the sacred nectar of creation upon which Vishnu floats between his coming into planetary time again and again. The Shakti feminine principle is addressed as Devi, Shri (or Shree), Bhavani, Ammathayeh (Tamil) or just plain **SHE**, although in Sanskrit there are no capitals.

(See a special note of the strong sentiment felt by the devotee when using the genderless word Sri, in section **LAKSHMI**). In addition there are other terms of loving respect, hence confusion in the Western mind of polytheistic beliefs.

Why then has the pronoun He appeared in the text as if one is referring to a patriarchal Deity as seen by many, especially modern feminists, in intellectual rebellion against such exclusive male semitic chauvinism? Or the use of the word God, or Lord (the closest equivalent in English for isvara) used even by Indians in current books and Indian magazine articles of today?* The word appears in India not in any sense to imply a feudal attitude of the 'Lord of the Manor' syndrome. And there certainly is no concept of a patrician Lady supervising the universal creation when She is honoured. Certainly as I approached this dilemma of pronouns infused with cultural layers of meaning, some bound to be the residue of centuries of colonial domination in India (which has to be remembered is not all European Christian plus British missionary activity but Islamic as well) I felt it not only proper to follow Indian convention up until now... but also to follow the heart of the matter. The way in fact many of my close Indian friends acted even though they may hardly ever have set foot in a temple to follow ritualistic aspects of a daily 'practised' faith. Nevertheless they sincerely bowed a head and placed their hands in Namaskaram in reverence to a concept, a power, that cannot be explained in explicit words.

Out of reverence and respect I have done the same.

At the highest reaches of Hindu comprehension there is no subservience of the feminine (what happens on earth is the doing of mankind's patriarchal makings). There are no matters such as the strictures of St Paul upon women with which to contend, or theological constraints upon giving witness within church and actual assembly of bishops and priests. In fact, in the language of Middle English the term 'Lord' implied guardianship. It is therefore comforting to note that **SHRI** or **SRI** as the Universal Mother and the inseparable Consort of the Lord is seen as acting in a similar role (as quoted in a book devoted to tracing the roots of the Sanskrit definition of the feminine principle—more powerful ultimately than the male). In **Shakti—in Art and Religion** edited by **Dr Nanditha Krishna** for Chennai's C P Ramaswami Institute of Indological Research, 1991, there is an explanation of Shri. She plays 'a unique role as the guardian angel of the soul.'

She and He and It are everywhere along this padayatra into the land which is India. Ultimately beyond language, that energy, force, presence is beyond gender!

* My own conversion, or rather abstention finally from using this term half way through the final draft is explained in PANTHEON.

An ABC of Indian Culture

Abhayam
Advaita
Ahimsa
Akasha
Alvar
Anand
Arati
Ardhanariswara
Arranged marriages and
    other matrimonial
    matters
Arul
Arya–aryan
Asceticism
Ashoka
Ashokan pillar
Ashramas
Astrology, palmistry,
    auspicious days
Asuras
Asymmetry
Atithi
Atma–atman
Attar
Avatar:
    Matsya
    Kurma
    Varaha
    Narasimha
    Vamana
    Parasurama
    Rama
    Krishna
    Buddha
    Kalki
Ayurveda
Ayyanar

Bauls
Beggars
Betel leaf
Bhagavad Gita
Bhagavan Sri
    Satya Sai Baba
Bhagwan/
    Bhagavan/Bhagwati

Bhakti
Bharat
Bhava
Bhikshu
Bhoodan–Bhave
Bhumi
Bindu
Birth control
    and family planning
Bishnois
BJP/BSP
Bodhisattva
Bombay now Mumbai
Boons
Brhm
Brahma
    Brahmacharya
    Brahman
    Brahmin
    Brhmvidya
Buddha/buddhi
Buddhist art
Buddhism and Indian
    politics
Bureaucracy

Calcutta now Kolkata
Calligraphy
Caste
Caves
Chidambaram
Chola
Christianity
Coconut
Colour
Communist parties
Conch shell
Coorg, coffee, cardamon
    and cinnamon
Core concepts
Corruption
Cow
Crafts/silpa
Cricket
Crorepati
Curry

Dalit
Dance
Darshan(a)
Deepavali–Diwali
Desire to please
Devanagari
Dhaba
Dharma
Dhoti
Dikshitar
DMK
Dowry
Dravidians

Education
Ellora
Epics
Evil eye

Fakir
Fasting
Festivals
Fillums
Financing India
Fissiparous tendencies
Five-year plans

Gana
Gandhi
Ganesh
Ganga Ma
Garlands (see Mala)
Gayatri
Ghalib
Gham
Ghazal
Gnow
Gold
Goonda
Government
Grace/krpa
Gufa
Guna
Guru

Halo
Hanuman
Havan/homa
Henna
Hijra
Himalayas
Hindi Wallah
Hindu
Hindutva
Hinglish
Hiranyagarbha
Homilies

IAS
Indigo
Indus Valley civilization
Intuitive knowledge
Islam
Istadevata
Itihasa/history

Jains and jinas
Jajmani system
Jallianwala Bagh
Jodi
Joint family
Jyoti(r)lingas

Kabariwallahs
Kalamkari
Kalidasa
Kalpa
Karttikeya
Kashmir
Kathakali
Kautilya
Kerala
Khadi
Kirtan
Krsna... and krpa
Kumbh mela
Kumbh abishekam

Lakshmi
Language and attitudes of
    mind
Lok Sabha
Lotus

Magadha, Mithila,
    Madhubani and the
    Mauryas
Mahabharata
Maitri (Mitra, Mittra, Mithra)
Mala
Mangalsutra
Mantra
Manu
Mehndi
Miracles
Monsoon
Mudra
Mughal empire
Muhurram
Murti
Music
Muslims

Nada
Naga, Nagas
Names
Namaste/
    Namaskaram/Namaz
Narayana
Nastika
Nataraja
Nayan(m)ar
Neem
Nehru
Netaji
Nimbu Pani
NRIs
Numen

Om
Onam
Orthodoxy

Paan
Palimpsest
Panchayat
Pantheon
Paradox
Parsis

Philanthropy
Pilgrimage
Pollution
Population
Poverty
Prana
Premonition
Puja
Purusha/Prakriti
Putliwallahs
Pyjama

Quaternities
Quit India
Qutb Minar

Raga
Railways
Rajputs
Raksha Bandhan
Ramanuja
Ramayana
Ramazan (Ramadan)
Rangoli
Rasa
Ravana
Regional cultures
Rsi/Rishis
Rta/Rita

Sabha *et al*
Sacred thread
Sadhana
Saffron
Samadhi
Samskaras
Sanatana dharma
Sandalwood
Sandhya vandanam
Sannyasi (sadhu)
Sanskrit and
        Sankritization
Saptapadi
Saptarshi
Saraswati

Sari
Satchitananda
Satya
Satyagraha
Secular Society
Shaking the Head
Shal(a)bhanjika
Shiva–Shakti
Sikhs and sikhism
    (and khalsa)
Silk
South Indian Kingdoms
Spices
Sthita–pragnya/prajña
Subrahmanya
Sufis
Susvagatam
Swadeshi/swaraj
Swastika
Symbols

Tamil Culture
Tandoor
Tansen and Tyagaraja
Tantra
Tapasya
Tattva
Temple at Tirupati
Third Eye of Wisdom
Tilak
Tolerance
Touching the Feet
Trees
Tulsi

Unity in Diversity

Vac
Valmiki
Varanasi or Kashi
Varna
Vasishta
Vedas and Vedanta
Veena
Veerappan
Vibhuti

Vidyalaya
Village Guardians
Vishnu
Viswakarma
Viswamitra
Viswanath temple
Vrata

Women

Xenophobia
X-rated videos

Yajnavalkya
Yantra
Yoga
Yuga

Zero
Zimmi

■ **ABHAYAM** (n. *Sanskrit*)

As a term for that **fearlessness** just mentioned, **the moral courage** to 'stand up to be counted' runs as a deep and subtle concept much more capacious in intent than the single word implies. Daily affirmations to exercise this quality of will, acceptance of vilification from peers and the crowd when political correctness is the order of the day, even the energy to participate, to sit on a committee raising vital issues in the community, are all implied depending from whichever angle you are coming.

◆ And for Indians although the word itself may not even pass their lips it is encoded in the sense of all the early morning rites in the privacy of the home before the family shrine, enacted with devotion by the mother while placing a newly-plucked flower at the foot of the Deity, female or male.

◆ It is embedded in the stories grandparents or teachers will tell about Rama and Krishna in his shepherding mode (so like Christ addressing His flock in The Sermon on the Mount).

◆ It suffuses the *slokas*, chanted by heart in quatrains or couplets of Sanskrit during the more ritualistic daily temple rites.

When last in Ahmedabad at the end of 1996 my friend referred me to the **Bhagavad Gita,** which every day is read by millions of Indians as the **Bible** must similarly have served its devotional role in mediaeval Europe.

The first verses of chapter 16 depict Krishna as the serious Deity, mentor in a demanding intellectual debate with **Arjuna**, the noble warrior who is prevaricating about fighting the eternal war against those unrighteous forces (this time his greedy and arrogant cousins) that plagued not only Indian society in the Punjab several millennia before Christ, but are familiar to all of us across centuries, racial divides and cultural diversities (see **BHAGAVAD GITA** for its spiritual and practical content).

This time it is the symbolic battle of Kurukshetra–about to begin, but the **BHAGAVAN** Krishna as spiritual guide, has to instruct this eager and noble young man (whose name means *the shining one*) on how to discriminate between the impulse born in every personality to search for perfection and the obstacles every single one of us encounters in obstructing our reaching the goal–for the struggle is not only external, the warring history of this planet.

It is within each human that the battlefield lies.

The greatest epic ever conceived in world literature (refer to **MAHABHARATA** from now on identified as MahaB) succinctly points out in its approach to the **Kaurava v Pandava** struggle (Arjuna being one of five brothers in this clan, the 'goodies') that humanity is a mixture of both tendencies: 'Nothing is wholly good or wholly evil'.

And so in Sanskrit, the ancient language which is still widely used daily throughout the country, most especially in devotional worship, unlike Latin which has diminished in Christian liturgical use, the chapter begins:

abhayam sattvasamsuddhir
jñanayogavyavashitih

Krishna enumerates the qualities which men and women of all cultures and in all ages have sought to attain or been encouraged by social rules to maintain for the good of society as a whole.

'**Fearlessness**, purity of mind, wise apportionment of knowledge and concentration, charity, self-control and sacrifice, study of the scriptures, austerity and uprightness...' this was the Socratic resolution to defy the blandishments of his friends to flee Athens in the delayed wait in prison before the potion of hemlock was brought by the prison warder for him to drink.

Professor Sarvepalli Radhakrishnan translated and explained once: '**Abhayam is a temper of the mind, and not acceptance of belief, nor a practice of a rite.**'

Towards the end of the 19th century another great Indian who brought Hindu philosophy back into its rightful place in the global arena despite an Anglo-Saxon colonialism sitting heavily in alien might upon the Indian mind–**Swami Vivekananda** whose contribution is acknowledged under **ADVAITA** (also **BHAKTI, DARSHAN**) had this to say about the word's earliest usage.

Strength, strength is what the Upanishads speak to me from every page. This is the one great thing to remember, it has been the one great lesson I have been taught in my life, strength, it says, strength, O man, be not weak... stand up and be strong. Aye, it is the only literature in the world, where you find the word 'Abhih', 'fearless', used again and again; in no other scripture in the world is this adjective applied either to God or to man. ABHIH, FEARLESS!

He goes on to recount his vision of the great Emperor Alexander encountering a **SANNYASI** in the forest as he marched down into the plains of the Punjab in 325 BCE. 'Astonished at his wisdom' and with blandishments of gold and honours he attempted to take him back to Greece.

Impervious, the stark naked ascetic stood his ground. The Emperor then takes on a sterner countenance threatening to kill the sage if he does not come. The sannyasi only laughs in his face for how can that be? 'Who can kill me? Me you kill, emperor of the material world! Never!'

For I am the Spirit unborn and undecaying; never was I born and never do I die; I am the Infinite, the Omnipresent, the Omniscient; and you kill me, child that you are!

'That is strength, that is strength...' comments Vivekananda and the Upanishad texts as a whole, echoed in the Gita passage, Chapter 10, Verse 2:

This is the language of the greatest of Indian scriptures, the most demanding falling upon you, falling like a sword-blade, strong as the blows of a hammer they come.

At the end of the 1800s this was the stirring call to his demoralised Indian compatriots, to paraphrase Vivekananda's vast store of **Lectures from Colombo to Almora** (Advaita Ashram, 1956).

It is an ancient struggle of the inner self that takes Indians back to the **VEDAS**; Greeks back to the **Iliad**; Christians back to the parables of Christ and the forces of light in Milton's **Paradise Lost.** The fall of Satan, once an angel but corrupted by the insidious forces of darkness, the shadow side of life, lost souls continually at war with the 'shining ones', marks the constant need for alertness, character marked by compassion, freedom from covetousness and greed, for those who follow the Buddha's message of the golden mean, the middle path. Verses 2 and 3 of the Gita's chapter 16 enumerate Krishna's similar distinctions where gentleness, modesty and constancy of behaviour free from anger are the desired norm.

■ **ADVAITA** (n. *Sanskrit*)

literally means '**not two**', transposed into philosophic terms it is the Vedantic (end of the Vedas) theory encapsulated in the texts known as the Upanishads that holds the view = **DARSHAN** = that the divine, the creator, gods and goddesses, whatever **that** is termed, is an indivisible **ONE** of which all humans and consciousness is embedded. This is a major component in the systems of philosophy which make up the body of Indian thought (refer to **DARSHAN**) and is called non-dualism, the Sanskrit prefix negating **DVAITA** = another system which developed in later centuries, again to counteract the rarefied intellectual concepts–at cosmic level–which Adi Shankaracharya (born at the end of the eighth century CE and regarded as India's pre-eminent saint-thinker) developed in a comprehensive reform. He walked the length and breadth of the land to unite it through four spiritual centres. The sage's name means auspicious, also associated with Shiva, whose 108 names include **Sankara.** *Adi* = original or first, *Acharya* = preceptor or learned scholar.

> *Through sheer power of intellect he demolished a whole structure of error and bigotry. He reconciled many traditions by viewing them all from the height of ADVAITA, thus re-establishing the authority of the Vedas. Combining vast learning and relentless logic with a profound mystical experience of the unity of Being this Seer in his immortal commentaries... developed a system of ideas that shaped for good Hindu beliefs and attitudes and is now acclaimed as the peak of human thinking by philosophers the world over.*

(T M P Mahadevan for Founders of our Living Faith booklets, National Council of Educational Research and Training, New Delhi, 1970)

An Indian writing more humbly in **The Indian Down Under**, a monthly newspaper produced in Sydney for Australian-settled Indian **NRIs** (non-resident Indians) explained the terms in this way:

Dvaita–that God is elsewhere

Advaita–that the God is within us.

As I have said in the Foreword the word **God** hardly appears in this exploration of Indian viewpoints because it resonates with so many undertones and individual perceptions from Christian roots.

Unfortunately **advaita**–the term–comes alphabetically as one of the first stepping stones in a particularly rocky boulder-strewn pathway into India. It should really be one of the last! At least then the slow build up, even if they are personal interpretations, of the truths about India will have given some foundations to what many regard as highly abstruse metaphysics, not exactly the kind of conversational level one would have with friends over a beer and a barbecue at the end of a hot day in Australia! To mention **Advaita** would surely end all conversation, but India's turn of mind is more attuned to philosophical matters. I have had astonishing random conversations (sometimes even in halting English but also with the help of my Hindi teacher of the 50s) with supposedly 'illiterate' villagers–a Western term that totally denigrates the wisdom such people possess in an ancient but still very vibrant and robust **oral culture,** conversations that embrace a truly philosophical attitude, totally integrated with their peasant earthiness.

They are aware of cosmic thinking, the concepts rishis embedded in all cultural expressions whether by simple parable expounded through travelling bards (as in ancient Greece) and saint-musicians through the spider's web of pathways, pilgrimage routes, tree-shrine stands. Peasants gather of an evening after the physical labour of the day to mull over life in general. The stars, galaxies, forces beyond description are all part of that framework which we, the generation of the virtual reality electronic/celluloid epics, **Star Wars** and **Star Trek**, and the real Reality (a very Indian phrase) as seen and relayed back to our infinitesimally fragile blue and white bejewelled planet earth from Voyager II, and the Hubble telescope, are only just beginning to comprehend.

But our younger generations, breaking free of institutional religions and the orthodox framework of the Christian church, **are** moving into this philosophic arena–as are our own Western scientists, not only those of the 'pure' science of physics but microbiologists, neuroscientists, *et al*.

Half a century ago when first encountering India–the real Reality and not the theoretical framework of studying at the foot of the guru in Oxford–our Western views were still embedded in certainties–that 'one and only truth' syndrome. Scientists also disliked heresies as much as the theologians of old. If you questioned their theories on matter, creation, you could as a layperson be almost crucified for daring to scrutinise the prevailing wisdom. Today's existence all around us is a very different matter. Humility is creeping in. One often hears a famous scientist admitting on a TV documentary: 'we just don't know'. Such an equivalent Sanskrit phrase–**neti**, is examined in the section on the Upanishads. People (and not only the young) crowd into lecture theatres to listen to astrophysicists today who are surprised at the range of the lay public attending. Why are we here? What is out there?

Long before Shankaracharya, early Vedic thinkers, an eminent Tamil scholar Dr V Raghavan once explained in the old Madras (such a clean and garden city then), came to the conclusion that there was only one Reality trying to manifest itself, in a multitude of forms, the 'I-ness' of each individual and that individual's **ATMAN** (soul, spirit) in old terms, that particular genetic DNA imprint and consequent personality (in modern terms) all just part of a greater wholeness.

'An individual is constantly making an effort,' he went on, 'to unite this ego–I-ness–to the complete Reality. Through cause and effect, **KARMA**, we ultimately attain that goal through constantly making our own destiny.' He emphasised these last words. 'Absorption into Reality comes about by constantly building our own faith, shaping the future by our own efforts, our karma–dharma, not by another's direction or papal authority.'

This is the Law of Karma, as spelled out in the Gita... the purpose of human life is to realise this truth, to become united with this source of creative **energy**.

He startled me with the phrase **Thou art That: Tat (That) twam (you, thou) asi (are).**

As an inhabitant of a predominantly Christian but rapidly secularising civilization I was intellectually challenged. I was only at the beginning of stretching personal perspectives and perceptions that would accept that the God of my orthodox upbringing was not just a Father, 'Our Father which art in heaven...' but a Principle of Creation, whatever that Ultimate Impersonal Absolute is which the Upanishads refer to as Godhead, that is not only **out there** but **within us**, each atman inherently part of that **(paramount) paramatman.**

Quite often sages turn to parables to explain the obscure higher reaches that such deep thinkers who developed the Upanishads attempted to ascend–and did–according to the belief of many Indians not only today but in all the massive body of commentaries and spiritual disciplines that have followed. Human beings at ground level, however, in this reality clouded by maya find obscure semantics pass way over our heads. It is just as the biblical passage in Corinthians states:

For now we see through a glass darkly.

The way the Christian mind is conditioned from childhood there is a **dualistic view (dvaita**, almost the same spelling). The Bible separates out **The Father, Son and Holy Ghost**. The mystic vision fuses them all.

Purushottam Mavalankar laughingly chided me on the Western habit of always wanting to categorize everything:

You westerners have card-index minds. You always want to compartmentalise everything. Take a lesson from us. Indians I know love to confuse you by seeing everything as interlinked, as part of the whole but isn't that what your modern scientists are discovering...?

'Everyday when I set foot on the floor,' he continued, 'I say this prayer getting up from my bed:

Oh Lord who gives Energy to this world

who is the Creator

I bow to you

It is just a reminder that we are not alone in the world, *or not here for ourselves alone,'* he emphasised. 'By this prayer the thought is ingrained into my daily life that I am that, *Tat twam asi–Thou art That'.*

That phrase again. And how scientific, that impersonal pronoun. The Impersonal Absolute as it has come to be known.

Professor Radhakrishnan had spoken many times of this 'sense of unity that lies behind the manifold universe, the changeless truth behind all appearances, transcendent over all and immanent in all.' (see his introductory essay to **The Bhagavadgita**, Allen and Unwin, London, 1967).

However, it was an even greater shock as a nominal Christian half a century ago (as it is still to many brought up in this background even today) to follow Shankaracharya in his search to worship also at the foot of the Mother **Bhavani.**

Indeed ALL, even SHE is part of the ONE. **Advaita!**

Conclusion

Stumbling up the rocky pathway like Bunyan's Pilgrim, the vulnerable personal **atman** needs a staff in the ascent. This is the dualism stage of understanding, **dvaita**, in one's spiritual progress up the long hard road, a painful learning process for each individual in the sometimes daunting process of **samsara**, that recycling development of the soul through many reincarnations.

◆ Such aids are the many **ISTADEVATAS**, individually chosen forms or **MURTIS** representing the Ultimate One in particular aspects, depending on the different stages of understanding or enlightenment each individual has arrived at. They are to be found in the Hindu **PANTHEON**, or in a guru's teaching or a saint's flashes of intuitive insights expounded in soaring musical praise of the name–**nama.**

◆ These are but shrines on the route to give strength, renew energy in the struggle to understand. They are distinct (dvaita) but not separate from this Force. Division of territory between faith and reason (philosophy) is always at the end of the day (or the long night) fused by the Hindu sages into **The One–all part of the whole for the spiritually evolved advaitin,**

The same God whom the ignorant man saw outside nature (Dvaita), the same whom the little-knowing man saw as interpenetrating the universe (Vishishtadvaita) and the same whom the sage realises as his own Self, as the whole universe itself (Advaita) all are the ONE and the same BEING, the same entity seen from different standpoints...

The Complete Works of Swami Vivekananda, (Vol III, Advaita Ashram, Calcutta, 1960).

(refer to **ALVAR, BHAKTI, DARSHAN, RAMANUJA**).

Swami Vivekananda (1863–1902) believed like the philosopher of 600 years earlier, **Ramanuja**, and his own saintly contemporary mentor **Ramakrishna** that Divinity is indivisible and many all at the same time. He made history even at the height of colonial times by addressing the historic World Parliament of Religions in Chicago in 1893. He was sensationally successful in introducing the concept of **VEDANTA** embracing advaita–the perennial philosophy–of Hindu belief to a receptive Western world (refer to **DARSHAN** also) but there are many other great sages and saints who are as 'insightful' without subscribing to this advaitin intellectual metaphysic.

■ **AHIMSA** (n. *Sanskrit*)

Non-violence; the 'A' being a negating term as in Greek... agnostic, atheist, amoral, etc. It also means respect for life. This concept has always been part of the Hindu, Buddhist and Jain ascetic and philosophic tradition but has come into global prominence because of its use as a very potent **moral** weapon by Mahatma **Gandhi** in his **political** demonstrations against the might of the British Empire in India in the 30s (see **SATYAGRAHA**).

It does not just mean non-violence, refraining from causing hurt. The positive side is that it implies active love, by detaching from one's own negative feelings even the **desire** to cause hurt and trying not only to turn the other cheek, but actively to change the protagonist. Gandhi used to exhort his followers when fighting the British in order to bring independence to India: **Hate the deed but not the doer.**

■ **AKASHA** (n. *Sanskrit*) pr. *aakaash(a)*

is a fundamental concept in the Hindu view of humanity's place in the cosmos. It means **ether, the spatial entity of invisible 'matter'** = gaseous, protons, neutrons, etc, that scientific exploration continues to break down into infinitesimally smaller components through the amazing developments of nano-technology.

In the modern English-language press for daily use in India amongst an average readership where no emphatic scholarly signs are given and where several terms are becoming increasingly familiar to foreigners (raga in music, for instance) it appears as akasa, akasha, aakash, aakaas. In this text—once the emphasis is known to be on the first long ã–it will remain as akasha. It will appear many times and most dramatically at the very core of the sanctum sanctorum of the majestic south Indian temple, **CHIDAMBARAM** where that most famous and evocative icon, **NATARAJA**, represents the fundamental of principles of cosmic astrophysics in the form of the dancing Shiva, a shrine beside him dedicated entirely to the concept of ether.

■ **ALVAR** (n. *Tamil*) also pr. *aazhvaars*

poet-saints of south India who as followers of Vishnu address lyrical hymns to Rama and Krishna as avatars of this Deity (see **AVATARs**). From the 7th–8th century CE to the following mid-millennium they form part of the great upsurge of the **BHAKTI** movement alongside their spiritual compatriots the **NAYANMARS** who sang adorations of the Lord Siva.

Both played seminal roles in galvanising south Indian reforms and imbuing a profound sense of belonging to an ancient civilisation, cutting across caste and gender definitions and ritualistic 'apartness' even in the last millennium, bubbling up into the north, influencing those who were singing the devotional bhakti message there also.

Untouched physically by the later Islamic subjugation of the north, certainly very intense from the 11th-16th century, the southern Tamil sense of Hindu joyousness and affirmation of faith was so markedly expressed in the syncopation and gaiety of the musical forms of these singing saints (shorn of the melancholy wistful beauty of a northern raga) and amplified by the vigorous disciplines and astonishing intellectual glories of the dance.

1956

With my young children I took a heroic journey in June to the south to immerse ourselves not only in the lively hill station of Kodaikanal amongst ground-down Cambrian mountains far older than the Himalayas and contemporary with Western Australia's geology where I now live but in Dravidian culture so passionately espoused by the Tamil and Telugu peoples.

We were in a new pulsating atmosphere even if dripping with sweat despite 4–5 showers a day!

In the literature and poetry we discovered Tamilnadu's quite effervescent saints–12 famous **Alvars** whose outpourings are collected in what could be described as the Tamil prayer book–4,000 verses in the **Vaishnava Prabandham**; 63 Saivite saints including (the priest told us) four women–known as **Nayanmars** and fashioned in visual remembrance at the Kapalishwar temple at Mylapore which we first visited after that initial train journey (turn to **RAILWAYS**). Now renamed Chennai, other temple cities in its environs also depict in stone and bronze these wandering saint-singers, most especially at Chidambaram on the furthest wall behind the main shrine. A **DIKSHITAR,** a special category of priest needs to show the visitor from overseas.

In homage to the Divine these Tamil saints of both persuasions composed poetry, sang it in the temples where the inter-relatedness of all daily life converged–private worship from home shrine to the last evening **ARATI** (pr. aarti) before the shrine of the powerful goddess Meenakshi or of Nataraja, the Dancing Shiva; the market place and the hubbub of open stalls and wandering hawkers; the eating outlets sizzling in seductive aromas; the symbiotic relationship of the multitudinous art forms from the lovingly-woven heavy silk garden colours of saris to the resonating metallic penetration of cymbals, the expression of pulsating footwork stamping the echoing mandapa hall in honour of the Deity, while scholars, ordinary people searching for peace of mind and absorption into beatitude, and pupils listening to priestly chanting gathered into the lined shadows of pillars, slatted along the flagstone colonnades by the brilliant yellow sunshine.

In the general melee and murmuration, these inspired saintly poets spread their egalitarian messages in sonorous beauty appealing to high caste and low, breaking the barriers of hierarchies so predominant in the untouched brahmin traditions of the South.

The 12 earliest Alvars are still honoured in Karnataka, their birthdays are celebrated, their bronze statues are placed near Vishnu shrines. A king of Malabar (from present-day Kerala) is among them as also **Goda**, a saintly woman. The most famous named Alvar is **Nammalvar**, interestingly a peasant of the land, of lowly caste. **Andal** yet another woman is still prominent in special worship even today. Born at some time in the 10th century, a temple just off the secondary route from Madurai to the southernmost tip of the sub-continent at Kanyakumari, is dedicated to her image and that of **Rangamannar**, south Indian terminology for Krishna. This is at **Srivilliputtur** where legend asserts that she was discovered as a five-year old in the sacred **TULSI** garden by a Vaishnavite saint **Vishnuchittar**, who recognised a strange quality of spirituality about her and took her into his ashram. The house where they lived became the foundation for a temple constructed over 600 years ago.

She captured my imagination because the strange thing is that Andal's life (so suddenly ended when she was 15) could have mirrored that of **Hildegard of Bingen** born a century later (1098–1179) but half a world away in Europe. Although born into a noble family, she was the 10th child, termed a *tithe*, given to the church at birth–in those days the possibility of feeding so many children a moot point. Hildegard had extraordinary visions (now ascribed to the strange phenomena of migraine) which were transmitted to the world through her quite astonishing ability (despite little formal education) to create music which has suddenly exploded upon our global receptivity through 'world music'–if only Andal could also be lyrically translated who knows how we could all appreciate her as likewise Hildegard about whom 11 books have been published in the last decade!

◆ Andal despite her youth composed a body of devotional poems, the **Thiruppavi** far in advance both in spiritual and emotional awareness than expected in such tender years. These saint-poet-musicians composed verses extolling the Lord as a devotional lover suffusing grace as devout as any of the Christian mystics of mediaeval Europe. Andal herself longed 'to marry the Lord' as Hildegard also did. Perhaps in their joyous total surrender Alvars can be seen as the equivalent of the full-blooded community singing of Gospel psalms, praise-chanting to that great Creator. That the numenistic sense of a Divine Presence is addressed in the masculine is of no consequence in the Indian psyche; only a convention, for the biological reality of the female principle is also fully accepted. The **Devi Bhavani Shri** (or **Sri**) in the form of goddess **LAKSHMI** or Shakti, is as potent a force as the masculine representation (see especial note in **LAKSHMI**).

◆ By the 11th century more philosophic great souls systematised the intellectual and poetic literature of the Tamil-speaking peoples. Such a one was **RAMANUJA** (Vaishnavite philosopher mid 11–12th century CE, died 1137) in disagreement with his southern predecessors' strong sense of divinity **without attribute (nirguna)** the gigantic daunting IMPERSONAL ABSOLUTE, a physicist's dream world for research exploration of energy and zero, **sunya**. Ramanuja sensed that ordinary humans want warmth rather than staunch intellectual stretching on the unemotional rack of philosophical challenge, the virtual scientific rationality of the strict monism of **Advaita**–of pure intelligence, consciousness, which the truly 'realised' rishis, yogis, saints, prophets, ultimately reach, as personified in Shankaracharya.

The surge of Hindu reassertion from Buddhist and Jain austerity also placed Hindu personal devotion–**bhakti**–at centrestage. On the back foot for at least eight centuries, where it had retreated into formalised ritual, Hindu concepts burst forth again, catching fire throughout the south and being taken even farther north onto the Deccan plateau where the Kannada-speaking saints of the Karnataka in full tide swept the message of hope and grace into Maharashtra.

◆ Even later reforming saints arose there in the 13th–17th centuries in a great swell of loving devotion seeking grace. Jnaniswara (The Deity of Wisdom), **Namadeva** (The Name of God), **Eknath** (The One Lord), **Tukaram** (a low caste **sudra**) and **Ramdas**, the humble cobbler sufficiently saintly to be revered by brahmins. **Janabai**, a woman and maidservant, and **Sena**, a lowly barber were also cult figures and composers of hymns. Vishnu is worshipped by them as the lyrical **Krishna**–spiritual lover.

◆ Strangest of all must surely be the story as told to me finally after 40 years of searching for **Vithoba** whose temple at Pandharpur lay, we were told, across our journeyings through Maharashtra. Confusingly encountered by our family foolishly optimistic that we could travel fast by road on top of the open world of the Deccan plateau from Bangalore to Bombay (of old) to catch the Frontier Mail night train to the north, the legend has become so real (in the material terms of this world in time and space) that today's pilgrimage to the saint's shrine (or so I thought) at Pandharpur on the Chandrabhaga river draws vast crowds. Walking the land in **padayatra** singing praise-songs to **Lord Vithoba** is a major part of the Bhakti movement today (see **PILGRIMAGE**).

Pandharpur became a hallowed gathering place, giving inspiration to a tradition of education and preaching of universal brotherhood. People such as Tukaram, Eknath and Namadeva braved persecution, crusading against inequalities and injustice while engaging with these pilgrims (see **BHAKTI, JYOTIRLINGA** and **REGIONAL CULTURES**–Maharashtra for the Pandharpur encounter).

Who was Vithoba? Was he an alvar saint-poet, a legendary devotional pilgrim? I had been shown the embossed silver **Padukas** (moulded like the wooden sandals Gandhi wore with one peg to anchor the big toe). The eager crowd kept shouting '**vasudeva**' as they were carried in a palki, each village group or community with its own. Now were they stand-ins for the deity? It took a lifetime to learn the intricacies of the Indian matrix, that mind enmeshed in a 'multiverse' long before the Western physicist planted this notion-theory in our common vocabulary encouraged by Stephen Hawking's popular books breaking the mould of old assumptions of a single universe–until now.

Such is that unique Indian vision that sacred image of wandering saints and great deity fuse and interrelate. **Krishna** (Vasudeva his 14th name) as Indweller, icon of Vishnu–and Vithala merge, and are called affectionately **Vithoba** by the singing **Varkaris** (pilgrim participators in this, their annual test of strength and faith).

I had a good deal to learn, swallowed as I was beginning to be, in this matrix!

◆ Acclaimed musicians such as **Purandaradasa (1480–1564 CE)** are also acknowledged as Vishnu followers, his music being very important to the Carnatic music tradition.

Conclusion

Alvars (and Nayanmars alike), women saints as well as men, are honoured right now, their images carried in processions and birthdays marked at joyous and lively festivals throughout the southern states, their **bhajans** or **kritis** (song poems) rendered to the **ISTADEVATA** in home puja. In some ways they could be described as secondary incarnations of the Deity so saintly is their reputation as well as the unique way some died while in a state of samadhi, deep meditation, knowing the precise time of their *shuffling off this mortal coil*–an intriguing **HINGLISH** phrase for death. Their messages soar in poetic imagery, sung in far-flung places, now translated beyond Indian shores into the universal.

■ ANAND

Joy, bliss, a sense of beatitude. It is *not* the outward show from ritual worship, etc, that counts in the soul's development during the progression towards release but the inner **heart**, that individual care for integrity which brings contentment and release... the **Indian psychology of bliss = anand.**

■ ARATI (n. *Sanskrit*) pr. *aarati*

The actual ritual worship at home and temple in the clockwise circling of flame in the lamps before the shrine and the Deity.

Indians are aware that **'lighting the lamp'** at prayer holds an inner meaning–**'illumination of the mind'**. As the equivalent of the human eye on the external world so the flame represents 'the inner eye' leading the ignorant, bound by short-sighted ego constraints, towards the liberating **marg** or way.

In many a home as dusk falls, in those fleeting moments between hazy daylight and velvet-smooth dusk, flickering oil lamps, *deepas*, are still carried in the hand through the darkening rooms to light the oiled wick in the niche where the Deity presides... **Istadevata,** that particular representation of the **ONE** preferred by a householder or individual**.** The flames replace the effulgence recalled every morning in the one real mantra to be chanted, **GAYATRI,** acknowledging the life-giving rays of Savitar–the Sun. A gentle cadence, a flowing song is sung, or temple nadaswarams crack the air, and gentle flutes bid goodnight to the Deity. From the flame blessing is taken by those present, hands as prayerful as Dürer's famous etching; a quick gesture wipes the flame over head and face, taking the evil off the head of those who worship, giving thanks for planetary blessings, gift from the galaxy where the sun centres our universe with its flaming creative energy.

■ ARDHANARISWARA (n. *Sanskrit*)
ardha = half
nar = man *nari* = woman
iswara = divinity

A truly remarkable artistic imagery in the Hindu acceptance of biological truth in conceiving the supreme energy, essence (or whatever the Absolute may be called) as half male, half female depicted as such in many visual forms of Indian art, folk as well as urban temple sculpture and bronze carvings. Conceptualisation also includes the Shiva/Shakti union or the upright phallic lingam set in the flat womb yoni with birth canal. In temple rituals such a shrine will be bathed daily with holy water, milk or ghee and marigold flowers with little thought for sexual implications which seriously disturbed Victorian missionaries on encountering such rituals, the liquid running along the canal slope graphically to be taken in the right palm onto the head as blessing.

■ ARRANGED MARRIAGES and OTHER MATRIMONIAL MATTERS

Take any leading English-language newspaper on a Sunday and spend an informative but frustrating hour (not because you won't find a spouse but because you won't understand the adverts!) in reading the matrimonial columns page after page. They need decoding, such is the variation in regional clues, **CASTE**, gotra, sapinda, acronym, salary and profession.

Although there are few statistics, it is generally accepted that most of India's population still arranges its marriages–alliances of families first and foremost rather than individual romances, and this is one way of effectively doing so.

Even though the English-language newspapers reflect only middle-class India, a vast proportion of the population who neither read nor write and therefore do not turn even to the regional language press, nevertheless if immediate family and trusted friends or the traditional matchmaker–a paid professional (a very bossy woman appears in Indian TV sitcoms as well as in a Western documentary) doing a search–are not successful in finding the right person for daughter or son, increasingly these people are using video and the internet. Someone will read for them! Even that traditional matchmaker has gone frighteningly professional. Seen on Mumbai TV this epitome of the large bag-lady with the wobbly-head and cheshire-cat smile available in emporiums for tourists where classic caricatures of Indian 'types' are replacing the Bharata Natyam dancers who enticingly wobble their jointed sections, this formidable personage has gone public rather than working quietly behind the scenes at the behest of the family sending messages to other families via the other traditional go-between, the village barber. But now TV is bypassing them all. As community TV firmly establishes a receiving dish in each village wonderfully scripted 'sitcom' serials take over accompanied by the hilarious laughter of Indians laughing at themselves.

Now professionalised, the arbiter sits on a dais presiding over the throng, men and women lined up either side of a bleak hall, seeking partners, sadly only able to choose in front of a voyeuristic crowd.

◆ Modern technology is even more sophisticated in catching up with finding that elusive soulmate. Women's magazines both in English and regional languages, directed mainly to the upper-middle class professional woman appear to encourage her to branch out into very carefully monitored **computer matchmakers.**

One such agency, under the management of a retired mariner captain (to give it respectability) sifts through personal looks, character, family background, short video clips; people are given phone numbers once the computer permeates through all the indices of compatibility. Here is territory beyond the boundaries of family alliances–the new dispensation–Western style individuality for 1% of the population... very little different from a new phenomenon in Western community newspapers and internet adverts seeking 'soulmates', unable ironically to find the appropriate 'match' in their nowadays mobile and rootless urban neighbourhoods.

◆ Increasingly, speciality magazines are supplying a service, advertising the fact that they are published in numerous editions, reaching lakhs (100,000 = 1 lakh), people who are out there searching for that perfect soulmate every bit as eager as the Mills and Boon readership yearn to replicate in their real lives what they read in the **billions** of pages of Barbara Cartland's novels.

New mobility and economic forces change the search conditions

◆ Even for nonliterate villagers life and work is becoming so mobile and change is so rapid, family confabulations are not working.

The drift to the city throws up all kinds of influences, family fractures, and chance meetings challenging the tightly-bound networks of old. In Kerala, for instance, it is not only professional brahmin upper and middle-class who are mobile and to be found increasingly in pockets of Australia, Canada and the USA, but also building construction labourers once of the lowest caste–now extremely wealthy–as well as technicians and other 'hands on' labourers who have moved in very large numbers to Gulf Arab countries. They have done the dangerous labouring jobs of creating the modern high-rise buildings in Kuwait and the United Arab Emirates; some have come back wealthy, disoriented, building extraordinary painted concrete blocks for homes amid the aesthetically pleasing traditional stone and brick homes embedded in the sun-flecked palm groves of Kerala. The traditional lines of inquiry which fanned out at caste level to settle a marriage arrangement are now in disarray.

◆ In addition such is the diaspora of Indians overseas (the **NRIs**) who may not have efficient networks or large enough communities in the USA, the UK, Europe, Australia or Canada in which to find that elusive partner that advertising is a useful arm in the search:

Decent marriage but no dowry bride. Should be beautiful, fair/charming/convented because she will find it easier to adjust in Germany, age between 26–27 years and very good family.

because as that Box Number family states:

We are very old established Brahmin family in Lucknow. Son very fair 1961/183/ Medicine working in UK. Soliciting urgent replies with full details and photo which will be treated with utmost discretion. Early ceremony wished...

◆ And there begins the momentary pause, the query. Why? Does the reading of his janampatra horoscope, the scrolls that can unroll to the length of the room with the life-map in intricate zodiacal sections and coded signs, indicate that something had better be done soon? Or what other factors come in to play when he was born in 1961 and is now 183 centimetres tall?

Natural human curiosity makes the visitor wish for a code to unravel all the clues! It is intriguing to discover that even Indians cannot explain the indicators beyond their own community columns. Regional caste, religious customs differ so widely that even if certain main criteria apply across the board, others are very particular to a certain group. Reference to a **'pooradam-star'** in a Tamil advert of a brahmin family is still a mystery until I meet the right category of brahmin, there being many criteria to measure birth influences by–not only the 12 zodiacal signs–but according to Hindu reckoning 27 specific stars per lunar month moving into dominant 'pulls' on the specific zodiacal position (explained in detail in **Dr S R N Murthy's** scientifically researched **Vedic View of the Earth**, Reconstructing Indian History and Culture Series, No. 14, D K Printworld, New Delhi, 1997). A diagram of the four lunar mansions and 27 influential stars may decode some adverts–but it raises more questions than it answers! (Turn to **ASTROLOGY** for illustration.)

◆ On one page alone in which approximately 150 families were engaged in this vital search, columns were sub-divided not only into all the major regional/linguistic communities but also under headings such as Finance/Banking; Government/ Defence; Hotel/Shipping/Airline; MBAs, IAS–ICWAS; Doctors; NRI–Green Card (a very important consideration for being able to work in the USA and bring in a double-income as a future spouse). That issue boasted 2,497 entries!

There are also the major religious columns of Hindu, Christian, Muslim families, subdivided down into Andhraite, Kannadiga, Marwaris, Khatris/Aroras; Mangalik, Kulalar Telugu, Velanadu Vaidiki, Scheduled Caste/Scheduled Tribe and occasionally, a sign of the times, Cosmopolitan:

European, 42 (looks 32), successful, good-looking, international aid professional seeks well educated, dark beauty, 20s/30s, who shares interest in nature, environment, travel, fashion, books. Must be French speaker or quick learner, and prepared to live between India or Mauritius and France. Direct correspondence only please.

Times are indeed 'a changin'!

In the 50s such an entry in the columns would have been inconceivable, as also those words incorporated into the paragraph, now even designated to a specific section, **Caste no bar.**

In my lifetime those three words map the changing attitudes of India. On the last visit, of approximately 150 matrimonials on a page, two-thirds carried that message. Other phrases also have crept in as indicators of social change and quite dramatic ones over what is now half a century of the new freedom **to be Indian.**

◆ caste/religion no hindrance
◆ divorcee (without children)
◆ issueless widow

- innocent divorced male; innocent divorcee
- wanted–smart educated ladies preferably with foreign citizenship

The Indian male is shifting his appeal also, no longer chauvinistically assuming he is everyone's Krishna! He advertises himself in many self-accolading phrases!

- Broad-minded, kind, gentle, moral life partner
- God-fearing (this self-description is appearing more and more reflecting the necessities of this **kaliyuga**-dark age).
- Sociologically there are desirable Gulf-returned executives
- Now not only caste, but religion, community, language, place are no bar also.

These categories have emerged to shape a new bride and bridegroom who this time at least will meet with some idea of what to expect, unlike only a few decades ago when many never cast eyes upon each other until the marriage ceremony... and every male preference was for a 'very beautiful pale-skinned or wheaten complexion girl of sweet, adjusting nature.' (see **ARYA–ARYAN** and **VARNA**–no matter socio-political polemics among a new generation of scholars the public appear still enamoured of fair-skinned daughters-in-law). Deep in the Indian psyche there is little difference in racial attitudes and prejudices than in Northern cultures. However, other dramatic changes are beginning to creep into the advert columns. 'Aryan' still resonates under the skin.

And yet there is still ambivalence deep down about the future of marriage (undergoing such rapid change as it is); the pressures on children in the future; the position of the woman; the new daughter-in-law; and with all the horror of bride-burning, a new phenomenon and a reflection of the unleashed greed of the last two decades which has with economic liberalisation increased its demands–dowry. Accelerated change unexpectedly crashes like a gigantic wave over all sections of Indian society whether rural or urban (see relevant section **DOWRY** and **FILLUMS** and their influence).

- In the light of the fundamental social shifts sweeping in with even greater rapidity as the millennium passed into history it seems hard to recall that in the early 50s orthodox Hindu women from very traditional backgrounds vociferously demonstrated outside Parliament in New Delhi against changes proposed in the new **Hindu Code Bill**. This was intended, after much deliberation, to adjust ancient laws on marriage, inheritance, the very heart of a society's functioning, enshrined in the **Dharma Sutras** or **Vedic Laws** to the prevailing needs under modern conditions. Such had not been undertaken in centuries due to alien structures such as rule from Islamic and European/British power.

I stood myself watching elderly matrons brandishing black umbrellas shouting their heads off at Congresswallahs trying to calm them down as they stormed into the Lok Sabha, Parliament's House of the People. Police and a few military were called to threaten them with arrest, a totally new situation for Indian male police–very few women having then been recruited. For these women what they knew, the framework in which they had grown up was a stable quantity; better the known than the unknown.

Women's magazines as published now were hardly known. **Shakuntala Rao Shastri**, editor of a well-known Bengali periodical **Mukul** and a double MA (in Sanskrit as well as English) from Calcutta University (with a further degree from Oxford) produced a quite enlightening book **Women in The Sacred Laws** (Bharata Vidya Bhavan, New Delhi, 1953) encouraged by an eminent leader, K M Munshi, many Indian men having given their women-folk reforming support. The intent of this series of books was typical of this period–of re-examining roots, retrieving knowledge which had nearly been lost under colonial disinterest and carried by recitations in oral culture. The actual words and their deeper meaning were hardly understood at all, being in Sanskrit like the marriage ceremony itself. New life needed to be infused in the rituals which were frozen like fossils in amber.

Indian women friends at the time were delighted because in the book and in the publicity given to the impassioned controversy of the Hindu Code Bill which eventually passed through Parliament, **Manu**, the towering law maker of the Samhita, of indeterminate historical age being referred to in Vedic texts but now believed to be contemporary with the fixing of the **MAHABHARATA** in written form got a drubbing. Manu is regarded in Hindu Vedic tradition as the **progenitor** of the present race of humans, having like Noah been saved in the deluge after the last Ice Age when the waters melted creating the Flood. His **Manusmrti** is the fundamental building block of Hindu law (**smrti** = empirical knowledge as opposed to **sruti**–divine revelation).

- Letters to the Editor at the time expressed these feelings: 'He needed his head examining like Rama does in questioning Sita's virtue! Why is it women always have to prove their virtue, not men? Manu did to Hindu culture what St Paul did to Christianity, he put women in chains.'

However, Dr Shastri did point out that in the foundations of Indian culture the attitudes were far more enlightened:

> ... laws of ancient India were so catholic in spirit and all-embracing, if they were taken in their true spirit they can cover the entire needs of humanity. At the time when these laws were framed, no country in the world produced better laws for womanhood, nor gave a higher status to women in society.

Conclusion

Even in modern families no matter how the marriage comes about the 'flavour', the ambience of Indian family life, is still based on the inherent qualities handed down generation by generation rather than the free-for-all alarming individuality of the total nuclear component in Western nations. A tropical climate may well have something to do with a sub-conscious concern with pollution and pure blood lines. Agni–fire, cleansing rituals, foetid air, sexual promiscuity fears, suppuration, all loom large.

A woman deep down is regarded in that ancient imagery as 'the vessel, which contains the curds of sacrifice'. Modern women may find that a heavy burden to carry as they breathe a new freedom of work in the professional world outside the house. At that level a feminist movement is growing and stating its case but it speaks responsibly and without the stridency of the West. It speaks with its own cultural voice and poses a question that many young Indian men face with ambivalence because within the family the son has been much honoured, and often spoiled by the mother in his upbringing.

'I find it very hard,' wrote one young wife, working equally hard in her profession in Kolkata as a film maker, 'to carry all this weight of purity. If only we could pass some of it over to mankind. Beyond legalities there is such a spiritual meaning for our fathers in the gift of the daughter–kanya DAAN'. (daan–donation)

Pollution, blood menstruating, fertility, that essence of woman that men fear in all societies, Shakti. Power of feminine energy. Hindu thinkers acknowledged it theoretically, intellectually–but emotionally?... There is the eternal question, across cultures in fact it is so deep a psychological fear of the power of woman that men, patriarchies, have had to regulate women throughout history–not themselves...

Another professionally-employed woman summed up the dilemma thus:

The **SHARAM**, the shame of the family, and the
obverse side appears always to rest on us, the
daughters, who then becomes the insecure, put upon
daughter-in-law, eventually the honoured mother.

[another word for sharam = *Lajja*]

As the new millennium establishes itself so does the influence of electronic technology. Indian knowhow in this arena of IT, WEB and text messages on mobile phones is creating a revolution in relationships undreamed of only a decade ago.

SMS (Short Messaging Service) arrived in 2002 bypassing prying eyes. The small screen on mobile handsets has established an anonymous channel of communication–and secret relationships... the mobile tool a 'courtship tool'. Research 'India Today' cover story October 14, 2002 and discover the provocative messages being sent out certainly across urban India—electronic courtships whether extramarital, flirtatious or deliberately provocative:

My mst ergnus zones are a
cktail of snsoy & d tactile
d brsh of lips over lng,
wet folds, deep prbing
xtasies & silences.

George Bernard Shaw, passionate promoter of a phonetic vocabulary, turn over in your grave!

Shobha De's Spouse is a must, hard-hitting, perceptive of modern dilemmas and imbued with commonsense. (Penguin, India, 2005).

■ **ARUL** (n. *Tamil* = grace; n. *Sanskrit* = **KRIPA**)

Some Western religious commentators disallow the **state of grace** to be a component for Hindus on the progressive path (or marg) to salvation.

The intervention of divinity in the sense of Christ 'coming down', God made man, to save sinners has not actually occurred if one considers Hinduism as a religion rather than a spiritual way of life. Hindus (and Sikhs) disagree in this interpretation. In the Bhagavad Gita, Krishna becomes that sense of divine:

I am the beginning, the life span and the end.

In the personal devotion, a direct almost mystical communication exists with the spirit of the Divine. This can occur through direct relationship with the chosen form of a particular deity representing a particular facet of the immense totality of Deity, or in deep meditation or the joyous uplift of community singing of the name of the Deity.

States of grace can hurry the process along if one believes in the transmigration of souls, a perpetual wheel it would appear to the uninitiated, or regeneration until the perfect state of 'realisation' is reached for the believer.

■ **ARYA–ARYAN** (n. *Sanskrit,* implies nobility of character)

As an adjective **arya** implies a quality of advancement to a higher level of all kinds of entities, not just human beings.

According to a book only published in the last decade, **Vedic Aryans and the Origins of Civilization–A Literary and Scientific Perspective** by **Navaratna Rajaram** and **David Frawley**, (Voice of India, New Delhi, 2001) in their reassessment as Sanskritists first and foremost of the foundation of India's history and society, there is this explanation of both terms:

Arya goes all the way back to the **RIG VEDA** wherein it
occurs thirty six times, generally as an adjective. It
never occurs as the name of a people but occurs as a
certain type of character or behaviour in people but
not a race... ARYAN is the evolved state of things which
derives from the Divine Word (Brahman). As such a
beautiful tree is Aryan, the order of the cosmos is
Aryan, the Aryan laws (Aryavrata) are the noble
spiritual laws that govern the universe. Aryan is not an
adjective that can be applied to a type of people only
but can be used for anything that reflects a higher
law...

Even in Radhakrishnan's 1956 edition of **The Bhagavadgita** the first page of Chapter II footnotes the Sanskrit word of Verse 2: **anaryajustam asvargyam**. The meaning implied: 'It is unknown to men of noble mind (not cherished by the Aryans)', that is not leading to heaven (svarg). He adds: 'the Aryans, it is contended by some, are those who accept a particular type of inward culture and social practice which insists on courage and courtesy, nobility and straight dealing'–qualities increasingly yearned for by electorates in democratic societies worldwide today!

So where have all the Aryans gone? Where did they come from? Where did they go?

Elusive as ever they appear once again to be a matter of conjecture! Like the 60s song–where have all the flowers gone–they are blown everywhere from Finland to Fatehpur Sikri.

Imagine the shock as I stand on this initial jagged stepping stone, at one time a stable slab of granite, now turned upside down and very wobbly! And, to boot, shifted around from east to west! These Aryans, so designated to distinguish them from those who have lapsed from law-abiding society, good citizens all were not a nomadic peoples out of the steppes of Russia as I had been led to believe for the last 50 years (hence so many Russian scholars also engaged in these linguistic/historical studies and a psychological reason for a rapport with India that John Foster Dulles perhaps never considered in the Cold War atmosphere of the 50s). If they did migrate at all it was from their original home in the Saraswati/Indus valley of northwestern India. If anything, they climbed up the formidable mountain passes into Afghanistan, old Persia, the Caucasus into Russia and beyond.

Reassessment: first arrival in New Delhi (and one needs to recall the euphoria then of the immediate post-freedom atmosphere when hardly anything was being questioned, Indians only too happy to embrace the reality of the day) and I began to delve into India's history. **Aryans** were a race of people, dominant, technologically advanced despite being nomadic, a bow-and-arrow, chariot-riding people. If the beginnings of India's history remained clothed in mystery then it still does even today! All one read (and still does) in many books was an approximate date when Harappa, Taxila, Mohenjo-Daro were thriving cities–approximately 4,500 years ago.

◆ The Aryans, this homogeneous race with an advanced language and a cosmic view of the universe overran a darker-skinned, Dravidian race and is the raison d'être for what now are the amazing brick-built advanced cities and harbours re-emerging from the arid soils that have so well preserved them archaeologically for us to puzzle about **their** inhabitants today.

The date according to this prevailing wisdom then was set at approximately **2500–1800 BCE**.

Archaic history: The literary culture of this period was expressed in the chanted quatrains of the **VEDAS**, which millennia later were finally written into books. These echoed the legends (or real history, no one too sure) of the warrior god Indra's metaphoric victory over the evil forces, the **dasyus**, darker-skinned, perhaps Dravidian or the original Neolithic tribal people. These were slowly marginalised and pushed to the perimeters of what eventually became a thriving urban civilization of petty kingdoms, flexing their muscles against each other all along the Gangetic basin.

Revolutionary thinking: All these theories are now turned upside down! The Aryans, not a race at all but a like-minded cultural group designated as such in the Vedas, personified the noble qualities of this word Arya eulogising an indigenous peoples who existed from time immemorial in the northern regions of the Saraswati/Indus basin. Like much of humanity elsewhere they probably migrated out, moving ever westward taking their distinctive culture, emblems and symbols (turn to **SWASTIKA**) and above all, language, out of Aryavrata into middle Asia and thence into Europe. Just the opposite of everything we ever learned!

In addition the **DRAVIDIAN** people are subsumed into the general Aryan fold due to a considerable shift in datings (see later), Dravida being regarded now as a purely geographical designation for those groupings now settled in the south–Tamil, Marathi, Telugu and Kannada-speaking. They too are not a distinct Dravidian race as previously accepted, according to this new thinking.

The Indus Valley script long guessed to reflect this earlier Dravidian race before its collapse and amazing disappearance under sand, rubble, and ruined cities, is now thought to be closer to Sanskrit, the foundation of the Aryan Vedic culture as it advanced to the sophisticated level of the Upanishad and Epics (Puranas).

The case for reassessment of all the previous data, which led to this entire sociological construct has come about from many quarters.

◆ A new generation of younger Indians at home and abroad, trained in a broad range of scientific disciplines other than linguistic studies, which had previously dominated.

◆ Since the still-acknowledged Max Müller (German scholar who lived in Britain) put Sanskrit on the map in Europe in the mid-1800s, the advanced technology of today has initiated this reassessment.

◆ The speeding up of computer dating and cross-cultural comparison between Egyptian, Sumerian and Indus Valley societies and explosion of new astronomical data is part of the new equation. Satellite photography uncovering previously unknown archaeological data and cross-referencing with computational outcomes also contribute new facts.

◆ The publication of Max Müller's correspondence to show how Aryan was constructed as a race (see **N S Rajaram's The Politics of History**, Voice of India, New Delhi, 1995).

As a result, a chronology which had previously been engraved in stone now faces radical adjustment and if the research continues to be backed up by hard evidence then most of the information given to travellers about earlier Indian history coming from the great body of written material up until a decade ago will be totally out of date. Already Vedic civilization interlinked with the datings of the collapse of the Indus Valley site and its 'invasion' have to be totally changed. A chart in the Rajaram/Frawley book readjusts a whole number of categories–not only the history of the Early Vedic culture to at least **4000 BCE** but Indian kings, compilers of texts in the literature and geological events.

This latter is crucial since it is the basis of much of the radical new thinking which is corroborated from a geological source I would have thought beyond question.

◆ **Dr S R N Murthy**, retired Director of the Geological Survey of India in his book **Vedic View of the Earth** published only years after the Rajaram/Frawley radical research proposition not only projects an even earlier emergence of Aryans in the Siwalik hill ranges (the footstool so-to-speak to the massive ranges of the Himalayas beyond the Jammu/Himachal Pradesh regions) as direct descendants of a 'Europoidal race' descended in turn from earlier nomadic cave-dwellers (Ramapithecus) and even early higher apes, well-preserved remains of which have been found in this 20 million-year old range. That would stir the Africanists and Richard Leakey no end!

But for me it is even more rewarding to find that research in satellite photography confirms the existence of the **Saraswati river basin**–once a formidable riverine irrigating system larger than the Ganga, so much so that Saraswati was eulogised so highly in the Vedas that she was over time (as happens in India) elevated to the status of Brahma's consort–as Goddess of Learning and the Arts. For so long a supposed mythological river said to flow again at the sangam (juncture) of the rivers Jumna and Ganga at the 12-year renewal of the **KUMBH MELA** (see **KUMBH**) where I had been at its first dramatic and tragic re-affirmation in 1954, near Allahabad, now Saraswati has emerged out of the shadows of what is seen as the reason for the downfall of Harappa, Taxila and Mohenjo-Daro advanced city civilizations. And this is the great drought–of several hundred years! This is now noted in Egyptian records as a slow attrition climatically all across the middle east affecting centres of urbanisation like Ur of the Chaldees in Mesopotamia (today's Iraq).

♦ It is always good to find myths justifying their existence. As a believer in the accuracy of oral history (I always warmed to Charlie Chaplin's sudden response to a question on this, that 'myth was a pinpoint of truth') many events in latter decades due to wide-ranging technological advances have proved the ancient history of Dwarka, Krishna's city in western Gujarat as well as the city, Heraklelon, under the sea off Egypt, by a French archaeological team in 2000 CE. It had been totally submerged in an earthquake over a thousand years ago.

Myth, Reality and Datings: I find datings in my lifetime have undergone such dramatic backward flips that the myths originally supporting a tenuous earlier story have indeed come true. That Vedic civilization may be pushed further back in time is not at all disturbing no matter the upset to long-established historical theory and power centres within universities. After all, the physical sciences are facing such upheavals intellectually from new heretical thinking all the time. I have never understood the reluctance of white European academics to accept anything unless empirically tested, thus refusing to accept the validity of oral history. A telling example–since arriving in Australia in 1976 and becoming involved with Aboriginal artistic culture through the pioneering Indian Ocean Arts Festivals I first learnt of 40,000 years of Aboriginal history, a continuum as consistent as India's. Now, due to the palaeontological finds of bones, skulls and artefacts, that dating has been pushed back to 80,000 years and, controversially, at the base of rock art overhangs in the Northern Territory, to 120,000 years. Thermoluminescent tests have yet to confirm this latter dramatic speculation.

♦ And on the Indian scene the **Bhimbetka rock shelters** (see **CAVES**) and **galleries** were not even a rumour on the art scene when linguistic researchers were at work in the 19th century nor when we drove in the adventuresome 50s to Bhopal and Sanchi. Just 40 km south of Bhopal in Madhya Pradesh they only emerged out of thornbush and jungle vine in the 1970s, consequently establishing evidence of an advanced Middle Stone Age Culture approximately 10,000 BCE as the Great Ice Age began to melt down. The lively paintings equal to those in Spain and France and South Africa show in natural-coloured murals considerable evidence of iron work in use in energetic hunting scenes, machetes, bows and arrows and long spears flourishing in the hunt of buffaloes, deer prancing, elephants being ridden. Riders rein in horses on their flattened cars (a painting device to overcome lack of perspective techniques, two-dimensional-depiction not being fully understood).

And this is for real, contemporary with the now emerging Saraswati civilization of the gigantic riverine area of the north.

New Publications: Booklists of just three New Delhi publishing houses are indicative of the widespread intellectual activity of a younger generation of Indian writers and scholars of diverse professional backgrounds intent on going back to primary sources–which incidentally entails knowing your Sanskrit to examine the Vedic texts which contain the clues to India's origins. The names of these publishers incidentally speak for themselves–**Voice of India, D K Printworld's Reconstructing Indian History and Culture, Aditya Prakashan** = adityas, sun deities–imperishable, their essence, the constancy of celestial luminescence in a scientific sense; and **prakashan** = publication. Armed as they are now with the new technologies mentioned earlier, they also seem to be more street-wise in dealing with the traditional eurocentric bias (even amongst earlier Indian academics) where in-built cultural assumptions of the late 19th–early 20th century conditioned the linguistic thinking of the time, according to some of the new authors.

Even **Dr J P Mallory**, of the earlier school of research who rounded up many of the disciplines (language, archaeology and even myth in his wide-ranging survey **In Search of the Indo-Europeans** (Thames and Hudson, London, 1989) is cautious on matters of race which had become a favourite theory with the rise of anthropology in the 19th century. It was also easily confused with **ethnic group**. **Nation** also became an important political concept with the advance of Bismarck's theories on nation-states and their autonomy at the same time. The idea of a state as an actor in its own right in relation to other states developed in the late 17th century after the Treaty of Westphalia (1648). In 1871 Bismarck merged 300 minor states under Prussian supremacy into modern Germany. Max Müller was part of this social environment.

♦ The Aryan Myth, Mallory writes 'influenced numerous intellectual currents of which the development of European linguistics was but one, **Leon Poliakov** (The Aryan Myth, London, 1974) has shown that the roots of this caricature reach back into 'near-universal longing of the peoples of Europe to secure for themselves an illustrious ancestry'. This new academic thrust was fuelled in Europe. There were religious motives as well, the strong reform Protestant movements, wishing to sever ties with Hebrew language studies and the Old Testament. If a link could be found with Indian and Iranian literature then ancestry more illustrious could be traced to an even more ancient ancestral fair-skinned blue-eyed race! Indeed, a misappropriation of linguistic research gave rise to racial prejudices, which ultimately led to the extremist horrors of Nazi Germany.

In a post-colonial world eurocentric notions of history and those angled perspectives are being churned up.

Yet another book re-examining in a more dispassionate way amid all the ruffled academic egos, the possibility of many sources of Indian civilization, **The Quest for the Origins of Vedic Culture** even if it is by yet another firangi, **Edwin Arnold** (OUP, Oxford, 2000) is worth reading, and also **The Saraswati Flows** by **B B Lal** (Aryan Books, Delhi, 2002).

Personal footnote: Twenty years on in Australia I have seen dramatic change in Aboriginal attitudes–from a gentle passivity amongst the parental generation who remember the heavy hand of colonial subjugation, to the quite amazing political 'nous' as well as confidence to speak out against being pushed around even psychologically any longer by **wajila** (white) cultural attitudes, brainwashing, or interference. So none of this vigorous questioning in India is of any surprise. The only question marks arise out of personal curiosity. Once, while flying over the Caucasus I studied the circular air route map between Delhi and Moscow. Finland, with echoes of cultural links, is only 3,500 km from Delhi, only a little more than Perth to Sydney. Yet Aborigines without any means of transport other than their feet traversed that same distance many times partly to collect the rich ochre in WA for their sacred ceremonies.

But as the flight, redirected from normal routes with Iran in turmoil way down below, crossed the Caspian and the steppes of Russia I considered the map again and the movement of peoples. Human movement has occurred from the beginning of time–even on foot over vast distances–and not only for conquest. Sometimes it was just for curiosity to see what lay on the other side of the hill.

Music and Art have known *no* boundaries. The form of the Goddess percolated as an idea in nearly every major culture long before Indian society really became a partially rural–partially urbanised Vedic society. People moved **all ways** as they still do today, accelerated in number and density by modern technology.

When one sees the landscape from the air no wonder the Indo-European language roots exist. Distances are comparatively short and once through the mountain passes there is a continuity of terrain. If 'arya' equates with aspirations and indexes of behaviour, the search for nobility, the transformation towards better ordered societies, then we should all rejoice. It is not just an academic exercise about which theory is correct. The Vedic rishis are certainly the first major example of an Indian society with an oral tradition which became the foundation literature for setting standards, a yearning for a dharmic society.

And if from that Sanskrit language that emerged as the channel for transmitting their speculations, **Sverige**–the word the Swedish people use for Sweden–is the exact echo of **Svarga** = heaven and Iceland has a dessert exactly the same as Indian **Kheer,** and Celtic myths echo with Indian symbolism (the **das aswamedha sacrifice)** then cultural links are wondrous in humanity's cross-referencing and we should rejoice that what indigenous peoples in India speculated about flowed out, and ever northwards as other influences along the same routes of movement flowed in. Artists have always jumped boundaries to share, absorb, transform.

In a perilous world we need a touch of the aryan, the ennobling, from wherever the spark ignited. A translation from the Rig Veda VII33,7 (quoted in Rajaram's **The Politics of History,**) reads as follows:

Praja (A) Arya (A) Jyoti Graha (A)
Children of Arya   seek light

Jyoti = light, **graha** = grasping, taking hold of something as in **SATYAGRAHA,** much promoted by Gandhi achieving enlightenment, luminescence… the message of India's most important mantra: the **GAYATRI.**

■ ASCETICISM

'The extraordinary norm', that is, emancipation from rebirth by cultivating desirelessness, is how **Franklin Edgerton**, Professor Emeritus of Sanskrit at Yale University, designates this especially Indian concern in his scholarly, but fascinating and readable book: **The Beginnings of Indian Philosophy** (Harvard University Press, Cambridge, Mass., 1965). On first encounter I took quite a shine to the good professor (totally unbeknown to him) partly because I too had an Edgerton in my name and partly because, despite his scholarly eminence, he wrote his footnotes with such humour and humanity you felt you could have talked to him over a south Indian coffee and still carried on a flirtation of the mind despite the august title and its even more daunting sub-title **A summing up after a lifetime of philological study and reflection.** This so inspired me to hope, if ever there is a reincarnation, to have the clarity of mind to become a Sanskrit scholar despite the disheartening number of grammatical rules to be learned! The depth of his scholarship is very moving. As a mentor there could be no better for Professor Edgerton goes to the roots of meaning, the very essence of a philosophical concept embedded deep in the vibrancy of a seminal word: **tapas** = heat in Sanskrit, implying **fervour, zeal** as well as **the warmth needed to hatch the 'cosmic egg'** which brought forth creation. Even ultimate Godhead has to undergo austerity = penance to bring forth creation.

Other faiths, civilizations and cultures have also promoted self disciplines–**SADHANA** = saa (the long emphasis on the first syllable, a characteristic of many Sanskrit words). Pilgrimages, fasts, Islamic attention to **roza**, strict ritual fasting at **Ramazan,** daily prayer rituals, and personal disciplines at Lent, such as in Catholicism, imply ascetic obligations. But no culture has aligned this discipline with a total view of a cosmic force in the universe as **SANATANA DHARMA** has done and to why such attention to discipline is vital not only for a human but to the planet for ultimate well-being–as we have now been made to realise through scientific evidence on the pollution of the atmosphere and poisoning of the environment by profligate industrial man. Human 'stewardship' such as even the Judaic-Christian ethics envisaged has been forgotten. In the philosophic searchings for what was **Truth**, the earliest thinkers in India understood the inter-relationship of all things and the enmeshing of human activity to that in the cosmos. The one affected the other as–to our cost–we now know. As in the physical so in the interflow of psychic forces, such as

♦ **Tapas**, penance, vegetarianism, meditation, yoga and the hermit on the lonely trail, is a far cry from the rambunctious, meat-eating robust peasant culture enjoying the good things of life that vibrates in the later Vedic texts and the two major Epics, especially the MahaB.

For at least 3,000 years of known oral literature, **'the extraordinary norm'** has sent out its electric current from that unknown original source. Perhaps the key to this lies with the haunting figure, seemingly cross-legged and meditating(?) on a Mohenjo-Daro seal, often referred to as the proto-Shiva, that great Yogi at the very centre of the Indian soul (see **INDUS VALLEY CIVILIZATION**) and has been consistently acted upon by modern political figures, **Mahatma Gandhi** and his fasts the ultimate exponent. Others like Morarji Desai who as an old, 81-year-old austere freedom-fighter elected as Prime Minister in 1977 in the wake of the traumatic Emergency period of rule by Indira Gandhi; Jayaprakash Narayan who gave up a passionate political career as a revolutionary fighting for freedom and true socialism to work peaceably with Vinoba Bhave in the early 60s on land reform was yet another high-profile figure who personified this principle of self-abnegation which appears strikingly absent in the world of contemporary politics, self-serving politicians and greed on the acquiring of the perks of office. He too was jailed after initiating in 1974 a mass movement of integrity opposing Indira's draconian Emergency laws.

Its force has led on to **SATYAGRAHA** type demonstrations worldwide and hunger strikes when political anger at oppression has exploded. As no words can sum up so succinctly the phrase he coined there is no apology for quoting Professor Edgerton's passage in full, 'Few can attain it'.

Despite variations of behaviour in how to seek and apply **the extraordinary norm** there is substantial agreement in the end to be sought. The aim 'is emancipation from rebirth'.

Perhaps the earliest account of it makes it the result of getting rid of all desires, except desire for the Self. The desireless man becomes immortal and identical with the world soul; 'being just the Brahman,* unto the Brahman he arrives'. He is then unaffected by any action; he is beyond good or evil deed. For him there can be no more involvement in the karma-controlled chain of rebirths. This is what is later called 'release' or 'salvation'.

Such is **moksha** or **mukti** (see **CORE CONCEPTS** and **QUATERNITIES**).

---

* Brahman = BRHM, the neuter word for the ultimate cosmic/force, not to be confused with Brah*min*.

Throughout the ages, Edgerton points out its followers have received, even from those who cleave to that *ordinary* norm, the homage of reverence, implying a recognition of its superiority, though it may be regarded as unattainable by the generality of mankind.

There is a footnote to this. Enlightened beings such as Buddha and Krishna and contemporary Indian thinkers such as the late Dr Radhakrishnan all caution against those who carry such activity–or rather non-activity–to extremes (such as sadhus who expose themselves deliberately for alms at major festivals or events like the **KUMBH MELA**). The latter has written against extreme asceticism:

We must not try to save the soul at the risk of destroying the human species.

In the Upanishadic texts that is amplified:

They enter the region of the dark who are solely occupied with the finite but they fall into a region of still greater darkness who are occupied solely with the Infinite.

■ **ASHOKA**
circa 272–232 BCE

who became a noble and compassionate emperor, ruling for nearly 40 years, inherited his northern throne as grandson of the great but tough **Chandragupta Maurya** in 269 BCE. Ruler of the first historical subcontinental empire rather than a regional petty kingdom.

Ashoka united a further substantial area in annexing large tracts of Orissa and Andhra and thereby staked his claim to be honoured throughout time. Forswearing the aggrandisement of the 'principalities and power' ethos due to his victory at Kalinga in present day Orissa he became lawmaker extraordinaire, establishing a sense of democracy, the notion of **samiti** and **sabha** (committee and assembly), **panchayat** (the rule of the five village elders to be elected) and **people's participation** in a constantly reiterated ethos of non-violence.

Ashoka is the first emperor therefore of a nearly united India, the annexed territories stretching from the earlier Mauryan Empire of which Alexander the Great had laid the foundation in the 4th c BCE (as he swept down the high passes of Afghanistan into Sind and the Punjab) down it is said to Kanchipuram near Madras. He steps out of the shadows of a previous legendary history to become part of the India we travel through today–the great law **Edicts of Ashoka** an abiding legacy on stone pillars throughout the north and Nepal. His famous **Lion Pillar** at **Sarnath** and others nearby in Bihar state, part now of contemporary Indian Government insignia.

And yet again he dissolves into the shadows when the zoom-lens of modern curiosity focuses in on him–a noble visionary without a form, not even an engraved shape to indicate his looks, the dress he wore, his family, his wife, his advisers–all vanished in the relentless lack of Indian documentation... and only his words remain. (Refer to **ITIHASA = history**).

But for his time and what then was expected of principalities and powers forever in rivalry, accumulating and losing territory, Ashoka is one of the great world innovators, a statesman rather than just a ruler. Gigantic rock inscriptions (such as at **Girnar** in **Saurashtra** in western India) deliberately engraved in the Prakriti language and Brahmi or Kharoshti script of the vernacular and therefore part of common day use, testify to this.

A miniaturised version of the extensive rock face which so astonished early British scholars trying to piece together the jigsaw of Indian history in the 18th–19th century stands outside the National Museum in New Delhi. It gives no idea of the original which first came to the notice of the outside world when the legendary Colonel James Tod came across it in 1822. Read **John Keay's India Discovered** (Windward Press, N H Smith, 1981) for an account as exciting as any mystery story of how the pieces were put together.

This is the description as noted down by Tod for his own astonishing account of travel a century and a half ago:

> The memorial in question, evidently of some great conqueror, is a huge hemispherical mass of dark granite, which like a wart upon the body, has protruded through the crust of the earth, without fissure or inequality, and which, by the aid of the 'iron pen' has been converted into a book. The measurement of the arc is nearly 90 feet.

It took 15 years for another traveller with the aid of brahmin scholars he took along to check some of the characters—each nearly two feet high, an engineering masterpiece in itself of engraving on this mysteriously polished and smooth rock—to 'read' the just rediscovered **Brahmi** script, a forerunner of **Devanagari** (refer to section on **LANGUAGE**). This remarkable British employee in the Bengal Mint, turned Sanskrit scholar, James Prinsep had succeeded in breaking the code, discovering names such as Ptolemy and Egyptian kings so enabling the edicts that were emerging from their stone-engraved captivity to enlighten others of the remarkable firm but benign ruler whose writ stretched from the high passes of present-day Pakistan to the Coromandel Coast and from far Gujarat to the Tamil regions of Madras.

Extract of Edict 18 on the Girnar rock: This is part of the statement that has now remained for 2,300 years carved laboriously at Girnar at the behest of an emperor who had been greatly shocked by the carnage at Kalinga in Orissa, which his policy of expanding territorial rule had brought about. One edict speaks of 150,000 injured and twice as many killed.

> King Priyadarsi, Beloved of the Gods, does not consider either glory in this life or fame after death as of great consequence, except in regard to the following, viz, that, at present as well as in future, the people of his dominions would practise obedience to Dharma and also that they would act in accordance with the principles of Dharma. On this account alone, King Priyadarsi, Beloved of the Gods, desires glory and fame...
>
> Whatever endeavours are made all those are made for the sake of the people's happiness in the other world and in order that all men should have little corruption. And, what is sinful is corruption. This comparative freedom from corruption is indeed difficult to achieve both for the poor and the rich if they do not make great efforts by renouncing every other aim. This is certainly more difficult for the rich to achieve.

In the 14th century the ruling sultan of the fifth city of Delhi, **Feroz Shah** (1351–88) visited Tobra village upriver in Ambala district. He had heard of the find of a significant pillar. At that time no one realised its import or what this script, which had some affinities to the Mohenjo-Daro pictographs (also, at that time forgotten and lost deep in archaeological topsoil), could mean.

In a quite astonishing operation equal to that of Stonehenge or construction of a small pyramid the ruler decided to have it transported to his palace in Delhi. Great amounts of silk-cotton

Scrolls and Spirals—Golden Ages—Dispersion

10,000 BCE		3000 BCE		350 CE		400 CE		600 CE
		Neolithic/Indus Valley/Harappan Saraswati Basin/Dravidian/civilizations				Small urban Kingdoms		
◆ Ancient indigenous settlements referred to as Aryan (this now disputed)				Mauryan empire				
						Buddhist ascendancy. Kanishka		and Emperor Harsha, Huns and Rajputs
◆ plus tribal people						Coming of Europeans		

10 c CE		11–14 c CE		17–19 c CE		19–20 c CE		20–21 c
Advent of Islam		Delhi Sultanates		Mughal Empire of Turko-Mongol origin		British Raj at its height		Independent India 1947
Tamurlane (1398) shatters central authority in Delhi		1498: Vasco da Gama arrives in Kerala. Babur sweeps in 1526		Aurangzeb dies 1707		Franco/British struggle… emergence of British rule		Civil authority in New Delhi. A nation comes into being

were gathered and wrapped around the 42 feet high column. As it was gently excavated it rolled over on its side. A wooden carriage with 42 wheels was constructed. Two hundred men assigned to individual ropes attached to each wheel hauled the pillar on the carriage and then pulled it to the Jumna where a long boat had also been built. Further engineering skills by winch were devised at Delhi. The Sultan did nothing by halves! This immense weight had not only to be placed *in situ* upright but he decided that in addition it would be more dramatic to have it placed nine storeys up on the roof! (see **John Keay, India Discovered**, Chapter 4.) It is still there.

Even British engineers 2,000 years later were impressed and marvelled at its surface so well polished by Mauryan artisans that they mistook its sandstone for brass! It took another half-millennium before its message could once more be made clear. Feroz Shah could well have pondered on what it said—which perhaps could be useful on all governmental portals even today, its message primarily the same in ethos as the Girnar Edict just quoted. Its long message ends thus:

My intention is that the noble deeds of Dharma and
the practice of Dharma, which consist of compassion,
liberality, truthfulness, purity, gentleness, and
goodness, will thus be promoted among men.
Thus saith king Priyadarsi, Beloved of the Gods...
(Taken from **Inscriptions of Asoka,** Publications
Division, Government of India,1957).

Associated with the law edicts of the great Emperor Ashoka is his conversion to Buddhism after the carnage of the great battle at Kalinga. Ashoka's troops won the battle but left a moral question—what point destruction on such a scale? This caused Ashoka to ponder his responsibility. Thus institutional laws were framed and 'posted' in everlasting stone inscriptions, laying the foundations for a democracy of its times where universal laws were firmly established for all to see (there being no instant communication as we expect). This sense of law which applied to one and all was embedded in the concept of dharma, and ran its writ throughout his entire polity.

■ ASHOKAN PILLAR

India's national crest and all official insignia is taken from the Ashokan Lion capitol discovered in the ruins of Sarnath near Varanasi in 1904, thanks to the initiatives almost a century earlier of a young British army officer, Lt. Alexander Cunningham, who took an interest in the well-known Buddhist stupa. He followed in the footsteps of other great scholars like Sir William Jones in Calcutta and Sir Charles Wilkins who founded the **Asiatic Society** and along with learned pandits began to reconstruct a story of India's lost history in the 18th century.

Four lions stand back to back facing the four cardinal points of the universe.
1. As emblems of power.
2. Four racing quadrupeds match them underneath—**a horse, an elephant, a lion and a bull** (echoes of Mohenjo-Daro bull on seal). These alternate with...

3. The Buddhist emblem of the universal law—**the chakra.**
♦ This cyclical frieze is symbolic of the cosmic movement in the universe as the animals and chakras wheel around the capitol, always clockwise.
♦ The chariot is associated with royalty.
♦ According to Buddhist belief this also symbolises the thread of unity in the wheels—a unity which underlies vicissitudes of human life.

The frieze rests on a **lotus with inverted petals, emblem of purity and fountainhead of life and its creative inspiration.** Below in the Devanagari script in Sanskrit is inscribed **Satyameva Jayate** from the **Mundaka Upanishad: Truth Alone Triumphs.**

Golden Age Spirals: In a strange symbolism, the chakra of law, the cyclical frieze, the chariots circling, the unified threads of Ashoka's pillar of national significance are frozen in time, always completing the circle. But Indian history with its great surges of creative energy has to be seen in a different visual configuration in which **PALIMPSEST** and **FISSIPAROUS TENDENCY** play their parts. Indeed this pattern has been referred to as 'a ferment of dispersion'. Visually it is my own device for 'seeing' Indian history.

John Irwin, noted Keeper of the Oriental Department of the Victoria and Albert Museum in the postwar decades disputed much of this art critique-received wisdom, certainly in relationship to the conjectured Persian-Hellenic motifs (including the supposed honeysuckle in the circling band of embossed stone on the Pillars, and Buddhist monuments such as Sanchi). He defends their **wholly indigenous origins** as being lotus motifs, as also on the famous **Sarnath Pillar** just noted. The four quadrupeds circling the abacus supporting the four majestic moustachioed lions are essentially an indigenous device according to Irwin, associated with royalty rather than the quaternity of four looking out to the four corners in 'a position of fixity'; they reinforce the chariot wheel (or chakra) itself signifying cosmic movement.

Thus Brahmanical Kings by driving a chariot parallel
to the course of the sun at their consecration
ceremonies were deemed to be aiding the rotary
movement of the universe and thereby revivifying the
forces of generation.

Symbols are really loaded in India! Everything is part of the whole.

It is as though India's particular geographic shape—that distinctive downward-pointing triangle—has become a test-tube fired in the laboratory of history, a cultural chemistry in which infiltrating or migrating peoples or invasive marauders coming and going and then finally settling after centuries of partial citizenship, all were stirred and melded. Centuries roll on—and in a pluralistic fashion—each comes to a cultural fruition evolving into an Indian-ness as a paradoxical fusion.

A personal note on Indian history, the difficulty of focusing and knowing where you

are in its lengthy unfolding spirals and scrolls, Golden Ages and final dispersions.

In Delhi when our family first arrived in India the capital was no more than an overgrown village of nearly two million people. Manageable and intimate, everyone at a certain educated level knew everyone else. Networks were efficient. The overheated goldfish bowl of the 'Diplomatic Circle' could be avoided and my husband thankfully was free of any diplomatic protocol or hierarchies. Indeed his first duty was to be plunged into Indian broadcasting circles of creative people, individual writers, producers, musicians, playwrights and the pioneering Unity Theatre, historians, politicians, talkers all!

It was the venerable Khushwant Singh who, chuckling roguishly, alerted me in a tirade against the new-established Planning Commission (its inaugural chairman another vigorous Sikh, Tarlok Singh) to the truth that, while encountering all the to-ing and fro-ing of arguments about Gandhian principles and the building of three major heavy industry steel complexes (all in north India where the only coal fields are) as the major national priority, lodged in my head for evermore:

*Let's face it, the greatest single heavy industry in this country is **talking**.*

Our home was however conducive fortunately to Indians of all kinds calling by to do exactly that–talk!–the BBC having acquired a reputation for 'open house' from my husband's predecessor, Bill Ash, who lived a Gandhian lifestyle. From intimate discussions over many a simple meal I gleaned my first intimations of how Indian history was seen by such already-established thinkers as **Humayun Kabir** and **K M Panikkar** whose small but incisive **Hindu Society at Crossroads** was published in 1955. Kabir had already published **The Indian Heritage** in 1949.

In the flush of what Panikkar called 'the renovation of the social energies' of his heritage, he had inveighed against the cumulative deadwood of Hindu society–largely a result, as he saw it, of being thrown on the defensive by the invasive legacies of colonial domination–Islamic and Christian European. He expressed a sincere yearning for a structured and thorough overhaul of all Hindu institutions to complete the processes that had intermittently occurred throughout the two millennia certainly of documented history since Buddha's cleansing simplicity from all the complex ritualistic accretions when the Hindu polity was already ancient in millennial years of indeterminate thousands.

Golden Ages became embedded in my psyche rolling through Indian history in what they called **circles** but which I continue to see as open-ended scrolls, a social entropy in fact which sets in every few hundred years but then regenerates in a new form. I see that now after recalling those enlivening sessions half a lifetime ago in the new India's golden decade of the 50s when politicians were honest, law-abiding, not given to gross displays of pocketing tax-payers' money which pays for their houses, sentries at the gate, cars and journeys overseas.

The diagram I made–quite intuitively–was my guideline, internal visualization, which kept me grounded as I began to travel around India. Too often one comes across 'heritage art' sites such as at Sanchi, Hampi, the Kashmiri Hindu temples which are unrelated to the immediate environment around them. For the traveller who has no idea of the continuity and patterning in the history it is difficult to understand them in their context. I have found since that other outsiders coming in to such a complex yet unified civilization and who have added to the configuration find it useful in keeping some semblance of mental equilibrium instead of being totally daunted by the onrush of such overwhelming length and volume of material.

■ **ASHRAMAS** (n. *Sanskrit*)

The four stages of life symbolised equally as a stretch of 25 years (see relevant section under **QUATERNITIES**). They give a social framework to a Hindu's life, and the ground for enactment of **dharma** and **karma** fundamental to the ethical view.

Again the symbols are simplified and the numbers rounded in the busy Indian mind devoted to creating some kind of anchorage in specific terms in the gigantic cosmological thinking that envelops a person, which could otherwise be overwhelming. A life is measured as a straightforward 100 years, each of the four **ashramas** measuring 25 years.

Brahmacharya	studenthood
	no distractions
	celibacy
	vegetarian food
	self-discipline
Grihastha	householder in which all the
	pleasures of social life–**artha**–are
	enjoyed. At the crucial retirement age
	of 50 (with the arrival of one's grandchildren!)
	a need for reflection and quietude sets in.
Vanaprastha	withdrawal to **vernal** = **vana** or **aranya** =
	forest retreats in meditation/yoga to
	consider the point of one's life with
	thoughtfulness and to behave as
	Buddha later taught, 'mindfully'.

Finally the stage of ascetic 'aloneness', the hermit **SANNYASI**

Sannyasi	taking **sannyaas** = self-control in an
	ashram, cave or hut by the banks of a holy
	river to live a very basic simple life but still
	contributing to social life in giving wisdom.

There is still a mistaken impression abroad from too many TV images of 'picturesque' or 'bizarre' India because certain extraordinarily unusual events do occur (extreme ascetic **sadhus,** for instance) that it is a land of **other-worldliness** where people spend an inordinate amount of time doing nothing but contemplating the next life. This is mirrored in the ashen-smeared yogi–the particular form taken by Shiva as Bhairav who frequents cremation grounds, echoing it is said that shadowy Mohenjo-Daro seal already mentioned.

But this is not actually so. Puritanism was non-existent in the Hindu view until Islamic influences and then the full weight of Victorian Christianity and British Empire social attitudes weighed down society with a heavy blanket of prudery, certainly at the turn of the century upon a middle class striving to come to terms with new Western influences especially in urban situations.

In ancient times, the **svadharma** (personal duty) of the second stage of the householder was laid down as **kama** and **artha**—it was accepted enjoyment of sex, wealth, possessions and power were a natural self-gratification. In fact, Indians faced with an influx of young Western hippies after the great student upheavals of 1968, seeking alternative lifestyles and practising sitars while attempting to embrace yoga and Maharishi Mahesh Yogi's TM, looked askance and with some amusement at this reversal of the orderly ashramic progression. 'They've got it all back to front, you don't give up life at the beginning. Meditation comes with the getting of wisdom, and that comes with age!' one friend announced, alarmed at the Beatles' arrival at a Himalayan ashram.

The hedonist view—**anandvad**—would eventually leave the person satiated and dissatisfied. 'It is a psychiatric truism,' an Indian once wrote to a newspaper, 'that profligacy turns the heart and mind to ashes. Each of us by the pain of his experience and the abuse of his body reaches the truth of the Ten Commandments without a 'Thou shalt not' religion, a negative injunction. Our Law of Karma is at work, always 'thou shalt do'. We have to take the long view—we learn, maybe not in one single life, that ego has to **self-realise** its own discipline.' I often wondered if such a Letter to the Editor would be published in a Western daily paper!

■   ASTROLOGY, PALMISTRY, AUSPICIOUS DAYS
(n. *Sanskrit* = jyotish)
Love. Finance. Are You Worried? Have you lost all hopes of achieving success in your desires such as: Choice marriage, enmity, domestic trouble, litigation, examination, promotion, health and all confidential problems. Do you want success? Consult world renowned astro-spiritualist and palmist who has created sensation (quick results—strict privacy observed).

Even Indians cannot resist the **quick fix** despite everything in their culture and 18 chapters of the **BHAGAVAD GITA** notwithstanding warning them there is no such thing in the long trail awinding through **samsara**. Time alone brings enlightenment.

In a subcontinent where until the first airconditioners were introduced in the 50s (the thought of **that** is now incredible but a BBC representative wrote a one-act play on this status symbol for an Indian theatre company, so revolutionary was it in 1952) one slept outside in the oppressive months of April-May-June, prickly heat and all. The monsoon saved one from going berserk, but as a European you suddenly realised how those of us from a northern hemisphere are hemmed in by four walls and a roof.

We are not people of the seasons and the stars. Trying to go to sleep on a charpoy on the lawn or a flat roof top under the intensity of an Indian sky (before pollution fogged it out) with shooting stars streaking through the velvety blue-black darkness—so penetratingly vibrant you felt you could touch it—one's mind naturally turns to thinking about stars. In 499 CE **Aryabhatta** compiled a treatise on mathematical astronomy. There was accurate knowledge of eclipses, a decimal system and measurements of planetary movement. A spin-off into astrology is a natural adjunct.

If the moon has a magnetic pull that has created the word 'lunatic', that also affects tides, the axis of the earth and slows its rotation—what of stars? Now astrophysicists tell us they too have magnetic pull... did those inquiring rishis searching for answers also find the climate and intense sparkle of stardust affected their thoughts? Certainly India has taken the study of stars to a fine art and mapping their conjunctions as an exact science. It is not just a question of reading a potted horoscope in the daily paper as a good many Westerners do, more for fun than caution. Each individual's birth chart is drawn up after comprehensive examination at many levels and extensive research into family sources.

◆   Worship of the **navagraha,** nine planets, a place set apart in many temples for the purpose is common. Certain days are regarded as having more good 'vibes' than others, depending on the position of the planets. *Shanivar* (Saturday presided over by Saturn) is said to cast inauspicious shadows upon people. Tuesday has better 'feeling'. Certainly a great deal more scientific thinking and accuracy of timings in the lunar year's calendar, with its magnetic convergences has gone on than in Western time measurements.

In many orthodox homes—no matter whether one is Hindu, Muslim, Christian, there is a sense that there is more in heaven and earth than meets the eye—and best to consult the great scroll of the *janampatra* drawn up by the family astrologer at a baby's birth. The 'houses' of the zodiac and much other information in chart form is there to be consulted before a person makes a journey, a major decision and certainly in finding a spouse. No right-minded person would wish to marry another whose horoscope was seriously out of kilter with one's own. It is doubtful if even a Westerner, once they knew about such incompatibility risks and the years of argument ahead **that** would bring about, would defy the stars either!

Going on a journey with all the hazards of travel not only in ancient days through tiger-infested forests needed morale-boosting. But today's terrorist-prone world of flight is no better. There are Indian friends who have been known to cancel journeys if the stars are not right. Major politicians such as Morarji Desai, Indira Gandhi, Narasimha Rao have all taken on board permanent astrological advice, consulting permanent astrological advisors. In fact David Frawley has likened the janampatra to a 'road map for our entire nature and life experience. It is the science of karma'.

◆   What is surprising is the fact that Indians themselves get taken in by spurious purveyors of star forecasting and it is a wonder that those who as guru 'stargazers' to wealthy businessmen, civil servants, state and federal politicians, even prime ministers, cannot correctly tell when **their own stars** are out of joint! I once sat opposite one who spent most of his time cross-legged in an airbus which fortunately had wider seats, his immaculately cream-coloured south Indian silk lungi and shirt a joy to behold in all its sumptuousness. Some in recent times, obviously contaminated by the Kali yuga in which we now live, have landed up before the courts and even been jailed along with their corrupt clients. Others appear to reach for the stars by flying global air routes ministering to the far-flung **NRIs**.

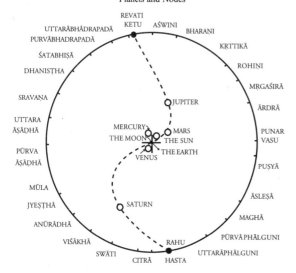

Stellar Arcs of the Formation of Luminaries,
Planets and Nodes

At US$100 a half-hour session no wonder frequent flyers are gathered giving them *carte blanche*. One day they may well be rocketing to the stars!

The earliest sages, however, assiduously studied the firmament and the constellation of stars and began to recognise a repetitive patterning. This enabled the first Vedic calendar to be established so that the priestly rituals and sacrifices which were becoming more than ever important in the social life of the third millennium BCE gradually were endowed with these heavenly sacramental influences. This starry pathway appeared regularly. In any one month it was perceived that 27-28 stars rotated in prominence. Each luminary was invested with certain qualities and influences within the four lunar 'mansions' of the month. One's birth star was particularly important in drawing up the life horoscope of individuals, as also are the arcs of the planets. Detailed investigation of these astronomical facts and speculative astrology is examined in **Dr S R N Murthy**'s book: **Vedic View of the Earth.**

A delightfully illustrated and well-laid out book is also worth seeking out to gain insight into the meticulous framework which gives meaning and security day-to-day, month-to-month, season-by-season to an individual Indian's existence. **Vimla Patil**, Editor of **Femina**, and lawyer, a vital woman and prolific writer has assembled **Celebrations, Festive Days of India,** India Book House, Bombay, 1994.

■ **ASURAS**

The negative powers in the cosmos; fortunately at the eleventh hour the forces of good summoned by the preserving forces–Vishnu and his **avatars**, or the fierce but equally benign goddess, Durga–finally overpower them, **but only just**. Originally the word was applied to major early-Vedic deities such as Indra and Agni, but shifted its meaning–implying **anti-gods** (root SU = benign, A = negating same).

■ **ASYMMETRY**

At an Indian Independence Day function in Australia one of the contributions sent in as a prize for the raffle being held on stage came in the form of a cheque from a local business dealing in Hindi film videos and equipment. The cheque–one of the prizes–was announced. **It was for $301.**

'Whatever are they going to do with the one dollar?' an Australian in the audience exclaimed. Is somebody's accountant slightly offbeat? No, this is **the principle of asymmetry in gift-giving** and it is very prevalent in the culture.

A bride if she is blessed with being in a very well-off family will be given 51 or 101 saris as part of her trousseau so the husband won't have to buy her any clothes for a good long time! Average middleclass trousseau would comprise 11, 15 or 21 outfits. In many cases she gets them from her husband's family also.

And in the Tamil south, certainly amongst traditional brahmins, if the women go visiting another family on auspicious celebratory or religious occasions, they prefer to go in a group of three or five rather than an even number. In Kerala however, three may be inauspicious, all very confusing!

In particular regional areas or within communities such as the Patidar in Gujarat or the Chettinad families of Tamilnadu (people dealing in money, gold, loans, for hundreds of years) there is such a tradition of keeping big ledger books assiduously recording in minute detail the gifts given either way, to make sure **who is ultimately beholden to whom.** Will this all now be stored on CD ROM, fed into computerised record or will these true moneylenders and dealers in money, whose brains are functioning computers anyway, that do not suffer the vagaries of India's powercuts, really trust all the new-fangled technology when they can really see-it-all-at-a-glance in these amazing ledgers with their fine blue lines and blessed with Ganesh's sign OM?

But why the imbalance?

Anthropologists have theorised way back to earliest societies, reflected all over the world in places as far apart as the west coast Canadian Indians of British Columbia to the **rishtedar** family gatherings in Pathan society. In these potlatches up the coast north of Vancouver where communities had time for creating artistic objects because their land and seas were replete with home-building material and the fish of the sea (unlike sparse societies that have to spend so much time on basics they have no time to luxuriate in the joyous pursuits of life) the potlatches served the purpose of circulating wealth through all the groups. A balanced sheet of gifts left matters static for the next time.

The scales need to be tipped up by that of extra one so that the person to whom the gift is given felt in honour bound to pay the 'debt' at the next potlatch–and so set in motion the processes again–**of being beholden**. Secondly, to a Hindu they will quote Upanishadic texts on zero–**an even nought has no intrinsic worth**. Coming into being brings forth a particle, the action, **one** (see **ZERO**).

Nought is sunya: empty
we are back to obscure metaphysics again,
and singularities
to a simple gift
of
one

■ **ATITHI** (n. *Sanskrit*)
A negates *tithi* = date(lunar)
◆ meaning 'without date', applicable to the person who wanders into the village without a time, date, appointment attached to that person. India being a land still of hermits, gurus, sadhus, bards and wandering minstrels, people on pilgrimage on foot (**padayatra**) there is always the need for that extra helping to be added to the family proportion of food.

A concept of hospitality therefore has arisen in the meaning of atithi embedded at the core of Indian culture (not only Hindu), the stranger in one's midst... According to a Vedic saying:
He who cooks for himself alone, and eats alone, eats sin.

In the law books or **sutras** detailed rules are laid down for honouring the unexpected guest on first arrival. If the guest was a distinguished person like a priest, a mentor, or a senior relation it was considered worthy to dedicate a cow in their honour, the word **goghna** appearing in Vedic times to describe this and incorporated into the first grammar written by Panini.
◆ In the Tamil literature the maxims of **Tiruvalluvar** quoted by proud Tamils ever since the first century BCE and still treasured at the annual congress now held around the globe from Melbourne to Toronto by the powerful international community who trace their ancestral origins back to Tamilnadu, there is this verse:
What for do the wise toil and set up homes? It is to feed the guest and help the pilgrim.
Where is even the draught of immortality, it shall not be tasted alone when the guest is in the hall.
No evil can befall the man who never fails to honour the incoming guest.
Behold the man who received the worthy guest with his best smile; Lakshmi [goddess of wealth] delights to abide in his home.
Behold the man who has tended the outgoing guest

and waits for the incoming one; he is a welcome guest to the gods.
Translation taken from **V S Aiyar, The Kural,** Krishna-Murthy Publisher, Tiruchirapalli, 1952.

In India hospitality is seen as part of personal dharma–the giving of sustenance (even a glass of water in such a hot climate) is a *must*. A hospitable man is referred to as **aatitheya**.

■ **ATMA–ATMAN** (n. *Sanskrit*)
Individual essence of Self. Never dies, nor is it born. It always IS. **Maha-atma** is derived from this term, meaning an individual great soul such as Ramakrishna, the Bengali saint of the last century, or Gandhi.
Mortal life is, to the Hindu, an existential expression of that eternal essence, bracketed by a series of phenomena, great transitions such as life and death.
(**Dr V Raghavan** late Sanskrit Professor, Madras University–**Traditional Roots of Some Leading Gandhian Ideas and Ideals**, Swarajya Annual Number, Madras, 1969).

An Indian woman friend put this more poetically–'our outward body can be seen as a change of clothes for that imperishable soul that continues in another reincarnation.' This she firmly believes.

The continuum remains therefore as a deep thread. It is the principle of life itself which never decays. It is **brhm** or **paramatman** (see **CORE CONCEPTS** and **PANTHEON** chart). Indians often use the symbol of water to explain this concept. Water is usually liquid **pani** (pr. paanee) but it changes into other states such as solid ice, soft snow, steam gases, cloud or even fog, very *real* no matter how insubstantial when analysed under a microscope. Where has it gone? Yet **fog** can virtually bring to a halt any kind of transport or human being trying to negotiate a real 'pea-souper' which has descended on a city. These could be likened to the individual and differing manifestations, the small atma, but they must not be mistaken as being wholly separate entities. They are still part of the **one greater whole**–the **Paramatman/Brahm.**

The form may change in the individual atma; the essence (the Atman) in this analogy of water, remains no matter the outward appearance which is **maya**, the passing reality. In this context there is no word for **atheist** in Hindu thinking even though there is–**nastik!** However, Dr Raghavan took issue: 'How can that be? Being born itself presupposes the fact there is a creative force no matter whether the word God is attached to it or not. That is the trouble with your word 'God'. The very fact that you have a consciousness to reason so, the very act even of denial is the assertion of its existence.' **Atman IS.**

■ **ATTAR**
fragrance = Essence of flowers implying fragrance
Heavy aromatic oil-based perfumes, sold in minute phials mostly in major cities. Hyderabad is a major centre for concocting such heavy perfume, but in the north Kannauj, one-time capital of Emperor Harsha (7th century CE) in central UP is the biggest

A

production assembly place–in the bazaar the traditional caste of **perfume makers = ghandis** say the industry goes back to the centuries just before the Christian era.

More than **30 different perfumes** are created from flower petals of many kinds–not just **roses = gulab**, the best-known. Boiled in copper containers and then steam-distilled with **sandalwood** and **khuskhus = vetiver oils** it has traditionally been stored in round leather 'bottles' that look like cannon balls. Attar is very expensive now due to the disappearance of the sandalwood forests and the fact that a lot of flower petals (40 kg in some cases) go into creating a tiny phial of perfume.

One particular fragrance is recalled by all those who have ever lived in the country for any length of time–that is the evocative and indelibly imprinted memory of the earth after the first monsoon rain soaks in–exactly as in Western Australia with similar geology, red laterite soil, long periods of parched earth and then 'the Wet'.

■ **AVATAR** (n. *Sanskrit*) a descent, a coming down.

To Hindus this means a descent of benign forces into planetary time from that of the cosmos to retrieve all the entities and qualities which are periodically overwhelmed by evil–which seems a perennial threat once quelled in one aspect and place able to take up the cudgels again in yet another destructive and insidious assault.

Vishnu, one of the great **trimurti** (see **MURTI** and **HINDU PANTHEON** chart) of the Trinity of Hindu philosophy and iconography is this benign force which pervades the universe before incarnation takes place. To symbolise this, Vishnu, whose name and its roots is still obscure, is given a thousand names–**visnu sahasra** (thousand) **nama** to express this **all pervasive** tendency. He reincarnates in ten materialisations or symbolic forms–*das avataram*–to overcome that evil when it is most pronounced. Although Satan does not exist in Hindu concepts of heaven and hell, dark forces and evil beings are ever ready to attack the good and for a period of time remain in the ascendancy. This has been pictorialised in all the artistic imagery, legends and myths since the beginnings of Indian society thousands of years ago.

◆ Vishnu is the redemptive deity, who incarnates himself, coming down to re-establish the ultimate law or **rta** (see **RTA**) and the ways of **gnowledge** (see 'to **GNOW**' as distinct from the verb 'to **know**'), maintaining cosmic order by stepping down into the world at periods when it is most threatened, and in a form suited to the condition of the earth as it exists at a particular time.

The symbolism in Hindu iconography depicts him most often as blue in colour, the Pervader being one of his many names, the colour of the sky, the firmament, 'the formless pervasive substance of the spatial universe' in which he resides. It would appear that India's 'exuberant artistic imagination' had already by intuitive processes recognised the realities of what now are confirmed by empirical means through scientific exploration and probes into the dark impenetrability of deep space as the Hubble telescope searches farther and farther into the 'edges' of our universe.

The quintessential image of Lord Vishnu carved in stone by some anonymous sculptor **1,500 years ago in** a recessed panel on the Vishnu Temple at **Deogarh** in the Vindhya hills region and then again between the 7th-10th centuries at **Mamallapuram** just south of **Chennai** speaks across time as a universal image, portraying scientific truths that are only just unfolding in our own century. They were there all the time, but we did not know the facts. The artists transmitted by some other means of gnowing.

Vishnu reclines on the protective serpent, Anant–'without end' (who looks like a comfortable dunlopillo mattress). The seven-hooded head of **Sheshnag** (its other name) cradles the Deity of Maintenance as he floats on this Cosmic Ocean (of amniotic fluid perhaps, it being the very protection of life and the membrane that envelops all living embryos). **Lakshmi**, his ever-benign balancing feminine energy, solicitously massages his feet, an ancient ritual for a good wife that was resurrected with great panache on a particular day in the 50s by certain orthodox priests on the banks of the Ganga. This was, however, met with considerable disbelief and scorn by women and appears to have sunk like a dead stone into the Ganga... 'Letters to the Editor' of Indian newspapers were very colourful!

Vishnu sleeps on...

But does he? The texts apparently call this pose or **asana** (with long first aa) = **yoganidraa**, 'slumbering wakefully', inert but ready to spring into action again after this restful interval between the dissolution (pralaya) of the galaxy in which our planet exists and a new creation of the universe at the end of this particular **yuga** or phase of colossal time (see **QUATERNITIES** and time intervals = **kala** pr. kaala).

Carved in all this consummate artistry within the astonishing cave at Mahabalipuram (its other spelling, see above) as the Pallava monarchs began to dominate the south and patronise the arts in place of the Chalukyas, even this very act of artistic accomplishment carries vibrations significant in themselves. This is the **living rock**, not some artifice built by man in stone and brick, but the all-in-the-round, part-of-a-whole Hindu view of such intensity it is as relevant in truths as that other famous icon of energy, **NATARAJ**.

Heinrich Zimmer, whose untimely death in 1943 in New York while teaching at Columbia University, cut short the book he was writing on the resonating symbols of India, should be read by all those interested in the intrinsic philosophy carried within Indian thought patterns, and the 'shorthand language' which Indian sculptors, painters, craftspeople and architects envisage with such skill.

In beautiful English which flows like poetry, edited with skill after Zimmer's death by Joseph Campbell and amplified by Dr Ananda Coomaraswamy, who in the early decades after Independence pioneered a new critique on Indian art, the book is one of the most readable in explaining the density and intricacies of India's incredible ability to restate old truths in relevant modern terms. Dr Zimmer explains Vishnu's inherent qualities in **Myths and Symbols in Indian Art and Civilization** (Harper Torchbooks, New York, 1962).

*In the infinite ocean all the seeds, all the
potentialities of subsequent evolution rest in a
dormant state of indifferentiality... Vishnu the
anthropomorphic embodiment of this fluid life is
floating... in and upon the substance of his own
essence...*

The extraordinary ability of Indian symbols and metaphors to retranslate themselves into modern terms is evident if one considers that water comprises 70% of our body structure, a watery mantle of amniotic fluid. And that in the very beginning of life that double helix of DNA molecules binding all life emerged as matter from a watery 'soup'.

*In the form of a luminous giant he is recumbent on
the liquid element radiant with the steady glow of his
blessed energy.*

♦ The idea of life being but a single linear progression—and then eternity—did not appeal to the earliest thinkers. The sense of the multitudinous explosion of life was there from the beginning in Vedic reflection and exploration of what was seen around them by the rishis, the sages... thus the belief in reincarnation. An Indian teacher once expressed it this way: 'the sun which sets here rises elsewhere'. The transmigration of souls, that individual atman, seemed a logical truth to arrive at biologically as the same bulb sends forth another green shoot each spring worldwide. Why not then the inner soul or atman sloughing off the dead skin, reemerging, growing forth again?

♦ And to accept that there is only One True God in visual form is to deny the very existence of that **huge Impersonal Creative Force**. They say **that** would circumscribe God's comprehensiveness as well as personality—male or female. Hence the Pantheon.

And even one Deity may also have many forms—ten major ones in this case—the **dasavataram**—conceptualised in the **ascending order of biological development**, a truth sometimes missed by the stranger overwhelmed by this entire concept of an exuberant multiform divinity.

DASAVATARAM: In those cosmic waters, the first incarnation swims as:

1. MATSYA: **The fish** which directs Manu, progenitor of our human race to construct a boat (where have we heard this before?) to escape the deluge which is approaching and to set off with the famous seven rishis (known as the **saptarshi**) with their human wisdom. It would appear that the seas rising after the melting after the last Ice Age approximately 17,000 years ago is a deep memory in the consciousness of human beings and their common account of this terrifying threat to the survival of the species.

2. KURMA: **The tortoise**, half in water, able to climb out as a vertebrate but in this avatar it dives to the bottom of the ocean for the Vedic gods in Indra's heaven to use as a pivot on which to place the legendary mountain **Mandara** (which like Mt Ararat was to become a place of safety for all that was to be retrieved from the flood).

To accomplish such retrieval the mountain became the churning stick which in some village homes is still used, a bulky pole set in a churn to grind the corn or rice. Upon it sits the Lord Vishnu to give direction to the struggle which is recounted in the **Satapatha Brahmana**, circa 1000 BCE and also in the Mahabharata, the enormous Epic (now placed in the light of new scientific findings in archaeological, astronomical and satellite photography at approximately 3000+ BCE).

Vasuki, a benign serpent provides the rope and to make the effort easier as **ASURAS** depicted as dark-skinned hairy, anti-Gods, pulled the rope the Gods of the Vedic heaven combined to tug at the other end. In some miniature hill paintings Kurma, the tortoise is a submerged shape, the pivotal base for this struggle.

Out of the ocean rose 14 precious possessions which had been lost in the thunderous fight in earliest times between the evil forces who even had the temerity to try to conquer the great presiding deity of Heaven—Indra.

1. **Amrita, the ambrosial nectar** = the essence of life.
2. **Dhanvantari,** the physician of the gods who is bearer of the ambrosial chalice (depicted in later Rajasthani miniatures of the Mughal period as a Muslim **hakim**!).
3. **Lakshmi**, Vishnu's consort and goddess of good fortune.
4. **Varuni**, goddess of wine (known also as **Sura**).
5. **Soma**, the important sacrificial elixir said to be 'enlivening', fermented from herbs, drunk by priests at the Vedic fire ceremonies, mythologised as the drink of the gods in Indra's heaven. (*Somvaar* = Monday is later to be associated with **Chandra** the moon which has in other cultures also been regarded as presiding over the watery elements and even scientifically known to control tidal flow, the rising of sap, even the unique fertility phenomena of coral spawning at the full moon around Easter when the Indian Ocean turns red at the Ningaloo Marine Park off Western Australia).
6. **Apsaras**, celestial dancing-spirits of the air personified as **Rambha**, a nymph.
7. The divine horse **Uchchaihsravas**, seven-headed to remind the devotee of time and the sun's course, driven and reined in by **Surya**, the sun god.
8. **Kaustubha** the royal jewel which Vishnu wears on his breast as an amulet.
9. The celestial **parijata** tree, *Nyctanthes arbor-tristis*.
10. **Surabhi**, the sacred cow of plenty, also white.
11. **Airavata**, the royal auspiciously white elephant, Indra's vehicle.
12. **Shankh**, the conch shell of victory, announcing the waking of the god in the temple every morning.
13. **Rama's bow**, symbol of sovereignty.
14. The deadly poison, **halahala**, spilled out of heaven along with the amrita which Shiva immediately drinks as it surfaces, saving humanity from further catastrophe. It has, however, lodged in his throat turning him blue according to legend. **Nilakantha** (blue-throated) is one of Shiva's thousand names. It is Shiva who claimed the moon to wear in his hair as it also floated as Chandra to the surface.

In traditional lore just to drive the point home the Indian continent is seen as resting upon the back of the giant tortoise, safe from all assaults. And when Vishnu sounds the conch its fundamental reverberation travels through space asserting the rule of law and his pervasive benign presence.

3. VARAHA: **The boar** (now biologically fully terrestrial) which digs into the muddy waters... to retrieve **Prithvi** the earth goddess nestled charmingly on the crook of its arm in a magnificent 11th century sculpture at the Khajuraho Archaeological Museum.

4. NARASIMHA: **The man-lion** (half beast-half man in the evolutionary process of time). Vishnu assumes this form to deliver the world from a tyrannical king **Hiranyakashyap**. He is depicted in some paintings/sculptures in all the gory details disembowelling the tyrant who seemed at one point to be invulnerable due to the quixotic blessings of Brahma.

The intricacies of behaviour in the Vedic heaven are to be wondered at. Perhaps the psychology of the early rishis who composed the first old tales, **the Puranas,** as well as the **Brahmanas** as commentaries on the Vedic searchings after truth wished to make sure those who listened in to the storytellers of the times understood the all-persuasiveness (such as of glib cult leaders) of the evil forces in the universe. All learning and the compiled philosophies were at that time handed down in retentive memory as an oral tradition. Hyperbole in the metaphors emphasised the struggle... and even the gods of Indra's heaven with all their divine powers were often under threat.

These four avatars are said to represent the First Age of Truth–**Sat Yuga** (refer **QUATERNITIES**).

5. VAMANA: **The dwarf** (now early man, being small). In the **Treta-Yuga** (the symbolic Second Age) when dharma slowly begins to lose its ascendancy as a force of law and morality yet another ruler, **Bali**, by the force of his penances and devotion (see **TAPASYA**) managed to defeat Indra the supreme deity of the Vedic heavens thus fulfilling this constant dire threat just mentioned.

Like rulers, real or imaginary, his abiding sin was **hubris**. Not only did he defeat Indra but he boastfully spread his dominion over the three worlds–the firmament, the earthly domain and the nether regions. His audacity alarmed the gods who appealed to Vishnu to come to their aid.

In the form of the dwarf, **Vishnu/Vamana** asked Bali a **BOON** (this old Victorian word is a part of the common parlance in India, close to morality and the logic of people's lives. A boon granted has to be kept, like a vow also. It is part of the social contract).

Bali is amused by the tiny Vamana. What threat could he ever pose to one so powerful as himself? Vishnu in disguise requests that he be granted as much as he can encompass in three strides. This Bali grants half dismissively only to be startled when Vamana suddenly explodes into gigantic proportions striding out beyond the stars to claim all the world's territories in his first stride, the cosmos in the second. Bali offers his head for the third, which Vishnu designates to the third infernal region, land of the ever-

threatening tyrants and rakshasas. Vishnu, ever magnanimous in overcoming evil, allowed Bali his adversary a grace out of respect for his ancestor who had in fact been a virtuous ruler and devotee of Vishnu. In **Kerala** at the celebration of the colourful festival of **Onam**, Bali is allowed a 24-hour respite to revisit his people.

One of the abiding components in India reinforcing the power of this ancient capacity for telling stories is the role of grandparents in recounting and passing on these living mythologies in which are embedded the ethics of what has been called by the late Stella Kramrisch (well-known art historian) **the complex matrix of the Indian mind**. This matrix takes in daily signals from many sources reinforcing these deep echoing symbolic truths–ancient tradition depicted in heroic films, TV series, in temple carvings throughout India, in well-illustrated comic books and in miniature paintings and wall murals in caves. Even advertising agencies use them as shorthand, immediate images that need no explanation, as do the popular calendars hanging in millions of kitchens and which depict the everyday human world of deities.

6. PARASURAMA: **Rama of the axe**, brahmin despite this martial stance, but not to be confused with the hero of the epic **Ramayana**. This avatar may well commence the historical period as a great man in time. Clearly at some sociological point in the history of the south the brahmins who were after all the educated elite of society who in fact compiled, recited and refined these dense mythological histories felt threatened by the powerful ruler/warrior **kshatriya** class (see **CASTE** and **KERALA**). It is surmised by some Indian writers that these defenders of the realm over-reached themselves as society began to establish regional and urban kingdoms.

A personal note

Certainly the Malayalam scholar, Prof. Vishnu Narayanan Namboodiri, at (then) Trivandrum's University of Kerala–who took me under his wing–believed this as he dilated over the ambiguities of his beloved State–its four Ms... the Miracle of its surroundings and its environmental magic; Marxism; its behavioural Madness and the Modernity of its seafaring peoples who had always travelled the oceans from when the first dhows were built. And that was way before Islam, back into Old Testament days and trade with King Solomon, Cleopatra, Egypt, Rome.

Over toddy under a palm tree which sent me into a greater mental spin than the rushed pace of his enthusiastically voluble talk and to the silent amusement of his long-patient and gently suffering wife, I learnt at first hand of the unique quality of Indian polity all through the millennia when Hindu traditions were paramount–that ultimately each ruler–kshatriya gave honour and respect to the ascetic, the learned brahmin seer, teacher, thinker, priest, mentor. Divine Right of Kings never obtained in India (substantiated in greater detail in **CASTE**)... that Indians have throughout history never taken out conquering armies subduing others… that it was the trading instinct and Buddhist preachers (with Hindu pilgrims accompanying) who sailed to Sumatra and beyond. Armies have fought thundering battles on elephants and with horses and chariots *within* India, but never sailed out to put to the sword other races and nations in a proselytising crusade.

The sociological truth of myth is a powerful force. Perhaps in ancient times the muscular warriors objected to their elite bands of thinkers–the keepers of the social conscience reining them in. So the brahmins seeing events escalating, appealed to Vishnu for help and once more he stepped down into human order as a brahmin to re-establish the status quo of this particular period. With his axe (a special dispensation from the great god Shiva, Indra's heaven now fading into the shadows of time beyond human accounting) Parasurama defeated the repressive tyranny of the ruling kshatriyas.

He later threw his **parasu** out to sea off the coast of Malabar to create the land (which is now known as Kerala) for the brahmin community–the quintessential brahmins of all of India, the **Namboodiri caste** of Kerala... but also for the Nayars, the very active warriors in a gesture of reconciliation according to my university mentor whom I learned on a later visit had become 'nameless' having taken sannyaas, in a temple in Thiruvalla.

Legend or factual history, symbolic truth is more important. Even today it is fascinating to witness the process of reshaping the legend to provide identity and self-esteem to an Indian flung out into the global arena in the current diaspora–an **NRI** in Australia recounting in the monthly Indian newsletter, **Samachar,** yet another version from the west coast of India tradition, this time a Goanese claiming this avatar:

People always seem to have come to Goa in search of peace though it seems the Portuguese never heard of PARASURAMA. Parasurama came here a long time before they did. This was after the battle of Kurukshetra, which is described with such great relish in the Mahabharata. Parasurama was tired of bloodshed. He needed to settle down somewhere where peace lay around like water, where peace could be lifted from the air, where peace flowered in the trees. The legend goes he therefore shot an arrow from his bow and hoped that it would land where peace existed in such quantities that nobody knew what to do with it. It landed in the Arabian Sea but Parasurama being a resourceful man paid a call on Sagara, the Indian Neptune and requested that the sea be swept back. Thus Goa was reclaimed from the sea.

♦ All the following three avatars are transformed by the staunch disciplines of meditation to experience 'self realisation' and a condition of beatitude and calm beyond an ordinary human's status. Some Indian sources suggest all three were historic rulers or sages (similar to Western prophets) of some eminence so that in a very Indian way they were incorporated into larger-than-life benign embodiments of the greater symbol of all-powerful reclamation of the forces of good–Vishnu (see **EPICS:** The **RAMAYANA** and the **MAHABHARATA**).

7. RAMA: **The ideal man**, hero of the **Ramayana**, son of **Dasaratha** King of Ayodhya, who at his father's death did not inherit the throne, his stepmother having caused conspiracy in trying to place her own son, **Bharata,** to rule the empire–yet another commonplace of history in all cultures.

As a result Rama spent 14 years in exile, his young wife Sita was abducted by deception by **king Ravana** of Lanka and in a fearsome battle aided by the simian deity **Hanuman** and his cohorts, Ravana was finally slain. Sita was rescued and in the first example of an aerial car **pushpak = bird, viman = vehicle,** an unintercepted ballistic missile of its day often seen in representations of the Ramayana, returned to coronation in Ayodhya. (In the original Vedic texts visionary words appear such as **agnibar** = fire arrow = missile, and **amogh shakti =** atom energy).

8. KRISHNA: **Man divine**–the dark-coloured lord, saviour of humanity, first the enchanting baby, then flute-playing entrancing lover, then depicted in many images as the serious shepherd of his flock–as teacher bringing the message of the gospel of compassion and responsibility and revelation in the **Bhagavad Gita** as Christ, the loving shepherd did in the Sermon on the Mount in Biblical times, so many Indian friends in my early instruction of matters Indian being fully conversant with Christianity having been educated in convent schools.

9. BUDDHA: As the great reforming princely soul turned **meditating ascetic,** created a new flow of powerful thought into the body of a Hindu way of life which had become atrophied by the vast stretch of time in which it had developed, encrusted by an outdated caste structure and precepts which had become the deadwood of meaningless ritual. The brahmin hold on society had overrun its usefulness. Most authorities have pointed out that rather than fight your opponent it is best to infiltrate and join him. Buddhism was waxing as a belief system. Thus the teacher/prophet was incorporated as the ninth avatar into Hinduism as the message gathered force from the 2nd century BCE.

It would be no surprise to find Christ and Gandhi become future avatars. They are already spoken of as such by Indians when discussing religion with a foreigner, a very popular subject.

10. KALKI: **The 'messiah to come'** riding in on a white horse at the culmination of this present dark age, the **Kali Yuga** (see **QUATERNITIES**) with a sword 'blazing like a comet'. This last manifestation has all the hall marks of Jungian theory, 'the collective unconscious'–symbols universally manifested in all cultures.

The biblical text of **Revelation, 19.11–16**, speaks of the future messiah with 'eyes as a flame of fire... his name is called The Word of God, and the armies which were in heaven followed him upon white horses... and out of his mouth greweth a sharp sword, that with which he should smite the nations...'. While not wishing to suggest an analogy between a semitic God bent on evangelical threats to those who do not believe, or convert to an exclusive faith which regards all those outside the Christian throng as in danger of damnation, with the inclusive Hindu view where deities represent universal symbols of humanist ideals and predicaments, such archetypal coincidences are quite startling to the newcomer to India.

Avatars thus bring a **cumulative** spiritual experience and inspiration, recharging truths to reflect the new insights born of developing awareness. The bedrock wisdom, **SANATANA DHARMA**, remains changeless: 'Absolute truth' laid down by one prophet in a historical past that cannot take on board scientific discoveries in human development is not valid.

■ AYURVEDA (n. *Sanskrit*)

A medicinal system unique to Indian thought and deeply embedded in the Hindu view of the Whole. The recorded beginnings of Indian medicine are so ancient they can be traced back to Vedic literature, itself of imprecise antiquity; many therapeutic plants would have been used by earliest tribal peoples.

Ayurvedic texts supposedly passed down to mankind by the legendary **Dhanvantari** (see in **AVATAR**) which have recorded the use of at least 1800 medicinal items derived from plant sources begin with the Atharva Veda expanding into systematised compendiums recorded in the 6th century BCE (according to some sources, 10th century in others). These are titled **samhitas** by sage **Agnivesha** and **Sushruta,** descendant of the well-known Vedic sage Vishvamitra and knowledgeable in surgery such as caesarean and cataract operations. They were also aware of analgesic herbal drugs. **Charaka** (circa beginning 2nd century BCE) systematised medical knowledge into a comprehensive science of life with accurate knowledge of anatomy, surgical instruments, embryology, and training of medical students, even the use of leeches. Later translated into Latin, this is the **Charaka Samhita**.

These analysts predate the founder of Western medicine, **Hippocrates** according to the well-known medical authority, the late **Pandit Shiv Sharma**, distinguished vaidyaratna (jewel of medicos) and President of the All-India Ayurvedic Congress after Independence. Given the task of resuscitating the position of traditional medicine after long neglect under colonial rule and prejudice on the part of western-trained Indian doctors he had to re-educate, pointing out succinctly that western theorists in early times had borrowed a number of known Indian remedies including **nagara** and certain **peppers**, as did the Chinese, Persian and Arabic (8th century CE).

It is surprising how at an almost prehistoric age Indians managed to identify, study and classify therapeutically nearly 2,000 plants of varying medicinal value which today still add to the ever-increasing volume of knowledge of world medicine. Even the latest and most popular hypotensives are but preparations or derivatives of the 2,600-year-old Ayurvedic Sarpagantha first mentioned by Sushruta in 600 BCE.

Decoctions from vegetables preserved by their self-generated alcohol (**asavas**) and advanced pharmacy were also developed in treating all manner of respiratory conditions and painful swellings. Indeed the drinking of the **somalata** is celebrated in the Rigveda and must be one of the first plants used for its medicinal properties even though scholars and medicos cannot agree on its origins. In regard to this Pandit Sharma wrote decades ago that a large number of vaidyas designate *Ephedra vulgaris,* the source of the popular allopathic anti-asthmatic drug, **ephedrine,** as the possible ingredient 'but it appears that the source of **somarasa,** the celestial drink which made the gods dance with joy, remained a jealously guarded secret, and has been lost to us forever'.

Statistics are only speculation but it is thought that at least 75% of India's population especially in villages turn to ayurvedic treatments and not only for reasons of cost and accessibility. According to **Charaka,** this science is concerned with restoring harmony in the bodily systems in order to live a long life 'in a manner useful to society'. Mind and body are intricately interwoven so that all diseases or failures of our bodies and minds are seen as the interplay of three basic factors or **doshas** (functions) Hippocrates refered to 'humours'.

VAYU or VATA wind, body functions, concerned with movement–related to breathing, speaking, central nervous system controlling all movements in the body and responsible for vocal sound.

PITTA bile, digestion, metabolism that regulates energy and heat production.

KAPHA phlegm, tissue formation and bodily mucous. The lymphatic system.

When balance of these functions is disturbed diseases occur.

There are said to be seven main categories in which a person's physiology can be placed, a permutation of the **tri-doshas**. Appropriate diet and lifestyles can be prescribed by expert ayurvedic practitioners to augment the characteristic qualities and strengths of the particular body-type.

♦ The belief is that due to imperfect digestion the essences of improperly processed food in the stomach get released as a contaminated bile in the body fluids. Diet, cleansing enemas and vomiting clear the system of such poison. The feeling of the pulse is a subtle indicator of most diseases.

♦ Daily oil massage for 20 minutes has always been encouraged in traditional Indian homelife beginning with the head and culminating in massaging the soles of the feet. Anyone–no matter how stressed out–will feel rejuvenated, 'calmed' as a result of this. Meditation is recommended with massage. This may sound easy certainly in India's middle class which can still luxuriate in the presence of servants, but even in Western time-conscious overburdened life styles, this system would be more productive than time spent on jogging!

True and professional practitioners (often giving free treatment to their impoverished patients) blame the brutal effects of Western allopathic treatments for many of the obstinate side-effect problems that land up on their desks as a matter of last resort. The gentle treatment with natural herbs at least leaves no trail of harm in its wake. Even AIDS victims in India now come within the ambit of ayurvedic treatment as well as TB victims trying out a number of herbs.

◆ From personal experience, Kerala provides a very ancient tradition of ayurveda and its rejuvenating massage, now enjoying a remarkable resurgence at such high-quality beach resorts as Somatheeram (traditional **taravad**-style architecture used in creating the individual cottages). This is at the far end of a pristine coastline of traditional fisherfolk communities living just within the palm line fringing the five mile long beach. It is just 10 km south of the crowded and tourist-swamped Kovalam Beach. Other southern States are also following suit as in Swamimalai, Tamilnadu near the great music festival celebrating **TYAGARAJA**.

The Kerala Government is promoting with considerable vigour state-run massage and ayurvedic treatment centres where traditional massage is given while lying on a teak wood massage table for a particular kind of 'drip massage'—a continuous stream of oil pours in a regular flow from a pitcher suspended overhead onto the centre of the forehead. This is known as **dhara**. Then there is massage with small linen bags containing cooked rice!

◆ Massage and oil treatment are closely linked with the vigorous footwork of walking over prone dancers. The masseur is supported by a frame-like wooden bridge along which he slides with his full weight, 'feeling' the body below with his feet as he glides backwards and forwards, the process lubricated by coconut oil. Reinforcing the Kerala tradition is the existence of the original centre of martial arts, **kalaripayatu** = unarmed self-defence in the kalari gymnasium. This needed massage and healing for strained muscles as it is a most strenuous discipline, said to be the inspiration for karate which the Chinese encountered in the very earliest trading into Cochin port a thousand years before the Christian era. It is indeed a curious aspect that this stylised art form of vigorous and stringent self-defence was studied by Buddhist monks to protect themselves in non-violent ways by understanding what are said to be the 107 vital body pressure points—some lethal if they receive a blow.

◆ Most of the sacred trees of India may well enjoy status because of their intrinsic medicinal qualities discovered over centuries of experiment. For instance, the tall, dark-green leafed **bel/bilwa** tree *Aegle marmelos* associated with the ascetic **Shiva** (and **CHIDAMBARAM** temple), fasts, prayers and austere meditation, was regarded as so sacred that it was forbidden to be used as timber for fire ceremonies or fuel mentioned in the Atharva Veda. It contains medicinal properties which have long

been used in ayurvedic cures for **dysentery, fevers and purifying the blood**.

Way back in pre-Christian times **Sushruta**, the surgeon, understood the properties of the banyan tree, *Ficus benghalensis*, so magnificent and gigantic a natural phenomenon it has held the Indian imagination's belief in its cosmic durability surviving through the mythic floods, and powering the environment from age to age. Not only are its leaves considered in iconography to uphold Krishna floating on the waters, but its juices Sushruta used to help in childbirth. Squeezed from the stem, drop by drop into the right nostril of a labouring woman, the banyan juice may well have an analgesic effect. The juice is said to be strengthening in the immediate months before childbirth.

Finally the Western world has woken up to the potency of this medicinal system, a 'treasure house' it is called, an export trade running into **billions of US dollars** to countries far and wide which has aroused fears in India that unless patenting of plants is organised quickly (notoriously difficult to achieve) this natural resource will be lost to the more sophisticated and well-organised multinational drug firms.

■ **AYYANAR** (n. *Tamil*)

An honourable term for the large terracotta riders on horseback seen so strikingly standing guard outside south Indian villages. Legend records their protective capabilities in riding the village boundaries through the night accompanied by what American Indians would call 'braves' = **veerans**.

◆ Potters of **Pudukottai** district in Tamilnadu are noted for their creations of these feisty night riders, sometimes painting them in eye-catching brilliant primary colours. Along the road to Gingee into the hinterland towards Tiruvannamalai are some of the most magnificent, close to the roadside, one proud warrior with southern turban and handlebar moustache astride a ten foot high white horse, flanked by modern police 'guards' in uniform with immaculately creased trousers, now joining the motley, their rifles and lathis, the mediaeval lances and spears at the ready, to ward off intruders. Some have become white-washed, well-tended shrines swept by a local village guardian (human!) presided over by Ganesh, the carer of travellers.

■ **BAULS** (n. *Sanskrit*) a tempest

poets/musicians from both sides of the Bengal border who follow the path of ecstatic bhakti as they wander the roads and weave miraculously without harm through the chaotic traffic of Kolkata and regional towns.

The name, pronounced baa-ul, literally means 'blown as the wind' and is thought to derive from **Vayu** of the Vedic texts, the winds of heaven. Bauls are consequently itinerant singers 'blown out of mind,' often dancing in happy madcap abandon like children skip-dancing out in the countryside as they spread their message in high soaring melodies. They play on simple **ektaras**, one or two-stringed instruments, with dextrous ease.

Bauls have now become famous in the West as a result of Peter Gabriel's promotion of **World Music** at international festivals in Australia, France, and the USA. They are said to have gathered together in groups about 600 years ago during a period of revolutionary upheaval in Bengal, expressing songs of revolt against the oppressive feudal landlords and the fanaticism of some Muslim rulers of that era. Women play an important role in this wandering community, many of the ballads dealing with the inner meaning of male/female relationships, and in other philosophic ways rejecting the patriarchal straitjacket of brahminical ritual resulting from vast stretches of history.

Living chroniclers, Bauls carry with them the immediacy of Hindu belief, so much so in fact that they have now been put to use in village upliftment schemes to sing of birth control and improvement of crops—all grist to the Village Block Development mill! To the humble people who listen worshipfully, their impassioned love of the Divine implies a complete identification in mystic terms, and always there is the familiar theme, a poignant sense of renunciation which ultimately brings happiness and an enjoyment not so different from the Christian sense of grace. Hindu and Muslim musicians intermingle, a musician of one faith having a guru from the other deliberately to defy caste and orthodoxy.

'You do not know', the baul will sing in Bengali, 'that you have opened shop and six thieves (**shara-ripu**—the **arrows of passion**) are stealing away the goods.'

1. Ploughman,
   are you out of your wits
   not to take care
   of your own land?

2. A squadron of six birds
   is picking at the rice
   grown golden and ripe
   in the field of your limbs

3. Farming the splendid
   measured land of this human body
   you raised the crop...
   the devotion to God.
   But passions eat at it
   like sparrows.

4. The fence of consciousness
   is down to dust leaving open gaps.
   Cattle clamber up and feast on your harvest.

Sung by a modern baul, **Jadubindu**, and translated by D B Bhattacharya, **The Mirror of the Sky** (Allen & Unwin, London, 1969).

◆ Summed up, these six thieves in the Bengali language are **madh** = pride of possession or conceit (or alternatively vanity, pride embedded in ego, from which all the other sins of bodily temptation originate):

matsarya—caprice or envy

moha—infatuation which is illusion (*a-gyan* = non—knowledge)

mudra (moodra)*—parched cereal-literally translated according to Baul tradition but implying **greed or gluttony = lobh** = satiation. Also applied to money greed.

moithun—lust for the flesh (kaam)

manksha—anger (from hot spices) It is at this level that the village Indian is transformed from the deprivation of his material life to another inner reality where music and belief and morality are totally merged (see also **TANTRA** for the related 5 **M** categories deliberately indulged in, despite taboos, in order 'to go beyond' their magnetic power to control individual behaviour).

It was the same with Tagore's artistic genius. He used the same yeast of music, poetry, and philosophy, which runs as a singular and perpetual ferment in the deep body of Indian culture. This quality of Tagore culminated in *Rabindra Sangeet*, his own personal statement in music of this continuing exploration of bhakti. Tagore referred to himself as a baul.

There can be no more emotional experience than sitting in a vast Kolkata crowd at a Ramakrishna meeting-house and swaying, responding, murmuring in approval with these emotional Bengalis while the joyous cadences of Tagore's singing words drift into the humid air. Here are poems of such gentle beauty, searching for god along the highway and in the golden flicker of leaves and grass in the sparkling sunlight, yearning in the heart for the long-lost lover and expressing an optimism which is also characteristic of those joyous and sumptuously disciplined **kirtans** of the south sung along the country roads by similar wandering minstrels.

■ **BEGGARS**

A great problem on the conscience of tourists and sensitive Indians who abhor their presence at traffic lights where they have a captive audience and where their bedraggled children sometimes presented so deliberately for effect, risk life and limb every day.

A crippled boy in Delhi in Connaught Place (a polio victim) kept watch over carparking: he earned legitimate baksheesh; he was treated with respect and sought out as well as his mates.

But at great Hindu melas or festivals and in temple cities where orthodox Hindus gather, beggars lined up in every conceivable and disturbing array provide the means for the wealthy to earn a heartless merit, by giving **daan** (similar word donation from same Indo-European language root) to absolve their caste and personal **dharma**—in this context, duty.

---

* Moodra (mudra) = false joy derives from mud = mood, the gestures of body and hands in yogic disciplines which induce the bliss of spiritual consciousness or fulfilment = *bhoga.* All other passions are only false gods providing transitory ecstasy such as drugs or promiscuous sex.

To outsiders who cannot, however, accept the bland excuse given that being born to this condition is retribution for a previous ill-spent incarnation, the beggar predicament is a blight on India's image, especially now that other Asian nations do not countenance beggars.

Such horrific sights as the maimed who await the unwary *firangi* outside major railway stations and airports drawn magnetically while one copes with baggage make Mark Twain's words on India ring with truth:

So far as I am able to judge nothing has been left undone either by man or nature to make India the most extraordinary country that the sun visits on his round.

Nothing seems to have been forgotten, nothing overlooked.

Unlike in Europe or the Americas where apart from the hapless homeless sleeping in cardboard boxes for all to see—and ponder on—the tragic side of human life is usually hidden away in institutions or homes, in India it all hangs out, suppurating sores, crooked limbs, blind babies, a Hieronymous Bosch perturbing underworld come to life.

Once near Hyderabad a party of West Australians including a doctor's wife had the salutary experience of being taken to a Muslim **pir's** shrine. Chained up to posts under large shade trees were mentally disturbed/possibly violently deranged people—but though they were under the stare of any passer-by, their families gathered around them in a circle, squatting on the ground, meals in triple-tiered heated metal tiffin carriers, goats wandering around cropping the grass in the nearby graveyard. All too obvious a permanent resting place but they at least had been saved from begging to stay alive.

The Australian doctor's wife sensitively wrote up that day's commentary:

Most people were sitting in the walled compound quietly, with an air of resignation. The jolt came as our eyes took in other aspects—to several of the posts driven into the ground were chained, padlocked adolescents, mainly girls. We witnessed one girl sobbing and heaving herself about and in the process of being manacled by several women to a pillar and at one stage they caught her long flowing hair and wound it round the pillar to still her and prevent her attacking her relatives.

Another young man was foaming at the mouth, writhing like a snake—he too was being tended by women who were wiping his mouth and stroking his forehead. Another girl just sat manacled staring blankly into the air. It was explained to us that these young people were either in a state of trance, deranged or clinically schizophrenic and likely to convulse. The village people believed they were possessed of the devil and that the dead Muslim saint would take possession over Satan (Muslims used the same Arabic world Shaitan) and they would be cured. This could take anything from hours to several days. So what is primitive? Our way of putting deranged people in isolation cells with no clothes and padded walls. At least here the family is supportive.

But you have to laugh sometimes! There are occasions where handing out some baksheesh is warranted for sheer ingenuity—even if now it's no longer the meanest of coins but inflation-driven rupee notes that pass hands. Beware the cheeky shoe-shine boys of Delhi but give them something... when you demur about having your brightly shining shoes repolished, they'll distract your attention and then in a flash nudge you to look down. Mysteriously a blob of cowdung is firmly planted on your shoe from sources unknown!

If consciences have to be salved as surely they must, for even the most indigent backpacker is richer by far than most begging kids, give to a reputable charity that cares for streetchildren otherwise, for sure, you will be haunted long after! Thinking myself hardened to such unpleasant encounters after long years to-ing and fro-ing to the subcontinent, the last spent joyfully being swept away by the rapturous cadences of Tyagaraja's compositions enroute to **Thiruvaiyaru,** I was following in the wake of my Australian-Tamil musician friend.

She was also taking the opportunity of doing a private pilgrimage to certain temple shrines as we drove across country from Chidambaram–Karaikal–Tirunallar where the Shiva temple houses an ancillary shrine to the planet **Saturn**. Although a very rational Hindu not given to rituals and superstitious influences, a visit to a respected astrologer on arrival in Chennai from Australia had confirmed certain concerns and she had been advised to give *pranam*—respectful devotion and prayers to this superior force.

It was necessary as part of this padayatra (by Hindusthan cab, as solid and roadworthy as a tank) to appease the murti of Saturn and its possible malevolent influence on her family and the seven years misfortune which can occur for those born under its zodiacal station and certain positioned stars. Our solicitous Tamil driver, a Christian, parked his spic-and-span cab beside a placid temple water-tank where a new roofed podium sheltered a brightly-painted **SARASWATI** (consort of Brahma) symbol of wisdom and the arts, especially music. Two and a half days on India's roads is nerve-wracking enough. There suddenly appeared a chance to enjoy half an hour of peaceful ruminations and with powerful binoculars ever slung over my shoulder, to indulge in some not-so-challenging bird-watching in a noisy grove of trees— you can actually see India's birds! Like the human population, they are clothed in myriad dazzling hues. Five wrinkled crones, crouched on nearby rubble piles, watched as I stayed behind, climbing on a wall, happy in silence.

Out of the corner of my eye, a warning movement squashed that hope like a massive flyswat!

The first entrepreneur lady in drab sari came up, rubbing her stomach. The Tamil version undoubtedly of *bimaar* (sickness) accompanied the pretence of woeful hunger. She holds her hands out. The whine takes on a permanence one becomes only too familiar with... I am on the back foot. Should I or should I not delve into the car to find my handbag which will then release I know full well a whole new set of energetic resonances. Or what about the stacks of fruit we have packaged, ready for a late

49

lunch?... She persists. The others who had been animatedly laughing and chatting (they don't look a starving group at all) now fall silent, still seated. They watch with interest.

A psychological game of chess is now underway which with the inevitable ability of the beggar trained in the world of hard knocks, she will eventually win.

Little children appear from nowhere. They crowd me. Did they materialise out of the midday shimmering heat? I give them our bag of oranges. At this the four other crones like Macbeth's witches lift their cranky limbs off the gravel, ambling over to add the melancholy drone of a whining chorus. Not even a rush. They slowly crowd me in. I signal in mime that I have no more food. They rub their tummies, magnifying the decibel level of the dirge. They know they have me on my own. So much for bird watching! No wonder to get any peace in this land you have to go on padayatra to meditate in the high Himalayas. Ashrams must have been conceived for this purpose alone—to achieve a private silence!

I climb in the car. However, a curly-haired young man with stave and Dick Whittington's poetic bag is tapping the window which is partially wound down—a fatal mistake—so I won't suffocate at high noon under a Tamil sun. He has a begging pot, rudraksha Shiva beads to remind us all of the great Deity and he is pretending to cradle a baby and rub his stomach also. He looks quite well fed... and anyway, where is his wife?

I get cross, patience evanescing with the heat and get out of the car (I need air) and give him a lecture—in English—about working for a living. Of all the inane things to do! However, being in south India where there is a greater fluency in English, a language that was never regarded as an instrument of colonial rule but a tool to be used for the commercial benefits it opened up, as well as the greater levels of literacy in the state, I noticed from his expression (and the tell-tale triple thread under his crumpled shirt—a sure sign he was of the upper caste and very likely to be educated) that he knew what I was saying. Relenting I give the crones a 20-rupee note to share. The women have slunk away with yet another 10-rupee note and are eating the oranges I gave to the children, who watch, ready for the next foray.

From behind a wall on the temple lane a quite well-dressed young woman appears. She looks well fed also. And here comes baby too—also quite well-rounded. 'Ma, ma', the chant is moaned, as the mother points to the baby's mouth.

Back in to the car I get. The siege is on. Where have all the paisa gone? Having peeked into my purse—an act watched with hawk-eyes by this professional husband and wife team—I realise I am down (or up, depending on which side of the poverty line one is) to 50 rupee notes only. The last 10 rupees had gone out the window to the baby. Then I start shouting. 'Jaa-iyeh'. But that's Hindi and I am in Tamil-speaking country where I have noticed despite compulsory Hindi exams in schools and public services, no one speaks it—or wishes to understand it. They laugh at me and shake their head, even courteously. 'Please go away'. 'No understand,' the young man says, which means he does! He

lopes away as the sound of nadaswarams, strident oboes, announces some activity down the lane. There are better prospects calling...

And then the little children, having got nothing, oranges disposed of by the older women, crowd round. I am now imprisoned in the car as they hop, skip and jump all over it, pulling sweaty fingers down the windows deliberately to smear them and collecting big boulders to stand on to try and prise the window (my breath of air) down with their tiny hands. I feared our kindly driver who had saved us from many near-fatal mishaps on hazardous narrow roads, along with my Chidambaram miniature Ganesh tucked away in safe-keeping in a pochette covered in vibhuti powder and rose petals the Dikshitar had pressed on the little bronze the night before when blessing the tiny figure right in front of the Nataraja as the last arati ended, would return to find his spotlessly clean white Ambassador scratched all over.

And then my companions are strolling down the temple lane. An entire tribe rushes over to encircle them for baksheesh. I leap out of the car and shout a warning. Everything about India suddenly gets at me. The heat, the poverty, the rubble never removed by an efficient garbage-collection system, the kids not at school, the knowledge that 60 rupees down being the score, will not fill the bottomless pit of human need.

Sixty rupees... long after, back in Australia, the face of the pretty little girl, about nine years old, who danced up and down, bright-eyed and seemingly carefree within the limitations of her lifestyle, came to haunt me as I drove my own car again. She had tried with a wily innocence to prise the car window down and then skipped away empty-handed to get a bigger stone to stand on with her hardened bare feet to wield more pressure! So like my granddaughters... and I found myself weeping as I drove, and had to come to a stop.

♦ **Sixty rupees** is the equivalent of **2 miserable Australian dollars**... and she got nothing. The pang that comes with that thought is now imprinted, like a branding iron, on the tissues of my brain.

■ **BETEL LEAF**
has been part of Indian diet for a very long time, the refreshing properties in preventing bad breath, for instance, mentioned in an early treatise dating back to the first century CE.

♦ **Paan** is chewed in India to aid the digestion. The leaf grows on a vine, is very succulent, and has pasted and folded within it all kinds of ingredients: lime, cloves, betelnut or areca, aniseed, **ilaichi** (cardamom) scented tobacco, camphor and sugar crystals. The paan leaf (not too different from the peepul leaf shape) is full of minerals. To keep it moist for the peasant working in 46° heat, it is carried in khuskhus grass containers which are kept moistened and fragrant.

♦ **Supari paan** from Lucknow and Varanasi has the darker-green leaf and is more astringent.

♦ **Meetha paan** wrapped in a paler and thicker leaf from Chennai is more succulent and sweeter. This is more often taken in the south. It is also more acceptable to foreign palates and well-worth chewing after a full Indian meal of richly-spiced curries.

In Muslim culture beautiful silver filigree boxes and containers were crafted for high society households. 'Taking paan' was part of the etiquette of visiting strangers or acquaintances, and mixing the ingredients to a fine shade of intermingling flavours was considered a sign of cultured upbringing on the part of the hostess.

However, as in most things, Murphy's Law obtains. There is a downside! Most Indian dental surgeons must benefit enormously. If a filling is about to be dislodged, the blockbuster arecanut which takes a good half hour to masticate into submission, will be bound to have done so.

In addition Indian pavements, arcades and outer verandahs suffer a smallpox splattering of red spittle marks from the deep red juices. Chewing betel leaf creates a considerable amount of saliva, as well as very red gums, a fact noted in the famous **Kama Sutra** (circa 5th century CE). The lover was exhorted to go and examine himself in the mirror before joining his friends and courtesans!

■ **BHAGAVAD GITA** (n. *Sanskrit*)
Bhagavad = the Lord, the Divine
Gita = song

is the sixth **parva** section or book of the longer of the two Indian epics—the **Mahabharata** (**Maha** = great; **Bharat** = original Sanskrit name for India). This was written down systematically in all its length over many equally extensive years somewhere between the 2nd century BCE and the 2nd century CE. The oral tradition could be traced back several thousand years earlier.

Most authorities believe because of its literary style, resounding language and the sophisticated philosophical arguments used by Lord Krishna as presiding and preserving divine protector of humanity, that the Gita as it is popularly called, may well have had an earlier existence circa 500 BCE or even much earlier if current speculation by a younger generation of researchers is correct. Its legendary author is **Vyas** but this again may be a general name for 'compiler' as there are references in other contexts to a Vyas. Certainly, from my own feminine, not feminist, point of view the MB has always seemed to concentrate on a masculine love of clannish struggles in pedestrian language when translated into English. The entire atmosphere of the Mahabharata is, in today's language,

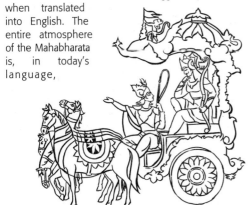

unmistakably macho, concerned with cousins flexing their huge muscles in a power game over land and property and then gambling it all away (see **MAHABHARATA**). But an Indian friend points out that behind the scenes are some very powerful women, and the MB could well be sub-titled 'Draupadi's Revenge' after the common wife of the five Pandava heroes!

However, the Gita's text is entirely different in flavour implying a lyricism and melodic ambience which is evident even after translation from the ringing modulations of the Sanskrit tongue in which it was first passed on to future generations from pandits (learned priests and teachers) and rsis (derives from the same etymological root as seers) who meditated upon the truths that shape society. From the most erudite thinkers to the bustling bazaar lanes of overcrowded cities where garish posters are to be found (religious homilies for the less literate) the Bhagavad Gita has through centuries captured the imagination of India, north and south—and now, in addition, many Western people. All Indian commentators declare it to be the one canonical text which has the widest acceptance amongst all sects of Hindus.

In my own personal experience the number of times Indians the length and breadth of the country have referred to it with direct quotes is beyond counting.

I recall it most poignantly, reflecting on the experience of the temple city of **Vrindavan** on the Jumna river with long time Indian friends after a picnic in the deep shade of a spreading mango tree. A crippled tiny Bengali widow, with her grey-white sari and shaven head, settled nearby. Even her eyes looked woebegone. She began quietly to chant from an equally crippled, much-thumbed book. The prancing horses and blue-skinned figure in a chariot on the cover marked it out unmistakably as the Gita. She almost intoned to herself. The passages were indistinct, but lost to the world, she garnered her hidden strengths. Her voice took off in mellifluous Bengali, surely one of the most sonorous languages in the world alongside French. In so doing she gathered a positive assertiveness addressing her Deity—the Lord Krishna.

In simple dignity, her beautiful voice defied the material neglect of her present condition eking out a meagre existence from begging at the temple gates where we had seen dozens of widows lined up, their upraised palms supplicating for pitiful *daan* (donations).

Such a contrast with a new experimental ballet of excerpts from the Gita choreographed in the 50s, those early days of independence and freedom to retrieve a culture that had had little chance to be nurtured in a full flowering in front of wholly Indian audiences. Its presentation didn't quite succeed as the depth of the philosophical argument and messages on self-discipline, affirmation and renunciation do not lend to dramatic stage action. Nor did it even in an Australian quarry in the expert hands of Peter Brook in a major theatrical nine-hour experience of the Mahabharata until the pale ashen-blue dawn crept softly over the cliff face as the upholders of dharma climb up towards their final release from the travails of this world.

The most telling moment in the early days encountering the Gita was in Kerala—again in a private home where I was taken to meet the old grandpa, a brahmin if ever there was one, impeccably swathed in his white mundu, southern style dhoti, seated on the rattan mat. I had heard the constancy of a background chanting all through the late afternoon while I chatted to my Malayalee mentor, a very lively, highly educated woman engineer (there are hundreds of them in this remarkably educated corner of India).

This seemingly haughty gentleman, a retired public service officer of the old ICS school, was the father of her husband; I felt really quite nervous being fairly new to India, not too sure if I was transgressing pollution barriers, aware that these were proud people who had had to deal with incoming Europeans of all kinds who had brought their own internecine conflicts for nearly 500 years onto south India territory (turn to **KERALA** and the Zamorin of Calicut—now Kozikhode).

He welcomed me onto another rattan floor mat. The daughter-in-law, although a highly professional female executive (way ahead of the Western world at that time) maintained her deferential stance in the doorway. Meanwhile, I crossed hidden social boundaries and became an 'honorary man'! I was dumbfounded by his bubbly humour which accompanied a learned PhD lecture on what the Gita was about—in impeccable English. And then after strong tea and wonderful Kerala savouries he began chanting...again!

What makes the Bhagavad Gita different?

Within its 18 chapters the message has now changed from
a) the Vedic hymns of praise to natural forces and their consequent wonder at the unfolding truths about the universe as revealed by the seeker-rsis, and the codifications and rituals that followed to give foundation to social worship in brahminical conduct of the fire sacrifice.
b) the speculative questionings in abstract philosophy towards the end of the Vedas.
c) the embedded caste structure and temple worship that developed over centuries.

The Gita, Indians assert, strikes a **new enlightened pathway** with stress on **ethical and spiritual development** of each individual.

◆ Logic says that to reach beatitude—a sense of tranquil stability, no one life is enough for that achievement. Only through many rebirths can one achieve the beatific vision. Certainly in my own lifetime I have seen profound changes in attitude to acceptance of a more cosmic vision, not only from nominal Christians within the European context as part of an entire seismic shift away from 'churchification', state religion and dogma. There has been a return to individual spirituality and a renewal of the long-lost mystic tradition. A postwar groundswell came to a head for our children's generation of flower-powered searchings for individual spirituality.

◆ This certainly coincided in Britain with an arrival of large numbers of Asians, the prominence of Indian music, a spate of new translations emerging with the Gita rivalling Chairman Mao's Little Red Book as required reading for our young Maoist offspring of the student upheavals of '68. Mao is now in limbo. The Bhagavad Gita serenely continues its publication impetus, spread to the farthest reaches of the British Empire, as wry an irony as the equally phenomenal spread of the Indian restaurant—even to the farthest Hebrides—when one considers the full force of missionary activity in India for the last 200 years!

An Indian likens the approach to this truth (which is the ultimate release from the world-wearying round of samsara) to that of perceiving a mountain. At first it cannot be taken in as a whole. Everest is not just the one view normally seen from afar. It has to be seen from many points of the compass. **Truth is therefore multi-faceted. Each view is true and yet not true in the complete sense.**

It is **Vishnu**, the all-pervasive cosmic entity acting through his incarnation Krishna who manifests the immensity of this concept in an explosive vision (see **DARSHAN**)—the Ultimate /Godhead = **Paramatman,** neuter in gender and equivalent to English word **paramount** via Latin.

◆ Perceptions in fact need refining over long periods of time just as a human sees things differently in the third ashrama or retirement stage of life than as a young adolescent, even though the same person.

These great cycles/chakras Indians think of in aeons, not centuries even, let alone decades!

The perceiver is determined by the cumulative effect of the **GUNAS** or qualities, specific 'bents' or characteristics known as **sattva**: pure tendencies; **rajas**: active powerful pragmatic business in the world; and **tamas**: inactive, lazy, dulled attitudes. Conflict in the make-up of human personality causes confused responses to the call of moral faith, ethical behaviour and intuitive wisdom. These need refining over long periods of historic time as the individual atma, slowly developing insights through many rebirths, gathers enlightenment.

◆ Krishna warns the believer that true wisdom, **jnana** (or **gnyana = gnosis =** intuitive gnowledge) is not to be attained by the outward displays of those sadhus and faqirs who publicly show off their austerities, **tapas** penances and extremes of asceticism (**tapasya**)—(refer to section to **GNOW** and the caricature frame depicting such practices in the frontispiece).

Only the spiritual devotion through **BHAKTI** worship will bring the spirit of detachment so enabling the worshipper from all castes, women as well as men to transcend the realm and magnetic pull of **PRAKRITI** = gross matter where all the contradictions of life enmesh humanity.

Fifty years of pondering the Gita has convinced me that it makes sense spiritually (and personally) in a world in need of independent judgement as populations become more educated, more globally connected visually by TV, electronically by the internet. When so much emphasis is placed—certainly in American culture which threatens also to infiltrate the global connections—on a seemingly god-given **right** to 'the pursuit of happiness'. The Gita's own emphatic message on self-discipline, ultimately leading to detachment is timely.

Bhagavad Gita = 18 Chapters condensed into one Frame

A much used bazaar poster for Indians represents in easily understood visual narrative the complex philosophy expounded by the Lord Krishna to Arjuna, the third of the Pandava brothers, on the eve of battle at Kuru-kshetra, the ground or field (kshetra) of the great clan of Kurus in the Punjab.

Arjuna (which means white), the shining one, is the greatest archer of all the brothers; generous, high-minded and handsome. But as he approaches battle, seeing all his relatives and elder statesmen who have taught him in his youth, ranged against the Pandava armies, he throws down his arms, confused and with no heart to fight.

Under each of the 24 panels a Sanskrit sloka or couplet from the Gita amplifies Krishna's long exposition of **dharma**, the moral duty and sense of righteousness which enables each individual to act through **karma** in serenity, without being swayed this way and that by false emotion.

'No human being can give up action altogether but he who gives up the fruits of action is said to be non-attached.'

Such a person has become **Jivan-mukta** (life release) achieving that serenity impervious to emotional stress and without recourse to tablets or drugs—or even the costly psychiatric visit!

This detachment is not to be mistaken for opting-out of engagement and concern for the world's woes but a harnessing of rightful action by following the path of a dutiful commitment without thought for personal rewards or self-gratification... the exact opposite of all the many rorts, frauds, power plays, insider-tradings, match-fixing, Olympic drug-induced attempts to 'win gold' about which law-abiding citizens around the globe wring their collective hands in the new millennium in despair at the disillusionment.

♦ In the Indian context **sincerity of motivation** (the Lord Krishna implies) through complete surrender **in the spirit of devotional dedication of the Divine** rather than **caste dharma** or **priestly ritual** and temple sacrifice, can bring that release out of samsara. **Here was a new egalitarian tone which lifted the spirit of one and all**.

'Pursuit of happiness', that American dream, so-called liberation from some imagined cage of restrictive inhibition or socially imposed structures 'is a sterile pursuit. You end up in a blind alley' is how my Hindi teacher put it once—but not strictly. He always used to chuckle gently in that Indian way as though life and what is served up could be taken on the chin if one learns **equipoise**—and *he* had lost all his money in a bank crash and came for an interview to teach Hindi via an American woman photographer when he had only a few rupees to his name and

was being supported by the Quaker Centre in Old Delhi. What he meant in his comments was that the Gita teaches that enjoyment comes only with discipline and responsibilities. Emphasis on human rights to the exclusion of these balancing components was a dead end.

The main thrust of the Gita's message can be encapsulated in the biblical phrase: **Be ye in the world but not of the world**:

The uncontrolled mind
Does not guess that the Atman is present:
How can it meditate?
Without meditation, where is peace?
Without peace, where is happiness?
The wind turns a ship
From its course upon the waters:
The wandering winds of the senses
Cast man's mind adrift
And turn his better judgement from its course
When a man can still the senses
I call him illumined
The recollected mind is awake
In the knowledge of the Atman
Which is dark night to the ignorant:
The ignorant are awake in their sense-life

♦ The Bhagavad Gita now dominates all Indian religious expression. Its thematic emblem, the Lord Krishna crowned, expounding its message to Arjuna the Archer who has laid down his bow refusing to fight his cousins, rides in a very warrior-like chariot drawn by the four horses of the senses. This constant image is today as resonant as it was then—if at all it existed pictorially in those pre-Christian centuries. It is to be seen in every conceivable kind of modern decoration, heading stylish hand-made notepaper in hotel boutiques of the 21st century, textiles, wood carvings, even incorporated into advertising gimmicks.

An **Upanishadic** text envisualises the imagery:

*Know the **self** to be sitting in the chariot*
*The **body** to be the chariot*
*The **buddhi** (intellect) to be the charioteer*
*And the **manas** (mind) the reins* (see **CONCH SHELL** section).

Every Indian knows what the symbolism means no matter the religious background. In this century in fact the Gita has become airborne taking to stratospheric flight in embracing communities around the globe. That is the measure of its universal message and the relevance of it.

The bible of Indian morality, and the high-water mark of its ethical system, the Gita reflects in its dense mass of Sanskrit and its luminous philosophical assertions India's special qualities and characteristics—a search for liberation from the bonds that bind us all to the anguish, pain, even the transitory pleasures of this planet earth, a search for our true **dharma** as human beings—our 'responsibilities', 'our duty'.

Arjuna, the shining one, the supreme archer warrior, one of the major characters in the Mahabharata and hero for the tightly-knit five Pandava brothers returned from exile is plagued with indecision as he sees his close relatives, his older teacher in the martial arts Drona, Bhishma the honourable elder statesmen of the powerful family of his cousins, the Kauravas who had so maltreated the Pandavas, lined up in battle array. He hesitates to go into battle. He throws down his famous bow in disgust and confusion. What to do? Krishna, now the divine teacher, then delivers the Gita, changing from solid Sanskrit prose to high poetry. He is shifting his stance from the earlier very human historic prince and scheming ally of the Pandavas to a new sense of divinity, clearly at a watershed of development in a changing society. Krishna, explaining to Arjuna that he can best fulfil his duty appropriately as a warrior in the battle against the greater evil proclaims:

All mankind
Is born for perfection
And each shall attain it
Will he but follow
His nature's duty

Krishna reveals the full magnitude of this force in the expanding form of a protective Vishnu—midnight blue of the cosmos, galactically growing with heads multiplying and a magnitude of arms and protective weapons flailing like so many windmills—the all-pervading god who dominates the firmament and maintains the cosmic **RTA** of what should be.

Painted depictions of this abstract concept are referred to as **Vishnu-rupa** = form or **DARSHAN**, a theophany of triumph over evil.

That duty is according to each individual's capacity—not necessarily bound by caste duty **jati dharma** or the ashrama stage of life responsibility but a more potent awareness, an **individual duty**—implying a free will to choose, wholly different from the Greek sense of fate which so haunted the steps of many an Olympian hero, or the Buddhist sense of impermanence. This is termed **svadharma** (see **KARMA YOGA**).

The ignorant work
For the fruit of their action
The wise must work also
Without desire
Pointing man's feet
To the path of his duty.

(All quotes from BG translation: trans. **Swami Prabhavananda and Christopher Isherwood**, Commentary: Aldous Huxley, Phoenix House, London, 1947.)

Circa 2nd c BCE—2nd c CE

During this great period of changing from oral to written culture this immense heaving body of Hindu thought seeped into every aspect of Indian life. It is the first thing that a Westerner notices in encountering India and coming into contact as friends with Indians. The message seems to be in relation to the body of Hindu belief as the Sermon on the Mount is to Christianity—in that many who would subscribe to little else in either New Testament or Old are moved and remember its verses about grace. Similarly, many Indians one knows who never set foot in a temple, or who decry the aloofness of temple functionaries and

their ritualistic formulas turn to the Bhagavad Gita—not only for solace, but inspiration as well. Here was the direct approach to the ordinary average Indian, now written down as the new millennium turned in the first century CE. It was on palm leaf, giving momentum to Hindu renewal after at least six centuries of Buddhist and Jain ascendancy.

◆ The late Dr Irawati Karve (one of India's leading women sociologists), in her fascinating sociological commentaries on Hindu society and its legends (**Yuganta**, etc., Deccan College, Poona, 1961 onwards), **Yuganta,** has detailed through a multifaceted examination of all the major characters, this slow transition from a historic and heroic saga of princely rulers bound by chivalric codes for the kshatriyas (even to returning conquered kingdoms, the symbolic display of power, superiority and status being the important point to have been made rather than forcible acquisition of territory) to a more defined caste system in which all groups participated, interlocked in providing services to each other. Teacher and learned thinker, the brahmin giving intellectual drive and spiritual guidance to protector and ruler who in turn must give deference to the superior brahminical sage and rishi. (This is one of the few societies in fact where the power of the ruler is not regarded as ultimate power, where the intellectual rigour of the ascetic marrying mind and spiritual excellence is still honoured with deeper respect than for principalities and power (refer to **AVATARS—Parasurama, CASTE** and **QUATERNITIES**).

◆ As Editor of the Pelican **Anthology of Indian Literature** John Alphonso-Karkala has pointed out, very soon the text loses reference to this symbolic battle at Kurukshetra which becomes peripheral and not central as the Gita was a later interpolation incorporated into the Mahabharata for religious compulsions to answer the Buddhist sway prevailing over society.

Throughout the text Krishna teaches the need to be free of attachment, to find that equanimity and steadiness (see **STHITAPRAGNYA** or **PRAJNA**). The Yoga of Meditation states:

No matter where the restless and unquiet mind
wanders
It must be drawn back and made to submit to the
Atman only.

Endnote:

For those who find puzzling paradoxes in the Bhagavad Gita, and who regard Krishna as a trickster, indeed posing not only Arjuna but all of us with the moral dilemma of 'just wars' or individual **dharma** (duty) which may implicate action which at the time appears to be wrong, it is worth searching out American philosopher **Martha Nussbaum's** publications. Giving the prestigious Oxford University **Weidenfeld Lecture (1996)** she dealt with this razor's edge of aspirations for unblemished moral action constantly tarnished by the conditions of moral existence. Her book **Fragility of Goodness** (OUP, Oxford, 1986) in examining the problem of 'cloistered virtue', (a Miltonic theme of mid-17th century) argues that the Platonic withdrawal, almost like taking sanyaas, virtually disengaging one from the contaminant of life and its compromises, is not possible for common humanity. Goodness in fact needs to be street-wise faced with so much peril in the dark era of **Kaliyug,** our dark age. Apostle Matthew spoke the same in the Bible: 'Be ye therefore wise as serpents, and harmless as doves'. The Gita's message would seem to be as equally realistic.

The Gita Goes Global

It is worth noting that the Gita has provided sustenance also to a number of African, Cypriot and other political fighters for freedom, who followed Gandhi's writings while imprisoned awaiting Independence from British Rule—eventually as a result of such treatment, to become leaders of their own nations! Nelson Mandela, Jomo Kenyatta, Martin Luther King, the Beatles even, have acknowledged their debt for the inspiration the Gita gave them when under duress, which must surely also have inspired Rudyard Kipling's most famous poem IF—a moral on the middle way of balance, even-handedness. Born in Bombay in 1865, his house still to be seen, Kipling must surely have imbibed the Hindu view of life, which an earlier generation of scholars did have the grace as well as the vision to promote in the late 1700s. Despite Christian missionary activity infiltrating Bengal most especially, Sir William Jones, that fine Sanskrit scholar who, with other kindred spirits, founded the **Asiatic Society** in Kolkata, promoted knowledge to the outside world as he began his dedicated study of **SANSKRIT** thus unlocking the mainsprings of Indian culture… and the profound beauty of the Gita. In 1785, Sir Charles Wilkins translated it into English. French and German scholars were also in the field. The Bhagavad Gita at last belonged to the world. Warren Hastings must have created many waves in the Calcutta British society of the day with all those East Indian Company men, surely astonished at being asked to finance its publication, Hastings giving his imprimatur in these words:

> I hesitate not to pronounce the Gita of a sublimity of conception, reasoning and diction almost unequalled; … I should not fear to place [it] in opposition to the best French version of the most admired passages of the Iliad or Odyssey, or for the first and sixth books of our Milton.

◆ In turn modern technology has caught up with amplifying this vision also into electrifying electronics or rather 'robotic animotronics'. Hitech Hare Krishna buffs have opened the **Iskcon Glory of India Vedic cultural centre** east of Kailash in Delhi to enhance the telling of the Gita from the static images of the traditional poster, to come alive for the 21st century child. The dramatic expansion of Vishnu's 'Universal Form' can now grip the audience with vivid animation and robotic techniques. Dinosaurs can take a back seat! A new kind of spiritual giant can now engage the baddies in a modern day Hindu Star Wars embellished with techno-savvy!

◆ In addition, the MahaB is presented in a *son et lumiere* fashion and the Ramayana told in paintings by global artists. To add to the cultural impact is a well-run vegetarian restaurant.

Perhaps the best known and most quoted sloka of the Bhagavad Gita is this and amplifies and makes sense of the whole dasavataram concept… the teaching of the Lord Krishna:

To deliver the good and to destroy the wicked
and to establish Dharma
I am born from age to age
Paritranaya sadhunam
Vinasaya ch dushkritam
Dharam sansthapan arthaya
Sambhavami yugeh yugeh

परित्राणाय साधूनाम्
विनाशाय च दुष्कृताम्
धर्म संस्थापन अर्थाथ
संभवामि युगे युगे

◆ I come into the world from age to age to restore the moral order—that is, to re-establish **DHARMA** whenever it is most needed.

■ BHAGAVAN SRI SATHYA SAI BABA

Sai Baba, claimed to be a reincarnation of a previous spiritual teacher called **Shirdi Sai Baba** (supposed to have been born in Maharashtra in 1838, dying aged 80 in 1918) was born eight years later. He locates his ashram, **Prashanti Nilayam**, in **Puttaparthi** village, **Andhra** and at Whitefield Ashram near Bangalore. Sixteen hundred centres exist in over 140 countries, 100 of which are in Australia. Followers believe he can perform miracles, not only simple ones such as materialising the sacred ash—**VIBHUTI**. I have had Gujarati families in Yorkshire and London swear blind to me that he 'materialised' in Kenya (his presence having left India) and that his 'energy' has cracked mirrors in their presence in Nairobi—this from seemingly rational, professional, educated people.

Be that as it may, Sai Baba is worshipped by millions of devotees as 'a living god'. Compared with many so-called gurus who have flooded into western countries in the past 30 years since the era of 'flower power' and alternative societies, often with drug culture links and who have set up spurious ashrams, Sai Baba has remained in India. He is undoubtedly acknowledged by a large Indian following as a truly holy person who, increasingly, is directing the wealth engendered by his presence to philanthropic objectives. One new hospital in Andhra has been built in an intriguing space-age style.

His trust also created a special project for 900 villages in arid conditions to supply drinking water. Funds come from followers all over the world. Recently one Japanese businessman donated 13 kg of pure gold. Sai Baba is reported to have said:

> The air that we inhale has to be exhaled. Otherwise the lungs will be damaged. Likewise, the knowledge you acquire and the money you earn should be used for the good of the society. Otherwise they are as worthless as the dust under your feet. You should repay your debt to the society which has contributed to your education and earnings. This is real Seva or Service.

(see **ASYMMETRY** and **ZERO**)

- **BHAGWAN / BHAGAVAN**
BHAGWATI (n. *Hindi*)
is another word for the supreme lord, the immensity of the divine presence, **bhagwa** being the word applied to the saffron robes worn by holy people. Increasingly, the world is having to come to terms with self-proclaimed bhagwans–fem. bhagwati–who since Independence appear to have grown in numbers along with India's phenomenal population explosion. For an outsider wanting to believe in Indian 'spirituality' as the century's antidote to its afflictions it is difficult to differentiate the legitimate from the spurious prophets of salvation of which there are many.

How to identify the bhagwan of integrity from the charlatan? Even Indians who are usually very sceptical of those who have made fortunes in an all-too-gullible USA (and even Europe) sometimes get taken in but a usual rule of thumb is to note the size of the Indian following compared with the international devotees in any gathering in India. Rajneesh and the young fat Divine Light Guru who married an American girl have been suspect in India from the start. Although Maharishi Mahesh Yogi has stood the test of time his devotees are mainly in the USA. Sai Baba is of a different discipline altogether but his predecessor namesake, Sai Baba of Shirdi, depicted wearing his saffron head-scarf lived and gave discourses under a neem tree (see **TREES**). This was in Maharashtra in the land of Shivaji (see **REGIONAL CULTURES**) where now the Shiv Sena's political writ intimidates, yet Muslims also held him in such high esteem they moved him into the local mosque for sanctuary.

◆ Perhaps the most controversial is the late Rajneesh, whose mala–necklace–with his photograph and *rudraksha* seed–beads–was worn by dozens of normally rational, professional people, distinguishing them out from the crowd in the so-called economically advanced nations. **Bhagwans** certainly did not seem to make much headway in Russia, China, or African nations. Many young Westerners wore saffron shirts and pyjamas. Some, including women, shaved their heads.

Rajneesh died still under a cloud of American as well as Indian investigation in January 1990. In India the Central Government Taxation Department was hot on his heels and innumerable derogatory articles appeared in India's English language press. Yet in Pune under the direction of German, American, Australian acolytes **Osho** (as this bhagwan is now called) is thriving still both in followers, mostly foreign, and in marble architecture which would surely have caused raised eyebrows from Vedic rsis.

They had a wholly different vision as expressed in the **Vishnu Purana** (6.5.78) or Vedic chronicles.

He who would understand the rise and dissolution, the coming and going, the wisdom and ignorance of all beings should be called Bhagavan... this great word **Bhagavan** *properly represents the Being who is the Supreme Immensity.*

And this is the power capable of overcoming the forces pitted against the noble aryas, the true dharma versus the unholy dasyus.

Footnote:
The Shirdi temple complex six hours from Mumbai is said to be the second richest temple trust.

- **BHAKTI** (n. *Sanskrit*)
Loving devotion... literally means 'participation' or sharing, that is the bhakta or devotee gives his/her share to the Deity. The Sanskrit root of the word **bhaj = to** serve, that is 'in the service of the Divine'; implying a giving-of-oneself.

The **Bhagavad Gita** describes such a one lyrically in Chapter XII, verse 13–20. A great sage once said: *Unless ritual is suffused with and penetrated by love, there is no worship.* The devotional worship of the **ALVARS** and **NAYANMARS** epitomise this initiating once again of a surge towards a **re-formed activist social ethic with emphasis on the loosening of social barriers and more upon individual worth in devotion to a personal Deity** and the **krpa (*arul* in Tamil)**, the grace that follows.

◆ **K M Sen** has pointed out in his evergreen pocketsize book **Hinduism** (Penguin, London, 1961) that of the three Hindu paths (marg) of worship:

◆ *jnana (gnyana) marg (knowledge) is apt to be dry and hard*

◆ *karma marg (the path of action and work and religious performances and ritual) has often been exclusive*

◆ *bhakti marg (the path of devotion) in which an abstract idea of the benign energy or divine 'comes down to earth' in the form of a personal god or goddess* (see **ISTADEVATA**) *to be lovingly worshipped, is the most accessible for the ordinary human. An image representing the abstract is the object to which prayer, music and personal attachment can be directed without in anyway detracting from the sense that the image is only a stepping stone, concentrating the mind on a Supreme* **Abstraction**.

◆ **The Age of Bhaktas** is put at CE 700–1800. Many saint-poet-musician-composers characterise this period of Indian history. Regional upsurgence occurs in the south, then Bengal, in the Deccan, in western India, a free-flowing movement which completed its many currents into the north with famous mystic poets–composers such as **Kabir** (14th–15th century) and **Meerabai** 100 years later.

◆ Bhakti movements seem to spring up spontaneously like molecular structures that reach a critical mass and explode with activity in the wake of the emergence of influential swamis/gurus or wandering hermits who gather around them followers given to ecstatic bhajan singing or worship after the teaching dissertations, parables, instructional advice, homilies, which may take place in a circle under a spreading tree as often as in the structured life of an ashram. Life-affirming **kritis and kirtans**, bhajans (songs of praise), lyrical poetry, ballads, all suffused with positive joy and majestic musical phraseology are sung in the vernacular for ordinary people rather than the high philosophy in Sanskrit for the elite. Not all are men or brahmins. Women and low caste saint-teachers are accepted and one mentioned in Sen's

Hinduism—Andal—was both! Her astonishing tale is told elsewhere (see **ALVAR**).

♦ Others, poets in the mystic tradition appear in temple centres dedicated to Shiva where rivers meet the Kaveri in Karnataka—at the **sangam**. They composed in the Kannada language religious lyrics known as **vacana** (see **VAC** = word) pronounced varchunu. **Dasimayya**, **Basavanna**, **Allama**, and **Mahadeviyakka**, a most unusual woman, are written about in a fully accessible book already mentioned—**Speaking of Shiva** (by Ramanujan). Much of these very personal approaches to an **ISTADEVATA**—a chosen 'materialisation' by an individual or family—as representing **the One Impersonal Absolute** (acknowledged but found to be too abstract for the ordinary individual to embrace warmly in the heart or even properly to comprehend intellectually) were in fact a reaction to this aspect of Hindu philosophy. After periods of intellectual emphasis there necessarily comes the swing to devotional intensity, and as in much mystic expression in the West the yearning for union with the Divine spills over into human erotic expression.

♦ In eastern India, bhakti worship was taken to its ultimate expression in the **Gita Govinda, Song of Krishna** as the cow-(*go*)-herd by the poet-philosopher **Jayadeva** of the 13th century. Translated by Sir Edwin Arnold in Victorian times, it was suffused with sensual spirituality in the lyrical sensuous love of the divinity, Lord Krishna in his earthly form and the yearning passion of his often frustrated Radha. The Victorian English were apparently shocked by its explicit nature. Read today it is mild, suffused with idealised romanticism compared with the stark-naked pornography which passes for literature in today's mass communication bound world.

In western India the development continued from the 13th to the 17th century in a great swell of Maharashtrian fervour as already mentioned. Amongst those devotees of Vishnu named in the **ALVAR** section, **Ramdas**, the lowly cobbler is well-known. A devout high-born Maharashtrian lady had given me a tiny booklet on the saint. With his compositions translated into English I had learned that being sufficiently of great dharma he was revered even by brahmins—so another stereotype of immutable caste hierarchies learned in Anthropology One (all theory) at Radcliffe was knocked on the head by the intricate human quirkishness of Indian complexities! The layers of my ethnocentric ignorance which had come to light in the first year in India began peeling away with a vengeance.

Personal encounter in the high country of Maharashtra.

That condition was given a further jumpstart when our family were totally delayed in the back blocks of Maharashtra by a long procession of exuberant, dancing pilgrims with laden bullock carts and conical palkis, like miniature temple-towers, carrying **padukas**—similar to the wooden chappals sometimes worn by ascetics—which honour their **Lord Vithoba**.

This motley group had been on the road nearly two weeks, women and children as well as men in monsoonal rain and hot sun, bedded down at nights with innovative canvas shelters—all on their determined way to **Pandharpur** on the rutted road we were taking from Hampi (difficult enough to reach even in the 90s) enroute from Sholapur to Mumbai. What caused immediate curiosity were the family **kalash** or pots of sacred tulsi or basil being carried as honoured objects in the middle of open farm carts.

♦ Pilgrims not used to seeing Europeans in the back blocks were only too willing to explain even if in halting English. This was their deity—the Lord Krishna (see **TULSI**).

♦ And then carrying with them also an air of festive occasions, they broke into music and dancing, gambolling around our car with oboe-like nadaswarams, brass cymbals, double-ended drums and bamboo flutes, laughing at our inability to make any headway. At least our young children were having a ball, India one vast adventure playground of the road so different from long boring road journeys in England!

♦ Chappals, sacred cows and jazzy music all reverencing some ultimate Force, joyousness, a million names for an ever-expanding population of divine 'presences'. Bhakti... intense devotion under the sky. Spontaneity of the heart's response, not circumscribed by priestly ritual, by even the domination of brick and stone and forbidden areas of architectural shrine... but an endless cycle, part of the encircling, starry firmament.

♦ ... The mind reels. Tulsi the God? My Christian fabric (inbuilt into upbringing) was being stretched all ways! No wonder people tell me of their overwhelming confusion—even mental exhaustion—on first encountering India. 'Where to begin?' 'It's scary! There's too much of it! My mind reels!' And then the body... 'How can they cope without running water? What of their hygiene? How do they survive all that dust, all that crowd of people?'

And then the magic seeps into the crevices of the mind. The urge to return develops impetus. A few more questions will be solved.

In this unexpected encounter it seemed thousands were kicking up their heels in a buoyant spirituality; now this particular march has exploded in volume, estimated to be at least 50,000 annually. Woe betide any hapless foreigners trying a cross-current dash across the black-soiled open land of cotton shrubs and maize crops of the upper Deccan. Pandharpur has apparently become a hallowed gathering place, giving inspiration to a universal brotherhood well over a thousand years along the bhakti **marg** or pathway.

♦ Further north **Meerabai** (also Mirabai, occasionally Mira Bai, 1498–1546) a princess, despite being married off in the traditional way into the royal house of Mewar, gave herself in a spiritual 'marriage' to the Lord Krishna. Legend in **Dwarka** still asserts that dancing in ecstasy, disturbing her noble family by refusing to consummate her enforced marriage, mixing with male and lower caste devotees (how horrified her family must have been) she is said to have been 'physically absorbed' into one of Krishna's **murtis**. Meera bhajans (devotional songs) have grown in popularity with the making of two films on her romantic life—one film involving one of India's most famous woman vocalists, M S Subbulakshmi (refer to end of **MUSIC** section).

In the north in Kashmir there was yet another line of mysticism as early as the 11th century and in the Gangetic region some, even Muslims, such as the humble weaver, **Kabir** who 'wrote' works of great lyrical force crossed the religious divide by appealing to common humanity.

◆ It has to be remembered that no matter how technically illiterate some Indians may be, the unbroken cultural continuum (which must be reiterated over and over again as a living quality even in today's India) enables expression through the spoken word. Oral culture and sung ballad combine to carry an exuberant, vibrant, colourful expression of faith, bursting at the seams with metaphor, simile and symbol.

Nama-Japa is one such form in which bhakti is expressed publicly, often seen by the traveller in gatherings along river banks, at temple centres or among simply-clad devotees circled in ashrams under a spreading tree. The frequent repetition of one of the revealed names of God—in the form of **shabda**, the word—and the shape of the word depicted in Devanagari script as **seed-bija mantras**, are 'thought forms' which when repeated in a mesmeric chant really do put the mind into over-drive.

◆ In this worship it is important to put oneself under the guidance of a true guru, serving the spiritual teacher in a spirit of surrender called **sharangati** (*charana*, Sanskrit = surrender; *gati* = way). Meanwhile the devotee would practice meditation. Staying with Indian families, one can wake up to a sunlit morning quietly brought into consciousness by the gentle voice of a woman in the household singing, chanting in this spirit of devotional concentration before the family shrine or puja area... almost a whispered reverence for the beneficence of the day, the tantalising smell of south Indian coffee brewing in anticipation of prayerful duty accomplished!

Another form is taking the lonely road of the mystic, often transported by ecstatic expression similar to the recently discovered body of women mystics in European literature and religious novices who composed their music in praise of the Lord in parallel fashion. Feisty women appear, such as Andal already referred to (see **ALVAR**) and Mahadeviyakka, devotee of Shiva, their equivalent, **Hildegard** of **Bingen** documented earlier, trained at a tender age in an austere church cell under the guidance of an anchoress, a western sannyasi.

It is only now on my last visit, this time to **Tiruvaiyaru** to honour **Tyagaraja**, that most famous of all composers in the south, that Andal has come to life for me, her murti now installed at **Srivilliputtur**, robed and garlanded, her hairdo magnificently shaped in the fashion of the times, precariously tilted; she stands alongside **Rangamannar**, yet another manifestation of the ultimate pervader of the cosmos—Vishnu.

Tamils have only recently begun to broadcast their culture to the outside world. In the 50s one had to dig hard to find the pathway to learn that Andal type special love for the **Lord of Tirupati**. There **Venkateshwara** resides (yet another symbolic name for Vishnu. They are endless—at least a 1,000 for the one concept!) Andal, plucked at the age of five from a sacred tulsi garden as a supposed foundling by a Vaishnavite saint.

And **Mahadeviyakka**? As **akka** (**elder** or **big sister**) she was initiated by an unknown 12th century guru into Shiva worship at the age of 12. The story becomes even stranger however. Courted by the ruler of that region, tradition says that she reluctantly agreed to marry him. But, poor man, little did he realise the strength of bhakti!... Mahadeviyakka's need to address her true 'lover' caused her to refuse sexual consummation with her earthly one, having dedicated herself already to Shiva.

A Lady Godiva of her time, undoubtedly rebelling against the social male tyrannies of mediaeval India and the straitjackets in which women had to abide, 'she appears' A K Ramanujan writes in **Speaking of Siva**, 'to have thrown away even modesty and clothing, those last concessions to the male world, in a gesture of ultimate social defiance, and wandered about covered in her tresses.'

> *Riding the blue sapphire mountains*
> *wearing moonstone for slippers*
> *blowing long horns*
> *O Siva*
> *when shall I*
> *crush you on my pitcher breasts*
> *O lord white as jasmine*
> *when do I join you*
> *stripped of body's shame*
> *and heart's modesty?*

Manikkavachakar. Yet another nayanmar of high literary repute and celebrated at Chidambaram with a festival in the Tamil month of Ani (June/July) has an especial appeal, sent as trusted brahmin emissary of high moral virtue by the Pandyan ruler of the time, to investigate the arrival on the coast 'of foreign traders selling fine horses' he paused to worship at the shrine—with grace descending. He forgot his fine clothes as prime minister, the splendid palanquin, the retinue of musicians and dancers in all their colourful finery. In the presence of the great God/Shiva he spoke these words:

> *Henceforth I renounce all desires of worldly wealth and splendour. To me, thy servant, viler than a dog, who worships at thy feet, grant emancipation from corporeal bonds...*

Tamil literature describes that despite being reminded by the courtly entourage of the treasure entrusted to him for the acquisition of such horses, he was so overcome by the mystic force of bhakti that he threw away his raiments, clad himself in a loincloth, his hair undone, adorned only by sacred ash (see **VIBHUTI**) and dedicated himself to Siva.* What headline would dominate the media today if certain prime ministers could hear the call of bhakti—but we live in the **Kali Yuga**, the age of disintegration of the old verities!

---

* Pandits tell you at **Chidambaram** that the saint literally 'gave up the ghost' in the temple, 'disappearing in radiant light', as also did another Nayanmar, **Sambandar**, at the tender age of 16. A superb 12th century Chola bronze of this serene youth can be seen in the **Australian National Gallery** in **Canberra**.

Conclusion

- One of the heartening aspects of the bhakti movements in India (and they have recurred many times over periods of hundreds of years) is their defiance of entrenched social orders—not that all is negative about the caste structure. Caste has been a stabilising force in the polyglot society which is India and has in economic terms enabled rich and poor to bond in the vertical alignments of the four main classes.

- Being expressed by its exponents in the vernacular language of the various regions rather than the classic Sanskrit formalised metres the lyrical poetry sung in beautiful music reached out to the ordinary villager and opened up the ancient philosophy in terms easily understood, in fact paradoxically returning to the original thinking and the sincerity of the searching hymns of the rsis several thousand years earlier. And such outpourings of joyous kritis, sung along the roads and by serene river banks still do.

- Such gatherings bring people on pilgrimage from all compass points of India (see **PILGRIMAGE**) for integrative influences in this 'shared common culture' as many Indians would point out, there being no geographical divisions between north, south, east or west when one is a *bhakta*.

On a recent CD recording (EMI: 147035) performed by renowned Carnatic vocalist, **M S Subbulakshmi** (refer to **MUSIC**) of the beautiful and meditative **Bhaja Govindam** composed by **Adi Shankaracharya** an early sage, yet another south Indian renowned for his sagacity as a Congress freedom fighter and first Indian Governor-General (1948–50)—one of the first to receive the nation's highest honour—the **Bharat Ratna, Chakravarti Rajagopalachari** pithily explains the difference which bhakti contributes in metamorphosizing knowledge into wisdom.

The way of devotion is known as Gnyana...

- *when **intelligence** matures and lodges securely in the mind, it becomes **wisdom***
- *when **wisdom** is integrated with life and issues out in action it becomes **bhakti***
- *knowledge when it matures becomes **bhakti***
- *if it does not get transformed into **bhakti** such knowledge is useless tinsel*
- *to believe that **gnyana** and **bhakti** are different from each other is **ignorance***
- *packed into this one hymn is the substance of all **Vedanta***

■ BHARAT pr. *bhaarat*

True name for India is **Bharatvarsha** going back five millennia or more to settlements of Saraswati valley region, an important clan being the **Bharatas** in the Punjab. The intricate sub-plots and aggressive battles in the epic **MAHABHARATA** focus on these tribes.

Sage **Bharat**, (pr. bharat, with short first a—whereas the children of Bharat are the Bhaaratas) is the first great legendary ruler in pre-history—whether mythological or real. Going way back to the edges of planetary time it is difficult in India to separate the two. Ordinary intelligent Indians often talk as if the myths and legends are *real* historical events. For instance my first surprise came in the 50s when researching my **Indian Music** book. A south Indian musician, a wonderful violinist, once spoke to me as if the legend was real of how Shiva came down to earth to teach the **tandava** dance and the extraordinary percussive rhythms, so intellectually demanding of the south Indian double-headed drum the **mrdangam** (see **tala** in **MUSIC**). Attitudes are the same to sage Bharat (**see David Frawley's The Rig Veda and the History of India,** Aditya Prakashan, New Delhi, 2001).

Baraat (no aspirate bh and emphasis on second syllable) is Hindi for the bridegroom's party to a wedding.

■ BHAVA (n. *Sanskrit*) pr. *bhaava*

States of being as created by dance expressions, musical ragas and the exquisiteness of performance in both these art forms, but also the aesthetic appreciation of certain intensities reached in poetry, or the finesse of the sculptural wonders of temple art and its symbolism and the 'charge' created by such aesthetic delight not only in the devotee, but the spectator—you!

Dr Kapila Vatsyayan has written in many other contexts of this ever-present urge in all the art forms to create a sense of **synoptic vision** = a binding together, a sense, that all the constituent elements must in the end be rounded off into a whole, which in itself creates this spiritual frisson.

That would seem to be the exact opposite of the many fragmentations of modern Western art experiments driven by individual, often anarchic forces exploding outwards, the random knowledge bombarding us today from a universe of Star Wars which threatens and sends signals of alienation and incomprehensibility. **Bhava** is the opposite—an aesthetic immersion in the total patterning of a meaningful universe as disclosed by the poetry, drama, dance, a painting or music of particular cultures.

Writing on the aesthetics of ancient Indian drama, the late **Dr V Raghavan** also points out that the ideal held up for the artist to emulate *'a harmonious emotional impression is also responsible for the Indian dramatist eschewing incongruities, discrepancies or idiosyncrasies in an individual character and trying all the time to do what is styled as the developing of the rasa. For this reason, too, the character as such is not the thing for him but the character as the vehicle of rasa. The bringing together of incompatible rasas is also to be avoided. Characters, story or plot take a secondary place; in fact, the story is in place not as a story but as a medium of rasa. Consequently, each play should have an emotional unity; the unities of time and place are of minor importance; indeed, in the sweep from the earth to heaven and over long passages of time that the Indian imagination takes, these two unities are left far behind.'* (**RASA** = inherent essence, literally juice, a flavour in relation to an art form which conveys the sense of bhava.)

Bhava embellishes any struggle that may be portrayed in the art forms of India with a benign resolution. It is often stated that there is no sense of tragedy in Indian drama. Aristotelian theories on progression of plot in a drama through conflicting forces to a conclusive resolution and the Greek concept of *agape*—suffering in which a fate loaded against an individual because of **hubris** = pride ended in tragedy, disturbed the Indian sense of bhava. Crushing fate did not bring the downfall for the proud **Kaurava** clan, according to Raghavan. Nor was the evil protagonist of the Mahabharata epic, **Duryodhana**, which means hard to conquer, undone by capricious fate. He too suffered from hubris—his overweening arrogance. '*The same ideal of achieving a harmony out of chaos, of producing restfulness out of disturbance, is also responsible for the avoidance of tragedy in the Sanskrit theatre. The tragic element and its poignant portrayal do, indeed, form part of Sanskrit drama...*'

but not as ends in themselves.

Rasa, Brhm Sahodre Asti...Rasa and Brhm are born from the same source/place.

- **BHIKSHU** (n *Sanskrit*)
  BHIKKHU (n. *Pali*)
  means literally a **sharesmen** or **almsman**. Those, who when the communities were formed after the Buddha's death, were given daily food by householders who considered it a meritorious act to keep the orders of monks/teachers in provisions in their individual **sanghas** (communities of study and worship).

The term is applied **mainly to the saffron-robed monks**, especially in SE Asia, who after withdrawal for about three months in the rainy season which they spend in meditation and discourses then emerge as wandering teachers/psychiatrists /general advisers to the populace.

This tradition is maintained in the contemporary urban world not only throughout Asia. It has spread far beyond in hundreds of thriving centres in the Western world, in response not only to the ease of mobility and modern travel but more to the disaffection with institutional Christianity amongst free-thinking, radical post-war generations.

- **BHOODAN/BHAVE**
  (Vinoba)....1895–1982
  Vinoba Bhave was a follower and inheritor of Gandhi's role in appealing for the harijan (outcastes) and the rural poor. He was a force for rural social reform in post-independence India, founding the **bhoodan** movement in 1951. This was after Communist-inspired disturbances in Telengana district of Hyderabad province, now northern Andhra Pradesh. A Gandhian disciple of 30 years' standing, Bhave was approached by pitiable landless peasants whose life held no redeeming features whatsoever. On the spur of the moment Vinoba Bhave turned to local well-to-do land owners to regard him as their **sixth son** pleading with them to give him his share of their land ownership in order to redistribute it to India's landless impoverished farmers. This was a great ideal, and to some extent he succeeded but cynics in the media often pointed out that the land given from a family holding was often the least fertile, the bad lands. His aim was to collect 50 million acres for free distribution; in the end approximately five million were collected.

Vinoba maintained Gandhi's tradition of being seen to undertake **padayatra** (pilgrimage on foot) across the face of India to focus media attention (and therefore the nation's millions) on this thorny question of rural reform, the landless, and the neglected isolated rural village community when early Planning Commissions of the Central Government gave priority to building up India's industrial base which had been severely neglected by the British colonial administrators.

Well over a generation on since Bhave's death in 1982 it is hard to encapsulate the quality of this noble soul. Like Pandit Nehru and Mahatma Gandhi, their personalities are so complex and essentially Indian, every statement would have to be encrusted with a dozen sub-clauses. Like a number of India's true saints Vinoba, or **Baba** as he was lovingly called by his dedicated band of young village-uplift workers, set a cracking pace with his spartan regime often beginning with spinning and prayer at 3 a.m. Volunteers laboured to keep up with his wiry frame and taut energy as he walked the weary miles following ancient traditions across the length and breadth of India, dying at the extraordinary age of 87, at Gandhi's famous central Indian ashram at Wardha, having chosen freely the **yogic way**, a spiritual aspirant, choosing to slow bodily functions down, virtually foregoing life.

In fact he willed himself to death. Though of seeming irrelevance today he stays here in his own right to remind us of a time when a true **arya**—a **noble soul** existed to remind India herself of her ideals rooted in antiquity. In a high-tech world of dotcom share trading where the nation's rich and well-heeled consuming classes are becoming richer as the gap ever widens from the static poor, the disgraceful squalor of city slums hardly seen anywhere else in true Asia, the neglect of education for those at the bottom of the billion people pile, great staunch dharmic souls such as Bhave are much needed to remind the nation of its true priorities.

One of the most moving and insightful accounts of his unsparing endeavours came from Taya Zinkin, a tough and no-nonsense correspondent for **The Guardian**. A contemporary of our fifties generation in India, she stood no nonsense anywhere and once ticked Morarji Desai off for standing at the bottom of a ladder while she climbed up in some new industrial complex being opened in Bombay where her Czech-British husband was a senior executive in Lever Brothers. 'In future', she snorted, 'I shall wear trousers on location!'

She was not the kind of person to go overboard about matters culturally Indian but this is extracted from a long account she wrote in 1954 for **The Illustrated Weekly of India** (June 20). His daily march pledged to a campaign to collect 50 million acres for the landless labourer by 1957, with only 3¼ million in hand was in Bihar in June, the temperature, pre-monsoon, climbing to over 40° in a humid shade.

She poured sweat as did everyone else on a 10-mile hike in scorching sun

The heat was terrific. I watched nesting birds pant, their beaks desperately open, tongues out as if they were dogs.

At six in the evening Baba came out of his room, a slim, frail wisp of a man with heavy glasses, a short loin cloth, a towel on his head and shoulders. His face looks even thinner than it is because of his Gothic beard and toothless gums.

Never before have I been at a meeting in India where there was pin drop silence. There were perhaps 200 villagers, but the silence was absolute. Infants did not wail, children did not keep threading their way through the audience as if they were playing Labyrinth, dogs did not bark, nobody sneezed, only Bhave's own cough punctuated a serenity beyond words. He spoke for a little while; he did not say anything startlingly new and his audience did not seem to be moved: smallpox-pitted faces were still, as darkness began to spread its cooling shadow on our group and stars appeared...

The next morning we got up at 3 and set forth at 4. Bhave in front, hardly grazing the soil in a rhythmical walk that seemed unreal in the light of the petrol lamp carried by one of his followers. The grey dust of Bihar seemed to cling to his brown ankles as if he were but an extension of the earth. Our halt was only eight miles away, a short march for Bhave who thinks nothing of 16 miles at a steady average of one mile per twenty minutes, rut, river, mountain, come what may.

Collapsed in a dripping heap on the mud floor, wrapped in towels to mop up the perspiration, Zinkin wrote:

Waiting for the interview I started a diary... in fear that afterwards I might not be able to recapture for myself this tremendous sense of complete, absolute, peace. This feeling, even if it is only fleeting, is so perfect that to have experienced it is the only thing that matters. One can later lose the peace, but the knowledge that it exists is more important than anything else. As I waited I remembered what the Chief Minister of Bombay had once told me about a very holy man now dead. 'His presence was enough to put an end to all desire; it created peace from within'.

◆ **Jayaprakash Narayan** better known simply as J P, was an ex-freedom fighter revolutionary against British rule in the 1940s who became Bhave's most influential supporter, transformed as he was by Gandhian philosophy and the fact that Bhave became the Mahatma's first chosen satyagrahi in 1941. He himself, in 1954, announced his own **jivandan**—giving of his life energies' to solve the land problem along with Vinoba at a major **sarvodaya sammelan** (*sarv* = all; *udaya* = upliftment, rise, *sammelan* = concourse of people) at the ancient Bodhgaya site.

◆ Many Indians would have liked to see him become prime minister after Nehru but in the early 50s J P followed an ancient tradition and withdrew. An editor friend was somewhat mitted by this, as he, like many others, regarded J P as a great political luminary with passion in his guts. J P had been an original fiery idealist (transformed ironically into a Marxist-Leninist in the 1920s by American educational ideas during seven years in Wisconsin-Madison). The editor, irritated, exclaimed 'How can he go back into himself like a tortoise!', an appropriate remark in India, the tortoise, being used figuratively in such a context of yogic holding-in—not a negative renunciation, rather a controlled energy.

◆ Because so many colleagues demanded an explanation when Westminster politics was just beginning to throw up two-timers and disloyal party politicians who thought nothing of crossing the floor of State Assemblies just for the sake of power seeking, J P wrote a small tract to explain what so confounded them: **From Socialism to Sarvodaya** as well as a book: **Socialism, Sarvodaya and Democracy** (Asia Publishing House, Bombay, 1965).

◆ Disillusioned already with top-heavy State socialism as demonstrated in Russia, and fasting in Gandhian tradition, J P was drawn to serious reflection on how to shift village life, the torpor, neglect and still evident impoverishment that party political democracy seemed unable to change. He spoke for that vast indefinable India whose predicaments, no matter all the good intentions, still went unresolved.

Somehow in reality worldwide, true community democracy is hard to come by. In the end before his untimely death J P worked closely with **E Schumacher** who had captured the imagination of organisations such as Oxfam and Australia's **Community Aid Abroad** with the world of intermediate sustainable technology and self-help. His seminal book: *Small is Beautiful* further captured world imagination in the 60s as well as his support of the **Men of the Trees** organisation.

Personal Footnote: In a private letter answering many questions from afar including our own mystification with J P's action Dr Zakir Husain, then Governor of Bihar, wrote:

As far as J P, I like him immensely. He is a jewel of a man—absolutely pure and genuine... His ideas about decentralization are very likely to find a more favourable environment in India than anywhere else, and I feel we shall soon look in that direction for the solution of our problems. Something along these lines has already been begun in Rajasthan and Andhra State.

The year was **1960**... Forty years on central bureaucracy may at last be listening.

■ **BHUMI** (n. *Hindi*) pr. *Bhoomi*

Bhoomi is regarded with devotion as Mother Earth. Among devout and traditional Hindus respect is paid to her each morning in a quiet prayer when getting out of bed, asking forgiveness for putting feet on her. **Prithvi** is also used as the name of a goddess honouring earth.

Sometimes travellers after long separation from the mother homeland kiss the earth on arrival, or did in the days before isolation in hermetically-sealed airports.

For so many indigenous cultures who see links go back uninterruptedly as does the profound Aboriginal sense of earth in Australia, the land is not to be **owned** but treated with care. Aborigines speak of **custodianship**, explaining idiomatically—**all people's mother this place**!

■ **BINDU, BINDI** (n. *Hindi*)

See **TILAK** (tika), and **ZERO** concept. The auspicious dot worn on the forehead. On women it does *not* signify marriage, nor as stated in some Western writing, is it a caste mark. The vermilion streak in the hair parting is a sign of being married in some communities.

Men wear a tilak usually in turmeric, grey vibhuti powder, or vermilion as a mark of attending temple and giving worship before the Deity. In Yoga theory two physiological **nadis**—channels of vital energy cross over at what symbolically is marked by **sindoor**—the Third Eye point where some Indians recall Rajput tradition at the time of Muslim persecution when blood was marked on the forehead of relatives from a cut on the thumb. That makes the wearing of a bindi as a fashion statement by Madonna and Naomi Campbell somewhat out of place!

■ BIRTH CONTROL and FAMILY PLANNING

◆ Vitally important to India where having one hundred sons appears in literature again and again as a Vedic blessing—perhaps a boon indeed in an essentially agricultural society—where tending the large and precious herds of cattle, and driving chariots was important..... somewhat different in 1953.

When my family first arrived in India the population was **360 million** and Delhi was **2.5 million**, enjoying a 'village' atmosphere where it seemed everyone knew everyone else. Now one billion people are fast catching up on China and increasing by **18 million** (the entire population of Australia) each year. Since 1956, 31 Australias, twelve UKs (55 million) have been dropped into the population. Delhi is said to be approaching 12 million if the outlying, rapidly spreading suburbs are taken into account. Quite alarming. Pollution of air is such it is a wonder that half the population have not expired of asphyxiation.

It is very little use mentioning statistics because they are not the important factor in the equation. Nor are individual attitudes. Hindus, Buddhists and many of the other religious faiths have no hang-ups about birth control. Muslims have some hesitations due to certain factors in past decades when insensitive handling of predominantly Muslim suburbs—and slum clearances around the Jama Masjid Mosque in old Delhi under Sanjay Gandhi's impetuous interventions—created political waves and much denunciation from mosque functionaries—also politically motivated. Even in Muslim countries, although orthodoxy quotes passages of the Qur'an which imply that control is not accepted, modern Muslims like Roman Catholics practice birth control.

◆ Taking India as a whole, government education and many varieties of voluntary programmes and persuasion have been assiduously undertaken—mostly in the economically advanced states, **and especially where women's education is given proper funding.**

◆ This is the crux of the matter rather than
a) government propaganda and poster campaigns seen everywhere with the visual nuclear family of mother, father, son, daughter on bill boards;
b) condom advertising in newspapers and on TV now, which provides many a chuckle. It is more freely expressive in lyrical terms—that vivacity of the Indian use of English again—than anything seen in western women's magazines;

c) The absolute necessity of children to care for the elderly being uppermost in any family's concern for the future...and especially male strength for agricultural work.

Having been in villages in Uttar Pradesh and Tamilnadu with social workers and seen the health records of families where every other child under five dies of malnutrition, diseases or accidents with open fires, and where some mothers have never menstruated for 15 years due to constant childbirth despite **all** the campaigns, thought turns to deeper causes of the malaise in family planning.

There are many factors in a predominantly rural population of far-flung villages and poor provision of mobile health clinics—insidious malnutrition of women, isolation and minimal structures of life insurance schemes, social security, pension, etc. **to buttress old age**, infirmity, inability to plough the land and bring in crops for a livelihood...

◆ First it has to be said that Indians have made heroic efforts in many inventive ways to master the complexities both in psychological factors as well as the dynamics of India's geographical immensity and far flung isolated hill, jungle and desert populations without the enforced programs of communist China.

Secondly, India's fitful start so soon after Independence has to be taken into account. **Rajkumari Amrit Kaur,** a high-born woman, an avowed Catholic Indian Christian, was appointed the Minister of Health in Pandit Nehru's first Congress Government. I can recall at the time the WHO Representative's repressed annoyance and frustration in getting the early schemes in place in various states in the initial birth control programs. There was lack of motivation and urgency.

◆ Experience with our family ayah who cared lovingly for our three children was a steep learning curve also at that particular time, as to how hard it was despite some programs in place to help her, when she came in despair one day asking for personal help. Having already had eight children, three of whom had died, she was pregnant again despite having tried to discover sources of family planning. We toured Delhi together with the help of our own fine Indian woman doctor.

For one reason or another this program or that was not available. We seemed to flounder in a sea of literature, pills, loops, advice for her husband, a senior bearer to an MNC Director—so he was earning a good salary as well as herself.

The consequence of considerable effort to find an efficient means of helping her was that she gave birth to her ninth child the same day exactly that the 16-year-old daughter gave birth to her first! We had attended her wedding precisely a year before. Scilla became a grandmother—aged 34. All the children were girls except one and the father obviously wanted to try once more for that elusive son... I had the unenviable task of taking a stand on behalf of Scilla who pleadingly requested intervention on our part to explain to him about the local clinics. This *would* happen just as my husband disappeared 'out of estachion' as the Indians say!

The result was sterilisation, legal as abortion also was at the time after the live birth of six children. But even that was difficult to effect as she had given birth at home and not in hospital... and no wonder, taking a look inside the government hospital where she eventually was operated upon.

It was a lesson also that no white Western person has any right to pontificate to Indians upon this crucial but complex subject. The dilemma goes beyond just birth and life matters—it is as profound as that of choice between slow, sometimes inefficient processes:

a) **of democracy** where citizens have options and need long-term education to come to suitable and appropriate conclusions, India's path. However, one ponders whether there is time for such luxury of approach. Everywhere one sees the damage to the environment of population pressure as compared with 50 years ago, in addition to the other stresses on employment, health facilities, educational improvement;

b) and the immediately more efficient methods **of authoritarian government** which **dictate** (even if it too has out of desperation to do so as in the case of China). Single child families are not just encouraged. They are enforced, despite enormous pressures in Chinese culture.

Democracy or dictatorship—two ways of responding to such urgency. This is the horns of the dilemma.

■ BISHNOIS

Very unusual community of Rajasthan in the arid zone near Jodhpur-Jaisalmer. They are true environmentalists motivated by the 29 (bis = 20 no = 9) principles laid down by their guru, inspired by the practice of ahimsa and vegetarianism.

Jambeshwar, born in 1451, was the son of a village headman. It is said of him that the hours of solitude spent tending the herds of goats and sheep bred a passionate love in the young shepherd for the land and the animals it nurtured. Then in 1476 he was a hapless witness to a terrible drought that ravaged this region. The inhabitants were led to strip the land of its foliage to provide fodder for their cattle. Consequently he drew up these principles for his people to honour as he realised that humans and nature must achieve a harmony of balance. Without trees the land is denuded, topsoil blows away, exactly what is happening in many regions of the world where land is being denuded of forest for timber industries.

Bishnois are the great milk suppliers throughout this region and way down from Bikaner to Jaipur, ubiquitous on their motorbikes now, with a rising standard of living compared with some of the other peasants.

Usually a Bishnoi settlement stands out in the harsh landscape because it is almost always surrounded by a grove of trees or neatly woven thornbush to keep their deer, goats and even the Great Indian Bustard—nearly extinct—safe from predators.

■ BJP/BSP

Bharatiya Janata Paksh or **Party,** a rightwing predominantly Hindu political force which achieved government at the Centre in the 11th general election of 1996 (see **SECULAR STATE** and **ORTHODOXY**). Under the leadership of **Atal Bihari Vajpayee**, it

lasted only 13 days but Vajpayee's reputation as a developing statesman and parliamentary orator gathered force.

The BJP has enjoyed a rapid increase in support in the Hindi belt of north India and parts of western India since 1984. It then won only two seats in the 543 strong Lok Sabha (House of the People). Up to 2001 it had won central government three times in a row. Its beginnings go even further back under another name—**Bharatiya Jana Sangh** (BJS) in 1951 when it was the political wings of the RSS extremist movement. That originated in **1925,** as one Indian journalist put it, a fanatical anti-Muslim street gang.

♦ Its growth as a national conglomerate in government with many disparate minor parties represents a major seismic shift in political culture. With the new millennium established, further experiment in parliamentary **coalition democracy** continues, the General Election of 1999 having brought about the formation of the **National Democratic Alliance** (NDA). The BJP-formed government as the majority party in a coalition of 24 parties, many only comprising a few MPs. This has constrained the ideological wing of the BJP which has had to come to terms with participants from the political left of centre and individuals from very different backgrounds than radical **HINDUTVA** politics.

♦ Prime Minister **Atal Bihari Vajpayee** surprised many of the party's fierce opponents with his level-headed tranquil guidance of the nation through some considerable crises especially with Pakistan. A leader of genuine integrity, he gave the impression of a gentle uncle; however, there is poetry in his soul and a passion hidden away until he begins to take the platform. Then he emphasises with wide gestures the depth of his feeling for India (see **GOVERNMENT** and BJP's unexpected but resounding defeat in 14th General Election, 2004).

1997

One strange bedfellow is the **Bahujan Samaj Party** (BSP). The metaphor should rather be female in the strange form of shakti, Ms **Mayawati**, mercurial BSP chief and intermittently CM of the UP who behaved in an extraordinary dictatorial fashion transferring without compunction hundreds of civil servants according to whim.

The BSP represents yet another minor regional party for the people at the bottom of the caste pile, the **DALITS** and landless bonded labourers of UP and Bihar who once gave their loyalties to the Congress Party and Mrs Gandhi.

To understand what is happening in this new political culture where rural India and regional State Governments are no longer part of what was a 50-year top-heavy dominance by the Congress Party (which became the Old Guard) having served honourably in the 30s and 40s struggles for independence from British rule, is to watch Westminster-style parliamentary democracy—especially the English system of first past the post wins—under scrutiny as in many ex-colonial independent nations. Devolution of power to regional parties is beginning to shift what were immutable principles imposed at Independence on Asian, African and Pacific Island peoples whose cultural roots were not British nor Anglo-Saxon!

Even the Celtic fringe of Scotland, Wales and Ireland has asserted ethnicity and language as needing recognition within the British system. Scotland now has its own parliament. Nigeria, Ghana, Sierra Leone, Zimbabwe, Malaysia, Fiji, Sri Lanka and the Solomon Islands in the Pacific have all suffered civil unrest under the imposed carapace of the Westminster-style parliamentary system.

Infinitely more complex a nation, the flexibility of Indian culture is still evolving a system where minorities—larger than many nations—have a say at the central core of the ruling party in government even though their regional base at state government level is an opposition party. Coalitions (often very disparate) have taken up residence in Delhi with power, perks and Government residences and cars to encourage them to retain this developing trend!

■ **BODHISATTVA** (n. *Sanskrit*)

can be broken down into these two words meaning wisdom/pure in the sense of wisdom/purity from **sattvic qualities** (see **GUNAS**).

A compassionate great soul such as a mahatma who opts to stay in the **samsara** cycle of transmigrations of earth-bound souls (**atma**, in active nirvana, Buddhists would state) to help other beings to salvation. A Buddha is one who has gone beyond this stage to become a **realised being**.

As the serene **Avalokitesvara** (pronounced Ava-lo-kit-eswaraa-**iswara** the manifest Brhm or Lord) this great soul strives with **dedicated compassion** in this particular grounded life to help other humans reach ultimate liberation—**Nirvana**. In the Buddhist universe their seniormost compassionate soul is **Ava-lok, the lord who looks down**. This concept of the embodiment of infinite compassion is dramatically visualised by a huge Ladakhi **murti**. This future Buddha-to-be is halo-ed by a thousand outstretched arms, an eye in every palm! For Mahayana Buddhists this is a symbol of the all-seeing power of such benign force. (Avalokita is a girl's name. No matter how melodious, daughters sometimes have to struggle to learn to write this multi-syllabled name in their first days at school).

◆ To see these benign visions in all their bejewelled glory you have to go to the Ajanta caves in Maharashtra—surely an additional wonder of this world lost to human knowledge for a thousand years when the original list was compiled as an arbitrary eurocentric seven! They were stumbled upon by accident in 1819 by an English army officer on a search for tigers in a horse-shoe shaped valley which had been lost to human habitation, overrun as it was by impenetrable thorn bushes and menacing beeswarms hanging in their thousands, in pendulous 'bells', from the trees.

Despite the presence of near-naked and fierce aboriginal-Bhil tribes, from that moment was set in motion the tortuous process that took over half a century (1820s onwards) bringing this incomparable treasure of Indian civilisation back into the light of day. (An account of this moving process including notebooks made on the spot like a TV documentary appears in **India**

Discovered by **John Keay**.) In the public domain at last, it took some time to understand the treasured extent of the artistic achievement.

As the jungle was gradually cleaned and bat droppings and other detritus removed, miraculous engineering skills of ancient masons and sculptors were revealed of over 1,500 years earlier. Living rock had yet again been carved into the round with precision, style, consummate polishing of surface to create Buddhist stupas (reliquary monuments), granite rock ceilings fashioned in imitation of carved wood beams, a garland of vivid painted depictions, some seemingly the fevered imagination of ascetic monks fired by the forbidden dusky beauties, apsaras (female aerial spirits) and nymphs dangling pearl-roped necklaces and sapphire-blue beads encrusted in delicate tiaras yet bereft of all raiment. Their dark pigmented bodies recline on verandahs and prop up columns which look almost Egyptian off a hieroglyphic frieze. (Indeed early art experts speculated that these wonderful galleries must be fashioned by the hands of a conquering Egyptian race! Indian capacity to accomplish such miraculous depictions must have been denigrated at the time by a superior colonial attitude.) The Ajanta cave paintings of quite astonishing expertise and aesthetic beauty in execution let alone mention of the immaculate style and ability to handle large crowd scenes and panoramic views like shuttered camera shots of animated movement in the urban townscape of the 5th–6th–7th centuries, are not frescoes in the Italian sense. The rock surfaces were polished smooth as much as possible and filled in with potters clay mixed with molasses and rice husk.

Lime plaster smoothed the surface even. Natural dyes, ground from the minerals in the rock, were then mixed with the red laterite. Soils are used—very much in harmony with Aborigines working the same hues in Australia in their rock gallery paintings of 25,000 years ago, or more—for ochres, burnt sienna, rich browns and yellow turmeric colours. But the Maharashtrian mountains also provide flashes of startling blue lapis lazuli, and azalea-leaf greens.

◆ And there in Cave I (painted it is thought in the second half of the 6th century CE) is a compassionate **Bodhisattva**—the unrealised **Buddha** awaiting descent into the world of suffering.

He dominates the temple portico behind, inwardly musing with droop-lidded eyes.

Despite the cliché eyebrows and the chocolate-box type bows tied around upper arms and securing the diadem-towering crown on the head, the all-too effeminate hand holding a white lotus—symbol of purity—the impression nevertheless of serene beauty is a haunting one, a long memory still resonating in the personal mind's eye from over 50 years ago. Then, Ajanta was only just opening up properly to visitors, electric arc lamps to light up the caves were still an experiment and the local dak bungalow was a hothouse minus fans, full of creepycrawlies. It was safest to carry the charpoy beds out onto the verandah—where in the grey light of dawn a local herd of goats found it playful to join us, munching bedroll sheets. Such is an awakening in India! But also another level of awakening. Until we came to Ajanta I had only seen the lifeless figures of such spiritual entities in museums. They were meaningless except for compassionate serenity sculpted into a facial expression. The Ajanta caves give the overseas visitor an in-the-round experience of Buddhist society, terraced living, an abundance of joy, the Bodhisattvas, many in the shadows, ready to intercede as well they might—certainly in Cave 1 where a cowering monkey-like human, gross cherubs, watching in curiosity, a lute player with repulsive physiognomy all seemed to be held at bay by the Bodhisattva's presence, defeating those **asuras** of the nether region of the mind that run riot through humanity.

Teaching those who remain in the endless line of recycled births and deaths is the way of the Bodhisattva. The present fourteenth **Dalai Lama Tenzin Gyatso** writes this in his own **Guide to the Bodhisattva's Way of Life—A Flash of Lightning in the Dark of the Night** (Journal of the Buddhist Society, Shambhala Publications, November, 1995):

Faith is very important in Buddhism, **but wisdom is even more so.** *True faith has to be based on reasoning... Without rational investigation it is impossible to distinguish whether the Buddha was speaking in an adapted or relative sense or whether his words are to be taken literally as expressing the ultimate meaning. This is why the sutras mention the four reliances:*

Do not rely on individuals, rely on the teachings.

Do not rely on the words, rely on the meaning.

Do not rely on the adapted meaning, rely on the ultimate meaning.

Do not rely on intellectual knowledge, rely on wisdom.

■ **BOMBAY**
now **MUMBAI**

is India's cosmopolitan city originally called after **Mumba Devi** the mother goddess of the earliest inhabitants, the Koli fisherfolk. Bombay prided itself on being internationally outward-looking, tolerant to most in-comers over at least 300 years since it came into the sights of the first Portuguese of the 16th century, and then given to the British by Catherine of Aragon as part of her dowry when she came to England to marry Charles II in 1665.

This deity is said to have lived in ancient times in a hut beside a tank where sacred lotus grew. Their touch cured ailments. Victoria Terminus now covers the site of her shrine.

◆ Now **16 million people** plus, Bombay once was along with Madras, titled as a Presidency of the Raj and regarded as having an upright impeccable administration—the cleanest in India. This was somewhat in contrast with its early history of suspect growth, impelled forward by the buccaneering greed of Europeans— Portuguese, Dutch, British all clinging acquisitively to its coastline and creeks; building forts and walled factories to fend each other off in the bitter rivalry for trade. This disrupted the local population, fleecing cultivators and artisans alike, pirates hiding in the creeks looting their produce in turn once it was aboard ships bound for the Mediterranean.

◆ **Captain Kidd**, notorious to children in English folklore, took on East India Company ships plying the route from factories in Surat and Bombay. He is said to have plundered one Company ship of a quarter million pounds worth of cargo—in those days a fortune. Finally captured, he was executed at the Tyburn gallows in London.

◆ As a result of the corruption and disgraceful behaviour of the English in Surat, much of which became a personal fiefdom for factory managers, the EIC appointed a **President**, Sir George Oxendon, to oversee what was the Royal Dowry—hence the title of **Presidency of Bombay**. (In the development of the East India Company from a business structure into an administrative one on behalf of the government in London, India by the end of the 17th century, had been divided up as Mughal power collapsed, into three presidencies—the other two Madras and Bengal, autonomous bodies with governing councils of senior merchants, able to communicate independently with central government in England.

◆ In very recent times Mumbai has hung its head in shame in the blood-letting riots that set the city aflame at the turn of the year into 1993 after the Ayodhya mosque issue and the mayhem that followed its destruction. An anger had pent up in certain sections of the Hindu community about their sacred sites desecrated over centuries by Muslim rulers who flexed their conquering muscles by carrying off stone-carvings from Hindu temples to build adjacent mosques—this from the 11th century onwards. Up till then it prided itself in its international cosmopolitan nature, not only in recent centuries but in ancient times when it was marshland but Egyptian, Roman and Arab vessels sheltered in its creeks.

◆ Basically tolerant, Mumbai was imbued with a secular ethos, given more in the past to making money whether by Hindu, Bohra, Parsee who helped with Jains to build up financial strength, philanthropic medical centres, flourishing art schools, museums and galleries. Buddhist, Sikh, Jewish, European, south Indian, Sri Lankan, huge conglomerates, MNCs from the USA, UK, Germany, Japan all create a cosmopolitan city......as well as visiting Arabs.

◆ Indeed there were some of us who never wanted to live in Bombay because it wasn't the real India—which of course is a nonsense when one considers in this complex, pluralistic subcontinent what is the real India. But being the nation's Hollywood (termed **B**ollywood from **B**ombay) approximately 1,000 films produced a year does cloud it in delusions of glamorous hype! Extravagant and implausible the plots may be but Bollywood is booming now at big film complexes in Britain— and not just for British Asians alone. Young Britons are queuing, Internet and Indian dance music fuelling the interest.

◆ One real problem has been the influx of illegal poverty-stricken migrants from Bangladesh (predominantly Muslim) considered to be one of the most impoverished nations—if not the most—in the world. Patrol of a border which in 1947 never existed is virtually impossible, and where both sides were Bengalis first before being either East Pakistani then Bangladeshi or Indian, or Hindu/Muslim. Playing upon parochial loyalties at local political level, the communal divide was exacerbated with terrible excesses in which construction and real estate developers played a part in trying to terrorise bustee slum dwellers off the land they had been forced to occupy over decades.

◆ The latest statistics show that roughly **50% of the city's population now lives crowded in less than 10% of the city area.** These slums are crammed into crisis proportions, a powder keg, while the rest of the middle class and the wealthy live in luxury by anybody's standards—some of the richest people in the world, billionaires in a US dollar criterion scale in the hundreds (and with real 24 carat gold in their safes—see **GOLD**).

◆ MNCs and NRIs have pushed the price of land, condominiums and apartment rentals to Tokyo heights with their encouraged rush to invest in real estate. Meanwhile, political parties despite all their declarations of patriotism in developing Mumbai turn a blind eye to its neglected public services—another basic statistic: 200 public toilets when 50,000 are needed —such is the inner political inefficiency.

The division between rich and poor is increasing alarmingly. Capitalism flourishes within the context of the new liberalisation and globalization... but with lost dharma... enough to make one wonder when a Marie Antoinette syndrome may finally overtake Mumbai. Indeed crime has as a product of the extravagant alternative cash economy-undeclared tax, proliferated in the last decade. Shoot-outs and extortion, now even Italian-style kidnappings, left at least 1,000 people killed in 1998. All kinds of businesses and dealers, professional people as well, pay protection money to Pakistan-based racketeers and gangsters. Local politicians and poorly-paid police are in collusion.

Three aspects of Mumbai stand out to be commended:

◆ **An efficient railway commuter system** despite terrorist attacks which could teach the rest of the world's cities a thing or two—when one considers the traffic, the organisational hazards, the lack of wealthy nations' resources and technological toys.

◆ **An indigenous system of supplying lunchtime food** direct from house to office in the quite extraordinary **dabbawallah network**. Thousands of tiffin carriers (triple-tiered metal containers neatly stacked in a simple frame with handle) from private homes get transported by rail to family members in offices across the city, servicing dietary complexities that must have no equal on earth. This operation is a modern miracle in the city's crowded commuter systems and a resounding credit for Indian ingenuity.

◆ **A courageous body of exercised Indians** of all communities working alongside each other—including Hindu and Muslim—to retrieve the honour of Mumbai. These people include women lawyers, Hindus representing Muslim clients, social workers (themselves paid a pittance), outspoken journalists and editors, honourable business tycoons, a body of artists and writers formed to counteract local political **goondas** (hooligans) at the time of communal rioting after the Ayodhya mosque/temple controversy aroused the national conscience in 1992–3... and a seriously increasing crime rate targeted the middle class.

In the cause of re-establishing **dharma**. Indeed, there is a need for a **maha-atma**. Gandhiji, where art thou now? Up-to-date information on the city is available at **www.inmumbai.com**.

■ **BOONS**

Vows, fasts (**VRATA**) for family welfare and special days for the individual's health and long life, are all interlinked in a view of life that takes a long perspective of what might happen in the next.

As a result of self-disciplinary rituals undertaken with hardship by humans, promises are made in return by deities in the thousands of legends, the consequences of which promises, the breaking of vows by humans, often inadvertently and not their 'fault' but brought about by the forces of a previous birth, ultimately and endlessly work out through the system of transmigration/**samsara**, of souls—the individual atmans. The Mahabharata and all the subsidiary texts, are full of boons requested of a superior power, vows made, fasts undertaken (**TAPASYA** with real fervour = heat) to effect an even greater boon.

◆ This was a word much used in Victorian English, very attuned to Indian ways of thinking no matter how militant Christianity and missionary activity in India had become in that era. Because society and family were securely embedded in the old verities, God's beneficence and anger at transgression (the concept of hellfire and damnation) were more real and boons were essential even in Western societies.

◆ Even deities receive boons! Often when they are in mortal peril the boon gives them immunity.

◆ **Indra**, the original Vedic supremo and personification of the greatest force of all, the firmament out of which comes thunder and monsoonal floods that could devastate as equally as drought, was always under threat from the undermining forces of the **asuras** = anti-gods. Indra granted boons to other deities further down the hierarchy of gods in heaven = **svarga** for help they might give in turn in order to preserve the status quo.

◆ Rama rewarded the monkey deity Hanuman with a boon which has made him immortal in the eyes of Indians. For his selfless service, devotion and bravery in overcoming Ravana, Rama on his return to and coronation in the kingdom of Ayodhya granted Hanuman anything he asked for. His response was a request to live as long as the Ramayana is read aloud and talked about—and as this happens all over contemporary India, Hanuman is alive and well! Consequently, at some public readings, an empty seat is kept on the public platform for the invisible presence of this wise deity—the result of this ancient boon.

■ **BRHM, BRAHMA, BRAHMACHARYA, BRAHMAN, BRAHMIN, BRHMVIDYA**—turn to sections dealing with **CASTE, CORE CONCEPTS, PANTHEON** and **QUATERNITIES**.

■ **BUDDHA/ BUDDHI** (n. *Sanskrit*)

The proper name for the 'Enlightened One' is the transliteration into English of the word for wisdom, wise, intelligent. **BUDDHI** = understanding.

1. History

Born into a Hindu royal family of the kshatriya class in Kapilavastu in the thriving kingdom of Magadha in northern Bihar, **Prince Gautama Siddhartha** which means **'he who accomplishes his purpose'** grew up surrounded by privilege and wealth in the 6th–5th century BCE. The dates of his birth are still under revision, and this particular question mark is typical of a fundamental difference between the Western view of time, specific, verifiable, or otherwise discounted if there is no empirical evidence in manuscript or archaeological dating*. Very different from this concept of time are the oral cultures as I am well aware in Aboriginal concepts in Australia. Akin to the Indian view there is a **passionately-held trust in the integrity of oral tradition** handed down by **strict rules** in the rituals of learning their song lines. The internal mental map of their country learned at puberty, accompanied by staunch ceremonies as a safeguard for nomadic lifestyle, must also have been necessary for the survival of early Indian neolithic communities.

Indians resent deeply the implication that because facts have not been written down, they are any the less accurate in historical time...indeed Indians remind the outside world that the adamantine adherence by brahminical tradition to the niceties of grammar and text related orally in the Sanskrit slokas was as strong a discipline as anything delivered down the ages in the Western predilection for **written** evidence. Arguments can still arise and become quite heated on this, a very cultural attitude and matter! (see **ITIHASA** = history).

◆ Up until now it has been accepted that the Buddha died peacefully at the age of 80, his *parinibbana* (death) taken to be in 483 BCE, without martyrdom unlike Christ being hounded as also was Muhammed in his early evangelism, having to flee Mecca. This was an achievement for such a far-off time when the average age of survival was so low. Perhaps this says something for the psychosomatic aspects of his life, his message spreading the word of living the **Middle Way**, the *summum bonum* of the **golden mean**.

2. Buddhist Faith

is in marked contrast to what has been termed 'the multi-foliate body of Hindu thought and the concern with **sanatana dharma** (*sanatan* = 'eternal or a continuous series of personal dharmic experiences'—the Hindu term for its distinctive way of life). Buddhist belief emerged out of this limitless body, encrusted as that was and weighed down in that era by at least three millennia of growth, never even getting rid of the barnacles clinging on to the main body because that's not the way of the Indian mind. Like some gigantic sea anemone, all tentacles waving in the waters—that **Ocean of Life** (see **AVATAR**)—whatever passes by is sucked in, absorbed and regurgitated into a Hindu form (that **PALIMPSEST** again!).

---

* The Indian Post and Telegraphs did issue a First Day cover for philatelists on **24/5/1956 to celebrate the 2,500th Buddha Jayanti**, his birthday so long ago.

The Buddha and those that followed, in the **sangha** (the body of the Church) cleansed the main Hindu concepts of centuries of dross but still retained the foundation pillars of belief (see **QUATERNITIES, CORE CONCEPTS**). Most people who follow the Buddhist way (and in many countries Buddhism is said to be the fastest growing religion) speak of its simplicity. The following skeleton framework to its basic philosophical concerns gives some idea of this perception:

a) **Mythological**—stories, myths and legends in the Jataka tales of the Buddha.

b) **Doctrinal**—exploration of ideas, concepts and beliefs **Four Noble Truths.... Noble Eightfold Path**

The Universe has evolved and functions according to **dhamma**—Pali language (dharma in Sanskrit) and is an expression of the Dhamma and Kamma (karma) law of natural cessation.

Three characteristics of existence: **anicca, dukkha** (duhkha in Sanskrit) and **anatta** being respectively impermanence, suffering or unsatisfactoriness, and egolessness or not-self.

c) **Ethical**—rules of behaviour—**sila, samadhi and panna**, being morality, mental culture or discipline, and wisdom respectively. Individual responsibility for own salvation in which compassion is stressed.

d) **Ritual**—rites and ceremonies **simplified**. No pantheon of deities or complex rites.

e) **Social**—ideas about social and community structure important. **Caste no longer exists** as a structure. Position of the **sangha in the community as a brotherhood seen as more important**.

3. Transformation into a Buddha

Prince Siddhartha's voyage of discovery to arrival at the **Four Noble Truths** which are the foundation stone of Buddhist philosophy—a more accurate term than religion—not being devoted to a personalised god who came as a divine intervention in the world as such was a long hard lonely passage, shorn of the luxury of his early years, the trappings of power and emotional security within marriage. All this took place within an area east of Varanasi up to the Nepal border, within the UP and Bihar states.

Certainly strange portents and events mark this passage as told throughout Asia in Buddhist legend and texts... a dream by his mother Queen Maya of her ascent towards heaven coming to rest with her handmaids in a beautiful hallowed place where she was bathed by wives of the Devas... the vision of a snow-white elephant (surely an echo of Indra's famous charge, **Airavata**, in the Vedic heaven of at least two millennia earlier?) carrying a white lotus, trumpeting and walking around her in this dream-like world between reality and this other reality, dissolving into a wispy **akasha** (ethereal substance or vapour) and entering her womb—another immaculate conception.

Prediction by divines at court who like rsis of old have insight into future events, foretold that a boy would be born who could become the most eminent of rulers in the worldly sense or the exact opposite—a ruler in spiritual terms of people's hearts; one condition was set that the latter course would only take shape if this young scion of the household were to venture forth into the real world, encountering its difficulties and unpleasant aspects.

But this soul in a previous Bodhisattva incarnation had been prepared to forego ultimate release from endless cycles of rebirth in order to come again into this historic period as a Buddha to retrieve good and protect humanity. This would be on a full-moon (**purnima**) night.

In the gardens of Lumbini nearly 100 km into Nepal—not dissimilar in symbolic Jungian terms of the way Eve was created out of the rib of Adam in the original Eden—the Buddha was born out of the side of Queen Maya. Of course, despite all the precautions taken by Prince Siddhartha's parents to prevent him coming across anything untoward, surrounded as he was as a child by a charmed existence within the palace walls, his curiosity—and of course his karmic destiny—encouraged the Prince to explore... the rest is history.

4. The Four Encounters

Consequently, this is what Prince Siddhartha was so shocked to see, once outside the palace precincts,

i **A shrivelled old man** crippled with age.

ii **A sick person writhing in pain**.

iii A funeral procession, **the shrouded corpse** being followed by the wailing cries of the bereaved. **A toiling populace** bowed down with sweat and never-ending work in the conditions of northern Bihar. (The word **Bihar** is derived from **vihara** = monastery. It is a land of paradoxes—and extremes—for its 70 million Biharis. It is a seat of India's most ancient empires, recorded at least as far back as the 6th century BCE; such was antique **MAGADHA**, a height of civilized sophistication, yet at least one-third of its now very impoverished population is aboriginal).

iv Led by the forces born within him to a sal tree *Shorea robusta*, Siddhartha sits in its shade where in a state of trance and troubled by this world vision of suffering and struggling humanity (not much different one could surmise from today!) he sees **a wandering hermit in a saffron robe** passing by. He explains his calling in the search for peace and tranquillity, leaving a profound imprint on Siddhartha's mind.

♦ Resolving to go out into the world to discover what answers there are to the nature of suffering he forsakes family, lovely wife and new-born baby Rahula, so named as a fetter by his father regarding his birth as one more earthly impediment to the search he knew in his heart he would have to make.

Imbued with sorrow at having to leave all whom he loved he sets forth secretly with his **loyal charioteer, Channa**, to accompany him so far to make his long pilgrimage of discovery of how to mitigate the conditions of humanity the truth of which has so perturbed his spirit.

Ridding himself of his fine raiments, once beyond the palace gates and out beyond the pale, he startles Channa by giving him his costly diadem turban, throwing away his body jewellery (hence the **elongated empty earlobes** to remind devotees who face his statues of how he gave up all wealth, even the heavy solid-gold earrings).

Finally with his gold sword he clasps his long hair bound in a top knot and with one swathe cuts it all off dramatically to the width of two fingers according to Buddhist lore. The hair then lay in flat curls and never grew again, the reason for depiction in later iconography of such **coils of hair**, and the protuberance on the crown of the skull—the **ushnisha**—which in later baroque Thai sculpture was to become even more exaggerated into a flame—the **vajra**—symbolic of the higher wisdom of the Buddha.

5. The Journey to Enlightenment...... Similarities occur again with the unfolding of messages of wisdom to humanity by other great souls.

♦ A withdrawal into meditation and a solitary lifestyle.

♦ Condemnation of those who ostentatiously undertake austerities supposedly to discipline the body to gain wisdom but like the priests and moneylenders of the temple who were castigated by Christ for their flaunting of faith, themselves more show than substance (as even today the extreme sadhu sects and fakirs in all their exoticism who so captured the Victorian mind).

After six years of undertaking such penances and austerities in the true Indian tradition for the attainment of *moksha* (release and liberation through self-realisation from the daunting cycle of karma) he discovered this way led only into a spiritual cul-de-sac.

♦ Temptation by Mara, the Evil One while meditating.

♦ Feet washed by a poor village woman seeking solace by worshipping a free spirit.

♦ Meditating for 49 days under a **peepul (Bodhi** *Ficus religiosa*) tree in silence.

♦ And thus came liberation while under the Bodhi tree, and the acquiring of supreme wisdom. Strange portents accompanied this self-realisation—a menacing flood and the protection by the sacred hooded serpent **Muchilinda** which acted as an umbrella for the Silent One and the tumult of an earthquake heralding **the Temptation.**

These recordings have come down the centuries in the fluent depictions in stone by nameless sculptors honouring these culminating events in the Buddha's struggle to attain wisdom.

In the statuary in later centuries the temptations and demands of Mara to vacate the Throne of Truth are depicted by the cross-legged Buddha composed and resolute, the hand mudra or gesture with fingers of the right hand pointing down, touching the earth seeking witness of his unwavering mind. The embodied earth emerged to give witness to this enlightenment.

6. Sangha and First Sermon

Now he must go out into the world and in typically Indian fashion—indicating the persistent brahminical influences which pervade the ambience of every Indian story of olden times—the great god Brahma appears in a vision exhorting Siddhartha to go forth and teach, gathering a body of disciples together who had accompanied him throughout these privations.

♦ The **sangha** or **brotherhood** was formed, laying the foundation stone of what eventually became the corpus of the Buddhist faith. (**There was no discrimination against women. Some become nuns. Caste was no barrier either.**)

- **The First Sermon** was given to an assembly of people seated on the ground in the Deer Park at Sarnath in UP near Varanasi. The message preached was that of the FOUR NOBLE TRUTHS and the EIGHTFOLD PATH—the Middle Way, which as the golden mean has marked out the Buddhist way of life. Thus was the **Dharma Chakra Pravatarna,** the **wheel of law** set in motion.

Neither the extremes of over-indulgence and self-gratification in the material life as Siddhartha had experienced in his early life, nor the extremes of asceticism he had undergone latterly had led to attainment of inner happiness.

7. The Four Noble Truths

are spoken of as noble–**aryasatya,** recalling again that Vedic concept of **ARYA:**

- All life is in a perpetual state of flux, **dukkha anicca** translated as anguished impermanence. Even happy events come to be seen as transitory, unsatisfactory and subject to suffering.
- This yearning for—and separation from—pursuit of happiness (as written into the American Constitution as a pre-requisite of a citizen's expectations) leads to dissatisfaction, tensions, even despair brought about by a slavish clinging to material possessions in excess of the necessities and even to emotional ties with family and friends, the hardest aspect of the disciplined Buddhist message to take on board.
- This grasping after fleeting and illusory happiness can be lessened, even brought to an end by **moderation, discipline of behaviour, coolness, aloofness**... all tools in the inner process of letting go.
- Extinction of dukkha through destruction of our ignorance, limited vision (maya), all this effort to control our wayward lusts, greed, desires to possess can eventually lead after dedicated training to that steady state—equanimity (see **STHITA-PRAGNYA**) or a **philosophy of compassionate detachment**.

8. The Teaching

The Noble Eightfold Path

is the key to escape this enmeshment which brings us back again and again to suffer the **dukkha** of this worldly existence in **samsara,** literally **perpetual wandering**:

Wisdom (**panna**)	Right Understanding
	Right Thought
Morality (**sila**)	Right Speech
	Right Action
	Right Livelihood
Meditation (**samadhi**)	Right Effort
	Right Mindfulness
	Right Concentration

This teaching was direct, easily understood by ordinary people not unfamiliar with the ideas of dharma, karma, moksha, maya (see **QUATERNITIES**) that were already embedded deep within Indian society.

Running through the entire body of Buddhist teaching that was to follow and fleshing out the skeletal frame is the emphasis on **right mindfulness, loving-kindness** and **compassion**; that true thought-understanding requires a deeper penetration of existence than just pure knowledge. There has to be that added dimension of wisdom—internal disciplines, purification of thought, the sense that personal freedom and **human rights** (so strongly urged in today's world) has also, in equal balance, a **responsibility** to society's needs. Such balance is a delicate acquisition. Simplicity rather than overload.

Buddha on the Internet might well take stock
of where the explosion of human thought
and communication is leading
in all its proliferation!

9. The Final Departure

- Into his 80s, trekking with his followers to the Himalayan foothills, and feeling very tired, he bathed and refreshed himself before lying down to rest in a mango grove in Kushinagar, northern UP, near the Bihar borders (see **Vaishali** in **PANCHAYAT** passages on ancient kingdoms and their 'feel' for **democratic republic**). The Buddha's final words before his parinibbana in the Pali text are written thus in English translation: *Behold now, bhikkhus, I exhort you:*

vayadharma sankhara (impermament everything that exists)
appamadena samppadetha = without delay strive on diligently...
'vaya' = decay
dharma sankhara = conditioned things formed by creation
appamadena = diligence, pamadena = negligence
samppadetha = strive on

- In more poetic language with the underlying implications: this quotation from **Sutta 16, Digha Niyaka** implies: **All things that exist, that are subject to formation are bound eventually to vanish. Strive on mindfully however, with diligence** (towards that **nirvana**, literally meaning blown out like a candle flame snuffed out, not being reborn, every new birth bringing further suffering (sadness or dissatisfaction).

The **social implications** of Buddhist teaching were profound and laid the foundations for India's own indigenous and deeply entrenched sense of democracy—despite what outsiders see as the great and perplexing divisions of caste, inbuilt wealth that seems to be immutably fixed and British-induced educational neglect of huge minorities. The Buddha worked around caste, condemned slavery, advocated the proper treatment of household servants, stating that they should be treated with the same consideration for personal rights as family members.

He was someone who could have walked into the UN assembly of today and outshone most delegates in that he was an advocate of non-violence before his time. He went further than most contemporary politicians

in roundly condemning also those who made weapons and traded in them. In his emphasis also on the inter-relatedness of humankind, the planetary environment, and cosmic laws as part of **one great life force**, Buddha is as much part of this age of ecology as any greenie.

Perhaps that is why so many young people worldwide become Buddhist. It is now declared to be the fastest-growing religion.

An allegory illuminating the intrinsic message of egalitarianism preached by the Buddha is told of his beloved disciple **Ananda** (= bliss) who was sent by the Buddha on a mission. Thirsty with the walk on foot he saw a beautiful young girl (**prakriti**—nature) drawing water from the village well. Ananda paused to request a drink but the young girl being of low caste sensing a mendicant of bearing and merit, lowering her gaze declared: Oh learned one, I have polluted it in the giving, whereupon Ananda immediately replied: Sister, I do not ask for caste, I ask for water!

10. What followed after the Buddha's Nibbana: Nirvana....mid-3rd century BCE

483 BCE has been accepted up until now as the passing of the Buddha but is now under revision.

Just as the Christian body of believers slowly was gathered into the Church, the painstaking work of narrating, classifying and compiling the teachings, parables, aphorisms of the Buddha was done by a few of his closest and most devout followers. Eventually major gatherings or councils to formulate the teaching took place at Rajgir in Bihar and later, under the patronage of the Emperor Ashoka. This literature was eventually written down in Pali (Palli = language of the village). The complex and difficult-to-master classical Sanskrit, a preserve of the upper caste priests, was abandoned. Prestigious seats of learning were established in northern Bihar at Nalanda south of Patna and in the south at Nagarjunakonda in Andhra Pradesh where thousands of teachers and even greater numbers of students gathered.

During the flourishing centuries of the Gupta empire, before Christ, the Buddhist dominance established

◆ **a common language binding heterogeneous peoples** even in Sanskrit which even spread into central Asia; and later Pali.

◆ **reforms against ossified rituals**

◆ **flourishing trade between individual kingdoms**

◆ **a great surge in urban culture** and a freeing up psychologically with a **greater egalitarian spirit**

11. Buddha as Avatar.... 2nd BCE = 2nd CE

Why has Buddha become the ninth in the line of the Hindu **dasavataram?** The pragmatic, straightforward teaching of the Buddha obviously made a direct appeal to the masses surrounded as they were in the sixth century BCE with a densely packed Hindu storehouse of accretions acquired over centuries of sectarian rules, caste regulations, priestly privilege from which they were debarred. Buddhists overseas (they are hard to find within India except as tourist pilgrims also at the major Buddhist heritage centres within eastern UP and Bihar)

tend to laugh it off gently explaining they regard themselves as entirely separate from the Hindu fold but the Hindu body, so elastic (that sea anemone syndrome again) tries to reabsorb as Christianity did with earlier animistic faith that had gone before—the Easter celebration and the egg of springtime festivity epochs before. As the Pantheon began to emerge visually and figuratively at the turn of the millennium, so Buddha's form also grew from the earlier abstract symbolism. Rather than recognizing the new preacher of an egalitarian way of life for its own time as an adversary it was best to incorporate this image of the great teacher as yet another stage in the development of a saving presence.

If you can't beat them, join them!

12. Where did the Buddhists go? (6th CE onwards)

However, despite the fact the Buddha's message spread widely and many conversions took place, the momentum returned to those in the Hindu fold through the bhakti movements north and south or were superseded by Islamic onslaughts and conversions from the 10th century on. Buddhism virtually left India as Buddhist pilgrims walked and rode over the high Himalayan passes into Tibet, Nepal, on and on into China and then to Japan, and through the dense foliage of tiger and leech-ridden valleys into Myanmar; or sailed out of the Bay of Bengal down to Sri Lanka and on to the far east.

Now there are only approximately 8 million Buddhists; the teachings and traditions are treasured as part of the Indian heritage but one of many strands in the total tapestry. Buddhist philosophy is now spoken of by scholarly Hindus as a heterodox philosophy—not one of the six main philosophies recognised as orthodox Hindu belief, drawing their sustenance from Vedic teaching.

■ **BUDDHIST ART**

Despite the fact that attempts were made to incorporate the Buddha into the overwhelming multiform conglomerate of the Hindu Pantheon, the legacy of Buddhist art at the cusp of time, which changed the global calendar has witnessed the man become the Compassionate One, standing in his own right, free in all the glory of the stonemason's craft.

Soon after his death and as Theravada Buddhism (which is predominantly maintained within India using Pali for its texts) moulded the monastic orders for teaching his message it was considered inappropriate to recreate the Buddha artistically in human form. **His immediate followers believed that his presence was too sacred and powerful to be made visible.** Besides which the Buddha had expressly forbade a personality cult. If you want to see me, he had said, go to my teachings. You will find me there.

A. Abstract symbols came to be used instead as reference to his person—depicted in all their glory in the consummate frieze sculpture at **Sanchi** in the restored gateways. Here a sociology of that faraway world in which Gautama Buddha lived can be seen in the marketplace scenes, the processions, the royal household, the architecture of buildings.

First, the abstract presence of Buddhism is represented by the Lion Capital and Ashokan Pillar of 250 BCE in the Sarnath Museum. Majesty and power reside in the strength of these regal creatures. They cushion the

Chakra, the **Turning of the Wheel of Law**: only the Buddha can set the wheel in motion.

The sandals: embossed with chakra wheel inlaid in the sole signifying pilgrimage and remembering the **Enlightenment**.

The Throne and/or **Bodhi Tree**: the present tree claimed to be from the sapling that Ashoka's sister carried from the original during the Emperor's mission to spread the word.

White Elephant: as a reminder of the **unusual circumstances** of his **birth**.

Stupa outline: a reliquary mound of earth bricked over as a chamber and enclosed in a railing forming a circumambulatory path = **pradakshina**, a reminder of Buddha's death and attainment of **nirvana** = a nothingness

Yantras or **mandalas**
- the rectangular base of a **stupa dome** or **chorten** = □ = earth
- the curved dome = O = air
- the narrow spire = △ = fire
- the crescent = (☽) =water

Chhatri or **umbrella: universal symbol** in India associated with **powerful rulers** from kings to holy people to viceroys.

Peepul leaf : to recall the Buddha's Enlightenment under the bodhi tree. (His first gesture after this momentous event was to express his gratitude to the tree).

The leaf once upturned has become an abstracted form like an inverted horseshoe (and possibly the reason for the Western horseshoe to have taken the lead from India and become associated with good luck). A cog wheel design inside the shape represents the rising sun.

Several caves at **Bhaja** in **Maharashtra** and **Barabar** near **Bodhygaya,** and **Ajanta** facades are carved with expert skill into this design; friezes elsewhere repeat the motif and even at the monumental **Mt Kailash Temple** in which nearly half a million tons of rock was carved out of the mountainside at Ellora to create the Shiva temple, the same shape appears. This time it is Shiva sitting cross-legged as a yogi framed in the aureole of the peepul shape, reclaiming the ground artistically for the Hindu faith, once more setting another golden age of artistic excellence in motion from the seventh century onwards until Islamic incursions and invaders put an end to the creativity with their fundamentalist attack on the dharma.

1st–2nd century CE: It was during the amalgamation of empire in the beginning of Christian times during the rule of the visionary **Kushan emperor Kanishka** that the first figurative representations of the Buddha began to appear in what is known as the **Gandhara** school of art. The famous standing **Buddha** of **Sarnath** inscribed in the third year of Kanishka's reign is put at 80 CE.

The sheer beauty of modelling, the inner contemplation of the meditating figure in yogic position, the plasticity of the surface depiction of diaphanous drapery, clinging to the Buddha's form turning it into ethereal substance, the teaching mudras or hand gestures, the subtle shift of the body reflect Indian art reaching a level of expertise equal to that being created in Greece at the time.

B. Sculpted Gestures (see **MUDRA**)
The most common mudras seen in the sculpted gestures as the Buddha meditates, teaches or provides a beneficent 'presence' are similar to those universal ones recognised throughout India and displayed in Hindu art.

Abhaya mudra: right hand raised in blessing: 'Fear not, for I am here'

Dhyanamudra: the gesture of meditation and composure, one palm resting on the other, upturned in the cross-legged lap asana = posture of yoga

Dharmachakramudra: of teaching the dutiful way of life, mindfulness, thumb and forefinger held up and touching in a circle.

Bhumisparshamudra: seated Buddha touching the earth with right hand taking witness from the earth of his enlightenment.

Art as a springboard for faith. Another contemporary manifestation increasingly witnessed in Europe and Australia is the month-long process executed by dedicated Tibetan monks of building up the colourful **sand mandala** beginning with ritual chanting and prayer, concentrated attention and potent meditation–in all of which viewers are invited to participate if they so wish. Then the four monks seated at the quadrants, start to build up the design. Long cone-shaped metal containers ridged on one side, are filled with different colours. Vibrating the cone gently along the ridged line with a metal spatula, the sand starts to flow evenly. The pattern builds up with absolutely accurate finesse carrying deep symbolism, not a line smudged. After the final ritual the sand is systematically scooped up, taken to a sacred river and consigned to the water... with dedication and prayerful ceremony. This has occurred several times in my home city—a new experience of globalization, thankfully not economic alone!

■ **BUDDHISM and INDIAN POLITICS**
The footnotes to Indian history are never ending! Yet another turn of the wheel has taken place with the collapse of the powerful Soviet bloc. The precarious shifts and turns of the Iraq-Iran-Afghan nexus and the alarming rise of fundamental Islamic terrorist activity all through the area to unrest in the inner Chinese Muslim provinces and hostage threats to foreign tourists abducted to the Philippines, present a gigantic political chess game. Some years ago a New Delhi byline in an English language newspaper under the name Ranjan Gupta read:

Buddhism Goes Full Circle in an Enlightened India
India, after a lapse of 2000 years, is to revive Buddhist links to forge new relationships in central and south-east Asia to bypass a hostile Islamic neighbourhood. Mongolia is the first country where

Buddhism is laying the foundations of a new diplomatic relationship after the collapse of the Soviet Union.

A vacuum therefore needed filling after this special rapport with the USSR. In an imaginative diplomatic move the Indian Government appointed the head Buddhist lama of Ladakh to Ulan Bator as ambassador where other ancestry leading down the centuries into India from Genghis Khan and the Mongol blood of Babur can also now be recalled in brotherly diplomacy.

Clearly a balancing act is necessary as the crescent of Islam spreads even further, flowing eastward over India's northernmost Himalayan ranges through the newly independent erstwhile Russian republics of Uzbekistan, Tajikstan, Kazakstan, Kyrgyzstan and Turkmenistan into the Chinese province of Sinkiang. They too are flexing their independent muscles. Buddhist societies in Tibet, Burma, and South Asia may well have to be a buffer. And so the ancient chess games of central Asia re-form on the board where once British imperialists and Tsarist Russians, Afghans and Chinese moved their jumping knights. The Buddha left a message for all this engagement of power play:

For one who clings, motion exists;
But for one who clings not, there is no motion.
Where no motion is, there is stillness.
Where stillness is there is no craving.
Where no craving is, there is neither coming or going.
Where no coming or going is, there is neither arising or passing away
Where neither arising nor passing away is, there is neither this world nor a world beyond, nor a stage between.
This, verily, is the end of suffering

from a sacred scripture of Buddhist teaching: **udāna** = utterances, in the Pali canon: **Inspired Utterances of the Buddha** edited by **John Ireland**, (Buddhist Publications Society, Sri Lanka, 1990). This volume contains 80 utterances attributed to the Buddha or his chief disciples on their self-realisation, a sublime state of bliss.

Where to find current Indian Buddhism in all its cultural/artistic glory is **Ladakh**—part of Jammu-Kashmir state, thus balancing out the strong emphasis Kashmir claims on world political conscionsness as being entirely Islamic.

La = pass, **Dakh** = land (of high passes). Leh, its capital has only become part of global tourism in the past 20 years. The flight from Srinagar is one of the most psychologically challenging over its forbidding blue-grey crusted moonscape peaks of the inner Himalayas.

An annual festival now takes place celebrating the Indus river, foundation stone of India's name and identity. This is the **Sindhu-Darshan Mela** (refer to **DARSHAN**).

■ BUREAUCRACY

The **babu** (now regarded as an officious clerk) gave India a bad name, an image of a nation smothered in a tangle of red tape. But let us face it—all nations suffer from obdurate government officials who regard you, as an enquiring citizen—an intolerable nuisance. But **babu** also had connotations of respect. Placed as an honorific after a name such as the first President of India, Rajendra Prasad, a truly homespun honourable Hindu in his khadi jacket and dhoti known as **Rajendra Babu**. A family elder might be referred to as **Babuji**.

And there is the obsequious (fearful) approach of an uneducated villager addressing a clerk of the court for instance as 'babu sahib'. There are niceties of detail at the bureaucratic babu level that only India with all its penchant for lists and categorisations can attain—and the following is one of them... and *not* a government department either...

Every occupant is presented with a detailed inventory when settling into nightly accommodation at the august Ooty Club in the Nilgiri Hills. This is just in case you feel inclined to walk off with a famous print on the walls without telling Management or the Colonel-in-Charge. And also if you feel inclined to pack up hangings, brass lamps, the most ancient of 19th century wardrobes—and clearly listed also... **one chimney**!

■ **CALCUTTA** now **KOLKATA**
founded 1690

is still alive! A phantasmagoria of 10 million volatile, talented, revolutionary as well as saintly Bengalis, radical demonstrators who specialised in turning over double-decker buses and trams in fighting the British for independence, Kolkata has been written off innumerable times as the city that should die—indeed several decades ago the Ford Foundation in a study concluded it was beyond redemption as a functioning city. Yet in 1990 it celebrated the 300th anniversary of its founding with aplomb! At night the population increases by 8 million!

It is quite impossible to describe coherently a city the size of some small nations. To do justice to her one would need to be as multi-armed as Kolkata's presiding benign deity **Durga** worshipped in colourful exuberance at the **puja celebrations** in September–October after the devastations of monsoonal rains.

◆ Kolkata provides a kaleidoscope of fitful impressions, a swirling universe of people, yet cursed by thousands of visitors and inhabitants during its 300-year growth from three undistinguished riverine villages now swallowed up in chaotic suburbs... cursed for its uninhabitable climate built as it is on swamp, in the proximity of salt lakes and fetid airs, beside a river Ganga that silts up with lethal sandbars down the Hooghly—its shipping pilots as a result the best in the world.

◆ Deluged nearly every year by volatile monsoons—you can almost catch a glimpse of the dark Kali—an alter ego of Durga—dancing with a similar demonic energy as the miasmic spread of city groans under wave after wave of refugees first in the savage amputation which was Partition and, in this new century, as well over a million illegal immigrants from an even more disrupted Bangladesh, especially after a series of devastating cyclones and floods, from topsoil brought down from the mountains from massive deforestation. Consequently, neighbouring Bangladeshis are dislodging settled societies in Assam, Uttar Pradesh and even distant Maharashtra. It also suffers from having as capital to service India's most densely packed state (nearly 800 people per square kilometre).

◆ Flying over the area once in a small impoverished Burmese plane, the great delta of the Brahmaputra and Ganga spread out below in an amazingly even design, a gigantic symmetrical mud fan, a crescent shape with brown silt leaking into the Bay of Bengal in a muddied flow clearly demarcated from an uncertain ocean.

◆ And yet its inhabitants still survive in a glory of the inner heart, treasuring the arts—despite the impoverishment in material possessions—probably more so than many an affluent nation. Bengalis are in the higher echelons of literacy attainment which is over 70% of its more than 80 million citizens.

◆ A 'surfeited muckheap' is Kipling's damning comment. From the charmingly civilised and homely Kenilworth Hotel—with its stairs and hall religiously washed down daily in the unmistakable disinfectant of British India—I watched the nature of the beast in the physicality of Kolkata's lethal climate, and the Kipling comment at work.

◆ Looking out from a bedroom window onto the vertical wall of one of Calcutta's last decrepit mansions, which undoubtedly will now have fallen to the bulldozers' implacable advance on behalf of the new rulers—the real estate barons, I watched a tree grow a foot in length in five days, emerging like a brawny elbow between two great blocks of stone masonry. The mildewed stonework and monsoon-battered stucco was home to a veritable carpet of vertical vegetation. So soon would the two pieces of wall be prised apart, then open to ravages of driven water invading the crevices, rapidly to crumble. And in the middle of the compound, ragpicker children, matted hair, faced with huge hessian bags, sorted out an unlimited detritus of other peoples' undoubtedly unhygienic refuse—the **KABARIWALLAHS**.

◆ Yet some of India's most gifted musicians, poets, cinema directors, actors, intellectual writers, politicians, saints, philosophers, business tycoons, innovators and powerful women have created a quite unique amalgam—Kolkata! And in a Marxist democratic state led by **Jyoti Basu, chief minister** since **1977** seeing the millennium in at 86! (He has since retired, but remained elder statesman with occasional prime ministerial ambitions).

An unusual history

Legend goes, when an Englishman employed as an Agent of the East India Company sat under an equally legendary tree (**peepul** or **tamarind** in two distinct places according to tradition) what became Kolkata, was born. The intruder smoked a pipe while considering how to resurrect the trading fortunes of the East India Company, then established firmly after nearly 100 years over in the west at Surat (1612), Bombay (now Mumbai, gifted in 1665 by the British government to the EIC) and down south in Madras (Chennai), 1640. He settled on an emporium in **Kalikata**. A riverine hamlet of fisherfolk and, according to British historians, the amalgamation of two other swamp-ridden villages—**Sutanati** and **Gobindpur;** thus was laid the foundations of an EIC trading post which even official Bengal appears to have accepted as the foundations of the city in 1690. Irreverent Bengalis prone to satire and healthy scepticism, assert this is typical of colonial European historians romanticising their own heroes in this case **Job Charnock**, when Bengalis were already trading along the river banks in the famous textile silks and muslins as well as *pith* (used in making Durga decorations at Puja time) and shellac referred to in a famous episode in the Mahabharata. Whatever the inconsistencies, anomalies, contrariness and paradoxes, the spirit of Kolkata flourished from that time onwards.

What is incontrovertible—the fitful fortunes under the Mughal emperor Akbar who had licensed a **firman** (an Islamic written edict) to trade to the Portuguese in 1577 was finally redirected by Emperor Shah Alam having fought all his brothers to succeed the Mughal dynastic throne after the death of Aurangzeb in 1707. His ruling allowed the English go-getting merchants of the EIC 'to trade free of all dues for annual payment to the Emperor 3,000 rupees...' Clive's treaty with an ineffective emperor ceded the whole of Bengal to the Company in 1765. And so another Empire was in the shaping... (Facts and figures taken from **J P Losty's Calcutta: City of Palaces**, The British Library, London, 1990 to celebrate 300 dramatic years of existence.)

This book and the late Mildred Archer's formidable array of tomes on Indian art of the period and India Office Library holdings in London, which document the heyday of Kolkata's wealth and sophisticated style and the **visual splendours** of Indo-British architecture, are surely compulsory reading for those who wish to understand the glories of Kolkata—the 'Rome of the East' apart from the lack of an ancient history.

◆ Today in the middle of **Chowringhee** it is almost inconceivable to conjure up the vision of those illustrative prints, gleaming white stone and marble palaces along this once spacious road, home to unprincipled British nabobs on the make with profits running at 45% as well as principled men of honour like Bentinck who was called 'that Pennsylvania Quaker'. He lived at such a simple level as Governor-General (1828–35).

Lithographs by Sir Charles D'Oyly depict splendiferous archways upon which huge imperial British lions pace in stone while elegant phaetons prance up and down, their British occupants laced up in crinolines defying with stiff upperlips the 110% humidity. Palladian columns and architraves give all the airs of a Bengal Roman facade—'dazzling splendours, towering peerlessly'.

Nor was the splendour confined just to the white 'goras'—fair-skinned intruders bent on making money as a nation of shopkeepers. An unholy alliance also existed out in the countryside between the EIC factory and the Bengali zamindars who collected the rents for the British dominion which was establishing itself. There were very rich Bengali merchants themselves, the Seths, the Seals and Dwarkanath Tagore, grandfather of the famous poet amongst them.

◆ Bengalis took head on the full force of western Christian and liberal humanist ideas bubbling up in the latter part of the 18th–19th centuries—not only in Britain but France during the Revolution. With such a rich regional culture of their own they absorbed and transformed the input, with little psychological disruption. Bengali culture, despite the physical impoverishment of an overwhelmed city sinking under traffic and people, is as full of vitality as ever, hidden away in the narrow lanes and stucco-peeling staircases, crumbling old mansions of a fine and harmonious architecture, in animated gatherings of poets under trees where everyone stands engrossed at the end of a working day looking in their flowing silk and cotton Bengali-style dhotis like so many toga-draped Roman senators. It is wonderful to stand on the maidan—a

vast 'lung' for the sweltering city by the muddy Ganga—listening to the mellifluous flow of one of the world's most sonorous languages, watching these culturally distinguished people.

Indeed they were—the **bhadralok**, the uppercrust intellectual elite known by the good Victorian term—**the gentility**, *bhadra* = manners; politeness, a very Bengali word not found elsewhere in the nation. The people who belonged to the bhadralok were the true **babus**, in the sense of true civilized gentlefolk, not the obdurate government clerk the British turned the babu into.

They have made Western culture their own Bengali palimpsest despite Macaulay's dismissive attitudes to their rich language in his famous speech promoting English. Through the emergence of Hindu reform movements—the **Brahmo** and **Arya Samaj** at the turn of the 'century'* they influenced the rest of India. An enlightened Vedantic message vigorously reinterpreted by **Swami Vivekananda** and the mystic saint **Ramakrishna** with **Rabindranath Tagore** singing his way in his own English translations of mellifluous Bengali—moved Western hearts to review their own attitudes to Indian civilisation, and prepared Indians to climb out of encrusted inward-looking ways, to take on the 20th century.

But amongst these assured peoples even the poorest taxicab driver or chaat-wallah pushing his humble barrow of fiery nibbles for the crowd to buy, can recite the poetry, or argue the political toss with as much erudition as the bhadralok. Surprisingly considering the stereotype of a Bengali no matter at what level of society as being an impassioned cultural orator, this included golf! The **Royal Calcutta Golf Club** (still so named) founded in 1829 is, after Scotland's St Andrew's, the oldest in the world. Such anomalies mask the maturity. A contemporary book reviewer, Pankaj Mishra, while commenting on entirely different matters Indian tackled the modernity of Bengali culture, recalling how both Rabindranath Tagore and Nirad Chaudhuri wrote 'witheringly of the shallow and gaudy Anglicization of socially ambitious Indians elsewhere'… 'In feudal north India there was none of the self-confident egalitarian spirit of the Bengal Renaissance.' Elsewhere, meaning the north, 'the meeting of East and West morally resulted in tackiness and a crude kind of snobbery.'

---

* **Raja Ram Mohun Roy** born in 1772 (spelled Mohan by Bengalis) was one of India's greatest secular reformers and an emblem of Bengali humanism. He is mentioned elsewhere as a gifted linguist, eclectic in his spirituality as a true Hindu would be, and is to be most honoured from a woman's point of view in working untiringly to abolish both child marriages and **sati**, giving support to the Viceroy of the time, Lord William Bentinck, to pass measures in 1829 outlawing both aberrant customs.

In 1828 Roy had had painful experience himself of the horrors of sati. The wife of his elder brother who died suddenly was forced to mount her husband's pyre. When the flames reached her she screamed and tried to escape the pain of the gathering flames but was pushed back by the crowd onto the pyre. She perished. Ram Mohun Roy had to witness this, an indelible impression which must have fired his own determination in other directions thus founding the **Brahmo Samaj** in **1828**.

In every way whether as an advocate for division of legal proceedings into two codes—criminal and civil law—even within the context of imperial rule in order to make the law intelligible to the ordinary Indian, his proposal to reinvigorate the ancient **PANCHAYAT village rule** and a **passionate plea for a free press**, indicates a modern man and a true democrat. He has been termed the **Father of Modern India**. Well known in Europe also, where he gave lectures and studied Christianity, he died of ill health in 1833 in Bristol, England.

A private note And tolerant as they are despite sudden volatility at street level, **Queen Victoria** is still allowed to sit amply comfortable as another Mataji in the Pantheon, gazing out over the one fresh air lung of Kolkata—the maidan where at the far end near the Writer's Building, **Thomas Holroyde,** Sheriff then of Kolkata, had declared her accession to the general public from the steps in 1837.

◆ The founding of the Asiatic Society in the late 1700s became a catalyst for an explosion of detailed inquiry. Indian history, chronologies, coins, archaeology, architecture, language, would all be gathered up by remarkable people working with Indian colleagues to piece together the cultural map of Hindu, Jain and Buddhist history. Misguided assumptions of superiority of Graeco-Roman-Christian civilization and the downright disinterest of English businessmen were about to be jolted. India was about to rejoin the world and in her own right.

◆ But then concerned at the growing power of Bengal, the British Government undid all this goodwill by the indefensible Partition of Bengal and worse (in its fundamental psychological divisiveness) initiated separate **communal** electorates (Hindu and Muslim). This was Curzon's doing in 1905.

◆ On a different note, find the several hundred acres of the extensive Botanical Gardens to gaze in awe at the very old banyan tree—the largest in the world, a span of nearly three and a half acres—its dangling roots become branches, a micro-climate in itself.. 'High overarched and echoing'…

There oft the Indian herdsmen, shunning heat,
Shelters in cool and tends his pasturing herds

Even John Milton had heard of its fame and recognised its amazonian nature in **Paradise Lost**!

◆ Bengalis can laugh at themselves although they do protest that other Indians ascribe characteristics to them that are exaggerated. Their version of a 'truism' goes like this:

One Bengali is a poet
Two Bengalis is an association
Three Bengalis is a political party

But note another version in **COMMUNIST PARTIES.**

■ CALLIGRAPHY

Because of the specific injunctions against artistic representation of Allah, and the Prophet Muhammed, the aesthetic temperament of Muslims has sought release in the pen, *qalam* or *kalam*. Handwriting, and all its architectural ramifications (often embossed in brick and wrapped bracelet-like

around minarets and towers such as the powerful decorations of the Qutb Minar in Delhi) is regarded as the highest form of art, a test of **fikr**, imagination, mathematical ingenuity and balance in design.

The kalam itself is a sharpened reed. The ink consists of lamp soot. Unable to depict figurative resemblance such as that of the Buddha or even the most abstract form of a Jain **tirthankara** (**messenger** bringing tidings of hope to humanity), or Christ on the Cross, Islamic artists created in calligraphy a new embellishment in the intricacies of angular upright or curved sloping lines of the Arabic script, a beautiful cursive language written from right to left.

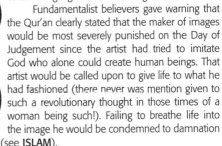

Fundamentalist believers gave warning that the Qur'an clearly stated that the maker of images would be most severely punished on the Day of Judgement since the artist had tried to imitate God who alone could create human beings. That artist would be called upon to give life to what he had fashioned (there never was mention given to such a revolutionary thought in those times of a woman being such!). Failing to breathe life into the image he would be condemned to damnation (see **ISLAM**).

Very early in Islamic development aesthetic principles were governed by precise rules which even to this day constrain many contemporary artists, sculpture of the human form being out entirely, religious art also severely limited in scope in painting. A secular art grew up and certainly in Mughal times both Hindu and Muslim artists, were able to paint miniature portraits of the emperors, the court assemblies, foreign emissaries and landscapes of exquisite bejewelled quality.

◆ Fluidity and lucidity of design developed over the centuries with such felicity of handling large-scale embellishment on solid form as well as in the detailed intensity of written manuscripts that calligraphy became fused in a unique form of artistic expression—a luminous device to reinforce the faith, urging those who viewed the Arabic script to contemplate Paradise. It is hard for those who are strangers to Islam and the Arab world to understand how the Arabic script is considered sacred in a very special way, having breathed life into the Qur'an.

Its use therefore in marvellously crafted raised stone and brick around minarets, framing doorways interspersed with delicate floral design tracery; curving around the inner ceilings of domes, lining the border of prayer mats and reminding the faithful in wall-hangings, parquetry, textiles (not to be worn), in abstract geometric design of its messages of order and law in Qur'anic inscriptions in mausoleum and mosque, home and wall-paintings and even a baroque form of convoluted animal depiction in which the form of the animal houses a compression of calligraphic alphabetic formations known as **tughra**.

Emperor Aurangzeb, the last of the Great Mughals, excelled as a master practitioner as did the last sad figure of its long line, Bahadur Shah II who spent most of his ineffective days absorbed in his poetry and script embellishment.

It is in the **Patna Khuda Baksh Library**, a renowned centre of Islamic learning, that treasures hardly known to the outside world are hidden away. Established in 1891 by a philanthropic Bihar lawyer after whom the library is named, it is hardly on any traveller's itinerary today and yet is a store house for rare gems to be unearthed. One holy book, a Qur'an written in 1269 using three styles and executed by the leading calligraphist of his day, **Yaqut-al-Mustani**, who was detailed to work at the court of the last Baghdad Abbasid Caliph is a treasured manuscript. It is written of him that 'a specimen of his calligraphy was as rare as a gem in his time'.

Also, like a sparkling illuminated manuscript of mediaeval Europe is the volume **based on the entire life of Emperor Shah Jehan, each page framed in the most exquisite of floral traceries and arabesques,** and despite inability to read the Arabic, most wondrous of all is that history leaping right off the pages of the **Diwan Hafiz** of **Khwaja Shamsuddin Hafiz-al-Shirazi**... complete with marginal notes in the handwriting of Emperors Humayun and Jehangir. Such graceful delineation is drawn with reed pen. The ink consists of lamp soot mixed in honey and myrrh to repel insects and add sooty lustre to the lines.

- ## CASTE

Castus is a Latin word meaning **pure** from which the Portuguese word **casta** is derived. Having rounded the Cape of Good Hope for the very first time in 1498 and been welcomed as yet another in the series of merchant adventurers by the Malabar Zamorin of Kozhikode (Calicut) the Portuguese introduced the word into India as they came to recognise certain defining codes of behaviour amongst the Indians with whom they were dealing—and attempting to convert in what was old Malabar, now the small coastal state of Kerala.

Varnam = rang = colour is the original Sanskrit term used for a differentiation amongst humans that is first mentioned in the late Vedic texts. In the Rig Vedic hymn 10:90 addressed to the **Cosmic Man = Purusa** referring to the Cosmic Sacrifice which brought about the birth of the human species, the question is asked:

when they divided the Purusa (as the victim of the Cosmic sacrifice)
...what did his mouth become?
What his two arms?
What are declared to be his two thighs,
his two feet.
(Edgerton translation)

The answer comes:

*the **brahmin** (priestly category) was his mouth*
*the **rajanya** (warrior) his two arms = **kshatriya***
*the **vaisya** (artisans, merchants) his two thighs*
*the **sudra** (serf) his two feet.*

Later texts sum up the categorisation thus, Krishna speaking in the Gita:

Seer and leader
Provider and server
Each has the duty
Ordained by his nature
Born of the gunas (qualities of personality)

Even later the divisions comprised wider categories **more akin to class** but uniquely and rigidly separated by certain daily rituals such as bathing, inter-dining and food preparation, and most especially marriage. Avoiding pollution became an obsession.

- ◆ The **brahmins** took on all the intellectual prowess of the race, first as priests in charge of the all-important daily ceremonies around the **hawan** (ritual fire) as wise sages, philosophers, moral guardians who were to be revered. They had no need of the 'dirtying of hands'. (Note **brahmin** ending now commonly used. **Brahman** refers to the ultimate formless BRHM. **Brahma** is the creative deity of the Pantheon).

A brahmin was one who composed and recited the 'brahman'—the word (a number of the early Vedic hymns are dedicated not only to **VAC** (pronounced vach) = word but **Brahman**—the original pregnant sound). In the later Vedic texts the **Atharva Veda** and **Brahmanas** created such a textual complexity only brahmins were able to master or conduct the detailed minutiae of ritual worship, and how correctly to intone the Sanskrit and details of the fire sacrifice which had become a popular ceremony. They were the custodians of the culture. In their minds and in the meticulous adherence to the codes of the society, their strictness and austerity expected of them, they were likewise honoured, and have been the secret key to the incredible continuity of cultural well-being enjoyed by Indians of the upper echelons.

- ◆ **Kautilya**—known as the Machiavelli of India who composed the manual of statecraft—the **Arthashastra** (300 BCE approximately) attempted to curb many of the privileges brahmins had created for themselves—they had immunity from punishment in cases of rape, theft and murder, yet to murder a brahmin incurred immediate death to the assailant. For a time they lost power in the period of Buddhist domination only to recover again as Hinduism flourished after Buddhism waned in the Gupta empire (3rd-4th century CE).

- ◆ The **kshatriyas**, as the warriors came to be known, were the protectors of society, not just aggressive fighters against those who threatened. They gave strength and support. Indeed in the very early days there was a strict code of chivalry. Having gained ground in conflict the code of honour obligated them to be magnanimous having made their point and in some cases to restore the territory overrun in battle! This is spelled out in the Mahabharata and if applied today would effectively put a stop to wars in the old Jugoslavia, in Somalia, etc., and bring nearly all the protagonists to account in The Hague Law Courts as common criminals!

Writing in **Gods, Guardians and Lovers** (ed. Vishakha N Desai for the Asia Society Galleries New York, Mapin, 1993) Michael Willis has some interesting points to make on this interrelationship of ruler class and the inspiration underpinning original Vedic society first, then mediaeval society from the mid-tenth century on, resulting in magnificent temples being built as a substitute for ultimate temporal power.

*A link between the god and king was thus forged through the application of the ascetic's sacred knowledge. From this the king received legitimacy and the **acarya** support for his order. The tangible product was a temple that advertised the power of the dynasty and its associations with a particular manifestation of the godhead...*

After the abeyance of royal sacrifices, power was seen as flowing down from the divine through whole or partial incarnation (in the case of Visnu) or manifestation (in the case of Siva). Kings no longer reached up through sacrificial effort but sought to associate themselves with the sacred as it was known and revealed in this world...

Regional princes made free use of imperial titles and competed vigorously with each other in the arts of peace and war. Yet, however powerful some of these princes became, no ruler was able to claim paramount status. In the absence of a recognized imperial center, there was no impetus to return to the detached role once played by the Pratihara monarchs.

Instead, as regional princes, their power, wealth and energies were focused in other directions unlike other monarchs in other cultures. Willis writes that maintenance and amplification of temple construction absorbed their powerful energies. In addition, throughout the long flow of Indian early history, those who came to organise an urbanised settled society of small kingdoms and agriculturists clearly understood they must bow to the cosmic laws of sanatana dharma spelled out in the oral transmission of the Vedic 'texts'.

The personification of this abstract code of coherent law in the universe—**Rta** (see **CORE CONCEPTS**, and **RTA**) was lodged in the **brahmin**, handed down within families, generation to generation, like pedigree breeding. Several thousand years on in social organisation rta was no longer a speculative concept of perceptive rishis but a cardinal law overarching the stratification of interrelated activities and responsibilities to each other—an ideal, later to become entrenched and unfortunately (as most human societies elsewhere also display) atrophied until reformers come along.

◆ **Kshatriya** power was, therefore, continually constrained in the texts by **reminders that rulers were temporal in the cosmic order of things and not absolute** as in other societies—even today, where military dictators enjoy considerable political acumen, and tenacity of tenure (witness General Saddam Hussein against all the odds, and General Franco).

There was full acknowledgement in all the codes, legends, parables that obeisance must be paid to those who concentrated their abilities on higher things—**the shining ones** concerned with the wider social dharma and moral fibre of its citizens. Such worldly temporal power stood therefore below that of the rsi, the seer through intuitive awareness, the teacher, guru, the hermit or

muni and the ascetic saint, a very different situation from that of other nations where the ruler, feudal warrior, robber baron, drug lord, hereditary monarch have been supreme.

◆ The brahmin was overlord without argument by virtue of that **ARYA** quality of nobility instilled in upbringing through:

1 **processes of tradition** handed down in accepted codes and rituals, father to son

2 ability by virtue of class dharma to **concentrate on learning** and applying Vedic teaching to all citizens

3 **strict upbringing in households to adhere to brahmin orderliness and discipline**

4 **separation from pollution** by customary social inhibitions

5 **sattvic food diet** and its cleansing influence on personality over time

6 a known statistic that many brahmins, women as well as men **live beyond the octogenarian mark**, a clear result of this bodily protection and lifestyle.

◆ The **vaisyas** came to be merchants and business communities who created the fluid in commerce that oiled society. With their mobility they kept all aspects smoothly running. They were also landowners and banias, the much disliked zamindars or rent collectors for the British regimes.

◆ The **sudras** were those who physically dirtied their hands, tillers of the soil, 'hewers of wood and drawers of water' to echo a Biblical phrase.

These major categories of class are very broad definitions as if society were viewed from a close-flying satellite. On a zoom lens **jati** (= **jaati**) is a differentiation more in common usage, meaning a **caste** more akin to a Scottish clan—and there are thousands. Their interaction goes on in well-defined ways of interdependence almost like guild systems at village level, and impinges even today on inter-dining, religious rituals, and considerations of who can marry whom. A **gotra** is yet another sub-division within a class, roughly translated = a bloodline clan, the Sanskrit root traces back to **gow** = cow! How important cattle were in that early Vedic society.

Reform of entrenched codes of behaviour

◆ With reform in the air as Indian leaders fought for Independence and the sense of a social democratic egalitarian society captured their vision, Gandhi (a vaisya) fought defiantly to rehabilitate the plight of untouchables who were often not even allowed to worship in temples for fear of polluting other worshippers. He renamed them **Harijans**. In the Constitution of modern India they are now referred to as **Scheduled Castes and Scheduled Tribes** numbering some 160 million and 70 million respectively (census figures). Politically, certainly in the heavily populated states of the north, they have taken on yet another persona and electorally became powerful under the nomenclature of **DALIT**.

◆ India's changes are so phenomenal in present circumstances with the emergence of a powerful middle class running into several hundred millions—with equally influential relatives scattered internationally in the India diaspora—together larger in numbers than the **total** population of the USA that it is almost impossible to keep track of social trends, and the spiralling effect of all this dramatic change into a liberalised cash economy affecting what were close-knit village structures of intercaste dependencies, based on exchange economies. Sociological theory may be one thing but western compartmentalism, trying to place the complexity of this continental 'unity in diversity' peoples into card-indexed boxes is well-nigh impossible. As a **firangi** it is dangerous to pontificate about caste. In the 50 years travelling the length and breadth of India I have discovered for every rule or 'fit' (a term used in classical sociology required reading of the 30s/40s academic discipline) there is a virtual opposite in India's diverse peninsula mass. I was myself made to fit into this 'fit' of perceived pointers in social change in a Marxist-dominated Department of Sociology at Leeds University in the 1960s while undertaking a study for the UK Government Home Office. The study was on social change amongst 50 Asian families, Hindu, Sikh and Muslim.

It did not work! For one thing cultural/spiritual factors counted as much as economic ones, and are more volatile in being measured by empirical criteria.

♦ In subsequent years I have re-met some of those courageous **Fifty Asian Daughters,** and their families. Much that they 'fed me' (their phrase!) they joked they had done so consciously as information they thought I wanted. Being old enough to be their mother I was aware at the time of their own anger at 'academic imperialism' of 'white academics gaining PhDs off their own backs', another of their phrases. One only has to see the hilarious, but very human and poignant British film **East is East** (premiered in mid-2000) made excitingly enough by a young British Asian playwright and a mixture of Indian, Pakistani and English actors (all British) to see how complex social change is.

Back in India the pendulum of change dramatically swings.

Horrendous reactionary caste hostilities still happen in the backward areas of India (Bihar and torched villages) in the ongoing fight between landlords and their militant Ranvir Sena bands scourging those Dalit villages supported by equally vitriolic Naxalites (revolutionary Marxist militia groups).

♦ On the other hand, although individual swallows do not make a summer, other dramatic changes occur. In the anonymity of contemporary city life and sophisticated political mores. A President (Narayanan, educated to be a lawyer) can come of untouchable stock and unaccountable technicians now man India's IT successes in industry and commerce making it to the top. A mixture of artistic flair and saintliness can release others from the chains of India's social divisions. An arts colleague known over the years whom I would term an **ex**-untouchable breaks the stereotype. World-travelled, a magnificent apartment in a prestigious part of Mumbai, with a home tastefully embellished by Kerala artistry in exquisite wood carvings and a family Ganesh of sculpted workmanship given homage and loving care in an intimate gathering every day, sums up all the disparities, confusions, paradoxes so bewildering to the newcomer to India. How to know that this man's father escaped his harijan status in

a truly Indian way that even brahmins would later make obeisance to him?

♦ His father, in a Western sense of speaking, 'took holy orders'. A call, as heard by those ancient rishis, lodged in his mind to go to Kerala to find 'his guru who would be waiting for him'. How to know *that*, except by a very common occurrence in India of telepathy? We are very sceptical of such areas of the mind. From a Western point of view such cannot be proven, and therefore does not exist! Shakespeare knew better when Hamlet spoke a remonstration to Horatio: 'There are more things in heaven and earth... Than are dreamt of in your philosophy'—and so do some who stay long in India and sense '**that other mind**' which the Dutch ballet dancer, **Beryl de Zoete** long ago wrote about under that very title.

♦ The Kerala story ends thus: the guru by serendipitous encounter 'recognised' the father, who then devoted years of study, meditation, insightful learning and proceeded from the **tamas** heritage willed upon him and his low caste status by entrenched tradition, to become a **sattvic**-clothed holy one... and people in turn heard about him on the myriad hidden networks of India and in turn came to pay homage and respect.
Even brahmins!

And so his son became educated, touched by his father's aura, with a special quality of his own, even in his dealings in Australia, the USA, the UK, Switzerland, a global messenger, but well-rooted, with integrity in his own Indian-ness.

♦ The reform faith Sikhism in mediaeval European times deliberately broke caste division also (see relevant section). In their hymns they praise earlier Hindus who broke the mould by their spiritual example:

Men praise Ravi Das the tanner who
every moment sang the one God's praises
Though of fallen caste he became the best
The four castes[classes] *came and fell at **his** feet*
Reform... or not?

♦ If this is so it is only now, freed of all trammels of imposed rule from outside—whether Muslim or British—that Hindu society can deal in a systematic way in transforming itself to modern needs. That now occurs through political processes in a democratic system. Since 1957 structural changes have dramatically changed the status of the low-caste. Virtually 50 per cent of government service posts are reserved for backward communities—40 per cent scheduled castes, 10 per cent tribal. In the north the **Mandal Commission** delivered its report on the very last day of 1980. Its investigation on how best to improve educational opportunities for the lower castes by positive discrimination in favour of the more disadvantaged sections of the community, that is the scheduled and tribal lower castes, was introduced in government memoranda in V P Singh's prime ministership in 1990 (The invisible subtle implications of these deep currents few foreigners can plumb are dramatically presented in **Booker Prize Winner Arundhati Roy's** novel **The God of Small Things** = see **KERALA** section). She has come too close to the bone, sufficiently stirring the pot to have a civil court case brought against her as author of the book, ironically in supposedly enlightened Kerala!

♦ The implementation finally of the Mandal recommendations brought about the demise of the Singh government. There was a backlash from upper class student agitation; their claim that such would divide Hindu society. Extremists indeed set themselves alight.

Currents flow this way and that as most ancient structures respond to the quest for an open society.

♦ The Supreme Court upheld the Memorandum of 1980 and by **1993** reservations in the civil service and educational institutions became law, subject to what is referred to colourfully as the **'creamy layer'** exclusion—that is sons and daughters of well-heeled lower caste individuals who may through previous good fortune have risen to high office or owned considerable landholdings. **Reservations are not for them...** or are they? Statistics show in the late 90s that in nearly a decade of so-called reform a new 'creamy layer' has emerged showing powerful Backward Castes such as the Yadavs and Kurmis in UP taking over three quarters of the loans made available to the **BCs**, so creating yet another fissiparous fragmentation and acronym—the **MBCs**, the **Most Backward Castes**!

♦ New books such as **Steven Parish's Hierarchy and its Discontents** subtitled **Culture and the Politics of Consciousness in Caste Society,** (OUP, 1997) provide guidance in this complex arena. From the Indian point of view reference should be made to the **Anthropological Survey of India**: **Peoples of India** project. (Caste is also discussed in QUATERNITIES).

And, appropriately titled, **Castes of Mind: Colonialism and the Making of Modern India** by **Nicholas Dirks** (Princeton, 2001) argues convincingly of our contemporary understanding of caste as a missionary-colonial construction!

■ **CAVES...**
10,000-8,000 BCE

have been regarded throughout India's history as sacred, as well as giving sanctuary from earliest pre-history, a cool place to escape not only wild animals but the onslaught of heat combined with monsoonal downpours. In central India at **Bhimbetka** in Madhya Pradesh and some only now being found in Orissa, they appear to have been retreats for animistic worship—very alike to those in Europe, Africa and the even more ancient rock galleries still being discovered in previously inaccessible canyons in northern Australia. The simple, yet at the same time sophisticated leaping deer (*mrga* = death-goers, the root **mr > marhaa**) depicted on the walls for shaman cults and the necessity of magic image—rituals to aid the hunter of the tribe successfully to kill his quarry—whichever continent—must have accompanied these visual invocations.

My fascination with caves and their importance in India's cultural development is, however, aroused from other grounds entirely—the sheer scale of their human engineering and artistic achievement, surely unique in world art. Indians should be justifiably proud of their existence but it is only recently that they have made their way into the national consciousness. Millennia later than the early hunter-gatherer imaging his quarry (and interestingly enough accompanied by riders on horseback very similar to the small tribal bronzes of today) apostrophied by hand silhouettes planted on the granite rock surfaces stating: I AM HERE, these Buddhist caves of the western ghats are very different places of withdrawal. Nor are they the magnetic Himalayan caves demanding staunch disciplines testing the meditative will and skills of sadhus and aspiring sannyasis who inhabit them.

These are caves for learned monks, teaching cells, advanced centres for established Hindu, Jain, Buddhist followers (and who knows what secular humanists of the time) to gather in fruitful discussion and teaching, a far cry from Plato's allegorical cave in his **Republic**, where people are trapped in a kind of Western maya. Imprisoned by their lack of wisdom to comprehend the platonic 'Idea of Good', these miserable creatures are chained, immovable, forced to contemplate shadows cast by the flames behind them. This symbol of their false reality was to be reinterpreted to them by the release of one of their number, himself symbolic of the philosopher who has to see the true nature of the cave reality before being released into the full glare of the sun—the real bright domain of truth and liberation. This 'philosopher' was to return to bring enlightenment to the imprisoned. The real reality is 'out there' but they are content with the shadow world they see. They refuse to believe him and just as Plato's guru, Socrates, was denied by the public in Athens, so too these cave dwellers, content in their blind ignorance, wish to kill this 'philosopher' who has seen the light. They are not in the least interested in the truth he has seen beyond their cave.

♦ How different these hermit Indians! Almost contemporary with the great era of the Greek philosophers of 400-300 BCE they created rock-cut temples filtering the sunlight in as it rose in the east, the massive rock faces of Deccan Trap basalts—given to fissures and alternating soft layers—easily excavated by the engineering masters of that time when Theravada Buddhism flourished and abstract symbols were used for the Buddha's representation.... and when Plato was writing.

There are said to be at least a thousand or more of these monasteries and architected chambers, **Karla**, **Bhaja** and **Bedsa** being the most prominent yet only now is the average Indian becoming aware of their significance not only for their very achievement in the limited technology of over 2,000 years ago. The dimensions of the majestic chaitya assembly hall incredibly carved out with geometric precision by mastercraftsmen leaves any visitor breathless—as does the steep half-kilometre climb!

But their cultural significance is overwhelming also. Every traveller should visit at least one. No Platonic prison caves, no

79

matter how allegorical, are here. Contemporary court life, divine beings and gorgeous apsaras (celestial dancers), serene bodhisattvas, architected pillared verandahs · and floral ornamentation run riot along the mural walls. The richness of human life invades the solitary spaces.

◆   At **Kanheri** in the Mumbai district colossal statues of Buddha reach seven metres high! It is very obvious at this site that a large settlement for monks was carved into the rock, many small caves fashioned into solitary cells, with stone benches and a verandah outside. Even more advanced and of later period in Hindu, Jain as well as Buddhist occupation, are the **caves at Aurangabad** see Carmel Berkson's books on the same and **Ellora**, Mapin, Ahmedabad, 1996. They will shake the Western traveller as well as the Indian tourist with his video-tour coach companions (and their litter-bug attitudes!) into some humility.

How could artisans working with simple tools and no steel scaffolding not only create a cavernous ribbed and arched ceiling (well-proportioned and symmetrical in imitation of wood beams) but with chisels fashion from the middle rock the smooth egg-shaped stupa? And the lines of identical Persepolis-type angular columns with up-turned lotiform bells, spirited elephants and their mithuna riders in multiples—all to be crafted in Mauryan Empire days before the Christian millennium? Such finesse, such style—and without electricity to aid them. A miracle of the second century BCE.

And for the Hindus who withdrew for creative meditation and discourse, a withdrawal from distractions of the world of Plato's material well-being, into that garbha-griha or wombhouse, their metaphor was in contrast for renewal of very positive energies in the world of Ideas, a 'cavity in mother earth' carved in the living rock.

■   **CHIDAMBARAM** (n. *Sanskrit*)
10th–16th century CE
Broken down into its constituent syllables this amazing temple 250 km south of Chennai comprises complex concepts. Put simply:
  chit = consciousness, that is ultimate awareness
  ambalam (Tamil) = a. the **place of ether,** that limitless space (sometimes likened to the cavity in the innermost heart)
  b. denotes *sabha* = assembly hall
ambaram (Sanskrit) = *amba* (the root) is equivalent to ambience or atmosphere.

This **place of cosmos**—in fact **the Universe** is described by **Dr Padma Subrahmanyam,** the famous contemporary south Indian classical dancer who studied for her PhD thesis under the guidance of learned pandit-priests at Chidambaram, as 'ether of knowledge or awareness' which resides as a world of itself in the cavity of our hearts. So the universe, so vast, is truly miniscule also, metaphorically residing deep in the heart/mind of each individual's consciousness (turn to section on **MIRACLES**). Her book: **Bharatha's Art, Then and Now**, (Nrithyodaya, Madras, 1979).

◆   Other than the **Orissa temple** to **Surya, the Sun God** and the **Madurai Meenakshi temple,** this vast Chola dynasty temple is India's most awe-inspiring not only because of the 50-acre scale (this figure differs depending on what you read or to whom you speak!) and its impressive gopuram gateways but also because of the intellectually demanding depths of the metaphors that lie behind its central shrines dedicated to **Nataraja–Shiva** in the form of the **Cosmic Dancer symbolising energy.**

◆   It also acknowledges Vishnu as Govindaraja in an L-shaped architectural device where the worshipper can face both shrines at once. This, the priests point out, is very unusual. Its glistening gold-plated canopied **Sivakamasundari** shrine is memorable in the blazing midday sun—a breathtakingly golden roof over the hall of dance. Fit for a dancing god. Unblemished. To the right of the shrine as the devotee faces the Nataraja figure is this golden goddess, to the left is the **Chitambalam Rahasyam** (secret, in the sense of mystery) shrine—no image or lingam, only empty space, surely the only shrine in the world embracing pure physics. A semi-circular arch holds a veil in place with a string of gold-washed sacred *bilwa* leaves. When drawn aside the invisible presence resonates like a frisson in ethereal space, the symbol of Shiva in his akashic formlessness—**as pure energy = ether (akasha).**

A Personal Encounter
If accompanied by a resident **DIKSHITAR**—the special class of brahmin priests dedicated to this most ancient edifice pre-dating even the present structure, the **sthala** or sacred place (locality) held dear by Tamils as **Thillaivanam**, then you may be lucky to acquire without charge a lively and comprehensive booklet by Dr S Meyyappan (retired Annamalai University professor and a member of its Poets' Association).

Not only do you learn about the legendary *thillai* forest (long gone—but this particular type of tree still grows in the saline swamps of the coast) where Shiva Nataraja performed the cosmic dance initiating energy into creation, but if that creation were seen as an embodiment (**PURUSHA**) of a human being, then this—the temple—is regarded as **the heart**. You are given also unusual insights into the depth of meaning just about everything carries in its essence which other sources omit.

By some mysterious circumstance the dikshitar who had been requested to look after my Tamil musician friend and myself surely did—and at a breakneck speed, trotting relentlessly through huge courtyards and the thousand-pillared hall where those powerful and artistically gifted Chola kings were anointed and 'coronated'—a typically apt transformation of English into Indian English! Up great slabs of stone and down into sunken shrines he strode effortlessly ever on to the farthest reaches especially to answer my question about the 63 **NAYANMARS** who are artistically cast in metal high on the last wall beyond the ultimate shrine. There at last he made sure on his business card (N T Anandathandava—his name meaning Siva's Dance of Bliss—grandson of Rajaganesa Deekshithar) that the four women saint-poet-musicians were written down for my edification. **Isai-gnyaniyar, Karaikkaal Ammaiyar, Manga-yat** (among women) **karasi** (queen of), and **Mahadevi-akka.**

And then he totally disappeared into the dark echoing colonnades! A crowd is gathering for the last of the six services. We are ready to collapse on the nearest flagstone, without food for half a day. It is nearing 10 p.m. A great commotion is pushing a throng of people, a huge heavy palanquin is lurching towards us carried on the bare shoulders of about 20 dikshitars. Nadaswarams are deafening. A glimpse of glinting miniature sandals—those of the barefoot dancing Nataraja, on a stool under the silver palanquin umbrella comes to a noisy halt right in front of us. They are on the way to the bedchamber where food for the gods will be offered. Flames are stirring on the thali trays awaiting the ablution.

As suddenly as he has disappeared Anandathandava is before us again determinedly ploughing through the press of people, insisting we follow. At the foot of the high altar, so to speak, we are bundled up steep side steps to find ourselves thrust into a corner of the main antechamber. There is Nataraja swathed this time in red sparkling saris, almost lost to view throttled in bejewelled necklaces and floral garlands. It is the **abhis(h)ekam** (ablutions) of the quartz crystal (**sphatikai**) lingam. There is much misunderstanding in a sex-saturated West about the lingam as an erect phallic symbol, almost universally translated as such with all the undertones of suggestive sex objects and sensuality. Yet in Sanskrit the true meaning of lingam is 'mark' or 'sign' indicating a deity (Shiva) without form (nirguna), Shiva as a totally abstract entity. Advaita all over again… and Shankaracharya. We were standing in the very innermost shrine where this amazing soul had brought the milky-hued sphatikai lingam over 1,000 years ago. My mind is reeling… I am standing where great souls have stood, singing, giving praise with joyous hearts—Appar, Sambandar 'who vanished in a glowing radiance created by Siva', Manikkavachaka, the prime minister at the 7th–8th century Pandyan court who was absorbed 'in a radiant flash' also… and Tyagaraja.

Our feet are awash in melted ghee, milk, Ganga water, sandalwood paste, and honey. The dikshitar now in the central shrine before Nataraja is agitating. Are we watching? Another dikshitar directs us further into the shadowy corner as this most sacred lingam, steady in a bronze saucer-shaped base, is about to be smeared in rice. A curtain is drawn in front of us. This we are not allowed to view, for reasons not explained. The final ablutions accompanied by rising cadences of chanting come into sight again, there is another surge forward from way down below in the central aisle. The **ARATI** is now being sung, the flames wafted in a clock-wise motion first to the Cosmic Dancer, then to the Goddess within her brightly-lit shrine-cell right in front of us, and then with much shutting of wooden lattice doors and darkening shrines elsewhere a black curtain is drawn across to the formless mystery. **Ignorance, the curtain, is lifted**.

The crystal lingam is carried on another thali to be offered up to the Dancing God as the saint from Kerala had done over a thousand years before, to be taken as the arati concludes on the palki to proceed to the various other shrines. An onerous task for

the priests who are not exactly heavyweights. The palki itself is supported by lengthy and very heavy teak poles.

Our dikshitar mentor is signalling. The curtain left-shrine is drawn aside again and held high to make sure we see the gleaming **bilwa** leaves. Then the final chants, the flames snuffed out one by one, he takes my miniature Ganesh, a constant in all my travelling, given long ago to me by another mentor, a Sanskrit scholar from Annamalai University. Ganesh had come from one of the temple stalls under the huge main gopuram. Now he had come 'home' and was being held in the dikshitar's palm for darshan, before the great Presence, returned again with a packet of sacred ash, rose petals and camphor.

The notices in the outer courtyard, hanging it is to be noted, slightly awry, state clearly that non-Hindus may not enter the main shrines. Yet seldom do things run true to form…

Dr Meyyappan says this:

All of us are aware that God is above all Forms. But how to convey that idea in a temple? Is it possible? Yes, it has been achieved in this Sthala by the 'Rahasya' behind the Deity—Nataraja with form. What exactly is that Rahasya, none has fathomed. That is why it is called Rahasya—secret. The curtain—the back drop is raised momentarily and there is an effulgence. The curtain drops. Supreme Truth can at best be indicated only by Effulgence. And this significance has been incorporated only in this temple.

Effulgence (another English word acquired in India! And turn to **GAYATRI**) must surely have lit our way. This is sheer 'modernity' a concept of 21st century physics. (see **Amartya Sen** on 'modernity' in The Argumentative Indian, Penguin, 2005).

The Architecture

Like Stonehenge the building of such a temple is mind-boggling with the quarries for the dressed granite blocks weighing tonnes some 64 km distant and on the far side of the Vellar river. In the **Nritta Sabha** (Hall of the Dance) built in 1178–1216 CE there stood the original shrine to the Goddess Kali in the tillai forests of old. Its 56 solid pillars are eight feet high, delicately carved at top and bottom. Everything is on a vast scale but like the Meenakshi Temple at Madurai it is a working temple and full of cow dung pats in the open spaces, mess from the thousands of worshippers throwing balls of ghee kept in water in a huge metal **hundi** onto images of the deities as part of specific rituals*, dead flowers, and other detritus (at least biodegradable until plastic inevitably has taken over).

---

* This is particularly so in the huge Madurai temple. One statue to Shiva and Shakti in domestic parley receives this bombardment. An Indian bystander explained simply to us: 'In one of the stories Parvati is angry with Shiva. This is a domestic dispute so we are on her side otherwise our wives will turn on us poor husbands! So we throw these butter balls at him to show our displeasure!'
How very real the gods are… such beatitude—'**beautitude**' in the guide book, another wonderful slip of the pen!

■ CHOLA

The Cholas stand out in resplendent glory as patrons of flourishing cultures in the 'deep south' around the Thanjavur region. In the ascendant as a lively sea-people going, trading with S E Asia and implanting Hindu culture as a result in Sumatra up into Cambodia and old Siam, they dominated the south in temple building, bronze sculpture, music. The explanation of their supremacy surely must come from the nature of the social contract with the large population of Tamils whom they ruled.

A pyramid of well-ordered administration appears to have existed, with considerable devolution, a model of modernity where villagers through their **SABHAS** and **samitis** (committees) enjoyed a good deal of autonomy, and democratic voting rights, the rules of which date back to a 10th century inscription on the temple walls at **Uttaramerur**—a village of brahmins (this is documented in full in **Romila Thapar**'s **A History of India**, Vol I, (Pelican 1966, pp.202-3): 'names shall be written on tickets for thirty wards... these packets shall be put into a pot..' to be drawn when all the voting is in. (**Archaeological Survey of India Report** (1904-5, p.138).

It was clearly specified how the result, the winning ticket, was to be disclosed to the large assembly—'the arbitrator shall receive it on the palm of his hand with the five fingers open.' Transparency a rule of law even in those days! Other south Indian friends have reported similar depictions in friezes devoted to more secular activities around temple podiums, the temple not only being a place of worship but central to civil administration, and law and order in a close-knit community—as is **CHIDAMBARAM**.

■ CHRISTIANITY

It is a salutary experience in early life to be told in no uncertain terms by a dignified Syrian Christian grandmother, her gentle green-grey eyes dancing with merriment, her skin paler than any southern European, that her ancestors were Christian long before my own in Britain. She was not referring to the conversions either by missionary Christianity in the hands of the Portuguese in the 15th century or from the first English missionary to go to India. William Carey was from Moulton Village in Northamptonshire. His plaque has been placed as a reminder on the village school, once his home.

> Shoemaker, Schoolmaster, Preacher, Scholar and Missionary Pioneer.
> While beneath this roof he conceived and developed the great missionary
> idea that has changed India and awakened World-Wide movements.
> He ministered to the Baptist Church in this village for over 4 years.
> Born at Paulerspury 17 August, 1761, he died 9 June, 1834
> And his body was buried at Serampore, India.

52 CE: Her emphatic gesture as she marked the air with a gesticulating finger was to reiterate that even if historians question the evidence there is no doubt amongst the faithful that **St Thomas—himself known** as **Doubting Thomas of the Apostles** arrived at Muziris (modern Cranganore) in Kerala and for seven years undertook padayatra carrying a large wooden cross as he preached his way across the southern peninsula to Madras in the first century. So much for demand for empirical evidence. The Apostle for reasons unknown was martyred, lanced in the side while praying in front of this cross, his bone relic displayed in the Church higher up on St Thomas Mount, in a southern suburb of Chennai.

So was founded the Syrian Christian church, the name taken from the Syrian believers who after the fall of the Temple at Antioch and having settled in Persia, were persecuted and travelled on to India from the first century after Christ's death. Now the **Marthoma** Church as it is called in Kerala is divided into several sects. Grandmother Verghese was right! It was much later in 563 CE when St Columba brought Christianity to the Isle of Iona off the promontory of Mull in Scotland (see section on **HALO**). According to the locals it was the people of **Kodungalloor**, a town of great antiquity where also seven centuries later India's first mosque was built by Arab traders, that first welcomed St Thomas.

1498 CE: Not until Vasco da Gama sailed in also to land on the Malabar coast at Kappad 14 km from Kozhikode did European Christianity arrive in India in force. A few Jesuit priests as overland travellers may have come earlier—a fascinating book written by Vincent Cronin recounts the intellectual encounters between such a Jesuit, Roberto di Nobili and brahmin colleagues, once he had mastered their language. He was much impressed by their rigorous intellectual beliefs and, for his pains, in courageously recounting these encounters, on return to Italy he was excommunicated for such freedom of thought!

The Zamorin of Calicut (used to visits from many enterprising traders and navigators—Chinese, Phoenician, Roman) was repaid for his tolerant hospitality by aggressive skirmishes and seizing of territory by the Portuguese, then in succession, other incursions from French, Dutch and British—not only in the name of trade but also the gospel. Put out by the presence of an estimated 200,000 Syrian Christians the Portuguese set about enforcing Papal infallibility; however, by 1653 the majority defied this imposition and rejected Papal authority remaining independent ever since. (The first Church for Europeans was constructed in 1510 by Franciscan Friars. This was in Cochin.)

Where the 'great Argonaut' lay buried, his epitaph is marked at St Francis Church in Kochi (Cochin)—his remains returned to Portugal 14 years later.

Only an uninspiring slab in the hamlet's rough road to the beach marks Gama's arrival. What was hearsay in the 50s on our first visit to Kerala and relayed by Syrian Christian friends with relish, eager with wry humour to put such a European intrusion in its proper religious perspective, is fortunately now properly documented.

Sanjay Subrahmanyam, now inaugural professor of Indian History and Culture at Oxford, has spent time in Portugal studying primary source records confirming the tale of the two Moors from Tunis who were already on the Malabar coast, ready to welcome the advance party making sure it was safe for Vasco da Gama to be rowed ashore.

And he was taken to a place where there were two Moors from Tunis, who knew how to speak Castilian and Genoese. And the first greeting that they gave him was the following;
"The Devil take you! What brought you here?"
And they asked him what he had come to seek from so far; and he replied:
"We came to seek Christians and spices".

The Career and Legend of Vasco da Gama (Cambridge University Press, Foundation Books, 1998)

Christian India Today

There are now just over **20 million Christians** of all persuasions—Catholic, Protestant, Baptist predominantly in the hilly north east regional states of Assam—as well as the Syrian Christian church of the South.

◆ India led the way ahead of the rest of the world by joining all the various expressions of faith into a coalition—the **Church of South India** in 1947 and **North India** in 1970.

Christianity is as indigenous a part of the spiritual fabric of India as all the other major faiths—Hindu, Buddhist, Hebraic, Parsee, Jain, Islamic, and Sikh persuasion. This is especially so in Kerala, underscored by the **Indianization** of much of the church ritual. In wedding ceremonies in Kerala, for instance, much of the form of the service is virtually Hindu, from the wearing of the **mangalsutra,** the sacred thread necklace (equivalent of the wedding ring) and the **minnu** (a gold pendant symbolically the size of a grain of rice) to church rituals in using oil lamps instead of candles, to worship in Indian music and dance forms—this even encouraged by ecumenical influences at the time of the Pope's first visit in 1964.

Controversy: Christian Activity... Conversion... Charity

In this land of finely-slivered social differentiation there is bound to be reaction to who is up, who is down... in the past secular India reinforced by all manner of modern democratic legislation has tried to embrace a new egalitarianism.

People have prided themselves on a so-called tolerance which many of the new, more militant politicized fundamental groups see as an inexcusable stance leaving the 'weak Hindu' prone to be 'walked all over' by more militant cultures—Islam converted people under the banner of jehad by the force of the sword; militant Christianity in the Crusades acted equally aggressively. This precedent carried on in peaceable ways admittedly during early colonialism. After Independence there was still a residual acceptance even of foreign missionaries until certain evangelical Baptist activity in the highly sensitive border-states of NEFA (North East Frontier Provinces) got out of hand, most especially as the entire area, now redrawn into a number of autonomous States (see **GOVERNMENT**) was riven with inter-tribal tensions exacerbated by geographical divides of dense jungle, deep ravines scoured by raging monsoonal torrents and mist-laden mountains.

Our generation in post-Independence India held radical ideas not only politically but at deeper levels about the established church and the need for redressing a whole range of spiritual arrogances. Activities of proselytising Christendom were therefore as disturbing to many of us in the 50s as to an Indian government struggling in its golden age of idealism and principled politicians to maintain a balance between acceptance of many faiths in its pluralistic society (an ideal upheld in its Constitution which had only been in existence just over half a decade!), and on the other hand to reassert its 'Indianness', the foundation stones of which obviously being **sanatana dharma** = a "Hindu" view of life.

A new generation of politically-minded Indians however is now increasingly irritated in a post-colonial situation of continuing subtle cultural domination or interference. After 700 years of Islamic domination (most of it ruthlessly enforced by power of the sword with Hindu temples desecrated, women abducted, Sikhs in later centuries persecuted and barbarically tortured) and 300 years of European intervention through trading, later to be sustained by a military presence including Franco-British antagonisms fought out on Indian soil, any further interference, no matter how unimportant, occasionally rankles.

How tolerant should Hindus be? Is it such a virtue after all? When powerful conflicting forces such as these exist, fuelled also by a restless population of young people especially unemployed youths, being uprooted from traditionally stable villages into the anonymity of huge and harsh city life, then there are bound to be disturbing extremities appearing in the political spectrum. (Turn to sections on **SECULAR STATE** and **TOLERANCE** and read **Rohinton Mistry's** haunting novel **A Fine Balance**.)

◆ Activities of the minority faiths and communalism come under scrutiny. Political violence can follow. Riots occur, sometimes in rent-a-crowd situations to score political points.

◆ Add to this another complex layer of India society with a culture all of its own—the huge number of tribal/aboriginal peoples, a spectrum of mini-cultures as diverse as the nation's other ethnic identities, approximately 8% of the total population. Their lives on the whole are bound by animistic faiths overlaid by a measure of simplified Hindu customs.

◆ Into this mix come a variety of Christian organisations—some impelled by educational/ medical charities of an indigenous kind doing 'good works' that are above suspicion. Their activities are spread evenly throughout India and work alongside secular/medical and Hindu bodies, Buddhist and Sikh and Muslim, trying to rescue the sad detritus and forgotten peoples.

Why then does one hear so much more in recent decades, allegations of attacks on isolated convents in central India, and converted low caste villagers in Gujarat and again, the north eastern states which show new Christian majorities?

The spectrum of zealousness differs from the loner, such as **Dara Singh**, failed Hindi teacher and abandoned by his few friends, arrested finally in a jungle village and brought to trial as suspect in the murder of the Australian missionary, Graham Staines and his young sons, finally convicted for murder in 2003 along with 12 other collaborators, and well-organised sectarian groups on the warpath in response to what is seen as an orchestrated foreign missionary activity. In addition overtly religious bodies now politicizing themselves into the newly-formed **shakhas**—branch meetings of committed Hindu activists and sadhus—to reassert **dharam sansad**, a return to the sense of **Hindu Rashtra**. This implied establishment of an assertive Hindu India is something really new in the political culture which for the last 50 years of freedom had emphasised a secular ideal of pluralism.

♦ Even the more mainstream parties invoke Mother India, figuratively portrayed on banners and posters as—**Bharat-Mata**, sometimes using goddess Durga's imagery of Shakti protection. Parties such as the RSS, VHP, Bajrang Dal, Shiv Sena, Hindu Jagran Manch have become more emboldened in attacking this 'tolerance factor' (see **HINDUTVA** and **SECULAR STATE**).

♦ The BJP government in 1999 sought a national debate on Christian mass conversions in tribal areas especially; this highlighted the many interwoven tensions. A vociferous backlash occurred in the English-language press. I happened to be in Delhi that January when the tragic torching of the Australian missionary jeep occured in Orrissa in which Staines' two young sons died also. The missionary had been working in a tribal leprosy centre. Throughout India there was shame and shock, disgust, protests, meetings, artists marching. A regular woman columnist challenged such extreme political activists with this message: Don't attack the Church... match its charitable work.

The Prime Minister undertook a much-publicized 24-hour fast on Gandhi's Martyrdom Day.

Calming voices came from indigenous voices in the south Indian church. Surely after 2,000 years, letters to the editors suggested, this body of faith could be accepted as entirely 'Indian'? Some of these sources also expressed concern at certain militant Christian activity foisted on India from outside. But it was in fact ironically an outside voice that expressed concerns that needed to come out in the open for the good of India's political development. The respected (and conservative) British weekly **The Spectator** spoke out more succinctly under an explicit headline **Christian Provocation** (Feb 6, 1999). **Jon Stock**, correspondent for the **Daily Telegraph** in India, detailed the disturbing outlets of the far-from-innocent Westerners whose crusade helps explain murder in India.

Listed were gospel missions in Michigan, South Carolina, Louisiana, Colorado all cited for raising funds to send evangelical missionaries—not noted for their tolerance of truth's validity expressed through other faiths—'to win India for Christ'. According to Stock's detailed research 'India is ripe for harvest'. This is how the Evangelising India for Christ Assembly in South Carolina sees its mission, spurred on by papal declaration in India of Millennium 2000 as the Year of Christ. Other missions in Colorado and Louisiana using 'prayer profiles' of the multitude of tribal identities, declared a virtual spiritual war on the darker forces which to their collective mind are satanic animism and Hindu worship of the phallus. It all sounds like the Victorian missionary attitudes of the 19th century, driven also by a frustration as the

correspondent explains, of coming to terms with the fact that after 2000 years of 'knowing Christ' that only 24 million of India's billion population are Christian.

Conclusion

One has to ask how many of these foreign congregations have any idea how ancient is Christianity as a layer of belief in this complex social structure. It is salutary to reflect amid the evangelical angst either side of the fence that many families of all classes and backgrounds willingly send their children to convent schools. Their quality of education is acknowledged. The Indian way of life being what it is, inclusive of all good influences in the spiritual sense, it does not seem to have been harmful. Go into any church in Kerala for instance and you know you are not in Rome. Nearly all the customs are totally Indian.

Inquiring of an eminent Hindu friend how she felt about her convent school background in Chennai, she rebounded with a chuckle: "I left their Christianity at the gateway on my way home!"

■ **COCONUT**

The very backbone of Kerala's wealth... but never sit under a coconut tree when sipping delicious milky south Indian coffee (a produce of the hill region on the horizon). Wayside cafes proliferate along the one coastal road; many are tucked away in groves. It has been known for a large heavy nut in full hard case to concuss the unfortunate traveller below! It has also been known for a coconut to fall on a bridal train ,during a Christian wedding photograph session—very auspicious but it could have been lethal, cracking the bride's skull just because the groom didn't shake the tree first!

Later, on a third visit to Kerala in the early 90s for a family reunion and a remarkably different Christmas at an ayurvedic resort overlooking Somatheeran beach where electronic church bells rang out insistently for four solid hours from a tiny Syrian Christian church enveloped in mysteriously dark palm groves, we were told of a Malayalam saying: 'There are 99 ways to use a coconut palm and the 100th will soon be discovered.'

An Indian friend once sat us down and challenged us to another brainstorming—think of 30 usages for this gigantic tough diamond. We got to 26 and ran out of inspiration. Try finding the other four...

1. A clean drink in a sterile container full of vitamins in the coconut water.
2. Soft white lining to be scooped out with a sharp piece of the outer shell is the most nutritious of all.
3. The nut itself to eat.
4. Desiccated coconut confectionery.
5. Tender terminal buds on plant can be eaten raw or cooked.
6. Copra made from kernel. Dried and edible.
7. Oil extracted from kernel good for hair shampoos.
8. Massage oil.
9. Margarine production.
10. Baby food milk.
11. Pharmaceutical skin creams.
12. Disinfectant.

13. Cattlefood.
14. Toddy-arrack. A lethal intoxicant!
15. Winding rope—seen manufactured along roadside.
16. Ditto, frond leaves as a mobile roof shelter when working on ground.
17. Mobile umbrella... and also hat for shade.
18. Roof thatch.
19. Womenswear buttons.
20. Ladle, spoon and other kitchen utensils made from shell.
21. Coir industry—door mats, rattan mats, kitchen carpeting squares.
22. Basketry.
23. Trunk of tree used for building construction.
24. Charcoal used from burnt shell, firing bakery kilns, goldsmith flames.
25. Canoe carved out of the trunk.
26. Auspicious fruit for use in worship.

◆ The basic shell is used as a bowl also for the **chutti**—the rice paste applied on faces in building up the 'wings' on Kathakali dancers cheeks.

Such domestic usages are not confined to Kerala, the land of coconuts. A Bengali friend relates that in the traditional kitchen many a housewife uses a cleaned half-shell as a sieve for the jalebi batter, the three holes being just the right size for the thick strands to fall slowly into the sizzling oil and fold into the sticky sweet.

◆ And in an all-India context the coconut rates supreme to mark auspicious beginnings in the company of the rotund Ganesh and to give thanks for successful completion of long journeyings. On the road south from Chennai is the much-visited wayside shrine on the right at Chengalpattu. Here people alight to pray to the Lord of All Beginnings and break a coconut on the slab of stone outside, before facing the hazards of the open road. On arrival safely back I have done the same four times in my life, delivered miraculously from half of India's population walking the road edges, dogs and hens darting under the wheels, buffaloes waiting until you are upon them in order mischievously to cross in lumbering fashion, unannounced road bumps, and new signs before rail level crossings ∿∿∿: 'Beware rumble bumps'. Indeed you could suffer concussion even in the new Express Video Coaches hurtling Indian tourists, already well-blessed, on temple pilgrimage at an astronomical pace. If you failed to slow down for these lethal—but effective—rumblebumps, a coconut would not save you.

◆ And consider the auspicious launching of ships... not with easily-broken bottles of champagne but with nature's solid cannonball of a nut. That is a feat for a cricketer's straight eye and a pace bowling hit!

◆ A staggering figure of 12,355 million nuts were harvested in the 93-94 year production (India Year Book—it makes you wonder who collated that figure!). Since then no figure has appeared. Perhaps they got tired of counting!

It is known that at least half a million people, mostly from the impoverished section of rural populations, find a certain livelihood from coir production. A new area of experimental usage (is this the 100th mark reached?) is in the manufacture of geo-synthetics—hard fibres to be used in road building, reinforcing asphalt surfaces, dykes, drainage surfaces that need environmentally suitable landscaping.

◆ Apart from all these day-to-day usages coconuts have deeper significance in representing life in its most bountiful and fulsome aspects.

It is no surprise that the religious terms used for such an earthy nut is raised to poetic levels, the **fruit of lustre = sriphal.** If a **MURTI** = representation in sculpted form of a deity, is not available this humble shaggy coconut can be raised to such substitution, placed on a **KUMBH/kalash** (pitcher) with mango or ashoka leaves, daubed with vermilion or sandalwood and worshipped as the istadevata's representation.

■ **COLOUR = rang** (n. *Sanskrit*)
= hence *rangoli* floor decorations in coloured powder. Brilliant colour figures very symbolically in Indian life and resonates through textiles and especially the vibrancy of sari silks, in temple worship, through craft, even in the visualisation of rasa moods in music. India is a memory of stunning colours even in the humblest homes.

Turmeric (*halad, haldi*) = yellow ochre, is most especially associated with the worship of the deities and can be seen being ground with water into paste by a functionary purohit in temples. He does this on a flat yoni from which it pours into pitchers ready for daily worship.

◆ When mixed with slaked lime powder it miraculously turns into **vermilion (*kumkum*)** also used in sacramental rites and for placing the dot **(bindu)** on the forehead in temple worship or in honouring a family visitor or at a reception.

◆ **White** from ground conch shells (auspicious in themselves); **red** from **alaktaka** (juice of a shrub); **black** from **kajal** (soot mixed with butter oil as eye black to protect and disinfect the eyes) are all regarded as pure colours.

◆ **Neela** = blue—associated with the colour of the deities (reflecting the firmament) and with the rare beautiful lotus, is especially revered.

The late **Pupul Jayakar**, one of India's great art 'philosophers,' chair of the many **Festivals of India** abroad and recipient of so many awards including the prestigious Padma Bhushan, 1967 for pioneering work in the early days of resuscitating rural art, indigenous design and village self-sufficiency, has pointed out a number of times that great art emerges 'from a simultaneity of sensory perceptions', in Indian tradition specifically designated as

rupa = shape	**varna** = colour
pramana = proportion	**rasa** = essence

Without **RASA,** the tincture, 'that element that quickens with vitality and the flow of life, artistic creation no matter how perfect in technique, remained lifeless—inert.'

■ **COMMUNIST PARTIES**

The first communist government to be democratically elected was in Kerala in 1957. **E M S Namboodiripad**, the highest of high caste brahmins, became the first Chief Minister of that state government. We happened to be in Kerala at the time. It was all very peaceful. Many Kerala friends chuckled with good humour, 'That will show those lazy Congress-wallahs! They are all corrupt. Had a monopoly for too long,' was the attitude. The chief minister's brother incidentally was at that time encamped in a rush hut beside the Ganga near Benares. A highly educated man like E M S, he had reached the stage of modern retirement and the Hindu third stage of **vanaprastha** but had escalated it into **sannyaas**, the fourth stage of life... to meditate and withdraw from everyday affairs. Nowhere else in the world could such a juxtaposition occur—each with their own integrity intact.

E M S (Elamakulam Manakkal Sankaran) died in March 1998, a fine old brahmin, aged 88, respected unto the end. Another of India's paradoxes, born an aristocrat reciting the Vedas at six years old, arguing the toss against obscurantists' ritual and becoming a passionate Marxist by the time he was concluding the brahmacharya stage. He was known all over India as 'a revolutionary in precept, Gandhian in practice'.

In fact while 'gone underground' during WW2 he was exposed to the impoverishment of the low-caste, to such an extent he ultimately disbanded extensive ancestral lands. The proceeds went to the CPI(M). He so angered his own uppercrust privileged community he was virtually ostracised, not even allowed to be present at the funeral pyre of his mother, a matter of insult and deep hurt. He was forced to watch at a distance.

Paradoxes abound. Many indigenous Christians—Syrian, converted, whatever source—voted Marxist.

For special books on the complexities of Communist manifestations in Kerala hunt out Professor **Tom Nossiter's Communism in Kerala, a Study in Political Adaptation** (1982) commissioned by The Royal Institute of International Affairs, Chatham House; and in Australia, Latrobe University Professor **Robin Jeffrey's Politics, Women and Wellbeing** (Macmillan, Melbourne, 1992).

Factionalism is rife among theoretical Marxists certainly amongst Bengalis but that may say more about Bengali culture than Marxism. As a result of this tendency there are at least seven different parties from strait **CPI** to **RSP** (Revolutionary Socialist Party) ready to slogan-shout on the streets! One of the first adages I learned (undoubtedly from my first mentor, Khushwant Singh) was: One Bengali is a meditation. Two Bengalis, a conversation. Three Bengalis, a confrontation.

■ **CONCH SHELL** (n. *Sanskrit = shankh*)

In temples all over India the deity may have slept well all night. As the sun rises bringing the warmth of the day, dispelling mists and grey shadows, in the half-light priests and musicians stir the god or goddess with the blowing of the auspicious conch, and in south India with the strident nadaswaram (oboe) as well. Not a living thing could sleep through that! Try blowing at the spiralled bulbous end but lips have to be compressed and pulled tightly in to eject breath sharply. Good luck!

The small musical party proceeds, through the echoing dark-pillared halls and sunlit paved courtyards, circumambulating the shrines.

◆ The deities are taken out of their niches, bathed and dressed—and still the fundamental sound of the universe flows out in reverberations. Perhaps this was also the notion Greek thinkers held of that basic 'music of the spheres'.

◆ The shankh is acknowledged as auspicious by all Hindus. It is one of the main attributes of Vishnu who holds it in one of his hands. Its presence as an artistic motif is as ubiquitous as the lotus, the fish and the rudraksha.

◆ Put your ear to the large conch and you may well hear the sound of the ocean circling its multiple spirals.

◆ In Bengal, craftsmen decorate them beautifully with incisions. Perhaps this is why the shankh is held in such esteem. Within its obvious visual **spiral** (and we now see that the galaxies are not full = circles or **chakras** but = spirals—open-ended) RSIS must have toyed with visual imaging and seen in this solid shell washing up on a few beaches in the Bay of Bengal an easily transportable symbol: holding the sacred **sabda** (sound = word = Vac) already well established as a profound entity in the very first sacred hymns. Cosmic space within its spirals was easily explained to those first villagers overawed by the immense stretch of the open Gangetic basin. Thus it was incorporated into **PANTHEON** iconography in later times.

Orissa, often left off the tourist beat, is a source of the last echoes of this original India. Despite its impoverished aridity it has astonishing examples of this long lasting visual continuum, especially amongst the high proportion of tribal people in the state who due to Pandit Nehru's policy were left untouched to develop at their own pace once given the basic governmental agencies of advancement in education, health, agricultural loans. Mini conch shells actually 'walk' through the mangrove mud flats at night, the molluscs still inside the shells. Rare large shells are also found on Orissa's isolated coastal strands.

Village art is securely grounded in the traditional knowledge passed on from grandmother to mother to daughter in the wall paintings in rice paste at the time of major festivals. The flowing nature of its ballooning outline appears prominent in the wall-length friezes sculpted with such artistry. On the enormous temple architecture conch shell design figures greatly. Apparently the foundations of the architectural alignment of the magnificent temple complex at Puri are in the shape of a conch. In the text this is referred to as **samkha kshetra**.

◆ The visual emblem obviously carries a profound sacred impulse to the viewer who clearly has heard its sound so often conveyed not only in temple but domestic ceremonies attendant on the deity. Something significant is happening when such sound accosts the ears.

Married women wear a pair of carved conch shell bangles (**churees**) made by a special artisan group in Bengal called shamkharis, and village women place their stylised rice paste depictions of the Trinity resting upon the conch. Weavers also incorporate the conch as a motif in the border designs of saris not only of tribal textiles but also in the beautiful much-sought-after but expensive modern Orissa **ikat** saris. It is significantly enough very similar in shape to some fat mangoes, an opulent symbol in itself of well-being.

◆ Armies sounded the commencement of battle to the riveting sound of massed conches. This is the Mahabharata description in Sir Edwin Arnold's Victorian-era translation of the great showdown at Kurukshetra between hostile cousins.

> *Krishna, with knotted locks, blew his great conch*
> *Carved of the "Giant's bone;" Arjuna blew*
> *Indra's loud gift; Bhima the terrible—*
> *Wolf-bellied Bhima—blew a long reed-conch;*
> *And Yudhisthira, Kunti's blameless son,*
> *Winded a mighty shell, "Victory's Voice;"*
> *And Nakula blew shrill upon his conch*
> *Named the "Sweet-sounding," Sahadev on his*
> *Called "Gem-bedecked",....*
> *From Sir* **Edwin Arnold's The Song Celestial**
> *(Trûbner, London, 1885)*

■ COORG, COFFEE and CARDAMOM

Once a state in its own right, this tiny distinctive region was absorbed into Karnataka, as the Kodagu region in 1956. This is the source of the sacred and beautiful river **Kaveri** (much cleaner than **GANGA MA**). It rises in spring water near the Kerala border at Talakaveri, flowing eastward to the Bay of Bengal. See a splendid book by **George Michell** and **Clare Arni, Eternal Kaveri** (Marg, Mumbai, 1999).

Coorg/Kodagu is known as the **coffee bowl** of India. It is unspoiled, has a climate that escapes Indian extremes, could be likened in parts to England's Berkshire countryside beyond Aldershot. Its people are upstanding and proud of their military generals and other managerial personnel (out of all proportion to the tiny state population). Its women tie their saris differently also, and are noted for their self-assurance.

An East India Company official introduced the idea of coffee plantations in the mid-19th century. Coorg now produces a major part of India's crop of coffee beans because of the combination of ancient rich soils, dependable monsoonal rains and constant warmth rather than harsh heat. **Robusta** and **arabica** are the delicious coffee brews of this region, exported all over the world bringing in approximately Rs10,000 million in foreign exchange.

Cardamom is known to Indians as **elaichi**—the Queen of Spices. Coffee can be flavoured with it (Arabs especially enjoy this taste) as can milk desserts such as **firni**. It leaves a subtle lasting after-flavour. Ayurvedic medicine uses the pod for digestive purposes and stomach upsets. The greener the pods the more aromatic they are but in curries the big dark Bengali elaichi are usually not eaten, there only for the subtle flavouring. Other important spicy flavours come from chillies, cinnamon, coriander, cumin, curry leaves... all embodied in a novel which allows an insight into traditional village life flavoured tantalisingly by the smell of Coorgi coffee, the sour tang of toddy and the aroma of the tiny green bananas fried in subtle spice—**The Scent of Pepper** by **Kavery Nambisan** (Penguin, New Delhi, 1997). Also a marvellous account of this unique culture tucked away in the ancient rolling hills of the south is by that intrepid Irish woman and her young daughter cycling the world—**Dervla Murphy: On a Shoestring to Coorg** (Century Hutchinson, London, 1985).

■ CORE CONCEPTS: PURUSH-ARTHA (n. *Sanskrit*)

Sanatana Dharma is how traditional Hindus refer to their world view which is not a religion or theology in the Western definition of such terms. The quest is the long search through righteous living for supreme union with the **Absolute = Brhmvidya = knowledge of Brhm = a singularity =** 🏃

Sanatana Dharma is the eternal law inbuilt into the creative process and

* applicable to all humanity, not just those who believe in a particular faith
* embraces all living matter also
* is the very essence of activating nature = prakriti
* upholds universes upon universes of incomprehensible infinity

It is in essence a very scientific view in close affinity to the way modern physics has reassessed creation with all the new thinking that has emerged with astrophysics research in the last two decades. (see Professor Stephen Hawking's book **A Brief History of Time**, Professor Paul Davies' **The Mind of God**, and Fritjof Capra's book **The Tao of Physics** which had great currency with students in the 70s in the search for new meaning not limited by institutional religions.)

1. **HINDUISM**

to use the word applied by the rest of the world but not by its devotees, possesses (or rather does **not** possess) some very strange characteristics:

◆ there is no 'beginning' in historic time.

◆ no actual revelation through a particular divine 'Being' as Jesus Christ is acknowledged by Christians, or a historical seer or prophet such as Buddha, Mahavir, Zoroaster, Muhammed, Guru Nanak in their relevant faiths.

◆ unknown rishis, saints, swamis, gurus, munis, sages have spread **the insightful word** over time. Other famous known learned people do exist—who have taken the knowledge further according to the expanded insights of their own particular age— **Adi Shankaracharya** in the 8th–9th century; **Sri Ramakrishna** and **Swami Vivekananda** in the last century.

◆ no overall body of church with a hierarchy of clergy exists, or even a sangh but rather an amorphous conglomeration of temple priests who were hereditary appointments of the brahmin class and not preachers, rather just functionaries in a temple, devoted to enacting the rituals with brahminical exactitude as well as knowing all the Sanskrit texts and legal codifications.

◆ sects of sadhus on a regional basis or specific followers of Shiva or Vishnu or Shakti spread the insights and visions of the rsis as handed down in parables in the oral recitations.

◆ there is no 'canon law' as laid down in Christian tradition by infallible doctrine and Vatican ordinance.

◆ there is no doctrine which has compulsorily to be accepted as the Nicene Creed for Christians.

◆ in fact there is no compulsory belief to be accepted as immutable law or self-evident truth as in Islamic tradition, never to adjust to world developments or undergo examination.

◆ each to her/his own comprehension is the intellectual freedom accepted in the limitless reservoir of literature devoted to elaborating on the one core concept of Dharma alone and its related subsidiaries—as propounded in the Vedic hymns, the Upanishadic speculative philosophy, the Puranic epics and parables (**purana** = old tales).

These lively human stories of the goings-on among the deities who have 'come down to earth' to live amongst humans sustain the faith through an overwhelming body of commentaries by saintly figures for at least 5,000 years, and in a constant updating through many artistic outlets.

Indeed no one person could possibly read and digest in one lifetime all this wisdom or even comprehend in the oral culture the handing down of the faith by listening to gurus at riverbank shrines, in ashrams, on the meeting place ghats in sacred centres, at huge melas. No wonder the idea of reincarnation took hold in the Indian mind to give time to absorb this vast store of wisdom as each individual—the innermost soul—atman expanded in 'realisation'.

And yet somehow this conglomerate unwieldy mass is '**quite spontaneously coherent in practice and self-driven**', in the words of **Nirad Chaudhuri**.

At least this one sentence in his book **Hinduism** puts the nature of the Indian paradox in a nutshell:

In the midst of anarchy, an astonishing cohesion; in the midst of diversity, unity; in the midst of intellectual freedom to believe and follow the individual marg or pathway, the most rigid social construction, caste, in which to place that believer—at one time not free even to cross the threshold of a temple if that way of ritual was the choice of actively doing one's duty, ordered out if one was of the lowly Sudra caste by an imperious priest.

2. **AN ASTONISHING COHESION—FRAGMENTARY PIECES—COSMIC WHOLES**

Serious students of Indian culture, thought processes and scientific concepts so holistically aligned with all art forms, as well as scholars, should be aware of the massive undertaking by **IGNCA** (Indira Gandhi National Centre for the Arts)... **A Lexicon of Fundamental Concepts of the Indian Arts: Kalātattvakosa**, examining at least 250 Sanskrit terms.

The first, dealing with eight of the prime **essences** 'which emerge in diverse disciplines ranging from biology, medicine to mathematics and metaphysics and which govern aesthetic theories and artistic expressions' appeared in 1988. Others such as **laksana** and **silpa** 'indicating process and manifestation at the level of form' were published in 1992 under the general editorship then of **Dr Kapila Vatsyayan** and of **Dr Bettina Bäumer**, German scholar and co-ordinator of the ambitious project. Mentioned earlier, the Lexicon is referred to a number of times in this book.

The first paragraph to the Introduction to Vol 1 of the Lexicon indicates the vast span, spatial nature and depth of Indian culture—all of a piece with the stars and abstract consciousness.

The Indian arts, both in theory (sastra) and practice (prayoga), are branches of a single living tree of Indian culture. They cannot be understood in isolation from other dimensions of thought and science, myth and ritual, spiritual and secular traditions. The underlying world-view has crystallised in certain concepts, reflecting the understanding of cosmos and man, of space and time, of circle and periphery, of the part and the whole, of body, senses and mind. So far, most indological and art-historical research has been done in single disciplines or in limited historical periods, but a serious investigation into the inter-relatedness of all these fields is still a desideratum. An interdisciplinary approach is the first prerequisite to understanding the relationship between the ancient sciences (e.g. Ayurveda, Jyotisa), philosophy, and the various branches of the arts.

Introduction: Bettina Baumer

Exhaustive—and exhausting—to those who attempt to understand. It is as if one were embracing the entire Universe. That is India!

3. **RTA** n. *Sanskrit:*

law in a very wide context, spelled as such in Sanskrit transcribed with the diacritical mark under the R = similar to the French rolled R but now in common parlance seen as **rta** in English

◆ that which sustains the universe at a cosmic level—for instance the ellipses of planets which have maintained that momentum and orderly encircling of our own galaxy and sun since its 'coming-into-being' = **Brhm** (neuter scientific concept)

◆ the power that keeps such entities as molecules, particles, gases, stars, gravity waves in their stable relationships

◆ the planet and its human development from cell to present hominid in a remarkable molecular patterning

◆ the individual quality of personality with its sense of moral law, and righteousness... 'where does the sense of good come from?' is the question asked

◆ an inherent law which acknowledges the 'essential being of physical properties'—its rightful essence such as flame is to fire, ice is to water.

Mahatma Gandhi used to quote a scriptural passage in relation to this profound concept which works in harness with Dharma:

THE SUN IS A GREAT KEEPER OF OBSERVANCES

His reasoning was that from the eternal **natural laws** that maintain universes upon universes in their 'ordered chaos', eternal **moral laws** exude from this natural inherent process, laws which have a common ground in all societies no matter how diverse. This is **sanatana dharma**.

4. DHARMA

Introduction

Derived from this vast comprehension comes the immediate sense of **Dharma**—personal, social, cosmological. This is the traditional first major building block of social behaviour.

'It is my dharma' is a common phrase as much used as 'It is my karma', by Indians. 'It is my dharma...' implies the outgoing duty, responsibility, the sense of right purpose as much as the previous phrases imply an incoming force that is 'out there'. Dharma is the ultimate sheet anchor for Indians of all backgrounds and faiths (I have even heard Indian Muslims use it, the phrase transposed to the teachings of the Prophet as relayed to humanity in the Qur'an).

It needs to be understood that adamantine but resilient concepts such as **dharma, karma, maya, moksha/mukti and atman,** loom large in the framework of India's social fabric. They are the building blocks of faith, ethics and social action. Just as European civilisation has emerged from layer upon layer of subsidiary cultures and an amalgam of scientific rationalism layered on Christian faith, itself layered upon earlier Graeco-Roman philosophy, logical thinking and Roman law, so the gigantic body of Indian concepts has grown from core building foundations that are an amalgam of neolithic animist, early indigenous Indian, tribal and incoming migrants, culminating in a massive intellectual speculation gathered into Vedic and Upanishadic literature.

THE BUILDING BLOCKS

A. DHARMA (n. Sanskrit)

dhri is the root.... to sustain, maintain, to hold in its rightful place or form

◆   The word has been likened to the Latin word **firmus/formus** = firm/form. The density of meaning is such that no one English word can fully translate the profundity of that phrase so often used even in ordinary conversation—'it is my dharma'.

◆   **moral law**, righteousness, harmony, order, personal responsibility and duty are all involved.

◆   at **cosmic level** dharma allied with rta refers to:

a)   the form of things as they are
b)   the power that keeps them that way
c)   an individual's personal duty to maintain
     this order, that is the moral law

In the Sanskrit texts dharma is said to be very 'subtle'—the knowing of good, the moral ground very difficult to acquire without the continual guidance of the guru, a tradition still held today in countless homes even in the most sophisticated of urban surroundings, invariably held dear by the women of the household.

The forms of all matter, objects, energy have inbuilt laws or structures as we now understand from scientific investigation, atomic measurement, analysis of molecular structures. We see a finite table made of wood. **That is the external outer reality. But the molecular structure if we had x-ray eyes** (which Australian Aborigines attempt to use in particular art forms) **would depict a deeper 'reality' of the wood.**

◆   **At personal level** dharma refers to a person's duty, responsibility to maintain the innate order, to strive for good and righteousness against **adharma**, moral disorder and evil. A person learns this through **smriti,** the 'heard' stories passed down through the ages from the learned and saintly people as well as the **shruti**—inspirational insights acquired through meditation, yoga, and intuitional gnowledge (*jñana* or *gñyana*), a direct revelation. (A Buddhist would speak of maintaining equilibrium from **dis-ease**).

A-dharma, is a more complex violation of the eternal cosmic law with consequent repercussions for that agent of evil through many rebirths. The Mahabharata echoes with examples of these consequences working their way through many generations. September 11, 2001 would, because of the magnitude and lack of forward declaration of war, certainly qualify. Ordinary sin in a daily sense is referred to as **paap**—its opposition **punya**—virtue acquires karmic merit.

This discipline inbuilt into daily action and thinking should be maintained at

a)   personal level either through puja in the home, yogic meditation, ritual worship by visiting the temple, a visit to or by a guru, etc.
b)   social level of class = **varnashrama** and
c)   an orderly progression through the stages of life or **ashramas** (see **QUATERNITIES: ASHRAMAS**)

Not that all this systematic course of action is always clear, or easy! K M Sen has pointed out that **dharma** is:

◆   neither an obedience to a revelation (supposedly god-given)
◆   nor a worship of God in accordance with the contents of that revelation
◆   The essential core of Hindu belief is free from all dogmatic affirmations on who or what god is—truth in fact transcends all verbal definitions thought up by humans. There is not just 'the one and only truth', a dogma propounded by the semitic religions. A true Hindu affirms this everyday in reciting the **GAYATRI** acknowledgement of true 'illumination' (move forward to this stepping stone).
◆   The importance of flexibility for redefinition in each age as human knowledge acquires new facts (always with the proviso that staunch examination of those facts should occur, leading to wisdom) is acknowledged by Hinduism, Jainism, Buddhism, and by followers of the Parsee and Sikh faiths also.

And at the same time it cannot be stated enough that this concept applies to all humans no matter their race, creed, culture. **Dharma** then is not static. **Rta** is what keeps it on course. Its great strength is to reinterpret its meaning to individuals and society in general according to the needs and attitudes of each age. **Modernisation is inherent in the concept.** Updating process through successive reincarnations (see **AVATAR**) and all the colourful literature of metaphor and myth that grew up and still is reinterpreted by the arts and festivals, TV and cinema in contemporary life is the quite brilliant process hit upon pragmatically to put the core messages across. For instance:

♦ The **Amar Chitra Katha** (eternal picture story) series of book comics produced for children and laid out in their hundreds on any city pavement 'book stall', is an easily accessible way for foreigners who are overcome and in culture shock to understand the exploding universe of Indian impressions! Just looking at the pictures of the parables and epics unfolding gives a clue to what Indians consider as important. See also **David Frawley's Hinduisum: The Eternal Tradition** (Sanatana Dharma) (Voice of India, New Delhi, 2000)

B. **KARMA** (n. *Sanskrit*)

Kri is the root

Kr means to act, **PRAKRITI** being the activating force of nature

C. and D: **ARTHA** and **KAMA**:

worldly material possessions, wealth, social wellbeing, and sexual enjoyment (kama) are well-documented (see **QUATERNITIES, ASHRAMAS**)... even more so in a re-issued publication of a 1969 book **Some Aspects of Indian Culture** (Publications Division, Ministry of Information and Broadcasting, Delhi, 1994) by the late **C Sivaramamurti**, one of India's most erudite as well as deeply sensitive scholars. As a Director of the National Museum in Delhi, his profound knowledge not only of the archaeological yardsticks that measure India's cultural development but his joy in elucidating the Sanskrit texts to guide us in today's everyday life were suffused with a personal *joie de vivre* in his jargon-free English. Even as he tackled these two signposts—**artha** and **kama**—'the wherewithal of life', one is made to realise they do not represent the all-too-shallow world of hedonistic pleasure. They really only belong to the second stage of life, that of the householder—**grihastha**.

As the next stage of life takes over, a hidden current seems to course quietly through many a bloodstream, a substratum of that ultimate withdrawal. This often erupts unexpectedly—a sudden passion for yoga or vegetarianism or fasting (and not just for a health kick) takes over your Indian friends' lives and certainly an insistent 'pull' to undergo the rigours of pilgrimage to far places—and often on foot.

This, however, is the symbolic ideal. In the contemporary world many 60-year-old-plus politicians have a knack of clinging onto power, monied entitlements and the 'goodies of life' with no sign at all of relinquishing **artha**.

The sensual pleasures of life—sexual fulfilment, good food, the company of loving friends, the enjoyment of sporting events, physical challenge, artistic portrayal in music, dance, painting, the aesthetics of pure worship—are not the free-for-all of boundless liberty and greedy self-gratification. Kama involves a deeper sense of fulfilment—a mutuality of giving and caring, an enrichment which comes from a maturing process of long-term commitment, and self-imposed responsibility.

E. **MAYA**: is often translated as 'illusion' but ignorance and clouded perception is a better description.

The major problem in the attainment of the universal goal of final building blocks—**moksha** (liberation from the round of rebirths and death) is the unfortunate existence and very recognisable fact of **maya**—the **film of ignorance** which limits our vision of our true human purpose in this particular incarnation. There may be echoes, an Indian feels, from a previous incarnation where the personal atman, honed through rebirth after rebirth, struggles through the painful disciplines of transmigration (**samsara**).

Struggling up the pathway of individual progress, very Bunyanesque, even at the level of ordinary factual knowledge, is a hard furrow to plough. To acquire wisdom needs a touch of grace as well as hard work in the karmic process. Sweeping away the clouds of unknowing, of impaired vision, of limited perceptions is a process it seems that is a universal condition. No generation seems better able to acquire wisdom, despite all the accumulation of worldly knowledge from who knows how many generations which have gone before.

The Bible in fact puts this condition poetically (but succinctly) in **Corinthians** 13 v 12. **For now we see through a glass, darkly.** The Indian view is that there is a **ground** of gnowledge (see to **GNOW**), a fundamental reservoir which is existent through the ages, like some gigantic computer of unchangeable awareness of truth, if only we could manufacture the right plug and maintain the right electric current within our will. Theodore de Bary refers to this in his **Sources of Indian Tradition** (Columbia University Press, New York, 1958**)** as 'the imperishable substratum of the forms of our existence, knowledge and bliss'— **sat** (true knowledge), **chit** (consciousness), **ananda** (bliss).

Yet all through the ages humanity has had to be advised against the deadly sins, entanglements of worldly temptations— **kama** (desire); **krodha** (anger); **lobha** (greed); **moha** (attachment); **ahankar** (ego). These add up to **avidyamaya**, the maya of ignorance.

Only slowly, slowly through stressful endeavour, ever vigilant like the seeker of the Bhagavad Gita poster narrative who seems also to face a Slough of Despond, do we acquire the ability to dispel ignorance or maya, not only a film over our eyes but a fog in our brains! Philosophers spent volumes of texts in wrangling over the inability of human reasoning powers and vision to distinguish between

♦ **Prakriti =** gross Matter, that which Nature stirs up with activity in the finite realm of planetary time and which enmeshes our individual atmans, and

♦ Subtle Matter, the inner reality of the universal Atman or Paramatman which should engage our attention.

If all this seems complicated, Professor Radhakrishan affirms that maya is an 'intellectual hobgoblin' and all it really means is that one should not be misled by outer appearances. **Nama Rupa**—name and form, the reality around us is all very well and good but humanity has limited perception of these. The inner essence is what needs seeking out, and only inner 'divinations' give a sudden flash of another elusive layer of consciousness (see **INTUITIVE KNOWLEDGE**).

F. **MOKSHA, MUKTI**: (n. *Sanskrit*) used to express the yearning for **release** or **liberation** from the processional round, the relentless treadmill of reincarnation that has to be undergone by each person's **atman** or individual personality/soul to achieve full **moksha**.

Indians may be touched with a bent for the metaphysical questions of life compared with more pragmatic Westerners but Indians are also realists par excellence and no more spiritual or other-worldly in their second and third ashramas. They want the good things of life as much as people in the high-consumption societies of the West. Indeed, those able to with middle incomes are having a field day scrambling to acquire possessions, the opposite of what is preached in the scripture and in the ascetic traditions—**aparigraha**—avoiding luxury in clothing, a surfeit of food, ostentatious possessions. The teaching is to take only enough as required in the householder stage of life with its enjoyments = **artha**.

Acquiring harmony, moral law, maintaining order is an innate urge within humanity's aspirations. Such goals have been upheld by all philosophies and human developments no matter how divergent the civilizations and in whatever period of history. Certain basic precepts have been put before individuals and recognised as time-honoured principles of good, acceptable behaviour... **piety**, a word hardly encountered in contemporary society.

G. **ATMAN** with a small 'a' is the individual soul maintained when the dross of human flesh is gone at the end of this life, to be reborn again and again in the crucible of fire, bound by the laws of karma, until the lessons of life have been learned, perfection and harmony finally achieved culminating in absorption in the total Atman.

This essence 'never dies, nor is it born'. It always is.

◆ **Essence** is often described quite vividly in parables—salt in water, for instance. As a tangible visible essence it is still there but not seen. Likewise we recognise water as liquid. It exists also in other states of tension or existential forms such as solid ice, soft snow, gaseous steam, or fog sufficiently solid to delay cars, trains, aircraft—all different externally yet possessing the same constituent elements.

◆ When the form changes by the transition, **the essence of water** is not lost.

It has been pointed out in a number of commentaries that tension exists for all sincere Hindus in balancing the injunctions.

a) to follow absolute **dharma** (the moral law) to reach the gates of liberating **moksha** and yet

b) abide on the other hand by the more restrictive **social codes of dharma**—that is the frames of reference inbuilt into the categorisations of class, the interaction of **varnashramas**. These after all are man-made, evolving over time out of the brahmin teachings as the sacerdotal rituals built up over centuries, the Indian equivalent of canon laws and 'churchification'.

As an individual begins to put a wise head on older shoulders that concentration of purpose that emerges from this social structure of dharma, karma, maya, moksha, mukti and the essential atman comes more easily, turning the mind to thoughts of righteousness, all passion spent, that even the aged prophet Isaiah (26:19) of the Old Testament, circa 7th-6th century BCE, who may well have imbibed wisdom from the east in the flow of trade and cultural interchange, sagely spoke:

The righteous themselves will possess the earth, and they will reside forever upon it.

Conclusion

As the Vedic thinkers advanced through their searches it becomes clear over a thousand-year period that their hallmark characteristic was that of universality—there was recognition that doctrinaire creeds, declarations of Absolute Truth engraved in stone encasements of earliest scripts did Truth a disservice. Ultimately, as physicists are now themselves pondering, it may ultimately be indefinable—not a categorical this and that, but a questioning negation—**neti, neti** says the Upanishadic search. It is **neither** this, **nor that.** We cannot know this vast **truth** all at once. Just as a baby has to grow into adolescence, then young adulthood to comprehend even a limited dispersal of maya, so one life may not be sufficient to reach full knowledge, full self-realisation. The Sanskrit text is this:

SATYAM EKAM
(Truth is one)   VIPRAH BAHUDHA VEDANTEH
सत्यम एकम
EKI DEV   विप्रा वहुधा वदन्ते
(One God)
एकि देव   but wise men interpret it in many ways

■ CORRUPTION

A-dharma is rife! It is the **kaliyuga!** Nothing is done by halves in India, so it seems. Most activity explodes, and exponentially at that; personal 'miscreants' (to use a favourite Indian expression) become larger than life. Thriller novels no longer need to be written. Fiction is out. Reality—even if it takes a decade to unfold—is in. But wait a minute... is it that India has joined the world? Or is it the seemingly endemic nature of the beast—its widespread existence, density due to a vast population so statistics take on a scale of their own? Are Indians so morally impervious to accepted standards of behaviour that the impression has got about at overseas export trade seminars that it is easier to do business with China, for instance, than with India. A 'too-hard basket'—how often have I heard that said while attending or addressing such gatherings.

◆ The more one considers the problem from afar the more the realization comes that India for all the old type 'greasing of the palm' to move the logjam of applications for licences, passports, driving licences, installation of a telephone connection, through the heavy weight of that population queue is often scrutinized through clouded **stereotypes** and **misconceptions**.

◆ Nearly every day in the last 50 years news electronically trips the switches of one's mind of startling global examples of corporate scandals, cleaning out pensioner funds and leaving investors penniless with little redress. Prime ministers are taken to court (not only in India). Corporate directors award themselves bonus payments and then a year later bankruptcy proceedings are filed and a liquidator is called in. Insider trading is rife. Drug

smuggling pays for armaments traced back to manufacture in wealthy countries that should know better.

♦ So what is new? When all is said and done, let who will, cast the first stone!

Those stereotypes and misconceptions

Paradoxes do indeed abound (note **PARADOX!**). Perhaps it is easier dealing with the pragmatic Chinese culture, but then one knows little of the really internal and personal activities of Chinese life. When officials are brought to court in corruption cases and found guilty they are usually shot to set an example. Little is heard afterwards of the aftermath. The world media has by then moved on.

♦ The one redeeming feature about India's problems is that they themselves are their own most stringent critics, with a vociferous press, undeterred by any autocratic governmental threat other than the law of libel. In recent years investigative journalism has taken on a **Washington Post** fervour as assiduous as any undertaken by Carl Bernstein or Bob Woodward.

PIL (Public Interest Litigation) has enabled the media to gather momentum in the search for the truths hidden in the dark and devious corners. And now there is a law similar to the Freedom of Information Acts in the USA and Britain.

♦ This legislative breakthrough and the gathering political 'nous' of journalists—including those who go on television with the fruits of their hidden electronic recording devices, giving another word **tehelka** to the English language have enabled all manner of corruption to come to light—in this case wads of money being passed to army officers to complete weapon deals with military kickbacks.

Other new phrases have entered the Indian-English vocabulary as a consequence apart from PIL.

Hawala: money-laundering in which much of the alternative economy was engaged. Huge assets acquired in India appear to flow freely through underground channels into Dubai, London, Antwerp, Geneva; this intricate international network flows back again to Dubai and Mumbai. The Madras Institute of Development Studies estimated in the late 90s that 40 percent of national income was engaged in this flight of capital out of India. This has since changed with liberalization on the economic front and people being allowed to take out more money on overseas journeys, etc. This has made 'black' money much less valuable to hold.

All manner of kickbacks have come to light that involved Swedish armaments manufacturer Bofors, Swiss banks, the late Rajiv Gandhi when prime minister since exonerated, defence deals, intricate wheeler dealings, underground characters, seemingly respectable uppercrust neighbourhoods such as Delhi's extending southern perimeter. It makes the era that my generation knew in the 50s seem a totally squeaky-clean innocent world.

Criminalization of politics is certainly a phrase I never heard until the early 90s. Then the Central Bureau of Investigation (CBI) was stung into action by the very nature of the degree of escalation and a vigilant press.

What also came to light was how many state politicians especially in the north have criminal records—in Uttar Pradesh alone at that time 106 members of a total of 403 MLAs plus 19 out of 100-odd ministers in Parliament! In Bihar and Madhya Pradesh there are similar instances. One, Mohan Singh, proudly went on TV to declare his dacoit past having killed ten people 'legitimately', for harassing the poor... a male **Bandit Queen** (see **GOVERNMENT**) for the real Bandit Queen, herself as a respectable **Phoolan Devi**, since assassinated.

The judiciary had been galvanised into action as the third arm of government into shaking out the 'white-anting' of the democratic system. The wheels of democracy do however turn no matter how slowly, in what **India Today** (April 17, 2000) referred colourfully to as **Alice in Plunderland**,.

Indeed it has taken over a decade for the wheels of justice to crank up. By the beginning of the millennium writs were issued on the Hinduja brothers after Swiss banks finally handed over details of their monies, Swedish account kickbacks for the Indian government to buy their armaments came to light. This also involved the acquiring of British citizenship by the Hindujas which caused the resignation of one of Tony Blair's ministers, Peter Mandelson. A donation to the controversial Millennium Dome in London of £1m was linked with this scandal.

Corruption is not only money-obsessed. In changes of government a tainted chief minister lands up with an elephantine cabinet in order 'to give berth to all the defectors who had made incoming government possible.' And what is even more disturbing was the reported attempt by leaders such as past prime minister, P V Narasimha Rao, to tamper with the parliamentary system by bribing legislators of a minor independent party for their votes in a confidence motion.

The case of Jayalalithaa

Jayalalithaa is a fascination. Even at the Tamilnadu Assembly election 2001 her political opponents mounted a demonstration float aptly titled with English wit—even in the heart of Tamil-speaking country—Jail–Lalitha. Street actors depicted her fraud trial (the Tansi land deal case) in which she was convicted of the charge of buying a big tract of government land and coastal properties (in which her companion **Sasikala** was implicated) for a fraction of its true value. For this she was sentenced to three years jail. Treading a political tightrope precariously despite her bulk she had six months to be legally re-elected to her constituency if her appeal against sentence was upheld. Almost to the deadline however the Supreme Court quashed her appeal. The chief minister's position out of reach, a front man was appointed: meanwhile her future in Tamil politics, only those who ride the Big Dipper will ever be able to predict, except she once again has had yet another appeal upheld (December, 2001), and in 2002 she became chief minister again! A very crafty lady! Thousands of her supporters danced in the streets of Chennai.

C

Rumours of personal wealth persisted for years, however, and 'buying' loyalty of the poor with free feeding of thousands at the ostentatious wedding of her foster son V N Sudhagaran, and the emergence from the shadows of a close female companion, **Sasikala Natarajan** whose own impoverished background suddenly disappeared into a flamboyant presence, heavy with gold ornaments and rumours of massive property buying in coastal real estate and farming properties, all began to accumulate critical evidence. No longer referred to as 'the Empress' she is lampooned as **The Booty Queen**. Indians are very sharp in playing with English flexibility of language!

It is best to let an Indian editor speak (India Today, May 22, 2001)

India can be a confusing place. One minute you are chief minister of a state, next you lose an election. And then, you are charged with corruption, convicted and sentenced to jail. You appeal, your sentence is stayed but the conviction is pending appeal. Meanwhile, it's election time again (one and a half years later) but you are debarred from contesting by the local returning officer because of your conviction. Regardless, your party wins a landslide. And you became chief minister again—no matter that you have not been elected. Such is the strange tale of the indomitable Tamil politician Jayaram Jayalalitha.

This is quite unique in Westminster-type politics anywhere throughout the British Commonwealth.

The electorate can well be forgiven for becoming increasingly cynical. Where is the redress not only for the really poor but those even of the middle class who are honest and pay their taxes to find them ending up in vast drainpipes overgrown with weeds, obscenely lining roads from Thanjavur for at least 70 km—supposedly meant to bring clear drinking water in village uplift schemes?

A flood of publicity, politically motivated, sinks without trace into parched river beds of people's hopes and faith in the democratic system when corruption starts at the top with a leader bitten by the Imelda Marcos bug. Having promised so much to 'her' people, the Empress was incarcerated in pretty much the same infested conditions in jail as the Tamilians, some little old women, seen making their home in these huge pipes while I was exploring the Thanjavur countryside in 1996. By January 2000 on the way back from the exhilarating feasts of Tygaraja music these circular 'tube' homes with fitted modern doors and gardens with vines obliterating the insipid concrete colour had become part of a Corbusier-style **GUFA** (cave) ribbon development along the same lengthy ditch!

In Tamil there is a saying: **makathu penn jagathilum illai = there is no equal to a women born under the zodiac star, Makam.** Such is the monthly star that presided over Jayalalitha's birth! Her devotees who still remain loyal refer to her as Rosapoo Amma (the rose of her mother) alluding in Tamil to her lighter complexion. **Varna** speaks also!

Dacoity: A wonderful Indian term for banditry is another matter and was in the 50s part of an ancient past-time with a certain mystique of Robin Hood encouraged in local legend, robbing the rich **thakur** (landlord) to give to the poor who provided cover, food and protection for the dacoit.

Anyone driving private cars then (as we and our friends did) through the badlands of **Madhya Pradesh** to visit the then isolated pre-tourist sites of **Sanchi** ran the gauntlet through deep ravine country and tiger-infested forests (wild animals still roamed freely and ate stray villagers). India had adventures of a different kind but even today moustachioed men walk around freely toting guns. The only difference is they also sit in the local state legislatures! Perhaps India, the collective electorate, should take a leaf out of its own antiquity and study once again that worldly-wise **Arthashastra**, a classical text on statecraft and the art of realpolitik 23 centuries ago.

♦ **KAUTILYA** (also known as **CHANAKYA** after whom New Delhi's Diplomatic Enclave is appropriately named) as the wily brahmin advisor to India's first real emperor of unification, **Chandragupta Maurya**, devised a manual in the 3rd c BCE as guidance for rulers and politicians of his time. Its general ethos followed the principle that ends justify the means. There is no new thing under the sun!

Surprisingly modern in tone, a millennium and half before Machiavelli bequeathed his name to the very same process in **The Prince**, the **Artha** (wealth, aggrandisement) **shastra** (law book) also examined how to control the venality of those who seek power and gain advantage for themselves; of diplomacy and treachery; civil law and all that is summed up by that Latinized English word that needs to be brought back into common currency—**malfeasance**.

And the solution according to Kautilya—**espionage** and **transfers** of those in charge after a period of time.

♦ Italian city states practised such methods while jockeying for power in Machiavelli's times; Chandragupta similarly while usurping the eastern kingdoms of Magadha (modern Bihar/Bengal). Maintain spies... keep watch on officials... never let them become entrenched in their own power bases... maintain suspicion... **and keep moving them around** as Chief Minister Mayawati who nearly bankrupted her UP State Government Treasury, undertook in the 90s with mass transfer of some 1400 IAS, staff, and police officers.

Conclusion

Before all perspective is lost about India's own shock to the system it is worth recalling that in a sense she is only catching up with many Western democracies who have suffered their own astonishing revelations of political chicanery in what has been called the **Decade of Greed—the Eighties**... financial wrong-doing its creed with insider trading rife in the USA; Board members of Guinness guilty of fraud and Baring Bank incompetence, the outright stealing of company funds and pension schemes, Japanese and Korean prime ministers and politicians imprisoned; Australian state premiers and cowboy business tycoons floating false paper money with Royal Commissions galore on police corruption, all appear to be part of the malaise of modern politics worldwide.

'Arraigning', 'nabbing', 'charge-sheeting', 'miscreants' 'rorts' and 'scams' are the daily vocabulary of the Indian press. At literary level India is now ready for its own blockbuster version of **Bonfire of the Vanities**, the American novel of the 80s. Will this be the next to be penned by Vikram Seth or Arundhati Roy or any number of India's talented writers?

Rasipuram Krishnaswami Laxman, the nation's pre-eminent commentator on political matters and the social foibles of these times of dynamic change in lifestyles has created a character referred to 'as the perennial figure of endurance and stoic neutrality.' In his checked coat (see illustration) and quizzical eyebrows, the Common Man watches bemused as first, in the old days, forage-capped Congresswallah Netaji inspired by his creator Samuel, equally trenchant cartoonist, played out his blatant rorts and personal agendas.

On a serious subject have a good laugh. Some of Laxman's inimitable cartoons are published in paperback, **The Best of Laxman** (Penguin, Delhi, 1990). A **Bhrashtachar Virodh Samiti** (anti-corruption body—another new phrase creeping into everyday Indian speech) has come into existence and a real live Common Man emerged in the late 90s in Maharashtra, that go-ahead lively state. **Anna Hazare** in a Gandhian-style fast focused attention on illegal transfer of government officers which has seriously inconvenienced others. Public reaction was very supportive. Miraculously public-spirited people still exist, *and* an investigative free press, to stand up for honesty, integrity. They certainly kept a finger on the pulse of India's heavyweight-state... **and the citizens of Pune have erected an 8-foot statue to the Common Man to honour his creator, Laxman—incidently brother of the equally brilliant novelist, R K Narayan.**

The Moral Climate

Where there is considerable corruption there is not only a **giver** and a **receiver** but a third party as well—the generality of society and its overall ambience. There is a certain morality, the bottom line, from which codes of behaviour and a sense of justice are established, setting the limit of what is tolerable. Corruption is a malaise which eventually undermines the whole of society. It is as though our moral tramlines have been dug up. In any country with huge populations of under-employed millions struggling with impoverished lifestyles, where few national schemes of health insurance or social welfare payment exist, **loyalty is therefore to the smaller group entity, the tribe, clan or extended family. Look after your own!**

Due to colonial rule loyalty was not seen as legitimate to an **alien** government known to be taking riches **out** of a country. Therefore there was a reverse system of **plundering** to redress the balance. The individual took what perks he could to benefit his own immediate family. This attitude became entrenched.

◆ As a result also of alien rule a huge bureaucracy grew up in which power, wealth, status were concentrated in hands of a tiny minority of Indians who saw themselves as an elite clinging to a narrow ladder with millions trying to climb up it. This is even more dramatic today. Media, TV, the cavortings of Bollywood, obscenely extravagant wedding festivities all highlight the alarming divide

between rich getting richer; the poor poorer. However, even rich nations suffer these same transgressions.

◆ Previous dominions/colonies have had alien codes subtly imposed upon them by rulers from overseas, undermining their own traditional and strong moral codes. They also had noted the 'perks' that the rulers enjoyed and expected to inherit as well. Past Election Commissioner Gadgil commenting on the sorry state of affairs in the mid-90s referred to India's *sharam* (shame) as being the Three Ms = **Money Power, Muscle Power, Minister Power** and the **Three Cs = Cash, Corruption, Criminals.**

He made the point that modern politicians are obsessed with power, not for what they can do for their country with such power but for what that political power can do for them, the opposite of President Kennedy's famous inaugural speech rousing Americans **to think of their duties as citizens as well as their rights.**

An afterthought:

◆ Even godmen go to jail! **Chandraswami,** a supposed holy man who held sway in the 90s over several leading politicians, stripped of his credibility as one such, swanning around the world (always a first class passenger) was exposed as passing fraudulently-acquired money this way and that. He chose the wrong man finally—the late Mr Patak in London, of the famous Indian condiment firm to whom he allegedly owed $100,000.

It is amazing, despite this sorry tale, how much honesty still prevails in circumstances that put our own societies (with higher living standards where there is little excuse) to shame. Our own family can bear witness to such honesty—lost possessions returned, open hospitality shown in the most woebegone circumstances where expensive equipment never went 'walkabout,' servants unfailingly honest despite temptations all around them.

■ **COW** (go(w) = n. *Sanskrit*)

Of course cows are holy! In such a devastating climatic assault as India's in the long summer months precious cattle (mentioned many times in the texts) would naturally need special care. What better excuse than to devise a sacred aura so that they would not needlessly be killed.

They were invaluable along with water buffaloes and far tougher than horses as draught animals pulling the traditional wooden plough. India has the largest cattle population in the world—approximately 210 million with 80 million buffaloes. Due to new methods of cross-breeding, education of rural farmers from go-ahead Karnataka, Maharashtra, Gujarat, Haryana and the Punjab, and technological improvements, India exceeds the USA in milk production.

Milk co-operatives have been initiated nation-wide emulating the really successful Anand experiment of the mid-50s near Ahmedabad (see **Anand–Amul Kaira Milk Co-operative** under **MIRACLES**).

For every step forward, however, there seems to be one back. Farmers say cross-breeding to improve stock is causing the oxen's hump to diminish—a hump that is vital to stop the plough yoke across the cattle's neck from slipping. India's zebu cattle are some of the hardiest in the world working under the relentless summer sun in a way weaker European cattle and horses cannot. Mysore farmers are now suspicious—they say unholy alliances in cross-breeding with European strains are making their own cattle slothful. **It is that tamas tendency creeping in when one is not watchful**... and it would be retrograde to go in for tractors, useless on limestone soils—and anyway the over 80 million draught animals save India a huge bill in fuel oil, as well as providing invaluable stacks of dried cow dung. And to see with what artistry and tender loving care these piles are devised in the outer part of a family holding is an indication of the total approach to cattle and the standing of that holy **Cow of Plenty Nandini** (also known as **Kamadhenu** or **Surabhi**)—so revered in the Vedas and coveted by sage Viswamitra when he saw it ruminating at rishi **VASISTHA**'s hermitage (see relevant section and **AVATAR-kurma**).

♦ And this is the reason why you may even encounter cows used as four-legged power by orthodox Hindu-orientated political parties wandering along pavements carrying political slogans printed on their flanks in vegetable dye, clearly patterned in Devanagari script!! **Gow-mata**, mother cow is invaluable in all she donates to humanity as a draught animal—the **zebu** hump oxen wandering over the face of India and its streets and cities in their millions, with their milk and attendant dairy products, their leather when dead, and food for non-Hindu Indians.

Read **Sarah Macdonald's Holy Cow** (Bantam, Sydney, 2002) for a wry Australian insight with fulsome laughter as partner of ABC TV roving correspondent in South Asia. A very moving ending embracing the 'heart' of India.

■ CRAFTS, SILPA (n. *Sanskrit,* pr. **shilp**)

The IGNCA Lexicon now being assembled on concepts in Indian arts and noted in **CORE CONCEPTS** describes **silpa** as a pervasive term, involving dexterity for both hands and mind in creativity and also techniques, ceremonial acts; also **'beyond explanation and therefore a subject of wonder'.**

A. **The general ethos and attitudes of the Indian framework and mind.**

In the West, industrialisation broke the framework of a long tradition in which artistic expression was seen as a whole. The mediaeval painter of the plastic arts, the stonemason, the weaver of the altar cloth or the kneeling stool in church, the fashioner of the candelabra were all of a piece.

The market place of modern commercial art, mass production, secularisation all contributed to a cleavage in the public perception of Art and how it was regarded as either 'high classical'—the domain of the Michelangelos of this world, the Leonardo da Vincis, the Picassos or Matisses—or primitive—that is **craft** the lesser art. A view of this activity being less 'intellectual', therefore emerged. If not inferior in construction or activity, nevertheless crafts were not on a level to be studied in universities as Fine Arts disciplines.

This fracturing of what is essentially an artistic activity that should be considered a 'holistic' expression of human creativity

without these artificial dividing lines fortunately did not occur in Indian culture surviving even colonial domination, and hopefully, will survive the impress of European attitudes introduced in the last century.

♦ The force of village culture, and the weight of the population still residing there despite accelerating migration to the city, may still influence the outcome of India's own modernising processes. These may not necessarily follow and imitate Western urbanisation and industrialisation patterns. Although tragically the plastic bucket and bowl have replaced the beautiful burnished **lota** in the village hut where one stands or squats on a simple stone slab to throw water over one's body—the basic Indian shower—there is still another fact to influence the permutations of social change through modernisation. In the West the Church and dogma remained so rigid that secularisation drained away religious inspiration and left society high and dry on a challenging but arid plateau of human **individuality**. The collective was forgotten. Tradition was deliberately cast aside as an inhibiting force.

The concept of 'developing' and 'developed' societies emerged as well—reflecting the Western view (not only economically) that the free-wheeling, free-thinking individualistic European world which also spread to the Americas and has a hold on multi-media expression in modern pop culture (music, and record companies, fashion, and advertising, TV and film) was 'developed', superior; whereas rural, predominantly agricultural societies still functioning within the discipline of the collective, that is 'the villages', were inferior, unsophisticated. This was the world of craft and a fine piece of wood design for furniture was not regarded as high art.

B. **'High art' and the lowly artisan where 75 per cent of the population are still villagers [Census 2001]**

The miracle is that, the religious (or rather the spiritual) has remained an influencing force, freeing individuals—and that is a paradox despite caste jati divisions—in the creative arena of their lives. Free of church dogma, hierarchy and priestly interference, Indians never had to undergo the inhibitive mechanisms of mental 'Spanish Inquisitions', to speak symbolically. In India it is nothing strange for the most urban of contemporary designers to turn to village art for inspiration.

From its very origins (even perhaps in pre-Vedic times) there was never any sharp distinction made between **high art** and **the crafts**. The craftsperson, the artist, the sculptor, the stonemason, the architect were all enjoined by sage Bharata who laid down first aesthetic principles in coherent form, to undertake the work in hand as a dedication to that ultimate principle **Brhm**.

Artistic style, the perfection of expression in an uncluttered way, was termed **silpa** in Sanskrit. The artisan was the initiated **shilpin**, as equal in status as the artist. The **silpa-shastra** was the treatise on how to make a form, whether an image of a deity; the layout of a temple, very symbolic and important; a simple jar for household use, a shape of perfect geometry, ergonomics at its best. As an aesthetic shape the pot = **KUMBH** has remained the same perfect shape for millennia (see following text).

Those rules have hardly changed to this day and for that one must be grateful to caste traditions which despite much that is socially unfair and inhibiting, still paradoxically give positive strength to the collective in threatening times of rapid change.

The stonemason's art is one such, seen in many places at work in Rajasthan where renovations to old buildings go on apace; and at the same time a brand new **Baha'i temple** of breathtaking beauty and simplicity created in south Delhi in the 1990s to excite beyond even the imagination and engineering skills of those who built the Sydney Opera House.

◆ Accuracy, finesse, sophisticated style can still exist in India amidst un-schooled village women in the poorer areas of Bihar. The Maithili/**Mithila** women painters who have never seen the inside of any College of Art personify all that Indian craft is about —they are embedded in a devotional tradition that stretches back certainly for 1,000 years. (see **MAGADHA, MITHILA, MADHUBANI** and **MAURYAS**).

This is the land of the Pandavas, Sita's birth in the soil, of Buddha, Mahavira, Ashoka. Great poets and compilers have emerged in its culture—**Valmiki** who codified the oral tradition of the Ramayana into literature in the 4th century BCE, a dating now under review. **Kalidasa** (India's Shakespeare) in the 4th century CE and **Vidyapati** (14th century CE) the mystic poet of the Maithili language who sang of love of the deity in erotic poetry in the manner of **Jayadeva's Gita Govinda**.

And to cap it all and reinforce the mixture of secular and spiritual that makes Indian culture so alive in ancient ways even in this century, the Mithila people of Madhubani (Forest of Honey in ancient time) and, one of its two major farming towns, claim that Mahatma Gandhi first spoke here of self-sufficiency to India's downtrodden masses when mounting the Independence Movement against British rule in the 30s. In those colonial days of exporting cheap primary produce to Britain for the factories of Manchester to manufacture into cloth to sell back to Indians at a higher price (meanwhile taking the profits) Gandhi preached the use of **handloom** and **khadi cloth**. This is now a source of a major craft industry encouraged by central and state governments through the **Khadi Gramodyog** shop outlets in all major Indian cities.

Textiles and the art of weaving—**tantu**—is referred to in the Rig Veda, and Indus Valley archaeology has produced evidence from textile fragments and **rumals** (handkerchief squares) of beautiful skills in design and sophisticated weaving technology. (Refer also to **INDIGO**). Note the trefoil design on the well-known limestone sculpture of a dignified bearded man, on what looks like a Roman toga draped over the left shoulder (National Museum, circa 2500 BCE, Mohenjo-Daro).

◆ In fact the making of textiles appears to have been clothed (literally) in sacredness from the very origins. *Tanto* from TANTRA is a term describing the ability for material to stretch, to expand. YANTRA a term applied to weaving, like the diagrams weave the mind through major concepts. GRANTHA describes the process of **plaiting, sutru** unstitched cloth traditionally worn in temples without buttoning or machined belts.

◆ This depth of background is important to understand. It attests to the continual live electric filament which sparks renewed energy into Indian village culture despite invasion upon invasion. It represents the continual renewal and persistence of living myth, which is really a symbolism for deeper human truths, and therefore flexibly responsive to each modernisation process in the turn of the gigantic cyclical spirals of Indian history. It explains the sophistication of thought which imbues all Indian craft in its myriad forms. **Stephen Huyler**, American ethnologist, has written about this in his richly illustrated book, **Painted Prayers—Women's Art in Village India,** (Thames and Hudson, London, 1994) and **Gifts of Earth: Terracottas and Clay Sculptures of India** (IGNCA and Mapin, Ahmedabad, 1996).

In addition **Yves Vequaud's** wonderful book **The Art of Mithila, Ceremonial Paintings from an Ancient Kingdom** (Thames and Hudson, London, 1977) explains at length the extraordinary resonance of craft which has also been written about at the Indian end by **Jyotindra Jain**, ex-Director of the National Crafts Museum in south Delhi and **Ajit Mookerjee** of Tantra book fame (see **TANTRA**).

Stephen Huyler has spoken of the special significance of the crafts in Indian art, of the force of rural, material culture and its reverence for the earth, perhaps best epitomised in its attitudes to the simple **pot, the lota, kalash, kumbh** throughout the great length of art development. **T**he Pot, 'cleansed and made pure by fire... the kumbh or common water pot represents fertility and prosperity, kalash, a pot filled with holy water and crowned with leaves symbolises the sacred cosmos seen in many illustrations and miniature paintings of Muslim tradition also.' It has not changed functional shape since artists first made depictions of its absolutely perfect proportions **about 6,000 years ago**.

C. Vedic continuities, Prajapati and Viswakarma

Huyler states there are more working potters in India—over three and a half lakhs (350,000)—than any other country in the world. All would accept their traditional descent from **Prajapati**, Lord of Creation. Here is the unbroken continuity of truth in the symbolic legend rather than factual history of the Western kind (**ITIHASA** elaborates on this). Initiated craftspeople still hand down their skills to apprentices as in the mediaeval guild systems of Europe.

◆ The craft of pottery may be very different according to region but potters everywhere subscribe to this commonality of concept and their intrinsic worth to Indian society.

Prajapati means **Lord of Creatures**, tracing back to the progenitor of all creation supporting the universe, predating even the present Hindu pantheon of deities. In the wider context of all the crafts **Viswakarma** is the Vedic deity personifying all crafts through 'creative power'. Viswakarma is still remembered and revered on one day of the year as the great architect of the universe described in the Rig Veda as 'beyond the comprehension of mortals'. Cheap bazaar posters propped up on mantel shelves even in England were my first introduction to a deity seldom seen in India—and interestingly enough his depiction surrounded by an array of tools was not only given reverence by Gujaratis but by the Ramgarhia Sikhs, a carpenter caste (their own definition, Sikhs supposedly no longer bound by caste). However, they still are part of the Indian ambience. Viswakarma to them is like a patron saint.

In the Brahmana texts (pre-Buddhist, 900-500 BCE) these shastras or codifications describe the entire world as a brilliant piece of divine handiwork—a silpa of the highest degree.

D. Government Intervention

◆ It is to the credit of the central government in New Delhi and state governments that the **All India Handicrafts Board** was set up in 1952. The initiatives of two redoubtable women **Kamaladevi Chattopadhyaya** and **Pupul Jayakar** in the mid-1950s helped to create the famous and much visited **Cottage Industries Emporium** (and its exports counterpart) at middle class level. From this mushroomed individual states emporia in a network throughout India.

From all these, money has flowed back to the artificer in the village, a Gandhian concept in helping make village India more self-sufficient. That at least is the ideal and certainly the myriad range of Indian crafts is a magnetic source for foreign currency earnings. Response is not only to the forceful marketing of tourism from overseas. Even internally Indians themselves in the new wealth of the middle classes are rediscovering regional artistic expression which a generation ago was hardly recognised due to the lack of mobility, communication and ignorance as a backlash from colonial rule. Even in the last decade further initiatives have been taken to heighten the exposure in bringing craftspeople from various regions on a rota system to practice in workshops in full gaze of the public, to be able to trade directly without the intervention of middlemen, as well as to receive prestigious awards from the President of India—honouring the excellence of design, style and taste.

◆ In the latter decade further widening of outlets to the public especially in the national capital have been initiated. Apart from the charming **National Crafts Museum** with its roster of leading artists from the states, the scale and scope of the 12-acre imaginatively presented colourful **Surajkund Crafts Mela** in the beginning of February in Haryana State south of Delhi and the **Dilli Haat,** near Safdarjung's aesthetically pleasing 18th century tomb to the senior Nawab of Oudh, have widened access and knowledge about the astonishing array of artistic expression.

Live demonstrations from within India and visiting international performing artists on the outdoor stage make this focal point a must for foreign visitors.

Artists co-operatives south of Chennai as well as the huge **Victoria Institute** within the city and individual village craft concepts in Rajasthan have been other imaginative regional responses as well as the **Hundi Utensils Museum** and vegetarian picnic complex at **Vishala** outside Ahmedabad. No visit to this city should occur without seeing the fabulous **Calico Museum of Textiles.** Symbol of this major trading centre in the subcontinent since the 15th century of India's gifted weavers and their textiles, and founded by the great industrial house of Sarabhai, it is the foremost museum of its kind in the world, with

stunning fabrics in a huge mansion—a museum in itself and a centre of scholarship and cross-disciplinary referencing.

Driving back through Rajasthan in the dried-out stony hills around Udaipur is another magic surprise, of this capacity to create vivid colour and stylish art in the bleak waste land— **Shilpgram**, a regional cultural centre for neighbouring states founded in 1986. Huts of various communities—fisherfolk in Maharashtra to desert tribes in Gujarat—are aesthetically built, sparkling with the fabulous crafts of village people still integrated in their cultures. In the late 90s a similar cultural village was inaugurated in Andhra Pradesh outside Hyderabad city at Shilpgram.

E. An explosion of creativity, a dizzying rainbow of colours and woven magic

◆ A list of crafts is quite overwhelming: clay and terracotta; cloth narratives = **kalamkaris**, easily folded to take on pilgrimage, narrating the Epics in a shorthand picture book style with Telugu script from Andhra Pradesh; metal work from tribal people in central India and West Bengal fashioning their ancestral images of deities, the **kul** (family/clan) **devtas** part Great Tradition, part local custom locked into agricultural spirits. Riders on horses galloping straight out of Vedic days and dancing women with hips swung in rounded curves, caught in mottled biscuit stone of Orissa as well, are echoes of an ancient Saraswati past 5,000 years earlier; bronze and bidri work with inlaid silver strips from the south and slippery fine silks splashing colour like a field of summer flower heads; gold and silver from everywhere; basketwork smelling of mown grass from the hill tribes of **Assam, Mizoram, Meghalaya**; teakwood carvings from **Mysore**; ivory— now banned, and sandalwood from Kerala; lacquered and painted furniture dangling wooden bells from **Gujarat** and the elegant veranda swings to catch the evening breeze, suspended on heavy ornamented and carved chains intricate with twined peacocks, elephants and long arabesques of foliage; painted boxes and papiermache and walnut wood carvings from **Kashmir**; vibrant red, green and spangled glass bangles from **Bihar** fashioned in fire and twisted and turned around a metal rod before your very eyes; lac turnery with animal resin applied on wood, hardened and then painted; tribal bronzes in dulled gold; exquisite **Bengali** rush and cane baskets and bamboo, smelling fresh and of damp jungles; stylish handmade paper and stationery harking back to Epic themes; and Puja festival necessities in **Bengal** made from **sholapith—a white porous core of a reed**—carved into intricate headresses and finery for the Goddess, such are only a **few** of the artistic gifts that express the interplay and intertwining of ancient into modern across at least 5,000 years of the continuum of folk memory—never broken.

◆ Of special mention because they are worn daily and are vital textiles in the employment of huge numbers of artisans—women as well as men in villages hidden away from the mainroad tracks taken by backpackers and tourists flying overhead—is the embroidered art of **chikankari** and **zardozi. Chikan** is said to be of Turkish original meaning 'floral embroidery'. It is of a very delicate kind.

When the first hot waft of the desert **loo** blows its prickly heat message across north India sensible men take to the loose-necked kurta flowing over pyjamas. Note the neckline and cuffs for white on white embroidery. This is the traditional **Lucknow-ee** running stitch, far more intricate than surface appearance indicates, tracing floral arabesques and filled in hatchwork which 'aerates' the cotton. Tucked-away filmy saris reappear from the depth of cupboards with the whiff of neem leaves which have kept them fresh through the winter cold.

Young girls in their early teens to elderly grandmothers gather in family parties to sew this fine work. It is said that, in the UP area of Lucknow alone, over 75,000 women are employed in such time stitching.

♦ Expensive **zardozi** comes into its own at the **shadi** (wedding) season but is being intricately worked all the year round by craftsmen, most of whom are culturally Muslim. Heavy embroidered wall hangings and opulent furnishings as well as royal household suitings and **shalwar-kameez,** and **lehengaa** ground-sweeping skirts, dominated Mughal fashions. Thousands were employed in the industry and still are—over 200,000 mentioned in the Bareilly district of UP alone. Chennai and Surat are other centres of the craft.

Making the thread is a tedious process of heating gold wire over a silver bar until a gold/silver alloy forms, pulled down over the tapered bar and through steel-plated holes of finely-graded circumference. Gilt wire emerges, gleaming like gold. This in turn has to be wound and twisted around silk thread. No wonder a blouse piece can cost the amount a zari male embroiderer earns in two weeks = Rs.45 a day Rs.700/Rs.1000. But a wedding skirt and overblouse might explode into well over Rs.50,000 (Rs. 50,000 = £500 or approximately $1,000 Australian—a great deal of money in India) taking six months of painstaking work to create the illusion of imperial grandeur for today's ostentatious weddings amongst the new rich.

♦ India's fabulous weaving expertise continues even today. One story comes to light in the '98 press of a Bengali weaver who captured Mrs Gandhi's attention. He modified a loom replacing the wooden shuttle with one of soft cane and by using a superior cotton variety developed in Kerala (Trichur district) achieved a muslin so gossamer light, a 1,000-metre length weighed just 4 grams!

♦ A far cry from this opulent world of urbane society with its expensive tastes is the simple but equally stylish world of tribal/village Indian steeped in its own integrity, fresh and energetic as it ever was. Take a **Warli** painting. Their tribal mud-walled houses are the canvas; a village culture comes to life in basic geometric designs that return into distant centuries of animistic worship, of women's business in painting the **chowk**, a seemingly wasp-waisted configuration, stylised into basic geometry of a woman giving birth—or even back to the beginnings of the wedding bed, covered in cloth till the tribal wedding ceremonies are completed and then unveiled to the young couple. Now on their canvases, sold worldwide, out of their stark and self-chosen frugal lives flows an explosive tribal world executed in rice paste, filled with extraordinary vibrant energy of the spiralling dance, daily life of the villagers, elegant animals straight from a Brancusi design. (The delightfully energetic as well as sophisticated legends sketched in rice flour and smeared cow dung from such a spare and ascetic tribal group, astonish!) See **The Warlis, Tribal Paintings and Legends,** edited by Yashodhara Dalmia in collaboration with artist Jivya Soma Mashe (Chemould Publications and Arts, Bombay, no date.)

So which is 'high art' and where the aesthetic division to mark out 'craft' as a less intellectually demanding, more lowly artistic discipline?

■ **CRICKET**

"It's just not cricket... that's not cricket!"

Such a phrase which has nothing to do with the actual playing of the specific game is, however, very much to do with establishing a truly English precept: 'Come on! Play the game' used when the protagonist is, indeed, 'not playing the game', that is abiding by unwritten subtle codes of behaviour we learn initially from the first reprimand as a toddler... but in 2000, sadly besmirched by greedy adults tainted in match-fixing allegations.

Emanating from cricket culture, and applied to behaviour that is simply 'just **not** done', it can only be understood by those touched by the bond of camaraderie that in a most unlikely fashion defied the dismantling of the Empire. After all Indians often had the upper hand with a flick of a fine wrist and a deceptive spin bowl... which prompts one to ask, is **googly** an Indian word? An 'off-break' ball, it first puzzled batsmen in 1902.

Indians in the genteel days pre-World War II understood such subtleties of behaviour implicitly because their own hierarchies of society, sense of dharma and propriety, strict codes of manners paralleled those of patriarchal patrician-ruled Britannia. In the traditional 5-day matches where fortunes waxed and waned with sudden and unexpected shifts, clothed in subtle nuances for aficionados to savour over a boxed lunch or tea from a vacuum flask, cricket was a 'gentleman's game' well attuned to Indian mores as well. Big money, adult greed, bookmakers and dissipated moral integrity that has tainted this hallowed game were unknown factors in those halcyon days!

Britain was no longer the Imperial Mother and could be deftly defeated at the crease. And strangely enough despite its patrician air cricket was paradoxically a game of the masses—where a boy with a strong Yorkshire accent such as Freddy Truman's unmistakable radio commentaries, averse to such a decadent language as King's English, could rub shoulders with an Indian who had trained his eyes dealing with a piece of wood and even a stone which flipped with erratic tendencies on gritty laterite soil. **Guli Danda** is a very Indian game as old as time itself. Our children, then aged four and seven, grew up in New Delhi learning to play it from the children in the servants' quarters in the leafy back lanes of India's capital. A toggle rather like a cricket bail was hit on its end by any old piece of hard wood (**danda**) so it bounced up and had to be batted immediately, a sure-fire training for 'getting the eye in'!

Where it all began

1550... As a structured game, cricket is first referred to in **1550** as having been played in **Guildford**, **Surrey**, developing out of bat-and-ball games which seemed to be popular in the southeast of England from even earlier times.

1721... In **Cambay**, India took up the cudgels (or the bats) and played the first game of cricket having, one supposes, witnessed over a century the English, who had first sailed in to Surat under the captaincy of William Hawkins, taking some athletic exercise, no matter how uncomfortable, in doubloons and frilled shirts, to shake down the quaffing of claret at breakfast time (in **that** climate!).

1897... **Ranjitsinhji**, a Saurashtra princeling, was the first Indian to be honoured in Wisden's Year List. He took this quirkish characteristic even further by playing **only for England**. He along with England's legendary **W G Grace** have been called '**wizards of the willow**'. And no wonder!

1932... A more professional approach occurred when the first Indian side to play a Test match—and the only one at that— in the UK filed into the august Club at Lords, the ultimate in cricket grounds, home of the MCC, the Marylebone (pronounced in illogical English idiom—Marybone) Cricket Club. Their real captain, the famous **Colonel C K Nayadu** (whose centenary was celebrated in 1996) had the temerity to show those Englishmen they meant business and went on to score a century.

1934... To honour this magnificent batsman, the **Ranji Trophy** was set up as India's most important domestic cricketing award. There have been many other gifted Indians cricketing in pre-war days—stars such as V M Merchant and Mushtaq Ali.

Cricket's future... watch out England and Australia, after 2001's pinnacle of success in Kolkata against a seemingly invincible Australian side. There are thousands of Harbhajan Singhs, Dravids and Laxmans in training—in the back streets of Chennai for instance! Night games for teenagers continue into the early hours; in vacations a crowd of maybe 2,000 using tennis balls vie for money sponsorship, sometimes up to Rs. 5,000 (no joke in Indian terms). These youngsters are honing their skills and 'getting their eyes in'.

Walking along the immense stretch of Karnataka's Tungabhadra Dam (a water spread of 145 square miles servicing 2 million acres of land) after a fascinating three days at the ruined capital of the mediaeval Vijayanagar empire, Hampi, a group of young Indian boys skipped around us, demanding: 'Which culture you from?'

We replied, 'Australia'.

'Very good culture!' came their immediate response, bright and very even white teeth flashing happy smiles. 'Very good culture! Very good cricket!' Out of the months of babes...!

An afterthought... Let dharma triumph over the evils of the last decade, too much money-grabbing, and the dismay of match-fixing, heroes' reputations sullied. Perhaps the eager youngsters we kept meeting in India will turn the game around and learn again to declare, '**It's just not cricket.**'

■ **CROREPATI**
the idiomatic journalese defining the new breed of billionaires too numerous within India to name personally. **Pati =** progenitor, father figures of the families now who are certainly worth at least a **crore** (10 million) are now propelling India into new confidence and a projected 8% GDP growth (2005). Mumbai, Bangalore, Chennai and Hyderabad (now dubbed Cyberabad because of an explosion of IT expertise, electronic engineers in demand for their very Indian mathematical aptitudes, so much so on my visit January 2000 a newspaper item announced Japanese recruitment running into several hundred) lead the way.

The US Fortune magazine ran an article on the Indians of Silicon Valley (Melanie Warner, May 29, 2000) detailing their astonishing prowess, centred in a supportive, closeknit and efficient networking group—all influential and very wealthy, nearly all having graduated from Indian Institutes of Technology according to the article—tougher to get into than MIT or Harvard! Many have climbed out of the rupee category into dollar and sterling monetary peaks, joining their **NRI** and Hampstead Heath brethren in the UK coming onstream as full-fledged Indo-British (no longer 'immigrants')—**Mittal** in steel, **Hinduja** in oil and business houses, numbers of **Patels** with supermarkets and photo-processing, **Patak** (condiments worldwide) and even a young Manchester University student, **Reuben Singh** making a name for himself in fashion—not to mention two new Peers, **Lord Bagri** (chairman, London Metal Exchange) and **Lord Paul** (steel). And of course there are growing numbers in India like **Narayanamurthy** of Infosys becoming crorepatis overnight. Soon there may be matriarchs also—crore **patnis**! However, **patni** does not quite reflect a new breed of self-made young women who are not necessarily wifely partners (patni) of these extremely wealthy men. Sanskrit never encountered this kind of economic **shakti**—a word will have to be coined.

A TV show—**Kaun Banega Crorepati** is tempting Indians, a copy of the American show **Who Wants to be a Millionaire**. Children are even playing the game in school, driving teachers crazy. It is heartening to learn that many who do win despite becoming instant celebrities, yet genuinely celebrated in their often humble surroundings, and foregoing a quite substantial tax burden on the winnings, a number of winners have been compelled by that inbuilt sense of dharma to donate considerable amounts (certainly in 2001) to relief efforts after the devastating Gujarat earthquake.

■ **CURRY**
Kadipatta (the 'd' pronounced like a rolled r) is correct Tamil for what originally was the term for the gravy (and not a specific dish) spices from the **patta** or leaf... The liquid gravy or spicy sauce thickens after 20 minutes of simmering, rendering down the different ingredients—mainly the staple ones of onions, garlic (except if one is a very strict Tamil Brahmin vegetarian as onions are said to heat the blood and arouse passions!), ginger, tomatoes, cumin, dhania, cardamom, salt, chillies (dried or fresh)

sliced fine, and/or mustard seed in ghee or vegetable oil. This is the **masala** = combination. It is not just a regular concoction because each household has its own permutation of spices from the nearly 30 basic ones in use.

There are a number of names in Tamil for what is originally a small shrub/tree indigenous to south India–**karivepilai** *(Murraya koenigii)* but now grown everywhere. Though in itself not lethally 'hot', in conjunction with the tiny green chillis, this combination makes palates tingle, causes grown men to weep, and has conquered the world globally, another Indian quip 'currying f(l)avour worldwide!'

Another joyous journey in the 21st century ongoing Indo-British interaction... **chicken tikka** has taken over from fish and chips as the popular takeaway dish.

Also the ultimate accolade from Harrods—promotion of Darjeeling tea with nibbles, Salmon Samosas and grilled masala paneer **'naanwich'** = an innovative naan sandwich!

◆ Ayurveda medicine used the new green leaves for many health reasons, containing as they do a number of useful minerals for the body—calcium, phosphorus and iron, vitamin C. Apart from embellishing cuisine taste, a freshly-plucked leaf concoction from shrubs grown in backyards, pounded in mortar and pestle and boiled with coconut oil, is a good hair tonic. Infused into boiling water, kari leaves help counter effects of dysentery and nausea.

◆ If your palate is burning due to hitting a hot chilli as well as a kari leaf make for the cucumber **raita** or yoghurt. Usually there is yoghurt on the table. It is far more effective than iced water!

■ **DALIT** (n. *Hindi*)
1. Literal meaning = downtrodden or oppressed
2. Political term of the last decade for the SC/ST scheduled caste/scheduled tribes = lower caste **shudras**, later Harijans and former untouchables. Over 150 million strong, their concentrated energies are now forcibly being expressed in politics.

◆ In a major editorial by a senior journalist, B N Uniyal, in **The Pioneer** newspaper in New Delhi (November 16, 1996) under the heading **In Search of A Dalit Journalist**, the chagrin of this non-Dalit journalist was self-evident:

◆ 'Let an Indian speak on this anguished subject for the consciences of all Indians who believe in the egalitarian ethos, the spirit of their democracy.' After getting nowhere in his enquiries based on a foreign correspondent's question, that night...

I went to the Press Club and asked several friends and acquaintances whether they knew any journalist who was a Dalit. Nobody did. A friend thought I was trying to act smart or score a point over others by thinking of writing on such a subject. "This is what is called one-upmanship," he said, admonishingly, "You want to show that you are the only one who is not a casteist amongst us!"

Another friend of long years told me that journalists are journalists and should not be screened on caste basis... Do you think any of us writes or reports as a Brahmin journalist, or as a Kayastha or a Jain journalist?" asked another friend. I admitted that that was not true, though I was by now becoming unsure of such an assertion. Does it really mean anything not to have any journalist amidst us from among the Dalits? I asked myself. I even wondered whether I could now trust a reply from myself to a question like that?

I came home and began leafing through the Accreditation Index, 1996, of the Press Information Bureau of the Government of India which lists the names of all the accredited correspondents who serve as the eyes and the ears of the nation in the capital city of Delhi. They are the ones who decide what is news and what is not; what is worth reporting of the day and what is not.

Though it is not they alone who decide what or whom to play up or play down... everything depends on what questions they ask at a Press conference and how they ask these. And, at the end of the day, it all depends on how they compose their reports.

The Accreditation Index was revealing. Of the 686 accredited correspondents listed in it, as many as 454 bore their caste surnames and, of them, as many as 240 turned out to be Brahmins, 79 Punjabi Khatris, 44 Kayasthas, 26 Muslims with as many Baniyas, 19 Christians, 12 Jains and nine (Bengali) Baidyas. I checked out the caste affiliation of the 47 of the remaining 232 correspondents at random. None of them turned out to be a Dalit either.

"There must be some,' said a senior official in the PB, but it is difficult to find out because they don't write their caste surnames. They must be wanting to hide their caste identity, you know. Who would want to be known as a Scheduled Caste?"

"What are you trying to achieve by making such an enquiry, anyway?" asked another, "Do you want to provide grist to the caste mill? Why do you think it is necessary to ascertain the caste of journalists? After all, most journalists are not casteists. You are not, for example, are you?"

"I am not sure," I said and hung up.

What would journalism be like if there were as many journalists amidst us from among the Dalits as were among the Brahmins, I asked myself. I was reminded of some lines of Maharashtra's Dalit poet, Namdev Dhasal....

One day I cursed that mother-fucker god
He just laughed shamelessly.
My neighbour, a born-to-the-pen Brahman
Was shocked.
He looked at me with his castor-oil face...
I cursed another good hot curse
The university building shuddered
And sank waist-deep.
All at once scholars began doing research
Into what makes people angry...

As a consequence there is a rise of the **Bahujan Samaj** Party in UP, one of India's most powerful but most backward states. Dalits are becoming exceedingly angry with both useless politicians and aloof bureaucrats.

■ **DANCE**
There are at least seven distinctive systems of classical dance but thousands of regional forms at folk level—tribal as well as village expressions. The chance to witness this particular profusion of vibrant colour, pounding rhythms and a gift for aesthetic style in presentation can be seen at the Republic Day celebrations in New Delhi on January 26 each year, at major regional festivals and especial state presentations.

In general:
◆ **Bharata Natyam** evolved in south India within the giant temple complexes of Tamilnadu.
◆ **Kathakali** (and **Mohini Attam**) as dance-drama with very stylised costumes in Travancore–Cochin, the earlier name for Kerala which was created under the states' reorganisation in 1956.
◆ **Kathak** in north India especially developed during **Mughal Court** patronage.
◆ **Manipuri**, a slower fluid dance expression emerged in **northeast India**.

In recent decades a new generation of dancers has brought into prominence **Odissi** and **Kuchipudi** dances styles influenced by sculptural forms on Orissa temples and Andhra traditions.

D

Aesthetic principles

The codes and guiding principles which govern **all these forms** were compiled by the sage **Bharata** into texts which were later written down in a voluminous treatise 4th c BCE–2nd c CE... **Bharata Natya Shastra**. Indeed they apply not only to dance but create the essential framework also for all the ancient forms of

- ◆ sculpture   ◆ literature   ◆ painting   ◆ poetry
- ◆ music   ◆ drama   ◆ scriptural epics

Tradition says that the sage received the knowledge of these principles and forms of the dance, their expression and the aim of raising human spiritual perceptions from the high god Brahma at the beginning of human history by direct revelation = **sruti** rather than by **smrti** (what is remembered or heard by tradition or handed down by written historical texts). This is quite matter-of-factly recounted by dance theorists and exponents as the means of arrival at the intellectual premise on which the techniques of all dance are derived.

History topples over the edge once more into legend. It is said that the ancient **muni** (**mauna**, Skt = silent) monk is credited with having produced the first drama with a celestial nymph **Urvasi** playing the part of the goddess Lakshmi. This was at a time when sages had free access to the court of Indra, the king of the Vedic gods 'when mortals mixed freely with supernatural beings—our first golden age' as a south Indian dancer once told me without batting an eyelid.

◆ These codifications embodied in the **shastras** are the systematic tabulations and principles which have governed the minutest aspects of bodily movement and expression in the execution of what is, ultimately, a **devotional dedication**—from fundamental dance positions, to glances of the eye, movements of the eyebrows, neck, shoulders, chest, wrists, elbows, **hasta mudras**—gestures of the hands, singly and together (a mime language of its own) to the realms of expressing abstruse philosophy and the metaphysics the dance is meant to embody. 'Authorised by canon, sanctified by tradition and stabilised by usage', is how the late Dr Narayana Menon, musician, well-known critic and one-time Director of Mumbai's Performing Arts Centre put it. 'These laws are as operative today as they were when first formulated over 3,000 years ago.'

Much longer in oral tradition perhaps, considering what is now known as the 'Dancing Girl' figure of Mohenjo-Daro and her stance, the codes are still held in narrow stiff palmleaf strips threaded into 'books' in the temple libraries of **Thanjavur, Thiruvananthapuram** (once Trivandrum) and **Madurai**—a lesson in encrusted history if given the chance to visit, and a salute to UNESCO in trying to allay the voracious capacity of silverfish trying to prove the second law of thermodynamics—no sooner is something created than it is subject to the forces of disintegration.

Even David Attenborough of BBC TV fame, lecturing in India some time ago, made known his admiration for the phenomenal ability to maintain such traditions and principles **without any cultural break in the continuum** despite all the political and social upheavals of India's history and with other cultural attitudes being laid on top of this embedded foundation. No matter the innumerable times invasion has occurred even before the focal point of gigantic temple complexes could give sustenance, the oral traditions in scattered ashrams and small shrines and caste disciplines of the rituals maintained the integrity.

Theory and Technique

Bharata Natyam derives its name according to Indian theorists from three conceptual divisions:

BHA = BHAVA outer expression of an intense inner experience and uplifting emotion.

RA = RASA flavour, juice, ambience

TA = TALA percussive rhythm

Together a harmonious totality of experience should occur with accompanying musicians and poetry, divine lyrics, sung by the **nattuvanar**—(often scholar/teacher/guru/vocalist musician all rolled into one) creating the spiritual atmosphere of dedication and devotion—and this is not necessarily to one Deity in particular but to the generality of **brhm**—that universal **wholeness**. Anyone participating in the explosion of music and dance in the hugely attended sammelans (gatherings) in south India at the end of each year, their winter, will experience a knowledgeable audience (in the old days men seated one side, women the other, now increasingly mixed) who are totally familiar with the entire framework—devotional as well as aesthetic.

All the Indian commentaries state that dance began as part of the temple worship; thinking is now that it could also have been part of the original Vedic fire ritual worship.

In the strict and even harsh training that has to be undergone—and endured—for longer than that of Western ballet, this sense of religious devotion and the framework of a yogic spiritual philosophy is very evident...

Now there is a slight shift... audiences are being 'entertained'. But in south India they are so knowledgeable they are still taken up into an ever-ascending spiral of transcendental joy. They are not on the outside as an audience intellectually dissecting the challenging mathematical graphs of vocalists but emotionally engaged in an artistic duel of exciting exchange of phrases, slides, skating rink figures of eight in the mind as virtuosos vie with each other in the fascinating configuration of tones, while dancers stake out the equivalent geometric designs to match the tonal graphs. Exhilarating... transforming, just watching the audience swaying with the dancer and her musicians. They, the audience, are part and parcel of the performance.

A moment in time with Rukmini Devi

Sitting in the corner of the open-sided **mandapa** or dance pavilion on polished blackened stone surface at Kalakshetra in a long-ago autumnal morning when pioneering dancer, **Rukmini Devi Arundale** was still alive, the fierce clackety-clack of tamarind stick on wooden block ricocheted into eardrums, hard-wiring the syllables of the drum beats into braincells, a computer imprint which surely must last a lifetime.

This was **Madras, Adyar** south of the river in the fifties. A famous dance school, a handsome woman describing their dance as a yoga, not just physical dance which at that point all the young girls as pupils were intent on learning in exhausting physical gymnastic stretches, twists and leaps and that crack, crack, crack, not of pliable drum skin of the majestic south Indian double-headed mrdangam—Lord of Instruments. 'Dance is yoga,' she had asserted. 'It is not just all these fluid movements, physical acrobatics some Westerners think, the abstract geometrical forms of the beginning of a performance, not the beauty of the central **varnam**—such poetry in our beautiful Tamil songs, or the balance between exactitude in the choreography demanded by the shastras, the flow of feet movements, the expressions of not just face and body, but the whole inner feel in expressing a portrayal. **It is an inner dedication to the God, that cosmic force...'**

'You have to remember we Indians live in our oral culture. Don't get misled by all the people you meet at your level, city people, who read and write.' (This was long before the impact of television, another natural extension in India of the oral.) 'If you want to understand our arts, not just dance you have to learn four words—**Bhava... Brahmananda... Rasa... Sadhana'— states of being engendered by the arts, the bliss of being- with-Brhm, the flavour of the art, personal disciplines in achieving all this.'** These are Rukmini's summing up, the words of a charismatic pioneer.

As green parakeets swooped in and out of the vast spreading banyan trees (one so massive and majestic in its 40,000 square feet that 5,000 people could seek shade within its dangling roots) in this fashionable leafy suburb, the young dancers still training their young bodies to the iron disciplines, here was an India raising itself in those Miltonic words 'like a puissant giant after long sleep', a new sense of release—finding itself again after centuries of dormant stagnation.

Her words are now branded into the mind for every time the magic of sound, visual delight in costume and choreography takes over to deliver yet another dance sermon in sculptural form. Long established in the 50s as a famous Bharata Natyam dancer, Rukmini Devi was one of the earliest pioneers of respectable middle class families allowing their daughters to train in what had become a disreputable and neglected art form under many centuries of Islamic inhibitions on any dance expression, and the further domination of British cultural norms. Originally a channel between temple and society for dance both classical and folk/tribal it is hardly ever secular. People dance their religion. Even my own children, dancing naked in a torrential downpour in their first summer experience of pre-monsoonal north India punchdrunk under the physical thumping of molten sky, opaque dust storms, horrendous nights of airless humidity and relentless sun, were expressing an elemental spiritual release as Shiva raised his foot with the first monsoonal touch of raindrop.

The saying in Sanskrit is:

    RASA   BRHM   SAHODRE   ASTI

rasa and brhm are born from the same place

The content of dance

Channels for these broad concepts to be put into effect are:

Nritta: pure dance in abstract, geometrical movement ('liquid architecture' according to Ram Gopal the famous dancer who bravely propagated Indian culture to the West in the unsympathetic 30s). This section at the beginning and end of the dance performance expresses neither mood, sentiment nor story. Musical **swaras** (notes) and **jatis** became progressively complex, a test for the debut of any young dancer.

Nritya: language of gestures—**hasta-mudra** are introduced. These create vivid image pictures and communicate ideas/story line and emphasise the mood already established. The **nattuvanar** sings the joyous poetry of devotion or the epic accounts of lives of the deities to expressive music.

Natya: dramatic expression is now added through **abhinaya**—mimed emotions—hasta gestures, facial expression, bodily movement. A totality ending in the **thillana**—brisk, scintillating with stunning sculptured poses.

◆ **Nritta** is a geometric patterning of mesmerising beauty... Euclidean equations formed in space danced to a demanding mathematic percussion. Seductive to the eye in the glorious shimmer and vivid glow of the stylised sari, the garlanded hair, the gold ornaments, the henna-defined red edging to the bare feet, the slap of rhythmic sound on wood, stone, earth, brick, wherever the gaiety of the dance takes one mentally and wherever the totality of movement is, the continual ringing of the ghungru anklet bells emphasising the drum beats intricately patterned in time and space, placing great emphasis on time measure and rhythm. Thus although some movements look as if they are being repeated, they may be in quite different, sometimes difficult, time-measures and rhythmic arrangements. The basis of the dance-movements are the **adavus**, the fundamental dance units. There are more than seventy of these units of dance-patterns as well as a series of endless variations. Each **adavu** consists of (a) the basic pose for starting, executing and finishing the movement (**sthanaka**); (b) the prescribed movements of the feet and leg (**chari**); (c) the decorative hand gestures (**nritta hasta**); (d) and the prescribed positions of the hands and arms during the execution of the movement. And in Bharata Natyam this exactitude in the geometry is what fires the critique—either way!

There is also the hypnotic call of the nattuvanar reiterating those very sounds or **jathis—passages of mnemonics**—drum syllables. **Thom tata kita naka jham tari kita taka.**

The central section of a dance performance tests further skills.

◆ **Nritya** is the interpretation of song lyrics, poetry and ideas through movements, gestures and expressions. It is a vast area of study centering on the use of the hasta-mudras, to communicate symbols, ideas, concepts, metaphors; action and narrative to the audience. There are 28 basic single hand gestures, and 24 basic combined hand gestures. Each of these has its specific varieties of usage. Learning the usage is like developing a rich vocabulary sufficiently explicit to 'speak' directly even to a foreign audience. A dancer's virtuosity depends on how refined and developed these hand-gestures are, combined with the myriads of facial expressions to convey emotional, physical, and intellectual states. In much of the mime these combined finger movements stated to number at least 4,000 differentiated gestures, bring eloquence as profound as literary embellishments to the abhinaya component in conjunction with body postures of torso and leg.

D

Bharata's text for instance mentions 36 forms of glances, and gives infinite detail of the number of movements of eyebrow, nose, lips, mouth, neck, etc. What permutations mathematically! And all the time there are the rhythms of insistent percussion chasing the footwork, and the story to be expressed in the emotive Tamil songs.

- **Natya**—it is in this area that **abhinaya** comes into its own. Without expression of that inner **sadhana** discipline a dancer may be technically perfect in nritta and nritya but nowhere in the final assessment.

- **Nava Rasa** theory. The shastras have clearly defined the major differentiations of nine (nava) moods, indefinable states of mind and/or feelings which not only dance and music can arouse in the viewer/audience. All artistic endeavour is capable of so doing according to the early Vedic theorists.

These are the main categories:

	RASA	sentiment	BHAVA	state of mind
1.	SRINGARA	eroticism	RATI	love
2.	RAUDRA	fury	KRODHA	anger
3.	VEERA	valour	UTASHA	bravery
4.	HASYA	humor	HASA	mirth
5.	KARUNA	pathos	SHOKA	compassion, sorrow
6.	VIBHATSA	disgust	JUGUPSA	aversion
7.	ADBHUTA	wonderment	ASHCHARYA	amazement
8.	BHAYANAKA	fear	BHAYA	fright
9.	SHANTA	serenity	SHAMA	peace

In so doing the dancer in Bharata Natyam takes on many roles, switching them fleetingly in the course of one dance. These roles, although not developed as in conventional drama require careful study, and dynamic or sensitive interpretations of the characters, as the dancer has to convince the audience of the characters' moods. A dancer's power of imagination and understanding of human emotions come into full play here. As an example, the child Krishna's pranks and antics. In a dance of that subject an elaborate mimetic interpretation is often given by the dancer of Krishna stealing butter, or stuffing earth into the mouth, changing roles to being in turn the mother reprimanding the child.

An Historic Occasion

In March, 1955, **Balasaraswati** arrived in the capital with her family (her grandmother, Veena Dhanamal, a renowned musician, her mother accompanying her as vocalist—herself a renowned dancer as well)* to receive her high artistic honour for services rendered to the dance as one of the very last traditional temple exponents.

The culture vultures of Delhi were agog. If foreigners had never seen a temple dancer neither had north Indians in those

---

*The hereditary line traces even further back to the great-great-grandmother. Kamakshi Ammal was a 'jewel' of the Tanjore Court dancers to the age of 75—in that time an astonishing age. Artistic activity like the Italian painters must affect personal adrenalin, encouraging longevity! The IGNCA has produced a CD-Rom—**Devadasi Murai** (Tamil = remembering Devadasis) a social history of their lives with stunning photography of south India temples and sculpture.

early days of rebirth. All one knew was that she was long past a dancer's prime and not exactly slim and vigorously youthful. But she was to dance in front of President Rajendra Prasad and his homely gentle wife, and a wide range of impeccable Diplomatic Corps, plus a flutter of Gandhi-capped politicians all wishing to make known their presence, seated and then busying themselves by reviewing the rest of the front rows.

And then everyone's large enveloping grandmother walked on. She stood centrestage looking like a drawing by Thomas or William Daniell in the early 1800s, her costume not the sleek brilliantly coloured pre-pleated sari of today; her hair a bit fuzzy and truly south Indian. To be kind to her one would say she was plump with middle-aged spread.

She took up her stance for the **alarippu**—the invocatory piece. The technique was there, the exactitude of the abstract **nritta**—but so was the bulk. She was in an artificial atmosphere far from the ambience of south Indian temples and familiar dedication of the dance to worship for she was one of the last traditional temple dancers—**devadasis**—given to deity. Yet she showed no signs of ordeal. The resonating flow of unfamiliar veena and the roll of the mighty mrdangam commanded attention.

However, a strange quality of lightness began to take over as Balasaraswati moved into **jatiswaram** and the rhythm established itself. It appeared to lift her up. It is a phenomenon of some fat people that they are light on their feet, floating almost. Perhaps cellulite gives buoyancy!

And then came the **sabdam** when the audience is introduced to expressive gestures and facial **abhinaya**. The dancer was taking over, the flute player and violin 'conversing' animatedly with each other and her elaboration of a hymn of devotion to Lord Siva settled in the air. **Bhava** was a palpable energy force. It could be tangibly felt in the charged atmosphere. Much shorter than most concerts, she was moving to where she belonged, the piece de resistance in the **varnam** where passages of pure dance and exquisite abhinaya alternate. She was singing as Parvati to the god who frequents Kailash in the high reaches of Kashmir where some authorities say Bharata Natyam in its most ancient form first was danced—when Shiva in his Himalayan abode initiated the vigorous **tandava**, so setting the world in motion again and outpacing Parvati who out of modesty could not stretch her leg so high in the gentler **lasya** mode.

The song of Kokils in the mango groves scents the air
The wind blows, the moonbeams torture me
Oh! Why this delay, why such misgivings in this love, my Lord
O Thou! Whom the Gods worship, whom Rishis bow to
Lord of the Universe—who bestows his grace on the weak
...Granter of boons, Merciful Lord of Kailash come unto me

Visually Balasaraswati was no longer the bulky frame. Imagination had brought a vision transported by **abhinaya** where delicacy of facial expression, the yearning look in the eyes, the rapturous interplay of Shiva and Parvati had captured the mind's eye.

She had also totally captured us.

Other dance forms different in style/content but the same in principle

These may differ in details of presentation and emphasis but they all adhere to the fundamental precepts categorised by sage Bharata as well as the aesthetic principles just described.

1. **Kathakali** (see separate section with **KERALA**).

2. **Kathak** derives from **kathakar**—a storyteller. Adopted by the court of the ruler of Awadh (Oudh), **Wajid Ali Shah** in the 1800s, it was developed further by **Shambhu Maharaj** and his family after Independence, rescuing it from the disrepute of the nautch dance of colonial times. A consummate dancer, Shambhu startled and entranced audiences with his extraordinary command of footwork—a speciality in pure nritta dance in Kathak. The 'conversation' and duel he would have with the percussion players of tabla and the deeper pakhawaj drum would bring the audience to an electric expectancy—'shabash' and 'wah wah' erupting like rocket explosions of verbal approval.

The virtuosity of his anklet bells as a rhythmic device answering the drum patterns until that final coming together on the main beat or **sum** with only one bell of the multitude ringing—and this all executed on a brass tray electrified us all. (**Ghungrus** attached to wide leather bands tied around the ankles are an indispensable adjunct to the sound of dance).

Kathak in its expressive form is still devoted to the same themes, the reference points of the lyrics still concerned with interaction with the world of the gods and that ever-present condition in India—unrequited love. The religious aspect, once suppressed at Islamic courts in the 16th–19th centuries is now brought to the fore again, renewed, in the narrative sections.

3. & 4. **Kuchipudi** and **Odissi** have both now established separate schools of discipline from BN. The former was re-established in the village of this name by Andhra brahmin men to rescue the corrupted temple dance.

♦ Emphasis is given to the curvaceous sculptural forms, carved in the temples of the region in soft sandstone and mottled red. Odissi makes even more obvious its sculptural origins, which some think from recent cave painting discoveries at Udayagiri near Bhubaneshwar may go back before Bharata Natyam to 2nd century BCE, the dancer very consciously coming to rest in that most constant Indian pose—the tribhanga thrust of shoulder, waist and hip in a continuum from Mohenjo-Daro to the free spirited nymphs (**SHALABHANJIKA**), to the modern dancer on stage emulating Radha castigating her Krishna for his dalliances. And meanwhile at her toilette, looking in an imaginary mirror she braids her hair, puts kohl on her eyes, has difficulty screwing heavy earrings in the lobes—so realistically mimed, women in the audience cringe with the discomfort!

In the invocatory dance she may well have bent in salutation to Mother Earth = Bhumi.

5. **Mohini Attam** became popular in Kerala in the 17th century but theorists believe its origins may be 600–700 years earlier.

It is a far more feminine expression than the masculine vigour of Kathakali, of the eternal and epic struggle between the opposing forces—the negative ones churned up in the symbolic waters of creation, the 'milky ocean' depicted in the Bhagavad Gita poster, and the forces of good which recovered the nectar, the amrita stolen by the asuras. Many of the narratives depict the hapless, helpless devas or minor gods appealing to the full power of Vishnu, sustainer of rightful order, before cosmic calamity occurs as the asuras capture the kalash or pot full of the brew of immortality.

Mohini appears as a female extra-curricular avatar to bewitch the asuras with her seductive dance of enchantment. So beguiled, the rakshasas and asuras surrender the kalash to her and the devas drink the amrita instead. Once more the universal order is saved from disintegration.

6. **Manipuri** dance weaves its way in circles in the raas leela dance throughout the social life of the northeastern hills people on purnima (full moon) nights, at every seasonal festival, on any auspicious day it would seem.

Krishna dances with the many gopis, each separated by Krishna replicating himself, painted in intricate detail with the deities of the **PANTHEON** joining the circle—in jewel-like colour on Orissa waxed palm-leaf **PATACHITRA**, a visual mirror image of the dance, each gopi the separated individual ego searching for the central divine.

A member in the audience once explained the deeper meaning of the raas leela—and we were not in a temple either but in the market place mandapa where all the villagers were gathered to watch the tinsel spectacle of glittering costume encrusted with mica pieces, tubular skirts in brilliant stiff brocades and scalloped starched muslin material unique to Manipur:

It is only when Ego is conquered, you understand, that perfect union with Divine is being possible. That is why we prepare bed for Radha and Krishna tomorrow.

Yes—India is very down-to-earth with a crashing bump even though concentrating on the firmament above!

But in the mind's eye the memory is etched over 45 years—of a delicate Manipuri girl lost in circlets of concentration, her dancing hair a sheen of ebony blackness, the longest ever seen, almost down to her knees, undulating with a life of its own as the dance rotated to a crescendo, eddying and swinging out with the full body of waves blown into spray.

Those four words of Rukmini's

All **four words** rolled into one. DANCE.

All dance forms are grounded in the same principles of that monumental manual of sage Bharata's—functioning in all their detailed laws (the shastras) and codifications within what really can be called a **moral/spiritual framework** of artistry.

Indeed the typical movement of the first section of the dance when the solo performer comes onto the stage and does **pranam** (obeisance) to the image or shrine bedecked with flowers at the side, and then to the accompanying musicians seated on immaculate durees or white sheets opposite, is that of respectful devotion. Never for one minute does the dancer turn the back towards the Deity. This in itself creates the ambience of worship.

♦ **Bhava**: refers to that heightened state of being.

♦ **Sanchari bhava**: means that once this fundamental state was fixed according to the particular form and section of dance/music then the performer was allowed to improvise, sanchari meaning mixed, returning always to the fundamental state at the close.

♦ **Brahmananda**: ideal state of supreme bliss, ecstasy, joy, serenity, tranquillity.

♦ **Rasa**: flavour, juice: in technical terms the particular effect certain tones of colour, sounds, etc. produce in the mind. The ambience that resonates as a result creating a particular heightened perception.

♦ **Sadhana**: the spirit embodied in a particular raga (modal structure, melodic combination of music), painting, drama to which a performer/artist/ musician has to strive through demanding personal discipline.

Even today music and dance principles have remained true to these major precepts. A musician's overall task for instance is to configure through sadhana the intrinsic identity or feel of the raga—melody—through his or her intellectual acumen in knowing the discipline and techniques but also being finely attuned at a higher level of spiritual awareness. For both musician and listener this led to ultimate spiritual realisation—transfixed in a moment of time = a Gnowing (see **INTUITIVE KNOWLEDGE**: *Gnyana*).

■ **DARSHAN(A)** (n. *Sanskrit*)

'Seeing', 'a view', which gives the beholder a special 'charge'. This is traditionally the word used in an Indian context for philosophy = a heightened perception of reality.

Insightful vision literally speaking, but **darshan can be given or received,** just as in the analogy of the Pope being carried in a palanquin down the aisle of St Peter's in Rome or at Easter when he raises his right hand, palm forward in blessing in exactly the same gesture as Shiva Nataraja, Vishnu standing, Buddha seated in meditation, the Pope is **giving darshan**. The nuns who genuflect in respect are **receiving darshan**.

Those who give are:

♦ **the deities** who similarly are presented in procession in the first temple arati in the dawn hours.

♦ **great souls—mahatmas** when they give blessings on their padayatras, now global.

♦ **charismatic humans** such as Pandit Nehru in a vast throng give darshan by their very presence and the psychological electric charge experienced even if the person receiving his darshan can hardly see him, let alone get near enough to feel the benediction.

♦ **gurus** are giving darshan all the time

♦ and **elders** also, especially much-loved grandparents. Many a time witnessing large family gatherings at airports, if such relatives come off the plane, all the younger relatives gathered to welcome them quickly touching their feet as a mark of respect. The grandparents quickly brush their heads blessing them. Such is **darshan**.

♦ **It can also be sensed in the abstract**. A devotee does not have to go to the temple, or take prasad (offerings in a basket or on a thali) to receive darshan. The visualisation of a Deity can bring a physical sense of energy transferred—such is darshan. And surely the most dramatic example in all Indian culture is the theophany of the Lord Vishnu in all ·his magnitude in the Bhagavad Gita. Krishna is delivering to the archer Arjuna the true 'view' = darshan of the ultimate truth in all its glory when Vishnu expands dramatically in form (see **BHAGAVAD GITA** section).

A philosophic view: Darshan is the nearest Sanskrit word used for the Greek word 'philosophy'. It actually implies **'a seeing'** meaning **'a point of view'**.

Towards the thousand-year-long period end of Upanishad enquiry into the nature of the universe and the meaning of human life within that framework, **six philosophies or** viewpoints crystallised in written form between 2nd century BCE to 2nd century CE. They each became separate schools of thought, all but one however, acknowledging the Vedas as the authoritative and valid bedrock in assessing truth, differing only in emphasis on certain points. They examined all the additional thinking and commentaries that many sages in intervening centuries had made.

1. & 2. Logic and a rational critique were brought to bear as much as in Graeco-Roman systems. **Vaisheshika** (founder sage Kanada) and **Nyaya** schools (sage Gautama) are in fact very dry and clinical. These two schools are similar in intent if different in emphasis, attempting to dissect in scientific rationalist style the constituent parts of the universe and creation, arriving even at the concept of the atom = **anu** in Sanskrit and this long before sophisticated development of scientific technology. In fact, Indian commentators describe these two systems as attempts 'to combine physics with metaphysics'. Amid such scientific investigation, the divine impulse was hardly mentioned, rather envisaged as a **First Cause**.

3. As in all things Indian, followers of these philosophies could not arrive at the truths they sought to embody by **pure intellect alone**. They had to be experienced as the **heart of the matter.** **Mimamsa** (attributed to sage Jaimini) could be called anti-intellectual in that its proponents were wary of philosophising. They believed a proper adherence to the ancient teachings of reverencing dharma and the accompanying rites and rituals demanded of a Hindu class dharma was enough for the *summum bonum* of human life.

4. **Samkhya** system (sage Kapila) implies 'enumeration', again more scientific an approach in gathering evidence. This school of thought is nearest to an atheistic view in not accepting a **'God'** as the creator of the universe in anthropomorphic **'form'**. As a scientist would, followers of the Samkhya way investigate the **force** that impels creation, from **PURUSHA** through **PRAKRITI**—abundant nature in all her **constituents**, seen as 24 evolvents = **TATTVA** of matter, elements (5), senses (5) very much as Greek philosophers concluded.

5. & 6. **Vedanta** (sages Vyas and Badarayana) and **Yoga** (founded by sage Patanjali) are better known than these four

schools. They are also inter-related, the one the theory, the other the practice through discipline and application of the theory of **Advaita/Dvaita.** These two points on the same compass investigate the relationship of the inner soul or **atman** of each individual to the gigantic nature of the ABSOLUTE BHRM, beyond gender.

What is real REALITY, an ever-present question mark which hangs over a Hindu search for mental steadiness amid the arrows of misfortune? The search for the essential **Brhm** led to a shuttlecock of speculation between the two ends of the spectrum—that a) no other reality existed outside of Brhm—and what ordinary humans recognise as the 'reality' around them is in effect a 'magic shadow show', brought about by **avidya =** ignorance which clouds our human vision, and b) those who follow the DVAITA = DUALISM path, the idea of the Christian God, a separate entity entirely outside and beyond the human soul.

Eventually enlightened souls come to see that multiplicity—the illusion of categories, separation, card-indexing minds—is **really** one. John Donne 16th century English poet, summed this up with his famous sonnet: 'No man is an iland intire of itselfe...'. We are all '**part of the maine.**' Liberation will come as the Gita says with God's grace and the discipline each individual applies in the search, progressing through each of the four ashramas (turn back to **ADVAITA** and **ASHRAMA**).

In the end all the deductive reasoning still led the Indian sages back to the realisation that there is a something—this consciousness for want of a better word—that gave unity to all the disparate strands. **But this was too much in the mind.** Despite material poverty in many places which may not have been so in the Age of the Rishis, Indians love things of the heart: flashes of joy and ebullience like the resonating colours around them, exuberance and that 'devotional vivacity' used as a phrase of inspirational English by an American art critic in New Jersey in describing a superb 1996 exhibition of Indian art the way it is lived in daily life.

Theodore de Bary has emphasised many times that to the Indian thinker philosophy is no mere intellectual game, a **darshana** or **vision of truth** at one level, revealed by a seer but at the other level, an **experience** realised and relived by the aspirant (**Sources of Indian Tradition**)... in fact an epiphany such as that which St Paul experienced on the road to Damascus.

Conclusion

Each of the six **darshanas is not a separation out** in the Western mode of card-indexing compartmentalising. Each is rather a segment on the circumference of the circle, the impulse one of unity pulling towards the central hub, Brhm, like the spokes of a giant chakra—another symbol!

A personal vignette in regard to this. One can only really learn when Indians speak for themselves... not everything is learned by a series of reasoned and orderly steps by what has been called 'the sequential linearity of logic'. There are quantum leaps of sudden revelation that scientist/communicator Bronowski, himself a gifted TV revealer of mysteries to the layperson, explained—not only in relation to Einstein's experiences but that of Mendel in 1856 who had guessed at the coupling of genes 100 years before the DNA double helix really was understood in 1953. He used the words 'truth often advances on you when least ready'; this is the Hindu **gnyana =** knowledge, **vidya,** a direct apprehension of reality = a **darshan** also.

The shining self is in the heart of all of us,

an elderly lady announced to me and half a dozen other passengers crammed in as she sat comfortably cross-legged on the train seat en route from Ahmedabad to Mumbai. She had been chanting a prayer of thanksgiving, perhaps like a Grace, before taking food.

We were sharing a vegetarian meal on a thali efficiently delivered by Indian Railways in the good old steam locomotive days. We trundled endlessly over major girded bridges where huge brown-watered rivers flowed out to the Arabian Sea. She was talking of her experiences on pilgrimage to Dwarkanath (Krishna's city) in the far west and the Swaminarayan temples around Ahmedabad. I thought she had said **changed** when talking of the good feelings pilgrimage once accomplished, brings on. No! She had said **charged** for she said it again.

*I have been **charged**, bijalee, electric 'shark'! As though someone has given me 'shark'. I saw 'the God', I felt 'good' all day.*

That is **darshan**... yet imagine such a conversation in a crowded, silent English Intercity Express courtesy of British Rail... or on Amtrak... or coast to coast in the plush Australian National Railway Indian-Pacific train from Sydney to Perth. Such is India!

■ DEEPAVALI-DIWALI

Literally means a 'row or cluster of lights'. A joyous autumnal festival which as a family celebration in coming together from all points of the compass, bringing and giving of gifts can be likened to the Christian joy of Christmas. Its origin is attributed to the coronation of the restored hero of the Ramayan (the other form of spelling—see **RAMAYANA**) to his rightful throne after 14 years of exile—'a removal of spiritual darkness from the world' according to followers of Vishnu by the Deity's seventh avatar. It occurs sometime in October–early November determined by the lunar cycle. The divine fire—Agni—flames on this night in the delicate **deepas/divas**, dispelling the darkness within.

This lovely beginning also of the Hindu New Year in many parts of India (but not in all regions, April celebrated in Kerala, Andhra Pradesh and Maharashtra) could go back to neolithic times after the end of the monsoon, the new sowing of crops, a rest from labouring in the field before the new moon and the coming on of the Indian winter in **Kartik** in the Indian calendar.

In Bengal this is symbolised by the 'night of **pitris**' (the souls of departed ancestors). Torches on long staves are lit and held aloft as beacons to light the way for the pitris. But not only for them. The goddess Lakshmi has to be honoured. Lights have to welcome her on the dark night otherwise she will pass by. Woe betide any household which does not light the way for the Goddess to enter the humblest dwelling with the rows of earthenware deepas filled with oil and rolled cotton wicks traditional style (a joy for our children to do each year). So simple, such warm beauty, flickering in niches and along verandahs and lining wall tops and at the foot of gateways to the wealthiest mansions and in the humblest *jhuggi bastis* (squatter colonies in the interstices of cities)... and much more welcoming than the sterile light bulbs that now without the motion of live flame, highlight entire houses. Another change for the worse... Diwali in the earlier decades had a dignity and graceful celebration with sparklers and family fireworks.

Ceremonial fire must be as old as humanity reverencing the incomprehensible forces of the universe. The earthenware lamp (**mitti ka diya**) is ubiquitous to daily life in India. Made from the very soil, the land on which we live, it is considered as **woman, nurturing flame** as **deepa lakshmi**, bringing light to the enveloping darkness.

Now big cities are battlefields. The last time after the worst flight from London to Delhi in 40 years of flying my sanctuary was the oasis of peace in Delhi's increasingly fraught city conditions of traffic hazards, crowded population and pollution—the **India International Centre** leading into Lodi Bagh with its beautifully-kept Lodi mausoleums, majestic trees, tiny squirrels and flashing emerald parrots.

♦ Arriving at 3 a.m. after an entire day's delay, the second night of Diwali continued with the thundering crack of alarming rockets and Chinese multi-pounders. Backlanes and open spaces, traffic intersections and flat rooftops were the battleground of the new single male 'terrorists' carrying on the non-stop sharp crack and whistle of higher and higher Indian decibel fireworks—and from every quarter. It took five nights slowly to peter out. Is this a measure then of the new affluence or the revved up hype of a new kind of youth culture?

♦ Finance, filthy lucre, is also part and parcel of the real world so silver, sometime gold coins, are left in a tray of milk for Lakshmi to note, and then pocketed by senior members of the family! Nowadays this is taken even further—big insurance companies, banks and shopping complexes enamoured of the commercial income spend flamboyantly on lavish decorations and illuminations on Diwali night before orthodox Hindu traders shut the old year's ledgers and set down the new transactions. Soon the Internet will impose a new order! Then— certainly in the Punjab—the gambling begins!

Bhai Duj (dooj) **ka tika** (teeka) is the ceremony following Diwali, the second day after **amaavas**, the night when there is no moon, called **duj**. This is when sisters honour their brothers if they live nearby. They carry a thali with a bowl of yoghurt, and vermillion or sandalpaste to mark the tika on his foreheard as blessing.

No way will electricity ever supplant the comforting warmth and beauty of the flickering flame. In northern hemispheres it is the bonfire which brings this same comfort to the deepest yearnings of a human being in the dark.

■ **DESIRE TO PLEASE**
There is a reluctance to say **no**—in order to keep the harmony, especially with strangers or newcomers, having possibly been attuned throughout history to accept incomers and to be hospitable to such people, as well as having to be deferential during long centuries of alien cultural domination.

♦ This often leads to an Indian saying 'yes' meaning 'no'. Businesspeople venturing into India need an Indian partner to help side-step such ambiguities (see **SHAKING THE HEAD**).

♦ **Keeping one's word and not causing offence to anybody is an important cultural norm.**

♦ An apocryphal story but where anything is possible in India who can deny its possible veracity? It was told to us in Madras during a DMK campaign at Chingleput, where the shrine of Ganesh attracts travellers to receive blessing for the safety of their onward journey and a coconut is broken on return to give thanks for safe deliverance. Current as a marker of social attitudes in the 60s, now no longer true but an indicator of how far rural India has moved, matured, is the story of the old Tamil farmer way out in the parched pink plains southwest of Madras.

After the first major general election following in the wake of Pandit Nehru's death in 1964, he and his fellow villagers were being avidly canvassed by various party officials. He accommodatingly promised his support in private to all 12 candidates in his constituency. Lining up in an eager queue to vote in the days before cynicism set in, he was seen to tear up his ballot paper into 12 pieces and place them one by one in the big, black battered metal ballot box.

When hauled up and told that his vote would be invalid he smiled genially and remarked: 'It does not matter. I have kept my word and displeased no one.'

No Problem!

■ **DEVANAGARI** (n. *Sanskrit*)
deva = deity *nagara* = city
script of the Sanskrit and Hindi languages. The one is symbiotic with the other.

The script implies 'language of the deities' (see section on **VEDAS**); the other, urban educated people speaking a refined, well-developed form of speech, i.e., '**cultivated**'. When I hear Sanskrit shlokas chanted the sounds become visual stepping stones, each individual solid phonetic, clear and chunky as their devanagari characters. (**Prakriti** is the opposite meaning = 'from nature', that is natural/not refined = common)

In fact **Sanskrit** itself means: सं स्कृत = **well done; pure; refined; well ordered.**

S + ⊙ = nasal sound, S Kr = T

कृ = **Kr** (root) = to do to act/ accomplish; **Sam** = with, together; ॢ is one of the additional signs added to a character as an abbreviated indication of the sound to be made (in this case Ra) rather than writing the full letter = R

Pronunciation: S as in sugar/ T as in tea, there being several fine shades of this sound whether with tongue on palate or rolled more like <u>thudding</u> sound.

• Entirely recited in an oral culture by an exclusive class of brahmins trained virtually from birth in a rigorous discipline—and this for hundreds of years in an oral culture, the language was finally standardised in a coherent if very complex grammar by the famous **Panini** in the 3rd century BCE.

• The script consists of **13 vowels, 35 consonants** with **some other 'melded' syllabic sounds**.

It is a logically phonetic language. Once the script is learned and mastered any word can be correctly deciphered and pronounced. Then you only have to learn its meaning!

The words hang from a bar, proceeding from left to right. (**Hindi** is founded on the same but more simplified principle). This is unlike Arabic/Persian derived vernacular (popular regional) languages such as **Urdu**. This runs cursively from right hand side of page to the left.

• All road signs in the north are, first, in Devanagri with Urdu script placed underneath in Delhi and UP because of a heavy preponderance of Muslims.

Some sounds which are aspirated (a bit like the **ch** sound in the Scottish lo**ch**) have a broken bar:

ध = dha; भ = bha

other **sounds** like OM = ॐ and BRHM = ब्रह्म
                                        B(r)...H...M

are more than words as such... a 'vast literature' could evolve—it has!—from just studying the roots and **CORE CONCEPTS** thrown up by the original reflections rishis conjured up about the theory of pure **sound/breath** (cf **PRAÑA: In the beginning was the Word**).

Twenty two pages of the **Lexicon of Fundamental Concepts** previously referred to are devoted to **BRHM**, the neuter Sanskrit for creation, to grow, develop! And in my Sanskrit primer there are five different ways of writing R. Most lazy English speakers who stumble even at the French R give up with a bad headache! See **Sampad & Vijay's The Wonder that is Sanskrit** (Mapin, Ahmedabad, 2002).

■ DHABA...

is a roadside stall or basic restaurant for travellers, a rest stop for drinking **chai** (milky boiled tea) in thick glasses. Tasty food cooked in front of you is safe to eat but don't look too closely at the washing-up facilities. They will put you off but our family never suffered runny tummies on long road journeys eating at these stops, resting on rope beds, or sitting up at basic wooden tables along with the hundreds of lorry drivers—these are their R and R stops. (Differentiate from **dabba**, the Mumbai system of delivery of tiffin carriers at lunchtime, an efficient world of its own—see BOMBAY—The word is without aspirate).

Flat wheatflour rotis are cooked till even Indian bacteria can't survive the sharp heat of the tandoor. Minced meat (keema) and lentil curries are better than many served up in 5-star hotels and in old Delhi, the back streets of Lucknow and Kolkata there are dhabas serving gastronomic delights only the locals can direct you

to, the temperature of cooking wiping out all germs!

Do **not** walk around the back to the loos. Best to hang in there until you reach the open road again and find a thicket of thorn bushes! Undoubtedly as soon as you obey the call of nature a young shepherd boy, still holding his shepherd's crook, while watching over his flock of black-tailed sheep or bleating goats, will materialise from nowhere. Beware!

■ DHARMA (n. *Sanskrit*)
root DHR = to sustain Duty, responsibility, the law   (see **CORE CONCEPTS** and **QUATERNITIES**).

This is a 'totality' concept, absolutely fundamental to Hindu thinking and colours the worldview of most of the other Indian faiths:

1. About the cosmos and this planet = **rta** (refer to this specific word).
2. And its place in the scheme of things = **sanatana dharma**.
3. And an individual's ethical behaviour within this scheme = svadharma — self-ethics.

As a word it has infinite subtleties of meaning being a seminal word in the deep core of the Hindu view of life—**Sanatana Dharma** at philosophical as well as ethical level where it is enmeshed with the concept of Karma. But it also resonates as a scientific philosophy, aligned with the latest views of quantum physics.

Dharma is:

• neither an **obedience** to a revelation in time or supposedly god-given

• nor a **worship** of a god in accordance with that revelation. The individual therefore has no need to go to an outside authority but must seek inner wisdom through meditation, thinking over the ancient texts, seeking out learned gurus, **satgurus** who have reached a higher consciousness and able to give guidance (refer to **BHAGAVAD GITA**, the **need for guidance**), as well as going on pilgrimage, undergoing fasts.

• the immutable right order of things known from **within**, it is a constant substratum of thinking even amongst the most worldly of Indians.

• **self discipline** is the **regulating factor** = svadharma

This most fundamental of Indian concepts is further elaborated threading throughout the text but most specifically in the **CORE CONCEPTS** section.

■ DHOTI

The dhoti about which a requiem was sung some years ago, is back! With the coming of coalition governments into power and the advent of regional power bases the dhoti seems to have become more prevalent in official photographs of cabinet ministers even if their own young have taken to the universal blue jean. Certainly on friezes of southern temples of 7th–8th century CE the populace is wrapped around in the self-same ancient cloth.

• Gandhi who even braved colonial smirks when he travelled to London in one to attend the Round Table conferences to consider India's demands for self-government, was making a definitive statement of cultural independence—why should Indian men wear a suit to prove their modernity when a hot humid climate demanded loose-fitting cotton. This unadorned seamless 4–5 metres of unstitched cloth was male national dress.

◆　Harrow-educated Nehru would have none of it and walked out of Western suits into his elegant rose-bud bedecked Islamic **achkan** (fitted knee-length buttoned coat with upright collar, now fancied by some Western men instead of the dinner jacket, another global 'cross-over'). A photo of Panditji in a dhoti would be an anachronism. Even in the most oppressive pre-monsoon heat wave in Delhi he must surely have taken to his cotton **churidars**–the crinkled pyjamas cut on the cross that look like many bangles (**churees**) rippling up a woman's arms.

◆　Its most elegant form in Bengal is in pale cream silk and the eye-shattering white of the **mundu** (sarong) in the south where many more of the middle class retain their Indian ways despite all modern living patterns of going to the office, attending conferences, appearing on TV, holding media sessions.

■ DIKSHITAR

An inward-looking community of priests attached to the **CHIDAMBARAM** temple.

◆　**Dikshitars** from the tender age of five are subject to an isolated life trained in pedagogical style to master the Vedic texts, understand the fine tuning of the Sanskrit language, the infinite variety of temple ceremonies and pujas, and to run the temple administration. This despite efforts in recent years by the Tamilnadu State Government to interfere due to what is regarded as irrelevant and outmoded religiosity and attention to the custodianship letter of the law (including retention of child marriage within their clan) in accordance with traditional 'texts' which in the oral culture can be tracked back for at least 3,000 years.

◆　Their sense of custodianship is readily apparent. They are clearly vehemently aware of their superiority. Watch them in action in Chidambaram on a working day which is everyday when, like the gigantic complex of the Meenakshi Temple at Madurai, it is asserted that at least 10,000 devotees stream through.

Clearly in the confusion and hustle and bustle, and the occasional volatile enthusiasm of the crowd pressing in to a particular shrine for 'darshan' from the installed deity, a certain degree of order has to be established.

It is the way it is done, however, that has often brought me up with a start—Dikshitars ever appear to be on the run, barking orders at compliant villagers if they get out of line when the Deity proceeds on a palanquin. Pushed and shoved back in no uncertain manner, the poor peasants who constitutionally can now enter the once forbidden hallowed precincts that as lowly castes until decades after Independence they were not allowed by the temple priests to do, still obey as if by force of habit—as though they had no right to address the great Deity directly but only after an enforced donation via the priests.

Admittedly that is the dikshitars' only income unless they take on part-time jobs using their hands (their womenfolk totally subservient as young brides of 16 to the domestic order).

Pandas and **purohits** are other brahmin functionaries who service families searching their ancestral records in Rishikesh or Kasi for instance, and performing particular ceremonies on these occasions or conducting worship in centres of pilgrimage and along the ashram trail.

Footnote. In other temples in south India one is entirely at the mercy of less aristocratic custodians. The only time I have ever been physically pushed, harassed or shouted at and prevented from entering a building (most often in search of magnificent and well-documented sculptural friezes) is by such functionaries. Priests they may be but they behave like the most revved-up sergeant majors!

I was not physically present in the worshipping shrines where Western dress is often a 'no-no', nor was I treading unthinkingly on sacred areas without permission. In fact it was mostly on occasions where Indian friends had invited me with them and led the way. They incidentally were abused also!

◆　Although such incidents are very salutary for the British who did just the same to Indians in barring them (and dogs) from entering the hallowed portals of the Bengal and Ooty Clubs (and many others) displaying some very suspect arrogant tendencies during the days of the Raj (beating a woman like Sarojini Naidu for instance with **lathis** on the Salt March) I nevertheless always hoped some explanation would be given by these temple custodians. But these were an embedded patriarchy of stubborn men who probably ordered their wives around in much the same way—born to rule!

■ DMK

Dravidham Munnetra Kazagham has its origins as a political party in the **South Indian Liberation Front** as far back as 1916 but its ethos and motivations are still embedded in the culture of southerners. Its political alignment was partly driven by **regional stirrings** against disproportional dominance in all the structures of life by brahmin society. This movement was concerned with social uplift of the two thirds of the low caste who not only could not enter temples in case they polluted the sanctuary but were denied access to education, political power, etc.

This was given further impetus in the founding of the **Justice Party in Madras in 1924.** Many reformers acknowledged injustice as Mahatma Gandhi's national message began to percolate into the general body politik. This was a regional crystallisation of political aspirations by a remarkable visionary known in South Indian style (see **NAMES**) by his initials, **E V R**, the **Periyar** (1879–1973). Periyar is an honorific term in Kerala and Tamilnadu for the seniormost man, that is = **the leader**. (The initials, in typically South Indian traditon, stand for his "home town" or **watan**, place of origin **Erode**, his father's name **Venkatappa**, **Ramaswami** his given name).

A Political Programme

It goes deeper than that bland title however, a subliminal message implying **great soul**. All over the south, E V R, a Kannada-speaking Hindu of the Naiker community was regarded as such, one indeed who displayed a Socratic abhayam if anyone did, despite Pandit Nehru depicting him as a 'barbarian'. This perhaps because of his singular espousal of anti-brahmin sentiment. A man of impassioned opinions he spoke out persistently against 'the contradictions and inconsistencies of the Brahminical facade of Vedic rectitude', denying the lower castes their rights as human beings. From all accounts he could be cantankerous and according to the **Dictionary of National Biography** he used some extreme methods to show up the flagrant stupidities of brahminical rituals even resorting to cutting off their sacred tuft of hair and thread, and slapping temple deities with his chappals!

In 1958 at Coimbatore he declared:

Almost all fine-looking animals and birds have become our gods. Ant-hills invite the gift of milk from our womenfolk. Why should the gods be undressed, bathed and dressed daily? Even the goddesses are undressed and bathed daily by the male priests! They need wives and concubines and are to be married every year! One god will wear a spear, another a bow and arrow. Others have the mace and the dagger.
This is supposedly to overcome evil.
If so, is it not time that our gods are properly equipped with modern weapons? Should not the bow and arrow be replaced by the machine gun and the hand grenade? Should not Krishna ride a tank instead of the obsolete chariot? There are certain things which cannot be mended but only ended. Brahmanical Hinduism is one such.

◆ The legendary and monumental C Rajagopalachari, affectionately known in the 50s as **Rajaji** (the golden age of honourable politicians who worked long hours for the betterment of their new nation) had decades before engaged E V R in the Congress Party Freedom Struggle (he had become President of the Madras Committee in **1922**) but his iconoclastic behaviour so upset the uppercaste establishment that Rajaji's Presidency Government under the British sent him to prison from where E V R was elected President of the Justice Party! This later became the **Dravida Kazhagam** (Federation).

He had led the anti-Hindi agitation in 1953. The founding of the **DMK** in 1967 was true fulfilment for E V R. Its main tenets of faith were the following:
◆ Political impetus towards Tamil autonomy.
◆ A general ethos of agnosticism similar to anti-cleric attitudes in France against priest-ridden Catholicism. It was asserted that brahmins used god and temples as channels for exploiting the masses, and government channels even under the British to form a north Indian hegemony through their bureaucratic 'knowhow' as a powerful arm of government.
◆ Justice for the poor and better redistribution of income.
◆ Greater freedom for women.

◆ Improving educational opportunities for lower castes.
◆ Unostentatious living.
He sounds like the Tony Benn of India!

The creation of the **States Reorganisation Commission in 1956** was the catalytic agent at **national** level for general disaffection in the south against neglect by the newly constituted central government after Independence. The whole of the southern tip of India felt this surge of Dravidian identity, most of all the Madras Presidency, about to become the State of Tamilnadu. And thus the DMK was formed under the leadership of C N Annadurai to assert wider issues than local brahmin/non-brahmin tensions. Some regarded the new leader as a defector from the main cause in order to gain power but that is politics. Times and circumstances had moved on. This Indian freethinker in Voltaire's tradition who roundly condemned the Indian Constitution 'as an instrument of Aryan oppression' had reached his 'use-by' date.

Southern Dravidian identity became increasingly a sensitive issue. Even if it was not true, there was a feeling that a Congress government favoured (or at least was totally dominated by) the heavy political weight and 'nous'—they were—of the numerically vast populations of Uttar Pradesh, Madhya Pradesh and Bihar. As India, now a free and entire state, sought to gain its own lost domain, matters of national language, true states' boundaries based on cultural/regional language areas and proportional representation in the Lok Sabha (the House of the People) all came to a head. In addition, Hindi was proposed as a compulsory test for entering government service. This proposal, put sometimes in a muscular way by northern politicians whose mother tongue was Hindi, would give them a head start at birth in any competitive national exam (see **IAS** section).

In 1957 on the first visit to South India we encountered real anger against northerners. Black flags were flying in many villages throughout Tamilnadu. The national flag was burnt by hot heads in Madras. That alerted the nation to take Tamilnadu sentiment seriously.

Even the commemoration of the 1857 **Indian Mutiny** to be renamed a **War of Independence** by new Indian historians redressing the way British historians had written up Indian history, got an airing in the Tamilnadu press.

Graffiti on walls was not so prevalent and unsightly as today but one large declaration dominated a stretch of road and our sights near the traditional Connemara Hotel approaching Adiyar.
Whose Mutiny? Whose Independence? Down with Hindi Wallahs!
Another slogan appeared:
Who gets all the big projects? Watch the Five Year Planners!

It was significant that impeccable English was used for all the world to take note, and not Tamil. Undoubtedly there were South Indians on the central Planning Commission but emotional sentiment when stirred can zoom into the firmament like a rocket as one witnesses daily around the globe as the concept of the nation state takes a steep dive into ethnic head-bashing.

D

Geography and distancing also play an important part in cultural perspectives. This ethnic/minority assertiveness has come to the fore globally as cultural factors have displaced marxism as explosive political triggers.

Just about everywhere from Chechnya to Cyprus (once again) ancient identities are demanding autonomy or at least federation of equals after centuries of neglect from the dominant majority. Just as British Columbia regards Ottawa, Scotland Westminster Government, impoverished Calabria central Government in Rome, and Perth Canberra (having nearly succeeded in 1933 in winning state secession by a 2/3 majority of voters in a referendum only to be thwarted by colonial government in Britain) so too Tamilnadu regards New Delhi and central authority 2,500 km away. Tamil film culture plays such a central part in the hard life of the ordinary toiling workers at the bottom of the pyramid that the fine line between reality in politics and the world of fantasy become fused. The Congress Party in the north was collapsing. The DMK was in the ascendancy, as the 1980s arrived.

Charismatic **fillum actors** such as **M G R (Ramachandran)** and his mistress, **J Jayalalitha,** already blessed with the aura of traditional epic roles as powerful deities on the screen, rocketed into political roles of power and the foundation of personality-cult **matinee idol politics.** They were building on the mass support given to **Muthurel Karunanidhi's** campaigns in the previous decade to force temple entry for Harijans—still denied entry to the 'high temples' a generation after Independence. This was of great impact in the more traditional south with at least 4,700 temples in Tamilnadu alone!

Tackling the obstructions and prejudice from another angle, the DMK Chief Minister in 1974 set about encouraging Harijans to lift their sights and educate themselves as temple **archakas = pujaris** or **priestly functionaries**—difficult enough even for brahmins as many archakas inherit the role from family lines born to the **agama** culture of temple rules and regulations, sacrifices or yagnas, learning of the Vedic slokas which are not uniform across temple culture. Shiva, Vishnu, Shakti all have their own forms and rites going back to the Puranas—even to detailed matters as to how to decorate the Deity for various festivals and pujas.

To the orthodox brahmin this political push was sacrilege; they pointed out Harijans could already be priests in many temples without elaborating that these were the village shrines to minor deities—the village guardians. Such deities were insignificant, part of the folk, the **Little Tradition** of anthropology, fading in comparison to the majesty of the great temples at Thanjavur and the famous Tiruvalur of Tyagaraja's annual music festival, a town very near to where Karunanidhi lived.

To the reforming politicised movement this was a hypocrisy like comparing St Peter's in Rome to a Welsh Baptist Chapel in the hierarchy of worship.

M G R formed the **All India Anna DMK** partly due to disputes over suspect financing, personality friction, a different emphasis but retained '**Anna**' in respect for the founder of the

original DMK, **C N Annadurai.** The party was hopeful that the miracle weapons, **thunderbolt vajras** and **Parasurama's javelin** that failed **Karna** in the **Mahabharata** epic of the fillum world, wielded in the politics of today would strike at the heart of those in the north. Delhi-baiting was a popular past-time even if **The Hindu,** a respected southern newspaper, cautioned against southern parochialism. The great masses, cinemagoers all, loved their filmstar politicians and seemed to believe them… until power corrupted the Empress Jayalalitha, all too human, forgetful of her shakti-dharma as Chief Minister. And Tamil interconnections in the deadly ethnic struggles of Sri Lanka with many criminals fleeing to Tamilnadu did not help either.

In 1996 the electorate woke up to reality. They saw around them the AIADMK ministers, relatives and close factory combines and industrial friends moving into palatial mansions enjoying fine lifestyles. A new maturity, a general election, the effects of TV coverage, the DMK wiped the slate clean with 172 seats gained from an earlier two only; the AIADMK lost 164 retaining only four. Democracy triumphs! But **E V R** would shudder with dismay at what free and privileged politicans have now brought upon his beloved Dravida.

A personal addendum:

Much of this account refers to brahmins often in a negative light. This is not meant personally. It reflects what Indians themselves write or express as an opinion in the supposed egalitarian democracy of the new India. Since parliamentary democracy and **constitutional clauses safeguarding the scheduled/tribal sections of the community have consolidated with the advancing decades,** the ethos of one individual, one vote as valid as the next is taking hold in political strategies as well as economically, even if wholly unsuitable or poorly trained personnel with little background of administration move into protected positions demanding competence in State and Federal bureaucracies. '**Discrimination in favour of'** is not an Indian phenomenon alone. It now is a democratic thrust for Afro-Americans and Hispanics; inbuilt into Aboriginal aspirations and contrarily the prejudiced racial arguments of newly emerging Australian/Canadian/French forces against immigration and welfare funding to minorities in the midst of new xenophobia.

◆ The elitist upper-crust nature of this class hierarchy as institutionally entrenched as the British House of Lords, but with subtle influences hidden away from public view like feudal court personnel that surround monarchy, has always been rooted in encrusted tradition which seldom reformed until other noble brahmin sages–saints appealed to that ultimate guage–dharma and righteous living. Even then extreme rituals embedded in the temple societies especially in the south were cruelly enforced by 'institutional' brahmins (a subject of films and novels now emerging in English by south Indian writers). This gave brahmins a bad name and accounts for an exodus in latter decades into teaching positions overseas as educational/ government professional opportunities narrowed due to quota systems imposed constitutionally as job reservations, university entrance and government posts began to gather momentum for the less-privileged classes.

♦ There are **positive** contributions which must also be emphasised even if in present-day India it is politically incorrect to do so. The learned teaching brahmin (female as well as male) has been one of the **essential forces of unity** throughout 5,000 years of developing society.

Rising above political power and chicanery of the kshatriya rulers, they concentrated on learning, passing that into the populace as ascetics who defied the blandishments of wealth and power for a more subtle influence–crossing regions and cultures and economic divides (a rich brahmin landlord in Kerala had affinity with a Bengali brahmin teacher, no matter how desperately impoverished as portrayed in the Apu trilogy of films).

The polity of ruling the kshatriya caste was balanced by that **mysterious adamantine thread of spiritual challenge** of the brahmin that Shankaracharya so appealingly embodied.

■ DOWRY

The cost of husbands is escalating!

And revolution is brewing. The new generation of professional young women figures they are overpriced.

The 21 year-old computer student, good-looking **Nisha Sharma**, rocketed into national fame and made headlines in leading newspapers world-wide in 2003. With remarkable courage she defied conventions beyond even what the TV soapies might have dared to write into a script:

The musicians were playing, the 2,000 guests were dining, the Hindu priest was preparing the ceremony and the bride was dressed in red, her hands and feet festively painted with henna.

Then, the bride's family says, the groom's family moved in for the kill. The dowry of two televisions, two home theater sets, two refrigerators, two air-conditioners and one car was too cheap. They wanted $25,000 in rupees, now, under the wedding tent.

As a free-for-all erupted between the two families, the bartered bride put her hennaed foot down. She reached for her royal blue cellphone and dialled 100. By calling the police, Nisha Sharma, saw her potential groom land in jail and herself land in the national spotlight as India's new overnight sensation.

Unfazed by the loss of her fiancé, Ms Sharma said that since Monday she had received 20 to 25 marriage proposals, by cellphone, e-mail and letter.

Legislation made this system of financing a husband (and his family) illegal over 40 years ago. The law is widely flouted, even ignored. The **Dowry Prohibition Act 1961** might as well never have been passed.

The flamboyance and flaunting of wealth at weddings is on the increase, an aspect of India which may well bring dangers as the gap between rich and poor increases with the massed strength of the consuming classes in the past five years. India's poor are becoming very knowledgeable due to spread of electricity leading to use of modern technology apart from transistors, and the growing tentacles of the visual–TV. New assertiveness is growing even beyond the cities where dowry demands paradoxically can be at their most exorbitant, certainly among the new rich. There is growing anecdotal evidence that a woman and her family are beginning to refuse marriage into 'demander' families seeking brides as commodities along with all the goodies. Some greedy families have even had graphic graffiti marked on their houses to warn negotiating families to beware!

♦ There is growing awareness via the oral culture of TV of abuses not only in dowry demands and consequent bride burnings but allied subjects which were never publicly expressed before–similar to Western society's inhibitions half a century ago. Wife battering, child sexual abuse, female deaths in suspicious circumstances, custodial rape–none of these assaults on human rights and dignity within what is supposed to be a sacrament of marriage in India was ever discussed. Now activist judges prompted by social outcries have handed down some outstanding judgements.

♦ **But nothing as yet appears to shift entrenched dowry customs.** The latest story out of Kerala quotes one fisher folk family and future husband demanding well over 2 lakhs = R.200,000 = just over £4,000 or $A2,000–plus scooter and TV (a good deal more to poor Indians than its seeming Western value). Gulf money slushes abound like an inland lagoon whipped up in monsoonal storms, a girl just completing school—as far back as 1993—was married with a dowry of 1½ crores rupees (1½ million).

♦ Some enterprising groups are organising mass ceremonies for peasant families in the wedding season (depending on auspicious planetary conjunctions) to cut down costs. And down in Kerala where the most comprehensive yet human survey of the factors that compound life of the daughter–inheritance, losing money 'out of the joint family unit', the ambivalence of male/female relationships across cultures and throughout history is the two decade research assiduously undertaken by **Jamila Verghese**. (Now republished in paperback form from Vikas, **Her Gold and Her Body,** New Delhi, 1999, speaks volumes in the title.)

Written in an easily comprehended style with some amusingly wry sketches the predicament of all women (most especially until they become economic units in their own right—and that brings heartache and hazards of its own!) presents a kaleidoscope which clarifies why around the globe a despairing lament is still raised when a daughter is born.

And yet how will the human race be generated without women as that honoured vessel—the kumbh, kalash, womb-house?

■ DRAVIDIANS

Until a few years ago this is what you would have read inscribed on the tablet above this slab of arid red laterite soil: 'Earliest Indian civilization–indigenous people said partly to be of negrito stock but source unknown'. Were they the original inhabitants of the long lost and mysterious **Indus Valley** civilization? The concurrence amongst Indian historians, archaeologists, social thinkers supported this theory.

As more archaeological diggings bring to light artefacts similar to Indus Valley Harappan–Taxilan–Mohenjo-Daro culture it is being realised how extensive this civilization was and how strongly intrinsic to the culture and worship of the Mother Goddess, the tree spirits and ascetic behaviour was amid the wealth and high standard of organised city site and living.

A Malayalam historian, **A Sreedhara Menon**, in his book **A Survey of Kerala History** (Sahitya Pravarthaka Co-op. Society, Kottayam, 1967) also has stated that a Mediterranean peoples in the face of aggression from the Greeks came to India in three distinct waves.

◆ Stop right there! New theories have dislodged this particular stepping stone. It can still trip you up. Confusion abounds and similar to the **ARYA-ARYAN** encounter, controversy dogs one's footsteps.

New theories based on reappraisal of datings due to advanced mathematical cross-referencing and astronomical research backwards into time; the symbiotic relationship between theories on India's foundations as a distinctive culture in which 'Dravidian' and 'Aryan' linguistic studies are inextricably linked; and the latest historical theories decrying the 'Marxist-missionary-colonial' bias of the past century in publications worldwide, have thrown all previous certainties into the tumble-dryer of historical speculation.

◆ The word Dravidian is now taken by many of the new younger generation of academics in various disciplines to describe a **geographical identity only**. One of the main protagonists of this reappraisal, Navaratna Rajaram dismissed the term quite cursorily in a nine-line glossary explanation, despite the fact that he comes of south Indian brahmin lineage (Maharashtrians settled north of Bangalore). He certainly resists accepting previous academic theories of Dravidians as a distinct racial-linguistic-cultural identity. Referring back to **Manu's** definitions in his role as Vedic progenitor of the race (if one dare use the word!) of **Bharatvarsha** and giver of the codes of law–Rajaram states 'they have always been considered part of the Aryan civilization'.

It is worth reading his book **The Politics of History** (Voice of India, New Delhi, 1995, chapter 4, dealing with Dravidian questions–**Emperor's Clothes**).

◆ Reading between the lines of a number of sympathetic articles in the contemporary press it does appear as though there is a conscious attempt to play down the artificial divide between north and south which has in some measure been falsely encouraged by previous linguistic studies especially by outsiders (**firangi**), early missionaries, and Marxist theorists as well as the divisive politics that have come about in current debates.

However, no matter the identity of Dravidians as an Indian society emerged from neolithic cave life, whether they were original inhabitants of the Indus Valley civilization (the previous theory for the past century) creating an advanced society, then overrun by another people(s), Aryans or not, invasion or slow migration changing their demographic realities, eventually dislodged according to their view of history, slowly drifting down into the narrowing peninsular, **travellers cannot escape the sense of a different identity, different feature, darker skin** of the Dravidian peoples **as they see themselves**… and their own passionate sense of pride in their language, **sangam** literature, their arts and the majestic Dravidian temple architecture (see **DMK, SOUTH INDIAN KINGDOMS** and **TAMIL CULTURE**).

To question this, especially the datings of the Sangam traditions the factual existence of which may well have succumbed to the tropical climate of the south–humidity, mould, termites–is to cause an adrenalin rush! Several of my Tamil friends have exploded at such reappraisals. One irate acquaintance relaxing in a new ayurvedic centre being promoted from Kerala Tourist Department (Malayalees equally aware of their distinctiveness) in the hills of the Nilgiris declared:

How dare those Aryans up north dismiss our literature as so short in time—the very thing they are claiming western scholars tried to do to their own Vedic timespan! It had reached such a height of literary advancement that even if actual records no longer exist, think of all that had gone before to attain such brilliance by the time records appeared!

At this point confusion reigns for those of us bereft of that indigenous knowledge of Sanskrit, Tamil, Malayalam, Kannada or Telugu languages. No doubt more will be heard from this very articulate people, **all Indians whether from north or south!**

Endnote: Several Internet websites vigorously present the sense of Dravidian pride completely oblivious to all this internal debate!

tamilnation.org/culture.kparathy
thehinduonline.com/hindu/daily
intamm.com/culture/south.htm
travel.indianmart.com/places/cities/
and an article detailed on
www.datanumeric.com/dravidian/page 001/

.....Discovery of Dravidian as the common source of Indo-European identity.

■ EDUCATION

This is still an unhappy area of India's Five Year Plans. Roughly 70% attend school between 6–11 with difficulties of monitoring this statistic despite compulsory education ideals mooted 50 years ago. Admittedly the new Indian government inherited a system of 14% average literacy and a budget which had spent *only* one percent of national income on education. That was to change with **Article 45, Indian Constitution** to provide universal elementary education... or so it was hoped. Yet well-known writer, H D Shourie in **The Times of India** (February 8, 1999) lamented the stark fact that India '**will enter the next millennium as the world's largest illiterate nation. Half of our total population** of more than 100 crore **is illiterate.**' What a contrast from the widespread village literacy documented for pre-British India by **Dharampal's The Beautiful Tree** (Other India Press, Mapusa, 1996).

However, the 2001 census figrures show there is improvement in that only under one third, approximately 302 million, are classified so.

The incredible statistic is given of those children in the age group 6–10 years who do **not** attend primary school = **35 million or more.**

Not only statistics are used to scourge all central governments for neglect of the education sphere—but **local indifferences, caste and class are to blame**, for the 'ramshackle' physical conditions of village schools—'crumbling, walls, leaking roofs, malnourished children...'. Having visited many of them the length and breadth of the country I grieve for dedicated teachers. I have encountered heroic men and women (impoverished by their poorly paid calling, brahmin and dalit alike) and their eager, open-faced pupils working in block-development villages still neglected by the distant state capital which channels both federal as well as state funding into education. Such meticulous tidiness with dirt playground swept clean each morning by the village kids as a learning of **seva** (the Gandhi-inspired teacher initiating that **sense of service** to these village seven-year-olds). Imagine our own spoilt children, who take luxurious standards of educational facilities for granted, being asked to do the same!

Other strong feelings are expressed about:
- Pupils not encouraged, **on the whole,** to think freely for themselves. Parrot repetition of teacher still exists because of the inbuilt cultural aptitude for learning by rote.
- Unruly behaviour of students if exams at college level become too difficult
- The great men of India at the beginning of this century, Gokhale, Tilak, Gandhi had all expressed a passion **for meaningful education which would be relevant for the needs of villagers**, a counterbalance to a bookish education instituted by British rule the aim of which was to train administrators, functionaries, clerks etc, for the Raj. In latter decades concern for basic education seems to have become invisible. India's great reformers could well wonder what has occurred in motivation recently.
- Present financing may have proportionately increased but when one considers the scale of the needs and demands—**the proportion of under 25- year olds being over 50% of the total population**—the mind boggles at how much of the budget **needs** to be spent on education—primary, secondary, tertiary and most important, technical colleges. The government faces daunting challenges with 700 million people over 35 years.

To its credit India has the third largest system of higher education in the world and over 15,000 international students also in 219 universities. The Indian Institutes of Technology have been praised (**Fortune Magazine**, May 29, 2000) for the excellence of their training. Particular universities likewise turn out gifted students capable of brilliant ideas, sophisticated concepts outstripping many student levels in the USA, UK and Australia. Clearly, although there are continual complaints of unimaginative and outmoded management methods and decrepit equipment, this is where the financing of education has been concentrated. There is no lack of graduate talent emerging into the international arena displaying:
- a clear scientific bent and mathematical prowess in mastering philosophically abstruse concepts—no surprise! (see **ZERO**).
- oral retention skills which must surely be now absorbed into genetic chemistry. The Indian brain has been conditioned for at least 5,000 years to transmit orally inconceivable tracts of poetic epics, storytelling parables, aphorisms, legal systems, the principles of aesthetics. All these intellectually demanding areas of human activity have been passed on by the strenuous disciplines of accurate word-of-mouth relay since far-distant antiquity!

The real concern expressed in my own travels meeting with a younger generation, who are testing the waters of a global village economy, is that its education was, ironically, too Westernised. **Modernity is not necessarily Westernization** as is stressed several times in other sections. Amongst the more thoughtful there is a growing desire to return to fundamentals of their own cultural tradition as they seem to become more appropriate to the unfolding scientific attitudes emerging among Western physicists and biochemists.

It is 30 years since **Richard Lannoy** highlighted this crucial quality in Indian cultural gifts so often unrecognised by those in administrative positions where power and decision-making are crucial and still heavily loaded with the influence of Western education based on national, linear 'factual accumulation', 'material' rather than 'spiritual'... and that does not mean 'religious', a subtle but serious distinction. It is all very ironic that when Western methods of learning are radically changing and shifting to what India's tradional learning processes knew from the very beginnings—the **gurukul**, the **music gharana**, the **forest hermitage ashram** or the **Buddhist cell** and university—all face to face in a holistic framework of **self-discovery** via 'net-surfing' motivation to assemble facts in a way relevant to the individual **shishya** (pupil, seeker) then true education occurred. Now India's system remains frozen in traditional Western systems. It is amazing that 35 years ago when his book **The Speaking Tree** (OUP, London, 1971) was published, Lannoy had the sensitivity as well as the intuition to foresee the West's arrival at the same

E

point but by mechanistic technology, the modern guru–the computer screen. That face to face encounter probing through a 'window' into the universe, the www of exploding knowledge! Maybe Indians in their lifetime will extract themselves from the inbuilt cultural ethnicity of American Microsoft information (so globally pervasive which a thoughtful Punjabi friend annoyed at its programme assault on the English language and spelling, attacked–I pinched myself that I am the Anglo-Saxon listening to her diatribe! She felt its computer influence 'was the slow drip, drip of an alien American culture, Indians should be producing our own 'windows', incorporating our own unique outlook and compass bearings in the beckoning but awe-inspiring reaches of the cosmos. But will the present classroom situation allow this to happen?'

The question of priorities is enormously stressful for any Indian government. It is all too easy to sit on the sidelines in comparatively wealthy nations and criticize. Indian governments have had to face major transformation all in the space of half a century with a colonial overlay that had also to be dealt with psychologically. Europe and the Americas have had the luxury of transforming into democracies undergoing disrupting change through a process of over 200 years.

That being said overhaul of rural education where professional people (who demand good schools) do not live, is, apart from real poverty, India's most urgent claim to attention.

- ### ELLORA
Late 5th–9th century CE

Cast in rock and stone, a miracle of human transformation of a mountainside in the stark western ghat range in Maharashtra, just over 200 km from Mumbai, a place of such powerful vibrations on the human spirit–a numenistic power sparked by the very wonder at the capacity of human beings to overcome all the odds in creating artistic endeavour, beauty, craftsmanship, engineering skills of the highest order when there were none of the labour-saving earthmoving equipment of today available to those artisans of nearly 1,500 years ago.

It has taken 40 years for the insight suddenly to dawn, a wiping-away of that maya of incomprehension, to understand afresh what this extraordinary artifice of the human hand, surely directed by the overwhelming vision-of-the-whole by the **architect Vishwakarma**, actually means.

Standing on top of the mountain in 1955 there were few people present. Now the Department of Tourism headcounts a million a year. The age of tourism had hardly begun and only the anvil-harsh clatter of rock cutters behind a large outcrop of granite and basalt gave any indication of human presence as we looked down on what surely should be a **wonder of the world**–a temple perfectly proportioned, **cut out** of the living rock. Mt Kailash (the adamantine core of central stability for the entire planetary existence, known also as Mt Meru) reared up from way down in the valley cut through the rock, Shiva's home where a plastic-smooth carving on the rockface deep within an overhang depicts his marriage to Parvati, as if it were a ceremony of today.

Statistics vary understandably because who knows what faced those planners, architects, stonemasons, labourers, carvers as they considered the intimidating rock face. But at least **400,000 tons** of rock, earth, rubble are said to have been cut out to create this extraordinary concentration of artistic expression.

Then, the scale, the immensity, the aloneness on the mountainside, the majesty of the sculpted figures fitfully lit by sudden splashes of sunlight dancing in the overhanging galleries, and natural caves that exist even today along the formidable escarpment quite blew the breath away.

But, now at a distance the wonder of another process occupies thought–a sociology could be written no matter how politically incorrect in affirmation of caste which made possible this extraordinary coming together of three of India's major streams of thought and faith–the Hindu way of life, Buddhists and Jain monks and teachers all to inhabit this strange abode where already there had been a 700-year-tradition of Buddhist retreat.

In the early centuries of Buddhist ascendancy in pre-Christian times places of learning, **viharas** or **monasteries**, had been established presumably in the readymade shelters of caves cool in the blast of summer heat, sheltered in the monsoonal storms which the very mountains created as they faced the trade winds out of the Arabian Sea. Interdependence of caste made this possible.

Hindu inspiration, social movement, saintly activity initiating reforms were emerging in the groundswell of the bhakti movement gathering force in south India especially during the ebullient, abundantly creative Sangam age of Tamil resurgence, so stirring another expressive mix (refer back to **ALVAR** and **BHAKTI**).

A complex interaction between spiritual, social, creative arts at a critical mass was about to explode.
4th–2nd c BCE

Similar to a previous **Golden Age of Chandragupta I** and his grandson–Emperor Ashoka–when much of the upper half of India was unified and prosperous, so now the wheel is turning into another creative period.

c 320–335 CE 606–647 CE

The **Gupta Empire of Chandragupta II** and his descendants inspired the materialization into plastic form of the by now established Hindu Pantheon of deities and their symbolic meanings; **Emperor Harsha** had unified the northern territories once again bringing peace amongst constantly quarrelling petty kingdoms. **The Huns** had swept in two invasive waves through the northwest into **Rajasthan** and remained to arouse Rajputs to a new awareness of cultural identity (see **MAGADHA**...).

Most important of all for the explosion of cultural activity along these bleak hills and cliffs–such an unlikely environment even today—**Chalukya and Rashtrakuta dynasties** in the Deccan just to the south established periods of settled rule (refer to **SOUTH INDIAN KINGDOMS**).

Suddenly all the forces were running in harmony.

◆ A dynamic and explosive devotional force of **Shaivite and Vaishnavite** saints primed by **brahminical disciplines**, and bodies of teachers, gurus, visionaries, already structured to write it all down to retain it as a force in the cultural memory (it has to be kept in mind that not all the ascetic devotees and inspiring thinkers came from the uppermost elite of Hindu castes—many bhaktas were of lowly origins).

◆ Add to this social geological strata a now stable segment of **kshatriya rulers** who bring stability and a flow of commerce not disrupted by civil wars or other social upheavals.

◆ Ellora and its surrounds and passes near Aurangabad lie on **major trading crossroads** through the Ghats. The Godavari river to the south apparently when in flood transported boats filled with goods right into the interior. In fact Palaeolithic finds in recent explorations indicate that early humans occupied this escarpment line 10,000 years ago. Further south **Bhaja** and **Karla** evidence centuries of Buddhist teaching high up in rock cut caves.

Perhaps then from the very beginning exchange of goods and the process of oiling the wheels of society had left residual knowledge in the area. Certainly at this point **the vaisya/bania merchants, traders, moneylenders** buttressed by the solid strength of rulers and their patronage then provided the sustenance for the fourth layer.

◆ The harnessing of an enormous manual workforce of **sudras** was made possible—the very breakers of rocks still at it hammering with rods and on anvils firing iron implements, as we stood looking down on the Kailash Temple—that cannot have changed in the past 1,500 years.

Thus an interrelationship and interaction of all four classes made possible this herculean task of four hundred years' activity to create Shiva's Abode—his lingam at the apex of an inner triangle where majestic female deities Ganga and Jumna stand guard, half stepping out from the rock face. Voluptuous **sapta matrikas**, the seven matriarchs sit in line guarding colonnaded walkways of hefty proportions, full-lipped, full-hipped female guardians, tree nymphs, shakti-feminine deities of such voluptuous proportions with towering headresses, like those enchanting spirits gracing the walls of Ajanta to the north east must surely have been a sore temptation in the midnight sleeping fantasies of so many ascetic Jain and Buddhist monks. **And everywhere the consummate engineering skills of those sixth-century architects and stonemasons.**

Questions and Conclusions

The question foremost in every visitor's mind as one stands gaping **under** the overhang (all the weight of rock above) decorated with superbly carved lotus floreate ceiling embossment of such perfect proportions—how were the proportions maintained, artisans suspended upside down chipping away at such obdurate unrelenting rock?

And how did those excavators and technicians bereft of all modern equipment know with such surety as they created this sanctified space envisioned in the early Vedic Shastras where exact measurement, geometrical alignments, an ordered universe was to be **cut out,** that the force of gravity would not cave it all in with the immensity of weight overhead? This is not free-standing form created in space unlike the marvels of Pyramid and Stonehenge engineering skills.

This is **space created into solid resistant form**. Sculpture emerges rounded and handworked 1,500 years before modern sculptors onwards used the same techniques (Rodin for one) to contrast 'living' stone/marble against fashioned form as an artistic device to heighten the aesthetic.

Shiva and Parvati relax in harmonious company sitting beside each other in almost languid regality. Beneath a remarkable artistic tour de force, some unknown stonemason has chiselled ten arms of the disturbing force of Ravana as though they are ocean breakers curling in to shore, energy and motion in rock-hard stone as though the sculptor was dealing in clay. One can feel the mountain trembling—but earthquakes apart, perhaps it will be standing another 1500 years from now incarnating that struggle 'which has not ended' of the demonic forces which ever threaten benign stability—as **Mulk Raj Anand** writes in an **Afterword** to a superb book **Ellora: Concept and Style,** by Carmel Berkson (IGNCA, Shakti Malik Abhinav Publications, 1992) that should be read by all who travel to wonder at the marvels of Ellora, singular in accomplishment in the whole of India.

■ **EPICS** (n. *Greek*)
Epikus = Epos, a word

Epics are different from parables or fairy stories. They are of **heroic proportions** and certainly the **MAHABHARATA** (great-India) fits the bill being the **longest single poem in the world**, compiled over a thousand years and known certainly in the oral tradition a millennia before the Christian era, being passed on from generation to generation, **all 100,000 two-lined stanzas long**. It is described as being seven times as long as the Iliad and the Odyssey put together. These datings are now under review again pushing the existence of these epics further back in time, circa 3800 BCE.

The **RAMAYANA** likewise, **24,000 stanzas of text**, is the earlier of the two but was eventually incorporated as Book 3 in the MahaB when **VALMIKI** (like **Vyas** in the bigger epic) compiled the vast unwieldy mass of legend-history-parable-lyric poem, statecraft manual, inventory of weapons in the MahaB and scripture in the Bhagavad Gita (the 6th 'book')—all to be written down in pre-Christian times.

To the learned, Ramayana is termed **adikavya: adi** = original, or first; **kavya** 'the pre-eminent poetical work in Indian literature to differentiate it from the MahaB which is **ITIHASA**—an historical account.
1574

Later, **Tulsidas** compiled the Ramayana into the vernacular popular language, closer to ordinary people's comprehension

E

rather than recited by educated priestly brahmins in high Sanskrit. This book, available in English translation, is called **The Holy Lake of the Acts of Rama** (ed. W B P Hill, OUP, London, 1952). It is written in the most lyrical and Shakespearean style language compared with the more masculine ambience of the greater work. In the Ramayana are wonderful passages of poetic observation of animal characteristics especially as the monkey armies manoeuvre to support Rama and rescue Sita from the clutches of wrongdoers.

Both epics combine to inspire countless subsidiary tales, drama, dance, ballets, modern tableaux, recitations in continuous 3-day cycles of devotional worship in the case of the Ramayana. This is undertaken either collectively, or privately in the home, most often initiated by the women of the household who have maintained the traditions over centuries. (Many Indian men who may become modernised, go to further training overseas, take to meat-eating, even beef, forgetting the rituals, are 'hauled back' in, to quote an Indian wife, when they return to India).

Indeed, these two epics carry the ethical value systems, and codes in more easily acceptable form to the populace than do the abstruse philosophies of the Upanishads or the speculative hymns of the ancient vedic deities now no longer part of the Hindu **PANTHEON** in which the 'qualities' of various aspects of godhead = divinity are 'materialized' into concrete form and symbol, concentrating the viewer's mind on a particular aspect of that divine sense.

All these multiplicity of messages gathered around particular characters carry the concept of **DHARMA** and ethical behaviour, such as:
- the **dharma** of a ruler
- human rights code
- the valour of a warrior and right behaviour (useful for armies to read today. For instance, having subjugated a rival kingdom a magnanimous ruler returned the land; the point of status had been made.)
- women's place in society and honour of women
- how a devoted wife should behave. Modern Indian feminism is putting this patriarchal view which suffuses the epics under microscopic examination as there appears to be no equivalent rules spelled out for husbands, or fasts undertaken for the welfare of the mother and wife **by the menfolk of the family!**
- citizens' duties, etc.

At a more subtle level the **Ramayana** has become the **Language of the Home**. The ideal archetype is spelled out and set before live audiences at festival time around October such as **Dussehra**—the autumnal ten days preceding Diwali when Rama returns to **Ayodhya**. Each major suburb in the big cities organises street theatre at Shakespearean level with few props to enact out the story. Most Hindus are encouraged therefore in everything they see and hear around them, now reinforced by another major oral tradition of television, to aspire to be like Rama, or Sita:
- the ideal husband/wife/son/daughter
- the ideal ruler
- the ideal companion, friend, brother

- the embodiment of virtue, truthfulness, bravery, caring

The sheer goodness of Rama is emphasised. Despite all provocation never an angry word is spoken. Whether Rama was a real historical king or not, he has now been elevated into the Pantheon, totally deified, so much so that modern Indians when they die are carried to the burning ghats to the sound of this chant:

Rama Nama Satya Hai
Rama name truth is

He (pronounced Hay) **Raam** was the last utterance of Gandhi as he sank to the ground, assassinated. These words are on the marble platform at his **samadhi**, by the Jumna in Delhi: हे राम

Scholarly commentators outside of India have been suitably impressed also with the scale of the monumental works. Professor Arthur Basham referred to them as **encyclopaedias of early Hinduism**. They are in fact regarded virtually as **'the 5th Veda'** (see **VEDAS**), the oldest literary work of mankind, a continuous oral tradition for 50 centuries.

If India overwhelms at times, so does its literature! The **epics** became vehicles in fact—not being written down for nearly a thousand years—to all manner of ancillary accretions to the main storyline, as an instrument to concentrate:

A The **composite mind of society on fundamental ethics**
B **Certain fundamental truths**, these being
- **SVA DHARMA**: the voice of conscience and individual (**sva**) morality (dharma)
- **JATI DHARMA**: the social conscience (as defined throughout the myriad caste differentiations)

Presenting the Mahabharata

Why is it then, that well over a thousand people would sit throughout a **nine-hour performance all through the night** until the first soft-brushed light of a pale blue dawn crept over a high quarry face stirring the eucalyptus trees with a light wind as **Yudhishthira**, King of Dharma, climbs the ancient Devonian rock face, stave in hand and a mongrel dog at his feet (very significant). There in the dawn silhouette he reaches **swarga** = heaven. All is well with the world... and this despite literature embedded so deeply in Indian value systems alien to many people's cultures outside of India, distant also in time and space. This in fact is Australian landscape, production by Peter Brook.

This was **Perth**, Western Australia. And why should people subject themselves to scaffolded seating, a buffet Indian curry meal served up appropriately by Community Aid Abroad at midnight on rickety tables under the twinkling stars? One could almost imagine being in an Indian bazaar, and then the less hardy souls creeping off to take a nap, Indian style in rugs on the unrelenting rubble ground at the edge of the quarry—to revive in time for the satisfying conclusion, there being no tragedy in the Greek sense of nemesis as discussed elsewhere. **Samsara** (transmigration of souls) allows a balance to be taken, another chance to redeem the faults and failures with the grace of Krishna's blessing if the heart is in the right place.

The question amplifies. Epics are universal in their appeal, relating

heroic events
in an **elevated style**
of some **literary elegance**
speaking of **universal themes**
pitched at **the popular common denominator**.
This is one definition of an epic.

But why then did not Jean-Paul Carrière of the Centre International de Crèations Theatres in France, and Peter Brook, noted for superb theatre productions transcreating across cultures, turn to gathering more of the Western tradition, even if pre-Christian? Why not turn to the **Iliad** or the **Odyssey**?

And why in **Bali** at the great ceremony held annually in the dry season, July–August, to honour the ancestors at **Galungan** each of the 18 **parvas** or books of the MahaB are enacted year by year in huge presentations in a football stadium, the atmosphere reminiscent of a Sydney football match with family throngs sitting through four hours with no interval. Riveted in attention even amongst little children, babies perched on grandmothers' legs, young men and aged, the throng of Indonesians, many Muslim or Chinese Christian were all lost in the elongated battle of Kurukshetra (traditional chariots combined with modern ballet), lithe young Balinese girls swaying in red and black costumes representing a visual forest fire, all dominated by the enormous split-gate architecture of a Balinese temple structure, itself symbolic of the gateway into the sanctuary of the divine beyond the reach of tribulation and human frailty? A big question mark.

Is it that India has found the resilience, flexibility, absorptive powers to allow a continuum of culture through time and space, not fracturing the cultural geology into separated layers? Is it that the **PALIMPSEST** works? The power of this epic is its capability like much of the dynamic images of Indian sculpture, such as the **NATARAJA**, to replenish itself in each age, its characters and message universal and ageless, cutting a gigantic swathe through history to become as relevant in modernity as in its own ancient era.

Unlike the Greek epics of the **Iliad** and the **Odyssey** which no longer vibrate in our day to day lives and which were fractured by Christian theological development and modern scientific theory, the **Mahabharata**, evolving through space and time in a civilization which even today conveys its messages through the resilient force of an oral culture to at least 75% of India's huge population, its village peoples, has accumulated like a glacier the rocky substances of innumerable regional histories and philosophies, mythological poetic truths, the wisdom of ages ... now with new scientific theories based on satellite photography, computation of genealogies, reassessment of climatic changes and geological evidence which has come to light the theory of an actual conflict and the emergence of verbal recounting has been pushed back to approximately 3000 BCE.

AND SO THE STORY BEGINS, a struggle for co-existence and the rightful sharing of ancestral land rights between two cousin clans—the **Kauravas** and **Pandavas**.

Traditionally the author is the sage **VYASA**, a protagonist himself in the drama; the string of tales within tales however also suggest he is **Vyasa, a compiler**.

1. These cousins, sons of Dhritarashtra **born** blind—a symbol of his own acts of short-sightedness throughout the epic and swayed like a similar like-minded King Lear) and his brother Pandu's sons in parable after parable, personify in their own compulsive conflicts the same foolish egos that rage within the spirit of mankind even today. **Arjuna,** one of the Pandava brothers (Hinduism's knight-in-shining-armour, his very name in Sanskrit meaning 'resplendent' or 'shining'), represents the forces of good in humanity—heroism, responsibility, integrity; and yet hesitancy to act in the face of bullying evil from the larger-than-life eldest Kaurava brothers—**Duryodhana** meaning 'hard to conquer' and **Duh-shasana** = 'hard to rule' who assaults and degrades **Draupadi**, the Pandava wife by trying to wrench off her sari.

2. Through foolishness, pride, selfishness, limited vision, the seductions of power and many more smallscale sins to which humanity is susceptible—universal messages are conveyed through the inspirational condensation of Carrière and Brook, with a cast of many nationalities, a lean Senegalese playing **Drona**, guru of the martial arts to both rival cousin clans despite being a brahmin.

3. Through mismanagement in dividing the kingdom a whole train of events is set in motion however, in which caste dharma, individual free will, personal goodness in the face of all provocation, treachery, unfair distribution of land and subsequent jealousies become the same entangled network of human incapacities we can easily recognise as besetting our own contemporary world.

4. Chicanery of politicians, aborigines bereft of 'their land', international power struggles, ethnic balkanisation that in the long view of history becomes meaningless, are all there, interlocked and reiterated to make an indelible impression—in all of its 18 books! Indeed the other major epic, the Ramayana, earlier in its telling became absorbed into the early 'books' of the later epic as its unbridled enlargement spread like a floodtide through Indian literature.

The Ramayana approx. 3100 BCE
In the minds of the Hindu people the **Ramayana** is ageless, belonging to an oral tradition as steadfast as that of aboriginal legend. The great Flood of the Bible is recalled and remembered in the early traditions of Vishnu, the Lord of Preservation in the Hindu Trinity of **Brahma, Vishnu** and **Shiva**. **Rama** is the **seventh avatar** or **reincarnation of Vishnu** who manifests the benign presence of creative energy in the universe when evil appears to be in the ascendancy.

The Ramayana was memorised in Sanskrit quatrains, and passed down from father to son, mother to daughter, guru teacher to devotee from at least the ninth century BCE. **Valmiki** compiling it half a millennium later around the period of Ashoka's reign undertook it in a typically Indian way. Seating himself, it is recounted, with his face towards the East and sipping water according to the rule he applied himself to the yogic powers through which he then clearly saw before him **Rama, Lakshmana** his brother and **Sita**, his wife.

> *He beheld by yoga power all that had come to pass, and all that was to be, in the future like a nelli fruit* on the palm of his hand ...Thus he came to set this fabulous epic down.*

The hero, Rama, is the embodiment of goodness. The son of the elderly king of Ayodhya near Benares, the world's most ancient 'living' city (now given its proper name **Varanasi**), and ill-starred in a classic case of stepmother jealousy; his regal father in those far-off times allowed even as a Hindu to take three wives. The story unfolds about Rama's exile from the kingdom he is to inherit from his ageing, abdicating father. The jealous machinations of the stepmother **Kaikeyi** force his father against him. Her ulterior motive is to see her own son **Bharata** ascend the **rajgaddi** or throne. Bharata refuses and places Rama's sandals there, but Rama has already been exiled; Sita his wife, and Lakshman his brother go with him.

Rama has been chosen by Sita as her husband in a contest from amongst all the royal suitors who come to seek her hand, a contest of superior moral as well as physical strength to lift the phenomenally heavy bow of Shiva. Only Rama was able to achieve this feat for he is really the Divine Presence of **Vishnu**.

Like a Greek tragedy Rama, Sita and Lakshman submit to the 14-year-exile commencing in a hermitage in the forest. Through many trials, sorrows and dramas unfold around a large theme, depicting the universal conflict between the forces of good and evil. Rama and Sita represent all the forces of the benign. Ravana plots to abduct Sita while Rama and Lakshman are away hunting in the forest.

Disguised as a mendicant, he persuades her into stepping beyond the magic circle of her protection. She is pounced upon and overcome, whisked off and imprisoned in **Lanka** where Ravana rules. She spurns all attempts by Ravana to possess her although he does refrain from physical assault. **Ravana** with his 10 heads and 20 arms flailing around with as many weapons is a symbol of the darker side of humanity—the sins of pride, arrogance, lack of compassion and sheer physical brutality in which the world abounds.

Finally, after many strange adventures, some involving the animal world, the wise Hanuman in an advance foray discovers where Sita is kept captive by **Ravana. Hanuman** is symbolised in the form of a monkey because these creatures are regarded as full of wisdom born of their cunning agility and ability therefore to overcome all obstacles that humanity faces on the long road to perfection. (Perhaps that is why that fertile Indian mind depicts Hanuman also as the patron saint of wrestlers!)

An army of monkeys comes to Rama's aid making a bridge. Hanuman leads Rama to Ravana's fortress across the boulder-strewn waters between south India and Lanka. After fierce battle Rama finally kills Ravana with a flaming arrow, and retrieves

---

* A yellow star-shaped fruit of transparency so its contents can be seen.

Sita. Reunited, they journey back the several thousand miles to their kingdom in the north, flying in their aerial car, **pushpak vimana** probably the first 'spaceship' in human art capacious enough to contain a city palace. **Good has finally triumphed**.

Grandmothers especially recount the Ramayana to their grandchildren as examples of the ideal husband and wife, holding up Rama and Sita—in fact the ideal archetypes of Indian manhood and womanhood.

RAVANA is an especially intriguing character often referred to as the Demon King, he is more in the frame of Milton's **Satan** in **Paradise Lost**, a **fallen angel** full of overbearing pride and arrogance. Hubris is his undoing. In paintings he occasionally is depicted with a donkey's head embedded in the crown of his own ten heads—an insignia of universal resonance. In English there is a view of the stupidity of a donkey—'as stupid as an ass'. So is Ravana, failing to understand where the obstinacy of his pride will take him.

The festival of **Dussehra** (which lasts 10 days = Hindi *das*) especially colourful in New Delhi and Mysore, celebrates the final triumph of Rama over the vaunting strength of evil, personified by Ravana. At the festival his gigantic effigy goes up in flames, fired by Rama's own arrow. Why the ambivalence?

◆ By penance—devotion to Brahma, the creative principle, Ravana had received a **BOON** that made him invincible against gods and men. With his learning (on his father's side he was a brahmin) and the superhuman power given him by his practise of austerities or **tapas**, he became, quite literally, big headed! **Four** of his heads are said to recall that he knew the **four Vedic books** by heart as a good brahmin would and **the other six** that he carried in his head all the wisdom of the **six philosophies** of India (see **DARSHAN**). His so-called immunity to death at the hands of human beings due to the boon granted gave him a false sense of his invincibility not realising that **Rama was a transitional being (in human form but elevated to more than human)**, having then the divine capacity to kill him.

◆ Throughout the telling of the redemptive tale and a close reading of a well-translated version (the Princeton Volumes—five now completed—slowly being produced from impeccable scholarship and assiduous care for the right translation of each Sanskrit word) Ravana presents a great deal of ambiguity as a personality. Sometimes in reading the nuances of the text, just as with Milton's treatment of Satan, you cannot help feeling sorry for this charismatic figure and those who surround him. Not all are evil and Lanka is shown to have a high degree of civil life. Like humans, he is a flawed personality yet as an Indian critic has pointed out 'in his own twisted way, honourable'.

Conclusion

These two epics come towards the end of the great explosion of thinking as an admixture of India's earliest peoples, began to formulate a composite culture. The building blocks:

the **Vedas**—hymns

the **Upanishads**—philosophical discourses

the **Puranas**—old stories and parables of less heroic proportions

Itihasas—'thus it was', that is **history**

Epics are not the **revealed wisdom** (*sruti*) of the race as passed on by the intuitive insights of the rishis in the **Vedas** but the **heard wisdom of human derivation** (*smrti*). In fact, both vast storehouses of the collective wisdom of the Indian race have been called **redemptive histories** because they deal not just with historical battles somewhere at the beginnings of India's unrecorded history but with moral struggles deep within the spirit of humankind—of integrity, moral courage, human nobility and wisdom, steadfastness in the face of threat, persistence to hold on when all seems lost, as well as dealing with creation and how it came about, dynasties of gods and genealogies of rulers, biographies of saints, adventures of human archetypes, warfare and states, craft manuals and weighty matters of human ethics—**dharma, dharma, dharma**.

Dr **Irawati Karve**, in her commentary **Yuganta, End of an Epoch** (Dishbmukh, Poona, 1969) and mentioned early in Bhagavad Gita section states that basically the Mahabharata is an account of the quarrel between cousins for the possession of **property** and **status**, and struggles for coexistence between the many individual hereditary kingdoms and feudal patriarchies, each somewhat isolated by jungle and inhospitable terrain in those far-off times. This is a theme universal to patrilineal societies and the shifting power plays while other weaker societies were being dispossessed—a theme as familiar today in the Balkans, or Africa, the Soviet Union or Aboriginal society in Australia asserting the right to retrieve land.

Note for overwhelmed travellers!

If trying to cope with the complexities of India alone is enough without taking on further dimensions at the literary level, turn to the pavement bookseller and buy a few copies of the comic books devoted to the Epics produced by **Amar Chitra Katha** (India Book House). They are well illustrated and very insightful in the way Indian children imbibe the fanciful goings-on in an atmosphere of suspended rationality, a world we hardly know where the division between the epics of the Greek gods, Hebrew theology, the bhakti of Christ's message and scientific wisdom could never amalgamate in such manner but remains compartmentalised even to this day.

And for good measure the Japanese are producing remarkably faithful CD Roms of the same.

■ EVIL EYE

Drishti — *Sanskrit* — **vision, seeing**

The 'eyes' have it! At one end of the cultural spectrum is the **ajna chakra**, the eye of wisdom situated in between the eyebrows—the place of understanding that blazes on Shiva's forehead when he emerges from deep meditation, so powerful it can destroy those in its flashing power. All cultures in Asia from Egypt to Sumeria subscribe to the concept of a 'third eye' that awakens inner vision—as also the obverse power of the Evil Eye.

Even the 15th century Pope Innocent VIII warned his Catholic flock to beware **Malleus-Maleficarum**—the malevolent devil from entering the human eyes and turning them into weapons against others.

Nazar in Urdu and **tohtkaa tohnaa** in Hindi commonly used in the north is a belief more prevalent than one might think no matter how seemingly modern Indians of whatever background and faith may appear to be. That someone may cast **'the eye of envy'** (*nazar* = eyesight) upon them or that they must be wary of the next step taken in their lives can be more than a passing fancy.

Extreme orthodoxy leads to consulting the family pandit or astrologer before undertaking a major journey such as an international flight, or even starting a project. It was well known that some of India's leading politicians including the late Morarji Desai and Mrs Gandhi, both prime ministers, consulted their own pandits.

They are not alone in this universe of chance in hedging their bets! Even in Euro/American cultures we are all a little bit wary of talking glowingly about a future event as though it were already successfully accomplished. Io talk about winning a competition before you have is asking for trouble.

- ◆ 'Don't count your chickens...'
- ◆ You are **'tempting fate'**
- ◆ You had better **'touch wood'** or murmur... God willing, often condensed to DV = *deus vult* (Latin) = **God wills it** (which interestingly was the Crusaders cry on going into battle in Palestine fighting Islam).

Throughout the south on small homesteads or at the bare, unlovely grey of grandiose building sites, will be the upturned pots upon which is painted a demonic face or distinctive scarecrow hung in baggy defiance of the evil eye.

How much more threatening must be the possibility of **nazar lagna**—'the evil eye put on you' in a less temperate climate where the odds are stacked higher. Physical hazards, disease, and in the case of India the additional burden of belief that in a previous reincarnation some earlier sin may still be working its way though the system is very prevalent and may unexpectedly put tripwires across your footpath.

Miserly wealth is also asking for trouble. Midas in India would not get very far unless at the same time he got rid of some of his wealth in giving **daan**, becoming a philanthropist. Good looks especially in young children who have not built up immunity are also not to be commented upon otherwise an envious eye may send the glance of disease, misfortune, a run of bad luck.

Children often wear a black thread around their necks in the early years to give the appearance of imperfection. Some married people feel there are jealous relatives around who don't want them to have a baby. This is when **tohtkaa/tohnaa** is an active force, a very real apprehension.

Amongst Muslim friends, and not only in India I have noticed black and green threaded amulets worn on the arm as **imaan zamaan** (spiritual protection) against inauspicious forces.

Some people within the family are born with the evil eye. There is the uneasy sense among relatives that whenever that person is nearby something untoward happens. Unfortunately the archetypal spinster aunt or the widow is regarded as this harbinger of misfortune.

If someone especially a young member of the family has come under sustained glances from this person a ceremony involving red chillies occurs—five are usual, taken and wiped over the person upon whom **nazar** has often been cast, and then thrown in an open fire. If they burn quietly then evil has been absorbed but if they crackle and spit then other remedial action must be taken. A friend spoke of her early childhood in a very educated household. A maiden aunt had eyes that always seemed to focus on her and 'pierce' her. She used to keep well away in mortal fear of nazar coming her way.

And another, a very sophisticated young woman who had defied custom and married across culture into a totally different part of India, was resident overseas with her husband for years—both in typically Western-style careers. She had a baby son—even more susceptible to evil envy than a first daughter.

Knowing that many of her Western friends would compliment both her and the baby, she placed a black tika mark behind his ear as a smudge, symbolic 'imperfection,' so that **nazar** would glance off such endearing features and all the inevitable compliments made by unknowing Western friends.

You may also, when encountering a group of traditional friends, hear an occasional crack and wonder what happened. My serene Maharashtrian friend who fasted on Tuesdays (causing me considerable anxiety early on in my days in Delhi when I hardly knew any of the nuances of custom and ritual which might inhibit one's natural hospitality) once placed her clenched fists at my head on my birthday and cracked her knuckles. Don't ask how it is done. All I know is that the evil had been taken away, off my head for the coming year, and she had cracked that evil for good measure.

'You will be in my prayers.'

She gave an ample smile and embraced me to her equally ample bosom!

◼ FAQIR

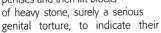

is a word now seldom used in India but still a term in the West. It is a misnomer. A faqir is a Muslim ascetic whereas the so-called holymen seen around doing penances are the Hindu sadhus. They undergo penances in extremes as the legendary faqir did on a bed of nails. Some tie cloth bands to their penises and then lift blocks of heavy stone, surely a serious genital torture, to indicate their indifference to pain—and implied sexual desire! A good many Indians especially of the middle class are sceptical about this declaration, as well as about those other sadhus who wear metal chains around the waist attached to metal-cupped chastity belts.

Others similarly attired may stand for as long as six years. One such resting his arms on a cushioned swing quite prominently placed for show at a religious mela at Varanasi, eyed me with considerable interest until our Indian companion muttered some Punjabi imprecations at him.

Others seem to appear out of the shadows at **Shivaratri**, again experienced with Indian friends at Varanasi. Matted hair, painted faces, strange waxed moustaches coloured white with **VIBHUTI**, elongated penises deliberately pulled and extended over the years in tantric rituals, they declare they are the manifestation of the great Lord of Destruction, Shiva whose birthday in February it is. Others think not.

Indeed, the Bhagavad Gita excoriates them. Buddha found their penances led into a blind alley. Gandhi ignored them. In no other nation do such extreme manifestations of spiritual discipline appear but flagellation in Christian ceremonies (in the Philippines, for instance, on Good Friday) and with Shi'a Muslims at Muhurram, certainly exists.

Ever known for their eccentricities, the English provide Thomas Coryate, friend of Ben Johnson. In 1617 he walked 2,700 miles to see Emperor Jehangir in his court then at Ajmer... and he was dressed as a faqir!

◼ FASTING (n. *Sanskrit* = *vrata. Hindi* = *upvas*)

is as old as India itself, part of that matrix of the Indian mind which exercises disciplines such as **penance, atonement, a stringent control of behaviour = tapasya**. (see **ASCETICISM, VOWS, BOONS, PILGRIMAGE**)

Deep within **dharma** is the commitment to **self-discipline** as the only way to overcome all the negative and disruptive forces in creation. **Penance** is used with qualification throughout the text. It does not carry the inherent overtones of Christian sin—doing penance to atone—rather in the Hindu ethical system penance is undertaken to strengthen character to curb ego. Some individuals do go to the extreme in self-abnegation, but **both** Krishna and Buddha decried such flamboyance and emphasised the inner heart.

◆ To bolster that effort a whole structure of rituals and legendary examples related to the activities of Deities—also in trouble overcoming the forces of evil—are there to make fasting a natural part of daily life. It is not a ritual set aside and brought in on special occasions.

◆ **It is just there, especially for women**. There are as many special **vratas** as there are weeks in the year. Some commemorate birthdays of the major deities of the Pantheon, some are regional, some acknowledge rites of passage, some are on **purnima** (full moon), others are for specific days.

◆ Even if Hindu, Buddhist, Jain, Sikh do not abide by these particular fasts, the two **ekadasi** will be kept, the 11th day of the lunar fortnight, twice a month (**das** =10, **ek** =1). They are especially auspicious, marking the halfway between the waxing and waning of the moon and the commencement of the bright **paksha** again after 29½ days.

◆ It is as though self-abnegation, foregoing the pleasures of food (and even drink) was a compact with benign forces that all may go well not only for one's own personal or family welfare; it is also the perennial paradox of Indian thinking, the law of opposites that, by foregoing, one adds energy to the sum totality of these forces to overcome that which is forever trying to undermine that energy.

◆ This concept is not of course the prerogative of Indian attitudes and spiritual fervour alone. Even in Western Christianity there are those especially in the Lenten period who observe fasting although even that has seemed to weaken with urbanisation and the breakdown of institutional church influences. In my own childhood it was quite normal to vie with each other as to what enjoyable thing would be given up for Lent. At school we would, especially if sweets were desired, keep each other to the vow—a very Indian word. Indian Christians it goes without saying are far more assiduous in marking this and other fasts than Western believers.

◆ **Islamic custom** has instituted the most regular and determined fast of all—that of **RAMAZAN** which again is a lunar month's abstinence, very testing to body first and then mind as the weeks go by and the Muslim observer of fast (roughly from the age of 12 upwards) becomes increasingly tired even though at the end of each day when the sun sets a good meal is taken. (This fast works backwards every following year by approximately 11 days—commencing Sept 24 to Oct 22, 2006, Sept 13 to Oct 13, 2007).

◆ Women are also more inclined to mark the fasts than their menfolk especially in the case of the northern **karva chauth** (the *char* = 4th day after the *ama(a)vas* = dark night of no moon, following Dussehra festival in October when welfare of husbands is paramount. Even deities fast! Parvati, having freely chosen Shiva in the 'free-choice' **swayamvara** wedding ceremony against her father's wishes—undertook severe penance—fasting to force his aloofness while in deep meditation. Much impressed by the strength of her austerities, supreme ascetic as he was in the form of **Bhairav**, Shiva did indeed ask her hand in marriage... after much prompting!

With great ceremony, all the women of the household dressed in whatever is their best raiment, gather around a thali, circular tray, or bowl filled with water awaiting the reflection of the moon. Once sighted, small gifts of sweets and new clothes are given to the married daughters. It is the one fast-festival when the newly-married daughter can leave her in-laws to come home and be feted.

In Britain, Sikhs and Gujarati Hindus alike appeared to commemorate it as well. If the sky was overcast they would phone friends in London or elsewhere to see if the moon had been seen—and then celebrate with special dishes and presentation of specially-grown sprouts in ten small earthen pots, all part of the ancient ritual. (One question always lodged amongst modern daughters exposed to corrupting feminist views in the West—they have however been aired in the new Indian women's magazines!—is there a fast observed by men for the welfare of their wives, without whom many men do not know what to do with themselves?)

Footnote: New Delhi evening in 1956

The American Women's Club (ever innovative and vigorous to embrace new trends so soon after Independence and promote opportunities in Indian development) was about to present its first fashion parade of Indian textiles and dress adapted for Western fashion wear—both for men and women. Dinner was to start earlier than the usual 9.30 pm traditional eating hour at official level in the Capital.

By 8.30 pm concern furrowed the brow of Fran Adams, indefatigable President of the American Club—a remarkable woman with deep empathy for Indian retrieval of its roots and cultural traditions. That was not easy when her husband held a senior appointment in the Embassy and Indian ambivalence existed about USA influence at that time, John Foster Dulles creating waves as Secretary of State in Washington, often chastising India for taking a neutral stance amid the Cold War tensions of that period.

Table after table for Indian officialdom and their guests remained empty. Was this a subtle way of getting back at America? Where was everyone? Other diplomats and European invitees were present and getting hungry!

Diplomatic calendars had been checked efficiently when choosing the date months ahead to make sure no other major event clashed with this night... no Indian festivals at a time of year cluttered with autumnal celebrations. That was a feat in itself before Pandit Nehru, in a fit of annoyance at India's lackadaisical attitude to energetic development, cut back the number of official holidays in a nation celebrating **eight major faiths**! There was a significant celebration virtually every week. That chance to take time off was cut down to official holidays roughly twice a month. There were also 50 national days to mark on the diplomatic cocktail party round.

What to do? Commence dinner for the other guests was the only recourse. It was not until dessert was being served at about 10 pm that the first eminent couples—all Indian—arrived... quite innocently unaware of the frisson that rippled amongst all of us...a sliver of a moon was riding high on a crystal clear November sky. Then and only then could the wives break fast and accompany their government-official husbands, ministerial partners and journalists. It was **karva chauth**. Best to consult a pandit next time for the fasting days!

■ **FESTIVALS**

Lannoy has fittingly referred to them as the **rhythmical oscillations** that punctuate the Indian year. India reverberates with so much colour and sound of festivals with so many books on the subject, it has seemed an unnecessary addition in this already culturally expanding universe. Throughout the text many references are made to various major rejoicings and religious celebrations. The same goes for India's unique **cuisine**.

The Indian Tourist Offices in major centres have increasingly detailed and excellent information on these national and state-wide celebrations.

■ **FILLUMS**

Going to the cinema must be the most popular form of entertainment for Indians—cheap in comparison with music or dance concerts, accessible in rural areas with mobile shamianas, a fantasy world beckoning, giving relief for a few hours from the hard slog of keeping alive and in good health. Film legend **Amitabh Bachchan**, with many recent international awards for his charismatic film career, stated at a glittering ceremony in Egypt 2001 that he was 'lucky to be part of Bollywood which **unites the whole of India in one thread'**. Such indeed is the influence of 'fillums'.

For millions it has been the **only** entertainment. Increasing mobility with the opening up of roads into villages, satellite dishes and cable TV, and a large and lucrative market in pirated videos may change this long-established format-driven 'fillum' world as new wealth spreads. Certain thriving states such as Karnataka and Maharashtra throw up new statistics showing increased purchasing power for peasant farmers. With new irrigation schemes at hand, and improving crop yields, and a burgeoning Indian industrial complex of factories making TV sets, etc. rural India in enlightened states is short-cutting the processes of development that Europe and the Americas went through... such as joining the global network—accomplished, startlingly, overnight when one considers from where the film industry has grown since the father of India's huge cinema industry, **Dhundiraj Govind Phalke**, lived to produce the first Indian feature film.

1913... and Raja Harishchandra was suitably based on the true Indian virtues of self-abnegation—**aparigraha**—extolling the monarch who gives up his family, his kingdom and personal possessions... just as Gautama Buddha and Mahavira had left their princely estates to search for enlightenment.

F

Even before this a few short films had been screened by the Lumiere brothers in Bombay's Watson Hotel in **1896**. Over one hundred years India has become the largest film-producing nation in the world, nearly **30,000 films** in over **40 languages** (the Arab world being a great market) emerging from Mumbai— (see **Theodore Baskaran, The Eye of the Serpent**, East West Book, 1996)—1,013 films churned out in 2001.

Since then however, **Bollywood** (logically it should now become Mully-wood after the re-naming of Mumbai) with all its hype has taken over and in latter decades fallen foul of over-commercialisation, criminal elements and a star system that emphasises pulchitrude before acting ability. Indian feminists declare that films have much to answer for in attitudes to women even today. Even Indian critics regard heroines as:

◆ one dimensional
◆ prepubescent virgins
◆ too love-struck for their own good

Despite the fact that most of the films run to set formulae, Indians refer to the 50s as a golden era of the art. As in much else, when **Mehboob Khan's** epic **Mother India** was made. (I was taken to its premiere in Delhi in 1957 by Pandit Ravi Shankar when Nargis was present—the glitz, glamour, crowd hysteria introduced me into a never-to-be-forgotten experience of raw crowd emotions going wild!) There was still an innocence, of a born-again India aware of its special qualities untarnished by the venality of politicians. The striving after effect with new technology replacing sincerity of storyline inside the movie house was not so prevalent either.

Themes

Great directors such as **Raj Kapoor** with 'Mera Naam Joker' and **Guru Dutt's**, 'Kagaz ke Phool', **V Shantaram** and **Bimal Roy** are recalled with nostalgia. They turned to regional literature for social themes which they blended in quite subtly with the regulation song and dance routines, the hero and heroine miraculously transported on some behind-the-scenes magic carpet to a Kashmir meadow (that was in halcyon days before 'the troubles' set in in earnest and tourists fled the valley). There they cavorted in between blossom-laden trees, with supporting

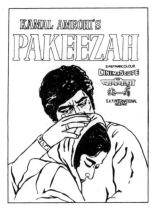

dancers to sing in high-pitched voices of unrequited love... and then the villain moved in to cast a shadow, usually combined with the wicked uncle, or a jealous mother-in-law. And there was priestly hypocrisy, untouchability, injustice, a bad woman (and now rape) thrown in for good measure.

As a good Shakespearean plot always possessed the value of light relief, a comic or a fool became the common man's jester to bring laughter to lighten the daily toil. Fortunately, as in all India's epic stories and dramas of later centuries, good overcomes evil—in the end, for that after all is the nature of the long haul, the personal search, the maintenance of Vishnu's realm of dharma, Krishna's grace enabling 'samsara' to release the individual atma. The concept of pride bringing its own downfall does not end in unmitigated disaster. **Hubris** and **Nemesis** are Greek words out of Greek culture—not Sanskrit.

The National Film Development Corporation was set up in the 80s paving the way for more courageous films, directed by others such as **Shyam Benegal** in Kolkata. They dealt with realistic themes—oppressed women, uppercaste landlords, Muslim-Hindu love themes across communal divides. The honest hero surrounded by the lack of integrity in society, wins through in the end—as does the wronged heroine. There is also the 'angry young man' epitomised in the earlier years by the 'smouldering eyes' of Amitabh Bachchan.

And 'the heroine' is interesting to watch. No longer a Sita who immolates herself in moral anguish in the fire of purification to prove her purity to her Rama (one always feels he needs his head examining in listening to the rumours of the crowd rather than trusting her virtuous nature) she has now become a fully-fledged modern woman—a shakti figure asserting her rights as did the late **Phoolan Devi** in the **Bandit Queen**.

By the 90s the realities of India crept in; the seductive come-hither of Hollywood in the 30s, Bollywood in the 50s, now ends in rape; heroines get kissed, but downright nudity in bed (despite Khajuraho temple sculpture) is OUT. Even the film, **Kama Sutra**, directed by an Indian woman **Mira Nair** miraculously filmed with taste and sumptuous style despite the subject, suffered few censorial cuts! In 2001 her **Monsoon Wedding**, the story of an Indian bride who has second thoughts about her arranged marriage, won the Golden Lion Award at the 58th Venice Film Festival, the first time an Indian and a woman, won the top prize. Punjabi friends in Delhi gloried in its ebullience. Laughter from all kinds of cultural groups rang out at its universal message. She deserves all the accolades!

Other well-known and talented women such as **Aparna Sen** (**36 Chowringhee Lane**), **Vijaya Mehta** and **Sai Paranjape** make films also, and not to a formula. Meanwhile Bollywood superstars have gone global, filming in the UK, USA and Australia's unique Outback, appearing also in stage shows to ecstatic fans overseas. Large **NRI** communities see to that.

It is TV in this decade which is making the running with the public all over India, villages as well as **people having access to satellite TV** in isolated areas as well as conurbations. **TV in total** with dozens of commercial channels some sending out unheard of electronic signals into the community at all levels—and with women directors and team script writers with sitcom social issues approached with hilarious satirical touches making psychological inroads film scripts never dared to address.

One stormy sitcom daringly investigated the question of 'the new woman'—independent economically, free-spirited, no longer assuming 'the role of maidservant' according to the woman

F

director, treating the husband, **pati**, as god as tradition demanded. Tara had her own desires and needs, even sexual ones, which the new-age Indian male should recognise. Gone is all romantic nonsense singing away in trilling tones in a Kashmir meadow.

And even more provocative, another 'darker' character is emerging—a daughter-in-law acting like a **demonic shakti** who can even question the values of her **saas** (mother-in-law) and look scathingly at the double-standards which have been encrusted in small town lower middle class India—those double standards allowing the man ability to get away with all kinds of misdemeanours... and this being watched in the most distant hidden villages.

Such is social dynamite.

1956 and the Cannes Film Festival transformed the Indian cinema world and its international status, but this now seems worlds away in the light of TV influence. **Fillums** became **film** with that infinitely moving trilogy that made **Satyajit Ray**, Bengali film director, world famous. Coming from a cultured family in the true Bengali tradition, his world of **Apu** beginning with **Pather Panchali**, made the world's headlines bringing great pride to the national scene, followed by other great Bengali artists, Bimal Roy, Mrinal Sen, Ritwik Ghatak being recognised.

New Ground Breaking!

One simply cannot imagine films like **Bombay Boys** being possible to bring to screen even a decade ago. Youthful **Kaizad Gustad** whose family came to Australia in the 80s and who liked to 'go walkabout' Aboriginal style—of 'no fixed address'—directed three young Indian men from Sydney, London and New York in a rambunctious comment on Mumbai life and the dubious thrills of its night life including 'gays', in a club, hardly the subject of earlier 'fillums' often referred to as '**Mumbai escapist masala**'. The Bajrang Dal or the Shiva Sena threatened Kaizad for 'denigrating Indian culture', similar to their targeting of painter M F Husain, and Deepa Mehta for her film 'Fire' which implied a lesbian relationship (more by default of abusive and boorish husbands). Of these controversies there is discussion later in the text.

Serious documentary cinema has also crashed into the mainstream, moving determinedly out of cinema art houses and there is also the delicious role reversal of famous **Shekhar Kapur** returning the compliment of Richard Attenborough's **Gandhi** by making **Elizabeth I** with very much a Mughal court setting. In 2001 another milestone was passed, overturning many Bollywood formulae—a period drama involving *phirangi guli danda,* a heroic villager and a nasty British colonial officer (the baddie) who play a tense cricket match which will settle whether the villagers in a harsh period of drought will be exempt from **Lagaan**—a punitive tax, Oscar-nominated for The Best Foreign Film Oscar 2002, it did not win, however it gained the best film award in Bollywood a few months later because of its significant social message.

It has taken off into local politics mixing metaphors even a nonliterate villager will understand—especially in Bihar where they repeat with anger: **This lagaan is not cricket!** Apparently

local babus are the baddies, imposing exorbitant fines on non-payment of taxes, not *maal guzari* (land tax) but impost on tractors and trailers. That is 'not on'.

But one thing never seems to change in the meaty histrionic melodrama of the real Hindi fillum—that pelvic thrust of the dance routine that seems to move in unison all along the chorus line until the final lunge of the full frontal male jerk—the tribhanga of the 20th century. Maybe when they reach three score years and ten they will all suffer degeneration of the lower vertebrae of the spine!

Age has pluses however... a repectable mantle placed on Bollywood by the British Film Industry. It has backed an A- level course for students with CD-Rom guide **Bollywood and Beyond** (BFI Ed. Resources). What next, Lord Curzon?!

■ **FINANCING INDIA**
Banking and other matters of business and changes in present circumstances.

1. **Coinage**

For efficient functioning and to keep a society content there has to be a lubrication of the cog wheels—that means a ready flow of cash.

Even in earliest times coins—and gold ones at that—have circulated and are still coming to light (only recently a cache of Roman coins surfaced along a beach of the Malabar coast north of Kozhikode, as also in the Madras region). Thousands emerged in Bactrian Afghanistan confirming the hoard of 20,000 that the doughty adventurer, **Colonel James Tod** gathered up from all over Rajputana in the 1820s. From these coins and the excitement of putting together the gigantic jigsaw in an archaeological detective story, India's history was retrieved. The coins established the linear genealogies but also indicated the extensive nature of India's trade.

2. **Rural economy in early times**

In the countryside the **jajmani** system operated. In a village with a balance of castes; there was what is known sociologically as **reciprocal obligations,** exchange of labour for payment in kind such as paddy, clothes or shelter. Feudal landlords—usually upper class as elsewhere in the world—by force of dharma were meant to provide in times of privation or emergency. The interaction was held in control by hierarchical tradition.

It was the **banias (trading** class) who constitute a section of the Vaisyas whose duty it was to oil the works. In this group a special regional community, the **marwaris**, had for centuries honed their entrepreneurial skills straddling the camel routes and caravanserais that led up to the high steppes of Asia and the Silk Route beyond that magic walled city of Jaisalmer with its wonderfully architected balconies of the **havelis**, the rich merchant houses built in solid biscuit-coloured sandstone profusely ornamented and crenellated, glowing in the afternoon sun. They came into their own providing the mechanics in a rudimentary form of banking as well as moneylending, credit, an export-import system long before the British and Parsees on the west coast, and especially the town of **Udipi** near Mangalore instituted the banking system as it is known today.

It is estimated that one-third of the ownership of assets in Indian-owned firms is in the hands of this distinctive community. There is a saying that a Marwari can buy in fact from a Jew and sell to a Scot and still make a profit, a fact for sure in all their USA and UK cornerstore delis! And that also of the Gujarati Patels (banias for sure!).

3. Mughal coinage and economic development

Writing on Mughal coinage in the extensive catalogue to the seminal Exhibition in London—**The Raj, India and the British 1600–1947** (National Portrait Gallery Publications, London, 1990)—**Dr Christopher Bayly**, Reader in Indian History at Cambridge University and Principal Consultant to the Exhibition makes the point that the Indian subcontinent had become a money economy very early in its history unlike much of southeast Asia and Africa.

Under the Mughals, revenue, official salaries and a significant proportion of rents and dues to overlords were paid in cash. The silver rupee was the basis of the system though gold mohurs formed a unit of account and a currency for hoarding...

Even then! No wonder the habit is so entrenched (see **GOLD**).

Bayly points out that with improved and settled agriculture as comparative peace settled on the countryside and a population estimated at roughly 100 million throughout their domain, bullion was imported by the Mughals from overseas—the New World—via the Europeans who bought the fine textiles and spices... 'the silver was coined in Mughal state Mints at all the major centres. This brought the Europeans into contact with the (largely Hindu) commercial classes of India who were also the purchasing agents for the manufacture of local artifacts. India's growing dependency upon the European bullion importers made her vulnerable to exploitation by the Europeans'.

4. Managing Agencies and Banking

Before the end of Mughal rule and the emergence of the **Managing Agencies** (the big channels for import-export trade of the British, unique to Indian conditions and colonial rule) some banks had been set up by the Marwari community to provide services to the Muslim Nawabs of Bengal.

The British system which overlaid Mughal bureaucracy inherited their expertise. Marwaris became not only agents in the ports but merchant bankers of a kind, eminent in industry (especially coal and shipping) and even to this day wield immense power and wealth in Mumbai and Kolkata and even down south. A cultural component, often forgotten when dealing with India's philosophic bent is this second part of their lives (see **ASHRAMA** and **ARTHA**).

5.

Jains are yet another strong, although minute, business community active in this commercial world as well as industry. There does appear to be a symbiosis. There are reasons for that.

There are certain distinguishing factors in the way of life of Jains that have shaped their particular involvement in society. Jain doctrine is founded in the fundamental principle of **ahimsa**—non-violence—in a much more everyday basis than Hindus. The appropriate way

of life therefore is a constraint on taking up many professions, and especially being involved in agriculture—refer to **JAIN**.

As also with the **PARSIS** many in this small community (approximately 3.5 million) **turned to commerce and banking to make a living** and in this century founded thriving industrial concerns—and with their gift for ending up with profitable enterprises, a tradition of largesse also became their hallmark.

6.

Another community which should not be forgotten in the financial equation are the **Sindhis**. Having lost entirely their homeland at Partition in 1947 to Pakistan and its southwest corner they are now part of the Indian diaspora in Hong Kong and the Arab worlds, as well as in Mumbai.

A description of them as 'Mr Fast-Buck-Maker' may be legitimate and they are not exactly shy in displaying big diamond rings and gold watches equally encrusted, a blatant symbol of wealth, but one million of them lost everything and have had to live by their wits. Some did find professional outlets but many service real estate and the garment industries and are primarily money merchants.

7.

Hundi and **Shroff** (the former a Hindi word and *shroff* thought to derive from the Arabic *saraf*—meaning a money-changer, and thence into **Urdu**) have been associated for centuries with the lending of money on a person-to-person basis, usually dealing with financing small businesses, rural loans, buying of cattle, farm machinery, dams, wedding costs, etc, the hundi system of bills of lading was a buyer's guarantee of payment after a specific time period to the seller and issued by a *shroff* (an agent). Having evolved into a surname, one, Kantisen Shroff, a constructive philanthropist, was nominated Business Man of the Year 1995.

However, great fortunes were made in past centuries by usurers; exorbitant interest rates of up to 35% are still charged to many small farmers who need immediate capital for new stock, at cattle fairs, for wedding cost loans and the burden of dowries. Just as the hoarding of gold as static wealth (see **GOLD**) is endemic in Indian culture, so too is the moneylender and his limpet-like capacity for survival, although the hold is lessening with widespread electronic communications, village knowhow and astute political awareness growing year by year, the effects of migration to towns and younger members overseas even if in low-class work in factory or mill. Their payments back to family are shaping a very different village India in some go-ahead states, breaking the back of an invidious system where Shylock as a symbol of heartless greed is nowhere in it!

8.

It was a **Parsi, Sorabji Pochkhanawala** who took financing India one step further. Community historian B K Karanjia has spoken with pride about him for he 'conceived the daring idea in **1911** of a banking institution wholly Indian in approach and outlook', the main objective being 'development of indigenous enterprises' rather than being a channel for the benefit of British firms back in the UK. Mangaloreans, now enjoying an economic renaissance along the coastal west due to the arrival of the dramatically engineered Konkan Railway, see this as a natural return to earlier heritage (cf. Udipi, next section 10).

F

9. **Chettiars** had instituted their own system of cashflow long before the British set up their unique system of Managing Agencies through well-known 'houses'. One could say that this south Indian Vaisya class community had instituted their own a thousand years earlier—in the eighth-ninth century CE as merchandising agents for the great Chola empire, financing their shipping supplies as well as being the exporting agency for diamonds from the Hyderabad mines of the interior. These enterprising families are now settled in the more inhospitable southern areas of Tamilnadu, especially the Ramnad district. In much earlier times this community appears to have incurred the displeasure of the local rulers—for reasons unknown—and they strategically withdrew, building their resplendent mansions (akin to Italian palazzo) as landmarks in the flat horizons of these parched pink plains. Eventually they too like the Fords and Rockefellers of the USA became latter-day philanthropists.

In **1923 Sir Annamalai Chettiar** was so honoured with an English knighthood, having founded the well-known university near Chidambaram that bears his name as well as the Indian Bank. His own Chettinad palace at **Kanadikathan** village is quite extraordinarily resplendent in architectural design, at least 110 years old.

Imposing palaces and mansions equal to any in Renaissance Europe can be seen (and some visited) throughout the Chettiar homeland between Pudukkottai and Sivaganga east of Madurai. The community is said to have owned nearly 100 villages, their architecture displaying great craftsmanship in the carving of woods and finely wrought furniture brought back in voyages from Burma, Sri Lanka, old Malaya, marble and other treasures imported from Europe, portraiture of ancestors that became part of the European influence when painters began travelling from England to India in the 18th–19th century.

The Chettiar Heritage (East-West, Madras, 2001) presented with 800 magnificent photographs by Muthuraman gives some idea of the glories of what once was. The authors–**S Muthiah, Meenakshi Meyappan and Visalakshmi/Ramaswamy**.

10. **Managing Agencies and the British Influence:** this is where the British really enter from the wings...

1876–77

With the proclamation of **Queen Victoria** as **Kaiser-i-Hind** and the amalgamation of power across the entire area of north India in particular under the new mogul Lord Lytton as Viceroy, questions of centralization emerged. The **East India Company** as a financing body for all the British factories and trading which had sprung up from the 17th century onwards disappeared. Central government from distant Whitehall in London took over, dissatisfied as the British Parliament had been with corruption and many a tale of ill-gotten gains by rapacious behaviour of Company officers.

By **1911** the capital of British India was moved to Delhi with as much pomp and circumstance as Mughal Emperors would have engaged in, a panoply of imperial Durbar for King Emperor George V and Queen Mary.

Industrialization and largescale empire trade necessitated a coherent network of banking. A unique system of joint stock companies registered in Britain was set up in the 18th–19th centuries as British colonialism took over with the collapse of Mughal rule. These channels of servicing the financial needs of industrialization, injecting British money into India (and taking it out!) became household names—Parry and Sons, John Palmer, Andrew Yule and Co., Jardine Matheson, Mackintosh. This was the era of what were called **Presidency Banks**. They had the advantage in port cities such as Chennai, Kolkata, Kochi, Mumbai of group management linked with Scotland and England with the economies of large scale operation in import-export, in centralized facilities, specialized knowledge of overseas markets in the ever-extending spread of empire to Hong Kong, Singapore, Australia.

Even though these agencies helped in the development of industries and increased the flow of money through the rural economies of grains, indigo, sugar, cotton and the important opium trade export by advancing funds as a banking system to cultivators, securing supplies and providing opportunities to market surpluses, in Bengal control over primary produce was subordinated to the needs of the new colonial power. From this infrastructure the system of **private banking** as we know it today emerged. However, **Udipi**, 60 km north of Mangalore (pilgrimage centre for the famous bhakti saint, **Madhva** and the even more renowned Udipi cuisine) still claims setting up the first four indigenous banks, especially pioneering the Canara and Syndicate Banks of the Mangalore region.

11. **After Independence**

Understandably after centuries of being dominated by alien rulers any Indian government wanted to rid itself of foreign entanglements. A real psychological urge to Indianize pervaded the atmosphere of nearly all Indian thinking when we first arrived in Delhi. Huge endeavours, such as the great dam at Bhakra Nangal and the Damodar steel works, needed foreign aid but it was based on government negotiation.

Private industry and commercial firms were hedged around (again understandably) by restrictions on imports while the Reserve Bank of India and federal treasury got their act together, **trying to protect indigenous industries and fragile new structures**. After several decades, however, and despite the massive re-organisation under successive **FIVE YEAR PLANS**, attitudes of mind inherent in bureaucracies and laggardly inefficiencies prevailed just about everywhere, certainly in the opinion of urban Indian business/industrial complexes trying to show initiative and encourage quality manufacture.

The flipside to this epoch was bureaucratic tardiness in procrastinating on decisions, passing files an adult game in government offices but unlike children's party games of passing the parcel the stringed files (and pink-red tape is still used!) were hardly ever undone; this meant a nightmare for enterprising businesspeople, especially those wishing to invest from overseas—one business director quoting demands for over 30 copies of every invoice submitted! **The Licence Raj** is the pithy term given to this period which halted many an entrepreneur in his or her tracks.

12. Nationalization of Banks and the Rural Sector

It was not until 1967 when Mrs Gandhi 'almost as a stray thought' it is recorded, while flying—as Prime Minister 1966–79—to a conference she was to address, decided to nationalize the banks in an effort to redress the imbalance suffered, partly by the financial demands of the huge cities and the obvious inclination for banks to concentrate on these profitable areas of the national economy. Thus rural India became a priority sector in 1969 when **fourteen major commercial banks were nationalized**. Trying to shift the mass of the populace who live in the shadow of 'the poverty line' increasingly haunts governments as Dalits find their voice—a fact recent general elections have highlighted. Small rural loans were encouraged but the running of banks, managerial styles and work rules were set in concrete. The banking heart throbbed for city life.

This lack of initiative from banks comes as a surprise considering how skilled Indians are in 'doing business' at ground level but the nature of the system and **personal experience of it is enough to blow a brain fuse**. However, much depends on regional cultures. Rural banks are thriving in parts of Tamilnadu helping women in non-farm income schemes and in community village initiatives in Maharashtra, Gujarat, Haryana, Punjab, Rajastan especially. Personal experience is recorded in **MIRACLES**—the **Amul** Kaira Milk Co-operative.

Evidence from the 2001 Census is beginning to show a major transformation however. Savings statistics indicate a rapid rise in bank deposits equalling 50 per cent of GDP—amongst the highest percentage in the world.

13. Advice to foreign travellers

As an indigent traveller who may not have the good fortune to be accommodated in a major hotel with facilities for changing money, or who may not have American Express travellers cheques or sterling pounds, **avoid a bank at all costs** unless you wish to cover a considerable chunk of Vikram Seth's novel: **A Suitable Boy** while sitting (if you are lucky) waiting for the sluggish wheels to turn!

Caught in Ahmedabad with **Australian** travellers cheques entailed a double two-hour session sitting on hard wooden chairs opposite a man lost behind three-inch thick red leather-bound ledgers lined with proverbial blue tracery. The cavernous light, inquiring faces of otherwise diligent staff who broke for **tiffin** and a *bidi* (smoke), the roar of central bazaar traffic, the blank stare first of incomprehension on the part of the moustachioed official, innumerable questions as to origin, destination; 'where is husband'; 'no children; yes!'

A disappearance, inexplicable, for *chai*, maybe his own as well as mine, 'for whom is the money?' 'How you like India?' 'You speak Hindi? Very good! Yes, money will be coming...' 'waiting for rate', rate not coming, further attention to ledgers, do I repeat questions again, how much longer, rising adrenalin, revert to yoga meditation, a young peon (a minor functionary/messenger) ambling in, an animated consultation, what to do about a loo, if I disappear do we start all over again? Go into a trance... For a third time, in a lifetime experiencing India, *that* proved effective...

Bound wads of rupee notes are suddenly 'materialized'. That Deus ex Machina again! (see **LANGUAGE** and **future perfect tense**, only operative in India!)

No explanations. Three hand counts by three separate minions, ledgers doubly signed, my own signature 'Thrice please'... a walk into the dazzling sun, dazed, almost run over by an erratic phut-phutting three-wheeler. **A time slot in one's life to be avoided at all costs.** However, liberalization policies do appear to be working... accounts can be opened from overseas with only one set of forms and by e-mail in no time at all. *Mirabile dictu!*

14. From the Indian Point of View

It is hard for anyone brought up in the privileged framework of urbanized Western economies—beset enough it is worth remembering with problems of their own—but which have had the luxury of developing an industrial complexity over a spacious period of at least 200 years, to understand the inevitable dislocations of a vast and diverse society at so many contrasting stages of development creating a uniform framework of infrastructure in a telescoped time span. Britain's economic development for instance and industrialization took place alongside the expansion of Empire with cheap commodity prices set by Whitehall in the 19th century. Britain's economic development did not have a Gulf War which added a *coup de grace* to Indian planning in the early 90s. Britain in those imperial days in fact *created* the global economy! Sterling was in fact the greenback of its day.

Someone once said back in the early Five Year Plan period of the 50s that India like the Red Queen in Alice in Wonderland, had to run to stand still. All problems had to be dealt with all at once with 17 million people being added year by year to the total population. The pressure on all aspects of economic development requiring financing is relentless.

But in the last decade dramatic changes to India's financing are taking place. New liberalization policies are taking off even if there are major bottlenecks but anyone who lives in federal structures such as Australia or Canada knows what that means even if all else functions efficiently. The harnessing of India's capital poses monumental planning challenges. Areas such as **Power, Roads and Bridges, Transport** and **Ports** are all in need of urgent attention and enormous financing. **Telephones**, the lack of which is a *cri de coeur* of most overseas companies now clamouring to do business with global networking ever on the increase, and privatization, a respectable word again in India, is of overwhelming import.

But again there is dramatic paradox. In thousands of villages especially throughout Kerala, Karnataka and Maharashtra the new yellow booths for STD phone and fax have burgeoned overnight. In some states an amazing and efficient network is organised, of handicapped people to run them—another example of India's inspired capacity to improvise.

15. Personal addenda and conclusions

Economic statistics are dry and have little immediate meaning especially when the traveller flies OVER them.

F

But driving head on into them can be very intimidating! An 11-hour journey from Cochin to Udhagamandalam (Ooty) in our mini-coach from a glorious family reunion Christmas appropriately in a Syrian Christian Kerala, also celebrating, was a nightmare journey.

Coming up from the coast of Kerala via jungle ghat roads now under renovation—fitfully and without states' co-ordination—is a test of sanity and skill in quick braking; hairpin bends in the Nilgiris via Coimbatore provide alarming encounters with hurtling lorries, charmingly painted with life-preserving deities and '**horn please**' signs but **no** mirrors. The law of the most powerful prevails but what if coach and lorry have to pass where late monsoonal rains have washed away the stone wall preventing a precipitous plunge into jungle valley below? Mercifully our remarkable young Tamil driver was named Ganesh: 3,000 km along such roads through four states of south India in three and a half weeks is a credit rating beyond anything McKinsey can envisage... and not even a flat tyre! On this crucial last leg of the journey we were encountering the complete clogging up of Mumbai's port facilities, incapacitated with sudden increased traffic due to the change in central government economic policies in freeing up regulations on export-import licencing. In the papers after a final safe arrival in Bangalore we read that lorry traffic had been diverted to Cochin—a road journey along two sides of a triangle, and a thousand kms further down the track! No wonder billions of rupees had then to be spent to open up the Konkan rail link already mentioned, an engineering marvel of Indian expertise (see **RAILWAYS**).

16. **A Moral Question**

The sorry tale of economic statistics which **are** accepted is saddening indeed in a nation that can hoard gold, 'in excess of 9,000 tonnes, the highest anywhere in the world'. A ready-reckoning would flood the digit window and probably blow the system when taking in the multiplying factor; 10 gms gold = Rs. 5,000! Such is the static wealth discussed in **GOLD**, where jewellery and family safes hold the money instead of investing it in creative saving-the-nation programmes.

Much can be laid at the door of ever-rising population density—and increase. In one 5-Year Plan 14 million new jobs were said to be statistically created while 17 million young people came on the market.

Another statistic population-wise: the active labour force between 15–50 now stands at **nearly 60 per cent of the population**. They also are active sexually and capable of creating an exponential population graph. Despite all the efforts educationally and by persuasion as a democracy (and India has to be admired for maintaining its integrity as such) a huge question mark hangs over this potential threat to stability.

There is hope. India possesses a very talented reservoir of trained and educated engineers, scientists, technicians, the largest population of such in the world... but is there the single-mindedness of politicians to apply urgent once-and-for-all methods to break the nexus of the following statistics: did the founding fathers—and mothers—of modern India fight for freedom in which at least 36 per cent of the population remains at the poverty line 50 years after gaining that freedom? Even younger Indian economists and increasingly editorials (one in 1995 headlined: **The British Can't Be Blamed Any Longer!**) are questioning why such obscene disparity between the flaunted disposable income of the few (the approximate 5–10 per cent) and the vast mass, especially those who constitute the really poor, those below the poverty level (measured in calories of nourishment set at 2,400 per day in urban areas, 2,100 in rural).

Admittedly the after-effects of colonial impoverishment of the rural sector (where India once was truly wealthy) may still be there but now there is a wealthy Indian population wholly engendered locally and responsible for its own behaviour.

So where have all the income taxpayers gone?

◆ In a culture that has so perfected the acquisition of single-mindedness of a yogic concentration for at least 5,000 years of training where ascetics in caves in the Himalayas defied icy conditions in their withdrawn oblivion to such physical onslaughts and sadhus sit immobile in the heat of the day in front of blazing fires to illustrate their strength of mind, there must surely be a moral challenge to the Central Government cabinet to get its act together likewise in single-minded concentration! India's wealth needs rounding up.

◆ Or is the ultimate question one of benevolent dictatorship, Confucian work ethic of autocratic China, the 'directed' democracies of Singapore, Malaysia and Korea, the only answer? When Europe and America developed economically the mass media and universal suffrage were not in existence. Capitalism had a free reign to act arbitrarily—to the detriment also of people. But is the free market now capable of that yogic single-mindedness—not just for personal profit alone but in motivating a shake-up India undoubtedly needs; **where is the sense of stewardship which launched the nation on that tidal wave of hope in 1947...?**

The wealth is there in India. There is more liquid money perhaps than in many of the middle-income nations such as Canada, France, Australia, South Korea, Malaysia, and certainly millionaires equal in number to Germany, Japan or the USA. **Dr Gus Hook**, Australian economist/demographer places the number in the coming decade at around 68,000 (see **GOLD** again). That is in American dollar terms! But there is then a final question. Apart from the giant companies and efficient industrial combines of Birlas, Tatas, Wadias, Oberois, Sarabhais, Shroffs, when will that 'black money', those recalcitrant taxpayers come in from the cold? It is estimated that less than **20 million taxpayers or thereabouts are contributing to India's financing**, a quite extraordinary statistic considering the burgeoning households earning over 40,000 rupees and the ostentatious housing popping up in wealthy suburbs.

Since the full impact of globalization and liberalization by the government of many tariff restrictions and financial controls, with tax indemnities for those who come clean about their incomes, plus an outspoken media, tenacious cultural behaviour may get cracked. An eminent economist, Professor Rao, retired Director-General of the

National Council of Applied Economic Research will then be happier. Over a decade ago he was writing articles and tracts pointing out that the **Licence Raj** as it had come to be known (some would say Nehru's gift and legacy to the new India) created its own forms of corruption–black money passing hands for one thing all the way down the line of bureaucracy to get that permit and get it quick.

If government interferes less systems have to become more efficient to survive. No subsidies means you swim–or sink.

'Feather-bedding' was the term overseas, many businesses suffering the same agonies in freeing-up trade, some going to the wall as competition stampeded local markets. That is exactly what India now faces with cheap Chinese goods infiltrating as the new decade gathers force–an unheard-of challenge to the bazaar shopkeepers of India. Maybe they will end up paying no tax at all with their backs to the wall!

17. Grihastha Ashrama Reigns!

The rapidly widening gap between the affluence of these new professional groups computer numerate and naturals for the Internet with their native mathematical skills and Indian savvy and those who were traditional owners of land is surely a future threat to social stability. As far back as late 1995, **the Economic and Political Weekly** warned that 'a proportionately **small** but numerically **large** and very powerful group of Indians had much to gain from globalization' while those landless peasants bereft of capital also 'are extremely vulnerable to attendant inflation. ' In addition...

...the industrial bourgeoisie with their freedom for unlicensed growth, unfettered by any obligations to the worker or the environment, large farmers with access to new technologies, new crops, new markets...

seem no longer to possess **'a morality of intention'** like their forefathers who took the burden of dharma seriously in the tradition of jajmani.

Unbridled affluence is very noticeable amongst the urban young. Each new revisiting highlights a widening dangerous gap of revolutionary proportions with no sign of a moral leader of national stature to affirm the constraints of sanatana dharma against the seductions of TV and its Americanized dollar-driven advertising promotions–or Indian magazines eulogising with inflated hype the huge condominiums... Platinum City in Bangalore for instance with no mention about what happens during the annual summer electricity cuts!

■ FISSIPAROUS TENDENCIES

A proneness to break away from the forces that pull towards the centre... centripetal.

1956

A phrase that came into prominence and dominated English language newspaper headlines in India as a result of the **1956 States Reorganisation Commission's** decisions to redraw the arbitrary boundaries of Indian States and Provinces created under British rule. The new criteria applied was realistically and logically based on cultural/linguistic lines, a demand surfacing urgently even by 1952. There had been a complex permutation of factors–dominance of Telugu communities (so they thought) by Tamils in the previous huge Madras Presidency, inflamed also by Communist Party sympathisers and a Telengana movement added fuel to flames. The old Hyderabad State was heavily Muslim, after two centuries of rule by Nizams–civil unrest culminated in fasts. A Telugu protester, Potti Sriramalu, died. Heads were bashed and the Telugu-speaking state of Andhra Pradesh was born. Half a century later a growing demand, cutting across party lines, for a separate Telangana state, resurrects Potti's ghost, and the creation of three new states elsewhere in 2000 CE adds legitimacy.

India's history has been on the whole characterized by spiralling **culminations** (as recorded in **ASHOKA**)–golden ages where the landmass was brought together (centripetal) under magnetic emperors–Ashoka, Harsha, Akbar and then Kaiser-i-Hind Victoria. Then, breakaway tendencies set in. Understandably centrifugal forces, Balkanization, as it was called in Europe between the two major World Wars and now again in what was Yugoslavia, make nation state governments apprehensive. This age-old fluctuation of gathering energies, a spiralling accumulation of forces including great visionaries and reformers over epochs and then the slow diffusion, revivalism, a return to the rituals, rules and regulations as a safety device, is part of the gigantic see-saw of Indian experience. Disintegration at the edges begins the century- long processes of crumbling, the loss of energy. That is why demands for a Sikh Khalistan-homeland, Kashmir independence, Assam autonomy and ancient ethnic 'tribal' hostilities along the delicate North East frontier still cause concern at government level. Ever since 1947, Naga tribal identity is proposing a homeland–**Nagalim**, a separatist dream of a landmass six times the area of present-day Nagaland which would swallow up Manipur entirely, one of the seven new states reorganized in this region in 1971, as well as part of Assam, a horror story for any Indian government aware of China and Myanmar just across the valleys. The result, crackdowns of considerable severity.

Centrifugal forces (Latin: *fugere*, to flee from) are at work everywhere in the political impulses of minorities. Basques, the Celtic fringe in Britain, Canada's Quebecois, the Ibo in Nigeria, Hutu and Tutsi, Chechen and Ukrainian, Muslim provinces in China Kurds and Shi'as in Iran all indicate these fissiparous breakaway tendencies from the old nation state concept. They seek a place in the sun and in the power structures, no matter whether a central government is democratic or autocratic or a military dictatorship. 'Ethnic cleansing' is a modern euphemism for the ultimate brutal coping with this recent phenomena most especially in the population upheavals of Bosnian, Serbo-Croat and Kosovo anguished reorderings, and closer home the Hindu pandit exodus from Kashmir, a decimating loss of land and identity.

A perceptive younger generation of Indians does however question the nation-state construct which is after all a European development that caused enough head-bashing and brutal wars of its own. Colonial policies imposed artificial nation-state ideas all

F

over the globe. India is the size of continental Europe. Is Europe a singularity… a nation state? Was India ever throughout its history one political entity? **BHARAT** and in an oblique way **PILGRIMAGES** presents a sense of a spiritual-cultural matrix. But in the modern world that still has to be administered–but how? Centrally or a confederation of states?

■ **FIVE YEAR PLANS**

The Tenth Five year Plan came into effect in 2002. The Central Government Planning Commission was set up after 1947. It has thought through and implemented nine such Plans beginning 1951 but from 1992-97 a number of crises, intensified by Gulf War repercussions and loss of oil supply has meant IMF involvement. Subsequently each year latterly had to have an individual Plan.

Systematic planning put India on its feet as an independent proud nation after so long under alien direction, enabling India to maintain its independence and psychological pride in doing things its own way and in an orderly fashion without interference from foreigners.

Heavy industries, the three first great steel mills, were given priority in a predominantly socialist economy. Agriculture was neglected but in latter plans about 20% of financing in Plans have been devoted to agriculture.

Such a structure independent of Cabinet with a forceful Prime Minister Nehru as its chairman was absolutely necessary to give some homogeneity to India's disparate states and a kickstart to the unproven economy.

It is easy for economists writing especially in commemorative issues examining 50 years of Independence **(The Economist, February, 1997)** to take to task Nehru's vision of socialist planning. That seems a harsh indictment to those of us who lived in India in the 50s so soon after she achieved freedom from economic forces skewed around to suit colonial needs and the policies of a very distant Whitehall dictating the terms. India needed regulations to prevent further interference and to establish a self-reliance in the Cold War period, neither tugged this way or that by Western free market forces or Soviet-style heavy-handed State control. There was a psychological need to be free of all outside constraints which has been a factor almost totally ignored by those governments who have not suffered colonial domination in the last 200 years. That includes the USA and the UK which dominated whole regions of the globe.

The miracle is that India considering her equivalent in size, cultural differences, and divisive language boundaries as equal to Europe's–has a common agricultural policy, overall industrial planning, an orderly economy, an amazing democratic process despite all assaults upon it and a people that recognize they are Indian first and foremost when outside forces threaten. Such plans have given a framework to this conscious development, and this time around a GDP growth of 8 per cent, up till the present just about 4.5. per cent.

F

GANA-s and GUNA-s

Gunas, not to be confused with **ganas,** the 'celestial hordes' used by Shiva to run and do errands for him in the **Puranic legends,** stories, parables, allegories. These brought down to earth vivid homilies of all the aspects of the immense and impersonal scientific concepts surrounding the Shiva metaphor in understandable terms for ordinary people.

In one such story which every Indian child knows, Parvati, Shiva's consort, magically created the figure of a young boy from rubbing the scurf off her body before taking her bath—perhaps with a turmeric root that is a cleansing abrasive used to this day in showering.

Having created a son, she requested him to stand guard at the doorway while she bathed. Shiva came by, unexpectedly, and tried to enter the room. The youngster refused to let him do so, blocking the entrance. Shiva became very angry and, in the commotion that followed, the boy literally lost his head. Parvati came to investigate. Horrified to see her decapitated son, she rounded on the headstrong Shiva and explained—and it needs some explaining!—that this was their son she had just created.

Bereft at this tragedy she threatened to use her shakti power to shake the worlds unless Shiva restituted the boy's head. The gods had gathered in dismay knowing the power of Shakti and pleaded with Shiva to placate Parvati. He despatched his **ganas** to search for the head of the first living being they encountered. That happened to be an elephant. So the young son found himself with this elephant head. Parvati gathered him into her arms, and Shiva named him **Ganesh** (**Ganapati** in western India and some other parts). **Ganesh** became **Lord of the Ganas,** who in later times take on a more malevolent quality as though they were similar to the hosts of hobgoblins of Western literature—the forces of the nether world that emerge in fairy stories and **Tolkien's Lord of the Rings** to plague humanity's footsteps.

Guna is a 'strand', three being the components thought to characterise all material nature and human personality (see **GUNA** further down the track). It is mentioned here because it is easy as a newcomer to India to get all these terms mixed up!

GANDHI
Mohandas Karamchand
1869–1948

October 2nd, Gandhi's birthday, is a national holiday. His name is prone, sadly, to be misspelled even in leading world newspapers as **Ghandi.**

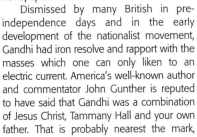

Dismissed by many British in pre-independence days and in the early development of the nationalist movement, Gandhi had iron resolve and rapport with the masses which one can only liken to an electric current. America's well-known author and commentator John Gunther is reputed to have said that Gandhi was a combination of Jesus Christ, Tammany Hall and your own father. That is probably nearest the mark, although Professor Radhakrishnan's remark about the Mahatma also rings true: 'that lonesome man who embodies the conscience of humanity'.

◆ For all those nowadays who would demystify the man and detract from his sanctification, Gandhi personifies that innate 'extraordinary norm' Professor Edgerton has singled out as uniquely Indian.

No matter how politically crafty or manipulative, no matter what terms of scepticism are poured on Gandhi now, he succeeded in galvanising the vast mercurial masses of India into a cohesive body which wore down the imperial power of the mightiest empire the world has seen. And he did it in a way which confused and morally undermined his opponent. With disarming humour he was able to explain to the English mill-workers convincingly the reason why he led the boycott against the very manufactured cloth they spun, downtrodden though they were themselves in the depressed 30s.

It was on August 9, 1942 that his **'Do or Die'** clarion call to the nation to fight 'bondage and slavery' stirred Congress Party followers to their utmost efforts in non-violent action to achieve Independence. "Freedom is not for the coward or the fainthearted," Gandhi had declared. '**Quit India!'**

As often happens with visionaries, in the end he was crucified by his own people, assassinated by an extremist Hindu antagonised by his protection of Muslims. In the traumatic riots and exchange of populations at Partition when East and West Pakistan were carved out of a land-mass that for well over 5,000 years had been whole and entire in ethos and essence, myth and epic.

◆ After his death, as Indian democratic processes took off and economic Five-Year Plans developed, many of his refreshingly original concepts of self-sufficient village economies and basic education, relevant to the masses and not influenced by British institutions and elitism, were quietly set aside and ignored.

◆ **Sarvodaya** is the Sanskrit term used by Gandhi [**udaya,** upliftment; **sarv** = for all]. It is a constant learning process undertaken by sympathisers and those who passed through his ashram, works in the service of truth, often the high-born volunteers had to learn 'the dirtying of hands', defying caste rituals in Gandhian attempts to raise the quality of village life.

1950s

Economic advisers from Britain, such as Nicholas Kaldor and Joan Robinson, were influential in convincing Nehru and the Congress Governments of the 50s and 60s that socialist economies, planning from the top, big industrial steel complexes should take precedence over decentralisation and village 'small is beautiful' economies.

Yet no one can gainsay that, without Gandhi, India's poor might never have made the gigantic step psychologically into the 20th century; identifying with the needs, expectations and functions of a modern secular democratic state. A glimmer of hope shone before them that set a pattern in government—and civil service thinking—that village India, low-caste India, minorities, tribal people (adivasis) and women could no longer be

G

marginalised. Development and extension service schemes now network throughout the farthest reaches of India; no matter how ineffective they are in backward areas like Bihar, a code has been imprinted on the Indian mind **of what should be**.

Eerily, these are the words Gandhi spoke at a prayer meeting on January 28, 1948. He was 78 years old.

If I am to die by the bullet of a mad man, I must do so smiling. There must be no anger within me. God must be in my heart and on my lips. And you promise me one thing. Should such a thing happen, you are not to shed one tear.

Two days later—January 30—at his afternoon prayer meeting he fell to that bullet. His last words:

He Ram. O God.

(**He** is pronounced **hay**)

And India wept.

୬୭୧୬ୟ୬ଓ୬ଓ୬ଓ୬ଓ୬ଓ୬ଓ୬

Gandhi in our times

After the initial homage to the passing of this charismatic mahatma in our lifetime, a new generation of politicians and economists were impatient with ideas of **gramdan**. This was Gandhiji's ideal of self-sufficient village republics, the cause of which was espoused by **Vinoba BHAVE**. Other related programs were regarded as too idealistic, irrelevant for modern needs, inefficient to operate. Even the institutionalised spinning each morning at the ashrams, which even hard-bitten politicians had to do if they visited Gandhi, began to be questioned. Highly sophisticated people like Pandit Nehru had to do menial servant jobs also, to instil self-sufficiency. These have disappeared as a personal discipline—and as a strength. Even Gandhi's wife **Kasturba**—unsung heroine that she was, had a big argument with her perfectionist husband and stubbornly refused to clean latrines in the ashram. When he lost his temper—he is after all not always a mahatma!—she quietly remonstrated: 'You are only human'. Much later when her difficult husband was concerned if she could lead a group of women in satyagraha (which she did) and risk being jailed she replies with humour tinged with asperity: 'I can survive anything when I have survived you.'

1954 onwards

The first criticisms began to appear. Nirad Chaudhuri, ever willing to be the gadfly stinging mainstream India into self-examination, published a major article in **The Illustrated Weekly of India** in the mid-50s questioning many of Gandhi's premises, almost a heresy in those early days of freedom. Central government, while defending the great man vocally as an icon, continued to ignore him in practical terms, applying from above many policies without heeding what villagers were saying. Gandhi would have had no part with such a policy.

Nearly 60 years on, Gandhi's name is once again on the lips of television and print media. Why is India's democratic society still negligent of the poor? One commentator, Subrata Mukherjee, writing on **Gandhi's Theory of the State** in 1998 had this to say:

It is generally agreed that one of the major consequences of colonial rule in India was the emergence and consolidation of an over-developed state and relatively under-developed society.

Subrata Mukherjee, **Gandhi's Theory of the State**, The Times of India, 1998

Gandhi was only too aware of this problem of Western-style states and their enormous powers of sovereignty running roughshod over minority sentiments. Over-centralisation in complex continental land masses needs other responses than a Westminster-system democracy suited to a small British land mass with high density, educated urban groupings sufficiently clued up to make their presence felt. Gandhi had always 'conceptualised a state composed of self-governing and self-sufficient village communities'. Indeed he once said: 'This cannot be done by imposition from without. The workers will have to be allowed to carry on the work themselves, more or less free of regulation by a central authority'. In go-ahead states this is happening.

◆ Perhaps the push once more, admittedly at central level, for renewed vigour in establishing **panchayati raj** (turn to **PANCHAYAT**) may redress the imbalance, built up in the last 50 years, between the huge neglected mass of villagers and city people.

Letters which emerged in Britain from auction in October 1996 (70 letters, hand-written in English on the back of envelopes and on scraps of paper in the last six months of Gandhi's life, fetching approximately £1 million) indicated his determination to shift the misery of India's hard-pressed, hardworking villagers.

We are on the road to showing the lowliest of villagers that (independence) means his freedom from serfdom, that he is the salt of the earth. Let us not defer the hope and make the heart sick... I wonder if we can ever be free of the fevers of power politics or the bid for power that afflicts the political world West and East?

This was his last prayer speech, on January 26, 1948. Alive today, he would be asking the same question in the light of contemporary political shenanigans. The villagers sick at heart may well become angered after half a century of waiting.

But perhaps Indians, suffering the jolts and traumas of events in recent decades, are having second thoughts. The level of corruption that faces India—different now in kind as well as degree from earlier centuries, linked as it is with international criminality and drugs—and cynicism on politics have brought headlines with this *cri de coeur*—**Gandhi where are you now?**

And the cynics?

Left-wing political theorists used to point a finger critically at Gandhi's connections with wealthy patrons such as Birla. Even high-born Sarojini Naidu stated flatly: 'No one knows how much it costs to keep Gandhiji in poverty!' Those on the right, such as the extremists, blame Partition and India's lost territory on him, mocking him as an appeaser.

G

Yet turn the question upside down and ask—without Gandhi, who could have galvanised the huge inchoate mass still embedded in a colonial cocoon of submission? Politics alone does not arouse a people. A burning desire for change has to be sparked alight by a leader arching over all divisions, who has an intuitive instinct in using timeless symbols that do not have to be explained, most especially important in India.

And how consummate to hone in on the infamous colonial Government **Salt Tax 1930** imposed by the British. This was a 2,000 per cent tax on an essential ingredient. Gandhi harnessed his satyagrahis—78 of them—to conduct a vividly dramatic protest march, 241 miles, over harsh terrain along the coastal route from the Sabarmati ashram, across the river of the same name, from central Ahmedabad city to **Dandi** by the sea. Once there, they dug for salt and took it freely.

With an 'instinct for political metaphor' this galvanised ordinary Indians, including many women, into serious mass protest, sending tremors into the massive foundations of the Raj. From then on the cracks spread in a slow attrition. Sixty thousand people were arrested—but the footprints to the future were indented by those uncomfortable wooden sandals of the sannyasi with just one peg—now on show in the Sabarmati Ashram Museum. (Read **Thomas Weber's On the Salt March: The Historiography of Gandhi's March to Dandi**, Harper Collins, London, 1997).

It is easy to debunk great men. One detractor was Woodrow Wyatt, a British MP who first met Gandhi on an All Party Delegation of MPs in 1946. He published the article **Even His Fasts were a Fraud** in **The Spectator** (Aug 9, 1997), on the 50th Anniversary of Independence. It seems to be a condition of our times, a time of few heroes, but one has to ask the question—without Gandhi where would India be today?

The electorate has shown astonishing maturity in recent elections, selectively ditching those politicians who have been the most brazen in their neglect of the very people at risk and whose cause Gandhi espoused. They have cut down the most flamboyant in a clean swathe, and have much for which to thank Gandhi. They are the heirs of Gandhi's gift—a vision to uphold them in the darkest moments when the Raj appeared entrenched forever. It has unfortunately taken nearly a century to get the message across (see **SWARAJ**). What an irony that at the 90s **Earth Summit** in Rio, the one name that reverberated through the sessions in which sustainable development rather than rampant market forces was seen as the holistic answer to the planet's environmental traumas was his. **Again and again, and in different contexts—Gandhi!**

A personal footnote along the pathway: On my 12th visit at the end of 1996, staying in Ahmedabad with our first-ever Indian friend **Purushottam Mavalankar**, I heard straight from the source—his late father, a dedicated Gandhian—about the man himself. **G V Mavalankar** had reminded his family many times of the essential truth Gandhi stood for; deep in his heart, no matter how cynical others might be, one does not undertake more-than-a-month-long fasts lightly:

My father used to say to us as boys that he felt immediately uplifted in the presence of a great soul, elated—but at the same time never feeling a small creature.

Swinging as we were on the Gujarati wrought-iron and richly carved **hinchko** (swing) in the afternoon sun, with the Harold Laski Institute across the garden, he recalled stories of Gandhi.

The erring model, smoking, he drank, led a normal life. He confessed to his father as a boy, never hid any of his failings. And then as he grew in stature he emphasised that practice and precept go hand in hand. There became no gap between what he preached and what he practised. It was in 1915, when he first returned from South Africa, that he was called Mahatma. Look at his experiments with truth. Each mistake he made in life led him to eventual success—he never made the same mistake twice.

He quoted Gandhiji (always chuckling) as saying:
*Don't worry over much about **new** mistakes.*
Learn from them
THEREIN LIES SUCCESS.

G

■ **GANESH**
On the new Indian-designed notepaper packets now to be found in upmarket tourist hotel shops (very expensive) and in the most unlikely bazaar bookshops (not an empty shelf in sight and some humble factotum attempting to maintain a semblance of order flicking a feather duster to push the dust elsewhere), a stylish sand-brown packet stood out.

With embossed design letter-heading in **DEVANAGRI** script, it was conspicuous in its tasteful simplicity. At every turn traditional and ancient symbols flash suddenly into focus in the most modern and urban settings.

In English at the foot of the paper it stated: An Invocation to Lord Shri Ganesh from Rigveda 2.23.

It read thus with literal translation under each group of Sanskrit words:

ॐ गणानां	त्वा	गणपतिं	हवामहे
OM gananam	tva	ganapatim	havāmahe
of demi gods,	*you, (are)*	*the master,*	*we invoke you*

कविं	कविनामुपमश्रवस्तमम् ।
kavim	kavinam upamasravastamam;
Poet	*of poets, the best of the praised Ones*

ज्येष्ठराजं	ब्रह्मणां	ब्रह्मणस्पत
jyestharājam	brahmanām	brahmanaspata
The Lord	*of the knowers of the vedas,*	*O brahmanaspata*

आ नः	शृण्वन्नूतिभिः	सीद	सादनम् ॥
ā nah	srnvannutibhih	Sida	sādanam
From our	*listen prayers,*	*your food (is best)*	*take seat in (our yagnaplace)*

O brahmanaspateh*! You are the master of the demi gods, the best of the poets, the best among the praised ones, the lord of the knower of the vedas, your food is the best. Please listen to our prayers and take seat in our yagna place. We invoke you.

You—Ganesh–the most improbable Deity, with your image now known worldwide amongst India addicts! A creation of that extravagant Indian imagination rooted in rural realities. Who is more omnipotent in sweeping aside all impediments in the very beginnings of human transport? As the early inhabitants tamed their tropical landscape a massive beast can tread through jungle thickets to face enraged clawing tigers and quell them with the raising of a hefty foot. Even criminals in Mughal times had their heads pulverised in such manner.

Ganesh, Ganapati—The Name

♦ The name derives from **gana** and **isa** (isvara): the **Lord of the Ganas**, the hordes of minor deities, perhaps originating from the mischievous, even malevolent spirits frequenting the world of earliest humans, sprites of that animistic world that weave in and out of Shakespearean magic groves of **A Midsummer Night's Dream** and **The Tempest**.

Ever watchful, Ganesh became the universal deity to overcome the obstacles that lie in the path of the unwary, ever ready to trip us up. An elephant is a symbol in itself of power, wealth and abundance (you would have to be wealthy in earliest times to own an elephant) and it can, with its remarkable wise countenance and power of recall, overcome all obstacles in its path.

As time went by, and realism and human development turned to a more sacrificial and ritualistic worship in praise of these mysterious forces, the ganas were harnessed into the Pantheon to do Shiva's bidding in the abode of the gods.

♦ By the time of the **Puranas**, the allegorical tales and parables which brought humanity back to base after the rarefied atmosphere and intellectual demands of Upanishadic philosophy, Ganapati has become all-powerful, the overcomer of all obstacles = **Vinayaka** (supreme leader).

Even the magnificence of Brahma, the tranquil calm of Vishnu and the burning inner fire of Shiva need guidance, such is the down-to-earth approach of Hindus in loving care for their deities. Be in Mumbai on the autumnal full moon day to celebrate the extraordinary vibrancy of **Ganesh Chaturthi** day to see the loving care taken in suburb after suburb in devising his image! Ever watchful, Ganesh has now become the universal symbol of power to overstep all the tripwires.

And what more powerful then, the massive elephant head symbolically attached to a rotund human form, but with a trunk more meaningful than most. Bent like the swastika, Ganapati's graphic sign implies the ability to reach the central point by getting around objects by 'the crooked path', the **viveka** = discrimination that lends to such wisdom. An elephant's trunk can, with fine discrimination, shift between lifting great weights such as tree trunks and (as anyone knows who has had a temple elephant bless them with a slobbery touch) delicately scooping up a tasty morsel from the palm of the hand. Over centuries of development, before even Buddhism and Jainism emerged, Ganesh appears to have gathered force as a combining symbol, accepted and deified by all cults, gathering in a wide spectrum of devotees, those who followed animistic protective guardians, ritual temple-going believers, high philosophy searchers looking for truth, the testing disciplines of yogic practitioners. As the **PANTHEON** established itself in all its exhausting manifestations and rich imagery, Ganesh took over the hearts of Hindus as the beginner of the day, to be bowed down to as the **Lord of All Beginnings**, embedded in the concept of original sound, **OM** and **VAC**. From breath which created word–sound, all categories came forth, and multiplied.

In Tamil, the sound syllable, stylised, takes on the outline of an abstract elephantine head; this sound mantra or meditative diagram device being closely associated with Ganesh... and from the word, speech, Ganesh is scribe. He sits down to place that longest of global epics, the Mahabharata on record, and he wisely rides a mouse (see **PANTHEON**) so that symbolically he can sneak into every nook and cranny, again a sign of his powerfulness.

To him who rides a mouse
holding the modaka** sweet in his hand
Whose large ears are like fly-whisks and
who wears a long sacred thread
Who is short of stature and
is the son of Maheshwara
Oh, Vinayaka, lord of obstacles,
I bow at your feet!

This translation is taken from a book to be highly commended. Written by two scholars, mother and daughter, **Shakunthala Jagannathan** and **Nanditha Krishna, Ganesha: The Auspicious... The Beginning** (Vakils, 1992).

♦ Even foreigners, travellers and backpackers upon the uncertain roads of the subcontinent have taken Ganesh to their hearts, carried upon their persons as an Indian St Christopher. And in some western homes also, Ganapati faces many a door to welcome those who approach the threshold. The deity has gone global, bringing a wry smile when one considers those sincere missionaries who laboured hard to convert the 'heathen'!... but others on the horizon could threaten in return, from yet another source, Hollywood and Disney. Robert Coleman, famed for Star Wars' special effects and 60

---

*The Lord of all Creation, identified in this manifestation as Ganesh.
**Modaka is also symbolic of the sweets made from the harvesting of grain and the earliest cults of peasants in the field, the harvest festival and corn dollies.

non-planetary characters, *'has an eye on the deity, seeing India's myths as a vast untapped source of epic film material'* (a news source in Australia). Indian producers, beware!

■ GANGA MA... Mother Ganges

The Holy Ganges, India's most sacred river.

Why? Obviously in the searing heat of pre-monsoonal north India, landlocked, without the coastal breezes of south India, water takes on a new potency; if a monsoon fails, water is vital and urgent for sanity as well as survival. Anyone who has suffered the assaults of living in the Gangetic plains for even one day, when the temperature hits 40° and stays at 30° in the night, knows first hand what even pouring a **lota** (pitcher) of water over one's head means, let alone a shower, and how even a tepid glass of water can taste like nectar. For this reason, **jal** (water) is regarded as a sacred element throughout India.

After a monsoon, such a vast, uncontrollable river would be revered by those earliest humans who had begun to settle in rural communities near its banks. Its floods could be miles wide, bringing down the silt which creates such fertile soil for every conceivable kind of crop. The Ganga rises nearly 14,000 feet up above Gangotri in the Himalayas in a glacial arch, entering the Gangetic plains at the holy city of Hardwar. At its source it is not really Ganga Ma but an even holier name: **Bhagirathi** (see later text), towered over by peaks nearly 20,000 ft high.

Whilst not India's longest river, the Brahmaputra overtaking her, in 300 miles she has thundered tumultuously down a descent of nearly 13,000 feet with another 1,257 miles to go to the Bay of Bengal! No wonder the mythology took on the full weight; only the strength of Shiva was able to contain and tame this turbulent Shakti force; through awesome gorges whistling with storm and blinding rain in the monsoon, tumbling over pristine snow and through dripping mist, gouging out and smoothing granite rock into chiselled boulders the consistency of hardened butterscotch, the waters frothed with milky chocolate spray. The echoes of lethal landslides resulting in endless rubble on the treacherous winding pathways, then the surprising quiet river bends create an unmistakable ambience. On sanded banks lone swamis and sadhus follow the trail of those earlier recorders of India's natural marvels, doing obeisance as they meditated in her honour, bathing in the icy blue waters while chanting her 108 names of beauty, blessing, auspicious qualities and redemption.

And then the torrent flows onwards again as **Shankha-dundubhi-nisvana**, making the sound of a conch shell and drum (her 19th name) until Ganga Ma reaches the plains of India proper (see **Slowly Down the Ganges** by **Eric Newby**, Hodder and Stoughton, London, 1966). Ganga Ma is a true mother sustaining (it is said) nearly 40% of India's population.

◆ From the holy Har-ki-pairi pool at Hardwar, hemmed in by temples, shrines, bazaars and pilgrims crammed on the ghat steps to bathe, 300 miles away from source she flows from only 1,250 feet above sea level, ever pushed forward by the daily surge of glacial meltdown and crushed soil. Seen from the air one could be forgiven for thinking there was an endless line of ants

moving along her banks, for even in winter months brave souls on a testing penance are scrambling ever upwards to her source; chanting her lovely names from the **Gangastottara-sata-namavali** (108 names of Ganga). The challenging pilgrimage leads beyond **Rishikesh** to the visible source at **Go-mukh** (cow-mouth), where the glacier breaks and arches into cavernous blue-grey misty waters, but this is retreating year by year, nearly 20 km already.

◆ Here the river is the **Bhagirathi,** and only downstream at **Deoprayag** (71 km from Rishikesh), where the river Alaknanda from Badrinath flows into it, so noticeably different in quality and reflective hue, do the different waters merge, indiscernible in becoming the one holy Ganga Ma.

◆ Bhagirathi (feminine) takes a Hindu's sense of myth (and perhaps the reality of poetic history) back to pre-Vedic times when this holy river is believed to have flowed for the Himalayan gods in heaven. This makes sense to Hindus who have overcome the rigours of the challenging pilgrimage, for local lore avers that the grey-white cauldron of waters that emerge from the melon-sliced glacial face (no way looking like the mouth of a cow) flows deep under the eternal depth of impacted ice from who knows what perennial spring in the womb-heart of the Himalayas. Some believe that the source-waters may well rise or join underground with those leading from the equally auspicious **Amarnath Cave** in the Kashmir Himalayas on the other side of the Nanda Devi range (see **PILGRIMAGE** and **TAPASYA**). This is another magnetic field for testing the faith of individual Hindus, and for tourists to reach the sacred cave where a so-called Shiva ice lingam becomes tumescent or diminishes depending on the waxing/waning of moons and atmospheric seasonal changes.

◆ Noone, geologically, has been able to trace the source. Perhaps satellite photography alone could 'sense' it down to its first trickle. Indians, no matter how modern, centred as they are in their millions in urban material surroundings, have not lost that capacity for remaining embedded in the natural flow of nature once they reach it on pilgrimage. Then it transforms into Prakriti, a resonating **numenistic** nature lost to the industrial West—now desperately trying to retrieve this sense of 'being part of nature' in environmental and Green Party movements.

◆ The Devprayag confluence is the entry point for the four most sacred shrines (**chardhamyatra**—see **TIRTHS**), at Badrinath, Kedarnath, Gangotri and Yamunotri. All lie in the new (27th) state created in 2000 called **Uttaranchal** (out of NW Uttar Pradesh) and a region considered auspicious territory. The struggles of pre-Vedic kings echo in all the named places of Gangetic pilgrimage, bubbling up and bursting into pilgrims' minds by the retelling on site as they sit in the golden evening glow listening to the recounting of the ancient tales and allegorical parables from swamis and gurus.

This is where Bhagirath<u>a</u> (masculine) steps into the story. He is the great-great-grandson of King **Sagara** who gives his name to the 7th of the 108 names **Ganga-sagaratmaja-tarika** (liberator of the sons of Sagara). A strange history is woven around Bhagiratha reflecting the hyperbole of India's mythology which

G

prompts one to raise sceptical Western eyebrows. This time his name reflects his unhappy fate 'born of poison' in the womb due to the nastiness of a rival wife to his own mother. Whether that affected his genetic structure or reflects in metaphor some phenomenal historic fact hyped up in oral culture and its transmission over centuries, the story states that childless as he was, he seeks a **BOON**—that word also again!—of a sage, who promised his first wife an heir; the other 60,000 sons who were nurtured as seeds by the other wife in a gourd to become embryos!

Of course, the only son becomes a hedonistic, wild youth, obviously in the classic syndrome of the sole heir abandoned by his father, Sagara. The other fanciful legion is sent out detailed by the royal father to observe the classic rite of guarding the **ashwamedha** horse–the ritual of expanding boundaries of their father's kingdom; however, to their shame they lose the sacrificial horse, which is abducted to the 'nether regions' (slightly different from the Christian hell).

Here **Kapila** the sage/philosopher is meditating. He is met later on (see **PILGRIMAGE** section: **Bengal**). A very touchy personality, a condition that is common to sages! As founder of the orthodox **Samkhya** school of the six Hindu philosophies (around the 7th century BCE) he may well be meditating in a highly intellectual way. Almost Jesuitical, devoted to enumeration of the essences of the natural world (see **PRAKRITI**) and the search for ultimate knowledge = **gyana** (identified with **PURUSHA**), Samkhya philosophy does not encourage belief in a personal God. Unfortunately Kapila happens to be in deep thought beside this grazing horse. The 60,000 sons crowding in naturally believe this man, unknown to them and inexplicably in this infernal region, is the culprit in losing the especial horse. They attack him. Aroused in rage, Kapila incinerates them all to ash. It is Bhagiratha, two generations further on, who supplicates an ageless Kapila to grant him the boon of releasing the Ganga holy waters from heaven to flow over the ashes of these doomed step-ancestors to revive them. This the irascible Kapila does grant, despite appearances (similar to the cantankerous **VASISHTA** and **VISWAMITRA** who, though born a ruler/warrior, elevated himself into the brahmin clan by dint of extreme **tapasya** disciplines, becoming one of the original seven sages saved in the Flood (see **SAPTARSHI**). Such acerbity recalls the academic characters of Iris Murdoch's and C P Snow's novels, especially English Literature scholars of Cambridge vying for one upmanship in those academic **Corridors of Power**!

The Ganga waters are allowed to flow via the toe of Vishnu or through the matted hair of Siva, depending upon the sect to which one belongs, to the great ocean waters, where Sagar the island shrine to Kapila marks the holy grail and release of souls, among them this considerable fraternity.

To fly over the mouth of the Ganga in daylight from Kolkata is a sight to wonder at–like a gigantic fan of grey mud, the sediment brought down by its waters discolours the incoming ocean in an even swathe several hundred miles out to sea from a stream just over a foot deep. The Ganges is such a mighty torrent it is capable of shifting 355 million tons of silt a year. No wonder Ganga Ma, so revered, has been given 108 names from just plain Ganga to 'a light amid the darkness of ignorance', 'born from the lotus-like foot of Vishnu', 'white as milk', 'possessing merit', and 'pure'.

◆ Many commentators have noted also a particular quality of Ganga water, no matter how difficult to believe when watching it flowing past. Despite all that now flows into it upstream from the urban detritus of at least 114 major cities–decomposing corpses of bodies cast into the water which cannot, by ritual, be cremated; chemical factory effluent, cattle excrement and agricultural fertilizer–it is still sipped by millions to absolve them of their sins and the consequences in many rebirths.

◆ It is also carried away in sealed pots to be stored in millions of home shrines for purification rituals. As Newby (and other records) point out, in the old sailing ship days of the great East India Company, the Ganga water taken on board as drinking water at Calcutta remained fresh and sweet, outlasting all other waters on the long voyages back to Britain.

◆ In fact the Maharaja of Jaipur, travelling to London in 1902 by the long sea route from Bombay (usually two and a half weeks voyage) to stay at the famous Ritz Hotel, had 8,000 gallons of Ganga water conveyed in two immense silver urns now on display in the City Palace of the Pink City.

◆ Doubting Thomases who are not true believers, still remaining sceptical of this hygienic act of faith, should read **Waters of Hope** by George Verghese (Oxford-Indian Book House, New Delhi, 1990). A supreme optimist, he firmly believes—given the political will and economic resources—the full length of the Ganges can be cleaned up. Then indeed can **feminine** sprites dance in joy again, their attributes throughout aeons of time, a metaphor for the life-giving fertility to the soil and the **husbandry** of agriculture—an interesting male balance to the feminine nature of the goddess Ganga whose other attribute of cleanliness may still be retrieved. But is the political will there? Another decade on, not much success has been in sight.

There are Western parallels. A good Victorian dictum heard often from English grandmothers in our childhoods–'cleanliness is next to godliness'–is achieved by millions upon millions day in and day out washing, immersing and bathing along the banks of Ganga Ma for at least the last 5,000 years.

Footnote on Developments

In a major article in **The New Yorker** magazine (Jan 19, 1998) Alexander Stille delivered some devastating scientific broadsides to optimism on cleansing the holy waters of Ganga Ma, pointing out that roughly **500 million people–one out of every 12 humans in the world**—let alone cattle, the source of raw sewage and detritus, live in the Gangetic basin and its tributaries.

The article not only raised concern about the degree of pollution but the deeper issue of clean drinkable water world-wide, and the moral dilemmas increasingly facing all nations and governments. Stille points out tellingly that 17 five-star hotels in Delhi alone consume as much clean water **daily** as 1.5 million slum dwellers could use in their *bustis* if they even had the luxury of a communal tap.

The article is worth a library search, for it has a joyous quality in his clarity of combining the hard core of scientific fact with the vibrant framework of Indian life encountered as he follows his research. This takes him to the equally vibrant **Veer Bhadra Mishra, mahant** (senior priest) at the **Sankat Mochan Temple**, above the ghats yet at the same time a hydraulic engineer professor at Banaras University. (In 1992, for his efforts to cleanse the Ganga of pollution, Mishra was conferred the UN Roll of Honour and later named one of the 'seven heroes of the planet' by **Time Magazine**).

What is more, to steep him further in a true sense of sanatana dharma, this academic priest occupies the ancient home of **Tulsi Das**, the 16th century rishi who composed the Hindi version of the **RAMAYANA.**

Mishra's professional encounter (spiced with a typically Indian chuckle) with the equally visionary and humorous William Oswald, Emeritus Professor of Engineering at Berkeley University, almost brings tears to the heart as well as the eyes at the thought of human endeavour in the face of intractable problems of a river system overburdened by the very weight of population.

Oswald is remarkable also in his turning, like Schumacher three decades before, to the **Small is Beautiful** ethos of looking at cultures and reinterpreting technology which makes sense of indigenous circumstances—such as not using grandiose electrical sewage plants which fail due to power cuts and monsoonal challenges. Oswald has conceived culturally appropriate pond systems. They will have the gargantuan task of dealing with 'fecal-coliform counts... **known to reach a hundred and seventy million bacteria per 100 millilitres of water—a terrifying 340,000 times the acceptable level of 500 per 100 millilitres'.**

Endnote: The most evocative record of the Ganga yatra must surely be William Dalrymple's TV Series (BBC Manchester 1999)—magnificently filmed, sensitively narrated with moments of sheer joy (a voluble Tamil professor regaling him with Wordsworth while bathing in a pool and a naked sadhu baba with Harley Davidson bike rigged with cassette player—pure India!).

■ **GARLANDS**
So ubiquitous in India, see **MALA**

■ **GAYATRI** (n. *Sanskrit*)
(Om) | bhurbhuva: sva: |
(Om) **tat saviturvarenyam** |
bhargo devasya dhimahi |
dhiyo yo na: prachodayat | (Om)
is regarded by many Hindus as the most sacred verse of the Vedas, repeated in reverence by millions every morning as they bathe, letting water course through their fingers, movingly spoken as they stand in rivers facing the sun, giver of life-enhancing energy, without the presence of which this planet would freeze up and petrify. These morning/evening prayers are known as **sandhyas**. As chanted the sound OM is added as invocation and

to give a ringing sonority to the customary ritual which has been added over the millennia. The towering personality of Raja Rammohun Roy (see **CALCUTTA**) devoted an entire text to **Gayatri**, the personified Mother of the Vedas.

Each daybreak when **Ushas**, 'Daughter of the Sky', heralds the dawn, Surya the sun, charioted with five horses brings life-giving light, enhancing human well-being. Early humanity realized fast that without the sun's warmth and enlightenment, there would be no sap rising, no energy, no benign force bestowing renewal of daylight activity—not possible in the dark when fire was first discovered to bring a flickering glow to the shadows. Anyone who has camped out knows the truth of this in outback Australia on a moonless night. Early Indians soon learned to pay homage and bow to this force in the **surya namaskar**, hands folded together in prayer, the morning salutation.

The root mantra, **AUM** (OM) termed 'the password of life' and referred to as the **bij** = seed, the fundamental sound first mouthed, precedes the benediction.

Personal Footnote: A steadfast friend, checking out last minute hesitations on my part as I stood on the final stepping stone, brought back from Chennai a movingly beautiful rendition not only of the **Gayatri mantra**, but of the **Pranayam mantra** chanted in meditation to open up the energising chakras of the body (and therefore the spirit) through breath-control (see **PRANA**) to the equally energising powers of the universe; and a prayerful devotion to the goddess Gayatri herself, adored for all her resplendent embellishments, 'hues of pearl, coral, gold, blue', her hands expressing mudras of blessing and holding all manner of attributes as metaphors of her powerful shakti potency. It is in such sound renditions that the transliteration in print with the colon sign placed after a word (see above–bhurbhuva: sva:) makes sense. This sign is called **visarga** and denotes an **emphasised aspirate**, like a 'kick-off' as the word ends.

In chaste, powerfully enunciated Sanskrit, this 1999 musical version, **sung by Pandit Jasraj**, was written by Sri Shyam Manohar Goswami for **Innervoice Times Music, India 1999**. Its modern translation goes thus:

Oh, Creator of the Universe! We meditate upon thy supreme splendour. May thy radiant power illuminate our intellects, destroy our sins, and guide us in the right direction.

Yet another with commentary in English and sung by **Pandit Rajan** and **Sajan Mishra** from the Banaras School of Music has been released by **Milestone** in a packaged series of four. This is titled **Chants of Gayatri**. But perhaps that translation which is most meaningful is the most direct–and simplest, Sanskrit word by Sanskrit word drawn from a publication of the **Bharatiya Yog Sansthan**, Delhi. Any physicist could relate to the devotional acknowledgement of the following. Imagination can supply the intervening spaces and put flesh on the skeletal spine.

PRAYER FOR ENLIGHTENMENT
This summary, the best and the essence of the Indian tradition, requires no Divinity or Deity in the semitic sense. **Om** is added as invocative of the source of all creation:

Om	(Invocation)
Bhur	physical plane
Bhuvah	astral plane
Svahah:	celestial plane
Tat	That (Brhm as mentor, or Paramatma)
Savitur	Sun as creator
Varenyam	Fit to be worshipped/venerated
Bhargo	Glory
Devasya	Of the shining one
Dhimahi	We meditate
Dhiyo	Intellect = Buddhi (in the sense of insight = illumination)
Yo	Which, who
Nah:	Our
Prachodayat	Enlighten

A final note: There are many translations into English. It is virtually impossible to transliterate the Sanskrit words to reflect accurately or plumb the depth of their density in cultural meanings. Occasionally **Savitur** appears as **Savitr** = the generator. This word is not to be confused with **Savitri** [name of a legendary heroine who, by devotion to her young husband Satyavan (who died in tragic circumstances) so pursued Yama, the god of Death, that he grants her a **BOON** which she used craftily to win back mortality for Satyavan.]

Let us adore the supremacy of the divine sun, the godhead, who illuminates all, who recreates all, from whom all proceed to whom all must return, whom we invoke to direct our understanding aright in our progress toward its holy seal.

A physicist's dream!

This entire mantra must surely be a scientific statement of truth. Indeed a physicist friend on hearing of the morning ritual immediately responded with an affirmation acknowledging the symbolic nature of the ritual also, of water trickling through the fingers raised in salutation to **Surya**. The very warmth and energy of the sun which makes life possible is equated with *flow*, a basic scientific truth of physics. No thing even if it appears to be solid, inert, or lumpen mass is actually so. It is at the same time in a state of flux, the metaphor of flowing water most apt. [For further reading refer to **Ram Swarup**'s **Meditations: Yogas, Gods, Religions** (Voice of India, New Delhi, 2000).

■ **GHALIB**
Persian Urdu poet
1797–1869

In north Indian literary culture Ghalib is one of its most notable unifiers, meshing into his Islamic traditions and delicate but magnificent Persian-Urdu verse Indians and Pakistanis, Muslim, Hindu and Sikhs, Punjabi and UP wallahs, no matter where they are. I have been in English-Asian homes where after good khana (food) individuals have begun reciting the poet's cryptic verses, to be capped with applause and yet another rendition, until all are taking part joyously!

At the time, as the 19th century gathered pace, the literary rivulets flowing from Ghalib's pen gathered into a force infiltrating the body of north Indian intellectual life, a world of private sophistication as active as any Parisian salon but about which British colonial life hardly had an inkling. Yet the lively cultural life of major urban centres such as Lahore, Delhi, Lucknow and Allahabad spread out even to the smaller mofussil towns. Even today, Delhi intellectuals and Rajasthani maharajas and their courtly circles, elitist bureaucrats, old wealth and new business tycoons of this age, Bengali poets rich and poor, peasant elders and village literates are still woven into this tapestry of **a vibrant oral culture**. Ghalib's sonorous couplets and quatrains encompassed all... even Madhya Pradesh Hindi-wallahs.

Personal experience on an ornithological foray near Bhopal on the way to visit Buddhist Sanchi for the first time as it opened up to travellers taught a good lesson. Never underestimate village India or fringe 'illiterates' by the uppity criteria of Western education. Over a salty brew of milky brown cinnamon tea, our party was sat on rope charpoys in the **panchayat** hall where we were swathed in true village hospitality. An elder was moved to poetic fancy in welcoming a Canadian (they had never met one before), as well as a well-known ICS Englishman, Arthur Hughes fluent in several regional languages, and retired 'into India,' two Americans who to the locals could have been off another planet, and the BBC, just as the first transistors were infiltrating even isolated outback villages. Regaled with Ghalib's poetic wisdom, even if jaggedly translated into awkward English inappropriate to the smoothly-flowing Urdu, it was obvious that illiteracy is a technical term. They were firmly and confidently embedded in their cultures of hundreds of years uninterrupted oral flow.

1797–**Mirza Mohammad Asadullah Khan Ghalib** was born in **Agra**. Mercifully, despite tragedy in losing a father and vital uncle—both involved as mercenary agents in the shifting politics of the Punjab and Maratha incursions of those times—the young boy Ghalib was brought up in his maternal grandparents' home. There he was exposed to excellent Persian and Arabic scholars, so that by the age of nine Ghalib could compose commendable verse.

But he was ahead of the solid culture of his time. The rhythm of his literary skills defied conventional forms that the literati of Delhi accepted. Despite a sell-out whenever his books of poetry were circulated, all his life he felt unappreciated—a true case of a prophet never without honour except in his own country.

Well aware he deserved higher accolades, his acerbic nature felt constantly short-changed. He penned these lines in Persian:

In eternity without beginning
My star has reached the zenith of acceptance;
But in the world, the renown
Of my verses will be after me.

How ironic. Now in symposiums, not only in his native land but worldwide, and wherever popular **GHAZAL** vocalists perform as well as the private poetry-reading sessions still very popular in India (whether Sikh, Hindu or Muslim communities) Ghalib's star is in ascendancy in the cultural firmament.

G

Privileged to know Ralph Russell as a co-lecturer at the Centre for International Briefing in south England, I was converted to Ghalib's sonorous poetry by listening to this well-known Urdu scholar from SOAS in London, whose love of Urdu and Persian was infectious. His various publications on Ghalib are worth searching out, as well as the biography by **Pavan Varma–Ghalib: The Man, The Times**. Yet another, **The Famous Ghalib**, Russell has added since (Roli, 2000). And more seem to pour off the presses from other sources, the poet standing taller than any of his time, surely a commentary on the fickleness of artistic appreciation.

Russia too has come to the party; the Moscow Institute of Oriental Studies, known for its scholastic excellence in Indian disciplines, has published a book by Natalia Prigarina: **Mirza Ghalib**, finally translated into English by Osama Faruqi (OUP, Pakistan, 2000) after 14 years!

♦ Visit also the **Ghalib Academy** near South Delhi's Nizamuddin Aulia's mausoleum to see the artistically neat calligraphy of his prolific letterwriting, his surprising passion for kite-flying and chess, as well as other memorabilia.

■ **GHAM** (n. *Urdu*)

Pain, an anguish of the heart much used in north Indian/Pakistani poetry and **GHAZALS** (light classical music with strong emotional vibes). It is the consequence of the yearnings of **unrequited** love, a condition of the subcontinent.

Is this a result of the prevalence of the arranged marriage system, which though on the whole as equally effective as the supposed love marriages of the West, can go disastrously wrong at times? Or because of a surfeit of idealism in the myths and legends, which are the ground base to the culture, and trying to equate the frailty of human love with the idealised love expressed at many levels towards the manifold deities of India? Perhaps this agonising emotion can be likened to the 'atmospherics' of the courtly ballads in Europe of the Middle Ages, when romance between the balladeer, often a knight on a white horse and playing a lute, serenaded the delicate lady on the balcony, virginal and inaccessible as she was. This has been visually depicted in so many European **Books of Hours**, illustrated in manuscript parchments, which glow vividly and sparkle with gold, no matter how old.. and also carries that sense of yearning for union with the Divine… mysterious… unattainable.

This is a pain born of lack of reality, love on a pedestal, a love that will never be amid the realities of today—of nappies, a husband home late for dinner in an urban world of frazzled tempers and stress, snoring at night and someone who grumbles that there are hairs in the washbasin again!

No wonder then that **gham** encapsulates an elevated meaning in the high poetry of an Urdu **mushaira**, taking on the mantle of a soul's yearning for union with the divine!

■ **GHAZAL** (n. *Urdu*)

What politics breaks asunder in group animosities, the arts can bind together in individual friendly participation and in an illuminating way. Announce a **shaam-e-ghazal** and Pakistani and north Indian lovers of fine light classical music will flock together for an evening of sweet melancholy steeped in this evocative art form. **This is their culture**, vocal music of cultivated poetry and romantic yearning, vivid in imaginative and emotional content, literally floating upon captivating ragas and across alienating political borders. (In recent years Jagjit Singh has been very popular with overseas Asian audiences, noted for the resonating texture of his voice, flamboyant surges on particular phrases well-known to the connoisseur).

♦ It could not be more symbolic of that synthesis of Hindu and Muslim cultural interweavings from Mughal times onwards.

Among the many social expressions of this absorption was the emergence of a joint language—**Urdu, derived from Persian and Hindi sources**.

1997

The 200th anniversary of **Mirza Ghalib** was celebrated. He has been called Urdu's greatest poet. See **Khurshidul Islam's** biography, **Ghalib, 1797–1869** (Allen and Unwin, London, 1996).

'Visionary saint, philosopher and scholar', Ghalib's poetry provides the high point of any ghazal evening with its soaring lyrical quality. Other poets, some Pakistani—such as the highly respected Faiz, Mir Taqi Mir, Zafar Faraaz, Quli Qutb Shah—plus the musicians, vocalists and instrumentalists from either side of the border—create the rich atmosphere of the north Indian **ghazal-gayaki**, this system which is as Mendelssohn or Tchaikovsky are in comparison with the demanding intellectual ragas of Bach.

♦ **Amir Khusro** (or Khusrau), a Turko-Indian musician of the 13–14th centuries who was a disciple of the famous Sufi guru Sheikh Nizamuddin, injected new lyrical styles of music into that of devotional India and popularised this freeing up into a secular romanticism. Ghazal—and the equally popular and more racy **QAWALI**—is very much in demand among resident Punjabis overseas who throng to such concerts and vocalise themselves in the enthusiasm and aroused emotions of the moment. They respond to fine musicians who display an elegant style = **bandish**, with explosive 'wah, wahs', 'shabash', loud clapping and audible sighing as a superb slide down the scale of particular notes sends the adrenalin racing! Scintillating ghazals are part of the magic of India.

■ **GNOW** (*Sanskrit* **gnyana-jnana** = knowledge)

A verb not to be found in the English lexicon, despite noun and adjective existing—**gnosis** and **gnostic** respectively. Agnostic is also a common enough adjective used in popular speech in these uncertain times. Even a pop group called itself so. It is doubtful they knew how close they were to Sanskrit in the gñ root and the negating prefix: a… **not to gnow**. It was a word first suggested by the late Professor Ninian Smart (then of Lancaster University) in acknowledging wisdom as different from factual knowledge. He was well known for his work especially in television on the world's diverse faiths.

ज़ The last letter in the Indian alphabet is this Devanagari character: which is a mixture of gya and nya. The word for intuitive wisdom is **gyana** in Sanskrit, but sounds more like **gnyana**. It often appears in print as **jnana**.

◆ The Greeks who created the English equivalents acknowledged other means to acquire wisdom, differentiated from straightforward knowledge realized from assembling facts.

External objectivity is one level; the inward search of the mystic is another. A holistic view in the approach to truth is a way taught by Swami Vivekananda in a book titled **Jnana-Yoga**, an assemblage of his lecture tour of Indian cities. (Available at Ramakrishna centres.)

Expounding the **Vedanta** (end = **ant** of the Vedas) and using texts from the **Katha Upanishad** he points out that the external worlds of phenomena are not the only source of understanding the truth of our existence.

Knowledge without love and love without knowledge cannot be. What we want is the harmony of Existence, Knowledge and Bliss Infinite.

SAT-CHIT-ANANDA, in other words…

◆ Elsewhere, Vivekananda foresaw a century earlier, the desperate search amongst so many individuals for a more integrated way of living, and the rise of irrational cults desperately searching for simplistic answers in a complex alienating materialist world. He sensed that the intellectual rationality even of a great seer such as Shankaracharya, even in the Indian context, 'throwing the scorching light of reason upon everything' needed to be 'joined with the heart of Buddha, the wonderful infinite heart of love and mercy'. He concludes:

This union will give us the highest philosophy. Science and religion will meet and shake hands. Poetry and philosophy will become friends.

Searching for that inner sense of one-ness, of being 'grounded', he quotes Plato as acknowledging the need for this 'other knowledge'—inspiration which comes to people through poetry. Vivekananda continues:

Ancient Rishis, seers of truth, were raised above humanity to show these truths through poetry. They never preached, nor philosophised, nor wrote. Music came out of their hearts.

One is aware in India that saints and seers sing their truths, as did the **ALVARS** of more recent times, as do the many **BHAKTI** followers of today. It is more openly acknowledged that through the oblique avenues of artistic forms, music, poetry, dance humanity can complement the 'world of reason with other means of acquiring true **wisdom**'.

◆ It has virtually taken a century to witness the stirrings of a new approach amongst scientists schooled in Western rationality; now increasingly phrases such as 'provisional knowledge' are used by eminent physicists such as Australia's Professor **Paul Davies (The Mind of God)** to qualify the finality of knowledge. That ultimate truth can never be measured in concrete terms brings one round to Vivekananda lecturing in London in 1896 (**The Absolute and Manifestation,** Simon & Schuster, London, 1992) taking one back to the sixth century BCE:

When the scientific teacher asserts that all things are the manifestation of one force, does it not remind you of the God of whom you hear in the Upanishads:

*'As the one fire entering into the universe expresses itself in various forms, even so that One soul is expressing itself in every soul **and yet is infinitely more besides**.'*

Do you not see whither science is tending? The Hindu nation proceeded through the study of the mind, through metaphysics and logic. The European nations start from external nature, and now they too, are coming to the same results... science today is telling us that all things are but the manifestation of one energy which is the sum total of everything which exists...

◆ It is this intuitive search using the other lobe of the brain in harness with that of hard fact—a **complementariness**, that is what gyana is all about, and very close to the understanding of India's inner life—a swastika zigzag, the erratic sudden flash of comprehension through poetic visions, dreamt insights, artistic leaps of the imagination ever ahead of the commonality of the times, scientific inspiration as devious and alarmingly 'irrational' as the flash of forked lightning (refer to **INTUITIVE KNOWLEDGE, VEDAS** and **YOGA**, especially passages on **consciousness**).

A Western scientist in a broadcast lecture recently reminded his unseen audience with pithy exactness: 'Data is **not** information; information is **not** knowledge; knowledge is **not** wisdom.' This is worth thinking about. **To gnow** has a different dimension in the mind from **to know**. Professor Ninian Smart was right!

■ **GOLD**
is of high-carat worth to every Indian because its real purity in content implies those eternal unsullied **sattvic** qualities (refer **GUNAS**). When defining this untarnishable metal, a **carat** (a weight just over 200 milligrams in **gems**) is a 24th part in assaying the purity of the mineral content after the impurities of rock and dirt are extracted and through which it flowed and then cooled millions of years ago. **Then it is 23:999 carats in the minting process**. To watch gold poured is a breath-taking experience, most especially when the thought crosses one's mind that way down under one's feet a liquid circle cast a tenuous ring around the planet's southern hemisphere before the cooling-down process began. This formed eventually into the supercontinent of **Gondwana,** from which South America, Madagascar, India and Australia have drifted apart over a 160 million years. Through the fabric of these soils are woven threads of gold.

On maps of eastern India the name **Gondwana** still appears where Orissa is now delineated as a state. The Kolar Goldfields, east of Bangalore, and the Kalgoorlie mines of Western Australia's Eastern Goldfields share part of the same heritage. At one time the Kolar fields had the deepest mine in the world, 2 miles in depth; quite an experience to travel down its two-stage shaft for BBC Overseas Service programmes. Despite air-conditioning, the

G

temperature was hot, the claustrophobia worse, the sense of dripping rock, echoing hollow shafts, the living rock 'moaning' and shifting—all quite overpowering. In fact a profound sense of matter—energy like an invisible current making itself manifest—envelops puny human spirits; the deep earth, **Prithvi**, ever shifting her bulky frame on those mysterious tectonic plates.

And now to add to the mystery a Hindu shrine at the bottom of that shaft, to honour the Englishman Alex Cave, who was appointed from his post in the British Army in India by the Indian Government **after** Independence to be Superintendent of Mines until 1956 when he migrated to Western Australia, his family now living in Perth.

GOLD HAS STANDING

◆ **Spiritually:** being a pure **sattvic** metal which never tarnishes, unlike silver, and which, even if a baby wears nothing else, certainly in south India is tied on cord around the stomach. The rubbing of skin against a chunky piece of pure gold is said to absorb the medicinal qualities of the gold. A pioneer in cardiac medical surgery, Dr Purshotam Lal is using implant technique technology—Goldstent—in his Metro Hospital in South Delhi because gold is anti-bacterial, being 'negatively-charged', so reducing blood clot formation, according to the good doctor. Is the fact of the negative charge the source of the belief that gold does not 'ping' like silver bracelets and pendants when travellers check in at airports and pass through the security frame? If so, gold smugglers have it made!

◆ **Historically:** a hammered piece, beaten flat and moulded as a template into the form of a mother goddess in all her implied fecundity, dug up by chance in a Bengali field being ploughed, perhaps for 40 centuries by peasant farmers, is dated at approximately 2000 BCE. It gleams as pristine as it was when first beaten. Other examples found in the tumuli at **Lauriya-Nandangarh**, north west of **Patna**, are dated around the 7th century BCE. They testify to the spiritual significance of gold and its early symbolic use in worship. One of the most compelling and famous examples is that of the **14th–13th century BCE Harappan Sri Mandala** figure of the goddess Sri. This figure of the female, with heavy golden orbs hanging from her ears and necklaces with the geometric **yantra** of triangles on her torso, establishes the antiquity and fundamental strength of mathematical concepts intrinsic to Indian philosophy.

◆ When first representations of the Lord Buddha were finally created, as well as the incomparable Chola bronzes of Tamilnadu a thousand years later (11–13th century CE), earlobes are depicted hanging down like looped ribbons, reminding the viewer by sculptural metaphor of the high status of these Beings, vested in fine gold and red raiments, and at one time weighty pure gold earrings!

◆ **Physically:** gold functions efficiently as a 'liquid' resource, easily transformed into ready cash in times of need; easily transportable; welcome anywhere as a stable currency exchange and about which every Indian can find out the day's price immediately; more stable than banks, which sometimes even today can collapse. After a good monsoon some farmers, despite encouragement to 'get their money moving' in rural savings banks, put their welcome wealth into gold bars or jewellery for which 'official' gold is set aside.

◆ **Economically:** a curious situation endemic in Indian culture—it would seem since 'time immemorial', a phrase current on an Indian lip everyday of the year—is that gold has been endowed with a higher intrinsic price than anywhere else in the world. Even today no government has yet been able to grasp the nettle of gold, its worth within India approximately 10% more than in the rest of the world, yet often becoming just static wealth, locked up in home safes. This has been a matter of serious concern to government finance ministers in that the hoarding of gold, though a national savings of sorts, represents static wealth hidden away in the community. Or it is smuggled into India and absorbed into the 'black money economy', a quite extraordinary separate economy where government and society is not reaping the benefits of working capital at all—or taxes!

When the austere, Gandhi-inspired Morarji Desai of Gujarat, one-time Finance Minister and Prime Minister of India was in power several decades ago, he tried very hard to shift this static asset, but even the repeal in 1990 of the **Gold Control Act of 1962** which prohibited Indians from possessing 'unwrought' gold (i.e., bars, nuggets) could not wean Indians of this habit of storing it away for an 'unrainy' day—the vagaries of the monsoon and attendant drought being a vital part of India's annual GNP well-being or downfall. This is especially so among the 75% of India's population that still lives a village economy. Indeed, demand for gold after plentiful monsoonal rain can rise substantially—up to 40%.

If the enormous statistical increase year by year is anything to go by, the estimate from **The Gold Companion** is that at least 18,000 tonnes is held privately! Currently if that was converted into liquid assets, as proposed by the State Bank of India in 1999, it would slash the nation's annual trade deficit considerably. The amount of gold sequestered away, much of it by women who regard it as **streedhan**—wealth donated or given on a woman's marriage or on family occasions and entirely her personal property—is currently worth at least 140 billion dollars.

The World Gold Council research shows India is the world's leading consumer of gold. A rider which states that only 51% of this gold was bought through 'official' channels says it all! The research was not far wrong. On average, at least one third of the total quantity comes in **'unofficially'**. The decline in the unofficial figures may be due to the increase in the amount of bullion **NRIs** (non-resident Indians) are allowed to bring back to India when visiting relatives or investing in property due to the liberalization policies of the central government.

◆ **Artistically:** it is used as a pure gold-plating as a matter of status, prestige and spiritual merit—on great domes of the Sikh Golden Temple in Amritsar, the Hindu temple roofing of Viswanath in **VARANASI** and the magnetic pilgrimage temple at **TIRUPATI**. All are of great spiritual significance being the vital canopy over the central shrine deep in the womb of the architectural plan—the **garbha griha**. This is the **axis mundi**,

G

around which all temple activity circulates in **pradakshan** as also in the ultimate shrine to **Shiva-Nataraj** at **CHIDAMBARAM.**

♦ **Socially:** the exchange of gold between families at **marriage** and as gifts to the young couple is such that the poorer sections of the population push themselves into loan debts at exorbitant interest rates. The demand for gold for this purpose continues unabated each year as India's population increase soars by approximately 17 million annually. A major factor in national gold trends in the future and economic considerations for gold mining companies and manufacturers world wide is the enormous number of weddings annually—over ten million, all with dowries!

The Gold Companies Bulletin, in stating that the standing of a family in many communities 'is still judged by gold that is exchanged as the Bride's dowry', puts the basic gift of gold in jewellery as at least one set of earrings, one nosepin, one ring, one wedding necklace (the **mala** or **mangalsutra**), two bangles—**all** 22 carat gold (Muslim society, although not wedded to such a systematic dowry system, still abides by **meher**, a form of wedding gift in jewellery or gold). That is a substantial outlay. Even the poorest families will have to aspire to 'do their daughter proud' for fear of what mean-minded in-laws may do to her psychologically, if not physically, when she moves into the predominantly traditional joint family. Understandably, when one investigates the average income at rural level, this leads to long years of debt and repaying the money-lenders their exorbitant interest rates for the wedding loan. For the middle class other factors are at work.

♦ **Weddings.** Economic liberalization and the surge forward economically by the 200–300 million strong consumer class adds another alarming manifestation—the 'greed syndrome'. Commented upon in many Indian newspapers, something new has happened in modern India—the excessive and obscene display of wealth at weddings. Among the super-rich, gold merchants had better watch out. Competition is building up—from diamonds, once a Western girl's best friend. That the poor do not riot on the spot in peasant revolts, similar to those which took place in mediaeval Europe due to the alarming divide between rich and poor, is a miracle of acceptance of ancient ways and the concept of personal dharma—what happens in the present being a consequence of what occurred in a previous life. But for how much longer?

♦ **Donations to Temples:** these also need to be taken into account as part of the pilgrimage dharma-karma cycle, of penances undertaken as a result of a psychological stress factor, a boon granted after prayers to a deity and the **vrata** or vow accomplished—an area of private life hardly known to economists who theorize in the West. The vast temple complexes which draw pilgrims from all over India to acquire merit as potent as any Muslim going on **Hajj** pilgrimage to Mecca, are reputed to have enormous holdings in diamonds and gold. **This also constitutes static wealth.** But the growing numbers of billionaires, those new **CROREPATIs** who need secure money to reinvest are certainly not sitting on their gold ingots! They are investing back into the country of their birth, building condominiums, hospitals and investing in technical colleges.

♦ **Artisans:** Because the holding of gold bars was prohibited until very recently, the investment of personal and family capital on the whole has been directed into jewellery. Jewellery gave clues to **personal status and wealth, region, even religion**. For instance, miniature mango pendants fashioned in the necklace indicate a Hindu bride, a crescent moon is undoubtedly an Islamic symbol. There is also the fine filigree work and what is called 'granulation', which is one of the oldest techniques used by the consummate artistry of the goldsmiths of India—a race apart who surely must trace their ancestry through the filament line of caste and guild in an unbroken thread that may be at least 6000 years of history in fashioning gold!

The range of Indian jewellery, with its finesse in the execution of design, sparks admiration in craftspeople across the world. The utter simplicity combined with the explosion of tinkling bells with green, red and white enamelled base and semi-precious stones glinting from the surrounding gold—all to enhance the burnished glow of brown skin, with extra ornaments, **nath** (the nose ring), hair ornaments, the turban **sarpech** (a fleur-de-lys kind of shape) stiff necklaces and flexible ones on gold thread with tasselled drawstrings dangling down the back—all are part of the skills, acknowledged by experts overseas.

Annually now, 70 million Indians purchased at least one piece of gold jewellery, and India still tops the list of world fabrication in carat jewellery creation roughly one-fifth of the nearly 3,000 tonnes created! (1999–2000) … and created by a significant industry that may involve nearly two million goldsmiths.

♦ Annually **nearly 560 tonnes of gold** is transfigured by hammering, beating, moulding and carving with fine instruments to be sold on the domestic market—**its internal worth the equivalent of 11 billion US dollars or more!**

Personal Humiliation—A Fast Learning Curve

A visit to an Indian jeweller with an Indian woman can be quite a daunting experience, especially if one had been conditioned to a wartime Europe where gold ornaments virtually disappeared, having been sold off for vital supplies and family food. An austere England, under the laws of rationing (egalitarianism that actually worked), allowed production of gold wedding rings of only one quality—9 carat gold!

Deep in the heart of Old Delhi, with its narrow dim lit lanes, thronging masses and old Brahmin bulls munching whatever is eatable in the refuse, we plunged into a Vermeer-like atmosphere of slatted light. My Indian friend Suvira checked in with the Sikh jewellers, his forebears having been 'in the family' for generations in Lahore before Partition. After the political upheavals, slaughter and mayhem he too had fled, to start life all over again in the overgrown Punjabi village of two million people that Delhi was in the 50s.

A paper was signed, a key appeared and we stepped further into the mottled half-light into what looked like a ship's boiler room, with heavy safe doors and wheeled locks on huge valves. Out came traditional antique gold earrings, faceted gold flashing like diamonds. It was decided that the old fashioned cumbersome hooks would be clipped off the malleable 23-carat gold and remade, along with part of the multi-tiered dome-shaped earrings, into two sets of a more contemporary design. I then began to see what Indian measurement was— **rattis, marshas** and **tolas**.

Very cautiously, all the separated gold was placed in the weighing pan with tweezers to check how many **marshas** there were. Indian gold measurement goes back to the beginnings of time; the ultimate fraction of a unit is a seed from a hardy bush *Abrus precatorius* out in the drylands of Rajasthan. This is called a **ratti** = 1/8 marsha, **marsha** = 12 tola.

◆ A ratti looks remarkably like a ladybird of the same colour but with one black 'quiff' at its head instead of dots over its body. Each ratti miraculously seems to weigh the same—0.27gms. 10 tolas = 3.75 troy oz = 116.6 grams.

◆ The dictionary definition of a **carat** is said to derive from the Arabic **qirat** perhaps from Greek, certainly from the Mediterranean where the **carob plant** produces a seed, like the ratti, of uniform weight which was used in earliest times also as a measure.

All pieces weighed, some was carefully placed back in the original envelope with a receipt recording weight. This was old gold to be used another time. The gold left in the brass pan was so soft it could easily be shaped and worked in front of one's own mesmerised gaze. No self-respecting householder would let such antique wealth out of sight.

In those early days after Independence, the Sikh owner figured a **firangi** must be wealthy. He tried to tempt me with two filigreed 23-carat churrees (bracelets)—**two for 130 rupees**. Unnerved in my naiveté and in a cultural void banded by my austere post war 9-carat gold English ring, I had the nerve to ask instead if I might first see anything in the nature of 18-carat gold, for a future gift of cufflinks. I was already being extravagant beyond my husband's means. A withering look flickered and was held psychologically in thin air. Diplomacy however, prevailed. But then, adding insult to injury, I produced silver wedding earrings for mending. The look of disdain this time was very salutary. For the first time, I realised what it was like for Indians to be on the receiving end of an icy stare from some English memsahib. It was then the learning curve took off. Meanwhile my friend had produced family heirlooms, which assuaged the sensibilities of the goodly Sikh. They were old brocade saris to be melted down, the heavy gold thread retrieved from the ashes to be put to further creative purpose.

The final touch; the gold shavings from the cutting of thinner, less bulky earring hooks for smaller ear-piercing were sold to the gold merchant to offset the cost of making three pairs of earrings—four rupees in all at 1950s prices!

◆ It is stated in the Gold Companies Bulletin that 250 million women each own an average of 20 saris and 20 grams of gold equalling 27 million metres of cloth and 5,000 tonnes of gold.

Afterthought—I should have bought those churrees: 130 rupees was regarded as an extravagance in 1955, at 16 rupees to one pound sterling exchange rate; now one pound buys roughly 50 rupees!

And a further afterthought—When the first Muslim invaders raided Mathura a thousand years ago and ransacked all the magnificent Hindu and Buddhist sculptures they took away as loot (one of the many words incorporated into the English language; **luthnaa** = to steal) five large golden images with ruby eyes and a **murti** = deity of solid gold weighing 1,120 lbs and decorated with a 3½ lbs of sapphires!

◆ **Smuggling**

Plus ç'a change, plus c'est la même chose.

...According to an estimate given by the Reserve Bank sometime ago, a million ounces of gold, valued at nearly five crore rupees, are smuggled into India annually [a crore = 10 million]. Across the Punjab border from Pakistan 10,000 tolas of illegal gold finds it way into the country everyday, according to another official estimate. Calculated at current gold prices, this means that the amount of our currency drained away through gold smuggling at present is almost Rs.5 crores a month. Persons arrested in recent months in connection with gold and currency smuggling have included a Briton, a Frenchman, a Cuban, a German Jew and Pakistanis...

Gujarat newspaper, source unknown, 1957, kept in personal diary

An arrest in Amritsar village at the time proved suspects were also Indian: Hindu and Sikh had their hair and beards trimmed and shaped in the Muslim fashion, and the Pakistanis in cahoots with this village group had 'adopted' the appearance of the Sikh peasantry to be able to pass inconspicuously in and out of each other's countries.

◆ **Fifty years on:** Nearly half a century later, little has changed except that the smuggling is on a highly efficient scale; high-powered instant communication by phone and internet aid and abet criminal elements in Mumbai, and motorised dhows ply out of the world's wealthiest townships—Dubai and Muscat. Here gold drips in serried rows in the airport duty-free shops and bazaars at probably the cheapest price per ounce in the world.

Most official estimates put the amount of gold smuggled into India each year as one third of the yearly circulation of gold. Smuggling proportionately keeps pace with legal imports despite all efforts on the part of finance ministers.

◆ **NRI's Influence...** Under the new dispensation of easing up red tape and regulations, NRI's (non-resident Indians) can bring back increasing amounts of the precious metal. This may well be used for investment or buying property in India for a new middle class lifestyle coming and going on a commuter basis between homes in two countries.

Throughout history, wherever there is gold imported there are smugglers. It is discussed in gold circles that of 80% of imported gold from NRI sources, 90 per cent of that is organised and paid for by smuggling syndicates, reimbursing NRI airfares and hotel bills—always one step ahead of the authorities! The gold is then resold for illicit dollars. The Ministry of Finance (whose sources these are) cannot win!

G

◆ **and Arraigned Politicians:** who have already appeared in **CORRUPTION**, especially Jayalalitha, dubbed the 'Booty Queen' by the Tamilnadu press. Arrested for embezzlement over a decade ago, a vast amount of this national static wealth was discovered in the police raid on her ritzy mansion. Allegedly, over $20 million worth of property was seized, including what at first seemed like good political dharma, the purchase of thousands of TV sets for villagers in Tamilnadu. Many however, had not reached their destination. In addition, to general astonishment, there appeared:

◆ 30kg of gold bars and diamonds
◆ 100 diamond studded watches
◆ 400 diamond churees
◆ and a giant golden sword!

Move over Marie Antoinette and Imelda Marcos!

Personal Encounter

On a high bluff in Maharashtra, looking out to the purple glow of dusk as the sun slips over the horizon to Africa and Oman and other points west, a sleek dhow travelling at quite astonishing speed leaves a curled wake, a give-away to any prowling customs boat, but no such craft patrols in these limpid grey waters. The motorised dhow glides into the isolated cove and for once there does not seem to be an unexpected Indian ready to pop up behind every bush—an experience most foreigners find very disconcerting when travelling by slow country roads through even the most isolated outback areas, just when the insistent call of nature demands the screening of even the scrawniest bush!

Small crates are being unloaded, flat boxes of big fish, pumpkins, but why there, not a jetty in sight, no nearby lorries to take away the heavy loads in a quick getaway?

Smugglers should beware of amateur ornithologists from Australia and Britain with several pairs of powerful binoculars chasing osprey and rare sea eagle haunts in unlikely places. However, without mobile phones to alert a shaky police force who need official monetary incentives from central government sources to outweigh the black money from Mr Big in Dubai, another shipment is surreptitiously off-loaded. We did not have mobile phones then!

In the last few years gold 'biscuits', in the compact size of a 20 gm Cadbury chocolate bar have been found stashed under heavy bunches of dates in open dhows; 24 bigger 'biscuits' weigh a young English woman down as she puts on a specially designed waistcoat with matching inside pockets, staggering suspiciously through immigration off a plane out of Bombay, this time to meet her Indian boyfriend in Hong Kong enroute who knows where? (She was arrested). Small tola-'biscuits' slit into fresh fish stomachs in another fleet of dhows; a thriving line across frontiers on the international road from Bradford, Yorkshire across Europe and the high frontiers of Asia, and down the Khyber into Pakistan and then India until balkanization once again in history's turn of the wheel and wars in Iraq stopped the early riders in gold bars. Iran and Afghanistan temporarily disrupted the flow, and an international world of curious loners in the yachting fraternity calling in at the Maldives and thence up the Malabar coast occasionally 'nabbed' or 'charge-sheeted' (to use this wonderful Indian English). But others get through.

And all for the love of imperishable gold.

■ **GOONDAS** (n. *Urdu*)

are becoming far more dangerous as modern India catches up with the rest of the world. Urban violence is increasing, both in burglaries and volatile acts of individual kidnappings and hijacking of planes. At one time, in our early days living in Delhi, hooligans might have ransacked a shop or overturned a car, drunk on the night of **Holi** (an Indian bacchanalia) and appeared in the newspaper the next day as a 'miscreant nabbed'.

Now a new idiom is creeping into the English language press as a reflection of loutish behaviour (again not particular to the new India)—**criminalization of politics**; goondas are paid to do somebody else's dirty work.

A gun-carrying mafia, they shoot to kill in Mumbai, in a murky world of drug smuggling from Afghanistan via Pakistan. They are allegedly linked to wealthy Indian businessmen resident in Dubai in the Gulf. And some are even sitting in state parliaments of Madhya Pradesh, Bihar and Uttar Pradesh!

■ **GOVERNMENT**

is a federal system divided between the centre and states/union territories.

The Demography of Government …The Facts

One should compare India with continental Europe rather than with individual nations. States are more akin to countries, each speaking roughly the same language within their boundaries and enjoying the same dress styles and customs—except that Europe has one Roman script, India many.

◆ There are **28 States, 7 union territories** and **18 major languages** including English and Sanskrit, plus hundreds of dialects. union territories (some ex-European enclaves such as Pondicherry and Daman and Diu) are too small to be states. The three latest states created in 2000 are **Chhattisgarh** (ex Madhya Pradesh), **Uttaranchal** (ex UP) and **Jharkhand** (ex Bihar). Delhi has now been designated the 29th state as the National Capital Territory.

◆ Whatever government, further changes will occur with the recent shift, as 50 years of independent government passed in 1997, with well-developed trends towards regional politics in coalition at the centre replacing the stability of a monolithic Congress Party assuming power in the euphoria of freedom after alien British rule.

◆ State Assembly elections do not coincide with major national elections. Staggered elections are absolutely necessary in such a complex and unwieldy population as India's—the largest single democracy in the world, an astonishing **nearly 675 million registered voters, almost half under age 35**. A large proportion are formally nonliterate and have to vote by symbol and thumbprints. The dynamics of the operation are inconceivable for small nations such as Australia or Canada whose very populations would be lost in states such as **Uttar Pradesh (166 million), West Bengal (80 million), Madhya**

G

Pradesh (61 million), Bihar (83 million) and Maharashtra (97 million).

◆ **LOK SABHA** is the House of the People: By the turn of the millennium it consists of 545 members, **one fourth of which are members from two states only, UP and Madhya Pradesh**, representation being proportional according to state populations. That has especial significance for other regions especially the south when matters of lobbying, planning financial and large scale project allocations are concerned, bearing in mind the necessity of proximity to central government power bases and top ministry civil servants in such cases.

South India accounts for only **1/5th** of the **545** seats in the lower house—from **Tamilnadu, Kerala, Andhra Pradesh and Karnataka.**

Two Anglo-Indian members can be **nominated** by the President if under-represented.

◆ **RAJYA SABHA**: The equivalent of an upper chamber, is elected indirectly to **245 seats—233 representing the States and Territories** and **12 members**, people of eminence from arts, science, sport, being nominated by the President. Similar to the USA, 1/3 of its members retire on expiry of term every two years.

The Indian system is therefore a blend of the USA federal and the British parliamentary system with constituencies and all the trappings of Westminster-style electioneering to which Indians, no matter how far-flung the village, behave as though they are temperamentally born to it, members of parliament being elected on the first-past-post criterion.

President's rule can be imposed on a state or the nation if political instability threatens. This became increasingly likely in the past decade. One could say India is now ruled **acronym**-ically, the last two general elections of 99 and 2001 producing central governments made up of 18–24 different parties (known by their initials–BJP, RSS, CPI, etc.) and a few Independent members to form what is now called the **United Progressive Alliance (UPA)**, the dominant grouping, the **Bharatiya Janata Paksh** = party, the **BJP** now surprisingly dumped into Opposition in the 2004 election. Can it work? Curried politics! Maybe India is leading the way as a coalition tendency is opening up political rule to reflect a growing sophistication among media and internet-wedded citizens sceptical of the monolithic parties which do not reflect the many minority aspirations in modern democratic open societies. India appears to have a genius for organic growth and survival, a cosmos of its own reflecting the nature of the galactic cosmos of ordered chaos, each Indian voter a **benevolent anarchist!** For that is the true nature of an Indian, a free-thinker both intellectually and spiritually. Despite the power politics of today, bureaucracy has to be commended for keeping India functioning no matter how much it is maligned. The process of democracy does move forward despite all the machinations in recent times of politicians.

In fact it is quite remarkable that 569 previous 'native principalities' (princely states in the Raj) ruled by Rajas, Nawabs and Begums with influential British Residents wielding power behind scenes, have been absorbed peaceably.

◆ One begins to marvel at India's capacity to allow for flexibility. The Lok Sabha is circular after all, very significant as a symbol of no hard edges, given India's philosophical ethos. A rectangular two-party system chamber at Westminster, a democracy with first past the post winners as the supreme ethos of the UK-style democracy does not suit India's deep-rooted plural society.

◆ With the rise of the BJP has come the associated growth of assertive Hindu ideologues in small fringe parties, in recent years becoming increasingly vocal and confident of their evangelical role in restoring the rationale and glories of the original Vedic sense of identity. They are to be watched because occasional outbursts of xenophobic behaviour do occur, an alien element in the Hindu polity to those of us who lived in India in the immediate glow of freedom attained.

◆ **The BJP and its allies**–has tempered much of the hotheaded emotion that shows up in the smaller noisy rogue elements:

Bharat = as already explained is the original word for the Indian landmass.

Jan, Janta = the public in general, the populace or citizens, the same root in Sanskrit = **ge**neral, **ge**nerate, **ge**nus, **ge**nitals, **ge**nder, all to imply creation of that assembly. **Paksh** = party.

The **Shiva Sena** regional party is strong in Mumbai and Maharashtra, partly for cultural reasons–the charismatic figure of **Shivaji** the 17th century heroic guerrilla fighter who led his army = **sena** in many victories over the last of the Mughals, and caused trouble for the British who were beginning to fill the vacuum.

In addition there are various smaller associations such as the **Vishwa Hindu Parishad** (World Hindu Council), founded in 1964 by RSS supreme ideologue M S Golwalkar, which have affiliated with and carried a type of extra-curricular activity forward in the backwash of the staged 1992 Babri Masjid (mosque) demolition, responsibility for which has been assigned to the **Bajrang Dal**, under close scrutiny in 1999 and referred to in the press as a paramilitary wing of the VHP, set up in **1984** by those who wished to see the mosque at Ayodhya 'liberated'.

A Major Achievement: Minority Treatment

One major exception stands out, a visionary achievement, pioneering ahead of what even Western nations, with plural societies have been able to institutionalize.

Within the body politic there are approximately **139 million scheduled castes** and **68 million tribal people** (2001 census figures). They constitute the most vulnerable citizens in such a huge nation. Seats in the Lok Sabha are retained for them, which is more than Aborigines in Australia are able to acquire.

It was Pandit Nehru under the guidance of the Mahatma and those statesmen-politicians of the Independence movement who drafted India's Constitution, who put into effect the first **affirmative action policies** long before the phrase emerged in Europe, the USA or in relation to Canadian Inuit and native Indians and Aborigines and Torres Straits Islanders in Australia.

◆ Both categories, as well as those previously tarnished with the label untouchable, pariah, chandala, sudra, etc. and those

G

partially modernized or jungle/desert-based tribal semi-nomadic peoples are given:

♦ **Constitutional protection**
♦ **Special representation** in both Sabhas
♦ **Protection from previous exploitation and temple prohibitions**
♦ Education discrimination **in favour** of reserved places
♦ **Special quotas in government** service for those suitably qualified and a whole range of other welfare measures and agencies to empower weaker sections of society (an example to tiny populations such as Australia of how to deal with its own minorities–Aborigines just 3.5% of the total population with never a chance of being represented in Parliament by the normal procedures of the Westminster system).

♦ Atrocities still occur (and are even acknowledged in government handbooks) in less enlightened areas of the country—bonded labour still exists and villages are torched if landless peasants dare to rebel against oppressive Thakurs—powerful uppercaste landlords. Such has been the case in Bihar and Madhya Pradesh, but attempts have been made to address the long-term issue.

♦ On the whole, considering the enormity of the challenges India has had to cope with in only half a century, all accumulating relentlessly, it is quite frankly a miracle each time one visits India to find despite all the negatives, exotic or bizarre happenings (which the foreign media delight in highlighting) that India is still one country under one flag.

THE NATIONAL FLAG: Pandit Nehru said that the flag should be a symbol for freedom to all people, a message that India 'wishes to be friends with every country in the world.'

♦ Horizontal tricolour in deep **saffron** (uppermost) for **spiritual sacrifice** and **renunciation** (the extraordinary norm again); the **white band** in the centre for **purity** and **truth;** the **green** at base for **faith** and **fertility** without which life is not possible.

♦ In the centre is the Buddhist **Dharma Chakra**, symbol of the Wheel of Law, from **Ashoka's Lion Capital** at **Sarnath**.

♦ **The 24 spokes** of the wheel are also symbolic. In Samkhya philosophy twentyfour **tattvas** are listed as principles of life matter—divisions of material nature, such as the five gross elements of ether, air or wind, fire, water, earth, the five senses. The spokes are also symbolic of the different paths to the same central Unity.

THE NATIONAL ANTHEM: Rashtriya Geet begins with the words Jana-Gana-Mana-Adhinayaka:

Thou art the ruler of the minds of all people...

The anthem is actually addressed to the **Dispenser of India's destiny**. It was translated into English by the poet/author himself—**Rabindranath Tagore** in 1911 (Dec. 27)

♦ It has an intriguing history going back to the early days of the Raj when the second only gathering of the **newly-formed Congress Party** was held in Calcutta. The King Emperor George V was due to arrive on December 30th from New Delhi where the third Imperial Durbar had been held to declare the new capital of the expanded Empire (Curzon's mistake as Viceroy in dividing Bengal was to be revoked also. Bengalis were to be placated and the Bengal Presidency was to come into existence).

♦ In a letter written to Tagore a month earlier by an influential friend in government circles suggesting to the Poet Laureate that he might compose a song 'to the King' the reaction of Rabindranath as a passionate loyalist of a different kind, was swift—and creative. Angry though he was at the suggestion, he did indeed compose a long dedication to **Bharata Bhagya Vidhata = Victory to Thee, O Dispenser of India's Destiny**. The embryonic future anthem was born. That Dispenser, almost an androgynous 'eternal Charioteer' watching over the fortunes of this ancient peoples along 'the rugged road of history amid all the tribulations and terror' when, 'thy trumpet sounds to hearten those that despair and droop', **is no British monarch! And Bharat is no Fatherland**.

♦ Tagore turned the prompting into a poetic composition as a paean of praise to the Divine. It was signed Brahma Sangit, addressed to the ultimate **Ruler of the Universe = Param Brhm**. The British could make of it what they wished! No English King George in the following sentiments! One verse comments on the country's plight at the time addressed to that eternal Mother. As a true Bengali did he have the formidable Durga/Kali concept in mind?

My country lay in a death-like silence of swoon.
But thy Mother-arms were round her
and thine eyes gazed upon the troubled face in
sleepless love through her hours of ghastly dreams.
Thou art the saviour of the people in their sorrows
Thou, O Dispenser of India's destiny

♦ It was published in the **Modern Review** in 1918 and such grew its popularity reflecting the psyche of Indians everywhere as the movement towards Independence gathered force that Bengali revolutionary, **Subhash Chandra Bose** (whom the British feared far more than Gandhi) chose it for the anthem of his National Army rendering it in Hindi when he defied the Raj and escaped the country in World War II.

♦ Another famous Bengali **Bankim Chandra** wrote India's other national song (equivalent to Land of Hope and Glory in relation to Britain's National Anthem) = **Vande Mataram**. As the latter suggests, India is seen as Motherland and some would prefer to sing it as **NETAJI** did as the anthem:

I bow to Thee Mother...
the Mother, giver of boons, giver of bliss!
Terrible with the clamorous shout of seventy
million throats...

In those days *that* was the population!

CONCLUSION—A FIFTY YEAR PERSPECTIVE FROM JANUARY 26, 1950

This was when India became a Republic and its constitution was finalised. When I look back over the decades, five aspects of India's democratic development come to mind, and a reminder that there are no new things under the sun. A small book, given to me by an Indian friend, a passionate democrat who admired British democracy but felt India had to create its own form and 'shake off Westminster', is still as relevant today as it was soon after the Republic was declared.

1. First, the book. **K M Pannikar**, then well-known as a diplomat and historian, had published **Hindu Society at Cross Roads** (Asia Publishing House, Bombay) in 1955. His optimism for his beloved nation was boundless. He had expounded this several times that here for the first time in Indian history, its total society was subject to human ordering. '**Mass communication** has buttressed **government interference** and made possible **comprehensive change systematically** and **equally to everyone**.' His thesis has held good over these past decades, continually being reinforced with an electorate showing considerable political 'nous'.

2. As my visits accumulated and changes became more visible, I have become aware of a new assertiveness on the part of a younger well-educated Indian generation who, in some areas, show increasing irritation with those from overseas who love to pontificate about the failures and flaws and the glaring material defects that still occur in India for all to see (unlike in Russia which for decades was closed to the prying eyes of the world press, even as China is today).

The survival of democracy has been written off many times by foreign correspondents, most damagingly 30 years ago by **The London Times** correspondent Neville Maxwell. Indian friends were hurt and annoyed by his prominent article on the editorial page—yet no military regime or dictator has taken over as elsewhere among many of its Islamic neighbours, so why single out India just because she was attempting to model her own form of democratic policy? **Modernization does not mean Westernization**. India models itself and has remodelled itself, with an acceptance of organic change sufficiently flexible not to crack the ancient template.

The three points I feel strongly about in this regard are these:

♦   There is no set model of democratic development. Each nation is an amalgamation of disparate strands of environment, geography, size, culture and religious influences.

♦   In today's conditions, the development of the polity under the full glare of battalions of the world media swooping in with TV cameras rolling whenever crisis threatens is part of a process unheard of in earlier centuries.

♦   Universal suffrage is already functioning unlike in Britain in the 19th century when the electorate itself was not fully represented, MPs could buy and sell their pocket boroughs and an elitist land owning electorate could legislate (admittedly within parliamentary conventions)—conditions wholly different from the disciplines imposed upon a modern day government such as India's in the 21st century.

There was a leisurely air about social change, factory acts and Chartist movements as the 19th century reforms gathered pace. A French revolution hurried things along. However, **India's democracy has been expected to function smoothly virtually overnight**.

None of these conditions existed when Britain and the USA were experimenting in earlier developments after Cromwell's overthrow of Parliament and the American Civil War. Imagine Japanese, Indian and Nigerian camera crews flying in during the aftermath of such major upheavals and commenting upon the conditions of those times! Would the new America or the old Britain have countenanced such impertinence?

3. The expectancy has been that India's post-Independence development would also be a Westminster model. Why should this necessarily be so when it is a vast pluralistic sub-continent set in a particular socio-environmental mould at least 6000 years in the making? Due to a national temperament forged in such pluralism, an embryonic democratic foundation laid by Emperor Ashoka, (see **PANCHAYAT** system) and an intellectual embrace of new arrivals and new attitudes (inclusive rather than exclusive), India seems naturally disposed to working out its own singular form of devolution of the democratic system.

4. **Reasons for Optimism:** Despite the fact that:

♦   Major crises still occur; one example is the **Emergency** in 1975 imposed by PM Indira Gandhi due to Punjab Sikh troubles and calls by J P Narayan (nationally respected political sage—see **BHOODAN**) to bring in the military due to her misrule, the electorate kept its head, rebelled and went to the polls in 1977, ousting her from office, then reinstating her in 1980.

♦   Kashmir is in a permanent state of rebellion (or at least disaffection) stirred by Taliban-trained terrorists.

♦   Statistics add up to huge numbers of marginalised people such as:

   ♦   450 million poor people with at least half below the poverty line
   ♦   30 million jobless
   ♦   several other disaffected border states, such as Assam, defying central government
   ♦   millions of women nonliterate and not formally educated
   ♦   12 million child labourers, according to unverifiable statistics

Nevertheless the Indian electorate has proved itself, despite chicanery and poor leadership in some State Assemblies, to consist of **remarkably mature voters;** increasingly level-headed and movingly patriotic with a touching belief that democracy, despite its limitations in improving their lot rapidly enough, does work.

In fact, **India Today** (June, 2003) pointed out that the nation has endured **in the past 16 years alone** 107 elections. Since the first ever election after partition which cost Rs. 1.5 crores that sum has escalated 900 times. How unlike China! I have yet to hear an Indian complaining.

Intellectual freedom is the resplendent gift of Indian cultural impulses throughout the ages. One could in fact declare that—in a very wide generality—each Indian is the **supreme benign anarchist**. I have said it earlier. It needs repeating. No dogma or creed inhibits individuals and their bubbly **sense of humour** is able to laugh at themselves, a sure sign of **tolerance** and a saving grace in Indian life.

G

◆ They have stayed with the secular ideals of the founding fathers (and mothers) who suffered imprisonment and all manner of humiliations, to be free of alien rule. The **overall calm in which 14 general elections** (since 1947) **have been conducted,** bearing in mind the extraordinary stresses and strains of organising 590 million registered voters, deserves supreme accolades, especially in the light of the November 2000 US presidential elections and the soap opera atmosphere of its protracted result.

RECENT TRENDS—THE STATES HAVE COME TO TOWN!

Regional, rural, backward-class India is flexing its muscles. Not just constitutionally (they would be there anyway) but in a far subtler way. With the steady erosion of the power base of the Congress over the last two decades an intriguing and vigorous new strength from regional parties in a way unmatched amongst Western democracies is asserting itself from the base of the pyramid—out there in the far reaches of India untutored in the elegant sophistication of parliamentary behaviour personified in Pandit Nehru's eloquent figure with his single daily rose in his Nehru-jacket buttonhole, these people have begun to claim their inheritance.

Now no matter how long the disparate groups of politicians forming three coalition governments in rapid succession survive, they will have caught a glimpse that no other Parliament has up to now achieved. The emergence of a polyglot mix of nearly 30 parties has realised new horizons unparalleled in previous Parliaments dominated by the worldly-wise Congress-wallahs who had been fired in the crucible of the Independence Movement and who were also high-born, many professional brahmin parliamentarians born to rule.

In relation to my many questions on these trends in 1998, a respected south Indian friend, ambassador to Asian and European countries, explained:

India itself is a coalition, so it is not unreasonable to have a coalition government, at the top or in the state capitals. What is hard to achieve is a basic consensus on the nature of governance and the fundamentals of the polity… But India is churning, it is in a social revolution of a peculiar kind, with large numbers of the hitherto marginalised groups now claiming a share of the cake as well as the oven producing it.

5. **Pilgrimage** as a unifying factor is seldom considered in assessing the forces at work in modern India yet its influences run deep, if obliquely. An intricately rooted tradition in Hindu (85% of the country), Buddhist, Jain communities but also strong in Islamic and indigenous Christian, its impact on modern Indians is quite remarkable. In the Hindu sense, visiting the four 'quadrants' literally walking the land of India as Shankaracharya did, undergoing privations and supreme physical tests alongside people from everywhere across the subcontinent breeds a secret sense of 'being Indian', being unified in a common endeavour (see **PILGRIMAGE**).

'I shared a lonely hut with people from Tamilnadu' laughed a young Punjabi girl, a Sikh. *'There were bed bugs everywhere high up on the way to Kailash! For the first time I realised these people were **Indian**, not just a different race speaking Tamil. They even were wearing old trousers like me because of the hardship and the terrain and we all in the end ate the same rice and chappatis...'*

◆ And in afterthought but most important of all—
We said the same prayers. Even if I am Sikh I know the Gita by heart. What difference is Krishna from what Guru Nanak teaches in the heart. We all had a good laugh. Politicians try to divide us. We realised deep down that we all were Indians on the same path.

EXPECTATIONS ARE RISING–GOVERNMENTS BEWARE!

◆ A slow but sure foundation of egalitarian outlets is happening despite the glaring disparities of income.

◆ **backward/scheduled classes** experienced a steady rise in parliamentary representation from **13 per cent** in the early 1980s to nearly **30 per cent** in 2001.

◆ the powerful presence of **regional satraps—powerbrokers** who in some cases have had Chanakyan careers as chief ministers manipulating the huge northern states like ancient Persian governors = **Kshatrapadhvan** = rich country protectors. Eventually this term became the word **kshatriya** (refer to **CASTE**) and then condensed further to **satrap**.

The late **Phoolan Devi**, archetypal symbol as the Bandit Queen of oppressed womanhood, was elected to Parliament after release from prison. A typical Indian paradox. She may have been an ineffective parliamentarian, but who knows the longterm outcomes. She was there! Her story is India's, a weird mix of reality, myth, an over-the-top personality, with the unexpected triumphing! The much-abused low-caste village girl turned feisty **dacoit** of the notorious bandit brigades of Madhya Pradesh's Chambal ravines, later shot some of her high-caste oppressors. Eventually she turned herself in, was convicted, gets sent to Delhi's famous Tihar jail. A Bengali woman film director investigated, feeling Phoolan Devi was more sinned against than sinning; Phoolan is released, becomes a world-wide renowned heroine due to the film **Bandit Queen** made on her life. Suddenly enters politics and wins, representing the **Samajwadi Party** for five years. The story does not end there. In 1997 a further warrant is sent out from a UP court in Kanpur. She goes underground, supported by her **Eklavya Sena** activists. Later, returned to parliament, she is shot on her way to her nearby home—assassinated in broad daylight. After years 11 suspects were arrested. One, Rana Pankaj jailed, later farcically to escape with escort accomplice, both disguised in police uniform!

Eklavya was the name in the Mahabharata of a son of a forest tribe, hence the relevance, being outside of caste, who longs to learn the arts of the kshatriyas but is spurned by Drona, lapsed brahmin teacher of martial arts in the MahaB. Undeterred Eklavya returns to the forest, makes an image of Drona which he worships in all sincerity, praying for the gifts of the warrior—a sure eye, a clear aim. This he achieves by his own singular efforts, but is discovered by Drona on a forest journey

G

with his Pandava clan pupils. In a contest of archery Eklavya outshines them all, even Arjuna. Drona is troubled by this and though acknowledging his prowess, demands a fee—Eklavya's right thumb. Without demur, this humble young man cuts it off with his sword in one stroke thus disabling his firing arm. So blighted, he can no longer aspire. In the epic it is one of the most poignant of stories, the aspiring young man yet another symbol of those marginalised by their birth, now transferred into a modern day metaphor.

◆ **Nearly 40 other women took their seats in Parliament in 1996,** some very colourful (and not in dress alone) amongst them a humble Bhagwati Devi, another elected MP, her early life spent as an impoverished stone crusher. If only Panditji could now walk into Parliament!

It may be a walk of another kind that he, either from agnostic disposition outwardly or from constraints of dharma and time, never had a chance to undertake, busy as he was for all his allotted time in traversing the land mass meeting crowds upon crowds of ordinary human beings. That is the hidden secret of India's togetherness: PILGRIMAGE—on foot!

FINAL FOOTNOTE: Perhaps the IAS will have the last laugh. An apocryphal story at the last general election may be a symbolic truth…

When a group of visiting MNC bosses arrived to take a **dekho** (**dekhnaa** = to see or look, Hindi contributing yet again to English!) about investing in the new economic liberalization, they balked at the possible 'political instability' of the relay of coalition governments. A miffed member of the PM's office retorted:

*That is not true—India has dynamic stability. That is to say, despite the instability, **decisions still get taken.***

And on matters governmental try a website: **samachar.com or bharat-rakshak.com**

… but take heart… a preliminary search (*Khoj*) of **India** gives four million plus websites!

■ GRACE = KRPA = (n. *Sanskrit*)

Those saintly lone individuals of the **sannyas ashrama** (stage of life) who take to the open roads proclaiming praise of the Divine, outside of caste sing in joyous terms (like the Bauls of Bengal) of the grace which comes unannounced: '*Winnow, winnow*' sings Chowdayya of the Ferrymen…

Look here, fellows
Winnow when the wind blows.
Remember, the winds
are not in your hands,
Remember, you cannot say
I'll winnow, I'll winnow
tomorrow.
When the winds of the Lord's grace
lash,
quickly, quickly winnow, winnow,
Says our Chowdayya of the Ferrymen

Again taken from Ramanujan's excellent **Speaking of Siva,** (explained in **BHAKTI** section), where other translations from the

free verse called **vacana**—see **VAC**—in the Kannada language appear.

◆ That miraculous flash of benediction comes with no warning. 'Harvest it when you can' is the message of all India's sages.

All mankind
Is born for perfection
And each shall attain it
Will he but follow
His nature's duty

Krishna, the good shepherd and teacher, elucidating to Arjuna the Yoga of Renunciation in the Bhagavad Gita gives humanity hope through His grace:

'Therefore, no one should give up his natural work, even though he does it imperfectly. For all action is involved in imperfection, like fire is smoke…'. However, Krishna continues his benign message—united with him

you shall overcome all difficulties by my grace. But if your heart is full of conceit and you do not heed me, you are lost.

And then Krishna addresses today's Indians as much as Arjuna's confused state:

Give me your whole heart
Love and adore me
Worship me always
Bow to me only
And you shall find me
This is my promise
Who love you dearly
Lay down your duties
In me, your refuge…
Even if a man simply listens to these words with faith, and does not doubt them, he will be freed from his sins and reach the heaven of the righteous.

(Translation Prabhananda and Isherwood).

■ GUFA

is 'the cave', an architectural wonder constructed from the fertile imagination of **artist M F Husain** in collaboration with one of India's leading architects, **B V Doshi,** in **Ahmedabad.**

The **GUFA** must surely rival the Sydney Opera House, New Delhi's Bahai temple, and Brazil's new capital as one of the world's most expressive pieces of advanced sculptural architecture, built in the late 20th century, but even more suitable for the 21st century.

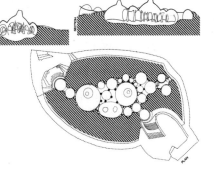

It says much for India's creative spirit and flexibility in cultural expression that such way-out innovative concepts can come to fruition and actually be constructed despite the containment of its cultural roots embedded in millennia of traditional rules laid down in codifications—**the shastras.**

◆ Looking like a crashed spaceship of elongated proportions half-embedded in the earth of educational grounds, its lizard-like swivel eyes protrude as portholes to let in shafts of sunlight to illuminate its 'womb-house' interior in a golden glow. It bears all the hallmarks of artistic genius, which indeed it is. The redoubtable, irrepressible Husain whom we came to know as a friend, buying one of his paintings when he held his first exhibition in a private home in Delhi, and Doshi, one of the new generation of innovative architects in the 50s created this, the cave as an inner space womb-house, so important a symbol for Indian culture. Both experienced strange dreams before its form materialised into that of Vishnu's second avatar, KURMA the tortoise. A hazy floating shell crystallised into a stunning mosaic, gleaming white, crushed ceramic pieces from shattered china cups with India's gift of artisan handpower creating the carapaces. Laid on web-like inner shallow domes these were architected in glass wool created by computer diagrams, 'resolving stresses to a minimum requiring only an inch thick ferro-cement shell' according to Yatin Pandya, Ahmedabad architect.

◆ And within... here is India at work again, that juxtaposition that the traveller encounters at almost every other turn of the road, ancient and modern so dramatically interacting. Conceived by computer skills, **yet constructed by tribal hand labour** weaving the random undulating spaces of the mysterious chambers, shadows cast as in a childhood fairy tale amid the lithe and bending earth columns which support the carapaces and carry stresses into the sand and gravel base hardened in granite.

A forest of columns, and in their shadows, sculpted figures reminiscent of Husain's early beginnings as a carpenter—archetypal horned forms and spirited nymphs larger than life prance out of spatial curves, stirring primeval memories of hidden menace in a Hans Andersen forest. Impossible to describe, the gufa has to be experienced... Indeed **Balkrishna Doshi** has written in his article published in **Indian Architect and Builder** (Vol. 8. no. 4,1994) of spontaneous experiences that the building process itself invoked:

I must tell you about an event that took place when the building was constructed. The tribals who had worked to construct it were so deeply affected by the technique of construction, the form of the building and the way changes could be made naturally, that they felt they were reliving their own ancient ritual of Pithora Bava. So, what they did was to perform a dance, following a puja and the sprinkling of sacred colours.

These nocturnal rituals lasted for nine days. But on the first day, hearing the chanting of sheshnaga (Lord Vishnu's resting place on the thousand hooded cobra) Husain suddenly stood up and holding a long brush, climbed on the domes. He feverishly painted on the

domes, a cobra connecting the two large rotundas. He then asked me to get this cobra glazed in black mosaic. On the ninth day, the tribals declared the prana, the breath of life from Pithora Bava, had now entered the Gufa.

◆ And dancing into that **prana**, the shakti energy personified, **Mallika Sarabhai**, dynamic channel herself of the most ancient traditions and the most contemporary of dance experiments, weaving her own patterns over the carapaces at the Gufa's inauguration—home, art gallery, learning space for Husain to inhabit.

Nearby and defined also by a 100 ft by 15 feet corridor, Husain's other astonishing creation—his **Theorama** of India's **eight major faiths** plus today's growing **Humanism** standing as the ninth panel along the walled boundary.

■ **GUNA** (n. *Sanskrit* = thread, strand)

Beyond the literal definition **gunas** become very important in **categorising** three dominant tendencies in nature and the material world and used especially in relation to human behaviour. The teachings of Krishna in the Bhagavad Gita characterise the **three gunas**, the qualities with which one is born, in these categories:

sattva = goodness, purity, **rajas** = passion, activity, **tamas** = darkness, sloth.

Chapter 14 of the Bhagavad Gita is devoted to an exposition of what the **gunas** constitute:

sattvic 'the shining one can show the Atman by its pure light; yet sattva will bind you to search for happiness, long for knowledge'

rajasic 'the passionate will make you thirsty for pleasure and possession, rajas will bind you to hunger for action'

tamasic 'the ignorant bewilders all men tamas will bind you with bonds of delusion, sluggishness, stupor.'

This concept is a very important component in Indian thinking, influencing daily life in very private ways especially to a dedicated follower of **sanatana dharma** (see **VEDAS**). Gunas are regarded as the fundamental constituents of the natural world = **PRAKRITI** = the rope that binds us all in the natural phenomena. On closer inspection the rope is seen to be made up of these three 'strands' which shape our personalities.

◆ **Sattva** or purity, the ascending tendency in all creation is something towards which all souls should aspire, a cohesive 'United Nations' type of impetus bringing groups, tendencies, forces in nature as well as behaviour together in **harmony and balance**. In iconography and art forms **the colour white is symbolic of sattva.**

◆ **Yoga** suggests in a very modern way that **sattvic** food is very much healthier on the whole and less likely to bring on the scourge of the modern world—diabetes and heart attacks—than going all out in a splurge for the meat-eating **rajasic** or, worse still, the **tamasic** food, over-rich, fatty (all fast foods you can think of) undoubtedly leading to sloth. In the perilous heat of India, dietary knowhow was quite obviously important. Food putrefies quickly as most travellers know by painful experience. Best to follow Krishna and take the sattvic path. The effect of the searing heat must surely have influenced the philosophy of a life in which inhabitants have to come to terms with **grishma**, a very onomatopoeic Hindi word expressing the summer season in May-June-July. Then everything is **agg**ressive! You **gr**it your teeth, feel **gr**oggy, **gr**ound-down with a**gg**ravation, **gr**owling with sodden flesh, adding **gr**ist to the mill of **gr**ishma's onslaught! It would appear from the texts of the Gita, the Puranic epics and the ayurvedic and yogic treatise that **guna**, **sattva** and **tattva** [the 24 enumerated elements, essences and evolvents of life] are inter-twined, almost like a Sanskrit genome imprint on each individual personality somewhat akin to a personal thumbprint we carry uniquely from the beginning of time in the infinite variations of the natural world.

♦ **Rajas**, the energetic qualities most frequently embodied by rulers, rajas, warriors, active brawn and burly masculinity of life, is symbolised by the colour red, which interestingly corresponds with Western colour theories about the **vibrant red spectrum**.

♦ **Tamas**, dense mass, spells inertia, anything which expresses dullness, laziness—in today's slang, a 'couch potato'! *Black or dark blue is the colour used in paintings to represent this quality—the **centrifugal** one discussed under **'fissiparous tendencies**—a pulling away from the cohesive forces, certainly the disintegrating force on the galactical scale of entropy. Is this why 'black holes' are defined as such?

And of course no sooner is one statement made than PARADOX raises its head again just to confuse the traveller. Dark blue is also the colour of the auspicious firmament—applied to the representation of Rama and Krishna, the blue-skinned deities.

■ **GURU**

Chaitanya, a 14th century Bengali poet and saint of the bhakti movement, stressed personal devotion in relation to the Benign. This was to be channelled via individual worship to an **istadevata**, a personal representation of divinity—in the form of a **murti**, such as **Devi**, **Shiva**, **Krishna** or **Rama**—chosen by an individual (not necessarily the same as that preferred by family or clan = *kuldevata* tradition). But he stressed also the need for guidance of the **guru**:

The guru is the skilful helmsman
Divine grace the favourable wind
If with such means man does not
strive to cross the ocean of life and death
he is indeed lost.

Individual responsibility—in the sense of **Christian free will**—is at a premium. It is up to you and your own intentions and tendencies (refer back to **GUNA**) to lift yourself out of the mire of karmic logic/law, entangled in the **maya** of blinkered vision. Fate in the Islamic sense of **kismet** does not really exist for

Hindus. Like John Bunyan's Pilgrim beset by many obstacles in the Slough of Despond, most humans, says Chaitanya, need guidance, a spiritual preceptor. That is why the integrity of an acknowledged **sattvic** person with proven wisdom, compassion, vision is treasured by hundreds and thousands of Indian families.

If a guru is not traditionally known within the family circle then an Indian—no matter of what level in society or personal development along the lonely individual **marg** or way of progression through life—will make all efforts to seek out that **guru**.

♦ **That guru can be a Holy Ma as well as a man**

♦ The search often entails a demanding pilgrimage, great personal physical and financial hardship, often on foot in rough circumstances to reach a sannyasi, a muni, an acharya, hidden away in unpublicised abodes.

♦ Sometimes by chance that guru crosses one's path—literally—and is 'known' immediately… a 'meant-to-be' encounter. Several of my Indian friends have attested to such encounters. Pandit Ravi Shankar's came out of nowhere. Known as **Tat** (sackcloth or burlap) **Baba** (honoured father-figure) he apparently sent in one of his chelas (pupils) to the room where the young Ravi was somewhat disconsolately practicing.

♦ Or like a very well-known international gallery director whose family were originally of the lowliest background in a more static caste-conscious era the father was known for his goodness, his beatitude, his saintly behaviour. In Kerala that soon became manifest and even brahmins acknowledged his **sattvic** nature and sought out his wisdom. His father, according to the son, was **impelled** by inexplicable forces to go up to a person on the wayside and acknowledge him as his guru. And that person was such!

This is not at all uncommon, where mysterious forces, call them psychic or powerfully amplified by yogic concentration—an area of mental/psychic/spiritual life developed extensively in Indian culture—has been virtually ignored both in European and specifically Christian daily living until the post-war decades. Perhaps that is the secret. If training and daily usage are such then over several thousand years that part of the brain must have developed skills the West applied elsewhere—the **SWASTIKA** versus the line, the all-in-the-round all-at-once g(n)yana rather than the empirical linear measuring of factual knowledge.

Psychologically, to be open to belief in these possibilities which appear to function amongst Indians with apparent ease allows forces to operate otherwise strangled by the scepticism Westerners apply. Indians of all kinds testify to these legitimate happenings, some quite inexplicable by Western standards of rationality.

♦ These are personal experiences which have to be taken on trust, beyond explanation of coincidence.

♦ Given to scepticism in the early days of wandering through India, trained in rationality, a rigorous education my grounding and four years of applying mind rather than heart, building brain fibre rather than a heart muscle, one was inclined to tread cautiously. A stereotype blocked the view—all this mysticism was said to be a

G

---

*A complete aside: Such a-sattvic conditions can be calmed by the use of the old-fashioned Planter's Chair (now called Australian chair!) Very useful in outback heat in a Federation-style house (i.e. colonial bungalow) to 'aerate' the legs on the extended arms while cooling off on an Indian-style verandah (yet another word derived from Hindi!).

flimflam like flossy candy. Gurus don't just direct themselves to a person. Haphazard happenings don't just occur in a patterning as instructional devices in an ordered karma—or do they?

◆ All one can testify is that too many Indians in chance encounters have opened doors to my understanding which indicate that they do; that **heart** has to be developed as well as **brain**; there has to be a harmony in the harnessed personality—and the ultimate visual image of the guru, the supreme teacher of the Gita stands in the chariot (the **ratha**) holding the reins. On many a glossy bazaar poster the four horses are even named in the **Devanagari** script.

Maan = mind	Chit = consciousness
Buddhi = wisdom	Ahankar = Ego

But study is not the only way in the **guru/shishya** pupil relationship.

A visionary flash of insightful wisdom can occur—a spark of mental energy as potent as electricity which itself was an unknown force when Shakespeare was penning his works in the flickering light of a tallow candle and a majority of humanity bedded down like the rest of the mammalian world soon after sunset. To turn a switch on and bright light appears would be as unbelievable to that world as our own approach to neurological feats scarcely understood today but which 500 years hence may well be commonplace, put the computer in the shade, and bring the yogic guru power intrinsic in the harnessing of the 'other mind' into an acceptance not possible as yet.

◆ Indians of all manner of backgrounds tend to dismiss Western scepticism. 'What do they know. We have been at it, investigating, for 5,000 years,' is a statement reiterated many times. But they do have a quiet chuckle at the naiveté of many who come to India in search of the ultimate exotic release in mind-blowing spirituality. 'Beware of charlatans' was breathed at me like dragon fire on first arrival by none other than alter-guru Khushwant Singh. I thank him for his advice! Charlatans are many, some now in jail—and even Indians can be fooled—in fact a new millennial guru to whom **India Today** devoted a major article elicited this letter from an irate reader in November 2001:

> *The story of Sri Sri Ravi Shankar was a waste of precious space. If you wanted to break the monotony of the Afghanistan war, you could have chosen many other topics. Who needs a 45-year-old self-styled "guru" to teach the Art of Living? I, like most others, learnt it at the knees of my mother, from teachers, elders and my senses. Bored socialites, the idle rich and misguided foreigners may find this man a passing fancy but please do not insult the intelligence of your readers with such matters.*

◆ Being a guru is by no means an all-male preserve although the place where a disciple came to learn wisdom rather than just education either in the guru's home or ashram seems to have been very much a male preserve (turn to **VIDYALAYA**).

Matajis and women saints are legion, their charisma and shakti strength implicit in the Hindu acceptance of the androgynous deity in all its symbolism. The goddess image, the earliest fertility icons dug up archaeologically even today, still resonate in Indian culture in household ceremonies, artforms, festivals, in Hindi and Tamil fillum culture. Even tough politicians like Indira Gandhi take on a spiritual charisma as also non-Indians such as Mother Teresa; Mirabehn Slade (an English admiral's daughter and follower of Gandhi); Dr Annie Besant; the French 'Mother' of Pondicherry; and the Irish sister Nivedita, gifted disciple of Swami Vivekananda, whose famous book *The Web of Indian Life* astonished Indians in 1905 when it first was published in Calcutta with an introduction by Rabindranath Tagore. The acceptance of the feminine power to hold and sway audiences, to be accepted as intellectual guides across the stepping stones to enlightenment, is taken for granted.

What is remarkable is how homely—in the old-fashioned sense of the word—they all look, comfortable, safe, everyone's wise grandma.

Another Personal Footnote

Contrarily a friend can just say, 'Let's go for a walk' through a leafy suburb of Delhi. Somebody's sister has just 'blown in', **a-tithi**, without date. Her comings and goings are just like this for she is a Holy Ma whose sister is an upper middle class lady of some sophistication, well known in the cultural life of the capital, and whose American husband helped export Indian fabrics of superb quality to international outlets. Their 'art museum' home is in this suburb.

News of **Mataji's** arrival spreads with that electric spark that is quite remarkable along mysterious networks. People flow in from all areas, educated and well-dressed, hard put to sit for two hours on the spread sheets of the lounge where fabulous artworks do sit at ease. One could be in Emperor Ashoka's era with the burnished Buddhas sitting in compassionate silence, except no artisan had fashioned them at that time, only symbolic abstract emblems of sandals, umbrella/chattris, chakra wheels then allowed to signify the Buddha's benign presence as a major guru for all time.

And there are scruffy people out of the night air with impoverished chadhars thrown around their shoulders. Over a hundred people are suddenly crowded in as though telepathic messages have sparked from the wink of Shiva's Third Eye.

A very comfortable middle-aged matron is settled cross-legged in the middle of the sofa, her sister (out of another world yet able to straddle this—and supplying a vegetarian buffet for all in the back family room after the gathering) sits beside her as though presiding at a committee meeting. A no-nonsense air, far from other-worldly, prevails. **This is Mataji!**

And then the chanting begins, a thousand names for the God, whichever Deity's syllabic mantras, it does not matter, for in the end they are all One. The rhythm picks up. It calms the mind after losing a husband of nearly 50 years-standing a few months earlier, my first visit (after his going) to the land to which we both gave our hearts.

And then the discourse in impeccable English, of such articulate nature, the flow as magnetic as a Robert Frost poem where there are miles to go before we all sleep, as

G

steady as Whitman singing on the open road, mindful of divine sparkle in beneficent nature in cadences of Tagore's singing poetry, or Thoreau's peaceful retreat at Walden Pond in a New England wood.

◆ Interspersed with Hindi, shifting from one to the other like changing gear on a bicycle ride, she talked of the Devi—her force in our lives, her protective nature for those who give their hearts and minds to her, of what her symbolism means, of compassion and effort to do unto others as we would be done by, this dark age of violence in the Kaliyuga and the benign violence of **Kali** in her energetic form, a very different persona from the benign aspect of the serene **Lakshmi** goddess.

Whatever would those early Christian fathers like William Carey have said who came out to India and set up the first printing presses in Bengal to 'convert the heathen' when now so many Westerners are relinquishing institutional Christianity? It is hard to control the mind with yogic singularity in India. Too much drama is happening all around one, colour, noise, vivid devotional sounds—this time the **sahasranama**, the thousand names of Vishnu. But Shiva also has many titles. It is all so overwhelming in scale—and I end up clinging to a lifeline thought while trying to remain serene amid this chanting throng.

It is this... principalities and powers are passing shadows... who would have then thought that such practices and the word guru would have become a matter of common parlance and acceptance in the heartland of the British Empire—London itself? A whole generation of white Westerners not only have taken over ashrams in India, backpacking through Asia, they dance in startling abandon saffron-robed and heads shaved down Oxford Street, through Paris, sell vegetarian food in New York. Did ever those first Portuguese iconoclasts who actually fought disbelievers on the very soil magnanimously donated to them by a tolerant Zamorin of Kozhikode, foresee how the chakra wheel would turn with such historical irony, Goa the magnetic centre for mind-blown New Age Western youth.

It **is** all mind-blowing. It is India! The bhajan takes over the flow of thoughts as an aura settles quite manifestly around the solid comfortable everyday figure on the sofa. **Hari-Krishna, hari**...hari...

Hari in Sanskrit, the **remover**, tracing its linguistic root back to Upanishadic times, at least 5000 years ago... **that which takes away**, removes the mental film of ignorance, the misguided belief that this reality around the room full of real people is the **real** reality, the mistaken belief according to the texts (and Dr Radhakrishnan's interpretations) that any material substance can exist in itself apart from **Hari**—that is Vishnu.

People ease their creaking joints. Some come to the front and do **pranam**, touch her feet in passing. **Pada-dhuli**, pada the same Indo-European root as the Latin *pedes* = feet; *dhuli* = dust.

How many times in India has one seen this, the taking of symbolic dust on the head in the gesture of bending, touching the ground at the feet of some one who is reverenced—elderly parents arriving off a plane at an airport being greeted by well-dressed children who have reached middle years themselves; eminent musicians by their pupils; even a son, a young boy of a hereditary household guru who initiates an orthodox family into compulsory caste rites would merit such a gesture from the elders of the household who would touch his feet and 'take the dust onto their heads' in supplication.

◆ No wonder the search for learning, education is so honoured in India.
◆ and yet in this land of the benign anarchist, there is still room for dissent (while acknowledging the authority of the GURU.
Even the Buddha, supreme guru had cautioned the shishyas (the seeker-students):
Don't follow me blindly,
Verify things for yourself!
◆ No wonder in the texts it is stated **the guru is greater even than the gods**.

त्वमेव माता च पिता त्वमेव
त्वमेव बन्धुश्च सखा त्वमेव
त्वमेव विध्या द्रविणं त्वमेव
त्वमेव सर्व मम देव देवम् ॥

Oh Guru! You alone are my mother, father, brother, friend, the knowledge and wealth. You are everything to me and God of all Gods.

- HALO (n. *Sanskrit* = *prabha*/light)

Figurative representations of Hindu deities and the Buddha began being sculpted in the round as the first millennium turned and Buddhas (standing and seated) were framed at **Mathura** and **Sarnath** with warm mottled red sandstone halos on the supporting background of stone. These are called **prabha valaya**, 'the one with an aura' in the sense of a glow emanating (**prabha**) and **valaya**–something circular like a churree bangle or ring, thus a halo.

One fifth century CE depiction in a virtual sheath of filmy robe carved miraculously in the stone, eyes cast down in inner composure is imposed upon an elongated aureole stretching down to the Buddha's ankles. Links between Rome were fitful and tenuous and confined to coastal regions south of Chennai and along the Malabar coast although some southern rajas apparently employed Romans as bodyguards so knowledge of the Christian halo in art representations could have seeped through the trade links but very slowly. Trade and cultural exchange with Greece was more constant so the freeflow of art forms and the possibility of mutual awareness could occur both ways.

A most resplendent halo against dark background and unusually dark hair of the Buddha with mendicant is to be seen at Ajanta also fifth century CE (see **The Buddha**, by **Pupul Jayakar**, Vakils, Bombay, 1982 but is also reproduced in most accounts of Buddhist art).

Writing of the presence of St Thomas in India in the 1st century CE and the fact that King Alfred (who by legend burnt the cakes even though most children in England will never remember why) is said to have sent Sighelm the Saxon nearly 800 years later to south India, **Jon and Rumer Godden** state in their book **Shiva's Pigeons, An Experience of India** (Chatto and Windus, London, 1972):

Certainly it was from India that several of the Christian church's best-known customs and ideals came: the revering of relics, asceticism, and the Buddhist rosary and halo...

- The concept of an **aura,** however, predates even the specific halo, going way back to Vedic thinking, circa 4000 BCE and those particularly holy meditators—the rsis, munis, sannyasis and yogis referred to in Vedic hymns as 'The Shining Ones'. Practitioners of the sattvic qualities (pure, cleansed, uncontaminated) taking only vegetarian food, unencumbered in the mind by drugs or sex, maintaining physical disciplines of the body regularly and conserving semen for inner 'energy', thus reaching ultimate super-consciousness, such highly evolved personalities are described as emanating a 'glow', a radiance that indeed does create an aureole, an electric charge so to speak, sparking in molecules around the skin's surface… a therma-electrical field which emanates from all matter–living or inert.

Advanced technology known as kirlian photography (used in Russian sports research to monitor the metabolic/fitness assessment of athletes) now shows aura-imaging of the electrical impulses of the body surface by technical means.

Clairvoyants claim that an advanced consciousness could actually see these bio-engineered energies reflected in different colours according to personality. We will have to await a further advance in technology for rationalists to take that on board, but exploration of the multiverse at quantum level is galloping ahead of our comprehension as ordinary mortals. Ajit Singh (The Times of India, February 6, 2002) reports under the title: **Action Spurred by Heartfelt Prayer:** Recent Studies at the University of California… claim that the whole universe, or rather, the multiverse at the quantum level, is a conglomeration of electromagnetic vibrations of various frequencies. Our body has also been found to be an electrical system exhibiting two types of electromagnetic fields… our skin exhibits a high frequency energy field… (which) radiates a luminous aura which engulfs the whole body… and acts as a screen against any onslaught of unfavourable vibrations from the outside…' So what is new? The Vedas say all knowledge is there, but like the onion, it has to be peeled off, layer by layer. It has taken at least 21 centuries of knowledge to validate empirically what some individuals were attuned to see as others have the gift of a voice capable of superb tone to sing.

- **HANUMAN**

is the deeply revered simian-shaped deity, profoundly associated with the fortunes of **Rama** and his brother **Lakshman** in their 14-year-exile and their search for the abducted Sita, young consort of Rama. Hanuman is not only sculpted in bronze or stone in the round and placed in his own shrine in temples but more often throughout the country embossed on stone and daubed with red vermilion by the wayside, under trees, watching over terraced fields of rice. In the legends he is described as being of a yellow complexion 'glowing like molten gold'. The ancient texts speak of his face being 'as red as the brightest ruby'.

It may still appear strange to those from far-off shores imbued by their own cultures (especially from those of Semitic roots) even if they are no longer of any specific religious persuasion to discover animals elevated to such divine status in Hindu mythology. And in very real day-to-day worship, imaged as an **istadevata** in human form, anthropomorphic to be exact, even though in legend the son of Vayu (wind) and a celestial apsara.

Ganesh has already appeared as the powerful symbolic elephant deity; **Sheshnag** will appear as the protective cobra associated with Vishnu, and later under another name with Buddha. Strangely enough the sacred cow remains as such, in her own right and not even a 'vehicle' like **Nandi**, the bull for Shiva. You might have deduced looking at the symbolism of all this that the Mohenjo Daro bull so famous an embossed seal symbol would have logically been elevated to the ranks of

Ganesh and Hanuman but Shiva took over the potency symbol of generation and powerful fertility in the lingam (refer to **PANTHEON**). There are other animals frequenting heaven, but only in the sense of being associated with the major deities like Lakshmi's peacock, Indra's elephant, Ganesh's mouse.

Today's Hanuman

Almost to the point of tedium it is stated that Indians' cultural propensities are such that specific symbols are the natural vehicles to express a raft of modern scientific and moral concepts of the most abstract metaphysical kind. This yearning to visualise, this gift of their civilization, is handed down in all these specific images. They lie at the heart of not only the Hindu faith, but also at the composite multi-layered Indian way of life (See later reference to Lucknow, the infertile Begum and temple at Aliganj).

Animals are part of the creative tissue enfolding planetary life as much as humans and flora. If one accepts the gigantic role of the Impersonal Neuter: **Brhm**, the scientific inexplicable creative force that still eludes all empirical definition, DNA discoveries and neurological research notwithstanding, then all material manifestations of **prakriti** = the natural world are part of the symbiotic balance with **purusha** = the original cosmic force that emerges from the non-manifested **Brhm**.

The qualities that Hanuman displays are healing ones associated with medicine and herbs; moral courage and steadfastness; devotion to duty, and in so carrying out that duty, a **sharp ingenuity**. Knowledge is certainly improved by experience!

◆ Anyone who has watched the rhesus monkeys scattering rapidly from their army bivouacs on the tin rooftops of the Shimla bazaar will appreciate their ingenuity, watching for the least careless move by these stupid human creatures buying bananas in the jostling crowded bazaars. My young daughter, strolling and dodging between buyers and sellers, was astonished to lose her bunch of bananas and hill-grown grapes wrapped in newspaper and thin string to a brown mass which shot by, deftly lifting the lot. We had been warned sufficiently about the unpleasant consequences of being bitten by a monkey—a long needle shot into soft stomach tissue was at that time the only recourse to prevent rabies. Best to let go and not argue the toss when a monkey wants what you hold.

◆ But how did a monkey know what was going on in the interior of our hotel rooms in Clarke's Hotel (as the building was called before the government acquired it)? Right atop the ridge we lived out the heat of a flaming summer way down below, the children transferring to a hill school, going on ponies everyday in old style for three months.

Teatime for a young Michael and Caitilin was a plate of their favourite banana sandwiches on brown bread, which had just started being baked (before India knew the joys of crusty rolls and all the sophistication of today's delicatessen pastries now available in upmarket stores). Hardly had the tray been brought in by the room bearer than a brown ball of fur hit the air like a meteoric projectile, snatched the sandwiches and leapt out again, the children too startled to scream! Another time when the fly screens were open (monkeys have the good sense to watch careless humans in our forgetfulness) a large male rhesus loped in, unbeknown to myself and took off with my large jar of Pond's Cold Cream, a lifetime remedy for sun, dry air and wrinkles. By chance a crowd soon gathered around the godown at the back of the hotel. The monkey had managed to unscrew the top of the jar and was plastering his face with cream. Did I have a simian 'stalker' who had been watching my antics for the past month?

◆ In the epic Ramayana Hanuman is depicted not only for using this inborn intelligence (after all are we hominids not genetically connected with the apes?) but he displays total devotion to Rama, and has always been associated with Rama as Deity ever since.

And in the struggles that ensued, Hanuman's defying a curse on him, returned. He was able to assume a gigantic leaping across the ocean stretch between south India and Lanka, co-ordinating the monkey army, under their general Sugriva's command. He reached Ravana's fortress where Sita was incarcerated, firing it with his immense tail (set alight by Ravana's wicked rakshasa forces). This most admired Deity is regarded as the Supreme Symbol of that characteristic most sought after, and which begins this continuum through the alphabet...**Abhayam— moral courage embodied in physical fearlessness.**

Ancient Times…

In the old days amongst the warrior cultures of the **Rajputs** and the **Marathas, Hanuman** was called upon by the guerrilla forces going into battle to defend their fortress hill domains from the marauding Muslim force of emperors such as **Aurangzeb—** last of the great Mughals but impelled by territorial imperatives rather than strategic common sense to extend beyond the **limits of army supply.**

Slogans such as **Jai Bajrang Bali** rent the air—Long live **Bajrang Bali**—yet another name for the Deity, because Hanuman was blessed with a physique as strong as a diamond = *vajra*.

… and Modern

An aberration indeed then to discover that this very same slogan was invoked during the anti-Muslim riots in Mumbai after the Babri Masjid mosque demolition—and now it has become a politically-driven slogan by a goonda (hooligan) splinter-group, significantly calling itself the **Bajrang Dal** (refer **HINDUTVA**). **A hundred years ago the great visionary Swami Vivekananda stated that India needed to return to its ancient anchorages, so morally degraded had it become. He held up Hanuman as the ideal example to follow.** That was prescient indeed for these times when politically motivated religious slogans get taken for piety.

Two personal footnotes to the mysterious presence of Hanuman—and his tenacity of purpose

1. LUCKNOW: A strange tale was told to me early in the piece and in the most unlikely of cultural settings when M C Chalapathi Rau, then editor of the **Lucknow Herald** and an agnostic if ever there was one, took me on yet another learning curve through the city where he had worked for a lifetime, Andhra-born though he was.

Now losing its elegance, Lucknow, though Hindu to its hidden roots, is steeped in old-world courteous Muslim culture, most especially under the baroque reigns of the **Nawabs** of **Oudh** in the 19th century; it is still plural in attitude. And there a Hindu temple is dedicated to Hanuman by **Begum Rabia**, a wife of one of the Muslim nawabs.

Not having born any children and all advice and prayers being of no help she was advised to follow popular legend and go to pray at **Hanuman-Bagh** where Sita was said to have spent time after her triumphant return with Rama for his coronation. When the populace began gossiping about Sita's suspect virtue while kept captive in Lanka by Ravana, even Rama began to entertain doubts and fell foul of the gossip, so repudiating her. Hanuman himself kept guard over her in her miserable state, and this was the spot. The Begum followed the advice, keeping vigil and praying that she may conceive. According to the traditions related to me by a Muslim teacher at the temple, during her pregnancy she had a vision in which Hanuman appeared, requesting that she build a temple at this sanctuary—now called Aliganj.

Every year a great mela is held at the site to which Muslims as well as Hindus come—with fervour. Hanuman's image is installed there. According to the authors of **Hanuman in Art and Mythology** (**K C Aryan** and **Subhashini Aryan**, Rekha Prakashan, New Delhi, 1998) Hanuman is addressed by the Muslim devout as **Mo-Atbar Madadgaar** = a reliable helper.

2. IONA: In a totally alien cultural context, discovered on holiday in an unexpected corner of the British Isles, one of those examples of India's gift for visual shorthand impregnated with condensed messages no matter how abstruse! On the most westerly point of a westerly isle off the west coast of Scotland lies bleak and windblown Iona where St Colomba first set foot in the sixth century (563 CE).

When one considers the distances in that first Christian millennium the likelihood of Scotland and south India interchanging cultural coded messages is quite astonishing. Yet in the 12th century abbey there is a wholly unexpected echo of an ancient Hindu temple at Kanchipuram not far from Chennai. On its aged wall there is embossed on the arch flanking the south window beyond the Choir and Sanctuary and lotus scroll—a curious small carving of embossed stone—a **curled cat** almost kittenish about to spring and an **alert monkey**.

The notes for visitors state (using the colonial spelling) that these same motifs are to be seen in the door of the Conjeevaram temple, which one is not defined. India's anonymous artist/ artisan/ stonemasons, revelling in the profusion of India's thought patterns, illustrate their amazing capacity to manipulate the simplest of imagery to the purpose of India's complex philosophy. **The cat with humped back about to spring, the monkey alert and ready to jump...as Hanuman ever was.**

Apparently there was certainly terminology related to this imagery in the south during the great age of **BHAKTI.**

♦ In texts there was apparently a distinction made visually in the emphasis within various personal pathways of devotion and the experiencing of divine grace.

1. The one is described as the cat-hold (***marjara***)—the image being of a soul being held by Deity, as a cat gently carries its kitten. This was said to be more the quality of the southern bhakti devotion.

2. The other is defined in the iconography as the monkey-hold (***markata***), the symbol implying that the human soul must take the initiative clinging to God as a baby monkey clings to its mother for dear life, implying a very tenacious activating faith.

NB: For those who wish to research the phenomenon of such animal-as-deity symbolism, an entire issue of the now out-of-print **India Magazine** (December, 1992) was devoted to Myths, Manifestations, Meanings of the Monkey God—not only in India but with the spread of this ever-popular deity in Thailand, Indonesia and even China.

■ **HAVAN/HOMA** (n. *Sanskrit*)
Sacramental fire ritual dating back thousands of years to Vedic ceremonies; marriage, temple worship, purification, and the final consummation of the body on a sandalwood funeral pyre. A special altar, demarcated in its geometric exactitude, defines the ritual fire. Interestingly enough, given notice, fire departments allow the construction of such 'altars' in Western contexts—restaurants, theatres and community halls used for Hindu weddings—a move in global crosscultural awareness to be welcomed.

■ **HENNA** (n. *Urdu* from Arabic n. *Hindi* = **Mehndi**)
is so much part of women's celebrations, a seemingly endless array of private and public festivals in which beauty, style, decoration, the desire for embellishment sparkle in an infinite display of the Indian gift of design, and it is there for the asking—leaves from the privet bush.

Dried and powdered green, at first the dye produced when water is added turns reddish brown... and then amid the hubbub of feminine chatter the artistry begins. And not only professionals—many a woman proves the equal of those stonemasons who engraved arabesques in precious stones on Mughal buildings or carved foliate designs on temple friezes and colonnades.

Especially at weddings, hands and feet, despite the malleable flesh, are traced by using a squeezed cone like icing on a cake with delicate lacery of mango leaves, intricate designs which will last at least a fortnight, and become a cooling agent as well in the steamy heat of summer.

■ **HIJRA** (n. *Urdu*)
Beware of having a baby in India, especially a son! The **hijras** will surely track you down and harass you until you pay them off and if you are a **gora**—pale-skinned they will demand an additional bonus.

Fortunately Punjabi friends had warned and advised on how much backsheesh would be expected—but then in India life follows the crooked arm of the swastika. The unexpected is always around the next bend—never the expected. A fortnight after our youngest son was home from birth, Christopher was asleep on the verandah in his bamboo cot. The slatted sun of a Delhi winter glinted among the pot plants and splashed cerise bougainvillaea. Raat-ki-raani ('queen of the night' jasmine) was just about to burst from bud to heavy-scented white blossom. The air was sharp with winter dryness. A murmuration of distant talk, laughter, cycling hawkers calling their wares from glass bangles, milk, bamboo stools to gimcrack plastic toys (the bane of all parents), they were all wandering in and out of the compound, providing a general hum of morning activity after the baby bath, and all its paraphernalia was stowed away. And then the hairdresser chances by.

In those immediate days in Delhi the luxury of a hairdressing salon, Western-style, did not exist. Where was the need? Indian women showered their hair, oiled it and prepared food in the open courtyard while drying their glistening black locks that danced with palpable energy in the warmth of the sun. So the bicycling hairdresser was quite a welcome sight for European females. Blow drier—a crude one in those days, basin, rollers and all—were stowed in a brown leather suitcase strapped onto that pillion-seat of multitudinous uses. And so after birth and lassitude it was a luxury to be lathered, massaged, rubbed and rolled up in curlers... **when an eerie silence wreathed itself around our compound like curling blue smoke from embers.**

Everyone had disappeared! Even the hairdresser had excused himself into the inner reaches of our tiny guest-house type bungalow.

And then a blatant sound of cymbals and drums thudding stopped at the compound gate—not locked even in those Delhi days when everything seemed secure and only jackals at night jumped through the walled hedge onto our lawn. Were they women now flouncing down the drive in flared lehngaa skirts of Rajasthani hues, the **chunni** floating in the air all a-glitter with cheap silver braiding? Or with their muscular arms waving, clattering **dumru**, the wasp-waisted monkey-wallah drums, were they men?

◆ With mauve make-up, blackened eyebrows, lipstick heavily smeared on, all six dancers looked positively ghoulish. They were **hijras**—commonly mistermed **hermaphrodites** when—more accurately—they have been emasculated in a particularly brutal way—not abusively but out of necessity before modern medical procedures made a more humanitarian method possible. Hijras are truly **eunuchs**, a **sub-caste or community unto themselves** who threaten villagers and the more ignorant when babies are born that they will abduct them unless they pay up, but who in a basic way solve one problem for society. If an infant is born deformed or with both male and female genital organs they take the child into their own 'families' and provide them with a future accepted identity, less hypocritical than our own far-from-open acknowledgement of the perturbing sexual realities that can occur.

◆ Traditionally this community finds its space in a particular niche of India's all-accommodating way of life. And spirituality has to be there, being India. The Mother Goddess presides over their

calling—and in so doing gives them the power of her mysterious demonic energy—hence the real terror of their curses in a land which still believes in this other life beyond the day to day—where boons, vows, curses, penances retain their validity and potency.

And so they danced on the verandah, awakening Christopher with their raucous behaviour, loud-mouthed rudery, banging drums; threatening to pick him up—with only myself under a crown of shampooed hair in rollers, a sight as incongruous to them as they were to me! No one else stirred. A few faces peered around doorways watching the unfolding of events, amused undoubtedly at the stranded predicament of Memsahib! They all appeared six-foot-tall amazons, bony structured and physically menacing. I had also been warned that if I did not readily comply (husbands are never around at crucial moments such as this or when having to cope with the ayah's husband about methods of birth control) they might flaunt their 'operation', a flash of Indian loin, the castrated private parts, by lifting their skirts and dancing away with ribald laughter.

'Polychromatic, heady-scented' is how a TV documentary on their plight once put it, with an overdose of cheap musk perfume, sense-assaulted—that is also India. Enough was enough. The baksheesh was given, not sufficient, more argument, my hair rollers feeling pricklier by the moment, more rupees found—and then I flounced off, baby safely in my arms. For a moment they sat, indecisive... but having berated all the population gathered in the servants' quarter and with our noble and protective bearer, Garib, faithful to the BBC for at least six incumbents, re-emerging, they left.

◆ On reflection the misfortunes of life, the raw deal of fate surely demand compassion. It is for them as most things are in India a survival of the fittest. Anyone who lives through the 'operation' performed by other hijras and not a surgeon must surely be the fittest, described in **A Son of the Circus** (J. Irving, Bloomsbury, London, 1994) as very basic. No anaesthetic, a shot of alcohol or opium, the tying of a string around the penis and the testicles, 'to get a clean cut, for it is with one cut that both are removed' while a portrait of the Mother Goddess gives strength, and the man-woman grits his-her teeth.

The worst is to come. The wound is allowed to bleed, purging the maleness in the body which is regarded 'as a kind of poison'. Hot oil is applied to cauterise the wound—but worse still, that is probed to shape it into a kind of vagina. Hijras regard themselves therefore as neither male nor female and (especially in Mumbai and Kolkata) now earn more money, as prostitutes of a third gender. Many take the surname Nayak, which is Hindi for actor.

Since that first encounter they too have 'come out' even though they are not homosexuals. In Lodi Bagh while staying at the India International Centre and having survived the riotous nights of Diwali, I walked around with binoculars innocently birdwatching on my last visit. I was alone, the jogging crowd of middle class Indians totally missing on a Monday morning after the first electric rainstorms of January had washed the dehydrating look of winter dust away. A hijra approached and demanded my bangle and earrings. That would **never** have occurred a generation ago.

The **chaat** boy with his barrow, roasting lentils watched expectantly, my Hindi totally disappearing with the suddenness of the encounter. I flounced off this time, expecting further harassment when a muffled 'guardian' virtually hidden under brown knitted scarves appeared with walking stick and pipe—undoubtedly an old ICS officer on his morning constitutional. He waved his stick. Caste hierarchy or gallantry still held sway! The hijra loped off, laughing defiantly.

Endnote: Reviled as a community by most people, maybe that defiance is being put to constructive use at last. Now in Tamilnadu an obscure temple town, Kooragam, comes alive at full moon time (around April-May) to enact marriage ceremonies for thousands of eunuchs. This ceremony is, as usual, based on a pre-Mahabharata legends demanding 'perfect male' sacrifice, the character chosen requested to marry before his death. Understandably unable to find a bride, as Deity of compassion, Krishna steps in transforming into the female Mohini, who marries Aravanan. Thus, all the hijras 'marry' Krishna. Their existence is legitimized—and they are happy. With the new century established a eunuch, Asha Devi, was elected mayor of **Gorakhpur**, a city north of Varanasi. Others have followed—that is indeed a 'coming out'. By 2002 a eunuch had become an MLA in Madhya Pradesh. Another clapping 'her' hands with her troupe was contesting the state assembly seat for Moradabad, in traditional style. She had 22 rival candidates! Such is India.

In 2003 Varanasi witnessed an extraordinary convention of eunuchs (30, 000 said to have gathered boisterously) to discuss their newly-emerging political clout; terrorism and other political matters.

■ **HIMALAYA**

It is not affected speech to pronounce this word properly. **Himal** means 'ice' in Hindi. We English, as usual, got the accented vowels all wrong (HIM-A-LAY-a), whereas the emphasis should be on the second syllable—a long A (HIMAAL-ay(a)).

♦ The psychology of the gigantic mountain barrier, young in geological age compared with India's southern Devonian range—the Nilgiris—has been India's great strength and cause of enrichment—for those who did succeed in struggling over the intimidating passes (many at 20,000 ft and enough to squeeze the oxygen out of human lungs) must have collapsed in thanksgiving at reaching the fertile and welcoming valleys beyond. Infiltrators have struggled in across the crescent since neolithic man came out of the cave.

♦ Trekking has now brought many outsiders of other kinds to northern India and its awe-inspiring mountains. They and those fortunate enough to have flown from Kolkata due westwards along the line of the highest range—the rooftop of the world—or rounded a bend of the sweet pine-smelling rough paths north of Nainital or north of Darjeeling will understand the unique *frisson* that shivers the body on first sight of the Himalayas.

Capped with the candy-pink glow of the first warming rays of sunrise, their aloof splendour is a vision of that 'other world' beyond humankind. Plumes of snow spray wrap their hard grey rock necks like fluffed-out ermine capes, howling winds shake the spumes of glistening crystal, frozen waters blown off peaks like shards of shattering crystal glass, deep purple valleys where no human habitation has ever existed send a shudder of intimidation through the soul.

The magnitude of range on range, and space of open sky, the dizzying heights and challenge to human survival was territory for legend. Surely Everest on the Nepalese side of the border—so tall to early inhabitants who first sighted it where it touched the firmament, must to them have been the stepping stone to heaven. Even seen from the window of a modern jet the elation is just the same. And the awe.

1. **Swarg**—the Sanskrit word for heaven is echoed in northern climes, an echo from those first Indo-Europeans whoever they were, in the name for Sweden—**Sverige**.

But more resonating than **Everest** in the psyche of Indians from an ancient pre-Vedic memory is that smooth-peaked, flat-topped broad cone—**Mt Kailas** which has remained sacrosanct from the defiling presence—and detritus—of the modern plague of climbers who are fast ruining Everest with litter, a logjam of people blocking others on the mountain, and a consequent increasing death toll.

2. **Mt Kailas** and **the Holy Lake of Mansarovar**—pinnacle of special padayatras and the mythological Mt Meru, the axial mountain upon which the subcontinent 'rests' have, as specific factors consecrated this Abode of Gods, a permanent imprint deep within the Indian mind. Most often it is recorded that Kailashpati (Shiva) first lost in meditation within the Himalayan solitary splendour and then married to the benign Parvati daughter of Himavan, king of the mountain, presides supreme.

As the roar of avalanches comes crashing down, magnified by the rush of turbulent waters gathering force in the melting snows from terrifying glaciers, themselves mountainous in their leading edge, slithering forward inch by inch, the presence of that **prakiti, unassailable Nature** of the Vedic rishis, is a vivid reminder of how helpless a human being is in the face of such primal impregnability.

3. The Vedic rishis peopled the Himalayas with Indra's heaven, home of that great carpenter and tool maker, **Viswakarma** (see **PILGRIMAGE**).

4. Holy men and ascetics, rishis and yogis of Vedic times have withdrawn into the icy caves to test the strength of their resolve and the body's immunity stretched on the rack of penances in the penetrating cold—or on the special pilgrimages to Amarnath high up in the westerly Kashmir ranges where Shiva's natural ice lingam is a source of worship to endless files of pilgrims in the accessible summer months.

5. **Puranic times** (nearly 5,000 years ago) saw Krishna Dwaipayana the vyas or compiler of the epic of equal magnitude—the Mahabharata—imbibe much of his inspiration here, along with the part-historic/part-mythological Pandava clan associated with the Garhwal and Kumaon valleys. Yudhisthira then King of Dharma finally ascended into heaven here with the dog who had adopted him, trotting at his weary heels.

6. Valmiki's Ramayana mentions the river sources—and there are many holy rivers that flow down the steep slopes carving deep into the rocks—the Ganga only a foot deep at Gangotri gurgling through gorge after gorge in her steep descent to Hardwar; the Brahmaputra at the eastern end; the Indus north of Kailas, in Tibet running an incredible northwesterly course along a gigantic slope of the Himalayan rift until it does a sharp 90° angle turn north of Nanga Parbat to turn southwest at the Hindu Kush (China so close) down the steep passes into Pakistan.

7. And the day-to-day world of 21st century reality— monasteries, yaks, Tibetan traders, nomadic shepherds moving up and down-hill between summer and fearful winters to graze their sheep and goats, lone pilgrims and Tibetan monks criss-crossing perilous tracks, modern buses and helipads bringing in provisions to the most isolated tourist outposts unthinkable even 10 years ago, startling signs of the times with plastic water bottles blowing in the wind—and well-heeled Indians, retired army officers, ministerial personnel, south Indian ladies, young eager Sikh women and fat Bengali merchants all undertaking the hazardous pilgrimage barefoot to pay homage at the ashrams spreadeagled around the foot of that abode of the **ultimate Yogi**—undertaking a crossing at 19,000 feet and 4,444 steps down a terrifying rockface to reach where the sages even today sit crosslegged by the icy waters of **Lake Manas** (see **PILGRIMAGE**).

Endnote to Modernity: A double-edged sword shaking these regions into a more subtle disturbance

For how long the unsullied beauty, the compelling majesty and the soaring spirit alone in a flower-studded high-range meadow with just sure-footed sheep on perilously sloping green hemlines to the grey shale skirts covering ever-extending sky-driven peaks?

Himachal Pradesh one of India's newer states after 1956 (created from many small royal principalities) and namesake of this ancient sacred terrain has to make a living for its nearly 55 million inhabitants—the population of Britain. Agriculture is erratic in such a dramatic landscape and hard labour for a hardy hill-folk of mixed Tibetan, Mongol, Vedic origins. Though rich with hydro-electric power, minerals, horticulture, a stable population and a dramatic improvement in health and literacy (doubled in two decades from 32% to 78%), its growth rate suddenly dramatically improved, the state government has turned to domestic and foreign tourist promotion to maintain the momentum... and like Everest, the terrain is beginning to show signs of stress as so many people trample its once unpolluted slopes. Now the detritus of human intrusion begins again unfortunately to show.

This state could become the emblem of the entire Himalayan region, trampled underfoot by the onward march of the tourists, both from overseas in the soaring appeal for, and promotion of, trekking tours. And also from within Indian society—not only from huge numbers engendered in the local tourism industry for mountain sports of all kinds—but also from the ancient tradition of padayatra to the sacred centres of retreat. Another kind of retreat is taking over also—from the newly rich consuming class wanting to build homes in the salubrious air to escape the suffocating pollution of the cities down on the plains.

The concrete piles, a builder's paradise, climb up with no thought for the aesthetics, piles of rubble left, greenswards filled in with unsightly tarmac. Detritus and litter are everywhere, blown plastic bags lodged by fitful gusts in stately deodar and pine trees, plastic bottles and rubber raft bits and pieces bobbing in what were once streams only messed by occasional dead sheep. And what of sewage pollution and the steady rise of electricity needs?

And the environmentally sympathetic architectural lines of the traditional housing and temples, with their sloping roofs of slate tiles and stylish wooden verandahs ideally honed to survive heavy snow and the flow of monsoon waters... will all this be allowed to collapse for ugly 'boxes' to put tourists in?. Gone are the ornamental niches, intricately carved wooden frames to verandahs and arched doorways. A world as ecologically satisfying in its cultural enclosure as the Himalayas, unique in its eco-system, is under threat... being ravaged. Shiva's throne is again being shaken by the Ravana of technological progress, without the discipline of any aesthetic principles at all.

- **HINDI WALLAH**

A pejorative term for the annoying ideologue who pushes the language issue to extremes.

At Independence it was obvious India needed a national language other than English, the mother-tongue of the erstwhile foreign ruler. As a derivation of **Sanskrit, Hindi** was the obvious choice. It also was the one language spoken by most people, but still less than half the population, then about 350 million. The Hindi Press is now 51% greater in circulation than its English language counterparts. But most of these Hindi speakers are in the north and middle India.

The suggested compulsory exam when sitting for the **Indian Administrative Service (IAS**, previously the famed **ICS**) set the cat amongst the pigeons in the 1950s. South Indians felt they would be at a distinct disadvantage, their mother tongues being Tamil, Telugu, Kannada and Malayalam. In addition, state politics and power games at federal level added additional suspicion. Mostly in their distinctive uniform—white Gandhi forage caps and baggy north Indian style dhotis, a whitewater cascade of cloth fluttering, such Hindiwallahs were a delight for the cartoonists' incisive humour as they threw their collective weight around, bearing in mind the huge populations of the northern states of Uttar Pradesh, Madhya Pradesh, Bihar, plus Haryana, the Delhi region and parts of Orissa.

It is the ultimate irony that with the rise in the last decade of a huge middle-income population English has so reasserted itself again it has become a legitimate 'Indian' language (see **LANGUAGE**). This accounts for ironic situations in Parliament when Hindiwallahs encounter their anglicised colleagues. In the last decade even a chief minister of the Hindi-speaking UP state remonstrated with the Service Chiefs—usually very anglicized:

H

Aap bharatiya hain, to Hindi main baat kijiye ... You are Indian, so please speak Hindi.

■ HINDU

is a distortion of the Sanskrit word **sindhu** given originally to name the Indus. Apparently, in ancient Persia the letters S and H appear to have been almost indistinguishable. Sindhu was heard as Hindu. The state of Sind in Pakistan retains this origin. The many travellers who came in, down the bleak passes, like the Iranian king Darius in 516 BCE, appear to have referred to the local inhabitants of the Indus as **Hindus**. Greek and Roman travellers transposed the word yet again to Indo > Indus > India, the land (**stan**) of Hindus.

It is not an accurate term to describe the religion. That came by the indigenes themselves only about 600 years ago; **sanatana dharma** is used in the indigenous texts for the faith. This is why Hindutva is an anomaly as a political slogan with supposedly religious overtones lauding the Hindu essence.

■ HINDUTVA
essence of Hinduism

an awkward term for an equally awkward concept. **tva** is Sanskrit suffix meaning **ethos** of a particular noun, ie, **sattva** which is **satya**—truth... ethos of Truth.

A sign of the times, the **politicization** of Hinduism (a misnomer used by outsiders for a way of life which is not a religion), an entirely new and dangerous trend in India where ironically democratic processes and free speech have allowed fundamentalist extremism to acquire validity.

1. The Hindu faith has never been a proselytising one demanding allegiance, excluding 'the other', insisting on acceptance of declaration through creed, dogma or Holy Books (as the semitic religions do) that a particular creed is 'the one and only truth and all others are false'.

Tolerance of other views in the amalgam which is the collective process throughout India's known history is its hallmark, an impulse noted in the Ashokan edicts, a will to take note of disparate groups, to incorporate them into the overall fabric as India developed (see both ORTHODOXY and TOLERANCE). That is the great strength of the Hindu philosophical viewpoint and its derivative faiths, but it is also seen as a weakness by a new breed of Indian commentators and active supporters of their spectrum of politics, fed up with being railroaded by evangelical Christian and Islamic movements worldwide, these radical groups free to get away with virulent attacks (and even outright terrorism leading up to the Twin Trade Towers attack, September 11, 2001 in New York). Aggressive exclusivist Semitic-sourced faiths are seen as having been inimical to the practice of this inherent pluralism in the development of its society and history, conversion a weapon to wield through verbal and political crusading as well, taking advantage of India's very tolerance—and a faith that allows an inherent intellectual questioning.

2. The British have often been accused by Indian politicians of the pre-war Independence movement of a 'divide-and-conquer' policy. Certainly the separate electorates set up before Independence did encourage a separatist mentality with a resultant emphasis on **sectarian issues**.

Ironically modern democratic processes have, worldwide, encouraged minorities to assert themselves. India has not been immune from this emotional injection of regional nationalism, or **identity assertiveness**. Certain politicians for their own ends in widening their power base, declare that the Hindu view of life is too tolerant by far especially of those adherents to proselytising religions which encourage a sense of apartness such as orthodox Muslims who demand recognition at Constitutional level of **Islamic law for certain civil codes**.

3. In this regard the existence of **Pakistan** just across the northern horizon (and the derivative running sore of **Kashmir**) with the actual hostilities that have erupted as a consequence on both soils has been the catalyst for right-wing, specifically Hindu-oriented parties to emerge and combine forces in the last decade. They are firmly convinced that the nation at Partition endured a cruel amputation that should never have been.

4. Having lived through the passionate debates of the Hindi-as-a-national language agitation and the 1956 States Reorganisation, I personally feel this religiously emphasised Hindu identity reaffirmation is psychologically inevitable but hopefully, like lancing a boil, it will run its course and the mature middle ground will prevail (see **SECULAR SOCIETY**). Taking the long view of history it is as though a part of the Hindu psyche has been utterly suppressed for so long it had to burst out in wholly aberrant and obnoxious ways—the Hindi language question following so soon on the deep anger about Partition may well continue to smoulder especially as continual and intense change from the new communication technologies threatens all settled older generations and launches young impressionable generations (and not only in India but worldwide) on a whitewater rush through unknown rapids of swirling globalisation, disrupted societies and family breakdown. Add to this a large proportion of unemployed restless youth with nothing constructive to do except be paid as a rent-a-crowd.

Virtually a millennium has been spent at the mercy of 'other' people, incomers who admittedly eventually settled and became Indian (the Muslim Mughals) or stayed long enough in the case of some British families of many generations to serve and become part of India—but who in the end 'went home' despite a deep affection for the country and its people. Over 80% of the population is classified statistically as Hindu: many of these may be secular agnostics but embedded in a culture which has been on the defensive for at least 700 years of rule by strangers who came in from the semitic heartland of the Middle East and Mediterranean civilizations.

From this there must be a backwash... and backlash.

5. Certainly a decade ago, the word **Hindutva** appeared to encourage sectarian tendencies. Against this canvas, 1990–1992 were seminal years with a politicized march on **Ayodhya**, a **yatra**

with all the trappings of a Bollywood version of the Ramayana, a chariot on a float and horses prancing. Vengance was being wreaked on historical domination, reflecting the heart cry of the **Sangh Parivar** against the decrepit mosque built deliberately five centuries ago on the significant site of a previous temple (as many were all over north India in the early sultanate regimes). But Ayodhya had especial significance associated with the birth of Rama. Such was the symbolic **yatra**–a true Hindu pilgrimage as a dramatic political BJP statement by L K Advani, then home minister in the central government. Ayodhya combined everything.

The visiting traveller might dismiss these legends as so much mythology. After all, does Zeus play any part in modern Greek politics? Beware dismissing what may seem irrelevant to the India of today! This is where India's symbolic and mythological past accumulates psychic forces totally unbroken in the cultural continuum, erupting dramatically from time to time taking everybody offguard. Such legends have a habit of reverberating with force down the millennia, taking on modern vestments and clattering like Parasurama's axe to claim the present political domain! One never knows what the tripwire will be that will re-alight passions that have lain dormant for decades... Ayodhya like Glastonbury, in England, has the power of **NUMEN,** that psychic force no rational scientist can measure—yet capable of arousing measurable political mayhem. The nephew of Mohammed Ghazni certainly attacked temples in the 15th century; the first Mughal Babur in 1528.

Is this then the new Hindutva puritanism? What does Hindutva really imply? A Supreme Court decision, December 11, 1995, almost as important a date in recent political history as that of December 6, 1992 when the Babri Masjid mosque was vandalised.

◆ After the Shiv Sena election victory in Maharashtra, a defeated candidate filed a case against a new chief minister and the use of the word **hindutva** in his party's political campaign, it being unconstitutional to use heavily-charged religious symbolism. The Supreme Court in its findings dismayed many avowed secularists who passionately believe in Nehru's and Gandhi's ethos–that India's constitutional premise, unlike Pakistan (the Constitution of which declared an unrepentant Islamic state) had embraced the exact opposite. **India was not a Hindu state**. The misuse of the word Hindutva politically implies that it was.

The Supreme Court in its authoritative wisdom however stated that **Hindutva** cannot be 'assumed to mean and be equated with narrow fundamentalist Hindu religious bigotry.' All of which prompts several questions: **How far back does one have to take history to be pure–a true Indian–in the sight of the political bigots? What is the essence of being Indian?**

Are only good Hindus good Indians?

In a nation where eight major faiths have found a true home and where in demographic figures they are huge majorities the size of independent nations, this is dangerous politics, anathema to ancient sages like Shankaracharya who embraced all humanity as part of the giant cycle. Surely 'ethnic cleansing' Serb style is not

India's pathway into her promised future? Nor is the India "harvest of faith" declared by Christianity. Nor is extreme Islamic zealotry, Muslim organizations' avowed intent to convert by subversion or openly declare a militant jehad on all **infidels** = nonbelievers in Allah, both inconceivable actions in India's cosmic view.

Postscript: On the other hand, it is hard for those of us who have never suffered the degradation of 'being ruled' in a colonial sense to climb into the minds of those who have, to feel the resentments and residual anger of those now nominally liberated yet who still feel sidelined in the world forums. This is most especially so in the case of India and its relationship with the Western press which seldom if ever carries bold positive headlines on a major success story coming out of the subcontinent. This fans further resentment and national chauvinism.

Because of the nature of my husband's posting as Representative of the BBC to India and Pakistan, both of us were only too aware of the nature of the beast...the yearning to be reported in a positive light, to be judged on modern progress...but the inevitable conditions of the profession, the outsider journalist on a 36-hour assignment retorting to our remonstrations:

*But who would want to write about dams, when 10 million people are bathing in one dip at the Kumbh Mela? That's **news**!*

The 'extraordinary norm' wins out every time–the 'exotic', the 'picturesque', the downright bizarre, because the sheer human eccentricity of India's freedom to behave in public as it so wishes and for all to see, is on such a scale that the world's press responds. The enormity of disaster, monsoonal floods, ferry boats overloaded and overturned, villages torched by caste intimidators, cyclonic batterings, multinational gas leaks, exaggerated religious fasts, aging cow 'homes' and gurus galore are all the grist for milling, eyecatching news story. Many times my husband was approached, almost invariably in the gentlest and most gentlemanly of remonstrations (only one intractable minister, unbending in a cool aloofness so uncharacteristic of the genuine warmth of personal relationships; the verbal protest was not for the BBC's short-comings, but the world press in general.

This had its personal repercussions; on return to the UK and in the midst of short tempers at the showing of Louis Malle's famous series of documentaries on India on the BBC–'art' films almost entirely sensationally devoted to the bizarre aspects of India's daily life–my husband's protests received remonstrations 'from above' that he had been a more effective representative for India to Britain, than Britain to India!

■ **HINGLISH**
Sometimes referred to as **Inglish** when written as a term in India, fairly takes your breath away with its inventiveness and witty turns of phrase!

Certainly for our family holding a reunion from the USA, the UK and Australia for a Christmas in Kerala, the gasps and exclamations did not spark like crackers in our small coach only for the alarming negotiated escapes our young Tamil driver—fortunately named Ganesh—adroitly manoeuvred going up to Udhagamandalam (Ooty) on the steep ghat roads. The onslaught of truck after truck hurtling down the hairpin bends from the plateau of the Karnataka Deccan—bringing goods down to the steamy jungles of Kerala and the ports of the Malabar coast, was alarming enough! But no, the hurtling impact, as we stared over the tree tops and precipitous slopes of a very dodgy road under constant repair due to the previous monsoons, was the array of large billboards cajoling the motorised public on bend after bend—in good Victorian homily style (see **HOMILIES** and **LANGUAGE** examples).

A cautionary tale in particular caught the eye first! A polite police notice for roadworks ahead—which incidentally the interstate carriers completely ignored. KINDLY BARE WITH US.

◆ Inadvertent or deliberate, the masterly use of the English language by Indians has made it a unique language of their own. That is understandable, knowing the absorptive qualities of Indian culture for one, and 300 years familiarity for another with English travellers from the time they adventured overland, intrigued by the 'exotic' tales out of the East. Besides, Indians seem to possess an innate mastery of language having to be conversant with so many of their own.

◆ And they love puns! Watch satellite TV and marvel at the skills of their advertisers, pirouetting in a verbal display of witty double-entendres on the square box. It happens in major languages such as Tamil, Bengali, Hindi but is most obvious in English, using it as though it belonged without question in India. One article from **Savvy**, a modern woman's weekly, on child musical prodigies cutting their own albums: 'Aditya Narayan at four taking the mike and moving in sync = **Taal Order**' (see **MUSIC** for pun on keeping the beat or **taal**!). The British Council opening of a Second Language Teaching Centre in Kolkata aimed to help the Indian student speak the ways the Brits do—referred to as **Tips of the Tongue..** or **Mayor Culpa**, a headline in **India Today** referring to the shenanigans between Jayalalitha and her arch rival's son, curiously named **Stalin**. He was at the time Mayor of Chennai. Sudden asset wealth 'disproportionate to known income' had initiated a court probe as well as raising media eyebrows.

◆ And while on the subject of 'Indian-ness' a neat pun appeared in a headline to an article speculating on what is the official dress code—there being, as expected, a sartorial pluralism as well, not only above the waistline but in what covers the legs—pyjamas, churidar, dhoti (differently styled in the UP, Bengal, Tamilnadu, Kerala) or formal trousers. Highlighted as **protocol breeches**—a visual caricature below dealt a blow at the **breaches of protocol etiquette**!

◆ Watch Indian TV advertising. It is scattered with a play on English words, as also in a more serious but wry mode the Hunger Project Indian newsletter commenting on the still prevalent patriarchal structure of society stated:

the people of India suffer from 'son stroke'—a fundamental belief that daughters are inferior to sons.

Not only are Indian writers of English using it as **their**

language with an array of acclaimed novels sometimes with record-breaking contracts (for instance Vikram Seth's **The Suitable Boy** and Arundhati Roy's **The God of Small Things**) but also younger Indo-British of migrant stock in the UK, aware of immediate colloquial nuances, are surging out into mainstream popular culture away from elite readership into such genres as **Punjabi rap lyrics** or equally deft cross-cultural forms and serious as well as immensely successful comic drama—**East is East**, **Balti Wars** and **Goodness Gracious Me**. Their own parents, often nonliterate in their own mother tongues of Urdu, Bengali, Punjabi, let alone English, at least rooted them in their own subcultures first.

None of this should be a great surprise. Indian civilization has been orally transmitted for so long that a very sophisticated and verbally skilled people are masters of telling tales. Handling language in an oral culture has to be articulated, full of exuberance and abundance of riches to hold the audience's interest when there were no texts to reinforce the act of remembering.

The storyteller's art has therefore to be one of symbols to capture the imagination. Play on words holds the attention. Humour adds spice. And a nation that in the higher echelons (where the literary text prevails) can quote chapter and verse of Shakespeare (surely the greatest punster of all) is going to be master of the language which is still a national language despite all the reinforcements added to Hindi. However, there is a downside.

◆ Government bureaucrats—both British and then Indian—spawned an officialese that is almost beyond belief. An example of this was quoted in an English language newspaper by the Federation of Consumer Organisations of Tamilnadu, who in desperation sought help from the British Council: **This was the 191 word sentence**—again legalese—which began most Indian insurance policies! Nearly 50 years ago **Sir Ernest Gowers** had tried to stem the tide of verbosity at source—in Britain!—in his famous bestseller: **Plain Words**. In 1951 the British Treasury to its credit, and in a fit of postwar broomsweeping and cleaning, encouraged Sir Ernest into further combat in an **ABC of Plain Words**, to unravel the gobbledygook of civil servants. But it is a losing battle. Indians, with their besetting characteristics of articulated exuberance and verbal vitality, may have engaged the right man, British Council adviser appropriately named **Cutts**, to continue in similar vein the onslaughts on such thickets of profusion.

He was later engaged in workshops to train Tamil civil servants to carry on the good work on what he termed '**a predilection for proclivity toward prolixity**'!

Endnote: Indian author makes news in Ireland in 1794!

In the mid-nineties, **Michael Fisher**, Professor of History at Oberlin College, Ohio, retrieved Dean Mahomet (the man's own spelling) out of the shadows of history as the **First Indian Author in English: Deen Mahomed** (1759–1851) (OUP, Delhi, 1996). A quite extraordinary resilient young man, he followed his young patron, an Anglo-Irish ensign, Baker (to whom he was majordomo in the Bengal Army) across northern India in the 1780s and then migrated to Ireland in 1784. There in Cork he showed an astonishing acumen, putting himself through school to learn genteel ways under the patronage of the Bakers and the rich gentry. He took up writing in English bringing out his book **The Travels of Dean Mahomet**. At the same time, having eloped with a well-born Irish girl, he established an acceptable lifestyle and property amid Cork society! Since then, yet another Indian, a Ladakhi caravanwallah, Ghulam Rassul Gaiwan, has also emerged with some lively tales about English Sahibs—**Servant of Sahibs**—in 1923.

Further Endnote: A teastop enroute to Chennai on my last visit

An encounter in deepest Tamilnadu with vivid English as it is spoken in the exuberance of the moment by an ordinary passerby, a student inhabitant of Tindivanam. My musician friend has, while waiting in our hired car, been dispensing sweets and fruit. A little Muslim girl is too shy to accept so I get out to find her mother. The young man makes way, opens the door for me (am I still a memsahib in today's India?). The window is wound down. He thrusts his hand in to shake mine so I take it. 'Welcome to Tamilnadu!', he ebulliently exclaims with a stentorian flourish. I introduce my musician friend Jeya, returning as we are from Tyagaraja's **aradhana**. He looks intently through the window. **'Veery handsome lady'**, he bounces the words in and with another pregnant pause, considering her from the far side of the car, the bazaar meanwhile crowding in to take part. **'Kwaality personalitee!'**

Such élan! Such surety of language!

■ **HIRANYAGARBHA** (n. Sanskrit)

is a very scientific concept of the early Vedic thinkers who visualised the cosmic process of creation > expansion to grow out of the primordial seed = the cells within the egg. Precisely what one sees in an age of electron microscopes and such

scientific 3D films as the Smithsonian Institution's **Cosmic Voyage**. There, 'the golden womb, that primordial egg born from the waters' is plain to see.

A most dramatic and pleasingly contemporary painting of this is to be found in **Ajit Mookerjee's** ground-breaking book **Tantra Art** (Karma Gallery, New Delhi, 1966) which inspired the seminal **Hayward Art Gallery** Exhibition in London bearing the same name. This drew thousands of people.

Despite its modernity this painting—of the Kangra School—in gold was however, executed in the **late 1700s**.

■ HOMILIES

There lurks in Indian society a goodly streak of Victorian ethic, prone to deliver the short text in full, to the crowds that pass by, or suddenly on a hairpin bend when the mind's eye should be concentrating on the possibility of a florally-decorated truck mowing you down, or it may be very subtle indeed when first encountered, until the message brings you to a dead halt—throughout Delhi.

◆ The latest surprise, while bleary-eyed from overnight travel, is not the elephant just in front at the traffic lights munching its breakfast of long stalks of sugarcane, brushing the windows of the car come to a halt alongside it. One gets used to being stationary at a red stop signal in the middle of the capital, behind the ample bottom of a pachyderm. It is the fact that I suddenly notice in my bemused state the letters stencilled in the face of the red traffic light—**RELAX**.

In Indian traffic, mind you! Now which bureaucrat thought that up, got it past the boss and had all the red composite faces stamped throughout Delhi, I can't imagine!

Interestingly enough, considering the angst of contracting malaria (now making a comeback) there are wry comments such as that on the very effective mosquito-repellent **Odomos** tube: 'ANYTIME… ANYWHERE… only rub a small amount in… DURING POWER FAILURE'. A comment indeed when the **pankhaa** overhead no longer twirls at highspeed blowing the mozzies away.

There are a lot of homilies up the mountain to Udhagamandalam, so many in fact you may go over the edge while taking your eye off the road to read this:

Helmet or Hell Met
It's your Choice!

◆ Over entrances to buildings, in Government offices, on fancy notepaper with that ubiquitous chariot and the symbolic four horses, there are these short, pungent messages that dear Queen Victoria would most surely have approved–**Action is thy duty, reward is not the concern.**

It's all because of **sva-dharma**. There are no human rights in India. You are duty-bound (**dharma**) to think of your **responsibilities** to self (**sva**), family and community. You are as likely to be exhorted from the back of a lorry as an elephant. **Horn please!** It's old hat. In Syrian-Christian Kerala lorry drivers seem to enjoy punning instead:

No Jesus, No Peace
Know Jesus, Know Peace

■ **IAS**

Indian Administrative Service = public service cadre. The comprehensive survey of all previous treatises on the political science of administering states–the **Sukra Niti** (= science of wise conduct) is ascribed to approximately 9th century CE. Written well over a thousand years later than the far better known–**Arthasastra** (pr. shaastra, the treatise on material gain = *artha*) compiled by **KAUTILYA**, minister to the emperor Chandragupta, circa 322–298 BCE and knowledgeable about Alexander the Great's incursions into India and attempts to overthrow the small regional kingdoms of the northwest, the Sukra Niti goes into remarkable detail about how just about everybody involved in social policy should undertake their administrative responsibilities. 'The chaplain, the deputy, the premier, the commandant, the counsellor, the judge, the scholar, the economic adviser, the minister and the officials should, like the king and especially the chaplain, give evidence of good demeanour...

well-versed in ritual formulas and practices, learned in the three Vedas, diligent about religious duties, conqueror of his sense-organs, subduer of anger, devoid of greed and infatuation.

Such well-meaning advice might well bring wry smiles to the North Block and South Block at the top of Rajpath in Delhi if faxed through to all government departments. Even more so at state level and declared each time a State Assembly is opened. A reminder of what was considered right behaviour 1200 years ago would indeed be timely as the brand new millennia starts with a clean sheet!

1951

The **All India Services Act** instituted the **Indian Administrative Service (IAS)** as inheritor of the prestigious mantle of the **Indian Civil Service**, popularly known as the **'heaven born'** ICS. By 1947 it was almost totally Indianised and strongly Brahmin and Rajput. It had come a long way from the Public Service Commission set up in **1886** in colonial times to permit Indians to participate at higher levels in running the country.

The IAS on the whole has maintained the high integrity and impeccable behaviour of its predecessor—many retired members of whom are still alive, writing their memoirs as sprightly octogenarians, sages of their generation. To them must be credited the wellbeing of the nation and its gradual emergence as a united entity during the hazardous years up to 1956 and the reorganisation of the states.

July 1997

It is only in the last half decade that disturbing signs of corrosion of the high standards expected has come to light, enough to arouse comment in editorials. At the installation of the then President of India, Kocheril Raman Narayanan, he made a previously unheard of plea:

Today there are signs of the weakening of the moral and spiritual fibre in our public life with evils of communalism, casteism, violence and corruption bedevilling our society.

Ironically, as democracy has become rooted (not only in India but elsewhere) those in positions of authority are subject to pressures of strong party politics and buying votes. Costs of election campaigns and raising funds open a Pandora's box for abuse, most especially in current circumstances of coalition governments, with three general elections in as many years. [Refer back to **GOVERNMENT** and costs].

A new force has appeared in this process where colonial autocracy no longer administers without having to seek the mandate of the constituency, or a monolithic Congress Party in central government did not have to concern itself with breakaway factions forever manoeuvring and involving those IAS within state government intrigues and cross party deals.

♦ Despite the fact that many Indians quite publicly deplore what they see as the loss of administrative integrity with so many officers implicated in the well-publicized scandals and the **sickliness** especially **of the UP and Bihar bureaucracies**, considering the enormous unwieldiness of the continental mass, the temptations to escape through bribery and other monetary fiddling the surrounding poverty in certain regions, the miracle is that India is still democratically functioning.

♦ Governance continues while politicians squabble. One fact that surprises considering the stereotypes held overseas of a nation weighed down under an inert body concerned with the letter of the law rather than the spirit, and desks groaning under stacks of files, is how few civil servants administer India considering the population... just about 5,000 appointed at last count. Amongst these are some very formidable women, highly educated, worldlywise, who glide into rooms with the assurance of centuries of sophistication, grounded in their cultural traditions, family roots and the knowledge that their decorative arts—not all sculptured on temple walls but vibrantly alive on themselves—can visually stun as they settle down at the boardroom table!

♦ **A postscript**: Indians avidly watched the **BBC TV** series send up bureaucrats in Whitehall–**Yes Minister**! On a return visit and at dinner with journalist friends, the evening came to a halt temporarily while all the guests fell about, in deep rapport with John Mortimer's rapier wit.

There is now a Hindi avatar! Both book and TV series are a natural, bureaucrats in both countries fashioned from the same colonial source. **Ji Mantriji** (by **Alok Tomar**, Penguin/BBC, 2000) and the teleseries will introduce you to archetypal characters who frequent the corridors of power **permanently**. Politicians can be voted out of office but **Mathur** and **Kaul** are secure in their government houses and pensions and the mighty **Jugran Dayal**, Cabinet Secretary, could take over Whitehall in a bloodless coup, such is his finesse.

■ **INDIGO** = *nilini* (n. *Sanskrit* = *neel*, *Hindi* = blue) (colour)

Know your market! To combine business acumen and exquisite artistic skills is something demanded of exporters today—otherwise they sink without trace... but the Indians who first experimented (when Europeans were painting themselves with woad), with the cotton they grew in plantations from Gujarat, across north central India into Bengal, must surely be given the accolade of business 'nous', not for the year, not for a decade, nor a century but for at least four millennia circa 2000 BCE.

◆ They were expert in cultivating the finest quality of cotton on this planet.

◆ They fine-tuned the dyes, in an intricate process and perfected the art of 'fast' colours, locking the dyes in place, a secret, intricate, tedious art of fine judgement of proportions and properties and their effects under sun bleaching, evaporation, steeping, adding mordants—metallic oxides—to facilitate the 'dye-binding' itself, a coating on the fibre, cotton being notoriously resistant to dyes compared with wool and silk.

◆ They obviously chatted up their customers to be perceptive of their needs—lungis for the Javanese, colourful turbans for the high-ranking in Arab countries and the Levant, exquisite muslins for Egyptians.

600 BCE

◆ In Graeco-Roman times the word was out to buy Indian cotton. And another 2,000 years later in the 16th and 17th century once those Portuguese had rounded the Cape, the midnight blue of indigo across blue's own colour spectrum to watery-flecked greys, green-blues to lilac, excited households in Europe so used to dull autumnal shades of woad and flax. Customers could not get enough.

◆ By the mid 18th-century, 'how had the Indians come to the stage of virtually clothing the world?' This the question put in the catalogue to the landmark exhibition: **Master Dyers to the World** initiated as material evidence of such wondrous creations and researched by **Dr Mattiebelle Gittinger**. This **1982** exposure of the story and examples of Indian textiles was promoted by the **Asia Society in Manhattan** and primarily mounted in the **Textile Museum in Washington**. It astonished the public that crowded in.

The answer came, from the catalogue Introduction:

Essentially through the beneficence of nature and their own genius. Paramount was the Indian superiority in cultivated and processing cotton; second their remarkable capacity for seemingly endless product differentiation...

That is, sensitive awareness to customer need.

The skills still are there, returning amongst today's talented young designers despite chemical indigo dyes perfected in Germany in the last century. A new delight in vegetable dyes is evident amongst the wealthy consumer classes, forcing the issue onto designers and printers of cloth. The beneficence of nature certainly has given small farmers the edge, for it is estimated that about 300 nature plants are known to dyers in India for the complex process of colouring cloth. And that knowledge can be tracked back to indigo-dyed fragments discovered in ancient Egypt and in the Graeco-Roman worlds before the Christian epoch **(fragments of plain cotton have been dated circa 1750 BCE at Mohenjo-Daro).**

◆ The Greeks had certainly coined the word **indikon = the shrub of India**, for the cloth traded out of Gujarat. It was here that the branching shrub grew, with its bitter bean pod used for medicinal purposes against bronchitis. **Linnaeus** in his famous plant research had codified the plant as *Indigofera tinctoria.*

◆ John Irwin, one-time curator of the Indian collections in London's **Victoria and Albert Museum** in a monograph of over 40 years ago acknowledged this when he quoted the Vulgate edition of the Bible in which the Prophet Job is said to have commented: 'the lasting value of wisdom is such that it may be compared with the dyed colours of India...' In contrast, European treatment of textiles indicated very 'crude methods' until the late 17th century.

◆ The demand was such by the 16th–17th century as Europeans caught the India fashion craze that the Textile Exhibition catalogue quotes the market needing approximately **30,000 camel loads of textiles and compacted dyes to be annually escorted across the land routes from India to Persia.** Some of the consignments continued onwards to the Mediterranean world and even to northern Europe. Even today indigo is exported in considerable tonnage predominantly to Russia, and **indigenous medicinal products are manufactured from the anti-toxic properties of both leaf and bean.** Products encourage hair growth, are a laxative, a tonic, an antidote for intestinal worms, and a cure for bronchitis.

The Dyeing Process: leaves provide the colouring. Their density of dye matter depends on knowing the shrub (like pruning roses), for instance how to cut the branches close to the ground, how to wrap them in tight bundles and pack them into water tanks to steep. Timing, density of packing, draining, allowing to ferment, re-soaking, beating to oxygenate the fluid into flaky substance, eventually to form a paste, washing again in lower tanks stepped down like canal locks and finally boiled and moulded into a gritty sticky pastecake. These are all part of intricate tedious processes which are far from haphazard.

The dyer has to have that innate sense of timing, be able to 'read the dye', know when to increase the density by adding more leaves to the infusion once the first batch is removed. **Mordant— a metallic oxide**—facilitates in the binding process, as equally exacting in judging proportions in the dye fluid to aid the process of coating the fibre, so affecting density of that resonating blue.

Then there is the painter's finely-tuned handling of the **kalam = pen/brush**, now a handblock which designs those most beautiful of interwoven arabesques of foliage which cover the Coromandel coast wall-hangings and purdahs; such beauty, such delicate multi-coloured flowers against blue-green indigo leaves, one can almost bury one's senses in a summer garden of delicate perfumes. Europeans were mesmerised as they landed in Surat and Calcutta in the early trading post days. Fortunes were made as their organising minds harnessed the impoverished farmers and artisans into factory assembly-line methods, often against their will.

1771

John Prinsep for one, the progenitor of that powerful and illustrious English family in East India Company days, arrived in

Bengal and set himself up as an indigo planter turning the skilled Indians of upriver Bengal to his purpose—and his fortune.

Books ascribe to him the introduction of the indigo trade and painting on fabric to England. However, the truth is otherwise. He undoubtedly increased the volume of exports as well as possibly to China through the power and monopoly of the EIC agencies. He also undoubtedly was instrumental in passing on the knowhow of indigo fast dyes for the beginnings of the English textile manufacturing industry which was finally to undermine this ageless Indian textile trade at source.

But it is the ill-paid farmer on his small-holding who was at the total mercy of the factory owner, as also the dyer and designer who are the unsung heroes of this trade which has finally proved as resistant to colonial take-over as are its dyes.

Finally selling out his indigo factories to the EIC, Thoby Prinsep the son and his family returned in affluence on the proceeds to live in style in Holland House, the family mansion in what is now Kensington High Street, London near the Commonwealth Institute. It is comment enough upon the rapaciousness of such colonial monopolies and the treatment of the humble villager at the bottom of the pile—often ending in spearings, shootings, kidnappings noted by magistrates of the mid-1800s—that as the Bengal Renaissance emerged, protest and reform were beginning to articulate the inequities and demands for a free India. This was dramatically voiced in a revolutionary drama, by **Dinabandhu Mitra**, presented in Bengal. Its title was **Neel Darpan**. The year was **1860**. Its protest centred on the torture of forced labour—the actual creator of the artistic skills—and the exploitation of farmers (who normally were engaged in agriculture for their own needs) by the **'nil kuthi sahib'**, kuthi referring to the huge mansions the English indigo sahibs owned.

- **INDUS VALLEY CIVILIZATION...** of indeterminate dating, variously set at 10,000–5,000 years ago

This stepping stone is very unstable and most probably will demand a complete realignment! The course of the pathway has already changed, verified by new factual evidence coming to light even as this is written, from ongoing excavations in Anatoler, Turkey. The Indus Valley is no longer the correct nomenclature, changing subtly to the **Harappan civilization** and now **SARASWATI** (or Sarasvati, depending on how you pronounce your Hindi consonants).

If only the pictographic script which heads the famous seals (which haunt me on the wall of my living room) could speak their secrets! These moulds in fine clay, so much more aesthetic than those available today, were brought by my husband from the Karachi Museum as replicas on one of his BBC visits to the then new Pakistan. Most of the famous sites of this civilization were suddenly no longer Indian from where it got its name, **Indos**, a Greek way of speaking from the Persians who somehow had to say **Sindhu**. And then the nomenclature got anglicized.

Even in the 50s there were as many questions as there were answers about the history of India. Books published before the

60s still refer to **2,500 BCE** but the diggings still being excavated at its major city sites—Mohenjo-Daro, Taxila and Harappa, all now in Pakistan—are pushing the datings further back into history. Its beginnings may therefore as some recent Indian commentators have stated go back to circa **3,500 BCE** and be intermingled with the receding dark-skinned neolithic cultures of that epoch. As a thriving civilization it petered out without any factual record about 1800 BCE according to most authorities. That is a theory now discarded by many of the new school of historical research both in India and internationally.

1. **Mohenjo-Daro**, **Harappa** and **Taxila** have yielded up over 2000 seals since the 1850s, when Alexander Cunningham pioneered the then new science of archaeology on the subcontinent followed by Indians still little recognized in the West who discovered much about these buried settlements of the now arid regions that constituted this amazingly modern city civilization. People like Daya Ram Sahni in 1921 and R D Banerji in 1923 were so totally eclipsed by the colonial bias of the times when Sir John Marshall and Sir Mortimer Wheeler dominated our generational knowledge. (Refer back to **ARYA–ARYANS** and the problem of historical slanting in what is fed to each generation, succeeding ones granted the wisdom of hindsight).

2. Despite the prevailing wisdom handed to us by the experts and their publications of Aryan 'invasion' theories—nomadic tribes strong in iron technology with superior weapons, chariots and horses sweeping in over centuries and subduing those Dravidian darker-skinned people of the Indus and their luxurious well-planned cities—there was a big question mark over the prevailing dating set at 2500 BCE.

I used to ponder the artistic achievements. How long had such technical developments taken in handling, polishing, executing with such finesse? Artefacts had emerged out of those buried cities with such artistic competence—the swung hips of the grey limestone torso (the first template of a dancing deity with the raised leg broken off?) in the National Museum in Delhi; the beaten silver chalices; the self-assured 'noble' with his pronounced beard, high cheek bones and trefoil embossed shawl over one shoulder; the gold ornaments and beaten gold tantric goddess—what did all these treasures rescued from the rubble indicate in the length of development in manipulating material within the culture? I secretly revised my own dating (very politically incorrect then!) when lecturing back in Britain to the Farnham Indian Orientation courses—it was at least 3,500 BCE! I find therefore no difficulty in accepting even earlier datings due to recent archaeological finds, as well as astronomical computations made possible now with the explosion of enhanced technology. As has been discussed in the **ARYA–ARYAN** section, datings all over the planet are undergoing reassessment. Some of the most dramatic are those concerning Aboriginal people in Australia, which have been pushed back 40,000 years in some places to 80,000 BCE!

The Nature and Extent of the Indus Valley Civilization

3. Walk through the capital's National Museum. Here is evidence, even if scant, of a very wealthy society which traded

extensively. Mesopotamia, and a Sumerian civilization were not so distant. For me echoes pulsed fitfully. I had as a child living in Iraq for a year been through those museums in Baghdad and they had captured my imagination even then.

Then on my first visit to Ahmedabad I was suddenly made aware of the exciting excavations of a huge harbour complex at **Lothal** to the west. They have extended over the decades—warehouses, inner docks, artefacts, pottery linking this area with similar dyes used in the firings on pottery in the Punjab and down to Maharashtra began to throw light on a far more extensive urban peoples that was even first envisaged—and now it seems even further is contemplated in the submerged remains that lie off the Gujarat coast in Dwarka. Here the National Institute of Oceanography wishes to create an underwater theme museum about one kilometre from where other lower levels of Krishna's city are also emerging. A proposed undersea tunnel would take visitors to a preserved temple, still intact. This sounds not dissimilar to the astonishing finds by French marine archaeologists off Egypt's Alexandria. **Myth becoming history seems to become increasingly familiar in breaking down resistance to accepting the validity of oral traditions**.

And that tradition is pulsating with the word **SARASWATI**. Even I plunged into unexpected realms of mythology amid the trauma of an early visit to the **KUMBH MELA** when I encountered my first dead person mangled in the rush of pilgrims to bathe with the naked babas, and was made aware as I tried to encompass the scale of Indian mythology that the sacred river 'flowed again' at this most auspicious conjunction of planets at the **sangam** = conjunction of waters—hence the legend of the waters rising. Is this a similar physical response to cosmic magnetic 'pulls', *neap* and *spring* tide responding to the moon's influence?

◆ Fortunately with the explosion of new scientific research many, even mathematicians and geologists, are also Sanskrit scholars. This is a critical component in re-examining Vedic and Puranic (old, ancient stories) literature. Cross-referencing accelerated by computer technology has yielded up many clues on the use of the Sanskrit **Saraswati** and its riverine connections. 4. From an actual river 'presence' (and all that meant in life-giving terms in such a perilous climate of flood and drought) to a Vedic abstract force to ultimate elevation as a personification of beauty, creativity, the arts, education and ultimate wisdom in the end-of-the-Vedas period and embryonic formation of the **PANTHEON**, **Saraswati** now re-emerges—in outline again. Researched satellite photography has revealed previously unknown dried-out watercourses of a fabled riverbed, of which the Indus is only a tributary. This coursed through **7,000 square km** providing a rich source for civilization to flourish. Now it is proving even more gigantic, spreading water courses flowing down a gentle geological gradient sloping through Rajasthan and Gujarat to the Rann of Kutch which in Vedic times was under water, becoming a navigational bay for trade. Maharashtra and the Godavari river system—**over one and half million square kilometres** are also now linked. No wonder great societies prospered!

In fact, archaeological diggings currently being undertaken in southern Rajasthan, north of the much-visited tourist city Udaipur, are bringing to light 4,500-year-old habitation sites of what is termed the **Ahar** culture. These farming people, with advanced living standards for the times, were able to make copper tools as well as fine pottery, seemingly in advance of Harappan society.

And then Catastrophe

5. A major climate disaster, the drying of the river around 1900 BCE as the Ice Age retreated, and **not invading Aryans**, is thought to have brought about the demise of the Indus Valley cultures—which with that of the Vedic Aryans provides the first known layer of literature of the Indian pluralistic **PALIMPSEST** that like an immense sea anemone when touched by new inflow brought to it through the prevailing current of times, curled its tentacles to embrace the foreign body and digest it.

Perhaps now it is easier for our generation than any earlier ones to take this onboard as a very distinct possibility. We are faced with global warming, desertification, salination, the scenario of islands such as the Maldives submerging as seas rise. El Niño effects and torrential floods, with volcanic eruptions make the planet look positively calm half a century ago. A slow attrition by drought, so extensive both geographically and historically, is now advanced as the current theory for the collapse and disappearance of this mighty fabled river and her unknown people for whom it was that Vedic life force.

And the script? That other 'literature'?

Those challenging 'characters'—upended fish, geometric-lined rectangles, six-spoked wheels that appear also on pre-Christian Celtic urns, 'singularity' figures like Jain murtis, cheese-grater shaped spoons in deep vases and 'barbecue' tongs, all configurations that look as though they graced somebody's urban kitchen, the pictographic frame to some of the world's most aesthetically beautiful miniaturized art—as stylish in simplicity and balance of form in space as a Brancusi sculpture or a sparse Picasso line drawing.

What are they? I have seen them not only on the flat ceramic seals but on the cylindrical brass 'rollers' in the dramatic **Corbusier Museum** display in **Kuwait**, extracted from recent desert finds, as also in **Bahrain's** delightful and instructive **Craft Museum**. The actual process of rolling the embossed cylinders on red sealing wax to attach to the hessian bags on grain is depicted. The well-known humped bull, as modern as any contemporary artist's work, flat-backed unicorns, a buffalo that could be wallowing in the Indus today, strange altar-like Olympic cauldrons, rhinos with studded raiments and the seven **matrikas** (mother devotees) all worshipping a triple horned 'head dressed' figure in a tree shrine—these have challenged intensive scrutiny from Aryan Finland's Professor Asko Parpola at the University of Helsinki to scholars in the Dravidian language schools of south India.

◆ Enthralled by Freya Stark and Gertrude Bell in my childhood and taken to see the Sumerian cuneiform script tablets in Baghdad, which seemed to my immature mind such a painstakingly cumbersome way of writing, this mystery of a more aesthetic way of communicating has a peculiar magnetic pull. And to me that haunting cross-legged figure, referred to nowadays as the proto-Shiva, **Pashupati Mahadev**, the great deity sits there with corrugated sleeves, a crown of sharp buffalo horns, a triple-leaved branch sprouting from the centre of its head–who conceived your idea? What are you saying to us? And still no word comes!

To keep up to date with new archaeological and geological theories as well as reassessment of where neolithic cultures and prehistory may have merged with what became known in the past decades as Aryan or Dravidian culture, read the new books being published by **Voice of India** and **D K Printworld**, both in New Delhi–and especially **Bhagwan Singh**'s **The Vedic Harappans** and several publications by **K D Sethna** (**The Problems of Aryan Origins: From an Indian Point of View**, Aditya Prakashan, 1992, 1994). In addition archaeologist **B B Lal** has again reassessed the Saraswati river valley civilization and given the earlier Aryan theory another blow to its vitals! (**The Saraswati Flows On**, Aryan Books, New Delhi, 2001).

■ **INTUITIVE KNOWLEDGE** (n. *Sanskrit = gyana*)
   leading to salvation
   buddhi = awareness, intelligence, consciousness
   This differentiation is recognised by all Indian rsis, sages, compilers of the orally transmitted wisdom century by century and thence into 'texts'. These were written down on the palm-leaf 'sheets', probably having inserted the personal viewpoints of the sage, giving the text additional **darshan** on the way.
◆   Intelligence, says the Indian (not just high-powered gurus and sages) is not to do with the gathering of facts and figures alone, the measuring of entities, which has so dominated Western thinking in the last few hundred years.
◆   Rational knowledge has to be in equal balance with that which comes by the crooked route, the swastika emblem, and the sudden flash from **darshan**, 'awareness' or presentiment, an instinctive sense of rectitude (refer to **SWASTIKA**).

Nirad Chaudhuri, in his 1979 book **Hinduism** (B I Publications, New Delhi), astutely dissected the paradox of the Vedic scriptures. First he pointed out that despite the 'sanctification of worldliness'–for instance the systematic structure of ashramas, kama, delight, eroticism, the worldly ways, 'they (the Hindus) always regarded true knowledge as not being achieved by intellect or scientific empiricism but by intuitive realizations… Empirical knowledge was deprecated to such an extent that one Upanishad said that worldly people pique themselves on intelligence and learning but remain in the maze of ignorance.' Rsis had moved beyond that confusion:

Behind all manifested phenomena which was subject to change, and therefore also to destruction, there existed consubstantial with them and yet inaccessible to the senses an

◆ unmanifested ◆ attributeless ◆ unchangeable
◆ and all-pervasive element which was eternal and indestructible.
   Kavi = poet being the term originally applied to the seers,

Chaudhuri emphasises the remarkable ability such visionaries had in laying the Vedic foundations by combining their training in acute sensibility with '**an intense emotional temperament**'. That is the quality that always warmed the cockles (whatever *they* are!) of my heart in everything Indian–as though these people knew instinctively how to combine both sides of the brain—in harmony.

◆   In this regard to see how subtly prejudiced has been the world of language in Western attitudes all one needs to do is travel the deductive linear route of A plus B leading to C through **Roget's Thesaurus**, first published in **1852**. Move on to **I, intuitive**.

There is all the ethnocentricity, bubbling up from the very core of scientific concentration in assembling all known alternative words (and of course in the mid-19th century wary of any feminine input!). **Intuition, gn**owledge reached by the crooked ways of poetic truth, the deep wells of mythological symbol, the Jungian collective unconscious cops a real hiding! Alternative adjectives that still reside within its section even in the editions published at the end of the century dismiss such knowledge as:

impulsive, gratuitous, unreasonable, illogical…
and moving on another level to the downright derogatory—
inconsistent, unsound, invalid, untenable, inconclusive, fallacious.
In fact, 'unscientific', despite the fact that the Latin roots mean **in-tuitus** (to look into)—exactly what scientific research aims to do. But the tide is turning. Perhaps one day **to GNOW** will, after all, slip unheralded into a 21st century lexicon! (see also section on **CORE CONCEPTS** and **VEDAS**).

Indians are not at ease with placing philosophy as an academic study in its own watertight compartment with little relevance to what happens in the day to day life of an average person especially when it ties itself in semiotic knots. The search for knowledge (that is, self-realization) takes place in the marketplace, the ashram, meditation at home. (See **CORE CONCEPTS, DARSHAN** and **VEDAS**.)

◆   The residual image that recurs again and again when travelling through Indian landscapes in this dramatic theatre playground along its roads is of the holy man or sage sitting with ordinary people gathered around, dispelling philosophy and usually with wit and a few belly laughs. Villagers sit in earnest, listening; the image transferred to an American shopping mall or Australian country town open reserve is one of total incongruity!

Despite all the vast range of his intellectual expositions of Indian philosophy—very demanding of the mind, Dr Radhakrishnan used to say that all Indians seek **darshan** from their sages, not intellectual knowledge **alone**. It has to be of the heart as well as the mind—harnessed as in true yoga. Insightful wisdom. A **gn**owing, a roundness with both halves of the brain in harness, which must be of deep satisfaction to most women coming from other cultures to India for the first time and seeing their Indian sisters carrying this emblematic reminder everyday—the third eye of intuitive wisdom in the **bindu** dot emblazoned on their foreheads, no matter now that it be a sophisticated decoration matching their saris.

♦ It is everywhere in art motifs from temple wall frieze to the daisy head dot on a textile to the puja, the metal tray circling the deity in the niche with flames in the five small bellmetal lamps—the **niranjanas,** symbol of purification, the mystic bindu in the centre, to the most demanding intellectual speculation concerning creation at the ● **zero-sunya** (see **QUATERNITIES, VEDAS, YOGA** and **ZERO**).

♦ **Intuition** as a key to unlocking the hidden mysteries of life's encounters and true meaning has been a constant quality of Indian intellectual life. Obviously then for artists, the visual interpreters of this philosophic-spiritual framework, intuition buttressed their imagination to create the evergreen symbols. Stella Kramrisch, internationally known for her understanding of Indian art, acknowledges this:

> *The Indian artist sees the image by direct intuition... so evoking the presence of God. Statues and temples are stages on the Road. The pilgrim is meant to see them as he moves from image to image and into the sanctuary, going steadily forward from the light of day into deepening superluminous darkness. He is also intended to see them as he moves around them in magic circles of recognition and understanding. Such rites of approach by movement and of circumambulation fix and define the form of the image.*
>
> The Art of India

■ **ISLAM**

In Arabic, **ISLAM** means **submission or surrender to the will of God. Muslim** means **the one who submits,** hence the bowing down when the first prayer or acknowledgement of indivisible divinity is recited in Friday communal prayers in mosques all over the world. Islam is said now to account for **one-sixth to one-seventh of the world's population as its adherents.**

Allah from the Arabic **Al or Ul-illah** means the Supreme God. Obedience to His Laws and physical prostration five times each and every day are the mental configurations deep in the Muslim psyche.

♦The **Kalimah** or First Principle, the prayer all Muslims declare with reverence each day and which indicates their essential Islamic identity is this:

> *Laa-ilaaha il-lal-lah; Muhammed rasoo-lul-laah*
> *There is no God but Allah; Muhammed is his Messenger!*
> 570 CE

Islam bows down in worship to a single all-powerful God, Allah, a force without personification manifested through the Archangel Gabriel (Jibreel in Arabic) to one **Prophet, Muhammed ibn Abdullah ibn Abdul MutTalib** who was born according to tradition, in Mecca in 570 CE (from which year the Islamic calendar is counted) and died in Medina in 632. This revelation which was miraculously sustained over a period of 23 years was taken down by Muhammed's followers on 'scraps of parchment and leather, camels' shoulder-blades and ribs, pieces of board and the hearts of men', and collected into **114 chapters called surahs,** which have been compiled into the Muslim Holy Book, now spelled **Qur'an** in respect to the Arabic phonetics. (Many Muslims now spell Muhammed with an 'ad', but still pronounce as the 'u' in rudder.)

Much to his own astonishment, illiterate though he was (as is recorded in the accounts by scribes with him), when commanded by the Archangel to 'read' the testament of Allah, Muhammed did so in a vision, the words exposed on parchment and held in front of him in the cave at the base of Mount Hira where he was meditating. But over time, once the Prophet's standing became secure and those convinced of his genuine qualities had followed him away from the cynics and disbelievers of Mecca (who just like the Pharisees held suspicions of Christ's saintly qualities and abused and crucified him) to Medina, the building up of a society to express this new Islamic vision understandably involved temporal processes of law and order.

Such processes were buttressed by Muhammed's continuing recitations of visionary teachings, often quite involuntary as he went about his business. Over decades after the Prophet's death, in the social process of establishing what it was to be a Muslim, Arab tribes in fervour and energy spread the message through foreign lands so having to defend their new-found way of life against those long-established cultures of Judaism, Christianity and Graeco-Roman Byzantium.

An admonitory tone seems to have set into the accompanying commentaries and the sharia (law books), almost a buttress to give the faithful strength against opposing society. The Last Day of Judgement, Paradise, the flames of Purgatory are very real, described more explicitly than the Bible in passages of the Holy Book, a far cry from the general attitudes of Hindu or Buddhist thinking. Here is a Prophet in time and space, known as the Messenger, speaking and relating of an abstract entity, the One, not even a trinity. **In Arabic text "May Peace be upon Him" is added after the Prophet's name as a mark of respect.**

It is useful to see the Prophet as Muslims describe him for he is a shadowy figure in the western world where old misconceptions of 'Mohammedanism' die hard. All artistic representation forbidden in Islam both of Prophet or symbols of Allah, details of Muhammed have been historically given by Ali, his son-in-law.

Born of the distingushed and dominant Quraish tribe of Mecca:

> *he was of medium height, neither very tall nor very short. His complexion was pinkish white: his eyes were black, his hair was thick, glossy, and beautiful. A full beard framed his face. The hairs of his head were long, falling to his shoulders. His gait was so energetic that you would have said that he tore himself from the rock with each step, and yet at the same time he moved so lightly that with each stride he seemed not to touch the ground. But he did not walk proudly, as princes do. There was so much gentleness in his face that once in his presence it was impossible to leave him; if you*

were hungry, you were satisfied by looking at him and thought no more of food. Any man suffering from an affliction forgot his troubles when in his presence, charmed by the gentleness of his features and his discourse. His nose was straight, there were gaps between his teeth. Sometimes he would let the hair of his head fall naturally, at others he wore it knotted into two or four bunches. At sixty-three years, no more than fifteen hairs on his whole body had yet become white with age....

Taken from the text of Tabari's **Universal History in Baghdad** 923 CE and quoted, as also the following passage from the **UNESCO Journal, Courier** Aug/Sept 1981, commemorating 15 centuries of the **Hegira** (or **Hijrat** from the Arabic–hijra = flight) of the Prophet and his followers from Mecca to Medina after a threat of assassination from those who opposed his new message.

....It was reported that his long arched eyebrows were divided by a vein which throbbed visibly in moments of passion.

An echo again of that Third Eye of Wisdom?

◆**Thus 622 CE becomes Year 1 of the Islamic era**. An Islamic Year is based on the lunar phases = 354 days. And so the Islamic calendar began.

The Qur'an

The Holy Book is more than the Bible is to Christians. The Arab root of the word means 'to recite' or 'to address' meaning 'a recitation' as it was from the earliest visionary revelations the Prophet received 'from above'. The Prophet did once explain how these revelations occurred. Over a long period—a span of 23 years—nearly a generation in time the Prophet received visionary flashes of Allah's spoken word:

They happen in different ways; sometimes Jibreel takes the form of a man who speaks to me as a man speaks, sometimes he is another kind of being with wings, and I remember all that he says. At other times it seems as if a bell were ringing in my ears—and when this stage of ecstasy fades I remember everything perfectly as if it were engraved on my memory.

Kept in most homes, the Holy Book is wrapped in plain cloth and placed on a high shelf above people's heads so that no-one turns their backs on it, a mark of disrespect. With permission it can, however, be on display in a proper setting, roped off with prayer carpet placed in front of it in non-Muslim settings of an educational nature. The Qur'an is declared the literal Word of God, a **living reality**. (In Britain Pakistani Muslim pupils were astonished to see some English students in Religious Education lessons treating their Bibles as though they were ordinary books to be thrown around in stupid behaviour in class.)

◆ Any study of the Qur'an has to accept that to Muslims **it is the final word—the truth of which cannot be extended or elaborated upon nor can it be questioned** or even put under the scholarly microscope for re-interpretation (unlike the Dead Sea Scrolls or other Biblical texts). To Westerners familiar with the process of reinterpreting the Bible at the core of Christian civilisation as archaeologists, Hebrew linguists, scientists wrestle

with changing concepts and reassessments of texts, the **dilemma of literalism** at the core of the understanding of the Qur'an does provide an intellectual and religious challenge.

◆   **The Hadith**

A collection of the Prophet's sayings (also referred to as **sunna** = custom or usage) in explanation of the revelations of Allah—and other matters in building up Islamic society—as a supplement to the Qur'an. Arab culture it must be remembered is very respectful to its male elders. Patriarchal tradition is central to this culture hence the prime importance of Hadith. In any problematical situation or personal moral crisis reference can be made not only to the Qur'an but to this whole tradition of juridical interpretation.

Shi'a and **Sunni**: The categorising and grouping of these ordinances has brought about a major division into two sects in Islam, the **Shi'as** and **Sunnis**. This is much the same as happened in other religions that are equally rich in doctrinal and theological disputations. The Sunnis are the followers of the accepted texts and customary laws which were subjected to detailed analysis and verification in the immediate generation that followed the Prophet's death, the Shi'as finding authority in a later generation tracing their allegiance to Hussain, the Prophet's grandson.

◆   **The Indian Experience**

There could not be a faith, in its philosophy, content, ways of worship and mores of presenting itself to the world at large, more diametrically opposite to everything you can imagine in the realm of the Hindu worshipper.

On the one hand is a **universe** exploding in multiple forms, a **PANTHEON** of deities (female as well as male!). A vast whirling mass of myths and Puranic legends—galaxies unto themselves—pulsate in and out of daily life. There is no clear demarcation, a line drawn in the sands of time to say where history in time begins, and the far horizons of imagination take over. Myth is accepted as **real** history (see **ITIHASA**). What a contrast with the bald simplicity of Islamic faith and Sultanate architecture in India!

Daily life is also specifically mapped out for the devout Muslim. The injunction to abide by the prescribed **Five Pillars of Faith**—the **shahada** proclamation of belief in Allah (see **KALIMAH** prayer); **salat**, prayers of a certain order recited five times a day; **zakat**, alms to be given to charity set at 2.5 percent of income; **saum**—fasting for one lunar month known as **ramadan;** and **hadj**, pilgrimage to Mecca at least once in a lifetime (note: **ramaz** = burning, the root implying 'to bake a sheep in its skin'). The one Islamic way is clearly defined; the wayward are clearly noted in the close circle of a village.

It is therefore a miracle that the two ways of life, the Hindu with accretions of history, customs celebrations, rites of passage, three times the length of the 1400-year history of Islam and the 130 million+ Muslims (an approximate statistic) can exist alongside each other in the subcontinent. It is the one country where despite 700 years virtually of Islamic domination (of one kind or another and in large tracts of the land, a near totality very briefly under Emperor Aurengzeb) **that it did not become an**

Islamic state. **One had to be carved out, an amputation, instead 1400 years after the Prophet rode up to Heaven**. On the whole despite that devastating upheaval and the intermittent bloody riots of recent times brought about often deliberately by power-hungry local political extremists of either side or neglect of the real minorities in the big cities, there **are** amicable friendships, interaction and joint celebration of each others' festivals, and a common view of 'being Indian' for a large section of the population.

◆ It would however, be foolish to take a totally sanguine view. As far as my own experience goes I **cannot recall any recognition publicly by Muslims of wrongs done in the past**. A Muslim friend summed up this sensitive area of national life. He was a gentle and respected AIR station director and he said it in mixed company over dinner: 'Yes, we are like vinegar and oil. You have to shake the bottle occasionally to get the mixture well and truly blended.' At least some British do acknowledge certain evils of the Raj, but Islam as a semitic faith is even surer of its destiny. To apologise for past wrongs as some British have, as Australians are increasingly accepting as necessary for reconciliation with Aboriginal citizens, as an American President has officially stated in relation to slavery and the damage suffered by Afro-Americans, seems to create a total blind spot for Islamic thinking.

Yet they assume a defensive position in relation to perceived discrimination despite Constitutional safeguards in public service either in lack of advancement encountered in their chosen profession or also inability to gain employment. This is the claim from their point of view. Other Indians point out that many Muslims have achieved positions of eminence and political power, too many to be just token acknowledgement of a minority. Indeed as numbers go demographically they are a huge numerical component in India, larger than half the nations of the world!

And there is a factor hardly yet investigated by social historians—**Muslim nostalgia for lost Empire**. The passing of the Mughals and that proven structure with the ascendancy of Islamic principles in Indian culture of the widest cultural impact in north Indian customs, art, music and religious reform (see **SIKHS**) was obliterated from public analysis in the messy and attenuated downfall of Mughal rule. Colonial ascendancy of another Raj totally alien and out of Europe swamped and preoccupied Indian thinking which united Hindu and Muslim against the common enemy until the escalating events of Independence dramatically ended British rule. One wonders if this is yet resolved. It has taken the British over half a century to overcome their own nostalgia for the **Raj**! The rise of the Taliban has led also to a radical grouping of various Islamic youth organizations, their hidden agendas a matter of real concern. Declaration of a desire to turn India into a Muslim nation, as the demographic increase of the Muslim population (more averse to birth control) increases quite noticeably, is to be found explicitly on websites.

Fanatical Islam exists once again at the extreme radical right as the pendulum swing of history sweeps the spectrum as it seems to have done in earlier established faiths.

Islam is no different but one has also not to stereotype as a result of what modern technology can create in the physical manifestation of such extremes–September 11th is the watershed example of scale and density of impact of the fanatic end of the fundamentalist spectrum which as a spectrum can also intimidate the peaceable learned pir and the Sufi mystic. Self-flagellation, austere simplicity, and suspicion of the sensuous arts–music, dance, pictorial representation and erotic expression of any kind–have always been part of an ambivalent attitude to human activity and exploration of the psyche in Islamic and Christian doctrine.

Taliban students of the *madrasas* (schools expressly devoted to Islamic studies) in the last decades are said to have originally been in revolt against the corrupt core of their own rotten autocracies (some of whose rulers were clearly seen to be enjoying the fleshpots of Europe and Thailand, and Mumbai in India). The denial of the Palestinian homeland further twisted the spinal cord into a painful extreme reaction. But it has also to be remembered that all the semitic faiths have seen themselves as the one and only 'possessors of The Truth' and therefore of salvation. Place another layer of human tribal–or is it even more fundamentally a biological imperative?–the 'them' and 'us' syndrome upon a sense of boundaries and separation as even the Romans had towards the barbarian over the ramparts... Hadrian's Wall in Britain an example—and the 'other' soon becomes a heathen, Pharisee, gentile, infidel, kafir–'beyond the pale' (the palisade) even in mediaeval Yorkshire.

◆ A concept emerged as Islamic teaching elaborated on the Prophet's words in the Qur'an, and doctrine developed (just as St Paul and the Apostles applied to Christ's teachings). In the Hadith commentaries learned 'people of the Book' conceived a concept of **Darul Islam,** the realm (**darul**) of peace, envisaging the heart and homeland, the very core of Islamic cultural/political/economic identity following the guidelines of the Five Pillars as laid down by their Prophet.

When such a society was the majority, true believers, an Islamic region, the concept of **Darul Hur(a)b** evolved. This is difficult to translate literally in English, with its in-built ambiguity even in Arabic, **hurb** literally meaning war, the realm of war. Recent events have brought this ambiguity into a global spotlight where fanatical terrorists have taken it literally to mean physical assault–suicide bombers and aircraft loaded with innocent civilians to become guided missiles of the most lethal kind, attacking the 'satanic' enemy of Darul.

The more peaceable section of Muslim society would say that such a term as hur(a)b implies personal moral conflict of self-purification, a waging of a mental assault on behalf of converting hearts and minds to the true faith, not a physical crusade as Christians also undertook and when Papal and Vatican councils at the time of the Spanish Inquisition put non-believers and deviants to the stake, to burn alive, because of their 'heresies'.

In the Indian situation with its own painful history and experience of invasive onslaughts, pillage and torture as means of conversion (and ask the Sikhs about their historical experience!) Darul Islam and Darul Hur(a)b take on a new significance. It has been pointed out to me that such concepts may apply to Muslim states when that is the majority society as in the case of Arab nations, Iraq and Iran. Jehadis (a term now part of global chatter) may well carry attempts to extremes in real physical hostility to the other while exercising extreme disciplines on their own fundamental Islamic groups (as in Afghanistan). But how is this to be applied in plural societies (which most nations are increasingly becoming) where ever-increasing populations of Muslim migrants are still minorities? Are they then going to subvert the majority by creating movements for autonomy, separate entities, a sense of social apartness within the main bodypolitik? Already nations such as Russia, China, the Philippines, Nigeria have encountered such threats resulting in political civil conflict. Muslim intellectuals are not very vocal in discussing such matters–the prime question being: How can an Islamic state exist within its host state? Kashmir being a prime example with 5000 years of being a Hindu/Buddhist culture–now 50,000 of the Pandit Community having been culturally threatened, fleeing south, displaced or decimated. In all conscience, one has to ask how minorities are treated in Islamic nations?

On my last visit to the UK in 2002 there had been rumblings again from a radical Islamic section of the growing Muslim population there, pushing for a separate **Islamic Parliament**… and **that** in the land of the Mother of Parliaments! No other migrant community has shown such a tendency. Most, even Jewish, have integrated totally over centuries and become part of the host citizenship. Understandably many Britons took exception to such moves.

Sectarian violence in India because of an accumulation of Islamic terrorism in Kashmir and elsewhere occurs now as a reaction, breeding a new phenomenon with Hindu fanaticism in response, seldom seen in its very long history of dealing with 'the stranger from over the hill'–the incomer.

It does seem that after consolidation sometimes over centuries as in Kashmir, due either to further infiltration and considerable conversion (Mindanao, the central Asian Republics of what was once southern USSR and the Uighur area of western China) a conscious move is made as we are seeing today to establish separatist Islamic states throwing over plural secular ones. Surely like Booker T. Washington in the America of 1895, long before a multicultural society became a political platitude, it could be agreed that, "We can be as separate as the fingers yet as one hand in all things essential to mutual progress."

A Final Personal Footnote: A sight as moving and profound, however, is that seen at Delhi's International Airport when Haj planes fly in from the Gulf after the pilgrimage. Squeezed wafer thin by the press of pilgrims, it is quite an experience as thousands of multiform people in the simple habit of seamless cloth (ihram) unsewn as custom demands, pass by, many henna-haired to indicate having attended the Hadj–Bangladeshis, Chinese, Malay, Japanese, Indonesians en masse, being the largest single Muslim country in the world, now 180 million. And

new–Australian and New Zealand citizens with their growing Muslim populations from countries in turmoil in the Middle East– every shade of skin colour, physiognomy, turbaned head or pillbox hat, now sinking as one on prayer mats unrolled from under the arm as the midday prayer time approaches. Towards the west they turn being east of Mecca, their heads down on the rectangular shape above the niche which is woven as an outline in the carpet piece representing the **mihrab**–the entrance to the sanctuary in all mosques.

Hadj, the fifth pillar of Muslim commitment to Allah, means 'resolve', a test of the individual Muslim's willpower and discipline to undertake what is eventually (despite all modcons, in tents, plus air-conditioned coaches as transport for the three million plus pilgrims expected nowadays) a very exhausting pilgrimage. It is a unique demonstration of human community.

◆ Some prayer mats have woven into the pattern that fundamental shape of India, the pot, a water pot with its slender gracefully curved spout, sustainer of life in remembrance of the harshest landscape of all, the interior of Arabia. Those who genuflect will first wring their hands symbolically on the **ibrick** as if 'washing' in desert sands, as they by ritual have to do before prayer. And a general chanting without embarrassment sussurates through the perennial clatter and rapid-fire shots of Indian conversation in public places… **an extraordinary sense of brotherhood–not even that, but a sisterhood as strong and potent**. There are large parties of women in the double cotton piece habit, with shawls over their shoulders, the few without veils being from more liberated Indonesian and Malaysian cultures. However, it is the first time I had ever seen a husband leading his young wife onto an Australian bound plane, encased totally in black, including gloves despite our summer heat! It is an annual trans-global migration of people embraced in one faith that actually does appear to live up to its egalitarian principles certainly in its own religious racial space if not in the economic, social and gender ones.

■ **ISTADEVATA** (n. *Sanskrit*)

See **MURTI**–the self-chosen deity. The representation of the ONE (Deity) in image form is the channel to help the ordinary worshipper to focus the mind on the abstract metaphysical concept that lies behind the materialisation in form.

Each individual devotee or family has by tradition certain chosen deities (see **PANTHEON**) with whom there has been an especial empathy. For example, some women feel a real emotional pull to **Krishna** as the baby; many Bengalis automatically, because of cultural input not only at family level but also community-wide, honour the goddess concept in the powerful image of **Durga-Kali**. That in no way precludes the worship of other deities, or regards other manifestations as inferior, as chosen by the individual in the family.

■ **ITIHASA** (n. *Sanskrit*)

…really does mean **history** to the majority of Indians, differentiated from **sruti**, the inherent core concept of sanatana dharma—truths of existence revealed through meditative reflection, consequent revelation, inspired transmission.

Itihasa belongs to the other channel, **smriti**. This passes on the **wisdom** (vidya, vid = to <u>kn</u>ow) of the race. **Smriti** is 'what is remembered', the **puranas** = old tales and legends = folk history.

This 'handing down' occurs daily through

- wandering gurus preaching
- bards singing along the routes through the landscape
- family puja
- grandparents telling stories
- school
- mothers
- fillums
- AIR early morning texts
- village plays
- and TV dramas

This body of comment is regarded in Kautilya's **Arthashastra** (the science of material well-being and the social polity) as the **fifth veda**—the **dharma shastras**. Social wisdom and ethics are embedded in them, laid down as signposts by the famous sages, Manu, Yajnavalkya, Narada, Bhrigu, Visvamitra, Baudhayana amongst others.

And in contemporary life, cabinet ministers with flair can evoke that intrinsic sense of unbroken identity, in being Indian, by dropping a simple phrase into the pool of thought in the year 2000. Jaswant Singh, then Minister for External Affairs, declared: '**It is the function of foreign policy to enable the nation to regain its national smriti**'. Using the analogy of Krishna chiding Arjuna at the beginning of the Gita as he hesitated to take up arms until by the last 18th canto he can also declare to Lord Krishna: 'I've regained my smriti', so the Minister is suggesting that Indians as a people tested by the trials of Kargil and the horrific fighting higher than any previous world battle in the rarefied air of the Himalayan peaks against the invasion of a Pakistan Army testing Indian resolve on the UN borderline, can establish their integrity in recalling these old verities learned throughout history—the smrtis.

So what is implied by history for average Indians? Do they have a sense of history in the context of what is studied in Europe or the USA? Forget the Indians who populate the big cities, speaking English, reading the English-language press delivered at their breakfast tables, the modernised, seemingly Westernised elite who have gone on to universities or higher professional training in the UK, the USA, Canada, Germany, France, Russia or Australia. They are the opinion makers, the leaders and the administrators of this huge land. But they are still only one-quarter of the population. Real dates are still in the murky past.

1500–900 BCE

Further excavations in the last decades at **Dwarkanath** and at **Hastinapura**, 60 km north of Delhi have yielded evidence of possible historical facts, and a major conflict (the **Mahabharata War** at **Kurukshetra**) almost two millennia before our present one, and a memorable flood about 500 BCE. These are acknowledged dates but the only ones.

518 BCE... It is acknowledged that King Darius swept out of ancient Persia to conquer the settled communities of the northern Punjab, and that **Alexander of Macedon** marched his legions through this same terrain two centuries later never to reach Hastinapura of MahaB fame, let alone Delhi in 327–25 BCE.

But where is the rest of India's visible pre-dawn history? Were the pastoral settlements and small kingdom towns of Vedic society and Ashoka's capital at Patna contemporary with Graeco-Roman times and the Coliseum or the Parthenon? The more one delves into 'the shadowy' records as Professor A L Basham describes the Indian condition, the more one comes across these phrases as written by Indians themselves **in relation to their culture**:

- 'Little is known of what happened'
- 'Khajuraho remains an enigma' (and this is in the 11th–12th century CE!)
- 'Hundreds of years later it is this unresolved mystery'
- 'Why was most of the work abandoned?'
- 'No answers are available'
- 'In spite of the scarcity of historical material, there is a wealth of subsidiary material, especially of Chinese origin'.

It is the **Chinese pilgrims** of later Buddhist times, and the Islamic scholar travellers such as **al Biruni** (circa 1030 CE) and the prolific and **adventurous Muslim Ibn Battuta*** (1304–68), the **coming of the Portuguese** and **Italian Jesuits** in the 15th century who put pen to paper and recorded the life and times they encountered in India, for history to be revealed to us latecomers. But where are their Indian counterparts? Sanskrit texts there are but they very soon become philosophy rather than history.

Turn to the Other India

Embedded in its innumerable mother tongues, the vernaculars spoken by the vast majority of the population who do not read the English press, at least 700 million Indians ground the nation, anchoring it in the **folk history**, the age old tales of the **Puranas** where rsis and sages and later the compilers of the two **EPICS**, Valmiki and Vyas carry the 'history' into daily life.

And that's where I encountered the Maharashtrian 'historian'. A far cry from the lecturing scholar, the business seminar, the economist nudging India slowly forward, a gentle balding man sits in simple biscuit-coloured khadi wrapped around him like a shawl. Acolytes encircle him. Villagers in their hundreds gather in the dusk. Parrots shriek and flash green between the emerald mango boughs. The time of **go-dhul** brings a certain aura, tranquillity. Women with children astride a thrust hip stand on the shadowy edges, framing the mass of flattened white-coiled turbans. My Indian friend lays down her dupatta on the dusty earth for us to sit on for no rain has fallen since October and this

---

* Designated 'the greatest traveller who ever lived' Ibn Battuta is thought to have covered the equivalent of at least 120,000 km—and this in the 14th century! He started out at the age of 21 from his Moroccan birthplace fittingly with the sea beckoning at Tangiers, and for 30 years travelled even as far as China, having been a judge for a number of years in Delhi circa 1330 CE, and sent as ambassador by one of the Indian Sultanate rulers to China. His four-volumed diary was published in translation for the Hakluyt Society, Cambridge University in **1958**.
(Read also **Alberuni's India** in Edward Sachau's English version in two volumes in Trubner's Oriental Series in 1888.)

is now the time of the koel that calls hauntingly deep in the leafy boughs after the bacchanalian festival of Holi. We are in Maharashtra where village women are strong, uniting in social movements to better their lot.

Anjuli begins translating softly in Marathi as the guru history teacher (he actually is such!) takes hold of the collective imagination. **The scheme of Great Time** sits hidden in the background of everyone's minds. This is the all-India binding, hidden away from the city theorist. A stray anthropologist or a wandering journalist might however pick up the clues. Swami Vishnushivananda explains about the 'compassionate sages Valmiki and Vyasa who wrote the itihasas for the enlightenment of ordinary people... **'You'**, he emphasises with a sharp gesture like a classical Indian dancer in all her glory:

Through beautiful stories, analogies and parables these two scriptures are the history of our race. They present the essential teachings of the Vedas and the Smritis in an imaginative form. Take for instance Shakuntala...

◆ ...Yes! Take Shakuntala, a nymph who was the daughter of that most celebrated of India's ancient sages **VISWAMITRA** (who appears at the end of this ABC). Is he legend or real history? Is he symbol of some very sagacious elder who did actually exist? And her story is not only part of legend but also now part of literary history, the subject of Kalidas's famous drama **Shakuntala** made known in the West in the last century by Goethe who was entranced by its literary power.

The nymph lives in a hermitage having been saved by a hermit, by name **Kanva**. Wandering in the forest in her idyllic life (the earlier India) a king **Dushyanta** (as in all fairy stories) falls in love with her beauty as he passes by. Acting with alacrity, he persuades Shakuntala to marry him and plights his troth with a ring.

Lost in her thoughts on return to the hermitage another irascible sage (they appear plentifully in the legendary histories!) of the name **Durvasa** is visiting her guardian Kanva. Shakuntala fails to pay him the respect he is due and gets cursed into the bargain. As a consequence, of course, many vicissitudes befall her, the ring slips off her finger when bathing in the river, the king fails to recognise her or their natural gandharva 'marriage' in the forest. Eventually after many more impediments and adventures he searches out Shakuntala who by then has given birth to **Bharata**, founder of the race from which India takes its name: **Bharat**.

And it is from this long lineage of rulers out of the shadows of pre-history that the story of the struggles of Bharata's descendants take place in their great story: **Mahabharata**—which is history of a kind, genealogies now creditable and recognised as such. This formidable epic echoes with signals like the pulses of ancient stars receding at the edges of the known universe faintly heard across space-time when our great astronomic discs decipher their mysterious radio wave signals into reality. So likewise the epic transmitter from the obscurity of unrecorded history, into the legendary oral history of the gigantic epic, into archaeological history—fact, a gigantic stride also across silent millennia. That is **itihasa**!

From Kashmir to Kanyakumari villages plug in to this other electronic current that is India's astonishing power of oral transmission, unifying and binding across distance, culture, vernacular script and language. In the darkness of this Maharashtrian village with its fitful and blazing electric bars we could have been anywhere on the landmass, in similar circumstances, the gentle sage wandering off on tangents of good Victorian homilies about **sukra nitis**—the science of wise conduct (return to **IAS**)—using the story of Shakuntala as a launching pad for his ethical teachings... not at all like Caesar's **Gallic Wars** of my Latin lessons, a history of a kind also, or the proof now evidenced in archaeology that Homer's epics were 'real' history. Just so Navaratna Rajaram and David Frawley, in their new mathematical and astronomical computations, begin to give shape to a shadowy **Battle of Ten Kings** in Vedic times (approximately 3730 BCE) pre-dating the Kurukshetra War (3100 BCE).

◆ Foreign commentators may get irritated at the recurring difficulty in delving into Indian history in an effort to discover the origins and movements of these mysterious clans and lineages that appear and reappear in the itihasas. There is no concise, clearly defined and well-documented chronology of events, as the West understands the term. Early Indian history has still to undergo painstaking research; documents that do exist are often uncatalogued and will provide absorbing material for study for those who have the patience to wade through the Sanskrit texts that finally turned oral folk-history into literary record. Long silences cloak the national memory around the Vedic period. No Egyptian hieroglyphics to imprint a record; no Sumerian script in cuneiform engraved on tablets; no temple architecture remaining, no sculpture, little art. Did everything get eaten by termites, documents turn to mildew in monsoonal climates?

Much nearer to the Christian epoch—fourth to second century BCE—this great transmission was finally written down from the long and architectonic stanzas committed to memory, a feat quite remarkable, measured in a thousand years or so.

And later on these texts passed into the vernacular to be understood by all.

This lack of historical sense does not seem to worry Indians. Their history lives with them. Constantly I was brought up sharply in India by this total lack of linear time; reality was concertina-ed so that centuries melted into nothingness and what had gone before, measured in thousands of years, pulsated with the same immediacy as contemporary events. Villagers used to talk to me as though **'presences'** still walked the earth, when Shiva first danced his rhythmical steps of creation.

And what is to come in the future within the great question mark of history beyond the edges of our mental horizons exists also in their minds. Immortality appears to stretch all ways, from afar off in the past, through the present, into the future so that the long thread of continuity binds them to the revolving wheel of birth and death and the endlessly recurring cycle **samsara** as effortlessly as the laws and principles of the cosmic *perpetuum mobile* which our scientists can now demonstrate, incomprehensible measurements of space/time.

A Personal Memory: This immediacy of the ancient world was brought home to me while trying to master my Hindi in the spring sunshine on the more public lawn of our new house in what was then Delhi's brand new Chanakyapuri colony on the Ridge. India's astute theoretican of statecraft (under his other name) was being remembered by newly-built foreign embassies dotting the then barren landscape. My teacher was struggling with my linguistic tardiness when another distraction came along as we could easily be seen by every wandering passerby! Except this was a blind musician! He just had the sixth sense to hear an **angrezi** voice and halted.

This one-time peasant farmer, like many of his impoverished Sikh/Hindu brothers after Partition, had taken to the open road as an itinerant musician to earn a meagre living. Playing his plaintive sarangi strings, he unfolded an ode in flowing Urdu—translated fortunately on the spot by my Hindi teacher—Alexander the Great, the subject, as if he had only marched into the Punjab yesterday!

> *Oh man! Give up all the worldly affairs and fix*
> *your attention on God.*
> *Oh man, in this short life what can you do?*
> *What did Alexander the Great take with him*
> *when he died?*
> *Both his hands were empty, stretching out of*
> *the shroud.*

- **JAINS**

Jina = victorious

are a small community of about $4^1/_2$ million people who, in proportion to their number, have shown a remarkable business acumen and, along with the even smaller Parsi community, wield financial industrial power and dispense philanthropy in the higher echelons of business.

Jinas are victorious souls, 24 in number, pre-eminent being **Mahavir**, contemporary of the Buddha and born in very similar circumstances, 14 auspicious dreams preceding his birth to a ruling family in Bihar, not so far from where Buddha spent much of his life preaching. Born **Vardhaman**, Mahavir (great hero) renounced his home life aged 30, and left the palace and worldly riches in similar circumstances. He is said to have worn only two simple pieces of white cloth which he gave away when 'tempted' by a hermit as Mahavir meditated in the forest. Thus he was left unclothed and was given the title **Digamber** ('clothed in space' or 'sky clad').

Approx 6th century BCE

Mahavir is accepted within the faith as the last of 24 **tirthankaras** (see **TIRTH**) = fordmakers who because of self-discipline 'cross over' the stream of many lives and the wayward ego (the **ahankara**) to reach that state of being beyond temptation—in fact, in charge of themselves.

Travelling the roads of India certainly in the Gujarat-Rajasthan and Mumbai hinterland, a newcomer to the country may well be startled to encounter an absolutely naked pilgrim with entourage, usually carrying a chhatri (umbrella) over his head to shield at least that part of the body from the sun. These are followers of one of the two major sects—the **Digambara** (sky-clad) seen to be clothed by the blue ether of the firmament, symbolised by the extraordinary 10th century statue of the naked Jain saint **Gomateswara** at **Sravanabelgola in Karnataka;*** the other the Shwetambara (white-clad) because of their white unstiched wrap.

With no acceptance that a Deity of personal divine power exists to answer prayer or intervene in the world of humanity, Jainism places the onus of **responsibility for good action on individual effort and personal discipline.** The undertow in a personality which has carried over from previous reincarnations can be instigated and given new direction by **SADHANAS** (pronounced saadhnaas)—austere disciplines.

By living simply, even austerely dressed in plain white cloth recycling material usage, bathing economically, not using electricity—in fact 'walking lightly on the earth' as a learned Jain muni, **Acharya Tulsi** once described their prevailing attitude, there are certain distinguishing factors that have shaped their particular involvement in society. Jain doctrine is founded in the fundamental principle of **AHIMSA**—a non-violence lived in a much more everyday basis than amongst Hindus who also accept

this teaching but in more general terms and which was so stressed even in a political framework by Mahatma Gandhi. As a consequence Jains are strict vegetarians; if they are members of the particularly extreme sect of monks their asceticism proscribes even cooking or lighting fires or eating root vegetables because insects in the soil might be killed in the digging. Likewise white-clad Jain monks and nuns can be seen walking through bazaars or on pilgrimage (most often in western India en route to the Jain centres of Palitana in Gujarat and Mt Abu and Ranakpur) flicking small fans of peacock feathers or flywhisks to prevent stepping on any insects or breathing them in. All living organisms are deemed sacred—even cockroaches!

Cooking rituals, emphasis on fasting, the carrying of a wooden bowl for food to prevent the use of fire take austere living to the extreme. From all this it can be deduced that the life of a **kshatriya** either defending society in ancient times as a warrior bearing arms, and dealing with horses, or being a farmer in the fields with cattle, dealing with cowdung fertiliser when it can be saved for that useful purpose, rather than burnt as much-needed fuel, was not exactly the appropriate way of life for a Jain.

As also with the **PARSIS** many in this small community turned instead to commerce and banking to make a living and in this century founded thriving industrial concerns—and with their gift for ending up with profitable enterprises, a tradition of largesse also became their hallmark. Philanthropic foundations, art galleries, hospitals, cancer-research centres, educational colleges, are part of the heritage for modern India which such money-spinning communities have provided as a part of their concern for **dharma**.

Where finance is concerned in northern India there is bound to be a Jain involved—for sociological reasons evolving out of the very nature of their somewhat austere faith, and over a very long period (this is explained in **FINANCING INDIA**). Jains held prominent positions in Mughal society, for instance appointed as bankers and financial advisers to those Muslim rulers who formed the sultanates of north India 400 years before the Mughal Babur even appeared on the scene in the 1520s.

Jain society flourished again a thousand years later in Karnataka under the powerful and artistically creative dynasties of the **Gangas, Chalukyas** and **Rashtrakutas**, none more so than the commissioning of the free-standing meditative statue by **Chamunda-raya**, warrior and eminent chief minister to the later Ganga kings (see **SOUTH INDIAN KINGDOMS**). This is surely, at over 17 metres high (nearly 60 feet), the world's tallest free-standing statue.

The only clothing in **Gomateswara's** uncircumcised nakedness is that perennial symbol of Indian art, the flowing vine or plant, springing from around the saint's feet and curling with a wonderful quality of carved perfection almost up to the shoulders. At certain auspicious times every 12–14 years a major festival—**Mahamastakhabhisheka**—occurs (the next in 2005 CE) necessitating that other astonishing creativity of the Indian builder—bamboo scaffolding which reaches behind the statue up to the top of the head. In the puja (before thousands of pilgrims)

---

* This site in Karnataka north west of Mysore is spelled many ways—**S(h)ravana**, = the naked ascetic on the hill, **Belagola** = pool of water at the base, **Gomateswara** = the handsome one.

an inordinate amount of coconut milk, gold coins and other symbol-laden properties are poured over the saint in a gigantic anointing ceremony. The somewhat smaller, naked Jinas in temples appear as 'singularities'—so stiff and basic in outline to reflect the Jain search for the ideal, an **entity**—complete detachment from the external world. Another Indian paradox considering the Jain involvement in high finances. This is yet another component in India's intellectual hobgoblin puzzle.

◆ A **jina**, a truly ascetic hero was described as a spiritual conqueror who practised the **Four Virtues:**

goodness...gentleness.,. devotion... contrition
(sorrow for misdeeds)

Endnote. Chandragupta I, founding emperor of the Mauryan empire over two millennia ago, gave his imprimatur to the faith by abdicating power to become a Jain ascetic, taking up residence in Sravanabelagola, thus cementing Jain influence in the Karnataka.

■ **JAJMANI**

is a socio-anthropological term for the interconnectedness of village life going back thousands of years in **the interlocking of caste reciprocity**.

Each caste discharges duties and functions somewhat similar to barter in early European history before a cash economy drove human relationships.

There are 'hierarchies of prestige' in the process—who does what for whom, with an almost trade union precision in not crossing subtle work boundaries. And in some cases ritual purity comes into the equation—certain religious rites of shaving hair 'for the taking of the sacred thread' when a son comes of age at about 7 years old. Not any old barber can do the job. There may be traditional 'enduring relationships' going back generations between families.

Nowadays almost everywhere cash economies are taking over as they did when industrialization swept in through Western countries 150 years ago. However, tradition being so much more entrenched in India, certain residual reciprocity continues in many more socially isolated regions.

■ **JALLIANWALA BAGH**

refers to the infamous massacre which occurred in Amritsar in 1919 on what is one of the most significant days of the Punjabi year—**Baisakhi**, the beginning of spring when everyone takes to wearing **peela rang** = yellow coloured turbans, cholis (blouses), saris. It is even more significant for Sikhs. On Baisakh Day 1699 the last Sikh guru **Gobind Singh** founded the body of the reformist Sikh faith—the **Khalsa** (refer to **SIKHISM**).

◆ Amritsar was crowded that day for a horse fair. It was **April 13th**, the day after martial law had been declared by the British authorities in response to civil unrest throughout the Punjab. Two Englishmen have gone down in history as symbols of a low watermark in British colonial affairs. Even Winston Churchill who later had a blank spot about giving Independence to India had this to say in Parliament after the tragic consequences of that day.

We have to make it clear, some way or other, that this is not the British way of doing business.

These two Englishmen who are often confused in identity by the remarkable coincidence of their names, **Brigadier-General Reginald Dyer** and the **Governor of the Punjab, Sir Michael O'Dwyer** still cause embers to flicker in the historical memory of Punjabis. They are held accountable for the brutality of the events of that day, when **379 people** in the large crowd herded into an enclosed open bagh or garden were slaughtered at point-blank range, and **well over a 1,000 injured or maimed** and left callously in their agony by the British troops, most of whom were Gurkhas who were ordered to fire on the crowd by Dyer.

The space, though open, was completely enclosed with no exit so that when the firing began the crowd had nowhere to escape, and **many Hindu and Sikh men, women and children** though they tried to climb the high walls to escape the fusillade were innocent victims of a harsh military action—ostensibly legal for this was Dyer's technical defence when later he stood trial as instigator of the massacre. He pointed out that because of the threatening situation from terrorist activity in Amritsar, he had declared martial law the day before, banning all public gatherings which had included an address by **Gandhi** in the gathering momentum of the **Swadeshi** Freedom Movement. **Tilak** the famous Maharashtrian freedom fighter had declared **'Swarajya is our birthright'** like a battle hymn of the American Republic, equally zestful in its struggle against colonization. The crowd had wantonly ignored this. It has since been pointed out by those who have sifted through the evidence that many who died were villagers from outside Amritsar who because of Baisakhi had come in to enjoy festivities. In an age before widespread transistor radio, news on the hour which we take for granted, or TV, many in the crowd would not have known of the bans and illegalities until much later. Dyer admitted he deliberately fired on the civilians 'to strike terror' into the Punjab.

What led up to the sad and sorry sequence of events lies at the heart of political misreading and sensibilities of human aspirations, slights, colonial neglect of the psychology of 'subject races'. Khushwant Singh writes in one of his first essays as historian of the Sikhs—**The Sikhs Today** (first published 1959):

The Montagu-Chelmsford reforms were a blow to Sikh expectations. The community which had done more than any other in the war (in supporting the British) which paid 40% of the land revenue of the province and formed 25% of the electorate, was treated with less consideration than other minorities—particularly the Muslims (who with a population of 10% in Bihar) were given 33% representation.

The British always deny it, but the charge so often levelled at the colonial administrators—and not only in India—is that of the inherent policy of **Divide and Rule**. Sikhs had been the backbone of the Indian Army whose regiments had fought valiantly alongside British, Australians and Canadians in the trenches of France in WWI. And although the crowd at Jallianwala Bagh was perhaps predominantly more Hindu than Sikh, the Punjab as a whole, a proud people, felt angered, their neglect by the colonial power rankled.

♦ Dyer a typical army man of that day, born in India, said to have 'a short temper', and an upright disciplinarian wanted decisive action instead to 'Show the Flag'. A woman had been murdered. Railway and bank personnel had died also. The Punjabis needed to be taught a stiff lesson but his military stance became one of those defining movements in England's colonial history. Undoubtedly Sir Michael O'Dwyer was of the same frame of mind in consulting with Dyer... and thus the hapless soldiers were marched in. Dyer was eventually exonerated but died several years after. And then 20 years on, history inexorably takes another twist.

♦ For his outspoken support of Dyer, Sir Michael O'Dwyer then 75 years old, the man who ruled the Punjab, was shot dead in WW2 at Caxton Hall, Westminster, by a clean-shaven Sikh, **Udham Singh**. In what is regarded as one of the most dramatic of the many trials that took place in India's struggles towards Independence, this one is full of mystery. Not only did Udham Singh who was hanged in Pentonville jail on July 31, 1940 plead guilty under a name-change to **Mohammed Singh Azad**, but he harangued the Judge when sentence was passed and he was asked if he had anything to say: *I say down with British Imperialism.*

Justice Atkinson ordered the press of the time not to publish these 'fiery statements' (there were many others). A banning order of 100 years was placed upon Mohammed Singh's case papers! Only now after 56 years have they been released. Clearly Udham Singh with his assumed Muslim name regarded himself as a freedom fighter on behalf of all Indians, no matter their faith. He patriotically shouted:

I shot O'Dwyer on behalf of India.

His remains were exhumed and returned to the Punjab in early 1970s. Naturally Punjabis honoured him. He was yet another Sikh martyr fighting the Oppressor.

The visit of the British Queen in 1997 with an official recognition of this dreadful event made some amends despite the lack of an outright apology. The fact that she was allowed to wear special socks in the Golden Temple rather than going barefoot which is customary ruffled some feathers as did a flippant remark made by the Duke of Edinburgh but on the whole the Sikhs were magnanimous in their response.

■ JODI

A pair, a true partnership not only in human terms. Indians have a capacity to think in pairs = the **mithuna** couples that twine around the sensual panels of Khajuraho temples (to which all tourists flock!) to the more philosophical binding/bonding of Shiva/Shakti, Radha/Krishna, Rama/Sita. The **androgynous deity** is surely the ultimate symbol in a cultural acceptance of balance in the **law both of opposites** and its other side— **complementariness.**

In recent surveys, the romantic cultural ideal entertained by thousands of women and ironically portrayed in an ecstatic sensual relationship on hundreds of glorious temple friezes throughout the ages, may be closer to a measure of attainment in real life, certainly for the new middle class moving out of a strict joint family framework. In this physical situation the mother-son relationship even after marriage remained dominant. For the young couple to show intimate affection was frowned upon; loyalty remained to the elders. Overt affection was seen as a threat. In idiomatic Tamil today 'a good pair' who are made for marriage with each other are referred to as **nalla jodi**.

■ JOINT FAMILY... and its extension

Technically speaking a **joint family** is one where:

♦ All members of the patriarchy live under one roof.
♦ Importance of elders in the hierarchy is upheld.
♦ Usually three generations, a pool of labour under one authority.
♦ Separate bedrooms but in summer most of the family sleeps on roofs—men one side, women the other. This is in traditional village situations where homes are still old style.
♦ Use of a common kitchen.
♦ A common inner courtyard.

With a father, his sons (and their wives) and all their children it is usual to hold a common bank account if the family is economically at that level.

There are many physical variations in these permutations. Obviously in the new urban situation this intensive physical closeness may not be possible now that people are increasingly hemmed in Western style into small boxes, the new cheap municipal housing that becomes a visual blight architecturally in all the overburdened cities. .

An extended family widens the permutations and allows a degree of privacy especially for the several daughters-in-law who in a joint family as stranger sisters-in-law have to endure a pecking order, rivalry, lack of support if the husband is weak and still in a warmer relationship with the mother than with the new wife.

♦ Individual family units may live in close proximity but separate homes.
♦ Separate kitchens
♦ Engage in other work than the common family farming or small-scale business
♦ Share finances at the same time as running a private account
♦ Of course Indian conditions and responses to the norm are infinitely varied as in every other aspect of life.
♦ In some northern hill regions polyandry has been practised.
♦ In Kerala a matriarchal system has existed for hundreds of years. Only now under modern conditions and with increasing urbanisation and the topsy-turvy economics of recent years where Gulf money has made the less educated manual workers extremely rich is the system of business concerns, property inheritance handed down from mother to daughter (see **KERALA** section) beginning to follow the more common norm. Land reforms under a Marxist government and in Mizoram and the common law India-wide have shifted the emphasis.

There are mixed feelings amongst younger generation of Indians about the joint family.

There were undoubted strengths:

♦ **Security plus warmth plus support** both psychic as well as financial

♦ **A complex of buttresses** against ill fortune if one member was unemployed (rest of family would support his dependants)

♦ **Children surrounded by emotional security,** a wide adaptable bonding, much love.

But many younger Indians, enjoying the first flush of higher education, technical training, a slight edge in financial independence and greater personal freedom complain about the following:

♦ Mental suffocation
♦ No privacy
♦ Innovators looked upon as deviant
♦ Natural suspicion of strangers

In fact the system did lead to an attitude of family (and **kin = jati** like Scottish clans) against 'the rest'. The sense of community took second place to that of family pre-eminence. Immediate personal concern is for family members and their jobs. One may well ask: **who is one's neighbour**? In fact there is hardly any time for friends or neighbours amid the everyday family preoccupations.

In an age of economic materialism with emphasis on individual aspirations and modernisation in the market place—with success or failure even at village level, in the agro-business, in selling farm machinery, in the intricate network of trying to improve one's family crop, all dependent on individual flair, and adaptability to the never-ending pressure of constant change—it is a wonder that the joint family still exists. Many Indians are moving into this social pressure cooker as did populations during industrialization and the dramatic urbanization of the west 150 years ago.

But as elsewhere in Asia as has been pointed out in other sections, **modernization** does not necessarily result in **westernization**. It is acknowledged that the joint family served its purpose as an insurance for security and protection in old age in a land where few comprehensive social security schemes exist.

The extended family shifts the emphasis slightly from living physically in very close quarters in one unit to living under several roofs preferably nearby and beginning to cook on separate chulas (earthenware stoves which are often outside anyway in courtyard areas) except on festive and ceremonial occasions. Then they all come together again. While some common funds may be retained for running business and small-scale ventures (or even huge concerns) separate money accounts are kept for private purposes without having to consult central family authority for permission to spend.

It is a fascination to encounter so many flexible responses Indians make in their deeper feelings and resolutions of family structure and psychological matters, no matter how great the tensions and passions aroused.

♦ Novels by **Ruth Prawer Jhabvala** (Polish, married to an Indian architect), **R K Narayan**'s gentle satires and latterly **Vikram Seth**'s blockbuster **A Suitable Boy** provide lively insights into the inner workings of such close emotional interrelationships which can also be very positive.

The sense of family, its importance in the scheme of things, is anchored in the **bedrock of dharma** first at the philosophical level of 'being part of the whole', secondly at the level of personal **svadharma**, within the framework of living one's individual life in the **quaternity of ashramas**, the sense of **obligation and responsibility for parents**, of taking on board the education of brother's children as if a member of the family unit, even if as an individual you are succeeding in going beyond the common farm holding (if you are lucky enough to have land and water resources) with a small-scale enterprise. Or even if you are an extension of the family overseas, earning a good salary.

Maintenance of a resilient physical structure of the joint/extended family is the name of the game. If they do not wish the new breed of rebellious youngsters to defy outright family authority or even in extremes to run away—as has happened in the UK situation, or in divorce a few years after an imposed arranged marriage protected as the young now are by national laws applying to all faiths—then successful families have to be very flexible, perceptive and open to mutual discussion. The hilarious poignant **East is East** film produced by Asian-Britons in the UK (2000 CE) illustrates these predicaments—very close to the bone!

♦ Some remarkable transformations have taken place in overseas conditions but these can also now be encountered in India's huge cities. In Yorkshire, ever-enterprising Punjabi Sikh families have bought terraced back-to-back houses in the once-cobbled, now upgraded inner-city suburbs. English architectural privacy has been reordered overnight and whether a local planning council knows about it or not, archways have been knocked into joining walls, and gates put into garden walls, making one home out of three houses! Many Sikhs, being of the carpenter Ramgarhia caste, have created interiors never envisaged by the English of Victorian times who built these solid edifices. Though there is a degree of privacy in living conditions in two-terraced houses becoming one with a common kitchen for festivals and central family occasions (and a consequent saving of gas and electricity bills) such extended family innovations enable them to enjoy the best of both worlds—a commonality, mutual help, baby-sitting problems solved, and yet still able to withdraw into privacy—a rare luxury back in India—when the urge is there.

At urban level this is paradoxically even easier for some Indians **in** India. The very wealthy can enjoy large older traditional homes which can be subdivided, providing what even Australians increasingly do in the spaciousness of landscaped suburbs with quarter to a third acre plots. Granny flats built apart from the main house, sometimes at the bottom of a large garden, enable younger family units and elderly parents (from either side) to interact without intrusion in helping each other when needed.

Personal Endnote. In one traditional home in Ahmedabad an eminent son of the first Speaker of India's newly-independent House of the People, G V Mavalankar, has shared a true joint family

J

with three brothers, their wives and families for over half a century. It catered for at least 25 people daily as well as servants in each family. On one visit after his father's death, we encountered his widow still continuing the joint kitchen. Every evening all the individual components came together for dinner around a large table in the central ground floor of the house. All four sons lived modern involved lives around this hub, lives no different in outer aspect from any urban family in New York, Paris or London.

Little has changed since then, except one brother and his family moved to Vadodara so one of the upstairs apartments now is home to one of Puru's England-returned sons and his wife and two children.

We sat on the traditionally carved Gujarat board swing the size of a single bed hanging by intricately carved chains, shaped as stylish peacocks. We were 'eating the cool evening air' as the Hindi saying goes (**hawa khaana**). The koel fluted a song in the deep green shade of neighbouring mango trees while the sun set across the Sabarmati. The air was punctuated with gentle laughter and witty conversation sharp with Indo-Anglian reference points and humour—yet as Indian in family structure as 6,000 years ago when the **grihastha** stages were most probably laid down.

Burra Paribar, Bengali-style

Across the continent in a yet more prolifically populated Bengal rich in cultural genes if impoverished by the burdensome weight of so many people and constant illegal migrations of the world's poorest—the climatically assaulted Bangladeshis—is this the largest family unit globally? Who knows!

Searched out in 1959 and discovered with the help of the then All India Radio Station director, Tini Chatterjee, 80 kilometres down Kipling's Grand Trunk Road leading west out of Kolkata—and then a **bund** road perilously dividing waterlogged paddy fields driving north until across a wooded area arose a gigantic mansion as large as any Florentine palazzo.

Identified in a census after Lord Curzon had decided to partition Bengal, the **Nandi** family was **several** hundred strong even then in the early 1900s. Much inquiry along the bund had led my own search for **burra paribar** (the big family) into the hinterland—and there it was, all of a unit with its own private temple architecturally constructed beside it, the size of a country mansion in Europe and just about large enough for the Nandis all to squeeze in now that they were **nearly 600 strong**. The octogenarian patriarch and his wife were still alive and active, both miraculously able to be looked after by 598 descendants! When we visited there were 48 separate kitchens and dozens of huge rice storage sheds, bazaars in themselves.

Terms of Kinship in this Bengali Family

Yet another contemporary JHALANIS, comprising five generations live in Delhi, 21 family units living in one apartment block of seven units, seven kitchens, with its own parking lot of at least 20 family cars.

Every member has a **different** name to mark out the hierarchy on both **husband's** and **wife's** side. Uncles and aunts are not just that! You have to know whom they belong to! They are not just Grandpa and Grandma, nor Aunt or Uncle.

Financing Extended Families

Such family units make international financing around the world remarkably efficient, discrete, safe from the hazards of using impersonal brokerage or paying bank fees and exchange charges. Three generation families founded in trust at second and third cousin level have tremendous advantages in the new global economy. An extended family can financially extend with ease also—building up rapidly a cash flow and a sound capital base, being virtually self-sufficient and resistant to volatile market forces.

Known personally are Sikh and Gujarati families encircling the globe like Shakespeare's Puck, with money flowing freely between cells in Montreal, Manchester, Jullundur, Mombasa, Ahmedabad, Singapore, Hong Kong and across to Vancouver, a large centre for Punjabis many who have links into Australia's Queensland and New South Wales pioneer family communities. They put down vigorous roots in the 1880s showing personal initiative in 'following the Raj,' as the banana and sugar plantations were established by British settlers often with their own intimate connections with India as retired administrators or army personnel, preferring an Australian climate to returning to the grey damp of 'home' in Britain!

♦ **Cousin brothers** is a very Indian term which in a village community embraces such close friends they virtually are **bhai** = brother. It is a term much used when I talked to families in Australia's Pacific coast town of Coffs Harbour en route to Brisbane. Their grandparents had benefited in their later settlement from community links across the vast stretch of Pacific Ocean. With rapidly advanced capital, consolidation was easy. Money in cash does not have to move physically. Accounts are adjusted within the common family budgeting and relatives visit at no cost, plane fares and length of stay a matter for local settlement of debts outstanding between individual family members.

No wonder in the early days of UK settlement amongst the uncomprehending poorer British families in the back streets of northern mill towns these Britishers watched Indian (and Pakistani) families grow wealthier by the week, neighbours seemingly 'frequent flying' before even such a bonus scheme was introduced by international airlines... and concluded that they were all fiddling income tax! A joint/extended family can amass savings very rapidly compared with scattered nuclear families, Western style. They also find it hard to accept the excessive individuality of the nuclear family Western culture encourages without the corresponding sense of balance in the emphasis on responsibilities and obligation. This was the pungent comment of a dignified Sikh, his white beard ruffled with his rueful laughter.

' *Too much private rights. Not enough obligation!*'

■ **JYOTIRLINGAS** (n. *Sanskrit*)
Jyoti(r) = small flame
linga = Shiva's 'mark' or sign in Skt.
The term for the 12 sacred sites which consecrate the ground where **shivalingas** are believed to have 'sprung up' in swift shafts of light—points where Shiva graced the soil of India 'with his living

presence' as a rather shy Indian man explained to me somewhat euphemistically. I later found out in all innocence that this meant where Shiva's semen fell—according to legend!

These centres of numenistic power are dotted around the subcontinent and draw large numbers of pilgrims, not only Saivite worshippers. Many other temple centres exist to honour Shiva but these twelve are especially venerated, their 'hallows' reflecting the architectural styles of their region:

1. Weighty colonnaded architecture at **Rameshwaram** way down south.
2. The gold-canopied and twice re-built **Visvanath** temple in the heart of Varanasi's crammed bazaars and clogged narrow lanes.
3. **Kedarnath** (already of great antiquity in the first century CE) near **Dharamsala** in the **Kangra Valley** set in dramatic scenery, watched over by the Himalayan sentinels of the Dhauladhar range, clothed in unblemished mantles of white snow. It is at **Kedarnath** behind the 8th century temple that **Adi Shankaracharya's samadhi** is commemorated. Far from his Keralite origins, the saint 'shuffled off his mortal coil', a piquant turn of Indian English (see **LANGUAGE**).

The other **nine** sanctified places are :

4. **Somnath** on the coast of Gujarat south of Dwarka itself of a particular magnetic pull being one of the four 'points of the compass' instituted also by that vigorous sage, Shankaracharya, to create an imperceptible psychic unity to the sprawling landmass through arduous **PILGRIMAGE**.
5. **Srisailam** mountain near the banks of the Krishna River in Andhra Pradesh. A temple was built here at a later date, part of the patronage of the wealthy Vijayanagar Empire.
6. **Omkareshwara*** and
7. **Mahakaleswara*** at Ujjain are both in **Madhya Pradesh**, the latter of unusual importance as being in line of the prime meridian running from Sri Lanka up to the *axis mundi* of Vedic legend, Mount Meru. Ujjain scholars claim the setting of the annual horoscope almanac comes from here—the ephemeris or constant base chart for the heavens which shifts annually needing adjustments in the setting of horoscopes consulted by millions of Indians.
8. **Grishni or Grishneswara** lies close to the awe-inspiring Ellora Caves.
9. **Bhimshankar** is claimed way over the other side of India near **Guwahati** in **Assam** (although a site near Pune in Maharashtra lays claim also in this name).

The last three are to be found in this west coast state as well.

10. **Trimbakeswara**, not far from the source of the river Godavari, south west of Nasik.

---

*Do not be put off by what appear to be names too intimidating in their length (especially in the south) to be pronounced. Their constituent parts can be separated out such as **Omkar**eshwara. **Omkar** = sound of Om, the fundamental breath–sound of the cosmos. **Iswara** = deity, but when joined with other syllables becomes **eswara** as in Mahakal**eshwara**, **Mahakala** being the Great Time measurement.

11. **Vaijnath** or **Baidhyanath**, near **Hyderabad** but also claimed for the north east as **Vaidyanath** in the Bihar **Santal Parganas** district.
12. **Nageshwar** (near Hyderabad) but also listed elsewhere as **Nagnath** between Dwarkanath and the Rann of Kutch.

All very confusing for the firangi! It is, one soon learns, best not to ask too many questions hoping for a linear sequence of rational explanations as one travels around. Best just to listen…
- It is the Puranas, the old legends that hold this kind of knowledge together. These parables consolidate the distant Vedic teaching, then the Upanishadic philosophy, often too erudite for the ordinary person, too abstract to comprehend. These **numinous** sites are part of oral history, steeped in other qualities that enrich a person's understanding of life, not just factual truths of location.
- A living rock anywhere can become invested with meaning if an auspicious event in the distant past happened in the vicinity. A Kerala friend on pilgrimage to Kedarnath, doubly blessed as being also one of the char-dham (four holy places, the other three being Badrinath, Yamnotri and Gangotri) explained his own 'frisson' received quite physically from what are regarded as 'naturally energized rocks' (his phrase). For an extra donation to the temple purohit of several hundred rupees, the devotee can do pranam to the Shiva Lingam away from the crowded concourse of pilgrims allowed a fleeting glimpse,

An electrical charge seemed to pass through his body.
It was quite physical, something like a mild shock. I shivered—and it wasn't from the icy cold either!

He chuckled with that very catching Indian wobble of the head.

Personal Endnote: Lost in the back of beyond in middle India's outback, dusty red earth, ravine country, bandits and half of the country's cobra population (so it seemed, and scorpions), we took a wrong turning on dirt roads and found ourselves following the Narmada river, landing up with no knowledge of the auspiciousness of the location at Omkareshwara… an adventure and a half, before four-wheel drives existed, one of those crossover points into the Indian mind which has relevance even today as people, stirred by real anguish, protest about the damming of the Narmada, as sacred as Ganga Ma. It is associated similarly with the mighty Shiva, and geologically more ancient. But even if only part of this stepping stone, it will appropriately be placed here, as an important point, a **TIRTH** or ford to the ever winding padayatra of my personal journey. First it was the physicality of the land. To travel by car is hazardous at the best of times. To find yourself

off the beaten track is to compound the dicey game. We had had Buddhist blessing in Sanchi but no way then was my husband, a true BBC man always wanting to get to places in the straightest quickest possible line, going to return the way we had come, crossing the fast-flowing river by perilous wooden raft, crammed with a country bus, a lorry, several cars, buffaloes, villagers and our Ford car, the bonnet overhanging the planked open sides. Villagers cracked open a coconut for us on arrival at the 'terminal', a tumble-down jetty washed by racing waters as the force of the river brought us downstream. The peripatetic Vinoba Bhave had been in the vicinity, Gandhi's famous ashram not too far away. The earliest carvings at Amaravati took shape in the second century in these environs. The neolithic caves of Bhimbetka hardly known about in the beginning of our own travels through these inaccessible (then) badlands of Madhya Pradesh are symbolic. No tourists ever ventured as there were few facilities. Even now state tourism is only just beginning to take off as the Narmada takes on new significance with marble rocks, holy sites, rapidly expanding numbers of pilgrims seeking out the route the Pandavas of the Mahabharata are said to have followed to the **Panchmarhi caves** (five shelters), in their exile.

There is a wild beauty in this tiger country, stepped down waterfalls amid heavily-forested rocky terrain. And then by chance the bitumen picks up again… and there are wandering sadhus with next-to-no-clothing, a cloth bag each, wooden bowls and huge iron tridents—the **trisul** associated with Shiva. Time is like a shuttle weaving in and out of centuries. A lone hermit, or is he a muni (an ascetic who practices **mauna** = silence) rests placidly on an exposed granite mound, in self-denial at not enjoying the shade of an expansive tree nearby.

◆ And then we lurch into a scruffy bazaar with a hot tea stall and a crowd gathers around telling us which way to go—to a cave! Why would we want to go to a cave when we are trying to get back to a mirage of a main road from Bombay as it was then—to Mandu, Indore, Ujjain and hopefully, in another century, home in New Delhi….?

Of course, the zig-zag path that dominates my life, that swastika shadow which marked many a pathway, took us to the cave instead, much to my long-suffering husband's disgust, with only sadhus to stare at him and no one to give us clear directions. The cave was musty with bat odours, pendulous hives of swarming bees were hanging ominously in a nearby sal tree, the dark stone sculpted forms and fading marigold petals strewn in ghee around the floor had little meaning then.

Who was the shadowy figure seated in lotus position framed in what looked like a billowing protective serpent? And was that a beard and a stave like a bishop's crook? Certainly not Shiva or Buddha? A woman was sculpted again out of that numenistic living rock. My husband was agitating, generally irritated with all the misdirections by middle-India villagers who had hardly seen an angrezi in years.

'You go straight'. You do, and come not to a 'bifurcation' (a favourite Indian term) but this time a 'trifurcation'. We end up sitting on the banks of a river, at a bigger town that I too could not

pronounce in those days—**Omkareshwara**. Chapati and dal was the only sustenance to be had, the smoothed rocks beaten down by centuries of dhobi activity, our haven.

◆ It is only half a century later that enlightenment comes (we did get home three days behind schedule but safely with Ganapati in our car and a broken coconut for blessing!). A tiny booklet put out by the National Council of Educational Research and Training series **Founders of our Living Faiths** came my way by accident in a backstreet bazaar bookshop when I was looking for another out-of-print publication. (India is a wonderful receptacle for all the books unavailable anywhere else in the world because it has a huge readership, despite many people not able to read). The booklet was for children. It was about that ubiquitous sage Shankaracharya. He was surfacing once again. I learnt all kinds of unusual facts in simple terms—and most important of all about the fore-ordained journey he was to make to the same cave on the banks of the Narmada.

From Kaladi in Kerala where I had been (again by accident) he had bade his concerned and widowed mother goodbye, a boy only **eight years old** (like Guru Nanak centuries on), renouncing the world after a mysterious crocodile nearly drowned him until his mother accepted his *vairagya*, renunciation. Born around 788 CE, he died, like Christ, exceedingly young, aged 32. And so, promising his mother to return when death was imminent (he would know by that sixth sense of inner wisdom), he

> set out northward in search of a guru. Coming to the banks of the Narmada, he found the teacher he sought, Govinda Bhagavatpada, the disciple of Gautapada. The sage was living in a cave, attended by learned and wise disciples. Shankara announced his arrival and Govinda, rising from samadhi, questioned him: 'Who are you?' In reply Shankara described his real 'I', the supreme self, in ten verses (Dasashloki) which declared the identity of the atman and the Brahman. Govinda was delighted at this exposition of the essence of Vedanta, formally accepted Shankara as his disciple, initiated him into paramahamsa sannyasa.

from **Swami Sivananda, Sixty Three Nayanmar Saints**, Divine Life Society, Madras, 1980

So the sculpted man with the beard may well have been the sage-guru, the living-rock lady with the pitcher Shankaracharya's mother. Yet no one thought to explain to us. All that any of the young men in the bazaar want to do is to chat you up and practice their English! At the end of the 'cave day' as I called it (not to arouse the adrenalin of my husband at the time), we treated ourselves to an unexpected swim in the clean waters upstream where elegant grey herons were somewhat startled by our energetic splashing on that late steamy afternoon where the great sage-saint must have walked lightly on bhumi, Mother Earth, amid the flash of pied kingfishers, snow-white spoonbills and the perky orange hoopoe.

Now *another postscript*: Irrigation is as much part of Indian culture as any artistic endeavour, being a necessary adjunct to agriculture, itself under the assault of a tropical sun. As the population and the big cities grow, state governments are desperately seeking sources of clean water. That means even sacred rivers such as the Narmada are under serious threat, hundreds of big and small dams envisaged to drain its waters away. Such projects, some already under way, will remove in total 200,000 tribal and village agriculturists from their ancient lands.

The very nature of the Narmada's dramatic falls through pristine gorges and the famed marbled rocks has encouraged central government engineers to respond to the increasingly strident demands for electric power and clean water from Gujarat as well as middle India. The frightening expansion of Mumbai with an annual quarter-million rural or semi-employed labourers migrating into its boundaries in search of jobs is yet another chronic claim on these resources.

It is as though sacred and profane are in total conflict, contradictory forces, the material needs of self-contained condominium townships for high-tech professionals, cybercities demanding 'modcon' facilities, hydro-electric dams to block the Narmada's sacred free flowing waters, the most vital commodity—clean drinking water for the nations burgeoning millions—a truth that cannot be denied. Water needed... and more.

Can even the wisdom of India's greatest thinker (for this is how he is referred) come to the rescue after all the controversial demonstrations on the dry river bed, the uprooting of thousands of tribal people from their total environment to alien regions in Gujarat, the stormy meetings….?

Endnote: Extensive coverage of this thorny question is taken up in a book worth reading—**Taming the Waters** by **Satyajit Singh** (OUP, New Delhi, 1997) subtitle: **The Political Economy of Large Dams in India.**

J

■ **KABARIWALLAHS** (n. *Urdu*)

must be this world's original systematic recyclers, long before other people felt the world needed cleaning up. They are, because of the caste structure, lowly scavengers and scrap merchants. Steptoe and Son is just not in it nor the rag and bone man with his horse and cart of my childhood deep in the heart of the countryside in England. No matter how welcome he was clearing awkward metal fittings, old furniture, bedraggled mattresses, car batteries that no one wants to handle, kabariwallahs undertake the most demeaning tasks more efficiently. They filter other people's junk and detritus into constituent parts, rid railway stations of litter, dismember cars and distribute the parts, dispose of old tyres and even reprocess plastic, the bane of all clean-fill minded shire councils. **Hail Kabariwallahs! Zindabad!**

In Maharashtra's go-ahead state, enterprising cooperation with Oxfam and Australia's Community Aid Abroad has brought inspirational revolution to a panchayat of women ragpickers; they have formed a co-operative to collect from individual houses instead of rubbish dumps, etc, income from this banked to earn interest to generate other activities. **Self-help and new dignity! Ragpickers take charge.**

■ **KALAMKARI**

is the actual process of painting on cloth with the pen = *kalam. Kari* derives from same root which supplies the verb *karnaa* = to act, work.

Now in resurgence as an art form and in high demand worldwide, it nearly died out when the skilled craftspeople of Andhra Pradesh in the districts of Masuliputnam and Srikalahasti on the Coromandel coast suffered deprivation as the East India Company patronage collapsed, the former designing for multi-purpose cloths, the latter specialising in temple hangings.

There was considerable trade in the traditional painted cloths to China and the East from the 15th century onwards; furnishing, chintzes in glorious florals, bedcovers and 'throws'–called Palampore (from the Persian **palang-posh**–bedcovers–where they were very popular) bonnets and dress materials all derived from this laborious dyeing process which took days to resist-dye.

Originally their design and usage was for aiding the guru/saint tell his stories in the temple precincts such as Tirupati. Mythological figures from the **EPICS** covered the entire cloth like an ancient 'cloth comic'.

Persian/Mughal preferences shifted design emphasis to the abstract floral; now experimental modern design and pastel rather than traditional reds, burnt sienna, indigo and purple, are being used–with that innate sense of style Indians of all classes possess. **Patachitras**–a painted story on cloth–is another form of this craft. A little-known village in Orissa off the main Puri-Bhubaneshwar highway, Raghurajpur is becoming famous in retrieving such an ancient religious tradition, hardly known about to outsiders a generation ago.

■ **KALIDASA**

was regarded as a genius in his time, circa 400 CE. At the court of King **Vikramaditya** also known as Chandragupta II at **Ujjain** he was one of the famous **navaratna** (like Akbar's nine jewels, an indigenous tradition honouring poets, writers, artists, musicians). His standing especially in north Indian literature is as Shakespeare's in English literature, most especially for the richness of his Sanskrit poetry and its multitudinous resonances.

As well as the long poem **Meghaduta**–The Cloud Messenger–his most famous poetic drama is **Shakuntala**–a complex tale of sudden love and romantic tragedy that has by force of the Hindu philosophic impetus to end happily (see **ITIHASA**).

Long before Jules Verne or H G Wells, Kalidas was a truly contemporary visionary whom Hollywood and George Lucas would surely have been elated to recruit for he had already forestalled them long before **Star Wars**! In the story of Shakuntala's bewildering search for her lost husband ancillary plots erupt... a mob of giants for one, determined to plague Indra's heaven, the Vedic deities being a constant even in the beginning of the Christian millennium when Kalidasa probably regarded Christ as yet another benign avatar in the long procession of great souls come to restore dharma to this planet. Indra is jealous of rsis who become powerful with the moral fervour of **TAPASYA**–ardent penance. Trouble has broken out. The minor gods seek **Dushyanta's** help so he takes to Indra's aerial car. Finally deposited in a halfway 'space station' in the sacred Himalayas–the abode of the sage Kashyapa who gave his name to Kashmir–he encounters his unknown son whose demeanour however strikes a chord. In a few moments he finds his long-lost love and embraces her passionately. They all kneel before the awe-inspiring sage who blesses them and they actually live happily ever after!

The interesting thing is that as far back as mid-Victorian times the story of Shakuntala was better known to people in Europe than it is today. Goethe was so moved he penned a response to it. Schiller also was influenced by Kalidasa's genius.

In an article by **Thomas Salman** written in 1867 for **The Gentleman's Magazine** edited by one **Sylvanus Urban, gent**(sic) (one wonders if this is a typical English whimsy acting as a pseudonym) Kalidasa is praised for his place in India's mighty literature, the secrets of which were only just being unlocked through the translations of Jones, Wilkins and Monier-Williams as well as by German and French scholars. A caveat added by Salman states:

The familiar canons and traditions of the European drama must be suspended in judging it. (Readers) must not be alarmed at dramas in seven and sometimes ten acts, with half a dozen prologues, and taking some five or six hours to perform.

Peter Brook's nine-hour presentation a century later of the **Mahabharata** pales into insignificance when Victorian readers were facing such a histrionic assault, with this final warning: the audience must be 'prepared for a strange mixture of divine and infernal machinery, for a state of society where polygamy is *de rigueur* and other oriental trifles common'.

K

■ KALPA (n. *Sanskrit*)

A time cycle of galactical immensity, (see diagram). Completely incomprehensible, kalpas are now the territory of modern astrophysicists coping with ever-disappearing universes on universes.

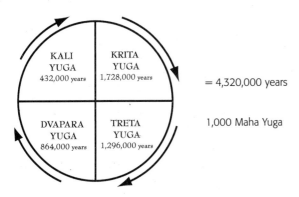

A KALPA EQUALS THE SUM OF THE YUGAS

A **maha yuga** (the Great Yuga) a visual representation of time (not to scale)

It is an approximation and using Western millions (not lakhs). Refer without fail to **QUATERNITIES** and **YUGA**.

(10 times the duration of one Kali Yuga in which we now find ourselves)

= 4,320,000 years

1,000 Maha Yuga

= 1 single day of Brahma
= 4,320,000,000
= 1 KALPA after which creation is overwhelmed, terminating in a DELUGE (myth of the Flood).

Happy birthday universe!

LUCKNOW, April 8

How about wishing the universe a happy birthday? One more year has passed in the life of the universe and it turned 1,95,58,85,098 years today, according to the Vedic calendar.

The present day universe, the ancient texts proclaim, was created 1,95,58,85,097 years ago by Lord Brahma. Interestingly, the life of the present universe as stated by Hindu seers also correlates, to some extent, with the calculations of modern scientists.

Today also marks the beginning of the year 2054 of the Vikram Samvat. Humanity has endured 5097 years of the Kali yuga (era of Kali) and yet another year dawns in the full life-span of 43,42,000 years of this much-maligned era.*

Some accounts double this figure to 8,640,000,000 human years. No matter!

The astronomical figures are only symptomatic of the extraordinarily modern reaches of space/time in which the Vedic rishis were exploring so very long ago.

And this account from **The Hindu International,** April 19, 1997: **Happy Birthday Universe.**

(Measurements are in lakhs = 100,000)

Kalpa maintains **RTA** = the implacable law, i.e., crop cycles, biological rhythms, regulating principles governing the whole intrinsic order of nature.

---

*For inspirational and poetic explanations of India's stretch of imagination in contemplating the unknown cosmos (5–6000 years ago!) read **Heinrich Zimmer**'s seminal book, '**Myths and Symbols in Indian Art and Civilization,**' a must!

■ KARTTIKEYA

The dark-skinned belligerent deity associated with Mars, he is also known as **Skanda**, and in south India, as **Subrahmanya,** a name still alive amongst the Tamils, the syllable su indicating **'the most auspicious'** essence of Brhm.

With another of those explanations that tend to raise the Western eyebrow, legend said he was the son of **Siva/Rudra**, born 'without the intervention of a woman'. Siva is said to have cast his seminal fluid into the cosmic fire; Ganga embraced its scattering. Other legends do confusingly acknowledge Parvati as mother also, along with her other improbable son, Ganesh or Ganapati born of her rubbing scurf from her skin while taking a bath, and 'forming' Ganesh into his shape.

Karttikeya's vehicle is a peacock and as deity he presides in the many shrines of south India's Saivite temples; so outlandish are the legends that symbolic meaning must be telling us something with Karttikeya's six heads—one tale allows the force of Siva's Third Eye on the surface waters of a lake to produce six offspring. The wives of the original rsis took care of them but Parvati (feeling that maternal urge which appears to have had no natural union with Siva's force) took these six youngsters in her arms one day.

She hugged them so tightly that they were squashed into a single form but the six heads remained. No wonder India is credited with the first magical fairy story literature in the **Panchatantra**—which spread into the fanciful fables of a Greek Aesop.

■ KASHMIR

Between October 20 and 22, 1947 fully-armed tribesmen from the NW of Pakistan and other Pakistan nationals infiltrated Kashmir in motorised columns aiming to occupy Srinagar and decide the fate of a predominantly Muslim population especially in the treasured valley. But the ruler of Kashmir was a Hindu raja and Kashmir had a significant if lesser population of Hindu Pandits, including by lineage the Nehru family whose ancestry went back at least 300 years. This is an important factor often forgotten in trying to unravel the complexities, distortions of truth at international forums and what is assumed fact by the international media half a century on.

Disputes over the territory of Kashmir–two-thirds controlled by India but with a mainly Muslim population–have triggered three of the four wars between India and Pakistan since 1947... (1947, 1965 and 1999 with 1971 an internal dispute between West Pakistan and its eastern wing leading to the founding of Bangladesh with Indian intervention). Skirmishes are common across the disputed Line of Control that divides Kashmir between India and Pakistan... a separatist campaign being waged until national elections in 1996 included Kashmir for the first time in nine years has claimed more than 30,000 lives since 1989.

So goes an amalgam of foreign press reports over the past decade. Served up in various shuffles of the political assessment by the Western media, the impression given to the newcomer is that Kashmir must have been an autonomous territory acquired in suspect circumstances by India with an imposed UN intervention, hence a ceasefire line as in the Jugoslav upheavals.

Putting Kashmir Into Context

No mention of the ramifications of Partition in 1947; the ad hoc responses to multifarious regional pluralism complications at the time; and the psychological traumas on all sides with the mutilation of a subcontinent, once a cultural whole in an ineffable, inexplicable way that defied political boundaries imposed by arbitrary colonial domination.

No mention either that despite a predominantly Muslim population in the vale of Kashmir, India's own population of Muslims has remained through 50 years of Independence increasing in fact year by year.

Anyone who dares raise their head to pontificate on this fated territory is bound to be shot down by whichever impassioned terrorist takes the first pot-shot! Where even rumours amongst West Indian lapsed orthodox Christians–the Rosicrucians–aver that Jesus Christ visited Kashmir and the lost tribes of Israel had settled there to multiply with Ladakhi–(at one time predominantly Buddhist), Tibetan, trans-Caucasian, Afghani tribal, Sunni and Shi'a–a volatile mix, anyone's assessment is legitimate.

1946–47

Mohammed Jinnah, lauded founder on the Pakistan side of politics, wore the heavy mantle of a London Inns of Court lawyer–the letter of the law rather than the spirit. With evidence now at hand of his obsessive belief that India's ideal under the leadership of Nehru and Gandhi **with whom he had been a colleague in the Congress in the long haul to freedom**, the

ideal of secularism amid the welter of faiths on the subcontinent could never work, is disturbing. That is what led to the creation of the new Islamic State, a **homeland** in his vision, to which all Indian Muslims would naturally migrate... so he thought.

But they did not despite Jinnah's view that the divide between Hindu and Muslim faiths was too great; that the philosophy of life, social customs, were so diametrically opposite that this new land of peace, **Pak** = 'pure', would be a haven, the ideal of a true constitutionally enforced Islamic society. Yet 130 million Muslims still live in India as Indian citizens–blood brothers and sisters in some instances across the border. (After Partition, Major General Habibullah headed India's Sandhurst in Pune at Khadakvasla. His brother was in command of the Pakistan Air Force at the same time.)

♦ Fifty years later at the commemoration of Independence for both nations a British Labour MP, young then, but a member of the All Party Delegation to India in 1946, **Woodrow Wyatt** writing in **The Spectator** (Aug 9/97) repeats how Jinnah held this notion that as **'the British were the heirs to Muslim rule in India, it should be handed back to the Muslims'. Together with the British** (and he almost convinced the Viceroy Lord Wavell of this) they could rule India indefinitely **'and stop this nonsense about Independence'**. Wyatt knew Jinnah well. He was after all personal assistant to Sir Stafford Cripps in the Cabinet Mission to decide how to unwind the processes of Empire. ·

1954

Coming in as total neutral, not even aware in those immediate but far-off days of the 1950s about the basic facts of Indian history as a subcontinental geographical entity of some mysterious force, perennially replenishing but inaccessible to empirical analysis–my first amazement was to discover and climb the hill overlooking Srinagar, Kashmir's capital on our first leave after a year in Delhi and for our young children's sake to escape its steaming heat.

And the 'hill'. It was named **Shankaracharya Hill!** And there was one of India's holiest Hindu shrines of Sharada (goddess of learning) said to form one of the **trikona** = three corners or tricorn of the Sri Chakra Mandala, ⚠ the bindu being Kashi the city, the three points of the compass being **Kanyakumari** in the far south, **Nepal**–and **Kashmir!** Here was installed the 'throne of omniscience' which the great Kerala philosopher was allowed to ascend as unifier of India for the **trikona contained what was the land of Aryavarta = Bharatvarsha.**

In that ninth century on his arduous travels which had taken even our car three days through the burning brown plains, the foothills of Jammu province, Islam was only just emerging within the Arabian peninsula.

♦ Throughout millennia long before the Prophet had been born (only a century before Shankaracharya himself) Kashmir Shaivism had flourished, hence the ingrained traditional society of Kashmiri Pandits (including the agnostic Nehru). That then must surely trace origins back to earlier times. It is from Srinagar in fact that one of a Hindu's most testing pilgrimages up to the craggy Amarnath Cave with its frozen ice-lingam sets out, a summertime yatra now undertaken under even more hazardous conditions due to Islamic militants shooting pilgrims, despite a state government (also predominantly Muslim).

◆ **A Personal Political View**… biased undoubtedly… as most people's views are! Standing on this very unstable and rugged boulder stone I make no bones about how many others I have stumbled over to reach a few conclusions nor, having visited Kashmir and Jammu–its other half-entity this side of the mountains–three times since 1954, in feeling very strongly…
a) that the Western world has forgotten that Kashmir has for ever and a day been an integral part of Indian culture
b) Indian governments have failed in pointing this out, reiterating legalistic arguments a foreign public does not understand and is bored to death in hearing
c) I blame my own people and the UK government in washing their hands of what had been imposed on the subcontinent so in 1947 creating a permanently running abscess even though the British argument can rightly state that Jinnah, Nehru, Gandhi and the Viceroy were all part of the equation.

Kashmir then was inextricably part of the Indian ethos when long before Islam's partial dominance of northern subcontinental culture, and the politicalization under European influence, Indians saw themselves neither as Hindu (a word not known in earliest time), Buddhist, Jain, Parsi or Syrian Christian but as regional peoples acknowledging a Vedic tradition and a sense of land–**Aryavarta**. The Pakistani argument would appear therefore to be fundamentally flawed in regard to what constitutes **Indian Nationhood**: the British by arbitrarily partitioning the subcontinent messed up Indian cultural realities. My education had only just begun on Indian soil.

For instance, Chinese pilgrim travellers in the 7th and 8th centuries CE record Kashmir as part of the extensive empire of Ashoka during the third century BCE. They also document hundreds of Buddhist stupas as well as images of the Buddha, monasteries, grandiose temples and viharas. A seventh century king, **Lalitaditya** appears to have been a patron of some munificence to the arts in general, but especially to the massive temple at **Martand**, parts of its thick walls still standing, others at last being restored. **Martand** like **Konarak** in Orissa was dedicated to **Surya**, the Sun God who appears elsewhere in Kashmir. A Vishnu temple in the small town of **Bij Behara** 5 km from Srinagar possesses a most unusual depiction of the Preserving Deity. The murti is carved as half male, half female (**ardhanari**). This form of the androgynous concept of the divine impulse is usually portrayed in Siva rather than Vishnu images. **Ishbar** is also a locality of Srinagar, surely a word derived from Sanskrit root *ishwar* = divinity.

◆ The idea of **India** as such is still being debated and part of the irresistible attraction for outsiders. Is India alone a political entity? Was India India at the time of the Mutiny = Sepoy Revolt of 1857? In fact was India a total political whole in the way it is now, when Harsha, the Guptas or as far back as Ashoka in pre-Christian times, held sway? What bound it then into a sense of unity that the greatest unifier of all, Shankaracharya, could roam

north, south, east and west establishing the four fundamental **mutts** of learning–and meet kindred spirits in the ninth century CE all over the subcontinent terrain?

Most historians appear to say that India in those times was an **idea**, a **civilization**, rather than a nation state which anyway is a recent political construct even in Europe in the 19th century.

◆ With the inheritance of the administrative offices, boundaries and traditions of the previous colonial power, the shadowy areas of the high ranges abutting the Hindu Kush and China's Sinkiang regions alongside Myanmar, provided 'the wild card' of regional politics and break-away tendencies seeking what is thought to be 'real' political power in autonomy. This was thrown into the political pack for the newly independent Indian government inheriting this cursed Partition. Pakistan also was left up in the air, with predominantly Muslim territory right next door. If it had been awarded to the Pakistan hegemony because of this population component would Kashmiris have been happy under rule from Lahore/Islamabad, or would it eventually like Bangladesh have thrown off the hated Punjabi domination? How would Britain have felt if Scottish nationalism had been so volatile and aggressive for some reason at World War II's conclusion that it had been carved out into an entirely autonomous State? Or the USA lost Texas? Imagine Australia without its western state which nearly seceded by referendum in 1933–soon put a stop to by Whitehall, Australia then a Dominion, India proposed to be one. Over the past decades I have jumped Stepping Stones by leaps and bounds on the Kashmir issue.

Sisir Gupta's comprehensive book, **Kashmir, A Study in India-Pakistan Relations**, (Asia Publishing House, Bombay, 1966) is worth reading for its coverage of the entangled beginnings forgotten too readily when what has been one clearly-defined physical locality due to its unique geographical features is severely lacerated and torn apart, and with an East Pakistan also created out of Bengal and which belonged nowhere. A nerve network was mangled but still existed in the racial memory so that both nations' strategies–economic as well as military–were inextricably entangled in the same cat's cradle of ancient trade routes, Himalayan passes, river systems, racial pluralism (despite Jinnah's tunnel-view of how a society could suddenly become homogeneous because of one factor alone–Islam). British advisers and politicians, Jinnah's implacable stance, Gandhi, Nehru, Congresswallahs and fundamentalist Muslims will all stand guilty at the bar of history. But there, for the grace of God, go all of us!

Whichever way one of the two nations moved after 1947 or metaphorically sneezed the other like a Siamese twin responded–mostly with suspicion, and then with downright hostility.

International players cannot be absolved either. The Cold War of the 60s and a powerful Soviet Union crouching on the northern side of the Himalayas created another agenda, Kashmir being the first recipient state in south Asia of traffic coming through the main Himalayan passes from China and Russia's Islamic Republics. Geopolitical manoeuvrings were in everyone's

K

thinking and make understandable the deep-rooted suspicions of each other which have made such a tangled mess. The perennial game of political chess played out by the West even in the epoch of the 1800s with the Afghan Wars and Tzarist Russia, Napoleon and British imperial interest appears now to be played out in the same inscrutable chessboard mentality as then, with another permutation of nation-states.

1947

Going back to the moment of Partition it has been intriguing for me to learn through new archival releases that British officers at the time were still with army units either side in the entire wind-down process of Empire. They put a brake on the newly-formed national armies acting and failed to report much of what was happening in the Valley as also did Field Marshall Auchinleck. In addition, the Director of the Indian Intelligence Bureau was about to make his own decision on citizenship by moving to Pakistan! Further evidence released from the British Archives in 2003 show even their withholding of military movements to Nehru's new government.

Meanwhile that prevaricating Hindu ruler of Kashmir having held off for so long to play all the options suddenly read the writing on the wall as mayhem broke out to the west in his domain. He needed Indian Army help—and fast. So he acceded to the new Indian Government to become part of the new polity to the south over the Banihal Pass where Jammu as a locality was essentially 'Indian' and had a greater Hindu population density.

But the matter did not end there. Nor was that accession simple. Although the Maharaja of Jammu and Kashmir had stated his intention of setting up an interim government with **Sheikh Abdullah** as **chief minister**, the Sheikh being a Muslim accepted by many Kashmiri Muslims as leader of the **Indian Kashmiri National Conference**, this also queered the pitch.

Over time a question of semantics arose. **Azad (Free) Kashmir**–renamed by the insurgent Pakistanis–remained in their hands. The four northern-most districts quickly opted to become part of Pakistan—Gilgit and Chitral not having been directly administered by the Maharaja but under British jurisdiction; Balistan and Muzzaffarabad already occupied. The Pakistani Government with problems of its own, tried to have the settlement issue brought before the UN to decide, fiercely resisted by all Indian Governments over the decades just as British Governments resisted similar 'interference' in the civil war within Northern Ireland—another region artificially separated in partition.

Consequently the antagonisms, killings, terrorism and hatred have continued over decades becoming as entrenched as the Irish troubles, the Palestinian conflict between Jew and Muslim, and African tribal conflicts. The tourist industry which was bringing new wealth to a notoriously backward and geographically isolated area of India has been killed off along with innocent Kashmiris. In2005 due to the threat of worldwide terrorism moves to a peaceful settlement have at last been initiated.

Tourism

With the economy woefully disrupted it is a very noticeable sociological fact throughout India even in the most southerly beach resorts for instance–how many importuning Kashmiri traders there are, living on their wits, pleading with every tourist who passes the shop front: 'You please look. No need to buy.' Of course there is need to buy! People should be prosperous in the Valley despite the rigours of the winters which enclose it in a suffocating isolation, people keeping warm under their wool *pherans* and often being lethally burned as a result of the *kangris* they tuck under them despite being filled with red-hot charcoal.

Tourism, and the ubiquitous sound of hammering of boatbuilders between bridges as one glided into Srinagar in a slender **shikara**, was a sign of how global tourism was beginning to shift the tectonic plate of Kashmir's lopsided summer economy–beautiful houseboats with their idiosyncratic architecture and intricate woodcarvings took shape between battered four-storied mansions and riverfront vegetable stalls.

Back into Historical Kashmir

Instead of all those dry law books perhaps Jinnah should have read the **chronicles** of **Abul Fazl** who penned so prolifically the life of the Mughal Court in Emperor Akbar's times. In **Bamber Gascoigne's** **The Great Moghuls** (Jonathan Cape, London, 1971) he gives a touching insight of the Muslim of the openhearted spirit, expansive and compassionate. A bit of a time-server according to the other chronicler Badaumi, yet ironically too orthodox by half for the Emperor.

Even if Abul Fazl went to the other extreme in giving the **ulemas** (the clergy) high blood pressure, at least the emphasis throughout his writing is on religious toleration–he practised what he preached, having a Hindu, a Kashmiri and a Persian wife–and within the space of one paragraph he calls the Muslims of Kashmir 'narrow-minded conservatives of blind tradition' but praises the Hindu priests of the same province for not loosening 'the tongue of calumny against those not of their faith.' His stated aim in studying and describing the culture and philosophy of the Hindus, was so that 'hostility towards them might abate, and the temporal sword, be stayed awhile from the shedding of blood.'

How prophetic... Much blood undoubtedly has been shed....yet here was the capacity for the human spirit to rise up to the heights, rather than to diminish into narrow sectarianism.

Lying on the rooftop of 'Ma Sutherland's' luxurious houseboat so totally on its own magnificent mooring at the far end of an almost uninhabited Nagin Bagh in 1954, with expanse of green lawn and the same majestic spreading chinar trees, leaves more luxuriant than the sycamore, and imprinted on so much Kashmiri art, books on Kashmir's history became compulsive reading despite this soporific hedonism... reward certainly for a hard-pressed husband who had worked assiduously for months for the BBC in the burning plains far beyond the only access then by road, the Banihal Pass 10,000 feet above sea level. And again in 1984, the half-remembered horror stories needed recalling. Was the history so blood-drenched? Down below the familiar sound of quacking ducks, tethered on long strings bobbing around among the rushes seeking fodder, soon to become the same for us for a future supper. Meanwhile saffron-coloured night herons with beady orange eyes silently waited for plump frogs.

K

Like Tudor grandees of old, propped up with floral cushions and framed with walnut-carved parapets and raised 'decks', a-flutter with pennants—we read the houseboat library with its smell of cedar permeating fingered pages of many previous occupants thumbing through the P G Wodehouse volumes, with James Elroy Flecker's lyrical **Hassan the Confectioner** in the time of eighth century Haroun-al-Rashid, Caliph of Baghdad (a contemporary of India's greatest intellectual, Shankaracharya, and a great traveller in the age when Sindbad the Sailor is thought to have turned his Omani dhow eastwards to Canton in China).

The distant calming slap, slap of a heart-shaped paddle as a woman crouched on the flat prow of a pencil-slim boat gliding through the floating gardens gathered up some of their vegetable bounty; a silent sentinel, **Butterfly**—the famed embroiderer in his homespun brown caftan and loosely coiled white turban waiting patiently in his gondola, a mediaeval painting of Mughal sepia tints surrounded by the delicate frame of floral arabesques in the lakeside greenery; Kashmir indeed was the way all those Mughal emperors regarded it—their paradise. A summer garden home to bring sanity to the fevered brow—and underwear embroidered with monogrammed initials and chinar leaves, Butterfly a most persuasive fellow!

And in fact my amoebic-dysentery ridden husband did recover remarkably in three days—probably psychosomatically but also from the ruthless but expert pounding of a Kashmiri massage from a **hakim** medic—who used also to deliver homilies that we were 'people of the Book' and should therefore have empathy with their predicament as like-minded people of the Qur'an. The assumption was that we 'Christians' would have immediate rapport with Muslim attitudes in the face of the 'infidel'—the Hindu.

The shadow side embedded within the Kashmiri psyche was totally muted by such deceptive luxury. And then I stumbled over an old leather-bound disintegrating history book of Kashmir. The 'dark shadow' so well known to psychoanalysts began to cast a chill across the lotus lake of that glorious summer of 1954—as I began to read its early history, and then again 30 years later. A trail of blood and treachery seems to be endemic from the beginnings of known history. The Aryan settlement is only conjecture. The nomadic flow of the neolithic must have gone on into the shadowland of history. In the last thousand years feudatory claimants have slaughtered indiscriminately, alarming murders of immediate relatives in ruling families redolent of the blood and guts of English Tudor times and Europe's own gory history within ruling dynasties, disputed successions and usurpers such as Henry I and Richard III. Pathan rulers in previous centuries were equally ruthless. Murder, mayhem, rape and pillage echo down the ages, an ultimate irony in a country so blessed in serene beauty as the Valley of Kashmir before its glorious lakes were lined with houseboats and its waters polluted by sewage. (See **LOTUS** for personal encounter and how physical the seduction, the impression of utter bliss every sojourner feels in the heart, increased if one comes by road necessitating the precipitous drive into paradise on earth as the Mughals also experienced as they toiled up the formidable landscape on elephant and in hand-carried palanquin.)

And Today

Economically, strategically, philosophically, politically India and Pakistan appeared to be on an irrevocable course of constant conflict. It is as though the British left an infected abscess which would flare up every decade in the body politik, no matter how many lancings, colonial history and interference still laying a blight upon all present attempts to solve what should never have been. All of us who have had the privilege of enjoying Kashmir's natural blessings (despite its precarious economic livelihood, and compulsive traders plaguing any firangi in sight before the harsh winter sets in and the cash flow abruptly stops) grieve at the present impasse.

Politically both have had to come to terms with an increasing Kashmiri yearning for autonomy and a new sense of nationalism as elections increase expectations.

Do Muslim Kashmiris (apart from fundamentalists and terrorists) see themselves as Indians? Or—increasingly, to put it as an Irishism—as 'not Pakistanis either?'. And what of all the other Kashmiris? The decimating exodus of the Pandit class; the virtually tribal nomadic Gujar shepherds shot as well as Hindus by the zealot jehadis; Buddhist and the predominantly 'secular' Indians of Jammu on the otherside of the mountains, way down below the ringed once-enchanted Valley? And Ladakh high up above.

Analysing material from the archives 50 years after this overwhelming fracture of what once was an ancient geographical cultural unity, a salutary account emerges as this compendium finalizes. Retired Army Colonel **J K Dutt** presents facts that shift all the previous assumptions I certainly imbibed from those earliest seminal days in Delhi. In more sceptical terms than our immediate post-war generation encased in an understandable idealism, Dutt sees Nehru in a different light from my own, clouded by that post-war 'golden era' somewhat adjusted (see **NEHRU**). Nehru's 'artful ground plan' calls for many explanations which so far have never been answered in the campaign to regain territory that now has been fought over innumerable times since Partition.

An in-depth analysis unfolds an intriguing scenario, almost reflecting a Shakespearean drama. Let there be no mistake that Nehru was a highly intelligent man, he was erudite, he knew law, he hailed from the best stock...

But he had set his mind on one thing. 'His aim was to become independent India's first prime minister for life, no matter what the consequences.' He had realised, Gandhi having expressed grave doubts about the Congress Party going political, that only one man stood in the way; already the supreme patriot Subhas Chandra Bose who could have stopped Partition as well as been mandated prime minister (see **NETAJI**) was **awol** (in old Malaya, leading, according to a colonial British government, a traitorous campaign alongside the Japanese)... out of the way!

That man was Mohammed Ali Jinnah. And one of the three bargaining chips was Kashmir, as well as relevant portions of the

K

191

Punjab and Bengal. Why then when armed militants, and Afghanis invaded, occupied what is now Azad Kashmir and nearly overran the Valley, did not the full force of India's military (as well as an inactive navy) not liquidate *'enemy hold on our land?'* J K Dutt poses the same questions we often asked ourselves even in earlier days before so many fragmented parties plagued the politics of the J & K state assembly in Srinagar–Jammu forgotten as part of the integration by outsiders when prising open the endlessness of Kashmir's tragic story. How many times had Muslim Kashmiri traders sidled up to us hoping for good business by assuming a camaraderie due to the fact we 'were people of the book' and therefore 'our friends', not one with 'those others'. Heaven knows how many beautifully embroidered chinar leaves would be stitched on immaculate white cotton tablecloths way down by Third Bridge while we were primed over salty cinnamon tea in samovars on the politics and cross-examined on Sheikh Abdullah, then imprisoned in Kud half way up the mountains and where we had stayed en route in the resident **dak** bungalow.

And how many monogrammed pyjamas and dressing gowns, ruched dresses for our daughter Caitilin, and table settings galore for friends would be cajoled out of our soporific state of mind amid the kingfisher and lotus-budded luxury of our quite un-real existence while Butterfly in his brown pheran and coiled white Byzantine-style turban, floated away, to send them down to Delhi when the winter snows hemmed the Valley in. Always it was assumed we were 'our brothers'–even me. But then women and political thinking is a curious notion to orthodox Muslims!

After the futile 2001 Agra Summit between President Musharraf of Pakistan and Prime Minister Vajpayee, Dutt writes of the future solutions to this seeping abscess.

The choices vary from the utopian through the theatrical to the pragmatic.

1. Pakistan vacating POK (a Grimm's fairy tale).
2. A plebiscite agreed 'thus setting the path for Kashmir's independence'–(a halcyonic theme for a Bollywood movie).
3. Converting the present LOC (Line of Control) into a formal Indo-Pakistan border, aided perhaps by honest brokerage by the UN (the most pragmatic common sense solution) after the Taliban defeat in Afghanistan, and Pakistan's traumatic change of role, having harboured so many extreme training centres for young Muslim terrorists for so long. And while on this subject yet another book to read, this time with a more unusual perspective (that of a secular Islamic ethos long established in Turkey) by a Professor of International Relations there, **Turkkaya Atov**. Amongst other aspects of Kashmir he examines the role played in the last decade by radical Islamic Al Qaida trained terrorists (and the involvement of the drug money networks of central Asia) in the hijacking of the indigenous insurgency agenda. The book: **Kashmir and Neighbours: Tale, Terror, Truce** (Aldershot, 2001). Could Osama bin Laden escape into Azad Kashmir?

And from the other side of the LOC, a well-praised overview: **India and Pakistan in War and Peace** (Books Today, New Delhi, 2002) by **J N Dixit**, former Foreign Secretary and highly-regarded diplomat, at one time Indian High Commissioner in Pakistan.

And the world wonders how better used could that military budget be on both sides by impoverished peoples in both lands expecting an improved life in health and in educational opportunities.

■ **KATHAKALI**
katha = story *kali* = play/drama
is the histrionic and cultural dance form of Kerala, encapsulating nearly 2,000 years of evolution, layer upon layer of cultural ebullience embracing that earliest human expression of ritual dance propitiating threatening as well as benign natural forces, to its most recent contemporary presentation in European-style concert halls to uncomprehending but mesmerised overseas audiences.

◆ Each layer still exists separately and is still performed in differing regions. Driving through the countryside as our family has done on three separate visits, the traveller has every likelihood of encountering quite haphazardly some amazing animated theatrical or ritualistic folk drama being presented–emblazoned in psychedelic colours and extravagant costumes.

◆ Animistic blood sacrifices, mysterious magical folk dramas, feminine energies focused around the powerful goddess Bhagawati, snake deity worship, bhootas (local ghost-spirits) and minor 'presences' in village ceremonies, and traditions outside such specific visual arts and temple culture, all make up the rich fabric of the dance in this exceptional region. One unique other strand is rooted in the gymnasia–the **kalari**.

This discipline thought to have been the precursor of karate (taken in the continuous navigation to and fro with China) is amplified in **KERALA** section. **Kalaripayatu** is quite terrifying to watch, sharp-edged curled swords in soft metal flung out at the opponent who jumps away with agility in time (enough to make the hardiest audience flinch). Such stringent discipline provides a rigorous backbone to the arduous bodily training characteristic of Kathakali.

◆ The beginnings most probably began with the simple storytellers centred around the small village shrines in primordial times. This hereditary class were known as **Chakiars**, temple functionaries who, it is thought, absorbed the infiltrating Vedic culture which came with the steady migrations from northern India. Brahminical society and those already part of a Nayar (Nair) military peoples ready to defend its coastal regions apparently enjoyed entertainment called **Chakiar Koothu** which later developed into **Theyyam**.

◆ Rulers, up to the eighth century CE known as **Perumal**, introduced a sanskritized text, rendered however by a 'playback' narrator who sings in the vernacular Malayalam language of northern Malabar where this part-magical, part-ritualistic, earliest animistic expression of fundamental forces transfixes the locals one of whom in their midst, often from the humblest group is chosen to be the vehicle for the goddess to become incarnate within, rekindling a direct spiritual bond with neolithic India.

◆ Masked dancers at this level enlarge their personalities in terrifying and visual ways–with powerful eyes symbolically

K

outlined in black in the shape of a scorpion with curled tail, enormous head pieces, sometimes in conical fashion, taller than the dancer's own height.

Gorgeous decorations cover the entire body, crimson flowers, tiny moulded metallic leaves and glass stones encrusted as a crown on papiermaché with billowing skirts add enormous dimension. It is quite terrifying to watch in the flickering light of the great brass oil lamps such a dancer, the hub of a spoked wheel of coconut stems lit in flaming torches. As the crescendo of chenda drums heightens the twirling dancer amid the flames, I was petrified. What if the folk hero caught fire?

Krishna Attam, yet another dance/drama based on the epic of the Krishna avatar refined the choreography and presentation in the midcenturies of the last millennium. The flamboyant masks of earlier periods were transformed into the elaborate painted faces of today.

Maharajas and feudal landlords became patrons of their particular regional dance ensembles, which flourished. Some even became trained in the dance. The Zamorin of Kozhikode became a proud and noted patron of his palace dance ensemble and that led to further development–**Raman Attam**–portraying the life of Rama, yet another avatar of Vishnu (see **PANTHEON**). The reason... a neighbouring raja had requested the Zamorin's palace ensemble to perform to entertain guests at his daughter's wedding. The Zamorin refused to oblige so the other Raja took up the challenge and created a more dramatic dance-drama injecting the vernacular in a well-blended mixture of modern components with traditional. Regional poets were put on their mettle to present poetic ballads for performance.

Mahakavi Vallathol

And here I was in the presence of this unbroken continuum so often referred to when theorists try to encapsulate Indian culture, the 'presence', contemporary poet, a literary legend in Kerala, addressed with respect as Poet Vallathol. It is not very often that one can drop in on a renowned and innovative literary 'great', as dawn breaks in the soporific grey of monsoonal Kerala–and find him on a verandah, being shaved. And–with characteristic charm, and Indian hospitality for the **a-tithi**, myself come unannounced 'without date', be asked to breakfast during the ablutions! This is Kerala in 1957, the year of the first Marxist government voted in by democratic means anywhere in the world where half the population is, ironically, Christian–of many traditions–long before Portuguese missionaries ever set foot on Indian soil in 1498.

It is also India before the onslaught of tourism. Then, there was only one hotel on the beach at Kovalam. In Cochin (now Kochi) the only worthwhile hotel was the Residency on Willingdon Island overlooking the spacious and fascinatingly busy harbour before it expanded into one of India's most prestigious hotels, the dining room positively cavernous and redolent of the recent British Raj hung with mournful sepia photographs of British rulers on horseback forever reviewing troops at durbars with the kings of Travancore-Cochin. The night before in Trichur I had been given a folded bed on a balcony where 23 Indians (all male) were bedded down on floor mattresses, there being no hotel, just a basic hostelry.

I had come down via Munnar in the High Range where a handful of British planters still existed on the tea estates and lived life to the hilt on rugby weekends where dinner was at breakfast time and breakfast in a haze of whiskey (for tough muscular players who would have done Kathakali proud) at teatime. No one knew in those days unless they were a dance guru, or an impoverished dedicated member of a dance group (and Kerala being what it is there were, astonishingly, hundreds) where **Cheruthuruthi** was. Directions to me were as manifold as the great goddess Durga's weapon-brandishing arms.

The road 'bifurcated'. But despite failed windscreen wipers in a torrential downpour and a heavy head from Trichur's existential 'night-out-on-a-balcony-of-snores' (plus Indians at morning ablutions around a common water tap below the balcony, clearing their mucous and chewing twigs of the antiseptic neem tree for cleansing teeth which entails a good deal of noisy spitting) the right route was found running alongside a majestic river amply flowing with chocolate waters between steep red-earthen banks. Hidden in prolific tropical vegetation **Poet Vallathol's** creation of the 1930s–his famous **Kala Mandalam**–loomed in the half-light, thudding to the unmistakable mathematics of the drums.

Shadowy groves of dense palms framed traditional style natural stone, rammed earth and red brick buildings, gracefully roofed in the jutting-prow style of Kerala architecture.

Tall and still lean and distinguished, **Mahakavi (great poet) Vallathol** didn't bat an eyelid when I was led in with a volunteer rugby-playing driver (who had never been culturally attuned to watching any dance, let alone Indian) in tow. Eighty years old–but I did not know that at the time nor would have believed it if I had–he was a hobgoblin of vitality in body, in mind, and clearly in spirit as he took my hand, held onto it, and commenced a gallant flirtation for the rest of the day!

The letter of introduction explaining who I was, from an old friend and one time BBC broadcaster in London, the late Dr Narayana Menon would arrive weeks later. No matter. Indian hospitality in unexpected circumstances is legendary–putting the rest of the world to shame–that his bubbling sense of humour took wings of fancy. Malayalam poetry addressed us with haughty brahmin insouciance. Such intellectual prowess! He nevertheless had a twinkle in his eye and an octogenarian zest that seems to be a characteristic of Kerala life where laughter resounds, cartoonists and satirists a dime a dozen. No one need starve. Life is on the whole good. That must be the reason. Despite the fact that he was deaf that did not seem to detract from a 'conversation' in body language as should befit someone who towers above everyone else in this world of gesture...

K

The early decades of the twentieth century produced three of the greatest Malayalam poets known popularly as the Grand Trinity of Malayalam poetry–Asan, Ulloor, Vallathol. It was the golden age of romantic poetry and never before were three Malayalam poets of such brilliance as contemporaries, from whom generations of young poets continued to draw inspiration and guidance.

Mahakavi Vallathol's contribution to the literature and culture of Kerala had been unique. Vallathol's was a many-sided personality and his achievements both in the literary and cultural fields are great. It was due to his untiring efforts that the great dance-drama of Kerala, namely, Kathakali was revived and earned world-wide fame...

Although nurtured in the Sanskrit tradition, Vallathol, along with his illustrious compeers, freed Malayalam poetry from its Sanskrit norms of literary composition and composed beautiful, simple lyrical pieces in Dravidian metre, which the readers could enjoy. These poems were distinguished by the freshness of the imagery in them, by a sensuous quality which thrilled readers and a melody which made exquisite songs.

S Balasubramanyam: *India Weekly*, London, November 1978

Fortunately I did not read this until decades later and as no one in north India had explained the true measure of the man whom I had tracked down, when he took my hands, I followed–unabashed.

Training

It was 5.00 am in the lamplit darkened massage room. Burnished brown bodies were already lying on the ground on coconut mats in the traditional-styled partially open-sided exercise hall. Massage experts had been at work for half-an-hour, holding onto two wooden rails like a mini-bridge, sliding over these young dancers from a standing position, the full weight of their bodies pressing down along the lines of the adolescent torso with that Kerala expertise in robust massage, feet feeling their way as sensitively as any hands, pressing into curves and pummelling muscles, sliding with oiled grace–backwards and forwards.

Other dancers practised rolling eyes endlessly, fluttering eyelids, eyebrows arched and down, arched and down, a few with heads in a bucket of water gargling. And then to a command they all rose as one, rubbed oiled bodies down and off we went again, the master guru respectfully accorded **pranam**.

Next for what seemed hours upon hours, shorn of billowing skirts and towering headgear young men rehearsed set patterns of gruelling leaps and vigorous passages of story line, ever dancing on the outer edges of the feet, a stance particular to Kathakali. And then hand in hand again, following the Master, we were amid a flurry of costumes–red, green, whites,

black, red beards and golden aureoles–and the art of makeup. Such a contrast of broken coconut shells, ground vegetable dyes, old mugs full of water–and bodies laid out on white sheets, white rice paste mixed with lime and gauze on hand to build up the winged extensions framing the cheeks–like improbable birds of the jungle. The basic red pastes and greens the artist can apply himself and then the mastercraftsman takes over, with a 'chopstick' piece of bamboo with tied muslin bag of soggy **chutti**, the rice paste and lime mixture. Stylised patterns lined with black collyrium are moulded round facial contours. This process may take several hours. The dancers can withdraw self-absorbed in a yogic trance. When the cheeks are firm and winged, the dancer **has** become Deity or Demon. Transformed.

Gods and mythological heroes, baddies and goodies are given basic colours according to their types or **GUNAS**.

1. Sattvik = Krishna, Pandava brothers, Indra, the benign
   Paccha preserving characters wear green paste with black framed eyes, arched eyebrows, clam-like thick red lips, a white bobble of chutti on the nose and another for that Third Eye, placed on a stylised red and green forehead.
2. Rajas = those characters with asuric (malign)
   Katti tendencies such as Ravana, Kamsa and Kaurava brothers turn red. The bigger the bobbles the worse they are, but they still retain some aspects of nobility, albeit fleetingly.
3. Tamas = are beyond redemption. Red and black colour
   Thadi predominate. Black beard-like ruffs around the neck, blood-shot eye from tiny seeds placed under eyelids as an irritant, and blackened teeth with eyes in black, viciously pinning down the victim as they glare from their white framed cheeks, reflect true evil–in the shape of gross Dussasana, aggressive, intoxicated with lust and power, the Kaurava who humiliated Draupadi the common wife of all five Pandava brothers, forfeited in a game of dice to be at Kaurava mercy. (White thadi symbolises strength/helpfulness such as the wise Hanuman.)

The daily routine builds up relentlessly from the age of 10 studying under the guru for about 12 years to achieve mastery over basic techniques such as the hand gestures, 500 words to memorise from subtle differences in 24 mudras and their combinations. Even then to master leading roles may require another 10-plus-years' experience on stage.

Sense of time and place have evaporated with the morning mist no longer carpeting the slow-moving river…and Vallathol is still the lively brahmin… Now long passed away, let us hope with residency in **Narada's** heaven along with the sages, watching over his beloved Kerala, passionate patriot that he was. And whose hand is he courteously holding now?

South Comes North

Dusk is falling in the north of India. **The Kala Mandalam** by chance is making its first appearance at the open grounds of the old Freemason's Hall in Delhi; torn down for modern buildings but then the atmosphere was closer to village India with tall bell-metal lamps flickering in the gloaming capable of holding a bucket of oil at a time, the ravens cawing, bats on the wing, hooded vultures brooding atop tall eucalyptus. An air of expectancy.

Major masters are appearing with famous teacher **Kunju Krishnan**.

The ear-splitting sounds now of the **chenda** and **maddalam** startle every one in the audience. Magic is weaving a spell round the stage and through the fitful shadows. Out of the dim light of the stage and the wafting oilwick lights a colourfully decorated cloth is held up for curtain-call. Long silver finger nails dramatically claw the top, tearing it down. Children cling for parental protection, taut and scared. The palace musicians watch carefully, proud **Chellappan Pillai** and **Chennithala Kochu Pillai**, immediately recognizable Kerala names.

Slowly unfolding as drama is the Mahabharata fought out 5,000 years ago on the very plains of Panipat not so far from this city—but a suitably condensed version. The final act has begun. Dussasana seemingly unconquerable, an insult to humanity, is about to be confronted. Heroic Bhima is pacing up and down, eyes flashing, eyebrows working apace—all that exercise now come to fruition. With the brawny strength of club expert and wielder in battle, he the only husband capable of defending the much-abused Draupadi.

A blood-curdling cry rends the air from the rear of the grounds. We all freeze in terror. Through our ranks two figures hurtle in frenzied leaps, red beards flaring, guttural sounds and hoarse cries boasting the law of the bully, the rabble-rouser, the world's tyrants, those brutes of the market place with their coarse vulgarities. The frenzied dance of **Duryodhana** and **Dussasana** takes on the grotesque mantle of that hidden world of the predator, seemingly invincible. Our children are transfixed, now standing on chairs to absorb every detail of the confrontation. Good and bad. Bhima and Dussasana. A flurry of fighting, maces cumbersome as they arc to home in on the kill. For half an hour the drums are thudding in a crescendo reinforcing the imagination to feel the bludgeoned flesh. The nattuvanar's narrative floats up to the velvety star-spangled heavens. Are there witnesses there to mark this final last battle? A gurgling gasp of death sinks with the combatants as a huge Duryodhana watches on; green Krishna lithely dances in. Bhima now has the moral ground... and the glutton Kaurava son sinks to the ground, disembowelled, a whole lot of red cloth sausage shapes sickeningly pulled out of his stomach by Bhima who sinks his face in the 'blood'—avenged.

Characteristics that mark KATHAKALI out as different from other major dance forms

While the principles of **Bharata's Natya Shastra** apply in regard to **nritta, nattya, abhinaya, nava rasa**, etc. there are differentiations in presentation and technique that make Kathakali unique (turn to **DANCE** for terminology).

From the very beginning when the actual 'curtain call' occurs and long silver fingers glint in the oil lamp flickerings, the ambience is suddenly larger than life. The **paccha** characters, the Deity and Consort representing **paramatma**, the **paramount spirit** give darshan to the audience.

1. It is true theatre in the round—whereas **traditional** presentations in the other dance forms are mainly solo.

2. It has been called one of the greatest 'theatres of imagination' in the world. It certainly is for outsiders! Without the guidance for the **Indian audience** of the narrative in Malayalam poetry of great lyricism and beauty, much of the gesture language is full of such density of meaning that it is lost on the strangers. Imagination is heavily taxed because often it is static in long passages of narrative.

3. At least dancers in the other traditions have learned to present an explanatory demonstration of an episode not only for the stranger in the midst but for other Indians who may know a legend in general but not all of its detailed ramifications.

Only one program ever explained the density of the verse required to fill the bare Elizabethan basic stage with no props. Much of the rich subtlety of Malayalam poetry is lost as a result.

Ravana is transfixed by the beauty of Rambha the nymph who appears as one of the 'jewels' in the churning of the celestial ocean. Sent by Indra to seduce Viswamitra, the sage, she was cursed, poor woman though it was the great Vedic god's fault (what's new!) and was turned to stone by the impregnable rishi. Though remaining so for a 1,000 years, she must have been restored to life as the Ramayana states that Ravana was so overcome, he ravished her! Poor woman.

The Malayalam text runs thus:
Like a piece of gold in the river bed seen through
the waters of the blue Kalindi,
The beauty of her golden form gleams through her blue
garments.

4. Battles become symbolic—fought on behalf of humanity, a moral ethos being presented in the Malayalam commentary on events as they unroll before the eyes of the spectators. It is not therefore just a secular drama, but more akin to Europe's mediaeval morality plays.

In dance technique its regional quality certainly manifests itself. The strenuous nature of some sequences demands wiry elasticity of the Kerala men, reminding one of its source in the ancient and rigorous martial-arts tradition of the Nayar warriors.

With the monumental headresses glinting mica and gold paper, the exaggerated face make-up, the magnitude of costume, the scale of the visual, these personalities on stage have become **archetypes**.

Thus victory for righteousness is firmly staged—and in traditional presentations that commence at dusk and continue in the open air village square till near-dawn, that may take nine hours to achieve! This reiteration of an affirmative faith in the basic values of Indian life demands stamina... as do pilgrimages, attendance at major melas where you contend with over 10 million others for limited space (and may get trampled underfoot, refer to **KUMBH MELA**).

K

It must surely be an example of the adamantine strength of the Indian mind over matter to be so sure!

ABHAYAM again!

■ KAUTILYA

Pre-eminent lawmaker (circa 300 BCE), a wheeler-dealing diplomat administrator, he compiled the **Arthashastra**, a realistic and sometimes cynical statecraft manual on how to run a state, during a very active period of structuring a coherent manual of social laws, systems of philosophy and realpolitik for the **Emperor Chandragupta**, predating Ashoka by a generation.

Regions and satraps were amalgamating under the one power, now referred to as the Mauryan Empire. But how long did that empire last? And then what happened to 'India'?

◆ During this time the famous Greek diplomat Megasthenes visited Chandragupta's court and commented on the richesse of social life he found there.

◆ **Artha** is exactly that—wealth, community well-being, individual ambition climbing the political/administrative ladder and joining the right clubs, enjoying the perks of office—well over 2,000 years ago. What's new?

◆ **Chanakya** is Kautilya's other name, hence Nehru's fixation to build a colony exclusively for diplomats on the barren ridge west of New Delhi, was called **Chanakyapuri**. Our family although not diplomatic moved from a humble little bungalow near Lodi Gardens because of the addition of our third child, to a new house in Kautilya Marg, Chanakyapuri—a double whammy of his hovering spirit.

The sad thing was that this Diplomatic Enclave concept significantly cut diplomats off from Indian neighbours. Over the decades a fortress mentality has increased this situation. Perhaps this reflects the perilous nature of modern politics and the volatility of terrorism. In the innocent era of 1953 on our family arrival in India we had the Chinese Embassy opposite with only two sentries—Indians—at the easily accessible gate; the next residence but one was the American ambassador's, our small 'mews' cottage was behind the main Indian naval attaché's home; down the road were Tunisians, Canadians and UN officials. At festivals all the families interacted. There was no aloofness. At Holi our eldest son—then 8—with his Indian schoolfriends ambushed the American ambassador in his car, squirting red powder and liquid over it! Chanakya (Kautilya) would **not** have approved.

■ KERALA

There are no apologies for singling out certain states or cultural regions for special attention in this compendium. They appear for various reasons specifically in **REGIONAL CULTURES** (Maharashtra, Gujarat and Orissa)—our family spent time there; my own personal and professionally cultural interests such as a sponsored ICCR visit took me there; or close Indian friends and a yearning for Indian music (and its audiences—so very important) in its rightful setting as with Tyagaraja's commemorative festival on my latest visit. How can I write about regions (but they are

now very few) I do not know personally?—Ladakh, the small hill states of the North East and Andhra Pradesh. Every other state in one way or another I have seen at ground level, by car, train or even camel and bullock cart! And old friends over nearly 50 years have with generosity of heart as well as mind opened up the treasure trove of their grounded culture, taking me into regional homes with regional experiences—a privilege indeed to enter, sometimes into the kitchen where the family sit down to eat, laugh, watch the TV, comment on the day and their own politicians, crooks, ideals, the outside world, hopes and failures. And we have laughed, an ever-saving grace on the inside of Indian life!

And such a privilege has also led to meeting those Indians who do not speak English, are far from the sources of power, who are on the receiving end of much frustration, lack of opportunity, shortage of amenities the consuming classes assume as of right. Yet they too are redeemingly grounded with tenacity in a culture that stretches so far back it has indeed become 'hoary'—their favourite adjective!

So Kerala comes into focus because one way or another I have been there five times from following my husband on his first BBC visit in that seminal year of 1957 and its first Marxist government to a hair-raising drive 43 years later across the crest of the Nilgiri mountainous roads into the eastern Wynard and Kuppamudi Coffee Estate beyond Sultan Battery—such a truly evocative name of struggles long ago…and here a luxury plantation hideaway now called **Tranquil** specialising in the burgeoning Kerala massage ayurvedic industry… all thanks to Shakuntala Devagnanam now part of Australian life..

◆ When **Parasurama**, sixth avatar of Vishnu, threw his axe to claim more land along the Malabar Coast from the encroaching Arabian seasurges (and, some assert, from the same tendencies of local rulers, their defence-mechanism warriors and power hungry encroachments) he must—as the then most recent manifestation of **Sri Vishnu**—have showered manifold blessings upon this emerald-green land amid the glinting silver and rainbow colours of the coastal seaspray.

Keralites worldwide as part of the 20 million **NRI** phenomena wax lyrical about the land of their birth and still retain the legend as though its antiquity legitimates the telling of it. But even the reality does. The lord of scientific-laws-of-equilibrium—Vishnu's at work in the universe maintaining the totality of planetary molecular/atomic particles and their sub-totals, no loss to outer space, the recycling of Stephen Hawking's notion of entropy, energy ever running down (yet biological scientists say he has taken no account of rebirth and cellular expansion of biological/botanical building up our planetary entity in a perennial see-saw process of equilibrium). So maybe the Hindu concepts are closer to the scientific truths after all—or as they are 'realized' so far.

Recorded in the Puranic texts, this pervasive quality of Vishnu to maintain the stability of the universe is in this manifestation, placed in the combative arm of **Parasurama** (quite something for a brahmin, unless he was on a yoga regime!). But, according

K

to Indian historians, probably the legend is a symbolic key to what happened in unrecorded history when a flexible social class structure still existed in a geographical area last to feel the full impact of the downward drifting, patriarchal society of Vedic times.

It had taken them centuries to settle in the Deccan around the second millennium BCE.

Already compartmentalised into caste strata, the earliest Dravidian society of Kerala must have really been threatened by this incoming social system. Who knows how many recalcitrant kshatriya foot soldiers of a new ruling class, feudal lords following on elephants, discovering the fertility of a land, began to throw their considerable selective weight around? Parasurama's axe it is said entered the sea in atonement for the sin of killing so many kshatriya soldiers.

Indian historians have suggested some early conflict arose as the class structure formalised and the India beyond the mountains filtered in bringing a tussle for power between Brahmin and Kshatriya. Something must have happened (so the conjecture goes) to reassert brahmin dominance over the defending Nayars, so much so that over the next three millennia that powerful force of scholarly learning and spiritual discipline went to the other extreme (in social discrimination as only trends can do in India). Up until the latter part of this century in many areas, an outcaste person in Kerala had to carry a bell, thus warning any uppercaste Brahmin landowner walking leisurely along his rice filled 'bunds' (pathway divisions of impacted earth) that the polluting shadow of the pariah would not fall on him. That would necessitate lengthy ritual and bath, or visit to the temple to negate the mishap and loss of dharma. Such became the encrusted deadwood of ritualistic belief in the land so remarkably transferred into modern flexibility as Kerala is today. (Such distorted ritual and caste consciousness has devastating effects even on indigenous Christian society as **Arundhati Roy's** fees-breaking 1997 Booker Prize-winning novel: **The God of Small Things** (Flamingo, London, 1997) only too grippingly, if convolutedly, illustrates.

What happened according to Malayalee historians who continue to reiterate this viewpoint, and local informants, was that both **Brahmin Namboodiris** and the **Nayars** who were away fighting for the kings of Travancore and Cochin or guarding their coastline which attracted seafarers from all over the world (Chinese to Carthaginian) lived in an interesting symbiosis. India's leading social anthropologist M N Srinivas has explained how the ones in their **illams** leased their extensive landholdings to the others, the Nayars in their **tarawads**; all the sons except the eldest (who married a girl from his own caste) had liaisons with daughters of the Nayar castes... the children of these one-step-down unions brought up in their mothers' family homestead–the tarawad–patriarchal and matriarchal intertwined. (see **Survey of Kerala History** by **Shreedhara Menon**, Sahitya Pravatharka Co-op Society, Kottyam, 1967).

♦ In approximately 5th–4th century BCE, partially recorded by the first Egyptian, Greek and Roman commentators, this region was an emporium of legendary wealth flush with money, in the records of **Quilon** (now **Kollam**). Clearly the port was a haven to the navigators of King Solomon, and later in pre-Christian times to Roman, Greek and Phoenician traders. It was told to me by a Kerala Nayar scholar that the gates of Carthage Fort in North Africa were architected in Kerala sandalwood. Jews had fled to Kerala from Syria and Babylon even earlier, in the 6th century BCE. By the 9th CE there was a considerable Jewish population in Kollam.

The Free Gifts of Land and Sea

Even if you were impoverished either **by design** as an ascetic long before the equally legendary **Shankaracharya** came on the scene in **Kaladi** near the **Periyar** river or **by force of circumstance as** a tribal whose lineage might well go back to a Dravidian (of unknown source?) or even earlier Bronze Age negrito neolithic, you need never starve!

♦ All you had to do was shake a **coconut** tree and hammer the fruit with a heavy stone. There within it was life-giving nourishment–and refreshment. Everyone tells you in the steamy heat of midday that the milky water has chemical properties which cool the blood; scrape the soft white lining that becomes the crunchy nut to benefit from the most nourishing of all its constituent parts.

♦ Fish catches were prolific also before Japanese trawlers with their fine-mesh seine nets appeared off the coast. Fish leapt out of the water at the golden sand edge (I have seen that happen on isolated beaches). Now coastal fisherfolk communities living in their thatch bamboo/coconut palm huts on the beach-edge coconut groves are suffering real impoverishment from the massive impact of Western technology. Watching the tedious two-hour haul of a circular net cast off the beach from a country boat at Somatheeram south of Kovalam, I was dismayed by their fruitless exertions–only a few hundred miserable fish in the catch.

♦ **Rice** husbandry recorded several thousand years ago grew in sumptuous green abundance.

♦ **Banana** plantations are indigenous. Try fried raw bananas and sardines in grated coconut with a few spices and buttermilk for a meal fit for Parasurama... even if he was a brahmin vegetarian!

♦ Who knows when the **spices**, protein-giving cashew nut and areca, tamarind roots, and tapioca all evolved. The major cashew-nut trade had flourished in ancient times.

Name it, Kerala grows it. Even **toddy** (fermented palm sap = arrack) could send you on a high. Try it once for the experience but having sipped only half a glass with a Sanskrit university scholar watching on, mesmerised, expect the world to swirl around its orbit for at least four hours. If you attempt to lie down, the result is even more de-stabilising!

The Kerala Mix

Into all this gastronomic sufficiency stir the uniquely Indian aromatic kadipatta (the **CURRY** leaf) of the south and encounter the extravagant vibrancy of Kerala–red-hot fish cuisine beating even Bengalis on what they consider their own renowned patch of cooking–fish. In a Syrian Christian home I hardly noticed the tiny green chillies embedded in the baked fish until it was too late. My head swam like the toddy, tears oozing and a palate traumatised for four hours!

♦ Along the road edge of daily life there is a constant blaze of colour. Other forms of local theatre and masked drama such as the flamboyant headpieces of **Theyyam Thira** with its surrealist masks and trance rituals, encountered startlingly in a small temple courtyard south of Mangalore, is very close to the bone, calling forth ancestors, propitiating basic forces of good with real asuras, the anti-benevolent entities that appear throughout India's legends and **EPICS,** emblazoning the verdant green landscape and immaculate white shirts and **mundus** worn ubiquitously at festival, Onam boat race and wedding rites.

♦ As explained earlier (**KATHAKALI**) the Kalaripayatu martial arts—often quite terrifying—has ancient lineage also, beginning around 520 CE with formulation by a Buddhist monk of methods to defend the philosophy of ahimsa with self-defence. **Kalari** (Sanskrit = the gymnasium ground); **kavu** = shrine to the presiding deity, **Paradevi** (paramount goddess) to be bowed to at her altar, the *poothara* as dawn breaks, the spiritual framework encasing all the arts guarded by the brahmin guru-priest). Hallowed places, secure in the Hindu socio-philosophical framework of society, totally discounting the stereotype of Hindus being all brain and no brawn, over-spiritual by half! Now a performance art even involving women, a team from Singapore have shown Australians how tough they can be, but imagine the surprise for airport security when they walk through presenting *kattaram, kettukari, vaalu, palisa, lathis, maduru, urumi* the most lethal of all—respectively daggers, staves, swords, shields, long poles, goats' horns and curled sprung-swords!

♦ Watch a display of Kalaripayatu especially when wielding the lethal **urumi** weapon which has to be used with caution. It is a rolled flexible finely fashioned steel blade, the working of iron being such an ancient engineering skill in India's knowhow—as witness the untarnished iron pillar at the Qutb Minar complex south of Delhi. It is hard not to flinch as the whine lashes through the airwaves along with the swish of steel unrolling.

♦ And then add to this one of the world's most unusual family traditions of marriage—a matrilineal system of inheritance with a typically polysyllabic southern name—**marumakkathayum** only now adjusting slightly to modern urban living. It has been suggested by Kerala scholars that wars between rival empires in the south in the 11th century weakened patrilinear inheritance. Compulsory military service and prolonged absence of men forced women to assume responsibilities for family and society.

A **Matrilineal System**

Such a joint family on the mother's side was called a **tarawad**—sharing a common kitchen. The women of the household all claimed a common ancestress. **Such families were almost always of the Nayar caste.** Their husbands who came to live in the tarawad were often higher caste brahmins or upper caste kshatriyas but their children remained of the Nayar caste. Land ownership enabled women to be economically independent. The financial straits for daughters in rural patriarchal societies, where 'kept' women were a plague on resources, until

this century of women on salaries outside the home, did not exist for Nayar women.

♦ **Nayar** and **Menon women** were free to marry several husbands, children of the union raised by the larger joint family. Husbands were visitors! Indeed in the old days it depended on which pair of sandals were placed out on the verandah of Nayar establishments as to which husband came in for the night!

Business and property were handled by the mother's brother (that important avuncular male, worldwide) but I have been told that many a matriarch was a powerful force to be consulted when property was to be divided, or marriage and the upbringing of children became a matter of family concern. The women also indulged in learning martial arts, and were art patrons, as well as being educated in an Indian tradition of learning long before convent schools added to this remarkable dimension of intellectually advanced young women.

Such a system which spilled over into some **Muslim communities** explains the standing of women in Kerala society, their high educational attainments even in very early times and their release from the tyranny of mean-minded in-laws.

♦ Even some **Moplah Muslims** (also **Moppilah**), who came by trade from Arabia around 7–8th CE who were totally different from those who swept into the north 300 years later, also lived in a matrilineal system of joint family. This probably came about in the early days when Arab traders married Hindu women. Although wives converted to Islam, social customs were maintained, as also in many Syrian Christian families. Kerala is an intricate mix of tolerant diversity on the whole despite the strict boundaries maintained between different communities.

The early Moppilahs in fact mirror the symbiotic relationship created by seas that crash out the shores of this beautiful land, between inhabitants and navigators who came to trade, most especially Arabs (long before the Prophet ever existed). Later times exacerbated by modern politics did create animosities and killings.

♦ In the backwaters teak logs soak for a year. They are brought down from the forests up on the Deccan south of Mysore. Then go to **Beypore** very near to Kozhikode to watch the skills of a plural society in ancient and modern industries. This unspectacular coastal port (if you can call it that) is one of the most ancient places in the world to build totally modern boats sealed with wooden nails and resin-packed coir, all natural products of the land, much sought as dhows by Arab neighbours not far across the waters. (Australian boatbuilders are also perfecting this art, replicating their heritage of earliest sailing ships).

At Beypore watch also the sheer muscle power of the Moppilah *khalasis* whom many a tough Australian wharfie would salute as they launch by hand a 400-ton dhow or even more horrific, use brain as well as muscle power in disposing of shipwrecked hulks without any machine technology. They use only a solid pole, ropes and pulleys.

Jewish Community

There are now approximately 6,000 Jewish people left in India, infinitesimal compared with other communities, Jew Town

K

in Kochi having emptied out to Israel. (A small community called **Bene Israel** live in **Maharashtra** having taken true Kannada names ending in 'kar'–Walrulkar being one family name. As White Jews they believe their ancestors set sail from Palestine when Nebuchadnezzar reigned but were ship-wrecked on the beaches of Malabar. They still practice the rituals of their fathers despite a lack of rabbis to maintain a pristine tradition. In consequence many of their customs are Indianised).

◆ And then came the **Portuguese, Dutch, French and British**. One would think such an influx of influences from that aggressively strong European culture would have swamped such a tiny state. **But no!**

Modern Influences, *essentially Indian*

A wave of Marxist governments essentially Indian in temperament, totally unlike any Soviet communism and state top-heavy administration, which have implemented extensive literacy and health programs, alternating with Congress rule when the highly-educated populace gets fed up with certain politicians; Gulf money for the underclass of low-caste construction workers, manual labourers, plumbers, carpenters, etc. and the professional middle class engineer all working their guts out in Dubai, Kuwait, and Oman... that is the Kerala mix! The largest number of women engineers graduating annually anywhere in the world–approximately 400 annually–also marches out of the state.

◆ And then one has not even begun with the brilliantly colourful performing arts and festivals now revived in all their flourishing array. In steamy April, the Trissur elephant parade of 101 gold-caparisoned elephants (refer to **ASYMMETRY**), the elegantly stylish and elongated-necked snake boats with over 50 rowers a boat and the Onam festival occurs when king Bali is allowed to return (refer back to **Vamana AVATAR**). Even women's teams participate dressed in saris! The frenzied cheering of their local village teams on the banks of the Pamba River, booming conch shells, oarsman chanting in praise of **Padmanabha;** the candle-framed holy of holies, the main Thiruvananthapuram temple; high-browed brahmins shaven-headed but for their **kudumis** (topknots) 'to pull us up to heaven' chortled famous editor and political cartoonist, Keralite par excellence, the late Shankar Pillai–with his mop of white hair untouched are all part of a gigantic daily theatre. In many a household visit, one is aware of such brahmins gently reciting the sacred Sanskrit texts in shaded corners of their homes, hours on end.

◆ The tantalising aroma of spices floating up in the air from disturbed gunny bags in the ancient warehouses of Kochi and Kozhikode (why do so many nouns begin with K in Kerala?) just adds the topping to all this cultural extravaganza. And yet it is always framed in the utter simplicity at the heart of Kerala's essential home-based piety and family worship, clothed in the immaculate white of sari and mundu, no matter how poor. The citizenry who appears to wash at least three times a day, are forever scrubbing clothes in the canals and lagoons at **all** times. They all appear to be of one class—so pristine clean is the entire state, until modern tourism brought its concomitant litter (I once mistook a lowly peon at Kochi AIR radio station for the Station

Director—he appeared so well turned out). But now one's concern after so many visits begins to grow at swelling populations despite successful birth control campaigns. Frayed edges of the social fabric as well as the physical environment indicate the growing stress levels. All is not harmonious in nature's paradise.

Fortunately Kerala culture never fractured, so resilient must it have grown over centuries of looking outwards as traders and seafarers, accepting only what was worth taking such as the enriching and divergent architecture--Dutch-style churches, Portuguese cathedrals, French mansions up in Mahe and that British hybrid colonial architecture which has provided an unmistakable and comfortable style throughout Malaysia, Singapore, Australia and Sri Lanka.

Yet another topography, that of the mind exists–grown out of the topography of the environment. This marks one culture of a particular group of people out from another. It appears particularly so of the majority of India's advanced states not only industrially but socially in relation to health, education for women, literacy rates and general well being. They are all coastal seagoing peoples–Gujarat, Maharashtra, Tamilnadu, Bengal. There is no doubt the liveliness of Keralites and the dazzling nature of their art forms has been partly fashioned by the outward-looking nature engendered by maritime traditions.

Historians also mention a considerable high literary culture with poetry recitation in which women poets as well as men participated. Foreign wives came in by ship and some brahmins ate meat. Women have clearly maintained an advanced status despite their shy demeanour in this part of this world... and still do, enjoying now every opportunity in education with near-complete literacy. Even contemporary men sing their praises–with a delightful degree of hyperbole!. This is an Indian male writing:

They were women of great valour, made famous in our songs and folklore. Unniarcha–her very name gave us a cold thrill. Our women are proud, imperious matrons in a matriarchal society and rule over the life and conduct of the young. Age confers on them great authority and majesty. Who is not a Coriolanus among men, though proud and turbulent, who would not stoop like a willow before these Olympian mothers and see in them the honoured mould wherein our trunks were framed?

Taken from Indian journal **Indian Perspectives** devoted to Kerala Culture 1996.

In all this extravagant eulogy, there surely has to be a dark side. One or two glimpses come through the slats of the tarawad and illam shutters.

The **Malayalam movie industry** gives some clues in recent social themes also reflected in novels by writers both local as well as foreign. Most especially Arundhati Roy's **The God of Small Things** and Janette Turner Hospital's novel **The Ivory Swing** (Hodder and Stoughton, Toronto, 1982) conjure up a sombre world of undefined menace, ghosts and disturbing forces hovering in the shadows of coconut palm groves and lonely

K

caves, where those most ancient **animist cults** still exist–and function. This is the resonating echo from **neolithic** and **tribal communities** propitiating their presiding forces–the tree and rock spirits and the **naga** nether world of intertwined snakes later to be incorporated even in the highly complex Dravidian civilization they espouse.

Oppressed daughters caught in abusive marriages never acknowledged because of family hypocrisy driven by shame; incest and the menace of uncles; abiding superstition and animist ritual, even to blood sacrifice; an ambivalent world of stone-slabbed serpent shrines under expansive trees and behind the speckled shadows; greed and sudden extravagant wealth with demanding dowries out of all proportion; and now with the flood of Gulf money the modern blight of alcoholism and 'granny dumping' unheard of in Indian society previously (which has prided itself on respect of the elderly and care for ageing parents). Such blights still exist in paradise–highlighted by the totally incongruous polychromatic concrete boxes which are the contemporary architecture–a builder's paradise of homes for the Gulf-returned. (Gulf money constitutes half of the state's **total bank deposits** from **NRKS** = non-resident Keralites, Rs. 40,000 crores in 2000.)

Tourism—At What Cost?

◆ Kerala State Tourism promotes this idyllic homeland in a two-page spread in a welter of glossy outlets especially airline magazines. Silent lagoons, swaying palm trees, golden beaches.

◆ Modern crafted houseboats styled in that unique Kerala tarawad shape like an upturned ship's hull with miniature curved roof-end prows. Superb workmanship of artisans in rosewood, teak, sweet-scented sandalwood.

◆ The comfortable launch gliding through intricately linked backwaters, a sociological lesson in how people work and live un-reeling along the communities, strung ribbon-like, garlanding the river banks.

You lean back, vulnerable, quaffing an airline freebie drink, almost within a sound's reach of the swish of palm leaf in the warm seabreeze, the mesmerising ring of a temple bell. The message:

No speed limits, lots of parking space and absolutely pollution free

But read the fine print amid the quite legitimate hyperbole (mine included). One sentence sent a shiver down the spine remembering the innocent joy of a grand-daughter then aged 18, who gazed out meditating in the early dawn on a cliff edge at Somnatheeram with bending palms and water sparkling in champagne bubbles of sunlight; then she exclaimed: 'Granny–this is absolute paradise, for real!'

The words: **Slice it open on a speed launch!**

Oh Kerala, beware! Are the backwaters to pander to high speed boats, water skiing exhilaration, erosion of banks upon which people live? Pollution free!

Coconut–the god-given gift, provided me on my last flight another gift–a visual lesson in geographical aesthetics. A pattern of regular chakras is laid out carpet like with this bird's eye

view–palm tree after palm tree, palm-oil bush frond, banana trees and bamboo clumps, all grow in a perfect symmetry of opened umbrellas, a hub and daisy-like divides along the spinal fronds–and then the patch-work squares and rectangles of vivid green ricefield; a lacery of grey silver rivers, and the containing edge of yellow sand, white crashing wave and green-blue water.

Endnote: Turn to **PILGRIMAGE** for an account of the extraordinary **Sabarimala Hill** shrine event dedicated to honouring **Lord Ayyappa** in the hilly terrain of the central Western Ghats.

And for those who wish to explore more of these lively Malayalees and their culture read two publications by noted historian **Sanjay Subramanyam, The Career and Legend of Vasco da Gama**, (Cambridge University Press, Cambridge, 1998). With his knowledge of Spanish and Portuguese he has been able to source original records in Lisbon… and an easy read, **Binoo John's 'The Curry Coast', Travels in Malabar 500 years after Vasco da Gama** (Konark Press, New Delhi, 1999).

■ KHADI

Only a few years ago if you had walked into a khadi gramodyog shop, even in central Delhi shopping district, you might easily have walked right out again. A few minutes' scan of the fustian atmosphere, shop assistants in their saggy sack-like jackets and inelegant saris not exactly out of any of India's leading couturiers (a growing and talented band of young designers) and more engrossed in talking to each other than serving customers, or preoccupied with bureaucratic-thick quadruple accounting of what they had just sold to some visiting politician was off-putting enough to send a would-be customer straight out to the tumble-dryer action of pavement life outside. Khadi had since Independence become a politically correct 'must' for high-necked sleeveless jacket or winter kurta to wear with baggy cotton pyjamas on political platforms with the emblematic white forage cap.

If you bought a piece of the hessian-coloured or limp creamy fabric unimaginatively draped in a window that inevitably was a catchment area for drowsy flies, would you end up, you pondered–especially if you were from overseas, looking like a sack?... On second thoughts, better not to…!

Despite caring for what happens to India I have never yet worn a khadi dress or skirt–partly because you would have to be an anorexic model to do so. But forget all this as of India's 50th Anniversary of Independence, 1997! The national material with its honourable history is making a comeback.

1917–1918

Mahatma Gandhi returned from South Africa to his native Gujarat. The Satyagraha Ashram at Sabarmati across the river from Ahmedabad was set up. World War I was ending. India had supported its colonial Mother in her wars in Europe. Jawans and officers had died horribly in the French trenches but what difference had that made, an increasingly restive set of India's politically-aware men and women were asking, the way India was treated–still a subject race?… Very little.

Anger began to rise and resentment coagulated increasingly leading to political defiance of unjust measures and British complacency. Gandhi arrived, the right man at the right time, to harness those incalculable semi-dharmic cultural impulses that quicken the Indian heart and steel its temper and bodily disciplines regularly throughout any individual year—hardship in pilgrimage, astonishing self-denial unknown to outsiders, a home puja daily.

Gandhi had the secret intuitive sense of how to focus all this dynamic psychic energy of an inchoate mass of unwieldy Indians yearning, undirected, to be patriots. This he specifically channelled in the next two decades, building up a crescendo of moral defiance symbolised in specific visible appeal to a heterogeneous populace, uniting all in an astonishing 'being Indian'.

And then **JALLIANWALA BAGH** occurred. A fuse was lit ... Indian patriotism was fired... Gandhi had that felicity of imagination to harness the collective imagination with simple emblems with which everyone had an immediate rapport, not just in their simplicity of function in a work-a-day world but in their resonances throughout at least 4,000 years of cultural messages.

The **charkha**, or **spinning wheel**, a few pieces of wood and some string, a basic technology Schumacher must have glowed over. **Small** is indeed **beautiful**! Spun off what anyone, the poorest villager indeed, could assemble was **KHADI**. Sabarmati Ashram not only became the nerve centre of the growing Freedom Movement... as Gandhi preached so he spun. Gandhi channelled the latent mood of unrest into productive manufacture—a cotton spindle, then to be hand woven into cloth to exemplify the need for Indians to regain their pride through an ancient textile which had brought fame in international markets from the Mediterranean to China long before Europeans were out of the **woad** stage!

Here was an astonishingly 'backward' weapon to take on all the power of the Raj and its manufacturing giant factories in Manchester that bought India's cheap cotton and then sold it back to a suppliant Indian market at a monopolistic profit.

Although khadi in the long run can have hardly made a significant dent in that market it is yet another case where the economic logic of the accountant's bottom line 'forgets' at its peril the force of significant elusive psychic symbols. Self-help and even a trickle of money in the buying of khadi as it took on politically defiant symbolic overtones financed a myriad poor artisans in scattered villages throughout the conglomerate territories that make up the nation.

♦ And amongst those who bought this readily noticeable textile woven from a simple charkha on the basic Indian loom that is changeless in its 'time immemorial' sturdiness, there was this symbolic bridge, a proud sense of togetherness—that amorphous quality referred to in a number of places: **Indian-ness**.

The keen eye of the contemporary professional designer such as Ritu Kumar and colleagues including the integrity of elderly Gandhians still working in the field (she mentions **Lal Bhuta** of the Khadi Bhavan in Mumbai) could still appreciate that here was a '**fabric not produced anywhere else in the world**', an exclusive fabric that needed to be promoted and marketed in India and launched in the international market! But the material while still remaining khadi needed some injection, small improvement, in cross-weaving from wool, silk, even polyester over the 'dead bodies' of some protesting purists to make the material more malleable.

And lo and behold! With Gandhian inspiration (unlike some people's assessment of Gandhi, he was never a rigid doctrinaire and believed both in acquiring and accepting new technology if it was relevant in improving impoverished village or urban living conditions) innovation in recent years has led to sell-out exhibitions of the new khadi. Designer khadi has arrived with stunning colour, lightness of swing and ability to fold gracefully—that fine difference between wearing a **sack** or a **svelte shift**!

A stunning presentation—**Tree of Life**, a history of indigenous textiles by Ritu Kumar, was last seen by an amazed London audience of designers in 1997. Take note of Kamal Wadkar and Devika Bhojwani also experimenting in blending the handspun cotton with other constituents—silk/wool/polyester to make the finished product no longer 'baggy'. Quilted coats by Asha Sarabhai, stylish jackets by Raghavendra Rathore, new style minimalist designs for the slim creatures of Mumbai by David Abraham and Rakesh Thakore are beginning to build up an Indian couture enterprise of its own as also Rina Dhaka through Selfridges in London. So walk into a Khadi Bhavan and buy—helping over 8,000,000 weavers, their families and their artistic acumen survive.

■ **KIRTAN**
is both an assembly gathered for the purpose of devotional singing of **bhajans** = hymms, most especially associated with the passionate outpourings of those imbued with the sense of **bhakti**, addressing Deity not as a remote scientific concept but as a personal god. Sikh **gurdwaras** (places of worship) resonate with the singing of these joyous songs known in the Punjab as **kirtans**.

Even in very earliest times music of various cultures does not develop in isolation. A nomadic shepherd can be a carrier even on a simple flute of different melodies. With the free-flow interchange of musical instruments across the top of Asia 6,000 years ago or more and the more recent migrations, the flamenco music of Spain, the Moorish stringed instruments of North Africa, the lutes of Egypt and stringed sarangi-sarod-lutes from Turkey to Iraq, Iran and in to northern Punjab all carry echoes of each other. The Romanies carried the fiddle out to the Danube basin and on into west Ireland.

In more immediate centuries **Hazrat Amir Khusrau**, the Persian aristocrat—musician-poet-humanist at the early Islamic Sultanate court of Khilji, made Delhi home. He not only invented the present form of the sitar from earlier Persian stringed instruments but pioneered new forms of the raga he found in India—the khyal, a poetic line composed as a melodic device to

K

advance a delicate and ornamental embellishment as improvisation carried the raga forward (refer to GHALIB, SUFI).

This form was further advanced by Mian **TANSEN**, one of the brilliant cultural 'jewels' at Emperor Akbar's court.

◆ All kinds of delicate ornaments (**pakad** or special phrases particular to each raga) are added as well as running glides or **taans** to embellish the delicacy and emotional tug of this devotional and classical romanticism. It is suggested that the poignancy so notable in the sarod and flute and·sarangi which often accompany the vocal poetry come from that region, the Kush in central Asia where Khusrau's parents originated and where he was born. Musical traditions meet and stir the creative spirits of Russians, Uzbeks, Turks, Persians, even Afghanis.

◆ Khusrau was a true Indian, especially 'proud' he declared 'of the people of Dilli' but he treasured his roots from the Kush.

■ **KRISHNA-KRSNA** (n. *Sanskrit*)
also *Kishen* reflects the difficulty of transcibing the fine slivers of Sanskrit phonetics into English
कृष *krs* = to scrape away
The meaning of this eighth **AVATAR** of the complex Deity who brings stability to the universe, Vishnu, is **redeemer of humanity** (see **PANTHEON**). In a footnote to his own introductory essay to **The Bhagavadgita** Professor Radhakrishnan quotes Adi Shankaracharya's commentary that the root of this name–**krs** implies a divine benign force that scrapes away or draws out all sins… **papam krsayeti nirmulayati**.

◆ Krishna is surely India's most popular deity, certainly in the north where his birthplace near Mathura is a centre of major pilgrimage. Brindavan's skies are pierced by the spires of dozens of Krishna shrines and temples.

◆ Grandmothers and mothers most especially turn to Krishna for inspiration, solace, and the telling of his many endearing exploits to the children in the family. Because they are so human, Krishna can create empathy in the worshipper whereas the Lord Shiva is distantly majestic and almost scientifically impersonal, overpowering in intellectual demands. Vishnu in all his majesty as the universal saviour had to 'come down' in historic times as Krishna to be approachable as the eighth avatar–regarded as the most powerful. In this reincarnation Krishna has grown in stature in later centuries, claimed as the only 'direct manifestation of the Lord Vishnu' by many Vaisnavites. And yet the historic Krishna is shrouded in mystery. The name first appears in the Vedas but not attached to a specific deity. Legends grew up in the Chandogya Upanishad and the Bhagavata Purana a millennium at least before Buddha's birth, adding a wondrous array of fables and parables about:

◆ his naughty but loveable **childish** pranks
◆ his very human **amorous** dalliance with milkmaids–**the gopis**–and his beloved Radha who had a very hard time of it maintaining her supremacy. The depictions of this handsome **lover** playing seductively on the flute are legion in Indian art. **Lila** (pr. *leela*) is a Sanskrit word associated with this manifestation. It refers to the joyousness of **divine play**, the spontaneous impulse

in affirming the creative capacity of the cosmic divine, personified in Krishna's circular dance with the gopis.

◆ Krishna's deeds of **valour** (which appear to extend through centuries on the human time scale) overcoming this threatening **raksasa** or malign force or that tyrannical king–especially **Kamsa** who like Herod tried to kill Krishna at birth by having all male babies slain in the region (Krishna was spirited away like Moses) because it had been foretold that he as ruler would die at the hands of Vasudeva and Devaki's eighth son.

◆ then in the millennium before the Christian era Krishna emerges as the **teacher** delivering the intellectually demanding 'sermon on the mount,' scaling the heights of the Gita's arguments for social responsibility, discipline and foregoing of self.

◆ and then this total transformation into **Deity** as Vishnu, the expanding image of whom bedazzles Arjuna, the noble archer, in the final message of the Bhagavad Gita, bringing the hope and salvation of grace.

◆ And yet, at the end, there are still puzzles and questions about this chameleon Deity.

His Yadava tribe decimate themselves in feuding to such an extent Krishna **the historical ruler** leads them west to settle in Dwarka in western Gujarat where recent excavations have proved the existence of at least four layers of historic cities known as Krishna's domain.

Yet despite protective divinity he too is slain by a hunter mistaking him for a deer–in his heel, like Achilles–his vulnerable spot. Is this then a metaphor for illusion or retrieval through parable of oral folk histories echoing truths of a very antique time? Indeed there are many echoes in Greek and Christian mythology also as the legends unfold. Certainly by the **fourth century BCE Krishna** is established as an influential Deity–and yet twice he gives ambivalent advice to his allies the Pandavas, encouraging Yudishthira, the symbol of Dharma, to tell a half-lie which brought about the dishonourable death of Drona his kinsman and **Bhima** to deliver a below-the-belt blow, very un-kshatriya behaviour, to shatter the thigh of his life-long adversary, **Duryodhana**.

◆ Finally, suspension of rational belief has to occur when fable takes on all the characteristics of overdrive in Indian exuberance. Tales are recorded of Krishna's other lives when despite marrying Rukmini this time around he is credited with having 16,000 wives and–take note again–180,000 sons!

Krishna is accepted in these several symbolic manifestations–endearing **child, lover, warrior, the Lord as Shepherd of his flock and teacher,** and finally **Redeemer**… but deep within lies the ambiguity of the volatile anarchist that he is–the Hindu Pan enticing seductively with his haunting flute, a healthy counterbalance to Rama, who has always seemed too bland a male, too good to be true!

♦ A fascinating book to read is **P K Varma**'s **Krishna, The Playful Divine** (Viking, Delhi, 1993).

Krpa, a Sanskrit word, is much spoken about in the Gita. **Grace abounding** which Krishna out of love and compassion will confer upon those who turn to him with a loving open heart, compassion (*karuna*, Sanskrit) part of the blessing and emotional equation, A K Ramanujan explains in **Speaking of Siva.**

'All true experience of God is KRPA, grace that cannot be called, recalled or commanded'...It is 'an unpredictable experience' (see **ARUL**).

■ **KUMBH MELA**

Most of the momentous happenings in the annual exuberant round in which the lives of these colourful major deities are commemorated in **melas/pujas** appear to begin in extra-terrestrial time and space. That does not mean they are not rooted in reality the way we experience it day by day in the material planet on which we live.

Charlie Chaplin once commented (when asked a question on the real meaning of one of his last major films, the allegorical cinematic drama of a post-war Everyman tale, **Modern Times**), that myth, fable, legend are but '**a poetic pinpoint of truth.**' For the largest conglomeration of peoples that gather for a special act of faith even more than the annual Hadj pilgrimage for Muslims at Mecca which now reaches several million on site each year **all at one time**, the **KUMBH** is just this–a huge poetic symbol of the truth about the constant struggle to defeat evil. The event recalls cosmic battles, sin and matters of evil doing, the perennial exertion to preserve the benign, ever under threat, a legendary tale from the **Srimad Bhagavatam.**

♦ This reality is no new thing to us of the 21st century which has experienced more than its fair share of evil forces reinforced with use of technology to make satanic torture, mayhem, genocide, paedophilia and global organisation of child abuse, terrorism, volatile shootouts ever more powerful, and cult zealots with lethal poisonous gas enough to paralyse the Tokyo subway system, part of our daily intake of visual imagery in the media. Children in our midst can never have been less innocent, more wordlywise accustomed as they are to television news–a daily shock to the system, most especially the mind-blowing destruction of September 11th, 2001.

The Legend

The Indian reality has ever been thus–a relentless struggle of the darker forces against all that stands for ahimsa, gentleness, the loving strands that bind. The Kumbh Mela symbolically mirrors the battle between the negative influences headed by **Bala Maharaj**, descendant of a powerful King–**Hiranyakasipu**–famous for his own fallen angel status and power to disrupt the heavens, and Indra's legions of demi-gods responding with forces of the benign high in the firmament above the Himalayas.

Due to a sage's curse (and that can be so powerful it can upset the equilibrium even of Indra's heaven) the demigods lost their psychic powers. These asuras showed every sign of intervening when the flood came and heaven's treasures were lost in the Ocean of Milk (see **AVATAR: Kurma**). In the squabble that ensued as recounted in the **Skanda Purana**, Jayant, son of the Vedic god Indra managed to hold onto the sacred **kumbh** and flee into the planetary firmament but those **asuras** (always depicted with eye-tooth fangs, coarse dark brown features and thick-set wrestler-type bodies) chased him, fighting furiously for 12 days and then finally got hold of the pitcher. In the struggle **the amrit fell on four places** now most auspicious for pilgrimages–**Nasik in Maharashtra, Ujjain in Madhya Pradesh, Hardwar and Allahabad in Uttar Pradesh.**

Very early in India's history, Shankaracharya is said to have organised the Kumbh Mela in these four cardinal points as a device for unifying the body of Hindus throughout the land. When certain planets come in conjunction and the sacred **Saraswati** river is believed to flow again with their magnetic pull into the **triveni** confluence of all three (with **Ganga** and **Jumna**) at Allahabad then the devotee who bathes at this sacred sangam meeting point is absolved of thousands of rebirths. Also in historic times the seventh century CE Emperor Harsha who encouraged a mini-golden age at the end of the rich Gupta Empire is said to have visited the great event six times, renouncing all his belongings and distributing all his wealth each time to his poorer subjects (see **MAGADHA** section).

The Reality and Personal Experience of Tragedy

♦ So it was only three months after arriving in India that I was almost literally thrown in the deep end with the Press Corps at the first Kumbh Mela to be held at Allahabad after Independence when **Jupiter** and **Aquarius** influenced the dark heavens over this land. In his homespun way as an orthodox Hindu, President Rajendra Prasad attended unexpectedly. Police were called away from a crucial area to circle the VIP party just at the **sangam** area where the naked Naga Baba sadhus were high on bhang, becoming obstreperous, and asserting their traditional right to bathe ahead of all the millions of pilgrims as the planets came into conjunction. Then sacred **amrit** flows again, so abundant 6,000 years ago when the legends were laid down and citizens manifested **arya** qualities of nobleness. Goddess Lakshmi, lady-luck style, had retrieved the amrit by entrancing the asuras (anti-gods who had entreated her to act as arbitrator in its distribution). All had ended happily for the powers of good–once again... but not this time at the sangam for at least 400 of the two million people attempting to bathe–the **snan** or auspicious dip–at the one time. They were trampled to death right in front of us.

♦ The millions have grown since then and still they come. By January-February 2001 when the 12th year had come around again Army statistics estimated that roughly 70 million people had gathered in awe-inspiring numbers during a period of 44 days to give witness to the eternal struggle between the forces of good and evil. Vishnu taking on the form of an enticing apsara Mohini (in another reincarnation–Lakshmi) had lured the asuras with other temptations away from the amrit. Meanwhile down on the ground where drops of the amrit fell, strength came to other forces–the Indian Army, detailed by the government to supplement the police and volunteer 'sewaks' (scouts and other volunteers) in organizing with quite astonishing efficiency. It is a 'military' operation under such weight of numbers, grid-system tented cities, mobile latrines, soup kitchens, everyone as they enter the roads to the sangam area under constant surveillance and inoculated against typhoid and cholera.

Personal footnote–February–March 2001

I can well understand the outburst from **Francois Gautier** (correspondent for the French press in India) on the Western media coverage of this extraordinary event.

Capturing the attention of the Western audience bombarded with a plethora of media signals is a major problem. My own husband agonised over this within the BBC Current Affairs programs half a century ago. 'Exotic', 'bizarre', 'picturesque' is the Indian stereotype…

The Kumbh Mela… demonstrates once again to which extent Western journalism, when it is applied to India, harps on the anecdotal, the superfluous, the derogatory, deforms everything and transforms what is beautiful and noble into a show of freaks and fanatics. And wasn't that the headline of **The Independent** *of London: "A freak fair?"*

News agencies in Europe and the US are only interested in the photos of Hollywood stars (Madonna, Demi Moore, Richard Gere, Pierce Brosnan, etc) who are going to descend on the Kumbh Mela, even if they will be totally lost amongst the millions of (real) devotees…

*…Isn't it strange that at the time of globalisation and standardisation of the whole world, at a time when the civilisation of Coca-Cola and MTV reigns supreme from Rio de Janeiro to Manila, from Paris to Shanghai, at a time when man's collective consciousness is universally lowered to an idiotic level by American television soaps–**Bold and Beautiful** or **Friends**–nobody in the West finds it extraordinary that 80 million souls converge by plane, by car, on horseback, on foot towards a place which they consider sacred, to pray to That which is beyond us, to this immanent Force towards which men have aspired to since millenniums?*

But not at all! What does the Western press do? It publishes photos of nakes sadhus, or stretched out on beds of thorns; it harps on the ban of Cox & Kings's unethical marketing of the Mela, or speaks of the VHP's fundamentalism. Always these images which denigrate India, always this colonial superior spirit which perpetuates itself in the negative vision which Western journalists have of the Indian subcontinent.

That has always been India's problem in comparison with China that defies the West, curbs press movement, closely supervises all commentary, resists interference and the internet–and therefore, in a curious way, commands respect from a somewhat cowed Western media. How ironic that India, an open democracy, receives the full blast from Western editors and correspondents back in their cocooned offices, air-conditioned rooms, travel privileges, free whiskey/sodas. I have seen it all–close-to!

Kumbh: (Hindi = waterpot) the pitcher of plenitude is almost as ubiquitous as the lotus in Indian art themes—from folk paintings around doorways, at weddings as far apart as Rajasthan, Orissa, Kerala, Gujarat–to the beautiful incised niches of pietradura semi-precious stone adornment in Mughal buildings.

Like the lotus the kumbh, being non-figurative, is equally adaptable for Islamic art where human form as sculpture or painting is forbidden. Beautifully fashioned, its pregnant shape under the rim depicts the enriched **cornucopia of a good life**, the coconut sitting in a floreat of mango leaves in the neck of the pot–often decorated with the auspicious swastika emblem. A delight in perfect shape and colour, to the eye simple in style and balance, symptomatic of the Indian ability to achieve beauty so effortlessly and to enhance a commonplace kitchen object with spiritual meaning.

■ **KUMBH-ABISHEKAM** (n. *Sanskrit*–a bathing)

is the ultimate 'ceremony of ceremonies', the sense symbolically of one's spiritual state being cleansed with pots of holy water.

Dr V Raghavan in his many writings described the entire ceremony as prescribed in the **Agamas (sacred knowledge handed down by traditional texts)** as most especially concerned in the **detailed rites** relating to every aspect of temple worship:

*The learned pandits who have been initiated (**diksha** = initiation) undertake at least a **hundred rites** in the bathing of a single Image in its installation or in the penultimate bathing from a scaffolding on high of a renovated or new temple, from its **Vimana stupi–the uttermost metal finial** that protects the sanctum sanctorum deep below, to the fire pits where the sacred homa/fire ceremony is lit. Every chant, every act, every spoonful of ghee, rice, water has to be just so.*

At the end of 1996 at **Marudamalai**, a 12th century hill temple, abode of **Lord Muruga**, near Coimbatore one such ceremony took place, circled by a great concourse of people far below. According to press reports the Deity, the dark-skinned son of Shiva, named also as Skanda, was 'uprooted' after a thousand years to be kept in safe custody while renovation of the stone work had taken place over a period of three years. The **abishekam** was a **six-day celebration** with the construction, blessing and lighting of **27 fire pits (homakundams)** by especially learned acharyas to propitiate the Lord on being installed again, the vibrating mantras whereby the divine presence is drawn back as a magnetic pull into the murti resonating through the vast mass of people.

- Holy water carried **from 16 rivers** had also to be sanctified in a puja, then with elaborate ceremony taken in procession up the scaffolding steps over 100 ft high where with great efficiency engineers of the 20th century world had installed an overhead pipeline!

- **Promptly at 7 am** (and it shows where Indian priorities are where the gods cannot be kept waiting) the river waters cascaded down from the pitchers carried on high amid chanting of Sanskrit slokas. The overhead sprinklers were turned on...

- And then the other India reasserted itself. Despite police reinforcements due to the presence of so many VIPs, industrialists and politicians, the thousands anxious for the holy shower, rushed forward trampling down the barriers and free-standing neighbours. The stampede was on, a number of spectators badly injured.

Such is the unmistakable sanctity of Kumbh, river water and ritual... testified by a resident Australian-Indian:

Yet most astonishing and humbling of all were the millions upon millions of poor and lower middle-class which with pure devotion and unerring faith and belief in a higher intelligence, came to gain some of the precious pot-full of nectar. They came during the Kumbh Yogh when the waters were the purest and sweetest and most magical in their mythical powers, to remove the stigma of bad-karma and flesh-polluting sin.

If looked upon in a scientific point of view, waters are known to become charged and controlled by the pull of the alignment of the planets. The whole hypothesis behind the power of 'magnets' have not been scientifically proven but still work for a lot of people. This 'charging' of the waters brings about the same sort of effect as magnets or acupuncture, releasing the bad and emphasising the good. This sort of effect is also said to be used by the moon, which controls the tides of the sea using a sort of 'charge'.

K

■ LAKSHMI

Churned up from the cosmic ocean of **amrit** as Vishnu reincarnates himself over and over again to preside over the tug-of-war between deities and asuras, she emerges, like Aphrodite did much later in Greek legend from the scattered spray.

Mild and seemingly gentle in her radiant beauty, as **Sri**, Vishnu's balancing half, her feminine energy redeploys itself with similar forceful preservative influences as she progresses through the Dasavataram, ever at Vishnu's side as consort, but under different names (see **PANTHEON**). Strangely no temples are dedicated to her but she is the focus of universal worship all over India at the major all-continental festival of Diwali… and she shifted a long-sustained cultural stance!

Personal note: It is on this stepping stone that I have to admit to a radical change of attitude, a virtual turn-around in response to an impassioned comment by an Indian friend whom I deeply respect. We have been in dialogue for some time on philosophic issues concerning English language usage in India (and by Indian writers in English as well as by outsiders such as myself) when dealing with translations of profound Indian terms that are not just matters of specific language but are 'halo-ed' in fundamental cultural dimensions.

Such is **Sri** and such is **the Lord**, Lord Shiva, Vishnu *et al.*

I have remained obstinately attached to the respectful use of 'the Lord Vishnu, etc' as following the convention used by gurus and pandits themselves when addressing overseas audiences. But my editor wrote this:

There are titles we are expected to understand. 'Monsieur', 'the Rt Hon.' Or 'H M the Queen'. You would be doing a sterling service if you introduced in reverse Sri (Shri) to Western perceptions!

It is such a beautiful word, with such a gentle, gracious meaning, a happy meaning and it is gender neutral!–Shri Vishnu, and Shri, his consort… A Sanskrit scholar will explain the nuances–Shri Rama, Shridevi, Shrimati. (see introductory **note to the Reader**)

The way this devotional approach to a term is so lyrically expressed has convinced me of its legitimacy as yet another Sanskrit word which should pass seamlessly into my native language alongside all the less dense terms–raga, guru, yoga, mantra, asana, ayurveda, swami have done!

And while on genderless issues it is worth taking note of **Ram Swarup's** book **Meditations: Yogas, Gods, Religions** (Voice of India, New Delhi, 2000). He points out in relation to Western religious traditions that 'the very word 'God' was neuter in its original Teutonic home. But when this word was adopted by Christianity after the Teutons became Christians, the word became masculine. The word 'Allah' has a similar history.

The **lota**, present at puja ceremonies, often on a bellmetal tray and decorated with a floret of ashoka or mango leaves on which is cosily bedded a coconut, is the harbinger of all that Lakshmi stands for, the 'electricity' of her auspicious 'presence' and plenitude.

Lakshmi is to be honoured, most especially as the goddess seated on a LOTUS. In this protective role she is the channel for benign influences–not just the gold shekels she appears in the imagery (most especially in Thailand's Hindu shrines) to be releasing upon the head of the devotee from the palm of her downward-pointing right hand. Yes, at the lustrous Festival of **DIWALI** when every home should be lit up to welcome her she brings good fortune as the goddess of wealth. But in the cosmic order of things her force is to protect her devotees with well-being and fortune of a less material kind. Merchants, however, as they open their account books for the New Year (incidentally, celebrated at different times in the calendar by Bengalis, Kashmiris, Tamils and others, constellations of worlds within worlds) do keep an eye out for that extended palm and a possible golden shower! For **Sri** is indeed auspiciousness incarnate.

■ LANGUAGE and ATTITUDES of MIND

In all cultures we often do not say directly what we mean, clothing our words in ambiguities–hence the length of time it takes to iron out political treaties that are binding, industrial agreements that sometimes take all-night sittings to find the right written formulae for accord, legalistic jargon that takes a page to express one simple thought.

There are additional dimensions for not reading the right signs when dealing with different cultural indicators–and radically different ones at that, such as the Indian view of life, creation and our place as humans in this framework. For one thing, time is at the cosmic level. For another, the concept of **samsara**, transmigration of the atman-soul through many rebirths runs counter to the sense of urgency in European civilisation with its biblical sense of one life–a linear progression with not much time left to get things done… or to reach 'perfection' if that is what you wish to do.

Over 60 per cent of Indians are now designated bilingual (one other language other than the mother tongue) or even trilingual, many having taken the English language and made it their own, another overlay in the **PALIMPSEST**. This should not lead to the assumption that they will be meaning the same thing, however. Grammatical structure, for instance, interacts with **CORE CONCEPTS** thereby shifting the emphasis of a sentence. Perhaps this is what Noam Chomsky is on about and why he is so popular in India and far more widely known among the generality of the population than in a country like Australia.

1   Many a business seminar taking on board how best (and efficiently) to cope with the challenges of doing business with India, considers 'attitudes of mind' a major stumbling block. All is not what it may appear to be on the surface. How to read the signs? Indian love of manipulating two languages at once, quite unconsciously and without having to pause for grammatical

thought about order or construction adjectively or adverbally, indicates a subtlety that is not face-to-face 'businessspeak'!

Aligned with nodding the head between the two distinct polarities of **yes** and **no**, Indians allow themselves the option of not hurting anybody's feelings by this adjustment. Harsher European clarity, a direct and well-defined-if-blunt NO—or YES—is not the Indian way!

2   Two languages blended together fluently, flowingly, all in one go... this is a remarkable capacity of Indians when talking to each other in a regional language. If they also speak English they incorporate it into the flow of conversation. Such an example in Bengali of this flexible handling of language is this mother's statement:

Jishnu roj shokāle uthe music practice kore, breakfast kheye, dānt brush kore, uniform aur sneaker pore, suncream lagiye, schoolbag niye schoole jaye...

Jishnu gets up every morning, practices music, eats breakfast, brushes his teeth, wears uniform and sneakers, puts on suncream and goes to school with his schoolbag.

The ebullient over-the-top Sikh popstar **Daler Mehndi** en route to perform in a 1999 concert in Delhi had this advert placed in the English-language media (plus translation for the Australian tour):

Mastiyan Chha Gayin... Romantic joy is spread around

1.   *Coca Cola Tour Daler Da Aagaya*...: Daler's Coca Cola Tour has come

2.   *Your city Nu Rock te Refresh Karanvaste*...: To rock and refresh your city

◆   Even simpler—a question put to me. *'Aap lunch key liyeh free hain*? ' Are you free for lunch?

◆   And an exclamation by a winner on the TV show *Kaun Banega Crorepati* = Who Wants to be a Millionaire ...' *Is se to meri life hi change hogayeeji* = My life has changed because of this'.

3.   There are further open-ended possibilities in phraseology to do with 'coming' and 'going'.

Rather than using the inverted question mark: '**You will come to my home tonight for the party, won't you?** Expecting the answers—yes, or no, the order of the Indian sentence is:

◆   *Tonight/to my home/you will be coming/isn't it?/no?*
There are distinct possibilities then that you might, or you might not, depending on immediate circumstances, there being many if you happen to exist within the multiple exigencies of a joint/extended family with so many calls upon your time and energies. Once back in the homestead even for a modern Indian working in an office, to turn around and go out again to see a friend at the end of the day, go to a committee meeting, frequent a cafe is all too much. Best to stay in the airconditioning if you are lucky enough to have one, or collapse by a fan. And besides, Indian hospitality is so compulsive (good dharma) as well as innately warm-hearted (that **a-tithi** principle!) that it doesn't matter anyway if you come late, and unexpectedly. There are usually in traditional households enough unemployed members

of a family or retainers (if but one humble servant) to jump to, to put together another helping of food... none of that Western rudeness in showing annoyance that you weren't given any forewarning and 'look at the time' attitude. Besides, Indian khanaa stretches further, a pilau is flexible!

In fact the Indian answer to 'Aren't you coming this evening?' would be: *'Hanji'* (**yes**, acknowledging the question is being asked), *'I am not coming'*, rather than a downright rude, *'No! I am not coming'.*

4.   The miracle is that despite the Spike Milligan/Peter Sellers attitude of English people trying to imitate 'Hinglish'–as nothing to the embarrassment of our own miserable efforts at Hindi–Indian writers have built up a consummate and articulate English literature of their own. **Nirad Chaudhuri's** impeccable classic English referred to by some literary critics as a 'mixture of the Elizabethan Bible, Gilbert Murray classics and the evening news on radio'; **Rabindranath Tagore's** lyrical poetry (Nobel Prize for Literature); the racy ease of **Khushwant Singh's** novels to the Tolstoyian command of **Vikram Seth's** masterpiece... and a thousand others, editors in their dozens, too many to mention, all indicate this mastery.

A Madhavan, poet manqué who became a distinguished diplomat and Director of the **India International Centre** has a fascination for the proclivities of the English language as used by his Indian colleagues. Over the years his occasional articles have with wry humour appeared in the English-language press. I had many hours privilege at the Farnham Centre of International Briefing sharing ideas on this matter with him.

5.   '… Indian writers have a sense of humour' he points out, 'well able to laugh at their own foibles, with that most Indian of phrases: *You do one thing*... suggestive rather than directive *Please do this*, is too peremptory. One of his articles tackles Indian English.... *'He has gone for taking meals,'* shadows the Indian construction, a great favourite which will not easily be dislodged. Nor will *'You came today, isn't it?,'* he pointed out in one of his wry essays. As if one didn't know! ....and with the rising Welsh inflexion echoing in the inner ear.

And there are the wonderful phrases he notes in 'officialese'–coming right out of the British Raj days of administrative instruction in **Tottenham's District Office Manual**, directed towards that loyal band of Indian clerks hidden behind rising mounds of pink-taped-files, with their elastic garters strung taut across the paper bulges threatening to slide out.

6.   Madhavan notes the Indian preference for the passive voice: *'You are requested to present yourself...'* And another example: *'I am to say that'*... well, go ahead and say it!

7.   *'Do the needful,'* is a beloved classic which is perhaps indispensable. But the limit for Madhavan is: *'This may kindly be got done...'*–a whole essay, he rightly comments, could be written on the official subjunctive, *'may'.*

8.   Because of India's characteristic absorptive gift, Victorian officialese must have surely influenced other areas of the gifted ability to harness English to her own purposes. Latinised polysyllabic words survive, fossil reminders of Miltonic solidity for

instance. Beware an Indian seeking to help you on the road if you have lost direction: **'you go straight...'**

Two kilometres down the track the road is sure to **bifurcate**. The dilemma is there, typical of Murphy's Law, an Australian idiom for life's deliberate tripwires that daily come our way. With a name like that, Murphy was Irish. The Celtic soul being very close to the Indian, **bifurcation** would be something the Irish would readily understand.

And if as a result of indecision when you come to the juncture you should run into a recalcitrant lorry hurtling along behind its Sikh driver, you might well **'shuffle off your mortal coil'**, a phrase that appeals to Indians' sense of classicism (it being embedded in Hamlet's most famous soliloquy). I had never heard this turn of phrase nor registered it as part of modern English currency until I landed in India; but surprisingly reinforced **in England** by a premonition note left by my husband's brother on the eve of his death just over a decade ago.

Tucked deep inside Lutyens pinkish-red Secretariat that overshadows Parliament perhaps there is an Indian civil servant long forgotten in a brown cell of an office, whose whole job in life is 'doing the needful', concocting phrases which will strike at the basic dharma deep in our souls, pre-poning (another word now commonly used in India) our decisions to act, rather than procrastinating, by **post**-poning, hoping that the hard work and discipline will be needfully done!

Postscript: Noted on my last visit–acronyms have been updated also and Indianised from Yuppy to **Puppy** = Punjabi Upwardly mobile Professional Youth. And there is the overseas, more disturbing **ABCD** = American Born **Confused Desi (of the desh** = of the country India) who with the **chutnification** of their American food may be really churned up culturally!

■ **LOK SABHA** n. *Hindi*
is the **House of the People**, literally the Assembly Place (Sabha) in the significantly circular Parliament House in New Delhi. At the last election there were **545 MLAs** elected from constituencies in **28 States** and **seven union territories** which claimed **13 members from that total**.

The **Rajya Sabha** is the equivalent of an Upper House, elected from **State** Legislators plus 12 nominated from the intellectual/arts world by the President.

Foreigners learning Hindi sometimes confuse the word **log** which also means 'people' with **lok**, the connotation of which is more embracing of the world at large. **Hum log** is more idiomatic, referring to **'we people'** as a smaller group.

■ **LOTUS**
Nelumbo nucifera species
referred to as **padma** in Sanskrit, **kamal** in Hindi, this stately flower taller than the Egyptian one, has become a timeless symbol of beauty and purity despite its origins in the murky waters that nurture it. **That** is its symbolic significance.

Trailing as it does in multifoliate carvings in sculpted friezes around temple walls or in a pink haze of delicate swaying rhythm

in miniature paintings or around majestic Buddhist **toranas**, gateways, at **Sanchi** or **Udayagiri**, the lotuses, calyxes, bending buds heavy with potential flowering, the tough, sinuous winding stems, and arched petals flow like great rolling waves in a constant continuum.

This is the Indian metaphor for teeming fertility flowing in design in every aspect of the visual arts as well as delighting the eyes and the assaulted body under the relentless sun-scorch by the undulating inner movement of a pink carpet of blossom on a distant lake in Kashmir.

No wonder the lotus is the national flower. The lotus and India are so part of each other, just as the Himalayas and Ganga are a perpetual environment shaping the continent before hominid ever roamed it. So the lotus has become an **archetypal emblem–a metaphor in art for all that is pure and benign**, personalised as artistic representation emerged in the immediate pre-Christian centuries, in the form of the goddess **Lakshmi, Vishnu's consort.**

The lotus grows out of the fecundity of a monsoonal tropical nature; a **ritual symbol** in the magical and meditational diagrams of puja, with worship in the home or at congregational festivities and at times of personal blessings and ritual family celebrations; an **icon** for poets to use as a measure for the beauty of the beloved–'lotus-eyed' as Vishnu, **also a fascination for modern graphic designers**; a **yogic symbol** for the final thousand-petalled expansion of psychic energy exploding out of the **seventh chakra** into super-consciousness and the flowering of self; and as a **name for men as well as women**–Kamal, Pankaja (literally born from the mud), Pushkar, Rajiv, Padma, Kamala, Nalini, Padmini, Mrinalini. And as **Avalokiteshwari** comes trippingly off a daughter's name (**ava** = down; **lokit** = who looks, locates; **iswara** = the deity) associated with **Padmapani** = the lotusbearer, one is led through its beauty and grace, pink, white and the smaller rare blue to the gods and their attributes.

The Lotus Metaphor–many popular images
1. **First Brahma**, creative force, seated on a very comfortable pink cushion and born aloft on the lotus-stemmed umbilical cord growing out of Vishnu's navel. Inert though the redemptive deity may be, Brahma has set forth yet another cycle or giant **kalpa** of creation.
2. **Then Vishnu** holding as one of his attributes the very essence of potentiality if one has had the privilege of watching over a period of a week such a flower come to fruition in all its wonder from its fulsome bud. Because it can close its leaves–and therefore prevent evaporation of its fluids in the heat of the day–it seemingly can regenerate itself, becoming therefore an emblem of prolonged life and rebirth as the avatars of Vishnu also suggest.
3. Likewise with the tranquil goddess **Lakshmi**, the gentle feminine nurturer (a far cry from the pounding energy of Shakti and the ambivalence of Durga/Kali). Lakshmi is also the harbinger of wealth and good fortune and most often depicted in popular bazaar art standing or seated on a fully-opened pink lotus.

L

4. **Yoga Art**: A spiritual aura has surrounded this flower from the very beginnings of Vedic literature, as the inner world of the human spirit was minutely examined and analysed and the yogic sense of energy centres or chakras was visualised in diagrams, the fully-opened lotus with all its perfectly spreading 16 petals of the **Sri Yantra** was seen as a means of conveying these truths... of the final sense of fulfilment, a burgeoning from aspiration to achievement, potential to completion.

Each chakra point of the major seven in the human body is presided over by a governing deity. Through tapasya austerities and prayers the gods can be invoked. In **padmasana** the meditating yogi is at the most serene stage, relaxed but alert to psychic energy flow from one chakra as it flowers, to flow upwards to the next to the final flowering of 'a thousand-petalled lotus' (as depicted in many Rajasthani paintings of the 17th–18th century).

5. **Tantra** is that final explosive chakra of **gnowledge (gnyana)** as the petals curl open in all their glory–from the ascetic end of the spectrum to that of India's most secret and occult expressions, the tantric worship occasionally in sexual congress to reach out to union with the mysterious Goddess.

6. **Self-consciousness**–and as the petals finally fall this imagery is used, likening it to the stripping away of the layers of self-hood, in which the atman is wrapped–until the final singularity emerges in pure nakedness when Atman is joined to ONE. (Read **Ajit Mookerjee**'s many works on Tantra).

7. **Medicinally** Ayurvedic medicine extracts essences from the lotus to aid concentration and as preventative potions for allergies. The seeds can also be eaten roasted as **makhanas** (spicy puffs), the stem as a vegetable and the rhizomes ground down into a nutritious starchy substance.

8. **In sculpture, royal authority and power** is represented by the upturned lotus bell–**kamalpushpa**–atop Ashoka's law-dispensing stone columns. **Indian architecture** from the very beginnings in the Buddhist caves and stupa gateway carvings, 2nd century BCE onwards, interweaves the panels of teeming local life of those far-off times with the tensile strength of the lotus tendrils. (Of interest is the fact that very ancient Celtic artefacts now surfacing in European archaeological diggings have stonework friezes of lotus calyx and tendrils, almost carbon copies of Indian motifs.)

Never linear, always rolling in waves of open-ended spirals, they merge into philosophic concepts of creation, a linear rhythm to convey the continuity of movement and growth in all nature... and that tendril theme continues around friezes and floral decorations from Ajanta caves to Agra's perfection of form in the hands not only of Hindu but Jain and Muslim, Buddhist and European to the pre-eminent symbol of all–the opening nine-petalled lotus of Delhi's astonishing **Baha'i Temple** with all its expectancy of 'that which is to be'.

◆ This very process is so adroitly expressed in yet another formula–in **Bharata Natyam** dance hand gestures. Books on symbolic Indian art, especially meaningful for the outsider, are **Ritual Art of India** as also Ajit Mookerjee, **Tantra Art, its** Philosophy and Physics and Zimmer's richly-textured **Myths and Symbols of Indian Art and Civilization**.

❦❧❦❧❦❧❦❧❦❧❦❧❦❧❦❧

1954
A **personal encounter**–struggling up endless bleak brown mountains, driving solo with a very sick husband laid out with amoebic dysentery and an alarming temperature, a seven-year-old son alert in the passenger seat as Indian-army-lorry spotter as they careened alarmingly down the endless hairpin bends head on into our upcoming traffic, we climbed out of the steambath heat of the Kashmiri foothills to Jammu–up, up to the 10,000 foot Banihal Pass–before the lower tunnel was excavated. Three days and a stop over at the dak bungalow at **Kud** and we were over the top.

In a rare season of peacefulness before the blight of terrorism withered Valley society there lay a long slope down into emerald green meadows, saffron bulb fields coated in a sheen of silky grass, tiny plots of maize standing high and then the long straight road with a line of fluttering poplars, statuesque sentinels heralding the approach into Srinagar. And blessed relief–cool zephyrs spirited off the surface of cooling lakes the effect like burying one's head in a reviving refrigerator.

And then **Nagin Bagh**. One more Indian miracle of those gentler days before 'the troubles'. Admittedly, a rare privilege before tourism brought huge coachloads, litter wafted across waters, pollution of sewage and plastic mineral water bottles floating on canals. And in that golden arrival at the furthest end *one* houseboat beside a green, green greensward–and enormous cooling **chinar** trees, solid and shady like gigantic sycamores of Europe.

Just 10 houseboats on the silent waters... and there through the cedar frame windows balancing in delicate harmony on the tip of a **bending lotus bud**, tight with potentiality, an iridescent blue/green kingfisher, poised in alertness, a flash of beauty in a bed of starry pink lotuses and mottled green leaves wafted in yellow sunlight. No wonder the lotus is India's pre-eminent symbol of that ineffable quality so hard to define, a magic of hallowed territory, caught in the equally magical title of Rumer Godden's novel **Kingfishers Catch Fire** (Macmillan, London, 1953).

◆ **The Vedas** even describe **the very rare auspicious blue lotus, neel kamal**. Once given one in Delhi, we all marvelled at its symmetry, the cool 'blush' upon its blue petals, the sensuous texture, the perfection of curve only to be rivalled in the man-made conception of the Taj Mahal dome and its inherent mathematical perfection of line flow.

◆ The Vedic texts also talk of the ever bending, flowing, moving entity of lotus stems as **generations of humans, flourishing in unbroken continuity**... as it was for us, so for many wanderers throughout history, peoples seeking more fertile soils who have undertaken the wearisome journeyings. Finally they reached these high valleys of refreshment where Mughal kings 5,000

L

years later resuscitated their Mongolian blood thinned in the debilitating heat of Delhi's summer oven...so many peoples must have taken delight in and bowed to Padma's beauty, attributing divine qualities just in the simple joy of looking at her day by day, a natural attribute for the divine to use as pedestal, the **pankaja lotus stalk**, standing tall in axial erectness, a symbol (especially in Buddhist iconography) of perfection above the muddied water where we live in imperfection!

In the beginning, when the cosmos emerged in the golden egg, **brhmand,** and creation, as humans understand it to have developed, took form, a lotus emerged from Vishnu's navel. Brhma, no longer abstract but human form as depicted in the **PANTHEON** sits upon that lotus seat. What depth of symbolic meaning!

As indeed the most recent manifestion created by Iranian-Canadian architect Sahaba and built with bamboo scaffolding by heroic Rajasthani migrant labour—women as well as men. People flock to worship at Delhi's Baha'i temple.

L

MAGADHA, MITHILA, MADHUBANI and the MAURYAS

No wonder the Hindiwallahs of the inland Gangetic basin speak with pride of **Bharatavarsh**–their India! This particular region, must be one of India's oldest recorded settlements, stretching back further in legend than its existence in known history (**ITIHASA**) from the Buddha's birth (5th c BCE in Lumbini, now Nepal) to Ashoka's seminal reign (3rd c BCE) developing the flourishing Mauryan empire of his grandfather–**Chandragupta I**.

This was 600 years apart from the later Gupta dominion of Chandragupta II (4th–5th c CE). How far did the Mauryan overlordship reach? Well, nearly the whole of the subcontinent had a sense of a pyramid of identity bound by certain Hindu, Buddhist, Jain rituals and a common view (those **CORE CONCEPTS**). At the apex a series of emperors followed, for the first time achieving central administrations of a sort, ruling by royal decrees.

Background Briefing

Individual kingdoms and satraps tacitly accepted this networking, as it would be called today, paying homage and revenues but free to rule their own domains in exchange for overall protection. A sense of 'India' has been shaping itself not as a political entity but more of a philosophical one. Pluralism was too strong a force–and an asset (see **FISSIPAROUS TENDENCIES**). A flourishing agricultural economy and a spirited cultural ferment interacted in a true Indian inclusiveness. Nalanda was a famous Buddhist learning centre (a university of its times), attracting huge numbers of Buddhist pilgrims from further Asia. Chinese tourist chroniclers of their day commented upon the buoyancy of trade as well as thriving cultural pursuits. A high watermark came with the overt stirrings of democratic rule–the **PANCHAYAT**, of councils at **Magadha's** resplendent capital, **Pataliputra**. This stretch of land had everything going for it for at least 600 years. And it fittingly ended in style with yet another emperor, **Harsha**, much neglected by the outside world, yet one to note, obviously imbued with the Vedic roots of this widespread culture even if he himself embraced Buddhism. Here also **VALMIKI**, the great literary sage had lived, and expounded his wisdom on the epic Ramayana several thousand years earlier. Yet no matter in what century, as the **Madhubani** women painters of **Mithila** indicate, the signals coming from this constant background noise of the culture are all of a piece. A beautiful book by **Yves Vequaud, the Art of Mithila, Ceremonial paintings from an ancient kingdom** (Thames and Hudson, London, 1977) alerted our generation to the wondrous creative spirit of these humble women.

Recognition of the importance of ritual art virtually 'hidden from history' as **Partha Mitter** points out in his book **Indian Art** (Oxford, 2001) is at last acknowledging this important, compelling and astonishing continuum for so long marginalized by the heavy hand of colonial attitudes from the West. Intellectual snobbery is fading even on its own grounds–that artificial compartmentalization of superior fine arts and the more lowly folk and applied arts (see **CRAFTS/SILPA**).

◆ But oh! For a Greek or Roman artisan mason to fashion life-like busts of these formative Indians. Ashoka is faceless, Harsha is faceless. Kanishka of the Kushanas from Bactrian Asia (the Caspian Oxus) beyond northern Afghanistan, is headless! His statue, heavily carved torso, heavy boots, heavy sword, is one of the very first (and few) of a ruler to be found in the Mathura Museum south of Delhi. Most are even more powerfully built yakshas or supernatural beings or Buddhas. Now tourist hotels are named after Ashoka, Kanishka, the Mauryas–a shift in emphasis from earlier days of the Imperial Hotel, the Cecil and Claridges, Delhi's only watering holes of the 50s.

Kanishka and the Kushanas took Indian names and embraced Buddhism. Sanskrit was adopted as the court language. Yet another layer in the palimpsest was laid down, chronicled in the Chinese texts as a cosmopolitan melting pot of those late Mauryan times–Indian, Chinese, mainly Buddhist pilgrims, central Asian and Graeco-Roman Mediterranean peoples all visiting for learning or trade, with some eventually settling, becoming Indian. The sense of excitement in the piecing together of this magnificent stretch of history before much of its wealth was carried away in those devastating raids by Mahmud of Ghazni, a fierce Afghani zealot converted to Islam at the cusp of the second millennium, comes in a very human transmission by **John Keay** in **India Discovered**. Here is India forming as a powerful idea, however, the term 'Indian' as cautioned previously, needs to be used sparingly. In **Sunil Khilnani's** succinct book **The Idea of India** (Penguin and Hamish Hamilton, London, 1997) he points out rightly that before the 19th century no residents of the subcontinent would have identified themselves as Indian in the political sense. It is to Harsha, reluctant emperor by default, that I took quite a shine over 40 years ago at that historic **KUMBH MELA** of 1954. An Indian journalist friend Prem Bhatia, rediscovering his own history in the new independence days was investigating the hearsay amongst pilgrims at Allahabad's spiritually significant sangam site. Now after searching for details all these years, the internet provides some of the answers and notes Harsha's gift of administration in binding a huge area of embryonic political India together.

Harsha came to the throne in Kannauj upstream from where we were gathered, after his brother-in-law the ruler was murdered in this regional kingdom of the Pushyabhutis, one of several hierarchies vying for paramountcy in the Gupta era of Magadha. Harsha's sister had been abducted in the fracas. Having retrieved her and to restore order, Harsha assumed the reins of empire in 606 CE–for 41 years. From various accounts his quirkish benevolence filtered down through the sieve of fable and hearsay. Chinese accounts of the time attest to Harsha's hospitality to that inveterate Chinese traveller **Hsuan-tsang** who crops up in and out of India's real history, surely the first Asian correspondent to make himself known to the world.

A man who can retain his identity as a resonating symbol of selfless generosity in a region rendered politically unstable by the sixth century CE invasions of the central European/Asian Huns and the sacking of Prayag nearby, where local petty rajas

M

appealed to him for protection in this vacuum, and yet can visit the Kumbh Mela in all humility–in our perspective, 1400 years on, must have something going for him! Although not consciously suppressed by colonial dominance, certainly cultural/spiritual details of Indian history had been in general totally ignored. For me, Harsha and his artistic personality came into focus when I stumbled across the human being at the Kumbh Mela. No longer was he one more name in a dry history account

◆   However, no illustration, no statue was reproduced. At least Kanishka's sole blurred image is embossed on a gold coin, bulbous crown Byzantine-style on his bearded head and a truly Pathan-size nose.

Accounts did tell however of visits by Harsha to successive **sangam** auspicious immersions where he had divested himself of all his vestments and rich finery to give to those impoverished subjects the sight of whom had so moved him. Consequently he had travelled back to his court virtually naked like the so-called holy babas, the Naga sadhus of his day. In his 41-year reign, three such gigantic gatherings of the **Kumbh Mela** would have taken place.

He spent much of his life on horseback 'listening in' to what his constituents had to say, rich source material for the plays he wrote, and the poetry he composed. Transmitted across the centuries is the fact that as a ruler, he led morally, promoting dharmic harmony in such a pluralistic conglomerate of peoples. Historians give this a dry clinical term–'doctrinal fraternity'. I much prefer the spirit of the man knowing that his capital Kannauj was a richly artistic centre until this last great Hindu emperor of the north was defeated in his push south by the rising power of the southwestern **Chalukyas**.

Then the axis of power tilted into that downward pointing triangle of the Carnatic and this intriguing ruler disappears illusively into the mists that rise of an early morning under the open skies of the Gangetic flood plains. He continues to remain tantalisingly immortal, part of the language he obviously loved. A Bengali professor friend tells me that as a child the phrase **harsha bardhan** was in common use in his school playground. The idiom implies generosity of an uncommon degree, an almost reckless nature, so if a child had some extra inviting delicacies in his tiffin carrier for lunch which friends might eye longingly, he would toss off the phrase in the vernacular: **I'm not going to do a harsha bardhan! You can't have any!**

Now if only the Madhubani ladies would paint the Emperor a face in the inimitable style they give to their so familiar deities, I would rest content!

Search the www.historyofindia.com. Books–*Harsha: A political study,* by **D Devahuti** *(OUP, Allahbad, 1998) and **The Dramas of Shri Harsha** (microform) trans.,* **Bela Bose** *(Ketabistan, 1948)*.

■   MAHABHARATA... *one of two defining* **Epics**
3100 BCE onwards
The word **itihasa** is applied to the Mahabharata–history, 'heard wisdom' = **smriti**, that which is passed down in an oral

culture of perhaps 3000 years before our common era, eventually **written down** in the great literary period of several centuries before the Christian calendar.

If India (Bharatvarsh) is vast–spatially, emotionally pulverizing, physically draining–then what of a tale that calls itself **Mahabharata? Majestic... big... the land of Bharat**.

And what if an international theatrical event emanating at the Avignon Festival in the late 1980s, a **nine-hour production** by Peter Brook from the French text of Jean-Claude Carrière is considered **only a condensation** of a massive text couched in the grandeur of Sanskrit slokas (quatrains) which easily outruns the Greek epics, the **Iliad** and **Odyssey** put end-to-end, **at least seven times over**? It is indeed the longest story ever told, 100,000 verses, carried in the minds of men primarily, generation upon generation in an entirely oral culture certainly for several thousand years before writing on palm leaf was introduced.

In a civilization which has honoured Holy Utterance–**VAC =** the word (and the vocalist in music) and remained uniquely within its oral culture, abiding by its exactitudes for empirical evidence for future generations as much as for its sonorances, it is rewarding to find another outsider, a young French Vedic scholar able to capture this capacity to carry the tradition with such steadfast accuracy.

Jean Le Mée (cited in Rajaram and Frawley's book **Vedic Aryans**) is quoted in a vivid turn of phrase describing these incredible feats of memory recited so consistently: 'an unbroken chain of generations travelling like a great wave through the living substance of the mind.' This reminds me of an earlier passage from the French lyrical visionary, Romain Rolland of the last century who recognised this spaciousness of not only physical or demographic India and its surging population, but the inner roaming psyche 'existing' for Rolland 'in a kind of feminine space' as if Father Time were a woman.

Indian TV went even further than Brook in the 80s with a traditional version, a production of several hundred episodes which stilled the nation every Sunday morning for years. And even this too was but a skeletal simplification of a massive chronicle becoming uniquely Hindu because of the Lord Krishna's watchfulness in leading its moral debate.

The Mahabharata is India writ large rolling out of the mists of antiquity in pre-Gangetic soil, **real but of unrecorded** beginnings, gathering volume over **50 centuries** (and that according to some Indian sources is a conservative estimate) in all its oceanic spaciousness. Indeed it is regarded as the 'fifth Veda' and titled as such by many Indians.

A Universal Story
It is now contained in a gigantic **14-volume English translation** (and many other abridged versions). The actual details appear under **Epics**, the struggle of **mostly** good against **mostly** evil forces but differing from Western heroic tales in that the spatial dimension encompasses many reincarnations. As in general humanity the waters of morality become extremely muddied at times between the major protagonists, the cousin **Kauravas** and the **Pandavas**.

For an unbroken continuum meaningful also in contemporary culture only Aboriginal Australia with its own legends and symbolic totems can outpace this feat of memory—but certainly not the complexity of philosophical debate which adds lustre to the essential story of two branches of one dominant royal family. Descendants of the Kuru clan, they are plagued with rivalries which culminate in an 18-day war at **Kurukshetra**, an 80-square mile plain now part of the national heritage north of Delhi in Haryana State (and where hundreds of designated pilgrimage sites now exist).

Kshetra = a ground, farming land, family dominions. Just as today land rights of tribal people versus incomers stirs the very soul of human societies, arousing passions, bitterness, bigotry and misguided actions—**political** at the social level, **personal** because of individual desire to 'own' land and pass on to children, **economic** because of human or corporate greed and dispossession of those whose identity is rooted in the very soil of ancestral 'belonging'. So the rivalries and warring factions carry the thematic development of the Mahabharata through such a sweep in time and space that the MahaB is regarded as the story of humankind.

Certainly as a woman I find it heavily weighted in its masculine emphasis, the 'goodies' being the five Pandava brothers (**panch** = five, a significant Indian number, see **Panchayat**) with their common wife Draupadi, and the 'baddies' the Kauravas, the 100 sons of the elder brother in the Kuru clan. There was one daughter—**Duh-salaa**... imagine! There are powerful women who play pivotal roles influencing action from their menfolk but the flavour or **rasa** of the text is still the language almost entirely of the warrior male. However the women do not act entirely in traditional mould of the dharma patni, the dutiful wife.

In Indian parlance both lineages would be regarded as **cousin-brothers** in that both branches were virtually brought up in one gigantic household (similar to that of the 600-strong **Nandi** family visited in the Bengal countryside and mentioned in **Joint Families**).

Both warrior lineages (and this is important in the moral dilemmas faced by individuals as the story develops) shared the some mentor in their martial arts training. **Drona** (interestingly enough a brahmin turned kshatriya) was guru to both. Rivalries, the canker of jealousy, that urge of the male gene to prove supremacy ricochets through the text along with the swish of arrow and the clatter of chariot.

However, no matter the supposed date of the ultimate battle (now set by Rajaram and Frawley circa 3100 BCE, see **ARYA-ARYANS**), given such rivalries, the MahaB is also a compendium of India's vast store of moral legends, Aesopian parables, real genealogies, statements on and theories about political machinations and manuals of battle formations (geometric mandalas) and martial arts all necessary for such masculine 'doing-deals'.

◆   Indeed one 'book' concentrates entirely on the art of clubs as a weapon of defence and attack; another describes the performance of the sacred horse sacrifice in defining the boundaries of the ruler's dominion, especially that of the **Samrat** (the overall sovereign) amongst many kingdoms jockeying for power in the early settlement on the plains of the Punjab. Irawati Karve, the sociologist has drawn comparisons with early Greek civilization amongst the first small kingdoms; and the city-states of mediaeval Italy. In world history, what is new? Indeed **Samrat** is now creeping in as a term in the media to describe the current governmental position in a confederation of regional party alliances.

Historical Context
3rd–2nd c BCE to 2nd c CE

In the great period during which these memory banks were transformed into permanent literature, written down in Sanskrit by the learned ones on palm leaf, compilers must have been in great demand. That is where Vyas often referred to as the author, comes in. In fact he is part of the 'text' as narrator/compiler of what predominantly is of Vedic origin. Paradoxically when first encountered by overseas visitors its most compelling visual impact may well be in south India in faraway Kerala's **Kathakali** dance-drama or the Andhra travelling shadow puppeteer theatres with the mythological characters made out of goat or buffalo-skin towering as high as a human. With their Telugu-Tamil speaking artists they may well have travelled also by the big boats in the very earliest centuries to Sumatra to lay the foundation of shadow puppets there (now a part of cultural performances in modern Indonesia and Thailand).

In later decades the **Bhagavad Gita** has become a volume known in any major bookstore of any major city worldwide and is read by hundreds and thousands of foreigners who exist outside the culture of the Hindu Indian. It is not only in this especial text that the MahaB is marked out as different from other epics in world literature. In the subtext of many of the other '**parvas**' or books, that flavour of the Gita, that wrestling with the moral dilemmas of the ordinary individual (and to which women can also relate, beyond the immediate world, no matter how chivalrous, of warrior society) compels attention between the boring dryness of battle upon battle description.

What marks the Mahabharata then as possessing such remarkable qualities?

◆   Its LONGEVITY
◆   Its PERSISTENCE over AEONS of TIME in its appeal
◆   Its RESILIENCE of meaning
◆   Its UNIVERSALITY of message, applicable even today and equally relevant to the world's trouble spots that seemingly possess no resolution—Northern Ireland; the Israel-Palestinian antagonisms of a millennium; the Kashmir crisis; Rwanda.

The MahaB unfolds its message at two important levels which intertwine through flawed and benign characters who become very real people—as 'in the round' as Hamlet, King Lear, feisty Portia or quicksilver Prospero. Remember the term **redemptive history** (see **EPICS**). It encapsulates in its many subtle levels a **dharma-yuddha–the ultimate internal struggle, the true war of righteousness**, that applies to all societies in all ages. Interestingly enough, this intensity of concentration on morality/virtue is how the epic is relayed in popular culture of cinema and comics.

Even those quarrelling cousins are not totally black or white, but shades of grey unlike the 'ideal types' depicted in the other major epic, the Ramayana. Driven foremost by **pride** of different qualities, some show greed mitigated by heroism; weakness for gambling forgiven in the unfolding process of personal struggle through profound moral resolution; dogged faithfulness, misapplied with brutish strength—even to kicking an opponent when broken in defeat. Each and everyone, as in the humanity which listens to the tale unfolding, faces the constant double-edged challenge... nobility of the human spirit which rises suddenly and heartwarmingly from the most unexpected quarters amid a cesspool of perennial human depravity. That paradox seems to be a constant no matter which society or what age or which religious ideal. Hence the universality of this epic far beyond its own cultural boundaries.

Tension in the MahaB is between:

a. **Svadharma: The strong pull of the personal situation and behaviour.**

In India's case this is where caste codes and demands intrude, reinforcing family expectations in personal morality—emphasised by rituals in home puja or daily temple attendance and rigorous abiding by customary rules, duties and obligations, ritual being an essential part of daily culture.

b. **Sanatana Dharma: The concern for higher universal dharma.**

This is the consciousness-raising pull towards social reform, drawing the individual beyond the narrow confines of self, family, social caste.

Prompted by saints, enlightened gurus and the democratic forces inherent in Indian philosophy at its least caste-constrained, this pull has worked effectively in shifting the masses into thinking of social well-being as a whole—hundreds of individuals have lit the way from before even the Buddha. Ashoka, Harsha, Shankaracharya, Guru Nanak, Bengali reformers who are legion, the 'greats' now finally passing who fought in the Independence movement to place a forward-looking Constitution on permanent record in striving for reconciliation and co-existence in diversity—strangely the contemporary message of this new age. Dadabhai Naoroji, Lokmanya Tilak (a true revolutionary), Badruddin Tyabji, Chittaranjan Das, Lala Lajpat Rai (Lion of the Punjab), Raja Rammohun Roy all marched India into the turn of the 20th century with reform in heart and head.

That double tension is a constant in Indian daily life but one of the above did once declare: **Unless ritual is suffused with and penetrated by love, there is no worship.**

Only at the end when the warring spirit relinquishes its raging does the King of Dharma, Yudhisthira, eldest Pandava, become absorbed in the heavenly abode, **svarga**. Human dharma and cosmic rta then become one.

■ **MAITRI, MITRA, MITTRA, MITHRA**

It may appear to be drawing a long bow as Australians would idiomatically say—with a touch of scepticism in the voice—to link the equally Australian principle of **mateship,** the fundamental ethos oft-quoted in literature and trolled out by politicians—with etymological links across a gigantic stretch of time with **Mitra**, Vedic principle and presiding deity of friendship and solidarity between humans.

In the vast 'aloneness' of the Australian continent and its noted indifference to humanity, mateship was an essential comfort. Now it is an essential component of national identity and has come to embrace women as well! 'She's a good mate' embraces women in a non-sexual way and probably carries more force and is longer-lasting than romantic love.

♦ **Mitra** appears in the earliest Rig Vedic hymns emerging in that founding society as the presiding genius of original light, the daytime deity ruling over **this immediate human society** and its proper functioning (based on trust, loyalty, 'his word is his honour' theme) as **Varuna** the other Vedic concept, does over **night and darkness,** a more mysterious world of the gods. Franklin Edgerton and Alain Danielou both comment on Mitra, Edgerton allowing for that speculative search as the rsis also drew their long bows wondering about the origins of the universe—cosmic man = **purusha**; the mysterious quality of consciousness, **sachitananda**. These 'disconnected riddles' which comprise the **first hymn**, 'the answers to which are mostly unknown' as Edgerton comments, deal most importantly with Holy Utterance, that volatile essence of sound. Verse 46 states:

> They call it Indra, Mitra, Varuna, Fire (Agni); or it is the heavenly Sun-bird. That which is One [neuter] the seers speak of in various terms; they call it Fire, Yama, Mātarisvan.

A healthy society could only function properly if there was a sense of solidarity when faced with the unknown 'other world'. Friendship, trust, loyalty are the essential building blocs, otherwise society falls apart. That principle is as true today as it was then. Mitra was therefore the symbolic focal point during that earliest of cultural developments.

This force re-emerged in ancient Persian culture in the worship of **Mithraism**—the Light of the World personified in **Ahura Mazda**, eventually to develop into **Zoroastrianism** (refer PARSIS).

♦ Then by Parthian trade in later centuries Mithraic beliefs were taken across the Bosphorus and like a cultural relay race over centuries picked up again in pre-Christian Roman society. Mithraic cults flourished. Roman legions, belligerent in their loyalties one to another, essentially bonded in mateship (as surely as Australian pioneers in the harshness of the outback assault) as they marched through Europe carrying the Roman Empire and its ethos with them even to the farthest limits of Hadrian's Wall in Britain's north. In the long march they set up shrines to Surya the Sun, eternal celestial light casting luminosity onto earthly society. Without the herald of the dawn's early light where would world humanity be in its proper functioning?

Mitra—spelled several ways—disappeared from the Hindu Pantheon but remains as a caste name. Once indicative of kshatriya origin, valorous warriors, it now is a sign of the kayastha community of clerics in northern India, those 'writers' who keep the records of society as did the British 'writers' appointed to the East India Company, yet another layer in the unplumbed depths of India's capacity to create **BUREAUCRACY**.

Not many of us can trace a genealogical tree back to the beginnings of the Vedas, the Rig Vedic hymns circa 4000 BCE! Such is the origins of mateship however, **Mt** the Sanskrit root of that profoundly necessary friendship, comradeship, the solidarity of humans alone in the cosmic void.

■ **MALA**

A garland or necklace and a favourite name for a girl.

As far as garlands go, this must surely be the land of the original **F**lower **P**ower! Go south despite the temple cities of the north and most especially Kashi where garlands galore are used in every conceivable spiritual rite of passage, and flowers sail in tiny leaf boats with a single light taking a prayer with them onto the rippling waters of the Ganga, or thick marigold garlands are draped in respect around the portrait of the gurus of the Punjab Sikhs at Amritsar.

But around Chennai's **Kapaleeswara temple** is the world's most abundant flower market–Pu-Kadai. From early morning young girls crouch in the half-light deftly knotting those firm sweet-smelling jasmine buds with a twist of banana stem twine. Great rush baskets of heavy scented, gloriously coloured flower heads are dispensed through the suburbs via the **phulwallahs** to grace the framed photographs of ancestors in the home shrines (no matter how humble), or to be twisted in spiral garlands around the great wooden props of a marquee for a wedding, or a carpet rangoli in the foyer of a major corporate building for a special 'happening', and always to be taken from the perfumed bazaar alley of flower stalls to be presented at the foot of the murti in veneration and love.

Overnight great truckloads come hurtling down the Nilgiri hills or from flower farms in the interior, bringing them during the cool hours, without refrigeration. Yet one is never aware of huge flower farms. This one thing mystified my musical friend and myself in all the kilometres we covered in six days driving though inner Tamilnadu. Even the poorest girl walking to school or the woman winnowing the grain by the road side had her braid or bun bedecked with a glorious purple spray–an unknown flower, with not a sign of cultivation in the more arid parts and isolated rural homesteads. Did a phulwhallah do a midnight cycle run to create this *Veni*?

A garland is not always created out of flowers. That personable prime minister whose 13th century Chola bronze resides in the National Museum in Delhi, and who appears in **BHAKTI** with its powerful influence throughout the ages in Indian psychology and in **NAYANMAR**, having forsaken his Pandyan ruler's orders to search for some lost cavalry horses because of a sudden mystic impulse to give up all material lifestyle out of devotion for Sri Shiva, smears his body with ash (**VIBHUTI**). He takes as his only clothing Shiva's **rudraksha**. Even before this

episode of renouncing the world, Shiva had bestowed blessing for another garland laid at the feet of his **MURTI**.

Manicka-vach(h)akka was that prime minister's name: *With love as the string and his nectarine words as the gems, he made a garland and offered it at the guru's feet. The Lord was highly pleased with it and called him* **Manicka** *(a gem)–vachagar (vachakkar = words of wisdom), since the hymns sung by him were like gems in wisdom.*

Thus writes **Swami Sivananda** in his booklet **Sixty Three Nayanar Saints**. The guru was Shiva in disguise as a brahmin. The saint came to Chidambaram, rolled on the ground in ecstasy and received **moksha**, 'merging himself at the feet of Lord Nataraja' literally being transported out of body, out of mind, to other realms. The garland indeed is a powerful symbol.

Shiva's garland of unusual/indented seeds of *Elaeocarpus ganitrus* (very alike to Australia's quondong) is so auspicious the seeds are regarded by devout Hindus as destroying the sins of many rebirths. This fruit looks positively prehistoric. It is! Believed to have existed as far back as the dinosaurs it certainly is traced back to the Puranas in the Hindu use of them as neck mala, perhaps even then banded with gold, black and red thread intertwined.

Legend recalls that the Vedic deity **Rudra** (pre-Siva) wept tears for all living creatures (echoed even at **Shivratri** depending on the full moon in February when he lets loose all the hibernating animals from his bag after the long winter). Where the tears fell, moistening the earth, the berry-bearing rudraksha grew.

◆   The Sabarimala pilgrims we kept running into in Kerala were wearing the 108-seed mala to remember the equivalent Saivite names they were chanting.

The mala can become personal, blessed in a ritual ceremony, and should not be exchanged. Lakshmi watches closely over those who wear the mala, bringing good fortune.

Indira Gandhi, as prime minister was not so lucky. She is supposed to have worn a mala of 108 extremely auspicious **ekamukhi**. The berries vary in their facets or mouths (**mukha**) and thus in degrees of granting blessings, depending on the ridges dividing the facets, the ekamukhi believed to possess chemicals that seep into the body by rubbing against the neck *so preventing blood pressure.* She, after all, was assassinated!

■ **MANGALSUTRA**

was originally a *taali* = red thread (also yellow in the the south) strung with black beads, as essential to a married woman as a Western wedding ring, blessed at the hawan sacrament of marriage and placed around the wife's neck by the groom.

Now gold, the simplest of joining devices interspersing the black, or increasingly fancy, incised beads, make up fashion 'statements'–'gone ethnic' according to fashion writers–all part of the new middle-class materialism. Even fashionable Muslim and Christian women are buying them.

The original joining device which hangs pendant-like at the loop of the necklace, often a traditional plump mango design or sunburst globe was said symbolically to represent the lingam and the **vati**–receiving chamber of the **yoni** = womb. That would not be at all surprising in Indian art design!

Traditional women wore it close to the skin to ward off the evil eye, not as decoration to attract attention.

■ **MANTRA** (n. *Sanskrit*)
 sound syllable....

The divine presence can be summoned up by a chanted mantra, the potency of **VAC** (sound) or in a △ = yantra, a geometric design or configuration to help concentrate the wayward mind in meditation. And if that sounds esoteric, walk into Gujarat villages and see women paint such remarkable designs in rice paste on their brown mud walls as contemporary (yet traditional) as any highly paid art in the West or to mould geometric embossed clay on their clay ovens and pots with these potent insignia.

The late French Sanskrit scholar, **Alain Danielou** has best described the Indian capacity to embrace the whole with its contradictions and paradoxes in his large tome **Hindu Polytheism** (Bollinger Foundation, New York, 1964):

It is only through the multiplicity of approaches that we can draw a sort of outline of what transcendent reality may be.

◆ Because that transcendency will always elude our confined means of knowledge (which modern physicists at the cutting edge of research discover **is** elusive, befogged in **maya**), Danielou writes that "this divinity cannot be grasped or understood for it begins where understanding fails yet can be approached from many sides... (through) a 'near approach', an **Upa–nisad**". The non-linear, hopscotch jump into comprehension is condensed into the sign of the swastika = 卐. Either way, it doesn't matter in the timeless Indian view.

Acknowledging that divinity and the comprehension of this 'immense' reality has been defined as 'that in which opposites coexist', India's earliest thinkers applied three criteria in trying intellectually to discover the truth of creation. One was an empirical method using logic, an almost atheistic scepticism (which will surprise many a Western intellectual); secondly a cosmological examination involving intellectual scientific investigation and the disciplines of yoga; and metaphysical examination 'using the semantic study of language', and abstract forms in sound and space, that is basically geometry.

These differing approaches in explaining the nature of the universe were regarded as points of view = a **DARSHAN**. Again, quoting Danielou:

Each one is real within its own field and aims towards the utmost limit of the reach of our faculties in a particular direction. The builders of the 'points of view' are not spoken of as thinkers or prophets, but as seers (rsis).

This kind of approach in seeking the truth about our very existence without dogma, creed, or church as a springboard, or divine representation may seem difficult for those imbued by

Western culture. But a Hindu is close to a scientific comprehension beyond the specific.

Though in its manifest forms, divinity is of necessity multiple, in its ultimate essence it cannot be said to be either one or many. It cannot be in anyway defined. Divinity is represented as that which remains when the reality of all that can be perceived has been denied. It is **neti, neti,** *'neither this nor that'.*

Hence the abstract sound syllable especially heard daily throughout the land, a travelling resonance for visitors anywhere. For instance, locked into the other ascetic images of Siva the Supreme Yogi is **the chanted mantra**, the device for concentrating in quietude, centring the mind. One such, playing on the very syllables indeed of **hamsa**–the sacred bird vehicle, the gander* associated with Brahma, the deity of Creation (see **PANTHEON**).

The temple is not just a place of ceremonial **pradakshina** both for worshippers taking a clockwise circumambulation around all the shrines first, or the main Deity being paraded on waking and before being 'bedded' after the last arati or nightly ritual; nor of puja and visual imagery. It is a place of **sound**, reverberating along its colonnades, and resonating halls. ''*The song of the inner gander,*' Zimmer writes, '*has a final secret to disclose. 'Hamsa, hamsa' it sings, but at the same time, 'sa-'ham, sa-'ham''. Sa means this and 'ham means I; the lesson is 'This am I.'*

◆ Stylised hamsa embroider so many temple friezes in stone to remind the devotee that sound mantra and visual symbol are one and the same, a metaphor for free flight, to soar aloft to self-realisation through disciplined inner development. Then there is final absorption in the Ultimate, spanning spatial infinity which even Icarus could not master. But–only if we learn to centre the mind.

■ **MANU**
 is the pre-eminent example of what is seen as a historical presence or what is yet another metaphor. This is a difficulty facing any Westerner armed with criteria of where empirical evidence lies to prove 'reality'. So what is 'reality'? Turn immediately to **ITIHASA**, the Indian view of history, if you wish to remain clear-headed!

Manu has plagued me all these years exploring the nooks and crannies of India. How many times have I checked his supposed dating and the **codifications** in his name, the **Manusmrti** which weren't just an academic set of social laws handed down like Hebrew Mosaic law.

◆ They sprang to life in no uncertain terms as I arrived in Delhi. **WOMEN** were demonstrating in a way I had never expected these graceful, supposedly submissive, spirits to behave. Orthodox believers in Parliament were re-examining Manu codifications before re-drafting the Hindu Code Bill. And women

---

* Some English texts refer to hamsa as a swan. This is incorrect. It is *Anserindicus, the bar–headed gander.* Those of us in Delhi in the 50s had the famed ornithologist Dr. Salim Ali as our mentor!

too were divided, some shouting outside Parliament, brandishing umbrellas. Patriarchal impositions, Manu's hand in 'ancient times', hilarity about the extraordinary details of a similar codification, the **Kamasutra** of **Vatsyayana** the circa 3rd c CE classic on the art of love.

◆ So who was Manu? Or are there many, each appearing throughout the Vedas, the later Puranas when codes take shape, until somewhere around the second to first centuries BCE the **Dharmashastra** on social behaviour took shape, the **Manusmrti** earlier than **Yajnavalkya's** of the 4th c CE Gupta period.

Dowson's **Classical Dictionary of Hindu Mythology** records the hyped-up version of the progenitor of mankind, **swayambhuva**, self-born 'who existed nearly thirty million years ago'; he floats in as one of the **saptarshi** (the seven sages) saved in the Hindu version of the Ark (see **MATSYA AVATAR**); his name is personally attached to the social tradition of **SMRITI** (heard, not revealed) that became written in the pre-Christian era. Clearly the discussion of dharma and how a person lives took shape in Vedic times. In the MahaB, Manu takes on a mythological presence, the life and times of such a progenitor of the human race, recorded as 4,320,000 a remarkably scientific connotation (retrace to **KALPA**). So what is 'reality'?

A plethora of books are now appearing investigating the subtle conditioning factors of such ancient influences. Sage Publications (Mumbai) carry many titles on the growing investigation **by women** authors such as **Leela Dube: Women and Kinship** (1997); also see **Kalima Rose: Where Women are Leaders** (Vistar Publications, New Delhi, 1992). Mentioned earlier also **Jamila Verghese: Her Gold and Her Body** (Vikas, Delhi).

■ **MEHNDI**
....from Urdu, **HENNA**, derived from the Arabic word **heena**. A form of body decoration, especially considered a beautification of the female form, which is applied throughout the north African Muslim world, the Middle East, and into the South Asian peninsula. The dried green leaves of a privet-like bush (*Lawsonia inermis*) are mixed with lime and water to make a paste, then packed into a cone for squeezing like icing a cake. Most often applied to young women before their marriage by family members, the designs are intricately beautiful, sometimes symbolic certainly for Hindu ritualistic decorations, including swastikas and lotuses, whether drawn by free hand or stencilled on the body, around the breasts, or palm or upper hand or on the soles of feet. Once the mehndi is washed off the reddish-orange design remains like a tattoo for nearly two weeks. In the sticky heat of monsoonal summer, henna is said to be a cooling agent in hair, on the palm of the hand and soles of the feet.

■ **MIRACLES**
India is perhaps the only country in the world along with China that can cause a real pathological love for it or hatred of it. There is no middle way, of sanguine emotion–bland and uncommitted this way or that; or on the other hand, wafted

lyrically into the Milky Way stream of magic or body-blowed below the belt with, literally, bile in the gut and convulsive frustration about to devastate the inflamed aorta.

I have been at times ready to hit my head quite physically against a wall, more to stop **thinking of having to cope**, burning tears of angry frustration have added a delicate lacework of decoration to a throbbing temple–alas, no pineal gland of kundalini energy sent me zooming however as a result into calming self-realisation as some Indian official blocks one's path; or an Indian Airlines plane unaccountably rests on the tarmac with 'no refreshment allowed before take off ' announced pedantically ad infinitum; or the bus goes without you; or the suitcase comes lurching off the carousel, caught in some roped package which is bursting at the seams, tipsy as a bibulous party.

And then a miracle occurs. Such as on Howrah Bridge, Kolkata after a remarkably efficient comfortable, unbelievably smooth journey on the Rajdhani Express–one of India's inter-city crack trains. But no steam locomotives to bring the one-time romance of India's gigantic railway system back in all its powerful glory.

◆ **The Miracle Of Howrah Bridge—and then the pathological magic takes over**
Three red-turbaned authorised porters swooped on our array of luggage and raced off amid what seemed like two million people into the maelstrom of Calcutta outside. We had stepped off the impressive Rajdhani Express from Delhi, a 19-hour overnight journey. I trailed behind trying to photograph a nervous husband ever-fearful of losing luggage, so I appeared more Asian than the Asian wives–far more than three paces behind! The porters were making for the illegal taxi ranks (they charge more to obvious foreigners like us) lying around the corner from the official taxi queue itself–'an hour's wait' according to the cowboy of a taxi driver, a real goonda up-to-no-good young Bihari, who rounded me up hastily. Before we had even time to negotiate a fare, he launched himself with élan past a startled policeman who blew his whistle ineffectually. At the rate we were moving, whirling like a possessed dervish between all that moves on Howrah Bridge I had no chance to make a bargain to the new Kenilworth Hotel (small family, refurbished, not your concrete box of a tourist one put up in haste, sterile and all-chromium).

In the centre of the bridge, in the lunch-hour traffic jam and under the noonday sun, a sudden thump caused me to look out of my window. **The rear back wheel had come off**, stuck in a tram line as our driver recklessly had overtaken four lanes of traffic, in the face of another four coming towards us. A tram was determinedly bearing down upon us at the same time.

We had 10 pieces of luggage (too much winter clothing from two months in UK), 40 kg overweight too, in the boot and on top of us. Notwithstanding such extra weight our cowboy leapt out and proceeded on an attempt to jack up the back axle!

I do believe my husband was in a state of shock for when I matter-of-factly took the advice of a stalled motorist beside us–'You'd better get out'–he did ... and without demur! All the tram passengers had likewise disembarked stoically to survey two

M

red-faced 'angrez' as had all the buses bulging forth with Bengalis in their squeezed masses. We then undertook a foolhardy attempt to carry heavy suitcases across the traffic lanes, now all at a total standstill, between lorries, handcarts, stalled cars, other taxis, thousands of bicycles, to the pedestrian lane at the side. And then India's miraculous capacity to cope with such situations materialised.

A porter appears from nowhere to line up the luggage. The grapevine had stretched back the length of the bridge to undisclosed sources of transport. An empty taxi arrives somehow weaving between static cars, lorries, buses. Unlike in the West, seeing our predicament, they actually tried to manoeuvre a space for his noble vehicle. Unbelievable! But that is not the end of it. Our cowboy deserts his stranded and destabilised steed and an irate tram driver trying to move the taxi off the line; he leaps instead into the seat beside our new driver to demand commission for his services up to this point. By this time male adrenalin is working. The only time I ever heard my husband roar like the proverbial Sahib was then... In the untangling traffic, some turning around miraculously in U-turns a London taxi driver would applaud, we sped through–to discover by a miracle of serendipity Padma Subrahmanyam and her dance entourage–family and musicians–resting also in the pleasant calm of this homely hotel before a major performance at Government House. Years before we had met in Western Australia when she had performed as India's cultural representative at our pioneering Indian Ocean Arts Festival. That night by chance we were translated into a magic performance in the spendour of Curzon's one time regal habitat....

We had never once looked back from the lace-curtained rear window to the chaotic centre of Howrah Bridge. Cowards!

◆ **Miracle Two–a humble massage lady**

A crunchy, diminutive woman with wrinkled skin and hands, deep furrowed face and barefooted with tiny rings on her toes. She **thinks** she is in her late 60s—no birth certificate has ever surfaced. She is a massage lady to keep body and soul alive, married as she was at 12, cohabited at 15, lost her **jawan** military police husband at 25. Life is precarious in India. Little compensation, pension schemes rare or non-existent. Then the previous year she had a massive stroke and was paralysed. She was taken to a **vaid**, a healer in the ayurvedic medical system. A learned one, he said some mantras, and prescribed a pigeon a day as diet!

They gather in flocks near the **Jama Masjid** mosque in Old Delhi–a bit like St Mark's, Venice or Trafalgar Square.

Pigeon broth was cooked each day. This she was fed and then the meat with a little rice. **She was cured**–and now look at her as she presses with all her energy, breathing deeply, perspiring with the effort. I get qualms listening as I sink deeper in to the ground. She is bright-eyed, brave, on her own, making her way across the city via three buses–enough to bring on another stroke in itself, especially when boarding a Delhi EXPRESS BUS, privately owned with unlicensed drivers who manoeuvre on the horn and mow down at least one person a day as they career through the jampacked traffic.

Some of her energy flows into me... I pray that she may escape many rebirths into a leisurely life enjoyed by those dusky Ajanta beauties!

◆ **The Miracle Breakfast**

We were sitting anxiously in the early flight Indian Airlines plane on the tarmac at Delhi domestic airport waiting to go to Bangalore.

We were waiting all right! A lot of tapping under a wing, no refreshment, no communication from the pilot, the endless whirring of ineffective air conditioning, a dearth of air hostesses ... Half an hour had gone by since we boarded. And having got up at 5 a.m. to be at the airport an hour before flying time there had been no time for breakfast for our party of West Australians. Already hardened travellers, three weeks on the roads from Ahmedabad via Jaisalmer's beckoning walled-town on the edge of the Thar desert to Bikaner, Jaipur, Delhi... They remained astonishingly stoical.

Businessmen, Indians all, were getting restive. We all had a hollow feeling in the stomach. The airhostesses appeared with tiny plastic cups with plain water in them to assuage our thirst. Oh for a cup of delicious Darjeeling tea in this land where tea is grown! Another 20 minutes ... there were murmurings of discontent. Why no information? What is happening? Please to tell! The airhostesses picked up the bad vibes. How helpless one feels. Why does one ever fly? The captain then announces peremptorily:.

You are deboarding. Please take all your luggage. There is mechanical fault. You please go back into main lounge. Snacks will be served .....

The intercom shuts off. Finito! No apology. A distinguished looking Indian stands up with alacrity:

No we will not deboard. No snacks. We demand full breakfast.

A *frisson* like sharp lightning sparks energy in the early morning lassitude quivering all the way down the plane aisle. An airhostess looks painfully confused. She had no training to deal with incipient passenger mutiny. This grey-haired Indian in a safari suit of impeccable style is now waving his briefcase. That ambivalent stage takes over of cowed passengers suddenly feeling challenged to act, have we the courage to cross the rubicon and launch forth on the unchartered waters of non-violent protest, do we support this lone voice? Once you are upon your feet the impetus has begun. Democracy is standing up to be counted!

No snacks. We demand full breakfast. You tell control tower!

There is still an ominous silence from the cockpit. Our stomachs are stirring at the thought of 'full breakfast'.

'Please to deboard!' comes the command. *'Report to AI office for snack vouchers'.*

Clearly the fine-browed well-groomed Indian is either an IAS officer (too young to be the heaven-born ICS, although there are some still around) or a man of substance. He has either done too much flying that week suffering the exigencies of erratic monopoly air travel or he is used to taking command, when the balance is tipped over and India gets the better of you. Now there are others beginning to feel courage warming the cockles, whatever **they** are, of their hearts. The chant gathers force:

No snacks! We demand full breakfast.

The airhostesses look lamely on. This time the captain, a decent-enough looking guy emerges way up front.

Please will you be getting down! Please report at the AI counter. I have communicated your message.

Now we have to gather up all the inconvenient extra pieces of hand luggage, awkward-sized parcels that poke other passengers which we hopefully had hidden away with the glorious thought that this would be the last time we had to cope with narrow aisles and minimal luggage racks. Thirst is beginning to harass the dry mouth. The seats are so narrow. The aisle is even worse. Is this how purgatory would feel? We clamber into the lurching buses. Mutinous spirits are amassing. Our guiding light is talking to nearby travellers; plans are gathering force as we are off-loading and led through the check-in counters all over again—out into the main concourse with no information about our gloomy future. Three officials at the IA office booth look stony-faced. Our distinguished spokesman is there in front. He wheels around and faces us, one and all:

*You please make your feelings heard. Let us **gherao** them!*

It almost sounds like **guillotine**. It could mean **garrotte**! It actually means **surround**.

No vouchers. No snacks. Full breakfast. Two hundred of us gather in a mass and surround the unyielding officials. And so the full-throated chant goes up while all the luggage is also off-loaded in the middle of the concourse. Other passengers for other planes look distinctly sympathetic. Our tummies are rumbling no end. It is now 9.30 am. We were all on the road by 6.30 a.m.

The refrain gathers body. I have never actually demonstrated before except in an Aldermason-anti-H-bomb march. That was silent. This is quite a jolly shout. It makes you feel good! And it certainly makes the three facing the hundreds look distinctly uncomfortable. Suddenly they disappear leaving an empty cubicle. This infuriates our leader who waves his briefcase again, looking ready to charge.

How much longer does patience last before it goes wham-bang? And snaps?

And then the miracle happens. A rotund IA official appears at the desk and waves the din down:

*You please collect these vouchers and your luggage and proceed to main dining room. **There will be full breakfast**. Replacement plane leaves in one hour.*

A victory for democracy! A victory for the lone Indian voice! A lesson learned. I always had regarded Indians under stress as passive sufferers, not spunky enough to oppose obstructive officialdom. I was wrong—and thank you Mr Indian Official whoever you were at this distance in time (before airlines were privatised) for the breakfast **also miraculously conjured up for over 200 people**—full Western, full Indian, porridge, cereal, rumble-tumble eggs, bacon, toast, Indian fruits, hot steamy Indian soojee, coffee and tea, tucked into to such an extent that when the flashing sign for boarding beeped its red message some of the old guard were determined to finish in style, defying all instructions until fully replete.

At Bangalore we somewhat sheepishly ploughed our way through the disconsolate passengers who not only suffered **their own delay** in the onward flight to Bombay **but an additional hour** added to the three while we ate contentedly musing upon Indian initiatives of a rare kind... and a miracle of 'jumping to', food suddenly supplied... only India could do that when the heart relents. British Airways on a similar ghastly flight experience years later couldn't match this by the aeronautical equivalent of a bargepole!

A Miracle of an Inordinate Degree

That India is still all of a piece is a major miracle! Unity—but not uniformity. Consider the layers upon layers of the huge sub-continent.

- **28 States** plus Delhi and 7 Union Territories with individual states the size of nations, indeed some nations within a nation, the latest **Chhattisgarh** carved out of Madhya Pradesh, in 2000 CE with a population of 18 million, the size of Greece!

- **18 major languages**, nearly half with **different scripts** plus English.

- **8 of the world's major faiths**—Hindu, Buddhist, Jain, Parsee, Jewish, Christian, Islamic, Sikh... these religious populations larger than many nations—800 million Hindus, 120 million Muslims or more, 25 million Christians, 16 million Sikhs—so it goes on!

- There are said to be 80,000 different ethnic/cultural groups.

- **At least 80 million tribal people**, in isolated mountainous or jungle terrain.

- Despite all these exponential challenges (which even China cannot surpass despite being a more regimented society with one common script) the nation's achievements in a self-reliant economy, an impressive industrial base, a wide-ranging smallscale artisan infrastructure plus astonishing advancement in software computer technology and expertise, need to be acknowledged. In implementing such projects as the experimental Remote Area Business Network with telex facilities, satellite earth stations and mobile telephone links unheard of before, makes the nation a force to be reckoned with worldwide. Management skills and world-class scientists and technicians have created a new level of social skills to such an extent that the apocryphal story goes that on his first visit to India, Bill Gates of Microsoft asked the then Prime Minister H D Gowda if some special genes were present in the structure of Bangaloreans! Another Cyberabad is gathering force across the border in Andhra Pradesh—Hyderabad, several satellite 'electronic' cities emerging. This entire infrastructure supported by a middle-income population that exceeds that of the USA or the European Union.

- Extremes seldom seen elsewhere of rich and poor in huge numbers, which, if they were mobilised—and inclined to terrorism witnessed on other continents, could create civil war and social mayhem that would make Naxalite activity in Bihar appear child's play. But India has survived intact.

M

It is to the credit then of any Indian government that sanity and maturity have created a measure of stability amid the tossing waves of India's contemporary politics. The resilience of the ordinary, much oppressed Indian in the lowly income groups of this complex land mass is truly phenomenal.

Another Plus...

India, in all its history, has never invaded another country, nor forced people to believe what they could not. India was also far advanced in astronomical and mathematical research even in Vedic society. **Baudhayana** of that time and **Bhaskaracharya** (circa fifth century CE) led the way for mastering the philosophical concepts of **ZERO**, trigonometry, algebra and calculus. Such capacity for handling numeracy is a gift of its people, giving it an edge now in the 21st century of information technology, space research and astrophysics.

- **A Socio-Economic Miracle–utterly butterly Amul...** (in Hindi *Amulya* = priceless)

Thus goes the jingle advertising the butter you see on your Air India/Indian Airlines platter, the cheese you may now find as tasty as any from Europe, Australia or New Zealand, the dried milk powder for Indian babies, interstate daily milk supply, improved cattle feed, and well over half a million happy farmers in Gujarat. It was not always so.

The White Revolution, as it is now referred to by Indians outside of Gujarat, only really got going in the early 50s. The milk supply of Bombay came under review on Independence. A scientist described it as being the bacteriological equivalent to London's sewage. With Independence, bold men planning in the backrooms of government felt there needed to be a total revolution from the old order of the open market–low prices for the producer/high prices for the consumer, with the middleman taking the profit in between.

Kaira district 50 kilometres southeast of Ahmedabad on the way to Vadodara is unusual. Over centuries its farmers were not subservient bonded labourers or subject to feudal landlords. Gujarati culture has always had a different emphasis with its trading history going back well over 2,000 years; their women by tradition, even if not formally educated, have been encouraged to trade also through textile-design and embroidery, earning money for the family **as well as keeping the cattle**. It defies all Marxist economic theories, in the past denying any cultural input into their simplified economic equations. Entrepreneurship is inbuilt into the culture, influenced by its geographic accessibility to ancient global markets, and caste mobility. (See mention of Patidar Community in **REGIONAL CULTURES**–Gujarati, and David Pocock's book **Mind, Body and Wealth**, Basil Blackwell, Oxford, 1973).

Kaira District, where the Co-operative Milk Producers Union (popularly shortened to Anand–the district headquarters) was set-up, was a centre of the Quit India Movement.

So the spirit of the place was primed for a miracle.

The co-operative started with **six villages** and 250 litres of milk collected a day ...

In 1956 I trekked across Rajasthan before any major roads existed west of Udaipur first to get our car through to my husband flying up on BBC visits to the All India Radio stations north of Bombay, secondly for him to give a lecture at the Harold Laski Institute in Ahmedabad, finally to see the elegantly beautiful Mrinalini Sarabhai dance an experimental ballet (yet another exciting manifestation of advancing independent India responding once more to new influences five decades ago).

There was also the additional incentive of being given a run-down of great enthusiasm by friends in New Delhi about the manager appointed to oversee an unusual pioneering in village India. 'Indomitable', 'indefatigable' were scattered into the introduction. His name was **Verghese Kurien**. You have to be possessed, part-mad, painstakingly diligent to take on such pioneer work when at all turns in a supposedly free market initiative major diary combines such as Nestlé tried to block the entire project from getting off the ground; when these same dairy firms advised that experiments in marketing buffalo milk, cheese making, processed baby foods were not possible in Indian conditions, the 'bacteria' for buffalo milk cheese-making not being present in the milk, that Indian staff were not trained sufficiently in condensed milk techniques to go ahead and mop up surplus in the flush season of milking...so...this is what I wrote on my return to the UK for the January 1960 edition of a London Indian periodical called **Envoy**, started by Krishna Menon:

There was something about the young South Indian, Verghese Kurien, that made me sit up. He had one of those deceptively flippant attitudes to foreigners. He made me feel that I was asking too many unnecessary questions. Knowing myself, probably I was! But I did notice that in his small compact frame, hidden batteries, stored with latent energy, charged when I mentioned a new well-packaged butter different from the white bazaar butter which we had been used to in Delhi.

Mr Kurien glowed in his fierce south Indian pride. 'I help to manufacture that butter. Come to Anand and see.'

Go, I did—Anand is 80 km from Ahmedabad. I shall never regret it, despite the fact that to reach this then gaunt and lonely region of western India entailed the most harrowing journey in a saloon car I have ever undertaken, over trackless wastes and roads which the Chief Engineer of Delhi warned me were 'only jeepable' and where in one wide **nullah** the car had to be lifted out bodily by 10 village men as it began sinking in the pebbly bed—forced then to drive another 35 km to find another crossing over rutted paths driven miraculously by the BBC driver.

The dairy project at Anand has not been called 'one of the most inspiring enterprises ever launched in India' for nothing. Mr Kurien, its manager, and all the other zealous workers there had every reason to feel proud; it not only seemed to be one of the cleanest and most efficient factories but it combined everything that Gandhi would have wished for—he was never against modern technical progress as many of us in the West mistakenly believe, but only against the dehumanising aspects of monolithic structures in industrialization that divorce the villagers from their own soil and their own integrity.

M

Here was a first-class milk-processing plant drawing its daily sustenance–milk–from **125 small villages involving 40,000 farmers**. This was decentralization really working. No farmer had been uprooted. They were continuing to live the life they knew best but they were living it better. Because Anand is a co-operative the major share of the profits, which are now considerable since further products like dried milk (extremely difficult to manufacture because of the high fat content of buffalo milk) and condensed milk are reaching the market, are returned to the member farmers not only in cash bonuses and rewards for unadulterated milk, and better cattle, but in the building of cattle compounds (instead of keeping cattle right next door to human living quarters). **All manner of improvements had flowed from the one basic development even through the 1960s.**

Mr Kurien, ticking over as energetically as his factory machinery, was eager to show us just how this was brought about in the villages. We were swept into one village after another at milking time when the cowdust lay heavy like sunrays in a quiet room, and the first oil lamps were flickering in the exhilarating coolness of dusk (now it is all electrified). His deputy took over the explanation.

In this village there are living 3,000 people. Three hundred and ten are members of the Co-operative. You have to remember, isn't it, that we have only just started. Some farmers, it is so, are hesitant at first. They see government credit and gram[village] co-operatives not functioning properly. Here is just another co-operative, they say. Will it peter out also? But they catch on quickly when they begin to see others having the benefits from our real commercial co-operative.

*First there is the immediate one of ready money. Formerly they were paid half an anna for one pound of milk. Now we are paying them three annas a pound. You see how much exploitation there was before. And each milk producer is getting his money **twice** a **day**. If his milk is better quality he gets more than average payment. You see we are not fooled by watered milk. We pay by **fat** content, not **weight**. Come and see.*

Quite frankly, I was amazed at what I saw. Was this possible in an Indian village with all its lack of amenities, its long tradition too of adulterated milk for sale in the bazaar, its absence of any modern organisation for transport such as we take for granted? I was standing inside a newly whitewashed building with long files of villagers lined up, each with his own small pitcher full of milk, in front of three men: a collector, a sampler and an accountant. The collector took and measured the milk, the sampler selected a test-tube of it, placing it in a small machine which whizzed around to produce the fat content, and the accountant then paid the correct amount. Milk below 6 per cent fat content was just not accepted at all. As a result the fat content of the milk brought in has risen to 7.2 per cent.

This complicated but educative process was going on in a 1,300 square mile area when we visited Anand. Since each producer earned on an average about one to two rupees a day,

over 40,000 rupees was having to be distributed daily in small change as there were no banking facilities in the back of beyond. Yet the painstaking effort of collecting milk (in this climate it cannot be left standing for more than three hours) and distributing money will be infinitely worthwhile if the moral is borne home on the farmer. An Indian peasant is no fool when he is shown a clear case of cause and effect.

By the late 60s, Anand had become the largest milk co-operative in the world, a model for other state dairies, initiating the concept of a 'milk shed' stretching from Maharashtra to Bihar taking in most of the states in between. By then Australian and New Zealand Governments had also implemented plans to train technical and quality control staff, who also in a chain reaction were in turn to take these improved dairying techniques to other 'developing' countries. Gandhi would have rubbed his hands with glee!

In 1973 I was back in Gujarat again on a mission, collecting artefacts for a major teaching exhibition in Yorkshire–**East Comes West**, a part of its aim to create a rapport with the many Gujarati families settled there. Standing outside the new cattle feed station just launched and reading the plaque on the wall expressing thanks to **Oxfam** and the citizens of Glasgow and Clyde Valley for the £50,000 they had raised, so helping to build this factory, I was overcome by a sense of real frustration in that only I was seeing the results of their generous donations. In my hands were the pellets of vitamin reinforced feed, ready for packing into 70 kilo sacks to be shipped to far places. Behind me were the young team, girls as well as men, from all areas of this multilingual nation, working in the laboratories–explaining things to me with such enthusiasm and conviction. 'These people do not need our patronage: they need our comradeship in help in order to help themselves' is what I wrote then.

200,000 buffaloes benefited also by this great act of giving by people in Scotland, tucked away in their city homes and tiny hamlets, people who have no conception of Indian conditions at all. Such an act of the imagination seen in these concrete terms on a sparkling hot morning in Gujarat, with green parakeets screeching and long-tailed monkeys loping through the dried lands, made my head and heart sing.

1996

Kurien was still in charge having received the prestigious **Magsaysay Award**. 'INITIATIVE not FINITIATIVE that's what we need mor e of in India,' he exclaimed, bounding around the room with yo-yo intensity. 'It's not good enough to start something, you've got to have the ability to follow it through and keep it ticking over.'.... and surely all at Anand had done just that. Nearly a **thousand societies** and **half a million members** exploded in these decades into over **70,000 societies** and **nine million members**!

◆ Chidambaram–the miracle of spontaneous dance

This is a personal miracle because it took over 20 years for both my husband and myself to visit the gigantic temple complex of **CHIDAMBARAM** together. We had an especial 'feel' to do so having called our home in London after the temple because of the deep interest we felt in Indian music and dance. From the very first classical music concert at Diwali within a few days of our first arrival in India on a crisp and brilliantly golden day in November we had crossed that mental rubicon many Westerners certainly in those days still regarded as a musical barrier–a jangling cacophony of sound.

And dance in all its forms had entranced us on first encounter. Dr Narayana Menon had then ignited the spark, explaining there were as many priest-musicians to play at the morning 'awakening' of the massive shrine to Shiva–Nataraja at Chidambaram as there were days of the year!

That type of miniscule information tends to lodge amongst the molecules of my brain and gather its own momentum. For me, I was none too pleased when in our first long drive back to Madras with children from Trivandrum my husband, like many a man, decided we had to go direct from A to B. He had to deliver a lecture to the British Council and Indian teachers of English by Radio the next day. My impetus, on the other hand, is the open-ended swastika. Take to the crooked path. Chidambaram beckoned. Only 300 km to the southwest but with monsoon rains, dangerous edged roads (in fact no edge at all between dirt, sand and gravel) and narrow width (Five Year Plans had not caught up with the traffic improvement in this early decade of the new India) we drove straight to Madras. But the mind fretted–and then in 1979 **Dr Padma Subrahmanyam** stepped in with a pounding rhythm and her attendance as India's official artistic delegate to the pioneer Indian Ocean Arts Festival, Western Australia.

Padma has been called 'a formidable dynamo of daring and initiative'. Having studied sculpted dance forms and theory in many temples and with scholars and temple pandits in south India for at least 12 years she had the **DIKSHITAR** temple priests–usually haughty and aloof, a race of privileged learning being the keepers of the intricate world of Hindu temple hierarchy and ritual–in the palm of her hand. And the temple devoted to the dance, where the gleaming magnificently aesthetic Nataraja, Shiva of the Dance, presides is Chidambaram!

And so after the Festival a few months later we found ourselves with Australian friends of India, the Westrips, Joyce born in Bangalore and an old Bishop Cottonian, in Madras sharing a journey with Padma and her family. The karmic cycle was potent–and complete.

♦ She was to dance at the Centenary Celebrations of Annamalai University, prestigious Tamilnadu seat of traditional learning and many eminent scholars. And where is Annamalai?–**very close to the town of Chidambaram and the immense temple.**

We followed in the wake of our learned and enchanting guru down that 300 km road I had been denied 22 years earlier! She had already inspected the vast marquee where she was to dance the next day, an astonishing example of India's capacity for artistic expression even at the lowliest of levels–the whole area, larger than two football pitches, it seemed to stretch into infinity, with every upright strut (and there were hundreds) swathed in garlands and ribbon. Obviously in a land where manpower is

supreme such fine detail of beautiful embellishments is just a matter of course and of subtly-wafted flower scents mingling. The magic again!

Padma, wishing blessing before her performance, visited the sanctum sanctorum of the Nataraja–having gained permission to approach the innermost shrine where Shiva in all his golden glory set the world turning again in gigantic creative processes as he raised his foot in the motion of release–and energy flowing out (turn to **NATARAJA**).

(turn to **NATARAJA**).

And the miracle was already dispelling maya! This was the one day of the year when Shiva danced out of all the swaddling clothes of red saris and huge sparkling diamonds that normally throttled and hid that magnificent bronze icon of scientific truths. Followed by a retinue of every conceivable kind of priest with all our menfolk stripped to the waist but allowed to retain their Western trousers (a liberal dispensation compared with Kerala where Indian dhoti, lungi or mundu would have been demanded) we followed in her wake.

Moved by the Deity's presence, Padma and her close family seemed inspired. Suddenly animated Tamil spilled all around us. It transpired that because of our own devotion to Indian arts and their promotion **we were to be remarried by the senior priest in front of the shrine!** Everybody appeared to be running. Ghee, milk, rice and tulsi 'materialized'–and within minutes–another mystification as if conjured by magic.

And so, dutifully my husband of 34 years and I held hands before the Shiva lingam, repeated some Sanskrit slokas, cast rice and other edibles, milk poured over our hands and bowed in namaskaram. The last arati was now to take place so, withdrawing, somewhat dumbfounded and overcome by the sudden course of events while nadaswarams stridently shook the heavy evening air, a cluster of other functionaries rang temple bells, garlanded the lingam, carried trays of tiny light diyas and brass lamps, scattered holy water and chanted at breakneck speed the formula slokas (very different in atmosphere from our own simple spontaneous ceremony). The night ceremonies were over. The shrine curtains were pulled together. A last glimpse of glistening gold–and Shiva could remain in equipoise, half way between the static and the about-to-begin.

We were dispersing, Padma now quietly meditative after animated whispered talk with some of the learned priests. The long dark colonnaded areas lay in shadows as the throngs dispersed; distant clatter of bells in other shrines ceased their ringing sounds. Echoes of hurrying footsteps resounded along the smoothed flagstones. We were by the tall flagstaff pole .... **and then Padma, just in her ordinary sari took pranam of the stones beneath here, turned to look back at hovering deities in her mind's eye .... and began to dance, possessed of a palpable energy addressing the golden pole as though it, itself, was the living presence.**

"She is 'married' to Shiva," whispered her brother. *"She has deep feeling, a true devotion in the dance."*

There was nothing more to say. We stood transfixed. Some village women, small children and a peasant man passing out from the evening worship caught sight of the vision–and sank to the floor.

Sixteen years later it is not even Padma in all her glory dancing, carried away into another world, entranced, that still vibrates in Shiva's inner eye of wisdom, a momentary glimpse of the sublime but rather the look of awe and wonder in one woman's eyes as she sank onto the flagstones in a devotional obeisance.

The Goddess was dancing before her. Potency was in the air. An epiphany had occurred .... for that all-believing village woman also ... and many years later wisdom dawned on me, that sometimes we are not meant to take the crooked path each time we are so impelled .... not until the karmic time is right. And that had taken nearly 25 years to gestate from that frustrated journey with a husband deadset on reaching Madras in a straight line!

♦ A Miracle On The Road That Kim Travelled

Collective gallantry is not dead or it certainly wasn't in the golden era many of us enjoyed in New Delhi in the 1950s.

For the sake of young children, in typical memsahib fashion, the home and husband were temporarily forsaken for the healthier summer atmosphere of Shimla. British ghosts still whispered in the deodar trees in their appropriate stately magnificence. Geoffrey Kendal's **Shakespeareana Company** was touring in the vicinity adding to this haunting Raj ambience, as also did the little Gaiety Theatre repertoire (still oh! so British).

The Cathedral on the Mall and the mock Tudor architectural frontages were the ultimate backdrop of, confusingly, middle class Britain against which the Indian Army stationed in Shimla to protect the as yet mountainous track to Tibet (unmotorable then) paraded on a Sunday morning. Resplendent in their uniforms and dashing military moustaches you could have sworn you were in Aldershot, Surrey quaffing beer after church on a Sunday morning instead of flirting with distinguished-looking Sikhs out for their constitutional. Kipling could have walked right back in and taken his place with all of us, even welcomed by Indians (see **PARADOX** and discounting what Harvard professors say!).

And then a very Hindu occurrence came about—that 'other India' to be commemorated down on the plains, then steaming with awesome humidity.

The event to be marked–**the first total solar eclipse after Independence**. After the Kumbh Mela this was the next impressive mela in which anyone with the least curiosity about the Hindu view of life as practised at ground level far from the abstruse metaphysics of scientific philosophy would be able to observe and participate. It was to be marked at that most numinous site of symbolic clash and intervention of divine protection–**Krishna** at **Kurukshetra**, the ground = *kshetra* of the Kuru clan.

In mythology anti-gods **Rahu** and **Ketu** as stellar bodies associated with the ascending and descending phases of the moon are regarded as disruptive to order in the firmament, Rahu swallowing Ketu in his tail, and trying constantly to devour sun and moon, so causing eclipses. Already people were on the move from all over India in their bullock carts and rustic buses (no video coaches, sleek with modcons for the burgeoning middle class of today!). Ever curious to understand all my guru had ever clarified for me I took a deep breath and a pilgrim bus (there being no other transport) 9,000 ft down in to the sauna bath of the Punjab plains. So be it!

Donning shalwar/kameez for convenience as well as modesty, though not a familiar garb for Western women at that time where 'going native' was still an attitudinal 'hangover' on the part of some British expatriates if one ventured into sari or any kind of Indian dress, I set off. But I had been presented with a truly traditional shalwar gathered on the cross in remarkable fashion on drawstring like true pyjamas in which **four waistlines** would have felt comfortable. Kawal Singh, Khushwant's wife, had insisted I wear the pyjamas as the most sensible for travel. (She was right and a generation following on revolutionised these residual Raj attitudes for all time. Now everyone wears them.)

And so I clambered into a very crowded bus, mostly hill people as passengers–**pahari log**–and a few true peasants carrying domestic belongings for the untested mela–big wicker baskets containing squawking chickens, a tiny lamb, pots and pans, a veritable veggie market and cloth-tied bundles of clothes.

Stared down by about 60 pairs of eyes, nevertheless with great courtesy a seat was cleared for me, firangis still being a source of curiosity especially at this level–probably unheard of before. At the moment I sat down on the hard double 'bench' a young man, brash Punjabi student that he was, took the opportunity to slip in beside me. The matter rested there for some time and the interest of other passengers subsided. However, not only were all female antennae at full extension. I was also aware of those eyes behind me, ever watchful!

As we lurched down the dramatic hairpin bends to Kalka (stopping every so often for a good deal of retching and road sickness, the bends enough with a speeding driver to turn any stomach Coney Island loop-the-loop) each lurch encouraged a warmer proximity on the part of my seated companion. Sliding along the wood was inevitable anyway in those conditions.

I should never, however, have answered his conversational ambits, practising his college English but even the proverbial aloofness that my churning stomach dictated seemed to have no effect as I increasingly helped to hold up the rickety metal structure of the side panels by melting into them.

Silence reigned at the rear. A break for *chai* at Kalka didn't help. Neatly and with deft aplomb he manoeuvred to the same position again with a comfortable nuzzling-up feel about him. We had reached the Grand Trunk Road. The one-sided conversation took on a more intimate tone. I silently prayed for that Third Eye of Shiva to shrivel his vital parts but in all of India's myths and parables *that* does not appear to be a scriptural option. Even the turbulent power of Devi in Calcutta was far distant. She can quell even the mighty power of Shiva.

But I didn't reckon with more humble forces.

Suddenly this young student put his arm around my shoulders and gave me a Punjabi squeeze. 'Getting fresh' was the term used in those halcyon days of a relatively innocent world.

M

Equally suddenly mayhem erupted from behind. Everyone was shouting at once at full rural decibel level. A village male cuffed the ruffian on the head. The bus lurched to a rattling stop. The driver now part of the fracas clambered back amongst chickens and kitchenware to find out what the **tamasha** was all about but with everyone shouting instructions or providing a running commentary in broad Pahari dialect I couldn't understand there was a moment of sudden irresolution I still recall...because now I know what taking someone by 'the scruff of the neck' actually means, so clearly is the movement imprinted in memory in that single still moment between two activating forces.

And that was a propulsion of this young male through the cleared door, turfed out onto the roadside of India's most famous route to the high passes and beyond—now into Pakistan. Belongings or none, he was left—forlorn—to find his own way to a holy dip. He would need it to reinstate dharma!

An elderly Sikh, shyly bent down over the empty seat and whispered in English: 'Please forgive us! **Sharam.** He brought shame on us... but may I be asking, where is your good husband?'

My lame answer in the state of perturbation being experienced, was pregnant with many unanswered questions for all those rear pairs of eyes and ears to digest: 'He is with the BBC in Delhi.'

SILENCE... but thank you, busload of Indian villagers wherever you are and good dharma to you!

◆   ... and while on the road, **a Minor Miracle** every day for those who drive in Indian traffic. A taxi driver's wisdom and warning: **You do not need a licence... You need good brakes, good horn and good luck!**

◆   **A Miracle Of Efficient Organisation**

Surfing on the crest of a sound rolling in on the drums as the sun slowly turns the hazy sky of a Delhi winter into crimson streaked with evanescing trailing ribbons of grey, the meticulous lines of cross-marching regiments send a shiver down the spine.

This is Indian street theatre of a rare dimension outpacing even the British at their own game! **The Beating Retreat**. It is on a par with the Edinburgh Castle Tattoo.

If the organisation of the four-hour **Republic Day Parade** on **January 26th** every year is a stunning example of meticulous planning by the Indian Army, the Delhi Police and the City Administration, then the Beating Retreat is the ultimate accolade to efficiency, a declaration to all and sundry not only in India, but those external commentators who invariably record

◆   the anarchic India falling apart at the seams, mudslides, flood and pestilence

◆   the 'picturesque' and bizarre sadhu watching the photographer's every move with praying-mantis beady eye, calculating how much to demand as the camera shutter clicks to a close …the exotic …

◆   or the overwhelming mind-blowing complexity.

...that here is order, impeccable accuracy, every back ramrod straight, each step as if a machine piston moved a thousand knees as one.

Annually every Jan 26 Jan 27 Jan 28

Every traveller should move with haste to join the millions thronging central Delhi's Rajpath where confluences of humanity meet below the rising hill of Lutyens' famous red sandstone architecture. To witness this assertion of India's cultural identity is to experience India at its most impressive.

Youthful gymnastic enthusiasm, tribal dancers, the rainbow-saturated colours emblazoned in people, costumes, imaginatively designed floats from individual states punctuated by tartan capes swirling as the military bands maintain the pace between schoolchildren folk dancing or parading in equally disciplined ranks (in '99 they were, aged 10–11, impressively rollerblading).

And then there are those who have received honours for heroism, handicapped children swaying slowly in the howdahs atop majestic painted elephants heavy with spangled drapery. The Camel Corps' impeccable ranks that leaves a thump in the heart—the tallest of Rajputs moustachioed and crested with starched turbans and cock's-comb pugris pleated and flared, lances shimmering in the morning sunshine, with pennants fluttering as they are held high... to be caught again in silhouette, motionless in the gloaming of the final Beating Retreat two days later.

The finale—'**Abide with me**', almost an echo, then rolling out, arouses that sense of **palimpsest** again as the massed bands reinforce the poignant diminuendo... from British sources! And in conclusion—the lone trumpeter now a shadow, high up on the roofed rampart of the North Block tower, sounds that tear-jerking finale as the flag is lowered in the silence and a flutter of pigeons homing to their own stations on the roof ledge… and then 'an explosion of frothy incandescent blooms'....fireworks.

◆   An unknown staff reporter summed it all up once in impeccable English—another miracle of Indian mastery of such subtle nuances in this malleable language. 'It leaves the viewer' he wrote 'standing **in the cool of spent emotions**... under the mild bright blade of a crescent moon.'

■   **MONSOON**
Hindustani from Arabic = **mausam** = weather
Indeed 'the season' is a truer definition, imprinted deep within the psyche of anyone who has lived continuously in India, especially the landlocked area of north India and the arid Deccan without feel or breath of life-restoring sea breezes. Only then can one appreciate that early Vedic call to the rain-god **Parjanya**. Without the monsoon there would be no India.

It is one of the earliest **hymns 5:83** in the **Rg Veda** (Edgerton translation):

Like a charioteer lashing the horses with the whip, he manifests verily his rainy messengers. From afar roars (as) of a lion arise. When Parjanya makes the rainy mass of clouds
The wind blow forth, lightning flashes fall, plants shoot up, the heavenly light-space overflows. Refreshment is produced for the whole world when Parjanya favours the earth with his seed.

The hymn says it all.

Potency, fertility the **bija** seed. The lusty stallion. The **maruts,** granters of rain from **Indra's** heaven. **Varuna** and earlier gods at the edges of time, roaring, thundering, implanting the embryo. The great water vessel pouring. Flooding. India, the tropical germination, overwhelming, nature bursting forth like the Ganga in flood, out of control. It is all there, very different from Europe's cool clarity, the northern hemisphere of ordered crops.

The last lines of the hymn begin:

You have rained down rain: now kindly check it!

... you have inspired hymnal devotion for creatures (priest-poets)

There speaks the anonymous rishi contemplating his new home some 6,000 years ago.

To stand under a corrugated iron roof and listen to the staccato machine-gun fire clatter of huge pellets of rain, caught in a heady-smelling warehouse of ginger corms in old Calicut is a psychic transformation. But Delhi after three years unabated with two weak monsoons was an inebriation of every nerve cell and bodily fibre when out of towering blue-grey cumulus, India's bellowing elephants—so often in painting tradition symbolising the coming of the rains—break through the storm clouds. Sparking snakes of lightning flash. Thunder cracks, shuddering through solid trees of Lodi Gardens. Our children defy all danger to dance on the lawn, naked, as the giant torrential first drops pour down.

Indians also go berserk as adults—writing feverish love poetry. Tansen the musical genius of the Mughal court composed raga **Megh Malhar** so appropriate in its wistful joy for this season. The legend is that his skills were so powerful and his voice so magical that his singing of this raga 'called forth the rains' (**megha = cloud; mal = dust; har =** taking away, stealing).

This is one of the most evocative of north Indian ragas, described as 'lustrous like the rare blue lotus.' As the parched land gasps for watering sustenance so the lover yearns for the consolation and embrace from the beloved, human first, implying the Divine ultimately. As the torrential rain swamps land, village, humans so the poignancy of enforced separation (**viraha**) from the beloved is portrayed, not only in evocative tones and in yearning quatrains but in the **ragini miniature paintings** depicting the moods of ragas. Lightning slashes across indigo blue sky. Huge ponderous clouds coagulate. Peacocks strut their stuff. The lady with her tanpura is cast down, all forlorn.

Note: the symbols + (plus) and –(minus) preceding a note indicate that the pitch is raised or lowered by a microtonal interval.

Acknowledgement: pianist John Barham

This is 'the season' of seeking out lovers and swings = **hindola**, keeping cool when it is hot and sticky. **Hindola raga** is very romantic. So many miniatures, sparkling gems of painted pigments and gold, embellished jewelled portraits of Radha and Krishna cavorting amid burgeoning nature, tumescent leaves curling to the weight of luscious rains feeding the roots of tropical plants, say it all. The cloud—megha—becomes the metaphor messenger blown by tropical storms to greet a lover, parted in distant terrain.

This is also 'the season' of joy when the farmer out on the dry lands beyond Hampi's extraordinary bouldered hills, iron stone burning hot with the sun, rubs his hands with glee; when the burdened peasant woman for once can watch the harsh dried runnels in the cracked earth near her mud hut (yet beautifully rice-paste decorated home) in Orissa and relax. The **kalash** will fill from fresh water without the aching grind of carrying it back from a distant well. Money will be flowing in from the crops that will now sprout rapidly and Diwali, four months ahead, can truly be celebrated. And the peacock will strut... the way a memory is still retained in that first long car journey to Kashmir. The first monsoon, but light and miserable that year, had reached Delhi. A rise before dawn, car packed to the rooftop, excited children, a huge ice pack, and one of the first new water containers to remain cool for 12 precious hours... and up the Grand Trunk Road en route to reach the cooler foothills before the now moist heat of the day made us stick to everything, no airconditioned cars except for the very rich! Miles and miles of sugarcane, reaping the first full flush of new irrigation channels from the storage of the Bhakra Nangal dam upstream; camel trains of cauliflowers stacked high on their wooden-wheeled carts (no rubber tyres until a decade later) lumbering down to the old Delhi markets.

And then the **mor** (**mayur** in Sanskrit) in all his male splendour, came out on the roadside, prancing, dancing, stamping his feet in a curled stance, the Kathakali dancer of his species, the aureole tail shivering and shimmering its splayed feathers, the auspicious blue-green-orange eyes beckoning us onwards. We ground to a halt. Bicycling villagers laughed massive displays of white teeth, pleased at our amazement, 'You like our national bird? It is sacred, no shooting, please.' They even inspected the car humorously to see if we had guns for shikar. And then shook hands, amiably, confusing me even further in the learning curve, having been warned on first going to India to do 'namaste' in greeting.

'Indians don't like touching so don't shake hands'. One learns...

c. 400 CE

India's greatest known poet Kalidasa clearly was overcome also by the impact of India's enormous skies when he penned **Meghaduta, the Cloud Messenger**, the touching poem of a yaksha who because he neglected his duties (**dharma** of a social kind) in attending upon **Kubera**, the representation of wealth, is exiled for a year leaving a new bride. Sending messages to her from the mountains that divide north from south India, upon the peak where he ponders in lonely misery

a cloud that charged the peak in mimic fray
as an elephant attacks a bank of earth in play.

Jayadeva in his 13th century love poem **Gita Govinda**, as poet to the court of the King of Bengal, uses familiar imagery of all those very air currents the monsoonal season stirred up in his own tumultuous weather environment. After all Cherrapunji, not so far away in the northeast has an average of 1,080 cm of rainfall—very different from arid west Rajasthan with just over 10 cm!

The wind from the Malayan range seeks Shiva's mountain,

to plunge in its coolness
As if tortured by heat from the coils of the serpents dwelling there in its caves
(the hollowed roots of sandalwood trees)

Endnote: Vouching for the truth of the terror of flying through monsoonal clouds and for vivid descriptions of the monsoon laced with hilarious Indian humour read ***Alexander Frater****'s delightfully funny **Chasing the Monsoon** (Penguin, London, 1991). It is compelling reading. Endorphins will vitalize your frame!

■ **MUDRA** (n. *Sanskrit*)
originally used in reference to 'a seating posture' or 'final closure' when undertaking yoga, a gesture after the breathing, the stretching of muscles, the exercise of bone comes to rest in the completed **asana**, the hands rest in equipoise, in the deep lap of **dhyana = meditation**. Another is the **abhaya mudra** reminiscent of the Pope preaching to the massed crowds in St Peter's Square in Rome at Easter, **his right hand raised with open palm forward** in the same gesture of blessing: **'Fear not, for I am here.'** (see **DANCE**). Because dance was part of temple worship, and presented narrative in mime it is assumed the mudra was the crowning seal to the ritual.

■ **MUGHAL EMPIRE**
It comes as a surprise to discover that there were 17 rulers in India who could rightfully be called Mogul, Moghul, or Mughal in the dynasty that epitomises yet one more extraordinary cycle of consolidation in India's long, long history. This setting in motion once again of the Golden Age **chakra** begins with **Babur** in **1523**, with his incursions in search of territory he felt legitimately his own, to compensate for his lost birthright of Ferghana and Samarkand (in today's Uzbekistan Republic).

Coming from a line of shifting power bases in central Asia north of the Himalayan—Tibet barrier, which had often probed tenuous thrusts into northwest India in previous centuries, and with Turko-Mongol blood in his veins, he perhaps felt he was coming home when he finally defeated the Muslim Lodi sultanate on the legendary battlefield of Panipat in **1526**—itself symbolic and redolent of ancient battles 5,000 years earlier.

This then is a second wave of Islamic settlement very different from that of **1026 CE** when **Mahmud** of **Ghazni** landed on the Gujarat west coast, plundering Somnath temple, killing (it is recorded) 50,000 devotees, an Afghan terrorrist of his time.

Babur laid the foundations, quite miraculously despite the few years he sojourned in India longing for the cool sweet air of the mountain country and the muskmelons of his birthplace, of an entity far more important than the fitful Muslim sultanates of the previous 300 years. Considering the disparities of race and creed with the Hindu/Buddhist/Jain/Muslim mix of the 14th–15th–16th centuries, Babur was more than a pillaging warrior despite his ancestry. He had a literary, even a poetic soul. One of the first things he did on finally reaching Agra was to create a garden with running water and he complained there was no ice in this hot land of 'Hindostan' (see Spear's **A History of India**, Vol 2). It is even stranger considering his ancestry, his two most famous ancestors being—ever on horseback—cavalry nomads…

Chengiz Khan 1155–1227 ravaging lands as far as eastern Europe's Dnieper River was grandfather of Babur's more immediate ancestor **Timurlane**. A man of many spellings (also see English dramatist Christopher Marlowe's **Tamburlaine**–the tale of **Chaghatai Timur Turk**) he had ruthlessly sacked Delhi in 1398… galloping in at the head of 'ninety thousand Mongolian horsemen.'

Pyramids of heads are recorded as being left in village after village, the Punjab countryside soaked in blood.

How To Remember Who Followed Whom
On encounter with this prolific **dynasty** the unfamiliar traveller can suffer a total mental block. Too many powerful men (and astute queens also wielding power!), too many family feuds, tombs galore for the Muslim custom of burial (Hindu rulers for millennia cremated and lost to ash and smoke curling in the air, not a headstone in sight to signify where Ashoka, Chandragupta, Harsha may have lived and died).

♦ I found my brain reach saturation point taking BBC visitors to the Taj Mahal again and again—but what a privilege! Emperors were a jumble until one day, trying to remember the right order of those who were contemporary to the significant age in Europe that led also to a golden Renaissance, the initials of these elusive rulers settled into an appropriate acronym, like completing a puzzle. The acronym Bha-jsha… **B**abur, **H**umayun, **A**kbar, **J**ehangir, **Sh**ah **J**ehan and **A**urangzeb = **bhajsha**, a very Persian sounding word! (Indeed, shift the aspirate and lo and behold, a Persian word emerges… **badshah** = ruler, king!)

Then fissiparous tendencies set in once again, disintegration at the edges in Maharashtra, the Deccan, upper Punjab, decadence and a lost sense of purpose amongst rulers who followed with only love of show and pleasure to while away their days. Delusions of grandeur (despite empty shell structure), dissolution and disillusion followed as the British in Bengal and Madras filled the vacuum and the last of the line was exiled to Burma. **Bahadur Shah II** died in **1862**—longing for a handful of India's dust to scatter on his foreign grave.

Language
The difficulty of transcribing the spelling of this dynasty lies in English not being a phonetic language unlike the Persian/Urdu, which employs only three consonants, MGL, to spell Mughal.

Urdu was the composite language eventually evolved from a

mixture of Hindi syntax of the indigenous populace with the introduction of lyrical Persian vocabulary at court level–especially the nouns, verbs mainly remaining from Hindi roots. A majority of the Muslim population were Hindus converted at rural level so the language of rulers, soldiers and administrators, fused over 300 years or more with the popular dialects. Persia and its civilization had an enormous influence through the Mughal settlement in India. Even as far south as Thanjavur, Spear recalls a European missionary using Persian as the language of the court administration to converse with the local raja.

Mughal:
ک ر = کر = meem
غ ن = غ = ghain
ل = ل = laam

The Mughal Legacy of Cultural Splendour

Over the years fortunately many books on the Mughals have emerged but in India especially some charmingly illustrated pocket-size booklets one can actually carry around, not at all like the very important three volumes commissioned by Emperor Akbar–the **Ain-i-Akbari**, and the **Akbar-Nama** by the leading Indian intellectual of his day–**Abul Fazl** (translated heroically and published, some 2,500 pages by **H Beveridge** in Calcutta in 1907!). Books that I have found very helpful are **Bamber Gascoigne**'s classic **The Great Moghuls** (Jonathon Cape, London, 1971), **Louise Nicholson**'s **The Red Fort** (Tauris Parke Books, London, 1989) and the fund of illustrated information in the London National Portrait Gallery publication, **The Raj**, during the 1990–91 exhibition of that title... and (by an Indian editor) **P N Chopra**, **Social Life During the Mughal Age** (Agra, 1963).

♦ Symbolic of the difference which marks Mughal Islamic society from that of the earlier **Afghani** Muslim **Lodis, Khiljis** (who did take Indian Rajput and Kashmiri wives) **or Turko-Syrian Ghaznis** is the very nature of the huge building programmes and the arts instituted by **Emperor Akbar** once he had established his name–**Akbar** means **great**, and **Akbar the Great** he doubly was in his long half century reign.

Conclusion

It is estimated that at any one time the Mughal Emperors ruled over approximately **120 million peoples** who could rightly be called Indian; they and their cohorts represented only 20% of a faith that included many Hindu converts from lower castes, as well as those threatened by the sword to conversion, and those taken in slavery.

And yes! The Mughal line of descent still exists... in an obscure suburb of Hyderabad (still redolent of Muslim culture) the **great granddaughter of Bahadur Shah II** still lives. Elderly Begum Laila Umahani and her considerable family appeared in colour photographs with an article about them in the **November 1998** issue of **Discover India**. And the lines continue with the Begum's two surviving sons, and grandsons. **Babur lives on!**

Why a 'Golden Age of Mughal Rule'? It's Cultural Flowering

What was it then that enabled the **Great Moghuls**–as they are often called in the West–to add such a sparkle to history, to transcend in fact the narrow confines of their own ethnicity and weave a tapestry suffused with vivid colours contributed by many Indians whose ancestry was very different?

1. From Babur onwards each emperor appears to have a **conscious destiny**, a love of documentary response akin to that of the Normans, a sense of purpose in history like William the Conqueror. In fact the chronicles that Abul Fazl recorded in Akbar's reign have been the Indian Doomsday Book of that 16th century age. Babur and Akbar both turned to the pen to record their daily lives and what was about them–**the Baburnama** and the **Akbarnama**. They were prolific–very Indian as well. I know, myself! Such expansiveness is a very Indian quality where zero becomes infinity in no time at all.

2. **Strong administration** all the way down the line from the internal palace daily regime in **protocol** as to who could approach the Emperor and where, very hierarchical but useful in giving the proud Rajputs a sense of place and importance in the reconciliation process after battle, as provincial governors. They as nobles were incorporated as other Hindu governors were into the imperial hierarchy, responsible for recruitment of their own forces to maintain order regionally. For this they were rewarded with cash salaries from the central treasury. **Dr Christopher Bayly** wrote the following explanation of the efficient bureaucracy which was the result of inspired thinking on the part of all the Mughals on how to run an empire long before the British who are usually credited with its creation–Parkinson's Law and all that!

The Mughal empire was a construct of the pen as much as of the sword. A skilled Persian-writing bureaucracy comprising Hindus as well as Muslims dispensed imperial justice, kept records of rights and, above all, collected the land revenues. These revenues, systematized and reassessed during Akbar's reign, were paid in silver rupees ... High productivity in agriculture and a flourishing internal and external trade in manufactures were necessary to keep money flowing around India and into the imperial coffers.

After 1765, when they became revenue managers of Bengal, the British adapted the Mughal system of land revenues to their own purposes...

The Raj Exhibition Catalogue

3. **A unifying spectacle** in the **Durbar** and the daily presentation–a **darshan** in fact showing the Emperor to his people. (In contemporary India this could be likened to the Republic Day parade, on January 26, involving a far-flung citizenry, creating a sense of pride in a physical 'coming together'.

4. **An effective salary system** probably for the very first time–and in cash, which flowed in ready silver, collected from an effective taxation system way out in the fields and from crop produce, to top officials. In this organisation the Hindu community of **Marwaris** played a leading part (see **FINANCING INDIA**).

5. As a result of this less haphazard payment system than the spoils and looting of earlier hit and run Sultanate Afghani raiders, a **dependent cavalry** was enlisted at all points of the compass and the local rajas rewarded with land grants according to numbers recruited–second nature to the Rajputs. Indians of all

M

cultures were brought into the system. There was a shift in emphasis from the harsh militancy of earlier Sultanate rule when even **zimmis**, those who were regarded as beyond the Book (Qur'an) idolaters and polytheists in the eyes of the orthodox ulemas or law-makers, though they fell within the protection of the law, still had to wear distinctive marks on their dress to distinguish their non-Muslim background and also as landowners or peasant farmers or business people, had to pay the **jizya** or poll-tax. Such indignities Indians had to suffer as indigenous peoples in their own land!

6. **Celebration of the arts** which employed thousands of artisans.

Carpets, textiles as wall hangings, personal vestments, the embellishments carved upon the solid wall were all pervaded by the same lyricism so expertly fashioned in the miniature painting. A delicacy of execution channelled that inner Mughal yearning for the verdant gardens they had relinquished in cooler Asian environments. Only Kashmir could reproduce that Monet/Manet quality of the resplendent garden of many hues.

♦ **A stunning architectural programme**—the Red Forts in Agra and Delhi, Sikandra the distinctive and majestically constructed mausoleum for Akbar on the Delhi-Agra road. The Jama Masjid in Delhi; Jehangir's Tomb and Aurangzeb's Badshahi Mosque; the Shalimar Gardens in Kashmir on the outskirts of Srinagar, a favourite summer house for the Agra and Delhi Court whose long journey by lumbering elephant, palanquin and horse cart must have taken an entire month; and baroque imambaras in Lucknow in the 1700s. Interspersed with solidity of shimmering marble and lustrous pink sandstone; the incredible delicacy of those chiselled *jalis* (*jaal* = mesh) that not only allowed free flow of air but the aesthetic play of light and shade beloved by the Mughals. So very different from the muscular and heavy architecture of the earlier Muslim invaders who never settled and became 'Indian'. Compare Tughlakabad (Delhi) or the Ahmedabad Islamic inheritance with the delicacy of embellishment in later times. One is a bull-necked Boxer facing the world in aggressive macho stance. The other a courtly connoiseur of fine taste. Both had a cruel side but so did Tudor England! A critical mass gathered with Mughal genius with a renaissance as in Europe at the very same period. 'Ripeness is all' as Shakespeare rightly reminds us. And a remarkable synthesis—'INDIAN-NESS' again.

♦ **Encouragement of fine textiles**—the giving of shawls for instance to an honoured guest was part of royal etiquette and even continued as a custom of gift-giving by British Viceroys. Catalogues on the history of textiles of the period list at least 140 different terms for the different woven chintzes, cottons, muslins, wool, silk weaves traded out of India. In fact India was a major world market in Mughal times, rivalling Europe.

On my eighth visit to that ultimate miracle of construction—the Taj Mahal, I had the luxury of just sitting on the grass, watching the world go by, and contemplating the indescribable. Of course it is for the eloquent poignancy that created the Taj Mahal that Shah Jehan will be forever

remembered. Who knows how conscience-stricken a ruler of his time can be, raised as an imperious ruler, born with the testosterone factor of his Mongol-Turkish forbears that he subjects his wife, **Mumtaz**, whose Arabic name means 'Crown of the Palace', to accompanying him on his military campaigns in the most rigorous of conditions. That she dies at the age of 39 giving birth to their 14th child is no surprise! A seachange comes over Shah Jehan. Two years of mourning are announced. He loses impetus and interest in the affairs of state.

And an idea is born—a mausoleum of such perfection that only 20th century corrosion threatened it, yellowing the marble, eating away at the fabric, chemicals, from a power station, the demands of our technology age, over 200 local industries also haphazardly allowed to establish themselves higgledy-piggledy around Agra—the final insult to a vision of kings...from 1632-52—its main architect a Persian, Isa Khan.

And look at the neck before the white marble of the dome discolours. Built during 20 years of the most painstaking artistry and careful geometry and mathematics, engineers of the 17th century have so perfected a dome within a dome, that the outer shell is able to soar, a 'necklace' of moulded and ribbed carved stone alone anchoring it to the cylindrical base, grounded in red sandstone that can only be seen high up from the minarets. And atop in all its delicacy the frilled splayed finial with its golden bobbles, a far cry from Humayun's dome—plain but aesthetically pleasing in its own way.

Here in Agra one never fails to experience the electric 'charge' as though standing in an artistic Cape Canaveral waiting for a visual 'lift off' such is the miraculous effect of soaring beauty despite the weight of stone (12,000 tons in the dome alone) covered with non-porous, translucent marble.

♦ **Even extravagance had its place** so long as the Treasury remained filled in its coffers by a stable working society not disrupted by the internal conflicts and invasions of previous centuries. **Love of gems**—in its way a symbol of power in a land susceptible to symbols. A temptation of larger than life proportions, even the harnesses of Mughal horses dripped in emeralds, rubies and pearls. But the Rajputs sitting on a pile of glittering earth they could mine with ease, had set the trends centuries earlier; cultural qualities were more **Indian** than compartmentalised as **Hindu** or **Muslim**.

7. **Language etiquette**, courtly gesture flowed out in many streams. What has become known as UP Muslim culture, the Lucknowee gentility of Urdu gatherings and polite society of today, all finds its tradition in these standards laid down by Mughals. As also in the **intertwining of musical arts** so noticeable in Hindustani musical traditions even today—Muslim vocalists singing Hindu devotional bhajans, Hindu and Muslim instrumentalists intertwined in marriage, adopting Hindu and Muslim gurus in a commonality of artistic expression in the **gharanas** (musical schools confined to certain family dynasties).

8. Akbar's court shone with not only the narrative paintings which recorded the times in luminous jewel-like miniatures (often Hindu themes painted by Muslim artists) but musicians whose

guru calibre is still referred to by contemporary instrumentalists and vocalists. A long line of Muslims, the **Dagar** brothers to this day are still rendering a mode of music **dhrupad** that traces its roots in **Vedic plainsong**. Its solemn development has been referred to as a 'votive atmosphere', indeed it is in its measured grandeur (see **MUSIC**).

Perhaps in the dance an indication of the great divide in attitude between the two cultures shows up. **Kathak** dance has already been noted in the **DANCE** section, symbolic of the secularisation of its content, taken out of temple context in worship of Krishna, into the more seductive presentation at court. Ananda Coomaraswamy, whom we all read for guidance on first arrival, summed up this divide in a pithy sentence: 'For the Mughal courtier life was a pageant, for the Rajput and the Brahmin (who functioned within this system) life was an eternal sacrament'.

♦ **There was a shadow side to the magnificent artistic achievement and the resplendent standards of living for the elite**—even higher perhaps than that of today's rich.

Within royal families and the prolific number of hangers-on the quixotic and volatile nature of relationships was in the extreme. Sibling rivalries for thrones often led to violent death. Fathers were incarcerated in prison, or exiled like Shah Jehan to an island at Udaipur Lake. High-ranking officers were poisoned. The eyes of architects are alleged to have been torn out after the Taj Mahal in all its perfection was completed. Food from the palace kitchen was double sealed and marked after tasting inspection before reaching the table. The zenana fared no better. With nothing but gossip to occupy minds, and giving birth after servicing the royal males, or to accumulate exotic items of jewellery as reward, treachery threaded its way like a sinuous reptile, sowing suspicion and intrigue...

There was always the vaults below, proof that neither the splendours of the Court nor the consolations of religion could satisfy every woman... some of the caged birds tried to slip out between the bars and, being discovered, were led down to a cell where there was a pit—over the pit a silken rope dangled from a beam.

Taken from a book now out of print: **When Kings Rode to Delhi** by Gabrielle Festing (Blackwood, Edinburgh,1912) the human face of history captures the imagination even today.

The melancholic quality of Islamic culture

It has always struck me listening to north Indian music, even listening to Urdu poetry translated for me by friends, and becoming increasingly aware of the volatile personalities and tragic events that were played out behind this pageantry and opulence, that a thread of melancholy runs through this transplanted Muslim culture.

It is not only Nur Jehan's poetic elegy for herself but the melancholy eyes which stare out from the exiled last Mughal King of Delhi that says it all. Captured with moving clarity and attributed to P H Egerton, the striking photograph in the earliest days of the new technology was taken in **1858**.

The lonely Emperor Bahadur Shah II had reluctantly agreed to remain in Delhi as Emperor for his rebellious followers, caught up in what the British saw as a mutiny of Indian army troops in 1857, but his loyal subjects saw as a sepoy revolt against invidious conditions.

Bundled off to Rangoon by the British incipient Raj, the deposed emperor died a few years later, aged 87, sorrowfully lost in smoking his hookah, and his poetry, his haunting epitaph even quoted today by many an Urdu-speaking friend—and not necessarily Muslim.

Kitna hey badnaseeb Zafar dafn keh liyeh
Do gaz zamin bhi na milikueh yar main
How unlucky is Zafar that it could not be found two yards of ground for burial (**dafn** = burial; **badnaseeb** = unlucky; **key biyeh** = for; **do gaz zamin** = the measure of a dug grave, **na milikueh** = not to be found)

He must have pined for his beloved soil, land of his resplendent ancestors far to the west. The radiance of the Mughal halo so often depicted in the miniature paintings, flickered out, a flame first torched by that full-blooded Mongol, Tamburlane, founder of the dynasty.

■ MUHURRAM

is a traumatic reminder of another set of tragic events in Islam's forward march. Each year the **Shi'a** sect commemorates the martyrdom at Karbala in Iraq, of **Imam Hussain**, grandson of Prophet Muhammed and the possible poisoning earlier of his brother **Imam Hassan** during the inflamed rivalries for succession to the **sixth Abbasid Caliphate** in Baghdad.

♦ Forty years after the anniversary of the death of the Prophet, Hussain was coincidentally killed on this same date while challenging the corrupt ruler, Caliph Yazid. The Shi'a sect especially, who trace their lineage from Hussain's bloodline, (his father **Ali** the Prophet's son-in-law), commemorate this day with fervent lamentations.

Meetings are held in preceeding evenings to recall the incidents with elegies (**marsiya**) especially for the benefit of the younger ones. A mourning procession takes place on the 10th day with large and elaborately hand-decorated **tazias** or floats, and with the chanting of hymns and ballads. Some of the participants are so moved that tears stream down their faces, and they flagellate their own bodies to 'suffer' along with Hussain. No weddings, TV shows or musical recordings take place around this time. The commemoration is likened to a lacerating experience following a funeral cortege.

♦ The tazias are sometimes huge in dimension, constructed often in bamboo wrapped around with coloured paper and tinsel. Each represents Hussain's mausoleum. The procession taken through the streets is quite a sight to see, especially in Lucknow where the resplendent **imambaras** (enclosure of the Imam)—a quite unique Indo-Islamic architecture—are the focal point for the processional culmination.

Hussain's martyrdom became one of those resonating community symbols very similar to those tribal marches of the Orange Order in Northern Ireland and Catholic remembrances of a similar order and oppression by William of Orange, the English king replacing a Catholic James, at the Battle of the Boyne.

◆ A focus for the disaffected, many of whom were the marginalized–in this case the non-Arab followers, (hence the strength of the sect in modern Iran) not privileged to be part of the establishment in the fold of early Saudi Wahabi Islam. Being non-Arab they were taxed despite being Muslim, or suffered social discrimination. In later times when power and aggrandisement followed in the wake of Islamic conquests, and divisions between rich and poor, those with status and those on the outside, became marked, Shi'as though accepting the main tenets of Islamic faith, looked askance at the orthodox Sunni jurisprudence or even some aspects of the Qur'an. They turned for inspiration to the **imam** in their own community–a charismatic teacher/leader to whom they personally gave allegiance–right up to this day.... **the Iranian Ayatollah Khomeini a powerful symbol of the force of this concept of the Imam even today.**

■ MURTI

= materialization, that is an **image** or **statue** (not an idol–a word which nowadays has derogatory undertones) of an **abstract concept** or **formless (nirguna)** idea of Divine Being.

Hence **Trimurti**, the trinity of the Hindu pantheon of gods and goddesses–**Brahma, Vishnu, Shiva**: Creator, Preserver, Destroyer. The most famous in this particular form of murti must be that magnificent chiselled face of rock-cut art within the cave at **Elephanta** (circa 450–750 CE) handled by stonemasons with such finesse on this island off Mumbai.

The giant head of Siva is **benign in the role of Brahma; meditative as Vishnu** facing the viewer; **fearsome as the earlier Vedic form of Siva, the thunderous Rudra**, the three aspects of deity seen as fused into one form. Is this an echo via coastal trade with the Indus peoples of antiquity with the triple-headed Harappan 'gunny bag' seal images?

◆ In the iconography of the Deities the **additional arms** and **even heads** in the case of Ravana in the Ramayana epic give a vision of superior strength and immense energy. Just as Picasso's split heads intensify the anguish, or the differing aspects of the face in question, so Indian sculpture and imagery embellishes and amplifies the essence, the concept, the idea rather than depicting a natural representation.

◆ These devices enable the artist to give expression to a wide range of symbolic attributes to the murti which encapsulate in their compressed form an enormous reservoir of concepts both philosophical as well as oral (almost like the Christian parables in visual form). **They become visual shorthand of abstruse, highly intellectualised philosophy.**

◆ **Objects** the deities hold in their hands are their attributes, **symbols of their power**, a further extension of the idea into the stories about these deities, e.g. Vishnu's chakra or discus to slay evil foes in yuga after yuga–aeons of time, or the **ankusha** (the elephant goad) held sometimes by Ganesh to signify his overlordship of the cosmos, as well as a metaphor of prodding humanity towards the pathway of righteous dharma.

◆ **The lotus** on which many deities sit in repose symbolises

divine creative energy–16-petalled. Sixteen is, in the Indian view, 'the perfect number'.

Murtis carry reverberating codes through millennia, as vibrant today updated sometimes with a contemporary sharpness, quite astonishing when one thinks that even when they were fashioned into sculptural iconography they embodied concepts already thousands of years old! Surely a fitting example of this is the engaging painting skill displayed by the artist village women of **Madhubani** (Forest of Honey)–a region so-called because of its flourishing agriculture in one of the first northern kingdoms known to Indian history–see **MAGADHA**.

The painted 'materializations' of **PANTHEON** deities and the legends encrusted on the concepts they embody, as well as village wedding scenes, abstract mandalas and cosmic designs astonish people from overseas. So exuberant are these new depictions, murtis of a different kind from those expert artisans of the 10th century Chola period or the fluid sculptured rock of the Deogarh masons (500 CE) that the Madhubani women (they are the artists, not their menfolk) became internationally famous overnight. Early paintings disappeared to private buyers. Some art critics may term their representations as 'naïve' or 'folk art' but that is far from the truth. Symbolic as any Matisse or Chagall, they are expertly handled with a technical finesse that belies the basic conditions of an earthen hut floor on which they may be executed, not so much because of 'primitive' conditions but because, like the equally world-famous Aboriginal artists of Australia, these women are used to crouching on the ground to execute domestic tasks.

It is however that indefinable **'gnowingness'**, a cultural wisdom beyond intellectual acquisition, beyond formal education (many of these artists may only have had two to three years of primary schooling) that gives them an enchanting sophistication equal to any western abstract art.

■ MUSIC
of the Classical Kind...Now...

His hand is feeling the air with articulate fingers as though rounding an invisible but statuesque form while the vocalist begins to give shape to the raga's first statement. This is the **alaap** and the music is of the south, **Carnatic** so it will be explored with alacrity as the drums are waiting to add depth to the statement. Percussion is of great artistry in the South.

The one dominant note extends endlessly in still air, the melodic line pennant-thin as yet, a prayer flag of sound lifted up on currents as the octave is explored, **five particular notes to this evening RAGA** with a slight and subtle difference, a half-tone less, in the descending order, a tinge of pathos curls around the mind, and then again the ascent further into the octave above, wafted on warm air across a valley of profound expectancy.

It is hard to distinguish which is human voice and which is at the moment placid violin echoing each new phraseology permutating those five full tones and shimmering around them with slivers of **grace**–half or quarter tones sliced so thin they

M

could be those beaten silver films that float as the ultimate decoration on Indian *phirni* dessert or sweetmeats.

◆ A few svaras are lifted up again with his right hand stretched, palm upwards as though seeking to touch a pedestal to place them there. There is a slight dip of tone… and the heart turns a somersault. The rasa, the flavour, the juices are flowing. The very soul is coming alive.

The dominant note is returned to again and again like great curving patterns of some ice skaters returning to base after a complex pirouette.* The pace is quickening, the patterns more complex but ever placing in the mind's eye the special phraseology of full and shaded tones of that raga, fixed in the composition of some ancient lineage, with certain specified sequences, intricate permutations and mathematically precise grammar. Such a framework of stringent discipline. Vocalist fuses with violin and flute, becoming one amalgamated instrument. That is intended. This is the measure of a musician, that inward search as the Vedic shastras, **the principles of aesthetic art declared vocal music to be the ultimate yogic dimension,** the pinnacle, the voice an instrument to achieve unity in that **PRAÑA**–breath–the creative **Brahm**. Without breath we would have no life, dehydrated as inert matter. The hands reach out again, 'thinking', shaping other configurations. And always that touch of pathos each time the particular **pakad**** in descent, skating around the dominant keynote, is touched in a glissando. Without **RASA** there is no art.

This is what Indian musicians refer to as **dhvani**–a creative reverie, a resonance in the entire psyche, not just mind but the entire being, as though one were a resonating string of the long veena responding in perpetual motion to the playing of the main strings above, never struck but ever responding in empathy.

Is this science? How to analyse, because is it beyond intellect, beyond sensory response, more like a yogic flash of intuition, direct perception, the constant search of all the Indian arts in creating that ambience–rasa–that flavours all the art forms, the ultimate aim a magnetic union, a kind of reaching out beyond this massed audience to timeless realms–a music of the spheres which finally science has proved is there–pure sound related to breath–**praña**.

◆ A radio program mentioned elsewhere following Voyager I in its space probe to planet Jupiter startled me with three insistent tones as the space craft passed through Saturn's rings, tones like whales whistling and birds fluting fitfully as they settle in the shadows of the night. Incredibly moving. A human voice begins to explain in scientific terms that radiation trapped in encircling magnetic field creates molecular impulses, elemental music in the dark empty spaces of the universe. It is as though the Indian

musicians are trying to reunite with this original source of all things, where creation begins.

Suddenly one is jerked out of this reverie of beauty into the adamantine demands of mathematics as graphs of rhythmic divisions from the resonating **mrdangam**–that Lord of Sound–thud into the forefront of comprehension. **Yantra patir mrdang = Yantra** = instrument; device to bring about some result; **patir** = pati, lord = husband; **mrdang** = double-head south Indian drum. Soon this will be followed by the divided double tabla of the northern Hindustani system. And here is another dimension of an unusual concert–north and south systems interacting as one in the hands of masters, but Hindu and Muslim also, a felicitous aspect of Indian music despite all that may crash in with precipitous consequence in the political sphere.

Everyone is nodding heads in idiosyncratic fashion, as affirmation of the anchor beat, heavily emphasised **sama** (sum), the end and beginning of great curves of percussion bars, the **tala,** an octave of ruffling waters as the breeze gets up, an angler hauling in that substantial beat again. The hands all around, musicians on stage, knowledgeable members of the audience, come down, clap, fingers counting out one, two, three like crabs waving–then another clap on the 'off beat' or a flap in the air, hand turned palm upward, then thud goes the **sama**, the main beat leading the rhythmic cycle. You feel like dancing … such syncopation and all the musicians are smiling at each other, acknowledging a well-rendered passage here, a nifty piece of fast drumming there. A ruby and a diamond ring flashes, gold on the other finger, this time the fingers are curled, counting out the tala one, two, three and then down comes the palm again, a sweet smile of acknowledgement from vocalist **Balamurali Krishna** to his mrdangam player **K Padmanabhan**.

He sits cross-legged swathed in sumptuous biscuit-coloured silk, stylishly embroidered in dark brown tracery, the shade of milky south Indian coffee. His eyes are now shut, the face twisted almost as the melodic line, now complicating in geometric graphs, accelerating, reaches up the higher octave-searching again, inward, upward, outward. He shifts slightly, settling in on the durree encircled by his musicians, one foot now keeping the tala as though it were a disembodied member attached to a hidden metronome.

Hariprasad Chaurasia, luminary in the **Hindustani** north Indian tradition, answers on his sensuous flute accompanied by **Zakir Hussain**, as equally famous now as his own astonishing tabla player father, the late **Ustad Alla Rakha**, long-time partner with **Pandit Ravi Shankar** in earliest experimental promotion of Indian music to Europe and the USA in their pioneer concerts when we came to know them well after friendships in India when they were an unknown factor in the world music scene.

◆ The conversation **jugalbandi** has begun as the liquid beauty of flute builds on the phrases and improvised passages echoed in the south Indian violin, the drone reinforcing dominant and fourth and fifth full notes, adding depth to a meditative raga–**Panthuvarali Ramakriya**. It is redolent with **taseer**, a lingering elongation of the notes, providing an elevated sensation.

---

*And Yo-Yo Ma, famous cellist, making a Canadian film (1994) on Bach suites for his 250th centenary engages Jayne Torvill and Christopher Dean, Olympic skaters, to do exactly this–exquisitely with a sarabande!
**Characteristic grouping of the special notes of a raga to which a musician repeatedly returns as to an anchorage after the many extempore passages of free improvisation.

In an unbroken swell, the long curl of a wave, it crashes on the **sama**. Now the precise and dramatic brilliance of Zakir asserts a challenge to the percussion, all combine in a **kacheri**, a mixture, a kedgeree of such interrelated, far from random, tones, implied harmonies, driving rhythm it is hard to remain still.

A reminder in that voice when velvet richness combines with absolute impeccable mastery of all the technical grammar, of another great master, **Ustad Ameer Khan** who could put one into a deep yogic trance as his voice floated out in abstract patterns of ever increasing ingenuity... this is *taseer*, an elevated mood lingering as do the notes, haunting the mind.

On Australian shores the waves curl over in this translucent brilliance as the swell builds up into substantial surf, then scatters in shimmering, glistening droplets of sharp diamond-white, green-blue, shadowy purple, pure emerald glints. Such imagery sweeps in to Delhi's Siri Fort concert auditorium as a similar sparkle of sound crashes into the auditorium.

And Then … India, Newly Freed–A Concert Under the Stars

Another vision forms of long ago, the very essence of what Indian music is about–a world away from the formality of the Western concert yet as equally valid, intellectually demanding, emotionally fulfilling.

There is a towering figure in musical genius, a guru in white **sherwani** and tight **churidar** pyjamas sitting in the middle of a crescent of his pupil musicians–all brilliant exponents of his legendary **gharana** or school of music with its own idiosyncratic rendition and performance.

India as a gigantic entity is so new in the 1950s, fresh and alive to itself, exciting new expositions and self-evaluations are happening every week and one is fortunate to be alive in the right place at the right time–for surely nowadays there are not many concerts in the traditional style running through the night until the first lightening of the indigo blue heavens spells dawn .... and the assembled array of talent gathered under the scalloped arches of the **Diwan-i-Khas** in the Red Fort in Delhi where once emperors had graced the Peacock Throne, shuffle out in a trance into the gathering dust, heat and noise of Old Delhi and the sound of the Jama Masjid mosque's call to the morning first prayer.

In an inspired masterstroke of theatre the public were allowed to lie on the lawns or sink into deep sofas (for the VIPs who were legion that night under a star-studded blackness of an Indian spring night) when **Ustad Allauddin Khan** took up his **sarod**, surrounded by his son, **Ustad Ali Akbar Khan**, then a young sarod player in his late 20s, likewise his brother-in-law, Bengali Hindu **Pandit Ravi Shankar** (85 years old in 2005 CE), on sitar married then to his guru's own daughter **Annapurna,** a fine **surbahar** player, her instrument of cello-like richness and depth.

Other younger members of this creative family and tiny grandchildren completed the crescent as the dynamic interchange played on through the night, each brilliant musician a foil to the other, building up a raga for over two hours, almost impossible now in Western-style concerts where time is money

and costs and an office job intrudes upon next day–everyone in a 21st century hurry!

♦ This lone Bengali musician (an eclectic Muslim) surrounded by his clan where Mughals trod added grace upon grace note to the consummate artistry of the expanding raga, playing in willow-green shade and casting a reverie across this limpid pool of sound, first one artist making a musical statement, the other echoing some of its phraseology but augmenting with embellishments that are not just accidental improvisation, but correctly structured according to the demanding rules of each raga, the particular relationship of the right tones, the shimmering down the permutations of notes allowed in a long *taan*, stretched out in a sliding *mir*, a glissando, and always keeping within that grammar of the tala.

♦ Liquid melodic patterns, demanding duet-duels between percussion artists, variations on an eternal theme, searching for (and stating) beauty, harmony, a coming to rest... an image of India at its purest that recurs as the music surges out into the spaces beyond enclosing concrete, the haunting sounds across a Himalayan valley beyond Shimla where the final purity of a flute catches the sad-sweet heart of Indian life, the image of a swirling pool and the inward pull towards the centre, wisps of blue-smoke as the melodic line extends through the impenetrable shadows of the majestic deodar pines.

♦ India may have dreadful pollution in its cities; a metallic poison of car exhaust; three-wheeler phut-phuts going crazy playing dodgems at the fairground roundabout in a daily nation-wide traffic jam; it has searing poverty, encrusted corruption; self-serving politicians galore; selfish businesspeople weighted down at weddings in obscenities of gold display; two million malnourished women and children; men still pulling–and–pushing excessively weighted handcarts. The sadhu laid out amid the lines of beggars at a pilgrimage centre or mela (fair) with his elongated penis on display, enlarged by tantric rituals, a bowl placed beside his powdered and clay-caked body for offerings–and for all-believing village women perhaps followers of a Shiva sect even to kiss this 'member'. They may receive blessing of fertility by so doing (as if India needed that!). **It is all the levels that puzzle, horrify.**

♦ But the music plays on into another realm where Indian beauty, a magical quality affirms those old verities that have reverberated all the way down millennia in an even flow from those earliest Vedic chants, and grounded in other disciplines–that India also honours and abides by to this day–'**an abstract and spaceless theme singing through time**'. These are the late **Yehudi Menuhin's** words describing Indian music when he first became President of the Asian Music Circle in Britain, an event of note itself after years of neglect and ignorance throughout centuries of colonial domination–when music was referred to as 'mere noise, and nasal drawling', 'a cacophony of sound'. With Ali Akbar and Ravi Shankar suddenly arriving on the scene, courageous work was done in bringing Indian music to eager young audiences whose ears were already taking in changing Western sounds shifting ground with electronic guitars,

Stockhausen and John Cage. Spatial music based on intervals, a new world of computerised sound, Phillip Glass, Peter Gabriel and WOMAD, all then lay ahead.

Menuhin wrote the following in one of Ravi Shankar's first programme notes when he too was running the gambit of his own Indian critics who accused him of 'jazzing up' India's traditional musical forms to suit Western tastes—as though **Khusrau** and **Tansen**, great cultural gurus had never existed centuries earlier to reshape and breathe new life into the raga system of that day.

> *Humanity is very gradually beginning to conceive, instead of isolated things and phenomena, a world in terms of the relation between all things and phenomena. Our knowledge is gradually approaching the stage at which art and science are indissolubly wedded in each act. Not until this process is complete can humanity as a whole achieve harmony. To an extraordinary extent, this marriage is to be found in Indian classical music, which is still mainly a votive offering. Indians believe in its therapeutic quality, as well as in its spiritual effect. By the same token, they have not submitted to our even-tempered scale. Our own chromatic-tempered scale, which has its beginning with Bach, has served us well in portraying ever more intensely and dramatically the passion and emotion of the individual.*

Having gone down that pathway to the extreme, Menuhin pointed out the change in Western music seeking out the more abstract and less personal.

> *Here, I feel, is where the eclectic and highly evolved character of Indian music has finally become significant to the western ear. Indian music has always stressed the relation of man to the universal. For this purpose, the modal composition—cast in one mood on a fixed base of which the intervals are carefully matched and selected, together with a particular rhythmic pattern—is capable of achieving a progressive and irresistible hypnotic effect, in the sense that it liberates the higher mind from the limits of the physical form.*

- There are times when strangers, listening to this music, are concerned that they have gone off in a trance, or fallen asleep and lost track of the music itself. This does not worry Indians themselves. They are used to the hypnotic effect Yehudi Menuhin perceives, and the liberating quality of the reverberation of certain notes in a raga, as well as the idiomatic phraseology of the **pakad** (phrase) basic to each raga which the mind expects to hear repeated in permutating variations.

There is no need to worry! Music is after all considered by the Indian theorists of the **shastras** (the aesthetic principles and codification texts) as yoga—a search for that unity of pure sound spoken of earlier. **Nada Brhm** the Absolute conceived as sound recognised physiologically in **YOGA** in the chakra centres of energies from solar plexus to the top of the brain. So meditative withdrawal is par for the course!

- **Ustad Hafiz Ali Khan** another famous sarod player of a different gharana regretted in the 50s the passing of this period of all-night sessions when musicians could take their time, a more spacious era when a raga could be elaborated, examined, augmented over a time frame of 'two hours'.

> *The spirit of dedication is gone and leisure, which came admittedly with the old feudal patronage system, nevertheless allowed the very foundation of learning. Leisure is too expensive a luxury these days!*

Endnote on Annapurna Devi: Now in her 80s this gifted player of a seldom-heard richly-toned surbahar, a more majestic instrument than the sitar has lived as a recluse since her one-time husband Pandit Ravi Shankar early on in this romantic tempestuous marriage (she was only 15) waywardly followed the path of many an artist, trailing hearts in many continents like an earthly Krishna.

Jealousy of her fine gifts contributed also to the fracture of relations. For a long time she has lived in seclusion in Mumbai but continues to be held in such respect as guru to many now distinguished musicians who learned the traditions of the **Maihar Gharana** (a school of music) of Madhya Pradesh at her feet—artists such as the incomparable Hariprasad Chaurasia and Nikhil Banerjee.

It is a miracle indeed that we were privileged to hear her play while still married to him, and in combination with her emerging brother the equally famous Ali Akbar.

Her own musicianship is the stuff of legend, her illustrious father reluctant to teach her due to the tragedy of her elder sister's experience, also a gifted vocalist. Married off in traditional fashion, her mother-in-law (true to stereotype) resented her talents and burnt her musical instrument. So the young Annapurna listened determinedly from 'behind the door' so to speak when her brother in turn came under Baba's tutelage. One day caught in the act of playing, her father put her through her paces. She responded, genius inbuilt into her system. Accepted in special ceremony into the gharana her father and she made **pranam** (though Muslim) to **Saraswati**, potent presiding force of music, the arts, and knowledge.

Her father Ustad Allaudin Khan (awarded the highest national honours including the Padma Vibhushan) died in 1972 reputed to be 110 years old.

Grammatical Structure … Its Components

One does not look for modulation, chordal sonorance and reverberation to give depth in Indian music. There are no equivalent forms, either, to a symphony or solo instrumental concerto. As in everything Indian, the fragment is seen as part of the whole. This is vital to the philosophy of the Hindu view of life, it affects every cranny of existence and thought patterns. Such a concept gives cohesion to the dissonances, which most modern Western music does not possess. Linked with this is the flexible Indian scale which is anchored to a **fixed doh**, called **sah**, but not to a fixed keyboard or tempered scale. The precision of Indian musical configurations which fill out the vertebrae of the ascending and descending scales of a raga (these usually differ slightly) are almost mathematical in their permutation of the notes particular to the raga. On this base a whole pyramid of improvised relationships between these certain notes is built up, and particular phrases are reiterated over and over again on the emphatic beats, to remind the listener of the subtleties of **RASA** to be created.

This is how the early texts defined raga in Sanskrit:

योऽयं ध्वनिविशेषस्तु स्वरवर्णविभूषितः

yoyam dhvani viseshastu svaravarna vibhushita
which is resonance/sound specific also musical arrangement adorned

रंजको जनचित्तानां स राग कथितो बुधैं

ranjako janacittanam sa raag kathio budheh
pleasing (fills with joy) people hearts that raag is said by the scholars

'(That) which is adorned with specific sounds and musical arrangements (**svara varna**) which fills the heart of people with joy is called raga (melody, particularly musical mode)'.

ॐ৬ॐ৬ॐ৬ॐ৬ॐ৬ॐ৬ॐ৬ॐ৬ॐ

SVARA-SHRUTI

Svara is the full tone or note. **Shruti** or **sruti** (Sanskrit: to hear), a microtonal interval of which there are 22 in the Indian 'octave', as follows:

SRUTI (22) or SHRUTI	Sa	Ri or rch	Ri k	Ri i	Ri j	Ga i	Ga j	Ga k	Ma	Ma k	Ma i	Ma j	Pa	Dha j	Dha i	D k	D	Ni k	Ni i	Ni j	Sa	Ri k
SVARA (7)	Sa	Ri or Reh				Ga			Ma				Pa	Dha				Ni			Sa	
DIATONIC Sol/Fah scale	Doh	Ray				Me			Fah				Soh	Lah				Te			Doh	
CHROMATIC 12-tone scale	C	Db	D	Eb	E				F	F♯ G			Ab	A				Bb	B		C	

Peggy Holroyde, **Indian Music** (Allen & Unwin, London, 1972)

Using Western visual means for clarification, this is an arbitrary and pictorial image of the Indian chromatic scale of 22 intervals within the octave of seven pure, substantive tones, the **svaras**. It is by no means the musical truth. Nor is the scale sung in consecutive order. Its importance lies only in the way an individual musician uses the satellite **srutis** as major or minor tones (in our sense) to approach a svara note, either by curling towards it or slurring away from it, or again by using the many sympathetic strings and resonances (of the gourds) on their stringed instruments to overlay the serial line of full tones with a host of connected quartertones or semitones—depending on how sharp or flat they are compared with our less acutely differentiated scale-system. The diagram is provided to help those familiar with Western keyboard systems visually to get some idea of the basic scaffolding and fine shading of tones an Indian musician can shape with a raga.

The Voice

The long sustained note. That is good grammar. Technical perfection, no wobble, the larynx wide open. Praña. That original Vedic theory, all of us part of a gigantic molecular invisible energy field of ether. The art of vocalists is considered the ultimate rendition of music, the right pronunciation, pure exact *vac* = word sound of utmost significance to Vedic theorists, known as **uchchaaran**. Quality of voice as in Western music is not considered a criterion in judging eminence; but this musician is caressing the tones, he is adding the soul, *soz* that makes him a great musician, not just a master of grammar. The sharp-tone percussive beat is now answering those abstract sol-fa syllables, the **ga-ma-pa**. Shortened, another grammatical device to judge his quality of mastery of the almost mathematical phrases. **There is no notation**. This is computer brainwork. They are answering each other, the vocalist twisting and turning those dha, ni, sahs, tumbling over each other, musical leaves blown by the force of his praña, rolling up and down three octaves now as the raga expands.

What gaiety! Sweet conversation not only with mrdangam and ghatam so clear you can track down the fast finger touches and get lost in the mathematical graph—such yogic concentration you lose the physical reality of the world around you.

This is a sweet meditation. Raga Brihadeeswara ... Iswara ... the deity is being addressed and the musician Balamurali Krishna is taking a mental circumambulation around the majestic colonnaded shrine at Thanjavur where he is known to have composed the pallavi spontaneously in his mind (and retained it—no notation again). Yet every convoluted phrase, embellished with a slide down the octave is reiterated in total perfection by the singing violin. As the mind and heart lurch in unison responding, a sough of approval escapes across the mesmerised audience, all those Indians swaying, shaking shoulders to the rhythmic pulse, right palms slapping, a very audible replication—and everyone on stage nods, smiles in acknowledgement, and climbs further heights of disciplined training, born of 30 years of dedication. Ravi Shankar once stated in concert, explaining to a London audience then unfamiliar in the late 50s with the intricacies of the Indian system that the best music is conjured out of 99 per cent perspiration, one percent inspiration! **Riyaaz** is the term for that concentrated disciplined practice, 4–10 hours Ravi once said 'of one's waking life **every** day'.

◆ **Reaction from an audience has a marked effect**, encouraging further passages of inspired improvisation that sets everyone in a state of ecstatic expectation, musicians egging each other on, audiences exploding in cries of '**wah, wah**', '**shabash**' in the north (a Persian word for 'excellent') a far cry indeed from sober Western audiences listening in appreciative silence. Once in a major concert of Ustad Vilayat Khan at London's South Bank, in the Queen Elizabeth Hall full to overflowing to hear a moving and lyrical rendition of a major majestic raga **Darbari Kanada**, Saeed Jaffrey actor and TV star but an early friend of humbler AIR days, excitable personality that he is, became understandably carried away, ejecting approving commendations as the climax grew with drums galloping apace like pedigree horses in full flight, manes of slivered mathematical cross rhythms trailing. A very irate and pukka Englishman in the row behind tapped Saeed on the

M

shoulder, admonishing him to be quiet. He could never have been in India ....and with chagrin, a subdued Jaffrey, too polite to throw the gauntlet down, sat rigid with frustration. I felt the Raj was being played out all over again. It was **A Passage to India** this time in reverse–Indian cultural norms trying to assert themselves in the UK!

Despite the pace of modern life, a new order of global concepts and all the attendant stress, there still seems to be a remarkable resilience–and dedication–to long hours of study in the same guru-shishya relationship, iron discipline and an inward spiritual compass bearing as strong as any in the past. And, rewardingly, the resurgence and restatement of very ancient traditions, which still maintains the importance of vocal music, as the **prime** instrument. The fixed texts = **dhruva** = truth or deity, **pada** = lines, are very profound **bhajans** = popular devotional praise sung in dignified manner in a special dialect of the vernacular called Brijbhasha.

Dhrupad

For instance, the emergence in the last decade of the young **Wasifuddin Dagar** of the famous **Dagar Brothers'** lineage who reintroduced the most classical of **Hindustani** musical forms– **Dhrupad,** the Bach fugue of Indian music–to the general public in the 50s is one contemporary example. Wasifuddin is the **19th generation in a direct family line of Muslim musicians** who have perfected this most demanding vocal music, which has its origins as Wasifuddin explained in the mystical reverberations of the sacred Hindu sound syllable 'OM' in the **Sama Veda** text where only 3 or 4 notes were used in the chants and where the syllables of the few words were intoned.

A raga in dhrupad is developed in slow, serene measured phrases using these syllables as launching pads for elaborate improvisation of a purely abstract kind based on the phonetic sounds. A text is then sung at the end, first 'grave and profound, an act of worship ... my music is a magnet which pulls me towards that bliss in which I lose myself and find God' says Zahiruddin Dagar, another member of the clan. Such repeated phrases have hypnotic effect. *Bandish* which means 'bound down' (same root) that is, a fixed composition when repeated can take off with a life of its own, 'sending' an audience with its expectation 'heard in the ear' before it actually occurs.

Searched out in his home in South Delhi, overrun by an extended family of many young children, his mother running the household, resident French musicians studying the music, all is tradition and modernity at one and the same time ... no fustian tradition enclosed in inward-looking orthodoxy here, amid typical quite overwhelming hospitality to the stranger who comes in without date. He plays for half an hour for me personally amid the clutter of other visitors, family, babies, young nieces bringing plates of Indian sweetmeats, cousin **bhais** wandering in and out. Wasifuddin's day is one long dedicated practice apart from concerts and now international interchange of knowledge which he finds very exciting.

Carnatic Music … The Stamp of Feet and Grace Notes Swinging

Music in the south is governed by the same aesthetic principles and forms as Hindustani music. The difference is in the emphasis, and some slight changes to a few specific forms.

Raga, tala, pakad (characteristic phrases of each particular raga), bhava (a mood with spiritual content), svara (sol-fa notes) and gamakas (microtonal grace notes that embellish the full tone) and taans (dramatic swooping glides) are all part of both systems and abide by the same strict grammar.

What is different is the mood, the affirmative joy of a faith never under threat. To put it succinctly, such music is a dancing Bach! I find it very hard to resist the urge to dance even in the most formal of Carnatic concerts when musicians of the calibre of **M S Subbulakshmi**, nod their heads to her percussion musicians to take up the theme. The more austere vocalist **Semmangudi Srinavasa Iyer, Dr L Subramaniam** or **M S Gopalkrishnan** (incomparable violinists) really get going, transporting one into a firmament of sparkling melodies throbbing and swaying to insistent percussive talas, while presenting the joyous compositions of the famous Carnatic TRINITY–**Shyam Shastri** 1762–1827, **Tyagaraja** 1767-1847, and **Dikshitar**, 1775–1835.

◆ The grammar of structure is immaculate but classical syncopation of sheer joy impels every foot to swing, the head to affirm the beat. Fortunately with so many CDs of good quality now on the market I can dance the light fantastic with abandon in the privacy of my own home!

One of the most succinct yet articulate summaries of the history, grammar, the 'heart' of this Carnatic system is to be found by e-mail posted by **Mohan Krishnamoorthy** of Melbourne Australia: **Shastriya Sangeetam**, at mohawk@labyrinth.net.au

Pan Indian and Global Music Trends

Since Independence quite astonishing changes are taking place. Collaboration between musicians from both backgrounds something so unusual and rare previously is commonplace now. Not only younger musicians influenced by film and pop music are stepping out to join forces with their Western counterparts which modern jet travel has made a daily occurrence. Even famous **traditional** artists, noted for their impeccable background in training in the guru/shishya system with its integrity of learning are stepping out into the **global world music** arena. And this occurred long before WOMAD (based in Bath, England) was formed as a major platform for global exchange and major festivals of world music. Like their Western counterparts they are quite naturally enveloped in the global opportunities of intercommunication that the computer-driven internet, electronic media world of e-mail and fax networking provide. Modern technology is running electronic rings around even the most traditional of musicians. There are now hundreds of genuine and unselfconscious collaborations. One stands out in 2002 in Delhi. The Finnish Embassy sponsored with the ICCR an evening of collaboration with classical Finnish musicians and talented **Kamal Sabri** on **sarangi, Shafat Ali Khan** playing full blast on tabla with an extraordinary Finnish guitar player Jukka Tolonen, so gifted he would, in his own genre, match Pandit Ravi Shankar and Ustad Ali Akbar in theirs. A gift indeed if this recorded concert **Striking**

Notes, featuring **Minna Raskinen** on the **kantele** could be tracked down. The Finnish national instrument has an intriguing history said to have travelled northwards with the Scythians as a nomadic people who finally landed on Baltic shores.

At popular level, Punjabi **bhangra** has exploded on the club scene not only in the UK but Canada and Australia with its driving drum rhythms–**Apache Indian** (but Anglo-Punjabi!), **Bally Sagoo** breaking all records with the first ever Indian language song called **Tum Bin Jiya** to make the 1997 charts. **Balwinder Safri**, **Jonny Zee**, and the **Sahota Brothers** (all five) who are as solid Punjabi as any Indian-born mob. Yet to-ing and fro-ing with India or native-born, they all have injected popular Indian music into a total new polyglot expression that is not just bland pop. Global immigration has had a profound effect, as also has politics. Many are experimenting with European jazz groups, collaborating in compositions with American chamber and symphony orchestras (although attempts at harmony by simultaneous 'echoing' of Western instrumentation is not altogether satisfactory) and setting up schools of Indian music worldwide. Even the Royal Festival Hall as well as the Royal Albert Hall have responded to all-night Indian music concerts, inconceivable even a decade ago. An array of Indian musical luminaries glittered in London in September 1998. **The Eternal Spirit** concert gathered famous musicians from north and south from 7 p.m. to dawn, quoting Khusrau for its theme: **'we can silk-stitch into one, two tunes however apart they might be.'** India indeed came to town in ways that no Viceroy, nor even Gandhi or Panditji, could ever have foreseen! But Sir William Jones of the late 1700s and Bengal's Asiatic Society would have rubbed their hands with glee for they were the honoured few who respected Indian culture, Jones writing the first book by a Westerner on **Music of India** in **1793** (since reprinted, Nabajiban Press, Kolkata, **1962**).

A Coda–and time to move on after this all-night Indian resting stop

M S, otherwise known as the great classical 'nightingale' of modern times, **Subbulakshmi** of the Carnatic system also is one of India's most celebrated women singers, **Lata Mangeshkar** her alter ego of the more popular film world. M S, who died in 2004, has drawn tens of thousands to her concerts both in the north as well as her own Tamil south where her devotional personality and the philanthropy of her artistic services and performance fees is legendary. At the same time she is a genuinely humble person for her eminence.

A book worth reading is **Kunjamma.... ode to a nightingale** by **Laksmi Vishwanathan** (Luster Press, Roli Books, New Delhi 2003).

To attend a concert in her own home-town, Chennai, must be one of the true global 'moments of all time'. To savour the challenge of the most precise and dramatic of musical interchanges between a number of instruments and a vocalist or instrumentalist who throws them the melodic line, while the audience can wallow in the sensual assault of south Indian women laden in great coils of heavy-scented jasmine garlands in their jet-black braids–a

ritual–and the resplendent sheen of rainbow coloured saris, the rustle of silk, the gleaming hair which is washed daily and smoothed with coconut oil–it is literally, heady stuff!

The audience sits cross-legged on the lawns under the stars on a balmy night of humidity, everyone swaying in unison in their immaculate white shirts no matter what level of class, caste or income; this is another experience of a communal yogic kind–all bound in a concentration on a single point–following her voice on a melodic line of delicate fine-lacery in its beauty yet surging in tremendous power in the main *statement of intent.*

A kriti Saroja-Dala-Netri of master-musician Shyamashastri places the sanskritised Telugu verse on the melodic line–'**samagana vinodini guna-dhama syamkrishna-nute'**–(roughly translated) *'chanting of the Sama Veda/which is wonderful/the treasure house or repository of all the gunas/is fully realised'.*

This line is expanded, augmented in sheer devotional fervour, the meaning implying that the individual who is a repository in equal proportion of all three **GUNAS** in total balance, equipoise, that constant sought in all philosophical searches in India possesses a treasure house in being personally fulfilled.

The one line is taken in many ways with *alamkaras* = ornamentations, equivalent to what happens in another art form, architecture... free-standing goddesses in temple niches surrounded by all the carved embellishments of the architectural discipline, foliate tracery of the lotus tendrils and leaves curling along the frieze, flying apsaras above, the grace notes of the stonemason's art. Here in the music the equivalent violin, voice and mrdangam, and veena, a geometry of thistle-down sounds lifted up again and again in spiralling graces, spiralling on currents of heated molecules, are framed in the adamantine steel of the kriti discipline.

◆   But it was a far more mundane domestic moment where I caught an insight into the constant presence of that 'other force' at supper when the brahmin cooks (on the trot!) brought in the food and spooned the rice on our **thalis**, a spoonful was placed at the righthand side. M S smiled enchantingly, 'You leave untouched! It is for the deity!' How close those numenistic 'presences' are in this land.

Such beauty heard in reality has fortunately been recorded for all time in a **UNESCO Classical Indian Music Series**. Forty years ago I was privileged to stay in her Madras household with her late husband T Sadasivam (her manager) while gathering material for my Indian music book. Her ultimate generosity was made manifest... being allowed to sit unobtrusively (but invited to do so) in her puja room in the soft warmth of dawn while she practised on one of her many exquisitely crafted veenas, burnished wood and carved ivory peacocks like figureheads of a galleon, her musicianship in full sail. Each morning practice a hard taskmaster, relentless, never to be foregone and devotion fused into the one when finally both instrument and musician performed namaskaram to the divine impetus of all beginnings–Ganapati.

A quiet, solemn moment of total shanti–peace frozen in time.

■ MUSLIMS

....constitute a population of 140 million plus, approximately 14 per cent of the total population. India is the second largest Muslim state in the world if measured demographically. Muslim influence culturally and artistically, politically, spiritually has been integral to Indian development throughout half a millennium at least.

A Warning Note… a very sensitive subject where honest opinion (and balanced) is at a premium, it is probably best to let Indians speak for themselves. Unfortunately the overseas media tend to put anything to do with Islam, Muslims, Kashmir, mosques being built or destroyed on ancient Hindu temple sites, under a monolithic heading as though Muslims all subscribe to one political viewpoint; accept homogeneous attitudes to 'being Indian'; and have similar ancestry.

◆ This is patently not so if one follows not only the intricacies of Indo-Pakistan politics but global Muslim antipathies as well as agreements (Iraq and Iran are clear examples of discord). Indian Mohajir migrants into Pakistan, Bangladeshi refugees within India, the considerable divide between south India Muslim politics and Muslim League politics in the north–the latter a shifting sand bar of evolving views as far apart as the newly termed 'secular Muslim' parties determined to rewrite the old agendas and show an 'Indian-ness' of identity compared with the polemical Islamic orthodox of the Babri Masjid Action Committee, all these are only a few of the many shades of political division.

◆ Just as Christianity has shown no sense of homogeneity and has warred against itself and created bitter factionalism (northern Ireland a prime example) there is no reason to lump all Muslims within the same fold as both the extreme Hindu political parties have learnt to do in the last fraught decade, or sub-editors in the Western press tend to do, seeking simplified headlines.

Unfortunately questions of who is a 'good Indian', a representative Indian, a 'true Indian' have been bandied around (see **SECULAR SOCIETY**) more by rabidly obscurantist politicians seeking power at state level than for genuine reasons of finding out the complex truths of identity and citizenship. Instead of asking themselves why such a huge number of Muslims remain in India and have not chosen to migrate to Pakistan (it cannot just be the physical/economic hassles of giving up 'home,' house, jobs alone) local politicians continue to play on people's basic emotions, appealing to the lowest common denominator.

◆ Manipulation of minorities for power-play purposes has been the name of the game for all political parties from colonial times onwards; fanning of the flames burst into a conflagration momentarily in the Mumbai riots (a shaming factor for the internationally inclined city's self-image). Like a forest fire though, winds can change direction abruptly and engulf the arsonists who set the flames alight.

The process from 1000 CE onwards was often ravaging to Hindu society. The slave kings of Asia Minor are still known popularly as idol-breakers. These were often Turkish mercenaries, converted or purchased slaves whose fortunes turned them into real rough riders into history.

From then on northern India has experienced 700 years of different Muslim ethnic groups flowing in.

Cultural Input

A Muslim, Sayed Saeed al Shafi, writing in **Indian and Foreign Review** (September 1981) had this to say:

It is well known that India was in constant touch with the peoples of the Mesopotamia, and its contacts with the Arabs pre-date the advent of Islam. History testifies to the fact that Islam came to India as a religion and as a culture centuries before it came as a political force. In fact, there is hardly any area of human endeavour towards which Muslim Indians have not made a definitive contribution: specially significant are the realms of art, architecture, crafts, music, mathematics, sciences, jurisprudence, literature and law, as also the field of city-planning and development of gardens. It was on the soil and climate of India with its age-old traditions in art and architecture and town building, where the Islamic art found its zenith.

Muslim thought and the cultures that the diverse subcultures brought with them have been likened in their strengthening capacity to overall Indian-ness to being like an alloy which is stronger **than its constituent elements that go into its making.**

If Pakistan, and politicians either side of the border could leave people alone, a new identity could surely grow as elsewhere in plural societies, especially Canada and Australia, where people accept and embrace multi-identities quite unselfconsciously for themselves. **But so long as Pakistan can find no identity for itself except in projecting 'hate India' on the screen as a backdrop to its own definition**, it seems as though this constant abrasive background noise will **continue to influence attitudes towards Muslims in India.**

A Personal View and the Current Intertwining of Communities

As an outsider looking in and with a long life spent in four main cultures and a few months in yet another (the UK, the USA, India, Australia and a mission for the Runnymede Trust, a Quaker organization in Britain to report on the Indian situation in South Africa in the 70s at the height of apartheid–the people I met not only Indian but renegade white Afrikaaner South Africans such as Bishop Naudé of the Bröderbond) I am aware that all plural societies have to contain ethnic separatist tendencies in one form or another. Communal tensions in all manner of permutations are the bane of every form of democratic society in this century. The tendency had been building up ever since colonial empires collapsed. It would seem that only authoritarian regimes such as Stalin's hold on the USSR; Mao's China and Tito's Jugoslavia, could hold together the demands for ethnic autonomy, later seen in the total **balkanization** (a term I knew in my early school history!) of the Balkans and the break-away Russian Muslim republics… as well as that threatening western China.

Such minority assertiveness now has free play and keeps manifesting itself in many different aspects even along this personal padayatra, perhaps because of the many intriguing responses I have encountered; from the total assimilative push to be the all-American guy or gal of the 40s when I was an impressionable college teenager there, to Britain's painful coming-to-terms with racial influx of the 50s–70s decades; to Australia's maturing harmony and push for reconciliation with Aboriginal citizens as we turned the millennium.

Official apologies are in the air worldwide. For the USA, on matters relating to slavery; in Canada, with indigenous Indians and Inuits; in Britain, with the totality of the Celtic presence (a semi-autonomous Parliament for Scotland, Welsh language taught in schools, and attempt at peace between the two Irelands). Old antagonisms were often due to lack of opportunities to gain access to the channels of national power, education, work opportunities. They were also due to the concept of majority rule in democracy without giving respect to minority cultures and recognising the enrichments to the totality by the plural diversity, Indonesia a case in point where outlying island cultures have been at the mercy of Javanese overlordship, both political as well as military.

Indians have always prided themselves at recognising **unity in diversity** (many stepping stones have plaques engraved with Indian experiences on this matter). But partition of the subcontinent appears still to leave a wound that suppurates with cumulative lesions for which the British must take most of the blame. Recent publication of Whitehall archives concerning what really happened behind the scenes in deciding on partition makes sorry reading–deception, perfidy and deliberate with-holding of information by British military command for the new Indian army.

Ethnic, religious and cultural diversity is now of worldwide importance in the politics of nation building but so also is demographic development–as Fiji has found to its cost. What happens when an introduced Indian component takes over the indigenous population numerically? Muslim numbers in India are huge in comparison with other worldwide minorities in plural situations and increasing. The fact that many Muslim Indians fought and went to prison alongside their Hindu, Buddhist, Sikh (or whatever faith) compatriots in fighting the British in the Quit India campaigns (and as agrarian revolutionaries the Wahabis in Bengal were some of the first in the late 19th century) a whole new world of Muslim politics exists since the upheavals of the last few years. The horrors of the 9/11 Twin Towers cataclysm and the volatile world of fanatical suicide terrorists has engulfed global society; individuals face many personal dilemmas.

This has implications for the geopolitical realities of an India currently bordered by an arc of some very hostile Islamic countries broadcasting evangelical messages intent on subverting 'idolatrous Hindu believers'. (This kind of inflammatory electronic assault is apart from those other missionary extremists, sourced most especially in the USA, engaged in virulent propaganda —see **CHRISTIANITY**).

Such factors lead to four questions which demand honesty and have probably been masked in the current debates about the ethos of 'a secular society'.

◆ **Have Muslims therefore come to terms with loss of Mughal Empire and earlier Sultanate domination? In so doing have they acknowledged publicly the wrongdoings that undoubtedly occurred, that everyone knows did occur?** Even Thomas and William Daniell had made comments as painters and explorers of India for a British public to see before photography what India looked like. Arriving in Gaya in March 1790 they stopped at a small town, Madanpur, where they found a desecrated temple. This is what they wrote:

> its situation is so recluse that it might have been expected the Hindus here would have escaped the insolence of Mahomedan usurpation; unfortunately for them it happened otherwise for after suffering in common with their countrymen from these intolerant invaders, they had the mortification to find their principal temple... polluted and their sacred idols defaced.

From **Early Views of India, The Picturesque Journeys of Thomas and William Daniell**, 1786–1794 (by **Mildred Archer**, Thames and Hudson, London, 1980).

Confronting truth openly is really the Gandhian way of defusing evil no matter how far back into the past. It is a painstaking task of which Australians are only too aware in relation to policies enacted out on Aboriginal people in times past.

◆ **Secondly, can modern Muslims broaden the base of Islamic thinking** to embrace modern science and education with a new intellectual vigour that manifested itself centuries ago when Islam led the world in scientific discoveries? It is just that embedded concept of submisssion, 'Muslim' an Arabic word for 'one who submits' which so influences all attitudes of the faithful to new concepts trust in the **freedom of the individuals to embrance reform**.

◆ **Thirdly**, can Muslims without diminishing their own particular view of the universe (very similar to the Christian on the march) accept that **there are other avenues to truth and experience of the divine?** That Hindus are not blaspheming 'idol' worshippers? That terrible destruction of Hindu temples occurred and mosques were deliberately built out of their rubble–as, being the nature of political conquest, Christian churches were built on the ruins of mosques in true crusader spirit in other geographical contexts.

Is it possible for a sizeable minority of a cohesive Muslim community that has migrated for one reason or another, not necessarily in conquest as in the sultanate days of northern India, to accept citizenship of a totality in a major indigenous culture such as Britian, without being influenced by the commentaries after the Prophet passed away? These commentaries termed shariat, speak of **darul islam**–a majority Islamic society–and **darul hrb–land of strife** (phonetically pronounced h(u)r(u)b) thus implying hostile society, that is 'consider your majority as an enemy'.

Personal Endnote: Encountering the devotees of **Ayyappan** (son of Shiva by Mohini, according to local legend) on my visit to Kerala during the same period as their 41-day long pilgrimage, I was quite astonished to encounter Muslim colleagues amongst the throng. In their marigold-garlanded mini-buses, which trailed us from Madurai to Kanyakumari and up the spine of Kerala to Erumeli. They were all Keralites, pilgrims at one but growing rapidly as a following beyond the exclusive domain of this tiny state (**PILGRIMAGES**).

Endnote: Understandably there are a number of younger Indian writers emerging, wishing to bring out into the open the suppressed anger of years. The unwritten rules of official 'secular society, composite culture' ethos muted this expression previously. Some publications appear appropriately under the **Voice of India** and **Aditya Prakashan** imprints–S R Goel's **Hindu Temples: What Happened to Them, Vol II–The Islamic Evidence**; and K S Lal's **Indian Muslims: Who Are They?** (Note: **Aditya** is yet another Vedic term for the sun in the sense of luminosity behind all the phenomena that transmit light–stars, dawn, sun, moon, etc. **Prakashan** = publication.)

Anger has to be released, as we in Australia well understand, with all the evidence emerging 50 years later from Aboriginal source and all the personal bitterness being expressed of the stolen generation, before society can move on in harness. Perhaps we need Krishna in the chariot, holding the reins!

And another endnote! It does seem that beyond political rhetoric ordinary humanity can be encouraged to tread beyond the boundaries of distrust, hatred of 'the other', political exacerbations of diversity. A **pir** is a Muslim saint, often a **SUFI** who appears across these barriers because of his gentle holiness appealing to all religious persuasions.

In south Delhi on a hilltop grove now no longer pristine as it was in the 12th century but polluted by the clatter of the Mathura Road leading south with all its overburdened traffic, and the decibel level of horns, the tomb of **Abu Bakter Joshi** draws pilgrims in their thousands including non-Muslims.

The shrine popularly known as the **Matke Shah** is very colourful with brightly-painted **pitchers filled with offerings of grain** and **gur** (jaggery) representing the supplications of the pilgrims seeking spiritual help. This symbolises the Pir's miraculous defiance of a mock offering of the ruler **Prithvi Raj** (see **PUTLI WALLAHS**) about whom the Pir had made critical comments. This 'prasad' the Pir prayed over and it transformed into grain and gur. Pirs today seem to hold little political sway.

Further endnote 2005: When all is said and done about Indian complexities, both social and political, remember that a much respected fine scientist and a 'gentle' man (as was the first Indian **Muslim** President of India, **Dr. Zakir Husain,** eminent scholar) is A P J (Avul Pakir Jainulabdeen) ABDUL KALAM. From a humble South Indian **Muslim** family of seafarers and boat builders, he was chosen by his fellow parliamentarians to the nation's highest symbolic post.

M

- **NADA**

Indians have developed a profound and complex sense of sounds and a scientific awareness of the physics of vibration interrelated with energy.

Nada is the primal, cosmic sound (see **OM** and **PRAÑA**).

Nada-Bindu is the original seed-bija from which the universe in which we exist has expanded and is accepted by yoga and ayurveda practitioners as the energy channels in the body from which psychic power can be harnessed by training and study under a yogic guru. Again, those early rishis ever searching for the true explanation of creation would have felt very much at home in a modern assembly of physicists. Their understanding of what is not seen or materially obvious, yet exists, is quite remarkable considering how little measurable scientific theory existed in 4000 BCE. They had already formulated this as **anahata** = unstruck sound is that which in normal life cannot be heard by the human ear. Only those dedicated to meditation, yoga, concentrating intensely on musical training may have occasion to become aware of what has been referred to in the West as the **music of the spheres**.

◆ Ahata is manifested sound, the result of an impact, as in music, the striking of keys creating measurable vibrations.

- **NAGA, NAGAS**

are not just snakes, threatening reptiles as outsiders might see them. Enshrined in random groups of stones carved or embossed on slabs placed under trees or in groves especially in south India, they are 'forces' to be reverenced.

They have become symbols, metaphors resonating with deeply significant meaning. Not only do they represent **the coils of time** associated with Shiva, but in artistic symbolism they are seen as the **transients** able to move between water and land, associated with the cosmic ocean, the waters of dissolution and paradoxically of creation in the DNA—nucleic acid, principle of our watery birth out of the **cosmic ocean. HIRANYAGARBHA** the Golden Egg symbolic of the birth of the cosmos, is aswirl in the primordial waters of life, just as the human foetus is before the waters of the womb break. Out of the waters, biologically, snakes provide the linkage between this, our original 'home' and **prithvi** = earth. They are seen as 'keepers of life energy stored in springs and pools', according to a fine photographic book by **Sunil Vaidyanathan: Temples of South India, A Photographic Journey** (English Edition, Mumbai, 2002).

◆ **Ananta**, the endless many-headed snake is there to support the life-preserving principle of the inert Vishnu, between reincarnations, and renewal, the curved inflated hood like the crest of a rising wave about to break—implicit with potentiality.

The only time a serpent is deemed malevolent appears in the Puranic tales of Krishna subduing **Kaliya** in the Yamuna river near Vrindavan, south of Delhi. This is not to do with the eternal struggle between good and evil as in the Biblical allegory of the Garden of Eden.

Art theorists put the imagery down to a truth of antiquity of the emergence of Krishna in the Hindu pantheon to suppress the no longer relevant nature divinities of an earlier animistic worship of aboriginal India, as Vedic society developed and urbanised. Be that as it may, the strength of nature divinities appear as strong as ever, certainly in the shadowy groves of Kerala… as well as in Malayalam legends.

The Lord of Snakes, Nagaraj, is believed to have appeared before the **Parasurama avatar of Vishnu,** when the sea had receded leaving a barren strip of country, not the Kerala we recognise today.

Parasurama in **TAPASYA** (fervent penance) prayed for further guidance to make this land fertile. All the throng of snakes did Nagaraja's bidding burrowing away under the soils, improving their quality, the snake and its sexual energy symbolism being ever a potent force of fertility and kundalini energy. The serpent deity is propitiated in many parts of India, not just the Dravidian south, by barren women seeking to bear children. Its healing powers have also been incorporated through Greek culture into the medical logo of intertwined snakes familiar in Western medicine.

A personal note at **Mannarassala** near Alappuzha (old Allepey) according to local legend and accepted 'rationally' by middle-class professional friends....

The family seat of Parasurama's brahmin disciples Vasudev and Sridevi, where they lived out their lives, became yet another 'hallow', part of the 'sacred geography' noted in **PILGRIMAGES.** The **Mannarassala Temple** is built there on the site of the illam, a unique place of pilgrimage especially for childless couples. The extraordinary fact is not the reputed age of the temple (believed by Keralites to trace back at least 3,000 years) but that a priestess called the **great mother–Valiamma–**presides over the worship. She inherits the role in a matriarchal line befitting so much that occurs in Kerala culture and personifies the old woman who in the legend pleads for the birth of a son. Giving up all else, her powers perceived as almost divine, Valiamma dedicates herself to serving the snake god, tradition taking this role back to an ancient source when Vasudev and Sridevi, the family ancestors, childless themselves, saved scorched serpents from a forest conflagration and healed their charred skins with melted ghee, honey and oil. For such service, the great snake god, **Nagaraj** the five-headed **Chiranjivi** was born their son—as well as a human boy to carry on the line! Nagaraj would reside in the depth of this place to be watched over by the senior mother of the illam. And so it is even today in the place which means 'earth cooled after the fire', **mannar** = earth, **asala** = a cooling.

But it is not only in the south that the **naga** is honoured (and who knows from how distant a signal pulsing from the up until now acknowledged roots in Indus valley culture, **Naga-bearing seals** having emerged from those mist-shrouded sources as archaeological digs continue… refer to **DRAVIDIANS**).

◆ The early faiths of India have all been touched by veneration in the cult of the serpent–Shaivism, Vaishnavism, Jainism, Buddhism. As the pantheon depiction took hold in rock sculpture the snake curls its way around the torsos of nearly all the major deities, in harmony with their bodies—in the matted hair of the

N

northern Siva catching the full forces of the Himalayan torrent of Ganga Ma; a waist belt for Ganesh; Vishnu's couch Ananta—indicating the endlessness of creation; a snake ring for Kali.

♦ **Nagapanchami** is the festival giving veneration to a multitude of nagas in July/August. But how drugged are the live cobras our family witnessed being propitiated? We kept our distance, faith not as firm as Indian companions, who accompanied the priest in placing prasad in the shrine.

♦ 'Never take fright! Let a snake go its way,' is the advice given as we travelled the length and breadth of the land. However, Indians do get bitten—and die—and even the snake-charmers' village outside Delhi is not immune to deaths despite the declaration of snake-wallahs they are immune or carry special earth balls impregnated with 'snake spit' (their term!). Having been shown the grey 'golf ball' fuzzy with bits of hair, I felt I would rather abide by the old adage... **Discretion is the better part of valour.**

And yet another reminder of Kashmir's strange and lengthy harbouring of Indian folklore, so ancient that associations may go back to pre-human times when land masses were still undergoing radical change, and only reptiles and the fish in the sea commanded the chain of development. In one **purana** the snake is credited along with the sage Kashyap in creating the valley that gives such melancholy beauty and his name to Kashmir. Names of towns such as Sheshnag and Anantnag serve only to reinforce the echoes coming in from unknown sources, like radio signals from outer space. But with the ubiquitous 'where' and 'who' the source of the abiding legends?

Personal Encounter

However, beware of embracing too benign a presence if proximity allows a sudden encounter... apocryphal stories abound of garden hoses mistaken in the dusk for dormant snakes on lawns but on a country road in the southern Deccan in the setting sun we slowed the car down to investigate a pile of coiled rope in our pathway.

As I climbed out with the door half open this inert coil reared up, erect, hood inflated, 10 feet away, no more. Fear froze me. A villager striding home on the other side of the road, in a flash of graceful motion dived for a big boulder sitting on the arid scrubland and heaved it with all his might. Astonishingly it landed on the first coil of the lungs and broke the cobra's spine.

Even quicker, the cobra turned on itself, lunged and gripped the nearest coil in its fangs, deadly poison oozing into the bite... and committed suicide. It took months to erase that image and the pain of its own **suffering**... and years to find the physiological truth as to whether it could be immune to its own venom—or not? Indians say 'yes'. Westerners, zoologists, as usual remain sceptical.

■ **NAMES**

Do not be intimidated by south Indian names. They especially are dauntingly polysyllabic. One Australian exporter of Indian pulses to India (believe it or not, coals get exported to Newcastle in many different cultural forms!) is dealing with **Shanmugampillai Subramaniam** in Coimbatore. If faced with a

long name like this, take a deep breath and break up the name into its constituent syllables. Most are names derived from the major deities in their many aspects.

Narayana(n) (pronounced Naar-eye-an-a) for instance is a very common name—both as a 'given' name for Hindus or as a **surname** in Western parlance, and an alternative for Vishnu. The word is derived from:

Nara son of the original Being created by Brahma in the waters = *nara* of creation. *Ayana* place of motion, in this context, where movement of cells first began.

Once the constituent syllables are realised to be names or words in themselves then you can trip the light fantastic and speak the name liltingly such as the following names of great south Indian percussion musicians who indicate another cultural formula.

Certainly amongst a considerable number of upper caste males (this does not apply to women) in the south what we would presume passingly to be the **first or 'given name'** at baptism is a **family place name** or **father's name**, the **second**, the given name, the **third**, the **caste**—but to confuse the traveller from foreign parts, this often is dropped altogether!

As follows, the names are single words divided here by syllables to clarify their meaning.

Family Place Name	Given Name	Caste Name
the famous late kanjira player		
Deva/kotam	**Sundara/raja**	**Iyengar**
deity/place	beautiful/lord	Vaishnavite brahmin
or village	(either Vishnu or Shiva)	
the even more famous mrdangam player		
Palghat	**Mani**	**Iyer**
(place in Kerala	jewel	Shaivite brahmin
in southern hills)		
expert ghatam-claypot-player		
Umayalerpuram	**Kothanda/Rama Iyer**	
(place in Tamilnadu	synonym	Shaivite brahmin
/town or city)	describing	
	Rama's beauty	

But this system of naming does not always run true to form. Take for instance the brilliant violinist known worldwide...

Father's Name	Given Name	Caste Name
Lakshminarayana	**Subramaniam**	**Iyer**

whose equally famous but more unorthodox violinist brother is L Shankar.

Lakshminarayana	**Shankar**	**Iyer**

If either had a son one should start off with Subramaniam, the other with Shankar and become

Shankar	Ravi	Iyer

Shankar is one of the many names of **Siva, the auspicious** as **giver-of-joy**.... he could be called in a short-handed way **S Ravi** which would make it simple for all of us.

♦ The female members fall outside this patriarchal system. They are named after natural hallowed forces such as **Shakti**, or emblems from the world of nature, **Padma** = lotus, or deities and their alternative names.

Do **not** fall into the trap of asking **people** what their **Christian** name is unless you have found out they are actually Christian. (There are over 20 million Christians in India, most especially in Kerala). Otherwise they may be Hindu, Buddhist, Jain, Jewish, Parsee, Muslim, Sikh or Anglo-Indian–so that would be very ethnocentric of you!

Family Trees

A South Indian Tamil lady explained her difficulty in constructing a family tree, even in the highly literate brahmin community, where you would expect it most to be possible. This is what she said:

In Tamil culture especially, the daughter marries a maternal uncle if available, or a first cousin (that is a father's sister's child or mother's brother's child). You would have to construct a three dimensional hologram and anyway you only know your ancestors by force of the oral tradition passed down through the families. There were no parish registers for registering marriages either. Anyway because of our theory of reincarnation we are not really concerned with that sense of history! It is immaterial.

♦ **Sikh names** derive from the founding of the body of Sikhs by Guru Gobind Singh in 1699. This was called the Khalsa, a word meaning pure. At this ceremony, those who became Sikhs took the name **Singh** if they were male, **Kaur** if female to signify the breakaway from caste. Singh means Lion, Kumari is an honorific name for woman.

Singh is part of the forename and in actual fact the surname is the sub-caste name borne by a whole family, or the village name–such as **Kairon**. (Sikhs disassociated themselves from caste but in the Indian context these names, such as **Sondh, Gill, Dhesi, Sambhi, Sandhu** have crept back to common usage). To add further confusion, however, these sub-caste names are dropped and a man who started off with a first name **Piara**, then the distinctive **Singh**, then his sub-caste name **Sambhi**—Piara Singh Sambhi—may eventually be known as **Mr Piara Singh**, or **Sardar Piara Singh**, sardar or leader as honorific.

Sometimes other names derived from trade guilds or confederations which grew up after the disintegration of the Mughal Empire–Ramgarhia for instance–are used as surnames. When two sardarjis (an affectionate reference to a Sikh) find themselves with identical names they will often adopt descriptive epithets in good humour as third names–such as **Singh Dhiddal** (with a paunch) and **Singh Ainki** (with spectacles).

♦ **Muslim names** are often the combination and permutation of the 99 names of Allah, each meaning a different and principal attribute of Muhammed.

Every Muslim has a tribal name based on the name of the area from which he has come, or from the founder of the clan. This is the equivalent of a surname. If this could be accepted as such it may solve some of the confusions which arise from too many Alis and Khans. The word Khan constantly causes confusion. It is not a surname in the Western sense. Khan means the head of a tribe, such as the famous Gandhian Muslim **Khan**

Abdul Ghaffar Khan. The first is the title, and the latter is part of the name but *not* the surname. He was often referred to as the Frontier Gandhi.

One Muslim father expounded further:

Many an Islamic parent names their offspring in the hope that as they grow up they will mirror the attributes of the word chosen as name.

Amir or Ameer means leader or wealthy… Adil is just. Sadiq is truth… Ghulam Rasool, servant of the Prophet. Qureshi, the Arab tribe of the Prophet's ancestry, Abraham or Ibrahim being the progenitor, is the most aristocratic name of all to bear.

After the prophet died there were four **khalifas** (caliphs) of Islam namely: **Abubaker, Umar, Ali** and **Usman.** Many Muslims name their sons likewise. **Ahmad** is another popular name. This was a name of Prophet Muhammed.

■ **NAMASTE**
NAMASKARAM: is the south Indian form
NAMAZ *Urdu*

Greetings between people with hands folded together (like Durer's famous etching) and then a bow of varying depth. The words are Sanskrit-Hindi, stating '**I salute the divine in thee'**, originally in the temple at the shrine where the **murti–statue** of the Deity was situated.

It is also a dance **hasta-mudra**, hand gesture of salutation to Nataraja usually placed at corner of the stage.

♦ As Hindus cup their hands to the Deity in worship, bowing in **namaskaram**, fingers being together in the shape of a lotus bud, so Indian **Muslims** bow down in **namaz = prayerful submission to Allah.**

But this is more formalised. Each prayer should be undertaken at five specific times a day. And even that is ritualised into thirteen specific positions from kneeling with nose and forehead touching the ground to standing facing towards Mecca with thumbs touching the ear-lobes.

The secular greeting to a Muslim is a saluting touch to the forehead (the **adaab**) and a slight bow. To be courteous as Lucknowees would be one could add the greeting:

Assalam-o-alaikum: Peace be on you… to which the reply will come:

Wa alaikum-us-salaam: And peace be on you.

Khuda Hafiz—when saying goodbye to a Muslim friend this phrase means 'May the Almighty protect you'. It has more meaning than just saying goodbye.

■ **NARAYANA**

….is yet another name for the Impersonal Absolute, Consciousness–Brhm the Mind of God, and of Vishnu in material form. In the world of symbols the ammonite fossil in India's sacred rivers–the **salagrama**–is carried by individuals, or worshipped under trees as signs of this material form.

My south Indian music guru, the late T K Jayaram Iyer, joyful violinist, first showed me his **salagrama** which was from the higher reaches of the Ganga and had been blessed in many sacred places. To him it represented the presence of the living deity, Narayana, at his concerts. He always kept it close to hand in his pocket.

'That which resides in all Beings'. That is Narayana.

- **NASTIKA**

A person who does not believe in anything beyond what he sees. Late Sanskrit scholar/writer Dr V Raghavan asserted it was not possible to be an atheist in the Hindu context. Actual existence, virtual reality so-to-speak, means one's thought processes and existence are part of the universal energy. You might try to deny the existence of God as envisaged by many Christians but you cannot deny the existence of physics, concepts of energy, the natural laws of the universe, the fact that your own 'awareness' is part of a greater **whole**... 'a superior reasoning power' as Einstein once put it, 'revealed in the incomprehensible universe'. That to him was the concept of God.

Astika–'it is'–is a true orthodox believer in the validity of the Vedas and the teachings of the many rishis who built up the rationale and basic tenets of belief from the original searchings and speculation of Vedic hymns. **Panini** the ancient grammarian gave his own version of **astik** = he who believes in life after death is 'astika'. Buddha also believed in incarnations and rebirths so he cannot be called a 'nastika' asserting a belief in 'nothingness' at the end of the day.

Nastika came, however, to mean a person who followed heterodox faiths such as Buddhism, etc, faiths that did not ascribe to the Vedic orthodox schools of philosophy, nor recognise the validity of the intuitive revelations and consequent formalised teachings (**not** creeds) that developed from these. (see DARSHAN)

- **NATARAJA**

....Natya....Lord of the Dance. From Sanskrit root *nat* = to represent visually. How remarkable that a dancing god, executed in bronze somewhere around the 10th century CE, under the visionary patronage of the royal Cholas in Tamil kingdoms (as generous and far-sighted in their patronage of the arts as the Renaissance Medicis or Tudor and Stuart monarchs in Britain) can spring forth again into our new millennium... a resonating icon fashioned by an unknown artisan with such consummate intellectual command of the concept that this is.

Symbol of creation in the rhythmical vibrations of this most famous dance—**ananda tandava** (bliss dance)—and of destruction ringed as Nataraja is in the aureole of flames, it has become so resonant in the collective global mind now that even Western scientists have appropriated Siva's name in areas of physics devoted to energy research. Certain apparatus in laboratories at the UK Atomic Energy Authority Culham Laboratories devoted to nuclear fusion energy

(to offset the extravagant use of the planet's fossil fuels) and particular chambers devised for bombardment of sub-atomic particles in California have been given the 'Shiva' name. And this even before **Fritjof Capra** wrote his **The Tao of Physics** (refer to **Journal of the Royal Society of the Arts**, Lecture by Dr Pease, UK Energy Authority, August 1981, pp. 584–596). For those scientfically interested in this concept, search out May 24, 2002 issue of **Science**: vol. 296, article by **Paul Steinhardt** and **Neil Turok: A Cyclic Model of the Universe**.... A continuum of bang and crunch.

◆ **THE CONCEPT**... Nataraja portrays Shiva/Siva paradoxically in his 'imaged' form as cosmic energy. Yet the word **Siva** means **auspicious** and **Sivam** in Sanskrit designates the concept when still or in **passive form of inner withdrawal**. Indian thinking delights in sparking like blue electricity along the double edge of permanent paradox–for that is what life is. The inert pale Siva and the unbridled energy of the dark Kali in symbiotic unison is a commonplace image (with hidden depths of demanding intellectual challenge as well as visually aesthetic balance in terms of its artistic expression). Zimmer once again is very useful in giving clear evidence on the complex metaphysics of this–in **Myths and Symbols in Indian Art and Civilization**.

One has to remember that Siva emerges in a process of **augmentation**–from existing indigenous beliefs in a symbolic form (or unknown deity?) thought to be embedded in an ascetic aura (see **INDUS VALLEY CIVILIZATION** seals) and amalgamation with the **Rudra** of early Vedic literature. This is long before representational sculpture emerged, and the **PANTHEON** literally took human shape. **Rudra** (Skt) = to howl, and somehow came to mean the remover of pain, although as a concept Rudra represented the fearful aspects of the natural world, forces out of control in thunder, tornado, fire, lightning. Yet Rudra was also paradoxically benign, giving shelter (which would diminish pain).

By a process of osmosis, typically Hindu in motivation, Rudra emerges into Siva.

◆ That very earliest image of **Rudra**–not a visual one, but orally chanted in the Vedic hymns–was one of metaphor... tempestuous storms and cyclonic forces roaring most probably out of a wild deity, howling and raging as a typhoon out of the Bay of Bengal. Such power had to be propitiated. Vedic hymns implored Rudra to be compassionate and benign. In seeking this tempestuous god with his anarchic energy transcending human boundaries, forest flames of energy determined to leap beyond the limits society carves as breaks to prevent primeval bush fires spreading and engulfing human beings, the Hindu appears to accept that destruction is **not negative**.

As a Western poet has realised: **there can be no beginnings without endings**

◆ **SIVA AS COSMIC DANCER... endless entropy cycling round into explosive rebirths...** as such must then be the most satisfying and aesthetically beautiful icon that can come out of another age, and a totally alien culture yet have relevance to the scientific thought and technological discoveries for a new millennium... new shifts in comprehensions which embrace a world of sub-atomic particles, quantum physics, quarks, black holes and gluons–a realm despite TV documentaries and the arts of explanatory graphic design that is beyond the comprehension of most of us. Yet Indians seem quite comfortable in accepting these cavernous intimidating empty reaches of the cosmos (see **KALPA**).

One has to ask the question–in reverence–as to how it is that an image, embracing the comprehensive notion of destruction, a wiping out of consciousness at the end of time, fashioned in such aesthetic beauty, of balance, in the difficult art of 'cire perdue' (lost wax) moulds, can speak across the epochs to us and crystallise these abstract concepts in a visionary flash of understanding.

Artists were striving in the earlier millennium of the common era, stretching the collective imagination in the most demanding of conditions against sheer rock face, adamantine granite conditions at **ELLORA**. In the seventh century CE in western India, Siva is beginning to bend and twist his body in a transforming liquid movement as though such rock was malleable clay.

Here is temple sculpture in all its unbridled strength of youth reaching out to express almost wayward physical energy yet harnessed to a hint of inward reflection and the joyous bliss which the growing bhakti impulses of south India are wafting northwards, a reassertion of the rich Hindu expression of personal devotion to a specific Vaisnavite or Saivite manifestation. To stand at the foot of the Kailash temple or in the sharp-edged almost architected verandahs overhung by a mass of frightening rock visually harsh in contrast of intense shadow and eye-shattering sunlight breaking the sharp-edge columns (also of massive proportion) and then to encounter these first experimental dancing Sivas 'rupturing the bonds of earth' (to use **Carmel Berkson's** evocative phrase) is to marvel at the capacity of human spirit to translate imagination into artistic reality once again. And to overcome the mountain's immensity, the challenge in front of all those who stood here 1,300 years ago.

◆ **THE EMERGING FORM = swarup**

As Berkson pointed out in her definitive book on **Ellora, Concept and Style,** never before had an artist sculptor created such an animated portrayal of the Dancing God. Imbued with the vitality charged with personal devotion of bhakti in Ellora. The sculptor's 'inflated imagination' is

unconstrained, subordinating all hesitation. He adores his god, he asserts the enormous force, the tremendous grace, the light-hearted abandonment of gravitational pull as a sign of his desire and delight.

Indeed that unknown Michelangelo forces form into high-relief rough-hewn but virtually in the round, defying all the challenges of limited tools, no electricity, no motorised back-up in the enormity of the laboured effort ahead....in 700 CE.

A still imperfect twisted torso, coiled like a thick rope, arched like a taut bow, a cylindrical exaggerated pipe of an arm, yet dimpled at the elbow, defies all the traditional limitations and proportional measurements as laid down in the artistic codes. 'Dancing his way into the higher realms' Siva's face remains serenely intent on expressing that inward yogic-centred mind, lost

in the potent energy about to explode. It is as though the artist was trying to climb inside the spirit of the god.

To stand in the early light of day at Ellora as saffron-robed monks search out the serenely-seated Buddhas hidden deep in the shadowed caves; to watch impoverished women flashing red and green and yellow tie-dyed saris as they cajole straggling herds of goats along the narrow ledge of a mountain path, unconcerned as they are about artistic aesthetics as they unselfconsciously carry with them that ineffable Indian sense of style and innate grace in their own rhythmic gait, is to be swept away on tides of elation in the inexplicable essence of India's magic.

The force of visual impact, that gift of some unknown stonemason so great, artistic imperatives demand a retracing of steps... a second look at that expression, a Siva listening to a distant drum. Arms that grew outwards from rock face in astonishing ingenuity, now broken off by time or marauders, the face impelled upwards, the expression now blurred by erosion and centuries of monsoonal damp and the dry nights of the ghat terrain, the shadowy other Siva at the end of the colonnade, exaggerated hulk of shoulder thrust out, the feet travelling in a remarkable opposite direction, this then is the template from which the perfected form, carried forward in a more pliant medium, will appear complete and eternal, the ripples of rhythmic dance no longer held in his mind alone...

◆ **INTELLECTUALLY IN COMMAND (of evergreen symbols)** Dance in Indian eyes is **matter in motion**; Nataraja within his deepest essence is a mass of **creative particles** suddenly flaring from random chaos in outer space surging into **molecular patternings,** structures in **constant motion** in what appear through illusory perceptions–maya–to be **static matter**. As an Indian once pointed out–a table is a form of **static wood** to the human eye–its inner structure is something else. The Hindu sees matter as stored energy. In the substratum of all our existence on this earth, static though it may appear, a blue globe in space, there is a fundamental 'restlessness'.

Wherever energy takes centre stage this artistic image zooms in across centuries and continents, across unknown languages such as Tamil and from a view of life totally alien to our roots in Graeco-Roman-Christian civilisation. And did Sydney Carter, post-war English composer of a new kind of joyous hymn, **Lord of the Dance,** respond to the same distant resonances which in that artistic anonymity of a **Chola** dynasty of the 10th–12th century danced to the pervasive vibrations of the melodious **veena**, such a familiar instrument for south Indian dance? The **devadasis** perhaps still uncorrupted in that far-off time as they gave service to the great Deity in their temple duties of dance, pounding the ground in the mathematical choreography of the intellectually demanding **Bharata Natyam**, reiterated the profound messages of energy in response to the deep vibrations of the veena, the echoing chambers of the fashioned gourds curling around with a palimpsest of sound through the resonating colonnades of temple architecture.

◆ **SHIVA'S ICON**... this image of Nataraja has been called 'one of the most powerful plastic realisations of theological thought ever achieved in art.' (Information sheet, **National Gallery of Victoria,** Melbourne).

Fritjof Capra, writer and physicist has explained this ceaseless flow of energy which is Siva Nataraja as an 'infinite variety of patterns that melt into one another... The metaphor of the cosmic dance thus unifies ancient mythology, religious art and modern physics.'

◆ **Dr Ananda Coomaraswamy** has written extensively of the density of thought behind this one perfect icon; 'a complete circle so united is rare in such bronzes. The circle issues from the mouths of a pair of dolphins (**makaras**). The halo symbolises the **pranava,** the mystic word AUM which is a generalised symbol of all possible sounds of the logos...

The hair on the head is braided, the upper part tied together to form a crown (baddhaveni) terminating in a crest of peacock feathers, and at the back a circular knot (sikha chakra) the lower braids falling loose (lamba veni) and whirling in the dance. At the base of the crown is a human skull–symbol of Siva's destroying energy.

A SYMBOL has been described as a condensed representation of a cluster of ideas. Even a Westerner unfamiliar with the depth of Hindu philosophy can still respond to implied meaning in the hand gestures or **mudras**–the **pancha** (five) **krityas** (*kri*-to act, to do) which Shiva, firing the imagination, indicates to the devotee.

The Fivefold Activity of the Supreme Being according to the Tamil/Sanskrit texts:

1. **Srishti** = pouring forth creation–suggested by the onomatopoeic **dumru,** drumming in the upper right hand the source of **nada,** the coming into being with breath > sound > word = **vac.** Vibration, nada represents the first stage of evolution, the very sound shristi having an electric sizzle about it as it should... for it is the **Big Bang** Creation.

2. **Sthiti** = maintenance and preservation indicated by the upraised hand the **abhaya hasta: Fear not, for I am here.** Stability of the universe implied.

3. **Samhara** = destruction of all matter from the single flame held aloft in the upper left palm (the cyclical burning away of galaxy upon galaxy by the gathering force of the sun predicted by modern astrophysicists). This is the purifying process by fire, salvation before another rebirth of the universal process all over again.

4. **Tirobhava** = veiling, concealment as signified by the **dwarf-asura**–anti-god cowering in submission under Shiva's foot.

Muyalaka (Tamil) or **Apasmara** (Sanskrit = not-knowing or heedlessness), the dwarf creature often referred to as illusion more correctly represents the egocentric nature of the human which is ignorant, bound up in a blinkered vision about the **real reality.** Muyalaka in fact represents 'the **six enemies of enlightenment = kama,** desire; **krodha,** anger; **lobha,** greed; **moha,** attachment; **mada,** conceit; and **matsara,** jealousy. Ego is humanity's problem state, the source of feeling separate from the divine in whatever form.

Many Hindu thinkers regard **a-vidya** = ignorance as the cardinal sin which this tiny figure represents. Self-disciplinary sadhana is the only way to rehabilitate such ignorance.

5. **Anugraha** = the sense of release bestowing grace in the left lower hand pointing to the raised foot kicking out and away from ignorance, so freeing the soul of these illusions and freeing the devotee from the fetters of the narrow prisonhouse of the ego pinned down by Siva's other foot, in bondage to a mistaken material reality.

Dr V Raghavan standing in front of his own icon of the Dancing God in Madras explained not only these important five components that the aesthetically satisfying image embodies but yet another depth beyond the obvious. The empty shrine at **CHIDAMBARAM** which represents ether, is echoed by that cavity in the human heart which automatically 'breathes' the very life-blood through our bodily systems. In so doing it whispered the mantra, **HAMSAH SO-HAM SVAHA:** 'I AM THAT: THAT IS I: SVAHA' (a ritual utterance at the end of an offering of prayer or substance to the Deity)... 'When one dances, your heart automatically beats the **hamsa**. So Shiva is dancing in that cavity, in absolute enrapturement.'

Apart from these major 'pointers' there are other embellishments to the compressed iconography, such as Ganga caught from flooding the world by the mass of swirling hair, becoming symbol of Shiva's descending grace.

◆ **TECHNIQUE**... to those who travel, make for Swamimalai, near Kumbakonam halfway between Thanjavur and Chidambaram. Here in the shadow of **Shri Murugan's** temple the art of the 'lost wax' technique–*cire perdue*–is still undertaken, the fashioning of these bronzes hardly changed for 1,000 years since the Pallava dynasty first encouraged the art. And then the 11th century Cholas in all their glory. First the icon is fashioned in moulded beeswax by craftsmen who claim 800 years of family ancestry. Then the special consistency of sand from the Kaveri river is packed around the mould and wired like a fat cushion to dry in the sun, later to be fired in a hollow on the earthen floor as in ancient times; the wax form melting leaving its impress; and then the expert hand pouring the **panchaloka**–the auspicious five metals = **brass** is an alloy, **lead, copper, silver and gold** into the fashioned hollow, a molten flow in one swoop. When cooled its humble blanket of clay is broken open for the polishing and filing, and the 'opening' of the murti's eyes.

M S is playing her veena, at practice as dusk falls and her home, its traditional wood carvings, even the brass lamps, softly disappearing in the shadows A single **diya** flickers. **Raga Sankarabharana** (Sankara yet another name for Shiva = auspicious) affirms itself as a major Carnatic raga, establishing that C major solfa note. She is singing in the higher register.

Lalata netre	One eye on thy forehead
Chandra sekhare	The crescent moon on thy brow
Alahala kantha	The fearful poison in thy throat
Mangala murti	Embodiment of all that is auspicious
Kailasa-pate	Lord of Kailash (the mountain)

Tripura-dahana	Destroyer of the Three Cities
Sri bhakta jana priya	O Fortune, Beloved of thy Devotees
Guna nidhe	Treasure of all gunas (qualities)

.... and at a later date, a resplendent Bharata Natyam devadasi, Balasarawati gives form to the words—**and the gods are dancing**.... all this 500 years before Copernicus and Galileo.

■ NAYANMAR

refers to those south Indian devotees of Shiva who turned often to the open road as singing saints in the **BHAKTI** movement—at the same period as the Vaishnavite **ALVAR** saints. From the 8th to 9th century CE both streams of strong individual worship gathered force, and continue in pockets all over the country, even today.

◆ **Manikkavachakar** (note the root from the Vedic hymn to **VAC** = Sanskrit = holy word in the sense of 'In the beginning was the Word'), prime minister of the Pandyan court (circa 700 AD) who encountered a visionary electric current of mystical awareness is one of the first of the **Nayanmars**, strongly revered even today by Tamil remembrances.

The prime minister was so overcome by devotional love for Siva he renounced public life. Imagine today such happenings in the Western world or, for that matter, the Indian!

◆ **Basava(nna)**, king's treasurer, is equally well-known in the 1100s for his succinct poetic sayings, *vacana*. Again note the root = spiritual insights. Born in the then state of Mysore, he wrote in the Kannada language.

Such defiant freethinkers, some born brahmin in the 12th century but critical of brahmin adherence in those times to unnecessary form rather than the true spirit of their calling, reinforced Basava's message which stirred the spiritual cauldron of his caste colleagues as well as unsettling the political establishment in which he was employed. Indeed, revolutionary followers dismissed with a sense of mystical universality the strictures of brahmin society lyrically documented in **A K Ramanujan's Speaking of Siva**.

Similar to the European mystical traditions their poetic devotions to the **bhagavan** (the lord) are redolent with sexual references although the separate tantric devotional tradition developed those allusions much further. Along with their male colleagues women 'gave themselves' to Siva in what in the literature is referred to as the **Virasaivism** movement (virile—is derived from the same root). Some went the whole way discarding clothes to become themselves without definition by external indicators.

■ NEEM

(Azadirachta indica)

has been declared the wonder tree of the 21st century, much sought after in Australia in the fight against salination due to its water retention properties. This multifoliate tree provides more than shade along the hot roads of India and the leafy suburban avenues of many big cities. If the assertion is true that the air around the tree is free from bacteria then in today's pollution a forest of neem needs planting.

It has many medicinal properties as well. Its dried leaves stored like camphor balls of old to keep the woolly bug from eating holes in prized cashmere shawls and cardigans stowed away in those old-fashioned but wonderful commodious domed trunks discovered in dark corners of many a modern Indian home. Indeed, its potential globally in integrated pest control has aroused interest in Europe and Australia.

Look on a bathroom window ledge if you have the privilege of staying with an Indian family: there will be a bunch of dark brown sticks bound together—the neem twigs in their prime to be chewed instead of using expensive toothpaste. The astringent juices keep the gums extremely healthy and the teeth sparkling. A sannyasi chewing such on a train and noisily hawking mucous with the spit going out the window in well-aimed globules (again that paradox of private cleanliness and offensive public hygiene—or total lack of it!) explained:

The juice is very bitter. Worse than quinine! It is taken by many of us, even sadhus (so even he made the distinction!) *to cool down the body and the blood—in order to help the mind not be distracted.*

What he was trying to say as we rattled over brown river after brown river on solid railway bridges not yet swept away by post-monsoonal flood waters on Gujarat's indented Arabian coastline south of Kaira was that neem juice helps subdue those rajas-red tendencies (see **GUNAS**) that lead thoughts astray—such as **sex** rearing its ugly head! It is fortunate that the railroad spit did contain strong anti-bacterial properties and that neem is used in the Indian battle against intestinal worms. Every part of the tree is useful and antiseptic. Oil from the nuts, leaves, flowers and the wood itself, all can be harnessed to clear ulcerated tissue and dermatological problems. I have had Indians tell me in villages that tender neem leaves chewed daily are an antidote to snake bites and scorpion stings!

Endnote: A report cautions India not to take this multipurpose tree for granted as it has done in the past. After research being undertaken in India (in use against malaria and as a possible natural contraception) the bulk of patents have been taken out overseas, only a tiny number in India. The matter of herbal property rights being acquired in bulk by big pharmaceutical conglomerates is of concern to Asian and African governments.

■ NEHRU, Pandit Jawaharlal

1889–1964

1st Prime Minister of Independent India 1947–64

It is very hard to write either of Gandhiji or Panditji as both were so affectionately called with the suffix **'ji'** to denote this reverential love for great souls. The inhibition is especially so when one has actually experienced what is now history—two generations ago! Seeing the Prime Minister of India driving around in his low-key small Hindustan car (how different from today's political aggrandisement) and watching him from the press gallery in Parliament, he was a real but still distant person–held in awe, statesman as well as politician by suffering the tapasya of being gaoled again and again by the British and consequently a fine writer and historian.

♦   It is hard in our cynical age of the new millennium when the Big Brother media now watches closely every move of heroes put on pedestals not to see them as mere mortals with feet of clay. Indeed, there is no belief in heroes or heroines anymore, most famous people, even inviolate monarchies such as the British now seem to be all too human like ordinary mortals, shorn of their mystique. And yet to wander through the **Nehru Memorial Museum** in New Delhi is a walk through a time capsule when heroes and heroines still were able to exist for us, the people.

For his time and place in history, Pandit Nehru is a **great soul**–there is no doubt about that, just for the very transformation of his own inner self though pain, hardship after such ease of birth which by dint of intelligence, inner dharma or miracle he brought about. Kashmiri Pandits–handsome by physique–are regarded as highly cultured, endowed with artistic sensibilities, their women some of the most beautiful in the world. Professor Arnold Toynbee referred to his 'captivating personality'. There is no doubt about that, nor his elegance and masculine grace, a distinction that touched women from afar. His equally infectious zest drew children as to an Indian Pied Piper. Watching him 'work a crowd' at Shankar's ambitious art exhibitions for children was fascinating.

Torn between two worlds, by all the norms of psychiatry you would imagine that he would have been a divided self. Or is it India's miraculous gift of being able to accommodate multiple identities, that layer upon layer of plural cultures that started when India began as an entity? It was Panditji after all who resurrected that beautiful classical term to describe this process–**PALIMPSEST** which in fact was the 'virtual reality' of his own complex identity.

He straddled his own aristocratic Indian upbringing, school at Harrow, college at Cambridge, studying law at the Inner Temple, Western dress encouraged by his own famous father's predilection for it, and then absorption into Gandhi's swadeshi movement without a hair turning it would seem on that elegant high brow–the white forage cap, accompanied by that ubiquitous rosebud daily worn in the high-necked **achkan**. Seven years in all in England in those most impressionable years provided hidden depths later to this layered personality. Nehru indeed once referred to himself as 'the last Englishman to rule India'.

Let one of his sisters speak. **Krishna Hutheesing** writing in **Dear to Behold: an Intimate Portrait of Indira Gandhi** (Macmillan, London, 1969) explains even the derivation of the name–and the Kashmiri heritage, useful to remember when assessing the Kashmir problem, which must have been a permanent anguish for Panditji.

We were Kashmiri Brahmins. Our ancestor Raj Kaul came to the court of Moghul Emperor Farruksiar, who was charmed with his learning. Farruksiar presented him with a house in Delhi on the banks of a nahar (canal), and our family became known in Delhi as Kaul-Nahar, which was corrupted to Kaul-Nehru. Eventually Kaul was dropped and our name became Nehru.

My great-grandfather Lakshmi Narayan Nehru became the first vakil (lawyer) of the East India Company at the court of the last Moghul emperor, but in the Revolt of 1857 his son's family was divested of its property and had to flee from Delhi, along with a multitude of refugees. On their journey to Agra, one of our uncles and his little sister were suddenly surrounded by English soldiers. Kashmiris are often very fair, and the soldiers mistook the little girl to be English and accused our uncle of kidnapping her.

He might have been subjected to hanging, but fortunately his knowledge of English saved the situation.

Nehru's grandfather had three sons, one of them Motilal much spoiled by the grandmother after her husband's death leaving Motilal in the charge of his lawyer uncle the Raja of Khetri:

As a boy Motilal had a violent temper–the famous Nehru temper which we all share... at college in Allahabad he tended to be a leader in wild capers, but when he took up the profession of law, he passed his examinations brilliantly. He liked Western ways and Western dress, which was not at all in conformity with the preferences of most Indians.

More radical Indian fighters for freedom were sceptical of the father **Motilal** and his Western ways denouncing him as a **firangi** in thought as well as dress although more often than not they themselves were in the elegant Kashmir black 'forage' cap, **achkan** (long tight-buttoned coat) and **churidar** trousers (called that for the wrinkles in the fold of the cotton leggings like the churree bangles on a woman's arm)... **Persian** in every seam... again one has to ask–what is Indian dress? That used to surface occasionally, some Indians resenting his 'western' indoctrination educationally.

A personal thought on Indian-ness

Nirad Chaudhuri once spent an hour mesmerising our dinner guests, lecturing them–as he was wont to do while standing, shaking his right index finger, castigating the new rulers in the Capital for their false values and Western posturings. He upset one of our Punjabi guests by pointing out that the shalwar-kameez she was wearing was not Indian, having been imported by Turkish Muslims in the 10th century! Yet she was Hindu. One of our Indian journalist friends at a later date had his tie cut off in a frenzy in the Punjab in Sikh-Hindu stirrings during the States Reorganization Commission and the tussle over the new secretariat in Chandigarh then being built. A tie was considered 'non-Indian'.

My own husband once faced an unruly mob in Bangalore 'wanting Goa' before finally the Portuguese understood the realities of an Independent India... and left. We were in a taxi enroute to the airport to fly home to Delhi. An excited student with scissors waving ominously shoved his head through the open window. 'We want Goa. You are firangi? You wear tie? That is **phoren**. They got Goa!' 'I am only too happy for you to have Goa,' my husband laughed, pulling his tie off and handing it to the young student who was totally nonplussed. Everyone ended up cheering us on in our stalled taxi, beaming brilliant white smiles while clearing a pathway! It was only as we drew away that I noticed some were wearing the revolutionary jeans just beginning to appear in Indian bazaars. Are they 'Indian dress'?

Nehru miraculously rose above all this pontificating. The miracle is—and the question remains—given this forceful conditioning into Western ways, and more importantly, thought patterns, how it is that Nehru was so able to communicate with the impoverished peasantry. A psychic rapport existed beyond doubt which no cynic can discredit with specious phrases. Having seen it once out in the back blocks of Madhya Pradesh in the Hindi heartland when he was castigating local politicians (and not too gently either) in front of their flock of voting low-caste labourers, 'hewers of wood and drawers of water' about such bigoted behaviour, pushing Hindi down other Indians' throats (and that was like going willingly into the lion's den), or stumbling across a curious 'invasion' of migrant Rajasthani building labourers who had come to have morning 'darshan' on the lawn outside his home (where we all waited in similar fashion), the sudden silence as he passed, such a slight frame, through the crowd brought a catch to the throat. Reverencing quivered and rustled as a perceptible current along those who hemmed him in. This was **darshan** indeed!

Maybe the secret communication could occur because he like Gandhi straddled so many inner levels—the two both embodiments of that absorptive quality of the Indian matrix. He always spoke out like Gandhi did also, proudly so of Indian-ness—mere imitation of others, especially that forceful European culture, was no good.

'You cannot be a gardener,' he once tellingly exclaimed, 'if you only collect pot plants!' You have to make incoming forces something of your own.

The darkened eyes (from what unexpected sadness, a wife taken so early from sickness and he so often in prison fighting for India's cause, with little of the joys of a normal married home life), the perfect Rama's bow of a top lip (another marvel of India's genetic heritage, seen in many a Buddha or Chola bronze representation), the finely-honed face, occasionally the roughspun khadi clothes were all constituent parts of an inexplicable whole. The Indian **PARADOX**—with charisma framing it, this time for real, in real history... seen with one's own eyes... which of course one day will become myth.

Remembering the sight of such a charismatic figure, it is the humanity of the man that resonates across nearly 50 years, that sudden winning smile and bubbling joy when in the presence of Indian children of all kinds, and his vision—despite all criticism from Indians themselves, of a determined independence in more than just foreign policy, decried by a Western press blinded by the Cold War between Russia and the USA.

First his **passionate belief in the democratic way to deal with his countrymen and India's pressing problems**. Many a time even we longed for him to become a benevolent dictator when watching longwinded debates in Parliament, a yearning to see him end the luxury of interminable discussion and just get on with the job, health, educational needs, caste discrimination and

population growth all calling out for urgent resolution. Yet Nehru (and Gandhi) are surely the architects of every Indian's political 'nous' and maturity of approach in election after election today.

Perhaps he was in temperament more of a teacher than a dogmatic and determined leader. What has come to light in a recent book is the twice-monthly communication from 'the boss' to his far-flung States' CMs. Quoting one such: 'He read the Prime Minister's letter, the loved—and dreaded—fortnightly letter that all chief ministers received regularly. Couched in beautiful language characteristic of Jawaharlal Nehru, it was a treat, a beacon light, a timely and educative pointer to the tasks ahead. It contained news, views, fancies, fantasies, literary gems, words of profound wisdom—and much more. It challenged and inspired a few perceptive chief ministers. As for the others, who were impervious to everything save their own interests, they probably thought it a waste of time and attention, though no one said so.'

Laying a firm base for industrial development despite my own critique about the sad neglect of village uplift and agricultural society in the back blocks and backward states of India. If the nation today has become a major industrial complex and world marketing power—surprising many—it is because Nehru insisted on encouraging India to become **self-sufficient in manufacturing**, defying and jousting with major powerful forces outside of India in the early days of Independence.

Formulating the philosophy of non-alignment and in 1955 along with President Sukarno of Indonesia signing the Panchshila (Five Principles) agreement at Bandung. Misunderstood by many Western journalists as anti-American, it appeared to many of us in India of the 50s right and proper that India should get on with the job of building up its own independence from interference after three centuries of just that from all kinds of European sources.

Allowing his own country to make its own mistakes. Recent books typify the love-despair relationship caring Indians have even to this day with their leader. Whilst acknowledging his generosity of spirit, 'credulous liberalism' which unfortunately allowed lesser political personalities such as some chief ministers to take advantage of his own integrity, and his driven sense of history, they anguish over the legacy he left—no real heir to inherit his passionate ideals. Even while he was alive the question kept being asked: **After Nehru, who?**

The shade from his gigantic banyan tree stunted all growth under it. But perhaps that is a historical inevitability that happens in all societies. Eden was no match after Churchill and disappeared, a lame and broken man after the aberration of Suez. At least, like Churchill, Panditji had the gift of oratory—the scratchy recording which at midnight ushered in August 15, 1947, still bringing a lump to many a throat, Indian and foreign.

Long years ago, we made a tryst with destiny, and now the time comes when we shall redeem our pledge. At the stroke of the midnight hour, while the world sleeps, India will awake to life and freedom. A moment comes, which comes but rarely in history, when we step out from the old to the new, when an age ends and when the soul of a nation, long suppressed, finds utterance.

Note for readers:

For a well-crafted and perceptive look at this charismatic man, **Jawaharlal Nehru–A Communicator and Democratic Leader** by **A K Damodaran** (Radiant Publishers, New Delhi, 1997) is worth finding. Another book from an NRI, **Shashi Tharoor**, taking an 'outsider' perspective is appropriately titled **From Midnight to the Millennium**, (Arcade Publishing, New York, 1997).

And this is Nehru on himself:

If any people choose to think of me, then I should like them to say: this was a man who with all his mind and heart loved India and the people of India and, they in turn were indulgent to him and gave all their love most abundantly and extravagantly.

A look back and the longer perspective

I could be well accused of being too saccharine and **NETAJI** who follows certainly would not have agreed with such a kindly assessment of Panditji. As a fiery Bengali, he wanted total revolution. But there are young contemporary Indians who also look back–but with sharper eyes, far less willing to give Nehru

a) the benefit of the doubt in matters of corruption, citing favouritism also towards ministers such as Krishna Menon who earlier as Indian High Commissioner in London seems to have got away with murder in scandalous deals in arms, contracts involving jeeps which turned out to be 'unusable', rifles and ammunition costing the Indian taxpayer lakhs of rupees and jeopardising the lives of soldier *jawans.*

b) certainly those of us who lived in Delhi were aware of rumblings, especially amongst our media friends who found resistance to their inquiries in yet another minister's bad judgement in matters of investment.

T T Krishnamachari was the Finance Minister who had invested not for self-gain but as part of government strategy in companies owned by a controversial speculator (also known to be a Congress Party financier). These schemes went awry. After protracted resistance and judicial inquiry TTK, as he was called, was forced to resign but Nehru soon reinstated him in another ministerial post. There were other cases as well in which Nehru as prime minister appeared to:

c) **resist judicial inquiries** and make strange decisions in response to parliamentary efforts by Opposition to open up debate.

d) in that period we were too willing to balance such misgivings about his behaviour with the recognition that after the horrific trauma of Partition, Indian society needed calming, and politicians who had themselves gone through the crucible of fire in British prisons might quite honourably make mistakes.

e) there is anger also on his political judgement as well–serious ones on Kashmir, a problem 'essentially of his own creation' despite being a Kashmiri Pandit, of his abandonment of Assam when the Chinese army unexpectedly invaded the Northeast in 1962. 'My heart bleeds for the people of Assam' will sing through history as a verbal act of sophistry when so many died due to his indecisiveness, almost a wish 'not to know'.

f) and there are those beginning to question his interpretation of what a secular state implies–again with people dying because of his ill-judgement.

It is difficult to know where the truth lies even if one could delve into all the cabinet papers, not only in India, but also in Britain on such intractable problems as Kashmir. Archival material emerging from Britain makes one wonder if even the greatest of Indian sages could ever have prevented the amputations that occurred–with such a wild card as Jinnah in the pack, the British government as equally devious.

Who would be leader? There but for the grace of God goes any one of us. Yes, one can agree that in 1947 India did not need a dreamer as has been said to me many times. India perhaps needed a tough administrator like Sardar Patel great patriot also, of unswerving integrity. His deceptive Gujarati gentleness was tucked well away in an iron glove when vital political decisions were necessary, such as incorporating the princely state of Hyderabad quickly before another Kashmir occurred.

■ **NETAJI**

....affectionate term for a controversial Bengali revolutionary, **Subhas Chandra Bose**, whom the British in wartime India hated, regarding him as a traitor who secretly slipped out of the country to take over command (**neta** = leader) in his own version of Indian military uniform of the **Azad Hind Fauj**. In 1943 approximately 50,000 Indian troops who had surrendered to the Japanese in Singapore in 1941 were formed into a **Free Indian Army** and Netaji formed a provisional Government of Free India.

His escape from British police surveillance in Calcutta and a convoluted route to Hitler's Germany, then transference to a Japanese submarine in the Indian Ocean to Sumatra and by plane to Tokyo and his eventually mysterious death while similarly travelling, is the stuff of fictional thrillers.

The Free Army fought alongside the Japanese in Burma but Independence came to India before they could create a substantial foothold in northeastern India and the Japanese Government lost interest as their forces had to retreat. The Army surrendered to the British in 1945, subsequent trials coming to nought with the first independent Government in 1946. The cry *Jai Hind* used nowadays as a salutation was first promoted as a defiant slogan by Netaji.

To Bengalis especially, **Netaji** is a hero, a leader cast in the mould of a freedom fighter such as those who fought America's War of Independence, which had been sanctified by history–a fait accompli of resistance to an even earlier English colonial domination.

Now in modern India further light is shed in histories written by Indian scholars. **Bose** is properly rehabilitated with stature, his struggle for Independence though entirely different from Gandhian **SATYAGRAHA**, seen as legitimate in military terms when reason and peaceable struggle at political round tables over 50 years seemed only a stalling device. How many 'freedom fighters' became 'terrorists' because of political inertia by Governments in power?

Netaji was a passionate Bengali first and foremost—emotional but highly intelligent, fired with steady determination (the Irish, remember, of India!). And like the Irish, myths have grown up about the 'romantic patriot' concept—he won't lie down despite being cremated supposedly after a tragic death in a Japanese bomber flying him out of Taipei to Manchuria. His cremated ashes were flown subsequently to Japan after wartime surrender and still remain in a Tokyo temple—but some Indians still cling to the belief that like President Kennedy's assassination, Marilyn Monroe's death, and Princess Diana's total car crash we are not being told the truth. Despite the fact that by now if he had survived, Netaji would be 106, all sorts of theories continue to exist that he may have formed the Chinese People's Army, been spirited to the USSR, or be living as a godman recluse in a cave in India. A detailed and lengthy reassessment with archival material released, and written for the prestigious **New Yorker** by leading Bengali author **Amitav Ghosh** sheds new light on this powerful personality. In today's terms and in the light of the ANC experience in South Africa, many would regard Netaji as an honourable freedom fighter (**India's Untold War of Independence, The New Yorker, June 23 and 30th, 1997.** This is compulsive reading).

Personal endnote

Occasionally one generation's 'bogeyman' wins the plaudits of the next. I should not be surprised but still am. On my last visit to India in 2001 I met up again with Sanam Singh, elegant Sikh friend who with her late husband, respected and decorated **General Harbakhsh Singh**, had travelled back on the same P&O ship to the UK as our family returning to the BBC in London. She showed me his post-honours autobiography: **In the Line of Duty, a soldier remembers** (Lancer Publishers, New Delhi, 2000).

As an officer in the army in British India and with the Vir Chakra, Padma Bhushan and Padma Vibhushan, his distinguished career took him for a sabbatical year to the Imperial College Army course in London. Looking at his book it serendipitously fell open on a page devoted to Netaji.

I was lucky to have had an interview with him in Malaya and to this day I have yet to meet a more patriotic and devoted individual earnestly committed to the freedom of his country. If he had lived and come back to India he would have, undoubtedly, transformed the whole political leadership. What a great leader of men he was!

He had after all been born into a highly respected kayastha caste family and a very privileged background, completing his years at Kolkata's Presidency College with very high marks and in 1931 was President of the Indian National Congress but was rusticated from university due to an ill-tempered response to an anti-Indian slur cast on him by a professor.

■ NIMBU PANI (lime water)

is a stepping stone for health in a hazardous climate. It is a perennial cooling drink along with lassi and iced tea, more effective than any iced alcoholic drink in keeping healthily cool in humid monsoonal weather. The **nimbu** = lime is full of vitamin C… as also is raspberry cordial, some chemical in its properties as conducive as opium in settling upset stomachs and calming dysentery. Or try it with soda, if you're chary of the water!

Isabgol looks like frog spawn. It is a concoction Indians know **all** about to stop a runny tummy and when being solicitous at your predicament on suffering the first bout of **Delhi Belly**. Apart from a diet of yoghurt and mashed banana, there is little you can do but starve and shut your eyes while drinking this. 'Yukky' is the only way to describe it! Like porridge it plugs the system.

The only time I have ever suffered, and felt it would be better to be dead, I was given these crushed seeds soaked in water which had become a gooey mass, almost worse to contemplate than a rumbling stomach!

This indigenous plant (*Plantago ovata*) has been used in Indian medicine for millennia but if a fever develops, vomiting and threatened dehydration occur, a doctor and antibiotics may be absolutely necessary to stave off even worse—amoebic dysentery.

■ NRIs

are the diaspora of **non-resident Indians** numbering approximately 20 million, more than the total population of many individual nations and now assigned a day of their own in the Indian official calendar, January 9th to be observed as **Pravasi** (one who has gone overseas), **Bharatiya** (Indian) **Divas** (day). This day is symbolically significant marking the date on which Gandhi returned to his motherland from South Africa.

They are **not** the **gastarbeiter** type of migrants encountered in Europe; usually highly educated and professionally qualified, a large majority of NRIs have taken dual citizenship of the nations where they have settled during the last 40 years but still regard themselves as Indian culturally. The term is confusing and flexible. They are a segment of populations in the USA, the UK, Canada, Australia and Germany of increasing affluence and stand out as different in emphasis and lifestyle from those compatriots of much earlier migrations to the West Indies, Fiji, South Africa and Malaysia/Singapore in the British colonial period. (For instance in the USA, it is an often quoted statistic that 40% of its motels are owned by Indians, predominantly Gujarati and highlighted in the well-known film **Mississippi Masala**).

Eminent NRI in Britain, **Lord Swraj Paul**, chairman of many leading UK companies, became the first Asian to head a British university in the latter part of 1999—Chancellor of the University of Wolverhampton. Two delicious ironies in one stroke—Wolverhampton the spawning ground in the 60s of Enoch Powell's constituency and National Front racist activities. How the wheels of Empire turn! Yet another Lord—**Navnit Dholakia** has been **re-elected** president of the UK Liberal-Democrat party.

The stereotype of such overseas Indians is usually very narrow—of successful academics, businessmen and small corner-store deli traders and IT whizkids making fortunes. Far more exciting but still hidden away globally are the young creators in the arts who are doing amazing things both in radically experimenting with the wellsprings of Indian culture, as well as having a good laugh (especially in film making) at themselves—musicians such as well-known politicized musician Nitin Sawney who with Akram Khan choreographer and Anish Kapoor (Tate gallery remarkable sculptor) created a sell out challenging musical about the cosmos–KAASH in London–all in fact British.

A Personal endnote: In many ways as well as the direct investment encouraged by the Indian government with preferential treatment and special dispensation on gold imports, NRIs' bonus injection incrementing into the economy is a new phenomenon just beginning to make itself apparent, along with internal tourism by resident Indians rediscovering their own country. A sign of these new factors encountered by our own family reunion in Kerala was meeting up with triple generation groups of NRIs, who have saved up for the symbolic journey of their lives, bringing back children (now parents) who themselves may never have lived in India. They, in turn, are accompanied by their young babies or toddlers to meet grandparents in tearful reunions for the very first time.

One such grandfather engaged in conversation in Kochi was a doctor from Chicago who had taken up a residency in a hospital after long medical studies in the USA. He had not been back to India in 35 years nor had his Indian wife, also a professional biochemist. Seven members of their family including his new Irish-American son-in-law were discovering India really for the very first time along with 24 pieces of luggage. This brought about an exchange of mutual commiseration as we stacked 18 pieces into another elevator! (see also CROREPATI)

■ NUMEN
Latin: a divinity
is a word hardly understood now in Western culture impregnated as it is in the USA and Europe by white technologically-dominated urban society. Since industrialization uprooted rural communities and overran the countryside with concrete cities the sense of 'hallows' is in retreat. But perhaps the reasons for this flow deeper than the effects of at least 200 years of people moving off the land into artificially created green garden cities.

There is another more subtle factor. Christian civilization and especially its Victorian manifestation of patriarchal **hubris**, preaching human domination over the animal kingdom and land to be used as property, has continued to quell that sense of awe and aura, an acknowledgement of psychic energy that at least English poets recognised up to the times of Wordsworth, Keats, Shelley and Coleridge.

Perhaps that is why Indians of an older generation, schooled in British education responded so avidly to such poetry which recognised the **numinosity**, the psychic energy, of natural phenomena, places, trees, groves... it could be spelled luminosity in fact...

A sense sublime
of something far more deeply interfused whose
dwelling is the light of setting suns.
And the round ocean, and the living air,
And the blue sky, and in the mind of man:

A motion and a spirit, that impels
All thinking things, all objects of all thought
And rolls through all things...

This sense of numen, divinity which suffuses places, objects, natural phenomena is recognised visually in India way back in Indus Valley civilisation. The seals dug up at Harappa, Taxila, Mohenjo-Daro evidence tree 'spirits'.

Awareness of hallowed land, points of the compass, are marked out for all time in Indian mythology, art, temple locations, village shrines, simple stones daubed with vermilion on city streets. There are shrines in fields, on mountain tops. Even in the heart of the throbbing commercial empire of Mumbai, the large tree near the Gateway to India and the sophisticated Taj Hotel is festooned with the evidence of worship by devotees who come and go at random throughout the day.

Once an image is suffused with **numinosity** it becomes **dynamic** and conveys **darshan**. It retains a sacramental significance.

To a Hindu **prakriti–nature** is part and parcel of the whole, neither subdued by human forces nor in the ascendancy. **PRAKRITI** and **PURUSHA** are inextricably **partners** in the same spiritual quest and equation. American/Canadian Indian and Aboriginal sites such as the famous Rock–Uluru vibrate with numinous forces. Only now do Glastonbury and Stonehenge renew their mysterious auras with the social/spiritual changes of perspective brought about by the student revolutions of 1968, the coming of FlowerPower, the rise of the environmental-ecological Green movement, and the return to natural habitats, organic agriculture, awareness of planetary forces beyond human control in the 'alternative society' movements.

Many of these hallows are close to rivers, the analogy being that of the 'spiritual ford' referred to by many Indian writers and gurus, where 'the soul **crosses over** the river of **samsara** to reach the far shore of **liberation** or **moksha**.' A melodious cassette, **TIRTH**, presented by a famous Carnatic vocalist, T N Sheshagopalan states that 'this popular living tradition, **tirtha**, is undertaken to places made sacred by the presence now long gone of the Vedic sages who performed penance there'. Then swamis and other holy men began to visit them and they became:

Tirtha sthaana–an auspicious sanctified territory marked
by the presence of temples, bathing ghats, trees and
sacred wells–at Kashi, Dwarka, Badrinath, and Tirupati.

Such a shrine, or **tirthasthaana** of especial import or spiritual energy is **TIRUPATI**. There is a legendary tale told in many accounts (including the cassette text) of the great 18th century saint musician TYAGARAJA queuing at the shrine of Balaji, the affectionate term for Krishna in the manifestation of the Divine Child. Tyagaraja was so moved during this long expectancy of the 'darshan' to come in divine grace and blessing from Vishnu that 'he opened his heart in devotional song' such that the curtain shielding the **murti–image** was drawn of its own accord to reveal the supreme Shri Vishnu in all his glory.

It has been truly said (commentator unknown) that **India is a country where even the stones have nervous systems.**

Salagramas (refer back to **NARAYANA**) certainly do! Note: **Ajit Mookerjee's Tantra Art** discusses and depicts these 'linear vital energies' within rocks, hallowed and given worship as the Devi intrinsic in them.

Such stones even are the 'living architecture' of temples, only now becoming accessible to the traveller, for example, the astonishing shikhar-shaped monolithic temples of the **Masroor** complex in the lower reaches of the northern **Dhauladhar** Himalayas of the **Kangra Valley** in Himachal Pradesh. Dating back to the eighth century CE (approximately) they look like mini Himalayan peaks, energy running through unfinished surfacing of neat chiselled patterns before the artistic masons mysteriously moved on.

Even more explicit is the temple without a symbolic murti, no image to concentrate the focus of worship at all. The little-known temple in Kerala, the **Kadampuzha Devi** shrine, about the famous **Guruvayur Temple**, dedicates a special ritual to a hole in a rock, covering that aperture with **kattu thechi** wild flowers in what is called the **phulmudal** puja (covering with flowers), the rock hole embodying the principle of cosmic energy as represented by Parvati Devi.

Apparently so tiny is the temple and so sought after the darshan from such an undertaking that its rarity (the puja only performed during one third of the year) that even the rich and famous such as J Jayalalitha (displaying gratitude for winning her appeal against jail—see **CORRUPTION**) have despite the cost of the puja (over Rs. 30,000)—to take their place in the queue which now stretches to nearly 2050!

No wonder BHUMI (earth) has an especial place in Hindu iconography in the form of a goddess—Prithvi. Simple shrines bedeck the countryside, especially in the south. Many a stretch of emerald green paddy is watched over by her presence. Indigenous Australians would feel very much at home in this land. After all, they refer to their lands, their earth and sacred places (now recognized by state and federal laws) as **MOTHER**, subtly different from 'motherhood'... and India often referred to as **BHARAT MATA**.

■ OM = ॐ

pronounced as in home, and also spelled A-U-M in Indian languages for a specific reason, both metaphysically and phonetically, provides the Indo-European language root for the Latin: **omnes** = all; omnipresent, omnipotent etc, all-embracing as this ultimate mantra signifies.

◆ The **prime mantra** or **sound syllable** of the universe full of extrasensory potency, is sounded at the beginning and end of all worship and ceremonies in the chanting of the Vedic slokas or quatrains. As the swastika is a graphic symbol of Ganesha so AUM is his sound image. The concept of sound represented identification with the divine energy, a magic entrance into a 'realisation' beyond self consciousness.

◆ At its most abstract the view of using sound syllables for meditative purposes and yogic concentration is pure physics.

As my yoga teacher **B K S Iyengar** once explained in one of the first classes to present yoga in London encouraged by **Yehudi Menuhin** (then President of the **Asian Music Circle**) the sound emanates from the very core of human being.

The extended A-A is the sound when the throat is at its most open (like saying AH to the doctor), **U** as in 'ululate' projects this life breath—(see **PRAÑA**) through the mouth, and the only vibratory sound possible—as the lips close off breath and sound— is **M-M-M. It is a logical progression**. The theory of a universal ultimate original sound is similar to the Greek theory of the music of the spheres.

◆ Sound alone does not give the 'character' its potency. Its three curves have their meaning also, inter-related and calligraphically enmeshed, if somewhat obscure, related to consciousness and the dream world of awareness.

A personal note

Imagine the surprise one evening travelling under the immediacy of the Australian star-studded sky listening on the car radio to a science programme on ABC. The Voyager I spacecraft was passing through the rings of Saturn when a four tone, modal sound literally 'rang' and 'hummed' across space, a fundamental OM. A startling and thrilling moment when all theories across time from rsis intuitively reaching out to tone perceptions thousands of years ago and today's empirical and rational conclusions from scientific exploration, from Hindu philosophy to NASA, became one. And now one discovers solar winds of extraordinary force create music as they move around the planets.

■ ONΛM

A Malayali word for the important Kerala harvest festival after the heavy monsoonal rains. Moveable according to the position of planets and moon at the end of August through September, it heralds the Malayali New Year.

Thousands gather along the banks of the River Pamba to watch the graceful snake boats participate in what must be the most colourful as well as elegant boat race in the world, outpacing even Chinese dragon boat races in visual theatre.

Villages for miles along the river Pamba near Aranmula 50 km from Kottayam own individual boats. Nearby a temple dedicated to Krishna and Arjuna is linked with the legend that started the festival said by local Malayalis to track back through 5,000 years of history to a time when a wealthy Namboodiri of the highest of high brahmins (landlords in Kerala as well as spiritual gurus) fed a starving widow and some children from food in a boat which had floated downstream with no one to steer it.

■ ORTHODOXY

India has prided itself in its **TOLERANCE** over the ages and during its cultural development from so many strands of race, culture and creed. Nor is this just a passive tolerance for the sake of paying lipservice to a national goal. Both Nehru and Gandhi cajoled and reminded their countrypeople that tolerance implied activity, a generosity of spirit in trying to understand the other point of view.

Just as each nation has thematic and idiosyncratic qualities or **gunas** that mark it out—the constitutionally enshrined 'pursuit of happiness' in the USA; habeas corpus and the Magna Carta principles of law in Britain; la gloire, national glory in France; 'a fair go' delineating Australian fervour about an egalitarian society and mateship which refuses to allow class to define personal aspiration or behaviour, so India among its tenets of faith has stressed tolerance as one of those defining categories always emphasising 'unity in diversity'.

Perhaps due to modern politics and pressures to get votes (often by appealing in popular terms to the lowest common denominator of response) **orthodox** and **fundamentalist religious attitudes** are appearing increasingly in political life. This is a paradox of the free-for-all Westminster-style democracy which often ironically leaves many people virtually disenfranchised or marginalised by heedless majorities, in turn pushing the disaffected to extremes of the political spectrum. This is disturbing because as economic liberalization opens India up once more to global influences, and satellite TV and Internet swamp a nation two thirds of which is under 35 years old, ironically the extremes of the social spectrum may well strengthen as a defence mechanism against unwelcome foreign influences, some of which are admittedly disturbing and powerful in their message.

O

■ PAAN

♦ Chewing paan is an acquired taste for the visitor but well worth the acquisition after a rich and sumptuous Indian buffet when the eye and taste buds win out over wiser signals from an overburdened stomach.

♦ Paan is also a nightmare for the cleansing departments of overburdened civic authorities, the red splatter of discarded betel nut plus saliva a red-stained decoration of many city walls and pavements.

♦ Paan must also be a dentist's delight—plus and negative! The juices that flow while chewing the mineral-loaded leaf may be an astringent creating healthy gums and breath but the lethal chunks of arecanut which take a good half hour to masticate down to swallowing proportions can dislodge the most well-embedded of tooth fillings.

♦ What looks like a green samosa is, in fact, a heart-shaped betel leaf, well formed to be a platter for a number of 'charged' ingredients smeared on it by the roadside vendor and his pushcart or stall strategically lodged in a niche of a city wall or bazaar surrounded by all the bustle of pedestrians wanting a 'lift'.

♦ Grown like hops, especially in central India, the darker **supari** leaf is more bitter (and very much part of elegant Muslim society in Lucknow with its intricate etiquette including the giving and taking from a filigree silver paan box). Supari is the seed of the areca palm.

♦ The paler more succulent leaf of south India, Madrasi **meetha**, is sweeter and softer to chew.

♦ A number of ingredients each in their separate tins is smeared onto the leaf, folded in a triangle, pinned down by a single clove and placed delicately in the pouch of the cheek... then the mastication begins, bovine fashion!

Lime paste, cardamom, areca nut chunks, fennel and licorice, crystal sugar, and shredded coconut, sometimes scented silver-covered hunks of tobacco can all be circulated. Catechu (kattha) is especially healing, drying up phlegm, skin sores and healing gums. Chips of the acacia wood are boiled in water, evaporated into a gluey dark brown substance and moulded into solid blocks. Gulkand is a gooey mix, a jam made from rose petals!

Just when you think you did eat too much saffron-scented rice for your own good and distension will explode the stomach the half-hour chewing of the cud pays off, most especially if the tobacco is added...

AND LIFT-OFF OCCURS!

Tasting paan and putting the right balance of ingredients together engenders the expertise of connoisseurs, as much an art form as sampling wine in France or Australia. And no wonder, with a 5000-year history at least, known and talked about in the Puranas.

■ PALIMPSEST

A Victorian English word much-loved by Pandit Nehru to sum up what Indian society and culture was about. In his *Discovery of India* he uses it to define the layering of cultures from incoming peoples, one on top of another. That is India's history.

This is what he wrote while he was sequestered in a colonial jail:

... some ancient palimpsest on which layer upon layer of thought and reverie had been inscribed, and yet no succeeding layer had completely hidden or erased what had been written previously...

As each ethnic group settled, a sea change gradually occurred over generations, the layer at the base taking the impress of the new layer laid on top of it. It could be described as a social geology of history, just as special geological strata on a mountainside tell a story of what happened physically and climatically over aeons of time in the evolutionary story of our planet.

The palimpsest is India's story like a giant sea anemone stretching out hundreds of tentacles to all who came in over the highest mountain passes of the NW, by river and deep valley in the NE, and by coastal trade especially in Kerala and Tamilnadu. The tentacles curled inwards absorbing each culture, retaining identity and regurgitating into yet something else again.

Technically the term comes from the art of **brass rubbing with waxed paper** where the technician creates an image with charcoal on waxed paper from the embossed brass figure reproduced on the tombstone.

Chambers' Dictionary states: A manuscript in which old writing has been rubbed out to make room for new (Gk **palimpseston-palin**, again, **psāein**, to rub). Another English word we had to run to the Oxford Dictionary in our New Delhi home to learn about from India. 'Fissiparous' was the other!

■ PANCHAYAT = pānch, Hindi for five
a council = rule of the five elders of any village

♦ One of the earliest democratic societies in the world contemporary with the Greek concept of **Demos**. May even predate Greek idea which incorporated system of slavery in city society. Some Indians think that organised village communities may have already existed **4,000 years ago.**

The sage **YAJNAVALKYA**, noted seer of the Upanishadic philosophic explorations at the end of the Vedic period referred to the idea of law and courts which presupposes an already well-ordered and accepted functioning system. The **Arthashastra** also refers to village elders. The Mauryan Empire itself even before the systematic spread of the Ashokan Edicts had established a well-organised bureaucratic system. Villages functioned autonomously through a **sabha** = assembly. Division of labour was widespread so that the services of one group such as potters was balanced by the contribution of another group to the village economy, artisans being paid in grain.

8th–7th c BCE

Go to Vaishali in northern Bihar to find out. Modern archaeological diggings have unearthed foundations of what is thought to be a **Lok Sabha** of its day in pre-Buddhist times. Called the **Raja Vishal ka Garh** it is only the outline several bricks and mortar high of the Republic of the **Lichchhavi** clan recorded

P

in the Buddhist Jataka tales and in Chinese accounts of later centuries... **and now claimed to be the first duly elected assembly of representatives in the world.**

They speak of this mysterious group (of unknown origins) as 'dashing young fellows with their brilliant equipages and saucy manners'. They were clearly young 'blades' who were peacocks in their love of stylish clothes and fast carriages. But other accounts refer to them as 'wanton, insolent and utterly irreligious, a marked contrast to **BUDDHA** and his sombre-clothed disciples.' But they clearly believed in legal process, as part of a confederation of clans in this most potent geographical area, Vaishali being Rama's territory and the birthplace of **Mahavira of the JAINS**, as well as being so much part of the Buddha's domain.

Vaishali is 44 km north of Patna on a detour route off the road that leads to Nepal. It is clearly marked out by one of Ashoka's famous pillars with a single powerfully sculpted lion symbol of regal authority atop and facing to the north. This commemorates the place where the Buddha preached his last sermon before his **nibbana**. Also where his ashes rested is marked by a circular tin stupa.

Buddhist accounts refer to the **Lichchhavis** as exemplary peoples abiding by democratic rules of assembly, recognising the importance of quorums, moving resolutions in committee, etc–all the fine details in fact of how to ballot, vote, elect and maintain regional/local councils in a democratic way. **Vaishali: the Bygone Glory** by Shahid Akhter Makhfi (**Indian Perspectives**, November 1997, accessed from Ministry of External Affairs, External Publicity Division, New Delhi, and **On the Golden Trail of the Buddha**, Pran Nath Luthra (**Discover India** magazine, July, 1996).

◆ Land belonged to the village. Most councils were run by a **patwari**, a village headman usually the school teacher, a **vaid =** doctor, a **chowkidar =** village guardian, and dealt with all local concerns–settlement of boundaries, management of the village shrine or temple, cattle disputes, inter-village cattle fairs and festivals, public works or paths, communication lines running out like radial tyre spokes from the village hub (a distinct pattern seen from an aircraft flying over India).

◆ In spite of an effective money-raising bureaucracy set up by the Mughals in the first really settled period for hundreds of years, the villagers were left very much to themselves and their feudal rulers–except for raising taxes for central government purposes from a percentage of the crop yield.

In the last 250 years during British times although peace came to the countryside and top administration functioned efficiently, neglect–or rather lack both of funds and encouragement–occurred for self-government. District collectors and judges did travel extensively 'up country; 'out of station'–all phrases straight out of the Raj. Administrators were very conscientious and learned the vernacular language. However, Western legal systems and commercial ownership of property introduced alien concepts. It was not until I read a tiny book full of righteous dismay almost immediately on arrival in Delhi that I came to realise the subtle damage colonialism does to a people–and the book was written by an Englishman! But

no ordinary Englishman. **Sir Penderel Moon** of the ICS was one of those idiosyncratic free spirits that can exist in English society which allows for eccentrics. He had published **Strangers in India** (now unfortunately out of print) in 1945. Such was his vision (leaping beyond race, creed and colour) that Tarlok Singh–then heading the newly-created Planning Commission requested him to stay on in an advisory role, one of the few British administrators to be so privileged to do so. Luckily we came to know him and his impassioned feelings about the malaise brought about in peasant society by this alien imposition of private ownership of land as well as the profits drained out of that land which had been a rich country in production, only to be returned to British manufacturing. Stories were legion about Penderel and his escapades, not all apocryphal! His own heart was embedded in India. He did tell us of his own secret Partition role dressed up as a Muslim woman in burqa running messages across the new frontier into Pakistan to Hindu families in peril.

◆ It was the system however, that failed the villager. The psychic energy–**empowerment** the buzz word of the 1990s–had to wait until the early 1950s when India's first independent government set up the **Panchayati Raj** on October 2, 1959 in Rajasthan. This resuscitation of active village autonomous councils now spreading a network of participation into upper level district councils is functioning widely especially in effective, go-ahead states. Millions of people are involved in about 700,000 villages with **one-third** of the positions especially set aside for women, as also for scheduled/tribal castes.

That is not to say all are go-ahead and successful. Factionalism and caste bullies exist but the fact is that a good many bodies have given the villagers a sense of achievement in building their own schools, mending bridges, improving roads and drains, experimenting with new concepts taken straight from TV educational/farm programs. This is Gandhian ideas (and Nehru's dreams) actually functioning, training villagers to assess their own needs and stand up and fight for them.

A chink in the **samiti** village hall door gives an interesting insight despite cynicism in some quarters that much more could have been done. Noam Chomsky on a visit to West Bengal in 1996 (because the then West Bengal State Minister of Finance had studied at MIT as a student in the USA) visited a panchayat without warning. It consisted of 18 members, six of whom were women and seven scheduled caste and tribes. He found 'convincing evidence of direct participation and engagement in problems, a model of democracy.' Obviously a lively interchange took place. Peasants, agricultural workers had no idea what questions their noted visitor would ask. His experience bears out everything we also found in visits unexpectedly and on the spot in Maharashtra, Punjab, Bengal and Gujarat.

'They knew the answers, they thought the questions through, they replied with frankness and clarity supporting evidence with maps and personal notebooks, other people broke in–and that's democracy. You don't see that very often.' Reported in **Frontline**, February 23, 1996.

P

Resuscitation of **panchayati raj** in post-Independence India has been very important as a building brick in the ever-maturing political process far away from urban centres. Perhaps it was ever thus! Dr Padma Subrahmanyam, while on her **DANCE** researches in Tamilnadu, discovered temple sculptured friezes at Tiruvarur depicting local scenes of democracy at work. An example of *kudamulai* in the 14th century, of carved friezes portraying villagers placing palm leaf tokens (**olai**) into a pot (**kuda**) for voting purposes. Similar depictions have been found elsewhere.

- **PANTHEON** (n. *Greek*)
  Pan = all
  Theos = God
  330 million deities—that is the symbolic number Hindus themselves use just to give an impression of immensity of the divine impulse!

- ◆ A thousand names for one god—**VISHNU**.
- ◆ Multi-armed **MURTIS**, images of goddesses galore
- ◆ A hundred ways to worship and a total individuality of puja—devotional worship in the home and shrine
- ◆ What more confusing? Or is it?

Throughout this account of discovering what India is about, an attempt has been made to avoid the use of the word God. It is a word that has so many resonances and in Western faiths implies a very specific personification circumscribed by institutional religion, theologies and creeds, some directed by Vatican ruling. That is not what the Pantheon in Hindu terms represents, rather, hidden in the myriad expressions of divinity are profound attitudes—**a comprehensive view of life reinforced by a daily way of personal ritual** that starts from an entirely different reference point. For instance, the anthropomorphic beings that people the Pantheon stretch their influence through archetypal symbol and myth in very human lives recounted during centuries of incoming cultures, imbibing progressions through increasing intuitions this influx brought about plus widening knowledge moving flexibly over vast ranges of time and space. Their lives and adventures and magical stories of boons granted, austere penances undertaken, battles and victories against daunting forces of evil encompass Indians of all creeds, classes, castes, incorporating their perspectives in the generality—rather than marginalising them. Even Christians in the Indian ambience acknowledge Rama as a symbol of the ideal man, a moral ruler; Christ becomes an avatar of redemption; Muslim saints acknowledge the Hindu seer; and Hindus vice versa, even worshipping at Muslim shrines; Buddhist, Sikh and Jain know all the fabled stories which carry the ethical message.

When Ravana crumbles in flames at Dussehra, a shout of triumph goes up in the Delhi skies from millions on the open maidan, people of many faiths or not, in a universal sense of relief that benign forces embodied in Rama (Vishnu the Pervader who re-establishes dharma) have indeed prevailed. Our young children jumped for joy as we with our Punjabi friends, absorbed into this gigantic concourse, shouted in triumph as the gigantic burning of effigies lit up the dark sky over Delhi.

The fables that spring from this pantheon of very real and appealing Deities appear to have relevance for each new generation. In this head-on encounter one marvels at the virtual reality of the ever-replenishing myths and symbols that 'wrap-around' its peoples as **Richard Lannoy** has explained in his book **The Speaking Tree** (OUP, 1971).

Why?

- ◆ Because they possess a directness in visual simplicity of line in rock surface engraving, sculpture in the round, or free-standing bronze.
- ◆ They speak dramatically with sensual and emotional language to which any ordinary human can relate, even Westerners (used in the generic sense) from alien European cultures.
- ◆ Embellished as these are by density of meaning, they now embrace even contemporary scientific concept.

I **NATURALISTIC REPRESENTATIONS... To begin at the beginning...**

One of the great mysteries about expression of **sanatana dharma**, the proper term for the Hindu view of life, is the absence of all the artistic forms for a thousand years or more, knowing the inclination towards symbol as well as legend in visual expression on the Indian subcontinent. Such enlightenment would help explain the first representations of worship to a divine force. What happened after the Mohenjo-Daro seals? Such tantalising depictions of seven worshippers (lined-up devotees? kneeling before a tree shrine? A deity, three-headed human forms, the seated yogi)? And does that image reverberate down the millennia to the 5th–6th c cave sculpture of a triple imaged Shiva at Elephanta?

Epochs go by; terracotta and golden mother goddess, flattened plaques and bronzed abstract forms have been upturned by peasant farmers ploughing; or by bulldozers building the new multi-storeyed architecture of Indian cities. These are random finds however with no coherent structure to give social meaning to their presence. The Vedic deities remain abstract principles, distant from humanity, propitiated in mantra and fire ritual, by river bank and grove more likely than not. But there seems to be no concrete architecture to give them an earthly residence.

Textually carried in the oral **Puranas**, the diffuse and penetrating legends that gave sustenance and an enriching framework to people's lives, made the deities very real, indeed human in their exploits. The gods and goddesses had come down to earth for 2000 years, mentally treated with devotion—being looked after, cossetted, fed, bathed and taken out for walks like revered next-of-kin.

As the millennia concertina into the common era of the Roman calendar all is no longer **just legend**, entirely carried in oral culture. Epigraphic evidence of 'the idea' of a deity commences. But there is still no painting, no visual murti. Even the presence of Buddha up until the turn into the Christian era was signified by the abstract charkha, sandals, bodhi tree, or chhatri umbrella of dignity, carved in the earliest Buddhist stone gateways to architectural stupas.

P

◆ Evidence has been known for sometime of an inscription in Hittite cuneiform script in a cave in Asia Minor–not India–which is witness to a treaty between a **Hittite king Kurtiwaza** (who reigned circa 1370–1355 BCE) and others.

Mitra, Varuna, Indra, Nasatyan are the names of the Gods invoked as witnesses to the Treaty.

But not a sculpted figure or painted icon in Indian sight! This evidence of the richly prolific artistic expertise appears in the round only at the end of the **Mauryan golden age**... and even then the Pantheon, a convenient stepping stone, was only just beginning to take a visual shape...

II THE EMERGENCE OF A STRUCTURED CONCEPT: BASIC CHART

Behind all the forms or visual representations of the Hindu deities, be they male or female, a visual shorthand towards understanding the many-sided aspects of truth embedded in Hindu philosophical thought, there is the concept of a **creative Energy–Intelligence–the Impersonal Absolute** as it is called in Sanskrit, which is signified by the neuter noun, **BRHM**. To define by gender would circumscribe IT. Even THAT pronoun, learned rishis state, is diminishing.

As a device to make the pathway clearer to those who find such an expanding universe of deities confusing or mystifying:

NIRGUNA(no form)	BRHM	in Devanagari
a force beyond	ब्रह्म	script (the
definition,	or PARAMESWARA	language of the
in Sanskrit Brhm	(the paramount	gods or devas =
implies 'growth',	absolute spark of the	Sanskrit meaning
to 'develop'.	creative energy)	'pure')

Conceived as the ultimate oneness, wholeness or creative energy by all Hindus and which gave rise over the millennia to the monistic school of philosophy which concentrated on **Nirguna**, the idea of a **Principle** at work as the cosmos which was beyond description (see **ADVAITA**).

ॐॐॐॐॐॐॐॐॐॐॐॐॐॐ

The Vedic hymns and the great minds of those earliest centuries speculated on the binding unity of this ultimate.

Sitting on many a village charpoy over 50 years, talking to people on trains and in buses (and Indians love to talk but they do at the same time ask questions!) I can state without a doubt that–no matter their educational standing by Western criteria–they would be aware of the immensity principle, and the growth from amorphous **BRHM**, immeasurable, into a 'presence' in the phenomenal world = **BRAHMA** in which they live. At last the language and the image is taking shape! They hear the famous metaphor, vivid and captivating in its graphic imagery from wandering gurus, hermits, meditating teaching swamis, singing **BAULS** skipping along the roadside, pilgrims giving witness, glowing with darshan.

The Brhadaranyaka Upanishad explains:

As a spider emerges (from itself) by spinning threads (out of its own body) so too from this self [Atman = Brhm] do all the life-breaths, all the worlds, all deities, and all contingent beings rise up in all directions.

As the spider spins its web therewith, and then retracts (the threads) when it so desires, so is the world spread out by Brahma from Himself and will be again merged into Him when He so desires.

And this ineluctable flow and recession is recounted in joyousness. High philosophy of the Upanishads glows with optimism in creation. No cosmic alienation here! No gloom and doom, the detritus of planetary pollution as the 21st century turns its slow wheeling motion into the new millennium.

The world is God's revelation of Himself; His joy assumes all these forms...

says yet another text some 3,000 years ago–although in English translation there is always difficulty in defining God as **He** when God as a word has overtones that are not part of Sanskrit concepts, virtually scientific as a physicist would accept creative energy. But gradually this abstract idea of a beneficent consciousness became **form** to enable ordinary human beings to concentrate their minds by meditating upon an image. On taking on personifications, thus leading to the **Hindu pantheon of multitudes of Deities and Consorts**, mistaken in previous centuries for 'idols' in idolatrous worship. In fact these *murtis* or images are never seen as such by Indians, certainly not the educated people, nor even worshipped as such by a good many peasants and nonliterate villagers. Even they have an inkling of their **symbolic nature**, and how the male or female deity represents a particular facet or differing aspect of the **singularity** that energises the universe.

III THE PANTHEON REALISED
A. TRINITY
(with balancing feminine energies as consorts)

This Trimurti (or Trinity) of images expands like a population

B. SAGUNA:	BRAHMA	Savitri	Fem. Rig Vedic
(becoming form) with qualities and attributes and a vehicle as transport in the many stories or epics known as the **Puranas**.	the CREATOR symbolised by the dot or **Bindu** ⊙ Vehicle: Hamsa, bar-headed goose often mistakenly referred to as swan.		goddess of the Sun's energy
		Saraswati	Fem. goddess of wisdom, music, learning and the arts

| **VISHNU** Lakshmi on a lotus. (fem.) Vehicle: Garuda **Venkateshwara** in south India. | Preserver or **Sustainer** of the Universe coming down in different and biologically evolving forms to redeem mankind from evil. | Destroyer and Regenerator of cosmos after cosmos | **SHIVA** **Parvati** on a lotus. (fem.) Vehicle: Nandi **Devi** (Sth India) **Durga/Kali** (Bengal) **Ambaji** (Gujarat) |

explosion through very human stories related especially by grandmothers in the family circle to their grandchildren. The main deities to bear in mind are these relating to **Vishnu** and **Shiva**.

DVAITA: With the multiplicity of male and female balance **dasavataram** imagery develops in biological sequence (turn back to **AVATAR**), epics and folk tales turn the singular monism into the diversity of **dvaita** = worshipper and worshipped = two = dvaita. This is the final stage when the idea of deity now formalises into **murtis** to be addressed with ritual in temples as well as in homes. Krishna most especially comes into prominence as eighth avatar of Vishnu for worship in the home, as well as the Devi.

♦ From Shiva and Parvati separately two sons are created:

Ganesh: the ebullient elephant-headed corpulent deity is a class unto himself. Even the gods pay homage to him as son of **Shiva** and **Parvati**. He it is who bestows blessing on all new ventures, even those in Brahma's heaven.

Karttikeya/Skanda/Azagan/Murugan/Subrahmanya: one and the same deity, brother of Ganesh, Murugan formerly believed by the Tamil people to be a Dravidian god of war yet graceful and amicable is (alias Karttikeya) dark-skinned, Skanda known as the celestial general, slayer of malign forces. Throughout Tamilnadu there are at least seven extremely sacred shrines to this Deity fashioned in black stone, especially a beautiful temple in the mountain-top town of **Palani** due north of the Nilgiri hill station of Kodaikanal. Here the dark youth, clad only in a loin cloth and holding a staff symbolizes the mendicant seen just like this by many a traveller on the roads of India, having renounced all material possession in order to attain spiritual equanimity.

♦ **Shiva** is known by 108 names, especially **Mahesvara** (the **Maha** (great) **Isvara** (god), or **Pasupati** (lord of all animals like St Francis of Assisi) or **Mahayogi** (the great ascetic). But most important in relation to today's interplanetary realities, as **NATARAJ.**

♦ **Parvati** has also many names depending on which region of India she is worshipped... **Kali** (Bengal), **Ambaji** (Gujarat); **Shakti, Devi**–and most important again–**Sri** (explained in **LAKSHMI**).

The oneness of all the deities regardless of whatever name is given to them is symbolised by the hermaphrodite (androgynous) form Ardha/Nari (half-female) **Ardha/Nari/Isvara** (half female deity).

♦ Personally fortunate in having a close friend able to explain this rich exuberance of artistic expression very early on in the piece before confusion triumphed, the following analogy was made: It has been relevant in the understanding of worship ever since... like a flash of lightning it shifted an intractable Western viewpoint–and it made sense, a new **darshan** when Ganesh, worshipped first by all the major Deities, stepped in to remove all mental obstacles!

Take a father figure in a family. He is one and the same person in himself but the wife sees him one way, his son another. His mother holds a very different perception as does his sister of him. And will that be the same as his brothers? Or his friends. **But he within himself is one and the same**. *That is the way the personification of the Divine should be understood. All those deities are only symbols*–**istadevata**, *personal forms to address prayers to, to fix your mind upon–symbols to give a sense of direction but not taken for the totality of truth or whatever you want to call God.*

So it is with Siva/Shiva, or Vishnu, Devi or Shakti, Murugan or Saraswati, Lakshmi, or Krishna...

It is all very confusing at first and no wonder conscientious missionaries in the first encounters were alarmed at what they regarded as such 'flagrant idolatry.'

Shiva for instance is **Prajapati**, the **protector** of all creatures. **Pati** (Skt = lord, master) applied in most Indian glossaries in English to God as well as to husbands! This can be misleading. The use of the English **Lord** carries overtones of dominant Victorian Christianity with its confident sense of 'Master of all Nature', lording it over the animal kingdom with that superior sense of 'being in charge' as colonial viceroys and administrators were. Prajapati is a very different concept, more of **stewardship**, 'part of nature' in tune with contemporary ecological affinities.

One God, Many Names

♦ Not only is there Shiva of the 108 names; Vishnu in Shankaracharya's commentary encompasses a 1000, exploding into space as **Vishnu-Sahasra-Nama** (sahasra = thousand). And what of the hundred sons of **Dhritarashtra** in the **MAHABHARATA** where humans and deities seem to inhabit an amorphous world of interaction like next-of-kin? In one text Krishna is said to have 16,108 wives (why the extra 108 one wonders?–16,000 would have been symbol enough of his multiplicity of appeal... no wonder he is capable of 180,000 sons, And then there are a mere billion celestial spirits. India profligates. It is all too clear in fact that a mere billion plus present population is no new thing when 330 million gods are referred to by pandits **as yet another way of stating that the idea of Brhm the Impersonal is** infinite and beyond comprehension... an exponential graph of the universal atman in which we are all absorbed.

♦ Even in Kulu Valley at Dussehra celebrations, deities seem to emerge in their own right, not only from more than a hundred temples, but each valley and village, all to gather on their individual palanquins to honour Rama, here known as **Raghunathji**. Those who carry the palanquins regard their guardian deities as very human. They state that they know when the Deity needs a rest. The murti suddenly gains weight upon their shoulders, forcing them to stop–and rest also!

And God Is In All Things

♦ The representation of the Benign, the Impersonal Absolute made manifest may not necessarily be a personification, an image in the form of a human. Many Indian devotees acknowledge divinity in a tree, a stone by the wayside or under a specially sanctified place of **NUMEN**. Perhaps it was in such a place in antiquity, in time unrecorded, that its location became sanctified by a wandering holy person, sitting down and delivering wise messages to those who took time to listen. Or he/she may have died there, a Holy Ma being as accepted as the male saint.

P

The stone will be covered in vermilion, even clothed with bright metal foil and a red or saffron sari, absurd to some Western eyes. But the stone with eyes painted on it though a manifestation of energy running in rock—the very earth, **Mother Bhumi** (or **Prithvi**)—is regarded as a very real representation that needs to be treated with respect as much as any other (turn to **PURUSHA/PRAKRITI** and back to **NUMEN**).

◆ **Vishnu**, all pervasive and of the auspicious blue of the firmament presides individually over a later stepping stone reincarnating to pervade the modern scientific concepts of the universe appropriate to the ending of this padayatra journey (see **VISHNU**). In a century where science is pushing its own frontiers to learn where truth is—Vishnu of the DNA principle, the double helix emerging from the sacred ocean where he has lain, inert between great cycles representing what we are—blood, plasma, mucous, liquid roughly 65–75% of total body weight, fluids held up by a skeleton in a skin... Over millions of years single-celled protozoa evolved, non-cellular fluid within the human form—to create humankind.

◆ And the **Goddess**—she is everywhere—the most ancient of neolithic vitalities, from animistic tribal, all the **Prakriti** representations through to the ultimate formless energy of SHAKTIDEVI. She will be found from A to Z and the bindu dot of **ZERO**... the process of becoming. She first emerges in representational form alongside the primordial Being as SRI (see **LAKSHMI**), the two wives of the Vedic deity Aditya and later, Vishnu, an Aphrodite manifest in the spray of the ocean of nectar, then changing names with each avatar of Vishnu, as **Sita**, consort of Ramachandra, as **Rukmini** with Krishna, as **Lokamata**, mother of the worlds.

◆ **Durga:** As in the affairs of humankind, so also in the cosmos, the forces of Good have ever to be on the alert. In legend (but also in the reality of human affairs throughout history) no sooner are the forces of positive action established, than the process of entropy begins to eat away. The malignancy is ever-present, ready to strike again. In imagery the worshipper knows this force as **Mahishasura**, asuras, those dark entities of the Vedic tradition, an anti-god.

◆ **Durga Pooja,** autumn festival of Bengal, is the supreme celebration of such perennial struggle—and ultimate triumph. The shaktis of all the gods emerging as fires all rushed together, consuming in a flaming cloud which grew and grew and then condensed into the shape of **The Great Goddess Mahadevi or Durga**—an amalgamation of all their powers.

The deities of Indra's heaven recognising the power of shakti combined all their several strengths by handing over their individual symbols of power to Durga.

This is Zimmer's account of events in the Vedic **svarga (heaven)** from **Myths and Symbols in Indian Art and Civilization**...willingly abdicating their various masculine strengths and attitudes, (the male Deities) deliver into Shakti's 18 hands their various symbolic attributes, amongst which are:

◆ Shiva the ascetic who hands over his **trident–the trishul**
◆ Four-headed **Brahma** who gives up his **begging bowl** and the **magic of the Vedic manuscripts**

◆ The **God of Time** who yields up his **sword and shield**
◆ The legendary father of the Goddess–**Himalaya**–who presents her with **the lion to ride**

BRHM is beyond description; at the same time each view or 'darshan' has to be taken on board, considered, digested. It may not be meaningful for that particular soul but it may suit the state of mind of another person and therefore cannot be gainsaid.

For this reason Indians are both individually and at corporate level markedly tolerant. Throughout their 5,000 years of known history they have absorbed other 'darshan' from other cultures, taking the essence of that which is true to humanity as potentially valid, setting aside the superfluous, and then curling in like the sea anemone digesting and making 'the residual truth' their own.

To proselytise and forcibly attempt to convert others is an indefensible attitude. To thrust a religious doctrine in forced conversions is anathema in the Hindu faith—unlike the history of Crusades, Inquisitions, Holy Wars and **jehadi** fanatics and the Burning of Books, entire libraries of cultural wisdom destroyed in a-dharma. Every form of knowledge may break the confines of that imprisoning maya and needs quietly to be examined and reflected upon. 'This is the One and Only Belief. All else is heresy' is not the Hindu view or way to behave.

Conclusion: Some Indians even though born Hindu never set foot in a temple, never attend **puja** or temple worship, never address any one of the pantheon of deities represented in human or animal form. **Nevertheless they remain Hindu.** How is this possible?

It is useful to remember that this huge community of people is basically free to choose a personal **marg** = way of life, and a certain aspect of the ONE in the search for the BENIGN.

In the final analysis an Indian is also the ultimate, if benevolent, anarchist—not beholden to any one dogma, no infallible papal doctrine, no body of church fathers in the past saying this is to be believed, that view is heretical, if not subscribed to then put that disbeliever to the stake... and fire it. In this sense Hindus are closer to humanists. Yet in the shadows of their minds there is that ultimate framework of abstract notions, disciplines, **sādhanas**. The true anarchist knows the unwritten rules that govern the universe, that grounding, RTA.

❧❧❧❧❧❧❧❧❧❧❧❧

1. **The Philosophical Level:** this is the devotee pondering in private moments at an immense galactical level with awareness of universe upon universe of incomprehensible dimension.

This is the inspiration of **The Great Tradition** of the universal deities—of **Brahma, Vishnu, Shiva** and their feminine complementary deities, of the universal mother symbol of the Great Goddess **Mahadevi, or Shakti**. This level embraces **svadharma**—one's own particular dharma into which each person/soul/atma is born; it is based on social duties and obligations. Emperor Ashoka emphasised this in a Buddhist way as **Dhamma**—the social order without which a people or culture cannot function in a coherent and harmonious way.

P

2. **The Temple Level of Ritual,** social custom, ceremonies, superstition, sacrifices where a rigid attention to detail according to tradition and what the shastras order is upheld, certainly by the 'go-between' priests of all kinds.

The Little Tradition–local, regional deities not worshipped beyond their immediate localities. Very personal worship and religiosity. Immobility of factual ideas as compared with the ever-expanding scientific concepts of philosophy.

3. **The Individual Level of Bhakti Worship,** daily yoga, wandering mendicants, the Holy Ma carrying on discourses in ashrams or private homes, the guru and sannyasi withdrawn to lonely places to meditate and comprehend, groups of pilgrim musicians chanting the mantra–syllables of the great Trimurti as they march along the pathways of India, the yogi practising austerities for self-discipline and for harnessing energy before going out to teach in the ashram.

Hindu communities all over the world and across regions and languages within the country can identify with each other simply though this daily epiphany of patterned behaviour, **the personal puja,** taking **darshan** from one symbolic form or other of this myriad reflection in the Pantheon of visual representation.

Coming Down to Earth

Long ago Hindu **pandits,** learned men of the scriptures, explained the coming-down-to-earth which the Pantheon symbolises as they talked to a French scholar and traveller in India who encountered them in the 17th century. Bernier learned this. 'We have in our temples a great variety of images... To all these images we pay great honour; prostrating our bodies, and presenting to them, with much ceremony, flowers, nice scented oil, saffron...yet we do not believe that these statues are themselves Brahma or Vishnu; but **merely their images** and **representations**. We show them deference only for the sake of the deity whom they represent, and when we pray it is not to a murti, but to that deity...'

Images are admitted in our temples because we conceive that prayers are offered up with more devotion when there is something before the eyes that fixes the mind; but in fact we acknowledge that God alone is absolute, that He/She only is the Omnipotent Lord.

'To render accessible the world of the Gods' to ordinary humanity is the way Australian archaeologist Dr George Michell, has put it, working in that most numenistic of sites, **Hampi,** where every pillar has chiselled a part of that Pantheon, spilling out on every surface in fluid beautiful form in that once extremely wealthy Vijayanagar kingdom of sculptural magnificence. And these 'manifestations' are very real!... and some villagers really think they are. One newspaper headline read: 'Temple deity batting eyelid', following which 'people made a beeline to the temple to have a glimpse.'

Under the headline **God abridged: A divine series that makes the deities drawing room friendly, India Today,** magazine reviewed a new series of pocket books produced by Viking Penguin, India commencing with five major symbols of the ultimate sense of the divine, Vishnu, Krishna, Shiva, Devi, Ganesh with the rhetorical question: 'Have you ever tried to roll the universe up into a ball and expect ultimate truth in 150 pages of flawless English prose?' It gave thumbs up to this attempt, attractively designed, to encapsulate the infinite.

■ PARADOX

India itself is one gigantic paradox. Its inhabitants to their credit and our consternation nurtured on Greek and Roman logic and linear deduction, delight in the law of opposites!

◆ Five people crowd onto this stepping stone, articulating loudly... Bengali, American, Canadian English and two south Indians, one Tamil, the other from Andhra.

1. **A Bengali writer** addressed this phenomena in **a novel: The Flame of the Forest. Sudhin Ghose** explains:

Mother India's chariot is drawn by strange pairs: high intelligence and utter stupidity; generosity and cupidity, the desire to serve and the urge to thwart. Self-abnegation and exhibitionism.

The acute contrasts confuse and perturb. Meeting India head-on is an activity for the stout-hearted–but rewarding beyond measure in human warmth if the ford is crossed... Whatever truth about India is spoken, its opposite is sure to rear its contrary head somewhere else far flung in the vastness of this subcontinental complexity... and be as equally valid!

2. A Canadian novelist **Leslie Forbes** in her recent books–**Bombay Ice** (1988 and **Fish, Blood and Bone** (Weidenfeld and Nicolson, Toronto, 2001) also highlights the stark dichotomy. '*India seems to me to contain the best and worst of everything man has done in terms of humanity and inhumanity*'... and '*where all the centuries exist simultaneously*.'

3. Mark Twain as an American had his say on the subject:

So far as I am able to judge nothing has been left undone, either by man or nature, to make India the most extraordinary country that the sun visits on his round–nothing seems to have been forgotten, nothing overlooked.

India confuses, appeases, maddens, entrances by turns. There is the mistaken impression abroad for instance that it is the land of great spirituality, of saintly virtue, ashramic simplicity–in fact the Holy Grail for thousands of young Westerners disaffected by institutional religion and doctrine rather than devotion and integrity of the heart. This is patently not so. There are as many scams, sleazy moneygrubbers and greedy operators, hypocrites and dissemblers as those in Europe, Australia and the USA. **Bonfire of the Vanities** could easily be transposed into a Hindi film, the setting Mumbai and the Dawood brothers of Dubai and now Karachi its chief protagonists.

But the attempt to control wayward human instincts is a constant also despite the paradox of chaotic semblance at street level. The predisposition to search for individual fulfilment in **right dharma** is noticeable, so embedded in daily household puja or at the wayside shrine where the dudhwallah bringing in the dawn milk on his bicycle, his wife perched precariously on the pillion, alights for a moment to take **darshan** from the

P

vermilion-daubed Hanuman stone enshrined at the base of the antique giant peepul tree.

Imagine a Yorkshire milkman on his rounds stopping daily at the village church to offer prayers at the altar!

● These minute daily acts, tiny specks of spiritual yeast that encrust themselves in the folds of the brain, irritants causing constant reflection, do in effect create an ambience, the 'presence' of which cannot be gainsaid.

Amid the proliferation of a hundred ways to worship in ritual, Indians are at the same time solitary pilgrims encountered on the roads of India and as pilgrims in their own padayatras. Adherents of other faiths can be profoundly affected by this atmosphere. This pronounced characteristic of Indian culture is in itself a total paradox as that English professor so enamoured of India's profundity, **A L Basham**, commented upon decades ago:

> The ascetic idea contained within itself the negation of the very social values of orthodoxy on the lower level, and it is to my mind a wonderful achievement of the Hindu spirit of assimilation that these two disparate ideals could be fused into a single system of thought which even today is very much alive.

4. The contradictions remain in puzzling degree—and what more specific than the Goddess, a potent and very alive force in daily life. This is what a Tamilian whose most distant origins are in those sources has to say in a recent publication from Canada where he now lives. Prof. V Subramaniam, contrarily professor of Political Science at Carleton University, Ottawa not only writes on **Problem Recognition in Public Policy and Business Management**, he writes an entire book on **Mother Goddess and Other Goddesses** (Ajanta Books International, Delhi, 1993).

> Paradoxes form an integral part of theologies including Hindu theology, but the concept of the supreme Hindu Mother Goddess probably accommodates the largest number of them. One can identify off hand quite a few: She is virgin and she is also mother; she is a mother goddess but should not be physiologically a mother; she is the Saivite Parvati and a Vaisnavi; she is the Tantrik's orgiastic mistress, yet purest of the pure; she is bloodthirsty Kali and also the very embodiment of the merciful and beautiful as Amba or Lalitha; she is the invincible Durga and Shakti, but is also the weak Bharatmata in need of protection. This multiplicity of paradoxes, partly proves the continuous popularity of the Mother Goddess cult over the centuries …

● And where is the Professor of Business Studies at LSE or Harvard who will be writing a Western equivalent of this passage? This is India! A complex plural society when the world was still young, an India that cannot be homogenized into a coherence for American 'instant TV' presentations… which leads me to Queen Victoria and a profound **personal eye-opener**, a lesson in early wisdom, living through a paradox full of wry humour and irony which taught me also that not all Harvard professors are right in their judgements all of the time!

5. Here is the background in which Queen Victoria, my Harvard Professor of Modern English Literature, Professor Theodore Spencer, Chalapathi Rau one time revolutionary and radical editor of Lucknow's nationally-read **The National Herald**; and Kipling's Kim are, Indian-style, all of a piece!

Geoffrey Moorhouse in his inimitable and very readable style in **India Britannica** (Paladin, London, 1984) was describing the events of 1877 when Queen Victoria was titled **Kaiser-I-Hind** (Empress of India) at an astonishing Durbar called by Lord Canning, the new Viceroy—also of imperial Roman proportions.

Such a titular concept of a strange amalgam of Teutonic-Anglo-Saxon vintage in the middle of northern India to assert British dominion after the traumas of the 1857 Sepoy Revolt is weird enough.

> There can scarcely in all history have been an absentee monarch who touched as many distant subjects as Queen Victoria did with a sense of mystery approaching the divine; certainly there can have been none representing alien rule whose own person seemed increasingly exempt, as time went on, from the natural resentments of a conquered people. When the tide of Indian nationalism first began to flow towards the end of the century, the Queen herself was never associated by its leaders with the policies of her Government they had started to reject, and in this they showed a fine appreciation of where power really lies in a constitutional monarchy, whatever lustre is carefully maintained on the figurehead itself.

To some Indians of the time she seemed yet another manifestation of Shakti. To my generation as post-war Britishers, quite radical in our views in wanting to shed as rapidly as possible all the trappings of Empire, Victoria was more a benign matriarch. Until I drove Chalapathi Rau back to his home in Lucknow down Kipling's road that he had made famous—the Grand Trunk Road. Then a joy to drive in winter with burgeoning crops, high-standing sugar cane, a dancing peacock quivering its resplendent blue-green tail spread like a huge fan, brick-making kilns. The hazards then were the long lines of bullock carts bringing in the gobhi (cauliflower) loads. They hugged the bitumen for a smooth ride pushing us onto the dirt margin at the side. Lorries then were few and far between.

M C as this radical editor was known, had just come down from the heights of Shimla attending the Press Commission chaired by Dr Zakir Husain and he was roundly scolding me for never having read Kipling's **Kim**. This was punctuated with his great ripples of laughter. That took me totally by surprise from someone supposedly so left-wing, an agnostic from Andhra, avowedly a person dead-set to get rid of my predecessors —especially supercilious memsahibs! Yet he was a man of great warmth and humanity thwarted by his speech defect.

M C blamed my accidental American education for this glaring omission in my literary upbringing. Professor Theodore Spencer having roundly admonished me as a humble freshman,

P

and as his sole English student in the Radcliffe of 1942. He had fixed me as the representative of British Empire in his mind's eye, the USA having just been bombed into the war by the events of Pearl Harbor. He had dismissed Kipling as a poet of imperial pretensions. That had set an inhibiting draught of cold Boston air on my ever daring to open a book of Kipling's despite my wartime patriotism about things British–even in the USA!

M C had bought a copy of Kim in that most British of hill-stations, Shimla. Inscribing it with an infectious chuckle, he presented it to me… 'It's the best book on India to date!' he declared.

Early on a magical winter morning I drove M C through a Lucknow square nearing the newspaper house when a line of swinging, skirted rural women caught my eye just as the imposing statue of Queen Victoria on its plinth came in sight.

Astonished, I was to discover that despite nearly a decade having run since the declaration of a free India, such symbols of British dominion were still tolerated (they were finally removed much later, except the Victoria of Kolkata and Bangalore). Imagine the greater astonishment when one of the women approached the plinth. From a tiny cloth bag along with her food for the day–undoubtedly working as a migrant peasant on one of the many industrial construction sites then springing up–she stretched up, placed a few marigolds at Victoria' s skirted feet, did **pranam** at the street level, placed a few more flowers on the ground, all did the hand gesture of 'namaste' and walked on, singing folk songs raucously as they went.

Geoffrey Moorhouse, how right you were! Unbelievable now! Unbelievable then, except that M C smiled expansively with that gentle and wise humour of the Indian who has seen it all before, no new thing under the sun.

- ■ PARSIS

There cannot be a poor Parsi in sight!

The tiny community, now dwindling to about 75,000(census 2001), is lost in India's billion-plus population, is a living example of how a refugee group can make good, prosper and become more than above-average public benefactors in the space of just over a 1000 years, short in India's overall timescale.

Fleeing religious persecution in Persia in the eigthth century CE as the first Islamic incursions delivered a hammer-blow to their far too tolerant faith they first turned to agriculture on Gujarat's western seaboard. There the Hindu raja generously gave them food and shelter, similar to the response of the Zamorin of Kozhikode to the Portuguese.

- ◆ There they prospered with the living faith in their spiritual 'light'–**Ahura Mazda** the Creator whose Prophet, the Enlightened Messenger, saw the light at the age of 42–this was **Spitaman Zarathustra**, a somewhat hazy figure depicted like Methuselah with a long white beard, born at some time between 1700–1500 BCE.

The place and date of his birth are uncertain. One tradition says he was born in Azerbaijan, another near modern Teheran.

He died while praying at a Fire Temple he had inaugurated in Balkh, in Afghanistan.

The message he preached was similar to that of the Buddha, his approximate contemporary–that of **Humatra, Hukta, Huvarashtra**: Good Thoughts, Good Words, Good Deeds, but without the sense of anguish–**dukh**. The message from Zarathustra is a fighting one, that each individual is capable of maintaining the constant struggle against evil, not by withdrawing form the world with ascetic practices or mortification; rather just getting out into the market-place so to speak–and doing something about re-arighting the balance–with a strong message about supporting those most vulnerable, being a protector of the poor.

With the eternal flame (literally so despite all upheavals and exigencies) he built Fire Temples. Emphasis is quite striking on the **sacredness of fire**, central to the Parsi abstract symbol of God as **Arar Behram** a scientific concept, an element of purity = the flame. Similar to Hindu rites as they emerged in the fire = **havan**. Ceremonies at all major pujas regard fire as purifying, not to be worshipped as such, but to be used **in worship** as an emblem of destroying impurities. When fire is applied whatever it touches becomes pure, from molten gold to diseased forms, to the air in a home where illness has been prevalent. Taking the flame onto the head by sweeping the palm across the oil lamp at the arati, the last evening puja in a Hindu temple is a symbolic gesture of purification, removing residual evil.

Zarathustra must also have impregnated the community with good business sense. Migrating to Mumbai about 400 years ago they cut a clear swathe through their refugee status. Economic decimation and cultural dislocation in alien surroundings was not their *cri de coeur*. Just the opposite.... as witness the size of the huge book of two zestful female 'energies'–**Pheroza Godrej** and **Firoza Mistree: A Zorastrian Tapestry: Art, Religion and Culture** (Mapin, Ahmedabad, 2002).

And they never looked back!

Such a remarkable tiny close-knit community, they have prospered out of all proportion to total population–in every kind of industry and commercial undertaking to such an extent that (again out of all proportion to total population) they have become major benefactors to general society, especially in Mumbai and Kolkata, giving massive donations to hospitals, research institutes, libraries, art galleries–one hundred or a thousand-fold above what they were generously given in Gujarat.

By happy chance those who had been settled in Gujarat were not far distant to events consolidating the trading post at Surat where the British East India Company was pioneering a new form of shipyard. Parsis were employed. One **Lowjee Nusserwanjee Wadia** so excelled in his workmanship and management skills that he was promoted to the new shipyards in Bombay. This was in the mid-1770s. With his team of fellow Parsis, he went from strength to strength, in building a new dockyard and ships that a mercantile family concern emerged amongst the generations to come, recognised by the British Royal Navy and honoured as such.

Other innovative endeavours such as banking suited their joint family cooperation in pooling resources. **Sorabji Pochkhanawala** broached the revolutionary idea in 1911 of banking, and assuming responsibility in the civil administration of Bombay–**especially all these cultural qualities of openness, confidence and compassion for those in need by setting up philanthropic institutions. These mark the Parsi community out as a quite extraordinary one, distinct not only in the wealth it has amassed–but the way it has recycled that wealth back into society through civic responsibility.**

It is worth remembering that from this dynamic community came the first Indian MP to sit in the House of Commons at Westminster–over 100 years ago, from 1892–1895. **Dadabhai Naoroji** was the Parsi. Known to be very anglophile he was elected to the London constituency of Central Finsbury.

By some quirk of urban sociology Parsi families were either given names of professions as they moved into modern times or took it upon themselves to entertain the outside world with some outlandish ones concocted by themselves. With their sense of fun, laughter, ballroom-dancing, partying, delicious cuisine and generally enjoying the good things of life, it is on all accounts not apocryphal to state there have been people named **Mr Sodawater-bottlewalla** although I have never encountered that gentleman yet. Mr Masalawallah, Presswala, Engineer, Doctor and the famous Rustomji Cawasji Banaju who became a Bengali merchant prince (on a par with all the wealthy British nabobs) did–and do–actually exist!

The late great Sir Jamshedjee Jeejeebhoy is a prime example of Parsi get-up-and go.... rags to riches success story selling used bottles as a boy, made a fortune and was eventually knighted by Queen Victoria for his philanthropy.

■ PHILANTHROPY

The perceived wisdom on India by strangers in the Western world is on the whole conveyed electronically. Visual images branded in that inner eye remain as stereotypes very hard to obliterate. Drought and floods, communal mayhem, overloaded country boats carrying poor people across huge rivers overturning and leaving a trail of drowned victims, bizarre gurus and other 'exotics' are, along with mud huts and disturbing beggars and elephant deities of stone consuming milk by the litre, the typical images for media moghuls also–avid for selling their papers–to stir a satiated public in a glut of pedestrian daily fare.

Even cricket crowds on the sporting channels behave like no other densely packed mass of aficionados as they seethe in packed stadiums of young men furled in colourful flags and jerking up and down like the insides of a piano playing ragtime jazz. These then are the predominant images fed to the Western world.

Few outside of India understand that all is not poverty nor that India can stand on its own feet in many economic ways, nor that it is exporting in considerable strength, solid in an industrial/commercial infrastructure... nor is it known that the measure of real wealth held certainly in long-standing dynastic families is not paper money but liquid and often augmented in family vaults in diamonds and gold.

One may well ponder the dramatic and disproportionate contrasts and the need for a more equitable spread of wealth... but at least there is a long-established tradition of **philanthropy** that existed even before Europeans arrived, or Christian missionaries began preaching about 'loving thy neighbour'.

◆ **Social responsibility** is no new thing within the teachings of karma and dharma. The duty of distributing a portion of personal income in the Hindu/Buddhist/Jain/Parsi communities has always been a very strong component in personal dharma. **Daan** is the Sanskrit term for donation: the householder's duties laid down in dharmic injunctions.

For Muslims distribution of **zakat**, customarily a 2.5% proportion of savings for almsgiving is left to individual discretion or channelled through mosques towards religious education of students, support of the poor, and other needful causes. Hoarding of money at the cost of others' suffering is said to be contrary to the Islamic spirit. There is a month of the lunar year named **Zeqaid** when assessment is made for this purpose. (One example is on record of Muhammed's economist companion, Abu-Zarr Ghaffari, who used to stand on the crossroads of Mecca and ask for money from passers-by for the public treasury).

◆ Personal philanthropy has been very strong in Bombay Maharashtrian and Gujarati dynasties going back several hundred years. The Tatas, Birlas, Sarabhais have instituted hospitals, art galleries, endowed universities and other colleges of learning, set up trusts and scholarships, endowed temple constructions.

In Bengal where endowment of the arts is common, the Tagore family initiated Shantiniketan's Vishwabharati University and spread their wealth in many other ways in the 19th–20th century. In south India a good deal of wealth is donated on pilgrimage to temple funds but there is also a strong tradition of institutional philanthropy from wealthy family trusts.

The motivating ideals are very Hindu:
Shraddha = faith and dedication
Ekagratha = holding on to the one, concentration
Saka Virayam = spirit of togetherness
Shraman = self-respect
This is one area of public service.

◆ Philanthropy weaves a hidden tapestry through Indian society. Nor does it exist, tidily in a vacuum, to be dismissed cynically by political critique as a bourgeoisie salving its conscience. Some of the most useful work in arousing reformers in the political tradition has in fact been initiated by ascetics such as the Bengali saint Ramakrishna at the turn of the century and by the first great Shankaracharya in Kaladi, Kerala, as well as hundreds of unsung humble Gandhian-style citizens who have since the first whiff of the freedom struggle of the early 20th century stood up to be counted.

Spurious gurus notwithstanding (in recent decades due to the naiveté of Western followers) a chain of hospices as well as clean simple accommodation and networks of help in ashrams

P

have been initiated by many swamis and other spiritual mentors. Sai Baba has created hospitals designed in space-age architecture in Andhra, and in Bangalore as well as many other projects in south India. No fees are charged. Poor people are fed and educated.

Black money economy, endemic money corruption between politicians and business (not confined to Indian society however), greedy lalas, income tax evasion, false shows of throwing money as backsheesh to beggars lined up in horrendous array at temple festivals are the disturbing dark shadows of Indian life but genuine Indian concern can be ignited by visionary leaders in the community who command respect whether high-born, middle class, or from nonliterate humble backgrounds. Unsung heroes—and heroines—there are who slave their guts out creating schools for slum children, getting impoverished women educated and in conditions beyond belief in the modern West.

■ PILGRIMAGE
= a padayatra n. Sanskrit **Pedes** (Latin)

It is surprising that such an important component in Indian life is hardly mentioned in any sociopolitical assessment of the integrative processes in this huge and complex society. And yet it is such a subtle and impregnable binding agent that defies categorisation. Perhaps that is why it is ignored, too amorphous to tap into a short sharp sound-bite for the reporter on the run in a jet age of global crises and staccato TV news items.

Somewhere everyday, throughout the length and breadth of the subcontinental landmass, millions of Indians must be on pilgrimage given the conditioning to do so; the prodigious number of sacred places that make it possible; the profusion of faiths that encourage and have institutionalised pilgrimage; the regionally diverse commemorations, celebrations, festivals; the astrological awareness of planetary conjunctions that demand ritual marking of their profound impact—such as the gigantic encounter every twelve years of the **KUMBH MELA**—last held at Allahabad in 2001. And then there is the existence of so many saints, munis, learned sages who create inspiration for **padayatra** and a sense of the sacred.

Why: India sparks and resonates with psychic energy, more than most lands other than Aboriginal Australia which is scattered with very active sacred sites dependent on oral tradition (the **Song Lines**) and time-honoured legends still enforced by rites of passage.

What Western rational humanity, schooled as it is in scientific empiricism has lost—that ineffable sense of emotional energy, a 'luminosity' which responds to a 'spirit' presence in the living rock (very Aboriginal) or in a tree, a deep grove of palms, or symbolises the thunder or the awesome mountain presences as Vedic deities—Indians have retained. By some extraordinary capacity of absorption, a resilience or perhaps reluctance to jettison what has gone before but rather to superimpose new concepts upon old acceptances, the sense of **NUMEN** has not been discarded. A contemporary publication by physicist

Margaret Wertheim—The Pearly Gates of Cyberspace (Doubleday, New York, 1998) suggests that the openness and searching individuality of cyberspace may have some unusual consequences—reinstating a new source to supply 'soul data' and a 'sense of connectedness' with abstract knowledge and with other individual searchers. In the past, institutional religion, the imposition of faith by dogmatic clerics and formal academic learning intimidated such a private exploration of a spiritual 'heavenly space'.

Philip Rawson, Kapila Vatsyayan, George Michell, Heinrich Zimmer have all written on Indians' 'intuitions of the **immense'**, the sense of 'primal vibrations' that are part and parcel of everyday life that is not so in modern industrial urban society in the Western Christian world. It is not as though Indians are airy-fairy mystics, although that may be a perception stereotyped amongst some. India has produced its own fair share of brilliant scientists throughout history, great physicists like C V Raman in recent times. It is a mathematically talented race into the bargain.

Carl Jung has written much about this dislocating sense of loss amongst scientific man who 'feels himself isolated in the cosmos'. It is doubtful if Indians do. Alienation, a oneness, vulnerability in the face of the incomprehensible infinity of galactical space and time exercised the minds of the rishis to such an extent that they came to terms with this intellectual challenge long, long ago.

In this land there is no Genet adrift in the universe waiting for his Godot.

The great cycles of reincarnation absorbed this immense reality. The dynamic forces of archetypal symbols, chanted mantras and visual yantras and the psychic energy they generated are still part of daily life, not weird, esoteric or strange. People are still familiar with the archetypes and find in them a satisfaction which in a curious way impels the need for pilgrimage—a return to the source of legend. For instance Shiva and Parvati, married and presiding over the stupendous territory of pristine snow on **Kailash** (untouched by climbers, their pollution and sacrilege of the sacred) still commands attention. The daunting **parikrama** –(pilgrimage) for instance of Mt Kailash beyond the northernmost frontiers into Tibet is one of the great journeys to be undertaken by Indians of all kinds, rich, poor, middle class, basic peasant, non-Hindu even, some so aged it is a wonder they do not die enroute.

And if they do, like those who lie on planks waiting to die at **Kashi**, to roll silently into the Ganga, then they will die content, saved many thousands of rebirths according to their way of thinking.

Diana Eck, Harvard Sanskrit scholar and noted authority on Indian Studies refers to what she called the 'sacred geography' of India. Specific places through aeons of time, and the actual marking of them by people undertaking intrepid journeys to reach these 'crossings over' = **tirthas** = fords are not just physical points on the quadrant of this downward-pointing triangle. **They are spiritual/psychic fords, shaping and influencing personalities, once experienced, for life**.

And so through the actual physical hardship of **padayatra**, walking on foot, India becomes an intimately 'known continent'. And not through history as other cultures learn, this accumulation of 'belonging to a land', of ultimate citizenship but by this first-hand experience–this '**consciousness**' of terrain accumulated generation by generation within families, the folklore within families carrying specific knowledge, recognition of landmarks for survival of those who will enact the same parikrama in the next generation. It is a geographical enhancement that many a nature-lover or environmentalist of today is beginning to reclaim with ecological sensitivity.

Indeed in **C M Bhandari's** magnificent photographic journal of the **Kailash-Mansarovar** pilgrimage **A Journey to Heaven, Kailash-Mansarovar** (Devamber Prakashan, Delhi, 1998) he explains his astonishment on being given the Hindi translation of the original **Skanda Purana** text (the post Vedic 'old tales' and parables) titled **Manas Khand**, to discover the detailed and exact cartographic knowledge of these far-flung geographical features–as recognisable today as they were described then when sage Bhagiratha performed his arduous penance, thus able to bring Ganga Ma down to earth. These scattered land maps and trekking pathways are the invisible filaments threading psychic energy through the length and breadth of the land, presenting its inhabitants in a magical touch with a sense of their **Indian-ness**–ignored by foreign correspondents and some Westernised Indians at their peril.

Such cartographic 'maps' were sung in Aboriginal ceremonies also–their song lines branded into the mind at staunch rites of passage to be a guide to the land in such adverse environmental challenges.

✄ Climbing the Pilgrim Way... Abode of the Gods.
Kailash Mansarovar

Where Shiva was married to his eternal consort is one of the most venerated magnetic points to visit in India. It is, amongst many names, called **Triyugi Narayan** recalling the three ages (**YUGA**) over which Shiva as Lord of Destruction and Regeneration has **already** presided on this solitary conical dome with his benign Parvati–and those ages stretch the mind for they are galactical in scope. And there is the sacred **hawan** (place for the fire around which the divine couple had taken the seven steps to sanctify marriage) to be treated with veneration. Pilgrims still bring wood to replenish the fire which is said to have been alight continually for aeons. This fact is accepted without question! It is all so much simpler to accept without that nagging Western desire, obsession even, for the empirical evidence, especially when with the wisdom of years, you actually do learn that what was once myth eventually turns out to be actual fact. Pilgrims undergo inconceivable hardship on inhospitable mountain passes at 19,000 feet, through biting winds and unnerving sleet, Tibetan Buddhists taking the extreme austerity of **shashtaang**, measuring themselves along the ground, standing up, and then again lying their full length.

This often painful undertaking, in places an unrelenting uphill 3,000 feet ascent near Thanedar, and 4,444 steps down a precipitous rock face, makes Lourdes and Jerusalem as points of reference in the Christian pilgrimage appear as mere child's play. The actual circuit on foot of the holy lake where belief is that the cosmic egg, a symbolic image of the beginnings of our creation was hatched in earliest geological formations, is approximately **75 km** usually accomplished in two days if lucky.

The pradakshina(circumambulation) of the mountain is **52 km** with all the intervening linkages, plus 200 km to undertake by bus, pony and foot from Delhi. And the true devotee should accomplish 13 circuits of Shiva's ethereal throne. It is almost beyond belief to the Western mind considering the height of the trekking, women in shalwar kameez, some pilgrims lacking any mountaineering gear or warm clothing.

Most survive, miraculously. Is it the power of Shiva/Parvati or the human mind? A true Kumaoni, a man of the hills, one-time ambassador, C M Bhandari engages the reader stage by stage by way of truly magnificent photographs on this journey into the **mind**.

This is territory where the awesome Lake Mansarovar is said to have been born from Brahma's mouth; where Ravana sought boons against dying at the hands of a human; where Krishna and Arjuna held discourse; where Mahadeva Siva steps back into pre-Vedic dominion of the mountains. Huddled against the biting winds, the impregnable snowclad mountains are overwhelming in their immensity, not only of scale but spatial physicality. That in itself daunts and elevates the mind.

'If this is earth, then what is heaven?' says the pilgrim who undertook the 32 days discipline. She was as modern as any yuppy female executive in New York but the 'call' had come, a yearning to follow ancestral ritual, to undertake this discipline.

Mt Kailash gathers together all the forces as a vibrating centre of the universe, dominant, alone in its majesty, 22,000 ft high, the Mt Meru of Hindu myth, axis of the world, the place of enlightenment for the **JAINS** first tirthankar, Precious Jewel of Snow to Tibetan Buddhists.

P

How was this implemented?

'I am a changed person–and I admire our rishis for thinking it all up!' explained another pilgrim, a personal friend from Kolkata. 'A force impelled me to hazard the journey.'

What did he mean, this diminutive Bengali who was approaching his 50s, and who looked as though the least puff of mountain air would have tipped him into the nearest crevasse as he approached the giant glaciers, so fine were his wrists and slight his general frame.

The sages were wiser than you might think!

Over centuries it would appear they wove tales and spiritual parables that captured the collective imagination over at least five millennia–those long gone eras, retrieving the accretions of folk tales from neolithic and tribal sources centuries earlier. The Himalayas after all are pre-Vedic.

So the body of a loose canon of belief was built up.

Staging posts were set up, highlighting especially sacred events linked with astronomical phenomena. Sages further sanctified these hallowed grounds in earliest Vedic society, almost unconsciously establishing the cultural unity of the landmass, the four points of the compass known as **dhams**, divine abodes.

All these points of reference became centres for pilgrimage—for learning, for devotion, for meditation and withdrawal. And so ashrams now exist, dotted all over the landscape to engender a constant flow of circumambulating pilgrims to stay a while on the following cluster of mini–STEPPING STONES.

❀ **Vrindavan (alternatively spelled Brindaban)** derives its name from a forest of **vrinda/tulsi** = holy basil.

South of Delhi this is where all the legends of the young Krishna have accumulated, necessitating a 60 km **pradakshina** circuit to take in all the half-historical, half-mythical places in his country of Braj in which domain there are 350 temples alone (nothing is ever on a limited scale in India) in what has been called the **Divine Amphitheatre**. Here again Bengali widows with shaven heads, dressed in all-white saris undertake the further hardship of prostration termed **ashtangi** (eight points of the body have to touch the ground). We have seen them undergoing such penance along the verge of the Grand Trunk Road from Calcutta via Allahabad to New Delhi. Not even an express bus would dare run them down amid the thundering traffic.

❀ **Jagannath Puri in Orissa.**

Millions assemble at **Jagannath Puri** in **Orissa** for the gigantic Rath ceremony of the temple chariot parade. Pilgrims regardless of caste, creed, status, region gather in Orissa to take a walk along with the Holy One fashioned out of a trunk of wood. The truncated deities **Jagannath**, his elder brother **Balabhadra** and their sister **Subhadra** emerge, a Hindu version of American 'South Park' caricatures in the TV series, somewhat surreal, belonging to other worlds.

◆ Legend is that the culture associated with the triad was appropriated after Vedic, Buddhist and Jain cultures flourished in Orissa, certainly known to history in the third century BCE but with many Aboriginal overtones—especially with the highly unusual sibling Subhadra. Nowhere else in the Hindu pantheon does the Shakti take the form of a sister. It has been suggested that this incorporation harks back to Buddhist nuns who were always addressed by the monks as sister. Even the legend behind the origins of such a strange truncated deity tells of a large sandalwood log floating in to be carved eventually into Jagannath and his siblings.

◆ The recarving every 20 years of the triad involves the most ancient of rituals when artisans are sent out into the forest to find trees which have been designated with certain psychic signs as appropriate for this sacred carving task. According to respected art critic Professor O C Gangoly this task is associated with the Sabara tribal people in the dense jungles of Bhalukand and their fantastical depictions of their animistic deities.

◆ The carving 'said to be Krishna's bones' is wrapped in leaves that stay permanently fresh for the next two decades in the chest cavity carved out in the new log. The priest 'breathes soul' into this new murti. So real do Hindu gods become they take on human aspects, even taking a bath at the **Snan Yatra** Bathing

Festival before the monsoon breaks. They catch a cold and take to bed, disappearing for 15 days, which gives time for old paint on them to be refurbished. Then all three re-emerge pristine clean for the coming year. Where else would gods be so well treated?

In olden days the millions of pilgrims that gather for this ceremony were so obsessed by the desire to escape the endless rounds of rebirths that they launched a name into the English language–**juggernaut**–for the unstoppable vehicle under which it is said some of the more fanatical believers threw themselves to destruction as the cumbersome wooden wheels of the temple chariot crushed them, thus gaining merit. The wheel of Empire has with delicious irony come full circle with the Hare Krishna movement celebrating the Rath Yatra in Trafalgar Square. Hundreds of British Indians turn out to pull the Rath.

Sagara In **Bengal**

Surely only India would regard a king called **Sagara** who ruled over that controversial Ayodhya in ancient times as especially sagacious because he had 60,000 sons. No wonder India has a population problem!

Perhaps a leaf should be taken out of **Kapil Muni's** book for he is the holy sage lost in deep meditation in the far reaches of the Ganga delta where he had constructed a bamboo hut on a spit of sandbank now called **Sagara** where another teeming gathering commemorating some germ of truth in pre-history and fanciful legend honours his memory as well as his sanctuary, now a temple very much part of the pilgrimage ritual.

The story is a confusing one ranging over generations caught up in cosmic cycles of reincarnation–**samsara** which tests the credibility of the outsider, other than that of children willing to suspend the norms of rational belief if captivated by extravagant imaginations. Sagara nearly did not make it into this world of reality, poisoned in the womb where he remained for seven years as the result of this jealous act from a co-wife of his mother. The period in history clearly must be that like the Mahabharata epic of constant feudal jockeying for power amongst petty kingdoms, rajas seeking supremacy being its theme.

Sagara, wishing to regain his father's lost kingdom, does the traditional thing–he sends out the sacrificial horse in the ritual of the **aswamedha yagna** to roam the land in asserting his command of territory. His expectation that his 60,000 sons by his first wife Sumati, who 'brought forth a gourd containing 60,000 seeds' which were placed in urns of milk where they grew (often depicted in the narratives painted on cloth), would guard this ceremonial steed representing the power of the kingdom, suffered considerable shock.

◆ None too pious themselves, they failed to prevent the horse disappearing into the nether regions (not quite as infernal as Dante's) and were commanded by their irate father to dig their way down to recover it. This they did, retrieving the horse invested with so much symbolism and tied it to a post near a habitation.

There they came across Kapil the sage or **muni** in deep concentration. Thinking the learned one to be the thief they threatened him with their weaponry while he was at his devotions. Angry at being disturbed by this legion of males he opens his Third Eye of Wisdom and incinerated them all into a pile of ash which over generations becomes an impacted mound. It is Sagara's grandson who later intercedes on their behalf for pardon so that **proper ritual** can release them from their spiritual no-man's land.

Kapil Muni, **still ̇alive**, despite all these aeons rolling by relents enough to promise Sagara that his own grandson **Bhagiratha** will be instrumental in bringing down the holy waters of the Ganga as a boon to cleanse their charred ashes from their present impurity and purgatory.

◆ Moving forward through the centuries, **Bhagiratha** undertakes the yatra to Kailash (how far back these traditions and customs are reinforced!), performing such daunting austerities that Shiva grants this boon. Ganga Ma at source named after Sagara's descendant is allowed to flow down to earth, the Deity stepping down from his eternal seat to shield the earth below from the full force of the cascade in his matted hair, saving all below Rishikesh and Hardwar from drowning—a not uncommon occurrence in monsoonal floods.

Thus this multitude cleansed by the healing waters of the mighty river entered heaven—and so will all those honouring this extravagant tale who struggle into the crowded trains of Bengal when they finally reach the lonely point unprotected from sea, sun and sky. Just a few possessions in a cloth bundle, pots and pans slung over shoulders for cooking in whatever firewood is available (for 3–4 million people?) a little food and much faith, they are off-loaded into rickety ferries under the full midday sun.

◆ Exposed to the elements for days they settle down to watch the world go by (and it does, a microcosm of all strands of Indian cultural life) amid scenes of a stupendous mela. Huddled under old shawls and saris at night around rough fires when the cold sea winds blow, passing the time shopping from the bamboo constructed food stalls, listening to the homilies of sadhus, singing community bhajans to keep their spirits buoyant until the auspicious hour as the first orange yellow rays of the dawning sun dim the stars. The tide is sweeping in. A conch shell is sounded by the priest, and the shivering quivering pilgrims cry in unison 'Kapil Muni Ki Jai' = Long live Kapil Muni, as they rush to the water's edge to take their holy dip... this will absolve them of *all* their sins committed in this reincarnation.

But the ritual is still not complete! They have a kilometre to walk, damp and dishevelled to give **prasad** to the temple shrine reconstructed for the umpteenth time over the millenia as the sea slowly encroaches upon the site where the Muni meditated. They pass naked sadhus, and the vibhuti-caked head of a holy man buried up to his neck; a young teenage Shiva mendicant glowing under strange mauve makeup, clumpy **rudraksha** beads around his neck, most auspicious and now proved to have medicinal qualities (see **MALA**), a Shiva trident spike through his extended tongue, unable to draw it in because the upright spike is up against his nose; cows and calves to be donated to the temple's brahmin functionaries; conches booming; wet marigolds adrift in muddied pockets of shallow water; the smell of damp cloth,

salted bodies caked, smoking fires smouldering, agarbatti incense odour and stench of urine, a totally Indian smell... and yet, an inner flame afire in the eyes of those pilgrims around us, tears of fulfilment falling, a palpable energy from the entire spectrum of India on pilgrimage.

This is Sagar Island and a muni's spirit in no way dead unlike the groves of Athene and the tales of Apollo only a lifeless if perfect figure in a Greek museum.

✺ Amarnath in Kashmir

Nearly 14,000 feet above sea level in a grey gaunt valley with a huge gaping mouth of a cave, the annual Kashmiri summer pilgrimage, a strenuous and dangerous 50 km from Pahalgam is taking place. Pilgrims seek blessing from the constantly forming natural ice **lingam** of Siva at **Amarnath**. This stalagmite is a reminder that **Mahadev's** presence is ever there, amid all the Muslim mayhem far down in the valley, and was ever thus in a memory of India that disappeared over the edge of historic time perhaps 6,000 years ago.

It certainly has been a site of pilgrimage in very ancient remembered time. It is one of the most testing physical pilgrimages of all (apart from Kailash-Mansarovar) by twisting road in uncomfortable lurching buses on precipitous bends; by horseback or on foot or even carried if infirm, on a sturdy porter's back across narrow bridges, swirling streams, through boulder-strewn rubble meadows, snow bridges, desolate tracks, cumbersome glaciers treacherously moving forward over the years, the very symbol of implacable nature against which humanity is powerless, rock falls thundering down gorges, all are a test at the best of times. And yet people from all over India feel impelled to undertake the impossible.

There is a need to tread warily. Even summers can be treacherous when ice melts, air currents change into maelstroms of wayward energy, and winds of asura-like ferocity are sucked into narrow valleys without warning, biting and lashing as in a shark-frenzy, yet the number tested by such conditions is now well over 100,000 annually. In 1996 over 160 people died and 8000 had to be evacuated in icy conditions by the Army.

✺ Sabarimalai in Kerala

With each year the number of devotees of this cult increases. One estimate is 30%, pilgrims from all over the southern states now joining the Malayalam throngs, some officials stating that percentage as 60% of the total, all attempting to reach the **Sabarimalai** temple on that auspicious Sankranti day, **January 14th.** We had encountered them halfway through their 2-month long endurance test of abstinence from liquor, meat and sex as well as the presence of women between 10–50 years (pollution of menstruation).

According to northern as well as southern astrologers this is the time of the sun's transit from the Tropic of Capricorn to the northern hemisphere. In Gujarat, for instance, this day is celebrated as **Makara Sankranti** with roof-top throngs competitively flying thousands of kites trying to cut rivals down. Neighbours share their friendship with gifts of sweetmeats. In Maharashtra jowar (sorghum) sprinkled with salt and tangy lemon and fresh fruits is taken to other households. In the south **Pongal** marks the harvest festival of the first crop of rice. All the vitality of festival time and vivid colour in painted cattle horns and decorated carts reflects the honouring of the sun = surya.

But the commemoration of Ayyappa reflects something more—today's honouring of pluralistic India at its most rewarding. Part of the ritual in the testing culmination of the pilgrimage is the visiting of the mosque in Erumeli and a church at Arthungal in remembrance of the legendary association of the saint with an Arab Muslim, **Vavar** (said to have been a pirate) and a Syrian Christian **Veluthachan**. In fact, along the heavily congested coastal road up Kerala we were in virtual convoy with the marigold-festooned 'people-carriers' of the hundreds of these male pilgrims. At chai stops we kept gleaning further information as they all spoke fluent English, being extremely well-educated Keralites many scattered overseas because of the lack of urban development in an essentially rural state. They explained that in the reign of **Ayyan** of the second Chera empire, an Arab merchant named **Sulaiman** (circa 850 CE) introduced Islam into this coastal belt. A colleague of his, Bavar (or Vavar) was noted for his saintliness as also the Christian priest-hero given an entirely different name on internet information–**Kadamattathu** but this discrepancy is nothing strange in this land of multi-identities! Anyway, as behoves a plural society Muslim and Christian are worshipped along with Ayyappa at this ecumenical shrine!

The estimate of pilgrims at last count who have to undergo a strenuous and sweaty jungle hill climb on foot for about 6 km was one and a half million people chanting **Swamiye Saranam Ayyappa**–first to visit the image of the god up the steep gold-plated steps that lead to the sanctum sanctorum. So is he saint or offspring of Deity? Not one pilgrim could give a clear answer. But on my last visit a south Indian tells me that Ayyappa addressed as **Hari Hara Putra**–is a manifestation of the combined energy source of Shiva/Vishnu as Mohini, born to overcome the evil rulers of consecutive timescales (kalpas). That sounded very familiar.

It seemed the pilgrimage itself was of more importance, its comradeship bestowing a 'glow' of benediction. And then the **makara vilakku**, that miraculous glow provides the final spiritual burnishing before the rush home. This time the huge numbers took up every vantage point jutting out over the densely forested valleys. An outcrop of roped hillside and even mounds of fresh coconuts were trampled on by the press of people. The soil gave way. Coconuts rolled. Humanity rolled with the slippery surface, people crushing others.

Year by year the numbers do not abate, pilgrims who brave all, drawn by the yearning to undergo penance, dharma and moksha, and to witness the mysterious celestial light = *jyoti* which flickers in an aureole of 'camphor-yellow glow' atop the central ghat heights at Ponnambala–Medu.

❀ The lone British pilgrim... 1815

William Simpson was the first European to trek as far up into the Himalayas to reach the sacred pilgrimage site of Gangotri. As a professional landscape artist he translated images back to Britain of an India hardly changed even now from those he painted over 150 years ago beautifully presented by Mildred Archer in **Visions of India, The Sketchbooks of William Simpson, 1859–62** (Phaidon Press, London, 1986), but also to be seen in a place of honour in the newly refurbished Imperial Hotel in Delhi, which has become like an art gallery under the inspired direction of Jasdev Singh Akoi.

Like a number of British scholars of the time who 'had gone native' taking to Indian dress and accepting certain customs, Simpson observed the purification ceremony and took a morning dip in the Ganges at its source, drinking of its sacred water. Pennants were flying to propitiate the volatile deities of this sky-touching region where the Indus, the Brahmaputra, the Sutlej all rise, amid the eternal glaciers and snows. Constant snow winds and snow-blindness dogged Buddhist pilgrims coming over the Tibetan passes. Simpson even fell terrifyingly into a crevasse and was only saved by his pointed Indian-style arm sleeves catching on the jagged sides–hanging above the menacing darkness of a cavern below 'the icicles hanging down suggested teeth to my thoughts and it seemed like the mouth of a dreadful beast ready to swallow whatever came in reach.' His paintings in 1862, with mountains awesome as they dominate the valley, pilgrims ringing the temple bell washing their clothes in the streams, a saffron-robed lean sadhu begging, are all of a piece with the same scene today... but now multiply the numbers in the picture by a magnitude of one hundred.

❀ **Conclusion** The mercy of the gods may have to be called into question. With the arrival of more technology, the video bus, the phenomenal leap in internal tourism (60 million Indians alone touring India in any one year) encouraged by the showing of old M G R Tamil movies (extremely popular) as one speeds to pilgrimage centres, the strain on the environment and fragile unusual sites grows.

Some sacred hallows were intended only for the lone holy spirit and a few acolytes. Now people arrive in their thousands since the opening up of better surfaced roads, bringing four-wheeled drive ever closer before the padayatra imposes its own disciplines.

It is a worldwide problem. The Parthenon, the Pyramids, the Lake District, Uluru, all face the impact of too many tourists ruining what they come to enjoy. Suddenly state and union governments have woken up to the fact that its trees are in peril for firewood to keep pilgrims warm on a padayatra.. One day the banks will burst...

The great swamis and acharyas of India understood the positive forces inherent in pilgrimage. The interaction and subtle play of meeting points is intense–south Indian Tamils in the high and icy passes; bushy-bearded Sikhs feeling the intensity of humidity and thankful for sea breezes whooshing in at Kanyakumari; Bengalis queueing patiently for **10 hours** to catch a fleeting glimpse of Shri Venkateshwara at Tirupati; Malayalees at Kashi, Gujaratis struggling with the mountain air as they marvel at the purity of snow on the aloof sphinx-like dome of Mt Kailash.

It is these sociopolitical assessments of Indian pilgrimage which have been totally ignored by the theorists. And yet it is an invisible filament threading its magic energy through the length and breadth of India, **presenting Indians with a sense of their Indian-ness... once again.**

■ POLLUTION

A deeply entrenched attitude of mind, concerned not only with bodily hygiene but more importantly its spin-off—**ritual purity** including spiritual ramifications as well. Survival instincts must surely have played their part in the dramatic environment of India's annual climatic onslaught in the pre-monsoonal torrid humidity. When even the ubiquitous crows no longer caw harshly, their beaks scissored apart gasping for breath as Delhi swelters, there understandably had to be a framework of rules to prevent disease spreading. Putrefaction is a matter of hours.

Kitchens must be carefully monitored. Intrusion by strangers bringing in unknown bacteria must be stopped at source, shoes left at the threshold. Interdining was forbidden between those who were privileged and able to access clean water and who had the education to learn discipline in personal cleanliness and food hygiene, and those who were not. Hands became implements. At least they were washed.... and frequently, because who could vouch for cutlery? Who could meet with whom, dine with whom, bed with whom, were matters of serious consideration.

◆ **Mlechchha**, the Sanskrit word reflects its meaning. It sours the face. All the muscles of the mouth are pulled down in disgust. One doesn't even have to practice abhinaya to act vibhatsa. The physiognomy does it for you... **mlechchha** is a deeply entrenched attitude of mind.

◆ **Pinky**....potassium permanganate—an effective antiseptic agent used certainly in British households in India for washing salad ingredients bought from the open bazaar where invariably most food is covered in flies. Lettuce, fruit etc was left in a bowl pink with iron filings to cleanse the germs, a morning rite in my own home to keep disease at bay for our three children.

◆ **Madi**, ritual purity amongst communities after taking a bath became an obsession for those most fortunate who did not have to dirty their hands. An underclass of 'hewers of wood, drawers of water' emerged and became institutionalised as the contaminating lower class.

Attitudes—reasonable enough in the beginning—in such testing circumstances, became institutionalised.

Over centuries people were admonished with ever finer degrees of codification to the point of psychosis. Religious purification took up inordinate amounts of the uppercaste householder's time while the rest of society (conveniently for the former) dirtied their hands in menial tasks.

One brahmin lady spoke feelingly of the emotional effect on children of the sense of this 'taking the bath'. Within an orthodox life over-conscientious parents, especially mothers, could become emotionally 'distant', children kept at arm's length after the ritual early morning cleansing. If touched even in affection, so rigid were the rules, that their bodies became polluted again... another bath would have to be undertaken–and not just a quick shower. Prayers and rituals had to accompany to provide the magic cleansing process. How then to cuddle a child if the letter of the law rather than the spirit prevailed from an ultra-orthodox parent. 'The lack of emotional warmth was felt from childhood,' was the poignant reflection 30 years onward.

◆ On the other hand the 3-day isolation of a menstruating woman–banned from kitchen and cooking–was a godsend!

'We could do with more of this ritual today!' observed a hardworking young woman Mumbai executive stretched to the limits as professional executive and domestic homemaker–and with husband's parents living in, part of a loose joint family structure. 'Modern living has wiped out many of these strictures. That is good! However, they have not replaced the irrelevant with a more meaningful code of behaviour. We are all aware of the anomalies of private cleanliness in a sea of public squalor!' she summed up what many modern city dwellers experience.

Many Indian anthropologists as well as Western scholars have written tomes on pollution and caste. Dumont's **Homo Hierarchicus** is a set book in many a social anthropology course. It is still worth reading.

Endnote: After a fifteenth visit to India in 2001.

The ultimate irony (or **PARADOX**) will be the fate of entire city populations, contaminated first, poisoned later and finally asphyxiated by air pollution. It will not matter a twice-born's sacred thread how many ritual baths are taken if local, regional and central governments do not act urgently. **Prana**, breath, that original life-giving force will be the death of India in a leaden haze of toxic chemical components pumped out by 2-stroke engines of the city phut-phuts, lorries, tumble-down buses, illegal and irresponsible industries.

Politicians are the codifiers of today but they seem singularly lacking in the disciplined will of their forefathers. On this Stepping Stone I take my outspoken stand.

■ POPULATION

One Australian population total is dropped into India every year, over and above the billion which already live there...**17 million additional people.**

For all those of us who knew India soon after Independence when only **360 million** peopled the land in the 50s it is a matter for anguish. Those of us who keep returning see the ravages of such a weight upon the soil; the slow creep of an ineluctable tide of humanity up the pristine forested foothills, the terai where magnificently handsome tigers roamed, the detritus in the cities, the sorely-tried municipal services collapsing. Power cuts; sewage breakdowns; aged buses; roads and pavements unable to be mended (how can traffic be re-routed in jampacked cities). Where is clean water to come from? Hydro-electric schemes necessitate the forced removal of 160,000 tribal people. Where is the space to make rational decisions when year by year the relentless statistics climb.

Indian Governments of whatever political persuasion attempt to control such exponential growth within the limits of democratic debate. While achieving remarkable progress in advanced and educated states both in village health, rural education, panchayat rule, engineering projects of which any government can be rightfully proud, as well as in the development of a sophisticated industrial infrastructure as backstop for remarkable national advance, planners find every surge forward quagmired in the population swamp–people, people, people–hand power looking for jobs and a decent livelihood in an age of robotic technology and machines.

A young Australian friend has spoken of the 'sensory and emotional seasickness' when first plunged into India. The impact of a sea of humanity is so profound most Westerners are in danger of losing their stability of balance. Government sources are deeply worried. Projections indicate India will relentlessly overtake China as the world's most crowded land in the coming decades.

Culturally, when dealing with plural societies facing fundamental social changes, there are no simple answers to a complex issue such as birth control. Democracies, let's face it, are inefficient. Time is spent in debate when decisive action is called for: autocratic governments such as China with its 'one child' policy can brandish governmental decrees over the heads (and minds) of its citizens with ease. There is no argument. Finish!

◆ India has the unenviable task of promoting a long-term educational and persuasive policy which has obviously succeeded in economically advanced, predominantly urban societies such as the USA, Canada, Europe and Australia (where there is concern about zero growth). All these countries have had the luxury of coming to terms with Marie Stopes and her controversial promotion of birth control over 80 years ago!

Interestingly enough Hindu, Jain, Buddhist and Sikh communities do not have any hang-ups on the matter. Islamic society, as also Catholic Christian is another matter. But beyond religious attitudes and inhibitions is a major cultural divide, with affinities to traditional class identities still prevalent. There is the enormous gap between a wealthy educated middle class and the 30–40 million really impoverished Indians with little formal education.

◆ Advance in controlling family explosion is inextricably linked with those who live within **certain areas**, badly administered in particular regions of economical disadvantage or corruption where

1. **there are no personal pension schemes**
2. **no health insurance to cushion aged parents, where children may well die young, or are malnourished**
3. **where bonded labour (serfdom) still exists**
   parents see multiple births as an insurance against the future
4. **and sons are necessary! Who else will take on the task physically to plough the small holdings, millions of peasants husband throughout the land?**

Vitally related to the question of population is:

■ **POVERTY**

… and amongst those people are **some 30 million who are desperately poor;** the 2001 census showing 268 million just poor—in fact every fourth person virtually.

Over the years I have, with Indian friends, agonised over these issues as they grew increasingly annoyed and frustrated at a seemingly endless logjam in what needs to be done–and effectively. Particular points came up again and again, poverty and population inextricably intertwined.

1. The circumstances in which India's economy is developing from agricultural dominated to urban industrialisation and upmarket technology is very different from the Western experience.

2. Many European nations undergoing the same processes but as colonial powers in the 19–20th century were able to set the trade/economic agenda for the rest of the world. Commodity prices for textiles, primary produce were bought at minimal cost (in India for instance), sold high as finished product once manufactured. Industrial nations grew rich on the backs of colonial primary producers.

3. Foreign debt was not part of any equation then.

4. India is still paying the price of a colonial legacy both materially as well as psychologically,

Materially, India had been in world terms an enormously wealthy country for long periods before and during Mughal rule and in the pre-British southern kingdoms. That wealth was drained away to make the British economy the dynamo it was in Victorian times.

Psychologically, the introduction of an anglicized school system (those Britishers pushing for such a seemingly innocuous 'reform' in Indian schooling in the 19th century were actually called ANGLICIZERS!) and **Lord Thomas Babbington Macaulay's** famous **Minute on the Subject of Indian Education** in 1835 in which he denigrated much of India's literary heritage, seriously drove another wedge between educated Indian elite and unschooled villages who nevertheless knew their oral culture. **Geoffrey Moorhouse** in **India Britannica** describes Macaulay and his policies as having 'powerfully demonstrated a philistine streak'.

◆ It is interesting that two people who lived just over 150 years ago still send signals out to a younger generation of Indians–Macaulay despite his other reputation for humane legal reforms was appointed to the Supreme Council of India in 1834 by the other person, the Governor-General in Calcutta, Lord William Bentinck who is regarded as having implemented these policies especially in higher education which may have provided fine Indian administrators to serve Empire needs but which created an elite adrift from the village roots of culture and needs. This had never happened before but it very much mirrored English society of that era–a highly cultivated patrician society, and a feudal, ill-educated 'lumpen' poor.

◆ Unintentionally such a length of education has given India a leading edge now in the new IT technologies globally where English is now international. In this regard China is at a disadvantage. But this does not allay the fact that many Indian educated now are as aloof from village life as their British counterparts of a century ago. This explained why Nehru especially and many of his colleagues opted for economic policies for the base of India's pyramidical structure that did not speak to or consult properly those at the bottom of the pile as Gandhi and Vinoba Bhave had done.

Gandhi may well be proved right. Indeed, on my last visit suddenly discussion of the Mahatma's ideas was after 50 years of deriding them as not appropriate, beginning to make a comeback, some writers even courageous enough to challenge current orthodoxy among entrenched academia and finance department bureaucrats.

◆ In India's conditions progress and economic liberalism may have to reverse all the norms and trends and undertake massive job creation at rural level in small-scale industries running totally counter to every economic rationalist theorising in the luxury of their sleek Western offices. **Schumacher** decades back preached this in **'Small is Beautiful'** with a call for appropriate technology where the **handpower** lies in the villages. **Few economists advising Western governments in their aid programs listened.** Yet this is where 75 per cent of the population exists. Gandhi knew it. Pandit Nehru did. Shastri in his tragically abbreviated life as prime minister in the mid-60s did. Shastri was shaping up to be a remarkably effective PM but with a public none too sure then of his stature, stepping out as he did from under Nehru's shadow—a situation not dissimiliar from Attlee's after Churchill and Truman's after Roosevelt. All were small men physically, somewhat colourless or low-key compared with their charismatic predecessors and with little international glamour—to be proved otherwise to a fickle public. Since then most politicians have been more interested in playing cynical power games and, in Indian eyes, lining their own pockets.

So many opportunities lost in the interim period, in the national estate most inter-related with the culture of poverty—education. For the upper echelons in the world of universities and private schools life is full of opportunities despite occasional angst about standards and pressure of population to attain that ladder of success. It is at the lowly level of the village that a miserable legacy of neglect and apathy still affects the body politik and the national psychological health.

◆ Educational curriculums seem totally irrelevant to children of peasant farmers, small business families, artisans and hard-pressed mothers who need physical help daily from their children in fetching water, gathering firewood, shepherding their precious livestock, slapping cowpats into shape for fuel for the evening fire and family meal.

◆ Where is the vocational training which Gandhi had pressed for in his concept of Basic Education? This would have been a pragmatic discipline of training for the real world. The debate about this was alive and well in early Independence days. I even wrote a major article for the **Illustrated Weekly of India** (July 14, 1954) devoted to what had excited me at **Jamia Millia Islamia**, the national Muslim university (its student intake over 50 per cent non-Muslim)—that of a basic education inspired by its diminutive, Gandhian V C Professor M Mujeeb. An education devoid of the rigidity and conventions derived from British curricula had been a very refreshing experience. To spend a day with children immersed in creative art, and their own bank to learn basic mathematical skills, to be lively entrepreneurs was a stimulating novelty. Even such a model was only just emerging back in new thinking about teaching basic skills in Britain.

◆ In India the situation is however more complex. There is the Oxbridge level, thousands of graduates going on to all kinds of levels of excellence. There is interestingly enough a huge pool also of technocrats, engineers (hundreds of them women, far more in proportion to population than, ironically, in Britain) electronically trained personnel, leaders in software and computer knowhow. Institutes of Technology have won accolades from overseas for the level of excellence of their graduates.

◆ But where is basic education, vocational training, the 'dirtying of hands' symbolised by the basic artisan, mechanic, the plumber who fixes things and is worth his weight in gold? He too was bottom of the pile in the Macaulay educational system of the late 1800s even in his own country. That too favoured the patrician hierarchy of the British class system of Curzon's time.

A book worth finding, **The Beautiful Tree** (The other India Press, Delhi, 1996) written by a revered senior writer, **Dharampal**, addresses this issue—the subtle damage done to the mindset of those in power behind transient governments since Macaulay's British administration created the template in Calcutta nearly 150 years ago. It seems both things need to happen alongside each other… economic liberalization and widely-planned village employment based on a radically rejuvenated educational system.

◆ **China** is quoted as an example of a contrasting Asian society where (due to authoritarian government) an alarming population growth has been to some extent controlled; collective farming has mitigated fragmentation which has ruined many Indian families and sent sons into nearby towns to find other means of livelihood. **At least nearly every child has been given primary schooling** and **basic health programs** although many inner areas of China not visited by tourists have as many stinking drains, lack of flush toilets, and all the other social ills of poverty as India.

◆ **The socialist doctrines** of early Congress governments did not solve the problem.

◆ **Improvements in modern medicine** ironically compounded the problem by increasing the population longevity rates.

What is India to do? Child labour is supposed to be illegal. Yet desperate families put able-bodied children to work as did children in the coalmines of Britain in the 19th century before the Factory Acts. It is not only abject poverty that stirs deep emotions for any visitor from overseas; it is also the sheer scale of under-employment, migrant labour and mobility to and fro between arid areas of Rajasthan for instance creating dismal slum conditions in cities. The diamond market alone is said to employ over

P

90,000 such itinerant workers in Surat. There is little unionised labour, few safety conditions, little national insurance. It is the same in the piecework textile trade around Mumbai and Chennai.

Keeping a Sense of Balance

What Indians do object to is the disproportionate balance given to such portrayals, as though Indian governments had failed nearly everywhere in improving conditions for its billion people. This particular reaction came from a journalist, **Swaraj Paul**, writing as far back as the 60s in the UK edition of the **India Weekly**. It could be reiterated even more strongly today:

Notwithstanding the misleading impression created by sensational headlines in the world press that India is a land of famines and floods, snakes and snake-charmers, teeming emaciated millions of people living in nothing more than hovels and probably just out of their jungle existence, the reality is that during the last 23 years–years of independence and accelerated economic growth–substantial progress has been registered because of planned economic development, hard work of the people, proliferation of education at all levels and constant efforts to build a self-reliant and self-generating economy.

As Paul rightly asserts, India has made enormous advances. During the anniversary for 50 years of Independence in 1997, editorials in a sober frame of mind weighed up the failures as well as the achievements. In a telling editorial one headline read: **'We can't blame Britain any more.'**

The import of the article was that in certain areas India had failed. A man of great integrity and a friend of long standing writes: 'You had plenty of opportunity to see India at rest and at work with all its futile posturings and serendipitous redemptions–the same muddling through: the same populist slogans and the same evasions. In some quarters there is plenty and also the gall to display plenty...'

Amazingly, there are still honourable, well-meaning citizens imbued by dharma, Gandhian ideas, radical politics and a social conscience or spurred by missionary endeavours, etc. who still try to do their best to mitigate poverty. On this Stepping Stone I still stand–ANGRY

See Professor Amartya Sen's 'Voice of Conscience' writings which have earned him a Nobel Prize in Economics.

■ **PRAÑA** n. *Sanskrit*

is a very potent force in Indian thinking encompassing a gamut of concepts in a pendulum swing from the cosmic **vayu** = wind (energy) of space physics to basic human physiology = breath = vital energy.

This is one term in the IGCNA lexicon(see p. 7). Presented by scholar Pandit H N Charavarty it takes up 18 pages! That would cause a landslide from this Stepping Stone!

1. **Cosmic Level** = coming-into-being from *bija* = seed sown from desire/fervour/tapas leading to a directional flow from 'that first beginning' = *vayu* or cosmic wind.

2. **Metaphysical** = the progress from speculative Vedic hymns (Atharva Veda 11:4) addressed to praña to the harnessing of this concept eventually to the idea that sound from breath evolved into language amongst humans. This then formed the basic Vedic concentration on accurate sound–leading to the next step... **mantras, incantations, chants took on a magic potency.**

3. **Physiological/Human** = the unconscious process of breathing without which there could be no life.

4. **Yoga** = the theory as part of an eightfold path of mental /bodily discipline which developed over a long period of philosophical and scientific study. This concluded that control of breath = vital air, was paramount in healthy maintenance of other bodily mechanisms and functions = energy force (see **YOGA**).

5. **Impact on the arts,** especially music = leading to the theory that

   a) the vocalist was the supreme conduit of musical expression because of artistic implementation of prana.

   b) the expertise of a sculptor/artist in giving 'breath'–an inner 'lightness' to the static form–was the ultimate in artistic expression. This is referred to as the 'subtle body' of a **MURTI** or painting.

1. **Cosmic:** speculation in the fourth Atharva Veda on prana could be likened to that of modern physicists wrestling with how creation began. 'In the Beginning was the Word...' is the first statement of the Biblical Gospel according to St John. Without breath there can be no word… and, indeed, no consciousness to be aware of reality that envelopes us.

'And the word is with God...' Hindu theories speak similarly.

Holy Utterance developed into an explosion metaphysically constructed around the neuter gender of the Sanskrit word: BRHM **or Brahman** = to grow, develop. Over a thousand years onwards as the concept of the **PANTHEON** of **materializations = deities** emerged, Brahman then stepped down into the material world of our planet and took on the masculine word form: **Brahma** = creative principle.

2. **Metaphysical:** One of the very first hymns of the Atharva Veda is addressed to Breath: Prana.

Verse 1: *Homage to breath, in whose power is this All, who is the Lord of all, on whom all is based.*

Verse 26: *O breath, turn not away from me; you shall be no other than myself. I bind you to myself, breath, like the child of the waters that I may live.* (Edgerton translation)

Breath and pulse are virtually indistinguishable in the biological processes of the body. From the very first sowing of the **Universal Seed = the Cosmic Egg (see ZERO)** a pulse begins, life breath permeates the energy breath which pulsates throughout universe upon universe: 'It is prana that makes the semen throb with life'.

What literally **takes one's own breath away** is the startling capacity of the Indian mind to be at one moment way out in the cosmos embracing incomprehensible dimensions as well as

P

abstruse philosophy, and the next, telescoping the mind in that love of fine details (Indians must be originators of **The List**). Prana is seen not only as 'universal pulsation' but in a **functional** role also 'leading the air contained in the lungs outside to the extent of **twelve digits from the centre of the body**.' There's a fine point!

According to those who spend time on ritual and meditation on such yantras (diagrams), electric energy 'charges' the devotee running like a current from the image, enhancing consciousness. Neurological surgeons are now talking of multi-consciousness as brain surgery advances. Like physicists they begin to realize how little is understood in what happens in the brain!

Pandit Chakravarty explains these abstract concepts in clearer visual terms below:

The vital life-force is the external manifestation of Shakti which again is the feminine energy linked with Siva. The following diagram which is the central part of many ritual yantras will help to understand the idea:

- The centre is the *vimarsa sakti* (reflective energy of consciousness)
- The first circle is *samvit* (pure consciousness)
- The second is *prana*
- The square is the external world.

3. **Bodily Function:** Praña is concentrated in **nadi, triple layered channels, insulated states like electric wire, through which nervous energy flows through the seven chakras along the spinal column.** These are in a sense marshalling yards of all the energy lines running through the human frame which create the metabolism—such as DNA, oxygen, molecules, blood, lymph glands, protein, amino fluids. Harnessed, they are then dispersed. But without breath, oxygen cannot filter through the alveoli into the blood stream. Death follows. We know this to be true in our very speech. When agitated, people advise you 'to take a deep breath'.

4. **Yoga:** in its methodical harnessing—yoking—of bodily functions and energies to gain ultimate balance—follows an eightfold system (see **YOGA**). Prominent amongst these is praña = breath-control. The opposite effect is 'butterflies in the stomach' before an exam for instance. Emotional nervousness affects the rate of breathing, chanting evens out the rate of pulse and calms you down. Ability through deep breathing to sustain and master a rhythmic flow changes energies in the mind enabling a concentrated focusing of the usually random uncontrolled situation inside one's head; this has now been scientifically proved under laboratory situations.

In addition lowered pulse rate, blood pressure and other attendant improvements in body state and well being have been measured and acknowledged scientifically.

Yoga practitioners have always complained that none of us breathe properly, taking in the full quota of oxygen to the fullest stretch of the diaphragm. Deep breathing has to start in its depths, 'pulled up' consciously by active thought processes while centring the mind between the two eyes... then expelling the air down to the very depths of one's being. Learning to take in breath through one nostril and expelling it through the other is part of the discipline. After regular practice a 'lightness', a kind of mesmerized but creative calm, is achieved, that ever-sought-after state of equipoise.

5. **Artistic Expression:**

a) The ultimate in musical form is that of the vocalist, higher even than the greatest of instrumentalists India can and does produce.

The control of sound by voice was regarded by the earliest Vedic ritual priests as containing a real magic of its own. The breathing of prayer became spiritualised as Edgerton has pointed out in his **Introduction to the Beginnings of Indian Philosophy: 'to know the name of anything was to control the thing. The word means wisdom, knowledge; and knowledge, as we have seen, was (magic) power. So brahman, the 'holy word' soon came to mean that mystic power inherent in the holy word**.' Proper chanting, purity of sound became immensely important as did the knowledgeable brahmin in supervising such activity.

b) **'There are no bones in an Indian god.'** Chintamoni Kar, well-known sculptor, once explained to us in the middle of a temple complex. All around in the golden light, **apsaras** and **gandharvas** as creatures of the firmament floated in arabesques, while below, tree nymphs curved in their shoulder-waist-hip triple thrust–the **tribhanga** stance, framing the major deities in the niches.

The pulse of life, an inner breath gave rise in the beauty of their carved forms to that gentle lift of the stomach over the bejewelled lower garment, as though their graceful bodies with the heavy yoke-like shoulders were breathing. Insubstantial air in the heat of the day, but lifting up substantial weight of hefty stone carved sublimely to inward calm, faces transfixed, withdrawn into an inner awareness. These are not anatomical Greek **bodies with a skeletal structure. These are forms making breath concrete.**

Stella Kramrisch, has explained in **The Art of India** that visual art is movement translated into measured lines and masses '... figures are modelled by breath which dilates the chest and is felt to carry the pulse of life through the body to the tips of the fingers...' She explains further:

It was found that by the concentrated practice of controlled breathing, an inner lightness and warmth absorbed the heaviness of the physical body and dissolved it in the weightless 'subtle body', which was given concrete shape by art, in planes and lines of balanced stresses and continuous movement.

It is interesting to discover that when King Solomon prayed for wisdom to rule the Hebrews circa 10th c BCE he was doing so at the same time India's **rsis** were arriving at certain cardinal principles also about the conduct and scientific principles of life. Wisdom in Hebrew literature is depicted as a feminine personification. She is **'the breath of the power of God'** similar to **VAC** = word, speech and **BUDDHI** = highest faculty of intelligence = wise understanding.

P

■ PREMONITION

Although not particular to Indian experience and even authenticated during Western history, it is more openly admitted amongst individuals as a legitimate part of the normality of human extension into 'the mind beyond' as an Indian friend once referred to her own premonitions, not just once but several times when we knew each other. She had been aware her mother had died in the far south **at the exact moment**, later confirmed by phone in Delhi.

One can accept that Indians may be more open, less sceptical perhaps and therefore more prone to this **other dimension** because much preoccupation with harnessing and developing the power of mind exists in Indian structures and channels of energy. **Daily disciplines and psychic effort in austerities, fasts, sadhanas, as well as the specific disciplines of the YOGA sutras** have so focused attention on the usages and influences of the mind over matter than these possibilities of intuition and premonition are a logical outcome.

After all, century upon century of experimental study and sustained physical concentration have placed Indian yogic practitioners on the scientific cutting edge, only now under a more dispassionate examination by Western experts. As a result some of what appeared to be far-fetched claims in Indian conditions are no longer in doubt. Dealing with the influences of **mind over matter** was never a casual laidback occult practice as Europeans first in India seemed to believe. A very harsh discipline and scientific rigour was applied through yogic training and austere daily routines. Opening the door into that **other mind**—acknowledged elsewhere in the dance sequences by Dutch dancer Beryl de Zoete, who wrote under this title about her Indian experiences.

♦ In a quite remarkable way premonition is quite startlingly documented by commentators actually present at the time when 'happenings' occurred involving the famous musicians of the Carnatic Trinity. All experienced dreams, visions in their saintly, philosophic, musical lives. These were related to their shishyas, the pupils of the musical ashramas of the time and have become part of the folklore of Tamil culture.

Premonition for Real!... not just hearsay... but mysterious sounds are heard.

The most vivid description of such premonition is that related about that most pre-eminent composer of the singing heart and mind entwined in gorgeous devotional poetry and soaring ragas—**TYAGARAJA**. In an account written by well-respected musicologist Professor P Sambamoorthy he relates how in 1846 this towering eminence had a dream so well-documented that every Tamil lover of music could recount it about this master of his own **siddhi**—the most appropriate translation being the equivalent of '**giving up the ghost**'. (**Thyagaraja**, National Biography Series, National Book Trust, Delhi, 1970.)

Tyagaraja addressing the congregation at the bhajan session of singing communal hymns rather than private meditations, actually concluded:

On the coming **Pusya Bahula Panchami** *day a miracle will take place. Please all of you, come on that day.*

On the **chaturthi** day, the fourth day of the bright half of the month and the day prior to his demise, Sambamoorthy writes, 'he requested Paramahamsa Brahmanandendra Swami to initiate him into Sanyasa asrama. At first the holy sage refused saying that Tyagaraja was already a **Jivanmukta** (liberated soul) and there was no need to be initiated...' With further pleas the Swami relented.

After this, Tyagaraja said to those assembled, 'Tomorrow at 11 am Sri Rama has promised to take me back; please perform bhajana continuously from now on.'

According to Telugu-speaking tradition these are his words:

Giripai Nelakonna Ramuni Guri Dappaka Kanti
Parivarul Viri Surabhulache Nilabadi
Visaruchu Kosaruchu Charimpaga... in English translation:
Unerringly *I have seen Sri Rama who is installed on the hill with his attendants vying with each other in fanning him with flower fans....*

Tyagaraja concluded with this benediction:

He has promised to grant me salvation in five days. My body was thrilled, and tears of joy rolled down my cheeks for I could only mumble, not being able to give expression to my thoughts.

News spread like wildfire. Named disciples are given as being present in the large crowd that gathered. It was written that Tyagaraja in deep meditation withdrew into himself composing his famous songs, sung to this day: **Paramatmudu** in **raga Vāgadhiswara** and **Paritapamu** in **Manohari raga**.

As he sat in the samadhi posture 'the congregation heard a mysterious sound emanating from the Saint's head. Soon they saw a bright flash of light leaving his skull and vanishing slowly high up after proceeding in a northerly direction. The mortal remains were then taken to the Kaveri bank with all honours and to the accompaniment of music and interred in a place adjoining the samadhi of his Guru...

Homage to Tyagaraja

And it is here where Tyagaraja **knowingly** 'shuffled off his mortal coil' that first a shrine, a **brindavanam** brick construction that housed the sacred tulsi plant for worship was built and then a large temple in recent times; the annual and magnetic music festival at Tiruvaiyarur now takes place in January at this very location where a flight of steps leads down to the majestic Kaveri river.

PAY HOMAGE WITH JOY!

And indeed as the millennium turned in 2000 CE I did just this with my Tamil musician friend, Jeya, swaying with thousands of his devotees on the sandy bank where his spirit had found its fore-ordained release.

■ PUJA

1. Often spelled **pooja**, the autumnal festival season, especially evocative for Bengalis. Durga, the conqueror of all malignant forces, is honoured.

P

Each suburb spends artistic effort and dedication as well as money on creating representations of the powerful goddess, to be taken at the end of the devotional tamasha and prayers for final immersion in the Ganga. This is a time for family reunion, cleansing houses, much rejoicing and too many fattening sweets given as prasad!

If the newcomer has the stomach to overcome drain smells, stagnant puddles, dank litter and dingy narrow lanes in northern Kolkata near the Hooghly there is to be found a suburb at Kumartuli inhabited by unclothed clay models of the multi-armed powerhouse which is Durga—as well as Lakshmi, Ganesh, Saraswati. This is the home of the guild potter—craftspeople the **Kum(bh)ars**, their materials, the special fine clay and straw for padding. This is transported by barge as in the past hundred years, right to their doorsteps.

2. The **ritual** of worship at which special vessels and ingredients are used both in temple or home to honour and welcome the Deity. Five ingredients specifically are needed:

deepa a lamp or flame

dhupa incense or agarbatti

naivedya food offerings such as fruit, nuts, crystal
sugar

gandha perfumed substances such as rose water or
sandalwood

pushpa flowers gathered fresh each morning

Pradakshina is a phrase used if an Indian friend invites you into a shrine or to visit a temple which you may circumambulate clockwise before making **pranam–an honouring gesture.**

◆ Puja is more than just simple, personal worship, just sitting down in meditative position praying in general and individual fashion, **even if addressing a personal MURTI or abstract 'force' with true veneration by chanting MANTRAS.** Certain utensils, ladling spoon, lamps, bells, metal tray, conch and ingredients such as vermilion kumkum, coconuts, sandalwood paste have to be used in a prescribed order. Puja is the framework ligaments and gristle of the Hindu body giving cohesion to the fundamentally anarchic qualities of this individual belief system—lacking church, creed or hierarchy of priesthood to bind all these disparate elements together. It is a patterning of action, a structured process, known almost by heart like the intoning of the Lord's Prayer in Christian churches, understood all over the land no matter the differing cultural backgrounds, giving, as the **padayatra** and **tirth** do, a very potent sense of identity to those performing the sacred rituals at births, marriages, deaths, special festivals.

◆ It is worth acquiring **Vimla Patil's Celebrations: Festive Days of India** (India Book House, 1994), delightfully informative and colourfully laid out.

■ **PURUSHA**
n. *Sanskrit* masc. cosmic man as an entity and
PRAKRITI
n. *Sanskrit* fem. material nature
The two concepts which original Vedic thinkers arrived at as

the building blocks of all else in the framework of the universe, its creative expansion, humankind within it, the development of unique consciousness and assessment, seem inextricable. The one cannot be envisaged without the other.

The early texts state that **Purusha** gives birth to the **creative impulse** before the universe comes into being in the **fervour of desire**, but it immediately 'receives back life' as though at the point of that first conception–the Big Bang or the Steady State–all things happened at once, male/female barely distinguishable.

In later Vedic development Purusha became more associated with **rupa** = form, i.e. primordial man, an archetypal figure as a balancing force to **Prakriti** = nature, in all her material forms. Purusha is then a **singularity**, balancing **multiplicity**. Gradually the meaning embraced the 'inner man', a matter of spiritual essence in personality, as well as the archetypal human, purusha, from the division of his body coming forth the four classes.

The Rig Vedic hymn to the Cosmic Man, 10:90 describes this coming-into-being from Edgerton's translation.
From him the Shining One (the cosmic waters)
was born
From the Shining One (was born likewise) the
Purusha.
Being born (from the Shining One) he extended
beyond the world
Behind and also before...

◆ Prakriti is the force that binds the Cosmic Being into the **maya**—what is taken as **phenomenal reality**. It is the realm of matter which is experienced as a **three-dimensional energy field**.

◆ Prakriti is also the **material** from which **BRHM** (the base of all existence) appears in form as God = **Brahma**; and the qualities which are imprinted into this life-force = **GUNAS** = **sattva, rajas** and **tamas**, creatures of the empirical, knowable, measurable universe.

Postscript

Wayside shrines, vermilion daubed stones given life with two hypnotic eyes and tinsel paper covering, or a sacred tree spirit remembered—all these are more than a manifestation of pantheism, nature veneration as Western philosophy would categorise it. Rather they are collective symbols of veneration of the **totality** of the **Ground of Being**—all parts of the whole, the individual human acknowledging the creative processes which existed in cosmos and upon planets aeons before hominid evolved and was then able to evaluate his/her place in the **living essence of nature.**

■ **PUTLIWALLAHS** (*n. Hindi*)

These manipulators of wooden puppets (kat putli), putliwallahs as we firangis call them, are a familiar sight in Rajasthan and big cities such as Delhi to which they migrate in the lean times to eke out a living in what are traditional guild families. They have carried the oral tradition for centuries of tales built around the great folk heroes, certainly of the **Rajputs** whose mythical claims to be descended from the sun and moon and

P

sacred fire, members of the original warrior class of kshatriyas (and therefore twice-born) gives them especial nobility. The genes of later Hun invaders are also in their blood.

The coming of electricity to what were remote villages only a decade ago–and therefore the possibility not only of movies, but the quite lethal sudden impact of videos and TV has had a serious impact on these folk artists who in less fraught times, and when populations were not exploding in numbers, were the great communicators. They not only performed the old tales but carried news. Some sociologists refer to them as **integrators** in the social life of communities which were isolated before modern communication. Storytelling throughout the ages in all pre-industrial cultures was a transmission line between elite classes and that at ground level out in the fields. There was flexibility and updating as they moved across villages into towns and back again and up and down the social scale.

♦   Now they have a different role perhaps as **absorbers**–losing one form of communication to another as the government and state tourism send them as colourful tools overseas in promoting 'exotic' India. The Indian Council of Cultural Relations (ICCR) has in recent Festivals of India winged such bands of puppeteers to the UK, Russia, the USA, Australia. Their quite alarming experiences in some cases may well filter back into their ballads and new adventures for a future generation of **angrezi** tourists to come and see, transformed, stories of being lost on the roaring tube trains of London's Underground, cast adrift with no 'minder' to look after them, no English, vegetarian in Australia, trying to cope in the clatter of American cities with resident Indians of totally different class, education, even caste supposed to take care of them as strange almost as Europeans or Americans.

In the past their basic wooden framed theatre and colourful cloth decorations were the **locus operandi** for our children's parties on the lawns of bungalow compounds. Presentations were usually fairly static, the family members all harnessed to recounting in high-pitched voices the sagas of heroic battles of **Prithvi Raj Chauhan**, ruler of Delhi, fighting against the second wave of Muslim invaders under **Muhammad Ghuri who in fact defeated this hero in 1192** on the battlefield. There was terrible carnage. Previously Prithvi Raj had laid the foundations of the famous Qutb Minar, the tower south of Delhi. He had earlier abducted the daughter of another raja Jaichand–and from the wedding hall! Quite a character…

The clash and clatter of battles are also played out on cloth horses in which **Raja Jai Singh** in the mid-17th century subdued the Mahratta warrior and nationalist leader **Shivaji**, and brought him to Emperor Aurangzeb's court.

The wife lost under her dupatta often played the drum, the fierce-looking husband with flourishing moustache manipulating old fashioned and awkward wooden stringed figures, engaged in hand-to-hand conflict, much of the ballad is incomprehensible in its dialect. However, snakes slither onto the stage and threaten people, a crocodile emerges in an unlikely drama–presumably out of the **Narmada** river in the Shivaji campaigns, to strike terror in the villages. Women swoon, rajas in traditional skirts flounce in

to claim their ever-shifting territories in the quarrelsome clans of Rajput rulers jockeying for ascendancy.

♦   Meanwhile **bhopas** or minstrel balladeers from the Marwar area, closer to the Norse or Irish storyteller traditions (also fast dying out with the impact of instant media) present night-long epics. These ballads are based on the episodes in the life of a **14th century Rajput chief called Pabuji** depicted in a very solid, broad of beam chieftan in his petticoated skirt..

♦   On an appointed day balladeers and painters come together, a ritual offering of a coconut is made to Saraswati, and the first chart is made of the narrative to be painted in vegetable dyes. This double artistic activity is said to be at least 700 years old, the children of the bhopas learning the ballads as early as seven years old.

♦   In Orissa very detailed narratives are painted on compressed palm leaves. These are the **patta-chitras** (*patta* = flat surface, *chitra* = picture). Two personally-owned pattas painted by a quirky and probably mad artist in Kolkatta have all the hallmarks of a mediaeval manuscript. Lively scenes in sumptuous colours depict all manner of activity within the gigantic temple at Puri. Idiosyncratic touches of naughty humour, tiny personal interventions in comic strip narrative sequence give humanity to sacred themes just as monks in European monasteries did, embellishing golden capital letters commencing a sacred manuscript with Monty Python frivolity, the personal imprint of many an anonymous monk.

♦   South Indians, especially in Andhra Pradesh, have their own tradition of human-size articulated leather puppets manipulated from behind filmy screens—thought to be the most likely precursors of the **Wayang Kulit** traditional shadow puppets of modern Indonesia. Taken by the Telugu and Tamil speaking navigators of the 2nd and 3rd century CE, they straddle both traditions–Hindu and Muslim in SE Asia–with abridged versions of the two great **EPICS**.

♦   Many of these **entertainers**, including **women acrobats, snake-charmers**, amazing magicians who defy all scepticism are recruited to add a genuine village atmosphere to the 'art of the tamasha' which has come to town reproducing for the urban sophisticate the atmosphere of their childhood where nearly everyone still had one foot in their ancestral village, now only trodden in the artificial atmosphere of **Dilli Haat**. This is a popular commercial marketplace (**haat**) near Safdarjung's Tomb, south Delhi—but also more authentically to be stumbled across anywhere in country areas where cattle fairs are being held and people come from far and wide with their wares to sell. The annual February **Surajkand Fair** (noted under **CRAFT**) provides these people an outlet to show their artforms.

They survive with a moving dignity of age-old purpose in the **jatra** or street theatre tradition, trying to keep clean in the most assaulting of climates with all the odds against them especially when they settle in their hundreds in the Dickensian slum of **Shadipur**, now called Kathputli Colony. Fitful income, no social security payments, dangerous feats in some cases to perform–a pyramid of acrobats hardly one centimetre out of formation from that depicted in a second century BCE carving in stone on a railing pillar from **Barhut** (now in Allahabad Museum). That is the fascination of India, centuries juxtaposed, a continuum of culture dislocated not at all by the disruptions of history, conquerors coming and going from all points of the compass. The bhopas sit in the shadows invoking blessing from that 'other' world.

When I come on the stage–Shakti sits on my face. She of the veena, Saraswati sits on my tongue....

But now does electronic circuitry on the TV screen unravel it all in the flick of a switch? Or augment this *oral* tradition? There may be signs that such artists are appearing in TV magazine programs.

■ **PYJAMA**

The world must thank Indians for devising such a simple cotton trouser on a drawstring to beat oppressive heat. The early British, still open to persuasion from India's indigenous population, understandably took to the wearing of such loose fitting pants after the leg-clinging leather breeches and brocade coats of the 17th–18th century male. Such fashion was enough to drive one mad with prickly heat.

Mughal fashion with pyjamas is with poetic justice now seeping into the fashion houses of Parisian Armani and Italy's Versace. Even dhotis are seen on the catwalks. Gandhi's spirit must chuckle at couture coming full circle.

Banish the sticky jeans in monsoon weather and return to the civilised world of the **aligarhi** narrow pyjama or the khulla full straight leg that, made in fine Indian cotton, lets the air circulate... with kurta tunic and sleeveless, embroidered jacket it is one of the latest styles, probably 1,000 years old–and still 'cool chic', maybe it should be a 'cool chick!'

P

QUATERNITIES

The sacredness of the cow is a self-evident truth in the Indian context. It is not just a bovine animal, bringing vital dairy products as sustenance for humans and making possible agriculture through manure and ploughing. Reflective Indians (and there are many) who have a leaning towards waxing philosophical, if you are willing to listen sympathetically, sometimes refer to a **quadruped**, standing solid on all fours firmly based; this is the sacred **cow of dharma**; four square = □ a quaternity.

This kind of talk is a metaphor—equally so in the language of English culture, 'on all fours' an example. (A well-known grocery store, basing its reputation in Western Australia on trading at the cheapest possible prices, chose a logo under the title **Four Square** as a mark of its good foundations and integrity—certainly not appreciated with a cigarette brand of the same name in India!)

It is a metaphor for whatever is rooted in stability, the foundations solid and sure, planted in the earth. Indeed the **YANTRA** or magic diagram designated to symbolise earth, as the first constituent of the **five elements** recognised by science, is a **square**.

The quaternities begin in outer space:

1 **Yugas:** at cosmic level.
2 **Vedas:** coming down from Indra's heaven, sourced in the intuitive thought and poetic vision of the meditating rsis—human, transferred from this level in the course of millennia after millennia.
3 **Morality and Ethical Behaviour:** concepts of the Hindu view and way of life gradually formulated as a result of visionary reflection into basic **CORE CONCEPTS**.
4 **Ashramas:** or stages of an individual life through which life should progress.
5 **Varna or Class:** The separation out of this orderly progress in yet another categorisation according to an **ordered vocation** (later related perhaps to previous birth and 'attainment to perfection' in that life's fulfilment, or not).

Everyday life in India reflects how deeply embedded this visual imagery still remains at the heart of the culture, most significantly so, as envisaged by some anonymous sculptor in the 4th century BCE atop an Ashokan column, four **different symbolic quadrupeds** circling clockwise the lions of power (see **ASHOKA**).

Interestingly enough in the religious iconography used even today—in comic books for children, dance ballets, bazaar posters for festivals the Immense Being who sits cross-legged at the apex of the Trinity triangle, Brahma, Lord of Creation, **is depicted with the four heads**, embracing all four corners of the world, the cardinal directions, known to Western imagery.

♦   Four seems to hold this special quality as does also its square root, sixteen, the auspicious petalled lotus mandala of the **Sri Chakra the most powerful in energy of interlocking triangles**, has the outer rim of 16 petals, the inner rim of eight, powerfully auspicious numerals because of their squared possibilities (see **YANTRA**).

The crucial throw of the Indian dice game, is the **major throw of four** depicted in the Mahabharata. Ironically, yet dependent on free will, a person's individual capacity to choose his or her vocation in life is possible but rare—like the prevaricating Hamlet of Indian literature, **Yudhishthira**, the **King of Dharma**, the ultimate personification of the ruler in righteousness, the Hindu concept of the **chakravartin**, a kshatriya warrior by birth but so refined and spiritually 'graced' a personality, he aspires to be and can eventually become a brahmin. And so, just because this Pandava's leader's one fault is a weakness for gambling, he loses his kingdom, his wife, his wealth and possessions in a fatal game of dice; **Duryodhana**, symbol of greed and lust for power invites him to that game of games but pitting him against the unscrupulous cheating Sakuni. And so the gigantic cosmic cycles are likened to the spot-on, well-balanced four-footed krita when all is well with creation, the world, humanity, the Golden Age. . . and then in descending order of worth, the other three. . .

1. YUGAS:	KRITA	TRETA	DVAPARA	KALI
	♦ root: kr-well made	♦ root = tri/three	♦ root = duo two	♦ root = related to kal-aha = strife/ quarrelsomeness
	♦ well done	♦ dharma is bereft of one 'leg'	♦ dharma becoming less stable	♦ the worst dice throw
	♦ the fulsome Golden Age			♦ this age is Kaliyuga (the Dark Age)

Everything is slowly disintegrating and going downhill, not only at planetary level but as entropy in the galaxies, an incremental loss of energy over billions of years (see **YUGAS**). On earth, Bhumi, the square: □ ELEMENTS: Fire=tej Water=jal, Wind= vayu, Ether=ahankar, illustrated as △= fire,   ☾= water,   ✡= wind, ○= ether, space

Q

2. VEDAS	RIG	YAJUR	SAMA	ATHARVA
	• hymns of praise,	• similar hymns but arranged as formulae for ritual sacrifice ceremonies	• chants	• a strange mixture of philosophic hymns— very scientific on Time for instance
	• lyrical poems inspired by insight and philosophical speculation mostly on forces in Nature	• priestly liturgy and puja rituals	• musical texts	• magical incantations for protection charms
3a. ETHICS and MAJOR CORE CONCEPTS	DHARMA responsibility in righteous behaviour	ARTHA • full enjoyment of social life • material wealth to be enjoyed • KAMA and sexual fulfilment	MAYA ignorance in mistaking reality for the ultimate 'reality' • the 'cloud of unknowing	MOKSHA release, liberation from the cyclical round of many lives
3b.	RTA • universal order constant in cosmos • moral laws that are innate and eternal	KARMA • the law of action by which there is a sequential result in moral terms	ATMAN • essence of each individual entity or soul • in human terms the sense of one's inner self	AHIMSA • law of non-violence to all living beings • attachment to truths

hierarchies dividing humanity into general functions

4. ASHRAMAS	BRAHMACHARYA for the first 25 years, a celibate life spent in study	GRIHASTHA a householder enjoying the material pleasures of life	VANAPRASTHA commencement of idea of retiring 50–75 years	SANNYAAS withdrawal from all family ties to contemplate upon the real reality
5. VARNA	BRAHMIN the learned, spiritual leader	KSHATRIYA warrior, ruler, protector	VAISYA trading, commerce, business people	SUDRA manual labourers, those who work in the fields. 'Untouchables' emerged in later society.

Q

• These **philosophical building blocks of Indian thought and society** comprise a basically straightforward and simple analysis over a period of formulation and wise 'chewing of the mental cud', a two-three thousand year development. Final codification into the written texts of **Vedic hymns**, philosophical speculation in the **Upanishads** and in the categories of the law books, the **Shastras** took place approximately between 200 BCE and 200 CE. These are the authoritative texts upon which the **Smritis**, remembered traditional epics, Puranic legends, later commentaries by swamis, acharyas, gurus, are based. Smritis adapt themselves to the changing conditions of society without losing their fundamental integrity and essence. Just as Western law based on precedence reinterprets and responds to social concerns, behaviour and belief, the Indian oral tradition of 'handing down' a four-square set of codes can be very effective in bypassing caste restrictions and priestly codifications.

QUIT INDIA

August 8, 1942 is, according to politically-minded friends reviewing this list of signposts along the padayatra path, a **defining moment** in the struggle to become free of overlordship, of being told by alien incomers what to do. It shaped political culture like a lightning bolt (turn back to **GANDHI**).

In the ambivalence of remaining loyal to the war effort against a greater evil, Nazi tyranny, Gandhiji addressed the AICC in Bombay with a stirring call for the British overlords to **Quit India** and to his compatriots to make one last effort to get them out: **karenge ya marenge: do or die**.

To his dedicated political followers it was a renewed determination to achieve freedom from British rule come what may, a final push after long, long years of demonstrating patiently. Gandhi had also spoken words to this effect:

I want the English to remain in India but as friends–not rulers

Backbones were stiffened for that final push. Those old enough to have experienced wartime India can remember the electric atmosphere of defiance after that speech. Some did **die**. Others **defied**. **Demonstrated**. **Went to prison** continuing a general mayhem psychologically against the British presence.

And the British went. . . eventually.

♦ What is remarkable is that Gandhi's words came true. What so astonished many of us residents in post-Independence times was the lack of animosity on the part of Indians at every level to those of us who came from a nation that had ruled them and put their parents in prison. In five intense years travelling all over the subcontinent meeting people as disparate as communist students in Kerala and Bengal to top ministers, only one instance of what might be called hostility was encountered. And that ended in laughter. The moral leadership of Gandhi and Pandit Nehru allowed friendship to prevail.

QUTB (also Qutub) Minar (n. Arabic **manar** = tower)

Although the Eiffel Tower and the Leaning Tower of Pisa may be more famous, certainly in Asia the **Qutb Minar** is the most renowned and imposing of towers, built south of Delhi over two centuries (12th–13th–14th) inspired originally by the conquering invader **Qutb-ud-Din**. At his death it was completed by **Iltutmish** in CE 1230 and repaired after damage from lightning in 1368 by **Firoz Tughlaq** who added the narrower upper two storeys.

Hindu and Muslim cultures merge into the first hints of the synthesis of art forms, a forerunner heralding the miracle of architectural enrichment which the later Mughal period epitomises.

The visible confluence of the two major traditions can be clearly seen at this site with **Qutb-ud-Din's 'Might of Islam'** Mosque right nearby, constructed and enlarged by Sultan Iltutmish in the next century. Qutb's name means **Pole of the World: Axis of the Whole Universe.** Invaders thought well of themselves in grandiose terms in those days (see **R Nath, A History of Sultanate Architecture**, Abhinav, New Delhi, 1977).

The long cloisters are lined with intricately engraved red sandstone pillars which show every sign of Hindu artisans at work in earlier times. Lotus leaf scrolls and pods, familiar curvaceous triple-bending nymphs and the occasional Devanagari script give the game away. All this retrieved from Qutb-ud-din Aibak who plundered Dilli in 1188 CE[*] and ruined well over 20 Hindu and Jain temples in this south Delhi area. The resultant rubble was used to create the first extant mosque in the city which claims mythological origins, for this is the stamping ground of the Pandavas and even further back into legend, Indraprastha where the Vedic god is supposed to have conducted a sacred yajna sacrifice.

Archaeological digs indicate city foundations dating back a millennium BCE, and even possibly neolithic. This is also the land claimed by Tomar Rajputs and the Chauhans of Prithviraj fame, the latter being slain in battle by Ghori's army commander Qutb-al-Din Aibak, material for puppet theatre nowadays!

Mosques required a tower in earlier times for the muezzin's voice to carry over distances before megaphones were invented. The call to prayer, the *azan*, five times a day is a compulsory part of daily Islamic life. The three lower storeys are covered in beautiful Arabic calligraphy engraved by the past-masters of such technique, the Hindu stonecutters whose ancestors for over a thousand years had perfected the art of incising the red sandstone of northern Indian architecture. Here also Devanagari characters and floral arabesques appear amid the Qur'anic flow of words, because stonemasons used the ruined Hindu temple stones from nearby.

The upper two storeys are different, having been rebuilt and extended upwards from the damaged fourth storey, hit by lightning in 1368. Yet another name familiar in other heritage sites and roads in Delhi, Firoz Tughlaq commissioned an attractive patterning of creamy marble framed in resonating red when the setting sun's ray catch the stone against a cobalt-blue sky. Then one appreciates what consummate artists these warrior Sultanate kingdoms harnessed to the task of declaring their Islamic presence, yet another cultural layer upon the palimpsest of the Indian identity.

*A freed slave, Aibak was appointed by Muhammad Ghori as viceregal administrator of Delhi, thus founding the line of rulers that make up the early Sultanate–Khiljis, Tughlaqs, Sayyids and Lodis remembered in place names all around the capital.

Here also is the Iron Pillar now locked inside a wrought-iron fence. Of uncertain date it is known to have been transported (another feat that conquerors were able to dictate huge sources of labour to accomplish) in the 4th century CE. It has never rusted being of such superb quality and technical fashioning.

A personal encounter

In earlier times you could try and achieve your especial wish if, standing with your back to the column, your stretched arms enabled hands to meet. The weight of public tourism is such that perhaps authorities fear damage that 2,000 years could not bring about.

Despite the weight of feet walking day by day through the grounds the Archaeological Department has improved the site considerably and has added useful information, which includes a sentence even longer in its sub-clauses and phraseology than a ringing Miltonic prose mouthful!

'He, on whose arm fame was inscribed by the Sword, when in battle in the Bengal country he kneaded (and turned) back with (his) breast the enemies uniting together, come against him; he by whom having crossed in warfare the seven mouths of the River Sindhu, the Vahlikas were conquered; by the breezes of whose prowess the southern ocean is even still perfumed, he the remnant of the zeal of whose energy, which utterly destroyed his enemies (like the remnant of the great glowing heat) of a burned fire in a great forest, even now leaves hot the earth, . . . who having the name of Chandra carried a beauty of countenance like (the beauty of) the full moon, having in faith fixed his mind on Vishnu, this lofty standard of the Divine Vishnu was set up on the hill (called) Vishnupada c 4 AD.'

By the time I had penned this I was surrounded by a curious circle of young Indian men, bemused.

'Why you take such interest? Are you Muslim?' one asked.

'No,' I rejoined. 'This is all about the **Hindu** origins of the Pillar from the early inscription engraved on its surface in Pali. Long before Islam ever came to India!'

'Oh! You supporter of BJP?' They laughed.

How historical fact plunges into modern controversy!

Q

RAGA

is derived from *ranj* = emotion, colour (of a mood) there being nine principal ones (see **RASA**). A musical set of notes = swaras (not a scale) in certain defined and long established relationships, rules of organisation and development, amplified by decorative devices (swaying gamaks), sliding runs (taans) and wavering microtones (srutis). Pandit Ravi Shankar describes a raga as 'a scientific, precise, subtle and aesthetic melodic form with its own peculiar ascending and descending movement which consists of either a full octave, or a series of six or five notes'.

In various permutations all these and other arabesque embellishments, learned during strict discipline under a guru for a decade or more, create a melody, a mood, a meditation.

There is no notation to speak of, all the disciplined grammar committed to memory and learned through an oral tradition. Once learned then improvisation can take over. But the ground base, demandingly mathematical and as intellectually commanding as Bach, Schoenberg or Glass, creates the frame.

The Voice is considered tantamount in importance compared with instruments.

Ravi Shankar once joked that Indian music is 90% perspiration (i.e., practice and concentration) and 10% inspiration!

RAGAMALA PAINTINGS

are visualised music, paintings depicting the mood and conjuring up the essence of the raga in question.

Delhi's National Museum has gathered together over 1000 of these miniatures, mostly painted in the Himalayan kingdoms of the 18th–19th century.

RAILWAYS

Go by rail if you want to find out about India, warts and all, but first read **The Lonely Planet's** fabulous story–a true travel survival story by a UK traveller–Francois Baker–who survived! If after laughing out aloud, despite all, then read about **gricing** (now added to 'fissiparous' and 'palimpsest', 'coronated' and 'bifurcation' to my increasing vocabulary, thanks to India). 'Gricing' is as obsessive as bird watching, but chasing huge locomotives in India must be hotter and full of dangerous grit in the eyes. Never put your head out of the windows in India if you are lucky to be near a grilled window that does open–you may end up in hospital after 15 hours of misery with a tiny but nasty piece of coal dust from those fascinating steam engines that occasionally still exist despite being phased out in 1987. Then India lost its magic whistle heard at a distance as elephantine locomotives thundered through the night.

And either chain your luggage and packs to the rack, or sit on it–and don't buy any luggage remotely looking Indian, because some one of the **13,000,000** people now travelling daily on **7,500** trains will deftly lift it in full view of the compartment and disappear just as the train draws into a station–and get lost in the crowd before you can catch up with them.

This apart, taking an express for 24 hours will be something that is like no other country except perhaps China–but there so few, certainly in rural areas, will speak English the way all kinds of Indians and certainly young men now do. That is something that over the last 10 years has come as a real personal surprise. Usually it was well-educated middle class who tried out their English on the visitor. Indians on the whole are basically friendly. They also want to 'place you'–fit you into the hierarchy so you will be asked how much salary you earn, which culture you come from; are you married; if not, why not; how many children; which religion, and don't say 'none' because that will really start a major philosophical discussion!

And don't believe everything people tell you. Indian Railways are remarkably efficient despite the business of actually getting on the train–that is, if you are too mean-minded to decline using a porter who deserves all the backsheesh he can get for ruining his neck for the rest of his life carrying the heaviest suitcases some Indians fill (as well, admittedly, as my own).

And sometimes Indian express trains like the Chennai to Tiruvananthapuram run can arrive early–which happened to our young son on his return after 18 years away from where he was born to do voluntary service at a very basic level up in the tribal/poor rural area of the mountains of eastern Kerala. India's train track is astonishing and must be the most adventurous in the world with three gauges and wonderfully different music sounds under the carriage at fast speed but it is the narrow gauge up to Shimla, the little Blue Train from Mettupalayam to Udhagamandalam, and the Darjeeling track that take the breath away. Just even thinking of the engineers and labourers who laid in 1880 some of the precipitous track on this 'most spectacular railway in the world' almost in touching distance of Kanchenjunga–on sleepers some of which came from the great jarrah stands of Western Australia, makes one salute the physical heroism in putting substance into the vision.

The miniature train journey to Shimla on our first experience of the 'hot weather' in New Delhi (without air-conditioning) is as vivid as it was then–the overnight train with all the sounds of India, the great train whistles and whooshes, the early morning expectorations as people chewed their neem twigs to clean the mouth, and chaos at Kalka–and then this toy train. And the first stop at **Barog** where the Solan brewery was one of India's new industries beginning to expand and make profits.

♦ But it was the breakfast in this delightful mountain station that has stayed acutely detailed in my memory. Potted geraniums and bougainvillaea along the platform and the cool air miraculously transforming baked flesh and itchy prickly heat rash brought on by the misery of the pre-monsoonal humidity down on those relentlessly steaming plains made an impressive dent in the psyche. As we climbed slowly grinding and locking, grinding and locking onto the track as the giant loops took us higher and higher through 103 tunnels, we felt psychologically better with each number passed and clearly marked. And I can still taste the freshness of the English breakfast served up perfectly with crisp toast and properly cooked eggs–a perfection. It is not just trains you travel–it is restrooms, restaurants in south India and the cleanliness of their brahmin kitchens, the encounters with all of life lived on the platform, the mediaeval characters straight out of a Shakespeare play.

Delhi–Madras, three days, two nights, June, non-air-conditioned in newly independent India.

As the block of ice (organised by a thoughtful Northern Railway Board friend) melted and spread its coating of saw-dust over the public compartment by day, private coupé by night along with travelling companions less welcome, denizens of the dark shade under lowered seats to make a base for the crisp, clean bedrolls and pillows–large railway nurtured cockroaches enjoying a string bag full of fresh fruit despite the fact that it hung on a hook in the small shower with very smooth slippery walls, the distancing profoundly changed the India we had come to know after the years in our home in New Delhi. In the middle of the clattering dark, lulled to sleep by the regularity of the track rhythms underneath me I awoke, presentiment alerting every nerve end. As soon as I turned on the harsh compartment light, I froze, as did the largest cockroach I had seen, only its spindly antennae quivering slightly, at the end of my bunk. My husband still consigned to the steaming oven of Delhi, I had to act. Summoning up whatever shakti energy remained at 3 a.m. I slowly retrieved The Hindustan Times, rolled it up tight and aimed my cricket-trained arm. One hit….a boundary. My son cheered. It is also testing yourself if you have the luxury of travelling in your own coupé when a whole family bangs on the door, wakes you and your young children as the train lurches to a stop, gone midnight at Agra, and moves in unexpectedly with one large mortar and stone pestle the size of a large bucket (not the kitchen kind), an oil drum, five huge suitcases and several bedrolls and then sits on your bed as if that is also the day-time seat!

Even to newcomers such as our family after three years land-locked in the plains of north India, the elation of sea breezes so affected my then two young children they went crazy on the Madras sands. The ozone electrified their English genes! And all around very distinctive Tamils in their Persil-white shirts and lungis with their amazing command of English not seen as a colonial construction of oppression as often in the north but to be used internationally as a commercial and educational advantage. This sense of the sea, of an outward-looking attitude was so liberating even for me psychologically after being landlocked for so long in the northern plains. Ready access to the sea had been part and parcel of my island culture in the UK and I had not realised how part of my thinking it was until that first evening in beautiful peaceful Madras, a garden city as it was then. And there was the other side, those fisherfolk who lived in poverty under the palms in their thatched huts south towards Adyar. Their skins burnt blue-black through the centuries they are the people of the kattamaram (Tamil for 'joined logs' = catamaran, another infiltration in English). These roped logs are a dynamic art form in themselves, 3 or 5 logs side by side, carved in a special way to narrow at the bow where separate carved pieces are added. At the end of the day they are unroped to dry on the sand. Somehow these hard-working fisherfolk eke out a subsistence existence, so vulnerable at sea. Such disheartening catches we watched being laboriously hauled in with poisonous sea snakes as well and how friendly they were to Michael and Caitilin who romped around them.

And some statistics

When the national railway system hits the statistics ramp, figures explode in one's face! Almost too much to take in for what is one of the largest rail organisations in the world, with the most extensive rail junction certainly in Asia at Mughalsarai on the other side of the Ganga at Varanasi. Marshalling yards that can seize up like a traffic gridlock in London if there is a slip-up with Down and Up trains (one is never sure which that means) listed in the daily papers and broadcast on All India Radio–a mantra for travellers and listeners such as myself in that half-sleep on waking, shunted like the real Thomas the Tank Engine that comes into virtual reality in India–such as the **Fairy Queen** with its cowcatcher sweeping (ever upwards) on narrow gauge in eastern India. The shiny green engine was British-built in 1855 and was just in time to transport troops to Bihar to quell the 1857 Sepoy Revolt, now regarded as a war for independence.

◆ No wonder it is, then, the oldest preserved loco in India now spruced up and shunted out of the National Railway Museum and operational again on tourist heritage runs from Delhi in the winter months, so popular that Indian Railways is contemplating further heritage trains steaming out to earn tourist dollars! Or the romantic Blue Train to Ooty which celebrated its centenary in 1998. The imagination ranges far and wide in that comatose state listening in to the early morning radio incantation of up-train and down-train arrivals and delays, and in so doing, saluting the problem-solving expertise of laying rail up precipitous mountain edge, unrelenting granite rock, so different from temperate climates, the flat plains of Canada and the USA or the milder countryside and softened soils of the English countryside.

◆ And all this multifarious array from the exotic to the everyday locomotive pulls and shoves through:

◆ **7,000 stations** (Mark Twain in **A Tramp Abroad** referred to this 'perennially ravishing show' of daily life) , with **13,500 trains** stopping at them every day.

◆ **100,000 km** (at least) **of track** since the first locomotive steamed out of Bombay in 1853 on its experimental 20-mile journey. The East India line came into being. A delightful story is told that on the very next day, a well-known Parsi and one of the first Indian Directors of Railways, knighted by the British and with the resplendent name of **Sir Jamsetjee Jeejeebhoy**, reserved the entire train for a family outing from Bombay to Thana and back!

◆ **One and a half million tonnes of freight…13 million** people (three quarters of Australia's population) travelling each day and the stylish new **Shatabdi Express** inter-city trains along with the crack **Rajdhani Express** which even in ferocious monsoonal conditions can arrive in Kolkata from New Delhi **earlier than scheduled** (a personal experience).

R

◆ However, it is the opening up of the western coastline, for so long the inaccessible Konkan, that deserves the ultimate accolade. Slashed by creek bed upon creek bed–the chapped fingers of deep red-banked earth dividing thick jungle slopes and raging torrents of monsoonal swollen brown rivers from the steep western ghats into the Arabian Sea, this Konkan line of 760 km is surely the ultimate challenge to India's engineering skills.

◆ **2,137 bridges alone to construct in impossible terrain from Mumbai to Goa and down to Mangalore** and nearly 84 km of tunnelling, which eliminated two sides of a triangle journey over the Nilgiri mountains down to inland Coimbatore, and lorry traffic you would not wish to encounter as we terrifyingly did.

◆ No wonder other national governments in the region line up for IR expertise and Indian Railway officers speak with pride of the 'integrative force' and the 'powerful economic component' such a cat's cradle of linkages creates. In even these remote areas of the land this is as subtle a binding agent in modern India as those already described in **PILGRIMAGE**.

For a delightful mix of fact interlaced with personal anecdotes and good humour read **Bill Aitken's Exploring Indian Railways** (OUP, London 1994), the largest network in the world under a single management.

◆ Travelling back from Kolkata I was enroute to Patna to say goodbye to a courtly Muslim scholar, a true gentleman if ever there was one whom we had known over the five years our family lived in Delhi. We were about to return to the UK. I was scruffy, sweaty and exhausted from the two-day search in the Bengali countryside for India's largest **JOINT FAMILY**–the 600 Nandis. From this amazing experience I tumbled out of the train at Patna to be startled by a braided aide-de-camp saluting immaculately. I was the only white woman in sight with bundles and baskets, all set to find the only taxi (ever hopeful–perhaps non-existent!) or a horse-drawn tonga. I reckoned even local Biharis would know where Government House, Raj Bhavan, was. However I was, not only to the consternation of all the staring Indians on the platform (and in my carriage) but also to my own, whisked off in a white Hindusthan car, lace-curtained with the Governor's flag fluttering. And there was **Zakir Sahib**, Dr Zakir Husain first met four years earlier in Shimla when he chaired the Press Commission, a wonderfully warm educator, a sincere Gandhian who had many a time reminisced with my husband, and the delightful Vice-Chancellor of the Jamia Millia Islamic University at Okhla, south of Delhi, Professor M Mujeeb. The Professor and Zakir Sahib had funny bones that rubbed against each other. There we learned Indian history, quirkiness, political 'nous' and self-deprecation in a constant champagne bubble of laughter while sharing two old rickety charpoys under a deep-shaded mango tree while mosquitoes attacked my bare legs (no Odomos ointment in those days!) The old flit-gun had to be searched out. Alas, both wives spoke only Urdu, and never ventured out unless I made a move into the deep interiors where my hopeless attempts with ungrammatical Hindustani caused further ripples of laughter in this quarter.

◆ Breakfast on a silver tray with all the British silver in place and 'the Governor' taking tea with me was a poignant and heady experience, further heightened by being accompanied to the **Khuda Baksh** Library under the guidance of such a scholar in all his Muslim 'Indian-ness' showing the treasures of his heritage–a rare privilege, the icing on the cake before it all melted away into a memory still vibrant of courtly India, and the cadences of Arabic text being recited from the fragile yellowing pages of rare manuscripts freckled with iridescent painted scenes that glowed with gold.... and Akbar's personal signature.

And then the karmic strike for all the hubris of yet another flagfluttering drive as the solid chauffeur-driven motorcar, horn jammed onto full decibel blast, chases the overnight Calcutta mail, the daily 'down-train' to Delhi. Accompanied again by the upright young aide-de-camp, the sleeper compartment guard appears amid the crush of India's travelling public. The clerk of reservations assuming the latter half of my name must be a Bengali Roy, thus assigned me to a four-berth with three Bengali men. This situation was nothing untoward for the sleeper section.

Accepting the fact that there is safety in numbers I proceeded to establish the remaining top bunk as my domain and in the gloaming (all lights seem to dim until the train gathers full speed and electric current) tried to sort out my array of luggage on the perplexed travelling companions below. I hung up my ubiquitous binoculars (some wonderful birds in the Bengal countryside) on the nearest hooked chain…unthinkingly.

◆ A lurching grinding sound judders along the carriage, my fruit (presented in a woven basket by the Husain family) scatters onto abashed Bengali gentlemen still assessing this invasive **firangi** female, their teacups still full of Patna **chai** now flung sideways, brown swill on the murky floor. The train has stopped.

Several minutes later with everyone confused and at a loss in the middle of a darkened Bihar (no villages knew the luxury of electricity then), a knock on the coupé door, and it slides open. A uniformed Punjabi guard examines the upper section of the dim interior perilously near my bunk.

'What is this package I am finding here?'–his words rang out—and NOT in Punjabi. My binoculars are now the centre of attention. They are hanging from what I now decipher as an ominous box painted red. The emergency chain is dangling down. I have inadvertently pulled the emergency cord and the express down train has come to a halt for no good reason at all.

The guard takes a long hard look at me–a remark still undeciphered to this day is made down below–and then all four men break into rip-roaring laughter.

'*He says you should be forgiven as the British have forgiven all our Bengali babus and revolutionaries*': The ice was broken… Indian humour prevailed… and I never paid a fine!

■ **RAJPUTS**

When considering India as a nation militarism does not immediately spring to mind. For one thing India is referred to as **Mother India**, not a **Vaterland**.

R

Only at the magnificent Republic Day parades on January 26 each year is the ordinary civilian really aware of military might, the technological advances of military rocketry, and the long and strong military tradition built upon by the British Raj–indeed one needs to be reminded of the heroism of Sikh and Gurkha, Maratha, Dogra and Madras, just a few of the regiments who fought in Europe in the First World War winning Victoria Crosses in acts of great bravery on behalf of other people's very distant conflicts–and again in World War II in defence of British colonial power. Without doubt, however, the testing of atomic devices in Rajasthan–land of the Rajputs–has created another dimension of singular concern worldwide.

And without doubt some of the bravest fighters have been **Rajputs**. But their traditions like those of the Sikh Punjabis go way back into history **in defence of India** as it was forming into a major entity long before the coming of the British and the evolution of the Raj shaped the many regional identities into a modern nation state.

Ancestry
Charles Allen and **Sharada Dwivedi** recount in the **Lives of the Indian Princes** (Century Publishing, London, 1984) some facts on Rajput history that like much else to do with this stratum of Indian life **borders on the surreal–a stunning theatricality, daily life where the mundane for the ruling family was shot through like sumptuous interwoven silk with fabulous ritual**, where dynasties were measured in aeons, not centuries.

The young **Yuvaraj of Dungarpur** explains his own genealogy and that of Udaipur his northern neighbour as being founded in the State of Mewar in 800 CE... 'the rulers of the Himalayan hill state of Suket could contemplate an unbroken line of succession without adoption for almost 1200 years'. The Porbandar rulers on the coast of the Kathiawar peninsula (where Gandhi was born) claim that their last Maharana Saheb is 179th in succession! For pedigree the caste system has ensured India takes the Olympic medal. No wonder Rajputs claim descent from Surya the sun! Figuratively it appears as an emblem throughout their culture.

It is in Rajput territory of course that the backpacker, taking be-tasselled camel safaris or wandering between the evocative walled desert towns of Jaisalmer and Bikaner, may well suddenly be displaced on the narrow connecting roads by a file of awesome tanks and lumbering army lorries. The Pakistan border is less than an hour's drive away. But even in the 10th–11th century CE when William the Conqueror was landing on English soil bringing Norman culture to the Anglo-Saxons with the demise of King Harold, **the argumentative clans of Rajasthan**, in constant petty fights with each other began to forge a common identity as Turko-Afghani-Mongol hordes, in one grouping or another, began to threaten their small communities perched on high-fortressed rocky eminences.

The harsh environment, the geographical location, the protein food they ate, the genetic structure during even earlier centuries when they absorbed the invasions of Huns in 500 CE who had also overrun middle Europe–all these components

seem to have combined to give the peoples of Rajasthan a very distinct ethos compared with some of their neighbours. One simply cannot imagine Gujaratis jumping onto horses, chariots trundling behind, charging into battle array with beflagged lances fluttering, practically every day of the week! **They** are merchants and collectors of gold or well-disciplined ascetics, Jains and Hindus alike, latterly followers of their native-born Mahatma Gandhi. And the neighbouring Chambal ravines of Madhya Pradesh and its Marwar plateau of dusty red earth and harsh landscape is for dacoits and brigands galore. Uttar Pradesh is so part of the Gangetic basin its people are preoccupied tilling the soil, irrigating and ploughing from dawn to dusk.

◆ On the other hand the dry air of Rajasthan must create a frisson of a different kind, a stir in the blood for here is a strong warrior tradition–its very name meaning 'the land of the rajas', the **kshatriya** class of ruler chieftains, hot-blooded and valorous with an identifiable code of behaviour recalling a similar European tradition–chivalry, knights in shining armour (too hot for India's climate, however), hawks on gloved fists, women upholding a strict code of sexual behaviour, carrying the **sharam** or shame of the family if they succumbed to the blandishments of the stranger galloping in over the low range of hills. They also displayed considerable bravery, in times of dire stress, accompanying their menfolk into battle. Giving birth to a son was of major importance to defend the future or to ride off into a battle in his own turn not only against yet another horde of invaders, but relatives who had smudged the family honour, or were acquiring family lands on the sly, or usurping a title.

One of the oldest of these fiercely loyal clans that made up what was previously called Rajputana, the land of the Rajput princes (and which was literally so in the days of British rule when a degree of autonomy in internal jurisdiction was granted, with a watchful British 'Resident' living within each territory to give 'advice'), was the **Sisodias** of **Mewar**. In the language of the people they trace their descent too from the Sun God hence the presence of the moustachio-ed sun emblem (the moustache a shorthand sign to indicate a warrior, seen also in art depictions of the south).

Associated with this illustrious Kshatriya descent are the tribal **Bhils** who are said to have inhabited the Aravalli hills (from where a modern Indian export comes of greeny-blue floor slate for modern housing in Australia) since well before 2000 BCE! It is the Bhils whom legend credits with receiving **Guhadatta**–one of the honoured earliest historic chieftains as well as Maharana **Pratap** whose prowess in battle and his adventures when rescued (again by the Bhils) are now sung in high-pitched voices under the crystalline sparkle of a jet-black star-spangled firmament.

Tourism and the modern Rajput
Tourists can now sit around camp fires listening to Rajasthani musicians–very successfully promoted by the Rajasthan Tourism Development Corporation–while bards chronicle their dramatic ballads. The entire atmosphere is like stepping back into mediaeval Europe. A success story of modern India in itself!

R

The whole of its region has been one of the first in independent India to envisage the importance of global tourism and its benefits in modern currency income. Areas totally inaccessible and only serviced by run-down **dak** bungalows (the one-time staging-posts for the mail and rest houses with resident cooks for visiting British administrators such as tax collectors) and where only kachcha roads or tracks existed, enough to ruin even the solidity of a Hindusthan car, are now the one place to be visited if nowhere else in India by time-constrained overseas visitors.

As well-educated modernizing people bereft of their Privy Purses abolished in 1973 by Mrs Gandhi's Congress Government, Rajputs as a matter of survival have become very efficient hotel managers turning ancestral palaces into heritage hotels.

Now on a camel safari out of Jaisalmer, or on the two famous **Palace on Wheels** steam locomotive trains, while eating kababs and tandoori-red oven-baked chicken in the huge edifice of the Umaid Bhavan Palace Hotel in Jodhpur (built by the Maharaja in the 1930s to give local people work in a famine relief project) musicians with stringed **sarangi** and the rollicking percussion of fast-playing **tablas** and **pakhawaj** drums sing of the feats in battle and the tragedies of romantic love stories... so many starcrossed lovers like **Roopmati**, a Rajput Thakur's daughter, married to **Baaz Bahadur** a feudal lord of **Mandu** who, although a Muslim, was killed in battle by one of Emperor Akbar's generals. Petty jealousies, shifting land-ownership, overwhelming male pride, all make for the stuff of ballads—just like the Scots!

Cheeky young singers and dancers dressed in vivid red with gold edgings are also harnessed to the promotion not only in the land itself but now in Festivals of India worldwide—London, Moscow, Philadelphia, and around Australia. Feisty and flamboyant, they toss overloaded turbans, perfect white toothy smiles, hand-clapping to catchy rhythms twirling the flare and swirl of red-skirted Moghul dress for men, prancing like plumed horses to entertain with tales of honour, of love at first sight as a raja and his courtiers hunt at full tilt for black buck, leopards, even lions in ancient days, or tigers... and these mesmerising handsome beasts did indeed roam wild across modern roads for those of us privileged enough to drive in the lonely dark on the roads from Jaipur, Ajmer or Alwar soon after Independence.

The Artistry of Valour

A Rajasthani 17th century painting conjures up the scene. The sudden surprise encounter with a lissom daughter of a Thakur chieftain, bathing secretly in a river with her handmaidens. The young ruler is transfixed in his gaze. The falling in love at first sight... the unrequited love, the elopements because she belongs to a household of the wrong clan, the 'sharam' and dishonour, the anger and clash of an Indian Shakespearean tragedy.

A highwater mark was reached in miniature paintings, many now to be seen in the palaces of Udaipur, Jodhpur, Jaipur and more out-of-the way residences being constantly opened up for 'heritage' tourism. Resplendent white palaces in flat perspectives but in narrative juxtapositions that present a 3-D vision; grid-designed flat cities; pink lotuses arising erect out of still lakes;

golden roseate-streaked skies slashed by V-shaped formations of migrating storks; the blue Krishna in amorous dalliance cavorting in verdant pavilioned gardens with doe-eyed gopis yearning to become the honoured favourite Radha; peacocks and white egrets trailing delicate curled clouds and swaying flower fronds; and crimson paint everywhere—this is the visual vibrant valorous world the Rajputs inhabited, defended—and now promote. It is also the ambience recalled by Mirabai whose devotional **BHAKTI** bhajans lauding the Deity are still very popular today, even though as a Rajput of royal birth she lived 1420–1550 CE.

There are tales of valour amongst Rajput queens in the later periods when Sultanate rulers pushed out the boundaries of their empire from Agra and Delhi, edging farther and farther to the west and south, subduing minor kingdoms or marauding and abducting. **Queen Padmini**, a legendary beauty, one such, who courageously resisted the advances of **Alauddin Khilji**, Sultan of Delhi in 1303.

Chittor, the ancient capital of Mewar to the southwest and now a traveller's delight, is the epitome of this tradition. If a fort was about to fall under duress this custom demanded sacrifice—of a high order. The garrison would dress in saffron, riding out to certain death, the women in their bridal finery defiant to the last, flinging themselves on a funeral pyre. Akbar was determined to bring the warring fringes of his empire into a regularised hegemony of Mughal administration. Red hand imprints, embossed in stone are dramatic visual reminders of their ghastly sacrifice. They leave a melancholy psychological veil upon the mind. **Maha Sati Chowk** honours the Chittor women who performed the ritual of **johar**, self-inflicted immolation in fire, when their menfolk rode out beyond the ramparts, to be decimated by Akbar's superior forces in 1568–their sense of honour as equal to the pride of Hindu ancestry held by their men. Imagine the media headlines today if nine queens, five princesses and 8,000 other brave women threw themselves into the flames to avoid Mughal rapine.

Around the major cities can be seen the umbrella-shaped **chattris**, also standing in melancholy golden-stoned array in the blazing setting sun, one of the few physical reminders of cremated remains in India unlike Christian cemeteries which remember the buried dead. These canopied platforms (from which **kiosk** derives its meaning) record these remarkable women.

The seesaw of historical development in Rajput life is as fickle and contrary as waves lapping in a stormy lake. The divide between who was whose ally was never a clear cut one and should not be viewed always as Hindu/Muslim communalism whipped up by modern power-driven politics of today. Hindu Rajas fought fierce battles against other Hindus. During the great age of Mughal emperors, Muslim rulers appointed them as local governors. Indeed the Rajputs have been called 'the sword-arm of the Mughals'. It was the iconoclastic Aurengzeb who heightened the antagonism, pushing former Rajput allies into open defiance along with the Marathas and Shivaji as the empire disintegrated. Hindus had a tax on pilgrim centres reimposed, and the psychic energy which gave vision to Babur's line, began to dissipate with extravagant lifestyles at the tail end of Mughal emperors—in name only. The princes of Rajasthan became then the backbone of Empire for a time, owing allegiance to the British Crown but never under direct political rule, being responsible for the 554 princely states themselves, just under one third of India, a fact little known about the Raj. A few were personal friends with the English monarch whom they considered as an equal.

Household words in Britain in the 1920s and 1930s with their sporting prowess at polo and cricket—and ballroom dancing with Western society ladies—their ebullient joie-de-vivre and ability to feel at home in the West made them the easiest of Indians to get to know. Behind-the-scenes, however, they still honoured age-old Hindu traditions. Great travellers and eccentrics, they nevertheless installed Krishna as **ISTADEVATA** at the Ritz, possibly the one hotel which was flexible enough even in Lord Curzon's impeccably English viceregal days to house **two gigantic Indian silver urns** (now on display at the City Palace in Jaipur). These travelled to England with Madho Singh II in 1902 on board ship and incidentally made the Guinness Book of World Records—each cast in just over 240 kg of silver, to carry over 8,000 gallons of Ganga water so that the royal entourage, would not be contaminated as twice-born high caste with tap water from the Thames!

■ **RAKSHA BANDHAN**
is the binding of a **rakhi =** wrist band made of silk or cotton thread, or dazzling jewels, in a ceremony honouring brothers by the girls of the family. Male strangers can also be so honoured or the son in a family of close friends. In the first decades after independence when Indians were free to migrate voluntarily overseas their culture needed reinforcing and interpreting after being so long suppressed or ignored. Indian newspapers sprang up to aid this process. This is an account in one:

'Raksha' literally means 'to protect,' and 'Bandhan' means 'to tie.' On this auspicious occasion, a sacred polychrome piece of thread is tied on to the wrists of males by sisters or mothers, with the wish that this amulet may protect the wearer from all evils.
The popular mythological legend connected with the tying of the sacred thread (amulet) is that when Indra, the King of the Heavens, was defeated in an encounter with a Demon King, Bali, Indra's wife Sachi invoked Lord Vishnu to help her husband regain his kingdom. Thereupon Lord Vishnu gave Sachi a thread, investing it with supernatural powers, and enjoined her to tie it on the wrist of Indra prior to his launching a counterattack against Bali. This amulet gave added strength to Indra and enabled him to defeat Bali ultimately.
As this amulet was tied on the wrist of Indra on the full moon day of Shravan month, the annual commemoration of the event, now known as the Raksha Bandhan festival occurs end of July/beginning August.

The religious ceremony that precedes the Raksha Bandhan proper makes the occasion a colourful one. In traditional households after an early morning bath, the entire house is decorated gaily with flowers and mango leaves, and sisters recite these words: "That thread by which Indra tied down the great, strong demon-king Bali; Oh, brother, with that I tie thee to protect you from all evils. Oh, amulet, may you not fail; may you not fail."

These brothers, honorary and blood relation alike, are meant in turn to protect their sisters and send a present each year. Even in Mughal times there are tales of such honour, Rajput queens appealing to Muslim overlords to protect them. A rakhi sent to Emperor Humayun by the Rani of Mewar brought forth his help when her kingdom was under attack.

A personal note: Our daughter took an 'honorary' Indian brother in a charming Punjabi ceremony with close Indian friends and their son. Long after wherever we were located we had to remember to make an attractive rakhi and send it posthaste half way around the world.

■ **RAMANUJA**
of uncertain date, 11th–12th century CE
a famous south Indian philosopher-saint who represents the swing of the pendulum from searching after abstract truth of what is the 'real Reality' **to the return to personal devotion,** a warmth of heart which has occurred again and again in India's social development after centuries in which the monist, highly intellectual, virtually scientific view held supremacy—too esoteric by half for most people who may yearn for a more personal relationship with a divine presence.

Ramanuja spread this truth as he saw it in his wanderings through the landscape of Tamilnadu that though we may as human beings be broken down into infinitesimal numbers of particles and molecules, we are not just part of a giant incomprehensible Particle (a monistic view). What is seen around us, on this planet, **is real**, even if in our present state of exploration through the new rishi of the 21st century—the Hubble telescope—we are a **nothingness** when viewed from the 'edges' of the Universe upon universes.

R

◆ He taught that the individual soul/atman needs to relate to a caring concept of Deity which although at the ultimate level is a gigantic Consciousness/Atman, nevertheless is interlinked with each smaller entity (turn back to **ADVAITA, BHAKTI, DARSHAN**).

◆ The austere asceticism, intellectually demanding aspect of Shiva as akasha, ultimate creative energy, is not the personal **istadevata** of Ramanuja, rather **his songs of praise are to Vishnu,** the gentler force **who through the Rama-Krishna avatars** brought **loving grace** to human beings in this terrestrial reality. Indeed he has been compared with Plato rather than the more cerebral Aristotle or Aquinas, Plato being more disposed to the mystical sense of oneness (refer back to **ALVAR**). Nearly 40 years of his life were spent in such devotion in the temple town of **Kanchi** where incidentally six of the 63 **NAYANMAR** saints of the Saivite persuasion were born.

■ RAMAYANA

(of very ancient dating, still speculative)

Only 24,000 verses compared with the other major **EPIC**, the **MAHABHARATA**, the Ramayana has, along with the Gita, become central to modern Hindu thought and is read and reread in ritual community gatherings in non-stop musical chantings of the full text which take several days and nights to complete.

This occurs at **Ramnavami**, the ninth day of the bright half of the Hindu calendar month of **Chaitra** (after Easter) when devotional bhajans and celebrations occur in the temples dedicated to the hero of the Ramayana.

The Ramayana is believed to have emerged as legend even earlier than the huge historical epic of the MahaB both being regarded as **redemptive history**, the controversial figure of Rama as an existent king thought to have lived anywhere between 3,800–3,700 BCE in Ayodhya by which time he had become incarnate as the **seventh avatar of Vishnu**.

Within its unfolding drama of **Rama,** his young bride, **Sita**, and **Lakshman**, his brother, their banishment into exile, their adventures and alarming adversities, the search for Sita abducted by Ravana, her eventual rescue and the restoration of Rama's rule and coronation, rules for moral and social life are encapsulated in parables and subplots to be passed on generation to generation.

◆ TV serialisations have brought these major epics vividly back to life for a vast audience; historical battles and personal struggles of these legendary kingdoms of about 6000 years ago are seen as metaphors and allegories for today's contemporary battles for righteousness, battles of personal integrity and conscience and character training.

The classic Sanskrit recitation of ancient poet VALMIKI(pre-Buddha?) was later translated by eminent Tamil poet Kamban (11th c CE) and later, Tulasi Das (also Tulsidas) into Hindi. W D P Hill in his English translation of the latter version evokes the atmosphere of resplendent nature in the innocent beginnings of the world. (OUP, London, 1952).

From Tulasi Das' point of view composing the long poetic tale in 1574 was a means of conveying the overwhelming message of Rama's sanctity and grace with a missionary fervour available to all no matter their chance of birth. Orthodox brahmin pandits were aghast that such a sacred text should be re-issued, so to speak, in the vernacular. At first the Varanasi pandits refused to accept it, but in the very temple denied entry to me because I had smelled the jasmine garland destined for the shrine of Shiva, in the mighty Visvanath temple with its gleaming golden dome, strange happenings occurred.

On completion of his text despite all the arguments with the learned hierarchy, it was left in the temple. Hill in his introduction explains: *In the morning there were found written on the book the words 'Satyam Sivam Sundaram', and the same words were heard in the air by pilgrims who came to worship in the temple. Copies of the book began to circulate and the pandits were dismayed at their popularity. They asked the Samkara scholar Sri Madhusudan Sarasvati his opinion of the work and he commended it very highly. Then the pandits made their final effort. One evening they placed in the temple of Visvanath a copy of the Veda, beneath it certain* **sastras**, *beneath them a Purana, and below them all a copy of the* **Ramacaritamanasa**. *In the morning they found that Tulasi Das's poem had been moved to the top of the pile. The pandits were at last convinced and begged the poet's pardon. (Satyam = truth; Sundaram = beauty in the unusual pale form of Shiva upon whom the dark form of Shakti dances.*

◆ The setting for the lyrical verse, **Chitrakuta**, is in the border areas of UP and Madhya Pradesh—once the 'wild wood' beloved of English literature also, of **The Wind in the Willows** and **The Lord of the Rings** where natural forces hold sway. It is as potent to Indians, resonating in beautiful cadences, vibrant imagery, the sense of wholesome co-existence and harmony with the animal kingdom and humanity as is any Shakespearean flight of fancy in the culture of the English in **Midsummer Night's Dream, As You Like It** or **The Tempest**.

Amply forested regions, the peace of the foothills, the fresh-flowing river Mandakini reflect golden ages of an earlier innocence, before the Kaliyuga laid a shadow on land and humanity.

In this all-embracing experience—the **intuitive feel** of the Ramayana—only Indians who are intimately enmeshed in their mother tongue can fully appreciate the very **rasa**, the flavour of its haunting poetic beauty, which Kamban transposed into an idealised Chola countryside.

◆ The Ramayana is not all lyricism even though it is referred to by knowledgeable pandits as **aadikavya**—the **'first poetical work'**—to mark it out from the MahaB, a more factual historical recounting of ancient feuding and conflicts at family and regional level. Both are 'heard wisdom', tradition transmitted by extraordinary feats of memory in 'quatrains' of verse, along the oral culture network into every nook and cranny of the ancient land. And then Valmiki appeared on the scene. He injected long passages of homily and down-to-earth statements; Tulasi Das omitted these and though ironically composing during the consolidation of the Mughal Empire, he reflected the intense accumulation of passionate faith in the 'grace abounding' which the bhakti movements all over India had infused in the social mores and attitude of teaching.

Rama was no longer a factual hero but a teacher of social ethics bringing grace to all, high or low, rich or poor 'if they had but faith'. He personified **Rama Rajya** = enlightened rule, a phrase that now erupts in rightwing circles of the more orthodox Hindu-oriented political parties.

R

The Ideal King

Great kings generally possess the characteristics (of the five gods), ferocity, majesty, placidity, chastisement and tranquillity, and they are therefore at all times respected and honoured by their subjects.

That king who, taking a sixth share of the produce as tribute from his subjects, does not protect them as his sons, verily commits a heinous sin.

That king who rules his subjects in strict conformity with the established laws and looks after the hermits in the forests, obtains in return a fourth of that dharma.

(Translated from original Sanskrit by T S Raghavacharya) Present rulers could take note.

That constant in Indian counselling between guru and those who follow, the message of self-abnegation seems to have been lost in the global free-for-all of capital gains, economic bottom lines, downsizing and the scramble for political power. This is Valmiki again:

In this world virtue, material gain and pleasure are all to be found in the fruit accruing from the pursuit of virtue;...

If there is a case in which the three are not found together, one should do only that in which there is virtue, for one who is intent solely on material gain is to be hated and to be engrossed completely in pleasure is not praiseworthy.

(As quoted in Chapter IX, **de Bary, Sources of Indian Tradition** Vol I cited previously).

Another case of déja vu! and the **Bonfire of the Vanities** all over again. The message is equally strong in Tulasi Das—the sense of Kaliyuga and a fall from grace seeps into the undergrowth of the 'wild wood' of Ayodhya with a truly uncanny sense of current affairs. Part of the epilogue of **Ramacaritamanasa** is a litany by Tulasi Das which could be any editorial of today, reflecting the scepticism of the times, and the social and moral disintegration many now lament.

■ RAMAZAN or Ramadan

is the month most sacred in **ISLAM**. The revelation of the Qur'an was completed in this month. It is important to note that **the month-long fast moves backwards through the years roughly 10–11 days** depending on the days of the month in the Roman calendar. The Hijra lunar year is shorter by this number than the solar in use in Western societies so all Muslim Eids and other commemorations follow this rule also. Many businesspeople going to India fall foul of knowing this if they are dealing with Muslim colleagues and find all offices closed or severely limited, and no contacts (or contracts) possible.

In **2000** nearly all of the Christmas season for Muslim colleagues in the west, **November 27–December 27** was spent fasting from dawn to dusk. Leap years and moon rise do shift the breaking of fast. The best action is to find the local mosque and ask for exact times, because Sunni and Shi'a communities use different calculations and consult different Eastern mosques. In 2006 most Muslims began the fast on Sept 24; celebrating the breaking on Eidul-Fitr on Oct 24.

■ RANGOLI

is the domestic term as also **alapana** and **kolam** for the art of making 'embankments'. In fact each region has its own particular word for such ritual expressions of beauty.

♦ Such 'embankments' are decorative floor or courtyard decorations, some of the most intricate geometrical design, in white rice paste, others of quite fascinating detailed floral or symbolic composition in coloured sands as stopping points before entering the house.

Mostly executed holding tiny wet bags of rice paste between the index and third fingers, the women of the household deftly trace the designs over the bare floor or courtyard which has been previously prepared with clay or cowdung and mud smoothed down. These beautiful expressions of love, joy in creating artistic style and beauty without ever having attended an art school are passed down the female line from grandmother to mother to daughter.

They are **auspicious designs—mechanisms of energy visualised to represent the fundamental sense of divine energy** seen in many forms (that is the specific deities, female as well as male represented in the **PANTHEON**). They mark family occasions such as rites of passage or great festival occasions such as **DIWALI** when Lakshmi's footsteps are marvellously delineated in a quick swish of the right hand on the floor using moist rice paste like icing on a cake, from a door to domestic shrine and kitchen (which is cleansed annually before the ceremonies).

■ RASA (n. *Sanskrit:* flavour, juice, essence)

Literally means juice but as laid down by earliest Indian theoreticians **rasa** is the **essence** of an artistic form, for example, in the playing of a **RAGA** by a master musician, by the expertise of playing, the fine handling of the particular tones of that raga mode and the especial phraseology applicable to that raga, the emotions of the listener are fine-tuned to experience the special emotional experience—**the bhava**—to be aroused.

♦ **Nava rasa** = nine major emotions have been categorised in the early codifications of the **Bharata Natya Shastra**, a monumental work laying down the ground rules of the drama and dance.

Raudra	*fury*	Veera	*heroism*	Vibhatsa	*disgust*
Bhayanaka	*fear*	Karuna	*pathos*	Hasya	*comic*
Sringara	*romantic or sensous*	Adbhuta	*wonderment*	Shanta	*serenity*

This concept the sage **Bharata** had compiled out of divine inspiration 'at the request of the Deities' as is stated by Indian practitioners. Legend and actual history become thoroughly entwined when dealing with these aesthetic shastras and the sage in question—Bharata. The Hindu imagination takes flight with the sage, translated into Indra's heaven so linking the sacred rituals of daily worship, the street theatre of its time, to the era close to the Christian millennium when the historical theoretician compiled what is termed **the fifth Veda**. This was the result of an appeal by the minor deities to the post-vedic Brahma to provide guidance for those members of society side-tracked by the powerful upper classes who had mastered the sacred language of Sanskrit, monopolising the earlier four Vedas for their own benefit. They alone knew the Sanskrit grammar, and how to chant the slokas accurately.

The Great Creator then fashioned a new **Veda**, *known as the* **Natya Veda** *which would be conducive to moral and material welfare. That which should be read, the intellectual content, Brahma took from the* **Rig Veda**; *that which could be sung, the music, he took from the* **Sama Veda**; *the* **abhinaya**, *the mimetic art, he took from the* **Yajur Veda** *and the* **rasa-s**, *the emotional content, he took from the* **Atharva Veda**. *Brahma then bade Vishvakarma, the divine architect, to construct a playhouse in which the sage Bharata was instructed to put into practice the new* **Veda**. *Bharata soon discovered that the performances lacked grace without women. Brahma resolved this predicament by creating celestial damsels whose skilful movements embellished the presentation.*

Sarya Doshi, **Marg, Aspects of the Performing Arts** Vol 34, 3, (1981).

Clearly the fanciful imagery is a way of saying that all the aesthetic principles that infused all the arts had an interconnectedness which led ultimately to one **singularity— Rasa**, the keyword of Indian expressive culture.

Each and every form of expressing the inner soul of an individual, a society, a nation in present-day terms, is a channel trying to unite the **local human consciousness** to that other level—**superconsciousness**—for want of a concrete word for the ineffable expressed by the English Romantic poets such as Keats, Shelley, Wordsworth in the vague terms of Truth and Beauty.

♦ A force that exists beyond everyday ordinary experience is evoked by the **rasa** that inspires a perfect performance by whichever artist, female as well as male (the Shastra texts always speak in the comprehensive HE!).

The great Bharata Natyam dancer **Balasaraswati** (see **DANCE**) speaks of her own art form as 'a divine art', the constant theme and impulse of which was 'the purification of the spirit' for the spectator seeing good overcome evil in wondrous expression, evil being accepted in paradox as importantly part of creation as the benign. Rasa imbued in the individual beholder a transcendental experience... that ultimate flash of recognition in the audience, that momentary sense of being united with what the artist is trying to express. **A frisson. A tingle down the spine** when a musical phrase soars, a painting in one whole canvas encapsulates the entire world in meaningfulness, a phrase that rings out across centuries from a writer long gone... such is the enduring sentiment = **sthayibhava** in Sanskrit. **Steadfast**...

So Bharata clearly stepped out from late Vedic times and down from discussing the shastras with Brhm as **Creative Impulse** and gathered up all this conglomeration that ultimately creates the torrential moods of rasa in whatever performance form.

♦ **Touch the right note**
♦ **Perform the right dance** thus a sense of rasa and fusion with Brhm are born from the same place.
♦ **Evoke the right state**

Just as Aristotle in his own assessment of the dramatic process spoke of **catharsis, composure reached often after turmoil of emotions**, so the artist is the symbol for that gift in unlocking the door to a transcendental state through **sadhana** (the perfection of whichever technique through discipline). A **rasika** is such a finely-attuned person in whichever artistic discipline chosen.

Authorised by canon, sanctified by tradition and established by usage is how Dr Kapila Vatsyayan, authority on Indian aesthetics put it. These laws are as operative today as they were when first formulated over 3,000 years ago. Many of the palm-leaf manuscripts which finally contained this body of oral traditions are preserved but very fragile in the temple libraries of Thanjavur in Tamil Nadu and Padmanabhapuram in Kerala.

RASA in the everyday

Rasa does not function alone in the realm of 'high art'. As a force it pulsates at utilitarian level with equal influence. For instance, the simple tool made by the village blacksmith, the fashioner of iron, a stylish peacock is no less a channel for the woman in the kitchen slicing vegetables on the **boti** or **pakshi**, the vegetable cutter. Whimsically delightful (and how different from factory assembly-line plastic tools) the boti takes pride of place in the kitchen where the natural product is utilised by the expertise of the woman of the household (chefs come later!). Fashioned in many shapes, this one is an embellishment of something so mundane as an implement, a subtle allusion to the bird in the tree 'gripping a branch, slicing and abrading the fruit with its hard bill'. And what more appropriate a place for rasa to glow, the **'nutritive essence'**, in what is the 'metabolic centre of the family-community' = that is the sanctum sanctorum so guarded against pollution, the traditional Indian kitchen = **rasoi** where **rasa** that nutritive **essence** is prepared? (Acknowledgement to **Pria Devi**'s **Introduction to Aditi**, the sparkling Craft Exhibition catalogue to '82 **Festival of India** in London, a stunning personal experience.)

■ **RAVANA**
of the **RAMAYANA** is an especially intriguing character, more in the frame of Milton's **Satan** in Paradise Lost, a **fallen angel** full of overbearing pride and arrogance.
Hubris is his undoing. In paintings he occasionally is depicted with a donkey's head embedded in the crown of his own ten heads—an insignia of universal resonance. In English there is a view of the stupidity of a donkey—'as stupid as an ass'. So is Ravana failing to understand where the obstinacy of

R

his pride will take him? Often referred to by Indian writers as a 'demon king' he is strictly speaking not so, but an **a-sura** (not god) constantly trying to subvert the deities of the Vedic heaven.

By tapasya—devotion to Brahma the creator, Ravana received a boon that made him invincible against gods and humans. With his learning (on his father's side he was a brahmin) and the superhuman power given him by his practise of austerities or **tapas**, he became, quite literally, big headed! Four of his heads are said to recall that he knew the four Vedic books by heart as a good brahmin would and the other six that he carried in his head all the wisdom of the six philosophies of India (see **DARSHAN**). His so-called immunity to death at the hands of human beings due to the boon granted gave him a false sense of his invincibility, not realising that Rama was a transitional being (in human form but elevated to more than human), having then the divine capacity to kill him. Occasionally you cannot help feeling a certain sympathy for this charismatic figure (as with Satan's final expulsion in Milton's resonating epic poetry).

Ravana presents a personality of considerably ambiguity. Not all aspects are evil, and his Lanka kingdom is shown to have a high degree of civil life. Like humans, he is a flawed personality and, as an Indian critic has pointed out, 'in his own twisted way, honourable'. But of course in popular culture there has to be a 'baddie' so at Dussehra he is demonized and his gigantic effigy explodes in flames, on the final 10th (das) day of the festival, fired by Rama's flaming arrows to the full-throated roar of the massive crowds—including our young children in those early days, who found this victory over the vaunting strength of evil a far greater release of high spirits than the firing of Guy Fawkes and the saving of the British Parliament!

■ **REGIONAL CULTURES**

In my many wanderings both on my own or with Indian friends in recent years since the death of my husband, I recognise more and more that I have lived a privileged existence partly because of the nature of Derek's professional position with the BBC and the entrée that meant, and secondly my own adventurous nature that pushed me beyond conformist boundaries. This meant we were never tourists, certainly in those immediate years of India standing on its own. Tourism as a separate component of the economy did not even exist.

There were few hotels beyond the major cities. Dak bungalows, the old staging posts for magistrates, judges, administrators on circuit provided the sole solace at the end of a hazardous, dusty and often hair-raising journey. A book about these could be written—the Victorian whatnots, books of great antiquity, amazing khansamas, cooks, who came in out of the shadows even with the most unexpected traveller to create the best crème caramel in the world; or who were occasionally just the opposite. And there were friends scattered throughout the landscape and AIR personnel always ready to overwhelm us with spontaneous hospitality, personal help and enriching experiences so keen were they to show us 'their India', to envelop us in their total family embrace. That meant being warmly welcomed into

their own homes, many traditional joint families with older relatives continuing the flow of their rituals and daily lives unimpeded by yet one more additional member—or two! And our young children in earlier days were great ambassadors, causing the pouring out of a cornucopia of showering generosity and loving care.

In the accumulation of these amazing experiences I began to realize India was not a nation in the Western application of the word and the realities of European geographical boundaries. In fact, the landmass is an amalgam of many cultural nations, distinct in language spoken, script written, clearly identifiable dress, turbans, the way a sari is tied, recognizably different cuisine and permutations of spices.

There is unity, subtly hidden away as I have pointed out in **PILGRIMAGE,** far away from the political/economic hydra-headed India that causes such surprise and confusion at times to outsiders—that amorphous nature of the Hindu/Buddhist/Jain/Sikh way of life, with lack of central authority already discussed in **CORE CONCEPTS**. This continent is hydra-headed, yet united in the matrix of the Indian mind, linked through symbols, legends, artistic expression. That is what makes its regions so fascinating in the way they reflect the underlying unity even in their diversity.

I make no excuse therefore for arbitrarily singling out only a few particular regions, already explained in the **KERALA** section. **KASHMIR** also stands separately for obvious political reasons which cannot be compartmentalized from cultural realities. Punjabi identity crept into so many aspects of our daily lives in Delhi that its presence flows in naturally throughout the text; south Indians and Bengalis were so conspicuous amongst journalists, editors, broadcasters, musicians, that we learnt about those cultures by osmosis and their intense and sophisticated literary eminence influenced from many angles; the northeast frontier provinces in the 50s were such sensitive areas and though now autonomous states, terrorism and inaccessibility made them the one area of India our family never reached.

Uttar Pradesh, Bihar and Madhya Pradesh were so part of north India's ancient history and cultural discoveries as our horizons widened to explore the Buddhist trail and the beginnings of the great sculptural/architectural heritage. They were also accessible, even if challenging, by car, boat bridges, floating rafts, and narrow tracks and daunting nullahs. Tamil Nadu and the Carnatic (the southern region, anglicized thus from **karu** [the black—of a people and an area] *nadu* [the country] and **agam** [home]) have other reasons for retaining stepping stones(see **TAMIL CULTURE, TEMPLE AT TIRUPATI, SOUTH INDIAN KINGDOMS**). It is **Gujarat, Maharashtra, Orissa**—seldom visited by today's tourists, which are the unknowns, far from the trekking states of the Himalayan region and the pioneer of all tourism—Rajasthan. For particular reasons of friendship, serendipitous encounters, and professional reasons, we met Marathi and Gujarati people head-on and at a very basic level.

GUJARAT

If ever a people was clearly defined by environmental factors it is the Gujaratis. As a vibrant community they have always

R

looked beyond the horizon for opportunities to trade, spreading into every conceivable global arena. Today it is no different. The Gujarat state government in the late 90s considered itself the most investor-friendly in the nation according to publicity promotion. Hyperbole that might be and Maharashtrians would undoubtedly take issue! Certainly a good deal of development is still called for in the arid interior with its poor roads and isolated communications, exacerbated by the calamity and dimensions of the 2001 earthquake, its horrendous epicentre around the considerable town of Bhuj in Kuchchh, more popularly called Kutch in tourist literature which caused an alarming human toll, ironically on India's great Republic Day, January 26.

◆ But the real keys to understanding this get-up-and-go attitude of the majority of its doe-eyed, round-faced predominantly vegetarian people (who are not of fighting stock) is in archaeological diggings 80 km west of Ahmedabad. Lothal… another historical find retrieved into the light of day from that vast spread of the Saraswati riverine culture, circa 3000–1750 BCE.

◆ Emerging from diggings undertaken during the last decade, made accessible to the general public, its most recent contours indicate large foundations, well-made bricks, double-storied houses with baths, a drainage system as at Mohenjo-Daro. Apparent two-roomed 'shops' provide evidence of considerable trade and activity such as a bead-making factory, gold remnants, copper and ivory objects, all indications of exchange activities. They are people '**outward bound**'.

◆ One only has to take a look at a map of western India to see the proximity of the prodigious river system of the Indus flowing all the way down from the high ranges of the Mount Kailash region of the Indo-Tibetan Himalayas through Kashmir in a conical triangle with its five-river 'fan' that has made the Punjabis the enterprising active people they are (due to nutritional factors also from rich agricultural crops).

◆ Just over 200 miles up the coast and before the amputation of this Indian region into Pakistan these were peoples, races and territories all part of the same trading ethos. Their lives flourished on commercial enterprise, as much of the hinterland was arid desert and flinty soils. There was also the extraordinary inland shallow salt sea of the Rann of Kutch to contend with. In the drying out period after the monsoon it became a steaming marsh beloved by pink flamingos and the famous herds of wild asses.

◆ Underwater ruins discovered by chance in 2000 during an acoustic survey of water currents in the Gulf of Cambay by the National Institute of Ocean Technology may prove to be a 9000 BCE city similar to Mohenjo-Daro. Ruins of Dholavira also are challenging old theories, an off-shore ruin emerging under the Arabian Sea with a proposal for a 'tourist' tunnel to be built to enable visitors to view it.

◆ It was all so easy to send down the river the gunny bags full of rice and wheat from farther in the interior fertile tracts. Mumbai as a huge entrepôt port has only existed for several hundred years. It is now thought that Lothal was a great centre for exchange of goods, brokerage, moneylending, fixing things–that Gujaratis can do so well, to such an extent they are some of the wealthiest shipping magnates not only in India but in Britain, as well as being enterprising enough to corner the motel business/real estate throughout the USA. Remember **Mira Nair's** film **Mississippi Masala**!

◆ Gujaratis may be seen building up capital with all the family working non-union hours in the ubiquitous cornerstore worldwide but through much of their history along the seaboard edge from Lothal, Ahmedabad and down to Surat (now an echo of itself) they were very wealthy bankers, serving export-import roles for Mughal rulers. Surat became their chief port for textile exports and for incoming coffee from Yemen, Zanzibari cloves, dates from the plantations of Oman, sugar from Natal and Mauritius, and a monopoly of just about everything with East Africa. Archaeological diggings there have provided evidence of Gujarati settlements along the Tanzanian/Kenya littoral. Globalization is no new thing for them!

◆ Ship-breaking is a highly-developed artform in an unprepossessing tiny port, **Alang**, bringing in overseas currency of an inconceivable kind, globally one of the largest such operations in the world, exceptional twice-monthly tides in the Arabian Sea enabling huge tonnage to be dumped on the graveyard shore! This is the hidden wealth in Gujarati hands!

◆ In recent times **the polishing of industrial diamonds** has provided India with one of its largest export outlets, at least 10 per cent overall with an income of billions in US dollars. Such a trade uses a large workforce of hand labour and artisan skills.

◆ A Gujarati friend in Britain once explained to me with great pride when Enoch Powell was in full stride inflaming racial tensions concerning the large immigrations of Sikh Punjabis and Patidar Gujaratis–an enterprising farming sect in the Kaira region south of Ahmedabad (see **MIRACLE–Amul**) that his grandfather among others of his clan had provided considerable loans–a fact not much noticed in British history–to early British firms setting up operations in western India as the Raj took hold and grew in financial and political power.

◆ K M Munshi (alive and well in our earlier years in Delhi) another towering figure of Gujarati society along with Mahatma Gandhi, Sardar Vallabhbhai Patel known as **Loh Purush** (the Iron Man of integrity in the Congress Party at Partition), and Morarji Desai, once commented as acknowledged man of letters and historian on his own people:

The present activities of trading and shipping through the ages led to the rise among them of a well-to-do middle class which dominated social life, influenced politics, laid down traditions and shared with kings the patronage of literature. Acquisition of wealth became an important if not the sole end of life, and the display of it a great virtue. The cosmopolitan spirit of this class, born of international intercourse, did not favour an ascetical or exclusive outlook on life, but fostered the instinct of adaptability and catholicity of spirit. Social inequality was based as much on wealth as on birth and tended towards uniformity.

In fact this is symbolized by the way people of this region address each other without obsequiousness, with respect as **bhai** = brother or **behn** = sister.

♦ Life had more of an even-ness about it compared with other parts of India. Despite considerable wealth, Gujaratis seemed able to hold in balance the ascetic tradition without going overboard on religiosity or fundamentalism. Their faith up until recent times has seen more of a practical application in charitable, philanthropic and more worldlywise activities. Aberrations have crept into the body politic occasionally in state politics which were often tumultuous and in certain temple worship of the Sri Swaminarayan sect, said to be the wealthiest of all the hundreds in India. Strong on female pollution, religious leaders have been loath to sit near women, including high commissioners' wives, at official functions. Even I unwittingly polluted a male devotee by embracing him as well as his wife in front of others. He disappeared to have yet another bath, his wife jokingly upbraiding him for being so orthodox! (It is very confusing to know how to behave spontaneously in this country. At first cautioned never to shake hands or touch in greetings, I found myself embraced from the beginning—and not only by my women friends.)

Over millennia: Not only Indus Valley peoples, Sumerians and Mesopotamians, but East Africans, Greeks, Romans and Persians, Portuguese, Dutch, French and English have all become familiar aspects of a cosmopolitan scene. The interesting development is that short of a minority, vocal VHP/RSS element (noted in **HINDUTVA** and **XENOPHOBIA** section) which I once encountered drilling in ex-army khaki in the back blocks when being taken to some isolated villages linked to the Kaira milk co-operative project, political xenophobia of the Shiv Sena kind in its southern neighbour, Maharashtra, has not flourished in Gujarat until party-system politics of the Westminster-style and the existence of Pakistan on its northern borders, Islamic extremism, terrorism, and its concomitant Hindu politicization for a variety of reasons developed in recent decades culminating in horrific communal massacres involving over 12,000 people in 2002. This was the result of the firing of the Sabarmati Express train bringing back *Ram Sevaks* (voluntary workers in the service of Rama) from Ayodhya. A mob of 2000 Muslim extremists had allegedly incinerated 58 Hindu passengers. The result—political mayhem despite disputed facts, still disputed.

Races seem to have melded into a cosmopolitan attitude taken up interestingly enough in most recent times by the creative impulses which also seem to flourish in artistic excellence both at the most nomadic and tribal society level of the Kutch region (now so well known to overseas textile designers and even film people—**Moulin Rouge** an example of use of Indian fabrics in profusion) as well as among the wealthy, urban elements of Ahmedabadi society (echoing in its very name the coming of

Islamic people both peaceable and marauding). **Ahmed Shah** conquered the **Solanki Hindu** dynasty which founded the original capital in 1063 CE just as a Norman conquest was about to occur in Britain. Recall for instance the creativity and remarkable inventiveness in architecture with Husain's and Doshi's achievements in building the **GUFA**.

The complexities are there, however, those Indian contradictions and paradoxes hidden at the core. The wealth and opulence, the inheritance of the long history in textile trade (see **INDIGO**), the huge mansions and industrial operations, the magnificent Calico Museum, private art collections, international travel of a large number of middleclass families as well as rich gathering up their diaspora. But inside the home simplicity yet a very comfortable domestic economy with good nourishing protein food even if predominantly vegetarian—a society summed up imaginatively at the **Vishalla** refreshment complex outside Ahmedabad which houses an astonishing **Utensils Museum**. Every conceivable piece of kitchenware and vessel you could imagine (over 3,000, says the leaflet) and an area for eating in traditional style with folk culture as entertainment gives a unique experience for those who are not privileged to live in Gujarati homes. Sit cross-legged (even if a strain on unused muscles) at low log tables and clean your hands (your utensils) with special Gujarati antiseptic creamy lather—clay based. These upper urban echelons sit alongside the sparse people of the desert and semi-arid regions of Kutch and Kathiawar, Saurashtra as a whole where living is a constant struggle.

These other Gujaratis survive the flaming heat of summer, the exhausting aridity of the endless dun-coloured environment by colouring their embroidered clothes with glittering dyes of rainbow jewels and embossing their mud and wattle rondavels with clay and mirror work, a useful device also in the textiles to ward off, it is said, the evil eye. Displayed on the walls and chulas/ovens in yantra geometry designs they are highlighted in white rice paste. Painted lacquer-worked chairs in delicate Mughal geometric designs and arabesques, or antique heavy rosewood swings and benches with hammered-in brass inlay designs…. the vivid colours more so than in most other Indian cultural groups, almost in defiance of their surrounds and constraints. As also the wearing of some of the world's most clumpy silver bracelets, necklets, armlets, and toe-rings. Imagine going to the well to draw a bucket of water in 45 degree heat when the silver soaks the heat up!

Mrinalini Sarabhai and the **Darpana Dance Company** creative team so well known in Indian cultural circles for bold experiments on old traditional themes (reflecting similar and parallel architectural developments under Le Corbusier and Doshi's guidance and design) have harnessed the arts along with tourist and hotel promotion to tell this colourful history—**Gurjar Yatra** … a little known story to the outside world and not too well known even to Indians, tourism, strangely enough, neglected as an industry by the state government, as I learned trying to find my way to **Dwarka**. Proof of this, a solo journey by so-called luxury coach along the roadways of the hinterland.

R

Dwarka and its mandir (temple)

I was sent off by the Mavalankars once again after spending leisurely days swinging on their Gujarati *hindola* beautifully embellished with symbolic wrought-iron peacocks, elephants, trailing lotuses. I was virtually on pilgrimage, blessed by Purnima, yoghurt 'thumbed' on to my forehead in benediction, and their many Ganesh murtis clearing the way for safe passage. I needed such farewell! A 12-hour journey by 'express' coach all through the night, one day in Dwarka, and then a repeat journey in reverse, across the drab, sparse countryside of southern Gujarat. Perhaps this is why tourism is difficult to establish, major centres flung far apart. The family sent a very authoritative admin personage with me to make sure I boarded the right coach, arrangements being very haphazard, few locals speaking English, and there being no tourist bus terminal, not even a marked pavement stop on a crumbling sidewalk. All I was told when purchasing the ticket was that the coach stopped 'near a taxi stand'. Of course, when we arrived late afternoon, there was not a taxi in sight!

My Gujarati 'angel', a lady, was very authoritative, a true warrior Durga and most definitely on the warpath! Coach after coach with other destinations was dragooned to a stop and affirmatively questioned. Finally the right one with no apparent means of identification did come to a halt of its own volition. The driver was given a blast of invective for the inefficiencies of the system both in a hose-like power gush of Gujarati and then English. Suitably embarrassed, the driver leapt up and settled me, also suitably embarrassed, in the window seat of the front row set aside for LADIES (strangely enough, labelled in English!).

I was immediately under the scrutiny of 68 pairs of eyes, pinned down like a desiccated butterfly. One seat remained beside me–empty. Perhaps I could stretch out, embedded in my pillow and fortified by Gujarati delicacies provided by Purnima who was silently worried for me... but at the last minute a weeping young couple raced up to the coach while my Durga was upbraiding Gujaratis in general. A young man clambered aboard with four major pieces of luggage. (Shades of **RAILWAYS** darkened my mind.) Where was he to sit?

The young girl, obviously a working woman with her scooter, husband and luggage off-loaded from the pillion seat, was all in red, hands henna-ed. A recent bride!

◆   And that was so. The young man turned to me as he sat down in a volley of words from the coach driver. Did I mind if he invaded this female space? He obviously wanted motherly comfort, clearly regarding me as at least three times his age! I relented and all the other occupants relaxed listening in to the rapid conversation in halting English amid the tearful farewell. Yes, his wedding had been three days earlier and he was off to take up his post as the new catering manager of Tata's large chemical and concrete making factory further down the coast.

Soon my shoulder became his pillow for his lolling head as he sunk into oblivion. Throughout the following night hours despite resistance on my body's hard-pressed part, I was pushed further and further into the hard window glass and metal panelling. At a chai watering hole huge transcontinental luxury coaches equipped with sleeping bunks and upholstered armchairs astonished me, as their travelling public stretched under cascading shooting stars on derelict tarmac. Open holes scattered with lime behind a wall was the not-to-be-remembered toilet stop!

A peach-coloured dawn, the steamy heat of the Arabian Sea even at 6 a.m., biscuit-coloured houses and an oasis of palms greeted us as though we had been off-loaded into Arab terrain. Memories of Basrah sprang from unknown areas of the brain as I recalled a year in Iraq as a 13-year-old following my naval father.

No wonder this utterly bleak coast, so open to the natural elements, was also open to those hordes of evangelical followers of a militant Islam, enthused after the Prophet's death, to convert the 'infidel' to 'the one and only truth'. Sweeping in farther down the coast in the 10th century, they had engulfed Somnath, the famous temple and its legendary wealth, a magnet for looting with its 'unholy' gods to the moon, Soma and the Sun. **Suraj Mandir** (Somnath) is the site of one of the Shiva-hallowed sacred **JYOTIRLINGA** shrines.

◆   The imposing figure that came to collect me out of the spare and bare room in a bed-and-breakfast seaside 'haven'(it was spelled 'heaven' by mistake!) could have walked out of the 10th century also! The 'heaven' was nothing more that a plain concrete ant-hill, and the room was empty, except for a rope bed, one sheet, a lumpy pillow and plain set of drawers atop which was perched a speckled mirror!

Lean as an Ethiopian athlete and striding forth in Harappan robes, shoulder-length hair and beard, a swirl of cotton coiled upon his head, he barely touched the ground as he floated like a Masai hunter, encouraged by his imposingly long 'bishop's' crook, this Sanskrit scholar took me (somewhat breathless) under his wing, having been bidden to do so by the long arm of my Ahmedabad friends calling their friends on the coast. I could barely keep up with him in the dripping heat as he regaled me with the history of 'Krishna's city', 6000 years old according to the archaeological remains, a grey mass of uninspiring bricks deep in the ground. More impressive is the possibility that **Swarnadwarka** (Golden Dwarka) is intact under the encroaching sea (similar to the Alexandrian city discovered under the Mediterranean in 2000). Engineers are now considering building a tunnel to the true centre of Krishna's legendary abode, for world tourists to travel a few kilometres offshore to view this submerged city where once Egyptians, Arabs, Persians, Romans, Assyrians sailed in, to this gateway (*darwaza*). Is *dwarka* (a different derivation) a gateway into India in ancient times?.

◆   My scholar was more concerned to get me to the main temple by noon to see its huge pennant broken on the mast of the immensely dominating and unusual conical spire (nearly 160 feet high) so I was only allowed to pay a brief homage to the shrine of Adi Shankaracharya, not even a pause to rest under the shade of the only fulsome tree in sight, said to have been planted by the sage-saint himself over a thousand years earlier when he established this place as one of the significant quadrants of

R

worship to unify ancient **BHARAT** in these subtle philosophical ways. They are called **mukti-dhams** (centres of release or salvation).

My guide and guardian was also more intent on taking on the persona of a Shakespearian actor. Flourishing his crook he declared in stentorian tones to a startled crowd of pilgrims who gathered around to stare at me, the only firangi in sight, and to listen to his declaration:

*This is **King** Krishna's city! After he slew the mighty serpent of evil, Kansa, he left Mathura and migrated here with his Yadav people. All this happened in Puranic times, many thousands of years ago. This temple, whose shade we stand under, is at least 2500 years old. Take worship!*

With another thespian flourish of his crook, he launched into a quotation from King Lear—word perfect, I discovered later, but the analogy with Krishna, who was more a figure of triumph than tragedy passed me by. I sank on to the cool flagstones, thankful to collapse among the several hundred pilgrims now seated awaiting the midday temple bells signalling the noon arati.

◆ High up on a perilously narrow wooden platform, at the foot of the temple pinnacle, two young men hung on precariously to a rope ladder. One held it at base while the other climbed up. Suddenly the triangular white and red pennant flag galumphed out with a startling crack in the stiff sea breeze, the temple standing majestically on its 60 columns near the shore-line. The youths clung on unsteadily with the forceful pull of wind and canvas.

With little time to pause and wonder I was summoned to line up in a narrow file for women, impelled at speed into the darkened interior where the arati flames were already circling the image with the staring white eyes, encased almost totally in silver foil. The rapidfire chanting of Sanskrit shlokas, the echoing chamber, cymbals clattering, the crush and hubbub of shuffling feet, the force of the crowd propelling me out, again like flotsam, on a tide of swirling people was all too much after a sleepless night and the worst breakfast I ever had endured in India–'wadgy' balls of dried dough, achaar served up on a crinkled leaf plate wrapped in old newspaper!

It took all afternoon and a sticky sleep to recover from this bombardment of the senses only to be collected again by the Rabindranath Tagore figure, this time intent on taking me home, loping his way through intricate mediaeval lanes in the ancient city around the temple precinct. Through a stone doorway I faced a steep wooden ladder. He clambered up with the ease of a langur. I had to remember the agility of a childhood in a country cottage in the heart of Leicestershire where climbing a shorter ladder led into a loft from the ice-cold pantry, a loft full of intriguing curios stored away from all my parents' travels.

But this was Dwarka. I found myself in Tudor-like rooms, low-beamed ceilings, boarded floors on the slope. Here I met the family all crowded in to one floor, his wife, his aunt, his electronic engineer son, his pregnant daughter-in-law (how was she going to cope with such a perilous climb each day and a babe in arms?).

A gargantuan vegetarian thali was brought for me after much ado, other visitors being brought to meet me as much a rare exhibit as the artifacts being dug up nearby! I had to be fortified for the night journey of return–but also as they watched me eat with no escape under their scrutiny came the leading question–how to get his son accepted as a migrant to Australia? It was payback time! I felt as miserably inadequate–an ingrate–as those other itinerants, but traders of antiquity who sailed in from the Gulf, down the Tigris and Euphrates rivers from Sumerian or Babylonian times… to meet a yet more ancient Gujarati standing on some well-constructed dock ready to tie up the craft… And to negotiate that first mathematical transaction–an inherited business acumen that has been reinforced over centuries of perfecting the art–for that is what it is!

A personal footnote: How best to recompense for acts of care and kindness that come unexpectedly. No gift from Australia could ever reach safely. No time, no shop in sight to find a gift on the run as it had been throughout the day. The solution, surreptitiously to fold a few hundred rupees in my notebook paper and in the last namaste to give it with the right hand 'for temple funds'—hoping against hope it would make it into clearly impoverished, but honourable, family coffers instead.

Back on 'home' territory, there are such contrasts! I am waking up soon after dawn to the soothing chant of a gentle voice, my sweet-tempered motherly friend expressing the deep currents of her faith, the family **ISTADEVATA**, Krishna prominent in the simple shrine. I creep in quietly to sit behind Purnima and absorb. The prasad being presented, a gift of a single aesthetically beautiful hibiscus flower plucked from the garden, fruit, nuts and sugar crystals, to be blessed in Sanskrit chants and received back, divine grace bestowed in the giving and receiving like communion bread. (And a remembered warning for the outsider–do not smell the garland of jasmine so seductively beckoning before you present it in the shrine, temple or otherwise as I had done in my first visit to Varanasi's distinguished Viswanath Temple. You will be abruptly dealt with by the purohit with a vigorous push–out of the temple!).

By evening in another home I was drawn into family discussion of where to send their university-educated son and daughter for further training… Canada, Germany, the USA, the UK? The far-flung joint family members wherever domiciled will be ready to provide a home base. I was not even excluded from family financial discussions and questioned closely on my knowledge of the Gujarati communities with whom I had worked in England. And it is not the first time, neither here nor there that I have seen the head of the household, the seemingly quiescent mother become dominant matriarch, laughingly chiding a husband and asserting educational preferences, financial decisions and which family member in the diaspora will assume responsibility! No money transaction need ever occur. Debts incurred overseas can be written off against the costs taken on board on home territory when the far-flung members come on visits back to the motherland.

R

And the next day there will be the simplest of breakfasts, a ritual visit to the temple in almost mechanical speed for a special ceremony marking a point in the horoscope–janampatra, or a local festival, to one deity or another, sattvic food (vegetarian for the rest of the day), a flurry of visitors bringing sweetmeat gifts amid the amassing of wealth. This is, after all, Gandhi's home state as well as the location of his famous Sabarmati ashram. It is the nurturing ground of super-ascetic **JAINS**, with their beautiful temple at Palitana, as well as the home of many Bohra Muslims who strictly abide by many austere Islamic injunctions including refrain from financial speculation and brokerage. **Zakat** paid through mosque channels to the less fortunate than those who enjoy luxurious lifestyles is of greater importance. (They constitute a sizeable component, some 25 per cent of the population.)

And if one is talking of austerity what more its epitome than a prime minister who even *looked* the part–Morarji Desai, one of the band of high-minded fighters for freedom who followed even ritualistic symbols of purity in his daily life. This (claimed on good authority) included the taking of the **panchgavya**–the five products of the cow–milk, ghee, curd, dung and urine, taken in powdered form or drunk as a liquid. In earlier times many of the twice-born, such as Gandhi who had travelled across the **kalapani** (black water) on return from university or legal training in Britain, were cleansed in this fashion on the insistence of ritual-abiding mothers and a whole tribe of household women.

My closest Gujarati friend, Purnima in her gentle way summed all this up:

*We never were feudal unlike UP or Bihar. Either we were tribal nomadic people, like the earliest Gujjars who were beholden to no landlord and created their own community village, or we were entrepreneurs who owned our own home and piece of land. We call each other brothers and sisters–**bhai** and **behn**.*

ᔕᕮᔕᕮᔕᕮᔕᕮᔕᕮᔕᕮᔕᕮᔕᕮᔕᕮ

MAHARASHTRA

We were sitting cross-legged on clean white linen stretched across rush-matting (**paats**) laid on a packed earthen floor in a simple brick-walled hall in the middle of nowhere up on the stony plateau way beyond Poona–now Pune. We were awaiting a Maharashtrian feast in honour of All India Radio's first ever visit to initiate pioneering **Farm Forum** programs, encouraging improved agricultural methods in go-ahead states such as the Punjab–and here in Maharashtra.

English by Radio was then an immensely popular BBC contribution in extramural learning beyond the major urban centres hence BBC collaboration on this project. We were about to experience yet another miraculous activity in this land of continual surprises in improbable circumstances–that of conjuring up tasty food for the masses from sources inconceivable in the West. Even a barbecue is more sophisticated than an earthen chula (oven/hotplate) stuffed with orange-glowing coals.

In abandoned gaiety we were enjoying the company of Marathi literature's leading playwright **P L Deshpande** who was at his most expansive best, full of witty repartee both in English and his mother tongue, along with his AIR crew. Hilarity was bubbling also among the 80 or so farmers, some women members of the **PANCHAYAT** (one of the earliest established in the new Block Development Schemes soon after Independence) and various elders from the surrounding districts. We had spent the afternoon among these pragmatic farmers while **P L** (as he was affectionately called) produced the first live UNESCO sponsored programme based on a successful series undertaken in Canada. The village headman of this panchayat had been convenor and a paid secretary was the liaison to relay such questions from listeners and participators alike back to the central Mumbai AIR station.

P L Deshpande had recently returned from an exchange fellowship with the BBC Radio Drama Department in London. You wouldn't have thought such overwhelming hospitality in return was possible in these back blocks as we had trailed the line of AIR cars clattering across the fragile stony soils 30 kilometres beyond Pune where land lay parched yearning for monsoonal downpours. Neat piles of rich black earth lined the dirt track, brought in to enrich the degradation of decades of neglect under the colonial administration when farming had been directed to the needs of Empire rather than the immediate community of neat villages.

We were in what the Americans would call the 'boondocks', the Australians the outback, and the British would be at a loss to describe being too tiny an island to enjoy the loneliness of spacious wilderness in the total silence of crystal razor-edged stars, the blue-black firmament awe-inspiringly close in the darkness of terrain where no electricity cables then stretched light into the interior. Only the intermittent howl and yapping of pi-dogs (one of India's evocative sounds along with the sharp clack of the chowkidar's heavy wooden stave as he walks the nightwatch, guarding a suburb or doing the village rounds), gave any indication of distant habitation.

The flavours of the land: Shadowy figures silhouetted against the flickering petromax lamps suddenly stirred the atmosphere with delicate aromatic smells. Trotting cooks on the run have etched the memory indelibly after half a century as an engraving on stone. The delicate taste of the repast served that night floats back–half sweet, half savoury, so utterly Maharashtrian. **Jaggery** (brown molasses) and salt, sweet rice alternating with plain fluffy white mountains carried in huge degchis (metal cooking pots), pungent kadipatta (**CURRY** leaf) and infused in the crisp, fresh vegetables, the regional cuisine priding itself in predominantly vegetarian dishes, lentils and mango **koshimbir** (a salad) and **chatni** (the ubiquitous shaved coconut steeped in its own milk along with green chilli)–all this balance of tastes gathered together and served in a traditional sequence of dollops arranged artistically on our individual **taats** (platters). Each ladling spoon places the salt in a tiny scoop, a piece of lemon, the rice on one point of the compass, vegetables at 3 o'clock on the circumference and what I thought was dessert elsewhere in an Indian restaurant, **shrikhand**, a thick saffron-flavoured yoghurt came as a rounding-up of all these subtle sweet-sour flavours with ballooning freshly-crisp steaming puris with their own baked wheaten aroma.

And this was not all! Were we being served whole garlic bulbs? In the gloaming there was a platter presented to us, with everyone watching, of **modakas**—moulded dumplings, the steamed rice flour taking on a shiny softness, stuffed with a yummy coagulation of grated coconut cooked in jaggery. No wonder that in all the stories these are piled high in the upturned palm of all created forms of Ganesh as a sign of his love for good food, which symbolically means well-being and prosperity. He is the patron deity of this state, whose ebullient **utsav** (celebration) is marked every autumn all over Maharashtra and especially on Mumbai's beaches where each suburb vies against the other to create a resplendent murti of the deity. No wonder he has such an expansive belly as well, symbolic of all that well-being brought on by such feasting, replete as we also were that indelibly etched night. And even at this distance, my female mind still nags, never fully knowing the dynamics behind the scenes, how many chulas, how many wives not at the feast preparing the vegetables, how many sweating over the embers cooking puri after puri, such lack of chaos in the organization. Best not to ask! Just go out under the stars and learn to accept, learn to still that restless European mind forever dominated by the how? how? how? of mundane existence.

The dynamics of region and history: What is it about a region that makes it what it is, significantly different, go-ahead in advance of other areas—not just between obviously different nations evolved out of civilisations radically alien to each other but between states, districts within a country—such as Yorkshire, Western Australia, Texas, larger-than-life identities of the core culture they inherit? Heritage… that is one thing—but even nomenclature reflects an attitude of mind.

Maharashtra—the name gives it away, **maha** = great, **rashtra** = nation, state. Why is Maharashtra now the most advanced state in the Union of India? Kerala is more literate but much smaller in geographical area. Maharashtra is the third largest in this aspect but other factors play their part. Juggling a complicated toss of history, environmental terrain, location, chance cross-cultural influences, mythological perceptions, who has settled and remained from elsewhere. Why is it that distinct groups, whether ethnic by cultural traditions, or a predominant caste, within a region give a flavour (rasa) and an energy such as the Marathas did to this particular regional history?

Even **Percival Spear** in his Pelican **History of India** finds it difficult as a historian to explain why a distinct group of western India 'burst forth with such brilliance in the seventeenth century unless one surrenders to the 'great-man-doctrine' and attributes it all to **Shivaji** (sometimes spelled **Sivaji**). 'They were short, stocky, unhandsome in appearance but wiry and enduring, tenacious, enterprising and persevering. They lived in a poor country, had few monuments of the past and little taste for the graces of life.

Hitherto they had had no history but they had a sense of belonging which is one of the pre-requisites of national feeling.'

A long historical memory—and pride—is there. Mumbai, as the nation's dominating business metropolis obviously has been a major factor in pushing the headline: 'WE ARE NUMBER 1'. Possession of this city in the 1956 States Reorganisation caused riots and head-bashing between Maharashtrians and Gujaratis, Bombay Presidency as the region was in colonial times, being well-advanced and cleanly run.* A push to reforms, population control, women's self-help groups is yet another progressive characteristic. Under the imprint *Chaitanya* (vital force) at least 150 such groups have been given training in improving their family plots of land, in planting groundnuts for extra cash income (oil used in cooking), teenage clubs and even girls' cricket teams.

The emphasis on women's socio-economic advancement has always been there—and out of loans given, women have repaid four-fifths of them; at least one woman has bought a tractor and was driving it! Maharashtra women stand no nonsense. Indeed, Fanny Parks, the noted English woman adventurer who moved around India with ease in the early 1800s noted the prowess of Maharashtrian women who rode **astride** their horses unlike genteel memsahibs even in a later time. Nor were they expected to adopt purdah and they rode into battle alongside their husbands. In fact Parks remarked: 'were I an asiatic I would be a Maratta'.

Mumbai is not, however, the totality of Maharashtra. Attitudes of mind go back to the early seafaring exposures of centuries before, and to a sense of yeomanship that was fairly egalitarian in nature, as well as the charismatic figure, Shivaji, taking history by the scruff of its neck and defying the British, as well as Mughal Muslims.

◆ Maharashtra has been described as an **axial state**. As archaeological evidence in recent years exposes a much more extensive Harappan, Indus Valley civilization even further south than expected, it is seen as culturally significant, a transitional 'nation' between north and south, between Sanskritic language systems and those like Tamil, Telugu and Malayalam that may have their roots in a different Dravidian past pushed farther south by those robust cultures of the north slowly moving southward.

◆ 'It is a meeting ground where neither (traditions) may feel strange and both pause in their transition' wrote **Gopal Krishna**, a graduate of prestigious Presidency College, Madras and editor for many years of the widely read **Illustrated Weekly of India** which helped Indians at intelligent but popular level after 1947 get to know themselves again in their own right and without any alien overlay.

Even before the charismatic Shivaji, there must have been an awareness in language, a pride of race born out of the plateau

R

---

* See the darker more poignant side of life for the really poor in Rohinton Mistry's, **A Fine Balance**, a touching novel published by Penguin (Canada) 1995, and 'good on him' as Australians would exclaim. Oprah Winfrey chose to feature Mistry and this book as part of her American TV book club, seven lakh copies being reprinted as a result!

landscape of the Deccan, the precipitous demanding terrain, the divide of mountain, the early intellectual input that has been part of the Hindu/Buddhist heritage going back into pre-Christian centuries. Impregnable fortress after fortress, eagle nests of power atop unassailable bleak ranges speak of a sterner Indian culture than **ahimsa**. From the air, the terrain is contoured to the south in crocodile ridges, sharp escarpments themselves, geological battlements laid down millions of years ago, encrusted and sharp as the Maharashtrians' proud features. Nobody has yet done a study of the effect of 'cave culture' as it could be called, the impact that must have flowed out from the **Karla** and **Kanheri** complexes, **Bhaja** and **Ajanta,** the staunch disciplines it must have taken to climb up to those daunting pinnacles and hundreds of cavernous cells, centres of an incredibly rich and culturally artistic explosion during a continuous flow of a thousand years, virtually uninterrupted in its continuum from the 2nd century BCE to 900 CE.

The terrain demands dedication and devotion for any one who wishes to seek out the guru, the temple, the lay sannyasi from **Kolhapur**, an important centre of Shiva worship and famed for its leather *jootis* (slippers), or the Buddhist monks in **Ellora**.

Along the spine of mountains, steep gradients, innumerable gorges, there was little chance for a settled agriculture. Perhaps this bred a sturdy and enterprising race of people also, but what is interesting is that even before **Shivaji the leader was born in 1630** inheriting his father's kingdom in 1646 and taking to the horse aged 15 to fight his first battles and capture a fortress against Muslim encroachment from the spread of the Delhi Sultanates, there must have been traditions less rigid even in brahmin culture.

♦ A strong egalitarian thread runs through village culture—good education even for women (and in recent times, their political advancement has been to the fore in grassroots state politics), and in the last hundred years within the spiritual life of the people a whole chain of social reformers emerged. **Eknath, Tukaram**, and very low caste **Ramdas**, a cobbler touching leather as he made shoes, to the great literary giant **Tilak**—as well as the powerful Peshwas who administered under British rule.

Our own encounter with the thousands of literary pilgrims of Pandharpur, the spiritual centre of Maharashtra on the roads of its southern region was an eye-opener to us, bearing out this impressive literary tradition. It is a tradition that belongs to all the people and not for the elite alone as occurs in many other countries. The **varkaris** (vari = the annual coming, **kari** = the one who undertakes or does a pilgrimage) surrounded us on the narrow roads, joyously expressing their philosophic poetry as they danced in file, slowing us down so we never reached an old friend **Apa Pant**, one-time high commissioner in London who had been extremely helpful there at the height of Gujarati/Sikh influx from Uganda. His home Aundh, a source of historic devolution by his ancestors to village democracy (explained in detail in his autobiography: **A Moment in Time**, (Hodder and Stoughton, London, 1974) is typical of cultural identity in this state buttressed by this remarkable literary pride not only in the

Vithoba cult we witnessed, but in the **kirtankars**, spiritual balladeers epitomised by local poet-saints **Dhyaneshwar** (13th century) and **Tukaram**, a liberating influence despite his lowly caste (in the 17th century). Their works are sung full-throatedly in the annual pilgrimage (see **ALVARS**). The **tamasha** theatre tradition, a wonderfully boisterous revue-variety programme enlivened by wry humour and political satire is another binding agent. P L Deshpande was a master in this genre, the audience we encountered were rolling in the aisles, as equally delighted with the sending up of bureaucratic inanities as their own family foibles. It will be well worth the while of the visitor to seek out **Hemsuvarna Mirajkar** and her theatre group. Her mime of a wife dealing with a recalcitrant husband in sung mime is brilliant theatre in this genre.

Shivaji

Go back into history. **Shivaji** is on his horse, sometimes gloved in a chainmail gauntlet, arm raised with a curved scimitar overhead, riding out to fight all those who threaten his beloved 'Hindu homeland'. This is a powerful visual image, in recent times amplified as a resonating icon in the collective mind's eye by commissioning of his statues in Mumbai and other towns similar to those of Roman times when emperors **rode forth** ...as **Shivaji** did in the mid-17th century—against the conquering Mughals of Aurangzeb's armies sweeping down to Bijapur, where the largest domed mosque still exists, an architectural symbol of might.

The Maratha leader was then in mid-rule (1646–1680), tempered by the sword in his own upbringing. Born in a fort he died in a fort, Pune his base appropriately now home at nearby Khadakvasla for India's National Defence Academy.

Before he died, he made one of those conquering gestures that would reverberate down the ages in a tribal fashion akin to the Irish tribal sense of politics (for instance the annual Irish marches recalling the Battle of the Boyne). Shivaji undertook a ceremony sanctified by Hindu ritual in which he crowned himself **Chhatrapati**—Lord of the Umbrella, a paramount ruler. Such symbolism emerges again centuries later in our time with tensions between Hindu-Muslim communities. The sectarian politics in the rise of the **Shiv Sena Party** (its nomenclature an obvious indication of parochial loyalties), the defeat of a long reigning Congress Party state government and the emergence of a new chief minister, the now retired Bal Thackeray and his abrasive style of Hindu chauvinism (see **HINDUTVA**), which revolved around the resurrection of this militant image of a ruler fighting for his clearly-defined people's identity as Marathas defending their soil. New statues of Shivaji on his horse proliferated (where is such a Gujarati 'hero' so martially to be commemorated—it is inconceivable!)* Bal Thackeray often appeared in elegant saffron silk robes, swami-like seated in a red-plush chair enthroned like a latter day chhatrapati.

The Mumbai riots in the wake of the Ayodhya mosque destruction in which the poor of <u>all</u> communities suffered grievously eventually caused the law to indict him for activities 'inciting communal passions'. Fortunately, despite these tragedies, a population of approximately 80 million people show on the whole an exciting ability to go global with the largest involvement of foreign companies in joint venture of any of the 28 states. With nearly a quarter of the country's industrial capacity and long-established family enterprises such as the Birlas, Tatas, Mahindras, Godrejs, Wadias of ship-building, Mehtas, Iranis of steel and locksmith fame, other forces of cosmopolitan energy overcame the trauma of the riots, throwing off such parochial recidivism.

Conclusion

It is an energy that takes me back to my original and abiding impression in an upper loft of that panchayat ghar, thrust into a circle of 80 look-alike Shivajis, swathed in top-heavy all-white coiled turbans, and a few Muslims with thin beards. First we were greeted by the produce of the new orchards resulting from a broadcast a year earlier on how to augment their basic agricultural incomes, something they had never conceived of doing by themselves before, there being no village level workers or block development to give them direction or advice, let alone land reform, under earlier British rule. A stocky villager presented a battered plate on which were twelve uncompromisingly fresh green figs which he had just proudly harvested. If there is one thing you cannot do in India, it is to insult a villager's hospitality by refusing anything he proffers. So eat those figs we did under the stare of 160 eyes, my cast-iron stomach having to take the major share as my husband had just recovered from a bout of dysentery.

At that period electricity being non-existent in the villages we sat in the candescent light of a petromax lamp while they thrashed out the subject of Vitamins A, B, C, D, E (how intriguing to hear the English alphabet so familiarly used in voluble Marathi!) A dignified elder brought the gathering to order with a sense of quiet leadership as effective as any parish chairman. Then the subject of agricultural pests and rodents which in village granaries eat up perhaps a quarter of the stored grain came on air. Deep concentration settled like a gathering of yogis engaged in a **yajna** (sacrificial worship). While I admired the intricate detail of embroidered Kolhapur jootis piled up by the entrance and the Bombay Station co ordinator had had his say, it was their time to contribute, relayed back by tape recording to AIR, and convenors' notes to be answered the following week when they would be listening in.

And what to do in exterminating pests such as mice and rats? Pandemonium broke out, full-throated, energetic, and strong with laughter. Even the one woman member was cajoled into saying her piece but then a tall handsome 80-year-old raised his hand emphatically.

Had not the first broadcast beamed out a year earlier to a radius encompassing a hundred villages been blessed in a traditional manner by invoking Shri Ganesh, The Remover of all Obstacles? And is there not a story in the Puranas that tells of Shri Ganesh, Bringer of Success and Prosperity winning a race in heaven? All the important deities were to take part by riding on their vehicles, Shiva on Nandi the bull, Vishnu on Garuda the eagle, Krishna on the peacock; Ganesh rode on a rat's back and by using a certain degree of cunning enterprise, he circumscribed the world of Indra's heaven faster that all the others. He drew a circle in the earth and inscribed the name of God within the ring.

'God is the whole universe,' said Ganesh syllogistically.... 'He is everywhere. I have circumscribed His name and so I have circumscribed the Universe'.

The connection with the rat had its point. The dignified elder cautioned his colleagues about getting rid of rats. How would they escape the wrath of Ganesh if they did such a thing? A hubbub erupted. A voice boomed out in Marathi:

'That is a heavenly rat. Not one of ours. We need pest extermination'.

One can move only so fast with nonliterate (though not unintelligent) villagers without causing painful social upheaval. Russia and China overcame a peasant conservatism by ruthless government. Indians attempt real discussion, fair consideration for criticism, and persuasion rather than force. This democratic way is inherently more slow and inefficient in the early days of growth, but the psychological involvement of the villager seemed to me to be one of the most challenging aspects of India's development, and most rewarding.

Forty years on in Maharashtra people are winning. But the lively old man who had recently learned to write in a literacy class was asked to what he put down his own long 82 years as well as his strong white teeth. Vitamins A, B, C, D, E, perhaps?

'Oh! Ho! That,' snorted the patriarch, 'That's not because of vitamins. That's God's gift!'

R

৯৮৯৮৯৮৯৮৯৮৯৮৯৮৯৮৯৮৯৮

ORISSA

This eastern state south of Bengal deserves its own special mention to redress an imbalance at international tourist level and within the corridors of power at central government level at New Delhi.

Apart from dedicated art lovers aware of the architectural and sculptural treasures at the temple massifs of Konarak, Bhubaneswar and Puri, the myriad multinational merry-go-round of backpackers has on the whole swept past this neglected state. Even disastrous cyclones sweeping in from the Bay of Bengal,

---

* The only 'horse' statue and its conquering hero, with arm wielding an outstretched sword in the whole of Gujarat, is surely a Muslim ruler riding in to found Ahmedabad—Sultan Ahmed Shah in 1411? (So many monuments and domed Indo-Saracenic mosques as a result)—or even Mahmud of Ghazni from Afghanistan, a generation before William the Conqueror?

after the initial flurry of activity, leave a trail of miserable homeless, neglected even years afterwards, ongoing ancillary problems not properly addressed.

♦ In national terms also, apart from the Rourkela steel plant and the Hirakud dam to jump-start industry, Orissa gave the impression of having been passed by, embedded in a rural traditional lifestyle of simple thatched houses, browny-red dust roads, coastal rice fields and tribal areas enveloped in hilly tracks and jungle valleys. With only one mainline rail link, Kolkata to Chennai and hardly any interior road system, a fact hampering Indian firms therefore from investing, despite being termed by its own independent state government 'a storehouse of nature's bounties,' Orissa has been discounted as among India's poorest states; unemployment is high, there being little infrastructure in smallscale or servicing industries.

♦ Above all about nearly half of **Orissa's total population is classified as SCs** (Scheduled Caste–in the past read mainly Untouchable or Harijan) and **ST** (Scheduled Tribe). Such people as the Santal, Kondhs, Parajas, Gadabas and others have on the whole lived secluded lives in scattered impoverished settlements in remote hill areas and jungles cut off from mainstream national life. This is partly deliberate, so vulnerable are they to forceful urban culture.

Orissa is on the move even if the bureaucracy is mired in overwhelming natural disasters (and some questionable lethargy). My personal interest continues because of Australian involvement of an unusual kind, in which my home state and aerial survey companies and local geologists have played a significant part in collaboration with Indian central government and state planning bodies as well as Australian aid bodies. Geophysical flights in magnetic sensitizing photography on a vast grid system may give this neglected landscape and its marginalized inhabitants a raised awareness of mineral and aquifer wealth lying under their seemingly unproductive and leached-out soils but as yet the aerial reports are sequestering on state government departmental shelves.

It is noticeable within India how few **Oriyas** = Orissans cross one's path. Yet paradoxically, from the turn of two millennia ago Oriyas were skilful travellers. Renowned as navigators along with the Tamils, they led and advanced shipbuilding with enterprising Oriyas sailing out to the distant Javanese archipelago and beyond to Cambodia and Thailand. Not only were their ships sturdy, they were spectacularly crafted in elegance as are most Oriya crafts to this day. Orissan navigation expertise was apparently recorded by Ptolemy, the Alexandrian mathematician, geographer in the second century CE.

The Arts of Orissa

This quality appears to be innate as though some ancient gene tracking back to the original aboriginal inhabitants is still locked into mental processes undisturbed by the geographical isolation of the tribal peoples and protected by the deeply traditional culture of temple cities. The expertise thousands of artisans must have generated in unbroken family lines is a power

that can despite neglect and dilapidated temples be resurrected at a moment's notice.

Watch a village woman clad only in a sari and glass bangles begin to stir soaked rice steeped overnight into a paste. Within a few hours the rich brown-textured wall of mud and dung that she had applied the day before to cleanse the long low thatch hut had dried to a perfect canvas, and will now become an enchanting art frieze of lotus buds and floral scrolls, and geometric pyramid patterns of the heaped rice brought in from harvest. The stylized feet of Lakshmi will appear to give honour to the goddess to whom they all as peasants pay homage for the fitful abundance she has granted. Lively elephants prancing in skittish fashion, peacocks with elongated tails, symbolic kalash the pot of plenty, daisy patterns and stylized chequerboard friezes will enhance nature's earthiness.

Although I never had the privilege of living 'inside' Oriya family life, absorbing a way of life(i.e., culture) from the moment the morning worship is murmured, we encountered Orissan writers and artists *outside* the state who led us into their extraordinarily lively world. Everywhere there is this numinous sense of being part of the very earth that is one's integrated base. Perhaps that is because so much of the riverine area 60 km from Bhubaneswar is linked by oral tradition to the two major **EPICS**, Ravana having supposedly undertaken severe penance in the Prache river area to win over Sita. There are innumerable temples also dating from 10th to 12th century and holy pilgrimage places dedicated to the goddess and one unusually to Brahma, the only other to this creator-force being at Pushkar in Rajasthan.

Walk through the thatched village of **Pipli** approached by a meagre bitumen road along the Puri to Bhuveneshwar highway. Be stunned by the vibrant market stalls with the primary colours of a myriad appliqué bags, umbrellas, wall hangings, shamiana tented covers startling the eye amid the dun-coloured dusty surroundings. Expert basketmakers, men and women weave brilliant colours into hardy containers, large doll representations of those most famous triple deities **Jagannath,** his elder brother **Balarama** and their sister **Subhadra** (see **PILGRIMAGES**). All remain truncated with stumpy arms, it is said because the divine carpenter (see **PANTHEON**), in a typically delightful Indian way, was disturbed and left them unfinished!

The nearer one gets to the temple structures, artisans (*chitrakars*) can be hunted out who paint the famous **Patachitra** paintings on specially treated palm leaf and cloth (*pata*), whimsical 'manuscripts' in lively stylized comic-strip narratives of the legend of the triple-image dark god Vishnu and his siblings–such fantastic forms sold as **icon paintings** (*chitra*) to millions of pilgrims, a tradition kept alive for at least eight centuries and unique in Indian folk painting. (Our own two painted by an idiosyncratic artist who 'saw visions' have all the hallmarks of a mediaeval manuscript. All manner of activity within the gigantic temple to Jagannath follows a quirky comic-strip narrative, with a frivolous 'Monty Python' touch of humour here and there such as individual European monks used to add within the golden scroll capital letters of their illuminated texts.)

R

Lack of patronage since Independence nearly obliterated this tradition. Royal patrons had in older times encouraged village artists. At last an Orissan Art conservation movement has begun to resuscitate this rural tradition. Fifteen km from Puri hunt out the village of **Raghurajpur** and be astonished.

Which brings one to the magnificence of the three temples, of **Lingaraj** at **Bhubaneswar**; the **Sun Temple** at **Konarek** and the **Sri Jagannath Temple** at **Puri** where from time immemorial Vishnu in the form of Nilmadhav was the power of the universe (**Jagat Prabhu**) freely worshipped and approachable by all castes and creeds, even untouchables free to enter the shrine when elsewhere in pre-Independence India they were shunned as pariahs.

The Temples

Entirely different from the magnificent grandeur of the huge south Indian temple complexes with the entire population of the **PANTHEON** in painted profusion climbing up the stately gopurams, the Orissan complexes have an architectural form all of their own—the sanctum in which divinity glows deep within the garbha-griha (womb-house) in metaphor of the indwelling divine consciousness resting within every human soul. Towering over this sanctum is the vimana, conical and rigid outside like a gigantic fir cone, capped wih an enormous flattened ring of stone like a stylized pancake turban of the old South.

But it is really the quite remarkable scale of the embellishing sculpture, the love divine and natural lust for life, as expressed in the male-female joyousness of sexual union, the magnificent strength of the horses that pull the 13th century Konarak Sun Chariot and the finesse of the lyrical and sumptuous friezes all around that astonishes... for example the exquisite detail of the carved embellishment and the tactile 'feel' of the mottled sandstone, with huge **apsaras** or nymphs melon-breasted in their fulsome beauty, with long finely chiselled noses, playing musical instruments and dominating the roofline. As they survey humble mortals below, they leave an unforgettable impression of sensuous majesty. Then, a manageable population could live off the land with a sense of abundance. Certainly from the 7th–12th century records state that some 7000 temples were built—an industry in itself!

Every one of the 24 wheels of the Konarak chariot, each seven feet across, has finely crafted medallions on the spokes and hubs—deities, lovers, warriors, musicians, and all around the circumference of each wheel a rolling design of floral leaves entwined with stylized natural forms. All along the base an endless parade of hundreds of feisty elephants, jostling and playfully butting each other in this gigantic queue.

Sublime and aloof, having lost half his arms from vandalism, the **Surya** deity in his stylish scalloped travelling boots is the more remarkable for the fine detail of the leg raiment on his thighs—patiently chiselled with expert control in delicate panels, descending one after the other as though woven in the finest of fine cotton, again not one panel the same. Indeed, Krishna Kripalani, then Secretary of the Sahitya Akademi (of Letters), who became a close friend, declared to us that until we went to Orissa our life in India would never be complete, these complexes truly 'the highwater of Indian artistic accomplishment'.

Such wealth, such profusion, such flare, such tenderness of loving glances and ecstasy in the consummation... nothing was haphazard, nor crudely executed, delightful humour will out as monkeys playfully fool around, frozen for all time in vivid sculpture. Grace abounds from the earliest, now ruined, temples of the 7th century at Bhubaneswar through to the 13th–14th century at Konark.

the most splendid luminary in the firmament of Orissan architecture but is sadly the last flicker of the architect's lamp, never lighted again to dispel the gloom which soon enveloped this hapless land....

And where has all the talent gone? And hope so long to remain hapless when other states are surging forward?

Dev Prasad Ghose may well lament the passing for nothing much has changed since his article on the **History of Orissan Hindu Temples** was penned for the special issue of **Marg, A Homage to Orissa** (September 1955). But watch for new initiatives despite the 2001 census pointing to some inland districts around Koraput being 'India's absolute worst' ravaged by poverty. Can new initiatives be sustained? Such as the pioneer **Konark Festival** annually in December.

■ **RSI or RISHIS** (n. *Sanskrit* and English = see, seer)

A **seer** as indicated in the root syllable and pronounced with a rolled R. Someone who has withdrawn in the very beginnings of Indian society, even pre-Vedic perhaps, by tradition to the great forests of early India before they got cut back for firewood as the population swelled. There to live simply, aesthetically and thoughtfully in order to ponder the truths of the universe—how came the creation, the universes upon universes of which they were aware long before modern rocketry, space probes and satellite technology brought the rise of planet earth in all its blue and white glory from behind the moon onto our TV screens in 1969?

The very fact that there are so many similar Sanskrit or Hindi words to express a similar state as rsi is indicative of how revered rsis have been through the ages. Indeed they have been regarded as 'beyond the celestials'.

Sages, gurus, swamis, acharyas, hermits, mendicants, munis, pandits, sadhus, sannyasis, wanderers, pilgrims all reflect this emphasis, redolent of the constant search on the lonely road of **self-realization**. This, says the Indian, can only be attained by going beyond actual empirical knowledge to that superior trained mind of super-consciousness where the intuitive knowledge brings inspired flashes of true understanding of the nature of the universe, and the world within ourselves, often without conscious thought being employed. Suddenly something makes sense when least expected!.

The Hindu ark was filled with a precious cargo—a passenger list of great eminence, the **seven traditional rishis**, the *saptarshi* = sept = seven. They inspired moments of revelation after deep meditative concentration, composing the vast body of Vedic

R

poetry—which really was distilled philosophy in Sanskrit quatrains. They were all brahmins except one who (born a kshatriya) by intense austerities raised himself to become a brahmin. **Viswamitra** was this man, a character who clearly was of such intellectual strength he did not suffer fools gladly—nor his equals if the legends passed on about his acerbic struggles with another of these famous seven, **Vasishta**, are anything to go by.

These perennial quarrels appear again in the **EPICS**, especially in the Ramayana. Such are the implacable foes however that curses rain on each other, they are turned into cranes, boons are granted, penances undergone 'for a thousand years', seduction by heavenly apsaras is attempted on behalf of Indra's request to help keep the peace but the two old men are at each other's throats quite literally through the ages, only finally reconciled by the intervention of the materialised creator—**Brahma**!

The other seemingly milder rsis who behave in a manner more appropriate to their sagacity are **Bharadwaj, Jamadagni, Kasyap, Gautama** and **Atri**—all associated with the creation of the various Vedas. Linked with Vasishta in Rigvedic hymns is the equally celebrated rsi **Agastya** often depicted in temple friezes of the Ramayana, bearded and benign, giving advice and sanctuary in his hermitage to the exiled Rama. He is also honoured in the south as one who inspired the founding of the Tamil language… nevertheless he doesn't seem to have made it into the ark! Rather than assume a case of discrimination (again!) maybe the Himalayan glacial melting never flooded the south…

An informative book dedicated to the rsis is **Rishis in Indian Art and Literature** by **C Sivaramamurti**, (Kanak Publications, New Delhi, 1982).

■ **RTA/RITA** (n. *Sanskrit*)

One of the fundamental **CORE CONCEPTS** of Indian thought, it has been called 'the implacable law' originating in the search for comprehension of the cosmos... **firmly fixed are the foundations of rta shining in beauty, manifold are its beauteous forms.** Rigveda 4.23.9

RTA expresses:

♦ The metaphysical 'ground' of dharmic thinking about order and patterning in the physical cosmos and human consciousness.

♦ The right order in the universe according to intrinsic laws such as the ellipses of the planets or the flame to fire.

♦ Correct, straight as in a rite, ritual. (Refer to **VEDAS** and **CORE CONCEPTS** for greater elaboration).

♦ **DHARMA** and **rta** are closely related. 'When humans violate those principles of balance between rights and responsibilities, privileges and obligations they violate the ordered structure of the cosmos also, as envisaged by rta.' This was Gandhi's view.

♦ The universe, the world, human beings are all of a piece; Donne's famous phrase again—all part of 'the Maine'.

God would cease to be God if He swerved from His own
Laws
even by a hair's breadth

is how Gandhi once put his own ideas on this resonating statement.

SABHA
SAMITI SANGH SAMAJ SAMMELAN

- All these words indicate a gathering of one kind or another, a **committee** or **association.**
- **Samiti** is a council of elders
- **Committee** comes from the same Indo-European root of the Sanskrit.
- **Sabha** is the gathering of elected members of the populace and princes, not the whole assembly.

A record from Uttaramerur in Tamilnad, dated in the reign of the Chola King Parantaka, in 10th century AD, is one of the most valuable historical documents of the country. It gives in minute detail, the functioning of the village committees and records the qualifications and disqualifications of the candidates standing for election, the division of the village into various wards, the main village committees, various sub-committees and their respective functions. Such village committees looking after the administration of the villages, as recorded in thousands of inscriptions, reflect the functioning of democratic institutions in South India for over 1300 years. **Tamil Conference 1995** as reported in **The Hindu.**

Deliberative bodies, the **sabhas** and **samitis** come of a very ancient lineage, almost certainly even earlier than those that evolved in Greece which injected the word Demos into the English language 2,500 years ago. Apparently the concept of an **assembly ruled by categories or numbers** is found nearly 50 times in the Rig Veda, and it evolved as oral literature circa 4000 BCE.

Kings, rulers, monarchies were limited by considerable moral strictures **with the rule not of temporal law but the over-arching moral RTA of DHARMA.** The elected village **PANCHAYATS** were there to back such rule.

- Within the benign anarchy of individualism and freedom of belief deep in the central core of Hindu framework, the paradox is there of equally deep and entrenched respect of law so strongly stressed at a much later date in **KAUTILYA'S Arthashastra.** Prior to the coming of the British system of local administration there was clearly a quite coherent functioning of self-government in practice in many regions, far more than is understood by outsiders. 'That the Hindu culture and its rich civilization had survived the depradations of centuries, is particularly due to the system of self-governing local councils which exercise large executive and judiciary power', was how historian **Radha Kumud Mookerji** explained this fact as far back as 1919 in his book **Local Government in Ancient India** (Oxford, 1919).

This foundation of the nation's present village social structure (the panchayat) is obviously very sophisticated, developed so far back in time but now resurrected from the ashes of colonial neglect. No matter how faulted it can be in backward states and corrupted and threatened by the new criminality in state politics and mofussil inertia, the sense of **stewardship** (which used also to be a strong force in Christian community leadership before the age of self-gratification) provides a remarkably committed impetus to the successful functioning of these sabhas and samitis. Resonating deep within the psyche is the fundamental truth of this saying: **panchon main parmeshwar**, the Sanskrit contraction of **param-iswara**, the paramount 'presence' implied in the voice of 'the five' (= **panch**, **main** = in). That is the voice of the supreme deity. The concept of the rsi-guru-shishya(pupil-student) parampara backed this ability to speak out—Buddha indeed had advised acolytes not to follow the guru blindly. 'Verify things for yourself'.

SACRED THREAD

is another quintessentially Indian symbol, a triple-threaded twirled cotton loop knotted by priests in an especially important Hindu ceremony to initiate young boys into the upperclass system. In orthodox families even now the **upanayana** ceremony is of grave importance although gradually neglected among more recent younger generations except as much-abbreviated ritual preceding the wedding ritual.

For a child it is first properly *'heard'* as the **GAYATRI** in a ceremony (the **word** as has often been stressed, being held as of paramount importance) at the equivalent of the Christian baptism—the **mundan** ceremony when the first lock of hair is cut, between the age of two and five. This is a family ceremony in the presence of the family pandit or the guru/teacher/priest at a time when the child is approaching the first of the four stages of the Hindu's life on earth—that of the student or brahmacharya. In Hindu thought any child up to the age of four or five is building up images of people, values, what is right and wrong, how to behave, images which float in its consciousness but do not necessarily take on any coherence.

The taking of the sacred thread (itself symbolic, triple-threaded as it is) occurs therefore at about the age of seven when a child can correlate thoughts and events, and has some ability to understand the solemn vows undertaken as someone reborn: 'twice-born'. It is at this stage that the concept of what is to be a dutiful and right-living Hindu first impinges on the child's mind.

In traditional society it was at this stage that a high-caste child left home to go to the guru's house to study Sanskrit and the scriptures, hence the name **upanayanam**. It means the act of being led to the mentor or guru (cf. **UPANISHAD**). The thread is white to symbolise purity and the triple **tri** recalls all the threes that have global significance—**trimurti, trinity, triangle.**

- The ceremony is a true rite of passage more like a rebirth and baptism into the true faith—an elaborate ceremony, the auspicious time chosen for the son by the family horoscope reader, at which the Gayatri mantra was *whispered* in the young boy's ear under a cloth.
- This also was symbolic because in those times of antiquity when priesthood and ritual and the correct intoning of the mantras was all-important, the learning of this prayer which was to be recited every morning for the rest of one's life when taking a bath, or immersing one's self in the sacred river facing the sun and letting the water run through the fingers or at the temple holy tank, was of supreme importance.

S

■ **SADHANA** (n. Sanskrit)

with the emphasis on the long first syllable, is the practical discipline undertaken in a devotional sense which accompanies the ongoing inner spiritual quest for absorption in the ONE moving energy of the cosmos. **YOGA** itself is the prominent and effective discipline in harnessing the wayward mind's focus. But all caste-ordained duties and obligatory rituals of the old traditional social order in India, one's own **svadharma**, testing pilgrimages, undertaking fasts, even becoming vegetarian are all part of the sadhanas which aid the individual **ATMA** along the progressive self-realisation path to liberation.

◆ Such self-imposed dedications are not regarded as daily chores, a dreary exercise. In fact people speak of a sense of heightened enjoyment = **bhoga** the way young people speak of 'a high'–but reached without drugs.

◆ At the tantric level, sadhanas extend the psycho-physiological experiences through ritual after ritual, contemplating specified diagrammatic yantras (ceremonies of such antiquity traced back possibly to the origins of magical rites into the taboo world of fertility and sexual union) to ritualise the search for ultimate union with our lost origins in space and time.

Self-control as a part of this devotional discipline, a very important constituent of dharma, is likened to the tortoise seen embossed in the flagstones of some temple entrances especially in Maharashtra. According to the maxims of Saint **Tiruvalluvar** (see **TAMIL CULTURE**) in the **Tiru** (sacred) **Kural**–short aphorisms of Tamil literature, that individual is to be praised:

Behold the man who can draw
into himself his five senses even as
the tortoise does its limbs;
he hath laid up for himself a treasure
that will last even unto his seventh reincarnation.

■ **SAFFRON**

has been called 'the emperor of the aromatics'.

A bulb *crocus sativas* grown in Kashmir (and Spain) which is very expensive to harvest and therefore treasured in cuisine. Indeed the way the genuine burnt sienna-red stamens are treated and sold in tiny quantities in India in sealed containers to prove their purity, it is no surprise to learn that saffron is more valuable pound per pound than pure gold! Picking out the three red/orange stamens at the heart of the flower, freshest in the dew of early morning is very tedious and labour intensive. To obtain the best flavour, soaking half a dozen stamens in a tiny amount of water releases the flavour and the glorious kesar (saffron yellow) to rice dishes and **srikhand** dessert, especially eaten in Gujarat.

◆ As a dye it is not known how ancient its colour has indicated holiness but across a particular spectrum from pure yellow through mustard tones to orangey-red, the wearing of the saffron robe has been a mark of the sannyasi, the swami, the monk, the learned wandering mendicant hermit, not only in India but throughout Asia for as long as recorded history… the reason why in answer to the question so often put to me, that of the most famous Mahatma of all in this last century despite all his detractors and who has had the most political influence internationally—Gandhi—is why he never wore saffron-coloured cloth? … The answer—he was still a householder despite his absences at his ashram—not a sannyasi.

Saffron as a sacred colour is now being sullied by polemical usage, a new phrase creeping into English = **saffron politics.** This refers to the ideological spectrum of minor political parties attached loosely to the BJP who assert and emphasise Hindu **rashtra** (country) identity after a thousand years of psychological, cultural and political subjugation from alien domination, predominantly militant Islam and culturally dominant Europe, especially Britain. Belonging to the **Sangh** = organisation, **Parivar** = family, they fly saffron pennants and some even wear saffron to proclaim their identity in the **Rashtriya Swayamsevak Sangh, Vishwa Hindu Parishad, Bajrang Dal and Hindu Jagran Manch.**

■ **SAMADHI**

Those who reach this final stage in the yogi's disciplinary quest have gone beyond consciousness. B K S Iyengar, guru par excellence and mentor to the late Lord Yehudi Menuhin, writes this:

At the peak of his meditation, he passes into the state of Samadhi, where his body and senses are at rest as if he is asleep, his faculties of mind and reason are alert as if he is awake. Singing the praises of this utterly 'serenely balanced' state Shankaracharya described it as a 'going beyond' for those who have learned this concentration and saintly withdrawal:
I have no misgiving of death, no chasms of race divide me. No parent ever called me child, no bond of birth ever tied me: I am neither disciple nor master, I have no kin, no friend—consciousness and joy am I and merging in Bliss is my end.
SAT: CHIT: ANANDA, none other!

It is as though great souls **will themselves** to death yearning for the ecstatic contact with ultimate reality… with such tranquil joy as Vinoba Bhave did on **November 15, 1982.** '**He did not die a natural death. He invited it'**, wrote Vasant Nargolkar, fellow Maharashtrian about Vinoba's final days fasting, insisting on dying as a yogi at the Paunar Ashram, noting that other great Maharashtrian saints **Jnaneshwara** and **Ekanath** (significant names in their meaning alone) 'had put an end to their lives when they felt that they had fulfilled their life missions.' This is sanctioned by Indian custom, foregoing all nourishment till the end.

◆ Tyagaraja's own documented extraordinary 'realisation' has been recounted earlier. They are but a few of the hundreds known to have chosen their moment of death to this life (see **PREMONITION**).

◆ **Samadhi** also refers to the platform erected on the spot where cremation takes place such as Gandhi's and Nehru's near the Jumna River in Delhi, visited by a constant stream of people every day of the year.

S

SAMSKARAS

Sacramental rites of passage such as birth and marriage. **Samskaras** have a deeper meaning however, in Sanskrit, implying habits/traits of personality fashioned by certain impacts, impressions—this is not formal education but lessons in life-giving wisdom = to **gn**ow, according to my ever-patient Hindi teacher. Indeed rites of passage are a 'stepping over' to another level in the individual's advancement—acquiring **values** as one matures. Some Indian friends would tell me this process is more than that, more a karmic 'residue' from a previous life, re-surfacing and adding substance in the onward development of personal atman.

SANATANA DHARMA

Term used by Hindus for their faith which is not regarded as a 'religion' but a way of life. It means the everlasting **eternal law and order (DHARMA)** both for humans and the cosmos, embracing all peoples (and natural forces) no matter their faith or beliefs, the Hindu view being inclusive of all, very different from semitic faiths that exclude those who are not believers, beyond the fold (see **CORE CONCEPTS** and read the lucid account of the term in David Frawley's **Hinduism:The Eternal Tradition** (Voice of India, New Delhi, 1995).

SANDALWOOD (n. *Hindi = Chandan*)
Santalum album

Just as the visual rainbow of colours seduces the eye of the beholder in India, the cacophony of sound assaults the ear, so the very flavour not only tempts the taste buds but insinuates its lifelong tendril hold through the nostrils into the innermost recesses of the psyche.

When 'the wet' deluges the parched soils of Australia and I am driving on the corrugated dirt roads of the outback, India floats back again from the paste of reddened laterite—the pindan—turned into a quagmire. It is the same unmistakable smell of rain on dry ground.

Anyone who had the fortune to travel out to India soon after independence—leisurely and balmy days by P & O liner before the horrors of jet flight—awaiting a morning berth in Bombay's docks will instantly recall that waft of air on the humid night, a bouquet far more complex than wine tasting... jasmine and urine, dried earth stirred into a thick porridge by monsoonal downpour, woodsmoke and cow pat, mellow spice and dalda, hydrogenated vegetable oil in a distinctive yellow tin, frying in the the bazaar, cinnamon and pungent fenugreek—perspiration, perfume and pong—layered like rockstrata, indefinable yet unmistakable all at one inhalation—and **sandalwood**.

The background of aroma will be this—**sandalwood**. Funeral ghats smoking, bazaars full of finely carved masterpieces, temple worship and sticks of fragrant wood, hollow canals secreting oil, ground down on large stone slabs like spices in the mortar, by a temple functionary. A little water added, the paste will be used to anoint the forehead of deity and devotee alike.

Reputed for its medicinal properties also, antibacterial and cooling to the skin, sandalwood is part of the cultural fabric like turmeric roots are to the social customs of the nation. Usage in religious rites must go back to pre-Vedic ceremonies. In many such references descriptions of nature appear also in the 12th century Gita Govinda where Krishna, *for once* pining for his Radha, is comforted by the poet:

> Art thou sick for Radha; she
> > is sad in turn,
> All the cooling fragrance of
> > sandal she doth spurn.

SANDHYA VANDANAM

and the Gayatri invocation are the most important daily rites for orthodox brahmins to perform at dawn, midday and as the sun goes down; sandhya being at the junction of the day's triplex division. All orthodox upperclass Indians will at some stage undertake this purification ceremony, a **SAMSKARA** or sacrament going down to stand in a river or a temple tank, allowing the water to trickle through the fingers of both cupped palms, expiating their sins as they recite the Gayatri to the personification of solar energy—the effulgence of the Sun, giver of life on this planet and 'illuminator' of the intellect.

An Indian once wrote:

These observances develop in us a feeling that we are part of a wider scheme of things in which our own life is in rhythm with the elements... our daily pursuits are directed by this ceremony toward achieving what Huxley terms 'upward self transcendence'—latent in us are enormous energies if only we can harness them by physical and mental discipline. This course of thought led us to yoga.

The wide world has now discovered the universality of **YOGA** and its meaning beyond any particular faith.

SANNYASI (or **sanyasi**)

is someone who has taken **sannyaas**, a unique concept in Indian life. The root word from **bhara nyasa** implies **laying down a burden**—meaning that in approaching a Deity the devotee is in total surrender—'with no bargaining possible' (as an Indian friend put it). 'You live your best and leave the rest in serenity to the forces of the Deity.'

This is the fourth stage of life, symbolically the last quarter aged 75–100 years in which caste can be set aside, a symbolic 'funeral' rite performed, the individual virtually 'dead' to society. The individual is free to loosen family ties (a sense of letting go) and to follow the lonely path to salvation in complete renunciation of all local binding ties in order to embrace the entire world as one's own.

The need to think on higher things is a constancy in the social order. Indeed through the **ashrama system the ascetic is honoured and encouraged**. Indian society (not just Hindu) is in fact one of the few in the world which places the teacher-saint-ascetic above that of the ruler-raja who has to defer and do **pranam** (a bowing down in reverence even to touching the feet of elders, or more eminent or holy people) with hands folded in namaskaram.

S

The silent energy of the Gandhian fast, of civil disobedience satyagraha which ultimately undermined even the entrenched imperial rule of all-powerful Great Britain, indicates the power of the ascetic force symbolised by the sannyasi stripped of all material wealth and power.

♦ It would on the surface appear to be a male preserve. No mention is made in texts of women leaving husband and home for the open road. Wendy O'Flaherty, eminent US-based Sanskrit scholar notes this **'element of ascetic misogyny'**. However **Holy Ma-s** exist but they have all the appearance of comfortable plump grandmas than lean loners of the pathways into solitary confinement.

♦ **Sadhus**: In no way mistake the two. There may be great devotees who become sadhus but the exhibitionist sadhu who begs at great melas is, in my female experience, to be kept at a distance—for obvious reasons! Certainly a minority of these physical ascetics are quite clearly charlatans and tricksters, and suspect.

♦ A **muni** is also an ascetic who has given up speaking—withdrawn in silence = *mauna.*

■ SANSKRIT
Sam = with, together
Krita = to act, done, accomplished thoroughly

is the fundamental stepping stone which forms the distinctive clusters of Indian thought patterns (see **DEVANAGARI** and **LANGUAGE**).

Although considered a 'dead' language by some, not being a 'spoken' language in daily use, because of its essential nature in expressing the Vedic hymns and symbolic mantras, it still bubbles in the hidden channels of India's thought processes.

Sanskrit's Inner Meaning

As the word Sanskrit suggests, it was the means of expression of **'the cultivated'** urban society, of a sophisticated high order of civil life and the **instrument through which to retain that purity of basic structure and tradition** so beloved of brahmin belief—and lifestyle… something worked up, like a refined craft, till perfected.

'The interesting thing is' according to a Tamil brahmin friend 'that any day in our newspapers of the south you will see religious discourses and gatherings advertised or reported upon in which Tamil and Telugu is being used as the *lingua franca* but at least a third of the words will be Sanskrit yet easily understood by all kinds of people in the massed audience.'

Embedded into the Indian capacity to think all-in-the-round (**synaesthesia**, pattern recognition is Richard Lannoy's word for it), it must surely be Sanskrit's remarkable structural complexity and multi-syllabled words **that are virtual symbols in themselves**, condensations of the matrix, that are the key to such subtle capacity and deftness of expression.

Arthur Koestler, discussing the complex matrix of culture and language once suggested that attempts to translate Hindu beliefs and attitudes into the verbal concepts and categorical structures of Western language leads to logical monstrosities. (In fact, in reverse, All India Radio as a government arm in promoting Hindi as the national language incurred the wrath of its listening public in translating in reverse English technical terms into polysyllabic Sanskritized Hindi for its news bulletins.)

Koestler further pointed out that in Eastern philosophies 'symbolic and literal meaning were never separated', concepts and grammar remained fluid. He concluded that for many Indians this lack of definition of belief is very appealing—no creed, no dogma, no specificity in what should be believed as absolute truth, **BRHM** being referred to as the Impersonal Absolute.

Herein lies the paradox again—a law of opposites that arouses question marks in the Western mind. The Sanskrit language at one edge of the huge spectrum arc of language and meaning is refined like a precision tool with rigidly-defined grammar—and more exceptions to the rule than can be imagined!

♦ Yet at the other end of the spectrum one word can explode into a swastika-shaped **cluster of thought**, what **Richard Lannoy** refers to in another context as 'the simultaneous interconnectedness and all at-oneness' of things as he probes even further into the complex depths of India in his own profoundly thoughtful book, **The Speaking Tree**.

♦ But not only a word. A character can also explode into an entire philosophy. Such is ॐ.

Even in the sound sense, listening to Sanskrit well spoken has an extra dimension to it, a psychic effect, even if not a word is understood. Once on a public platform Professor Sarvepalli Radhakrishnan, master orator, commanded profound attention in his audience as he launched into a Sanskrit reference of such sonority, cadence upon heavy cadence, solid stepping-stones of sound, that by a strange psychic effect an inner meaning took over—one felt one knew what had been said.

Christopher Isherwood who with Swami Prabhavananda has also translated the Gita reiterates the demanding nature of Sanskrit in putting it into basic English because it is so 'compressed and telegraphic'. Yet it abounds in exact philosophical and spiritual terms.

A Mental Framework and Educational Implications

This compression and density has been considered by Lannoy, a synaesthesia, which encourages 'intuitive pattern recognition,' qualities of thinking which could well be of immense value in our present challenging rapid-change technologies overtaking society with a multi-media assault of all-at-one-and the-same-time daunting proportions.

India has an unrivalled opportunity to overcome some of the most intractable difficulties of underdevelopment in an entirely new yet readily accessible way, peculiar to itself (such as sophisticated Indian intermediate technology co-ordinated with de-centralised, small-scale community living) in other words, modernisation of the 'self-sufficient' village community…

Gandhi would have rubbed his hands in glee at such a statement. And indeed Lannoy's acute observations over 30 years ago on Indian thinking are becoming matters of reality with India's proven aptitude for all activities of the electronic media and the

S

internet communication which is far from linear in patternings. Their electronic experts are sought worldwide for they have 'come home' to an all-in-the-round system of thinking!

The astonishing thing is that supposedly 'illiterate' people (by our Western criteria of measurement) think in as equally sophisticated a way, philosophically, as any educated brahmin. Experience after experience with my long-suffering Hindi teacher in villages and talking to Indians at many levels indicated the density in thinking.

Translation of a simple ballad of a Punjabi peasant farmer proved that once and for all near Ludhiana. I was made to sit down on a charpoy string cot for a tall glass of hot and very sugary milky tea. Bonhomie overflowed as it was **Baisakhi**, the spring festival. The song was full of sentiments about unrequited love (again!) but laced with philosophical comment of considerable depth which filled my lined Hindi exercise book with words dealing with **BRHM**–creation–infinity–yugas and action in this world.

♦ A lesson for all time never to underestimate India's peasants and villages–now even more informed than when my own personal pathway took me on these early rural explorations–thanks to many a bird-watching expedition.

'The non-linear, cluster configuration of Indian thought,' Lannoy rightly explains 'does not proceed along a developmental line progressing to a climax, but is a spiralling from a germinating point, and swelling in value by return and repetition.' There is the bindu again, that potent⊙. This surely must arise from the remarkable density of Sanskrit construction and compression of layers of meaning in complex nouns.

Just so is the **RAGA,** and Indian painting which encloses multi-perspective; Indian **DANCE** forms; the auspicious symbol of the **SWASTIKA** with all its condensed meaning. Perhaps India is at a cusp of history if only it can take that step into the future without becoming entangled in the 'modernisation is westernisation' syndrome–rather that Indians stay true to their traditional roots. Lannoy again:

India is probably better fitted to meet, and more predisposed to face, the challenge of a future change of attitudes than almost any other country in the world.

For one thing as becomes obvious if one reads even only a few of the Vedic hymns, the Indian mind 'is at home among the non-visual velocities and relations of the sub-atomic and astronomical worlds.' However, Lannoy rightly adds one hesitation, that is 'at the present moment there is no sign that Indian educationists are aware that they are sitting on a gold mine of promising attitudes'–that is a capacity to cope with a 'multi-sensible world of simultaneous interconnectedness and all-at-oneness quite unlike the old mechanised industrialised world'.

In his prophetic view India consistently displays a talent which has been 'long repressed and vilified as archaic' mostly because of the Western fixation on rationality born of scientific thinking in its earlier confined stage, before recent multi-disciplinary influences redefined 'the linear progression of sequential logic'.

Perhaps this is why Sanskrit is said to be remarkable in its computer compatibility!

Modern Developments

That most scholarly Englishman of the late 1700s, Oxford graduate Sir William Jones, would have enjoyed this debate. Landing in Calcutta to take up his legal appointment under the Governor-General Warren Hastings he was clearly an example of the right person in the right place at the right time...1783.

Of a fine and delicately attuned mind (and a wife not lacking herself in bright intelligence), he turned his attention to learning the language and unravelling its multitudinous secrets. But he worked with such intense application and devotion in such a debilitating climate that he gave his life to India–quite 'out of his mind', dying sadly in 1794, very quickly of the addled condition as he sailed away having tragically lost his wife to India's climate also. He must have startled Europeans of that epoch who knew absolutely nothing about Sanskrit or the true depth of its culture when he described it as 'more perfect than Greek, more copious than Latin and more exquisitely refined than either.'

In an era when colonial Europe was globally dominant in its surge outwards, subjecting others in Africa and Asia to its supposedly superior civilization–both religiously, culturally and technologically, that must have been hard to take. At this historical point it was not realised that in fact Sanskrit was the **mother language of the Indo-European system** as it is now called which in turn stems from Greek and Roman languages which share the same Sanskrit roots–think of the Latin **omnes** and **omnipotent**. That **all-embracing** notion absolutely inherent in the sound **OM** as well as words like *paramount* wisdom, *steadfastness*, etc ...At least Jones had the good sense to found the **Asiatic Society in 1784**–and for this must be the first English person to be so honoured by the Indian Government Post and Telegraphs in the 50th Anniversary year of Independence on his 250th birthday with a First Day cover and stamp, his name in Devanagari:

SIR WILLIAM JONES
सर विलियम जोन्स

A Sense of Indian Identity

Sanskrit has over millennia given the subtle sense of identity to Bharatvarsha, to the land of those who spoke the perfected language–not only the monopoly of the brahmin priests who had mastered it and which gave power to their class as the sacerdotal managers of the correct chants (in perfect tonal intonation) and rites framing the all-important sacrificial fire ceremonies at the centre of the Vedic life. It also became the line of communication for the reflective thinkers of all kinds–rsis, poets, musicians, philosophers, lawmakers, munis, and teachers who codified the medical formulae and texts of Ayurveda, in fact those who gathered together the **shastras**.

Panini (circa 350 BCE) and Patanjali (5th century CE, see YOGA) by systematising the language made it 'the enduring, all-pervasive cultural unifier.'

But then paradoxically the decline set in. Buddhism and Jain influences were on the rise for nearly a 1000 years until the 8th–9th century CE. Then Islam was to enter India. Finally European domination established itself and much of the Hindu

S

culture was thrown on the back foot, entrenched in unchanging hidebound attitudes, psychologically thrown on the defensive. The sway of Sanskrit lapsed, virtually confined to the learned brahmin community which at least maintained the oral capacity of reciting it even in slokas, not understood at all by the ordinary person—even at their own marriage ceremonies, similar to the incomprehensibility of the Latin liturgy to modern Christian congregations. Other cultural influences such as Persian flowed in with the Mughals.

Finally Macaulay's famous edict regarding English, as infinitely superior to learn as a language as British dominion increased throughout India in the last two centuries, imposed English in preference to Sanskrit for teaching purposes in higher education. The decline of Sanskrit inevitably occurred. It began to be regarded by the ordinary person, as Latin and Greek in Europe, as an archaic language.

Revival At Last

Since Independence there has been an effort by the government and cultural bodies to re-establish it as a living language apart from its religious usage in temples, in Hindu philosophical studies and among a very learned coterie. Now one day in the year is devoted to extolling Sanskrit, to help Indians understand its importance so that its vibrating resonance will continue to echo through the voices of Indian history. In addition, a well-established **World Sanskrit Conference** now meets annually, and the New Delhi-based **Sanskrit Bharati** teaches conversational Sanskrit in courses promoted throughout the country and abroad.

Conclusion

◆ Referred to as the **Rashtra Sampark Bhasha** = national link language (**bhasha**) those who can speak it regard it as the fundamental binding agent of Indian culture transcending:

- ◆ diversities of blood ◆ dress
- ◆ varna = colour/class ◆ cuisine
- ◆ regions ◆ gender
- ◆ linguistic areas ◆ rituals and ◆ social customs

Stop Press: While travelling through Tamilnadu on my visit in 2000 a survey of daily newspapers (not just English-language) had disclosed—it was clearly a surprise—that **half a dozen discourses** are being held **daily** on Sanskrit to audiences numbering hundreds. Although such gatherings are in Tamil or Telugu at least a third of the regional language component is Sanskrit, which is easily taken on board by the masses. The point made—that in the earliest foundations of Indian-ness, Sanskrit (as its name makes clear) cultivated the purity of communication as a *lingua franca*—retaining basic structure and meaning intact as an anchor for all the vigorous mixing-up that went on between the local dialects of those earliest clans and their regional vernaculars.

SANSKRITIZATION is a term given to what is a matter all societies understand—keeping up with the Joneses! This mostly happens in the middle ranks of caste, especially in business and artisan groups who become wealthier, a matter of considerable scope in the India of today. Outer changes indicate rising status and capacity to mix with higher caste by observing the socio-religious rituals of upper-caste groups:

- ◆ Adaption of symbols of higher status
- ◆ Dress and food—increased vegetarianism.
- ◆ Ritual and puja in the home are all part of the process of upgrading one's social status
- ◆ Going on pilgrimage, religious affirmations in undertaking special rites at family commemorations and donations (**daan**) to priests at the major centres of pilgrimage and temple centres such as ostentatious feeding of brahmins on ordained days or at sacred sites especially river banks.

Introduction by better-educated members of the family to certain procedures of faith (especially on the return of **NRIs**) are ways of emulating Sanskrit-savvy superiors and certainly in many matters of orthodox as well as social issues of caste, systems are more fluid than given credence in what is regarded as a static Indian society.

■ **SAPTAPADI**

The seven steps (pedes) central to and evocative of the nuptial ceremony around the sacred fire—**hawan.** The marriage is given recognition by the solemnisation of this ceremony. The husband assists the bride in taking the steps with him while wishing her a long, healthy and prosperous life.

The seven steps symbolise the following vows taken by the couple:

Let us be together at all times.

Let us lead our lives together—we shall have the same resolutions.

Let us love each other.

Let us be united in thought and action.

Let our desires be the same.

Let us lead a righteous life.

Let us raise a good family.

■ **SAPTARSHI** (n. *Sanskrit*)

... the significant seven original **RSIS** who appear again and again in literature, sculpture and painting. (see **AVATAR MATSYA**) Symbols of the progenitors, the wise men, to guide the human race. In one of the **Brahmana** texts their names are given as **Gautama** (not the Buddha), **Bharadwaj, Viswamitra, Jamadagni, Vasishta, Kasyap and Atri**. But remember in Hindu concepts, there are powerful feminine forces at play also—**Shakti power** for one—such as the following...

■ **SARASWATI**

Originally embodying the concept of free-flowing waters, pools and rivers, **sarit** and **saras**, coursing through creation with these equally free-flowing energies like the once mysterious Saraswati river that is claimed to emerge from underground to join the Ganga-Jumna confluence at **Prayag**, site of the **KUMBH MELA** Saraswati is the consort of Brahma, a major force in her own right, as well as now emerging in satellite photography as a once vast watercourse, possibly 7000 square miles in area,

S

responsible, according to geologist S R N Murthy, 'for the sustenance and prosperity of the Vedic civilization.' (**Vedic View of The Earth, quoted in ASTROLOGY**).

In addition, the Bhabha Atomic Research Centre has discovered probable sweet water running in consistent channels (saline on either side) in areas known to Vedic history in Rajasthan which may, when analysed and carbon dated, prove the age of this powerful and legendary river system.

♦ Like all the other forms of the Shakti principle she exists in her own right as the **goddess of learning and the creative arts which includes science**. She is an example of this other powerful area of the Hindu view which balances out patriarchy in all its masculinity.

Saraswati is the conduit for **speech—the word = VAK** (in Sanskrit, pronounced **vaak**) to amplify Brahma's creative intelligence. The word activates the intellect, as it has been shown to do by language theorists recording the development of communication from early hominid onwards. Hindu symbolism interestingly enough reflects this truth. In the beginning was the word... speech led to knowledge, poetry, expression in the visual arts, learning and science. **The Goddess is credited with having brought the Sanskrit language and Devanagari script to mankind. Holding the veena she is also the presiding deity over music, her attributes, the palm manuscript for knowledge, holy water in a pitcher, the rosary for blessing.**

Male and female principles are also shown to be complementary to each other rather than confrontational, inextricably intertwined like the DNA helix in the Brahma-Saraswati balance.

She sits on a lotus. Both are symbols of aspiration and purity, a metaphor of the mind's aspiration 'to ride high' fulfilling its potential as, similarly, the lotus stalk lifts the exquisite shape of the opening flower above the mud and murky depths of daily existence.

♦ In February a special festival is held to honour her. In the home school books, rulers, pencils, musical instruments are laid out to be blessed on the day of **Saraswati Puja**. Both then and in the autumnal **Durga Puja**, the potters' quarter in Kolkata (Kumhartoli) is known for its artistic creativity, fashioning the life-size statues—very white indeed! Draped in gauze saris to cover their buxom figures modestly until dressed sumptuously in glittering saris and jewelled crowns to be worshipped, then taken in celebrating procession to the ocean where finally they are immersed in the waves.

Endnote: How many Europeans can recall a Greek legend to back up their philosophical view of life?... and most especially the 'getting of wisdom'? **Zeus**, 'the Father of Gods and men' took as his first wife, **Metis, Goddess of Wisdom**. She was pregnant. So what does Zeus do? He actually swallows her before she gives birth so that he would not be 'outwitted' by his progeny. What message does that send about the importance of wisdom?

Saraswati in contrast is honoured—not swallowed!

■ **SARI**

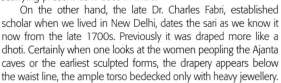

Six to nine yards of material, unstitched and of unparalleled beauty, has been worn by women for at least 5,000 years—defying all external influence and change. **Ritu Kumar,** prominent fashion designer writing in **India Calling** (India Book House, Bombay, 1994) says this:

There is no country in the world where a traditional aesthetic in apparel continues with such stubborn pride from the dim recesses of history into the hurrying, scurrying present as it does in India.

On the other hand, the late Dr. Charles Fabri, established scholar when we lived in New Delhi, dates the sari as we know it now from the late 1700s. Previously it was draped more like a dhoti. Certainly when one looks at the women peopling the Ajanta caves or the earliest sculpted forms, the drapery appears below the waist line, the ample torso bedecked only with heavy jewellery.

Watch a Gujarati woman drive a scooter in Ahmedabad's permanent traffic dodgems—in a sari... and marvel, for there are hundreds of these enterprising young women, miracles of vibrant colour in their helmets, with pallus fluttering, virtually circus performers surviving the impossible.

■ **SATCHITANANDA** (n. *Sanskrit*)

is a fundamental term and the ultimate goal for every Hindu. It will leap out at you as a word in the least expected places—a newspaper article on the amorality of current politics, a discourse of a visiting swami, a kinetic mobile, a piece of wired sculpture demanding consideration in a Mumbai art gallery, in a railway train being quizzed by a talkative group of male students, an old woman musing under a neem tree at Brindavan.

Sat = existence, the very **Being**, that we exist in the objective world enveloped in every entity that makes that world (from which **SATYA** = truth draws its meaning).

Chit = consciousness, that is the human capacity to be aware that **sat** is so.

Ananda = the bliss, ecstasy of **g**nowing that **sat** is so (see **GNOW**).

♦ Out of nothingness, **pralaya** (orderly chaos) a patterning of molecules and energy emerges... **Shristi**, creation from a spark of heat/warmth. **That one = Tad Ekam** (note the neuter) arrives. There is no other word for that transition from nothingness to something in the cosmos. (No one has yet satisfactorily explained usage of **tad** in Australian idiomatic speech.)

Chit is now even stretching the acceptance of human consciousness via astrophysics to a discussion on **The Mind of God**. What gives order = **RTA** to the chaos of the cosmos? What drives the universal patterning? Is there, as neurological specialists believe, multi-consciousness within the brain's one consciousness?

Ananda comes to those on the higher road when complete awareness flashes in a moment of intensified concentration. A fusion with that **force** brings a sense of bliss beyond even that experienced in sexual union with a beloved. This has been described many times in Indian literature by those who, through discipline, living a balanced life, undertaking ascetic yogic practice, then reach a sense of immersion in whatever constitutes the Cosmic Whole. That magnetic pull, the luminosity which gives an electric charge to the creative mind into space/time, also demands a return.

◆ Humans toughing it out in everyday life, trying their best to lead a life of integrity may also experience fortunate moments of ananda—fusion when everything comes together in a spontaneous satisfaction—a job well done, an artistic endeavour accomplished, a blues singer reaching that soaring high note with ease like Aretha Franklin or Mahalia Jackson, a sculptor surveying that final Chola bronze installed in the shrine with glory. **Sukritam**. Well made. An epiphany!

■ SATYA

..is **truth**...

from **sat**: the Supreme or Pure Existence before it became differentiated into **PURUSHA**—the male principle and **PRAKRITI**, the female principle = primal nature and the commencement of benign/malign forces in creation processes.

Sat being the root and referring to all that is existent then **satya** literally means **'that which is'**—in fact, the truth of the matter!

■ SATYAGRAHA

= grasping (graha) of the truth, satya**.**

This very Indian concept was transformed by Mahatma **GANDHI** into an effective political weapon which has, in an extraordinary way, travelled across geographical and cultural boundaries since Gandhi was assassinated, and become part of contemporary non-violent demonstrations of all kinds—anti-nuclear, anti-Vietnam war, 'greenies' clutching trees in the ecological struggles of the last decades of the 20th century.

The **satyagraha** movement was the essential spinal cord for the great struggles of the 30s and 40s in India's protracted political demonstrations against British colonial rule. Gandhi had declared many times to his followers: 'Hate the act or the principle of oppression; feel hatred for no being, even the protagonist'.

This idea and concept has been espoused worldwide far beyond India's cultural boundaries—a phenomenon most remarkable for its appeal to those leaders—later to become rulers—Jomo Kenyatta in Kenya, Nelson Mandela incarcerated in solitary confinement in South Africa, Martin Luther King in the USA during struggles for liberation from racial bondage. All of these leaders acknowledged their own debt to this philosophy, enhanced by Mahatma Gandhi, by reading his treatise and message of hope in **satyagraha**. This, despite beatings with lathis or long staves by the British police and Indians recruited also into the police in colonial times.

There is a Hindi word **sahishnuta (sahish = together)** which negates any idea of aggressive confrontation in tackling a deep-seated problem. It means a **sense of tolerating** but not just passively; rather an activating of one's attitude into trying to understand the other's point of view... very hard indeed if one encounters a totally macho intransigent and duplicitous opponent.

None of us, as adolescents in the 30s and embroiled in World War II of the 40s and gradually becoming influenced by the yearnings and ideals for a better world in which all peoples and races were truly free regarding each other on an equal footing, could ever have envisaged in 1939 when war broke out that India would become a totally free and independent nation in eight years. Nor that later such a force espousing non-violent 'people power' could bring down even an Indonesian president such as the entrenched Suharto.

◆ **Satyagraha** has had a remarkable impact in the cultural thinking of our times. Philip Glass, noted American avant-garde composer who has shaped a whole new chordal approach to music composition, created an opera entitled **Satyagraha: Product of a Great Soul**.

This was first performed in New York in 1981 based on passages from the **Mahabharata**. This opera completed the trilogy of Glass' two preceding works—**Einstein on the Beach** and **Akhnaten**. Program notes:

In Satyagraha, Glass and Constance Dèjon, his collaborator on the libretto, treat their philosophical subject in mythical style, evoking images of the birth of Satyagraha, its evolution, and its eventual resurrection in the 1960s in the American Civil Rights movement... Looming above the action, both figuratively and literally, are three figures crucially linked to the Satyagraha philosophy: the Russian novelist Leo Tolstoy, Martin Luther King, Jnr, and the Indian mystic and Nobel Prize-winning poet, Rabindranath Tagore.

Satyagrahis, those who undertake such strenuous protests as Gandhi did, leading to fasting and moral pressure without violence upon an often violent opponent, whether singly or collectively, can only be 'effective through personal purification of a most testing spiritual kind—true unto one's self through meditation, inner integrity and deep conviction.'

Indeed Gandhi used the word not in its literal Sanskrit meaning but as he called it 'a **soul force**', a cleansing of the inner personality before taking on the opponent in an effort to convince a change of heart, bringing about a peace honourable to both—far harder and much more protracted a process than having a free-for-all bash as Northern Ireland and the Middle East only too well exemplify.

■ SECULAR SOCIETY

When India was founded as a fully independent nation on August 15, 1947, it had to wait until the Constituent Assembly adopted its Constitution on November 26, 1949 (which came into force January 26, 1950) to become a **Sovereign Democratic Republic**. Underlining that statement was the unwritten declaration of secularism.

Conditioned from the beginnings of Indian history to tolerate pluralities, in recent years modern politics has encouraged communalism. This is not the fault of Indian politicians, rather a modern scourge of most Western long-established democratic societies, let alone fragile post-colonial African and Asian nations stamped with admirable democratic templates but sourced from alien Western cultures which have had the advantages of relatively homogeneous societies until recently, global migration by millions in search of work so changing the shape of societies in the northern hemisphere.

♦ The trauma of **Partition** and the constant aggravation from the carving out of Pakistan—an avowed Islamic state constitutionally totally different in ethos from that of India—has aroused adrenalin at state elections and narrow-minded and unprincipled power games during electioneering. On the obverse side of this is the constant awareness at national level of the **Unity in Diversity** theme which is constantly stressed in presidential addresses on Independence Day or Republic Day and by all national figures once in power.

Understandably, Islam and the Hindu way of life being as chalk is to cheese, there are many possible flashpoints, now exacerbated by recent nuclear rivalry of alarming proportions.

Communalism and nationalism seem to be constantly in opposition to each other as democracy emphasises the seeking of votes and local power games, as well as extolling tolerance for 'the other' rather than encouraging the whole. Yet the way ordinary people live Hindu and Muslim lifestyles are complementary, making up an entity—an Indian-ness greater than the two parts. A useful recent book which every thinking person involved with India (and Pakistan) could well read to their advantage is **Region, Religion, Caste, Gender and Culture in Contemporary India** (ed. T V Sathya Murthy, OUP, 1997), and Navaratna Rajaram's **Secularism, The new mask of fundamentalism** (Voice of India, New Delhi, 1995) for a very different point of view.

♦ **Prof. Rasheed-ud-din Khan** of the Indian Institute of Federal Studies has (as a Muslim) cautioned that Islam as a major component in the secular mix is not monolithic in India but, like Hindu societies

♦ *multi-regional*   ♦ *multi-sect*
♦ *multi-lingual*   ♦ *and multi-professional*
   In more popular language, there are Muslim communities (plural) rather than a Muslim community (singular).

He stresses the need to build a new Muslim identity in modern India. (**India Perspectives**, October, 1992). Unfortunately as 50 years of Independence passed with the ending of the century, other divisions exacerbated the nation-building process. Divisive communal issues have arisen with Christians, Buddhists, Dalits and Tribals as well, certainly in the new NE regional States.

In a nation which is virtually 28 culturally different nations in one, with eight major world faiths—**Hindu, Buddhist, Jain, Jewish, Zoroastrian, Christian, Muslim, Sikh in historical order of development**—it was imperative that India, having attained Independence in 1947, declare itself constitutionally a secular state. Quite genuinely Indians on the whole strive at personal level and at political level to promote and enhance, and strengthen this idea. 'India,' writes Professor Khan 'is bigger than a country, larger than a nation and more than a mere state. It is a defined civilisation with all its varieties.'

Extreme communal groups exist in the murky shadows, paying money to **GOONDA** criminal elements, to do their dirty work for them, in the political power games allowed by the democratic process, most especially at state and divisional levels. The needs of minorities and government response is a constant 'state of alert' but again this is far from India's challenge alone. Pakistan, Sri Lanka, Myanmar, Malaysia, Indonesia, China, all undergo the same political stresses. It is worth taking note of the UK situation also. How united is that democracy? After 300 years struggle Scotland at last has a partially autonomous parliament, but Ireland?

How to harness people's votes at such an impoverished level is, however, a malaise that faces new nations like India. Many a time while admiring the adherence to such democratic ideas, one yearns for a benevolent dictator to act swiftly... such an irony!

■ SHAKING THE HEAD

...is a very Indian habit especially in answering your questions, as though the skull is permanently on a wobbly ball-bearing base, like the dancing papiermaché figures on sale in the bazaar. Beware! The signals being sent out are opposite to the negative twist of the head from left to right and back which signals NO in Western culture.

Movement in short agreeable bursts from side to side means the person to whom you are talking, or just passing the time of day, is agreeing with you (even if not really listening to what you are saying). Often this emphatic head gesture is accompanied with the spoken exclamation: **Achcha** or **Haan-ji**.

Indians wish to please, especially the guest from outside their close community. 'Yes' may well mean NO when the person engaged in conversation with you wants to put you at your ease rather than hurt your feelings. Indian culture has a strong streak in it of honour to the genuine stranger who shows a sincere curiosity. Dharma underpins this with an outgoing courtesy and hospitality. Indian kindness can be quite overwhelming at times and may happen in the least expected situations.

'Naheen' meaning NO can be indicated by gyrating the head in a number of ways. You will soon learn to differentiate between

S

this signal and its verbal response and the Haan-ji or Achchaa emphasised on the last AA syllable. This signals YES. A rising inflexion may confuse the entire issue into a question!

■ SHAL(A)BHANJIKA

'The nymph who breaks the branch of the shala tree'—the shala *Shorea robusta* like the ashoka, banyan and peepul being especially sacred.

Yet another artistic metaphor linking the **TREE** to a profound concept inherent in feminine nature—**Prakriti**, the tree being a very potent symbol for masculine fertility linked to the **tree pole** at the centre of mankind's very earliest worship, and the nymph the personification of the quickening in nature, of sap rising.

Perhaps with the contemporary shock threat to the planet's ozone layer by industrial urban society's polluting ways, we are having to reconsider our own neglectful attitudes to the inherent sacredness of nature and the vital power of trees to cleanse the earth's atmosphere.

In India, carved by creative sculptors over at least two millennia, thousands of tree spirits people(literally) the friezes of temples in exquisite curvaceous forms, swinging their ample hips (no anorexic models here!) in the **tribhanga** bend, holding up lintels, filling niches, standing free in statuary, curving seductively as they embrace tree trunk after tree trunk. The **shalabhanjika** is the supreme example of India's exuberant approach to the sacred.

◆ The most famous must surely be the powerful female upholding part of a Buddhist gateway at the Sanchi stupa near Bhopal, between 1st c BCE to 3rd c CE.

◆ Perhaps that is a reminder to pilgrims that early Buddhist Pali accounts describe the birth of Buddha from the side of Maya Devi as depicted standing in this very pose, clinging to the shala tree in the middle of the Lumbini grove for support.

◆ Indian women will laughingly recount the well-known folk lore of the lovely young girl sent out to kick the flowering creeper or tree to make it fruit or blossom as the spring sap rises. Notes provided by Dr Thomas Maxwell, of the Faculty of Oriental Studies at Oxford University explain: 'in her playfulness this girl is an essential part of nature, of maya, her unwitting wantonness the very power of prakriti, the inherent dynamism of the wild... the quickening power of nature.' Indeed in the West in typical aggro fashion nature lore suggests that a woman hammering a rusty nail into the bark of a tree may 'quicken nature' to get a recalcitrant tree to fruit. A personal experiment following this advice in Australia produced one black olive on a fruitless tree. There must be a moral here!

■ SHIVA-SHAKTI...

(Purusha-Prakriti)

principle is the biological truth of creation, the balance in the cosmos which the rishis with their insights into the ultimate nature of being, built into the Indian view later incorporated into Hindu visual expression in the **ARDHANARISWARA** sculpture = deity part male/part female.

The principle is one of **complementary** rather than **equal gender balance** (how can that be anyway when there are disparities of sex, height, weight, shape, muscular strength?) leading to an inner non-representational unification without which there can be no human existence (turn to **PANTHEON**—Zimmer's explation of Goddess and **PURUSHA**).

Heinrich Zimmer has some fascinating contributions to make as a man interpreting this equation especially the puzzling (to a Westerner) imagery of **Kali-Siva** depicted in various asanas in his **Myths and Symbols of Indian Civilization** (see **WOMEN**). There are so many names all for the one Shakti, the abstract feminine principle—Bhumi, Prithvi, Uma, Saraswati, Parvati, Lakshmi, Ambaji, Kali, but the ultimate Devi is **Durga**, the obverse 'other image' of **Kali**. She is the unconquerable, sublime warrior maid who came into being out of the combined wrath of all the gods symbolized in a fiery cloud which grew and grew and then condensed into the shape of **The Goddess**—an amalgamation of all their powers, their attributes in her hands—another expansion in the meaning, an inspiration to the individual beholder to use imagination and disciplined thoughts to reformulate the image into a new relevance, within the prevailing spirit of the age.

Personal Endnote: For me it was an intellectual liberation from the constraints of an institutional Christian upbringing and at the beginnings of a fierce backlash from the feminist movement to begin to plumb the depths of Indian philosophy with such a powerful acceptance of the Shakti force. The push to equality rather than the truth of biological complementariness seems to have left a trail of embittered, lonely and confused, ideologically constrained women and a dramatic rise in young male suicides in the urbanised societies of the Western world—no matter how economically well-off or educationally advanced.

■ SIKHS and SIKHISM

from **shishya** a derivation from the original Sanskrit root **shish** for one who seeks to learn, a pupil, a disciple.

The name given to a sturdy and solid people who followed its first '**messenger**' Guru Nanak (mid 15th century). Sikhism emerged in the Punjab as a result of geography, history and genes. If one looks at a map of what India was before Independence and the enormous amputation it suffered at Partition when Pakistan was created out of what was the cultural homeland of a preponderance of Sikhs, you come to realise what an enterprising and resourceful people the Punjabis are in general—Hindu, Christian, Muslim, but Sikhs in particular.

Punjabis no matter what their faith, are a well-built, rambunctious people who love the good things of life, are not overly prone to asceticism and are vigorous sportsmen. Watching **kabadi** and **Punjabi wrestling** will soon put to rest the idea that India is a land of mysticism! Modern sports such as golf, tent-pegging and mountaineering are pursued vigorously (see Khushwant Singh's very readable book, **The Sikhs Today,** Orient Longman, Kolkata, 1959). They also enjoy, dubiously, quite a reputation with women!

S

Geography and Environment

Being in the traditional geographical pathway of invasions and trading routes into India for thousands of years (rather than the tenuous jungle routes of infiltration in the NE frontier until the shock of the Chinese invasion in 1962), Punjabis have had to become a forceful if not militant race of people.

Geography gave them good food resources with many rivers and ancient irrigation systems long before the British extended the canal networks. They harvested the granary of the nation and their cattle thrived also. So, genetically, they stand tall, with strong muscle power from a good dairy/protein diet. Nor are Punjabi women meek shadows of their menfolk; they can tell as many Rabelaisian jokes as the menfolk (known for their raunchiness) and enjoy a good deal of bawdy humour in their feminine song/dance gatherings before a **shaadi** party (wedding) as well as dancing the night away at times of seasonal festivities such as **Baisakhi**. This is the spring harvest festival on April 13th when the Sikh Holy Book is taken out in procession with much ceremony, and feasting afterwards. And now they can drink a straight whiskey alongside their men if they so wish, giving as good as they get in the male/female equation. Within the family walls a Sikh wife often quite literally wears the trousers.

◆ Indeed I have been present in a Sikh home in Yorkshire when a husband came home from his English factory work in a wool mill (having been recruited a decade earlier by a Bradford mill owner seeking hardworking labour that did not mind the unsocial hours of shift work the mills needed and which post-war English labour resisted). It was High Tea time on pay day. The dignified Sikh threw down his pay packet onto the kitchen table which his wife, casting a knowing look, took up, proceeded to apportion, handing back a few pounds for his 'pub money', putting the rest in a stylish tea caddy tin up on a shelf.

'You see who's in charge?' is all the Sardarji said. (Sardarji is a term of familiarity for Mr in the community). The stereotype is that Punjabis are all brawn and no brain, but that is not so, despite the Sikh delight in telling **'Sardarji' jokes** on themselves … as the following:

Banta Singh goes to a hotel and eats heartily. After eating he goes to wash his hands but starts washing the basin instead. The manager comes running and asks him, 'Prahji, aap kya kar rahe ho?' 'Brother, what are you doing?' To this Banta replies, 'Oye, tumne hi to idhar board lagaya hai: Wash Basin'. 'Well, you have yourself put up this signboard that says: Wash Basin.'

Khushwant Singh, chronicler of the Sikhs and reluctant intellectual, is their most ebullient teller of such tales. He confuses his admirers by hiding behind a naughty exterior, deliberately Punjabi in being provocative, writing risqué novels and gossipy columns to get a rise. It was once said of him after his return from the UK as Press Attaché to Krishna Menon as India's first High Commissioner that 'his bark was worse than his bite.' Typical of the Sikhs' forthright approach to life he also hides away a generosity of spirit little known to public scrutiny, generously supportive of those lone souls fallen foul of officialdom, who like

Bengali loner and intellectual gadfly, **Nirad Chaudhuri**, incurred the wrath of Nehru for his famous **Autobiography of an Unknown Indian**(Macmillan, London,1952). This cost him his career in All India Radio (overseen by a government ministry) and brought him to near-penury... when the French Ambassador and K S stepped in.

Because of the Sikh emphasis on the real world in which they emerged, breaking caste barriers in metaphorically 'dirtying their hands', reinforced by Guru Nanak's down-to-earth wisdom they have acquired the reputation of being more in the here-and-now than most Indians. Mechanics, carpenters, engineers, cultivators; the inside of a car engine is as familiar as a computer chip to them.

1469 CE

The Sikhs Emerge in History

Guru Nanak was born to a Hindu family of the **kshatriya** class. It is recounted that a Muslim midwife was at his birth. He must have been a spirit of his time, a yearning for reform in the air, Hindu society having been pushed on the defensive for centuries since the first arrivals of the Muslim Slave kings (they were **freed** slaves who made good!) from Turko-Syrian and Afghan expansion in the 11th century. Sultanates had been established throughout the north, temples ravaged, art treasures and sculpture defaced, women threatened. The result:

◆ socially inflexible and meaningless customs reinforced in the home
◆ rigidity of caste strictures on social interaction and interdining
◆ ossification over time of Hindu worship and priestly dominance of social expression
◆ at the same time the classless **BHAKTI** movement in the south was gathering force.
◆ Legend has grown around Guru Nanak that he was a precocious child... It is told that at seven months he sat in the posture of a yogi! Later as a twice-born Hindu son, being initiated by the family priest into a responsible young member of society at the (Sacred Thread) ceremony, he apparently cautioned those present not to be misled by custom, stating that possession of the triple thread with all its symbolism did not necessarily prevent man from doing evil. Possession of the thread could only have meaning by praising the name of **Ek Omkar—the One Creator**.

Aged nine, he already showed great ability to teach and discourse on the scriptures. With his constant companion **Mardana**, an elderly Muslim musician, and another Hindu peasant, he announced he was taking to the road, such a familiar aspect of Indian life, to learn and teach.

He travelled all over north India, then to the south, finally to Mecca, and Baghdad where he spent much time in intellectual discourses with Muslim divines. One favourite story is told that when in Mecca and in the habit of a Muslim, he had rolled himself on a durree on the ground and gone to sleep without realising that his feet were pointing in the direction of the Kaaba—holiest of holy places in the Islamic world.

A Muslim imam had noticed this attitude, a mark of real disrespect and had remonstrated with Nanak. 'Turn my feet then

S

in the direction where God is not', the teacher in Nanak had rejoined. Later in religious discourses with the **maulvis (spiritual guides)** of Mecca and to their questioning, 'who is better: a Hindu or a Muslim?' he had in great humility pointed out that God is more concerned with the spirit of the law rather than the letter. 'God reads hearts and not labels. Both Hindus and Muslims,' it is related that Guru Nanak explained, 'will be expelled from God's realm if they have not acted with nobility and compassion in their hearts; God judges people by deeds, not creeds.'

NB: Lying on the ground with feet stretched out pointing in the direction of someone—shoes or no shoes—is regarded as bad manners. Pandit Ravi Shankar once halted a London concert to admonish young Flower Power people littering the floor in front of the seated rows for doing the same. They had crowded into the concert some even smoking a 'joint'. They were given a gentle lecture for not paying respect to the finer instruments, if not the musicians. The famous musician resumed playing as they took up Buddha positions.

Guru Nanak's Teaching

As Guru Nanak's teaching developed and grew, he increasingly took on the roll of the messenger of the **Supreme Guru** proclaiming the Word—**sabad**—to a responsive populace. His sermons were straightforward messages often in lyrical verse form composed by Mardana, easily absorbed by inhabitants of the villages they passed through, summed up in the **Japji** or morning prayer.

There is One God,
Eternal Truth is His Name:
Maker of all things
Fearing nothing and at enmity with nothing.
Timeless in His Image;
Not begotten, being of His own Being
By the grace of the Guru, made known to men.
True in the beginning, true throughout the ages.

Encapsulated within this and again recalling the truth of physics and the search to define **mind/consciousness** is the **mool mantra**: the kernel of Sikh belief:

Before time itself
There was truth
When time began to run its course
He was the truth
Even now. He is the truth … And evermore shall truth prevail.

In a sense his hymns appear to be suffused with that devotional intensity paralleling the Bhakti movement of the same time in south India. Much of the dross which had accumulated around the body of Hindu belief, the proliferation of symbolic deities, the esoteric and obscurantist customs were cleared away.

Guru Nanak in a sense went straight to the heart of the Hindu view of the creative nature of Godhead, and in an amalgamation with the simplicity of Islamic belief in which God is without form, **nirguna**, created what radical Sikhs now claim **as an entirely separate faith**, not at all an offshoot or reform movement of the gigantic body of Hindu belief.

Symbolically, he broke with all the elaborate rituals refusing to wear the sacred thread as an upper caste Hindu by birth. He advised a brahmin disciple:

Make mercy thy cotton
Contentment its thread
Continence its knot
And truth its twist

Nanak died in 1539 just over a decade after Babur defeated the Afghan rulers of Delhi in 1526 and set in motion the great wheel of another historical golden age cycle, that of the MUGHAL EMPIRE.

The Gurus

The sense of being their own people with their own religious as well as cultural identity was carried on **by nine other gurus over a period of nearly 250 years**.

As peasant Punjabis and other Indians he encountered in his extensive wanderings warmed to the messages of a more socially open and robust society, the Gurus who followed added to the body of teaching and the praise-singing, a 'soul' music of that day and age. **Arjun**, fifth Guru, gathered together the hymns and preachings into the **Adi Granth**. This then became the focal point of worship rather than their own presence or personalities.

Over time, however, the Gurus have understandably been honoured, for several were persecuted, had sons walled up to die horrible deaths or suffered torture and beheadings at the hands of Muslim rulers while defending their Punjab lands.

It was also the moral duress imposed by religious edicts of iconoclastic Aurangzeb (1658–1707)—almost parallel with the final heroic **Guru Gobind Singh**—that set the pattern of rebellion by the Sikhs, to mark themselves out as such as a militant body, rather than have the mass of Hindu society suffer also for their stand against such oppression. Some very gory prints line gurdwara (temple) walls all over the world. They depict these atrocities to keep alive the memory of heroism in founding their faith.

1699 CE

The Khalsa

At Anandpur the last Guru summoned a great assembly of his people on what came to be called **Baisakhi Day April 13**—to be commemorated year by year from then on as the most important day of the Sikh year.

The assembly had been widely publicised not only in the Punjab; it involved people from widely different regions and backgrounds. At this gathering Guru Gobind Singh appeared on a platform before them with his sword and appealed for one among their number to come forward and offer his head for the faith and the cause of righteousness, not only of the Sikhs but of all the communities affected by the turmoil of the times.

There was consternation. No one answered. He repeated his plea once more, and then a third time. It was at this point that one in the multitude took his life in his hands and acquiesced to the Guru's demand for sacrifice. Five men, one after the other, disappeared behind the public platform with only Guru Gobind Singh appearing again with his sword dripping with blood.

Then he dumbfounded the gathering by bringing out all five men—unharmed and intact. He took these five as his beloved five followers—**Panj Pyara (Five Beloved)**. The five redoubtable warriors, **one a jat, one a kshatriya, and three of low caste origin**, who had offered their lives to prove their loyalty to the cause, were then baptised by him. This baptism consisted—and still consists within Sikh ceremonies—of the sprinkling of the holy water or **amrit** which is made from water and a special sugar stirred by a double-sided sword in an iron vessel—over the freshly-washed hair and eyes of the follower of Sikh belief. For this baptism ceremony nowadays, people must be properly bathed beforehand and clad in clean attire.

After this ceremony the Panj Pyaras drank a little of the amrit all together as a declaration of their equality one with another, saying after the guru: **'Waheguruji da Khalsa... Waheguruji di Fateh'** Praise be to the Guru (God) of those, the pure... Hail Guru of Victory (of truth over falsehood)—the suffix Ji a mark of affectionate respect.

These five were then initiated into the wearing of the five symbols of **Five Ks** (kakkas as they are termed):
1. KESHA **uncut hair**—a symbol of virile strength like Samson in the Bible.
2. KANGA **comb**—to keep the long hair tidy in a bun on top of the head.
3. KIRPAN a **short sword**—for defence only—a Sikh given sanction to fight back, especially with land acquisition and forced conversion by Muslim invaders. The last guru declared, 'when affairs are past other remedies, it is justifiable to unsheathe the sword.' **Kanda** is the double-edged dagger seen as a symbol of evenhandedness, used in the temple to stir the amrit.
4. KARA **steel bangle**—fired without a join and worn by both men and women to remind each believer that they are encircled by God.

It is quite an experience to share a doorway in torrential monsoon rain in Simla with a **Nihang,** a fanatical end of the militant Sikh defenders of the faith bristling with sword and scimitar, his pineapple-shaped puggri turban all a-clatter with metal chakras and other sharp weaponry. Nihangs roam the country side 'naked' (nihang), shorn of family ties, each one said to have the strength of **sava lakh**, 1¼ lakh men = 125,000!

At least this one had a gentle heart under his metallic exterior, a Sikh Sir Walter Raleigh helping my young family through the flood to safer ground—a mischievous glint in his crinkled eyes.
5. KACHCHA **boxer-shorts**—for mobility and brisk movement especially for the warriors Sikhs were to become, in establishing the right to their natural homeland, especially as Mughal rule disintegrated and British hegemony spread up to the Afghan frontier. The flowing dhoti was unserviceable in leaping on a horse in a hurry riding out to defend their villages. The kachcha is also said to remind Sikhs of the need for sexual discipline—which is just as well! One Sikh put it this way—the kachcha reminds one to curb 'unbridled libidinous energy'—that **tamas**, lower instinct!

Conclusion: The Khalsa (and its symbols) provided its devotees with an impregnable identity in the 17th century during a period when the Punjabis were under constant persecution from skirmishes with invading Islamic forces.

The Turban
The fact is that the turban cannot be equated with other forms of headgear. It is not as the fez is to the Turk, the stetson to the Texan, the akubra to the outback Aussie or even the bowler hat to the British. The British Army bowed its unyielding regulations to the force of Sikh feeling on the turban so that in the trenches in **World War I** the Sikh was not forced to remove his turban for the tin helmet and he died and won his VCs in the defence of British policies with his turban on his head. Previously wrapped cotton lengths were worn by farmers in the field to protect the head under the tropical sun. A Sikh's uncut hair demanded braiding to keep tidy.

◆ There is no mention of a turban in Hindu lore. The gods and mythological heroes are depicted wearing long hair, with or without beard (beards are generally worn by the sages). The headdress is generally golden **mukats** (crowns) with inlaid jewels, but **Charles Fabri** does trace back evidence of turbans being worn to the second century BCE (**A History of Indian Dress**, Orient Longman, Kolkata, 1960.)

Until say 25 years ago, the wearing of a turban was an important attribute of a 'gentleman', be he Hindu, Muslim or a Sikh. Headgear is removed indoors. In Asia it is the reverse—headgear is kept on inside a temple, mosque or gurdwara, the opposite of Western custom, as a mark of respect.

Gurdwara worship
Sikhs are essentially a sociable people. Congregational worship is important beginning as it did as a sign of social equality across divisions of caste, custom and creed drawing in people of Hindu, Muslim, Christian persuasion (and now overseas followers in modern times such as the **Namdharis** who wear flattened white head pieces rather than turbans).

The focal point of worship is the **Guru Granth Sahib** which is honoured not for itself but for the words and messages enjoined on the congregation by the One God = **ek Omkar** in its pages. At the simple ceremonies in the temple known as the gurdwara (gateway = **dwara**, to the guru) there are no priests as such. A trained teacher or **gyani** can lead the worship and hand over to any member of the congregation, women as well as men, as I have witnessed in gurdwaras in Britain.

After this the **karah prasad (a token of God's benevolence)** is distributed and eaten. This is similar in concept to communion food. Nanak instituted this ceremony, **langar** (hospitality) as part of his religious defiance of caste restrictions on intercaste eating and the idea of untouchability which had so damaged later Hindu social structure.

S

The Adi Granth or Guru Granth Sahib

Before Guru Gobind Singh died in 1708 (a year after his implacably different foe, Emperor Aurangzeb) he dismantled the tradition of human gurus, installing the **Adi Granth** which resides in all gurdwaras, opened each morning at a different page, and read aloud (at certain times it is also recited in typical Indian fashion like the Ramayana in continuous session—from beginning to end, through the night as well as day). As a collection of joyous hymns and teachings of the gurus it incorporates both Hindu and Muslim devotions.

One Sikh ruler who stands out in the sociopolitical sense is the quirkish character known as the **Lion of the Punjab**. **Ranjit Singh** (1780–1839) was well-known to the British of the time. He gave his people a sense of a **Sikh homeland** which has had ramifications in recent decades. Worth searching out is an account written by the Eden sisters of the then English Governor-General Lord Auckland in Bengal who was fixing the Pax Britannica on all the territories by then annexed from a corrupt East India Company. **Janet Dunbar**'s book **Golden Interlude** (John Murray, London, 1955) is a peephole into history, of what goes on behind scenes even on the most stiff-necked and august occasions. The ruler being of **jat** stock, was very forthright (even now considered a very bossy community by mild-mannered Indians).

And so in the words of the Sikh greeting: **Sat Sri Akal—Truth is Eternal** (a-kala = without time).

■ SILK

a sattvic substance

India and sumptuous silks are synonymous. In the middle of the bazaar in old Kashi (Varanasi, Benares) degradation, poverty, pollution assault the eye, the heart, the mind and the soul but then a flash of vibrant mustard yellow, brilliant emerald, kingfisher blue shot with limpid green catches the eye draped against rich brown skin, carried in a beautiful woven basket in coiled skeins atop the head of some young man in simple dhoti from dye vats to weave through the filigree of narrow lanes in Varanasi or pulled out on the simplest of wooden frames to dry in the sun. Everything is basic, of the earth, even the clattering looms in village huts are a defiance of every technology this century prides itself in—mechanical, commercial, hightech, hyped-up advertising. **Silk knows its own value**. The buying and selling of it in the lanes of Varanasi are astonishingly lowkey, especially if while buying one catches a glimpse of a humble weaver standing below the fat shopkeeper, with his simple rush basket of flowing silk a matter of tough bargaining, the fatter of the two winning and almost throwing the rupees at the bedraggled weaver.

◆ And yet fashioned from a loom so basic such liquid material probably is almost the same that a weaver worked with shuttle and skill certainly a 1000 years before this millennium. Weighty brocades of rare and priceless quality from Tamilnadu, Mysore and Benares, in muted colours from Bengal, printed designs taken from friezes on pillars of antiquity and thrown effortlessly over the shoulder as the final decorative statement of a nine or six yard sari, all these and many other distinctive regional design

and weaves bear testament to the continuum over millennia of Indian style, taste and the consummate skill in the flick of a delicate wrist born of guild and caste lineage tracing back to before written documentation.

Indian textiles—cotton as well as silk—were treasured from the Mediterranean worlds of Greece and Rome to those of the Far East when ships set sail in the second century BCE from Orissa and Tamil country to the Spice Islands, beyond the Malay peninsula. Even by Buddhist times in the fitful light of caves at Ajanta the painted wall murals indicate the sophistication of material worn by dark beauties, sparkling goblets in their hands, diaphanous silks floating in sunlit beams, pearls and other glittering hair decorations catching the light.

Most authorities believe that the original knowledge of silk weaving came from China. **Chinsukh** is the term originally used. The Silk Routes were famed in antiquity and led from Rajasthan, up the Hindu Kush over the high passes into the plateaux of inner China even before Buddhist monks trekked there from 5th century BCE onwards. Trade and cultural interlinks across continents are fascinating to follow through. In much later times silk (and wool) **shals** became **shawls**. A Persian word, shal, defined a whole range of garments flung around the shoulders. Thus the mango design travelled back with British Army personnel and families of administrators to become the stylish **paisley** design.

◆ Apart from the fact that temple cities were actually the swarming marketplace centres due to the daily flow of pilgrims (today the estimate is that 10,000 people pass daily through the majestic gopurams at Madurai) and regional rites of passage and wedding season ceremonies caused increased attendance for temple worship, silk was designated as **sattvic** = pure and non-polluting as a material to be worn by the deities when they are 'attired' (very realistically as real people in the temple ceremonies).

Sari miniatures with silver borders especially woven and bought deep in the heart of the Kinnara bazaar in Benares supply householders for dressing their miniature istadevatas.

Wild silks, honey coloured hues, mainly come from Northeast India, especially Assam and Bengal. **Tussar** is well-known via the government-established craft emporiums for thicker jackets for men to be worn in the winter. **Eri** is also from this region but is woven from cocoons which provide an unbroken fine filament of silk. Benares heavy brocades for weddings, major presentations and other major family transitions are famous. Gujarat has especial designs, intricate geometric tie-and-dye known as **patola**. **Ikats**—a different tie-and-dye weave of geometric borders, or sacred fish and geese similar to temple friezes—emerge from the most basic of mud hut homes in southern Orissa.

For the traveller some of the most easily accessible production lines, however, are the modern factories along the Bangalore-Mysore Road. Appointments have to be made if you wish to visit. But there is nothing like the mediaeval guild world and the chiaroscuro shadowed atmosphere of the heart of the gold and silver bazaar in India's oldest city. There, fat parents are

S

arguing while sitting in the open-fronted shops on white sheets with tough Marwaris about brocaded dowry items—pill box hats of golden peach brocade for men, eye-stunning sequinned red opulence for a bride's dream while lean and anxious-looking weavers carrying cloth-covered baskets unfold their latest creations—waiting to see what price they will fetch in the tough bargaining with the well-built lala merchant. (**Lala** = now derogatory term, a seedy film character too rich by half with unshaven stubble, fat tummy, ever belching. Jokes are made about them.)

■ **SOUTH INDIAN KINGDOMS**

This is a dry stone to stand on but a halt out of necessity. Every time I journeyed south (at least a dozen times in 45 years) my head has swum in a confusion of dynasties and dates. The culture is so locked in to a conglomeration of shifting power play even before the Christian calendar takes over, it is like being tossed around, a king-size wave of Indian history swamping you. And yet such insubstantial evidence leaves more questions than answers about which confederation of feudal chieftains permutated alliances, became powerful principalities, enlarged kingdoms even taking to maritime exploration carrying influence across the seas to Sri Lanka (Ceylon as it was then called) and southeast Asia (see **TAMIL CULTURE**).

The strange thing is that once in peninsular India where the southern states of **Karnataka**, **Andhra Pradesh**, **Kerala** and **Tamilnadu**, that downward pointing triangle, with **southern Maharashtra** and **Orissa** reflect or even instigate many of these electrical power surges of the human spirit; the uproar and upheavals in the north that left a trail of gutted embattlements, tombs and overgrown crumbled stone temples, have dissolved into equally insubstantial air, leaving little trace. The jostling between feudatory states which are even referred to in Ashokan Edicts as well as in the northern **EPICS** of the **MAHABHARATA** and the **RAMAYANA**—that is, the earliest **Cheras**, **Pandyas** and the first substantial dynasty of **Cholas** (not to be confused with those of later times who created the artistic splendours of temple-towns further south) are transformed both in style and ambience. Jostling throngs of locals as well as pilgrims from everywhere in the magnificent stately temple towns and along serenely-flowing rivers banked with shrines, musical centres and ashrams give constant movement to the countryside and its peasant farmers. Dotted with oases of Chettiar mansions enveloped in mango groves in the otherwise flat plains of Tamilnadu, and the shrines rather than forts, which crown the wooded hills of Andhra Pradesh, reflect a region saved from the depradations of the invasive Muslim forces of the north. A remarkable cultural continuum is maintained. As also on the drier Deccan plateau where a 2000 year Jain/Buddhist legacy of learning still exists visibly—a huge spiritual centre at **Nagarjuna** (the name of the turn-of-the-second-century CE monk) **konda** (place).

Every overseas traveller I have known who stayed even a short time in the south has remarked on the difference in the atmosphere, and it was my Punjabi friends who affirmed they would rather have a southern Indian family as neighbours any day—quieter, more law-abiding, cleaner—just better neighbours.

In the following centuries temple city after temple city emerged as focal points of the networks of trade and supremacy of one dynasty after another, each a symbol reflecting realms of glory and Dravidian surety in their roots of faith and belief systems. By the millenium the divine presences and their symbolic **PANTHEON** forms had rounded into physical sculpted shapes and fashioned into bronze icons, taking up their elegant stance emerging from the shadowy overhangs of the caves of Karla and Kanheri, Ahole and Badam, into the brilliant hues of a southern summer's day. From then on their presence dominated the devotional fervour of a south Indian worshipper's daily rites.

Dynasty after confusing dynasty as well as fluctuating permutating power

♦ In very rough order from 550 CE the **Chalukyas** of the northern Mysore region emerge with these first stirrings in carved sculpture on the living rock in the mysterious Jain and, Buddhist caves of the Western Ghats (turn back to **CAVES**).

♦ There follow in rough order the **Pallavas** (dominant ruler **Mahendravarman**—and the free standing **rathas** at Mahabalipuram prominent in artistic advancement) by the 7th century; the **Hoysalas** at Belur and Halebid in the west and the **Chalukyas** with a second dynamic push.

♦ The **Cheras** of Malabar spreading eastward interchanging with the **Pandyas** of the Madurai region and Chidambaram

And then the high-watermark of **Chola** glory in all the art forms of the Thanjavur and Kaveri basin regions; the gradual decline during **Nayak** rule until the final explosion of magnificence in building the **Vijayanagar** empire and its capital Hampi with its far-reaching global trading network way up in the Karnataka north of present-day Bangalore, its hub where **Krishnadeva Raya** reigned (1509–1565) over what is now modern Orissa and Andhra (Telugu literature flourished with his patronage being himself a playwright and interested in all the arts). Now at last many art books are devoted to this area—virtually unknown for us travellers in earlier decades.

A beautiful book **The Sensuous and the Sacred: Chola Bronzes from South India** by Vidhya Deheja (and others)—(Mapin, Ahmedabad, 2002) is worth reading.

Postscript:

Tamil-talk from friends never abates, so intensely proud are they of their culture.

The fluctuating fortunes of these many dynasties, their overlapping ascendancies over centuries, and uneven declines are partially due to an interesting feature of southern Indian culture pointed out to me by some of these individuals working not only in the field of the arts but those deciphering temple inscriptions and records—**a modernity in fact of autonomous assemblies at local level** which led to a subtle dispersal of power and a lessening of autocratic central government unlike the Muslim authoritarian empires of the north. The putting of the token in the pot as a democratic vote and geographic rather than political tussles diminished the hold of a king over his region. Such temples of the southern kingdoms were tremendous sociopolitical centres for the surrounding populace. In fact they have been referred to as **bio-organisms** in which not only spiritual matters are the main preoccupation.

■ SPICES

Enough is known worldwide now about Indian spices; restaurants having gone global with tandoori chicken and fabulous tingly cuisine before economists thought up the word 'global' or the microchip was invented to make it possible. But spices have whetted the taste buds far beyond what merchants could ever have foreseen in centuries gone by.

The holy cow came right back home into the Sahib's backyard in Britain of the late 50s—a delightful Indian irony since the colonial barriers at the gateway were dismantled. Could Lord Curzon have ever foreseen the slow ineluctable turn of the historical chakra? To acknowledge that his own third and fourth generation descendants would witness the de-sanctification of a Wesley Chapel in Bradford, Yorkshire in the 1980s in order that it be transformed into the largest tandoori restaurant in Britain would have been not only inconceivable—but heresy!

Well, it is so and surely Indians must relish these piquant ironies—of the spice trade in pepper, cashews of Kerala, cloves, cardamom, turmeric (haldi) and tamarind, cumin and castor oil, out of the heady bazaar atmosphere of **Kochi** (Cochin) and **Kozhikode** (Calicut) where mediaeval trade collides with the 21st century in every crumbling warehouse... and ginger, that most ubiquitous of all Indian flavours with garlic said to give strength. It sounds it! **Adrak**, Sanskrit for 'shaped like a horn' so called because ginger's knobbly shape is likened to the antlers of a stag.

It was spices that brought the Europeans, rivals all, to the luxuriant Malabar Coast in the 15th–16th century CE. India still produces roughly one-third of the world's 180,000 tonnes of pepper—'the royal prince' of spices, now challenged by Indonesia, Malaysia, Brazil, Sri Lanka.

But amid the Portuguese stone warehouses of Fort Cochin, the imposing Dutch facades, the ornate but lonely Jewish synagogue in Jewtown a stone's throw away from Mattancherry Palace on the seaward island—traders still go about their business as if intervening centuries had not existed. In immaculate white **mundus** and open neck shirts, despite the torrid temperature inside the old warehouses (non-airconditioned and cooled only by solitary circulating stand fans) they call the bubbling sounds of Malayalee auctioneers' shorthand. Nearly every afternoon, such is the overloaded nature of India's power infrastructure, unable to keep up with the leaps and bounds of modern economic thrusts, they sweat it out in the Vermeer-like shadows against brilliant sunlight as the Portuguese must have done 400 years ago when they presented the Palace (later to be renovated by the Dutch) to the Cochin Raja in 1555 AD. In the lower imperial bedrooms are incomparable frescoes as equal in beauty and colour as those at Ajanta but hardly known about, down a steep wooden ladder

hidden under a floor flap. The curator appears to think them erotic. Our family including grandchildren wondered why!

Candlepower and filtered shuttered light must similarly have greeted King Solomon's ships in search of sweet smelling incense from Mysore's sandalwood forests, teak, peacock—and these legendary spices of Kerala.

Postscript: A strange novel by **Chitra Banerjee Divakaruni, The Mistress of Spices** (Black Swan, Transworld Publishers, 1997) takes one into a surreal world where each Indian spice comes into its own 'personality', often traced back to the earliest 'texts'.

■ STHITA-PRAG(N)YA-PRAJÑA (n. *Sanskrit*, equipoise, balance)

The maintenance of stability. Sanskrit word of deep philosophical meaning conjuring up the image of **'a lamp in a windless place, a flame that burns but does not flicker'**, that is a sense of a tranquil mind, unencumbered by the tugs of any attachment (a very Buddhist search for the ideal lifestyle).

The root in Sanskrit = Latin, **status**; Greek, **statos, statike** = bringing to a standstill. English words based on this root are legion: s̲tatic, s̲tatue, establishment, s̲table, steadfast, stand.

The second part of the term is one of those Devanagri characters that foxes the English who are generally lazy about complex phonetics such as a subtle mixture of **nya** and a **G** that sounds like a **J = gnya!** ज्ञ

The message of the Bhagavad Gita could be summed up in this one word as well as in Rudyard Kipling's famous poem: IF: 'if you can keep your head when all about you are losing theirs and blaming it on you...'. A person in this supreme state of 'stabilised mentality' is likened to the tortoise found embossed on some temple entrance flagstones—when it withdraws its legs into its carapace, it is immune to sense distraction.

■ SUBRAHMANYA

is truly a south Indian name, one of the many describing **Skanda**, the second son of Siva addressed thus in antiquity, **a Purana named after him**. The legends state that he was born without the intervention of any female deity—not even Parvati, a case of immaculate conception in reverse!

Su is a prefix in Sanskrit for **auspiciousness**. The name thus implies **'dear'** or **'blessed'** by divine grace—of the **BRAHM**. This son is even more intriguing than **Ganesh** (Ganapati), first as an adolescent referred to under yet another name **Kumara**, or **Karttikeya** who rides on a peacock and the **son of the Pleiades**. No wonder strangers to India get confused by what appears to be polytheistic worship. In the Indian view such divine entities or aspects of the one godhead are too multi-faceted for single descriptions. Skanda, in his essential Being, represents the power of chastity in yoga where the male semen is stored. According to yogic babas, the ultimate control of sexual energy can be released through the energy-channel of the **Kundalini** up to the head chakra—the mouth-of-fire where it is consumed. From this suprahuman energy or **gn**owing-ness Skanda is born. Sexual power of this force can be directed to spiritual or intellectual channels instead. **Such is yogic power to create 'birth'. Murugan**, yet another aspect of this progeny of Siva is another matter altogether, darker and carrying echoes of neolithic worship forbidden to women.

■ **SUFIS** (n. *Arabic Suf* = wool)

An order of mystic-ascetic-poet-saints, some popularly known in Europe in early times as **dervishes**, captured in the popular imagination by their mesmeric spiralling dances and dramatic vestments, and reputed to have existed even before Prophet Muhammed experienced his own particular insightful visions. Certainly such orders of freethinking individuals were established in Arab and Palestinian lands by the 8th century CE. Some scholars feel that as Muslim culture spread through the whole Middle Eastern region after the death of the Prophet, these wanderers along the open lanes of communications and trade responded to the like-minded message of Islamic faith—belief in the one God and brotherhood **which the Prophet had preached**. (How precept and practice work out in society is a different matter—similarly so in the Christian world where brotherhood as preached by Christ was hardly so in many colonial/ class/ racial situations.)

◆ Islam seemed therefore a natural home to their own view of the world except that situated as they were in the Palestinian and Syrian lands they had also been influenced by those followers of Christian mysticism well-established by this time, cultural exchange, a symbiotic process within the great crossroads of trading that has occurred since time immemorial in the region of the Caspian, the Palestinian lands, Iraq, parts of Arabia and across the high lands of Persia.

1142–1236 CE

Many settled in Kashmir creating a musical poetical culture all of their own; others known as the **Chisti order** in north India attached themselves to the prominent hermitage of a saintly man **Muin-ud-din (or Moinuddin) of Ajmer**. His tomb later became the focus of Emperor Akbar's annual pilgrimage which had been undertaken to give thanks after his famous victory over the Rajputs at Chittor. For a detailed study of Khwaja Moinuddin as well as Sufi belief, spiritual disciplines, the annual Urs to which people of many faiths come, some in search of the miracles to which many worshippers attest over the centuries at this lively centre or **dargah**—look for the copiously illustrated book of **Laxmi Dhaul, Sufi Saint of Ajmer** (Apsara Publications, New Delhi, 2000).

◆ Another Chisti saint, known to have the power of prophecy, **Shaikh Salim**, lived not far from the imperial court then ensconced in Agra, Akbar having moved in from the Delhi of Humayun's time. Having no heirs despite a large harem and several sons having been born who had died in infancy Akbar, then in his mid-20s, was still without issue to carry on the Mughal line of inheritance. A remarkable portent of things to come was forecast by Shaikh Salim Chisti when sought out near Fatehpur Sikri by the anxious Emperor for blessing in this worrisome

concern for those who gossiped at Court—especially in the hothouse atmosphere most zenanas created.

◆ The prophetic words so optimistically affirmed to the Emperor came true. Three sons were born astonishingly in succession within four years of each other—**and survived**.

1569 CE...The first, **Salim** (named in honour of the Saint) later to become the next Emperor Jehangir; the second Murad in **1570**, the third in **1572**.

Such was Emperor Akbar's gratitude at the course of events and the repute of this saintly man that he decided a few years later to move the entire court to this numinous location, the humble village of Sikri at the foot of the hill, home of **Shaikh Salim**. Now in all of its deserted glory, the red-stone gem of a delicate architecture preserved in such pristine condition in the dry air, stands as symbol of this line of succession, a victory, **Fateh**, for sure for the line of Mughals 19 emperors in all; **pur**, a place where now the imposing and gigantic **Buland Darwaza** gateway, the loftiest in Muslim India looks out over the undistinguished countryside, silent now, a memory faded into the evanescent capriciousness which is the history of principalities and powers and their passing.

Described as 'one of the finest portals in the world' the Darwaza is carved with an inscription that mirrors the eclectic attitudes of Sufi influence at the height of Mughal ascendancy. After the recording of his titles and his conquest of the Deccan, the Emperor had carved in the warm red stone this passage which must have set the cat amongst the ulema pigeons (as Akbar seemed delighted to do):

Said Jesus (on whom be Peace!)
The world is a bridge, pass over it.
But build no house there.
He who hopes for an hour
Hopes for an eternity.
The world is but an hour.
Spend it in devotion, the rest is unseen.

Sufi Attitudes and Beliefs: Often clad in plain wool habits as a sign of giving up worldly possessions of fine raiment, Sufis withdraw into closed orders of acolytes attaching themselves implicitly to a particular **pir** or **saint**, more like monasteries in the West.

The tradition of **guru-shishya** being so strong an indigenous Indian concept, the devotional surrender of pupil devotee to a saint/mentor was no different. American author **Gail Godwin** in her book, **Heart** (Harper-Collins, New York, 2001) points out that the Sufi approach in matters of the heart was to augment the Buddhist ethos of 'cool mind, warm heart' to a more active 'thinking heart', a fusion in the Sufi concept of *himma*—the 'intelligence of the heart', with meditation geared to the pulsating rhythm of the actual physiological heart 'pump'.

In south Delhi is the shrine of one such charismatic guru—mentor to arrive—**Khwaja Hazrat Nizamuddin Aulia** (Khwaja indicates a person of distinction).

◆ Even to this day his **Urs** (a commemorative observance of the significant life of a Muslim **pir**) draws great numbers of

S

followers annually. Even orthodox Muslims (and others outside the faith) who abide strictly by the texts acknowledge saintliness as Gandhi did, no matter what the divisions of institutional religions. Such pilgrims come not only from within India—and even Pakistan—but from Iran and the Middle East. **Mushairas** or musical gatherings reach high emotions on such occasions— 'yearning conversations' as Ralph Russell, London SOAS (School of Oriental and African Studies) scholar, has called them. Professor Mujeeb of Jamia Milia University in south Delhi, a truly Gandhian Muslim with a gentle humourous disposition plunged us into such gatherings. Once more I took on the role of an honorary man in such an all-male congregation, fortunately almost incognito in a crowd intent on expressing heartfelt emotions as the moment took them, rising to render forth ecstatic Urdu verse which they all seemed to know by heart, the sea of heads wobbling in the sheer exuberance, an opening of a collective heart, on this momentous occasion. Appropriately amid the surrounding ruins of the **dargah** (sepulchre and mausoleum) is the grave of the saints, most famous disciple, **Amir Khusro** and **GHALIB**, poet still saluted in private home sessions wherever Pakistanis and north Indians gather in friendship overseas.

Saints Can Get Cranky Also!

It is a precarious act to cross a Sufi saint. Like the rishis of old they can bring down rulers with a potent curse—according to legend if not the exactitudes of historical fact. **Muhammad bin Tughlaq** fighting to enlarge his Sultanate mid-14th century CE, and creating unrest by raising taxes, ignored **Nizamuddin Aulia's** request for labour to build his sanctuary.

The saint declared that the Turkish-style fortress of Tughlaqabad seen as one now speeds to the annually seductive craft fair at **Surajkund** would become the habitation for nomadic Gujjars (one group of Indian Rom-gypsies) and jackals only... and so it did despite Tughlaq, away in the farthest reaches trying to put down yet another rebellion, brushing off the curse lightly when he heard of it, with his famous phrase: **Hunuz Dilli Dur Ast** (Delhi is still far off). Indeed it was. Succumbing to fever (some accounts say he was murdered) he died on the long march back.

Healing Kashmiri Music: A Personal Note

♦   In what now seems like a distant dream, in Kashmir's ongoing tragic circumstances, there was once a tranquil summer. Surrounded by the encirclement of mountains denuded of their last melted snow we listened to a Sufi musician a boatman's glide away from the formal beauty of the Nishat Gardens of Akbar in Srinagar.

Looking back with all the tragedy, the inordinate numbers of Kashmiris killed, the Hindu community of Pandits exiled, the Muslim militants intent on preventing any peaceful solution in their power games, were we in a dream (khwaab), or did we wake to a dreamlike reality on that night we first experienced **ghazal** music so redolent of Sufi sentiment with Ghalib's famous poetry....*Hain khwaab main hanooz jo jaageh hain khwaab main ...*

Punchdrunk from the body blows of searing heat down on the Gangetic plain where an egg would fry instantly on a car

bonnet, we sat down in 'heaven on earth' as this poignant land was referred to in Mughal days. Refreshment of spirit lay on us like thick balm. A special concert of Kashmiri music was being presented by the not-long established AIR station. Towering chinar trees enclosed us in shadows, their bold leaves (larger than sycamore) touched by the gold and crimson tints of Kashmir's approaching autumn. Placid waters billowed softly like grey shot silk melting into the shadows, a reminder of all the Hindu past, the **Shankaracharya** temple dedicated atop the hill overlooking Srinagar by that fibre-tough thinker.

One young man beginning to make a name for himself as a **santoor** player as well as vocalist let the ripples of this 100-stringed instrument flow as his voice addressed **the Beloved One, a bridal imagery of this Sufiyaana Moosiq**—yearning for union in the soul. And then suddenly we were brought down to a very homely atmosphere as half the population of the valley seemed to materialize in a hazy circle, so unused to local radio or expressions of music outside of the home or the hermitage in those long gone days of tranquillity... a quiet shuffle of people in long pherans and embroidered 'saucer caps', a few mischievous rogues of the trading community ever watchful of our stranger's presence, ready to touch us for an artful 'bargain' while silent women glided back home sitting crouched on the flat bow of their long shikaras after gathering vegetables from the floating gardens.

♦   Now famous, this Sufi poet and musician **Sheikh Abdul Aziz,** forerunner of another internationally-known santoor player **Shiv Kumar Sharma** on the WOMAD circuit, has stayed true to his Kashmir heritage. He is better known at the University of Maryland for his book **Romooz-i-Moosiq** than in his homeland—decimated as its arts presently are.

Writing in praise of his Sufi heritage he has given insights into a Kashmir now lost in the murky penumbra of terrorism spread through the valleys like penetrating smoke drifting from gunshot and metallic explosion as also another poignant poet of exile in the **Secrets of Ishbar** by **Subhash Kak** (Vitasta, New Delhi, 1996).

♦   Here was a healing balm. The Sheik quotes another Sufi thinker, Farid, of half a millennia ago in equally turbulent times: **I use a needle. Not the scissors. I sew, I do not cut.**

Akbar's chronicler-extraordinaire, Abul Fazl, refers to the Kashmiri sufis as the most honourable people of the Valley. As saintly selfless mentors who blended yogic practices, Buddhist 'mindfulness' and Jain austere diet such Sufis have also been referred to recently as harbingers of peaceful coexistence.

Given such an example of ancient tolerance these Muslim 'rishis' exemplified between the 13th–17th centuries one wishes that such attitudes could be resurrected for modern society today. Actual **written** history by learned poet **Kalhana**(the **Rajatarangini**—Rivers of Kings, early 12th century) shows that under King Laladitya(7th–8th c CE; prophet Muhammed born c. 570–632 in distant Arabia) Sufi influence may well have established itself in his prosperous and well-ruled valley. Architecture (the Martand Sun Temple), irrigation and flourishing agriculture presented a very different Kashmir from today. And even an enlightened Sultan, **Zain-ul-Abidin** proved so tolerant in the 15th century before the rot set in (see **KASHMIR**) that shrines and festivals were shared between Hindu and Muslim under the guidance of a saintly Sufi–Saikh Nooruddin Wali, popularly called Nand Rishi.

Endnote: Caught in the corner of the eye another of India's unexpected and magical flashes of street theatre—humanity in all its astonishing array, a statuesque and lean man well over six feet tall, loping with insouciance through the fray looking neither to left nor right through the total disarray of a traffic snarl-up within sight of Humayun's tomb in south Delhi.

Barefoot and a stave in hand, he was encompassed in a swirling green wool robe, a conical hood with an incongruous pixie bobble atop, a Muslim goatee the only indication apart from green of any affiliation. But the Sikh taxicab driver knew his man— a Pakistani **pir** visiting Nizamuddin's tomb and like-minded residents in the caravanserai style sanctuary that has grown up around this centre of pilgrimage.

Not one express bus ran him down. A miracle indeed when there was a casualty a day from these lethal vehicles of terror, now banned. Perhaps he too—almost walking on air—oblivious to present danger was in a dream within a dream, a free soul crossing frontiers of animosity, threatened nuclear rivalries, political chicanery between religious politics of the 21st century.

Long may he continue on his own Muslim-Sufi padayatra.
and Abida Parveen record her Sufi-inspired voice on CDs!

■ **SUSVAGATAM** (n. *Sanskrit*)
'**You are most welcome**', seen in the shortened form **sw** or **svagatam** in Devanagari script on decorative archways especially erected to welcome honoured visitors, dignitaries, or guests on official invitations. The additional syllable marked by the **सु** = su, gives emphasis of benign blessing to the word itself = **सुस्वागतम** su-svaa-ga-tam.

■ **SWADESHI/SWARAJ** (n. *Sanskrit* self/country self/rule)
(**swa** = self, own) is in vogue again, long after Gandhi resurrected it as an emotive political cry for **self-reliance** on his return from South Africa (see **KHADI**), and fitfully promoted by the government as a political message of **pride in things Indian** which also contains a certain xenophobic dislike of MNCs.

In 1909 Gandhiji stirred up controversy by writing what has been called his minor classic: **Hind Swaraj**. This was concerned with **swa** = self, **raj** = rule, dominion a matter of concern for a very fine Maratha **Lokmanya Tilak** also. Distinctive in the gathering force of political meetings defying British dominion as the first stirrings of the Independence struggle bubbled the Indian crowds, the luxuriant handle-bar moustache and flat black hat-turban marked out this proud patriot. Labelled by the British government an extremist too close to the likes of the great icon, Shivaji, Tilak declared: **Swaraj is my birthright**.

There were other great men of that time moved by a sense of justice, principled in their placing nationhood before the self-serving of many present politicians. Great architects of the idealistic Congress party in its beginnings—**Dadabhai Naoroji, a Parsi who actually coined the term Swaraji; Lala Lajpat Rai** 'Lion of the Punjab', and Bengali **Chittaranjan Das**. Gandhi followed in their footsteps emphasising India's right to return to her own roots and value systems and not to be messed about by a total domination of Western ideas not suited in some cases to her environmental needs. The essence of his message was that ancient call of the rishis to live in harmony with nature and what would today be heralded as **'the sustainable development'** message. The book met with contempt for such backward antediluvian ideas and was dismissed as irrelevant for the industrialising economy of India. So much for a sustainable economy.

■ **SWASTIKA** (n. *Sanskrit*)
su = well, *asti* = being, *svast* = auspicious
all being well meaning, as an overall concept, **when something is regarded as auspicious, fortunate.** A sense of infinite **wellbeing—material, physical and spiritual.**

Arriving soon after WWII when independent India was only six years old, it came as quite a shock to be transported soon afterwards out to a group of villages (now swallowed up into Delhi's megalopolis) to witness **a rural festival celebrating gau-mata, mother cow.** On what must now be one of Palam airport's land-gobbling international runways, in the days when you could walk onto the tarmac to meet friends coming down the ladder from sleek Comet aircraft, turbaned villagers had laid succulent veggies on the earth. They were also hand feeding a line of lucky cows with a mixture of brown jaggery—**gur**—and oatcakes.

With gaily-painted horns of blue and gold, yellow and red, 'Miss Piggy' cartoon eyelashes fluttering, they were skittishly prancing around at their unexpected luck at such good tucker. It was not so much this Hindu ebullience in the art of marking just about everything in the agricultural year, Mother Cow being far more valuable in ancient rural patriarchies than the derogatory western reference to 'a real old cow' = i.e., the wife, but the sight of **swastikas**, hand brushed erratically on their flanks that arrested attention... and with abruptness.

◆ Such a sign sent spine-tingling shudders through the nervous system. Imprinted on all our memories was that Teutonic image of mechanically goose-stepping stormtroopers, precision marching to Hitler's salute—this aberrant sign concentrating into its crooked arms all the evil Nazidom personified.

And yet to the Hindu the crooked arms embrace a venerated concept, to be worn as an amulet to ward off evil, emblem of the life-giving Sun God, golden **Surya**, arising in the firmament each day, galloping with the seven horses of the week to bring life, warmth, sunlight for chlorophyll and plants to grow—without which we would be a dead planet.

Over the years this symbol, a short-hand design for a highly abstruse philosophy, began again to reassert its true density of

S

meaning before Hitler in his demonic quest for a pure Aryan race (as if there could ever be one!) hijacked its true essence. In Indian sacred ceremonies and temple chantings 'swasti' can be heard along with **shanti**, the final amen, giving blessing at the end of puja.

♦   The crooked arms can be printed either way in Hindu art—it makes no difference to its essential metaphysical meaning. Its origins one presumes are in India with the Saraswati river basin peoples spreading with it throughout India and into Europe. In diggings the emblem has been found on pottery and shards at **Chogha Mish** in south west Iran dating back to at least 3,400 BC. The golden age of Iranian pottery is acknowledged to go back even further to 4,500 BC. The resonances of the swastika are therefore known to antiquity and have pervaded Indian art as well as the spiritual rituals, wedding rites, folk motifs and fine ceiling sculpture.

Its meaning:

♦   In the very earliest Vedic fire ceremonies the four cardinal points were always emphasised also as in the building of the hawan, fire pit, before the puja could begin. **The swastika is said to 'embrace' and hold in the energy of those cardinal points** but being open-ended, the branched arms were capable of expanding also into the cosmos. Firesticks used to be placed pointing outwards—yet another **QUATERNITY**.

♦   In the yogic vision the point/**BINDU** at the centre expands to the immensity of space expressed by the bent arms. That space cannot be defined by a completed □ or ○; only when sped around on its hub will the swastika take on the shape of a completed circumference, indeed a metaphor for the pulsating rhythms of creation—growth and fullness in all its plenitude when the circle is whole. And then the dissipation of energy into the void as the circumference fractures into bent arms and open spaces again. Constant fluidity.

♦   Yogis also have written that truth (that central Oneness) transcendent beyond planetary time and knowledge, cannot be reached along a straight line; truth is often arrived at inadvertently or by serendipity, in sudden flashes of illumination that take over the mind from unexpected angles—**the crooked path**.

Indeed Indians no matter of what spiritual background are averse to straight lines. The clarity of the Graeco-Roman world where deductive logic led our minds from A to B to C does not exist.

♦   Circles, domes, cupolas, circumambulatory passages around shrines, storage bins in courtyards, creations of the village potter's wheel are all **circular**. Watch people sit down on the grass to talk, or a student class gather under a spreading tree to listen to the guru. Like the Australian Aborigines they form quite naturally a circle. Mass-produced angular architecture and sharp points have alas come with Western architectural influence, including the horrendous 'ant hills' of cheap municipal housing in the nation's major cities.

♦   Surprisingly even in Australia the benign swastika has literally surfaced as design tiles in floor paving—of the old Customs House at Circular Quay in Sydney. The flooring was completed apparently in 1887, half a century before its evil manifestation

resurfaced again. So was there an Indian craftsman?

Fittingly, as a single motif, it appears on the original first edition of the **Collected Verse of Rudyard Kipling**. Supposedly arch-imperialist poet in India—now thankfully being re-assessed even by Bengali scholars undertaking PhD theses on the man, few people read beyond his most famous two-liner: **East is East and West is West**... to discover a remarkably enlightened conclusion for colonial **1889**. Search it out for a multicultural conclusion!

■   **SYMBOLS**

...play a remarkable and continual part in the development of Indian civilisation, carrying very sophisticated and interconnected thought patterns in their constant replenishment and abstract updatings, as visual shorthand describing complex resonances in Indian life, and pregnant syllables chanted to expand the mind into other realms of consciousness than the pragmatic and empirical.

At the philosophical level Indians appear to be constantly plugged into an electric current running directly from the dynamo of Jung's collective unconsciousness—a great reservoir of truths, visual or oral, outside time and space, but eternally present, unrecognised by individuals until a progressive stage of development = 'realization' is reached.

♦   This realization acknowledges the presence of archetypes, an original type or model prototype that exists in all cultures:

♦   **The Flood** and the rescue of the human race from obliteration (the Ice Age)

♦   the **Fallen Angel**—or unredeemed character representing forces opposing rta = Milton's Satan for one in **Paradise Lost**; **Ravana** in the **Ramayana**; several characters in **The Lord of the Rings** and **Harry Potter**.

♦   **Romeo and Juliet** syndrome. Heer Ranjha and many other legendary lovers unrequited

♦   **The faithful wife**: Sita, Draupadi, Savitri—and the faithful husband?...

The hexagram is a common and well-known representation of the biological interlinking of male and female principles—the fusion symbolising the perfect union of spirit (**purusha** = masculine forces descending from above, that is the cosmos) with matter (**prakriti** = feminine receptive energies, the earth receiving the thrust of fertility).

However, this symbol is in reverse—the dark triangle pointing upwards like the lingam when active, the feminine white triangle pointing downwards as the yoni = womb does in natural biology.

The pentagram is a most complex condensation of metaphysical philosophy, involving spirit/soul, intellect, heart, will, at the very core of the world view yoga encourages.

♦   The inner pentagram in miniature interweaves with the same corresponding powers of the universe according to the teaching of yogic gurus—**Kundalini** of a vast all-embracing kind, without words to explain such Divine Cosmic Energy.

♦   **Padmasana**, the lotus position, that yogic posture in which the Buddha is so often depicted, is the one most comfortable for concentrating on this intricate process, harnessing, releasing, reflecting the very pulse of life in these condensed representations of many clusters of ideas.

♦ The individual who achieves a basic harmony, a liberated person who is in harmony with other people, enjoys acceptance of human existence in the cosmos without a sense of alienation, who foregoes self-gratification to give generously, moving outwards into life and other people's lives, paradoxically receives in greater measure from **the energies of whatever one wishes to call the Cosmic Force** embedded (in the yogic view) in the solar plexus of the human body. There lies that network of nerves at the base of the spine behind the stomach, the fly-wheels in the nervous system of the human machine as **B K S Iyengar** writes in **Light on Yoga** (turn to **YOGA**).

■ TAMIL CULTURE and the Tamils

a seagoing people who spread their culture peaceably throughout southeast Asia and whose attitude of mind can best be epitomised in the recent idiomatic phrase: 'koncham (little) aadjust' with the emphasis on the first syllable…Very adaptable and that despite rigid rules of caste social behaviour at certain periods, the eternal Indian paradox.

A Tamil friend dilating with a wry smile on this flexibility and adaptability of Tamils in distant lands to accommodate themselves and become part of whatever culture in which they find themselves made this remark on 'koncham /kunjam aadjust': 'This is what the camel might say when entering the Bedouin's tent!' What he meant was that adaptability is self-imposed, the sea taking them out psychologically over the horizons. 'We aren't enclosed, land-locked like those northerners!'

And no wonder! Lying in the flat wetlands of the coast, **Poompuhar** north of Pondicherry was a great port in the huge delta of the majestic Kaveri river mentioned in the classic literature of the **Silippadikaram** before the Roman calendar of dating began.

The Interior Landscape and the Tamil Language

A K Ramanujan declared that Tamil **'as one of the two classical languages of India, is the only language of contemporary India which is recognisably continuous with the past'**, Sanskrit having lost its everyday presence as a conversational tongue for ordinary people (**The Interior Landscape,** Indiana University Press, 1967).

That is what makes it so singularly unique, explaining why all the superb art forms of Tamilnadu reflect its steadfast foundations in the **Agama** texts of codifications and maxims as reference points in all they express; why Tamils in their personal lives are so psychologically sure in the traditional modes of their daily home life, away from prying eyes. Here they continue ancient and meaningfully symbolic ceremonies, from the early morning bath, to the lighting of the lamp, to that first delicious steaming sip of milky south Indian coffee! And then the knowledge of those freshly-cooked **idlis** and **dosais** to come not forgetting the most scrumptious ingredient of all, the spoonful of tingling chutney in a dollop of yoghurt on the side of a **thali** plate or plantain leaf. *That* is the sparking plug that sets in motion humanity on a south Indian morning after the gentle chanting of domestic prayer and a flower plucked straight from the garden for the personal **ISTADEVATA**… as well as the ubiquitous flower garland of many for even the poorest women in the village.

1964

Perhaps now that an international **Association of Tamil Research** has been founded, its initial meeting interestingly enough in Malaysia's capital (the Indian Malaysian being predominantly Tamil from several 100 years of settlement during British colonial interference by bringing indentured labour for the rubber and tin estates), further discoveries into this rich store of Tamil culture can be made.

Unhappily for Tamil peoples, very little is known of the wellspring of their culture which of all India's flourishing and diverse mosaic is at least documented specifically in literature of a high order way back to the 3rd century BCE, but known in an oral tradition tracing back into an unidentified prehistory. (Recent excavations at Poompuhar visited on my last journey to the extensive Carnatic music festival in honour of Tyagaraja, suggest dates several centuries earlier.)

More readily known to the world is northern classic literature and its social roots interpreted by the Vikram Seths, Mulk Raj Anands, Khushwant Singhs, Nirad Chaudhuris and a whole array of literary giants in the north. Kamla Markandaya started a process in the early 50s of making known the world beyond the inner life of the south but **Tholkappi** who wrote the **Tholkappiam**, a work of discipline in stanzas of a didactic nature (**tol** = ancient, **kappiam** = grammatical work, including a compendium of various aspects of public/private behaviour) still remains a shadowy figure of prehistory, and is hardly known to the intelligent traveller from overseas.

Other noteworthy literature about which Tamils themselves enthuse, remains inaccessible in readable translation for a worldwide public.

Circa 5th c BCE….The Sangam Literature…

The sangams were literary academies for poets and other writers which gathered in Madurai regularly to present and discuss works. The **first sangam** exists by tradition but no literary works have ever been documented.

The second is the Tamil grammar just mentioned, the Tholkappiam.

The third sangam produced 'the eternal gem with a universal message' **Tiru-Kural** the renowned compilation of over 2,500 **kurals** (maxims or aphorisms) in the form of Tamil couplets composed by **Tiruvalluvar.** This holds an especial place in the Tamil psyche, cherished and quoted daily, even used on greeting cards for wedding invitations and retirement homilies.

Perhaps what has survived in compilations of this earliest literature, the **Sangam,** (in Tamil, **cankam**) and which was finally written down in the great period of scribes around **100–300 CE** (the same period that the epics and the Bhagavad Gita were finalised onto the page or parchment) is so sparse that this is the reason for ignorance outside of India. **A) First Sangam,** undoubtedly belonging to prehistory because of the very nature of its attainment which presupposes centuries of human development to reach such literary standards, refers to a period when activities of a literary body regulated and set standards. However knowledge about the first Sangam is indeed shadowy. Either geological upheavals, or the steady erosion of fragile palm records due to tropical climate, have left enigmatic signals as if travelling light years from outer space.

Certain structural rules were evolving in the literature, however, as to how it was presented.

- **Puram** writing signified attention to guidance in verse, directed to the **public/social arena** with didactic passages on how a king and his ministers should behave, how to administer urban life, in fact all the aspects of social life.
- **Aham** is the literary form referred to sometimes as 'love poetry'. Really it is versification dealing with the **private, personal arena**, including the emotional and often individual themes of love and what a person's own behaviour should be.
- **Veedu** literature is concerned with the final 'home'—the **individual's spiritual home**, seen as situated at the foot of the guru or deity.

Such love poems are as sweet and fresh with the dawn of time and young love as any so noted in English verse of the Romantic Poets (and so **'by-hearted'** in feats of memory by any educated Indian over the age of 60 brought up in English-type schooling when **learning by heart** was the order of the day!).

WHAT HER FRIEND SAID
The great city fell asleep
but we did not sleep
Clearly we hear, all night
from the hillock next to our house
the tender branches of the flower-clustered tree
with leaves like peacock feet
let fall
their blue-sapphire flowers...

Poet **Kollan Arici**, Third Sangam (circa 100–500 CE).

Ramalingar (born 1823 CE of the **Karuneekar** caste, hereditary village accountants) a devotee of Shiva declares:

Innumerable are the large galaxies of
undying worlds
wherein are contained
millions and millions of worlds
all of them put together
are as a millionth part of an atom
in the presence of the heavenly sacred feet
on the resplendent Golden Hall
So say those who know

to be found in India's **Sahitya Akademi** = Academy of Letters series... **Tamil Culture**.

B) Early poets called their inner landscape based on a visual imagery, **tinais**, divided into four distinct natural landscapes where Tamil people lived and worked before an urban civilization developed: there was the pastoral, **mullai**; hill country, **kurunji**; arable land, **marudam**, and the coastal tracts **neydal**. Each landscape was reproduced in literature music and dance, reflected in the atmosphere artists then created.

100 BCE

C) **Tiruvalluvar**: the poet saint who made a living as a humble weaver (like Kabir, a similar personality a millennium and a half later) was married to a pious and loving wife,

Vasuki. He was regarded however far above his status—**'a venerable sage'** of Tamilnadu—because of his workaday wisdom related to the common person, beyond caste or creed but composed in such an uplifting way that he has been likened to Seneca, Horace, Dante, Shakespeare, Robert Browning and William Wordsworth!

He certainly was a profoundly kind man because he came to be venerated by the local brahmins as he is today by Tamils scattered round the globe 2,000 years later. His homilies on how humans need to comport themselves covers just about every aspect of life—virtue and morality; wealth and pleasure: and love—'furtive' and 'married'! One very Indian quality, that of quite overwhelming hospitality, is quoted from him in **ATITHI**. A massive statue to the poet has now been erected at India's southern tip to face Swami Vivekananda.

D) At the turn of the millennium **Buddhist/Jain period > 500 CE... Tamil Idylls and Epics** developed the body of literature in a great surge forward.

- Over 400 poets with their individual isolated poetry emerge, as well as the two most famous longer works compilations, plus the constantly-referred-to Epic.
- **Pathupattu**—idylls like the Iliad in the style of sharp aphorisms sung by the bards and referred to as the Ten Idylls.
- **Etuthok(h)ai**—historical ballads in praise of kings and love lyrics: **The Eight Idylls.**
- **Silippadikaram** (**Silip** = anklet; **padi or pathi** = epic poem) of uncertain date, scholars differing on this matter also. This popular story for children growing up and recited by grandparents defies the rule that there is no real tragic drama in Indian literature. Unfolding a tale of an innocent young wife betrayed by her libertine husband who squanders the family wealth on a seductive courtesan; her faithful nature (a model held up for public appraisal in all the ancient literature!) allowing him despite his deceptive behaviour to return to the family fold.

They travel to Madurai, the capital of the Pandyan Kingdom. The husband takes one of his wife's anklets to sell for money and is betrayed by the court goldsmith who accuses him to the king of stealing it, so having him put to death.

Eventually all is made clear to the much-put-upon **Kannaki**, now the widow. She turns out to be more feisty than one would expect and marches into the city to the palace. Carrying the other golden bejewelled anklet of the pair she requests audience of the ruler and when asked her purpose, roundly accuses him of straying from the path of duty and justice by allowing such a thief to doublecross her husband. Such injustice! The king mindful of smudged dharma collapses and dies of shock.

The goddess of Madurai materialises to retrieve the situation explaining to the distraught Kannaki the reasons why all this tragedy has occurred due to previous actions in earlier reincarnations. The coda however to this lamentable tale is that after further self-scourging Kannaki is gathered up into heaven as a goddess, her saintliness to be remembered where once more she is reunited with her now celestially restored husband, but no longer in human form.

Resolution comes—but not in this life. However, the coda sums it up:

Even the gods pay honour to the wife
who worships no one save her husband
Kannaki, pearl among all women of the earth,
is now a goddess, and is highly honoured....

Alain Danielou trans. 1965

E) **Kamban**, revered Tamil **poet of the 11th century CE** spent every night studying Valmiki's original Sanskrit text of the Ramayana, translating it in thousands of lines the following day. Typical of the assiduous learning capacity of Indians, 10,500 stanzas eventually piled up on palm leaf, each painstakingly inscribed in Tamil and called the **Kambaramanyam (Ramayana)**.

♦ **The socio-economic aspects of cultural advance**

The age of exploration and rise of powerful dynasties was reflected back into the distant (in those days of basic transport) temple cities—of vigorous pulsating bazaar trade linked into China, the Spice Islands, Sumatra, Cambodia, and west to Egypt and the Mediterranean. Slowly the Hindu impulse regenerated as Buddhist/Jain cultural domination peaked during these early eras one after another in the flow of the **SOUTH INDIAN KINGDOMS**. A new millennium was dawning 2,000 years ago.

Artistic impulse to re-present **Devi**, the **Mother Goddess** (for instance the solid figurine dug up in a field and now in the **Madras Egmore Museum** is dated **approx. 1000 BCE**) and **Shiva** reiterates itself in great cycles of time. His striped terracotta-coloured temples and the legends of his prolific lingam scatter their fertile blessing throughout the peninsular. These are the two perennial symbols of that most Indian entity—that downward-pointing landscape of southern pink plains and sudden hills hardly touched by the Islamic impress or bureaucratic weight of Mughal administration, or British influence over central government.

Religious fervour clamoured for expression through
our myriad temples, rock carvings, paintings on ivory,
in the brilliance of exposition, the rainbow colours of
the dance.

is how one south Indian put it to me in Madurai, bursting with pride in her culture!

600–625 CE

The first true Dravidian-style temples are constructed with the royal munificence of the **Pallava** rulers. The **BHAKTI** poet/saint lyricists inspired a spirit in the land that makes the word **exuberance** overworked. How else can be described the visual landscape—except in the gifted phrase used by a New York Times art reviewer, Holland Cotter in another context trying to sum up the full rich encounter of a 1996 Exhibition in Washington—**Puja: Expressions of Hindu Devotion**. The phrase used—**devotional vivacity**—sums up this unique artistic **energy**, the very splendour of it all.

Driving by road is the true way to encounter south India—to be shaken by the massive size and scale of a distant temple, its majestic gopurams towering the closer you approach, to be stirred in the innermost core with the overwhelming, teeming, integrated mass of sculptured figures, now painted back into traditional polychromic colours—just to add to the eye-shattering effect, climbing up the huge **vimana** towers, the **PANTHEON** in all its representational profusion of that power in the cosmos.

And what is this colourful party in a field of gathered crops? A hobbyhorse troupe of dancers with turbans and red scarves, cymbals clashing, drums clattering, a farmer rejoicing for the bounty from a good monsoon. It could be Shakespearean times all over again, the horse like a boat into which the dancer had climbed, tassels and bobbles flying in circles as the horses pranced. The energy quotient spills out in all artistic forms even today, as though everybody is engaged—artisans obviously but villagers of all kinds, urban accountants, civil servants (whom normally one never associates with creative arts!) bankers, housewives, journalists. The very best jam session of jazz percussion I have ever enjoyed was in Madurai with classical Indian musicians and Mrs Mani, well-known vocalist from Bangalore, in a fusion music with one Western saxophonist. We could almost have experienced levitation with the throbbing syncopation and the accompanying mathematically demanding 'conversation piece', seven drums answering each other in a **tal vadya kacheri**.

F) **Divinity and deviance and bhakti devotion**… a mystical madness that suffuses the totally unconscious 'feminist movement' of the 12th–13th centuries—is an extraordinary tradition in the south. Female poet-saints from different levels of society and across regions (especially in the adjoining **Kannada-speaking region** of **Karnataka** interlinked in many ways with the strong **bhakti** movements of Tamilnadu) sought their own spiritual freedom from patriarchal social norms and rituals of the male-dominated home. Brahmin, prostitute, housewife, low caste artisan (often a weaver = spinster), married women with supportive husbands, or ashram-based sage-gurus broke out into the highly charged heroic = **virasaivite** movement.

♦ Even high-born women—Lingayat brahmins—took off, spiritual 'loners' (as did Christian women mystics **at the same time** in mediaeval Europe—an interesting historical point to consider) divesting themselves not only of prevailing social codes but garments shed in defiance of modesty. Nakedness, accepted socially in India amid male spirituality from that earliest virtually mental **singularity**—the outlined human being—to Jain saints in all their male glory to sexually explicit sadhus, is still shocking when practised by women. Yet to women devotees it is logically and rationally an acceptance of liberation—a realization of the true 'self' unclouded by male inhibitions, fearful of their own aroused sexuality—a peril all women have faced in their struggles to live, hassle free, since the first cave woman got dragged by her hair into cohabitation with the physically powerful male!

Many of these women are referred to with the prefix **akka, elder** or **big sister,** or **amma, mother,** such as Mahadevi-akka or Nagamma, and Lakkamma, a married saint who wrote a very potent erotic devotional verse to the lover deity = Siva. (A fascinating series of books is now emerging as modern Indian women, educated and freed economically and psychologically from old inhibitions, research the ancient texts and histories—such as Vijaya Ramaswamy with two books to her credit. **Divinity and Deviance: Women in Virasaivism,** (OUP, New Delhi 1996) and **Walking Naked: Women, Society, Spirituality in South India** (IIAS, Shimla, 1997).

In the coastal (and very well cared-for) town, once French, of **Karaikal,** the **Punithavathi Ammaihyar Festival** remembers the heroic devotion of the emaciated **NAYANMAR** saint who undertook **TAPASYA** of an inordinate kind … some devotees say because she is really an incarnation of Parvati and therefore married to Shiva? In essence she was, despite her earthly marriage, her husband (deserving of sympathy) forced into a life of celibacy. A **Mango Festival** in June recalls her married dilemmas when an unknown guest (Shiva in disguise testing her devotion) needs sustenance. She gives him a mango intended for her husband… and another… her husband returns wanting food. The mangoes are gone… but Shiva intervenes to explain the innocence of her fulsome gestures.

And a personal note: With my Tamil musician friend of the 'quality personality' (see **LANGUAGE**) we sought out the tiny temple devoted to **Punithapathi** (everyone knows where it is) to see the mural depicting her life, the mango saga, becoming ugly (to repulse the attentions of other men for her beauty) and finally 'walking' on her hands in **TAPASYA** to reach her Mahadev, to do **pranam**.

Ancient...

Travelling the length and breadth of the south by road over the last five decades, being present in large concourses of people, meeting villagers, living in people's homes (a great privilege), talking to ministers and impoverished students alike, one becomes aware of a gifted people secure in their heritage, sure of their identity. Custom and tradition are enacted daily, effortlessly across community. But it never was an inhibition and certainly never led to xenophobia. English became a second language. Now they lead the nation into cyber-space.

There is an inexplicable integrity in the air. Not that other regional cultures such as Bengali and Punjabi do not enjoy strong identities but Tamils have—**relatively speaking**—not been disrupted by history in the same way as those cultural entities of the north. In that region constant invasion has taken its toll. Even in the music there is a strand of Islamic melancholia from western Asia that suffuses love songs, whereas Carnatic music proclaims a joyous certainty; the strains of the sarod, a yearning for some lost identity in the high passes of upper Asia, a different Islamic view of the universe plucking at the heartstrings in quite a different way from the assertion of elated exhilaration in the South.

The heavy presence of alien incomer has weighed less upon this seagirt land where adaptability is **self-imposed**. Tamils have been noted for their intellectual prowess— thinkers, philosophers, medical achievers, mathematicians, engineers, saint-musicians (women included). Sacred grove and the electricity of numen flowed out to the courtyard of natural 'surround' at Mahabalipuram, south of Chennai. The rock-cut sculpture known as **Arjuna's Penance**, well over 1000 years old, is a permanent example of the engineering and artisan skills of coping in the most astonishing fluid terms of plasticity with the granite material of south Indian rock— called the toughest in the world, consisting of the 'finest crystalline granite'.

And there is always this passionate honouring of their language. A very distant descendant of a man born in 1876–M M Adikal–still lays a flower in her home shrine for him. 'He was a gifted communicator, a genius even as a student, with perfect knowledge of all our Tamil classics. People tell me the flow of his speech was likened to the strings of the harp! He did a typical Hindu thing–giving up his position as Head of Tamil studies at Madras Christian College and took to the open road like our nayanmar saints extolling this rich language. He gave up everything just to do that!'

Perhaps because of this assuredness there has been complacency on the part of Tamil people in 'putting themselves over' to the rest of the world. Kabir and Mirabai may be known to some Western readers of Indian literature but Tamils have been slow in translating their own rich poetry.

Even before 'the first' proponent of **ADVAITA** philosophy in modern times = Adi Shankaracharya restored monism and the fusion of the sense of divine and the worshipper into a oneness—Thou Art That—a youthful Tamil saint swathed in mystery, miracle and legend, walked the tracks of Tamil lands. His name was **Jnana** (ultimate knowledge) **Samp(b)andar**. From the age of three the muse descended on him 'by the benign grace of gentle Parvati' and from then on Tamil scholars do not blink an eye when they assert that he 'prodigiously composed extempore verses' on this viewpoint which is 'the pre-Aryan **Saiva Siddhanta**, a Dravidian revival' in the 7th century CE.

A sublime image of the saint as he came to be accepted–Sambandar–crafted by a Chola artisan in bronze in the 12th century caught my eye in the marvellous **'Vision of Kings'** exhibition curated a decade ago by Michael Brand in the Canberra National Gallery Exhibition, Sambandar now gracing Australia in all his youthful nakedness, as firm and beautifully proportioned as any Grecian Apollo, a tiger-claw amulet necklace to protect his vulnerable innocence of youth.

T

And then at the age of 16 yet another miracle to defy scientific rationalism according to M S Poornalingam Pillai who, as a new breed of Tamil scholar emerging as a result of education in the British Raj of the WWI period, was intent on making known these renowned saints—Sampandar being one of the 63 **NAYANMAR** bhakti poet-musician wanderers from temple city to temple city where their names are enshrined (see **CHIDAMBARAM**).

Writing in **The Indian Review** of the period (April 1915) with the intent of retrieving his Tamil culture for the outside world to recognise its most ancient pre-Sanskrit lineage, he documents the wedding of this 16 year-old who with his bride entered the temple at Nallur to solemnise the marriage rites—'and were seen no more. Thus his brief span of life which 'buckled in a sum of age', terminated as it opened in a miracle.'

♦ Swallowed into a flashing radiance emanating from Shiva's powerful aura as other saints are said also to have experienced, Sampandar is remembered not only for this miraculous merging into the infinite at such a tender age, but his strong advocacy of returning to the original Saiva Siddhanta–the purest path of **Sanatana Dharma.** He taught this perspective of India's core beliefs along with a famous lutist who accompanied him along with a woman vocalist singing his lyrics 'with her finest throat'.

This was at a time when the Jain and Buddhist faiths were at the height of their ascendancy and dominance in south Indian society, many rulers leading their village populace in conversion from their encrusted Hindu rituals and superstitions. Poornalingam Pillai writes that 'the Jains were Pharisees and extreme formalists' exercising great sway in the regions of Madurai.

To my astonishment, having always believed that Hindus were slow to anger and on the whole upheld a tolerant faith (see **TOLERANCE**) this scholar says of this resurgence promoted by such saintly fervour that the Jains 'having failed in their incendiary acts on the saint's pavilion' were defeated in a great concourse of debate on the validity of their respective faiths. As a result 'eight thousand Jains were impaled'. I hope he is speaking metaphorically!

For yet another lucid account of this 'purest Saiva path, Saiva Siddhanta' log on to **www.himalayanacademy.com**

❀❀❀❀❀❀❀❀❀❀❀❀❀❀❀

…and Modern

But at the end of it all, when the kings and saints have gone, it still is in the quiet backwaters of everyday life that the Tamil maintains the faith, nurturing the roots each day in a setting of personal quiet worship. Even at festival time (and it seems that every week there is some celebration, divinity, a birthday, a marriage, a parable to bring the divine into this merriment and daily extravagance) it begins in the simple activity of water and prayer-home activity…often on a plain wooden plank on a stone floor with—hopefully—a brass lota rather than a plastic one. The first bath of the day in style immemorial… the ritual of the oil bath before dawn rooted in ancient belief that in so doing the individual is cleansed of sin as efficaciously as taking a dip in the Ganga.

♦ Whispered prayers before the family puja cupboard will be given, the doors opened so the goddess or the dark Murugan can see the world outside and the measure of devotion from the family quietly sitting there, about to chant in unison.

And then the succulent feasting meal is laid out on the green plantain leaf (and Tamils will tell you that you can identify the exact region from where people come from the way which ingredients go where on the leaf) and most especially among the Chettiar community (see **FINANCING INDIA**). Amid the brilliant white of the puffy rice, the dark browns and greens of vegetables, the yellow of the crispy fried banana, the creamy sambhar and the reddish pepper water or rasam, in orthodox homes a small spoonful of rice will be placed on the right hand side of the thali or bright green leaf. And why? I learned from none other than the noble-spirited M S Subbulakshmi who gave me the privilege of staying in her home so very long ago. The sound of veena practice every morning to wake to, in quiet joy…

It is for the Deity. And **SHE** will bless you!

Postscript: At last several websites have appeared, one very informative, of historical as well as literary background material under the grandiose title Tamilnation, such is the immensely strong sense of identity of 70 million Tamils scattered world-wide. http://www.tamilnation.org

■ TANDOOR

♦ A clay oven in which bread dough and meat are cooked at high temperatures.

♦ An Indian spicy dish which has encircled the world… a cuisine phenomenon (which parallels the spread of Indian music), especially the ubiquitous tandoori chicken. Marinated in spiced yoghurt and the characteristic red (colouring) this form of fast dry cooking at extreme heat yet retaining moisture in the meat, accompanied by wonderfully squidgy roti (bread in a flat unleavened fish-shaped form called **naan**) has defied the Raj legacy and taken over the cuisine of every major town in the UK. What a delectable poetic justice!

Such is the irony of history! Even as WWII ended the only true Indian restaurant in London was Veeraswamy's just off Regent Street. And even here the normal way of serving curry was very British with a stir of curry powder in a stew with sliced banana and desiccated coconut along with mango chutney as condiments. And as for the USA, Canada, Australia, curries were unknown.

♦ The North West Frontier towns such as Peshawar, in pre-Independence India, were the source of this succulent dish. When Partition happened refugees brought their traditional dish to the famous **Moti Mahal** restaurant in Old Delhi.

T

European families made a pilgrimage to this sole source; a mischievous aspect of this visit was to take visiting American friends backstage afterward to see the chef with sweaty brows bent over the earthenware ovens sunk, traditional style, into the ground. Perhaps his salty perspiration added to the subtle flavours. Americans did a momentary 'about take' thinking about what they had just eaten!

■ TANSEN and TYAGARAJA

pre-eminent musicians of the Hindustani and Carnatic systems of classical times, lived respectively in Mughal times, **Tansen said to have been 56 when he died in 1589,** Tyagaraja 1767–1847 living in the full swell of the **BHAKTI** movement in the post-south-Indian kingdoms period.

◆ **Mian Tansen** was born Ramatanu Pande, a brahmin but during Emperor Akbar's eclectic rule this prestigious Muslim title was conferred upon him and he was regarded as one of the 'nine jewels' at the court… **NAVARATNA**. The power of Tansen's voice and its evocative capability in creating **rasa** was such that all kinds of legends now still prevail about the supranormal phenomena that occurred when he sang (refer to **MUSIC, MONSOON** and **RASA**). His humble tomb is in the grounds of 15th c Mhmd Ghaur's tomb in the Gwalior fort where also is the legendary tamarind tree, the leaves of which if chewed bestow the gift of a melodious voice. In fact his revered guru, Swami Haridas, had discovered him first as a boy on hearing a tiger's fierce growl. Amazed, he found a 10 year-old boy, imitating the tiger to protect a garden against pilferers.

One of these 'happenings' has re-emerged in contemporary India celebrated each Holi (the springtime bacchanalia) up in the Punjab as a newspaper item recorded in 1996 from Patiala.

A structure has come up about 40 km from here, on the Chandigarh Road. It is known as the shrine of Banno, the music queen of the 16th century, who is said to have sung the Raag Malhar to provide a soothing effect to Sangeet Samrat Mian Tansen when he was suffering from a burning sensation following his recital of the Deepak Raag in the court of Emperor Akbar.

Legend has it that when Tansen rushed to Banur town to seek relief, Banno Dhoban (a washer-woman), who was one of the top singers of her times, was drawing water from a well. She sang Raag Malhar. As soon as she started singing, clouds gathered in response and sent down showers to calm down the atmosphere, providing a soothing effect to Mian Tansen.

After about four centuries, Banno has come to be regarded as a goddess of music at Banur. She has been deified and is worshipped by a large number of devotees of the region who visit her temple to pay obeisance and pray for having their wishes fulfilled. On the annual festival day commemorated in memory of Banno during Holi, musicians gather at the temple and pay their homage … the historic well where Banno sang Raag Malhar has been converted into a pucca structure, which has added beauty to the shrine.

Tansen had a close association with Banur, then known as Pushpawati, or the city of flowers. This is supported by an important document, discovered by the Punjab archives department a few decades ago. It relates to Raja Ram Chand of Banur who had introduced Tansen to the court of Emperor Akbar in 1562.

◆ **Tyagaraja's** reputation appears to reach out year by year to an ever-growing audience and not just middle class people. In an astonishing manner this gifted human is as alive today as ever he was in the period just before the Sepoy Revolt in the north, when the British were making inroads in Tamil country totally oblivious to the dynamic cultures flourishing in the arts.

Saint-philosopher-yogi-musician, he appears a number of times throughout the text. **Tyaga** means **renunciation** in Sanskrit, a giving-up of egotistical attitudes. In the first half of January the latter part of the Tamil month, Marghazi, is devoted to music festivals and dance; go searching for his very alive 'presence', about 15 km from Thanjavur. For five days a huge gathering of music lovers gathers to pay homage to the great composer at his shrine beside the swift flowing river Kaveri, where he sang. This is his **aradhanayam** (an offering of salutation) in the form of a memorial festival which has been held there for over 150 years since his death in 1847 to celebrate:

1. a **musician** who is noted for the melodious sonority of his mostly Telugu compositions, this language of the Andhra state being renowned for tonal elegance. He was bold in experimenting in new forms for his over 700 songs composed I was told, in approximately 200 ragas.

2. a **sage** for the intellectual content (sahitya) of these poetic lyrics.

3. a **bhakta** for their profound devotional quality. At the time of our visit local newspapers spoke of Tyagaraja as the living incarnation of Maharishi Valmiki! This 'humble and pious, unpretentious Telugu brahmin', eulogized one publication, 'has been invested with divinity, as his murti is worshipped and his creations sung.'

Indeed it is, taken in procession through the streets from his modest home in the town to his shrine by the river steps where people join in his especially noted devotions. It is a joyous sight and experience in which to share, sitting in the

T

sand under a giant **pandal** swaying with several thousand grandmas, diamonds glittering in their earlobes and noses; enthusiastic music students; haughty brahmin aficionados; the wondering poor; political guards; busy-body local politicians—IF YOU CAN FIND ACCOMMODATION! We did in a new heritage venture–a sign of the times in the 'surging south' where Ayurvedic and Kerala massage centres for the stressed-out Westerner are proliferating. At **Sterling Swamimalai** four 100-year brahmin homes have been converted in a coconut grove, a five-minute walk from the deep and clean Kaveri river, where so many of the bhakti saints meditated, composed and sang. Run on sattvic lines, we ate the most delicious vegetarian food, home-cooked by young men who ran the centre immaculately–and with simpler sustainable energy, ecologically right, even for dealing with the plague of mozzies every dusk, frankincense being wafted on hot charcoal around the verandahs to choke their avid hunger for our blood. And then get out the Odomos!

■ TANTRA (n. *Sanskrit*)
Tan = to stretch, expand (pronounced taan)
Tr = root of word means rule-ritual
   is still clothed in secrecy in India, because much that is involved with sexual matters is suspect or subject to inhibitions perhaps absorbed from the Victorian British attitudes at the seat of power in Bengal where tantric practice was most prevalent and remains so, being the centre of worship of the **Mother Goddess Devi**, the dark side of turbulent power in **Kali**, the straight power of **Durga**, and the potent sexual energy of **Shakti**, the latter being intrinsically linked with the Tantric cult.
◆ This is a paradox in the land of the **Kama Sutra** literature, and where temples at **Khajuraho** depicting divine passion and **maithuna** (= sexually embracing couples) in truly gymnastic positions of coitus (are they possible with so many voyeuristic gandharvas and nymphs in attendance to give the bodies stability?) people the mountainous peaks of architectural temples devised by a truly liberated **Chandela** dynasty. Patronising the arts in such a profusion, 85 temples in 150 years within the same small radius, possibly outpacing several Italian dynasties in a later Renaissance period.
◆ Many continue to associate tantric rites with secret sexual rituals which the gripping novels of John Masters—**Nightrunners of Bengal** and **The Deceivers** (Penguin, Middlesex, 1952/55)—have highlighted, but basically Tantra as a mode of thought is more at home in the exploratory esoteric world of physics as diagrammatic paintings in Ajit Mookerjee's book **Tantra Art** exemplify. Tantric thought and intensity of meditation practices to harness brain-control lead its thinkers into the concepts and questions of 'laws of consciousness' now seriously being conceptualised by physicists, as also some Western philosophers have speculated… that 'the human mind emerges in TIME in order to order the random'.

◆ Study of tantric meditation, yoga, and TM, plus the advancement of technology in applying scientific measurement to brainwave research indicates that there is an enormous increase in **orderly patterning of the brain** during TM. The activity of **stretching** the mind = the root sound **taan** in Sanskrit takes one to a philosophical level akin to the triangular diagrams of infinity used in tantric meditation, trying to climb beyond the finite bounds of planetary time and space into that of molecular permutations coming together at random, a cosmic world of disorganisation 'out there' beyond our laws of physics, of atoms just running around, yet structures emerging, patternings creating order in chaos.
   1971
◆ Since the amazingly successful **Tantra Art Exhibition**, sponsored by the British Council in the Hayward Art Gallery in London and other galleries and symposiums in Britain exploded into public perception, opening up a whole world of metaphysical/artistic curiosity of what is ultimately 'a vision of cosmic sexuality', enormous interest has been engendered. **Ajit Mookerjee**, with his many publications, and **Philip Rawson,** then Curator of the Gulbenkian Museum of Oriental Art in the University of Durham, pointed out: **Tantra is not a belief or faith, but a way of living or acting.**
   A good deal of ignorance was dispelled in the West and a new correlation between physics, biology, metaphysics, the flux of change in the universe, Jungian concepts of universal symbols emerged for the first time in a coherent yet imaginatively devised exposition that drew a crush of people. Hundreds of young art students from all over Europe attended, as though tantra spoke to the world of the 21st century.
   But there is the other shadow side as well where worship of **Siddha philosophy** of supernatural powers; of the physicality of sex; the emphasis of the phallus (as with the Bengali saint Ramakrishna at one stage) gets mixed up with esoteric cults of the **Tantra Shastra**—systematised through codifications. Sexual congress with the partner in orgiastic ritual worship was combined with spurious notions that 'the more you have' the less eventually 'you need of sex.' Siddhi yogis intensify this entire aspect of yogic and tantric theory, deliberately enlarging their own phalluses for worship, occasionally seen at gatherings of sadhus in public display at such events as the **KUMBH MELA** or an eclipse of the moon at **Kurukshetra**. The initiate (it was stated by those 'in the know') learned supreme self-control through fullest play of sensuality. Well… nothing surprises where life in all its profound and puzzling energies is laid out bare for all to see!

༺ఌఌఌఌఌఌఌఌఌఌఌఌఌఌ༻

The reasoning behind other rituals to do with the eating of meat, and taking fermented drink, as well as the ritual sexual congress was to break through the rigidity of caste.

- At its basic level Tantra as **Richard Lannoy** has written in **The Speaking Tree** constitutes a special semantic:
1 **verbal** through **sound mantras** which cross all cultural barriers, being universal sounds and not specific words in an ethnic language or secret/sacred in the priestly ritual;
a **pictorial** through concentration upon **YANTRAS**—abstract mathematical/geometric diagrams.

In his writings **Philip Rawson** has recognised commonalities across cultures:

> Tantra contains many archaic elements. Some are as ancient as the Palaeolithic caves of Europe, and can be precisely matched with them. The great French cave complex of Pech-merle, for example, contains a chapel-chamber with female emblems which can be duplicated very closely at Indian shrines.

Similar depictions occur in Aboriginal rock gallery paintings in northern Australia. It is therefore more than probable that what we know as Tantra is an adaptation into later Indian life-patterns of very ancient and powerful images, practices and thought. Indeed, India is famous for the way it has preserved unbroken traditions of immemorial antiquity.

According to critiques of the London Exhibition the prevailing impression for viewers was one of mental exhaustion—as though coming to terms with the cosmic scale of the Indian mind was quite overwhelming. **It is**, considering the root of the word tantra—to stretch, exploding around every bend, up every gigantic mountain, inside the shadowy mysteries of the temple womb house for the deity. Too much for the temperate mind. According to Mookerjee:

> Indian culture, at least since the third century AD, has held an idea of the cosmos as being vast beyond human imagining, containing worlds numberless as the sand-grains of the Ganges, and developing through incalculable aeons of time. Indian mathematics and metaphysics have recognised number, both abstract and concrete, of an order of magnitude which only became familiar to educated people in Europe during this century…Even though its generalisations were made without the benefit of modern scientific knowledge they were never meant to be anything but colossal in scope. Meditation has the job of filling these abstractions with a valid content of reality.

Sometimes it is best to meditate and think no thoughts at all in this extraordinary land—just to keep sane!

> All beginnings are elusive
> all endings are definite
> The geometry caught in the mind's net
> does not have lines ending

(Poetic source unknown). Once quoted by the late famous crystallographer, Professor Dorothy Hodgkin, awarded the Order of Merit.

■ **TAPASYA**

Austere penance which creates **heat = fervour** of a spiritual, religious, nature, a concentrated energy enabling **self-realisation** to come into being. Krishna as the teacher, deplored those **FAKIRS** who underwent a mechanical type of self-flagellation of the body in this effort to achieve moksha, release from many rebirths before being able to be absorbed into perfection. Too much austerity was not the way to this release. As in all things moderation was the key to true attainment of this state of purification of the mind. A Bhagavad Gita bazaar poster depicts this very explicitly (see frontispiece).

According to Prof. Edgerton tapas 'occurs as a **cosmic force**. Occasionally it is a first principle itself, but more often the Creator **exercises tapas** 'in making the world.' The psycho-chemical theory in yoga is that by the mental discipline of tapasya a white heat of energy is engendered which can bring about such inexplicable influences (such as Gandhi's fasts 'unto death') so that what we call 'miracles' can happen.

- Throughout the centuries and in the mythological literature reference to such an individual saint, ruler, hero or even a woman devotee, undertaking such demanding austerities appears again and again, to such an extent that benediction comes from the relenting deities and **BOONS** are given as a consequence of such superhuman **power** over matter or events.

Not the same but often translated for **tapasya, penance** or **atonement = prayashchita** was applied politically to Mrs Gandhi after she was thrown out by the voting public after the Emergency she had imposed. Miscalculating that this extreme measure was warranted and had proved itself, by the efficiencies it engendered—trains running on time, public officials arriving at office on time, people buying tickets for trains, a lessening of petty corruptions, she felt the public would exonerate her, and called for their vote of confidence after two years Emergency (1975–7). In fact, democracy showed its triumphant spirit. The Congress was ousted for the first time in 30 years. Morarji Desai and the Janata Party succeeded in office for two years. Another split in this party, another ineffective government and Mrs G **having done penance**, was back again in1980. Having suffered (we are to presume!) she had to—so to speak—do her time. In fact she had atoned! And that was accepted quite naturally.

The political correspondent of the Ananda Bazaar Patrika wrote at the time that 'if the Indian people feel that she has undergone prayashchita they may forgive her for all that she did in the last 20 months.'

Endnote: Surely only this could happen in India … in 1993 after the Babri Masjid mosque demolition, vandalism and consequent communal rioting a tapas was undertaken for communal harmony. That is what the **Rolling Saint, Lotan Baba** declared in 1993. He undertook a 400km

T

pilgrimage from **Ratlam** on the central Indian plateau to a shrine of Vaishno Devi near **Jammu** in the Kashmir foothills, sometimes fast and sometimes slow, **his full length rolling sideways over the roads**, down steps, up gradients, through the flooded waterways, over the scorching tarmac surface of Rajasthan in 40° C heat. He covered an average of 20km a day. Only a few times was he really sick with fever. He wore very flimsy padding on his elbows and knees.

It took eight months of such **tapasya** done in the name of peace and harmony between antagonistic communities. He was accompanied by much devotion on the part of the local people from Ratlam who gave up their livelihoods to look after him, cooking, watching over his health.

An extraordinary hour-long documentary film made by award-winning Indian director Naresh Bedi deserves tracking down. It is an experience outside of anything you will encounter in a lifetime.

■ **TATTVA** (n. *Sanskrit*)

In the spirit of rational inquiry undertaken by the rsis in search of knowledge of what constituted the basic essences of life and this world, another whole list of categories evolved. They were termed **tattva** = evolvents, 24 in number, with the soul or Atman regarded as the 25th principle. (**Samkhya** philosophy concentrates on elaborating the fine detail of these categories–see **DARSHAN**).

◆ One could regard this as the pioneering scientific approach of early Indians to make sense of the material universe around them, closer to Western methodology but as Edgerton has remarked, each philosophical school, indeed Indians in general, 'revel in numerical categories' (see **GANA**).

Interestingly these sages reached the same conclusions as the Western world in five elements in the first enumeration and applied a geometric symbolism. (see **BHAGAVAD GITA bazaar poster** again):

○ akasha; ✿ vayu; ▽ tej; ☺ jal; □ bhumi,

ether = **akasha**, air, wind = **vayu**, fire = **tej**, water = **jal**, earth = **bhumi**, Greek and Roman thinkers at a later date arrived at the same definitions of four material fundamental constituents. The fifth, **akasha**, much discussed as **'that Imperishable aksara'** also defied description for ancient Western philosophers and came to be known, in Latin, as the fifth essence, **quinta essentia**, from which the English language derives **quintessence**.

How quintessentially Vedic in thought is Milton's affirmation of divine purpose, spoken like a rsi!

Let there be Light! Said God: and forthwith Light
***Ethereal**, first of all things, **quintessentially** pure, sprung from the deep …*

■ **TEMPLE at TIRUPATI**

Trying to decode an important announcement in the respected English-language newspaper, **The Hindu**, based in Chennai but read throughout the nation, started a detective exercise for me involving my Indian friends. What was this all about?

The decoded message

Venkat es(h)wara	=	'the birthless
n. *Sanskrit*		one'; that which
s pronounced sh		is naturally manifest;
Venkat	=	self-born, that is divine
eswara	=	iswara = supreme being

whose shrine is to be found atop the cluster of seven hills in an area called **Tirumala** (= auspicious hill) 20km beyond the main town of Tirupati.

◆ **Venkateswara** is the much revered manifestation of **Vishnu** in the incarnation of **Krishna** (known here as **Sri Balaji**). Almost hidden in form in the narrow shrine, his image is lost to view under bejewelled raiments and necklaced with precious stones and gold ornaments, swathed on festive days with tumescent floral garlands of jasmine, roses, and marigolds. Was ever a 'presence' so worshipped in such overflowing abundance for now, it is said, 20 million pilgrims flow through annually, herded through wire-netted cages, forming serpentine queues, day in, day out and only a shuffled glimpse possible in such a crush of the dark face–but that enough fulfilment. They stand in queues 24 hours a day, 365 days a years, so central is this shrine in its especial appeal and beneficent blessing. It may take the individual 10 hours of queuing through the cages (to control the crowd) to receive **DARSHAN** from the Deity in the shrine.

◆ Situated in southern Andhra Pradesh, Tirupati is the pre-eminent shrine for south Indians worldwide to visit once in a lifetime, and not only of the Hindu persuasion. Buddhist, Jain, agnostic, Christians and even Muslims all present themselves—and increasingly the curious explorers from the West—on pilgrimage to climb the steep steps up the seven sacred hills, the sacred **yagna** of **bhumi**, the soil.

For this reason it is also the wealthiest temple in all of India. There is pure 23:999 carat gold in those seven hills, ingots donated by wealthy merchants, small gold tokens of jewellery from a humble widow. Some Indians say Tirupati must be the wealthiest religious centre in the world—even when compared with the Vatican—5 tonnes of pure gold! And Indian hair, shorn traditionally by pilgrims, women as well as men brings in $70 million to one Bangalore factory wallah alone, an industry, via Italy, for Hollywood hair pieces. (Wall Street Journal, August 20, 2003—a fascinating article!)

It is also a great centre from which wigs are made—many pilgrims undergo the tonsure ceremony to 'cleanse' themselves before entering the shrine. The mundan is also a vow-fulfilment.

So why is Tirupati/Tirumal so auspicious a place? Why climb an exhausting 3,500 steps?… a tapasya in itself, to 3,000 feet, the one road jammed with India's ever-imaginative forms of wheeled transport. **And why then slowly edge forwards sometimes for 10 hours** (although several

T

hundred rupees will project the elderly, the foreign visitor in a hurry, the wealthy city dweller, into life in the fast lane!)?

IT IS SAID THAT... a familiar phrase, much used, that tends to let facts rest 'in the air'... that Tirumala was a pilgrimage centre way back in the sixth century BCE.

... and here comes another auspicious anthill in the almost surreal mythologies recounting the song-lines of the Indian landscape when in great antiquity VALMIKI meditated so long an anthill grew over him. In this legend a local farmer or chieftain who even has a name—Tondaman—stumbled across a huge anthill. A voice in the firmament seemed to ask that the ants be fed. A local raja who came to hear of this ordered milk to be sent. That would not be at all surprising considering many traditional women all over the nation put crumbs out to feed whatever insects are passing by, and milk is placed in dark groves in the south for the snakes to drink. Such was the amount of liquid that the red earth was washed away and, lo and behold! a resplendent MURTI of Shri Venkateshwara was revealed in its niche, already formed in stone, blackened and polished with antiquity.

And so it was said that ....the original shrine was established somewhere around the first century BCE, growing in substance around the eight feet figure as each and every pilgrim believed they had been blessed, their wishes granted by this most benign of the Trimurti. Fame gathered as the southern rajas—Cheras, Pandyas, Pallavas, Cholas came to pay their respects—and their fabulous donations.

It is also said that... a Pallava queen called Samavai (early seventh century CE) consecrated another silver image of the Deity... and the mystique of beneficence, sanctity took off, gathering an impetus that shows no sign of abating in the 21st century.

And then the saints come marching in. Shankaracharya, Ramanuja, Madhva... and that long procession of BHAKTI saints to add to the accumulating gloss of sanctity.

As Buddhism declined another golden age was cresting, a great wave of southern prosperity, an architectural explosion of wealth and dynastic patronage as rajas vied with each other in artistic expression of their faith to embellish Tirupati... its vimana, for instance, coated with pure gold leaf.

Decoding the names of the newspaper announcement that appeared in The Hindu news ad publishing the forthcoming Brahmotsavam, took time with a Tamil friend to make sense of a string of words which comprised:

Tiru (Tamil) = Lakshmi = Sri meaning auspicious, sacred

Pati (Sanskrit) = the lord/husband (who would be the lord anyway)

Devasthanam = deities: place (sthan) = temple

Brahmotsavam means the principal festival utsav to Brhm—the Impersonal Absolute—in the form of Vishnu. Annually 9 days end Sept/Oct.

Sri is the honorific as is Tiru in Tamil; the title with which to address a respected person as well as a Deity and the Guru in an aura of auspiciousness.

Swamiji many names of one person in the advertisement precede Ramanuja who spent much time at Tirupati teaching about Vishnu.

Viswashanti peace of the world (shanti = peace)

Sahasra a thousand—principal deities such as Shiva and Vishnu who are given a thousand different names symbolising aspects or qualities of their ultimately indefinable singularity.

Kundatmaka the firepit, homan (or kund) altar, is prescribed in the Vedic Shastras in great detail as to how to construct in the right proportions geometrically for the all-important sacrificial fire—the hawan—for offerings to the Vedic gods

Mahavishnu great Vishnu

Yagam major ceremony

Yajna Bhumi bhumi also means earth, yajna a sacred ceremony, i.e. the place of these especial fire rituals.

Dhwajarohanam flag raising ceremony near the central shrine, each temple having this architectural place for the pennant, and here adorned with sparkling gold plate in the slanting rays of the rising sun.

Garuda Seva (Garuda) is the vehicle half majestic bird/eagle, half human associated with Vishnu for the Deity to travel around the firmament (seva= service).

Ratha is the magnificent temple chariot replicating the temple itself and drawn with ship ropes through the streets amid a vast throng.

Chakrasnanam the seat or pedestal, shaped flat as a circular wheel of law (chakra).

In personal worship these images are treated with intimate respect but also with human warmth as part of daily family life, a charming quality reflected in the prayers. In the early morning a seat is offered for Ganesh or Vishnu to sit on to make themselves comfortable.

The words are chanted—Asanam Samar Payami = offering a seat...and indeed 'celestials' do descend to join mortals in these especial days and ceremonies such, according to the pandits is the concentrated psychic energy flowing in invisible vibration from such a concourse of mentally-focused prayer, chanting, emotional power exuded into the atmosphere.

1 A TIRTHA is the act of making a pilgrimage to a hallowed spot—literally a river bathing place or ford such as the sangam at Allahabad. The sanctified territory is referred to as a tirtha sthaana such as at Tirupati.

2 A cassette introduction to solemn and beautiful music under this very title, presented by a famous Carnatic vocalist, T N Sheshagopalan states that 'this popular living tradition, tirtha, is undertaken to places made sacred by the presence now long gone of the Vedic sages who performed penance there' (see TAPASYA and PILGRIMAGE). Then swamis and other holy men began to visit them adding to their magnetic 'pull', and, ultimately, a major temple site.

3 Historically it comes as no surprise to hit earth with a

thud of reality, to discover once more there is no defining moment to the Tirupati phenomenon. A Tamil lady in Chennai explained with unswerving devotion that the **murti** is truly the Lord (her words) who, beguiled by the salubrious landscape of the hills, took up the **padmasana yogic position**. So profound was his meditation over time Vishnu metamorphosed into stone so creating the hallows. Certainly **Ramanuja**, the Vaishnavite saint, **established the historic site**, the temple being built in the 12th century CE, the height of Chola grandeur and artistic vision.

More detailed information is provided on **www.tirumala.org** by Tata Consultancy Services. No matter what the exact facts, its resonating antiquity speaks another language to **50,000 pilgrims everyday**. And for now, **Sri Venkateshwara** stands, presenting one hand in **abhaya mudra**–a blessing!

■ **THIRD EYE of WISDOM** (n. *Sanskrit* = **aynachakra**)

The potent eye in the middle of the forehead, said physiologically to be the atrophied pineal gland in human biological development. Endocrinology states that the **melatonin** hormone in the pineal gland of other species is affected **by light** and **duration of light.** This has the effect of providing yearly clocks to mammals.

♦ It starts birds migrating
♦ Sets in motion the impulse to hibernate

Yoga practitioners, especially **siddhis**, believe they can reactivate the energy of that gland, the seventh chakra of energy, aynachakra releasing supra-consciousness, a chakra being a cross-over point of energy distribution. **Shiva** is referred to as **Tri-lochana**–three eyed, his eyes are sun, moon and **fire**–in the Vedic texts. In the mythology the ascetic deity, undergoing extreme tapas was tempted by Kama the god of love (and lust). Shiva became so angry at being interrupted that he opened this eye on his forehead, with this result as in the Vedic description:

The frontal eye, the eye of fire, is the eye of higher perception. It looks mainly inwards. When directed outward it burns all that appears before it. It is from a glance of this third eye that Kama, lord of lust, was burnt to ashes and that the gods and all created beings are destroyed at each of the periodical destructions of the universe.

The sublimation of Eros depicted in art as the crescent moon placed above the Third Eye has many analogies with psychology theories in the West and the harnessing in of sexual energies, transferring that powerful instinct to another kind of potency–of inner knowledge, g(n)yana which can bring balance to the deductive logic emphasised by Western thought and scientific rationality.

■ **TILAK**

...or tika sign on the forehead, between the eyebrows, dedicated to the Third Eye of wisdom of Shiva espesially, but to Vishnu also in many variations of the Vaishnavite design (see below). The tilak was a ritual mark in earliest Vedic times, applied at the time of the sacred homa (fire ceremony). This wide diversity of tilak indicating regions and sects of the many forms of Vishnu is described with diagrams in the **India Magazine,** October 1987.

For the followers of Shiva, this symbol is a **triple transverse line** drawn in ritual by the inverted thumb, middle and ring finger. Saivites used the **ash, bhasma,** or **sandal paste (mustard yellow)** to smear their forehead and bodies after visiting the shrine in a temple to this form of godhead. Vibhuti is also another word for the ashen-grey powder rendered down and sanctified from **cow-dung**, the white cow depicted in many bazaar painting associated with the goddess Lakshmi, bringer of good fortune and wellbeing, being also very sacred from earliest times in a predominantly rural society and a harsh climate.

The symbolism is obvious–dust to dust, ashes to ashes, so will we as mortals all return, a reminder in the words of our own burial service.

♦ For the followers of Vishnu, the tilak is very easy to decipher as it looks very much like the Roman alphabetic V except it has a rounded-end U. Sometimes the Devanagari characters for Krishna are delineated inside it, especially amongst devotees at the pilgrim centre south of Delhi near **Mathura** where the huge complex of **Krishna** temples are situated at **Vrindavan**. I have been told by a Krishna devotee that the **V** signifies those who are gently encased in this deity's 'caring' protection (the **Marjara** hold–see **HANUMAN**) and the links with 12th century Iona Abbey in Scotland. The **U** apparently signifies the stauncher Yogi who possesses the monkey, **Markata** tenacity to hold on tight, tough like Shiva.

■ **TOLERANCE....** *sahishnuta*

A heartfelt plea came as I stood on the last stepping stones pondering this life-long journey through a land that deep in the psyche is my 'other home' so far from my blessed childhood in far away Leicestershire that one ponders such a major cultural transformation, and how it came about. And now a north Indian cultural mentor of an agile and sensitive mind and challenging astuteness (how Indian all that is also!) has led me into a younger India, beyond the watershed of 50 years of Independence which all of my generation of friends have lived through.

Along with many others of his contemporaries going into print, he wrote an impassioned note sufficient to make me retrace my steps after my own troubled queries about a new dimension I felt was growing in today's political spectrum –that of **XENOPHOBIA** and emphasis on ethnicity … who is a true Indian, Hindu, Muslim, Christian, Dalit, can an Italian wife of an assassinated Prime Minister, though now Indian by adoption, be a 'true Indian' fit to lead Congress, etc, etc,?

The root cause of this problem is the clash between exclusivism and pluralism. It is not that all through history followers of the latter have not fought to defend themselves against onslaughts of the former but, over the millennia, it has been a losing war. Over the last 1000 years, first Muslims and then Christians ruled this land and, in two different ways, did what they could to destroy the indigenous faiths. Islam preferred the sword, Christianity soon turned to the pen. The latter was much subtler; it destroyed the indigenous schooling system so that the missionaries could introduce their own; and the new system, its ideology, its contents and its legacy–often referred to as Macaulian–still dominate the Indian English-speaking elite and its way of thinking.

◆ **A harder edge is developing in the debate**. When we first arrived India was centre-stage in world affairs, a leading player in the great human debates, consulted on moral issues to the annoyance sometimes of those whose own frameworks of reference had never been questioned before. Now she seemed to have withdrawn inward, become more parochial, concerned with ideological politics.

Tolerance was a constant in any debate in those heady days, a vast majority Congress Party seated comfortably in power. Tolerance was a quality of the Indian way of life, inclusiveness a central theme in a view of the cosmos where all, no matter their diversity, religions, and races were on the same journey–eventually–to the summit. As Radhakarishnan used to say, some pathways may be shorter and less tortuous than others. Nevertheless the summit was the same. **Satyam ekam viprah bahudha vedanteh**… Truth is one but the wise interpret it in many ways.

This basic impulse, inbuilt into the intellectual fabric of **SANATANA DHARMA**, may well have been the unconscious motivation of the 1950s embrace of the **Panchsila–Five Principles Declaration of Non-Alignment**, a deeply embedded need to 'understand the other person's point of view' heavily emphasised on a visit to the Mavalankar family in Ahmedabad in 1996:

*'You have to note the Sanskrit word **sahishnuta**–an active sense of tolerating, not just a passive acceptance.'*

Purushottam, long-time friend, had explained **sahish** = tolerant, an acceptance of other points of view; **anuta** = someone with the **capability of activating** tolerance through ways of living or promoting such an attitude. '**Tolerance**,' as Gandhi explained, '**Is an active mental attitude, going out into the market place in a mental framework of generosity of spirit to confront–and understand–the opponents' argument despite disagreeing with their 'point of view'**.

The traumatic horrors of Partition, never envisaged, needed calm and a healing atmosphere, tolerance of diversity after the divisive communal upheavals. Looking back over the decades and over 300 stepping stones I do recognise that in that immediate era after 1947 a general euphoria, the release

of freedom, cloaked the post-colonial ambit in which we all lived, the many subtle hangovers in language, attitudes, historical theories, even cultural forms. All this hidden-away influence shaped the 'perceived wisdom' we imbibed. I do remember at the time Indian artist friends such as Husain, Khanna, Gaitonde, Gujral, Chintamoni Kar the sculptor, all discussing in an equally impassioned way, in our tiny Chelsea-mews-like bungalow, into the midnight hours, how to remain 'Indian' in an 'international' art scene which virtually obliterated nationality yet the criteria of which (predominantly abstract) was a subtle American, European definition.

◆ It was a matter which had troubled me also in the writing of my **Indian Music** book in the early 70s when Indian musicians were only just beginning to make their impact and where the **Encyclopedia of World Music** devoted hundreds of pages to European origins and traditions, Asian and African an after-thought crushed into minimal space at the end.

The hardening edge

The ethnocentric force of Western culture is hard to combat … but a letter posted on the internet indicates Indian irritation at constant criticism. It had appeared in **The Washington Post** from an Indian writing in 1999 from Georgia about constant attacks on India's political parties of the right fundamentalist persuasion after vandalism on churches…

Hindus a Favourite Target.

An act of violence against innocents is an indefensible act and must be condemned. What I would like to know is if these people engaged in massive breast-beating exercises over each and every incident that happens in India have ever honestly pondered fundamentalists waging war in other countries. All we hear in such cases are human rights issues against the very people challenging such violent groups. A few years back, many churches were burned deliberately all around the United States, but no one raised a hue and cry about it to the level that has arisen even over a small incident in India. Could it be due to the stark reality that despite our liberal face it is still considered politically correct to point out that the majority of India is Hindu, and hence all such incidents of violence against non-Hindus are the work of Hindus implicitly and collectively? It is still considered politically correct to denounce Hindus' religion publicly. It is still considered politically correct to mention the demographic map of India in almost every news item, whereas the same yardstick is seldom applied to other countries of the world. It is still politically correct to implicate India for being against minorities just because it is majority Hindu. It is still politically correct, in almost every incident with negative connotations, to carefully point out the religious identity of an individual or group as Hindu…

T

The common perception is that the only way to get something published is to write something against Hindus or India no matter how unreal, unproved, unjust, vicious and fabricated the stories may be. Can someone please explain what is **Hindu fundamentalism***?*

◆ Two things spring to mind. A tougher edge has come with the second generation after Independence dissatisfied with its results and frustrated by continued cultural domination in the global communication systems. It is not dissimilar to my experiences in the UK of the 60s and early 70s where second generation children of their migrant Asian/West Indian parents began to assert a more militant stance in classrooms if they encountered history books biased by cultural myopia, or stood up to be counted politically, as also is happening in Australia at last among a more politically aware younger generation of Aborigines no longer content to be pushed around by a 'wajela' (whitey) mentality.

Conclusion: Is it also that democracies in the West expect more of India than other nations, and even Indians hold higher expectancies of themselves because of their very old traditions and ethos—of pluralism? Rooted deep in philosophical concepts this is very different compared with theocratic states adhering to staunch authoritarian religiosity such as in the crescent of Islamic states that curve around the Himalayan ranges. Compare also the nature of Indian democracy—an open society laid bare for all to inspect—warts and all!—with a China fiercely proud and resentful of any foreign intrusion. It even deals firmly with its own Muslim border state and the dissenting Uigers. No Kashmir … no autonomy there!

Perhaps the majority of Indians do know that their sense of tolerance, of not excluding those 'barbarians', 'infidels', 'pagans' 'heathens', descriptive terms Christians and Muslims have used in a derogatory sense over the centuries about 'the other', **is their great single hidden strength**—despite all the hazards as we become a global village. Yet another Ashokan Edict engraved on rock declares:

samanvaya eva sadhuh
synthesis, reconciliation, concord is 'the supreme' good.

■ TOUCHING THE FEET

Out of the corner of your eye, you may, at an airport, as guests enter a wedding function, when young musicians join their master gurus on stage, even when villagers deferentially meet a big sahib politician, notice a very swift movement as fluid as a curtsey dip. This is **pranam** (pronounced pranaam) touching the ground in front of a person, or doing obeisance at their feet. It is a mark of respect for elders, parents or a person of some significance and reverence for the guru/mentor. By such an act of humility you indicate the forgetting of self.

Touching the earth is another matter, acknowledging its sacredness, as many artistes do before entering or ascending the stage for performance.

■ TREES

are regarded with especial reverence as 'live' symbols of a divine presence. Perhaps now with ecology and environmental emphasis in our own urban-oriented global view we begin also to re-establish the tree in our mind's eye again as important to our survival.

Throughout India, tracing back worship even to Mohenjodaro society, trees have been focal points of sacred groves—threads, flowers, bangles are all placed at the foot of such majestic symbols of power, strength, growth, and life-saving shade. Even Mughal emperors, Muslims all, honoured the tree and are remembered thankfully even by foreign travellers who go by road, for the thousands of trees they planted along the pathways as they became major roads of communication in the opening up of Indian transport and communication systems from the 17th century onwards. Ashoka also did the same. Great souls have found enlightenment as Gautama the Buddha to be did in his long fast and meditation under the **bodhi/pipal** tree (its Hindi name also spelled peepul).

◆ Huge spreading trees have held a fascination not only in India for humanity. Their strength and 'living' nature resonate in the mind—but never more so than in a land so caught up in symbols and myth as India. And what more astonishing as a place of **numen**—a sense of **hallows** also familiar to the early Christian church—than the awesome spread of the banyan sometimes 30 metres at the crown under which a whole village could gather. The tree spirit later became part of animistic worship giving a sense of holiness from the creative strength of the tree, such that in antique Tamil literature as well as later Buddhist the terms **vriksha—chaitya—tree temple** refers to such a construction around its sacred trunk. **Rising sap** is a potent symbol of the universal fertility implicit in all creation.

Circa 70 CE.... Pliny of Rome had taken note from travellers during a time of increasing trade and cultural interchange with India when he wrote:
There is in India a tree [the banyan] *whose property it is to plant itself. It spreads out mighty arms to the earth where in the space of a single year the arms take root and put forth anew.*

◆ From very earliest Vedic society the invigorating properties of its sap—and of its seeds were understood, used in ayurvedic medicine infusion, as an aphrodisiac, the gum itself like Australia's red gum useful for healing open sores.

◆ **The Banyan, Vat and Bel** are equally important. The last also known as **bilva** has an interesting link with Siva. (See a 1994 publication, **Indian Medicinal Plants**—Arya Veda Sala, Kottakkal, Orient Longman, Kolkata—from which some of the facts appear here).

caste is. As tradition becomes a glaring contradiction in an industrialising India, so the general body of society will reflect subtle shifts—but the modernizing will (and should) be her own.

Even as far back as the 60s in the general national reassessment of itself, the Indian middle class was conducting its own self-analysis. Much of this process took place through the influential and high-level journalism of **The Illustrated Weekly of India** out of Mumbai. There was no TV discussion then and All India Radio was very much under the thumb of the Ministry of Broadcasting, forum-type discussion stilted compared with today's more forthright airing of opinions on Doordarshan TV let alone the commercial channels.

The magazine editor conducted several issues on current concepts of **caste** and **dharma**. One letter summed up the majority of opinion:

The ancient sages circa 3rd–4th century AD known as the Age of Legislators declared:

The Vedas (srutis), the Itihasas (smrtis = heard histories), the usages of good men, what is agreeable to the thinking self, and desire born of due deliberation, this is traditionally recognised as the source of dharma... There is a sense of democratic response to the surrounding ethos. Even as far back as the Mahabharata it is recorded in Sanskrit—

mahajano	vena	gatah	sa-panthah
great beings	by which	gone	that way

This was rendered by the sender of the letter as: **That alone is the dharma = panthah = the way (how you live your life) which is chalked out by the people, that is, the public at large.** The letter's final sentence: 'so willy-nilly, we have to move in tune with the zeitgeist... the spirit of the age'–that is the spirit rather than the letter of the law … **aadjust karanaa!**

♦ Such deep undercurrents of sentiment run as a powerful subtext to what appears to be prevailing norms and Vedic injunctions daily interpreted in customary rites all over India at the **'temple-level'** of culture where nothing seems to change in age-old only partially understood rituals. This is the area of Indian life most encountered in daily travel by the backpacker.

♦ Other currents gather force over ages sweeping out into the flood plains where the populace lives. Reform is then in the air and 'great souls' like Ramakrishna, Aurobindo, Gandhi, Tilak, Ram Mohun Roy take off.

♦ Vedanta could be said to be this reaffirmation of India's perennial philosophy—the original pristine unadulterated thought sifted through the sieve of those fine Upanishadic minds—the **SANATANA DHARMA**, 'the eternal way of ways, valid for all time.' Dr Raghavan referred to it as **'the bullion with which all the diversely current religions have to be linked and evaluated.'**

This Vedantic approach and the tolerance it fostered became the tonic note of the Indian symphony. Its permeation of the Indian mind was so comprehensive, that placed as he was on the stage of international relations, the modern Indian political leader, such as the first Prime Minister of Free India, adopted as his contribution to international relations the policy of non-alignment, of live and let live, and of friendliness towards all powers.

Indian Thought and Culture, by Raghavan on an Indian delegation, **Vedanta Kesari Publication, Sept 1971**

Of all the great sages of modern times in India it is Swami Vivekananda (so intimately associated with saint Ramakrishna and both identified with Bengal culture and the explosion of reform within the Hindu body at the end of the 1880s) who spoke of Vedanta. An Indian writer in Australia's **The Indian Down Under** wrote this in relation to both:

Swami Vivekananda restates in unequivocal terms the call of the Upanishads to be 'Abhih' to be fearless, dauntless and to become strong. A superhuman energy flows from the ordinary human body when spiritual strength is attained.

For too long this writer Kanaka Ramakrishna feels the West has concentrated on physical strength, then intellectual strength, neglecting the inner spiritual strength, the moral concern of the welfare of the atman: 'a modern man is more concerned with pleasures, comforts and achievements in external life, overlooking the more important aspect of internal life. As a result he lives in constant fear and suspicion.'

We are back to the first stepping stone again–the eradication of fear from the mind… and the overcoming of ignorance… not just of the mind. When reflecting on the Vedas, the word religion does not come to mind. Indeed the **sanatana dharma**–the dharma without end, is not even a philosophy in the Western sense of the word; **it is more a way of life, a spiritual search without doctrine, dogma, a Nicene Creed to be recited**, not **even a Church body** or leader equivalent to a Pope or Archbishop. Edgerton succinctly points out that there never was such a figure in ancient India (i.e., a Vedic philosopher). Even the later classical Indian philosophers would have been amazed to hear this said of themselves. Purely abstract speculation would have seemed to them pointless and incomprehensible. **Their aim is to point the way to human salvation.**

■ **VEENA**

India's most traditionally evocative stringed instrument (more so than the sitar which is an 'incomer'). It is associated with the goddess **Saraswati**–Brahma's consort and symbol of the importance of the **arts, music and learning**.

♦ Its lineage is very ancient, perhaps over 4,000 years and linked with the Egyptian lute, called a vena.

♦ It was said by the sage **Yajnavalkya** that: 'He who knows the art of veena-playing and **sruti** (note) **shastra** (artistic principles in this case) can attain god easily.'

♦ Of all instrumental sound that of the veena is said most closely to resemble the sound of the human voice.

The modern veena has 24 moveable frets comprising two octaves fixed in wax on a hollow wooden base. The fingerboard rests on two hollow gourds, one larger than the other usually cut down from the jack tree or pumpkin family, a product only of Pandharpur where we had encountered the Vithoba pilgrims, and also from the Hooghly region of West Bengal.

♦ It is a popular household instrument in south India and is often played by the women of the household in private daily puja.

■ **VEERAPPAN**

Could there ever be an account so quintessentially Indian as that of bandit extraordinaire–Veerappan? For his sins he made **The Boston Globe** and The **West Australian** in August 2000. Not bad for an outlaw on the run for 30 years, who is alleged, with his merry band of interstate renegades, to have murdered over 120 people, slaughtered over 1,500 elephants for the illegal ivory-poaching trade and decimated the dense teak forests of Bandipur and Mudumalai of their sandalwood trees worth Rs. 100 million in the illegal trade overseas.

Kidnapper's demands met …the Australian headlines read …(August 8, 2000)

*Two Indian State governments have acceded to demands for the release of a veteran actor kidnapped last weekend by a forest bandit. Veerappan, 56, sent the demands for the release of actor Rajkumar in an audio tape to governments of the southern states of Tamil Nadu and Karnataka, where police have tried in vain for years to arrest him. The demands included the release of prisoners in Karnataka charged under a tough anti-terrorist law, inquiries into alleged police excesses, better wages for tea and coffee **farmers and the installation of a statue of revered Tamil poet and saint Thiruvalluvar in Bangalore.** (My emphasis and turn back to* **TAMIL CULTURE***).*

This saint lived–it is now established–by the beginning of the Tamil calendar 30 years before Christ's birth! For my eldest son in Massachusetts who phoned, vivid memories had come to mind of a near-family encounter in our 11-strong Kerala Christmas reunion travelling the roads of south India for 3000km in a minicoach. Coming up from the coast at Kochi we had rested a short time in the great crossroads of the south, bustling Coimbatore. Only half an hour earlier two sheepish police superintendents had been released by none other than the 'brigand' as the local press refer to him–and with full publicity! And then like any adept Indian magician he vanished.

It is not the first time that state government officials from Kerala's high ranges of the Wynad through Karnataka south of Mysore down into Tamilnadu have been embarrassed by the ease with which Veerappan operates. A few days later on our way down the ghat road through the beautiful blue-gum shaded hills around Udhagamandalam (Ooty) to the hospitably-run Jungle Hut resort on the Mysore side of the mountain range, police check posts and army jeeps spelled excitement for my grandchildren.

♦ Veerappan had surfaced again, seen in the area with local tribal people who regard him as a mixture of Robin Hood saviour against police harassment and defiling of their daughters, and

dispenser of ransom money as largesse in their impoverished scattered settlements. In fact the bandit regards himself as an incarnation of Rama, defender of the faith and upholder of the rights of these downtrodden people. When a temple he had built to his family's **ISTADEVATA** was ransacked in 1990 by the police–according to locals–he struck again, killing 22 of a force in a mine blast while they were trying to track him down.

Our family went on a different expedition up the nearby mountain armed with binoculars. Bird watchers all, we were after the sight of more exotic prey as well as hopeful sighting of wild elephants–except that we had been warned to obey the rules never to approach a herd and to remain quietly unobtrusive. Only two months earlier a German couple suddenly coming in the pathway of a fully mature tusker (one that *had* escaped the bandit's depredations) approached it eager for dramatic photographs. Drama there was… the tourists were stampeded and trampled to death, shrill trumpeting alerting the Jungle Hut owners nearby. And now our midnight jeep safari in search of tigers (they had been seen in the area) cancelled, an army unit with full armoury of weapons was in the vicinity, searching for Veerappan.

Up the mountainous climb every crackle of dry twigs behind every bush became a real live 'baddy' about to jump out and hold us to ransom, Tom our grandson, then aged ten and Claire, six had cut themselves staves to resist. Sheer innocence of childhood! And yet in India you never know what speaks to the heart… with middle age approaching it looks as though Veerappan wants to call it a day. And India being India, like the Bandit Queen, I heard an editor in Mysore on my last visit speculating he might even stand for politics!

Inveterate show-off that he is, Veerapppan may push his luck too far. Incredibly, still roaming free in Karnataka's jungles, he abducted yet another state officer whose decomposed body was later found after an encounter with police in Chengai forest. This was stated in the press to be his 122nd victim which begs the question; 'How can a Special Task Force of at least 300 trained troops fail to capture him?'

He had in fact asked the Chief Ministeress for a film to be made of his life, no doubt hoping for a Hollywood sum for the film rights! But the money would be for his people who had given him sanctuary and who worshipped that great Tamil saint, Valluvar, Tirusahib. He too was low caste but he had given them the **Tamil Veda** which, unschooled though they were, they could qoute, line and verse 4000 years later.

Age and bad eyesight however brought the bandit out of the jungle in 2005. A posse of police ambushed him and shot him dead.

■ **VIBHUTI** (n. *Sanskrit* = **divine power**)

1. Is the all pervasive force that powers the universe.

2. Many paintings of Siva in his ascetic form depict him at cremation grounds, grey with ash, and burnt cow dung which is applied to the body, especially of Saivite sadhus.

♦ Original meaning is 'divine power' given to the devotee through the blessing of the 'divine essence' (implied in the meaning also) by the priest at the gateway to the inner temple shrine. This is in the **form of powder** placed on the middle of the forehead of the person come to worship and who brings a flower, a garland, fruit, sweetmeats or ritual balls of rice and saffron, etc. to present to the Deity.

This is offered up to the image and then blessed and returned to the worshipper as **prasad**.

◆ Hindus quote the Gita passage X: 41 to give credence to the meaning of vibhuti as a blessing. Krishna speaks to Arjuna of the power of his vital essence: 'whosoever being there is endowed with glory and grace and vigour, know that to have sprung from a fragment of my splendour'. Satya Sai Baba followers cite this as reason to believe the powder as springing from the skin.

Shiva is said, in the disintegration of the galaxies at the end of each **KALPA** that he alone can bring about, to have burnt even Brahma and Vishnu. He smeared their ashes on his body. In his aspect as the supreme yogi associated as an ascetic with cremation and funeral pyres, such ashes (**vibhuti**) are no mere burnt earth. They are at a deeper level (there is always this unplumbed depth in Indian belief!) reminders that yogis who reach the height of superconsciousness have burnt their energy centres or ascending chakras.

Yogis smear their bodies in the northern winter with the greyish white ash from the ritual fires before which they pray and meditate. It is said to protect naked bodies from feeling cold.

◆ Vibhuti has taken on worldwide significance with the encirclement of our planet with yogic and meditation centres and jetset swamis. It seems to be as commonly used a definition among non-Indians as guru and ashram. It is especially associated with the miraculous powers Satya Sai Baba is believed to possess in producing vibhuti from the palm of his hands, when surrounded by the huge crowds (not only Indians) that gather for his appearances in his ashrams in Andhra and in the Whitefields suburb of Bangalore where I had gone out of curiosity. Sitting in an impeccably clean ashram, next to an Indonesian lady to have her personal statue of the Virgin Mary blessed. Photographs of Satya Sai Baba have a curious quality of 'gathering' the brownish white substance if the glass is wiped clean, though rationalists and professional magicians unavailingly reproduce these 'miracles'!

◆ **Vibhut** is a ballistic missile that myth ascribes to Viswamitra who gave this first mention—a kind of contemporary engineering in his day—for Rama to use.

■ **VIDYALAYA** (n. *Sanskrit*)

Is the abode (**alaya**) of **vidya** (knowledge) personified as Saraswati so, a school. **Vishwa** (universe) **vidyalaya** is a university. The **guru-kul** ('guru lineage'), the system by which the guru teaches the **parampara** (tradition of gnowledge) of his or her lineage to disciples as if they are members of that family line. The really old traditional system of Sanskrit learning still takes place although some elders would say the stringency of discipline is not adhered to as in former ages. This was not just formal education in the Vedic texts as it would be today. Possibly one of the reasons for India's secret in maintaining such a **continuum of** culture and with such **a coherence** over millennia, despite waves and waves of incomers with new religions and racial customs, is this system of education disciple-ship, digging deep into its own cultural **awareness** as well as imbibing **facts**.

◆ A guru's presence was to be honoured with the utmost obedience, even to being a virtual 'servant' accomplishing the most menial tasks in order to indicate the degree of submission and devotion. Ravi Shankar has spoken of this, even the harshness of the guru's demands in order to test the mettle of the **chela/shishya's** character, as disciple.

◆ Then the **very personalised education** began.

◆ In an open learning situation, one to one with the guru imparting his knowledge, the **chela** went at his own pace. Few women broke into this male preserve unless exceptionally talented when male relatives would give tuition or a guru took the initiative in teaching not only the Sanskrit 'texts' but the deeper cultural wisdom. But it was possible… and did happen!

◆ Learning was connected to life outside the classroom, not divorced from the community.

◆ It is stated by Indian commentators that the **gurukul** system—**the guru-shishya-parampara**—'**could not be bought or sold**'. Money transaction was not in the nature of the system. Reverence, respect, integrity was the functioning currency. Pandit Ravi Shankar used so often to stress, '**Vinaya**'… which he explained 'is vital in a shishya's relationship with the guru.'

◆ Patronage from wealthy citizens kept the guru (and his family) alive.

◆ Such a system survived even the most intense of Islamic incursions and overlay of Muslim customs and conversion.

◆ Collapse of the widespread indigenous village schooling system only came as **Dharampal (The Beautiful Tree**, Other India Press, 1996) skilfully shows, under the systematic inroads of British missionary education (with Macaulay at the helm), in the early 19th century onwards and the concept of 'the school' was established with curricula, administrative bureaucracy, examinations. Even government-funded Sanskrit schools of today have lost their 'heart' in the pedagogy and the secular teacher's role is totally lacking status—and imaginative approach to knowledge described as 'Hindu' and about which, as referred to earlier, **Richard Lannoy** writes with such feeling in **The Speaking Tree**.

Subtle distinctions are made in Indian cultural teaching about what vidhya (knowledge) is (see **GNOW** stepping Stone).

On a truly meditative re-issue of a Subbulakshmi recording of a famous hymn dedicated to the 'way of devotion' composed by **Adi Shankaracharya** (CD EMI 147035) **Bhaja Govindam**, the late Rajagopalachari succinctly introduces the CD in his own words …

◆ when **intelligence matures** and lodges securely in the mind, it **becomes wisdom**

◆ when **wisdom is integrated** with life and issues out in action it **becomes bhakti**

◆ **knowledge**… if it does not get transformed into bhakti… **is useless tinsel**

V

- to *believe* that ***gyana and bhakti,*** *knowledge and devotion are different from each other, is* **ignorance**

'Packed into this one hymn is the substance of all Vedanta.' As is the message in the Bible in I Corinthians Chapter 13… **for now we see through a glass darkly… but the greatest of all (qualities)… caritas** = love, charity, compassion, grace abounding = **Bhaja Govindam.**

- VILLAGE GUARDIANS

….known as **gramadevatas**, these wonderfully stylised burnt-clay figures on horses and elephants vary distinctively from region to region.

Worship of village deities is still an important cultural function in the communal life of rural and tribal India. The sense of a personal deity is felt very necessary—certainly when villages were very isolated in the old days. As in Bali, where the **Devi** or **Goddess** watches over the terraced rice fields from a platform on a pole, the **sthan** (or 'hallows' = NUMEN) is usually a platform under a spreading tree and these figures reside there.

- Ceremonial processions are taken out in the agricultural cycle. Villages are still aware of the fragility of their livelihood and the season-to-season struggle with the monsoon. So any propitiation is worthwhile to pray for good monsoon, no accidents, safe journeyings.

The village potter is crucial to this community worship (see **CRAFT**) and the sense of well-being, protected by **watchmen** (**vira-s**) on the outskirts. Where guardian riders on tall terracotta horses (each with very distinct personalities) keep at bay the evil forces—**bhut/bhoot** or ghosts, the **evil eye** and other malevolent portents cannot hold sway.

In Tamilnadu and Karnataka some of these large terracotta **vahanas** (vehicles) are painted. Although made from the same red earth as pot vessels, for extra strength human hair is mixed into the clay as a binding agent. This is the responsibility of the potter's wife in conjunction with the village barber. She in fact also adds the detailed moulding to the figures. They are a collector's dream, but they carry within them great cultural significance and need to remain where they are—their dashing riders, kshatriyas all, with regulation moustache and individual turbans, clubs to bash a marauding demon out of existence, crafted sometimes with real humour. Now even the local policeman or English Sahib of colonial times has been added.

- VISHNU

the all-pervasive, preservative force in the cosmos and the balancing deity of the **TRIMURTI**, of blue pigmentation. Vishnu descends as an **avatar**, an **incarnation** time and again to redress disorder caused by malevolent energies inbuilt into creative processes.

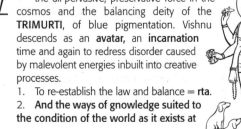

1. To re-establish the law and balance = **rta.**
2. **And the ways of gnowledge suited to the condition of the world as it exists at**

a particular time. Truth is not absolute. It moves and reshapes itself, **reforming** according to the temper of the times.

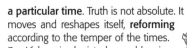

3. Vishnu is depicted ever blue in colour, symbol of the **pervading ether** of the **universe**, the formless substance of the firmament.

Heinrich Zimmer in his writings on the **Myths and Symbols in Indian Art and Civilisation** describes the atmosphere surrounding this amorphous concept of Deity:

In the infinite ocean all the seeds, all the potentialities of subsequent evolution rest in a dormant state of undifferentiation…Vishnu the anthropomorphic embodiment of this fluid of life, is floating.. in and upon the substance of his own essence…

As I have mentioned before, I see this as a metaphor now possible to express in modern scientific terms of the DNA double helix of our very substance for are we not, in large proportion, constituted of water, blood, mucous, plasma, liquid, roughly 65-75% of total body weight, held within a film of skin? **The ocean represents potential existence.**

In the form of a luminous giant He is recumbent on the liquid element radiant with the steady glow of His blessed energy…

as indeed his **murti** depicts in all the splendid plastic sculpture of **Deogarh** and **Mahabalipuram**, the deity reclining on **Anant**—the endlessness of time in the ocean of the sacred **amrit**. Vishnu is in sleeping mode, **yoganidra**—slumbering wakefully…but to my mind too bland as a deity. Shiva has always appealed more, being very demanding intellectually, as well as expecting relentless discipline on the part of his devotees. Hindus would refer to Vishnu as **Jagat Prabhu**. Literal translations as I have often pointed out of words such as **prabhu = pra = all-powerful, bhu** of the earth (**bhumi**) cannot cover concepts accurately by using the word Lord. Having had my own vision stretched by a sensitive and challenging editor and then discussed conclusions reached with trusted Indian friends and Anu Madan who helped with understanding the density of meaning behind Sanskrit words, I would hope that at least some discerning travellers will embrace these easily pronounceable Sanskrit terms like they have with ashram, yoga, raga, etc. in respect for cultural identity instead of clinging to false Anglicized/Christian words such as 'Lord'.

- VISWAKARMA

is the Vulcan of Hindu deities, the great **carpenter** and **architect** of the creative arts. Worshipped by many Sikh carpenter guilds, especially the **Ramgarhias** as their patron saint so to speak… the Vedic **Twashtri**, artificer and the all-seeing fashioner, not only of all the crafts but the very universe itself!

Bold bazaar posters of this Rig Vedic 'force' as architect even of the Universe show him with all the instruments a mechanic or engineer would need, nuts, screws, spanners to fashion the weapons of the Great Deities, the discus for Vishnu, the trident for Siva. Wait until the inventive artists of the bazaar catch up with modems and laptops of the electronic age!

■ **VISWAMITRA**

...also one of the seven famous **RSIS**, he too was an influential sage of earliest Indian legend, born a kshatriya but by dint of intense **tapasya** (and confused conceiving) eventually attained brahmin status. There is dispute about his ancestry; son of a king in the Rig Veda, he is described elsewhere as descending from another regal line.

What is always recounted are parable stories of his obsessive rivalry with, and jealousy of, **Vasishta**. Both these venerables had 100 sons, surely a symbolic sign of their 'powers' but enough to cause irrational behaviour! Their acerbic attitudes to each other and the curses they rained down disastrously wiped out both their progeny and remind one of the bitterness of scholarly rivalries between famous English professors at Cambridge University several decades ago! So–again–what is new?

■ **VIVEKA**

The power of discrimination to sift the moral wheat from the daily contaminated chaff of worldly existence.

A metaphor is used of the **hamsa** = sacred goose or gander that is supposedly able to sift water from milk with the aura of spiritual discernment with which it is associated due to the quality of **buddhi** = wisdom, intellect, experience, a benign blessing that leads to grace, such as the 19th century teacher **Vivekananda** realised.

Go to Mt. Abu where the saint spent time meditating overlooking the **Nakki** (nails) lake. Legend states the gods carved it out with their finger nails. A hill station Festival in June highlights Abu's famous roseate Dilwara marble temples, an ornithological sanctuary, the peaceful Vishnu temple atop the mount, tribal music and a night of spirited Rajasthani qawali devotional music, but as jazzy as hot gospel in the USA!

Such are the manifold layers of meaning carried by these seminal Sanskrit words that others immediately arise such as **vasana** = desire (pron. **vaasana**) which **viveka** dispels. Indians will quote the saying:
The less I have ... the more I am.
Endnote: In 2003 the 140th anniversary (**shraddhanjali** = giving of respect offering) of the saint's birthday occurred. It was recalled that as a young man the swami had been very sceptical as an agnostic of Ramakrishna, regarding him as somewhat of a madman.

■ **VRATA** (n. *Sanskrit.... a vow*)
has many levels of meaning being so ancient a word
◆ the sense of cosmic geometry, the circle, a completeness, roundness.
◆ something which happened, is created
◆ a rite in the sense of doing a penance or fast

Women in their role as carrying the traditional designs through centuries from grandmother to daughter to granddaughter are the channels of this sacramental vivacity and vision. At festivals, family rites of passage, community celebrations it is they, without intellectual training or conscious articulation, who design the wall paintings on their impoverished villages huts, or the rangoli patterns on urban thresholds and courtyards in a timeless cosmic energy embracing space–spatial designs of the **SWASTIKA** and the **BINDU**, the **LOTUS**, the shape of the mango.
◆ Often designed in coloured rice or grain this is said to be an auspicious act in feeding those ants and other insects in heralding daybreak while also creating artistic beauty.
◆ Messages from literature abound to reinforce the practice and indicate the power of vrata. The story of **Savitri** and her ill-fated husband **Satyavan** is as well known as Red Riding Hood or Cinderella to Western children, but of great spiritual depth. Savitri undertakes the threefold fast, foregoing food and sleep for three days. That strength helps her defy the ultimate test with death. Even her father-in-law tries to dissuade her but her reply is typically Indian **woman**, steadfast to the end... *Have no heed. What I do set myself I will perform.* **The vow is made, and I shall keep the vow.**

That being so, the king agrees. Vrata must be kept, 'I cannot bid thee break thy word... once given.'

Personal encounter with someone who did indeed 'give her word'...and undertook a vrata referred to as **sawa lakh**. Going on pilgrimage to undertake such a discipline is no easy matter unlike going in the comfort of a coach to Lourdes in southern France, even if there a Roman Catholic pilgrim may undertake fast or other penance; or even going to a more arid Palestine of old, walking the path to Golgotha before all the modcons of today's Israeli-added air-conditioning and taxis to holy places in Jerusalem. Nor is it the discomfort of climbing the mountain to St. Patrick's shrine in Eire, or those demanding ascents in Spain.

A quiet Maharashtrian lady, wife of a high-ranking All India Radio director, quite without warning took me aside at a very cosmopolitan dinner, talking of her undertaking, in prayerful tones, before going to Hardwar for the first time. 'You may wonder where I have been'. I had wondered as she was more than an acquaintance, often being a mentor on matters of deep cultural significance in her Hindu family life. She explained her undertaking–the **sawa lakh ritual** to lift whatever weight had been on her mind. That meant writing on individual scraps of paper the name in Hindi of her particular **ISTADEVATA** which happened to be Rama राम 125,000 times (a **lakh** = 100,000, **sawa** = a quarter = 25,000). Then each paper had to be wrapped in wheat-flour dough rolled in a ball. Placing them in urns she had then taken them on pilgrimage to Hardwar, dedicated the 125,000 balls each with a sandalwood or vermilion mark in honour of her chosen deity, done special puja, given donation to the priests aiding her, received **DARSHAN**–and felt herself blessed.

V

She and her companions then proceeded to the auspicious pool where pilgrims take a dip—**Har Ki Pauri**—and slowly one by one fed all 125,000 atta balls to the sacred fish. She could see the query in my expression. She chuckled. *'It is cheaper than going to the psychiatrist, you know! I was impelled!"*

Endnote: An intriguing word, yet another with common Indo-European roots linking us to Latin—and political correctness not doing its etymological homework—is **mannat**. Its Sanskrit root = **manus** (Latin for hand). It is used in the sense of **giving a pledge**, putting a hand on you heart so-to-speak, to the Deity for thanks for the boons which come in a symbiotic relationship with **vratas** (often a spin-off from the tough self-discipline encountered through fasting, a cleansing of the soul). And the political correctness?… chair**man** became ousted by headlong feminists, thought to be a gender-dominated word associated with the **man** of **man**kind… nothing of the sort! In early Roman government the leader of the senate was led by his hand (**manus**) to be seated in the chair of omniscience (remember Shankaracharya establishing such in the Hindu temple in **KASHMIR** overlooking Srinagar?) where the pledge of duty (**mannat**, by hand) was sworn. Hence chair-*man*!

V

■ WOMEN

Yama, the god of death, was standing at the gates of heaven and interrogating three women. 'What have you done with your life?' he asked the first one, 'I loved one man, but then I married the man my parents chose for me, and I never looked at another man.' 'Let her in through the silver gate!' Yama told his assistant. The second one stated that she only loved the man she had married. She was let in through the golden gate. Then came the third, a dancing girl. 'Lord', she addressed Yama 'I have never made a man unhappy. I have given pleasure and fun to so many that I cannot count them.' 'Give her the key to my room!' was the god's instruction to the assistant.

PARADOXES abound when considering the actual position in society of India's many kinds of women encased in general as they are by the mental 'chastity belt' of family **sharam** or **lajja–shame = honour**; their own self-perceptions; the deeper undercurrents; the range of backgrounds from tribal to Mumbai yuppic, from a nomadic wizened tough matriarch with her shepherd clan in Kashmir's high valleys to an equally tough-as-leather administrator in a senior post in government. Our family has encountered them all!… and the supreme paradox is that the dancing girl went straight through Yama's pearly gates directly, because she was sincerely performing her **dharma**!

Attitudes by outsiders to women in India, images of what they themselves feel they should be, imprinted by surrounding culture from childhood, backward areas that inflict a draining drudgery at one level and advanced education that encourages and makes possible, with breathtaking femininity into the bargain, at another–all these factors provide a confusing array of impressions and role models.

And we as Western women are but drooping wallflowers propping up the pavilion when an Indian woman in all her full glory, bedecked in jewellery and henna-ed hands, gleaming long hair vibrant with a life of its own dancing in the sunlight, the soft swish of sari folds and the gentle tinkle of churree bangles, glides–not strides–into a room! *There* is ultimate grace.

I have watched one such descend a curving staircase, her elegant neck as delicately stretched as an egret suddenly alert, a shawl effortlessly thrown across the opposite shoulder, the rustle of apple-green silk edged with sunlit gold as the hem line swirls as though caught in a breeze, a flutter like a windblown meadow of flowers along the 'fall' of the sari border which weighs the hem down, dark eyes pools of millennial wisdom passed down that adamantine line of family ritual and surety of aesthetic style, grandmother to mother and now to this charismatic presence of the granddaughter… wife, mother, entrepreneur, artist, politician/journalist… what isn't she?… and then felt the electronic frisson as all eyes in the foreign concourse followed her lissom form.

We were lucky indeed to get any of our husbands out of India!

The spectrum reaches such extremes, from the all-powerful and potent **shakti image** which has pulsated in the veins of India since myth and reality merged into what its people regard as history, to the 'doormat' label attached to the woebegone female figure stooping in an off-white sheath of worn cloth, scrubbing floors in the gloom of mediaeval housing, burdened under heavy pitchers on her head to be carried over rough tracks, or the young daughter-in-law (**bahu**) harassed about insufficient dowry and driven by the horrors of burning. These indeed are the women originally hailed with praise in early texts, ever-steadfast wives 'as shadows to the substance'. These latter are the flickering images off electronic media signals imprinted in the Western brain despite India having provided one of the most powerful, determined and manipulative women prime ministers of modern world politics (barring her English contemporary Thatcher counterpart).

But that is the nature of the ambiguities and ambivalence that surround **Sri** whose Vedic yantra is the supreme *One* which saints and great men of the past have extolled; Sri is in fact referred to as **vamanga** = the left part of the body (fem gender) considered weaker in men, so women—representing this vital strength in their shakti power—**are therefore in most ritual situations such as marriage or in temple seating, placed on the left side of a man in order to protect him.**

The Sri symbol of feminine energy as creative essence purely biologically has such a visual resonance for Indians, it is repeated again here.

The rationalisation of the symbol-theory is that the five ▽ **expanding downwards to interpenetrate the four thrusting upwards create an energy** of their own with the movement of the eye inward and outward representing the **twofold process of creation-expansion and contraction into the One.** This is contained in the **BINDU** = the powerpoint of the innermost fifth unpenetrated ▽ and dissolution.

】®】®】®】®】®】®】®】®】®】®

A. **On a recent journey from Ahmedabad to Udaipur** another mental canvas is brushed in thick vivid strokes, a patina adding further confusion to the overall painting… **amazons of Rajasthan**, aflame in red textiles—oranges, ochres, crimsons as well as yellows and greens, wide-hemmed **lehngaas** swaying at the hemline (some five metres in circumference) like waves lapping at the sea's edge, chunnis or odhnis (veils) flapping as uncontrollably as their full-throated laughter, triple-layered brass pots heavy with water, glistening and flashing on their heads as the sun lowered towards the horizon, striding along the tarmac of the desert road at the end of the day.

Not only were they aware of their charisma as they cavorted into the sunset majestically and with dignity but they appeared to be tossing Rabelaisian jokes back and forth like so many tumbled balls juggled in the air…

B. **And out of Gujarat** an even more startling sight. A line of 19, kohl-eyed women all in black cotton habits embedded with glittering mirrorwork in their swinging skirts, each leading a camel.

W

They also strode by, heavy with chunky, silver anklets sweeping aside the hemlines, massed silver necklaces covering the bodice, hardly deigning to acknowledge a group of foreigners saluting their Grecian theatricality. It was this party who admired them; we peripheral to their curiosity.

◆ Atop the camels and across the embroidered saddles upturned rope charpoy beds swayed, babies and young children clinging to each other and dogs, goats and lambs, cooking pots and household items clattering atop upturned legs. One elderly man, all in white, head swathed in cotton, turbaned with stature, led them in the dust track beside the road, striding forth with whittled bough as 'bishop's crook'.

Belonging to the **Lohar** community, their menfolk are blacksmiths by trade, of no fixed abode, tinkers of old. Now they are responding to the explosion of internal tourism for Indians—so they fashion stylish and unique wrought-iron artefacts to sell in wayside pavement stalls. Low down the scale of economic hierarchies, these women gave no indication, however, of being psychologically oppressed. Indeed it is difficult to know by what Western criteria any judgement could be made about their self-esteem or standing in the community in their self-chosen nomadic lifestyle.

◆ **There are a thousand faces of femininity in India, more varied surely then those of Europe, the Americas or Australia all put together, given the complex layering of Indian society vertically between, as well as horizontally within groups.**

C. At a date unknown, speculation ranging over several thousand years, the celebrated sage **YAJNAVALKYA** is associated with what is considered the oldest of the metaphysical philosophies, the **Brhadaranyaka Upanishad**, part of which is taken up with a theological 'tournament' of discourses at the court of Janaka, the ruler. (Some sources say he lived at the beginning of time, one of the original **RISHIS** 6,000 years earlier!)

At this contest philosophical questions of great erudition are batted backwards and forwards between brahmins like a tennis match of Wimbledon proportions. As a known dissenter Yajnavalkya usually delivers the final matchpoint but one of the eight contestants is a formidable woman, a feisty creature and scholar, **Gargi**. She is of considerable philosophical standing herself so she questions him—no less—about the all-pervading essence in the universe. Said she, *'Verily I,... as a chief's son of Kasi would string his unstrung bow and take in his hand two arrows to smite his enemies and stand forth* (to combat)—*just so I stand forth against you with two questions. Answer me then!'–'Ask, Gargi,'* he said.

Her abstruse question about what pervades all creation relating to ether/akasha and the imperishable, clearly had not been intimidated by an earlier riposte in which on answering her learned syllogisms, the sage had cautioned her: *'Gargi, do not question too much, lest your head fall off... you question too much.'* (**Franklin Edgerton, The Beginnings of Indian Philosophy, Selections from the Upanishads**).

D. Bearing in mind this past, the pendulum swing surely takes in a wider arc to greater extremities than anywhere else in the world. Where else such a custom as **sati** (suttee) the self-immolation of a widow on her dead husband's pyre? A convenient way sociologically in a rural society to relieve the economic burden of widowhood and the inability to contribute to agricultural production. Women have been burned in European history for ecclesiastical reasons (Joan of Arc an icon). Witches also. But men also were put to the torch, even Popes–for heresy. I do not know of any such case in India's history where men suffered the same awful fate!

This bizarre custom of sati was first outlawed in Bengal by the Governor-General of British India (then functioning from Calcutta) Lord William Bentinck in 1829 after much consultation with leading Indian reformers. British administration tried on the whole not to become entangled in interference with religious/social aspects of Indian home life which lay within its jurisdiction but **many Indian men to their credit** in the great wave of fresh air blowing through Bengali culture at the time—men such as **Raja Ram Mohan Roy**—demanded action against such aberrations which were never part of original tradition.

End of 20th century

Accounts of occasional sati in remote areas and more especially in Rajasthan (see **RAJPUTS**) for cultural reasons still surface and make headlines in an ever watchful Indian press. Such actions are roundly condemned causing a furore not only among middle class women. Such acts are illegal being unconstitutional in modern India but social customs as entrenched as they are in India are difficult to police and again–the contradictions–a fleeting glimpse on TV of miserable mothers-in-law in custody, awaiting trial!

E. Muslim encroachments at the turn of the millennium (10–11th century CE) further reinforced a misplaced pride in what were acts of astonishing feminine heroism in mass immolation defying the fierce onslaughts of the early Muslim incursions across north west India and the ever-present threat of abduction, rape and household slavery. This raison d'être in extreme social conditions cannot however explain the recent examples–rare though they may be in a population of a billion, but alarming enough to have brainwashed a young widow into accepting sati 'for the honour' of the family in a horrific enactment of a totally banned ritual burning in 1987. The girl's name **Roop Kanwar** at least now remembered in history rather than a hand imprinted on a wall as at Chittor.

The mental cruelties of dowry deaths have also been a subject of exposure by Indians themselves, men as well as women (see **Jamila Verghese, Her Gold and Her Body**, Vikas, Delhi, 1997 and **Girija Khanna** and **Miriamma Verghese, Indian Women Today**, Vikas, Delhi, 1979).

F. Since Independence women of all kinds of backgrounds have emerged as a powerful force in the body politik and, in recent decades, as an ever-strengthening economic factor. The presence of young women driving the modern Maruti car rather than the dumpy but long-life Hindusthan as well as manoeuvring the lethal

W

traffic astride the ubiquitous scooter not only in the serviceable shalwar-kameez but also the sari, can be an indicator of whatever one wishes to make of it as far as women's economic power in modern India goes. The number is now legion.

In the 1950s a woman at the wheel, though accepted (and without any of the mental constraints their sisters felt in Islamic Pakistan) was a small proportion of the motoring public. Seen in Bangalore in 1994 a young helmeted girl, braids flying, in stylish tight jeans, her boyfriend riding pillion in the office-going traffic! Not a head turned.

This new confidence and social freedom to move unrestrictedly has always been part of Indian society within the norms appropriate to the times. Only after Islam settled upon India bringing with it the strictures of man-made shariah laws similar to those of St Paul in the Christian tradition did **purdah** which in Arabic means a **curtain**, push women even of other cultural backgrounds back into the shadows and behind the screen.

The Modern Woman
The emergence of women into public life and politics was certainly encouraged by the Independence movement and Free India Campaigns of the 1930s when women went to prison along with their men and people like Sarojini Naidu moved great crowds with her poetry as well as her defiance of unjust British laws.

Pandit Nehru, Mahatma Gandhi, Vinoba Bhave, all as enlightened men encouraged women to come into mainstream life. Bengali intellectuals were very active at the turn of the 20th century and interchange of ideas took place between British liberal thinkers moved by the great sweep of revolutionary changes in Europe and a very advanced level of Bengali society—people of the calibre of Tagore and Motilal Seal were many among not only artistic groups but within the wealthy mercantile class.

In fact the government through its postal services has placed historic women in the public eye and commemorated their talents and bravery on stamps, **Meera** the first to appear in her poetic struggle against 'the dogmatic Hinduism of the priestly classes' (see **BHAKTI**). Others were reigning queens, turned warriors by widowhood—**Durgawati**, (16th century central India); **Ahilyabhai** of Indore (18th century); **Channamma** in Karnataka (18th–19th century); **Rashoman**, (18th–19th century) in Bengal, as well as the most famous fighter against the British during the mid-1850s revolts, **Lakshmibai** of Jhansi (central India).

It must be said also that many fathers in the past century were the force behind daughters aspiring to educational levels, as universities were founded. Even before 1947 they encouraged them into professional life as lawyers, business executives, engineers way ahead of their Western counterparts. Often mothers paradoxically were the inhibiting factor, brought up to be more traditional daughters-in-law for good families and surrounded by all the trappings of middle class gentility common even to the British Raj society as well, a much closer proximation in social behaviour and sexual mores between West and East in pre-World War II years than today.

Endnote to this assessment. In a paper delivered to a Jungian Society in 1979 and reported in **Harvest**, No. 25, Journal for Jungian Studies, London, **Dr Manisha Roy** speaking of **Animus and Indian Women** reiterates this very fact 'a woman in India is led by her father or father-figure to her academic intellectual life. So whatever animus drive she may experience, she also has strong support from external masculine figures'.

◆ **In recent years this new confidence in their own capabilities has not been confined to the higher economic classes either.**

Regionally there are disparities but in go-ahead states like Maharashtra and Gujarat, women have, even in the villages, organised radical grassroots reform movements and become powerful in the **PANCHAYAT** movement of local rule; they are also traditionally a power to be reckoned with at upper middle class level by foreign companies doing business with their husbands in the corporate structure. Many decisions are joint family ones where powerful matriarchs behind the formal lounge screens have a considerable say in advice given; in the Punjab where physically they can become tyrants within the home; in Bengal, Kerala and Tamilnadu, Andhra Pradesh and Karnataka where education is greatly prized and where astonishing feats of political prowess and astute Machiavellian manoeuvrings have become prerogatives not of the male but of the darker side of feminine ruthlessness—the Chief Minister of Tamilnadu in the early 90s had not been dubbed 'the Empress' for nothing. Jayalalitha, ex-film star surfaces many times in this book.

Obviously in an international city such as Mumbai young women are making their way like their Western sisters into many areas previously considered male preserves. They encounter exactly the same ambivalence, inhibitions and opportunities as their Western sisters attempting to break the 'glass ceiling'. A young film maker interviewed in Australia's **The Indian Down Under** newspaper (December 1995) explained:

Safina warded off the prevalent threat to a woman travelling at odd hours in India by covering her head with a scarf. Here she does not feel in any way threatened.

She made a conscious effort to educate herself on the technical side of film making, to counter the refrain her colleagues and others voiced regarding her dealing with 'machines'.

And that is liberation for Safina: 'tackling the problems head-on: otherwise you are caught up in the purdah of your own making,' she said.

One very robust but highly talented biochemist Vimla Majumder, senior executive in the brewery industry in Bangalore—where beer is a huge conglomerate in India (now exporting Cobra Beer to UK pubs!)—also spoke on an international network in more articulate terms than many Anglo-Australian or English women. Her view of management is that it must become more **androgynous** to take into account feminine values and gifts in dealing with management—an appropriate phrase for a culture which envisaged **ARDHANARISWARA**, a

W

totally appealing numinous archetype to those of us brought up within conventional patriarchal religions of the West.

◆ Within agriculture a remarkable female presence at another level made itself felt in Gujarat as far back as the 50s when the **Kaira District Milk Co-operative**, at Anand, was set up by one of India's quintessential managers, **Verghese Kurien**. This has already been recounted under **MIRACLES**. At this more humble level, far different from middleclass women (advantaged in so many ways) where non-literacy is rife, astonishing and exciting experiments are going on–in **western Orissa** for instance in **Sambalpur** district, again in dairying projects; in **Andhra Pradesh** and **Karnataka** in anti-liquor struggles; in **Punjab** and **Tamilnadu** empowering women to 'rise up as leaders', reinforced by constitutional amendments, increased parliamentary representation and a panchayat presence–all grassroots movements.

Submissive Power

There is a saying in India that women are 'unobtrusive scaffolding upon which families build their lives.'

If **Sita** (Rama's consort and the almost-too-good heroine of the Ramayana epic) is held up even to this day most especially by grandparents telling the old stories to their offspring as the epitome of the ideal woman, the ideal wife, the ideal caring feminine entity there is a dynamic, volatile energy which emerges from the shadow side of the anima. The paradox starts here.

This is Sita's plea as a new bride to Rama to take her with him and his brother as they face exile and a wandering life in the forests of Uttar Pradesh of that ancient time.

'Lord of my life, home of compassion, fair giver of bliss and wise, you who are to the house of Raghu as the moon to the lily, heaven without you would be hell! Mother, father, sisters and dear brothers, the loved ones of the family and the circle of friends, the mother and father of her lord, the guru, relatives and helpers, fair sons and noble who bring happiness, nay, all there is of love and kinship, O my husband, is to a wife without her lord a grief that burns even more fiercely than the sun. Body, wealth, home, land, city and kingdom—all these are naught but sorrow on sorrow to a woman deprived of her husband. Lord, without you pleasure would be sickness, ornaments a burden, the world as the tortures of the god of death. .... As a body bereft of life, as a river that has no water, so, lord, is a wife without her husband, With you, my husband, all is happiness, if only I behold your face like the pure autumn moon.

From **Tulsidas: The Holy Lake of the Acts of Rama,** trans. Hill,

Patriarchal law-givers such as Manu in ancient times (somewhat akin to St Paul who reinterpreted Christ's parables and gospels to the disadvantage of women whom Christ had treated equally) and male compilers of literature such as the many Vyases continued to hand down a meek and mild idealised image as symbolic guidelines to a polyglot population. Soon after Independence, in the new dispensation of women who had suffered imprisonment as freedom fighters, women began to research the texts themselves. Such a one was *Shakuntala Rao Shastri* who published **Women in the Sacred Laws.**(Bharata Vidhya Bhavan, Delhi, 1953). This book opened up a whole new enlightened world of women's rights protected by the shastras.

And then the dramatic swing in contrast to the all-powerful Indira Gandhi–India's **Shakti** as she was called–as one of the world's most dominating prime ministers.

The Goddess Image: Potency and Power Percolating into a Presence

Kali is no goddess of past mythology–a dried husk of the Greek Gaia/Demeter partnership of earth, and fertility and secret rites, themselves the source of a solemn and principal festival in the ancient Greek mythological year, lost now to history.

A scrawny and voracious hag though she may be in the dark tantric representation, all black and skeletal, drinking her victims' blood, a picture of frenzied energy chasing the massed and powerful army of ugly animal-like demons, she is still 'the other half' of femininity = MA, the Mother.

In both her puzzling forms she recalls the pulsations of an Indian culture long before earliest settlements produced the resonating Vedic poetry, Indra's noisy heaven and heroic epics.

◆ **Kali** springs to life, with all the panoply of festival, ritual, artistic interpretation, and deep-rooted worship, most especially among Bengali families not only in India but in the far-flung diaspora of Canada, Europe, the UK and Australia. She is very much alive in popular tradition, full of frenzied, blood-dripping imagery at the bazaar poster level, worshipped at Kalighat, and in the esoteric tantric rituals which are hardly spoken about, far-flung though they are throughout India.

Kali dances upon the pale-hued and prone body of her spouse SHIVA as emblematic of energy, creation and the balance of dissolution, disintegration and final destruction, endlessly holding the cosmos in their minuet dance of opposites, turning slowly in partnership from inertness to the spark of life–then the dying glow at the end of the cycle of turning.

Below her stamping feet is Shiva—entirely white, untouched by her electric energy, in a state of quiescence. It is a very disturbing image, common in Bengali bazaar posters and in paintings. But as the electric molecules flow, it is this **shakti energy, more potent and powerful than Shiva which will spark the great god into another galactical cycle of creation** when he will stamp his foot again in the tandava dance and set **rhythmic energy** in motion.

The Goddess and the attributes she holds

But what a puzzling goddess image to outsiders! "What a dreadful looking woman," an Australian once remarked. "Blood, brimstone, her red tongue lolling out of her mouth, skulls around her neck!"

Indians on the other hand see a reminder of time passing towards the ultimate death we all face but try to blot out of mind, and a benign Mother also who has to be tempestuous to counteract the evil of the world. They also are aware in the mind's eye of Kali's benign other half—powerful, all-conquering Durga.

What empowering archetypes to turn to give any woman a psychic charge!

1. In some images Kali holds the **noose** in association with Durga, to imply the destruction, the snaring of those who defy the established order of morality—and later to become an aberration among the **thuggees**—from which the English word 'thug' comes. They waylaid travellers before the advent of modern transport, as they walked the rough roads of 19th century India and strangled them with the Kali-blessed **roomal** handkerchief.

2. In the other hand of the goddess are **scissors** to cut the umbilical cord of life, or the goddess is brandishing the **ankusha**—the **goad** which is yet another metaphor, the **holding-in-check** of runaway elements of human nature, similar to the goad with which mahouts 'rein in' their elephant charges.

3. The third attribute is the rosary, the fourth **a cranium** full of the nourishing elixir of life.

And finally in some iconography she holds the **palm leaf folded texts** of learning and the Vedas.

What a far cry from the shades of meaning, culturally nurtured in images of the immaculate Virgin Mary 'uncontaminated' as Zimmer puts it, 'by the darker principle.' Or Joan of Arc in our own civilisation. Boadicean warriors there have been and other imprints in our own day of Iron Maidens such as the daunting 'headmistress' style of Britain's first woman prime minister, Maggie Thatcher. But the intricacies of the female in Indian thought are so dense and philosophically intertwined with the ever-percolating sense of fertility, that creative force of **prakriti** (see **PURUSHA**) and **Prithvi** = earth (Sanskrit nouns of feminine gender) that it is hard to disentangle where the influence of one begins and where the other ends.

Seduction and Fertility...

Just as this feminine entity, earth gives life to all living substance—plant, animal, human, gifts in the power of the Mother to give, so the vagaries of nature can also be cruel, turbulent, sudden.

The fertile motif is everywhere, not only in the specific flattened mound of a female figure, often before the shrine on a flagstone floor in a Maharashtrian temple dating back to the 3rd century CE, but even thousands of years earlier in simple terracotta moulds. This emblem is all exposed, legs apart, generative organs defined as a cleft, often headless and capped with a lotus, wide open to the forces of nature, fertility implied, penetration and consummation. This is tropically abundant India, prolifically overgrown with jungle potency, not the controlled sexuality of a northern climate. This is the embodiment of the life force—Lajja, Gauri, Aditi, Renuka, Prithvi.

This graphic depiction has never been suppressed in India. In a tropical climate perhaps it could never be. Nor in a nation where three quarters of its people are rural/tribal and fundamental nature is very pervasive. Luxuriant foliage, lotus tendrils curving in endless arabesque on temple friezes, melon-heavy bosomed tree spirits upholding majestic stone gates even at Buddhist **stupas** such as Sanchi, tendril-twining throughout century upon century of Indian artistic expression, the intimately conjoined maithuna couples at Khajuraho and Puri are constant reiterations of the sensuous forces of Nature—**demanding reproduction—prakriti-procreation in Sanskrit/Latin**. But in no way is any of this imagery erotic in the pornographic sense of deliberately provocative Western commercial messages to be implanted on the psyche.

The nubile young Lolita is very suspect in the public Indian tradition—even Krishna's harem of milkmaids dance the circular raslila with the gentility of a mediaeval minuet! The seductiveness of the **SALABHANJIKA** nymph holding up the sculptured railings of Buddhist art at Barhut (third century BCE, now in Calcutta and Allahabad museums) is one of the spirit rather than the body and even Krishna and Radha in coitus, with handmaidens in attendance are transformed into metaphysical explanations of the human souls' search for union and absorption in the divine, delightfully indecorous though the temple sculpture or the painting in its gymnastic feats may be!

Nevertheless Vedic texts are quite graphic in their metaphors, referring to DESIRE as the heat that engenders the EGG (see Edgerton). In the Upanishads it is stated: 'Woman is the fire, Gautam the phallus, her fuel; the hairs (pubic) are her smoke; the vulva is her flame; when a man penetrates her, that is her coal, the ecstasy is her sparks'. (quoted from Varma and Mulchandani's book **Love and Lust: An Anthology of Erotic Literature from Ancient and Erotic Literature from Ancient and Mediaeval India**, HarperCollins, Mumbai, 2004).

... and the Mother

♦ 'The Wondrous Essence of the Goddess,' as Zimmer termed her does not emanate from such dangerous immaturity and sexual licence but from **Durga**—the all-powerful female urge of creative benign forces...**Mataji, Ammai is the magnetic image that holds most sway on the Indian mind.**

In the ultimate analysis every Indian knows that women have been honoured in their culture **no matter the aberrations of historical circumstances**, and the dead wood of powerful chauvinistic tendencies inbuilt into the temple and caste when the rivers of inspiration and fervour ran dry before the next swing of the pendulum towards regeneration. This was when **pati**, a term applied in respect to deity in Vedic society, similar to the Latin **pater**, became encrusted with ritual and priestly domination. Pati came to be applied to earthly husbands also who were regarded by tradition as the god!

All over India the respect due to a woman is very marked. A young woman is referred to as daughter—beti; as a sister, didi, as an older woman, **ma**.

The living spirit still flares up from as far away as Kaladi where Shankaracharya in the gentle landscape of riverine Kerala yearned to be given insight. It was to Kali that he prayed for inspiration.

Who art thou, O Fairest One! Auspicious One!
You whose hands hold both: delight and pain?
Both: the shade of death and the elixir of immortality,
Are thy grace, O Mother.

♦ As also did a continuing line of modern saint-philosopher musicians and revolutionary politicians (intellectuals all!) seeking

W

Independence–most especially in Bengal. **Ramakrishna** (1834-1886) beginning life as a brahmin pujari, an orthodox household priest in Kolkata, soon had taken up service in the worship of Kali to whom he dedicated his extraordinary saintly life. A legend in his lifetime, his message through devotion to **the Mother** was that all faiths lead to the one goal ultimately. For a time he gave up everything, becoming one with the outcasts of society in a symbolic gesture similar to Gandhi's, later living as a Muslim and then as a Christian. **Vivekenanda** was his disciple and set up the casteless, outward-going philanthropic **Ramakrishna Mission** that branches all over India today. **Vivekenanda** himself, **Aurobindo Ghose**, **Rabindranath Tagore** all have made reference to this vital metaphor–the Mother–and, most intriguingly, **Bankim Chandra Chatterjee**, interpreted the history of Bengal–and India–in the imagery of Kali, benign and fierce, wise and sweeping all before her–as many Indian women do with great flair and feminine grace.

♦ What still amazes me as an outsider coming in from Western culture is the power of the goddess as a symbol of the **Essence**, the divinity in the life process as worshipped by **intellectual professional male devotee** as well as female across to the poorest bereft of any formal education worth speaking of–even the communities of semi-arid western Gujarat… **at the autumnal season of the great festivals of Dussehra** and **Diwali** and **Navaratri.** Those living a basic existence constantly under the threat of drought, forced migration due to desertification, a constant struggle for water as well as food, celebrate with swashbuckling gusto not only the presence of Shri Krishna (who is said to have recreated a whole community in coastal Saurashtra after persecution in the region of Mathura and Brindavan) but also the Mother Goddess **Ambaji**. The women, dressed in all their deep red spangled skirts, yellow, orange, purple tie-dye cholis and dupatta scarves, on village rooftops and cityscapes perform their undulating **garba** dance with gusto.

The pulsating rhythms of the dholak drum beat out echoed by their gathering momentum, multi-coloured batons (*dandias*) cracking furiously against each other. The atmosphere is electric. It is joyous also. A climax of handclapping, menfolk all part of the worship as they gyrate around a single dancer twirling with the earthen garba *deep* (a decorated cut-out design kalash on her head) seems to vibrate with feminine power transmitting an echo (even in the implements as well as the design, simple pottery such as these continually emerging from the rubble) of the Harappan civilization well over 6,000 years ago.

Does this then reside in the background psyche of many an Indian woman, a hidden force of empowerment, even despite her own diminished situation, a model to live up to in strength that emerges from nowhere to give her a sense that power there is, strive if she will? And that men still admit this in their psyches?

A splendid and sumptuously illustrated book **Devi: The Great Goddess** co-published by **Mapin**, Ahmedabad and **The Sackler Gallery, Smithsonian Institution**, Washington, DC (1999) under the direction of **Vidya Dehejia**, leaves no doubt of the **force**

embedded in the one word = **Devi** whose invocation as Mahashakti flows like molten lava:

Mind and words are powerless
to encompass your glory
whose extent is as immeasurable
as that of cosmic space
(**Subramania Bharti**)

Conclusion... Shakti Power and modern politics
1985

A significant cultural gathering occurred in Chennai, reading like a roll-call of South Indian brain power, to examine the concept of Shakti and follow through a panorama of her development iconographically, in worship, incarnations in folk religion, her presence in literature and powerful influence in cultural life from village festival to elite philosophical attitudes.

♦ This symposium is now in book form under the auspices of the C P Ramaswami Aiyar Foundation, Chennai, honouring one of the great thinkers of recent times. Grounded in the very old Sanskrit shastras and agama texts **Shakti–in Art and Religion** is edited by **Dr Nanditha Krishna**. The only sad aspect is the illustrations–a disappointment to encounter–presented in a dull governmental grey with none of the aesthetic flair of other art books.

♦ The gathering itself was yet another indicator of the impetus of cultural research which modern Indians can now enjoy and promote after such a long period of colonial inertia, and in **the full light of modern reinterpretation of the very old texts**, many by women scholars examining their own gender.

It always used to be a homily in India: **Heaven is under the sole of the mother's foot**. And especially if she had sons... but now a whole articulate, talented generation of young women of another kind is appearing in incredible numbers given the size of the overall populations.

♦ Yet many strong women feel a sense of frustration that men still set the political agenda for too long; that Mrs Gandhi when prime minister, like her counterpart in Britain, ignored those hapless women whose own lives were circumscribed by traditional mores; that women have long suffered under-representation at all levels of government; that the Jayalalithas of this world do great disservice to the cause of women's true emergence by holding power and office under false pretences.

Legislation on serious matters upholding women's interest–sexual abuse, discriminatory pay, matters of child labour and prostitution–all languish in predominately male parliaments.

But **Shakti, Kali, Durga** are watching, India's menfolk have to beware! Those in the orthodox camp like the Janata Dal Party who deride women who cut their hair as **par katee** = snip-winged creatures, may well find their own wings clipped! India's **Cleo** magazine has arrived at the pavement bookseller level... and the adrenalin is rising. With content unimaginable even half a generation ago–outspoken comment on sexual harassment at the workplace; child abuse; widow neglect and the social hypocrisy that still pervades the subject; the rise in alcohol drinking and domestic violence; incest, questions of which continent one is inhabiting take on an alarming urgency. **Doe-eyed malleable Sita is out of sync with a vengeance!** There is a whole new 21st century world marching in, the statistics declaring that 250,000 women managers are running big concerns as well as 500,000 smaller businesses.

A personal afterthought: is one foolish still to believe in the ideal inherent in this intellectual acceptance of a feminine divine force? It is worth considering the impulses that come out of founding allegories of great civilizations...The Garden of Eden story presents an Eve created from a rib taken out of the male body. This is the Old Testament story of Creation, as though the female deprived the male of part of himself, implying sacrifice on his part and eternal indebtedness on hers... and consequent guilt! The Islamic tale, despite the 'garment' metaphor of male and female complementing each other, is full of wariness of female assertiveness, not even a Mother Mary figure to soften the tone of Arabia's unyielding masculinity of the desert.

In the delightful version of the Brahma intervention the balance is equal—and applied with zest. The Indian Brahma even has a sense of humour (see next column).

Climb the last stepping stone to catch a glimpse of what Brahma had to say…

And while on this stepping stone, lest it be thought to be peopled entirely with the well-trained professional woman, the well-fed middleclass mother-in-charge, the well-heeled glamorous arts pioneers, all privileged, I want to remember the hundreds of women I have met at village level in far-flung places. Mostly unschooled in the formal sense, often eating only one frugal meal a day, hard-worked from dawn to beyond dusk, they too are keepers of the nation's conscience.

It took **Oppi Untracht** to spell out the moving accolade to their firm hold on India's cultural heritage in this passage from an article he wrote so long ago while photographing evocative **Ritual Wall and Floor Decoration in India** (**Graphis Journal**, 136, pp. 148–159 and 176–178, Zurich, Switzerland, August 1968)—and this before the equally evocative colour photography and publications of **Dr. Stephen Huyler**, especially **Painted Prayers**.

It is they who require the mystic ideograph to invoke the gods and make ritual contact with the supernatural, to close the gap between devotee and deity with a drawing or diagram… The traditional knowledge needed for their creation is passed on by the older women of the joint family household, who teach the girls from the age of five until puberty, so that as women they are equipped to give proper attention to these significant times and events. The folk arts of India have persisted in what is probably the longest unbroken tradition of any nation in the world, covering a period of perhaps three thousand years, and for this colossal achievement credit must go mainly to the real preservers—the village women.

In the Beginning

From the Sanskrit of ancient India comes this lovely legend of the creation of Man and Woman, rich in imagery, warm with human understanding and agreeably lacking in the harsh penalties of Eden.

The God of Brahma created the World. Out of the elements he made the sun, the moon, the stars, the mountains and forests and finally man himself.

But when Brahma came to fashion Woman he found that he had exhausted all the solid elements in the creation of Man.

So Brahma took the curves of the creepers, the roundness of the moon, the trembling of the grass, the clinging of the tendrils, the velvet of the flower, the slenderness of the reed, the lightness of the feather, the brightness of the sun's rays, the tears of the mist, the inconsistency of the wind, the timidity of the hare, the vanity of the peacock, the softness of down, the hardness of the diamond, the sweetness of honey, the cruelty of the tiger, the warmth of fire, the chill of snow, the chatter of the jay, the poison of the snake; and he combined them in Woman.

Brahma gave Woman to Man; and Man's joy knew no bounds for now he had found someone to share with him the pleasures of the world. But in the course of time Man came to Brahma saying: 'Lord, this creature you have given me makes my life miserable. She chatters incessantly, requires continuous attention, cries about nothing and is always idle'.

So Brahma took her back.

A few days later the Man was again at Brahma's door. 'Lord', he said, 'my life is lonely now that the woman has gone. I remember how she danced with me and how she laughed and filled my heart with joy. I remember how she clung to me and how sweet and comforting was her presence when the sun went down and darkness encompassed me'.

So Brahma returned the Woman.

A month later the Man again importuned him: 'My Lord, I cannot understand it, but I am sure the woman causes me more annoyance than pleasure. I pray you Lord, relieve me of her again.'

'Go your way and do the best you can,' answered the god.

'But I cannot live with her,' said the Man.

'Neither,' said Brahma, 'can you live without her.'

So the world started with Man and Woman and with them came love and jealousy, happiness, sorrow, romance and hypocrisy.

W

XENOPHOBIA

1. This is not a trait of mainstream Indian civilization, Hindu philosophy being extremely tolerant in accepting other faiths as approaches to the concept of human development and reaching out to truth in that development.

2. When Hinduism was influenced by periods of orthodoxy and emphasis on ritual daily living, reaction to incomers was more of **aloofness** than **downright prejudice**. Certainly in terms of social contact and at important rites of passage where ritual pollution had become in later social development a matter of greatest concern there was a sense of holding the stranger at bay, of forbidding entry to temple or kitchen and restricting inter-dining. A 'no-touch' situation–**mlechchha**. This was however more a negative reaction to the approach of the stranger and mostly within the Hindu fold rather than as protagonist or persecution of a religious minority. Some sources suggest **mlic**, the root, was to do with speech, this meaning separation–rather than pollution of a later meaning–due to reaction to those who spoke a different dialect or accent, as in the UK not so long ago–a matter of class snobbishness.

3. European macho behaviour has consistently pushed the Indian body corporate into stand-offs. Tagore succinctly summed up the British Empire sense of Christian superiority so prevalent at the turn of the century when English patricians like Willingdon and Curzon and Macaulay felt that they were bringing light to the heathen. He declared **'the torch of Europe's civilisation was not meant to give light but to start fires'**. Fortunately there were other English people who honoured what India stood for. This included even Queen Victoria who took an uncommon interest in Indian affairs (especially the progress of women) and roundly chastised her representatives in Calcutta for attitudes of snobbish superiority and 'red-tapeism'–which 'exists very strongly in the India Office' (Royal communication to Lord Curzon in 1900).

4. When we first arrived in India I suppose we all assumed that the new-found freedom was liberation from such parochial tendencies. Exuberance of spirit pervaded the atmosphere in the slow recovery from the horrors of Partition and the assassination of Mahatma **GANDHI**. There was a productive concern with getting on with the task of transforming India. And the Congress Party ruled monolithically. Bigotry had hardly a chance ... and under Nehru's magnetic personality on the world stage India went international. Now half a century after Independence the temper appears to be changing. With Kashmir a permanent abscess and the latent anger of many under-employed young men disenfranchised from any sources of power and excluded from the richly festooned pavilion of wealth and consumer possessions of the privileged, growing in their millions, here is a rich source for rent-a-crowd communal politics if the new, still small but very local Hindu fundamentalist parties wish along with their Islamic equivalents to stir a riot.

5. The RSS... **Rashtriya Swayamsewak Sangh** (National Volunteer Service Organisation) sounds like a harmless local citizens bureau of volunteers. But is this the tail that wags the dog? It represents fundamentalist Hindu cadres, brigades indeed of longstanding with military training even if only replica wooden rifles are used, as I witnessed by complete chance in Gujarat long back in the 1950s. It is noted for its summer youth camps, distinguished by wearing black forage caps and baggy khaki uniform–'a cross between the Boy Scouts and Hitler Youth Brigades' is how an editor put it to me in Ahmedabad. He added: Three characteristics mark it out

♦ Martial themes
♦ Discipline inculcated with religious fervour
♦ Loyalty demanded and to be declared to a **Hindu nationhood**...**pracharaks** (a harsh-sounding Sanskrit term) the zealots thus created as supposed keepers of the Hindu conscience. 'We don't go in for theocracies in this country even though Pakistan, and Islamic fundamentalism, might push some of our own extremists into this position,' warned a long-standing journalist, a lapsed Hindu 'humanist' as he called himself. 'You have to remember' he cautioned me on my last visit after the cataclysmic and seismic events of September 11, 2001 (like psychological tectonic plates shifting worldwide) 'that Gandhi was not assassinated by a Muslim. It was a right-wing Hindu, Nathuram Godse who shot him. He was given moral support by the RSS'. And suspicion rests on them and other similar parties when communal tension rises for any reason whatsoever. Goondas can be paid to defile a mosque or temple, causing riots, both Hindu and Muslim dying as a result of the mayhem. All one needs to do is push a stray bazaar cow around–and a typhoon can blow in from nowhere.

O Hindu awake! You have a noose around your neck!
is the RSS cri de coeur, a message which motivated Godse.

6. On my last visit the filming in Varanasi of Deepa Mehta's film **Water** unfolded an intricate script worthy of another film, this time on the stirred-up bigotry being played out in real life and daily about Mehta's avowed intention to treat honestly some touchy subject matter, in particular the plight and treatment of Bengali widows. This involved the interplay between the state government, city administrators, self-styled Hindu holy men, a student threatening a suicidal jump in the Ganga, Hindu interpreters of hoary texts on widowhood, media examination of the miserable conditions of penury many widows are left in at their main regional centre of congregation–Krishna's city of temples at Brindavan where they are fed on 2 rupees a day from a trust.

What caught my attention however were remarks made about the Indian film-maker Deepa Mehta. She is Indian but based in Canada. An NRI. **'Not one of us'** a young student declared to me with fillum-style bravado in the middle of Delhi as a group of youngsters ready for marching orders milled around me. I had accidentally dropped my Hindi vocabulary book to help me on my way. He had come running after me to deliver it back. *'Which country you from? You speak Hindi?* (how I wished he was right!) *Where you family? Your husband? Orstraaliah! Are you a journalist?* I guess a female on her own, wandering around with a briefcase is assumed to have some kind of profession.

X

My own question in reply set it all off, asking why so many of his friends were excitedly standing around waving saffron pennants.

It is on behalf of our holy Ganga Ma. **Canadian lady** *is bringing trouble for us. She made earlier film. FIRE. All about two women having sex. Not good!*

Amid the traffic roaring by, horns honking, cows meandering, I should by now have the wisdom not to continue conversations in this land where Khushwant Singh had long ago warned me that talking was India's single heaviest industry! Curiosity gets the better of me however and having spent most of my life trying to promote harmony amongst disparate communities by spreading knowledge of 'the other' I was intrigued as to why 'Canadian' had defined Mehta rather than 'Indian'. In some of the verbal slanging matches that make it into print the old guard scholars coralled at JNU (acronym for Jawaharlal Nehru University, Delhi) also refer to some of the new researchers going into print dismissively as **'NRI' historians**. Fascinating! **Who is more Indian Indian?** The young man didn't seem to know why he felt so irritated that the film maker was from 'outside', yet with such an Indian identity. But that was too complicated for simplistic political slogans he was about to chant about insults to Ganga Ma. **Bharat Mata ki jai.** Victory of Mother India! Even if Mehta was disingenuous by getting free publicity by being controversial (not unknown in the international world of the arts) I was still left with a nagging concern. **Xenos**, from the Greek actually means **guest** as well as **stranger**. Back to **A-TITHI**, the stranger unbeknown who comes from outside. Did not the Vedas of the Himalayan heights of Indian philosophy enjoin the stranger to be welcomed. The Kural of the Tamil people did likewise.

7. But on the obverse side of the coin, look at what happened to the Zamorin of Calicut who generously welcomed the Portuguese in 1498 with a gift of land. A second wave came in, built a fort and when they discovered they were not getting anywhere converting the 'heathen' they brought in the military and tried to claim the rest of the Zamorin's domain. So much for generosity! Perhaps too many strangers have come in and abused India's hospitality born of its predisposition to inclusiveness and lack of dogma, as Gandhi often stressed. When asked once by Professor Radhakrishnan why he was such an avowed 'secularist' when he so utterly identified with the Hindu philosophic view of life Gandhi had replied:

On examination I have found Hinduism to be the most tolerant of religions known to me. Its freedom from dogma makes a forcible appeal to me in as much as it gives the votary the largest scope for self-expression. Not being exclusive it enables its followers to respect all other religions ... and to admire and assimilate what ever may be good in other faiths.

8. Is it that this younger generation, now 50 years after Independence, still feel thwarted, that the unravelling of outside influences is still not done? All around the old commonwealth of nations as well as other ex-colonial territories civil wars are still fought (West African nations); land issues disrupt civil society

from Zimbabwe to Fiji and the Solomon Islands; fanaticism is whipped up from Pakistan to Uganda.

Proportions of population are tipping also in Asia and Africa. As the West 'ages', Asia especially shows up substantially younger populations in proportion to older members. In India 50% are under 30 years of age. A BBC broadcast explained the threat throughout the Islamic world of an increasingly larger proportion of youth with no jobs, disaffected with unresponsive governments, corrupt politicians lining their own pockets, with no access to power, an easy target for the fanatical zealots of the Right—for instance in the new autonomous ex-USSR republics of Uzbekistan and Kazakstan where new Muslim governments face real threats from fundamentalist Islamic militant youth organisations. **And the spread of cybercafes gives them a sense of a worldwide fraternity**. The pain and anger of young people frustrated in their higher expectations has given me the sense of many Indians not able yet to reclaim their inheritance despite 800 million of that billion-strong population being categorised by census as Hindu—a huge majority who should in no way feel threat from the stranger on the other side of the fence. (This was written six months before the surreal and barbaric events in New York—the doom of the Trade Center Towers—and the attack on the Pentagon, Sept. 11, 2001).

9. The nuclear proliferation with Pakistan, the hijacking of an Air India plane held in unbelievable conditions in a January winter on the tarmac surrounded by Taliban guards in Afghanistan; the constant drip, drip, drip, of inflammatory messages via TV and from extremist Islamic clerics preaching a new fundamentalism in an arc across the middle Asian plateau right through to the Philippines brings a new dimension into the political culture of India (see **SECULAR SOCIETY**). Muslims with the recent emergence of extremist Muslim radical student cells, a new phenomena in Indian civil society.

Is this supposed virtue of welcome to the stranger, the much vaunted pluralism, the secular state ideal so lauded by the majority of Indians during the last 50 years, now under threat by the darker forces, again re-emerging like that powerful Mahishasura, the dark buffalo assaulting all that stands for enlightenment. Do we all need the multi-armed warrior goddess **Durga** taking up the cudgels (in all her various weaponry) on our behalf?

After the (1990) Yatra by orthodox Hindu elements supporting restoration of Rama's supposed temple complex and coronation site (on which a later mediaeval mosque had been built probably deliberately by early conquering Islamic Sultans) leading octogenarian painter **M F Husain** came into the spotlight. A line sketch he had executed with imagination and delicacy **twenty one years earlier** aroused the ire of some for insulting the respected if aloof Hindu deity, **SARASWATI**. This time law suits were brought against the Muslim artist, his effigy was burnt and a militant off-shoot of the Hindu right-wing **Bajrang Dal** (see **HANUMAN**) invaded the artist's private gallery in Ahmedabad and vandalized two dozen of his most prized artworks. Hussain—no stranger to Hindu belief and a pluralistic

X

artist if ever there was one (see **GUFA**)—apologised if he had hurt Hindu sentiments.

All manner of arts people and sympathizers took to the streets calling for a national day of protest on Hussain's behalf as he had been attending another of his exhibitions in London at the time. **The reason for all this fanaticism: a virtually asexual sketch of a lithe and Botticelli-esque Sarswati beneath the waters, a chaste Aphrodite** gracefully holding aloft a lotus (her emblem) above the waters, a cute fish blowing bubbles. Far less harmful than Mumbai dance routines on TV or Michael Jackson gyrations promoted by Maharashtra's public relations son of avowedly ideologue Hindu Bal Thakeray, (one-time C M) in a most unlikely unholy alliance concert at the end of 1996.

I happened to be in India at the time having just visited the Gufa with Husain. I was later in Thanjavur to see its newly-cleaned magnificent 11th century temple, having been alerted by Padma Subrahmanyam (see **MIRACLES** and **DANCE**) to search out the beautiful sculpture of a near-naked Saraswati high up on the main Saraswati Mahal tower, as like many artists she was much exercised at this new component, political intimidation of artistic expression, a dimension more akin to European experience than India's. The deity was caught in the angled rays of the sun, highlighted in all her fulsome nakedness, except a band across her nipples, seated in padma asana under a chattri, the other playing her veena. The only ornament was a most unusual crown standing high on her head, the Tree of Life growing out of it. (see **HINDUTVA** and the new **Puritanism**).

A very old friend with whom I am in total agreement, a Bengali woman, in favour of Mehta's film being made, did on the other hand, stop me with her forceful interjection, partly in jest;

We've been pushed around long enough. I sympathise with these young demonstrators. Mehta went about it in the wrong way! She's out of touch with the subtleties of regional politics coming to town. For one thing she should have gone to Varanasi first, without publicity, talked quietly to the pandits there, without the press knowing. But film people want publicity to sell films before they're even made … and secondly, and this is far more important, what's wrong with standing up for ourselves? Look at China! The US respects China and pays court to her, a communist nation. Because China is strong. We are the largest democracy in the world, open to all to come and comment, your press most of all; and all we get is sanctions and stand offs. How many nuclear devices has China exploded?

Conclusion: Such emotion is understandable. Hindu society has had enough of being trodden on because it is based on radically different, unproselytizing impulses. But does that excuse these mindless acts of bigotry even against such a 'secular' artist as M F Husain? And after 21 years?

So many other sections are intertwined with this ongoing debate—**TOLERANCE, SECULAR, PALIMPSEST, CORE CONCEPTS,** the primal electric currents which run hidden below the template of what India is about.

◆ In the final analysis I return to the first plank that laid the foundation! **ABHAYAM**—standing firm. The traditional **Bharat Mata** a golden image of a Vedic age recalled by the xenophobes would have moved on, transforming, even if not a single Muslim invader or British mercantile prince had set foot on native soil.

◆ India has absorbed so many influences from outside and made them her own that to the outsider this **capacity to remain intellectually 'capacious' in attitude**—which surely is at the heart of those Vedic rishis and their constant searching for individual 'realisations' rather than creeds, dogmas, formulae (the quality that ironically most appeals to the iconoclastic Western young of today and on a similar search)—**is modern India's greatest strength**. It is a national characteristic that has threaded its way down millennia woven in adamantine threads in the fabric of the nation, an example to a majority of countries still struggling with the welter of ethnic identities searching for status within their own nation states.

◆ Mahatma Gandhi summed up India's ethos in his famous affirmation which I first encountered on stepping into the AIR building in Delhi for the first time with my husband. There it was engraved in the foyer.

I do not want my house to be walled in on all sides and my windows to be stuffed. I want the cultures of all lands to be blown about my house as freely as possible. But I refuse to be blown off my feet by any....

Would that Sardar Patel, the iron man of Indian politics who settled the Muslim enclave of Hyderabad at Partition with a fait accompli (a no-nonsense British approach in fact!) was alive today? All he would have advised against bigotry of this kind would have been a succinct: **Stay firm**. Be true to your ideas. You will survive. **Abhayam.**

■ **X-RATED VIDEOS**
–linked with question posed above.

India is awash especially in the big cities such as Mumbai with a market flooded with Asian and American pornography. Such is progress and the ease with which modern technology changes the nature of the **'erotic'**. This quality of, and activity in, human nature had always been more openly and healthily acknowledged in art, literature, the general ethos of life rather than its denial in Christian morality. Many more outlets were accepted even if 'philosophized' into the social framework by the esoteric practices of Tantric followers, and their ultimate culmination in a ritualised sexual union.

Although steamy cinematic scenes are emerging in an erratic progress to liberation, there is still an enormous area of society hedged in by deep inhibitions similar to Western societies of the 30s with all its false gentility and hidden passions. And then suddenly without warning a simple song can hit the charts about a choli blouse. In a film of the mid-90s called **'The Villain'** (**Khalnayak**) starring the nation's top actors a song slipped like cooking oil through the censor's hand—**choli keh peechheh**. The licentious hero cunningly eyeing the heroine as she demurely twists and turns to give full advantage to the cameras trained on

X

the tight fitting **choli**–and she certainly isn't suffering from anorexia!–asks her this provocative question–*What's beneath the choli?*

The trouble with all fundamentalists of all faiths is they don't have a sense of humour. And the trouble with many Indian men is the fact that despite openness on sexual matters in the early texts, and the entire cultural background of **TANTRA** and Kama Sutra explicitness, today's world sees them very repressed.

◆ **Eve-teasing** harassment, especially of student girls and tourist females is a major preoccupation of what one can only call the real 'goondas' of young male society in India's cities. It is a dead bore. An adventurous and sensible young Australian woman in her early 20s travelling in a rickshaw in old Delhi suddenly finds a young man on a bicycle coming up alongside and in the melee which is the permanent traffic jam she finds he is lurching towards her, grabbing both her breasts. It is a wonder he maintained his balance and a pity that she did not know enough Punjabi swear words to deflate his male ego and leave him in disarray amid the chaotic traffic. A far cry from the innocent days of yore (by which I mean the early part of the last century) or even the 50s when I happened to thumb through the library of **The Green Room** of the lively but tiny Simla theatre which had a very good repertory program due to the inspiring presence of the **Shakespeareana Company** of Geoffrey Kendal and his wife Felicity.

I picked up the memoirs of an English Lt General to see what Army experience in the Raj had been like, so naive in the immediacy of Independence. Writing on the 'darker side' of Indian life in 1912, this Army man was advising European women to take care in marrying Indians *'because no matter their similarity of position that is no guarantee for their sexual rectitude.'*

Someone had written in the book's margin: *'You fool'*!

◆ How ironic that in the 60s and 70s it was the other way around as Asian parents, migrating to the UK, were deeply perturbed by the sexual liberation then breaking out like a virus throughout British society, encouraged by the 'Flower Power' free-for-all and the pop-music industry. The new young advertising male had nothing to lose, and much sexually to enjoy in pushing imagery to its erotic limits, as also in today's cynical advertising game of promoting tourism, titillating the appetites of foreign tourists with the explicit sculpture of the abandoned couplings of Khajuraho. Contamination comes from Western culture flooding in on the electronically powered US and European technological empires; gratuitous violence of popular music culture (again predominantly young men); and all the Microsoft programming which even dominates the spelling and diminution of English grammar.

◆ The ultimate irony is that hard-core commercial sources promote pornography especially from the USA and Germany explicitly, blatantly and with nothing but commercial greed as the driving force, corrupting young Indians because of the easier access of technology. At least indigenous erotic art so avidly publicized now existed in a framework in ancient times. Now it is a nothingness.

And who amongst the young male 'radical Hindu' gangs hired to smash on behalf of correct **HINDUTVA** views, incinerates or trashes such video stores carrying these lucrative market–a 'forehn' influence if ever there was one!

X

363

■ YAJNAVALKYA

An interesting sage, celebrated and of truly great antiquity some 5,000 years ago or more, a major protagonist of the **Brihadaranyaka Upanishad** which Prof. Franklin Edgerton delights in presenting in his book: **The Beginnings of Indian Philosophy** and in which the sage appears outpacing any Oxford or Harvard intellectual of today.

Born with a halo because his father is reputed to have undergone 12 years of penance to achieve an heir with the blessing of Siva, this most revered sage is regarded as the father of Indian philosophy, having promoted the basic **CORE CONCEPTS** of India's metaphysical thought, modern physics of its day, as he took on scholar after scholar.

He appears to have been a freethinker (ever present in Indian culture from the beginnings of formulated thought) defying brahmin orthodoxy and the growing hierarchical hold they had on Hindu society. At the congress of scholars assembled at the court, Yajnavalkya reigned supreme in disputation. Despite his reputation for being extremely dogmatic, modesty not one of his virtues, he was awarded the prize of 1,000 cows, the horns of each adorned with pure gold coins given by King Janaka, himself apparently of philosophic bent (he is not to be confused with a later ruler, Janaka, father of Sita).

He clearly was ahead of his time and emerges as a real (rather than mythical) personage in historical time. Not only are his erudite and philosophical discourses recounted in the major Upanishads (see his encounter with **Gargi** in section on **WOMEN**) but he instructed his second wife **Maitreyi**, well-remembered several thousand years later by present-day Indians, in philosophical doctrine and intellectual encounter and counselled her when he decided as a good brahmin to renounce family life and wander off as an ascetic. She told him after his discourse on death and the fact that there was no consciousness afterwards that he had confused her to which both in typical philosopher's as well as husband's style, his immediate riposte as a male is:

I say nothing confusing... So be it!

■ YANTRA (n. *Sanskrit* root = **yam**, to sustain, support)

Geometrical designs (see **RANGOLI**) **and meditative configurations** which are the visual equivalents of the **mantras** or thought forms. For diagrams, Sanskrit texts, Devanagari script, and erudite explanation see **Alain Danielou**'s instructive tome: **Hindu Polytheism**.

As in algebraic and chemical equations and formulae, the basic theories and elements of the physical worlds are reduced to shorthand signs, so also that of thought patterns. Metaphysical theories and spiritual energies can be reduced to a combination of geometrical and floral patterns, set in an open lotus design with the four gateways out to the world (strangely a **globe** with '**four corners**').

Numerology of the △O□ has also been explored in the west by Hebrew scholars. 'Sacred geometry' is referred to in the **Book of Revelations** and the **Cosmic City of St John of the Cross.** The new Jerusalem, Glastonbury, the Pyramids, all embrace this mysterious truth of specific measurement that contain natural harmonies–that is they were 'meant to be'. Further reading: **City of Revelation: on the proportions and symbolic numbers of the cosmic temple** by **John Michell** (Garnstone Press, London, 1972).

Such contemplation on a specific form and thinking about its hidden messages, that the guru will explain, helps centre the wandering mind. These diagrams that are on a flat plane can expand (again considered a symbolic process of energy) into three-dimensional representations of a particular divinity = in modern computer terms, **virtual reality** and very much part of tantric philosophy. (**Jung** himself has interpreted the two Shiva-Shakti inter-penetrating triangles ✡ as representing 'the wholeness of the psyche of self, of which consciousness is just as much a part as the unconscious' (**Man and his Symbols**, Aldus Books, London, 1964).

■ YOGA (n. *Sanskrit*)

yuj or **yug:** related to Latin = **yugum** = yoke

is (a) **method or means**; (b) **an exertion, disciplined activity of postures**; (c) a **philosophy of life—one** of the six orthodox systems (see **DARSHAN**).

Yuj = to bind together: to hitch up as the harness of horses or oxen to a cart. Professor Edgerton and Dr Radhakrishnan both caution against translating **yoga** as meaning 'union of the soul with **brhm** (or **Brahman**) the Ultimate' as a sole concept.

Union–from its very sound–derives obviously from some Indo-European language root–as does **yoke** applied to the carved wooden piece which keeps two oxen **united** in ploughing, but **yukta** = disciplined, zealous in action.

◆ The entire force of yoga is intent in all its multi-layered disciplines in yoking bodily energy to efficient functioning of mind. Psychologists say that we usually only use 30 per cent of the human mind efficiently; another 30% is on automatic drive. What happens to the other 40 per cent of brain power? Yogis say they have the means to harness that energy into further constructive power.

All have to be 'harnessed together' in order to achieve ultimate composure leading to detachment from the travails of what John Bunyan only too well understood in his **The Pilgrim's Progress** (and it is worth an aside that in the bazaar posters illustrating the Bhagavad Gita, one panel of the 24 comic-strip type narrative portrays a lone pilgrim traversing a terrain unmistakably as daunting as the **Slough of Despond.**

The need to 'still the mind' is stressed in Chapter VI of the Gita.

When his mind, intellect and self (ahamkara) are under control, freed from restless desire, so that they rest in the spirit within, a man becomes a Yukta–one in communion with God. A lamp does not flicker in a place where no winds blow; so it is with a yogi, who controls his mind, intellect and self, being absorbed in the spirit within him.

Those who seek **vairagya**, a Sanskrit term for quelling the agitation constantly ruffling the surface of the mind like a gentle breeze, at other times a sudden storm, turn to the practice of yoga. It is an **Indian** thread crisscrossing the totality of society and not particular to Hindu culture. Allah Rakha, famous tabla player who exploded onto the Western world with Ravi Shankar, undertook exhausting yoga, Muslim though he was. In the early 50s when they came to our tiny bungalow to play, he told me of his years of self-discipline, especially physically, suspending himself from a ceiling beam to give strength to his percussion arms. Major General Habibullah when we first arrived and visited the military academy at Khadakwasla, used quietly to withdraw from the family room to spend time in yoga meditation. He was Muslim.

◆ The brain is like a telephone exchange zipping often unwanted random messages. To still it and 'listen in' to the more profound and creative signals seemed to be a preoccupation of the earliest sages and rishis. Perhaps the solitude of the forest life in **Yajnavalkya's Brhad** (great) **Aranyaka** (forest), and the enormous dome of the Indian night studded in its deep indigo with the crystal sharpness of stars beyond count inclined a person to seek composure–otherwise beyond was a chaotic madness too disturbing to contemplate.

◆ Yoga is quite essentially Indian. In typical fashion and with the assiduous research expected of any scientific discipline its early theorists undertook to categorise in the minutest detail the workings of mind, psyche and body. **Again one faces that characteristic quality of India which threatens to swamp** anyone involved–thrusting the macro universe of the interconnectedness of all things into a sudden telescoping all in one gigantic rush into a singularity of intense thought. It certainly is not a quick fix–a jab of a drug needle–to a momentary 'high' as some TM followers in the first heady rush of the 60s and the cult of following yogis like Maharishi Mahesh Yogi, thought it to be. Indeed the follower of yoga philosophy soon realises it is not a message of self-gratification.

◆ Yoga's implicit message is self-discipline from **within. You can't have everything you desire.** Nor is it as some suppose in Western societies, a gymnastic exercise in systematic and quite extraordinarily contorted wrap-around poses to squeeze the living daylights out of you! Such bodily disciplines have to be harnessed to a 'world-view' to make any impact on the totality of individual endeavour. Krishna in the Gita teaches this message.

'When the disciplined mind is established in the self alone I iberated from all desires, then is the person said to be harmonised.'

◆ The true follower of yoga has wrestled over centuries of development with the abstract idea of freeing the individual. The **inner personal soul/atman,** locked in this limited cage of skeletal 'awareness', needs freeing into '**that other dimension**', a state of harmonious **beatitude** which is the whole message of the Gita:

philosophic wisdom	= **jnana marg**
devoted love	= **bhakti marg**
strenuous action	= **karma marg**

These are all **complementary** and part of the **One. Paramatma. Forgetfulness of self**–that small ego which binds us to the illusory immediate world–is the key. Many have mistaken India's message as an **other-worldliness** especially when encountering the extreme manifestations and bizarre visual aspects of ascetics, when visiting melas and temple complexes. But this is not so. Yoga philosophy is very much in this world and leads to renewed but focused energy.

Self denial > **non attachment** or **vairagya** could be recalled in another biblical echo of the same message …

Be ye in the world but not of the world.

1. **Historical**: What must have been long in the minds of Indians and in practice was drawn together systematically into a text that is called **Yoga Sutras** by south Indian sage **Patanjali** who developed the work of India's great grammarian **Panini** and has himself become a legendary 'divine' (a statue of him wrapped in the coils of the snake has been carved–a reference to the yogic **kundalini energy** coiled around the base of the spinal energy chakra). The sutras were probably put into written form circa **5th century CE.**

Sutras are **aphorisms** shortened for memorising easily. This became the basis of one of the six systems of Indian philosophy but not in the intellectual or abstruse sense of another school known as **Samkhya**. It was eminently practical in following a systematic **bodily discipline** first, which encouraged a parallel **ethical** discipline of meditation and learning to abide in a framework of self control. The message–moderation in all things–the Buddhist **Middle Way,** the Greek **Golden Mean.**

This system has major pillars which give structural foundations to the ultimate construction of a personal philosophy in which meditation heightens that awareness.

2. **Bodily Disciplines**: the **shishyas** or pupil-trainees have first to apply themselves to the ten **virtues**.

1. **Ahimsa** = non-violence, no killing, oppose evil in the wrongdoer by moral resistance, not violence to the person.
2. **Satya** = truth-speaking and refrain from spreading falsehoods about others.
3. **Astheya** = abstention from covetousness.
4. **Brahmacharya** = celibacy.
5. **A-paragraha** = divesting oneself of possessions, non-hoarding.
6. **Saucha** = aiming at purity of body through good habits.
7. **Santosha** = continence of mind, serenity, satisfaction with bare necessities of life.
8. **Tapas** = austerities to be practised through the heat = fervour, yearning to reach the goal of eventual absorption in the **Paramatma.**
9. **Svadhyava** = **sva** = self; **adhyaya** = education in self-realisation and awareness that creation was intended for worship of a great 'Being' and not for personal worship alone.
10. **Isvara Pranidhana** = dedication (**dhan**-donation) to **Isvara** = deity as in bhakti worship.

Y

The practice of **asanas** or scientifically based postures, brought about pressure on certain bodily points of energy, cleansing the entire body of impurities and releasing poisons to be expelled from the abdomen. **Nadi**, the vein or pulse, is of great importance (not to be confused with naad = sound or nabhi = navel, centre of the universe, the hub of the wheel).

Practice of right breathing **pranayama** aerated and oxygenated the lungs, revived the nervous system. Adoption of a vegetarian diet reinforced these processes.

3. **The Four Pathways of Yoga:** (another **QUATERNITY**): After a student has trained himself long enough in the undertaking of the preceding 10 virtues–**and always under the guidance of the guru**–he can then turn to the physical discipline of the last: dedication to the divine force.

Karma Yoga Marg = the way of Action
Bhakti Yoga Marg = the way of Loving Devotion
Gyana (jnana) Marg = the way of Knowledge
Hatha Yoga Marg = the way of Bodily Discipline

Hatha Yoga leads eventually for those who become a total **yogi** or **siddhi** (a state of spiritual perfection) to **Raja Yoga**–the most difficult and dangerous of all in which mystic or occult powers have become part of the mythology handed down to the world outside India. Claims to supernormal powers are legion–levitation, becoming invisible, walking on embers, burial alive (have seen that, and the emaciated frame of the man after 40 days. He lived!) Even the Indian rope trick is part of the legend.

Siddhis are said to produce an aura of energy, known as **tej** (**teja**). Is this where the concept of a **HALO** arose?

4. **Asanas:** the postures evolving over centuries through balanced shapes controlling muscles, nerves, glands (scientifically studied), developed elasticity, resilience, endurance of pain and astonishing sense of vitality. They reinforced what is termed the **ashtanga**, eight (asht) parts (angas), successive self-disciplines which have to be practised.

1. **Yama** self-control curbing the instincts similar to universal moral commandments
2. **Niyama** disciplinary preparation
3. **Asana** postures
4. **Pranayama** breathing control: increases sattvic tendencies.
5. **Pratyahara** withdrawal of senses, defiance of the powers of desire
6. **Dharana** fixation of thought, neutral steadiness, resistance to distractions.
7. **Dhyana** meditation from which the word **Zen** is derived.
8. **Samadhi** fixation of psyche and release from bodily imprisonment. A **jivanmukti** such as all great souls with a detached mind full of love and compassion for all humanity–i.e., all the rishis, Buddha, Christ, etc.

5. **The Sapt-Chakras** of the human form

A **chakra** means a **nerve centre**, a crossover point in the spinal column where the **nadi** or **clusters of nerve cells** cross each other. **B K S Iyengar** aptly visualises the seven chakras as 'the flywheels in the machine', proceeding from the base of the

spine upward to the top of the skull and exploding out to 'super consciousness'.

A word of caution Beware however of sparking 'fly-wheels' that promise instantaneous access to the infinite mind, bypassing mantras, asanas, mental tapasya and sadhana as in the advert below. There are plenty of seductive adverts in the local press and in our first months in Delhi an American mediaman landed in hospital for a month with a fractured spine, having plunged in headlong (probably literally by standing on his head) without the taming guidance of a guru. 'Instant clairvoyants abound.'

Bhai Sahib is an adept with over 45 years experience in Meditation, Metaphysics and Modern Science. He has at long last discovered the Highest, the Purest, the Speediest and the most Effective techniques spelled out in a great detail as a Universal System, enshrined in the Sanctified Divine Doctrines of all the World's Faiths. Under this System, the awakening and flowering the lofty and Sublime superconscious Giant, the Holy Spirit within, is actually felt as a Vibrant Euphoric experience in myriad mystical ways...(Join such-and-such Yoga ashram, is the message.)

6. **'Serpent Power'** This is the area of **kundalini power** or super energy (**kunda** = coil) which even amongst Indians brings on a tone of awe and has been written about at length by one of those intriguing breed of English scholars who was drawn to India as though they had been born within its cultural context in a previous reincarnation. **Sir Thomas Woodroffe,** who took the pseudonym **Arthur Avalon**, wrote in 1918 of his researches through a Bengali brahmin family 10 generations removed at that time from **Purnananda** (born **Jagadananda**) whose written manuscript of **1526 is still in their keeping**. Purnananda obtained siddhi or total yogic realisation in Vasishtashrama some seven miles from Guwahati in Assam.

Born in 1865, son of an advocate-general to the Bengal government of the time, Woodroffe was one of those English brahmins, scholar of University College, Oxford–and there were a considerable number of them in this particular era. The photograph of Sir John at the Konarak Temple to Surya in Orissa must surely have perturbed British officials in Calcutta in those very pukka Edwardian days for in every respect here is a white Bengali brahmin even in the way the dhoti is layered! Perhaps his fellow legal friend **Pramatha Natha Mukhopadhyaya**, a Calcutta High Court judge, may have taught him how to tie it. The text of his famous book **The Serpent Power** which opened up the whole recondite world of **Tantra** and supreme union is summed up in the preface to his first edition written in Ranchi in 1918:

*We pray to the **Paradevata** (the Supreme Goddess) united with Siva, whose substance is the pure nectar of bliss, red like unto vermilion, the young flower of the hibiscus and the sunset sky; who, having cleft Her way through the mass of sound issuing from the clashing and the dashing of the two winds in the midst of*

Susumna*, rises to that brilliant Energy which glitters with the lustre of ten million lightnings. May She, Kundalini, who quickly goes to and returns from Siva, grant us the fruit of Yoga!

7. Snakes And Ladders: It was not for nothing the British discovered in the bazaars of Kolkata that the way or marg is indeed testing, fraught with difficulties to be overcome, from yogic diagram to a game they took back to their homeland.

The hundred-squared diagram was a visual device or **yantra**—a mechanism for illustrating the long hard slog up that marg or pathway to ultimate release or 'realization' where those most rare of infrequent luminaries, the siddhis, explode into pure Consciousness—in square **100**. Children hardly know its origin, or why square **99** is so perilous, where the snake's head slides them all the way down—to begin again. Oh! despair!

Yoga is a methodological channel to attain perfection—and indeed a yogic prayer runs like this: '*I salute **Adisvara** [the primeval — the first — Siva] who taught the science of **Hatha yoga**, a science that stands as a **ladder** for those who wish to scale the heights of Raja Yoga'.*

8. Yoga Incorporated! After centuries of colonial disregard for some of the unique systems of thought and scientific exploration in these ancient texts, those in India who genuinely promote yoga systems and disciplines worldwide had better beware! Amid a plethora of establishments mostly in Indian-trained **Western hands** (five different centres or ashrams within a stone's throw of where this is being written) there is a danger of yoga being taken over by corporate America.

Indeed, unless it follows its own disciplines of centredness, impervious to the blandishments of the Almighty Dollar, the spin doctors and wordsmiths overseas who fashion smooth advertising slogans—already some are abroad and kicking a yogic punch: **Spirituality for the Boss**. Books are being published on this very subject …

How to succeed in holistic management!
Total mind-quality control!
Feel good: exercise the yoga way!

◆ It is alleged that some USA company staff are now being programmed first thing in the morning with 20 minutes deep breathing and no thinking.

empty the mind … let the cosmos flow in … wipe the tension out

Respect for the workforce and genuine 'care management' are the buzz words out of yoga's age-old capacity to acknowledge the holistic emphasis on both sides of the brain long before Western physiologists began dissecting, measuring, probing. A more sober management expert from Kolkata where time is set aside for yoga meditation (as also in hundreds of other big Indian companies) had this to say while talking to a group of Australian business leaders …

Those who studied the power of the mind were aware of the rational, calculating combative ego side. But they acknowledge also the powerful existence of the other lobe—that which seeks co-operation, possesses quantum leaps of intuition embedded in the nerve endings. Acknowledges the interconnectedness of things. If we only realised how fortunate we are to possess this science our rishis perfected as our cultural right!

That flash of **darshan**, a **seeing** awareness, sensitivity to others needs. Interconnectedness. Perhaps Indian corporate bodies can retain the **real** quality of yogic '**centredness**'. Patanjali, take a bow!

Professor Radhakrishnan in a wry comment on the quixotic responses of human nature to that final attempt to reach absorption—dedication to Isvara—had this to say: Men demand **justice** for a wrong done by others. **Mercy and forgiveness** for a wrong done by themselves. Repeating aphorisms—pithy sayings—from the Yoga Sutra he reminded his students:

A yogi on the other hand should seek justice for himself for a wrong done and mercy for others likewise.

■ **YUGA**
one of the categories of Quaternity
Astronomical aeons of time in the Hindu view of the universe are visualised in a gigantic cycle of **KALPA**, the accumulation each time the cycle turns from the original point of creation—**see ZERO, the bija, seed, dot, particle, atom—whatever word one wishes to put a name to the point of 'coming-into-being'** until the final dissolution again when Vishnu once more reclines inert—upon Anant, the serpent depicting the endlessness of cosmic time.

Within each kalpa there are four unfoldings (see **QUATERNITIES** again!) in more manageable cycles of time, closer to our own geological timeframe. These are the **yugas**: Krita, Treta, Dvapara, Kali (see illustration in **KALPA** section).

◆ Each succeeding age is characterised by increasing loss of dharma and virtue, a spiritual diminution of law and order and physical deterioration. The cycle we happen now to be in commencing about 5,000 years ago is known as the **Kali Yuga, the Dark Age** running on **25 per cent of dharma**, deteriorating all the time down to the final conflagration. (It is worth recalling that in a series of broadcasts in the late 60s on the BBC given by Professor George Steiner, eminent European thinker and author, he used similar imagery. He summed up the light of Western educational culture as functioning in the dim glow of a **25 watt bulb**. His assessment of the deterioration of Western civilization shorn of its classical roots in Greek and Latin culture was in evidence all around us, most conspicuously so in our contemporary ignorance of even the literary allusions let alone their hidden meanings such as in Milton's great poem *Lycidas*).

The importance of dice, games and chance in time. The quaternity of yugas derive their names from the proverbial game of dice, itself such a vital part of what happens in Indian

---

* Basic **nadi** at seat of spinal cord which propels the other six nerve 'cross-over' centers.

Y

legends—not just chance but a force of karma from previous transmigrations (samsara) of the individual atman or soul carrying with it the electronic 'charges' of how previous lives have been lived (see the long discussion of the meaningfulness of what looks like my childhood game of Ludo when illustrated on Indian kalamkaris in **Richard Lannoy's The Speaking Tree**—a must for both Western and Indian readers.

The die, singular of dice, is cast therefore first in Krita; the perfect throw, the four-legged cow of the universe standing firm on its four legs and then in descending order of righteousness, morality, social responsibility, sense of the benign and individual goodness.

Treta the off-balance throw of three

Dvapara shifts the dangerous balance on two legs between perfection and imperfection

Kali the instability of attempting to remain upright on only one leg, **Kala-aha** (Sanskrit) = strife, dissension, all that is quarrelsome or bad influences

◆   Perhaps this vast concept could be likened to the Hawking theory of **entropy**—and the moment in time from which begins the long slow ineluctable slide downhill, losing energy until a black hole sucks us all in the Kaliyuga! A new imagery of the second law of thermodynamics having already recounted the predilection Indian theorists have in compiling lists, it comes as no surprise to find **Tulsidas** dilating on the misfortunes of living in this cosmic cycle, compiling page after page of points of this disintegration—where 'universal lawlessness, confusion of caste, religious mendicants amassed wealth and built houses' (only too true even in this day and age when many rishis have frequented

the West and evaded the Indian taxman!)... 'the world was full of envy, harsh words and avarice; no one was tranquil...' etc. etc.

Amid this litany of woe concerning moral and physical pollution even then which Tulsidas (and also a much earlier Valmiki) uncannily predicted, a strange category stands out.

Women's only ornament was their hair and they were never satisfied. They were poor and wretched and utterly self-centred... and hard with no tenderness in them.

Oh dear! Obviously they neglected their husbands, indeed a Kali Yuga!

◆   Closer to our own scientific empirical measurement, a quite extraordinary coincidence in measurements of time...

In 1993 an American paleobiologist **William Schopf** of the **Centre for the Study of Evolution and the Origin of Life** at the **University of California** believes that from examination of **bacteria fossils** in one of **Western Australia's** remote and isolated northern regions, near Marble Bar, life on earth had a foothold nearly 500 million years earlier than previously accepted. Present rocks with single-cell microbes were dated at approximately 3.5 billion years of age. Our planet earth is said to have solidified somewhere around **4.550 million years**. Did life evolve and diversify as these recent finds suggest less than a few thousandth of a millimetre long, organisms in tiny mineral grains—around that magic single day in the life of Brahma, **4,320,000,000** years ago in planetary time? Not far out!

Endnote: A wry thought... in Hindi **kal** (pron. cull) means both **yesterday** and **tomorrow**—something to consider seriously as an Indian view of cyclical time?

Y

■ ZERO

Just about every aspect of life reverts back to zero in Indian thinking, and perhaps–to use an English idiom–metaphorically back 'to the year dot', date unknown!

Conceptually the symbolic nature of the **BINDU** = the drop = **drapsa** (Sk. for semen) which began all of creation, which expanded from nothing = the void (**vyoman**) emptiness = *sunya* expands into the circular **ZERO** enlarging into the Cosmic Womb = **HIRANYAGARBHA**. This was depicted eventually as the golden egg ovoid.

It appears embedded in emblematic ways, in literature, in music, in textiles, spills over from science into philosophy, from yogic meditation into mathematics–and doing business without an abacus!

◆ Indus Valley fragments of cloth indicate zero already a symbol visually expressed symbolically in all the arts over and over again; **Baudhayana**, c. 2,500 BCE, called the first true mathematician; **Panini** circa 350-250 BCE onwards; **Aryabhata** I, 5th cent CE; **Bhaskaracharya**, mathematician and astronomer early 12th cent. CE.

The potentiality of the concept metaphysically (see **Rigvedic Hymn 129 to Creation**,) lies at the foundation of Vedic/Upanishadic philosophical systems and the mathematical texts: **Sulbasutras**, the most ancient in the world. The later numerical definition–the cusp between **sunya** = nothing = infinity becoming something = **anu** (atom or particle), eventually a dot in a decimal system of numbers, led to Indian civilization being very numerate and mathematically versatile.

The mathematics of zero

Dealing with the specifics first, the Western definition of zero usually assumes that it came via the Arab system of decimals in trading with Europe, even before the spread of Islam. The Latin word **ziphirum** is said to have derived from the Arabic **sifr** = cipher–zero–non entity.

◆ As mentioned in the **KERALA** section Arabs traded all down the coast of western India (cf. **Tim Severin, The Sindbad Story**, and his re-enactment with the Omani government of the dhow voyage of Sindbad to China, Hutchinson, London, 1982) They must have encountered a decimal 'blank' when counting money for such goods while buying spices! Professor Basham in **The Wonder that was India** has written: 'Indians had a clear conception of abstract numbers, as distinct from **numerical** quantity of objects or spatial extension'. A rudimentary algebra appears even at a definable **595 CE** date on a Gujarati inscription which records nine digits and a zero rather than the cumbrous Roman numeral system.

He further records that **Hindisat(va)** was a word used by Arabs to describe mathematics as an 'Indian truth', the concept of zero = **sunya** = emptiness, and consequently, infinity as being fully understood by Indians... Early mathematicians had taught that $x/o = \infty$, but Bhaskaracharya (*acharya* = learned teacher), had proved infinity was a correct supposition in philosophical terms, a cosmic truth imprinted in, and recognised by, Indian philosophy at least a millennium earlier. Basham explains:

Infinity, however divided, remains infinite represented by the equation $\infty/x = \infty$. By the 13th–14th century AD European systems had incorporated the Indian/Arabic 0 and encircled it = $\odot$ in order to make it into a uniform size with other numerals, 1,2,3, etc. eventually just becoming 0. In traditional Indian numerals it still remains a diminutive o.

Everywhere you turn there are visible signs of the symbol of zero. And thinking spatially is a fine art also as in chess, a game of real antiquity in India.

◆ From the very beginnings of artistic application '**potentiality**' has engaged not only those first **RISHIS** who composed the Rig Vedic hymns but interpreters in the plastic arts all along the centuries. In clay, for instance. In a footnote to a section of the **Katha Upanishad** Dr Karkala (**Anthology of Indian Literature**) gives this explanation to a passage describing the Great Self beyond the intellect, beyond the undeveloped, beyond the Purusha where there is nothing.

*Nothing: not negative, but positive; not one particularised thing but one thing that is everything-no-thing, **for example, a lump of uncarved clay**.*

A lump of clay is often referred to as a symbol of potentiality, so basic to the Indian potter. From it comes the pot, such a symbol in all its form of plenitude; within the substance of basic earth, **prithvi, prakriti, that simple wadge of clay is everything**–an explosion (which, of course is India in all its interconnectedness) happens all the time from nothingness.

◆ Zero appears also as **yogic diagrams**, flat and on the surface for concentrating the mind on one point-singularity = the • in the O to represent the coming-into-being = $\odot$.

◆ And thence, to the ultimate in **yantras**, the expanding three-dimensional **Sri Yantra**, △ most potent of tantric devices for the yogi to reach the final superconsciousness (already explained in **YANTRA/YOGA**)

◆ The **tika** on the forehead between the eyes recalling the exploding energy of Siva's **Third Eye** and the **atrophied pineal gland**, said to contain incipient energy and the possibility of being revitalised. Anyone going to the temple for the first **arati** may have a sandalwood tika placed on that central spot after ritual worship with fire in a brass lamp-holder. The very act of rubbing or impressing the **tika** at this sensitive **nadi** (the hub of the chakra wheel of the pineal criss-crossing nerve centre) is said to stimulate it and direct one's consciousness inwards.

Indian friends similarly will put a spot of yoghurt and rice grains on the forehead for safe travelling before the visitor undertakes a long journey.

◆ **Rangoli**—and all the other regional words for this form of intricate geometric decoration—will mark the centre as the zero or dot. The rice paste designs become symbolic spiritual designs expanding artistically.

◆ The zero is incorporated in innumerable **wall decorations** all over India, executed by women who have wisdom if little formal education, to know their ancient truths, handed down over generations (refer to **Stephen Huyler's Painted Prayers**, a

Z

photographic marvel of a book investigating such sophisticated domestic reverential art).

◆ The 'daisy' symbol-scientific concept turned into decorative device—is found on every conceivable kind of textile, fragments, even those extricated from deep within 6,000 plus year old soils, at Indus Valley sites to boutique motifs of today's young designers ✿.

◆ The same motif is expressed in the circular **raslila dances** of Manipur. Krishna and the many gopis, symbolic again of multiplicity in union with Radha at the centre, circle and circle.

Even the cosmographical ground-plans for temple architecture were based on the expansion of zero. The most insignificant measurement 'was determined by the specific laws of proportion ... to put structure in harmony with the mystical numerical basis of the universe and time itself'. This was recognised by **Benjamin Rowland** in his seminal book **Art and Architecture of India** (Penguin, London, 1953) brought out soon after Independence*. So many visual reiterations too numerous to enumerate, to the most urban reminder of Union = Parliament House, New Delhi, in all its circumference.

◆ **Philosophical/Metaphysical**: The fact that Volume II of the on-going multi-volumed project of IGNCA on basic Indian concepts in arts devotes **46 pages** to the explanation of **Bindu** (including primary source Vedic quotations) and **29** to **Sunya** says volumes in itself. Both are Sanskrit terms for **zero**.

Kapila Vatsyayan quotes these succinct lines from the **Hejavra Tantra** in order to define India's indefinable essence, that concern with **pralaya** = the undifferentiated moment of transition when creation is about to form in the single cell in the primeval soup in the depths of the earth or the waters on which the Lord Vishnu sleeps:

First the void;
Second the seed;
Third the emanation of the image;
Fourth the articulation of the syllable;
Fifth the fullness of the void

What happens at the cusp between the no-thing before universes expanded into our consciousness, at the beginning when **zero** divided into something, materialising and proliferating into **prakriti** over billions of years until the human brain could actually observe from outside and think about 'it', is still wrestled with by modern physicists seeking definitions. Perhaps there are none!

The prestigious Templeton Prize winner 2000, **Emeritus Prof. Freeman Dyson**, physicist at Princeton University's Advanced Studies Center (as also might well concur an earlier physicist so honoured with this religious accolade, Prof. Paul Davies) and an Anglican mathematical scientist, Dr. John Polking-horne. In an Australian TV science programme '**Compass**'

interview after the award announcement Dyson admitted that contemporary physicists are less arrogant than 50 years ago. 'Every time you solve one mystery two more open up' was how he put it. He went on in a vein the **RISHIS** would have felt very much at home with discussing on the same programme:

Atoms have weird properties—an atom has a 'mind' of its own ... as though there is a 'universal mind' beyond comprehension'.

It was in fact a physicist's definition of what could be called God.

We cannot prove that God exists but this concept is consistent with what we know about science ... In some sense the universe must have known that we (Life) were coming. The laws of the universe are friendly towards life.

His conclusion was that science and religion, long at loggerheads with each other, are only now at the beginning of understanding. Fly right in, **YAJNAVALKYA** in your **pushpak vimana** and join the debate!

'Non-existent there was not, existent there was not then.' Thus speaks an unknown Indian rishi across finite time to us today—circling, eclipsing, in following the laws of **RTA** Dyson speaks of in an infinity of space.

■ **ZIMMI** (*n. Urdu*)

A term used in the Islamic world to differentiate those citizens who are non-Muslim from those who are, certainly in matters of the **shari'ah** or social laws which are regarded as sacred in ordinary Muslim societies.

People of the Book, i.e., the Bible-Jewish and Christian—as citizens in the mixed societies early Muslim rulers encountered were regarded as warranting protection. Islamic law being very strict, it was not so difficult to maintain in the strictly Islamic heartland such as the Arab desert lands. With the enormous explosion outwards through north Africa into Spain, through Turkey, and Iran with its distinctive ancient Persian culture, and thence over a period of several centuries down into India, staunch rules over a cosmopolitan society were difficult to enforce, especially when Muslims were minorities in a majority situation—as in India.

Zimmis did fall within the protection therefore of laws introduced by the Sultanates in north India but those beyond the Book, idolaters and polytheists in the eyes of the orthodox **ulemas** or law-makers had to wear distinctive marks on their dress to distinguish their non-Muslim background and also as landowners or peasant farmers or business people, had to pay the **jizya** or **poll-tax**. Such indignities Indians had to suffer as indigenous peoples in their own land.

---

* Symbolism abounds! Alignment of shrines, walkways, the sanctum sanctorum follow the seven chakras of the human body along the spinal cord, the sanctum however slightly to the left as is the human heart. Detail of tiling also said to number 20,100 = to human daily breath count!

Z

AFTERWORD

THE PADAYATRA

The stepping stones do not end here. Other travellers will place their own slabs on **Pathway India**, an exploding universe in itself, around every turning something vividly unexpected, brilliant colours dazzling our vision. Edward Lear was not only a whimsical poet but a fine artist. In his Indian journeys (**Impossible Picturesqueness**), he exclaimed characteristically:

The way... drove me nearly mad from sheer beauty and wonder of foliage. O new Palms!!! O flowers!! O creatures!! O beasts!!...Anything more overpoweringly amazing cannot be conceived!!! Colours and costumes, and myriadism of impossible picturesqueness!!!...

These particular stepping stones are but a few personal signposts in the infinity hidden in the magic **O** of the Indian o.

AKHILANDA KODI BRAHMANDA NAYAKI

states the Sanskrit rishi

(to) that **nayaki** =heroine; i.e., the Devi = **Brahmanda**, = totality of the cosmos = Divine Energy; that presides over the millions = **Kodi** = crore of universes is **Akhilanda** incomprehensible infinity.

The Devi presides over the millions of universes of incomprehensible infinity.

INDIA—FROM ZERO TO THE EXPLODING WHOLE

One abiding impression remains constant. How very modern at the level of its philosophical view, how very contemporary in embracing what we would call 'scientific' exploration is the entire basis laid by India's most incisive thinkers… and so very, very long ago. With not even rudimentary technology let alone our advanced electron microscopes and particle bombardment chambers to enable accurate measurements and atomic clock time frames to be computed, how then did those **RISHIS** of such antiquity come to understand the immensity 'out there' and 'within' the mind of consciousness? They even took on board in metaphysical terms that which is seemingly static—**Jagat** = that place, location, entity which when examined closely is in a state of flux.

As long ago as 1947 in the Appendix to their translation of the Gita, Prabhavananda and Isherwood wrote:

Science also postulates a monistic universe. All matter is made up of different combinations of the chemical elements; and these elements are composed of combinations of identical units. Man is all of a piece with this world and with the most distant of the stars.

At my own distant alma mater, at the 1968 Commencement Address at Radcliffe College, **Professor George Wald**, Harvard Professor of Biology virtually echoed these sentiments.

◆ Speaking of the process of living organisms, the four elements, the generation of light in stars by the 'burning' of hydrogen to helium, the red giant process of a dying star in which a transformation into carbon, nitrogen and oxygen occurs, itself to constitute part of the infinite masses of dust and gases filling interstellar space from which in turn new eddies and condensations are formed—new matter, new planets, new creatures such as humanity—Wald came to this conclusion. A hushed audience listened.

Stars had to die that we may live … We are made of the stuff of stars...

Thank goodness some scientists are poets! Those amazing rishis of over 6,000 years ago would have concurred. Although only embryonic scientists, they had arrived at a similar sense of 'patterning' in their own meditations in the forest life under that sparkling, intense indigo dome of star-splashed night. Although seemingly concentrating on metaphysics, this foundation of Indian **CORE CONCEPTS**, the shaping of India's entire attitudes of mind (and therefore basis of society) whether it is the long vision of reincarnation that colours an individual's sense of place and social responsibilities to an untutored woman's design on her mud and wattle home in Orissa for a major festival, is the terrain on which these stepping stones are laid.

It is as though certain universal forms of which we are now becoming conscious by technological advances of science (the 'collective unconscious' symbols about which Western psychoanalysts led the search a century ago or so) are part of the 'patternings' already structured into the molecular forces of cosmic matter... such as the fossilised ammonite so familiar to the antique Palaeozoic rocks of northwestern Australia. Such ammonite spirals are picked up in the rivers of India by sages even today... they are worshipped as symbolic of the spirals of time, of the spiralling galaxies, of the uncompleted open circle of time regenerating and turning in on itself, yet never completing the circle fully, but flowing out in that aperture of the **spiralled conch-shankh**. They are carried on the person as auspicious symbols—**shalagramas**—representing Vishnu on the primordial waters of life, the ebb and flow of **pralaya** dissolution, to be followed by creation.

Now scientists are increasingly recognizing that there are basic shapes that we as humans unconsciously respond to because they are fundamental components in the structure of the universe. Even musical patterns and graphs of tonal structures such as Mozart's piano concertos are coming under scrutiny, the question being are there innate patterns and symmetries the brain appears to programme itself?

How astounding then to discover that on reaching Zero, that another entire world of visual spirals opened up—as though meant to be. US academic, chemistry professor Hubert Alyea, renowned for his communications skills, is frequently quoted for his subtle punch line from Louis Pasteur: **'Chance favours only the prepared mind.'** Already an ABC Science program had alerted me to new thinking about minuscule tubes in the brain connecting the matrix—**the micro tubules**—which could I suppose, be called the physiology of consciousness. These seethe with activity and 'seem to know how to interlock', increasingly coming under analysis according to the programme by advances in anaesthetic technology. **'A non-computable quantum universe in one's head'**. That sounded like Professor Dyson and how very Indian! I was floored! By chance that program was reinforced by my monthly issue of the **India Magazine** arriving, conspiring towards a density of 'patterning' fed into my already alerted mind. There was an interview with the eminent mathematician **Professor Sir Roger Penrose** by **Ranjit Nair**, a philosopher of science.

◆ Another stepping stone occurred as I hit **ZERO**—leading me as a result into the world of abstract mathematics. Having suffered the exigencies of an English school education which in my generation separated science disciplines from the humanities at a foolishly early age of specialization, I needed a lay explanation of these abstruse matters. By serendipity my near neighbour is a young physicist, Tim St Pierre, professor at the University of Western Australia. Being shown the Sri Yantra he leapt with fortuitous lateral thinking and pulled down from a working shelf **The Emperor's New Mind** by Roger Penrose (OUP, London, 1989).

How astonishing then to those not numerate wizards of mathematical artistry, but trained in visual designs such as myself, to discover a world of riveting, aesthetically pleasing designs that are inherent in the laws of nature which is, I suppose, what pure mathematics is. Not until computers were themselves designed to speed up the processes of collation and magnification was it possible to conceive an 'imaging' of this **infinity, a singularity** that yogis and Jains, Indian musicians, artists and dancers, all in one way or another have in this long journey been engaged in creating, and now envisaged by a Western scientist as pure mathematics. Seen as a simple equation it generates of its own

accord the following astonishing complexity—an illustration of this mathematics equation postulated at a very simple level.

◆ Previously hidden mathematical truths are laid out clearly by Penrose, a world known as the **Mandelbrot Set**, a set of points—a pattern—that first looks like a dot on a graph on the computer screen. This then 'grows', looking like a creepy-crawlie one might encounter in a dark corner in India, with trailing wisps of hair along the graph line (with which even the least numerate would be familiar). This 'beetle' as it is now referred to, is the Mandelbrot Set.

Four different views of the Mandelbrot set

From this configuration (p.98 in Penrose) the reader is led into an Indian explosion of infinity. Each 'beetle' in itself replicates the patterning yet, like a raga, is never reconstructed in exactly the same permutations. A world of infinite complexity, seemingly random, emerges with each magnification as though one was sitting in an Omni cinema being taken in ever awe-inspiring surges of energy into the heart of the galaxy and on and on to the blurred edges of the cosmos.

Those original seven rishis afloat as they were in their own Vedic Ark on the floodtide of the Sea of Nectar would have been in their element speculating on such familiar designs slowly delineating from their laptops! **Ad infinitum**...

Through magnifications one plunges into such a crevice that one could go dizzy with the entanglements that explode in the mind, let alone on the screen. And then the question arises...

Is this then a confirmation of Lannoy's comment (and others) that every single murti, carved or in bronze casting, every temple structure adhered most strictly to the codifications laid down in the Sanskrit shastras by those early thinkers of the principles of aesthetics **'to put structure in harmony with the mystical numerical basis of the universe'**.

Gargi, female philosopher of the Upanishadic symposium could well have asked the acerbic sage Yajnavalkya: **If this astonishing 'design' of infinitesimal chemical/molecular/ mathematical stuff of the universe is such, does that mean it is 'implanted' organically in every cell of the brain, wired into our visual imagery, so that eventually an Indian weaver will 'dream up the design'.** The sage was busy rowing however. So no answer came...

All one can ask standing in the modern framework of computer mechanics and electronic impulses is whether the natural structures of the heathland fern, the seahorse's tail as Penrose names these magnified configurations, which appear to be lifted off the border of a **white-on-white embroidery stitch of a Lucknowi chikan work sari** are all of a piece... an astonishing congruence is the inescapable conclusion. Which leads one to wonder whether Indians

Chikan design

have a special insight because of their unique disciplines, to **GNOW** these patterns almost without thinking.

1   **First in abstract mathematics** now possible to be visualised' in all its infinity of design, the very **'rule book'** which constructs the firmament we understand as 'out there'.

2   **The unconscious impulse of the artist to create aesthetic shape** and form as in the mango design of the Indian paisley shawl, or the above design so familiar to a village weaver,

3   **in the very structure of these natural forms** (the ammonite for one.

Traditional Indian culture and learning is so impregnated with mathematical concepts, the exploding graphs of an Indian **RAGA** for instance, building on the foundation of a very simple melodic grouping of given **svaras** and their microtonal embellishments, 'patterned' yet making unpredictable artistic shifts in their permutations so that their 'seahorse tails' of elongated taans, though adhering to the recognisable mathematic structure are never quite the same again in the free improvisation.

This is what the **Chandogya Upanishad** examines in a parable on the fig tree and its seed. The rishi asks **Shwetaketu** what he sees in the fruit of the tree, breaking it down into its very kernels until 'nothingness' is reached—but... as the rishi points out in a timeless way: 'from the subtle essence indeed, my dear, does this great fig tree arise'.

India is an entity Stepping stones have usually well-defined edges otherwise the seeker stumbles. Just over 330 signposts may specify one truth on this personal **padayatra** about this land which has baffled many—and even been designated a 'vast conglomerate, comprehensive in the widest sense, an amalgam of often contradictory beliefs and practice held together in One (whole) by certain powerful ideas and by a system of social regulations'. But the Indian writer (unknown) goes on:

It is continually forming about new nuclei; it is agglutinative in its growth, made up of many accretions, imperfectly adjusted to each other and to the whole of which they are parts.

It has also been said by a Muslim academic that India

is

bigger than a country
larger than a nation and more than a mere state
it is a defined civilization with all its varieties

So,

as the first anonymous author asks intriguingly
'Canst thou draw out leviathan with a hook?'

Just so, this compendium of core concepts, political attitudes, social codifications, Sanskrit condensations to represent a world of gigantic philosophies, shorthand symbols for equally explosive thought processes, is only parts of the whole—and each individual will arrive at a different set of truths,

their own 'hooks' to draw out a patterning
of leviathan India
which is more than the sum of these many parts
a few hundred signposts along the stepping stone pathway
of this particular,
my own personal
padayatra

,,,,,,,,,,,,,,,,,,,,

'All beginnings are elusive
all endings are definite
the geometry caught in the mind's net
does not have lines ending'

quoted by world-renowned crystallographer, the late **Professor Dorothy Hodgkin, Order of Merit,** in a science broadcast on Australian ABC radio. Source unknown, the stanza reflects her thinking on the random **order = rta** to Indians, of the cosmos.

Om Shanti shanti shanti!